名城遵义

Cultural Famous City

美在农家
The beauty in farmer family

新农村风貌
The outlook of new rural areas

Zunyi city is located in the north of Guizhou province, facing provincial capital Guiyang to south, bordering Sichuan to west, closing Chongqing to north, is the main region of middle-upstream of the Yangtze River overall development which is planned by nation and the middle of Guizhou industrial belt building. Zunyi is the second largest city of Guizhou, the total area of 30,762 square kilometres, the existing population of 7.3 million, governs 2 districts, 1 city, 10 counties (including two minority autonomous counties). The GDP of the city is 40.2 billion yuan, financial revenue of 6 billion yuan, the per capita net income of peasants is 2,319 yuan.

"Zunyi Conference" is famous in China and the world. "Zunyi Conference", a turning point in China's revolutionary history, because of the "Zunyi Conference" so Zunyi is well-known throughout the world.

Zunyi has unlimited scenery. Here are four national forest parks, one state level scenic area, two state level nature protection areas and six provincial scenic areas, nearly one thousand heritage points.

Zunyi has abundant products. Over 40 minerals now have been surveyed, 527 minerals points have been found and used, among which, coal, manganese, aluminium, mercury, pyrite, silica, nickel, molybdenum, barium are advantage minerals, and the reserves of the minerals occupy leading position in the province or in the nation. The capability of reserves the water is 103 KW per square kilometre in the city, 49% higher than the national average. The reserves of proven coal are expected to total 19.35 billion tons. In addition, Zunyi also is the granary in the north of Guizhou, and has huge variety of rare medicinal herbs.

Zunyi new rural building made notable results. Zunyi suited measures to local conditions, taking Four Things in Farmer Family "rich, study, happy, beauty" to guide farmers enriching and going to well-off , by the end of 2005 the establishment points of Four Things in Farmer Family accumulated over 1,500 in the city, building activity "Four Things in Farmer Family" caused great repercussions throughout the country.

Zunyi has continuously accelerated the process of industrialization. There are a number of high profile public enterprises and advantage products, such as Moutai Group. The city has more than 2,000 various industrial enterprises, forming the complete industrial system taking electricity, coal, electromechanical, chemical industry, building materials, automobile manufacturing, making wine, food processing as the whole.

Zunyi has convenient traffic and extends in all directions. Chuanqian Railway runs through the city from north to south, Chishui River, Wu River lead to the Yangtze River, Guizun highway connects to the provincial capital Guiyang, especially the opening of Zunchong highway, has finished a history of having no highway in our province, forming the transport network of Zunyi access to the Yangtze River and reaching the sea.

Zunyi is harmonious and beautiful. The city accelerated development social economic culture, and vigorously built "Peace Zunyi". The city has won the title of Chinese Historical Cultural Famous City, the Chinese Wine Cultural Famous City, China's Outstanding Tourist City, National Garden City, State Green Model City, China Habitation Environment Example Award City, National Health Advanced City, National Double-support Model City. Zunyi -- social harmony and health, is a beautiful and comfortable city. Zunyi has become city in the green, water in the city, people in the scenery, and the charm city in the West of China.

遵义市政府与市政府住宅一小区
Zunyi city government and a municipal residential area

总第17期 №17

贵州统计年鉴

GUIZHOU STATISTICAL YEARBOOK

贵 州 省 统 计 局
国家统计局贵州调查总队 编
Guizhou Statistical Bureau
Guizhou Survey Organization of NBS

中国统计出版社
China Statistics Press

（京）新登字041号

图书在版编目（CIP）数据

贵州统计年鉴. 2006/贵州省统计局编. -北京：中国统计出版社, 2006. 6
ISBN 7-5037-4902-4

Ⅰ.贵… Ⅱ.贵… Ⅲ.统计资料-贵州省-2006-年鉴 Ⅳ.C832. 73-54

中国版本图书馆CIP数据核字(2006)第026173号

贵州统计年鉴 - 2006

作　者/贵州省统计局
责任编辑/蔡启新
E-mail/yearbook@stats. gov. cn
出版发行/中国统计出版社
通信地址/北京市西城区三里河月坛南街75号　中国统计出版社
邮　编/100826
电　话/（010）63376907
印　刷/北京京都六环印刷厂
经　销/新华书店
开　本/850×1168毫米1/16
字　数/1093. 5千字
印　张/45. 56
印　数/1-1400册
版　别/2006年10月第1版
版　次/2006年10月第1次印刷
书　号/ISBN 7-5037-4902-4/F·2249
定　价/260. 00元

编者说明

一、《贵州统计年鉴——2006》是一部全面、系统反映贵州省2005年国民经济和社会发展变化情况的资料性统计年刊，是国内外各界人士认识贵州、了解贵州的重要工具书。本年鉴内容在《贵州统计年鉴——2005》的基础上增加了全省非公有制经济方面的主要统计资料和“十五”时期主要统计数据。同时，根据第一次全国经济普查结果对生产总值和社会消费品零售总额的数据进行了调整。

二、本年鉴为中英文对照版，全书内容包括24个部分：综合；人口；劳动、就业与社会保障；固定资产投资；能源、原材料消费；农业；工业；建筑业；交通运输、邮电通信；国内商业；对外经济贸易与合作；旅游；价格指数；财政、金融、证券、保险；人民生活；科技、教育和文化；资源、环境；体育、卫生及其他；非公有制经济；民族自治地区；经济强县；扶贫与开发；地县社会经济发展概况；全国各省主要统计资料。同时为帮助读者准确理解和使用统计数据，在每部分之后附有主要统计指标解释。

三、本年鉴中，如有统计口径等因素变化，我们均在表下加了注释，使用时请注意。

四、本年鉴数据与往年数据有出入的，以本年鉴数据为准。

五、本年鉴部分数据合计数或相对数由于单位取舍不同而产生的计算误差均未作机械调整。

六、本年鉴表中的符号使用说明：

“…” 表示数据不足最小计量单位数；

“空格”表示该项统计指标数据不详或无该项数据；

“#”表示其中的主要项。

本年鉴在编辑、出版、发行过程中，得到了有关单位的大力支持和帮助，在此谨致衷心感谢！

Preface

Ⅰ.Guizhou Statistical Yearbook 2006 is an annual statistics publication which provides comprehensive and systematic data series about the national economy and social development in Guizhou Province in 2005,It is an important reference book for personalities of various circles to know Guizhou province. Guizhou Statistical Yearbook 2006 was expanded by adding statistics on Non-piblic-owned economy,main statistics on the national economy and social development of Guizhou Province of each year in "Tenth Five-Year Plan".The data of GDP and Retail Sales of Consumer Goods are adjusted on the basis of the result of the First National Economic Cenus.

Ⅱ.This yearbook, in Chinese and English, contains the following 24 parts:General Survey;Population;Labor, Employment and Security;Investment in Fixed Assets; Consumption of Energy and Raw Material;Agriculture; Industry;Construction;Transportation, Postal and Telecommunication Services;Domestic Trade;Foreign Trade and Economic Cooperation;Tourism;Price Indices;Finance,Banking,Securities and Insurance;People′s Livelihood;Science&Technology,Education and Culture;Natural Resources and Environment;Sports,Public Health and Others; Non-public-owned Economy;Minority Nationality Autonomous Areas;Strongly Economic County;Anti-poverty and Development;Prefecture (County) Social and Economic Summary;National Main Statistic Informations Grouped by Provinces. In order to make readers using materials correctly, interpretation of major statistical indicators are attached after every chapter.

Ⅲ.The concepts,definitions and coverage of statistics of some data in the book have been adjusted,which are not comparable with former years,therfor some notes are added in the book.Users are alerted to the notes about the difference in the concepts,definitions and coverage of statistics when using and comparing data in this book.

Ⅳ.The data,which not tallied with the previous ,is subject to the data in the book.

Ⅴ. Statistical discrepancies in this book due to rounding are not adjusted.

Ⅵ. Notations used in this book:

"..." indicates that the figure is not large enough to be measured with the smallest unit in the table;

"blank space" indicates that the data are unknown or are not available;

" #" indicates major breakdown of the total.

Thanks for enthusiastic of many units and individuals to the compilation,publication and delivery of the Yearbook!

《贵州统计年鉴—2006》编辑委员会

张如飞（省审计厅厅长）
王黎明（省国资委主任）
蒋天才（省知识产权局局长）
初志忠（省储备物资管理局局长）
刘启云（省粮食局局长）
高　弟（省煤田地质局局长）
石　超（省招商引资局局长）
陈仁贵（省物价局局长）
董穗生（省食品药品监督管理局局长）
张梓钟（省质量技术监督局局长）
张建华（省烟草专卖局局长）
兰开锋（铁道部成都铁路局贵阳办事处主任）
潘　福（贵州电网公司总经理）
李向春（省机场集团有限公司董事长）
李德明（省通信管理局局长）
杨志文（省邮政局局长）
龙超亚（省中小企业局局长）
刘伦才（省农业机械管理局局长）
鲁智云（省国防科技工业办公室主任）
王　平（人民银行贵阳中心支行行长）
张庆民（国家开发银行省分行行长）
李　光（中国农业发展银行贵州省分行行长）
黄再红（中国工商银行股份有限公司贵州省分行行长）
崔宗河（农业银行省分行行长）
吴民豪（中国建设银行股份有限公司省分行行长）
张　铭（中国银行省分行行长）
彭士学（贵阳市商业银行董事长）
刘乃云（省农村信用社联合社理事长）
吕如庆（中国人民财产保险股份有限公司省分公司总经理）
柳福青（中国人寿保险股份有限公司省分公司副总经理）
廖　康（中国电信集团贵州省电信公司总经理）
王　志（中国联合通信有限公司贵州分公司总经理）
解　兵（中国铁通集团有限公司贵州分公司副总经理）
周　黔（中国网络通信集团公司贵州省分公司总经理）
袁　周（贵阳市市长）
卢守祥（遵义市市长）
刘一民（六盘水市市长）
慕德贵（安顺市市长）
刘晓凯（黔南州州长）
李月成（黔东南州州长）
班程农（黔西南州州长）
黄家培（毕节地区行署专员）
谌贻琴（铜仁地区行署专员）

Editorial Board

Wang Liming: Director of the Provincial State-owned Assets Supervision and Administration Commission
Jiang Tiancai: Director of the Provincial Intellectual Property Right Bureau
Chu Zhizhong: Director of the Provincial Hive Material Administration
Liu Qiyun: Director of the Provincial Grain Administration
Gao Di: Director of the Provincial Coal Mine Exploration Bureau
Shi Chao: Director of the Provincial Investment Promotion Bureau
Chen Rengui: Director of the Provincial Administration of Price
Dong Huisheng: Director of the Provincial Food and Drug Administration
Zhang Zizhong: Director of the Provincial Administration of Quality and Technical Supervision
Zhang Jianhua: Director of the Provincial Administration of Tobacco Monopoly
Lan Kaifeng: Director of the Guiyang Branch of Chengdu Railway Bureau of Ministry Railway
Pan Fu: General Manager of the Provincial Electric Power Company
Li Xiangchun: Director of the Provincial Airport Corporation
Li Deming: Director of the Provincial Administration of Communication
Yang Zhiwen: Director of the Provincial Post Bureau
Long Chaoya: Director of the Provincial Administration of Medium-scale and Miniature-scale Enterprises
Liu Luncai: Director of the Provincial Bureau of Agricultural Machinery
Lu Zhiyun: Director of the Provincial Office of Science Technology and Industry for National Defence
Wang Ping: Director of the People´s Bank of China Guiyang Branch
Zhang Qingmin: Director of the National Development Bank Guiyang Branch
Li Guang: Director of the Agricultural Development Bank Guizhou Branch
Huang Zaihong: Director of the Industrial and Commercial Bank of China Guizhou Branch
Chui Zonghe: Director of the China Agricultural Bank Guizhou Branch
Wu Minhao: Director of the China Construction Bank Guizhou Branch
Zhang Ming: Director of the Bank of China Guizhou Branch
Peng Shixue: Director of the Commercial Bank of Guiyang City
Liu Naiyun: Director of the Provincial Rural Credit Cooperatives
Lv Ruqing: General-manager of the PICC Property and Company Ltd.Guizhou Branch
Liu Fuqing: Vice-manager of China Life Insurance Company Ltd.Guizhou Branch
Liao Kang: General-manager of the China Telecom Corporation Guizhou Telecommunication Company
Wang Guochang: General-manager of the China Mobile Communications Corporation Guizhou Mobile Communication Company
Wang Zhi: General-manager of the China United Telecommunications Corporation Guizhou Branch
Xie Bing: Vice-manager of the China Tietong Corporation Guizhou Branch
Zhou Qian: General-manager of the China Network Telecommunications Corporation Guizhou Branch
Yuan Zhou: Mayor of Guiyang City
Lu Shouxiang: Mayor of Zunyi City
Liu Yimin: Mayor of Liupanshui City
Mu Degui: Mayor of Anshun City
Liu Xiaokai: Chief Executive of Qiannan State
Li Yuecheng: Chief Executive of Qiandongnan State
Ban Chengnong: Chief Executive of Qianxinan State
Huang Jiapei: Chief Executive of Bijie
Chen Yiqin: Chief Executive of Tongren

《贵州统计年鉴—2006》编辑人员

主　　编：陶谋立　冯育毅

副 主 编：王正潮　刘带春　张贵平　廖定华　钟赛梅　李洪刚

编辑部主任：杨大昆　刘　晴　聂坤琪

分 科 主 编：（姓氏笔画为序）

尤金福　白文英　李诗刚　邹陆华　陈景平　肖　瑶　邵　尉

张学进　杨　丽　周亚丽　胡　刚　龚　勇　程邦嘉　董安娜

编 辑 人 员：（姓氏笔画为序）

许大陆　冯金友　刘继海　肖高萍　范振新　周　蓉

周玲颖　徐　锋　程大利　谢小清　董建魏　董海燕

英 文 翻 译：邹　康　王朝晖

统 计 制 图：汪　兰

编 务 人 员：韦　博

Editorial Staff

Editor-in-chief: Tao Mouli　Feng Yuyi

Deputy Editor-in-chief:

Wang Zhengchao　Liu Daichun　Zhang Guiping　Liao Dinghua　Zhong Saimei　Li Honggang

Directors of Editorial Department:

Yang Dakun　Liu Qing　Nie Kunqi

Editor-in- chief by Section(in order of strokes of chinese surname):

You Jinfu　Bai Wenying　Li Shigang　Zou Luhua　Chen Jingping　Xiao Yao　Shao Wei

Zhang Xuejin　Yang Li　Zhou Yali　Hu Gang　Gong Yong　Cheng Bangjia　Dong Anna

Editorial Staff(in order of strokes of chinese surname):

Xu Dalu　Feng Jinyou　Liu Jihai　Xiao Gaoping　Fang Zhenxin　Zhou Rong

Zhou Lingying　Xu Feng　Cheng Dali　Xie Xiaoqing　Dong Jianwei　Dong Haiyan

English Translators: Zou Kang　Wang Zhaohui

Statistics Drawer: Wang Nan

Staff for Editorial Affairs: Wei Bo

目 录

CONTENTS

一 综合

General Survey

二　人口
Population

三　劳动、就业与保障
Labour Force,Employment and Security

四 固定资产投资
Investment in Fixed Assets

五 能源、原材料消耗
Consumption of Energy and Raw Material

六 农业
Agriculture

七 工业
Industry

八 建筑业
Construction

九 交通运输、邮电通信
Transportation,Postal and Telecommunication Services

十 国内商业
Domestic Trade

十一 对外经济贸易与合作
Foreign Trade and Economic Cooperation

十二 旅 游
Tourism

十三 价格指数
Price Indices

十四 财政、金融、证券、保险
Finance,Banking,Securities and Insurance

十五 人民生活
People´s Livelihood

十六 科技、教育和文化
Science & Tethnology,Education and Culture

十七 资源、环境
Natural Resources and Environment

十八 体育、卫生及其他
Sports,Public Health and Others

十九 非公有制经济
Non-public-owned Economy

二十 民族自治地区
Minority Nationality Autonomous Areas

二十一 经济强县
Strongly Economic County

二十二 扶贫与开发
Anti-poverty and Development

二十三 地县社会经济发展概况
Prefecture (County) Social and Economic Summary

二十四　全国各省资料

National Main Statistic Informations Grouped by Provinces

1

综　合

General Survey

One

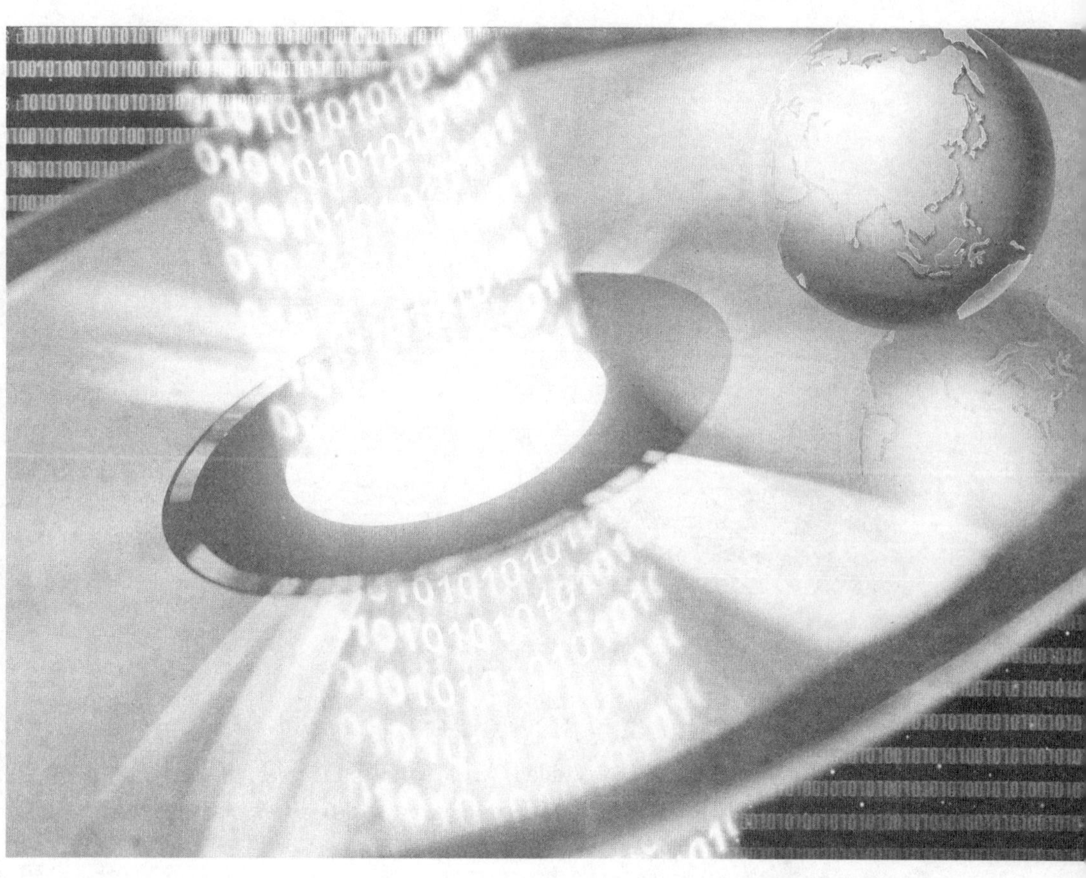

生 产 总 值
Gross Domestic Product

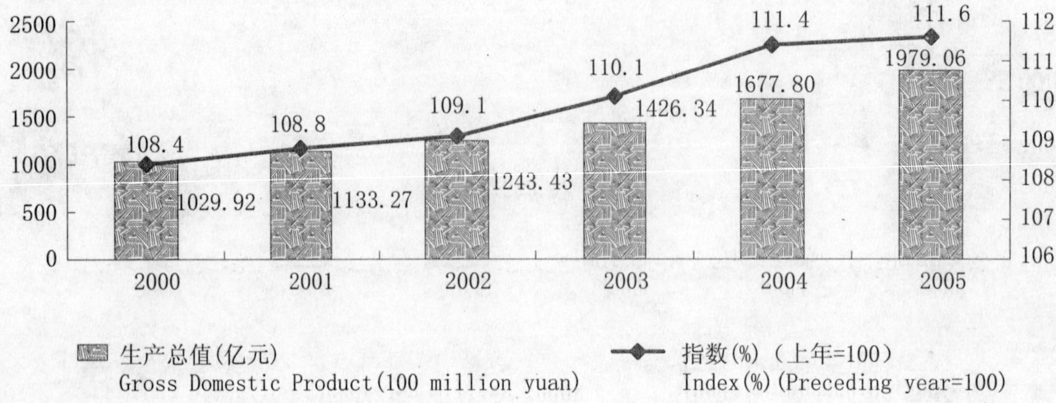

生产总值构成（%）
Composition of Gross Domestic Product (%)

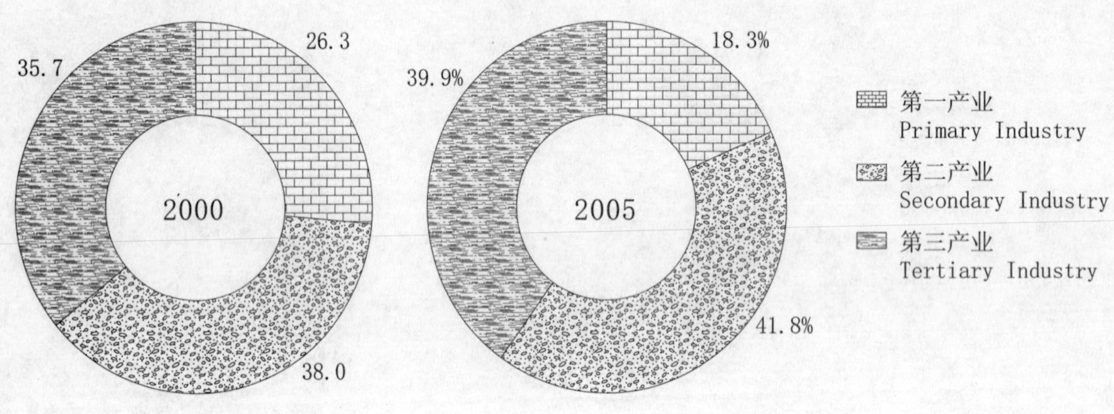

第三产业增加值构成（%）
Composition of Added Value of Tertiary Industry
(Tertiary Industry=100)

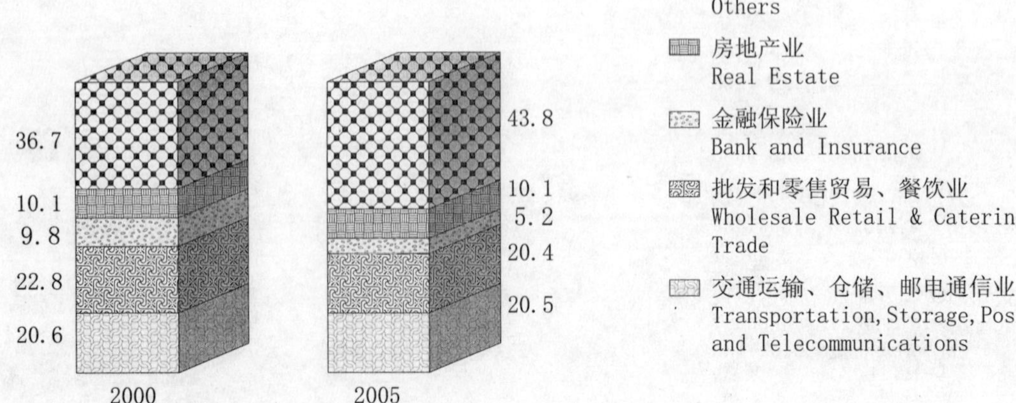

1-1 各州市地县名称(2005)

Name of Each State,City,Prefecture and County of Guizhou(2005)

州(市、地)名称 State(City,Prefecture)	县(市、区、特区)名称 County(City,District,Special Region)
贵阳市 Guiyang	南明区 云岩区 小河区 花溪区 乌当区 白云区 清镇市 开阳县 息烽县 修文县 Nanming Yunyan Xiaohe Huaxi Wudang Baiyun Qingzhen Kaiyang Xifeng Xiuwen
六盘水市 Liupanshui	钟山区 六枝特区 盘县 水城县 Zhongshan Liuzhi Panxian Shuicheng
遵义市 Zunyi	红花岗区 汇川区 赤水市 仁怀市 遵义县 桐梓县 绥阳县 正安县 Honghuagang Huichuan Chishui Renhuai Zunyi Tongzi Suiyang Zhengan 凤冈县 湄潭县 余庆县 习水县 道真仡佬族苗族自治县 务川仡佬族苗族自治县 Fenggang Meitan Yuqing Xishui Daozhen Wuchuan
安顺市 Anshun	西秀区 平坝县 普定县 关岭布依族苗族自治县 镇宁布依族苗族自治县 Xixiu Pingba Puding Guanling Zhenning 紫云布依族苗族自治县 Ziyun
铜仁地区 Tongren	铜仁市 江口县 石阡县 思南县 德江县 沿河土家族自治县 松桃苗族自治县 Tongren Jiangkou Shiqian Sinan Dejiang Yanhe Songtao 玉屏侗族自治县 印江土家族苗族自治县 万山特区 Yuping Yinjiang Wanshan
黔西南布依族苗族自治州 Qianxinan	兴义市 兴仁县 普安县 晴隆县 安龙县 望谟县 贞丰县 册亨县 Xingyi Xingren Puan Qinglong Anlong Wangmo Zhenfeng Ceheng
毕节地区 Bijie	毕节市 大方县 黔西县 金沙县 织金县 纳雍县 赫章县 威宁彝族回族苗族自治县 Bijie Dafang Qianxi Jinsha Zhijin Nayong Hezhang Weining
黔东南苗族侗族自治州 Qiandongnan	凯里市 黄平县 施秉县 三穗县 镇远县 岑巩县 天柱县 锦屏县 Kaili Huangping Shibing Sansui Zhenyuan Cengong Tianzhu Jinping 剑河县 台江县 黎平县 榕江县 从江县 雷山县 麻江县 丹寨县 Jianhe Taijiang Liping Rongjiang Congjiang Leishan Majiang Danzhai
黔南布依族苗族自治州 Qiannan	都匀市 福泉市 荔波县 贵定县 瓮安县 平塘县 罗甸县 长顺县 龙里县 惠水县 Duyun Fuquan Libo Guiding Wengan Pingtang Luodian Changshun Longli Huishui 独山县 三都水族自治县 Dushan Sandu

1-2 各州(市、地)行政区划(2005)

Administrative Division of Guizhou Province(2005)

单位:个(unit)

州(市、地)名称	State (City,Prefecture)	地级单位 Unit at Prefectural Level	#市 Cities	县级单位 Unit at County Level	#县 Counties	#自治县 Autonomous Counties	县级市 Cities at County Level	市区 District under the Jurisdiction of City
全省合计	**Total**	**9**	**4**	**88**	**67**	**11**	**9**	**10**
贵阳市	Guiyang	1	1	10	3		1	6
六盘水市	Liupanshui	1	1	4	2			1
遵义市	Zunyi	1	1	14	10	2	2	2
安顺市	Anshun	1	1	6	5	3		1
铜仁地区	Tongren	1		10	8	4	1	
黔西南布依族苗族自治州	Qianxinan	1		8	7		1	
毕节地区	Bijie	1		8	7	1	1	
黔东南苗族侗族自治州	Qiandongnan	1		16	15		1	
黔南布依族苗族自治州	Qiannan	1		12	10	1	2	

州(市、地)名称	State (City,Prefecture)	特区 Special District	镇 Town	街道办事处 Urban Subdistrict Office	乡 Township	#民族乡 Ethnic Community Township	居民委员会 Neighbourhood Committees	村民委员会 Village Commttees
全省合计	**Total**	**2**	**691**	**92**	**760**	**252**	**1610**	**20031**
贵阳市	Guiyang		29	40	49	18	422	1166
六盘水市	Liupanshui	1	30	4	64	50	142	1094
遵义市	Zunyi		164	14	62	8	276	1733
安顺市	Anshun		38	7	42	11	99	1837
铜仁地区	Tongren	1	69	5	95	56	132	2948
黔西南布依族苗族自治州	Qianxinan		76	4	50	3	77	2048
毕节地区	Bijie		98	6	146	77	165	3934
黔东南苗族侗族自治州	Qiandongnan		90	5	116	17	151	3249
黔南布依族苗族自治州	Qiannan		97	7	136	12	146	2022

注:贵阳市、六盘水市、遵义市、安顺市为省辖市。

Note:Guiyang,Liupanshui,Zunyi,Anshun are cities under the jurisdiction of provi nce.

1-3 “十五”时期各年主要社会经济指标

Major Social and Economic Indicators of each year in “Tenth-Five-year Plan” Period

指 标	Item	2000	2001	2002	2003	2004	2005
人口与就业	**Population and Employment**						
人口（万人）	Population(10000 persons)						
年末总人口	Total Population at the Year-end	3755.72	3798.51	3837.28	3869.66	3903.70	3931.12
#城镇人口	Urban Population	896.49	910.12	931.11	958.52	1025.89	1056.29
乡村人口	Rural Population	2859.23	2888.39	2905.17	2911.14	2877.81	2874.83
#男	Male	1968.00	1973.41	1993.15	2010.22	2022.22	2024.11
女	Female	1787.72	1825.10	1844.13	1859.44	1881.48	1907.01
年平均人口	Annual Average Population	3732.89	3777.12	3817.90	3853.47	3886.68	3917.41
就业（万人）	Employment(10000 persons)						
年末就业人员(包括外出人员)	Year-end Employees	1866.23	2068.01	2106.14	2145.00	2186.00	2220.00
#职工人数	Staff and Workers	193.97	189.17	188.47	188.70	192.67	202.02
城镇登记失业人数	Urban Registeration Unemployment	10.24	11.15	11.08	11.18	11.61	12.13
宏观经济	**Macroeconomy**						
国民经济核算（亿元）	National Accounting(100 million yuan)						
生产总值	Gross Domestic Product	1029.92	1133.27	1243.43	1426.34	1677.80	1979.06
#第一产业	#Primary Industry	271.20	274.41	281.10	298.69	334.50	362.49
第二产业	Secondary Industry	391.20	433.52	481.96	569.37	681.50	826.63
#工 业	Industry	328.73	360.73	395.45	473.38	577.40	714.24
建筑业	Construction	62.47	72.79	86.51	95.99	104.10	112.39
第三产业	Tertiary Industry	367.52	425.34	480.37	558.28	661.80	789.94
#交通运输、仓储、邮电通信业	#Transportation ,Storage,Post and Telecommunications	75.86	88.47	102.48	119.26	134.90	162.10
批发零售贸易餐饮业	Wholesale,Retail & Catering Trade	83.72	89.67	100.61	116.05	136.90	160.92
生产总值中	In GDP						
最终消费	Final Consumption Expenditures	920.46	1000.35	1085.75	1169.55	1367.94	1627.27
居民消费	Household Consumption Expenditures	754.57	791.03	851.27	912.56	1058.36	1230.07
政府消费	Government Consumption Expenditures	165.89	209.32	234.48	256.99	309.58	397.20
资本形成总额	Gross Capital Formation	489.19	629.24	682.22	789.80	894.34	1024.94
固定资本形成	Gross Fixed Capital Formation	456.26	575.89	663.89	768.76	871.46	996.24
存货增加	Change in Inventories	32.93	53.35	18.33	21.04	22.88	28.70

1-3续表1(continued)

指 标	Item	2000	2001	2002	2003	2004	2005
固定资产投资（亿元）	**Investment in Fixed Assets (100 million yuan)**						
全社会固定资产投资	Total Investment in Fixed Assets	402.50	533.74	632.44	754.13	869.25	1015.28
#基本建设	Capital Construction	151.89	238.81	312.62	384.81	477.83	528.85
更新改造	Innovation	93.57	118.55	120.79	140.54	152.33	180.57
房地产开发	Real Estate Development	46.58	67.01	83.01	104.95	121.66	154.12
其他投资	Other Investments	110.46	109.37	116.02	123.83	117.43	151.74
能源生产与消费(万吨标准煤)	**Total Production and Consumption of Energy(10000 tons of SCE)**						
一次能源生产总量	Total Production of Primary Energy	3875.92	3482.92	4286.06	6317.89	7791.23	8459.52
能源消费总量	Total Engrgy Consumption	4278.61	4437.90	4469.86	5534.49	6020.98	6428.60
#生产消费	Production Consumption	3200.95	3341.62	3318.02	4323.11	4800.76	5161.82
生活消费	Residential Consumption	888.56	883.69	925.70	956.93	969.18	1001.67
能源终端消费量	Final Consumption of Energy	3848.22	4149.84	4159.02	4998.69	5323.43	5981.64
农业	**Agriculture**						
年末常用耕地面积(千公顷)	Cultivated Land at the Year-end (1000 hectares)	1843.48	1832.28	1769.40	1750.54	1752.20	1753.50
农业从业人员（万人）	Agriculture Employment(10000 persons)	1372.12	1368.28	1353.92	1322.10	1288.49	1268.09
农林牧渔业增加值（亿元）	Added Value of FFAF(100 million yuan)	270.99	274.17	280.82	303.95	340.92	368.93
农 业	Farming	187.31	187.45	185.31	181.53	208.05	218.33
林 业	Forestry	14.03	11.85	12.42	17.62	16.20	15.85
牧 业	Animal Husbandry	61.49	71.39	79.51	87.79	106.25	122.16
渔 业	Fishery	3.16	3.48	3.58	3.96	4.60	6.15
农林牧渔服务业	FFAF Services				13.05	5.82	6.44
主要农产品产量（万吨）	Output of Major Farm Products(10000 tons)						
粮 食	Grain	1161.30	1100.30	1034.20	1104.30	1149.58	1152.06
油 料	Oil-bearing Crops	74.34	71.32	72.48	72.31	82.71	84.89
#油菜籽	Rapeseed	66.20	63.48	64.05	64.01	73.93	76.51

1-3续表2(continued)

指　标	Item	2000	2001	2002	2003	2004	2005
烤　烟	Flue-cured Tobacco	31.09	26.38	30.65	28.72	29.98	34.45
肉类总产量	Meat	124.06	131.70	145.02	156.99	171.06	187.01
水产品	Aquatic Products	6.24	6.89	7.46	7.96	8.85	9.46
工业	**Industry**						
全部工业增加值（亿元）	Total Added Value of Industry (100 million yuan)	328.73	360.73	395.45	473.38	577.40	714.24
规模以上工业企业	Industrial Enterprises above Designated Size						
增加值	Added Value	216.99	236.57	271.09	346.49	476.75	585.85
#国有经济	State-owned Units	175.83	188.97	217.70	256.35	340.97	420.87
非国有经济	Non-state-owned Units	41.16	47.60	53.39	90.14	135.78	164.98
#轻工业	Light Industry	82.16	87.66	88.20	116.72	147.79	177.19
重工业	Heavy Industry	134.83	148.91	182.89	229.77	328.97	408.66
产品销售收入	Sales Revenue	593.80	646.01	752.97	974.30	1325.95	1577.16
利税总额	Total Profits	87.44	94.30	104.74	135.87	201.21	232.49
主要工业产品产量	Output of Major Industrial Products						
原煤（万吨）	Coal(10000 tons)	3677.00	3731.39	5001.13	7802.50	9756.62	10615.20
发电量（亿千瓦小时）	Electricity(100 million kwh)	404.70	480.25	547.12	636.60	713.04	786.78
铝（万吨）	Aluminum(10000 tons)	27.19	28.39	33.22	41.31	42.29	41.99
钢材（万吨）	Steel(10000 tons)	150.93	138.61	177.79	192.97	203.22	214.85
轮胎外胎（万条）	Tires(10000 pieces)	255.34	279.74	273.52	301.56	355.96	371.66
磷矿石（万吨）	Phosphorite(10000 tons)	588.70	669.91	729.20	783.68	801.98	878.79
白酒（万吨）	Liquor(10000 tons)	8.38	12.11	12.67	15.04	9.22	11.74
卷烟（万箱）	Cigarettes(10000 cases)	187.35	180.79	177.84	183.19	194.74	208.21
建筑业	**Construction**						
建筑业企业从业人员(万人)	Construction Employment (10000 persons)	22.30	25.91	27.14	29.33	30.04	30.64
建筑业增加值（亿元）	Value-add of Construction (100 million yuan)	24.67	33.16	39.97	48.69	55.74	
建筑业总产值（亿元）	Gross Output Value of Construction (100 million yuan)	109.06	150.20	181.12	212.29	255.45	271.23
房屋建筑施工面积(万平方米)	Floor Space of Buildings under Construction(10000 sq.m)	1792.48	1945.59	2309.35	2519.79	2891.76	3152.82
房屋建筑竣工面积(万平方米)	Floor Space of Buildings Completed (10000 sq.m)	824.01	891.93	1054.27	980.28	1251.23	1149.49

1-3续表3(continued)

指 标	Item	2000	2001	2002	2003	2004	2005
交通运输	**Transportation**						
运输线路长度（公里）	Length of Transportation Routes(km)						
铁路营业里程	Length of Railways	1642	1644	1893	1900	1891	1986
公路线路里程	Length of Highways in Operation	34643	34617	44220	45304	46128	46893
内河航道里程	Length of Navigable Inland Waterways in Operation	2132	2132	2132	3322	3322	3322
旅客运量（万人）	Passenger Traffic(10000 persons)	53116	54665	55980	55074	58707	64450
旅客周转量（亿人公里）	Passenger-Kilometers (100 million passenger-km)	238.36	251.06	250.79	248.55	278.21	312.40
货物运量（万吨）	Freight Traffic(10000 tons)	15615	16344	17399	18224	19439	21771
货物周转量（亿吨公里）	Freight Ton-Kilometers (100 millionton-km)	404.07	439.30	486.03	547.01	610.28	646.55
邮电通信业	**Post and Telecommunication**						
邮电业务总量（亿元）	Business Volume of Post and Telecommunications Service(100 million yuan)	40.92	47.57	73.07	101.50	131.23	174.22
年末固定电话用户（万户）	Number of Telephones Subscribers at the Year-end(10000 subscribers)	157.30	211.28	274.32	332.40	387.60	466.49
移动电话用户	Number of Mobile Telephones Subscribers	78.50	168.90	246.90	331.10	440.00	509.42
国际互联网用户	Number of Subscribers of Internet Service	18	20	47	83	98	109
交换机容量(万门)	Capacity of Telephone Exchanges(10000 lines)	385.05	586.86	794.30	969.60	1149.10	1369.60
国内商业（亿元）	**Domestic Trade(100 million yuan)**						
社会消费品零售总额	Total Retail Sales of Consumer Goods	355.58	391.14	430.64	474.57	535.31	606.92
市	City	204.71	228.25	253.36	281.23	318.63	362.74
县	County	68.56	74.25	80.71	88.78	102.01	115.80
县以下	Below County Level	82.31	88.64	96.57	104.56	114.67	128.38
对外贸易（亿美元）	**Foreign Trade(USD 100 million)**						
进出口总额	Total Value of Imports and Exports	6.60	6.50	6.91	9.85	15.14	14.04
出口额	Total Exports	4.21	4.22	4.42	5.88	8.67	8.59
进口额	Total Imports	2.39	2.28	2.50	3.96	6.47	5.45
利用外资	Utilization of Foreign Capital						
签订合同项目(个)	Projects of Agreements and Contracts (unit)	59	65	55	70	68	61
实际吸收外资金额（万美元）	Foreign Capital Actually Absorbed (USD 10000)	19545	14010	9383	13191	13932	19568
引进省外项目(个)	Projects Import out of Guizhou Province (unit)	801	910	1082	1861	1824	1996
引进省外资金（亿元）	Amount Import out of Guizhou Province (100 million yuan)	33.93	48.53	57.30	104.00	130.00	232.50

1-3续表4(continued)

指 标	Item	2000	2001	2002	2003	2004	2005
旅游	**Tourism**						
入境旅游人数(万人次)	Number of International Tourists Inbound (10000 person-times)	18.39	20.55	22.81	7.70	23.10	27.62
#外国人	Foreigners	7.12	7.85	8.45	2.40	7.63	9.26
港澳台同胞	Compatriots from Hong Kong,Macao and Taiwan	5.30	5.95	6.53	2.83	6.69	7.82
国内旅游人数	Domestic Tourists	1980.00	2100.00	2200.24	1835.21	2480.37	3099.46
国际旅游收入(万美元)	International Earnings from Tourism (USD 10000)	6092.23	6873.23	7950.63	2893.91	8020.27	10141.36
国内旅游收入(亿元)	Domestic Earnings from Tourism (100 million yuan)	57.95	75.81	99.86	114.36	161.02	242.83
价格指数(上年=100)	**Price Indices(preceding year=100)**						
居民消费价格总指数	Consumer Price Index	99.5	101.8	99.0	101.2	104.0	101.0
商品价格总指数	Retail Price Index	97.3	98.4	99.3	100.0	103.2	101.3
农业生产资料价格总指数	General Price Index of Means of Agricultural Production	100.6	99.4	100.6	104.1	109.0	110.2
全部工业品出厂价格指数	Total Ex-Factory Price Index of Industrial Products	100.4	102.2	98.9	103.4	108.0	107.2
全部原材料、燃料、动力购进价格指数	Total Raw Materials, Fuels and Power	102.9	100.2	97.6	106.0	112.0	107.4
财政、金融	**Government Finance and Finance**						
财政（亿元）	Government Finance(100 million yuan)						
财政总收入	Total Financial Revenue	153.04	177.04	203.03	236.64	296.48	366.16
财政一般预算收入	Local Financial Revenue	85.23	99.75	108.28	124.56	149.29	182.50
省 级	Provincial Level	15.86	21.61	25.26	28.49	35.50	42.26
地 级	Prefectural Level	20.34	21.73	21.65	25.36	29.50	36.80
县 级	County level	25.54	31.69	37.30	40.65	48.95	64.77
乡镇级	Township Level	23.49	24.72	24.07	30.06	35.34	38.67
财政一般预算支出	Financial Expenditure	201.57	275.20	316.67	332.35	418.42	520.73
金融（亿元）	Finance(100 million yuan)						
全部金融机构存款余额	Total Savings Deposit Balance	1106.64	1341.11	1553.00	1898.62	2322.27	2777.54
全部金融机构贷款余额	Total Loan Balance	1064.82	1212.23	1403.92	1714.04	2020.04	2303.93
城乡居民储蓄存款余额	Resident Savings Deposit Balance	539.49	641.67	759.05	912.84	1094.55	1350.90
教育、科技、文化	**Education,Science and Technology**						
专任教师数（万人）	Full-time Teachers(10000 persons)						
普通高等学校	Regular Institutions of Higher Education	0.72	0.90	1.11	1.18	1.38	1.44
普通中学	Regular Secondary Schools	8.12	8.81	9.76	10.73	11.56	12.27
小 学	Primary Schools	17.48	17.32	17.79	17.94	18.08	18.37

1-3续表5(continued)

指 标	Item	2000	2001	2002	2003	2004	2005
在校学生数（万人）	Students Enrollment(10000 persons)						
研究生(人)	Postgraduates(person)	1002	1418	1973	2966	4457	6168
普通高等学校	Regular Institutions of Higher Education	7.98	10.82	12.27	14.94	17.99	20.68
普通中学	Regular Secondary Schools	157.20	184.60	212.81	235.30	249.34	254.96
小学	Primary Schools	500.21	490.17	484.28	476.87	479.41	473.76
学龄儿童入学率（%）	Enrollment Rate of School-ageChildren (%)	98.50	98.20	98.20	98.20	97.80	98.30
国家财政用于教育支出(亿元)	Local Goverment Expenditure on Education (100 million yuan)	34.74	49.35	59.32	64.38	81.45	102.00
研究与发展（R&D）支出	Expenditure on R&D	4.18	5.35	6.07	7.89	8.61	10.98
科技活动经费支出总额	Expenditure on S&T Activities	10.87	13.31	15.30	15.48	21.80	24.73
文化	Culture						
图书出版量（万册）	Number of Books Published(10000 copies)	10288	12767	15030	12364	8890	9993
杂志出版量（万份）	Number of Magazines Issued (10000 copies)	994	1210	1339	1039	1281	1349
报纸出版量（亿份）	Number of Newspapers Issued (100 million copies)	2.89	3.17	3.15	3.41	3.37	3.52
家庭、生活	**Household、Livehood**						
家庭	Household						
家庭总户数（万户）	Total Family Households (10000 households)	1004.20	1061.26	1048.44	1057.28	1069.51	1139.46
城镇居民平均每户人口(人)	Average Persons Per Urban Household (person)	3.11	3.12	3.16	3.11	3.05	3.06
农村居民平均每户人口(人)	Average Persons Per Rural Household (person)	4.52	4.47	4.45	4.42	4.41	4.40
婚姻	Marital						
准予登记结婚（万对）	Marriage Registration Permitted (10000 households)	28.02	26.81	24.60	23.43	22.36	21.13
离婚数（万人）	Divorce(10000 persons)	6.72	5.63	4.68	5.71	8.08	7.63
居住	Residence						
城镇居民人均居住面积（平方米）	Per Capita Net Floor Space of Urban Residents(sq.m)	17.60	18.40	25.47	25.20	25.50	26.40
农村居民人均居住面积（平方米)	Per Capita Net Floor Space of Rural Residents(sq.m)	19.75	20.43	21.14	21.62	22.05	23.50
人均生活水平（元）	**Per Capita Standard of Living(yuan)**						
人均生产总值	Per Capita Gross Domestic Product	2759	3000	3257	3701	4317	5052
人均地方财政收入	Per Capita Local Financial Revenue	228.32	264.09	283.61	323.24	384.11	465.87
城镇居民人均可支配收入	Per Capita Annual Disposable Income of Urban Households	5121.21	5451.91	5944.02	6568.91	7322.04	8147.13
城镇居民人均消费性支出	Per Capita Annual Living Expenditures for Consumption of Urban Households	4278.28	4492.25	4598.30	4947.62	5494.43	6156.27
农村居民人均纯收入	Annual Per Capita Net Income of Rural Residents	1374.16	1411.70	1489.91	1564.66	1721.55	1876.96
农村居民人均生活消费支出	Annual Per Capita Expenditure for Living Cost of Rural Residents	1096.59	1098.40	1137.56	1185.17	1296.34	1552.39

1-3续表6(continued)

指　标	Item	2000	2001	2002	2003	2004	2005
城乡居民人均储蓄	Per Capita Urban and Rural Resident Savings	1445	1699	2082	2359	2816	3448
工资	**Wages and Welfare**						
职工工资总额（亿元）	Total Wages of Staff and Workers (100 million yuan)	144.56	169.66	184.34	209.33	236.60	284.16
职工平均货币工资(元)	Average Wage of Staff and Workers(yuan)	7468	8991	9810	11037	12431	14344
环境	**Environment**						
环保投入资金（亿元）	Environment Protection Investment (100 million yuan)	10.98	14.74	27.14	30.70	32.84	33.26
#老工业污染源治理资金	#Old Industry Pollute Fountain Treatment	2.37	1.63	2.13	2.63	4.56	7.79
城市环境基础设施建设	Urban Environment Infrastructure Investment	4.11	8.01	19.93	21.80	22.13	18.01
环境污染事故（次）	Accident of Entironment Pollution(unit)	54	114	64	32	43	28
污染事故直接经济损失(万元)	Direct Economy Losing for Pollute Accident(10000 yuan)	39.83	151.80	143.30	43.30	38.20	57.90
卫生	**Health Care**						
卫生机构数（个）	Total Number of Health Care Institutions (unit)	8992	8791	7027	6499	6664	6571
#医院、卫生院	Hospitals	1878	1872	1857	1866	1850	1843
卫生机构床位数（万张）	Number of Beds(10000 beds)	5.80	5.91	5.99	5.93	6.13	6.18
卫生技术人员（万人）	Number of Medical Technical Personnels (10000 persons)	8.54	8.61	7.97	7.76	7.67	7.78
#执业医师	Doctor	4.57	4.64	3.15	3.69	3.69	3.55
市政建设	**City Construction**						
城市固定资产投资完成额(亿元)	Investment of Urban Basal Establishment (100 million yuan)		42.70	49.30	45.62	50.80	37.53
自来水供应总量(万立方米)	Volume of Tap Water Supply(10000 cu.m)		58386	58172	57314	65983	63705
排水管道长度（公里）	Length of Sewer Pipelines(km)		2425.86	2600.96	2902.00	4204.54	5204.51
出售水量（万立方米）	Water Volume Sold (10000 cu.m)		31827	35221	35720	35047	34511
煤气供应量(万立方米)	Volume of Coal Gas Supply(10000 cu.m)		9143	10871	14411	16929	19209
出租汽车总数（万辆）	Taxis(10000 units)		0.87	0.92	1.10	1.13	1.23
运营公交汽车数(标台)	Total Number of Operating Public Buses (unit)		4415	4376	4797	4722	4858
城市道路长度（公里）	Length of Paved Roads(km)		2716	2772	2923	3268	3518
园林绿地面积（公顷）	Areas of Green Land(hectare)		12728	28025	29336	29810	31160
建成区绿化覆盖率(%)	Goverage Rate of Urban Green Areas(%)		16.61	16.29	17.88	19.10	20.03
火灾、交通事故	**Basic Statistics on Fires and Traffic Accidents**						
火灾发生数（起）	Number of Fires(case)	667	720	785	673	2099	778
损失折款（万元）	Losses Converted into Cash(10000 yuan)	2786.47	1977.00	2099.65	1836.14	1429.33	1671.21
交通事故发生数（起）	Number of Traffic Accidents(case)	2593	4064	4258	5002	3395	3315
损失折款（万元）	Losses Converted into Cash(10000 yuan)	1899.62	2067.81	2420.65	2810.00	2353.00	2507.01

1-4 “十五”时期社会经济主要指标指数

Indices of Major Social and Economic Indicators of each year in “Tenth-Five-year Plan” Period

单位：%

指　标	Item	2005年比下列各年增长 Increase Rate in 2005 over 2000 or 2004		九五”时期年平均增长 Annual Average Increase Rate in “Ninth Five-year Plan” Period	“十五”时期年平均增长 Annual Average Increase Rate in “Tenth Five-year Plan” Period
		2000年	2004年		
人口	**Population**				
年末总人口	Total Population at the Year-end	4.7	0.7	1.4	0.9
就业	**Employment**				
年末从业人员	Year-end Employees	19.0	1.6	0.6	3.5
#职工人数	Staff and Workers	4.2	4.9	-0.7	0.8
宏观经济	**Macro Economy**				
生产总值	Gross Domestic Product	62.3	11.6	8.7	10.2
第一产业	Primary Industry	19.8	5.2	3.3	3.7
第二产业	Secondary Industry	80.7	12.7	11.5	12.5
#工业	Industry	81.5	14.1	10.7	12.7
第三产业	Tertiary Industry	74.4	13.9	10.0	11.8
人均生产总值	Per Capita GDP	54.8	10.8	7.2	9.1
生产总值中	In GDP				
#最终消费	Final Consumption	64.1	18.3	7.4	10.4
居民消费	Resident Consumption	51.1	15.7	5.8	8.6
政府消费	Government Consumption	123.3	27.0	13.1	17.4
资本形成总额	Gross Capital Formation	91.8	12.9	8.3	13.9
固定资本形成	Gross Fixed Capital Formation	100.0	12.7	18.1	14.9
存货增加	Increase in Inventory	-22.8	21.5		-5.0
固定资产投资	**Investment in Fixed Assets**				
全社会固定资产投资	Total Investment in Fixed Assets	152.2	16.8	18.7	22.0
农业	**Agriculture**				
农林牧渔业增加值	Value-Added of FFAF	19.8	5.2	3.3	3.7
工业	**Industry**				
全部工业增加值	Total Industrial Value-added	81.5	14.1	10.7	12.7
建筑业	**Construction Enterprise**				
建筑业增加值	Value-added of Construction	76.8	6.1	18.9	12.1

1-4续表1(continued)

单位：%

指　标	Item	2005年比下列各年增长 Increase Rate in 2005 over 2000 or 2004		九五"时期年平均增长 Annual Average Increase Rate in "Ninth Five-year Plan"Period	"十五"时期年平均增长 Annual Average Increase Rate in "Tenth Five-year Plan" Period
		2000年	2004年		
交通、邮电通信业	**Transportation,Post and Telecommunications**				
旅客周转量	Passenger-Kilometers	31.1	12.3	4.9	5.6
货物周转量	Freight Ton-Kilometers	60.0	5.9	8.6	9.9
邮电业务总量	Business Volume of Post and Telecommunications Service	3.3倍	32.8	45.3	33.6
年末电话用户	Number of Telephones Subscribers at the Year-end	2.0倍	20.4	42.8	24.3
移动电话用户	Number of Mobile Telephones Subscribers	5.5倍	15.8		45.4
国际互联网用户	Number of Subscribers of Internet Service	5.1倍	11.2		43.4
电话交换机容量	Capacity of Telephone Exchanges	2.6倍	19.2	28.9	28.9
国内商业	**Domestic Trade**				
社会消费品零售总额	Total Retail Sales of Consumer Goods	70.7	13.4	12.4	11.3
对外贸易	**Foreign Trade**				
进出口总额	Total Value of Imports and Exports	1.1倍	-7.3	-0.7	16.3
出口	Total Exports	1.0倍	-0.9	-0.5	15.4
实际吸收外资	Amount of Foreign Capital Actually Utilized	0.1	40.5	15.8	…
旅　游	**Tourism**				
入境旅游人数	Number of International Tourists Inbound	50.2	19.6	2.5	8.5
#外国人	Foreigners	30.1	21.4	6.1	5.4
港澳同胞	Compatriots from Hong Kong,Macao and Taiwan	47.5	16.9	14.5	8.1
国内旅游人数	Domestic Tourists	56.5	25.0	2.5	9.4
国际旅游收入	International Earnings from Tourism	66.5	26.4	16.0	10.7
财　政	**Government Finance**				
财政总收入	Total Financial Revenue	1.4倍	23.5	11.9	19.1
财政一般预算收入	Local Financial Revenue	1.1倍	22.2	17.0	16.4
省　级	Provincial Level	1.7倍	19.0	16.9	21.7
地　级	Prefectural Level	80.9	24.7	25.4	12.6
县　级	County level	1.5倍	32.3	16.1	20.5
乡　级	Township Level	64.6	9.4	12.8	10.5
财政支出	Financial Expenditure	1.6倍	24.5	18.5	20.9
金　融	**Finance**				
全部金融机构存款余额	Total Savings Deposit Balance	1.5倍	19.6	18.3	20.2
全部金融机构贷款余额	Total Loan Balance	1.2倍	14.1	15.7	16.7
城乡居民储蓄存款余额	Urban and Rural Resident Savings Deposit Balance	1.5倍	23.4	16.9	20.2

1-4续表2(continued)　　　　单位：%

指　标	Item	2005年比下列各年增长 Increase Rate in 2005 over 2000 or 2004		九五”时期年平均增长 Annual Average Increase Rate in “Ninth Five-year Plan” Period	“十五”时期年平均增长 Annual Average Increase Rate in “Tenth Five-year Plan” Period
		2000年	2004年		
教 育	**Education**				
专任教师数	Full-time Teachers				
普通高等学校	Institutions of Higher Education	98.2	4.1	5.2	14.7
普通中学	Secondary Schools	51.2	6.1	4.8	8.6
小　学	Primary Schools	5.1	1.6	0.7	1.0
在校学生数	Students Enrollment				
高等学校	Institutions of Higher Education	1.6倍	15.0	16.8	21
普通中学	Secondary Schools	62.2	2.3	7.7	10.2
小　学	Primary Schools	-5.3	-1.2	1.0	-1.1
文 化	**Culture**				
图书出版量	Number of Books Pubilshed	-2.9	12.4	-2.6	-0.6
杂志出版量	Number of Magazines Issued	35.7	5.3	11.5	6.3
报纸出版量	Number of Newspapers Issued	21.8	4.4	8.3	4.0
人均生活水平	**Per Capita Standard of Living**				
城镇居民人均可支配收入	Per Capita Annual Disposable Income of Urban Households	48.8	10.6	3.0	8.3
城镇居民人均消费性支出	Per Capita Annual Living Expenditures for Consumption of Urban Households	43.9	12.0	5.6	7.5
农村居民人均纯收入	Annual Per Capita Net Income of Rural Residents	26.3	5.2	4.5	4.8
农村居民人均生活消费支出	Annual Per Capita Expenditure for Living Cost of Rural Residents	41.6	19.8	3.3	7.2
城乡居民人均储蓄	Per Capita Urban and Rural Resident Savings	1.4倍	22.4	15.3	19.0
工 资	**Wages**				
职工工资总额	Total Wages of Staff and Workers	96.6	20.1	7.6	14.5
职工平均货币工资	Average Wage of Staff and Workers	92.1	15.4	10.8	13.9
卫 生	**Health Care**				
医院、卫生院数	Number of Hospitals	-26.9	-1.4	2.1	-6.0
卫生机构床位数	Number of Beds	6.6	0.8	0.2	1.3
执业医生数	Number of Doctors	-22.3	-3.8	2.6	-4.9
环 境	**Environment**				
环境保护投入资金	Environment Protection Investment	2.0倍	1.3	40.3	24.8

注：表中“城镇居民人均可支配收入”、“农村居民人均纯收入”指数已剔除价格因素。

Note:The indices of “Per Capita Annual Disposable Income of Urban Households” and “Annual Per Capita Net Income of Rural Residents” getrid of the price factor.

1-5 “十五”时期各年社会经济主要指标结构

Structure of Major Social and Economic Indicators of each year in “Tenth-Five-year Plan” Period

单位：%

指 标	Item	2000	2001	2002	2003	2004	2005
人口与就业	**Population & Employment**						
人口	Population						
城镇、乡村结构	Grouped by Urban and Rural Area						
城 镇	Urban Population	23.9	24.0	24.3	24.8	26.3	26.9
乡 村	Rural Population	76.1	76.0	75.7	75.2	73.7	73.1
性别结构	Grouped by Sex						
男	Male	52.4	52.0	51.9	51.9	51.8	51.5
女	Female	47.6	48.0	48.1	48.1	48.2	48.5
就业	Employment						
从业人员产业结构	Grouped by Three Industries						
第一产业	Primary Industry	69.9	81.8	80.6	77.9	76.5	75.2
第二产业	Secondary Industry	11.9	6.5	5.2	5.6	5.7	6.5
第三产业	Tertiary Industry	18.2	11.7	14.2	16.5	17.8	18.3
宏观经济	**Macro Economy**						
生产总值产业结构	In GDP						
第一产业	Primary Industry	26.3	24.2	22.6	21.0	20.0	18.3
第二产业	Secondary Industry	38.0	38.3	38.8	39.9	40.6	41.8
第三产业	Tertiary Industry	35.7	37.5	38.6	39.1	39.4	39.9
#公有经济	Public-Owned					72.5	72.2
非公有经济	Non-state-owned					27.5	27.8
投资	**Investment in Fixed Assets**						
全社会固定资产投资结构	Structure of Total Investment in Fixed Assets						
城镇	Urban	82.5	86.3	87.8	89.4	90.2	90.3
农村	Rural	17.5	13.7	12.2	10.6	9.8	9.7
#基本建设	Capital Construction	37.7	44.7	49.4	51.0	55.0	52.1
更新改造	Innovation	23.2	22.2	19.1	18.6	17.5	17.8
房地产开发	Real Estate Development	11.6	12.6	13.1	13.9	14.0	15.2
其他投资	Other Investments	27.4	20.5	18.3	16.4	13.5	14.9
#国有经济	State-owned	64.6	67.0	67.0	60.6	58.4	53.0
非国有经济	Non-State-owned	35.4	33.0	33.0	39.4	41.6	47.0
#公有经济	Public-Owned	71.7	71.7	71.2	70.0	65.8	56.9
非公有经济	Non-State-owned	28.3	28.3	28.8	30.0	34.2	43.1

1-5续表1(continued) 单位：%

指 标	Item	2000	2001	2002	2003	2004	2005
资金来源结构	Grouped by Source of Funds						
国家预算内资金	State Budgetary Appropriation	8.8	6.6	7.9	6.1	4.6	4.1
国内贷款	Domestic Loans	26.0	28.5	30.0	24.7	26.3	27.0
吸收外资	Foreign Investment	1.9	1.2	0.8	1.0	1.0	0.8
自筹资金	Self-raising Funds	44.5	46.3	45.4	52.3	48.3	52.0
其他投资	Others	18.7	17.5	15.9	15.9	19.8	16.0
农业	**Agriculture**						
农林牧渔业增加值结构	Structure of Value-added of FFAF						
#农 业	Farming	69.1	68.4	66.0	59.7	61.0	59.2
林 业	Forestry	5.2	4.3	4.4	5.8	4.8	4.3
牧 业	Animal Husbandry	22.7	26.0	28.3	28.9	31.2	33.1
渔 业	Fishery	1.2	1.3	1.3	1.3	1.3	1.7
农林牧渔服务业	FFAF Seryices				4.3	1.7	1.7
工业	**Industry**						
工业增加值结构	Structure of Gross Industrial Value-added						
规模以上工业企业	Industrial Enterprises above Designated Size	66.0	65.6	68.6	73.2	82.6	82.0
规模以下工业企业	Industrial Enterprises under Designated Size	34.0	34.4	31.4	26.8	17.4	18.0
#国有经济	State-owned	89.8	83.4	79.9	81.7	68.3	66.4
非国有经济	Non-state-owned	10.2	16.6	20.1	18.3	24.9	33.6
#公有经济	Public-owned	81.0	79.9	80.3	74.0	71.5	71.8
非公有经济	Non-public-owned	19.0	20.1	19.7	26.0	28.5	28.2
#轻工业	Light Industry	37.9	37.1	32.5	33.7	31.0	30.2
重工业	Heavy Industry	62.1	62.9	67.5	66.3	69.0	69.8
能源	**Energy**						
能源生产总量结构	Structure of Total Energy Production						
原煤	Coal	78.8	76.5	83.4	88.2	89.5	89.6
天然气	Natural Gas	0.2	0.2	0.1	0.1		
电力	Hydro-power	21.0	23.2	16.5	11.7	10.6	10.4
能源消费总量结构	Structure of Total Energy Consumption						
原煤	Coal	48.1	44.0	47.2	46.8	52.7	49.6
天然气	Natural Gas	1.8	1.8	1.6	1.3	1.1	1.2
电力	Hydro-power	35.7	39.9	36.4	37.7	32.3	35.3
建筑业	**Construction**						
建筑业总产值结构	Structure of Gross Output Value of Construction						
#国有经济	State-owned	70.6	73.5	73.8	77.3	77.0	76.6
非国有经济	Non-state-owned	29.4	26.5	26.2	22.7	23.0	23.4
#公有经济	Public-owned	93.4	90.9	86.5	86.1	84.1	82.6
非公有经济	Non-public-owned	6.6	9.1	13.5	13.9	15.9	17.4
交通运输业	**Transportation**						
货运量结构	Structure of Freight Traffic						
铁 路	Railways	22.9	23.7	25.0	27.3	28.3	28.3

1-5续表2(continued)　　　　单位：%

指　标	Item	2000	2001	2002	2003	2004	2005
公　路	Highways	74.8	74.1	72.9	70.7	69.7	69.3
水　运	Waterways	2.3	2.2	2.1	2.0	2.0	2.4
客运量结构	Structure of Passenger Traffic						
铁　路	Railways	4.2	3.7	3.5	3.3	3.2	3.4
公　路	Highways	94.9	95.4	95.5	95.7	95.5	95.3
水　运	Waterways	0.9	0.9	1.0	1.1	1.3	1.3
国内商业	**Domestic Trade**						
社会消费品零售总额结构	Structure of Retail Sales of Consumer Goods						
城　镇	Urban	57.6	58.4	58.8	59.3	59.5	59.8
乡　村	Rural	42.4	41.6	41.2	40.7	40.5	40.2
对外贸易	**Foreign Trade**						
出　口	Total Exports	63.8	64.9	64.0	59.7	57.3	61.2
进　口	Total Imports	36.2	35.1	36.2	40.2	42.7	38.8
国际旅游	**International Tourism**						
来黔涉外旅游人数结构	Structure of Tourists Visiting Guizhou						
#外国人	Foreigners	38.7	38.2	37.0	31.2	33.0	33.5
港澳台同胞	Compatriots from Hong Kong, Macao and Taiwan	28.8	29.0	28.6	36.8	29.0	28.3
财政、税收	**Government Finance and Fas**						
地方财政收入结构	Structure of Local Financial Revenue						
省　级	Provincial Level	18.6	21.7	23.3	22.9	23.8	23.2
地　级	Prefectural Level	23.9	21.8	20.0	20.4	19.8	20.2
县　级	County level	30.0	31.8	34.4	32.6	32.8	35.5
乡　级	Township Level	27.6	24.8	22.2	24.1	23.7	21.2
财政支出结构	Structure of Financial Expenditure						
#基本建设支出	Capital Construction	12.3	15.7	11.5	9.5	9.1	7.9
企业挖潜改造资金	Enterprises Innovation Funds	3.2	3.5	8.0	9.8	9.2	9.6
科技三项费用	Science and Tethnology Promotion Funds	0.7	0.5	0.9	0.9	0.8	0.8
城市维护费	Urban Maintenance Expense	3.2	2.9	2.7	2.6	2.5	2.5
税收收入	Taxes						
#国有经济	State-owned	52.9	47.6	49.8	45.9	43.3	38.3
非国有经济	Non-state-owned	47.1	52.4	50.2	54.1	56.7	61.7
#公有经济	Public-owned	60.1	54.6	55.2	50.3	46.7	40.9
非公有经济	Non-public-owned	39.9	45.4	44.8	49.7	53.3	59.1
金　融	**Finance**						
金融机构存款结构	Structure of Total Savings Deposit Balance						
#企业存款	Enterprise Deposit	38.8	38.0	35.2	34.5	36.2	32.3
财政存款	Treasury Deposit	3.6	3.6	2.7	2.4	2.6	2.2
储蓄存款	Urban and Rural Savings Deposit	48.8	47.8	48.9	48.1	47.1	48.6
农业存款	Agricultural Deposit	2.1	2.1	2.2	2.2	2.6	3.6
金融机构贷款结构	Structure of Total Loan Balance						
#短期贷款	Short-Term Loan	57.5	48.5	46.9	37.9	35.1	33.7
中长期贷款	Middle-Term & Long-Term Loan	36.8	45.2	46.7	51.5	55.9	63.6

1-5续表3(continued)　　　　单位：%

指　标	Item	2000	2001	2002	2003	2004	2005
科 技	**Science and Tethnology**						
科技经费筹集额结构	Structure of Funding for S&T Activities						
#政府资金	Government Funds	28.9	28.0	32.1	27.4	22.4	22.3
企业资金	Self-raised Funds by Enterprises	55.4	54.9	56.1	57.3	65.2	65.5
事业单位资金	Self-raised Funds by Institution	7.9	5.2	3.3	4.8	4.0	3.2
金融机构贷款	Loans From Finance Institutions	5.6	5.3	4.2	6.4	5.1	6.6
科技活动经费支出结构	Internal Expenditures on S&T Activities						
#劳务费	Service Fees	27.4	84.3	29.6	29.7	26.4	20.9
固定资产购建	Purchases or Coustruction of Fixed Assets	29.3	26.6	29.7	19.7	30.6	33.3
#研究与发展费经费支出	Expenditure on R&D	38.4	40.2	39.7	50.9	39.5	44.4
教 育	**Education**						
在校学生结构	Structure of Students Enrollment						
#大学生	Students Enrollment of Higher Education	1.2	1.6	1.7	2.1	2.4	2.8
中学生	Students Enrollment of Secondary Schools	23.6	26.9	30.0	32.4	33.4	34.0
小学生	Students Enrollment of Primary Schools	75.2	71.5	68.3	65.6	64.2	63.2
专任教师结构	Structure of Full-time Teachers						
#普通高等学校	Institutions of Higher Education	2.7	3.3	3.9	4.0	4.4	4.5
普通中学	Secondary Schools	30.9	32.6	34.1	35.9	37.3	38.2
小　学	Primary Schools	66.4	64.1	62.1	60.1	58.3	57.3
人民生活	**People's Livelihood**						
城市居民消费结构	Consumption Structure of Urban Residents						
食品类	Food	43.2	40.8	38.9	39.8	41.1	39.9
衣着类	Clothing	10.6	11.3	10.5	10.6	10.7	11.4
居　住	Residence	9.9	8.8	10.4	8.5	8.5	9.5
家庭设备用品及服务	Household Facilities,Articles and Services	7.4	7.8	6.1	5.8	5.2	5.5
医疗保健	Medicines and Medical Services	5.5	6.0	5.8	5.9	5.5	6.5
交通和通信	Transport and Communications	8.6	9.3	10.0	11.3	10.9	10.2
娱乐教育服务	Recreation,Education and Cultural Articles and Services	11.5	13.0	14.7	14.4	14.4	13.2
农村居民消费结构	Consumption Structure of Rural Residents						
食品类	Food	62.7	60.0	58.1	56.9	58.2	52.8
衣着类	Clothing	4.8	4.6	4.8	4.6	4.3	5.1
居　住	Residence	12.7	13.4	13.2	14.4	12.8	15.2
家庭设备、用品及服务	Household Facilities,Articles and Services	3.5	4.1	4.3	3.5	3.2	4.0
医疗保健	Medicines and Medical Services	2.5	2.8	2.8	3.9	3.6	4.6
交通和通信	Transport and Communications	2.5	3.2	4.3	4.2	5.4	6.4
文教、娱乐、用品及服务	Recreation,Education and Cultural Articles and Services	8.9	9.0	9.5	10.8	10.8	10.4
卫 生	**Health Care**						
卫生机构结构	Structure of Various Health Care Institutions						
#医院、卫生院	Hospital	20.9	21.3	26.4	28.7	27.8	28.0
卫生机构床位结构	Structure of Beds of Health Care Institutions						
#医院、卫生院	Hospital	95.0	94.6	96.2	95.1	94.8	94.5
卫生技术人员结构	Structure of Medical Technical Personnels						
#执业医生	Doctors	53.5	53.9	39.5	47.6	48.1	45.6
环 境	**Environment**						
环境保护投入资金结构	Structure of Environment Protection Investment						
#老工业污染源治理资金	Old Industry Pollute Fountain Treatment	21.6	11.1	7.8	8.6	13.9	23.4
城市环境基础设施建设	Urban Environment Infrastructure Investment	37.4	54.3	73.4	71.0	67.4	54.1

1-6 “十五”时期各年社会经济主要指标比例、效益

Major Indicators on Proportions and Efficiency in Economic Social Development of each year in “Tenth-Five-year Plan” Period

指 标	Item	2000	2001	2002	2003	2004	2005
人口与就业	**Population and Employment**						
人 口	Population						
人口出生率(‰)	Birth Rate(‰)	20.59	18.56	17.96	15.91	15.08	14.59
人口死亡率(‰)	Death Rate(‰)	7.53	7.23	7.21	6.87	6.35	7.21
人口自然增长率(‰)	Natural Growth Rate(‰)	13.06	11.33	10.75	9.04	8.73	7.38
就 业	Employment						
就业者负担人口(城镇)	Dependency Ratio(Urban)	1.92	1.88	2.13	2.03	2.03	2.12
城镇登记失业率(%)	Unemployment Rate in Urban Areas(%)	3.8	4.0	4.1	4.0	4.1	4.2
三次产业从业人员比例(以第一产业为100)	Industrial Structure (primary industry=100)						
第一产业	Primary Industry	100	100	100	100	100	100
第二产业	Secondary Industry	16.99	7.91	6.41	7.21	7.45	8.66
第三产业	Tertiary Industry	18.32	14.29	17.60	21.14	23.27	24.28
宏观经济	**Macro Economy**						
国民经济核算	National Accounting						
三次产业增加值比例	Industrial Structure						
(以第一产业为100)	(primary industry=100)						
第一产业	Primary Industry	100	100	100	100	100	100
第二产业	Secondary Industry	144.25	157.98	171.45	190.62	203.74	228.04
第三产业	Tertiary Industry	135.52	155.00	170.89	186.91	197.85	217.92
全社会劳动生产率(元/人)	Overall Labor Productivity (yuan/person)	5519	5480	5904	6650	7675	8915
第一产业	Primary Industry	2078	1621	1655	1787	2000	2171
第二产业	Secondary Industry	17638	32381	44261	47255	54695	57175
第三产业	Tertiary Industry	15367	17591	16073	15801	17008	19484
人均生产总值	Per Capita Gross Regional Product (yuan/person)	2759	3000	3257	3701	4317	5052
固定资产投资	Investment in Fixed Assets						
全社会固定资产投资相当于生产总值比例(%)	Proportion of Investmetn in Fixed Assets to GDP(%)	39.1	47.1	50.9	52.9	51.8	51.3
全社会房屋建筑面积竣工率(%)	Rate of Total Floor Space of Buildings Completed (%)	61.6	57.6	61.4	59.0	54.5	53.1

1-6续表1(continued)

指　标	Item	2000	2001	2002	2003	2004	2005
能　源	**Energy**						
能源生产弹性系数	Elasticity Ratio of Energy Production	0.93		2.53	4.69	2.05	0.75
能源消费弹性系数	Elasticity Ratio of Energy Consumption	0.33	0.42	0.08	2.36	0.77	0.59
每万元生产总值耗的能源(吨标准煤)	10000yuan GDP(ton of SCE)	4.31	4.09	3.77	4.08	3.59	3.25
产 业	**Industries**						
农 业	Agriculture						
每亩耕地生产的农业增加值(元)	Agricultural Valueadded Per Mu of Cultivated Land(yuan)	981	998	1059	1138	1273	1370
农业从业者人均耕地面积（亩）	Per Capita Area of Cultivated Land for Agricultural Laborer(mu)	1.34	1.34	1.31	1.32	1.36	1.39
每亩耕地农业机械总动力(千瓦)	Total Power of Agricultural Machinery Per Mu of Cultivated Land(kw)	0.22	0.24	0.26	0.29	0.30	0.38
每亩耕地用电量(千瓦小时)	Electric Power Consumption Per Mu of Cultivated Land(kwh)	51.29	50.65	54.00	61.02	115.25	114.90
每亩耕地化肥施用 量(公斤)	Chemical Fertilizer Consumption Per Mu of Cultivated Land(kg)	25.78	25.45	27.72	28.53	28.27	29.43
农业从业者人均主要农产品产量(公斤)	Output of Farm Products Per Agricultural Laborer(kg)						
粮 食	Grain	846	804	764	835	892	909
油 料	Oil-bearing Crops	54.18	52.12	53.53	54.69	64.19	66.94
肉 类	Meat	90.41	96.25	107.11	118.71	132.76	147.47
每亩播种面积农产品产量(公斤)	Output of Farm Crops Per Mu of Sowning Area(kg)						
粮 食	Grain	246	235	224	244	253	250
油 料	Oil-bearing Crops	97	95	96	96	104	102
工 业（规模以上）	Industry(above Designated Size)						
资本保值增值率（%）	Ratio of Per-tax Profits to Capital(%)	114.6	131.9	109.4	112.5	114.6	113.0
总资产贡献率（%）	Ratio of Total Assets to Industrial Output Value(%)	7.7	7.1	6.9	8.8	10.7	10.9
成本费用利润率（%）	Ratio of Profits to Industrial Cost(%)	2.3	2.9	3.1	4.0	5.9	5.5
全员劳动生产率(元/人,按增加值计算)	Overall Labor Productivity(yuan/person),(account by Value-added)	31751	35649	41604	41991	65629	89252
建筑业	Construction						
技术装备率（元/人）	Value of Machinery Per Laborer (yuan/person)	5270	5354	7952	7754	7979	7471
产值利税率(%)	Ratio of Per-tax Profits to Gross Output Value(%)	4.3	4.7	5.3	5.4	5.1	4.7
全员劳动生产率(元/人按增加值计算)	Overall Labor Producti vity(yuan/person)(account by Value-added)	11243	13013	14730	16548	20000	
交 通	**Transportation**						
铁路网密度(公里/万平方公里)	Railway Density(km/10000 sq.km)	93.19	93.30	107.43	107.83	107.32	112.71

1-6续表2(continued)

指　标	Item	2000	2001	2002	2003	2004	2005
公路网密度(公里/万平方公里)	Highway Density(km/10000 sq.km)	1966.1	1964.6	2509.6	2571.2	2617.9	2661.4
铁路货运密度(万吨公里/公里)	Railway Freight Traffic Density (10000 ton km/km)	1841.0	2033.5	1957.2	2201.6	2434.7	2366.1
公路货运密度(万吨公里/公里)	Highway Freight Traffic Density (10000 ton km/km)	19.01	20.33	16.79	16.91	18.27	20.08
每万人拥有公共车辆(标台)	Per 10000 Persons Possession of Buses (unit)		8.50	8.29	6.48	5.81	6.05
电话普及率(部/百人)	Popularization Rate of Telephone(include mobile telephone)(sets/100 persons)	6.36	11.11	13.90	17.40	21.40	25.00
国内商业	**Domestic Trade**						
社会消费品零售总额相当于国内生产总值比例(%)	Retail Sales of Consumer Goods as Percentage to GDP(%)	34.5	34.5	34.6	33.3	31.9	30.7
人均社会消费品零售额(元)	Ratail Sales of Consumer Goods Per Capita (yuan)	952.6	1035.6	1127.9	1231.5	1377.3	1549.3
对外贸易	Foreign Trade						
#出口总额相当于生产总值比例(%)	Total Value of Exports as Percentage to GDP(%)	5.3	4.7	4.6	5.7	7.5	5.7
每一来黔境外旅游者消费支出(美元/人天)	Daily Expenditure of Per Tourists Visiting Guizhou(USD)	331.70	161.35	160.19	160.19	159.17	160.09
财政	Government Finance						
财政总收入相当于生产总值比例(%)	Total Financial Revenue as Percentage to GDP(%)	14.9	15.6	16.3	16.6	17.7	18.5
地方财政收入相当于财政总收入比例(%)	Local Financial Revenue as Percentage to Total Financial Revenue(%)	55.7	56.4	53.3	52.6	50.4	49.8
金融保险	Finance and Insurance						
金融机构存款相当于生产总值比例(%)	Bank Deposits as Percentage to GDP(%)	107.4	118.3	124.9	133.1	138.4	140.3
金融机构贷款相当于生产总值比例(%)	Bank Loans as Percentage to GDP(%)	103.4	107.0	112.9	120.2	120.4	116.4
金融机构现金支出相当于现金收入比 例(%)	Proportion of Cash Outlay to Cash Receipt in State Banking System(%)	101.8	101.2	101.6	101.0	100.8	100.9
教育、科技、文化	**Education,Science & Technology and Culture**						
教育	Education						
学龄儿童入学率(%)	Enrollment Rate of School-age Children(%)	98.5	98.2	98.2	98.2	97.8	98.3
初中阶段毛入学率(%)	Enrollment Rate of Primary School Graduates Entering into Junior Secondary Schools(%)	73.6	82.0	87.2	94.2	98.7	98.7
高中阶段毛入学率(%)	Enrollment Rate of Juniorsecondary School Graduates Entering into Senior secondary Schools(%)	21.5	22.9	25.4	24.1	26.4	30.5
高等教育毛入学率(%)	Enrollment Rate of Senior secondary School Graduates Entering into Institution of Higher Learning(%)	5.9	7.3	9.0	10.0	10.0	11.0
教师负担学生系数(学生/教师)	Student-Teacher Ratio (student/teacher)						
大学生	Students Enrollment of Higher Education	11.08	12.02	11.05	12.66	13.04	14.36
中学生	Students Enrollment of Secondary Schools	19.36	20.95	21.80	21.93	21.57	20.78
小学生	Students Enrollment of Primary Schools	28.62	28.30	27.22	26.58	26.52	25.79

1-6续表3(continued)

指　标	Item	2000	2001	2002	2003	2004	2005
科技	Science and Technology						
R&D经费支出相当于生产总值比例(%)	R&D Expense as Percentage to GDP(%)	0.4	0.5	0.5	0.6	0.6	0.6
科技拨款相当于财政支出比例(%)	S&T Appropriate Fouds as Percentage to Financial Expenditure(%)	1.5	1.3	1.2	1.3	1.3	1.2
文化	Culture						
每百万人拥有艺术表演团体(个)	Number of Art Troupes Per Million Persons(unit)	0.75	0.74	0.73	0.70	0.66	0.66
每百万人拥有公共图书馆(个)	Number of Public Libraries Per Million Persons(unit)	2.38	2.38	2.36	2.33	2.31	2.31
家庭、生活、环境	**Family,Livelihood and Environment**						
婚姻	Marriages and Divorces						
结婚率（‰）	Marriage Rate(‰)	1.5	1.4	1.3	1.2	1.2	1.1
离婚率（‰）	Divorce Rate(‰)	1.8	1.5	1.2	1.5	2.1	2.3
生活	Livelihood						
城市与农村居民收入比例(以农民纯收入＝100)	Ratio of Annual Income of Urban Residents to Rural (rural resident=100)	1：3.73	1：3.86	1：3.99	1：4.20	1：4.25	1：4.34
福利	Welfare						
退休职工退休金、退职费相当于工资总额比例(%)	Expenditure for Retired Persons as Percentage to Total Wages(%)	28.27	28.89	32.98	31.86	32.43	27.66
离退休退职人数相当于在职人数比例(%)	Workers Who Have Retired or Resigned as Percentage to Employed Ones(%)	32.18	34.58	36.47	38.36	40.23	33.86
卫生	Health Care						
每万人拥有医生数（人）	Number of Doctors Per 10000 Persons(person)	12.2	12.3	11.3	11.2	12.2	9.1
每万人拥有医院床位数(张)	Number of Hospital Beds Per 10000 Persons(bed)	14.8	14.8	15.1	14.9	14.9	15.0
城市建设	City Construction						
人均公共绿地面积(平方米)	Per Capita Public Green Areas (sq.m)		3.02	4.06	4.49	4.53	5.32
自来水普及率(%)	Percentage of Households with Access to Tap Water(%)		48.0	74.6	77.6	84.8	88.4
燃气普及率(%)	Percentage of Households with Access to Tap Gas(%)		24.5	46.4	49.5	51.3	54.6
环境、灾害	Environment and Disaster						
环保投入占生产总值（%）	Environment Protection Investment as Percentage to GDP(%)	1.1	1.4	2.3	2.3	2.1	1.7
平均每起火灾损失（万元）	Average Loss of Per Fire (10000 yuan)	4.18	3.00	2.67	2.73	0.68	2.15
平均每起交通事故损失	Average Loss of Per Traffic Accident(10000 yuan)	0.73	0.51	0.57	0.56	0.69	0.76
平均每起环境污染事故接经济损失	Average Loss Converted into Cash Per Pollution Accident (10000 yuan)	0.74	1.33	2.24	1.35	0.89	2.07

1-7 贵州主要经济指标占全国比重

Percentage in the Country of Guizhou Main Social and Economic Indicators

指 标	Item	全 国 National Total		贵 州 Guizhou		贵州占全国比重（%） Percentage of the National Tot al(%)	
		2000	2005	2000	2005	2000	2005
土地面积(万平方公里)	**Area of Territory (10000 sq.km)**	960	960	17.62	17.62	1.84	1.84
人口（万人）	**Population (10000 persons)**						
年末总人口	Total Population at the Year-end	126743	130756	3755.72	3931.12	3.0	3.0
劳动就业	**Employment (10000 persons)**						
年底就业人员(万人)	Year-end Employees	72085.00	75825.00	1866.23	2220.00	2.6	2.9
#职工人数	Staff and Workers	14059.00	10942.00	193.97	202.02	1.4	1.8
职工平均工资	Average Wage of Staff and Workers(yuan)	9371	18405	7468	14344	79.7	77.9
国民核算	**National Accounting**						
生产总值（亿元）	Gross Domestic Product (100 million yuan)	99214.60	182320.60	1029.92	1979.06	1.0	1.1
第一产业	Primary Industry	14716.20	22718.40	271.20	362.49	1.8	1.6
第二产业	Secondary Industry	45555.90	86207.60	391.20	826.63	0.9	1.0
第三产业	Tertiary Industry	38942.50	73394.60	367.52	789.94	0.9	1.1
人均生产总值（元）	Per Capita Gross Regional Product(yuan/person)	7858	13985	2759	5052	35.1	36.1
固定资产投资	**Assets (100 million yuan)**						
全社会固定资产投资(亿元)	Total Investment in Fixed Assets	32917.70	88604.30	402.50	1015.28	1.2	1.1
财政	**Government Finance (100 million yuan)**						
财政一般预算收入	Local Financial Revenue	6406.06	15092.04	85.23	182.50	1.3	1.2
财政一般预算支出	Financial Expenditure	15886.50	33708.00	201.57	520.73	1.3	1.5
金融	**Finance**						
金融机构存款余额(亿元)	Total Savings Deposit Balance(100 million yuan)	123804.40	287169.50	1106.64	2777.54	0.9	1.0
金融机构贷款余额(亿元)	Total Loan Balance	99371.10	194690.40	1064.82	2303.93	1.1	1.2
物 价	**Price Indices**						
居民消费价格总指数（上年=100）	Consumer Price Index (preceding year=100)	100.4	101.8	99.5	101.0	-0.9（百分点）	-0.8（百分点）

1-7续表1(continued)

指　标	Item	全　国 National Total		贵　州 Guizhou		贵州占全国比重（%） Percentage of the National Total(%)	
		2000	2005	2000	2005	2000	2005
农 业	**Agriculture**						
粮食产量（万吨）	Output of Grain(10000 tons)	46218	48402	1161.30	1152.06	2.5	2.4
油料产量	Output of Oil-bearing Crops (10000 tons)	2954.80	3077.10	74.34	84.89	2.5	2.8
工 业	**Industry**						
原煤产量（万吨）	Output of Coal(10000 tons)	129900	219000	3677	10615	2.8	4.8
发电量（亿千瓦小时）	Output of Electricity (100 million kwh)	13556	24747	404.70	786.78	3.0	3.2
磷矿石产量（万吨）	Output of Phosphorite (10000 tons)			588.70	878.79		
卷 烟（万箱）	Output of Cigarettes(10000 cases)	3397.00	3877.80	187.35	208.21	5.5	5.4
能 源	**Energy**						
一次能源生产量(吨标准煤)	Total Production of Primary Energy(tons of SCE)	128978	206300	3875.92	8459.52	3.0	4.1
能源消费量	Consumption of Energy	138553	222468	2738.14	5718.83	2.0	2.6
每万元生产总值能耗（吨标准煤/万元）	Energy Consumption of Per 10000 yuan GDP(ton of SCE)		1.22	4.31	3.25		2.7倍
交通运输业	**Transportation**						
铁路营业里程（公里）	Length of Railways(km)	69000	75000	1642	1986	2.4	2.6
公路里程	Length of Highways in Operation(km)	1403000	1931000	34643	46893	2.5	2.4
#高速公路	Expressway						
旅客周转量(亿人/公里)	Passenger-Kilometers (100 million passenger-km)	12261	17467	238.36	312.40	1.9	1.8
货物周转量(亿吨/公里)	Freight Ton-Kilometers (100 millionton-km)	44321	80257	404.07	646.55	0.9	0.8
邮电通信业	**Post and Telecommunication**						
邮电业务总量（亿元）	Business Volume of Post and Telecommunications Service (100 million yuan)	4792.70	12198.90	40.92	174.22	0.9	1.4
国内商业	**Domestic Trade(100 million yuan)**						
社会消费品零售总额(亿元)	Total Retail Sales of Consumer Goods	39105.70	67176.60	355.58	606.92	0.9	0.9
对外贸易	**Foreign Trade**						
进出口总额(亿美元)	Total Value of Imports and Exports(USD 100 million)	4742.9	14219.0	6.60	14.04	0.1	0.1
#出口	Total Exports	2492.0	7619.5	4.21	8.59	0.2	0.1

1-7续表2(continued)

指 标	Item	全 国 National Total 2000	全 国 National Total 2005	贵 州 Guizhou 2000	贵 州 Guizhou 2005	贵州占全国比重（%）Percentage of the National Total(%) 2000	贵州占全国比重（%）Percentage of the National Total(%) 2005
旅游	**Tourism**						
入境旅游人数(万人次)	Number of International Tourists Inbound(10000 person-times)	8344.4	12029.2	18.39	27.62	0.2	0.2
国内旅游人数	Domestic Tourists	74000	121000	1980.00	3099.46	2.7	2.6
国际旅游外汇收入（万美元）	International Earnings from Tourism(USD 100 million)	1622000	2930000	6092.23	10141.4	0.4	0.3
国内旅游收入(亿元)	Domestic Earnings from Tourism (100 million yuan)	3175.5	5285.9	57.95	242.83	1.8	4.6
教育	**Education**						
普通高等学校(所)	Regular Institutions of Higher Education(unit)	1041	1792	24	34	2.3	1.9
普通高等学校专任教师(万人)	Full-time Teachers of Regular Institutions of Higher Education(10000 persons)	46.3	96.6	0.72	1.44	1.6	1.5
普通高校在校大学生(万人)	Students Enrollment of Regular Institutions of Higher Education(10000 persons)	556.1	1561.8	7.98	20.68	1.4	1.3
科技	**Science and Tethnology**						
研究与试验发展经费支出占生产总值（%）	R&D Expense as Percentage to GDP(%)	0.9	1.3	0.4	0.6	-0.5 (百分点)	-0.7 (百分点)
文化	Culture						
广播人口覆盖率(%)	Listener Rating(%)	92.5	94.5	76.2	83.3	-16.3 (百分点)	-11.2 (百分点)
电视人口覆盖率(%)	Viewer Rating(%)	93.7	95.8	85.3	90.5	-8.4 (百分点)	-5.3 (百分点)
卫生	**Health Care**						
医院、卫生院（个）	Hospitals and Township Hospitals (unit)	66095	60397	1878	1843	2.8	3.1
卫生技术人员（万人）	Medical and Technical Personnel (10000 persons)	449.10	446.00	8.54	7.78	1.9	1.7
医院、卫生院床位（万张）	Number of Beds in Hospitals and Township Hospitals(10000 beds)	290.80	313.50	5.51	5.84	1.9	1.9
人民生活	**People's Livelihood**						
城镇居民可支配收入（元）	Per Capita Annual Disposable Income of Urban Households (yuan)	6280	10493	5121	8147	81.5	77.6
农村居民人均纯收入	Annual Per Capita Net Income of Rural Residents(yuan)	2253	3255	1374	1877	61.0	57.7

1-8 小康生活水平基本标准及实现程度(2005)

Basic Standard and Level of Implement of Well-to-do life in Guizhou Province(2005)

指标类型	Item	权数 Proportion	小康值 Standard of Well-to-do	实现程度 Level of Implement
经济水平	**Level of Economy**	**14**		**99.1**
人均国内生产总值(90价)(元)	Per Capital of Gross Demestic Product(90 Price)(yuan)	14	2500	99.1
物质生活	**Substance Life**	**48**		**87.7**
收 入	Income			
城镇人均可支配收入(90价)(元)	Per Capital Annual Disposable Income of Urban (90 Price)(yuan)	6	2400	100
农民人均纯收入(90价)(元)	Per Capital Annual Net Income of Rural(90 Price)(yuan)	10	1200	62
居 住	Habitation			
城镇人均住房使用面积(平方米)	Per Use Space in Urban Areas(sq.m)	5	12	100
农村人均钢砖木结构住房面积(平方米)	Per Brick and Wood Structure Space in Rural Areas (sq.m)	7	15	100
营 养	Alimentation			
人均蛋白质摄入量(克)	Per Feeding Quantity of Proteid (g)	6	75	83.4
交 通	Traffic			
城市每人拥有铺路面积(平方米)	Per Flagging Road Space in Urban Areas(sq.m)	3	8	62.8
农村通公路行政村比重(%)	The Proportion of Administration Village Which Connected Highroad(%)	5	85	100
结 构	Configuration			
恩格尔系数(%)	Engle Coefficient (%)	6	50	100
人口素质	**Stuff of Population**	**14**		**42.9**
文 化	Culture			
成人识字率(%)	The Rate of Adult Literacy(%)	6	85	100
健 康	Health			
人均预期寿命(岁)	Per Life-span of Anticipation (year)	4	70	0
婴儿死亡率(‰)	The Death Rate of Baby (‰)	4	31	0
精神生活	**Spirit Life**	**10**		**92.9**
教育娱乐支出比重(%)	The Expenses Proportion of Education and Entertainment(%)	5	11	100
电视机普及率(%)	The Popularization Rate of TV set(%)	5	100	85.8
生活环境	**Habitation**	**14**		**97.7**
森林覆盖率(%)	The Rate of Forest Bestrow(%)	7	15	100
农村初级卫生保健基本合格以上县百分比(%)	The County Percent of Primary Health Care beyond Basic Check out(%)	7	100	95.4
总 计	**Total**			**84.9**

1-9 城镇小康生活水平基本标准及实现程度（2005）

Basic Standard and Level of Implement of Well-to-do life of Urban in Guiz hou Province(2005)

指标类型	Item	权数 Proportion	小康值 Standard of Well-to-do	实现程度 Level of Implement
经济水平	Level of Economy	21		100.0
人均国内生产总值（90价）(元)	Per Capital of Gross Demestic Product (90 Price)(yuan)	12	5000	100.0
第三产业增加值比重(%)	GDP Proportion of the Tertiary Industry (%)	9	40	100.0
物质生活	**Substance Life**	**37**		**100.0**
人均可支配收入（90价）(元)	Per Capital Annual Disposable Income (90 P rice)(yuan)	15	2400	100.0
人均住房使用面积平方(平方米)	Per Use Space of Housing(sq.m)	10	12	100.0
人均蛋白质摄入量(克)	Per Feeding Quantity of Proteid(g)	5	75	100.0
恩格尔系数(%)	Engle Coefficient(%)	7	50	100.0
人口素质	**Stuff of Population**	**12**		**100.0**
人口平均预期寿命(岁)	Average Anticipate Life-span of Population(year)	5	70	100.0
中学入学率(%)	The Rate of Enrollment of High School(%)	7	90	100.0
精神生活	**Spirit Life**	**12**		**100.0**
电视机普及率(%)	The Popularization Rate of TV set(%)	5	100	100.0
文化教育娱乐支出(%)	The Expenses Proportion of Culture,Education and Entertainment(%)	7	16	100.0
生活环境	**Habitation**	**18**		**50.0**
人均绿地面积(平方米)	Per Greenbelt Space(sq.m)	9	9	100.0
万人刑事案件立案件数(件)	The Number of Register Criminal Case of 10000 Persons(Piece)	9	≤20	-
总 计	**Total**			**91.0**

1-10　农村小康生活水平基本标准及实现程度（2005）

Basic Standard and Level of Implement of Well-to-do life of Rural in Guiz hou Province(2005)

指标类型	Item	权数 Proportion	小康值 Standard of Well-to-do	实现程度 Level of Implement
收入分配	**Income and Distribution**	**35**		**65.2**
人均纯收入（90价）(元)	Per Capital Annual Net Income(90 Price) (yuan)	30	1200	62.7
基尼系数(%)	Geordie Coefficient(%)	5	0.3-0.4	80.0
物质生活	**Substance Life**	**25**		**78.6**
恩格尔系数(%)	Engle Coefficient(%)	6	≤50	72.0
人均蛋白质摄入量(克)	Per Feeding Quantity of Proteid(g)	9	75	79.6
衣着消费支出(90价)(元)	Expenses for Dress Consumption(90 Price)(yuan)	3	70	40.2
钢木结构住房比重(%)	The Proportion of Steel and Wood Structure Housing(%)	7	80	99.4
人口素质	**Stuff of Population**	**9**		**19.4**
人口平均预期寿命(岁)	Average Anticipate Life-span of Population(year)	4	70	0.0
劳动力平均受教育年限(年)	Average Fixed Number of Year of E ducated Labour Force(year)	5	8	35.0
精神生活	**Spirit Life**	**12**		**95.0**
电视机普及率(%)	The Popularization Rate of TV set(%)	6	70	100.0
文化服务支出比重(%)	The Expenses Proportion of Culture and Serve(%)	6	10	90.0
生活环境	**Habitation**	**11**		**71.1**
已通公路的行政村比重(%)	The Proportion of Administration Village Which Connected Highroad(%)	3	85	100
安全卫生水普及率(%)	The Proportion of Household which Connected Sanitation and Safety Water(%)	3	90	7.0
用电户比重(%)	The Proportion of Household which Connected Electricity(%)	3	95	87.1
已通电话的行政村比重(%)	The Proportion of Administration Village Which Connected Telephone(%)	2	70	100.0
社会保障	**Social Security**	**8**		**86.7**
享受社会五保人口比重(%)	The Proportion of Enjoied Five Protective Population(%)	4	90	73.3
万人刑事案件立案件数(件)	The Number of Register Criminal Case of 10000 Person (Piece)	4	≤20	100.0
总　计	**Total**			**70.4**

1-11 “十五”时期各年生产总值

Gross Domestic Product Grouped of each year in “Tenth-Five-year Plan” Period

单位：亿元(100 million yuan)

指　标	Item	2000	2001	2002	2003	2004	2005	2005年比2004年增长(%) Increase Rate(%)
生产总值	**Gross Domestic Product**	**1029.92**	**1133.27**	**1243.43**	**1426.34**	**1677.80**	**1979.06**	**11.6**
第一产业	Primary Industry	271.20	274.41	281.10	298.69	334.50	362.49	5.2
第二产业	Secondary Industry	391.20	433.52	481.96	569.37	681.50	826.63	12.7
工　业	Industry	328.73	360.73	395.45	473.38	577.40	714.24	14.1
建筑业	Construction	62.47	72.79	86.51	95.99	104.10	112.39	6.1
第三产业	Tertiary Industry	367.52	425.34	480.37	558.28	661.80	789.94	13.9
农林牧渔服务业	Services for Farming, Forestry,Animal Husbandry and Fishery	3.52	4.34	4.77	5.66	5.85	6.45	7.3
地质勘查业、水利管理业	Geological and Water Conservancy	1.97	2.72	2.89	3.19	6.46	8.18	28.7
交通运输、仓储、邮电通信业	Transportation,Storage,Post and Telecommunications	75.86	88.47	102.48	119.26	134.90	162.10	9.7
交通运输和仓储业	Transportation and Storage	59.48	68.55	78.69	90.93	93.71	112.93	5.4
邮电通信业	Post and Telecommunications	16.38	19.92	23.79	28.33	41.19	49.17	18.8
批发和零售贸易、餐饮业	Wholesale & Retail Trade and Catering Services	83.72	89.67	100.61	116.05	136.90	160.92	12.2
批发和零售贸易业	Wholesale & Retail Trade	71.18	73.21	81.42	93.14	116.78	131.50	8.6
餐饮业	Catering Services	12.54	16.46	19.19	22.91	20.12	29.42	33.3
金融保险业	Finance and Insurance	36.07	37.24	41.45	48.01	60.30	71.07	14.5
房地产业	Real Estate	37.05	45.32	53.49	59.86	68.30	79.53	8.6
社会服务业	Social Services	27.33	29.10	35.97	43.46	45.57	55.72	24.9
卫生、体育、社会福利事业	Health Care, Sports and Social Welfare	18.29	23.51	24.83	30.05	30.43	38.72	26.2
教育、文艺、广播电影电视事业	Education,Culture and Arts, Radio, Film and Television	34.49	46.81	50.57	58.88	71.37	79.17	9.8
科学研究和综合技术服务业	Scientific Research and Polytechnical Services	4.18	4.16	4.31	5.23	8.97	14.23	56.5
国家政党机关、社会团体	Governments Parties and Social Organizations	39.30	48.37	53.04	61.94	88.60	108.78	15.4
其　他	Others Sectors	5.74	5.63	5.96	6.69	4.15	5.07	25.0
人均生产总值(元)	**Per Capita Gross Domestic Product (yuan)**	**2759**	**3000**	**3257**	**3701**	**4317**	**5052**	**10.8**

注：本表已按第一次经济普查资料修订。

Note:Data in the table are adjusted on the basis of the statistics of the first national economic cenus.

1-12 "十五"时期各年生产总值构成

Composition of Gross Domestic Product Grouped of each year in "Tenth-Five-year Plan" Period

单位：%

指 标	Item	2000	2001	2002	2003	2004	2005
生产总值	**Gross Domestic Product**	100.0	100.0	100.0	100.0	100.0	100.0
第一产业	Primary Industry	26.3	24.2	22.6	21.0	20.0	18.3
第二产业	Secondary Industry	38.0	38.3	38.8	39.9	40.6	41.8
工　业	Industry	31.9	31.8	31.8	33.2	34.4	36.1
建筑业	Construction	6.1	6.5	7.0	6.7	6.2	5.7
第三产业	Tertiary Industry	35.7	37.5	38.6	39.1	39.4	39.9
农林牧渔服务业	Services for Farming,Forestry, Animal Husbandry and Fishery	0.3	0.4	0.4	0.4	0.3	0.3
地质勘查业、水利管理业	Geological and Water Conservancy	0.2	0.2	0.2	0.2	0.4	0.4
交通运输、仓储、邮电通信业	Transportation,Storage,Post and Telecommunications	7.4	7.8	8.2	8.4	8.0	8.2
交通运输和仓储业	Transportation and Storage	5.8	6.0	6.3	6.4	5.6	5.7
邮电通信业	Post and Telecommunications	1.6	1.8	1.9	2.0	2.4	2.5
批发和零售贸易、餐饮业	Wholesale & Retail Trade and Catering Services	8.1	7.9	8.1	8.1	8.2	8.1
批发和零售贸易业	Wholesale & Retail Trade	6.9	6.5	6.5	6.5	7.0	6.6
餐饮业	Catering Services	1.2	1.4	1.6	1.6	1.2	1.5
金融保险业	Finance and Insurance	3.5	3.3	3.3	3.4	3.6	3.6
房地产业	Real Estate	3.6	4.0	4.3	4.2	4.1	4.0
社会服务业	Social Services	2.7	2.6	2.9	3.0	2.7	2.8
卫生、体育、社会福利事业	Health Care, Sports and Social Welfare	1.8	2.1	2.0	2.1	1.8	2.0
教育、文艺、广播电影电视事业	Education,Culture and Arts,Radio, Film and Television	3.3	4.1	4.1	4.1	4.3	4.0
科学研究和综合技术服务业	Scientific Research and Polytechnical Services	0.4	0.4	0.3	0.4	0.5	0.7
国家政党机关、社会团体	Governments Parties and Social Organizations	3.8	4.3	4.3	4.3	5.3	5.5
其他	Others Sectors	0.6	0.4	0.5	0.5	0.2	0.3

1-13 “十五”时期各年生产总值(按支出法计算)

Gross Domestic Product of each year in “Tenth-Five-year Plan” Period(Accounted by Expenditure Approach)

指 标	Item	2000	2001	2002	2003	2004	2005	2005年比2004年增长(%) Increase Rate in 2005 over 2004(%)
绝对数(亿元)	**Absolute Figure (100 million yuan)**							
地区生产总值	Gross Domestic Product	1029.93	1133.27	1243.43	1426.34	1677.80	1979.06	11.6
最终消费	Final Consumption Expenditure	920.46	1000.35	1085.75	1169.55	1367.94	1627.27	18.3
居民消费	Household Consumption	754.57	791.03	851.27	912.56	1058.36	1230.07	15.7
农村居民	Rural Households	450.16	470.96	506.10	532.60	386.84	449.45	14.6
城镇居民	Urban Households	304.41	320.07	345.17	379.96	671.52	780.62	16.2
人均城乡消费水平对比(农村居民=1)	Urban/Rural Consumption Ratio (rural households=1)	1:5.00	1:4.94	1:4.91	1:5.08	1:5.07	1:4.80	
政府消费	Government Consumption	165.89	209.32	234.48	256.99	309.58	397.20	27.0
资本形成总额	Gross Capital Formation	489.19	629.24	682.22	789.80	894.34	1024.94	12.9
固定资本形成总额	Gross Fixed Capital Formation	456.26	575.89	663.89	768.76	871.46	996.24	12.7
库存增加	Changes in Inventories	32.93	53.35	18.33	21.04	22.88	28.70	21.5
货物和服务净出口	Net Outflow of Goods and Services	-379.72	-496.32	-524.54	-533.01	-584.48	-673.15	
构成(%)	**Composition(%)**							
以最终消费为100	Final Consumption Expenditure=100							
居民消费	Household Consumption	82.0	79.1	78.4	78.0	77.4	75.6	-1.8
政府消费	Government Consumption	18.0	20.9	21.6	22.0	22.6	24.4	1.8
以居民消费为100	Household Consumption=100							
农村居民	Rural Households	59.7	59.5	59.5	58.4	36.6	36.5	-0.1
城镇居民	Urban Households	40.3	40.5	40.5	41.6	63.4	63.5	0.1
最终消费率(%)	Final Consumption Rate(%)	89.4	88.3	87.3	82.0	81.5	82.2	0.7
资本形成率(%)	Capital Formation Rate(%)	47.5	55.5	54.9	55.4	53.3	51.8	-1.5

1-14 资金流量表（实物分配）（2004）

Flow of Funds Table(Physical Transaction)（2004）

单位：亿元(100 million yuan)

机构部门交易项目	Institutional Sector Transaction	非金融企业部门 Non-financial 使用 Utilization	来源 Source	金融机构部门 Financial Institutions 使用 Utilization	来源 Source	政府部门 Governments 使用 Utilization	来源 Source
净出口	**Net Exports**						
增加值	Value-added		895.05		60.30		196.00
劳动者报酬	Compensation of Laborers	355.12		23.07		178.86	
工资和工资性收入	Wages and Related Income	327.16		21.91		172.24	
单位社会保险付款	Employer's Contribution of Social Securities	27.96		1.16		6.62	
生产税净额	Net Taxes on Production	278.53		7.39		1.51	243.23
生产税	Taxes on Production	288.73		7.39		1.51	253.43
生产补贴	Subsidies to Production	-10.20					-10.20
财产收入	Income from Propery	72.25	25.75	11.18	38.00		1.12
利息	Interest	34.35	4.36	11.18	38.00		1.12
红利	Dividend	37.90	21.39				
初次分配总收入	Total Income from Primary Distribution		214.90		56.66		259.98
经常转移	Current Transfer	63.86	43.70	57.44	21.62	91.96	346.31
收入税	Taxes on Income	26.85		0.47			22.55
社会保险付款	Payment to Social Security	27.96		2.48	6.90	6.62	37.19
社会保险福利	Social Security Welfare					44.59	
社会补助	Allowances					33.65	
其他	Others	8.05	41.70	51.49	10.72	2.10	280.57
可支配总收入	Total Disposable Income		194.74		20.84		514.33
最终消费	Final Consumption Expenditure					335.96	
居民消费	Household Consumption						
政府消费	Government Consumption					335.96	
总储蓄	Total Savings	194.74		20.84		178.37	
资本转移	Capital Transfer	2.63	34.64		0.12	50.92	29.69
投资性补助	Investment Allowances		24.76		0.12	50.92	28.05
其他	Others	2.63	9.88				1.64
资本形成总额	Gross Capital Formation	762.31		5.70		36.17	
固定资本形成总额	Gross fixed Capital Formation	767.63		5.70		36.17	
存货增加	Changes in Inventories	-5.32					
净金融投资	Net Financial Investment	-535.56		15.26		120.97	

注：该表未按第一次经济普查资料进行调整。

Note:Date in the table are not adjusted on the basis of the statistics of the first national economic cenus.

1-14续表(continued)　　　　单位：亿元　(100 million yuan)

机构部门交易项目	Institutional Sector Transaction	住户部门 Households		省内合计 Province		省外部门 Guizhou Province		总计 Total	
		使用 Utiliz-ation	来源 Source	使用 Utiliz-ation	来源 Source	使用 Utiliz-ation	来源 Source	使用 Utiliz-ation	来源 Source
净出口	Net Exports					-279.46		-279.46	
增加值	Value-added		526.46		1677.80				1677.80
劳动者报酬	Compensation of Laborers	277.33	878.30	834.37	878.30	50.29	6.36	884.66	884.66
工资和工资性收入	Wages and Related Income	277.33	842.56	798.63	842.56	50.29	6.36	848.92	848.92
单位社会保险付款	Employer's Contribution of Social Securities		35.74	35.74	35.74			35.74	35.74
生产税净额	Net Taxes on Production	27.53		314.96	243.23		71.73	314.96	314.96
生产税	Taxes on Production	27.53		325.16	253.43		71.73	325.16	325.16
生产补贴	Subsidies to Production			-10.20	-10.20			-10.20	-10.20
财产收入	Income from Propery	3.65	16.36	87.08	81.23	1.70	7.55	88.78	88.78
利息	Interest	3.65	7.40	49.18	50.88	1.70		50.88	50.88
红利	Dividend		8.96	37.90	30.35		7.55	37.90	37.90
初次分配总收入	Total Income from Primary Distribution		1112.61		1644.15		313.11		1957.26
经常转移	Current Transfer	34.95	94.60	241.22	496.23	292.28	39.25	526.50	527.50
收入税	Taxes on Income	17.64		44.96	22.55		22.40	44.96	44.96
社会保险付款	Payment to Social Security	8.34	1.32	45.41	45.41			45.41	45.41
社会保险福利	Payment to Social Welfare		44.59	44.59	44.59			44.59	44.59
社会补助	Allowances		33.65	33.65	33.65			33.65	33.65
其他	Others	1.97	7.04	63.61	340.03	281.28	4.85	344.89	344.89
可支配总收入	Total Disposable Income		1172.26		1902.17		60.08		1962.25
最终消费	Final Consumption Expenditure	750.57		1086.53				1086.53	
居民消费	Resident Consumption	750.57		750.57				750.57	
政府消费	Government Consumption			335.96				335.96	
总储蓄	Total Savings	421.69		815.64		60.08		875.72	
资本转移	Capital Transfer			53.55	64.45	13.53	2.63	67.08	67.08
投资性补助	Investment Allowances			50.92	52.93	2.01		52.93	52.93
其他	Others			2.63	11.52	11.52	2.63	14.15	14.15
资本形成总额	Gross Capital Formation	66.55		870.73				870.73	
固定资本形成总额	Gross fixed Capital Formation	69.35		878.85				878.85	
存货增加	Changes in Inventories	-2.80		-8.12				-8.12	
净金融投资	Net Financial Investment	355.14		-44.19		48.19			

1-15 “十五”时期各年城市公用事业基本情况

Basic Statistics on Urban Public Utilities of each year in “Tenth-Five-year Plan” Period

指 标	Item	2001	2002	2003	2004	2005
城市规模	**Scale of Cities**					
城市面积（平方公里）	Cities Areas(sq.m)	6082.55	6082.55	6210.99	6270.06	7002.55
#建成区面积	Developed Areas	627.02	617.58	661.17	656.02	706.19
供水管道长度（公里）	Length of Water Supply Pipelines(km)	4631.95	4553.32	4801.35	5108.08	5313.26
自来水年供水量(万立方米)	Annual Supply of Tap Water(10000 cu.m)	58386	58172	57314	65983	63705
#生活用水量	Water Consumption for Residential Use	23660	28982	28968	32400	31895
人均生活用水（升）	Per Capita Water Consumption for Residential Use(liter)	153.40	160.26	159.85	158.17	147.80
用水普及率（%）	Percentage of Population with Access to Tap Water(%)	47.95	74.58	77.59	84.80	88.37
煤气管道长度（公里）	Length of Gas Pipelines(km)	1274.52	1452.82	1489	1549	1930.50
煤气供气量（万立方米）	Coal Gas Supply(10000 cu.m)	9143	10871	14411	16929	19209
#家庭用量	Consumption of Coal Gas for Residential Use	5360	6653	6824	7747	8389
液化石油气供气量(万立方米/吨)	Liquefied Petroleum Gas Supply (10000 cu.m/t on)	49682	73417	84331	88122	79420
#家庭用量	Consumption of Liquefied Gas for Residential Use	46571	63297	73405	75881	65324
*燃气普及率(%)	Percentage of Population with Access to Gas(%)	24.45	46.37	49.54	51.27	54.59
市政工程	**Municipal Engineering**					
城市道路长度（公里）	Length of Paved Roads(km)	2716.34	2772.35	2922.82	3268.06	3518.35
城市道路面积（万平方米）	Area of Paved Roads(10000 sq.m)	3073.43	3423.70	3752.80	4448.80	4852.90
人均拥有道路面积(平方米)	Area of Paved Roads Per Capita(sq.m)	2.68	4.37	4.80	5.48	6.05

1-15续表(continued)

指　标	Item	2001	2002	2003	2004	2005
城市桥梁（座）	Number of Bridges(unit)	579	607	641	651	657
排水管道长度（公里）	Length of Drainpipe(km)	2425.86	2600.96	2902.00	4204.54	5204.51
污水排放量（万立方米）	Volume of Sewage Letting (10000 cu.m)		45791	46207	69537	51036
污水处理量	Disposal Capacity of Sewage	2450	1095	1306	7170	10754
污水处理率（%）	Treatment Rate of Sewage(%)	3.34	2.39	2.83	10.31	21.07
路灯盏数（盏）	Number of Street Lamps(unit)	81225	99047	121143	142257	185077
公共交通	**Public Traffic**					
公共汽车总数（标台）	Number of Public Transportation Vehicles(unit)	4415	4376	4797	4722	4858
平均每万人拥有公交车(标台)	Number of Public Transportation Vehicles Per 10000 Persons(unit)	3.85	5.58	6.48	5.81	6.05
客运总量（万人次）	Number of Passengers Carried (10000 person-times)	78737	78364	72214	81996	89589
出租汽车（万辆）	Taxi(10000 units)	0.87	0.92	1.10	1.13	1.23
城市绿化	**Afforestation in Cities**					
绿化覆盖面积（公顷）	Public Green Areas(hectare)	19115	35906	37329	39871	41736
园林绿地面积	Areas of Green Land	12728	28025	29336	29810	31160
#公共绿地面积	Public Green Areas	3461	3184	3507	2680	4267
人均公共绿地面积（平方米）	Per Capita Public Green Areas(sq.m)	3.02	4.06	4.49	4.53	5.32
公园数（个）	Number of Parks(unit)	87	125	101	102	98
公园游人数（亿人次）	Number of Visitors to Parks (100 million person-times)	0.32	0.34	0.42	0.73	0.63
建城区绿化覆盖率（%）	Coverage Rate of Urban Green Areas(%)	16.61	16.29	17.88	19.10	20.03
环境卫生	**Environmental Sanitation**					
清运生活垃圾（万吨）	Volume of Garbage Disposal(10000 tons)	1412	397	434	440	383
生活垃圾无害化处理率（%）	Treatment Rate of Carbage Innocuous (%)	3.19	10.85	11.25	18.30	26.67
清运粪便（万吨）	Volume of Disposal of Excrement and Urine (10000 tons)	193.7	14.10	17.60	17.80	27.20
公厕数（座）	Number of Public Lavatories(unit)	2379	1778	1550	1534	1762
水冲公厕比例（%）	Scale of Public Water-washnig Lavatories(%)	54.35	74.99	80.45	82.59	85.07

注：“*”指标不含电气在内

Note:The data with "*" excluded electric.

主要统计指标解释

行政区划　指国家对行政区域的划分。根据宪法规定,我国的行政区域划分如下:(1)全国分为省、自治区、直辖市;(2)省、自治区分为自治州、县、自治县、市;(3)自治州分为县、自治县、市;(4)县、自治县分为乡、民族乡、镇;(5)直辖市和较大的市分为区、县;(6)国家在必要时设立的特别行政区。

可比价格　指计算各种总量指标所采用的扣除了价格变动因素的价格，可进行不同时期总量指标的对比。按可比价格计算总量指标有两种方法:一种是直接用产品产量乘某一年的不变价格计算;另一种是用价格指数进行缩减。

不变价格　指以同类产品某年的平均价格作为固定价格,用于计算各年的产品价值。按不变价格计算的产品价值消除了价格变动因素,不同时期对比可以反映生产的发展速度。新中国成立后,随着工农业产品价格水平的变化，国家统计局先后五次制定了全国统一的工业产品不变价格和农业产品不变价格。从 1952 年到 1957 年使用 1952 年工(农)业产品不变价格,从 1957 年到 1970 年使用 1957 年不变价格,从 1971 年到 1980 年使用 1970 年不变价格,从 1981 年到 1990 年使用 1980 年不变价格,从 1991 年开始使用 1990 年不变价格。

平均增长速度　我国计算平均增长速度有两种方法:一种是习惯上经常使用的“水平法”,又称几何平均法,是以间隔期最后一年的水平同基期水平对比来计算平均每年增长(或下降)速度;另一种是“累计法”,又称代数平均法或方程法,是以间隔期内各年水平的总和同基期水平对比来计算平均每年增长(或下降)速度。在一般正常情况下,两种方法计算的平均每年增长速度比较接近;但在经济发展不平衡、出现大起大落时,两种方法计算的结果差别较大。

本《年鉴》内所列的平均增长速度,除固定资产投资用"累计法"计算外,其余均用"水平法"计算。从某年到某年平均增长速度的年份，均不包括基期年在内。如建国四十三年的平均增长速度是以 1949 年为基期计算的,则写为 1950–1992 年平均增长速度,其余类推。

企业(单位)登记注册类型　是以在工商行政管理机关登记注册的各类企业为划分对象,以工商行政管理部门对企业登记注册的类型为依据,将企业登记注册类型分为内资企业、港澳台商投资企业和外商投资企业三大类。内资企业包括国有企业、集体企业、股份合作企业、联营企业、有限责任公司、股份有限公司、私营公司和其他企业;港澳台商投资企业和外商投资企业分别包括合资经营企业、合作经营企业、独资经营企业和股份有限公司。对不在工商行政管理部门进行登记注册的行政机关、事业单位和社会团体,主要按其经费来源和管理方式进行划分。

国有企业　指企业全部资产归国家所有,并按《中华人民共和国企业法人登记管理条例》规定登记注册的非公司制的经济组织。不包括有限责任公司中的国有独资公司。

集体企业　指企业资产归集体所有,并按《中华人民共和国企业法人登记管理条例》规定登记注册的经济组织。

股份合作企业　指以合作制为基础,由企业职工共同出资入股,吸收一定比例的社会资产投资组建,实行自主经营,自负盈亏,共同劳动,民主管理,按劳分配与按股分红相结合的一种集体经济组织。

联营企业　指两个及两个以上相同或不同所有制性质的企业法人或事业单位法人,按自愿、平等、互利的原则,共同投资组成的经济组织。联营企业包括国有联营企业、集体联营企业、国有与集体联营企业和其他联营企业。

有限责任公司　指根据《中华人民共和国公司登记管理条例》规定登记注册,由两个以上、五十个以下的股东共同出资,每个股东以其所认缴的出资额对公司承担有限责任,公司以其全部资产对其债务承担责任的经济组织。有限责任公司包括国有独资公司以及其他有限责任公司。

股份有限公司　指根据《中华人民共和国公司登记管理条例》规定登记注册,其全部注册资本由等额股份构成并通过发行股票筹集资本,股东以其认购的股份对公司承担有限责任,公司以其全部资产对其债务承担责任的经济组织。

私营企业 指由自然人投资设立或由自然人控股，以雇佣劳动为基础的营利性经济组织。包括按照《公司法》、《合伙企业法》、《私营企业暂行条例》规定登记注册的私营有限责任公司、私营股份有限公司、私营合伙企业和私营独资企业。

其他内资企业 指上述企业之外的其他内资经济组织。

与港澳台商合资经营企业 指港澳台地区投资者与内地企业依照《中华人民共和国中外合资经营企业法》及有关法律的规定，按合同规定的比例投资设立、分享利润和分担风险的企业。

与港澳台商合作经营企业 指港澳台地区投资者与内地企业依照《中华人民共和国中外合作经营企业法》及有关法律的规定，依照合作合同的约定进行投资或提供条件设立、分配利润和分担风险的企业。

港澳台商独资经营企业 指依照《中华人民共和国外资企业法》及有关法律的规定，在内地由港澳台地区投资者全额投资设立的企业。

港澳台商投资股份有限公司 指根据国家有关规定，经外经贸部依法批准设立，其中港、澳、台商的股本占公司注册资本的比例达25%以上的股份有限公司。凡其中港、澳、台商的股本占公司注册资本的比例小于25%的，属于内资企业中的股份有限公司。

中外合资经营企业 指外国企业或外国人与中国内地企业依照《中华人民共和国中外合资经营企业法》及有关法律的规定，按合同规定的比例投资设立、分享利润和分担风险的企业。

中外合作经营企业 指外国企业或外国人与中国内地企业依照《中华人民共和国中外合作经营企业法》及有关法律的规定，依照合作合同的约定进行投资或提供条件设立、分配利润和分担风险的企业。

外资企业 指依照《中华人民共和国外资企业法》及有关法律的规定，在中国内地由外国投资者全额投资设立的企业。

外商投资股份有限公司 指根据国家有关规定，经外经贸部依法批准设立，其中外资的股本占公司注册资本的比例达25%以上的股份有限公司。凡其中外资股本占公司注册资本的比例小于25%的，属于内资企业中的股份有限公司。

行政机关、事业单位和社会团体 参照企业登记注册类型，主要按其经费来源和管理方式划分。具体规定如下：

(1)行政机关：包括国家机关和政党机关，原则上均列为“国有”。但有特殊规定的，如供销社等，则列为“集体”

(2)事业单位：包括经国家机构编制部门和有关业务主管部门批准成立的各类事业单位，不包括实行企业化管理的事业单位。事业单位的划分办法如下：

①由国家财政预算拨款或列入财政预算外资金管理以及经费主要来源于国有主管部门或国有上级单位的事业单位，列为“国有”。

②经费主要来源于集体单位的事业单位，列为“集体”。

③公民个人（或个人合伙）开办的事业单位，列为“私营”。

④上述以外的其他事业单位，如果其经费来源不明确，按管理方式进行归类。

(3)社会团体：包括经民政部门批准成立以及未纳入社会团体管理条例范围的工会、妇联等各类社会团体。社会团体的划分办法如下：

①未纳入民政部社会团体管理条例范围的工会、妇联、共青团、青联、工商联、科协、侨联等社会团体，国家拨款设立的基金会或基金管理组织以及经费主要来源于国有业务主管部门或国有上级单位的社会团体，列为“国有”。

②经费主要来源于集体单位的社会团体，列为“集体”。

③公民个人（或个人合伙）开办的社会团体，划为“私营”。

④上述以外的其他社会团体，如果其经费来源不明确，改按管理方式进行归类。

国内生产总值（GDP） 指一个国家（或地区）所有常住单位在一定时期内生产活动的最终成果。国内生产总值有三种表现形态，即价值形态、收入形态和产品形态。从价值形态看，它是所有常住单位在一定时期内生产的全部货物和服务价值超过同期中间投入的全部非固定资产货物和服务价值的差额，即所有常住单位的增加值之和;从收入形态看,它是所有常住单位在一定时期内创造并分配给常住单位和非常住单位的初次收入分配之和;从产品形态看,它是所有常住单位在一定时期内最终使用的货物和服务价值与货物和服务净出口价值之和。在实际核算中,国内生产总值有三种计算方法,即生产法、收入法和支出法。三种方法分别从不同的方面反映国内生产总值及其构成。

三次产业 是根据社会生产活动历史发展的顺序对产业结构的划分,产品直接取自自然界的部门称为第一产业,对初级产品进行再加工的部门称为第二产业,为生产和消费提供各种服务的部门称为第三产业。它是世界上较为通用的产业结构分类,但各国的划分不尽一致。

我国的三次产业划分是:

第一产业:农业(包括种植业、林业、牧业和渔业)。

第二产业:工业(包括采掘业,制造业,电力、煤气及水的生产和供应业)和建筑业。

第三产业:除第一、第二产业以外的其他各业。由于第三产业包括的行业多、范围广,根据我国的实际情况,第三产业可分为两大部分;一是流通部门,二是服务部门。

最终消费 指常住单位在一定时期内对于货物和服务的全部最终消费支出,也就是常住单位为满足物质、文化和精神生活的需要,从本国经济领土和国外购买的货物和服务的支出;不包括非常住单位在本国经济领土内的消费支出。最终消费分为居民消费和政府消费。

居民消费 指常住住户对货物和服务的全部最终消费支出。居民消费按市场价格计算,即按居民支付的购买者价格计算。购买者价格是购买者取得货物所支付的价格,包括购买者支付的运输和商业费用。居民消费除了直接以货币形式购买货物和服务的消费之外,还包括以其他方式获得的货物和服务的消费支出,即所谓的虚拟消费支出。居民虚拟消费支出包括以下几种类型:单位以实物报酬及实物转移的形式提供给劳动者的货物和服务;住户生产并由本住户消费了的货物和服务,其中的服务仅指住户的自有住房服务;金融机构提供的金融媒介服务;保险公司提供的保险服务。

政府消费 指政府部门为全社会提供公共服务的消费支出和免费或以较低价格向住户提供的货物和服务的净支出。前者等于政府服务的产出价值减去政府单位所获得的经营收入的价值,政府服务的产出价值等于它的经常性业务支出加上固定资产折旧;后者等于政府部门免费或以较低价格向住户提供的货物和服务的市场价值减去向住户收取的价值。

供水综合生产能力 指按供水设施取水、净化、送水、出厂输水干管等环节设计能力计算的综合生产能力。包括在原设计能力的基础上,经挖、革、改增加的生产能力。计算时,以四个环节中最薄弱的环节为主确定能力。

年末供水管道长度 指从送水泵至用户水表之间所有管道的长度。不包括新安装尚未使用的管道。

全年供水总量 指报告期供水企业(单位)供出的全部水量。包括有效供水量和漏损水量。

生活用水量 包括公共服务用水和居民家庭用水。公共服务用水指为城市社会公共生活服务的用水。包括行政事业单位、部队营区和公共设施服务、社会服务业、批发零售贸易业、旅馆饮食业以及其他公共服务业等单位的用水。居民家庭用水指城市范围内所有居民家庭的日常生活用水。包括城市居民、农民家庭、公共供水站用水。

用水普及率 指城市用水人口数与城市人口总数的比率。计算公式:

用水普及率=城市用水人口数/城市人口总数×100%

人工煤气生产能力 指报告期末人工煤气生产厂制气、净化、输送等环节的综合生产能力,不包括备用设备能力。一般按设计能力计算,如果实际生产能力大于设计能力时,应按实际测定的生产能力计算。测定时应以制气、净化、输送三个环节中最薄弱的环节为主。

供气管道长度 指报告期末从气源厂压缩机的出口或门站出口至各类用户引入管之间的全部已经通气投入使用的管道长度。不包括煤气生产厂、输配站、液化气储存站、灌瓶站、储配站、气化站、混气站、供应站等厂(站)内的管道。

全年供气总量 指全年燃气企业(单位)向用户供应的燃气数量。包括销售量和损失量。

用气普及率 指报告期末使用燃气的城市人口数与城市人口总数的比率。计算公式为:

用气普及率=城市用气人口数/城市人口总数×100%

城市供热能力 指供热企业(单位)向城市热用户输送热能的设计能力。

城市供热总量 指在报告期供热企业(单位)向城市热用户输送全部蒸汽和热水的总热量。

城市供热管道长度 指从各类热源到热用户建筑物接入口之间的全部蒸汽和热水的管道长度。不包括各类热源厂内部的管道长度。

年末道路长度 指年末道路长度和与道路相通的广场、桥梁、隧道的长度,按车行道中心线计算。在统计时只统计路面宽度在3.5米(含3.5米)以上的各种铺装道路,包括开放型工业区和住宅区道路在内。

城市桥梁 指为跨越天然或人工障碍物而修建的构筑物。包括跨河桥、立交桥、人行天桥以及人行地下通道等。包括永久性桥和半永久性桥。

城市排水管道长度 指所有排水总管、干管、支管、检查井及连接井进出口等长度之和。

城市污水日处理能力 指污水处理厂(或处理装置)每昼夜处理污水量的设计能力。

年末运营车数 指年末公交企业(单位)用于运营业务的全部车辆数。以企业(单位)固定资产台帐中已投入运营的车辆数为准。

城市园林绿地面积 指报告期末用作园林和绿化的各种绿地面积。包括公共绿地、居住区绿地、单位附属绿地、防护绿地、生产绿地、道路绿地和风景林地面积。

不包括:

1.屋顶绿化、垂直绿化、阳台绿化和室内绿化。

2.以物质生产为主的林地、耕地、牧草地、果园和竹园等。

3.城市总体规划中不列入绿地的水域。

公共绿地 指向公众开放的市级、区级、居住区级各类公园、街旁游园,包括其范围内的水域。其中居住区级公园应不小于1万平方米,街旁游园的宽度不小于8米,面积不小于400平方米。

Explanatory Notes on Main Statistical Indicators

Divisions of Administrative Areas refers to the division of administrative areas by the state. The Constitution of the People's Republic of China stipulates that the administrative areas in China are divided as: 1) The whole country is divided into provinces, autonomous regions and municipalities directly under the central government; 2) Provinces and autonomous regions are divided into autonomous prefectures, counties, autonomous counties and cities; 3) Autonomous prefectures are divided into counties, autonomous counties and cities; 4) Counties and autonomous counties are divided into townships, nationality townships and towns; 5) Municipalities and large cities are divided into districts and counties, 6) The state shall, when necessary, establish special administrative regions.

Comparable Prices refer to prices that are used to remove the factors of price change in calculating economic aggregates, so as to facilitate comparison of aggregates over time. Two methods are used for calculating economic aggregates at comparable prices: 1.Multiplying the output of products by their constant prices of certain year; 2.Deflation of data at current prices by relevant price index.

Constant Price refers to the average price of a given product in certain year, which is used for comparison of output value over time.As the output value at constant prices removes the factor of price changes,it reflects the trend of production development over time.Since 1949,with the changes in general price level,the State Statistical Bureau has issued nationally unified constant prices five times:the 1952 constant prices for 1952-1957;the 1957 constant prices for 1957-1970; the 1970 constant prices for 1971-1980; the 1980 constant prices for 1981-1990; and the 1990 constant prices have been used since 1991.

Average Annual Growth Rate Two methods for calculating average annual growth rate are applied in China,one is often called level approachor the method of calculating geometric average,which is derived by comparing the level of the last year of the interval with that of the beginning year;the other is calledaccumulative approach or algebraic average or equation method,which is derived by the summation of the actual figure of each year in the interval divided by the figure in the base year.

Usually the results calculated by the two methods are fairly close,but they differed sharply when uneven economic development occurred with striking fluctuations in growth.

The average annual growth rates listed in this statistical yearbook are calculated by level approach except for the growth rate of investment in fixed assets.The base years are not listed when the years are listed for average annual growth rates. For instance,the average annual growth rate of 43 years since 1949 is listed as average annual growth rate of 1950–1992 without listing the base year 1949.And the analogy of this is also the same for the rest of the years.

Registration Status of Enterprises Enterprises are classified into 3 categories, namely domestic–funded enterprises, enterprises with investment from Hong Kong, Macau and Taiwan, and enterprises with foreign investment, in the light of the registration status of an enterprise in industrial and commercial administration agencies. Domestic–funded enterprises include state–owned enterprises, collective–owned enterprises, cooperative enterprises, joint ownership enterprises, limited liability corporations, share–holding corporations Ltd., private enterprises and other enterprises. Included in the enterprises with investment from Hong Kong, Macau and Taiwan and enterprises with foreign investment are joint–venture enterprises, cooperative enterprises, sole investment enterprises and share–holding corporations Ltd. For government agencies, institutions and social organizations which are not requested to be registered in industrial and commercial administration agencies, they are classified mainly by their sources of funds and way of management.

State–owned Enterprises refer to non–corporation economic units where the entire assets are owned by the state and which have registered in accordance with the Regulation of the Peoples Republic of China on the Management of Registration of Corporate Enterprises. Excluded from this category are sole state–funded corporations in the limited liability corporations.

Collective–owned Enterprises refer to economic units where the assets are owned collectively and which have registered in accordance with the Regulation of the Peoples Republic of China on the Management of Registration of Corporate Enterprises.

Cooperative Enterprises refer to a form of collective economic units (enterprises) where capitals come mainly from employees as their shares, with certain proportion of capital from the outside, where production is organized on the basis of independent operation, independent accounting for profits and losses, joint work, democratic management, and a distribution system that integrates remuneration according to work with dividend according to capital share.

Joint Ownership Enterprises refer to economic units established by two or more corporate enterprises or corporate institutions of the same or different ownership, through joint investment on the basis of equality, voluntary participation and mutual benefits. They include state joint ownership enterprises, collective joint ownership enterprises, joint state–collective enterprises, other joint ownership enterprises.

Limited Liability Corporations refer to economic units established with investment from 2–50 investors and registered in accordance with the Regulation of the Peoples Republic of China on the Management of Registration of Corporations, each investor bearing limited liability to the corporation depending on its share of investment, and the corporation bearing liability to its debt to the maximum of its total assets. Limited liability corporations include exclusive state–funded limited liability corporations and other limited liability corporations.

Share–holding Corporations Ltd. refer to economic units registered in accordance with the Regulation of the Peoples Republic of China on the Management of Registration of Corporations, with total registered capitals di–

vided into equal shares and raised through issuing stocks. Each investor bears limited liability to the corporation depending on the holding of shares, and the corporation bears liability to its debt to the maximum of its total assets.

Private Enterprises refer to profit-making economic units invested and established by natural persons, or controlled by natural persons using employed labour. Included in this category are private limited liability corporations, private share-holding corporations Ltd., private partnership enterprises and private-funded enterprises registered in accordance with the Corporation Law, Partnership Enterprises Law and Interim Regulations on Private Enterprises .

Other Domestic-funded Enterprises refer to domestic-funded economic units other than those mentioned above.

Joint-venture Enterprises with Funds from Hong Kong, Macau and Taiwan refer to enterprises jointly established by investors from Hong Kong, Macau and Taiwan with enterprises in the mainland of China in accordance with the Law of the Peoples Republic of China on Sino-foreign Joint Venture Enterprises and other relevant laws, where the share of investment, profits and risks is stipulated in the contract.

Cooperative Enterprises with Funds from Hong Kong Macau and Taiwan, established by investors from Hong Kong, Macau and Taiwan with enterprises in the mainland of China in accordance with the Law of the Peoples Republic of China on Sino-foreign Cooperative Enterprises and other relevant laws, where the investment or provision of facilities, and the share of profits and risks is stipulated in the cooperative contract.

Enterprises with Sole (exclusive) Investment from Hong Kong, Macau and Taiwan refer to enterprises established in the mainland of China with exclusive investment from investors from Hong Kong, Macau and Taiwan in accordance with the Law of the Peoples Republic of China on Foreign-Funded Enterprises and other relevant laws.

Share-holding Corporations Ltd. with Investment from Hong Kong, Macau and Taiwan refer to share-holding corporations Ltd. established with the approval from the Ministry of Foreign Trade and Economic Relations in line with relevant state regulations, where the share of investment from Hong Kong, Macau or Taiwan businessmen exceeds 25% of the total registered capital of the corporation. In case the share of investment from Hong Kong, Macau or Taiwan is less than 25% of the total registered capital, the enterprise is to be classified as domestic-funded share-holding corporation Ltd.

Joint-venture Enterprises with Foreign Investment refer to enterprises jointly established by foreign enterprises or foreigners with enterprises in the mainland of China in accordance with the Law of the Peoples Republic of China on Sino-foreign Joint Venture Enterprises and other relevant laws, where the share of investment, profits and risks is stipulated in the contract.

Cooperation Enterprises with Foreign Investment refer to enterprises jointly established by foreign enterprises or foreigners with enterprises in the mainland of China in accordance with the Law of the Peoples Republic of China on Sino-foreign Cooperative Enterprises and other relevant laws, where the investment or provision of facilities, and the share of profits and risks is stipulated in the cooperative contract.

Enterprises with Sole (exclusive) Foreign Investment refer to enterprises established in the mainland of China with exclusive investment from foreign investors in accordance with the Law of the Peoples Republic of China on Foreign-Funded Enterprises and other relevant laws.

Share-holding Corporations Ltd. with Foreign Investment refer to share-holding corporations Ltd. established with the approval from the Ministry of Foreign Trade and Economic Relations in line with relevant state regulations, where the share of investment from foreign investors exceeds 25% of the total registered capital of the corporation. In case the share of foreign investment is less than 25% of the total registered capital, the enterprise is to be classified as domestic-funded share-holding corporation Ltd.

Government Agencies, Institutions and Social Organizations are classified into following categories by source of funds and way of management taking reference of the registration status of enterprises:

(1) Government agencies: include state and party agencies, classified in principle as "state-owned". There are exceptions, such as supply and marketing cooperatives which are classified as "collective".

(2) Institutions: include institutions of various types established with the approval by organization and staffing departments of the government, but exclude institutions where enterprise management system is introduced. Institutions are further classified as follows:

(a) Institutions whose main budget is listed in the government budget appropriations or extra-budget funds, or allocated from the budget of their competent government agencies. Such institutions are classified as "state-owned".

(b) Institutions whose budget mainly comes from collective units. Such institutions are classified as "collective".

(c) Social organizations established by individual or a group of citizens, which are classified as "private".

(d) Institutions other than those mentioned above whose source of budget is not clear. Such institutions are classified by way of management.

(3) Social organizations: include social organizations established with the approval from the Ministry of Civil Affairs, and organizations that are not covered by social organization management regulations such as trade unions, women´s federations etc. Social organizations are further classified as follows:

(a) Social organizations that are not covered by social organization management regulations of the Ministry of Civil Affairs such as trade unions, women´s federations, communist youth leagues, youth associations, industrial and commerce associations, scientists associations, overseas Chinese associations, etc., foundations and fund management organizations established with funds from the state, and social organizations whose funds mainly come from the budget of their competent government agencies. Such institutions are classified as "state-owned".

(b) Social organizations whose budget mainly comes from collective units. Such institutions are classified as "collective".

(c) Social organizations established by individual or a group of citizens, which are classified as "private".

(d) Social organizations other than those mentioned above whose source of budget is not clear. Such organizations are classified by way of management.

Gross Domestic Product (GDP) refers to the final products of all resident units in a country (or a region) during a certain period of time. Gross domestic product is expressed in three different forms, i. e. value, income, and products respectively. The form of value refers to the total value of all products and services produced by all resident units during a certain period of time minus total value of intimidate input of materials and services of the nature of non-fixed assets or the summation of the value-added of all resident units; the form of income includes all the income created by all resident units and distributed primarily to all resident and non-resident units; the form of products refers to the value of all final goods and services for final use by all resident units plus the value of net exports of goods and services during a given period of time. In the practice of national accounting, gross domestic product is calculated with three approaches, i. e. production approach, income approach, and expenditure approach, which reflect gross domestic product and its composition from different aspects.

Three Industries Industry structure has been classified according to the historical sequence of development. Primary industry refers to extraction of natural resources; secondary industry involves processing of primary products; and tertiary industry provides services of various kinds for production and consumption. The above classification is universal although it varies to some extent form country to country. Industry in China comprises:

Primary industry: agriculture(including farming, forestry, animal husbandry and fishery).

Secondary industry: industry (including mining and quarrying, manufacturing, production and supply of electricity, water and gas)and construction.

Tertiary industry: all other industries not included in primary or secondary industry. Due to the fact that tertiary industry involves in a large variety of industries in China, it is divided into two sectors: circulation sector and service sector.

Final Consumption refers to the total expenditure of resident units on final consumption of goods and services in a certain period, namely the expenditure of the resident units for purchases of goods and services from domestic economic territory and abroad to meet the requirements of material, cultural and spiritual life. It excludes the expenditure of non-resident units on consumption in the economic territory of the country. The final consumption is classified into household consumption and government consumption.

Households Consumption refers to the total expenditure of resident households on the final consumption of goods and services. The households consumption is calculated at market prices, namely the purchaser's prices which the households pay; the purchasers prices of goods are the prices the households pay when they obtain the goods, including the transport and commercial expenses paid by the households. In addition to the consumption of goods and services bought by the households directly with money, the expenditure on goods and services obtained by the households in other ways, i.e. the so-called imputed expenditure on consumption, is also included in the households consumption. The imputation expenditure of the households on consumption includes the following types: (a) the goods and services provided to the households by the units in the form of payment in kind and transfer in kind; (b) the goods and services produced and consumed by the households themselves, in which the services refer only to the services provided by the residential buildings owned by the households; (c) the services of financial intermediary provided by the financial institutions; (d) the insurance services provided by the insurance companies.

Government Consumption refers to the expenditure on the consumption of the public services provided by the government to the whole society and the net expenditure on the goods and services provided by the government to the households at free charge or lower prices. The former equals to the output value of the government services minus the value of operating income obtained by the government departments. (The output value of the government services equals to its current operating expenditure plus depreciation of fixed assets). The latter equals to the market value of the goods and services provided by the government free of charge or at low prices to the households minus the value received by the government from the households.

Production Capacity of Water Supply refers to the designed comprehensive production capacity of water facilities, covering the 4 links of water collection, purification, conveyance, and outflow through trunk pipelines. Increase capacity through transformation and innovation projects are included as well. The capacity is determined mainly on the weakest of the above-mentioned 4 links.

Length of Water Supply Pipelines at the Year-end refers to the total length of all the pipelines between the water pumps and the user's water meters, excluding pipelines newly installed but not used yet.

Annual Volume of Water Supply refers to the total volume of water supplied by water-works(units) during the reference period, including both the effective water supply and loss during the water supply.

Consumption of Water for Residential Use refers to the water consumption of households for daily life and the water consumption of public service facilities. The latter refers to water consumption for urban public services, including the consumption of government agencies and public institutions, military barracks, public facilities, wholesale and retail outlets, restaurants, hotels, and other units providing public services. Household water consumption refers to consumption of water for daily life of all households in the boundary of cities, including households of urban residents and farmers, and public water supply stations.

Percentage of Urban Population with Access to Tap Water refers to the ratio of the urban population with access to tap water to the total urban population. The formula is:

Percentage of population with access to tap water= (Urban population with access to tap water) / (Urban population)×100%

Production Capacity of Gaswork Gas refers to the comprehensive production capacity of the urban gas-works in gas generation, purification and delivery at the end of the reference period, excluding capacity of the reserved facilities. In general, it is determined by the designed capacity, and when actual production capacity is larger than the designed capacity, the capacity is determined by the actual measurement on the weakest link in the production, purification and delivery.

Length of Gas Pipelines refers to the total length of pipelines in use between the outlet of the compressor of gas-work or outlet of gas stations and the leading pipe of users, excluding pipelines within gasworks, delivery stations, LPG storage stations, refilling stations, gas-mixing stations and supply stations.

Volume of Gas Supply refers to the total volume of gas provided to users by gas-producing enterprises (units) in a year, including the volume sold and the volume lost.

Percentage of Urban Population with Access to Gas refers to the ratio of the urban population with access to gas to the total urban population at the end of the reference period. The formula is:

Percentage of population with access to gas=(Urban population with access to gas / Urban population) × 100%

Heating Capacity in Urban Area refers to the designed capacity of heating enterprises (units) in supplying heating energy to urban users during the reference period.

Quantity of Heat Supplied in Urban Area refers to the total quantity of heat from steam and hot water supplied to urban users by heating enterprises (units) during the reference period.

Length of Heating Pipelines refers to the total length of steam or hot water pipelines for sources of heat to the leading pipelines of the buildings of the users, excluding internal pipelines in heat generating enterprises.

Length of Paved Roads at the Year-end refers to the length of roads with paved surface including squares bridges and tunnels connected with roads by the end of the year. Length of the roads is measured by the central lines for vehicles for paved roads with a width of 3.5 meters and over, including roads in open-ended factory compounds and residential quarters.

Urban Bridges refer to bridges built to cross over natural or man-made barriers, including bridges over rivers, overpasses for traffic and for pedestrian, underpasses for pedestrian, etc. Both permanent and semi-permanent bridges are included.

Length of Urban Sewage Pipes refers to the total length of general drainage, trunks. branch and inspection wells, connection wells, inlets and outlets, etc.

Daily Disposal Capacity of Urban Sewage refers to the designed 24 hour capacity of sewage disposal by the sewage treatment works or facilities.

Number of Vehicles under Operation at the Year-end refers to the total number of vehicles under operation by public transport enterprises (units) at the end of the year, based on the records of operational vehicles by the enterprises (units).

Area of Urban Gardens and Green Areas refers to the total area occupied for green projects at the end of the reference period, including public green land, green land in residential quarters, green land attached to institutions, protection green land, production green land, roadside green land and forest in scenic spots. It does not include the following:

(1) Greenery and plants on roofs, balconies, indoors and vertical green areas;

(2) Forest, cultivated land, grassland, orchards and bamboo grooves that are for production purpose; and

(3) Water areas that are not included in urban master plan as green land.

Public Green Area refers to green areas open to the public such as municipal, community and neighborhood parks and roadside parks, including waters within parks. Neighborhood parks should occupy an area larger than 10,000 square meters, and the width of roadside parks should occupy an area larger than 400 square meters, with a width of more that 8 meters.

2 Two

人口

Population

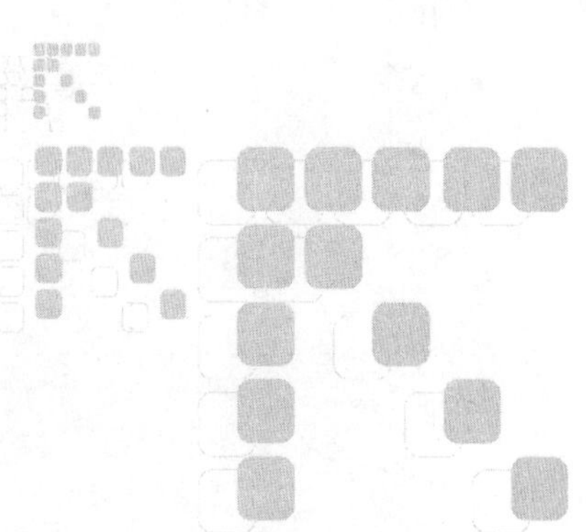

年末总人口（万人）
Total Population at the Year-end (10000 persons)

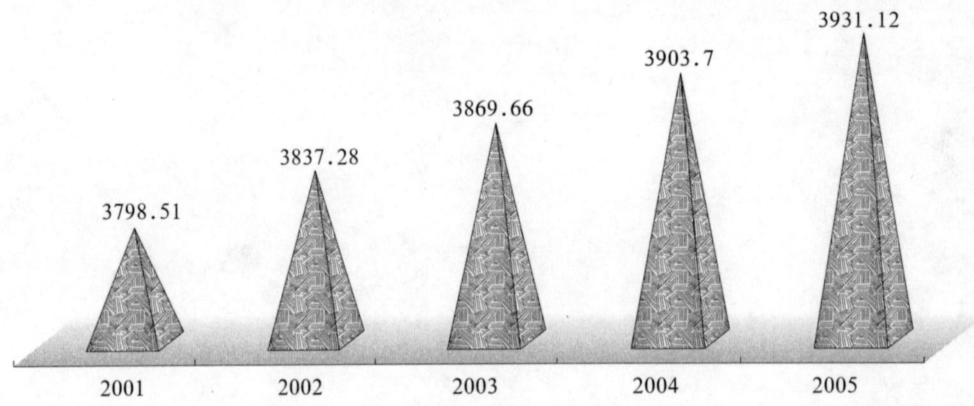

年末总人口构成情况（%）
Composition of Total Population (%)

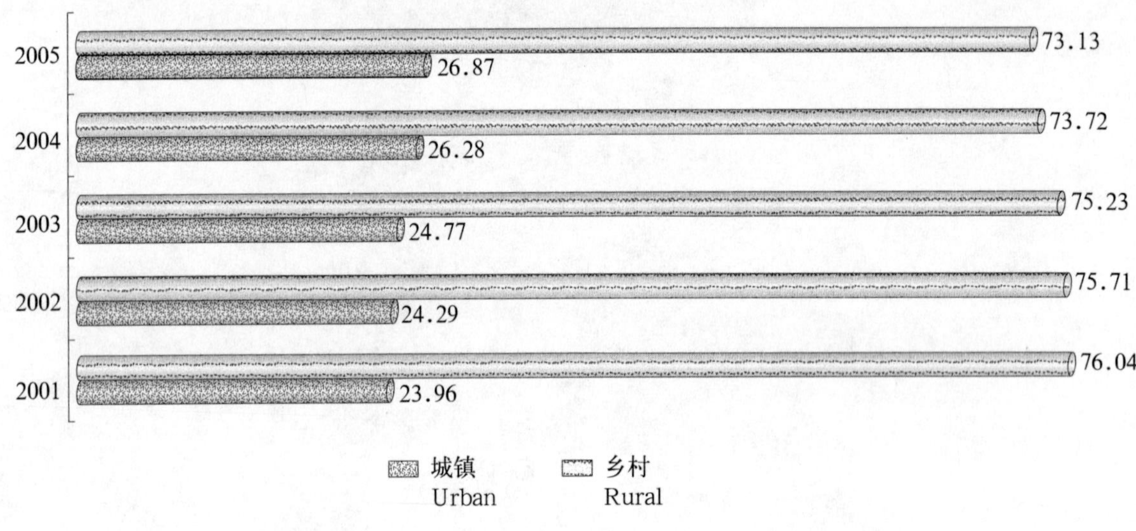

人口自然增长率（‰）
Natural Growth Rate of Population (‰)

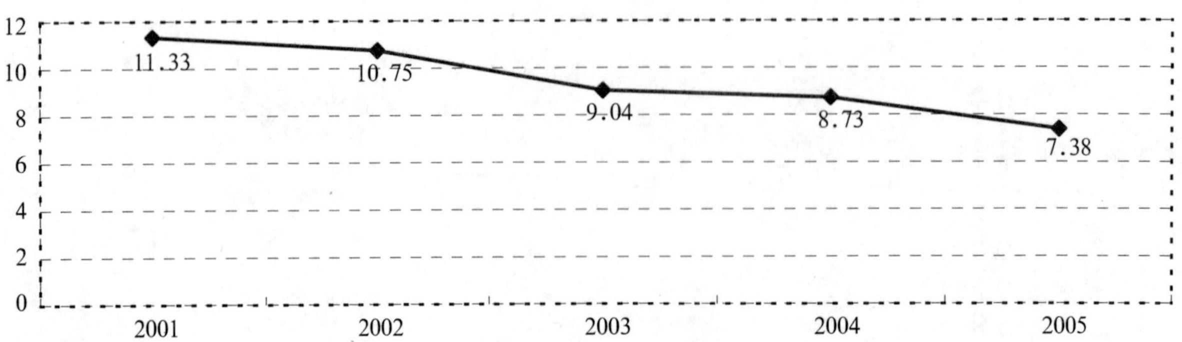

2-1 “十五”时期各年常住人口变动情况

Basic Statistics on Population of Each Year in “Tenth Five-year Plan” Period

单位：万人(10000 persons)

指 标	Item	2000	2001	2002	2003	2004	2005
年末总人口	**Total Population at the Year-end**	**3755.72**	**3798.51**	**3837.28**	**3869.66**	**3903.70**	**3931.12**
年平均人口	Annual Average Population	3732.89	3777.12	3817.90	3853.47	3886.68	3917.41
按城镇、乡村分	Grouped by Residence						
城 镇	Urban	896.49	910.12	932.11	958.52	1025.89	1056.29
乡 村	Rural	2859.23	2888.39	2905.17	2911.14	2877.81	2874.83
按性别分	Grouped by Sex						
男	Male	1968.00	1973.41	1993.15	2010.22	2022.22	2024.11
女	Female	1787.72	1825.10	1844.13	1859.44	1881.48	1907.01
性别比(以女性为100)	Sex Ratio(female=100)	110.08	108.13	108.08	108.11	107.48	106.14
年末总户数（万户）	Total Number of Household (10000 households)	1004.20	1061.26	1048.44	1057.28	1069.51	1139.46
家庭户规模（人/户）	Average Family Size(person/household)	3.74	3.73	3.66	3.66	3.65	3.45
人口自然变动	**Natural Change of Population**						
出生人数	Number of Birth	76.86	70.10	68.57	61.31	58.61	57.16
出生率(‰)	Birth Rate(‰)	20.59	18.56	17.96	15.91	15.08	14.59
死亡人数	Number of Death	28.11	28.44	27.53	26.47	24.68	28.24
死亡率(‰)	Death Rate(‰)	7.53	7.23	7.21	6.87	6.35	7.21
自然增长人数	Natural Increase of Population	48.75	41.66	41.04	34.84	33.93	28.92
自然增长率(‰)	Natural Growth Rate(‰)	13.06	11.33	10.75	9.04	8.73	7.38

2-2 五次人口普查人口基本情况

Basic Statistics on National Population Census in 1953, 1964, 1982, 1990 and 2000

指 标	Item	第一次 (1953)	第二次 (1964)	第三次 (1982)	第四次 (1990)	第五次 (2000)
总人口（万人）	**Total Population(10000 persons)**	**1503.73**	**1714.05**	**2855.29**	**3239.11**	**3524.77**
男	Male	759.53	868.48	1464.08	1676.88	1846.45
女	Female	744.20	845.57	1391.21	1562.22	1678.32
性别比(以女性为100)	Sex Ratio(female=100)	102.06	102.71	105.24	107.34	110.02
家庭户规模（人/户）	Average Family Size (person/household)	4.63	4.47	4.98	4.41	3.74
各年龄组人口（%）	Population by Age Group (%)					
0–14岁	0–14	569.61	665.31	1167.28	1058.47	1067.66
15–64岁	15–64	880.13	1001.43	1554.82	2031.25	2252.92
65岁及以上	65 and Over	53.99	47.31	133.19	149.39	203.93
民族人口	Nationality Population					
汉族（万人）	Han Nationality (10000 persons)	1109.84	1312.89	2112.95	2114.88	2191.17
占总人口比重（%）	Percentage to Total Population(%)	73.81	76.60	74.00	65.29	62.16
少数民族（万人）	Minority Nationalities(10000 persons)	393.89	401.16	742.34	1124.23	1333.60
占总人口比重（%）	Percentage to Total Population(%)	26.19	23.40	26.00	34.71	37.84
每十万人拥有的各种受教育程度人口(人)	Population with Various Education Attainments Per 100000 persons (person)					
大专及以上	Junior College and Above		231.04	388.40	773.00	1915.00
高中和中专	Senior Secondary/Secondary Technical School		780.86	2967.12	3936.00	5665.00
初 中	Junior Secondary School		3138.61	11412.50	14688.00	20639.00
小 学	Primary School		20577.58	28811.43	37379.00	43557.00
文盲人口及文盲率	Illiterate Population and Illiterate Rate					
文盲人口（万人）	Illiterate Population(10000 persons)			853.67	800.86	488.61
文盲率（%）	Illiterate Rate (%)			50.57	36.73	19.89
城乡人口（万人）	Population by Residence(10000 persons)					
城镇人口	Urban Population	109.91	203.55	540.22	623.17	844.51
乡村人口	Rural Population	1393.82	1510.50	2315.07	2615.93	2680.26

2-3 “十五”时期各年户籍人口变动情况

Changes of Permanent Residonts of Each Year in “Tenth Five-year Plan” Period

单位：万人(10000 persons)

指 标	Item	2000	2001	2002	2003	2004	2005
年末总人口	**Total Population at the Year-end**	**3676.63**	**3710.2**	**3747.68**	**3786.84**	**3831.19**	**3867.73**
按农业、非农业分	Grouped by Agriculture and Non-agriculture						
农 业	Agriculture	3144.98	3156.33	3175.18	3196.69	3224.62	3258.04
非农业	Non-agriculture	531.65	553.87	572.5	590.15	606.57	609.69
构成（以年末总人口=100）	Composition(total population at the year-end=100)						
农 业	Agriculture	85.5	85.1	84.7	84.40	84.2	84.2
非农业	Non-agriculture	14.5	14.9	15.3	15.6	15.8	15.8

注：本表资料由省公安厅提供。

Note:Data in the table are obtained from the Department of Public Security of Guizhou Province.

2-4 “十五”时期各年婚姻情况

Number of Marriages and Divorces of Each Year in “Tenth Five-year Plan” Period

指 标	Item	2000	2001	2002	2003	2004	2005
准予登记结婚（对）	**Registered Marriages(couple)**	**280239**	**268149**	**245966**	**234322**	**223621**	**211257**
初婚（人）	First Marriages(person)	543331	518046	471097	446895	415269	382143
再婚（人）	Remarriages(person)	15473	16296	19287	20207	30507	40371
#女性（人）	Famle(person)	7711	7957	9904	9214	15421	19916
离婚人数（人）	Divorces(person)	67172	56318	46780	57102	80804	76284
#民政部门批准(人)	Permitted by Civil Administration Department(person)	30848	17690	17812	25538	44074	45718
法院调判（人）	Sentenced by Court(person)	36324	38628	28968	31564	36730	30566
涉外婚姻（对）	Registered Marriages with Foreigner and the Citizen of Hong Kong,Macao, Taiwan	837	978	774	771	733	737
#国内公民（人）	Domestic Citizen(person)	837	978	774	771	723	732
#女性（人）	Famle(person)	816	961	756	758	708	706

2-5 “十五”时期各年计划生育主要指标

Main Indicators on Family Planning of Each Year in “Tenth Five-year Plan” Period

单位：万人(10000 persons)

指 标	Item	2000	2001	2002	2003	2004	2005
符合政策出生人数	**Number of Birth in Legality**	**55.35**	**53.49**	**57.25**	**52.16**	**52.27**	**53.19**
生育政策符合率（%）	Family Planning Rate(%)	72.01	76.31	83.49	85.08	89.1	93.05
领独生子女证人数	Number of One-child Certificate	44.10	41.74	44.68	48.32	52.43	57.63
独生子女领证率（%）	Acceptance Rate of One-child Certificate (%)	6.7	6.2	6.6	7.2	7.6	8.4
采取节育措施人数	Number of Contraception User	594.05	622.94	620.87	629.50	636.51	628.52
避孕率(含复合使用药具)(%)	Contraception Rate(%)	90.1	93.0	91.9	93.5	92.7	91.5

主要统计指标解释

人口数 指一定时点、一定地区范围内的有生命的个人的总和。年度统计的年末人口数指每年12月31日24时的人口数。

市镇总人口和乡村总人口

其定义有两种口径：

第一种口径（按行政建制）

市人口：市管辖区域内的全部口（含市辖镇，不含市辖区县）；

镇人口：县辖镇的全部人口（不含市辖镇）；

县人口：县辖乡人口。

第二种口径（按常住人口划分）

市人口：设区的市的区人口和不设区的市所辖的街道人口；

镇人口：不设区的市所辖镇的居民委员会人口和县辖镇的居民委员会人口；

县人口：除上述两种人口以外的全部人口。

出生率(又称粗出生率) 指在一定时期内(通常为一年)平均每千人所出生的人数的比率，一般用千分率表示。计算公式为：

出生率=年出生人数/年平均人数×1000‰

式中：出生人数指活产婴儿，即胎儿脱离母体时(不管怀孕月数)，有过呼吸或其他生命现象。年平均人数指年初、年底人口数的平均数，也可用年中人口数代替。

死亡率(又称粗死亡率) 指在一定时期内(通常为一年)一定地区的死亡人数与同期平均人数(或期中人数)之比，一般用千分率表示。计算公式为：

死亡率=年死亡人数/年平均人数×1000‰

人口自然增长率 指在一定时期内(通常为一年)人口自然增加数(出生人数减死亡人数)与该时期内平均人数(或期中人数)之比，一般用千分率表示。计算公式为：

人口自然增长率=(本年出生人数-本年死亡人数)/年平均人数×1000‰=人口出生率-人口死亡率

Explanatory Notes on Main Statistical Indicators

Total Population refers to the total number of people alive at a certain point of time within a given area. The annual statistics on total population is taken at midnight, the 3lst of December.

Urban Population and Rural Population. There are two definitions. The first definition (according to the administrative organizational system):

City population: Total population under the jurisdiction of city (including population of the town under the jurisdiction of city. excluding the population of counties under the jurisdiction of city).

Town population: Total population of town under the jurisdiction of county (excluding the population of town under the jurisdiction of city).

County population: Total population of country under the jurisdiction of county).

The second definition (classified by the permanent population):

City population: Total population of districts under the jurisdiction of city with district establishment and the population of street under the jurisdiction of city without district establishment.

Town population: Total resident–committees population of towns under the jurisdiction of city without district establishment and the resident–committees population of towns under the jurisdiction of county.

County population: Total population except city population and town population.

Birth Rate or (Crude Birth Rate) refers to the ratio of the number of births to the average population during a certain period of time(usually a year) which is often expressed in‰. The following formula is used:

Birth Rate=Number of Births/Average Number of Population×1000‰

Number of births refers to live births i.e. the births when babies had showed any vital phenomena regardless of the length of pregnancy.

Annual Average Number of Population is the average of the number of population at the beginning of the year and that at the end of the year. Sometimes it is substituted for with the mid year population.

Death Rate(or Crude Death Rate) refers to the ratio of the number of deaths to the average population (or mid year population) during a certain period of time (usually a year) which is often expressed in‰. The following formula is used:

Death Rate umber of Deaths=Number of Deaths/Annual Average Number of Population×1000‰

Natural Growth Rate of Population refers to the ratio of natural increase in population (number of births minus number of deaths)in a certain period of time(usually a year)to the average population(or mid year population) of the same period which is often expressed in‰. The following formulas are applied:

Natural Growth Rate of Population=(Number of Births–Number of Deaths)/Average Number of Population×1000‰=Birth Rate–Death Rate

3

Three

劳动、就业与保障

Labour Force, Employment and Security

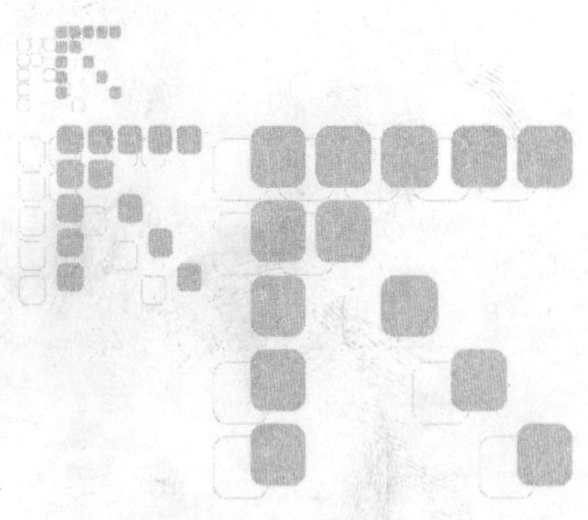

从业人员（万人）

Number of Employed Persons (10000 persons)

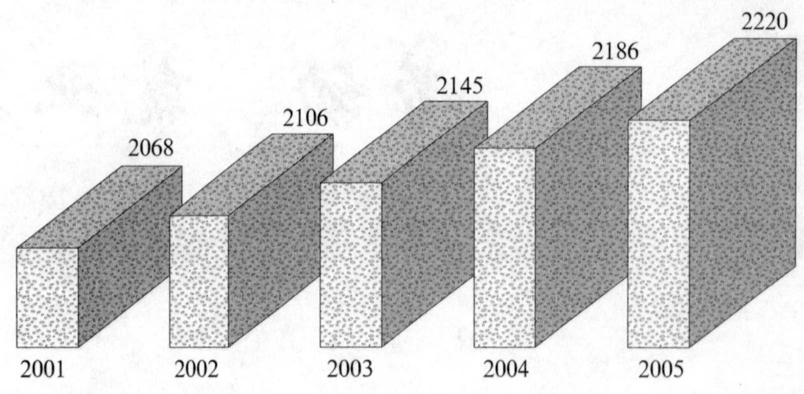

职工平均工资（元）

Average Wage of Staff and Workers (yuan)

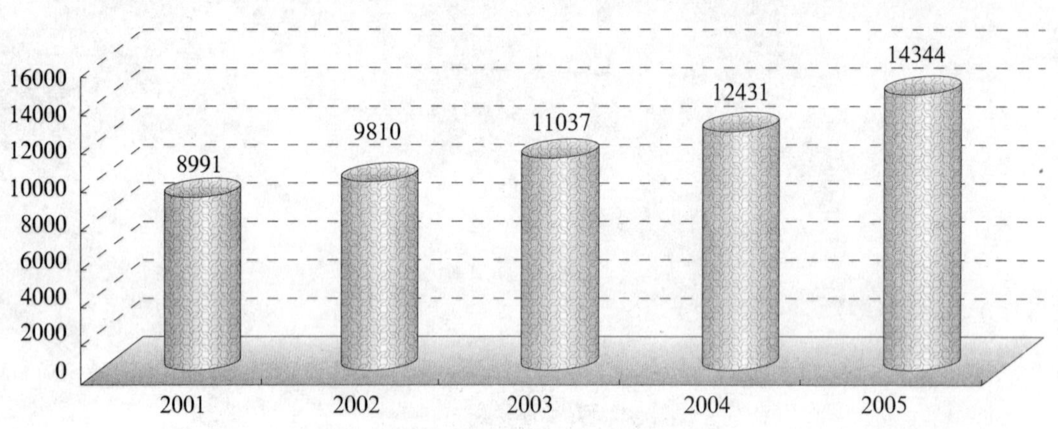

城镇新就业人数（万人）

Number of Newly Employed Personnels in Urban (10000 persons)

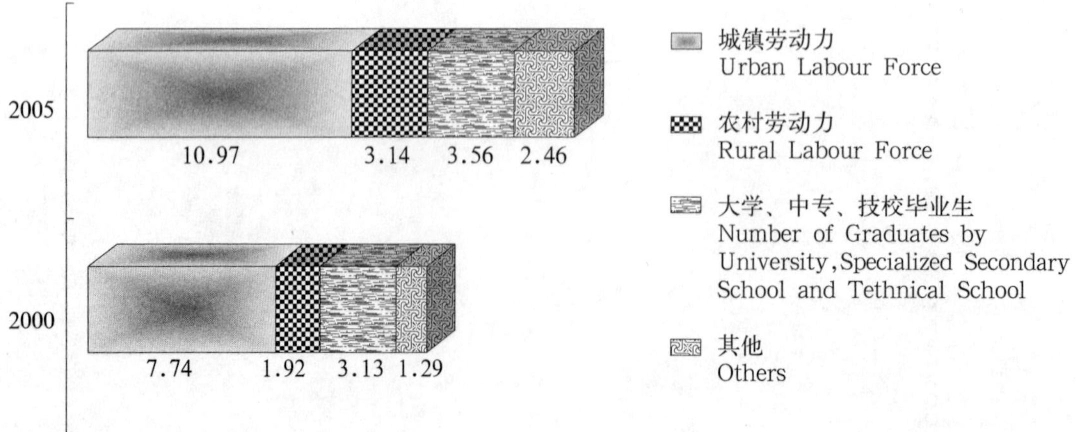

3-1 “十五”时期各年从业人员及劳动报酬

Number of Employed Personnels and Wages of Each Year in “Tenth Five-year Plan” Period

指 标	Item	2000	2001	2002	2003	2004	2005	2005年比2004年增长(%) Increase Rate in 2005 over 2004(%)
从业人员总计(万人)	**Number of Employed Persons (10000 persons)**	**1866.23**	**2068**	**2106.1**	**2145.00**	**2186.00**	**2220.00**	**1.6**
按产业分	Grouped by Type of Industry							
第一产业	Primary Industry	1305.28	1692.3	1698.39	1671.2	1672.29	1670	-0.1
第二产业	Secondary Industry	221.79	133.88	108.89	120.49	124.6	144.58	16.0
第三产业	Tertiary Industry	339.16	241.8	298.86	353.31	389.11	405.42	4.2
按城乡分(万人)	Grouped by Urban and Rural (10000 persons)							
城镇从业人员	Urban Area	267.15	246.75	257.19	402.29	418.00	434.00	3.8
#国有单位	#State-owned Unit	151.31	157.97	153.58	148.42	147.06	142.13	-3.4
集体单位	Collective-owned Unit	19.3	16.47	17.00	22.14	27.57	29.64	7.5
股份合作单位	Share Holding Uint	1.84	1.39	1.60	1.56	2.45	2.65	8.2
联营单位	Joint-owned Unit	0.65	0.51	0.49	0.44	0.48	0.68	41.7
有限责任公司	Limited Liability Corporations	14.91	17.12	19.72	20.98	27.24	36.99	35.8
股份有限公司	Share Holding Corporations Ltd.	2.94	4.22	6.30	9.37	9.28	10.62	14.4
私营企业	Private Enterprises	19.22	16.97	20.54	26.17	37.49	43.82	16.9
港澳台投资单位	Economic Units with Funds from HongKong,Macao and Taiwan	0.64	0.76	0.98	1.28	1.29	1.30	0.8
外商投资单位	Foreign Funded Units	1.23	1.07	1.00	1.50	1.28	1.65	28.9
个体	Self-employed Individuals	55.87	30.27	35.98	75.61	95.90	100.9	5.2
乡村从业人员	Rural Area	1599.08	1821.26	1848.95	1742.71	1768.00	1786.00	1.0
#私营企业	Private Enterprises	9.23	11.34	12.79	16.49	17.32	19.12	10.4
个体	Self-employed Individuals	27.86	66.18	58.00	80.97	72.96	78.20	7.2
乡镇企业	Township and Village Enterprises	230.47	253.60	265.00	216.30	222.60	234.90	5.5
职工人数总计(万人)	**Number of Staff and Workers(10000 persons)**	**193.97**	**189.17**	**188.47**	**188.70**	**192.67**	**202.02**	**4.9**
国有单位	State-owned Unit	153.55	148.87	146.96	141.75	139.57	140.50	0.7
集体单位	Collective-owned Unit	19.01	15.72	14.39	13.71	12.77	9.81	-23.2
其他单位	Others	21.41	24.58	27.12	33.24	40.33	51.71	28.2
职工工资总额(亿元)	**Total Wages of Staff and Wokers(100 million yuan)**	**144.56**	**169.65**	**184.34**	**209.33**	**236.60**	**284.16**	**20.1**
国有单位	State-owned Unit	116.41	138.12	148.69	163.02	177.62	202.40	14.0
集体单位	Collective-owned Unit	10.18	9.69	9.37	10.30	10.78	10.20	-5.4
其他单位	Others	17.97	21.84	26.28	36.01	48.20	71.56	48.5
职工平均工资(元)	**Average Wage of Staff and Workers(yuan)**	**7468**	**8991**	**9810**	**11037**	**12431**	**14344**	**15.4**
国有单位	State-owned Unit	7594	9308	10150	11390	12870	14681	14.1
集体单位	Collective-owned Unit	5444	6218	6566	7504	8630	10506	21.7
其他单位	Others	8325	8831	9681	10975	12103	14161	17.0

3-2 "十五"时期各年城镇新就业人数和失业人数

Number of Incremental Employed and Unemployed in Urban Units of Each Year in "Tenth Five-year Plan" Period

单位：万人(10000 persons)

指 标	Item	2000	2001	2002	2003	2004	2005	2005年比2004年增长(%) Increase Rate in 2005 over 2004(%)
新就业人数总计	**Total Incremental Employed Personnels**	**14.08**	**14.36**	**15.85**	**22.23**	**22.08**	**20.13**	**-8.8**
按主要来源分	Grouped by Main Source							
城镇劳动力	From Urban Area	7.74	5.71	9.05	15.61	13.92	10.97	-21.2
农村劳动力	From Rural Area	1.92	2.98	2.36	2.44	2.78	3.14	12.9
大学、中专、技校毕业生	Graduated from University and Specialized Secondary School	3.13	2.74	2.46	3.1	3.71	3.56	-4.0
其 他	Others	1.29	2.93	1.98	1.08	1.67	2.46	47.3
按安置去向分	Grouped by the Direction to Allocate							
国有经济单位	State-owned Unit	3.2	2.3	1.98	5.22	6.52	9.71	48.9
城镇集体经济单位	Collective-owned Unit	2.22	1.56	1.27	0.68	0.62	0.73	18.1
其他经济单位	Unit of Other Type of Ownership	1.71	1.31	1.9	1.67	3.37	5.76	70.9
其他劳动者	Other Labourers	3.95	9.19	9.66	14.66	11.57	3.93	-66.0
城镇登记失业人数	Number of Regisered Employed Persons in Urban Areas	10.24	11.15	11.08	11.18	11.61	12.13	4.5
城镇登记失业率(%)	Regisered Unemployment Rate in Urban Areas(%)	3.8	4.0	4.1	4	4.1	4.2	-0.1 (百分点)

3-3 单位从业人员变动情况（2005）

Changes in the Number of Staff and Workers on Their Posts（2005）

单位：人(person)

指 标	Item	总计 Total	国有单位 State-owned Unit	集体单位 Collect-iveowned Unit	其他单位 Unit of Other Type of Ownership
增加人数	**Number of Persons Increased**	**187081**	**118396**	**7979**	**60706**
从农村招收	Recruited from Rural Area	74118	42305	4776	27037
从城镇招收	Recruited from Urban Area	24961	11009	1089	12863
录用的复员转业军人	Employment of Demobilized Soldiers	3938	2548	153	1237
录用的大、中专、技工学校毕业生	Employment of Graduate from College, Secondary Technical Schools and Workers Training Schools	34429	24743	568	9118
调入人数	Number of Persons Transferred into	25032	21248	655	3129
#省外调入	From Outside Guizhou	758	678		80
其 他	Others	24603	16543	738	7322
减少人数	**Number of Persons Decreased**	**154570**	**91934**	**9685**	**52951**
离休、退休、退职	Retire and Resigned	25545	19297	1098	5150
开除、除名、辞退	Expelled and Discharged	13673	3701	872	9100
终止、解除合同	Contract Terminated	41926	18448	1775	21703
离开本单位仍保留劳动关系的职工	Remain Labour Ralationship	13279	9747	971	2561
死亡	Deaths	2664	2071	113	480
调出人数	Number of Persons Transferred out	24848	21192	641	3015
#调出省	To Outside Guizhou	524	389		135
其 他	Others	32635	17478	4215	10942

3-4 城镇单位各行业从业人员数（2005）

Number of Employed Persons in Urban Units by Sector（2005）

单位：人(person)

指 标	Item	从业人员 Number of Employed	国有单位 State-owned Unit	城镇集体单位 Urban Collective-owned Unit	其他单位 Unit of Other Type of Ownership
总 计	**Total**	**2105883**	**1467312**	**104138**	**534433**
按企事业、机关分组	By Enterprises,Institutions and Agencies				
企 业	Enterprises	1206865	576271	101904	528690
事 业	Institutions	618757	610929	2085	5743
机 关	Agencies	280261	280112	149	
按产业分	By Type of Industry	2105883	1467312	104138	534433
第一产业	Primary Industry	29618	29239	44	335
第二产业	Secondary Industry	829703	376309	64658	388736
第三产业	Tertiary Industry	1246562	1061764	39436	145362
按国民经济行业分组	By Sector	2105883	1467312	104138	534433
农、林、牧、渔业	Farming,Forestry,Animal Husbandry and Fishing	29618	29239	44	335
采矿业	Mining and Quarrying	108624	31504	2832	74288
制造业	Manufacturing	417190	160205	24944	232041
电力、燃气及水的生产和供应业	Production and Supply of Electricity, Gas and Water	65367	50308	886	14173
建筑业	Construction	238522	134292	35996	68234
交通运输、仓储和邮政业	Transportation,Storage and Post	87371	76781	3679	6911
信息传输、计算机服务和软件业	Information Transmit,Computer Services and Software Trade	16410	7093	83	9234
批发和零售业	Wholesale and Retail Trade	120644	63670	14689	42285
#批发业	Wholesale	70808	45419	4300	21089
零售业	Retail	49836	18251	10389	21196
住宿和餐饮业	Quarter and Catering Services	27455	11248	1207	15000
金融业	Finance	48666	23272	10940	14454
房地产业	Real Estate	38240	5796	2339	30105
租赁和商务服务业	Leasing and Commerce Services	24486	13690	2919	7877
#租赁业	Leasing Services	835	70	293	472
商务服务业	Commerce Services	23651	13620	2626	7405
科学研究、技术服务和地质勘查业	Scientific Research,Technic Serviced and Geological Prospecting	36088	30693	155	5240
水利、环境和公共设施管理业	Water Conservancy,Environment and Public Facilities Services	25209	23504	1350	355
居民服务和其他服务业	Services to Households and Other Services	7800	1861	1053	4886
教 育	Education	380138	374736	217	5185
卫生、社会保障和社会福利业	Health Care,Social Securities and Social Welfare	88767	86880	657	1230
#卫 生	Health Care	86395	84508	657	1230
社会保障业	Social Securities	940	940		
文化、体育和娱乐业	Culture,Sports and Entertainment	20299	18302	36	1961
#新闻出版社	News Publishing Company	4079	4033		46
广播、电视、电影和音像业	Broadcasting,Television,Film and Video Trade	7584	7297	36	251
体 育	Sports	1945	1731		214
公共管理和社会组织	Public Administration and Social Organization	324989	324238	112	639

3-5 城镇单位女性从业人员年末人数(2005)

Number of Employed Female in Urban Units at the Year-end by Sector（2005）

单位：人(person)

行　业	Sector	女性从业人员数 Number of Female Employed	国有单位 State-owned Unit	集体单位 Collective owned Unit	其他单位 Unit of Other Type of Ownership
总　计	**Total**	**679215**	**486474**	**29965**	**162776**
农、林、牧、渔业	Farming,Forestry,Animal Husbandry and Fishing	8479	8351	2	126
采矿业	Mining and Quarrying	20259	8002	424	11833
制造业	Manufacturing	143080	57892	8713	76475
电力、燃气及水的生产和供应业	Production and Supply of Electricity,Gas and Wate	19061	15110	233	3718
建筑业	Construction	29710	13870	5140	10700
交通运输、仓储和邮政业	Transportation,Storage and Post	26499	23069	1048	2382
信息传输、计算机服务和软件业	Information Transmit,Computer Services and Software Trade	5776	2618	20	3138
批发和零售业	Wholesale and Retail Trade	49967	25269	6560	18138
#批发业	Wholesale	24298	15482	1686	7130
零售业	Retail Trade	25669	9787	4874	11008
住宿和餐饮业	Quarter and Catering Services	15361	6181	713	8467
金融业	Finance	21866	10015	4318	7533
房地产业	Real Estate	12138	1905	712	9521
租赁和商务服务业	Leasing and Commerce Services	8547	5084	469	2994
#租赁业	Leasing Services	267	37	90	140
商务服务业	Commerce Services	8280	5047	379	2854
科学研究、技术服务和地质勘查业	Scientific Research,Technic Serviced and Geological Prospecting	10709	9569	42	1098
水利、环境和公共设施管理业	Water Conservancy,Environment and Public Facilities Services	11508	10625	773	110
居民服务和其他服务业	Services to Households and Other Services	3116	600	226	2290
教　育	Education	148367	145875	107	2385
卫生、社会保障和社会福利业	Health Care,Social Securities and Social Welfare	50842	49628	405	809
#卫　生	Health Care	49730	48516	405	809
社会保障业	Social Securities	406	406		
文化、体育和娱乐业	Culture,Sports and Entertainment	8061	7086	5	970
#新闻出版社	News Publishing Company	1486	1470		16
广播、电视、电影和音像业	Broadcasting,Television,Film and Video Trade	2752	2657	5	90
体　育	Sports	700	600		100
公共管理和社会组织	Public Administration and Social Organization	85869	85725	55	89

3-6 各行业在岗职工人数(2005)

Number of Staff and Workers on Their Posts by Sector（2005）

单位：人 (person)

指 标	Item	职工人数 Number of Staff and Workers	国有单位 State-owned Unit	集体单位 Collective-owned unit	其他单位 Unit of Other Type of Ownership
总 计	**Total**	**2020175**	**1405019**	**98076**	**517080**
按企事业、机关分组	By Enterprises,Institutions and Agencies				
企 业	Enterprises	1148711	541364	95866	511481
事 业	Institutions	597652	589992	2061	5599
机 关	Agencies	273812	273663	149	
按产业分	By Type of Industry	2020175	1405019	98076	517080
第一产业	Primary Industry	27635	27260	44	331
第二产业	Secondary Industry	790184	353350	59205	377629
第三产业	Tertiary Industry	1202356	1024409	38827	139120
按国民经济行业分组	By Sector	2016987	1405019	98076	513892
农、林、牧、渔业	Farming,Forestry,Animal Husbandry and Fishing	27635	27260	44	331
采矿业	Mining and Quarrying	106216	31063	2053	73100
制造业	Manufacturing	405280	153660	23746	227874
电力、燃气及水的生产和供应业	Production and Supply of Electricity,Gas and Wate	62552	47732	869	13951
建筑业	Construction	216136	120895	32537	62704
交通运输、仓储和邮政业	Transportation,Storage and Post	81968	71410	3674	6884
信息传输、计算机服务和软件业	Information Transmit,Computer Services and Software Trade	15448	6313	82	9053
批发和零售业	Wholesale and Retail Trade	117282	61744	14370	41168
#批发业	Wholesale	68265	43707	4181	20377
零售业	Retail	49017	18037	10189	20791
住宿和餐饮业	Quarter and Catering Services	26240	10242	1181	14817
金融业	Finance	45487	22265	10833	12389
房地产业	Real Estate	35700	5047	2304	28349
租赁和商务服务业	Leasing and Commerce Services	23800	13292	2876	7632
#租赁业	Leasing Services	824	70	293	461
商务服务业	Commerce Services	22976	13222	2583	7171
科学研究、技术服务和地质勘查业	Scientific Research,Technic Serviced and Geological Prospecting	35242	30118	148	4976
水利、环境和公共设施管理业	Water Conservancy,Environment and Public Facilities Services	22380	20681	1350	349
居民服务和其他服务业	Services to Households and Other Services	7613	1802	1009	4802
教 育	Education	364457	362455	208	1794
卫生、社会保障和社会福利业	Health Care,Social Securities and Social Welfare	85920	84123	644	1153
#卫 生	Health Care	83600	81803	644	1153
社会保障业	Social Securities	893	893		
文化、体育和娱乐业	Culture,Sports and Entertainment	19981	18016	36	1929
#新闻出版社	News Publishing Company	4042	3996		46
广播、电视、电影和音像业	Broadcasting,Television,Film and Video Trade	7435	7148	36	251
体 育	Sports	1936	1722		214
公共管理和社会组织	Public Administration and Social Organization	317650	316901	112	637

3-7 各行业职工中专业技术人员数（2005）

Number of Technical Personnel by Sector（2005）

单位：人 (person)

指 标	Item	合计 Total	国有单位 State-owned Unit	集体单位 Collective-owned Unit	其他单位 Unit of Other Type of Ownership
总 计	**Total**	677663	570514	15483	91666
按企事业、机关分组	By Enterprises,Institutions and Agencies				
企 业	Enterprises	214327	111065	14798	88464
事 业	Institutions	432479	428633	644	3202
机 关	Agencies	30857	30816	41	
按产业分	By Type of Industry				
第一产业	Primary Industry	10723	10649		74
第二产业	Secondary Industry	136135	68474	7771	59890
第三产业	Tertiary Industry	530805	491391	7712	31702
按国民经济行业分组	By Sector	677663	570514	15483	91666
农、林、牧、渔业	Farming,Forestry,Animal Husbandry and Fishing	10723	10649		74
采矿业	Mining and Quarrying	16358	6831	205	9322
制造业	Manufacturing	72234	33868	2387	35979
电力、燃气及水的生产和供应业	Production and Supply of Electricity, Gas and Water	14986	10374	105	4507
建筑业	Construction	32557	17401	5074	10082
交通运输、仓储和邮政业	Transportation,Storage and Post	9943	8507	592	844
信息传输、计算机服务和软件业	Information Transmit,Computer Services and Software Trade	4577	2190		2387
批发和零售业	Wholesale and Retail Trade	16765	9669	1100	5996
#批发业	Wholesale	12193	8354	571	3268
零售业	Retail Trade	4572	1315	529	2728
住宿和餐饮业	Quarter and Catering Services	1950	640	96	1214
金融业	Finance	24860	16326	4559	3975
房地产业	Real Estate	10099	1346	374	8379
租赁和商务服务业	Leasing and Commerce Services	4777	2630	224	1923
#租赁业	Leasing Services	68	5		63
商务服务业	Commerce Services	4709	2625	224	1860
科学研究、技术服务和地质勘查业	Scientific Research,Technic Serviced and Geological Prospecting	19639	17038	49	2552
水利、环境和公共设施管理业	Water Conservancy,Environment and Public Facilities Services	3486	3347	55	84
居民服务和其他服务业	Services to Households and Other Services	941	273	71	597
教 育	Education	317125	314180	77	2868
卫生、社会保障和社会福利业	Health Care,Social Securities and Social Welfare	64284	63044	509	731
#卫 生	Health Care	63745	62505	509	731
社会保障业	Social Securities	320	320		
文化、体育和娱乐业	Culture,Sports and Entertainment	8846	8702	6	138
#新闻出版社	News Publishing Company	1782	1782		
广播、电视、电影和音像业	Broadcasting,Television,Film and Video Trade	3708	3672	6	30
体 育	Sports	420	400		20
公共管理和社会组织	Public Administration and Social Organization	43513	43499		14

3-8 在岗职工工资总额（2005）

Total Wages Bill of Staff and Workers on Their Posts by Sector（2005）

单位：万元 (10000 yuan)

指　标	Item	合计 Total	国有单位 State-owned Unit	集体单位 Collect-ive-owned Unit	其他单位 Unit of Other Type of Ownership
总　计	**Total**	2841640	2024031	101975	715634
按企事业、机关分	By Enterprises,Institutions and Agencies				
企　业	Enterprises	1621885	812560	99909	709416
事　业	Institutions	829854	821741	1895	6218
机　关	Agencies	389901	389730	171	
按产业分	By Type of Industry				
第一产业	Primary Industry	30333	29998	39	296
第二产业	Secondary Industry	1102922	507190	54312	541420
第三产业	Tertiary Industry	1708385	1486843	47624	173918
按国民经济行业分	By Sector	2841640	2024031	101975	715634
农、林、牧、渔业	Farming,Forestry,Animal Husbandry and Fishing	30331	29998	38	295
采矿业	Mining and Quarrying	182032	50363	1714	129955
制造业	Manufacturing	543059	217230	19468	306361
电力、燃气及水的生产和供应业	Production and Supply of Electricity,Gas and Water	166261	119258	596	46407
建筑业	Construction	211570	120340	32534	58696
交通运输、仓储和邮政业	Transportation,Storage and Post	146450	135456	2751	8243
信息传输、计算机服务和软件业	Information Transmit,Computer Services and Software Trade	36262	14121	52	22089
批发和零售业	Wholesale and Retail Trade	118161	64960	11193	42008
#批发业	Wholesale	72523	45923	3922	22678
零售业	Retail Trade	45638	19037	7271	19330
住宿和餐饮业	Quarter and Catering Services	25477	8987	1092	15398
金融业	Finance	115091	59912	25467	29712
房地产业	Real Estate	34679	6201	1905	26573
租赁和商务服务业	Leasing and Commerce Services	31620	20163	2292	9165
#租赁业	Leasing Services	838	68	113	657
商务服务业	Commerce Services	30783	20096	2180	8507
科学研究、技术服务和地质勘查业	Scientific Research,Technic Serviced and Geological Prospecting	62955	55218	155	7582
水利、环境和公共设施管理业	Water Conservancy,Environment and Public Facilities Services	26724	25515	847	362
居民服务和其他服务业	Services to Households and Other Services	6908	2155	753	4000
教　育	Education	507562	501897	195	5470
卫生、社会保障和社会福利业	Health Care,Social Securities and Social Welfare	123803	121939	764	1100
#卫　生	Health Care	119976	118112	764	1100
社会保障业	Social Securities	1856	1856		
文化、体育和娱乐业	Culture,Sports and Entertainment	26100	24514	35	1551
#新闻出版社	News Publishing Company	8207	8132		75
广播、电视、电影和音像业	Broadcasting,Television,Film and Video Trade	7526	7207	35	284
体　育	Sports	3202	3032		170
公共管理和社会组织	Public Administration and Social Organization	446595	445804	124	667

3-9 各行业在岗职工平均工资（2005）

Average Wage of Staff and Workers on Their Posts by Sector（2005）

单位：元 (yuan)

指 标	Item	合计 Total	国有单位 State-owned Unit	集体单位 Collect-ive-owned Unit	其他单位 Unit of Other Type of Ownership
总 计	**Total**	14344	14681	10506	14161
按企事业、机关分	By Enterprises,Institutions and Agencies				
企 业	Enterprises	14519	15554	10531	14193
事 业	Institutions	14002	14045	9254	11259
机 关	Agencies	14373	14374	11470	
按产业分	By Type of Industry				
第一产业	Primary Industry	10989	11014	8955	9136
第二产业	Secondary Industry	14474	15103	9281	14728
第三产业	Tertiary Industry	14338	14640	12369	12658
按国民经济行业分	By Sector				
农、林、牧、渔业	Farming,Forestry,Animal Husbandry and Fishing	10989	11014	8955	9136
采矿业	Mining and Quarrying	17175	16106	8590	17870
制造业	Manufacturing	13471	14149	8230	13559
电力、燃气及水的生产和供应业	Production and Supply of Electricity,Gas and Water	26326	24237	6965	35441
建筑业	Construction	11152	11818	10161	10507
交通运输、仓储和邮政业	Transportation,Storage and Post	17812	18959	8250	11078
信息传输、计算机服务和软件业	Information Transmit,Computer Services and Software Trade	23228	21224	6538	24880
批发和零售业	Wholesale and Retail Trade	10209	10700	7629	10407
#批发业	Wholesale	10858	10838	9281	11229
零售业	Retail Trade	9323	10381	6960	9585
住宿和餐饮业	Quarter and Catering Services	9982	9127	9239	10623
金融业	Finance	25051	26132	23965	23982
房地产业	Real Estate	9770	12013	8335	9474
租赁和商务服务业	Leasing and Commerce Services	13676	15749	8173	12198
#租赁业	Leasing Services	10129	9570	3824	14260
商务服务业	Commerce Services	13807	15783	8684	12064
科学研究、技术服务和地质勘查业	Scientific Research,Technic Serviced and Geological Prospecting	18086	18385	10466	16392
水利、环境和公共设施管理业	Water Conservancy,Environment and Public Facilities Services	12040	12410	6296	12497
居民服务和其他服务业	Services to Households and Other Services	9055	11994	7154	8368
教 育	Education	13957	13996	10151	11190
卫生、社会保障和社会福利业	Health Care,Social Securities and Social Welfare	14575	14659	12085	9756
#卫 生	Health Care	14516	14601	12085	9756
社会保障业	Social Securities	21066	21066		
文化、体育和娱乐业	Culture,Sports and Entertainment	12975	13505	9750	8046
#新闻出版社	News Publishing Company	19673	19710		16326
广播、电视、电影和音像业	Broadcasting,Television,Filmand Video Trade	10132	10111	9750	10765
体 育	Sports	16607	17516		8614
公共管理和社会组织	Public Administration and Social Organization	14202	14211	11153	10522

3-10 城乡私营企业户数和从业人员数（2005）

Number of Private Enterprises and Employed Persons in Urban and Rural Areas by Sector（2005）

单位：人(person)

指 标	Item	户数(户) Number of Enterprises (unit)	城镇 Urban Areas	乡村 Rural Areas	从业人员 Number of Employed Persons	城镇 Urban Areas	乡村 Rural Areas
总 计	**Total**	**41484**	**28867**	**12617**	**506512**	**374145**	**132367**
农、林、牧、渔业	Farming,Forestry,Animal Husbandry and Fishing	1237	695	542	14330	8345	5985
#农、林、牧、渔服务业	FFAF Services	81	48	33	729	406	323
采掘业	Mining and Quarrying	3952	710	3242	30350	7428	22922
制造业	Manufacturing	7418	4544	2874	126336	71952	54384
电力、燃气及水的生产和供应业	Production and Supply of Electricity,Gas and Water	446	239	207	6113	3583	2530
建筑业	Construction	1532	1251	281	21386	18569	2817
交通运输、仓储和邮电业	Transportation,Storage,Post and Telecommunications	706	524	182	10204	7550	2654
信息传输、计算机服务和软件业	Information Transmit,Computer Services and Software Trade	2218	1828	390	13633	11482	2151
批发和零售贸易、餐饮业	Wholesale and Retail Trade	14350	11310	3040	113218	89328	23890
住宿和餐饮业	Quarter and Catering Services	987	537	450	10541	7176	3365
房地产业	Real Estate	2137	1841	296	21605	19739	1866
租赁和商务服务业	Leasing and Commerce Services	2147	1871	276	14965	13389	1576
居民服务和其他服务业	Services to Households and Other Services	1952	1552	400	19398	15788	3610
卫生、社会保障和社会福利业	Health Care,Social Securities and Social Welfare	175	153	22	2009	1572	437
文化、体育和娱乐业	Culture,Sports and Entertainment	281	223	58	2616	2257	359
其他行业	Others	1946	1589	357	99808	95987	3821

3-11 城乡个体工商业户数和从业人员数（2005）

Number of Household and Employed Persons of Self-Employed Individuals in Urban and Rural Areas by Sector（2005）

单位：人(person)

指标	Item	户数(户) Number of Enterprises (unit)	城镇 Urban Areas	乡村 Rural Areas	从业人员 Number of Employed Persons	城镇 Urban Areas	乡村 Rural Areas
总　计	**Total**	**431662**	**243245**	**188417**	**596604**	**336706**	**259898**
农、林、牧、渔业	Farming,Forestry,Animal Husbandry and Fishing	2159	480	1679	3588	921	2667
#农、林、牧、渔服务业	FFAF Services	150	16	134	208	20	188
采矿业	Mining and Quarrying	1863	490	1373	5910	1243	4667
制造业	Manufacturing	36205	19347	16858	59351	30920	28431
电力、燃气及水的生产和供应业	Production and Supply of Electricity,Gas and Water	234	85	149	406	205	201
建筑业	Construction	590	435	155	1138	770	368
交通运输、仓储和邮政业	Transportation,Storage,Post and Telecommunications	27274	16545	10729	35348	22082	13266
信息传输、计算机服务和软件业	Information Transmit,Computer Services and Software Trade	1846	1334	512	2601	1932	669
批发和零售业	Wholesale and Retail Trade	263432	143584	119848	331988	180384	151604
住宿和餐饮业	Quarter and Catering Services	43651	27220	16431	74766	47535	27231
房地产业	Real Estate	167	130	37	378	320	58
租赁和商务服务业	Leasing and Commerce Services	2720	2133	587	3702	2882	820
居民服务和其他服务业	Services to Households and Other Services	36003	22435	13568	52752	32794	19958
卫生、社会保障和社会福利业	Health Care,Social Securities and Social Welfare	2263	1611	652	3811	2749	1062
文化、体育和娱乐业	Culture,Sports and Entertainment	3686	2312	1374	7335	4219	3116
其他行业	Others	9569	5104	4465	13530	7750	5780

3-12 职业介绍机构情况

Basic Statistics on Careers Service

指　标	Item	2004	2005	2005年比2004年增长（%）Increase Rate in 2005 over 2004(%)
年末职业介绍机构（个）	**Number of Careers Service at the Year-end(unit)**	**353**	**410**	**16.1**
#劳动保障部门办	Run by Labour Department	300	351	17.0
其他组织办	Run by Other Organs	9	9	持平
公民个人办	Run by Private	44	50	13.6
本年末职业介绍机构人数（人）	**Number of Staff and Workers of Careers Service at the Year-end(person)**	**1255**	**1514**	**20.6**
#劳动保障部门办	Run by Labour Department	1065	1354	27.1
其他组织办	Run by Other Organs	30	22	-26.7
公民个人办	Run by Private	160	138	-13.8
本年登记招聘人数（人）	Number of Registered Job Vacancies This Year(person)	243654	258925	6.3
本年登记求职人次数(人次)	**Number of Registered Job-seekers This Year(person-times)**	**213496**	**194530**	**-8.9**
#下岗职工	Laid-off Workers	44388	36446	-17.9
失业人员	Unemployment	99198	88430	-10.9
获得职业资格人员	Person with Certificates	15127	16654	10.1
本年介绍成功人次数（人）	**Number of Placed Job-seekers(person)**	**109795**	**88077**	**-19.8**
#下岗职工	Laid-off Workers	27788	20600	-25.9
失业人员	Unemployment	56466	39927	-29.3
获得职业资格人员	Person with Certificates	8380	10934	30.5

3-13 企业下岗职工情况（2005）

Basic Statistics on Laid-off Workers of Enterprises（2005）

单位：人(person)

指　标	Item	下岗职工 Number of Laid-off Workers	#当年新增 Newly Increased in 2005	实现再就业 Number of Renew Employed	再就业率（%）Renew Employment Rate(%)
总　计	**Total**	**45341**	**2909**	**27671**	**37.9**
国有企业、国有联营企业、国有独资公司	State-owned(Joint Ownership) Enterprise and State-owned Corporation	27260	1930	27671	50.4
#中央企业	State-owned Enterprises	6146	656	3834	38.4
#亏损企业	Loss-making Enterprise	27260	1930	16410	37.6
城镇集体企业	Urban Collective-owned Enterprises	13648	831		
其他企业	Enterprises of Other Type of Ownership	4433	148		

3-14 "十五"时期各年社会服务及设施和民政事业发展主要指标

Main Indicators of Social Work & Establishment and Civil Administration Career Development of Each Year in "Tenth Five-year Plan" Period

指　标	Item	2000	2001	2002	2003	2004	2005	2005年比2004年增长(%) Increase Rate in 2005 over 2004(%)
城镇社区服务设施数(个)	**Number of Urban Welfare Facilities(unit)**	3450	3529	3961	4873	4406	4704	6.8
#社区服务单位数	Number of Community Services	45	39	81	122	127	149	17.3
城镇便民利民服务网点	Number of Urban Service Points for Civilian	8179	8163	8658	10662	11100	12004	8.1
乡镇敬老院覆盖率	Coverage Rate of Villages and Town Elderly Welfare Homes	61.8	56.6	56.9	54.6	55.9	55.8	-0.1
城乡各类收养性福利单位床位数(张)	Number of Beds of Welfare Home in Urban & Rural Area(unit)	16686	15546	16788	13834	14586	15629	7.2
城乡各类收养性福利单位床位利用率(%)	Using Rate of Bed(%)	59.6	60.6	54.9	62.5	65.9	63.8	-3.2
享受城镇低保人数(人)	Number of Persons Receiving Lowest Cost of living in Urban Area(person)	51798	306931	338723	425148	474805	492046	3.6
城镇低保生活保障支出(万元)	Expenditure of Lowest Cost of living in Urban Area(10000 yuan)	2147	7540	18322	24025	34596	43527	25.8

3-15 “十五”时期各年享受国家定期抚恤、补助、救济人员数

Persons Enjoying Regular Subsidy and Commiseration of Country of Each Year in “Tenth Five-year Plan” Period

单位:人(person)

指 标	Item	2000	2001	2002	2003	2004	2005	2005年比2004年增长(%) Increase Rate in 2005 over 2004(%)
合 计	**Total**	126408	115078	105867	105638	105434	104227	-1.1
伤残抚恤人数	Number of Persons Receiving Disability Commiseration	15396	14498	14996	14919	14941	15080	0.9
“三属”抚恤人数	Number of Persons Comfort and Compensated Bereaved Family	20386	14682	5607	5454	5479	5360	-2.2
烈士家属	Family Numbers of Martyr	13958	10195	3517	3249	3266	3161	-3.2
牺牲、病故军人家属	Family Numbers of Immolate & Die of Illness Armyman	6428	4487	2090	2205	2213	2199	-0.6
复退军人定补人数	Number of Subsidies for Exsevicemen	90626	85898	85264	85265	85014	83787	-1.4

3-16 “十五”时期各年社会福利单位机构情况

Situations of Social Welfare Institutions and Enterprises of Each Year in “Tenth Five-year Plan” Period

单位：个(unit)

项 目	Item	2000	2001	2002	2003	2004	2005	2005年比2004年增长(%) Increase Rate in 2005 over 2004(%)
总 计	**Total**	**1077**	**1248**	**1308**	**1294**	**1338**	**1421**	**6.2**
收养性福利单位	Adopting Social Welfare Institutions	733	883	891	856	876	892	1.8
国家办	Run by Government	57	57	62	64	71	69	-2.8
集体和民办	Run by Collective Units and Private Units	676	826	829	792	805	823	2.2
社会福利企业	Social Welfare Enterprises	201	226	230	200	200	228	14.0
国 有	Run by Government	16	16	16	15	15	17	13.3
集体和其他	Run by Collective Units and Others	185	210	214	185	185	211	14.1
优抚事业单位	Administration Agencies for Martyrs	40	40	40	40	42	44	4.8
救助类单位	Collecting and Repatriation Units	20	20	20	21	21	20	
殡仪服务单位	Funeral and Interment Institutions	36	37	43	50	67	83	23.9
彩票发行单位	Collecting Purse Units	3	3	3	5	5	5	0.0
社区服务单位	Community Service Institutions	44	39	81	122	127	149	17.3

注：“救助单位”2005年数据不含农场，故与2004年数据不可比。（下表同）

Note:Collecting and Repatriation Units in 2005 excluded farm in the table,So it is not comparable to the data in 2004.(the same to next)

3-17 “十五”时期各年社会福利单位工作人员情况

Basic Statistics on Persons Engaged of Social welfare Institutions of Each Year in “Tenth Five-year Plan” Period

单位：人（person）

项目	Item	2000	2001	2002	2003	2004	2005	2005年比2004年增长(%) Increase Rate in 2005 over 2004(%)
总计	**Total**	**9462**	**10940**	**11919**	**12339**	**17029**	**16822**	**-1.2**
收养性福利单位	Adopting Social Welfare Institutions	2214	2182	2291	2253	2477	2470	-0.3
国家办	Run by Government	1059	1068	1182	1180	1314	1283	-2.4
集体和民办	Run by Collective Units and Private Units	1155	1114	1109	1073	1163	1187	2.1
社会福利企业	Social Welfare Enterprises	4415	6156	6842	6689	8602	8846	2.8
国有	Run by Government	986	808	745	650	689	959	39.2
集体和其他	Run by Collective Units and Others	3429	5348	6097	6039	7913	7887	-0.3
优抚安置事业单位	Administration Agencies for Martyrs	385	375	375	383	383	359	-6.3
救助类单位	Collecting and Repatriation Units	1088	923	880	917	856	252	
殡仪服务单位	Funeral and Interment Institutions	977	861	861	1220	3612	3556	-1.6
彩票发行单位	Collecting Purse Units	21	38	54	72	78	85	9.0
社区服务单位	Community Service Institutions	362	405	616	805	1021	1254	22.8

3-18 “十五”时期各年社会福利救济主要支出情况

Basic Statistics on Social Welfare Relief Funds of Each Year in “Tenth Five-year Plan” Period

单位：万元(10000 yuan)

指标	Item	2000	2001	2002	2003	2004	2005	2005年比2004年增长(%) Increase Rate in 2005 over 2004(%)
总计	**Total**	**20483.70**	**27310.17**	**40470.30**	**51889.60**	**67901.20**	**107797.50**	**58.8**
优抚对象补助金额	Funds for Family Members of Martyrs and Disabled Veterans	12751.60	13726.40	15086.92	18687.50	20499.90	30953.00	51.0
国家支出	Government Funds	8765.20	9901.60	1192.92	15002.54	16992.20	25634.00	50.9
集体供给	Collective Funds	3986.40	3824.80	3894.00	3685.00	3507.70	5319.00	51.6
传统救济对象的国家救济金额	Funds for Family Members of Traditional Relief	1491.20	1596.06	1592.34	3151.20	3972.70	25114.30	532.2
最低生活保障支出	Expenditure for Persons Receiving Lowest Cost-of-living	2808.10	8322.71	19253.14	24846.30	35474.80	45290.70	27.7
城镇	For Urban Areas	2147.20	7540.11	18321.82	24024.90	34595.60	43526.50	25.8
农村	For Rural Areas	660.90	782.60	931.32	821.40	879.20	1764.20	100.7
收养性社会福利单位支出	Funds for Adopting Social Welfare Institution	3432.80	3665.00	4537.90	5204.60	7953.80	6439.50	-19.0
国家支出	Government Funds	2676.90	2910.50	3866.30	4852.70	7570.30	5911.00	-21.9
集体供给	Collective Funds	755.90	754.50	671.60	351.90	383.50	528.50	37.8

3-19 “十五”时期各年享受补助、救济人员情况

Persons Receiving Subsidies and Relief Funds of Each Year in “Tenth Five-year Plan” Period

单位：万人(10000 person)

指 标	Item	2000	2001	2002	2003	2004	2005	2005年比2004年增长(%) Increase Rate in 2005 over 2004(%)
城乡居民最低生活保障人数	Number of Persons Receiving Lowest Cost-of-living in Urban Area and Rural Area	12.03	35.47	39.31	48.28	51.65	56.77	9.9
城 镇	Urban Area	5.18	30.69	33.87	42.51	47.48	49.20	3.6
农 村	Rural Area	6.85	4.77	5.44	5.77	4.17	7.57	81.5
传统救济人数	Number of Persons Receiving Traditional Relief Funds	17.09	11.08	8.39	28.56	33.63	101.63	202.2
收养性福利单位收养三无对象人数	Number of Persons Adopted by Adopting Soci al Welfare Institutions	0.86	0.80	0.77	0.77	0.82	0.85	3.8
精减退职老弱残职工得到救济人数	Number of Laid-off,Retired, Elderly and Disabled Staff and Workers Receiving Relief Funds	2.20	2.18	2.04	1.97	0.00	1.80	-3.0
享受原工资40%救济人数	Number of Persons Receiving 40% of Their Original Wages	0.83	0.81	0.74	0.70	0.68	0.69	-2.0
享受定期定量救济人数	Number of Persons Receiving Periodical and Fixed Government Relief Funds	1.37	1.36	1.31	1.27	1.17	1.13	-3.6

主要统计指标解释

经济活动人口 指在16岁以上,有劳动能力,参加或要求参加社会经济活动的人口;包括从业人员和失业人员。

从业人员 指从事一定社会劳动并取得劳动报酬或经营收入的人员,包括全部职工、再就业的离退休人员、私营业主、个体户主、私营和个体从业人员、乡镇企业从业人员、农村从业人员、其他从业人员(包括民办教师、宗教职业者、现役军人等)。这一指标反映了一定时期内全部劳动力资源的实际利用情况,是研究我国基本国情国力的重要指标。

各单位的从业人员 指在各级国家机关、政党机关、社会团体及企业、事业单位中工作,取得工资或其他形式的劳动报酬的全部人员。包括在岗职工、再就业的离退休人员、民办教师以及在各单位中工作的外方人员和港澳台方人员、兼职人员、借用的外单位人员和第二职业者。不包括离开本单位仍保留劳动关系的职工。各单位的从业人员反映了各单位实际参加生产或工作的全部劳动力。

城镇私营和个体从业人员 城镇私营从业人员指在工商管理部门注册登记,其经营地址设在县城关镇(含城关镇)以上的私营企业从业人员;包括私营企业投资者和雇工。城镇个体从业人员指在工商管理部门注册登记,并持有城镇户口或在城镇长期居住,经批准从事个体工商经营的从业人员;包括个体经营者和在个体工商户劳动的家庭帮工和雇工。

城镇登记失业人员 指有非农业户口,在一定的劳动年龄内,有劳动能力,无业而要求就业,并在当地就业服务机构进行求职登记的人员。

城镇登记失业率 指城镇登记失业人数同城镇从业人数与城镇登记失业人数之和的比。计算公式为:

城镇登记失业率=城镇登记失业人数/城镇从业人数+城镇登记失业人数×100%

职工 指在国有经济、城镇集体经济、联营经济、股份制经济、外商和港、澳、台投资经济、其他经济单位及其附属机构工作,并由其支付工资的各类人员,不包括返聘的离退休人员、民办教师、在国有经济单位工作的外方人员和港、澳、台人员(1998年以后的数据均为在岗职工数据,其他相关指标如职工工资总额,职工平均工资等指标也从1998年按此口径进行了相应调整)。

国有单位职工 指在国有经济单位及其附属机构工作,并由其支付工资的各类人员。

城镇集体单位职工 指在城镇集体经济单位及其管理部门工作,并由其支付工资的各类人员。

其他单位职工 指在联营经济、股份制经济、外商投资经济、港、澳、台投资经济单位工作,并由其支付工资的各类人员。

在岗职工 指在本单位工作并由单位支付工资的人员,以及有工作岗位,但由于学习、病伤产假等原因暂未工作,仍由单位支付工资的人员。

职工工资总额 指各单位在一定时期内直接支付给本单位全部职工的劳动报酬总额。工资总额的计算原则应以直接支付给职工的全部劳动报酬为根据。各单位支付给职工的劳动报酬以及其他根据有关规定支付的工资,不论是计入成本的还是不计入成本的,不论是按国家规定列入计征奖金税项目的,还是未列入计征奖金税项目的,不论是以货币形式支付的还是以实物形式支付的,均包括在工资总额内。

职工平均工资 指企业、事业、机关单位的职工在一定时期内平均每人所得的货币工资额。它表明一定时期职工工资收入的高低程度,是反映职工工资水平的主要指标。计算公式为:

职工平均工资=报告期实际支付的全部职工工资总额/报告期全部职工平均人数

职工平均工资指数 指报告期职工平均工资与基期职工平均工资的比率,是反映不同时期职工货币工资水平变动情况的相对数。计算公式为:

职工平均工资指数=报告期职工平均工资/基期职工平均工资

职工平均实际工资指数 职工平均实际工资指扣除物价变动因素后的职工平均工资。职工平均实际工资指数是反映实际工资变动情况的相对数,表明职工实际工资水平提高或降低的程度。计算公式为:

职工平均实际工资指数=报告期职工平均工资指数[]报告期城镇居民消费价格指数×100%

社会福利事业单位 指集中收养社会孤老、残、幼的机构，包括由民政部门管理的社会福利院、儿童福利院、精神病人福利院和城镇集体举办的福利院及农村集体举办的敬老院以及优抚医院和具有收养能力的社区服务中心等。该指标主要反映在社会福利性单位投入的水平。

社会福利事业单位收养人员 包括民政部门管理和城镇、农村集体举办的社会福利事业单位中收养的老人、少年儿童、缺乏生活自理能力的残疾人员和精神病人。该指标主要反映收养性社会福利单位的收养能力。

社会福利事业单位 指以安置城镇有一定劳动能力的盲、聋、哑和肢体残疾人员就业为目的，享受国家减免税待遇的国有或集体企业。包括福利工厂、福利商业和服务业、假肢厂和安置农场等单位。该指标主要反映对残疾人照顾的特殊政策。

Explanatory Notes on Main Statistical Indicators

Economically Active Population refers to the population aged 16 and over who are capable to work, are participating in or willing to participate in economic activities, including employed persons and unemployed persons.

Employed Persons refers to the persons who are engaged in social labour and receive remuneration payment or earn business income, including: total staff and workers, re-employed retirees, employers of private enterprises, employers of individual economy,employed persons in private enterprises and individual economy, employed persons in the enterprises in the urban areas,employed persons in the rural areas,other employed persons (including teachers in the schools run by the local people,people engaged in religious profession and active army,etc.)

This indicator reflects the actual utilization of total labour force during a certain period of time and is often used for the research on China's economic affairs and national power.

Persons Employed in Various Units refer to all the persons working in government agencies of various levels,political and party organizations, social organizations,enterprises and institutions, and receiving wages or other forms of payment. They include fully-employed staff and workers, re-employed retirees, teachers in schools run by the local people,foreigners and Chinese compatriots from Hong Kong, Macao,and Taiwan working in various units, part-time employees, employees of other units working temporarily at current posts, and employees holding the second job, but exclude staff and workers who have left their working units while keeping their labour contract (employment relation) unchanged.This indicator reflects the total number of laborers actually engaged in production or other operations in various units.

Persons Employed in Private Enterprises and Self-Employed Individuals in Urban Areas Persons employed in private enterprises refer to the persons employed in the private enterprises which have been registered at the departments of industrial and commercial administration and are situated at a county town (i.e. a town where the county government is located) for business operation or at urban areas with the level higher than a county town. The self-employed individuals in urban areas refer to persons who hold the certificates of residence in urban areas or have resided in the urban areas for a long time and have been registered at the departments of industrial and commercial administration and approved to be engaged in individual industrial or commercial business, including self-employed persons as well as helpers and hired labourers who work in the individual households engaged in industrial or commercial business.

Registered Urban Unemployed Persons The registered unemployed persons in urban areas refer to the persons who are registered as permanent residents in the urban areas engaged in non-agricultural activities, aged within the range of working age, capable to labour, unemployed but desirous to be employed and have been registered at the local employment service agencies to apply for a job.

Registered Urban Unemployment Rate Registered unemployment rate in urban areas refers to the ratio of the number of the registered unemployed persons to the sum of the number of employed persons and the registered unemployed persons . The formula is as follows:

Registered urban unemployment rate =number of registered urban unemployed persons/number of urban employed persons + number of registered urban unemployed persons×100%

Staff and Workers refer to the persons who work in(and receive payment therefrom)enterprises and institutions of state ownership, collective ownership, joint ownership, share holding, foreign ownership,and ownership by entrepreneurs from Hong Kong, Macao, and Taiwan, and other types of ownership and their affiliated units,excluding the retired persons invited to work in the units again, teachers in the schools run by the local people and foreigners and persons coming from Hong Kong, Macao and Taiwan and working in the state-owned economic units. (Number of staff and workers in this yearbook include only fully employed staff and workers, excluding those who have left their working units while keeping their labour contract/employment relation unchanged).

Staff and Workers in State-owned Economic Units refer to the persons who work in the state-owned economic units or their attached units and are listed in their payrolls.

Staff and Workers of Collective Owned Units in Urban Areas refer to the persons who work in collective owned units in urban areas and their administration departments and receive payment therefrom.

Staff and Workers in Units of Other Types of Ownership refer to those who work in (and receive payment therefrom)enterprises and institutions of joint ownership, share holding, foreign ownership, and ownership by entrepreneurs from Hong Kong, Macao, and Taiwan.

Fully Employed Staff and Workers refer to persons who work in, and receive wages from their working units, as well as persons who have their work posts, but are temporarily absent from work for reasons of study or on sick, injury or maternal leave and still receive wages from their working units.

Total Wages of Staff and Workers refer to the total remuneration payment to staff and workers in various units during a certain period of time.The calculation of total wages is based on the total remuneration payment to the staff and workers. Therefore, all the wages and salaries and other payments to staff and workers are included in the total wages regardless of their sources, category, and forms (in kind or cash).

Average Wage of Staff and Workers refers to the average wage in money terms per person during a certain period of time for staff and workers in enterprises, institutions, and government agencies, which reflects the general level of wage income during a certain period of time and is calculated as follows:

Average Wage of Staff and Workers =Total Wages of Staff and Workers in Reference Period/Average Number of Staff and Workers in Reference Period

Index of Average Wage of Staff and Worker refers to the ratio of average wage of staff and workers at the report time to that at the reference time. It reflects the relative changing degree of average wage in money terms at the various of time, which is calculated as following:

Index of Average Wage of Staff and Worker = average wage of staff and workers at the report time/average wage of staff and workers at the reference time

Index of Average Real Wage of Staff and Worker refers to the average wage which has removed the factor of price change. Index of average real wage of staff and worker reflects the relative changing degree of average real wage, and indicates the degree of the rising or declining degree of real wage of staff and worker, which is calculated as following:

Index of Average Real Wage of Staff and Worker = Index of Average Wage of Staff and Worker at the Report Time/Urban Consumer Prices Index at the Report Time×100%.

Social Welfare Institutions refer to institutions taking care of old people without children, handicapped people and orphans. They include social welfare institutions run by civil affairs departments, children welfare institutions, social welfare institutions for mental patients, collective-owned old people´s homes in rural areas, convalescent homes and community service centers with the capacity of receiving those people. This indicator reflects the input in social welfare institutions.

Number of People Taken in by Social Welfare Institutions refers to the number of old people, children, totally dependent handicapped people and mental patients taken in by social welfare institutions run by civil affairs departments and those run by collective units in urban and rural areas. This indicator reflects the capacity of social welfare institutions.

Social Welfare Enterprises are collective owned enterprises which employ the blind, deaf-mute, and other handicapped people who are able to work in cities and towns and enjoy exemption from state taxes, including welfare plants, welfare commercial services, artificial limb plants and farms, etc. This indicator reflects the preferential policies toward disabled persons.

4

固定资产投资

Investment in Fixed Assets

Four

全社会固定资产投资（亿元）（按三次产业分）
Total Investment in Fixed Assets (100 million yuan)
(Grouped by Three Industries)

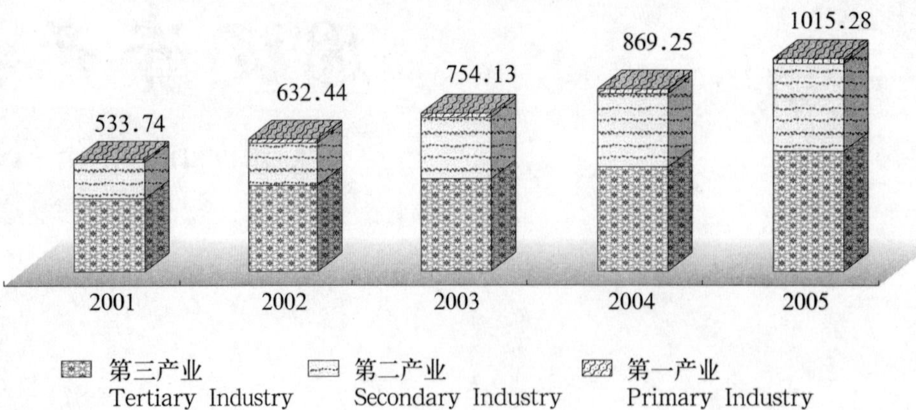

房地产开发投资额（亿元）
Real Estate Development Investment (100 million yuan)

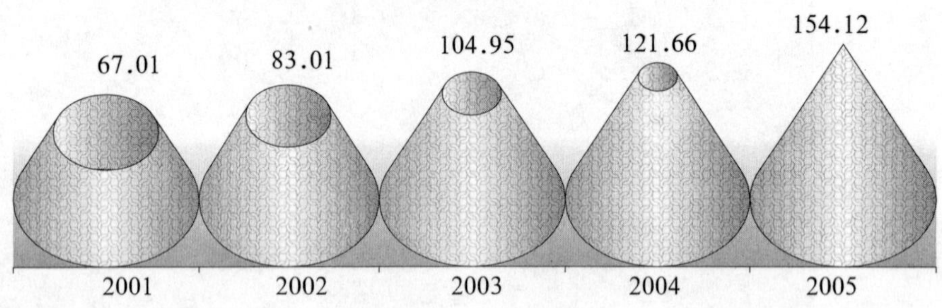

房屋施工、竣工面积（万平方米）
Floor Space of Buildings Under Construction and Completed (10000 sq.m)

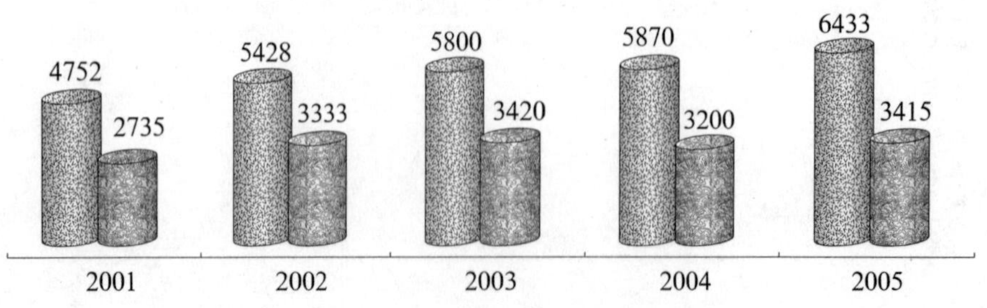

4-1 “十五”时期各年全社会固定资产投资

Total Investment in Fixed Assets of each year in "Tenth-Five-year Plan" Period

单位:亿元(100 million yuan)

指　标	Item	2000	2001	2002	2003
全社会固定资产投资	**Total Investment in Fixed Assets**	**402.50**	**533.74**	**632.44**	**754.13**
按隶属关系分	Grouped by Jurisdiction of Management				
中央	Central	66.52	127.54	161.53	187.42
地方	Local	335.98	406.20	470.91	566.71
按管理渠道分	Grouped by Channel of Management				
基本建设	Capital Construction	151.89	238.81	312.62	384.81
更新改造	Innovation	93.57	118.55	120.79	140.54
房地产开发	Real Estate Development	46.58	67.01	83.01	104.95
其他投资	Others	110.46	109.37	116.02	123.83
按经济类型分	Grouped by Registration Status				
国有经济	State-owned Units	259.95	357.69	423.88	457.10
集体经济	Collective-owned Units	28.45	22.45	18.86	39.26
个体经济	Self-employed Units	59.63	67.89	75.71	66.24
联营经济	Joint Ownership Units	0.55	1.44	1.64	3.16
股份制经济	Share Holding Units	29.65	48.80	58.16	119.15
外商投资经济	Foreign Funded Units	3.25	4.10	2.84	6.99
港澳台商投资经济	Units with Funds from Hong Kong,Macao and Taiwan	2.90	3.47	7.62	6.45
其他经济	Others	18.12	27.90	43.73	55.78
按城乡分	Grouped by Urban and Rural Area				
城镇	Urban	332.23	460.78	555.32	673.93
#房地产开发	Real Estate Development	46.58	67.01	83.01	104.95
农村	Rural	70.27	72.96	77.12	80.20
#农村个人	Rural Individuals	49.90	58.21	64.60	52.88
按资金来源分	Grouped by Source of Funds				
国家预算内资金	State Budgetary Appropriation	35.59	35.10	49.93	46.35
国内贷款	Domestic Loans	104.75	152.10	189.53	186.03
利用外资	Foreign Investment	7.57	6.15	5.02	7.90
自筹资金	Self-raising Funds	179.16	246.92	287.15	394.06
其他资金	Others	75.43	93.47	100.81	119.79
按构成分	Grouped by Use of Funds				
建筑安装工程	Construction and Installation	250.84	312.24	409.74	466.97
设备工具器具购置	Purchase of Equipment and Instruments	87.86	120.97	128.24	166.10
其他费用	Others	63.80	100.53	94.46	121.06
按主要行业分	Grouped by Main Sector				
#农林牧渔业	Farming,For estry,Animal Husbandry and Fishery	15.42	13.96	20.89	21.67
工业	Industry	135.07	173.07	201.39	291.41
#电力、燃气及水的生产供应业	Production and Supply of Electric Power,Gas and Water	75.05	97.75	117.72	156.74
建筑业	Construction	2.03	0.94	2.00	1.78
房地产业	Real Estate	55.99	76.65	95.05	149.62
按三次产业分	Grouped by Type of Industry				
第一产业	Primary Industry	15.42	13.43	20.26	21.67
第二产业	Secondary Industry	137.10	174.01	203.39	293.19
第三产业	Tertiary Industry	249.98	346.30	408.79	439.27
房屋建筑面积(万平方米)	Floor Space of Buildings(10000 sq.m)				
施工面积	Floor Space under Construction	4057	4752	5428	5800
#住宅	Residential Buildings	2735	3248	3859	3995
竣工面积	Floor Space Completed	2501	2735	3333	3420
#住宅	Residential Buildings	1862	2059	2593	2533

4-1续表(continued) 单位:亿元(100 million yuan)

指标	Item	2004	2005	2005年比2000年增长(%) Increase Rate in 2005 over 2000(%)	2005年比2004年增长(%) Increase Rate in 2005 over 2004(%)
全社会固定资产投资	**Total Investment in Fixed Assets**	**869.25**	**1015.28**	**152.2**	**16.8**
按隶属关系分	Grouped by Jurisdiction of Management				
中央	Central	218.71	229.35	244.8	4.9
地方	Local	650.54	785.93	133.9	20.8
按管理渠道分	Grouped by Channel of Management				
基本建设	Capital Construction	477.83	528.85	248.2	10.7
更新改造	Innovation	152.33	180.57	93.0	18.5
房地产开发	Real Estate Development	121.66	154.12	230.9	26.7
其他投资	Others	117.43	151.74	37.4	29.2
按经济类型分	Grouped by Registration Status				
国有经济	State-owned Units	507.74	537.71	106.9	5.9
集体经济	Collective-owned Units	38.41	39.78	39.8	3.6
个体经济	Self-employed Units	70.40	87.26	46.3	23.9
联营经济	Joint Ownership Units	2.06	0.89	61.8	-56.8
股份制经济	Share Holding Units	168.85	236.11	696.3	39.8
外商投资经济	Foreign Funded Units	8.00	12.33	279.4	54.1
港澳台商投资经济	Units with Funds from Hong Kong,Macao and Taiwan	8.26	7.64	163.4	-7.5
其他经济	Others	65.53	93.56	416.3	42.8
按城乡分	Grouped by Urban and Rural Area				
城镇	Urban	784.25	916.36	175.8	16.8
#房地产开发	Real Estate Development	121.66	154.12	230.9	26.7
农村	Rural	85.00	98.92	40.8	16.4
#农村个人	Rural Individuals	56.58	68.24	36.8	20.6
按资金来源分	Grouped by Source of Funds				
国家预算内资金	State Budgetary Appropriation	39.96	42.12	18.3	5.4
国内贷款	Domestic Loans	228.80	274.54	162.1	20.0
利用外资	Foreign Investment	8.77	7.86	3.8	-10.4
自筹资金	Self-raising Funds	419.49	528.13	194.8	25.9
其他资金	Others	172.23	162.63	115.6	-5.6
按构成分	Grouped by Use of Funds				
建筑安装工程	Construction and Installation	535.33	622.35	148.1	16.3
设备工具器具购置	Purchase of Equipment and Instruments	192.72	232.21	164.3	20.5
其他费用	Others	141.20	160.72	151.9	13.8
按主要行业分	Grouped by Main Sector				
#农林牧渔业	Farming,For estry,Animal Husbandry and Fishery	22.62	24.64	59.8	8.9
工业	Industry	348.75	414.38	206.8	18.8
#电力、燃气及水的生产供应业	Production and Supply of Electric Power,Gas and Water	198.73	239.75	219.5	20.6
建筑业	Construction	1.70	1.89	-6.9	11.2
房地产业	Real Estate	171.46	217.09	287.7	26.6
按三次产业分	Grouped by Type of Industry				
第一产业	Primary Industry	22.62	24.64	59.8	8.9
第二产业	Secondary Industry	350.45	416.27	203.6	18.8
第三产业	Tertiary Industry	496.18	574.37	129.8	15.8
房屋建筑面积（万平方米）	Floor Space of Buildings(10000 sq.m)				
施工面积	Floor Space under Construction	5870.00	6433.00	58.6	9.6
#住宅	Residential Buildings	3973.00	4626.00	69.1	16.4
竣工面积	Floor Space Completed	3200.00	3415.00	36.5	6.7
#住宅	Residential Buildings	2352.00	2658.00	42.7	13.0

4-2 “十五”时期各年房地产开发投资主要指标

Main Indicator of Real Estate Development of each year in "Tenth-Five-year Plan" Period

指　标	Item	2000	2001	2002	2003	2004	2005	2005年比2004年增长(%) Increase Rate in 2005 over 2004(%)
土地开发及购置（万平方米）	**Land Development and Purchase(10 000 sq.m)**							
本年土地开发面积	Land Space Developed This Year	203	287	398	375	278	248	-10.8
本年土地购置面积	Land Space Purchased This Year	289	576	291	624	657	520	-20.9
本年完成投资额（亿元）	Investment Completed This Year(100 million yuan)	46.58	67.01	83.01	104.95	121.66	154.12	26.7
#住宅	Residential Buildings	27.14	38.06	46.97	56.60	70.97	85.87	21.0
#经济适用房屋	Economically Affordable Housing	8.71	8.33	7.05	10.71	10.84	9.63	-11.2
资金来源合计（亿元）	**Source of Funds (100 million yuan)**	**73.54**	**94.32**	**120.06**	**154.52**	**176.72**	**233.72**	**32.3**
#国内贷款	Domestic Loans	13.90	14.78	18.47	26.01	32.63	49.30	51.1
利用外资	Foreign Investment	0.44	0.16	0.15	0.74	0.29	0.68	134.5
自筹资金	Self-raising Fund	16.52	24.15	29.40	45.13	48.89	63.91	30.7
房屋建筑面积（万平方米）	**Floor Space of Buildings(10000 sq.m)**							
施工面积	Floor Space under Construction	1015	1367	1676	2104	2443	2785	14.0
#本年新开工面积	Floor Space Started This Year	413	518	537	903	878	1008	14.8
#住宅	Residential Buildings	752	1017	1237	1580	1829	2113	15.5
#经济适用房屋	Economically Affordable Housing	208	225	203	252	293	299	2.0
竣工面积	Floor Space Completed	349	491	514	655	644	712	10.6
#住宅	Residential Buildings	288	400	410	512	529	568	7.4
#经济适用房屋	Economically Affordable Housing	119	115	82	87	71	82	15.5

4-3 "十五"时期各年全社会固定资产投资资金来源

Total Investment in Fixed Assets by Source of Finance of each year in "Tenth-Five-year Plan" Period

单位：亿元(100 million yuan)

指 标	Item	2000	2001	2002	2003	2004	2005	2005年比2004年增长(%) Increase Rate in 2005 over 2004(%)
总 计	**Total**	**452.57**	**583.94**	**603.81**	**833.68**	**940.43**	**1139.83**	**21.2**
#国家预算内资金	State Budgetary Appropriation	38.94	36.97	46.90	48.48	40.74	44.04	8.1
国内贷款	Domestic Loans	118.33	164.64	197.48	203.15	243.91	305.41	25.2
利用外资	Utilization of Foreign Capital	8.55	6.53	4.90	8.52	9.07	8.54	–5.8
自筹资金	Fundraising Oneself	192.17	263.49	230.76	423.89	442.32	573.44	29.6
其他资金	Others	94.58	112.31	123.77	149.64	204.39	208.40	2.0
基本建设合计	**Capital Construction**	**174.59**	**250.68**	**323.67**	**394.34**	**471.83**	**555.40**	**17.7**
#国家预算内资金	State Budgetary Appropriation	27.51	28.38	40.14	32.94	22.18	29.84	34.6
国内贷款	Domestic Loans	56.64	92.63	133.44	135.34	177.15	216.25	22.1
利用外资	Utilization of Foreign Capital	6.98	4.67	1.23	5.83	7.40	6.75	–8.8
自筹资金	Fundraising Oneself	50.93	87.10	111.49	178.10	183.00	236.91	29.5
其他资金	Others	32.53	37.90	37.37	42.13	82.10	65.65	–20.0
更新改造合计	**Innovation**	**97.21**	**128.92**	**129.38**	**159.40**	**171.29**	**197.96**	**15.6**
#国家预算内资金	State Budgetary Appropriation	5.11	4.57	6.21	8.63	9.28	3.15	–66.1
国内贷款	Domestic Loans	37.78	46.84	36.18	35.23	26.50	29.47	11.2
利用外资	Utilization of Foreign Capital	0.97	0.54	3.43	1.45	1.25	1.04	–16.8
自筹资金	Fundraising Oneself	45.56	68.38	71.31	99.18	115.18	145.33	26.2
其他资金	Others	7.79	8.59	12.25	14.91	19.08	18.97	–0.6

4-4 基本建设主要指标（按国民经济行业分）（2005）

Investment in Capital Construction by Sector(2005)

行 业	Sectors	施工项目（个） Number of Projects under Cons-truction (unit)	全部建成投产项目（个） Number of Projects Completed and Putinto Use(unit)	基本建设投资额（万元） Investment of Capital Construction (10000 yuan)
总 计	**Total**	**4968**	**2929**	**5288493**
农、林、牧、渔业	Farming, Forestry, Animal Husbandry and Fishery	100	69	36345
#农 业	Farming	25	20	7782
采矿业	Mining and Quarrying	73	22	226414
#煤炭开采和洗选业	Mining and Washing of Coal	52	11	181553
石油和天然气开采业	Extraction of Petroleum and Natural Gas	1	1	5216
有色金属矿采选业	Mining and Dressing of Nonferrous Metals	6	3	32849
非金属矿采选业	Mining and Dressing of Nonmetal Minerals	11	7	5266
制造业	Manufacturing	192	91	212301
农副食品加工业	Processing of Food from Agricultural Products	15	8	7368
食品制造业	Manufacture of Foods	11	7	6355
饮料制造业	Manufacture of Beverages	14	6	28363
烟草制品业	Manufacture of Tobacco	5	2	16956
木材加工及木、竹、藤、棕、草制品业	Timber Processing,Manufacture of Wood, Bamboo, Rattan,Palm, and Straw Products	3	1	4610
家具制造业	Manufacture of Furniture	1		607
造纸及纸制品业	Manufacture of Paper and Paper Products	3	1	21569
石油加工、炼焦及核燃料加工业	Processing of Petroleum,Coking,Processing of Nuclear Fuel	8	3	22943
化学原料及化学制品制造业	Manufacture of Raw Chemical Materials and Chemical Products	24	11	28608
医药制造业	Manufacture of Medicines	7	3	8914
化学纤维制造业	Manufacture of Chemical Fibers	1	1	1970
塑料制品业	Manufacture of Plastics	4	2	2717
非金属矿物制品业	Manufacture of Non-metallic Mineral Products	35	19	25538
黑色金属冶炼及压延加工业	Smelting and Pressing of Ferrous Metals	10	6	8418

4-4续表(continued)

行业	Sectors	施工项目(个) Number of Projects under Cons-truction (unit)	全部建成投产项目(个) Number of Projects Completed and Putinto Use(unit)	基本建设投资额(万元) Investment of Capital Construction (10000 yuan)
有色金属冶炼及压延加工业	Smelting and Pressing of Nonferrous Metals	6	2	2348
金属制品业	Manufacture of Metal Products	8	6	6529
通用设备制造业	Manufacture of General Purpose Machinery	4		2537
专用设备制造业	Manufacture of Special Purpose Machinery	6	1	1921
交通运输设备制造业	Manufacture of Transport Equipment	10	5	4682
电气机械及器材制造业	Manufacture of Electrical Equipment and Machinery	7	3	2905
通信设备、计算机及其 他电子设备制造业	Manufacture of Communication Equipment,Computers and Other Electronic Equipment	1	1	410
工艺品及其他制造业	Manufacture of Artwork and Other Manufacturing	2	2	553
电力、燃气及水的生产和 供应业	Production and Distrbution of Electric Power, Gas and Water	219	87	2003653
电力、热力的生产和供应业	Production and Distribution of Electric Power and Heat Power	163	69	1942643
燃气生产和供应业	Production and Distribution of Gas	7	2	7393
水的生产和供应业	Production and Distribution of Water	49	16	53617
建筑业	Construction	11	5	12295
交通运输、仓储和邮政业	Transport,Storage,Postal and Post	1672	1025	1199160
#仓储业	Storage	8	7	3994
邮政业	Post	7	4	4308
信息传输、计算机服务和软件业	Information Transmission,Computer Services and Software	94	70	58175
批发和零售业	Wholesale and Retail Trade	117	68	91696
住宿和餐饮业	Hotel and Restaurants	43	24	40030
金融业	Financial Intermediation	25	9	14851
房地产业	Real Estate	71	30	55790
租赁和商务服务业	Leasing and Business Services	21	11	32530
科学研究、技术服务和地质勘查业	Scientific Research,Technical Services and Geologic Prospecting	38	13	39647
水利、环境和公共设施管理业	Management of Water Conservancy, Environment and Public Facilities	580	295	575886
居民服务和其他服务业	Services to Households and Other Services	25	16	11643
教 育	Education	901	647	267844
卫生、社会保障和社会福利业	Health,Social Security and Social Welfare	200	129	73103
文化、体育和娱乐业	Culture,Sports and Entertainment	95	40	69365
公共管理和社会组织	Public Management and Social Organization	491	278	267765

注：本表资料为50万元及以上投资项目数据（以下各相关表同）。

Note;The Date refer to Investment of 500,000 yuan and over in the table(The relative tables in the chapter are the same)

4-5 更新改造主要指标（按国民经济行业分）（2005）

Major Indicators of Innovation by Sector(2005)

行　业	Sectors	施工项目（个）Number of Projects under Cons-truction(unit)	全部建成投产项目（个）Number of Projects Completed and Put into Use(unit)	更新改造投资额（万元）Investment in Innovation (10000 yuan)
总　计	**Total**	**1212**	**767**	**1805715**
农、林、牧、渔业	Farming, Forestry, Animal Husbandry and Fishery	6	2	2495
采矿业	Mining and Quarrying	112	74	131013
#煤炭开采和洗选业	Mining and Washing of Coal Mining and	93	66	118032
非金属矿采选业	Processing of Nonmetal Ores	12	5	9053
制造业	Manufacturing	596	336	907631
农副食品加工业	Processing of Foodfrom Agricultural Products	42	26	16320
食品制造业	Manufacture of Foods	25	11	18534
饮料制造业	Manufacture of Beverages	36	22	45571
烟草制品业	Manufacture of Tobacco	17	13	27254
纺织业	Manufacture of Textile	3		4394
纺织服装、鞋、帽制造业	Manufacture of Textile Wearing Apparel,Footware, and Caps	1		263
木材加工及木竹藤棕草制品业	Timber Processing,Manufacture of Wood, Bamboo, Rattan, Palm,and Straw Products	4	4	3304
造纸及纸制品业	Manufacture of Paper and Paper Products	5	3	3168
印刷业、记录媒介的复制	Printing,Reproduction of Recording Media	11	7	25871
石油加工炼焦及核燃料加工业	Processing of Petroleum,Coking, Processing of Nuclear Fuel	3	3	2000
化学原料及化学制品制造业	Manufacture of Raw Chemical Materials and Chemica Products	121	62	261101
医药制造业	Manufacture of Medicines	49	27	60444
橡胶制品业	Manufacture of Rubber	14	9	12278
塑料制品业	Manufacture of Plastics	16	11	7590
非金属矿物制品业	Manufacture of Non-metallic Mineral Products	80	50	66788
黑色金属冶炼及压延加工业	Smelting and Pressing of Ferrous Metals	49	31	116724
有色金属冶炼及压延加工业	Smelting and Pressing of Nonferrous Metals	27	11	145350
金属制品业	Manufacture of Metal Products	15	9	14968

4-5续表(continued)

行业	Sectors	施工项目（个）Number of Projects under Construction (unit)	全部建成投产项目(个) Number of Projects Completed and Put into Use(unit)	更新改造投资额（万元）Investment in Innovation (10000 yuan)
通用设备制造业	Manufacture of General Purpose Machinery	24	10	14326
专用设备制造业	Manufacture of Special Purpose Machinery	15	9	20746
交通运输设备制造业	Manufacture of Transport Equipment	15	6	9255
电气机械及器材制造业	Manufacture of Electrical Equipment and Machinery	12	7	9215
通信设备计算机及其他电子设备制造业	Manufacture of Communication Equipment, Computers and Other Electronic Equipment	6	2	17348
工艺品及其他制造业	Manufacture of Artwork and Other Manufacturing	3	2	2280
电力、燃气及水的生产和供应业	Production and Distribution of Electric Power, Gas and Water	114	55	374456
电力、热力的生产和供应业	Production and Distribution of Electric Power and Heat Power	88	40	360949
燃气生产和供应业	Production and Distribution of Gas	5	4	2758
水的生产和供应业	Production and Distribution of Water	21	11	10749
建筑业	Construction			3842
交通运输、仓储和邮政业	Transport,Storage,Postal and Post	23	19	44005
#仓储业	Storage	2	2	1878
信息传输、计算机服务和软件业	Information Transmission,Computer Services and Software	225	191	238164
批发和零售业	Wholesale and Retail Trade	27	19	20929
住宿和餐饮业	Hotel and Restaurants	12	8	4062
金融业	Financial Intermediation	2	1	3242
房地产业	Real Estate	1	1	1100
科学研究、技术服务和地质勘查业	Scientific Research,Technical Services and Geologic Prospecting	2		1461
水利、环境和公共设施管理业	Management of Water Conservancy,Environment and Public Facilities	54	31	37743
居民服务和其他服务业	Services to Households and Other Services	2	2	1150
教育	Education	10	10	1889
卫生、社会保障和社会福利业	Health,Social Security and Social Welfare	10	8	7221
文化、体育和娱乐业	Culture,Sports and Entertainment	6	2	8752
公共管理和社会组织	Public Management and Social Organization	8	6	13639

4-6 基本建设、更新改造投资新增主要生产能力（2005）

Newly Increased Production Capacity through Capital Construction and Innovation(2005)

生产能力名称	Productive Capacity	计量单位 Unit	数量 Amount
原煤开采	Coal Mining(10000 tons/year)	万吨/年	348
焦炭	Coke(10000 tons/year)	万吨/年	116.5
生铁	Pig Iron(10000 tons/year)	万吨/年	62.67
炼钢	Steel-making(10000 tons/year)	万吨/年	12
电炉钢	Electric Steel(10000 tons/year)	万吨/年	12
铁合金	Iron Smelting(10000 tons/year)	万吨/年	12
热轧钢材	Hot Rolling Steel(10000 tons/year)	万吨/年	37
冷加工钢材	Cold Processing Steel(10000 tons/year)	万吨/年	0.9
锻压钢材	Forging and Pressing Steel(10000 tons/year)	万吨/年	1
挤压钢材	Extrusion and Pressing Steel(10000 tons/year)	万吨/年	0.8
铅锌采矿(原矿)	Lead and Zinc Mining(10000 tons/year)	万吨/年	2
氧化铝	Alumina(ton/year)	吨/年	60
电解铝	Electrolytic Aluminium(ton/year)	吨/年	9000
铝加工	Processing Alumina(10000 tons/year)	吨/年	600
黄金	Gold(kg/year)	公斤/年	1000
磷矿开采	Phosphorite Mining(10000 tons/year)	万吨/年	30
水力发电	Hydropower(10000 kw)	万千瓦	52.41
火力发电	Thermal Power(10000 kw)	万千瓦	194.5
输电线路长度(11万伏及以上)	Transmit Electricity Line(110000 Volt-amper Level and above)(km)	公里	957.6
变电设备能力(11万伏及以上)	Transform Electricity Equipment(110000 Volt-amper Level and above)(10000 kv.A)	万千伏安	161.68
水泥	Cement(10000 tons/year)	万吨/年	223.8
平板玻璃	Plate Glass(10000 weight cases)	万重量箱/年	20
胶合板	Veneer(10000 steres/year)	万立方米/年	0.6
硫酸	Sulfuric Acid(ton/year)	吨/年	1448000
电石	Calcium Carbide(ton/year)	吨/年	120000
合成氨	Synthetic Ammonia(ton/year)	吨/年	35000
氮肥	Nitrogen Fertilizers(ton/year)	吨/年	184000
磷肥	Phosphate Fertilizers(ton/year)	吨/年	330000
钾肥	Kalium Fertilizers(ton/year)	吨/年	150000
塑料树脂及共聚物	Plastics(ton/year)	吨/年	15000
轮胎外胎	Tires(10000 tires/year)	万条/年	59

4-6续表1(continued)

生产能力名称	Productive Capacity	计量单位 Unit	数量 Amount
中成药	Traditional Chinese Medicine and Patent Medicine(ton/year)	吨/年	4772
食用植物油	Edible Vegetable Oil(Dispose material,ton/day)	日处理原料:吨	172
	Edible Vegetable Oil(Refine Oil, ton/day)	日精炼油:吨	66
啤酒	Beer(10000 tons/year)	万吨/年	15.4
白酒	Liquor(10000 tons/year)	万吨/年	0.86
机制纸板	Machine-made Paperboard(10000 tons/yuar)	万吨/年	1
移动通信基站设备	Move Communicate Group Stage Equipment(channel/year)	个/年	585
程控交换机	Program-controlled Exchange(10000 lines/year)	万线/年	0.85
新建公路	Length of New Highways(km)	公里	9243
#高速公路	Freeway(km)	公里	163
改建公路	Length of Reconstructed Highways(km)	公里	1184
新建独立公路桥梁	New Independent Highway Bridge(extending.m)	延长米	1281
	New Independent Highway Bridge(bridge)	座	11
新增(改善)内河航道	New Extend(Ameliorate) Freshwater Sea-route Mileage(km)	公里	23
新(扩)建公路客、货运站	New Construction(Expansion)Passenger Transport and Freight Station(units)	个	18
	(sq.m)	平方米	120045
民航机场跑道	Number of Civil Aerodrome Runway(line)	条	1
	Longness of Civil Aerodrome Runway(m)	米	2200
候机楼	Number of Waiting Building in a Aerodrome(unit)	座	1
	(sq.m)	平方米	2720
长途电缆线路长度	Length of Long-distance Cable(km)	公里	707
耕地面积	Area of Cultivated Land(10000 mu)	万亩	3.12
造林面积	Afforestation Area(10000 mu)	万亩	20.55

4-6续表2(continued)

生产能力名称	Productive Capacity	计量单位 Unit	数量 Amount
水库容量(总库容)	Capacity of Reservoir(100 million steres)	亿立方米	0.3
有效灌溉面积	Effective Irrigated Area(10000 mu)	万亩	9.29
除涝面积	Area Drought(10000 mu)	万亩	0.5
商业冷藏库	Business Cold Store(10000 tons)	万吨	1.06
粮食仓库	Grain Storehouses(10000 kg)	万公斤	7644
	Grain Storehouses(sq.m)	平方米	19232
高等院校:学生席位	Number of Students Capacity of Universities and Colleges(unit)	个	8897
建筑面积	Floor Space(sq.m)	平方米	37448
中等学校:学生席位	Number of Students Capacity of Middle Schools(unit)	个	159749
建筑面积	Floor Space(sq.m)	平方米	453798
小学校:学生席位	Number of Students Capacity of Primary Schools(unit)	个	82734
建筑面积	Floor Space(sq.m)	平方米	231797
其他学校:学生席位	Number of Students Capacity of Other Schools(unit)	个	13894
建筑面积	Floor Space(sq.m)	平方米	54730
公共图书馆:藏书量	Public Library:Totle Collections(10000 volumes)	万册(件)	51
阅览室座席	Seating Capacity of Reading Rooms(seat)	个	1215
建筑面积	Floor Space (sq.m)	平方米	10026
医院病床	Number of Hospital Beds(bed)	张	3767
宾馆、旅馆、招待所客房数	Guest Room of Hotel,Inn and Rest House(unit)	间	839
	Guest Room of Hotel,Inn and Rest House(sq.m)	平方米	28631
城市自来水供水能力	Tap Water Supply Capacity(10000 tons/day)	万吨/日	23.21
城市自来水管道长度	Length of Tap Water Pipeline Built(km)	公里	289
城市液化石油气储气能力	Gas Storage Capacity of Liquefied Petroleum Gas of City(ton)	吨	1025
城市公共交通车辆购置	Purchase Vehicle of Public Traffic of City(vehicle)	辆	240
城市道路扩建长度	Length of Expanded Roads(km)	公里	130.72
城市道路扩建面积	Area of Expanded Roads(10000 sq.m)	万平方米	280.86
城市排水管道铺设长度	Length of Drainpipe(km)	公里	17.37
城市污水处理能力	Disposal Capacity of Sewage(10000 tons/year)	万吨/日	1.89
城市永久性桥梁	Bridge of City's Permanence(bridge)	座	3
城市防洪堤长度	Length of City's Floodwalls(km)	公里	416.91

主要统计指标解释

全社会固定资产投资 固定资产投资额是以货币表现的建造和购置固定资产活动的工作量，它是反映固定资产投资规模、速度、比例关系和使用方向的综合性指标。

基本建设投资 基本建设指企业、事业、行政单位以扩大生产能力或工程效益为主要目的的新建、扩建工程及有关工作。其综合范围为总投资50万元以上(含50万元,下同)的基本建设项目。

更新改造投资 更新改造指企业、事业单位对原有设施进行固定资产更新和技术改造,以及相应配套的工程和有关工作(不包括大修理和维护工程)。其综合范围为总投资50万元以上的更新改造项目。

房地产开发投资 指房地产开发公司、商品房建设公司及其他房地产开发法人单位和附属于其他法人单位实际从事房地产开发或经营的活动单位统一开发的包括统代建、拆迁还建的住宅、厂房、仓库、饭店、宾馆、度假村、写字楼、办公楼等房屋建筑物和配套的服务设施,土地开发工程(如道路、给水、排水、供电、供热、通讯、平整场地等基础设施工程)的投资;不包括单纯的土地交易活动。

其他固定资产投资 指全社会固定资产投资中未列入基本建设、更新改造和房地产开发投资的建造和购置固定资产的活动。

城镇和工矿区私人建房投资和农村个人投资 城镇和工矿区私人建房包括市、县城、镇、工矿区所辖范围内的全部私人建房,不论其房主是否系本地的常住户口均应包括。农村个人投资包括农村个人建房及购置生产性固定资产的投资。

施工项目 指报告期内曾进行建筑或安装工程施工活动的建设项目,包括报告期内新开工项目、报告期以前开工跨入报告期继续施工的项目以及报告期施过工并在报告期内全部建成投产或停缓建的项目。

新增生产能力 指通过固定资产投资活动而增加的设计能力或工程效益，它是用实物形态表示的固定资产投资的成果。新增生产能力的计算,是以能独立发挥生产能力或工程效益的单项工程(或项目)为对象。当单项工程(或项目)建成,经有关部门鉴定合格,正式移交投入生产,即可计算新增生产能力。

房屋建筑面积 指从房屋外墙线算起的各层平面面积的总和,包括可供使用的有效面积和房屋结构(如柱、墙)占用的面积。多层建筑按各层(包括地下室)面积总和计算。

住宅建筑面积 指施工和竣工房屋建筑面积中供居住用的施工和竣工房屋建筑面积。

施工面积 指报告期内施工的全部房屋建筑面积。包括本期新开工的面积、上期跨入本期继续施工的房屋面积、上期停缓建在本期恢复施工的房屋面积、本期竣工的房屋面积及本期施工后又停缓建的房屋面积。

竣工面积 指在报告期内房屋建筑按照设计要求已全部完工,达到住人和使用条件,经验收鉴定合格,正式移交使用单位的建筑面积。

房屋建筑面积竣工率 指一定时期内房屋竣工面积占同期房屋施工面积的比率。

新增固定资产 指通过投资活动所形成的新的固定资产价值，包括已经建成投入生产或交付使用的工程价值和达到固定资产标准的设备、工具、器具的价值及有关应摊入的费用。它是以价值形式表示的固定资产投资成果的综合性指标,可以综合反映不同时期、不同部门、不同地区的固定资产投资成果。

建设项目投产率 指一定时期内全部建成投入生产项目个数与同期正式施工项目个数的比率。它是从项目建设速度的角度反映投资效果的指标。

固定资产交付使用率 指一定时期新增固定资产与同期完成投资额的比率。它是反映各个时期固定资产动用速度,衡量建设过程中投资效果的一个综合性指标。

Explanatory Notes on Main Statistical Indicators

Total Investment in Fixed Assets in the Whole Province Investment in fixed assets Amount of investment in fixed assets refers to the volume of activities in construction and purchases of fixed assets in monetary terms. It is a comprehensive indicator which shows the size, pace, proportional relations and use orientation of the investment in fixed assets.

Investment in Capital Construction Capital construction refers to the new construction projects or extension projects and the related work of the enterprises, institutions or administrative units mainly for the purpose of expanding production capacity or improving project efficiency covering only projects each with a total investment of 500,000 RMB yuan and over.

Investment in Innovation Innovation refers to the renewal of fixed assets and technological innovation of the original facilities by the enterprises and institutions as well as the corresponding supplementary projects and the related work (excluding major overhaul and maintenance projects) covering only projects each with a total investment of 500,000 RMB yuan and over.

Investment in Real Estate Development It includes the investment by the real estate development companies, commercial buildings construction companies and other real estate development units of various types of ownership in the construction of house buildings, such as residential buildings, factory buildings, warehouses, hotels, guesthouses, holiday villages, office buildings, and the complementary service facilities and land development projects, such as roads, water supply, water drainage, power supply, heating, telecommunications, land leveling and other projects of infrastructure. It excludes the activities in simple land transactions.

Other Investment in Fixed Assets refers to the construcion and purchases of fixed assets not listed in the investment in capital construction, investment in innovation and investment in real estate development.

Private Investment in House Construction in Urban Areas, Industrial and Mining Areas and Individual Investment in Rural Areas The private house construction in the urban areas and industrial and mining areas includes all the private house construction under the jurisdiction of cities, counties, towns and industrial and mining areas, no matter whether the owner of the house is registered as the permanent resident in the locality or not. The individual investment in the rural areas includes the investment in house construction and purchase of productive fixed assets by the individuals in the rural areas.

Projects Under Construction refer to projects having construction and installation activities undertaken in the reference period, including projects started in the reference period, or continued from the previous period, or completed and put into production or suspended in the reference period.

Newly Increased Production Capacity refers to the increase of designed capacity and project efficiency through investment in fixed assets, which reflects the accomplishment of investment in fixed assets in kind. The calculation of newly increased production capacity is based on individual project which operates independently and efficiently. When an individual project is completed and checked and accepted and put into production, it is counted as newly increased production capacity.

Floor Space of Buildings Under Construction and Completed refers to total floor space in each story of buildings calculated from the outside line of building walls,including both usable space and the space occupied by constructions like pillars or walls. The floor space of multi-story buildings includes the total floor space of each story (including basement).

Floor Space of Residential Buildings refers to the floor space of the residential buildings under construction and completed among the total space of buildings under construction and completed.

Floor Space Under Construction refers to total floor space of all buildings under construction during the reference period, including floor space of newly started buildings during the reference period, floor space of construction extended from the previous period to the current period, floor space of construction suspended during the previous period and resumed in the current period, floor space of construction completed in the current period, and floor space of construction started and then suspended in the current period.

Floor Space of Buildings Completed refers to the floor space of buildings completed in the reference period, which have come up to the designed standards and have been put into use.

Completion Rate of Floor Space of Buildings refers to the ratio of the floor space of buildings completed in certain period of time to the floor space of buildings under construction in the same period,which reflects the investment result and economic efficiency of the construction industry from the angle of the speed of project construction.

Newly Increased Fixed Assets refer to the newly increased value of fixed assets through investment,including the value of projects completed and put into production, the value of equipment,tools,and vessels considered as fixed assets,as well as the relevant expenses as investment in fixed assets.

Rate of Construction Projects Completed and Put into Use refers to the ratio of the number of construction projects completed and put into use in certain period of time to the number of projects under construction in the same period. This reflects the investment efficiency from the angle of the speed of projects construction.

Rate of Projects of Fixed Assets Completed and Put into Operation refers to the ratio of the newly increased fixed assets to the total investment made in the same period. This is a comprehensive indicator,reflecting the speed of the employment of fixed assets and the investment efficiency.

5

Five

能源、原材料消耗

Consumption of Energy and Raw Material

万元GDP能耗（吨标准煤）
Average 10000 Yuan GDP Energy Consumption(Ton of SCE)

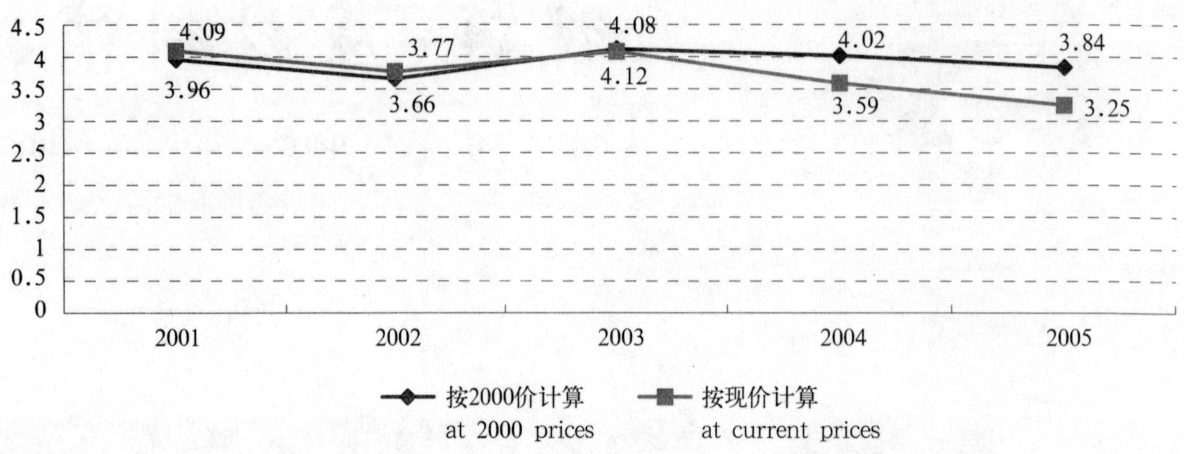

能源终端消费总量（万吨标准煤）
Final Consumption of Energy (10000 tons of SCE)

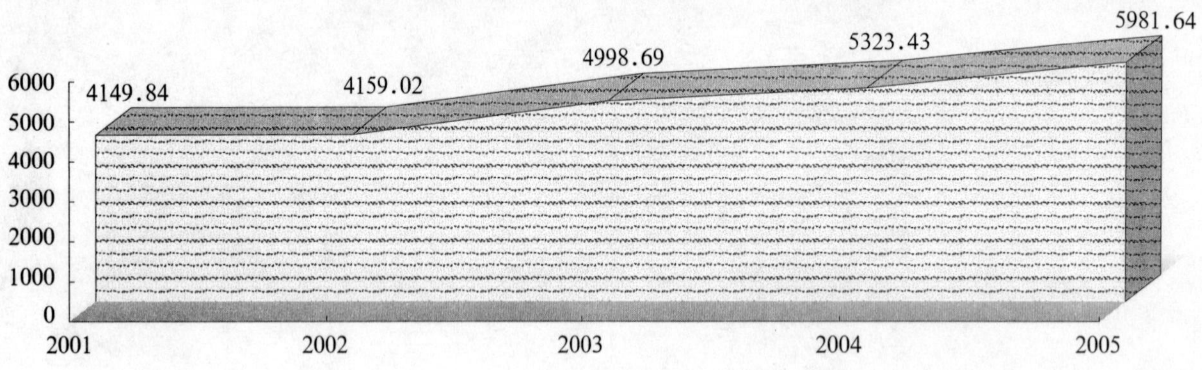

能源生产、消费弹性系数
Elasticity Ratio of Energy Production and Consumption

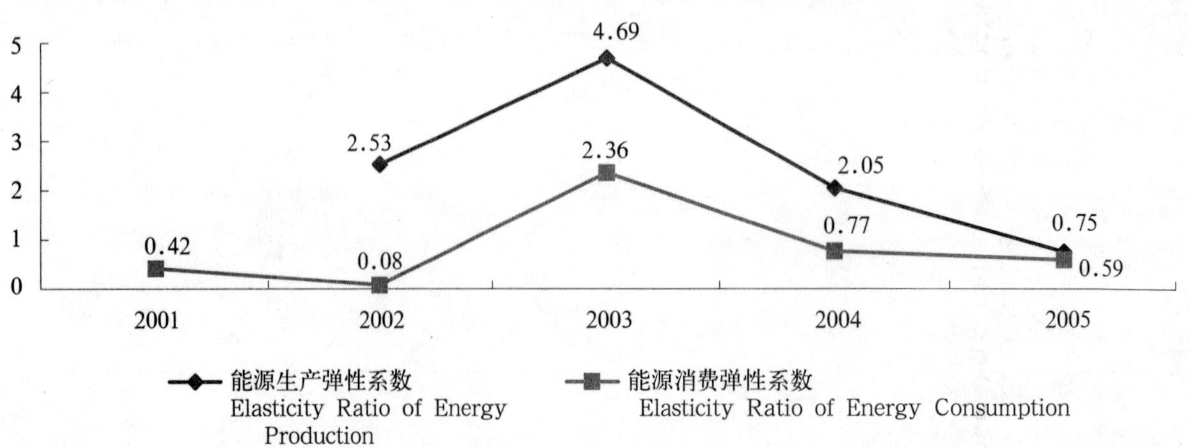

5-1 “十五”时期各年能源生产、消费总量及构成

Total Production and Consumption of Energy and Its Composition of Each Year in “Tenth Five-year Plan” Period

单位:万吨标准煤(10000 tons of SCE)

指 标	Item	2000	2001	2002	2003	2004	2005
一、绝对数	**Absolute Figure**						
一次能源生产总量	Total Production of Primary Energy	3875.92	3482.92	4286.06	6317.89	7791.23	8459.52
#原煤	Coal	3054.88	2665.33	3572.31	5573.33	6969.15	7582.43
天然气	Natural Gas	8.50	8.26	5.83	5.59		
水电	Hydro-power	812.54	809.33	707.92	738.97	822.08	877.09
能源终端消费总量	Final Consumption of Energy	3848.22	4149.84	4159.02	4998.69	5323.43	5981.64
#原煤	Coal	1852.20	1827.32	1961.46	2334.30	2803.36	2965.56
天然气	Natural Gas	69.46	72.86	66.55	66.18	60.59	72.35
电力	Electricity	1373.01	1657.32	1514.73	1884.21	1716.71	2109.61
二、构成(%)	**Composition(%)**						
一次能源生产总量	Total Production of Primary Energy	100.0	100.0	100.0	100.0	100.0	100.0
#原煤	Coal	78.8	76.5	83.4	88.2	89.5	89.6
天然气	Natural Gas	0.2	0.2	0.1	0.1		
水电	Hydro-power	21.0	23.2	16.5	11.7	10.6	10.4
能源终端消费总量	Final Consumption of Energy	100.0	100.0	100.0	100.0	100.0	100.0
#原煤	Coal	48.1	44.0	47.2	46.8	52.7	49.6
天然气	Natural Gas	1.8	1.8	1.6	1.3	1.1	1.2
电力	Electricity	35.7	39.9	36.4	37.7	32.3	35.3

注:电力、热力按等价热值折算(以下各表同)

Note: Electric power and heat are converted on the basic of equal caloric value.(The same as in the following tables)

5-2 “十五”时期各年综合能源平衡表

Overall Energy Balance of Each Year in “Tenth Five-year Plan” Period

单位:万吨标准煤(10000 tons of SCE)

指 标	Item	2000	2001	2002	2003	2004	2005
可供消费的能源总量	**Total Energy Available for Consumption**	**2738.1**	**2795.9**	**3192.9**	**4757.5**	**5197.4**	**5718.8**
一次能源生产量	Primary Energy Output	3875.9	3482.9	4286.1	6317.9	7791.2	8459.5
省外调入	Inflow from Other Provinces	262.1	292.0	298.7	334.4	349.6	420.1
调出省外(—)	Outflow from Guizhou Province(-)	-1382.1	-1027.6	-1372.3	-1906.1	-2794.6	-3309.0
年初年末库存差额	Stock Changes in the Year	22.5	48.6	19.6	11.2	7.1	148.3
能源消费总量	**Total Energy Consumption**	**4278.6**	**4437.9**	**4469.9**	**5534.5**	**6021.0**	**6428.6**
在总量中:	Consumption by Sector						
农、林、牧、渔、水利业	Farming,Forestry,Animal Husbandry,Fishery and Water Conservancy	242.7	241.9	245.7	274.7	283.2	288.1
工业	Industry	2563.2	2727.5	2694.6	3599.7	4041.5	4352.6
建筑业	Construction	44.1	37.8	38.4	46.3	52.1	56.4
交通运输和邮电通讯业	Transportation,Post and Telecommunications Services	178.5	176.1	176.0	212.5	233.7	273.5
商业、饮食、物资供销和仓储业	Commerce,Catering Services, Materials Supply and Storage	172.5	158.3	163.4	189.9	190.3	191.3
其他	Others	189.1	212.6	226.1	254.5	251.0	265.1
生活消费	Residential Consumption	888.6	883.7	925.7	956.9	969.2	1001.7
在总量中:	Consumption by Usage						
终端消费	Final Consumption	3848.2	4149.8	4159.0	4998.7	5323.4	5981.6
#工业	Industry	2132.7	2439.4	2383.8	3063.2	3344.0	3905.7
加工转换损失量	Losses in Processing and Transformation	323.2	187.5	209.7	408.7	541.6	276.0
#炼焦	Coking	159.5	141.1	151.0	194.3	125.1	1.4
损失量	Other Losses	107.2	100.6	101.2	127.2	156.0	171.0
平衡差额	Balance	-1540.6	-1642.0	-1277.1	-776.9	-823.6	-709.8

5-3 “十五”时期各年煤炭平衡表

Coal Balance Sheet of Each Year in “Tenth Five-year Plan” Period

单位:万吨(10000 tons)

指 标	Item	2000	2001	2002	2003	2004	2005
可供量	**Total Energy Available for Consumption**	**3376.6**	**2982.8**	**3746.4**	**6075.0**	**7196.0**	**8196.1**
生产量	Output	4276.8	3731.4	5001.1	7802.5	9756.6	10615.2
调出省外(—)	Outflow from Guizhou Province(–)	–935.0	–840.4	–1210.8	–1678.0	–2545.0	–2617.2
年初年末库存差额	Stock Changes in the Year	34.8	91.8	44.0	4.6	13.4	198.0
消费量	**Total Energy Consumption**	**5352.0**	**5157.4**	**5405.6**	**7105.9**	**8186.9**	**9189.7**
在消费量中:	Consumption by Sector						
农、林、牧、渔、水利业	Farming,Forestry,Animal Husbandry, Fishery and Water Conservancy	222.0	219.0	232.0	256.3	258.5	249.3
工业	Industry	3752.0	3589.0	3765.2	5364.5	6528.5	7556.5
建筑业	Construction	4.0	3.8	4.9	6.1	7.2	7.3
交通运输和邮电通讯业	Transportation,Post and Telecommunications Services	8.0	7.8	8.8	9.2	9.4	9.5
商业、饮食、物资供销和仓储业	Commerce,Catering Services, Materials Supply and Storage	132.0	129.5	139.2	153.8	155.6	149.5
其他	Others	174.0	171.0	192.1	216.5	220.5	219.6
生活消费	Residential Consumption	1015.0	997.4	1017.3	1009.5	1007.2	998.0
在消费量中:	Consumption by Usage						
终端消费	Final Consumption	2593.0	2558.4	2746.0	3268.0	3924.6	4151.7
#工业	Industry	1038.0	1033.6	1151.7	1616.6	2266.2	2518.5
中间消费(用于加工转换)	Intermediate Consumption (Consumed in Transformation)	2714.0	2559.1	2613.6	3697.0	4200.6	4980.0
发电	Power Generation	1368.0	1413.4	1430.7	2169.1	2643.9	3212.3
炼焦	Coking	527.0	438.9	456.3	534.5	361.9	328.6
洗选损耗	Losses in Coal Washing and Dressing	45.0	40.0	46.0	51.0	61.7	58.0
平衡差额	Balance	–1975.4	–2174.7	–1659.2	–941.0	–990.9	–993.7

5-4 “十五”时期各年电力平衡表

Electricity Balance Sheet of Each Year in “Tenth Five-year Plan” Period

单位：亿千瓦小时(100 million kwh)

指 标	Item	2000	2001	2002	2003	2004	2005
可供量	**Total Energy Available for Consumption**	**287.9**	**335.2**	**366.6**	**399.6**	**458.7**	**487.0**
生产量	Output	316.2	369.8	427.5	491.9	595.4	679.2
水电	Hydropower	91.2	101.2	101.9	59.2	98.7	109.7
火电	Thermal Power	225.0	268.6	325.6	432.7	496.8	569.6
调出省外(-)	Outflow from Guizhou Province(-)	-28.4	-34.6	-60.9	-92.3	-136.8	-192.3
消费量	**Total Energy Consumption**	**287.9**	**335.2**	**366.6**	**399.6**	**458.7**	**487.0**
在消费量中	Consumption by Sector						
农、林、牧、渔、水利业	Farming,Forestry,Animal Husbandry, Fishery a nd Water Conservancy	11.1	13.8	11.4	12.3	16.3	13.7
工业	Industry	225.5	265.2	281.7	323.9	370.5	386.8
建筑业	Construction	2.4	2.4	2.9	3.2	3.3	4.1
交通运输和邮电通讯业	Transportation,Post and Telecommunications Services	11.2	12.5	13.6	14.2	16.0	15.6
商业、饮食、物资供销和仓储业	Commerce,Catering Services, Materials Supply and Storage	2.6	3.2	3.8	5.1	3.0	9.0
其他	Others	7.6	6.1	6.4	7.3	7.1	6.6
生活消费	Residential Consumption	27.4	32.1	46.9	33.5	42.6	51.2
在消费量中	Consumption by Usage						
终端消费	Final Consumption	270.4	315.0	349.7	375.6	433.7	455.2
#工业	Industry	225.5	265.2	281.7	323.9	370.5	386.8
输配损失量	Losses in Transmission	17.5	20.2	16.9	24.0	25.0	31.8

5-5 “十五”时期各年能源生产消费弹性系数

Elasticity Ratio of Energy Production and Consumption of Each Year in “Tenth Five-year Plan” Period

指 标	Item	2000	2001	2002	2003	2004	2005
能源生产弹性系数	**Elasticity Ratio of Energy Production**						
能源生产比上年增长	Growth Rate of Energy Production over Preceding Year	7.78	-10.14	23.06	47.41	23.32	8.58
电力生产比上年增长	Growth Rate of Electricity Production over Preceding Year	18.25	16.93	15.06	15.07	21.04	14.07
生产总值比上年增长	Growth Rate of Gross Domestic Product (GDP) over Pre ceding Year	8.4	8.8	9.1	10.1	11.4	11.5
能源生产弹性系数	Elasticity Ratio of Energy Production	0.93		2.53	4.69	2.05	0.75
电力生产弹性系数	Elasticity Ratio of Electricity Production	2.17	1.92	1.65	1.49	1.85	1.22
能源消费弹性系数	**Elasticity Ratio of Energy Consumption**						
能源消费总量比上年增长	Growth Rate of Energy Consumption over Preceding Year	2.77	3.72	0.72	23.82	8.79	6.77
电力消费比上年增长	Growth Rate of Electricity Consumption over Preceding Year	18.22	16.45	9.38	8.98	14.79	6.17
生产总值比上年增长	Growth Rate of Gross Domestic Product(GDP) over Preceding Year	8.4	8.8	9.1	10.1	11.4	11.5
能源消费弹性系数	Elasticity Ratio of Energy Consumption	0.33	0.42	0.08	2.36	0.77	0.59
电力消费弹性系数	Elasticity Ratio of Electricity Consumption	2.17	1.87	1.03	0.89	1.3	0.54

注:生产总值增长速度按可比价格计算。（以下相关表同）

Note: The growth rates of GDP are calculated at comparable prices.The same as in the following tables.

5-6 “十五”时期各年生活能源消费量

Energy Consumption for Non-Production Purpose of Each Year in “Tenth Five-year Plan” Period

能源品种	Item	2000	2001	2002	2003	2004	2005
合计（万吨标准煤）	**Total (10000 tons of SCE)**	**888.56**	**883.69**	**925.70**	**956.93**	**969.18**	**1001.67**
煤炭（万吨）	Coal (10000 tons)	1063.87	1045.71	1065.70	1053.32	1046.95	1035.80
煤油（万吨）	Kerosene (10000 tons)	0.24	0.58	0.58	0.56	0.52	0.50
液化石油气（万吨）	Liquefied Petroleum Gas (10000 tons)	6.31	7.10	6.70	6.50	6.80	6.53
天然气（亿立方米）	Natural Gas(100 million cu.m)	0.07	0.06	0.05	0.05	0.40	0.41
煤气（亿立方米）	Gas (100 million cu.m)	0.51	0.51	0.55	0.78	0.86	0.91
热力（万百万千焦）	Heat (10 billion kilo-joule)	0.28	1.75	4.87	4.91	4.88	4.91
电力（亿千瓦小时）	Electricity (100 million kwh)	27.42	32.07	46.92	33.46	42.57	51.20

5-7 “十五”时期各年每人年平均生活用能源

Annual Average Per Capita Energy Consumption for Non-Production Purpose of Each Year in “Tenth Five-year Plan” Period

指　标	Item	2000	2001	2002	2003	2004	2005
平均每人生活消费能源(千克标准煤/人)	**Annual Average Non-Productive Consumption Per Capita(kg of SCE/person)**	**238.04**	**233.96**	**242.46**	**248.33**	**249.36**	**255.70**
煤炭（千克）	Coal(kg)	285.00	276.85	279.13	273.34	269.37	264.41
电力（千瓦小时）	Electricity(kwh)	73.46	84.91	122.89	86.83	109.53	130.70
液化石油气（千克）	Liquefied Petroleum Gas(kg)	1.69	1.88	1.75	1.69	1.75	1.67
煤气（立方米）	Gas(cu.m)	1.37	1.35	1.44	2.02	2.21	2.32

5-8 “十五”时期各年能源利用效率

Using Efficiency of Energy of Each Year in “Tenth Five-year Plan” Period

能源品种 Item	2000	2001	2002	2003	2004	2005
每万元生产总值能源消费量（吨标准煤）（2000价） Energy Consumption Per10000 Yuan GDP (ton of SCE)	**4.15**	**3.96**	**3.66**	**4.12**	**4.02**	**3.84**
每万元生产总值能源消费量（吨标准煤）（现价） Energy Consumption Per 10000 Yuan GDP(ton of SCE)	4.31	4.09	3.77	4.08	3.59	3.25
能源消费总量（万吨标准煤） Total Energy Consumption(10000 tons of SCE)	4278.61	4437.9	4469.86	5534.49	6020.98	6428.60
工业能源消费量 Energy Consumption of Industry	2563.16	2727.47	2694.60	3599.73	4041.52	4352.60
每万元工业增加值能源消费量（吨标准煤） Energy Consumption Per 10000 Yuan Value-added of Industry(ton of SCE)	7.99	7.79	6.93	8.17	7.92	7.43
每万元工业增加值煤消费量（吨） Coal Consumption Per 10000 Yuan Value-added of Industry(ton)	**16.69**	**14.73**	**13.91**	**15.94**	**16.04**	**15.68**
每万元工业增加值电消费量（千瓦小时） Electricity Consumption Per 10000 Yuan Value-added of Industry(kwh)	8975.71	9571.13	9431.74	9075.79	8989.16	8311.09
每吨能源生产的生产总值（元） GDP Produced by Per Ton Energy(yuan)	2407.14	2523.81	2732.70	2429.56	2487.85	2601.36

注:工业增加值、生产总值均按2000年可比价格计算。

Note:The growth rates of Value-added of Industry and GDP are calculated at 2000 comparable prices.

5-9 “十五”时期各年分行业能源消费总量

Consumption of Total Energy and Its Main Varieties by Sector of Each Year in “Tenth Five-year Plan” Period

行 业	Sector	2000	2001	2002	2003	2004	2005
工业	Industry	2563.16	2727.47	2694.60	3599.73	4041.52	4352.60
采掘业	Mining and Quarring	288.73	410.41	465.64	753.32	939.96	973.64
煤炭采选业	Coal Mining and Dressing	245.36	350.33	401.76	671.81	855.94	876.20
黑色金属矿采选业	Ferrous Metals Mining and Dressing	1.51	0.28	0.64	1.10	4.02	5.24
有色金属矿采选业	Nonferrous Metals Mining and Dressing	4.69	5.27	7.39	10.64	8.00	10.08
非金属矿采选业	Nonmetal Minerals Mining and Dressing	37.02	54.46	55.72	69.73	72.00	82.12
木材及竹材采运业	Logging and Transport of Wood and Bamboo	0.15	0.07	0.13	0.04		
制造业	Manufacturing	2070.40	1976.28	1877.86	2387.11	2467.07	2692.60
食品加工业	Food Processing	16.31	12.50	12.95	14.89	7.25	8.23
食品制造业	Food Production	9.81	3.53	4.03	4.87	6.33	7.10
饮料制造业	Beverage Production	23.08	10.74	12.13	14.77	14.80	16.50
烟草加工业	Tobacco Processing	48.05	27.50	26.52	36.87	17.24	19.58
纺织业	Textile Industry	8.48	8.40	7.77	9.32	5.50	6.55
服装及其他纤维制品制造业	Garments and Other Fiber Products	0.50	0.75	4.37	5.22	0.47	2.75
皮革、毛皮、羽绒及其制品业	Leather,Furs,Down and Related Products	0.03	0.07	0.16	0.23	0.04	0.04
木材加工及竹、藤、棕、草制品业	Cane,Palm Fiber and Straw Products	2.76	2.23	2.27	2.65	5.21	5.92
家具制造业	Furniture Manufacturing	0.27	0.26	0.30	0.41	0.14	0.19
造纸及纸制品业	Papermaking and Paper Products	11.80	12.36	13.25	15.50	9.03	10.17
印刷业,记录媒介的复制	Printing and Record Medium Reprodu(ction)	1.21	3.15	2.87	3.57	0.98	1.14
文教体育用品制造业	Cultural,Educational and Sports Articles	0.09	0.54	0.57	0.77	0.04	0.04
石油加工及炼焦业	Petroleum Processing and Coking	156.20	122.10	133.81	174.64	240.07	186.38
化学原料及化学制品制造业	Raw Chemical Materials and Chemical Products	369.65	438.95	410.24	487.25	555.73	608.13
医药制造业	Medical and Pharmaceutical Products	3.50	9.02	9.34	12.10	6.42	6.92

5-9续表(continued)

行　业	Sector	2000	2001	2002	2003	2004	2005
化学纤维制造业	Chemical Fibers	0.91	0.12	0.26	0.46	0.86	1.05
橡胶制品业	Rubber Products	15.41	25.14	25.40	30.95	24.61	27.96
塑料制品业	Plastic Products	2.47	3.01	2.85	3.53	2.90	3.18
非金属矿物制品业	Nonmetal Mineral Products	372.38	173.81	171.39	242.04	279.36	323.09
黑色金属冶炼及压延加工业	Smelting and Pressing of Ferrous Metals	526.84	548.30	507.10	635.21	705.35	814.53
有色金属冶炼及压延加工业	Smelting and Pressing of Nonferrous Metals	434.16	487.81	441.99	584.05	526.97	576.14
金属制品业	Metal Products	19.44	19.12	18.77	23.05	9.03	10.93
普通机械制造业	Ordinary Machinery Manufacturing	6.29	8.09	8.49	11.44	6.67	7.58
专用设备制造业	Special Purposes Equipment Manufacturing	3.29	4.56	4.70	6.48	4.04	4.71
交通运输设备制造业	Transportation Equipment Manufacturing	22.13	38.32	39.95	51.36	23.93	29.19
武器弹药制造业	Weapon and Munition Manufacturing	0.05	0.03	0.03	0.06		
电气机械及器材制造业	Electric Equipment and Machinery	3.98	4.39	4.39	6.71	7.86	7.74
电子及通信设备制造业	Electronic and Telecommunications Equipment	5.49	4.59	4.50	5.71	2.57	3.08
仪器仪表及文化、办公用机械制造业	Instruments,Meters,Cultural and Office Machinery	0.48	1.61	1.56	1.74	0.57	0.68
其他制造业	Others	5.34	5.28	5.90	1.26	3.10	3.10
电力、煤气及水的生产和供应业	Electric Power, Gas and Tap Water Production and Supply	204.03	340.78	351.10	459.30	634.49	686.36
电力、蒸汽、热水的生产和供应业	Electric Power、Steam and Hot Water Production and Supply	174.33	298.49	308.80	408.80	551.85	636.75
煤气生产和供应业	Gas Production and Supply	20.97	33.78	33.55	38.97	75.00	40.05
自来水的生产和供应业	Tap Water Production and Supply	8.66	8.49	8.75	11.50	7.64	9.57
建筑业	Construction	44.10	37.81	38.36	46.26	52.06	56.36
交通运输、仓储及邮电通信业	Transportation,Storage,Postal & Telecommunications Services	178.49	176.12	175.99	212.52	223.70	273.49
批发和零售贸易餐饮业	Wholesale,Retail Trade and Catering Services	172.47	158.28	163.37	189.92	190.31	191.30
其他行业	Others	189.10	212.59	226.14	254.46	251.04	265.11
生活消费	Residential Consumption	888.56	883.69	925.70	956.93	969.18	1001.67

主要统计指标解释

能源生产总量 指一定时期内全省一次能源生产量的总和。一次能源生产量包括原煤,原油,天然气,水电、核能及其他动力能(如风能、地热能等)发电量,不包括低热值燃料生产量、生物质能、太阳能等的利用和由一次能源加工转换而成的二次能源产量。

能源消费总量 指一定时期内全省物质生产部门、非物质生产部门和生活消费的各种能源的总和。能源消费总量包括原煤和原油及其制品、天然气、电力,不包括低热值燃料、生物质能和太阳能等的利用。能源消费总量分为终端能源消费量、能源加工转换损失量和损失量三部分。

(1)终端能源消费量:指一定时期内全国生产和生活消费的各种能源在扣除了用于加工转换二次能源消费量和损失量以后的数量。

(2)能源加工转换损失量:指一定时期内全国投入加工转换的各种能源数量之和与产出各种能源产品之和的差额,是观察能源在加工转换过程中损失量变化的指标。

(3)能源损失量:指一定时期内能源在输送、分配、储存过程中发生的损失和由客观原因造成的各种损失量,不包括各种气体能源放空、放散量。

能源生产弹性系数 是研究能源生产增长速度与国民经济增长速度之间关系的指标。计算公式为:

能源生产弹性系数=能源生产总量年平均增长速度/国民经济年平均增长速度

国民经济年平均增长速度,可根据不同的目的或需要,用国民生产总值、国内生产总值等指标来计算,本年鉴是采用国内生产总值指标计算的。

电力生产弹性系数 是研究电力生产增长速度与国民经济增长速度之间关系的指标。一般来说,电力的发展应当快于国民经济的发展,也就是说电力应超前发展。计算公式为:

电力生产弹性系数=电力生产量年平均增长速度/国民经济年平均增长速度

能源消费弹性系数 是反映能源消费增长速度与国民经济增长速度之间比例关系的指标。计算公式为:

能源消费弹性系数=能源消费量年平均增长速度/国民经济年平均增长速度

电力消费弹性系数 反映电力消费增长速度与国民经济增长速度之间比例关系的指标。计算公式为:

电力消费弹性系数=电力消费量年平均增长速度/国民经济年平均增长速度

能源加工转换效率 指一定时期内能源经过加工、转换后,产出的各种能源产品的数量与同期内投入加工转换的各种能源数量的比率。它是观察能源加工转换装置和生产工艺先进与落后、管理水平高低等的重要指标。计算公式为:

能源加工转换效率=能源加工、转换产出量/能源加工、转换投入量×100%

Explanatory Notes on Main Statistical Indicators

Total Energy Production refers to the total producuion of primary energy by all energy producing enterprises in the country in a given period of time. The production of primary energy includes that of coal, crude oil, natural gas, hydro-power and electricity generated by nuclear energy and other means such as wind power and geothermal power. However, it excludes the production of fuels of low calorific value, bio-energy, solar energy and the secondary energy converted from the primary energy.

Total Domestic Energy Consumption refers to the total consumption of energy of various kinds by material production sectors, non material production sectors and households in the province in a given period of time. It is a comprehensive indicator to show the scale, composition and development of energy consumption. The total energy consumption includes that of coal, crude oil and their products, natural gas and electricity, However, it excludes the consumption of fuel of low calorific value, bio-energy and solar energy. Total domestic energy consumption can be divided into three parts:

(1)Final Energy Consumption: It refers to the total energy consumption by material production sectors, non material production sectors and households in the country (region)in a given period of time, but excludes the consumption in conversion of the primary energy into the secondary energy and the loss in the process of energy conversion.

(2)Loss During the Process of Energy Conversion: It refers to the total input of various kinds of energy for conversion, minus the total output of various kinds of energy in the country in a given period of time. It is an indicator to show the loss that occurs during the process of energy conversion.

(3)Loss: It refers to the total of the loss of energy during the course of energy transport, distribution and storage and the loss caused by any objective reason in a given period of time. The loss of various kinds of gas due to gas discharges and stocktaking is excluded.

Elasticity Ratio of Energy Production is an indicator to show the relationship between the growth rate of energy production and the growth rate of the national economy. The formula is:

Elasticity Ratio of Energy Production=Average Annual Growth Rate of Energy Production/Average Annual Growth Rate of National Economy

The average annual growth rate of the national economy can be shown by the gross national product, gross domestic product and other indicators, depending upon the purposes or needs. The gross domestic product is used in calculation of the ratio in this chapter.

Elasticity Ratio of Electricity Production is an indicator to show the relationship between the growth rate of electricity production and the growth rate of the national economy. Generally speaking, the growth rate of electricity production should be higher than that of the national economy. Its formula is:

Elasticity Ratio of Electricity Production=Average Annual Growth Rate of Electricity Production/Average Annual Growth Rate of National Economy

Elasticity Ratio of Energy Consumption is an indicator to show the relationship between the growth rate of energy consumption and the growth rate of the national economy. The formula is:

Elasticity Ratio of Energy Consumption=Average Annual Growth Rate of Energy Consumption/Average Annual

Growth Rate of National Economy

Elasticity Ratio of Electricity Consumption is an indicator to show the relationship between the growth rate of electricity consumption and the growth rate of the national economy. The formula is:

Elasticity Ratio of Electricity Consumption =Average Annual Growth Rate of Electricity/Average Annual Growth Rate of National Economy

Efficiency of Energy Processing and Conversion refers to the ratio of the total output of energy products of various kinds after processing and conversion and the total input of energy of various kinds for processing and conversion in the same reference period. It is an important indicator to show the current conditions of energy processing and conversion equipment, production technique and management. The formula is:

Efficiency of Energy Processing & Conversion=Output of Energy After Processing & Conversion/Input of Energy for Processing & Conversion×100%

6

农 业

Agriculture

Six

农林牧渔业增加值及指数
Value-added of Farming, Forestry, Animal Husbandry and Fishery and Its Indices

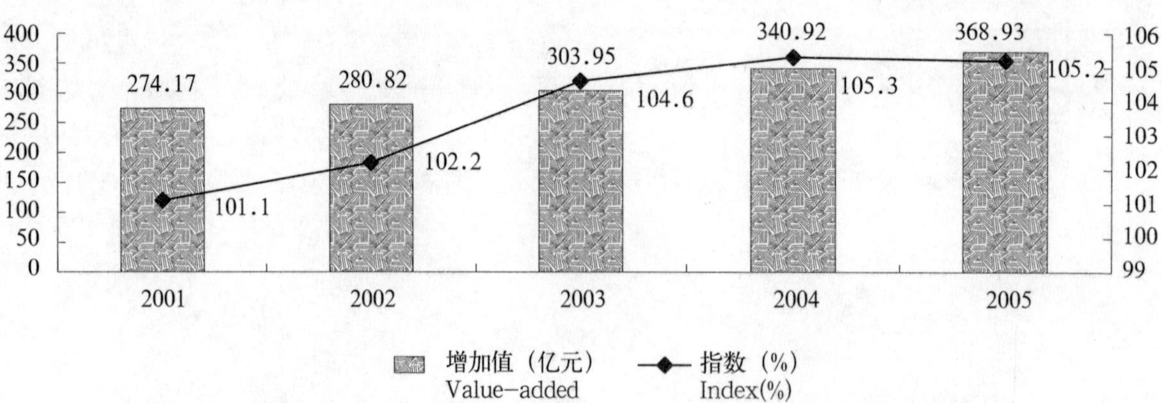

农林牧渔业增加值构成（%）
Composition of Added Value of FFAF (%)

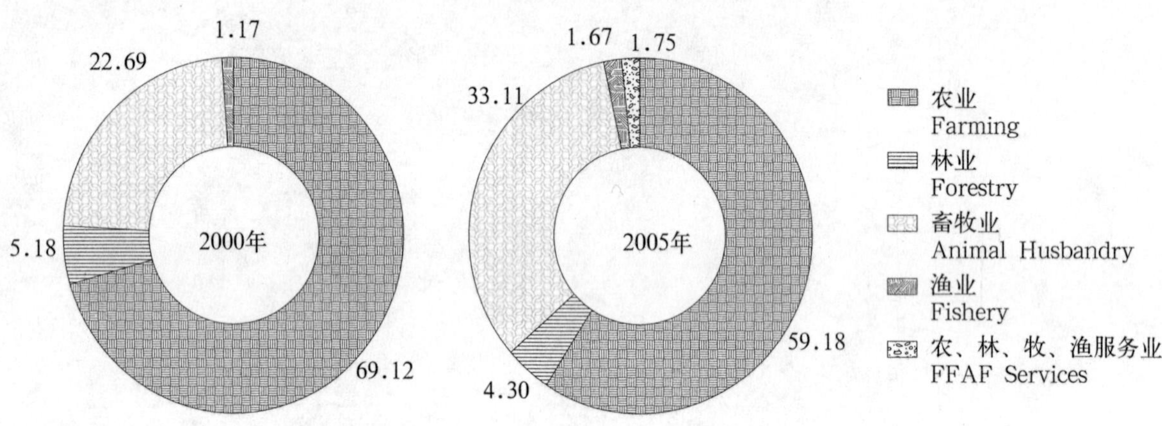

主要农作物产品产量（万吨）
Yield of Major Farm Corps (10000 tons)

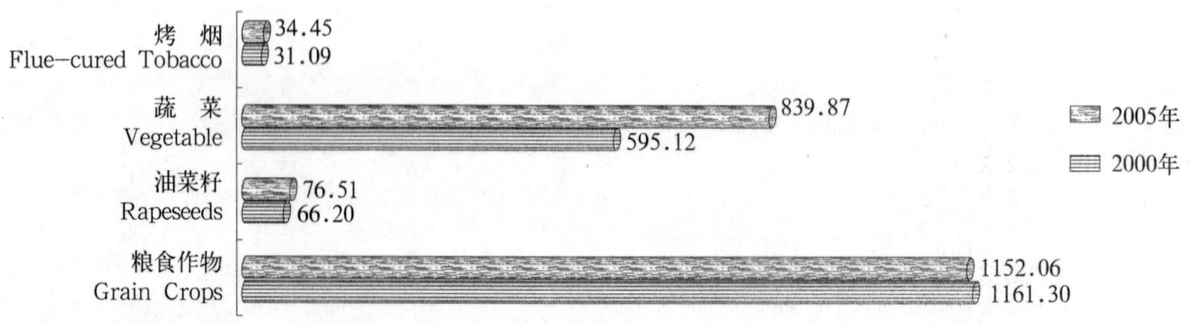

6-1 “十五”时期各年农村基本情况及农业生产条件

Basic Conditions of Rural Areas and Agricultural Production of Each Year in "Tenth Five-year Plan" Period

指　标	Item	2000	2001	2002	2003	2004	2005
农村基层组织	**Rural Grassroots Units**						
乡镇个数（个）	Nunmber of Township and Town Governments(unit)	1463	1460	1457	1452	1452	1451
村委会个数	Nunmber of Villagers' Committees(unit)	25696	24890	23898	22019	20070	20031
农村社会基础设施	**Basic Facilities in Rural Areas**						
自来水受益村数（个）	Number of Villages with Access to Tap Water(unit)	15633	15795	16041	15596	14378	14278
通公路的乡镇数	Township and Town with Highways	1463	1460	1457	1452	1452	1451
通汽车的村数	Villages with Automobile	20375	20149	19496	18078	16655	16856
通电话的村数	Villages with Telephone Communication	8218	11386	13602	14231	13493	14745
通有线广播的村数	Villages with Wire Broadcast	5936	6451	6945	6594	6121	6206
乡村人口与从业人员	**Rural Population and Laborers**						
乡村户数（万户）	Number of Rural Households(10000 units)	734.65	743.85	756.09	768.81	781.77	792.27
乡村人口数（万人）	Rural Population(10000 persons)	3123.46	3160.64	3193.36	3222.31	3253.63	3276.27
乡村从业人员	Number of Rural Laborers	1802.63	1821.50	1841.80	1874.88	1903.03	1934.16
#农业从业人员	Agriculture Laborers	1372.12	1368.28	1353.92	1322.10	1288.49	1268.09
耕　地	**Area of Cultivated Land**						
年末常用耕地面积（千公顷）	Regularly Cultivated Land(year-end) (1000 hectares)	1843.48	1832.28	1769.40	1750.54	1752.20	1753.50
#水　田	Paddy Fields	765.38	763.28	757.60	755.82	754.80	756.60
农业机械化	**Agricultural Mechanization**						
农用机械总动力(万千瓦)	Total Power of Agricultural Machinery (10000 kw)	618.63	647.93	699.41	761.99	797.18	1011.52
柴油机	Diesel Engine	486.20	504.16	549.89	595.33	612.50	708.90
汽油机	Gas Engine	32.65	32.56	29.04	28.31	23.13	24.46
电动机	Electromotor	97.64	103.42	115.47	134.90	157.88	275.38
其他机械	Others	2.14	7.79	5.01	3.45	3.67	2.77
农村主要能源及物资消耗	**Main Energy for Agricultural Use and Materials Consumption**						
乡村办水电站（个）	Number of Hydropower Stations in Rural Areas(unit)	798	795	721	786	782	791
发电量（万千瓦时）	Amount of Electric Power Generation (10000 kwh)	35811	39400	41921	48299	80541	93620
农用化肥施用量(折纯法)（万吨）	Consumption of Chemical Fertilizer(pure) (10000 tons)	71	70	74	75	74	77
平均每亩耕地化肥施用量（公斤）	Average Per Mu Consumption of Chemical Fertilizer(kg)	26	25	28	29	28	29
农村用电量（万千瓦时）	Electricity Consumed in Rural Areas (10000 kwh)	141821	139200	143356	160233	302913	302319
农药使用量（吨）	Consumption of Chemical Pesticides(ton)	8400	8329	8819	9024	9533	9764
地膜使用量（吨）	Consumption of Farm Plastic Membrane(ton)	12094	12397	14725	17188	18180	17243
农田水利建设情况	**Farmland and Water Conservancy**						
有效灌溉面积（千公顷）	Effective Irrigated Area(1000 hectares)	653.37	659.81	671.53	682.71	692.86	711.64
旱涝保收面积	Area that Ensure Stable Yields Despite Droughtor Excessive Rain	530.72	538.42	545.62	547.31	524.64	533.90
机电排灌面积	Area with Motorized Drainage and Irrigation Facilities	70.07	70.69	69.92	69.81	70.19	71.76

6-2 “十五”时期各年农林牧渔业总产值、增加值

Gross Output Value and Value-Added of Farming,Forestry, Animal Husbandry and Fishery of Each Year in "Tenth Five-year Plan" Period

单位：亿元(100 million yuan)

指 标	Item	2000	2001	2002	2003	2004	2005	2005年比2004年增长(%) Increase Rate in 2005 over 2004(%)
农林牧渔业总产值(当年价)	**Gross Output Value of Farming,Forestry, Animal Husbandry and Fishery (current price)**	**412.97**	**418.61**	**431.39**	**466.72**	**524.64**	**571.84**	**5.9**
农 业	Farming	279.62	279.95	278.88	275.46	317.69	335.53	4.3
林 业	Forestry	18.04	15.08	18.17	25.87	23.25	23.91	-0.1
畜牧业	Animal Husbandry	110.67	118.46	128.80	139.48	168.79	194.20	9.8
渔 业	Fishery	4.65	5.13	5.54	6.08	7.02	9.41	6.7
农、林、牧、渔服务业	FFAF Services					7.89	8.79	7.3
农林牧渔业增加值(当年价)	**Added Value of FFAF (current price)**	**270.99**	**274.17**	**280.82**	**303.95**	**340.92**	**368.93**	**5.2**
农 业	Farming	187.31	187.45	185.31	181.53	208.05	218.33	3.6
林 业	Forestry	14.03	11.85	12.42	17.62	16.20	15.85	-4.2
畜牧业	Animal Husbandry	61.49	71.39	79.51	87.79	106.25	122.16	9.7
渔 业	Fishery	3.16	3.48	3.58	3.96	4.60	6.15	6.4
农、林、牧、渔服务业	FFAF Services					5.82	6.44	7.2

6-3 农林牧渔业总产值

Gross Output Value of Farming,Forestry, Animal Husbandry and Fishery

单位：亿元(100 million yuan)

指 标	Item	2004	2005	2005年比2004年增长(%) Increase Rate in 2005 over 2004(%)
农林牧渔业总产值(当年价)	**Gross Output Value of Farming,Forestry, AnimalHusbandry and Fishery (current price)**	**524.64**	**571.84**	**5.9**
农业产值	**Farming**	**317.69**	**335.53**	**4.3**
谷物及其他作物的种植	Planting of Cereal and other Crops	224.32	230.65	1.6
蔬菜、园艺作物的种植	Planting of Vegetable and Gardening Crops	75.72	81.61	6.5
水果、坚果、饮料和香料作物的种植	Planting of Fruits, nuts, Beverages and Spice Crops	12.86	14.25	8.1
中药材的种植	Planting of Chinese Traditional Medicine	4.79	9.02	82.5
林业产值	**Forestry**	**23.25**	**23.91**	**-0.1**
林木的培育和种植	Cultivating and planting of forest	5.11	4.44	-15.6
木材和竹材的采运	Logging and Transporting of Timber & bamboo	3.60	4.15	12.0
林产品的采集	Collecting of Forest Products	14.54	15.33	2.3
畜牧业产值	**Animal Husbandry**	**168.79**	**194.21**	**9.8**
牲畜的饲养	Animal Raising	22.83	25.78	9.4
猪的饲养	Hogs Raising	121.10	139.25	9.2
家禽的饲养	Poultry Raising	23.77	27.96	13.2
狩猎和捕捉动物	Hunting and Catching Animales	0.09	0.09	持平
其他畜牧业	Others	1.00	1.12	7.9
渔业产值	**Fishery**	**7.02**	**9.41**	**6.7**
农、林、牧、渔服务业产值	**Gross Output Value of FFAF Services**	**7.89**	**8.79**	**7.8**

6-4 "十五"时期各年主要农业机械拥有量

Agricultural Machinery and Machinery For Possessing Farm Products of Each Year in "Tenth Five-year Plan" Period

指 标	Item	2000	2001	2002	2003	2004	2005	2005年比2004年增长(%) Increase Rate in 2005 over 2004(%)
大中型拖拉机（万台）	Large and Medium Agricultural Tractors(10000 sets)	2.40	2.72	2.16	2.71	3.33	4.14	24.3
大中型拖拉机配套农具(万台)	Suited Farm Tools by Large and Medium Agricultural Tractors (10000 sets)	0.16	0.20	0.31	0.45	0.40	0.47	17.5
小型拖拉机（万台）	Mini Agricultural Tractors (10000 sets)	5.50	5.36	5.26	5.18	4.77	4.83	1.3
小型拖拉机配套农具（万台）	Suited Farm Tools by Mini Agricultural Tractors(10000 sets)	0.75	0.78	1.02	1.02	0.95	1.03	8.4
农用排灌电动机（万台）	Number of Drainage and Irrigation Electromotor Engines (10000 units)	4.45	4.80	5.40	6.09	7.09	16.05	126.4
农用排灌柴油机（万台）	Number of Drainage and Irrigation Diesel Engines(10000 units)	6.74	7.20	7.80	8.51	8.56	11.30	32.0
联合收割机（台）	Combine Harvesters(unit)	31	52	60	81	93	130	39.8
农用运输车（万辆）	Transport for Agricultural Use (10000 units)	3.75	3.91	4.98	5.65	7.40	7.62	3.0

注：本表资料由省农机局提供。

Note:Data in this table are obtained from the Agricultural Machinery Department of Guizhou Province.

6-5 “十五”时期各年主要农作物播种面积

Sown Areas of Major Farm Crops of Each Year in "Tenth Five-year Plan" Period

单位:千公顷(1000 hectares)

指　标	Item	2000	2001	2002	2003	2004	2005	2005年比2004年增长(%) Increase Rate in 2005 over 2004(%)
农作物总播种面积	**Total Sown Areas of Farm Crops**	**4696.00**	**4650.70**	**4645.42**	**4634.19**	**4692.28**	**4804.10**	**2.4**
#粮食作物	Grain Crops	3151.30	3121.10	3076.07	3021.27	3034.50	3073.74	1.3
#稻 谷	Rice	750.50	750.00	734.64	720.46	716.51	721.67	0.7
小 麦	Wheat	567.40	520.50	498.43	474.27	429.17	410.63	-4.3
玉 米	Corn	727.30	721.80	703.81	686.30	706.45	719.52	1.9
大 豆	Soybeans	141.00	139.20	136.37	128.72	131.18	130.66	-0.4
薯 类	Tubers	702.50	724.00	740.78	748.24	786.79	820.65	4.3
#马铃薯	Irish Potato	477.50	494.90	508.58	519.40	551.25	574.86	4.3
油 料	Oil-bearing Crops	512.70	498.00	504.68	501.77	531.58	555.77	4.6
#油菜籽	Rapeseeds	461.30	445.49	451.57	451.36	482.43	504.77	4.6
花 生	Peanuts	44.30	45.70	43.92	43.25	42.39	43.32	2.2
麻 类	Fiber Crops	3.00	2.60	2.10	1.82	1.43	1.31	-8.4
糖 料	Sugar Crops	17.10	18.09	18.89	19.20	18.64	19.51	4.7
#甘 蔗	Sugarcane	17.00	18.06	18.84	19.14	18.58	19.44	4.6
烟 叶	Tobacco	213.70	202.13	217.27	207.20	206.79	222.71	7.7
#烤 烟	Flue-cured Tobacco	193.40	182.38	199.18	188.75	188.01	206.57	9.9
药材类	Crude Drugs	13.50	17.21	18.26	22.99	30.26	23.69	-21.7
蔬 菜	Vegetable	355.40	372.28	390.18	414.86	443.34	473.32	6.8

6-6 "十五"时期各年主要农作物产品产量

Yield of Major Farm Crops of Each Year in "Tenth Five-year Plan" Period

单位：万吨 (10000 tons)

指 标	Item	2000	2001	2002	2003	2004	2005	2005年比2004年增长(%) Increase Rate in 2005 over 2004(%)
粮食作物	**Grain Crops**	**1161.30**	**1100.30**	**1034.20**	**1104.30**	**1149.58**	**1152.06**	**0.2**
稻 谷	Rice	477.40	459.80	347.80	459.30	477.01	472.80	-0.9
小 麦	Wheat	103.50	87.70	87.00	74.60	76.80	73.00	-4.9
玉 米	Corn	342.20	319.40	343.20	319.90	333.90	344.29	3.1
大 豆	Soybeans	18.10	16.70	18.40	17.70	17.88	16.15	-9.7
杂 豆	Incidental Bean	21.40	20.50	22.40	21.60	22.72	21.61	-4.9
薯 类	Tubers	186.40	184.90	204.50	200.80	210.26	213.14	1.4
#马铃薯	Irish Potato	124.60	128.10	147.34	135.50	142.19	147.51	3.7
其 它	Others	12.30	11.30	10.90	10.40	11.01	11.07	0.5
油料作物	**Oil Plants Crops**	**74.34**	**71.32**	**72.48**	**72.31**	**82.71**	**84.89**	**2.6**
#油菜籽	Rapeseeds	66.20	63.48	64.05	64.01	73.93	76.51	3.5
花 生	Peanuts	7.45	7.21	7.47	7.48	7.91	7.34	-7.2
苎 麻	**Ramee**	**0.14**	**0.12**	**0.10**	**0.09**	**0.09**	**0.09**	**持平**
甘 蔗	**Sugarcane**	**66.66**	**65.11**	**73.98**	**75.74**	**65.76**	**67.76**	**3.0**
烤 烟	**Flue-cured Tobacco**	**31.09**	**26.38**	**30.65**	**28.72**	**29.98**	**34.45**	**14.9**
蔬 菜	**Vegetable**	**595.12**	**625.16**	**667.53**	**712.17**	**773.55**	**839.87**	**8.6**

6-7 “十五”时期各年主要农作物单产

Yield of Major Farm Crops Per Mu of Each Year in "Tenth Five-year Plan" Period

单位：公斤/亩(kg/mu)

指　标	Item	2000	2001	2002	2003	2004	2005	2005年比2004年增长(%) Increase Rate in 2005 over 2004(%)
粮食作物	**Grain Crops**	**246**	**235**	**224**	**244**	**253**	**250**	**-1.2**
稻 谷	Rice	424	409	316	425	444	437	-1.6
小 麦	Wheat	122	112	116	105	119	119	持平
玉 米	Corn	314	295	325	311	315	319	1.3
大 豆	Soybeans	86	80	90	92	91	82	-9.9
杂 豆	Incidental Bean	79	93	83	75	78	74	-5.1
薯 类	Tubers	177	170	184	179	178	173	-2.8
#马铃薯	Irish Potato	174	173	193	174	172	171	-0.6
其 它	Others	101	93	93	98	103	96	-6.8
油料作物	**Oil Plants Crops**	**97**	**95**	**96**	**96**	**104**	**102**	**-1.9**
#油菜籽	Rapeseed	96	95	96	95	102	101	-1.0
花 生	Peanuts	112	105	113	115	124	113	-8.9
苎 麻	**Ramee**	**47**	**42**	**48**	**52**	**64**	**69**	**7.8**
甘 蔗	**Sugarcane**	**2614**	**2404**	**2618**	**2638**	**2360**	**2324**	**-1.5**
烤 烟	**Flue-cured Tobacco**	**107**	**96**	**103**	**101**	**106**	**111**	**4.7**

6-8 “十五”时期各年茶叶、蚕茧、水果面积及产量

Toatal Areas and Yield of Tea,Silkworm Cocoon,Fruit and Aquatic Products of Each Year in "Tenth Five-year Plan" Period

指 标	Item	2000	2001	2002	2003	2004	2005	2005年比2004年增长(%) Increase Rate in 2005 over 2004(%)
面 积(千公顷)	**Area(1000 hectares)**							
茶园面积	Tea Field Area	44.79	47.14	47.25	48.09	52.32	59.73	14.2
桑园面积	Mulberry Field Area	9.24	9.15	9.10	8.12	7.47	6.25	-16.3
柞坡面积	Breed Tussah Field Area	2.75	2.60	2.30	2.90	3.10	3.18	2.6
果园面积	Orchards Filed Area	75.47	107.05	98.34	103.11	110.29	118.92	7.8
产 量(万吨)	**Yield(10000 tons)**							
茶 叶	**Tea**	**1.84**	**1.85**	**1.74**	**1.77**	**1.94**	**2.29**	**18.0**
蚕 茧	**Silkworm Cocoon**	**0.12**	**0.12**	**0.18**	**0.14**	**0.13**	**0.12**	**-7.7**
#桑蚕茧	Mulberry Silkworm Cocoon	0.12	0.12	0.18	0.14	0.13	0.12	-7.7
水 果	**Fruit**	**58.33**	**62.93**	**71.57**	**78.75**	**87.17**	**95.96**	**10.1**
#园林水果	Garden Fruit	31.10	36.43	39.66	43.78	47.18	51.42	9.0
#苹 果	Apples	0.77	0.79	0.94	0.93	1.03	1.02	-1.0
梨	Pears	4.77	6.66	8.24	9.79	10.84	12.37	14.1
柑 桔	Citrus	10.13	12.79	13.53	14.98	15.81	17.22	8.9
香 蕉	Bananas	0.99	1.03	0.84	0.85	0.89	0.87	-2.2
杨 梅	Red Bayberry	0.97	0.89	1.14	1.31	1.63	1.86	14.1
猕猴桃	Chinese Goosebeerys	0.59	0.99	1.06	1.13	1.18	1.21	2.5
柿 子	Persimmons	1.29	1.27	1.33	1.21	1.26	1.37	8.7

6-9 “十五”时期各年畜牧业生产

Statistics on Livestock of Each Year in "Tenth Five-year Plan" Period

指　标	Item	2000	2001	2002	2003	2004	2005	2005年比2004年增长(%) Increase Rate in 2005 over 2004(%)
猪牛羊出栏头数(万头)	**Number of Slaughtered Fattened Hogs, Ox,Goats and Sheep(10000 heads)**							
当年肉猪出栏头数	Slaughtered Fattened Hogs	1167.51	1229.99	1351.26	1533.68	1707.62	1911.34	11.9
当年出售和自宰的肉用牛	Ox by Sold and Killed	51.35	55.91	66.99	80.39	91.38	103.08	12.8
当年出售和自宰的肉用羊	Goats by Sold and Killed	165.47	179.15	200.65	223.73	248.80	280.26	12.6
当年肉类总产量(万吨)	**Total Yield of Meat(10000 tons)**	**124.06**	**131.70**	**145.02**	**156.99**	**171.06**	**187.01**	**9.3**
#猪 肉	Pork	105.05	110.93	121.59	131.40	143.10	156.19	9.1
牛 肉	Beef	6.99	7.58	8.97	10.13	11.38	12.50	9.8
羊 肉	Mutton	4.21	4.34	4.49	4.50	5.02	5.50	9.6
禽 肉	Poultry	7.32	8.03	9.04	10.14	10.76	12.00	11.5
其他畜产品产量(吨)	**Others(ton)**							
#牛 奶	Cow Milk	16920	20037	25272	33772	35626	37522	5.3
蜂 蜜	Honey	1567	1423	1736	1394	1784	1675	-6.1
禽 蛋	Poultry Eggs	65259	70049	79271	91162	99202	111106	12.0
大牲畜年末头数(万头)	**Large Livestock(year-end) (10000 heads)**	**731.49**	**746.12**	**771.04**	**801.88**	**839.88**	**873.81**	**4.0**
#役 畜	Draught Animals	518.08	521.05	531.47	537.36	564.74	577.43	2.2
牛	Cattle and Buffaloes	658.08	671.40	692.57	721.66	758.86	793.17	4.5
#黄 牛	Cattle	430.27	437.47	458.03	481.23	503.74	528.68	5.0
水 牛	Buffalo	227.05	232.94	233.12	237.77	250.34	256.29	2.4
猪年末数（万头）	**Hogs(year-end)(10000 heads)**	**1687.3**	**1730.7**	**1806.8**	**1904.4**	**2019.9**	**2138.0**	**5.8**
羊年末数（万只）	**Sheep and Goats(year-end) (10000 heads)**	**341.76**	**350.04**	**360.74**	**391.90**	**420.98**	**448.33**	**6.5**
山 羊	Goats	321.36	329.94	339.64	369.84	398.92	428.64	7.5
绵 羊	Sheep	20.40	20.10	21.10	22.06	22.06	19.69	-10.7
水产品（万吨）	**Aquatic Products(10000 tons)**	**6.24**	**6.89**	**7.46**	**7.96**	**8.85**	**9.46**	**6.9**

6-10 "十五"时期各年造林及林产品产量

Areas of Forestation and Output of Forest Products of Each Year in "Tenth Five-year Plan" Period

单位：吨(ton)

指 标	Item	2000	2001	2002	2003	2004	2005	2005年比2004年增长(%) Increase Rate in 2005 over 2004(%)
当年造林面积（千公顷）	**Areas of Forestation in this year(1000 hectares)**	**293.73**	**240.69**	**374.31**	**377.94**	**177.11**	**135.60**	**-23.4**
#飞机播种面积	Seeded Areas by Plane	30.16	37.50	32.18	17.66	6.95	3.41	-50.9
林产品产量	**Output of Forest Products**							
生 漆	Lacquer	1006	1047	1214	1221	1326	1328	0.2
油桐籽	Tung-oil Seed	116592	103697	96795	89857	87024	81669	-6.2
油茶籽	Tea-oil Seed	8195	9956	9685	9307	10112	10558	4.4
乌桕籽	Tallow-seeds	4180	4064	3910	3983	3450	2948	-14.6
五倍籽	Nutgall	1495	1469	1554	1641	1702	1943	14.2
棕 片	Palm-flake	4620	4787	4876	4688	4664	4733	1.5
松 脂	Pine Resin	4392	4118	4424	5682	5575	4882	-12.4
竹笋片	Bamboo Shoot	3593	4115	5105	7896	7909	9542	20.6
核 桃	Walnuts	7492	7010	7448	7578	8298	6840	-17.6
板 栗	Chestnut	7471	7810	8690	10426	11591	12286	6.0

注：表中"造林面积"及相关指标由省林业部门提供。

Note:The areas of forestation and correlative indicators in this table are obtained from Forest Department of Guizhou Province.

6-11 “十五”时期各年乡镇企业主要经济指标

Major Economic Indicators of Township and Town Enterprises of Each Year in "Tenth Five-year Plan" Period

单位：亿元 (100 million yuan)

指标	Item	2000	2001	2002	2003	2004	2005	2005年比2004年增长(%) Increase Rate in 2005 over 2004(%)
年末固定资产原值	Original Value of Fixed Assets(year-end)	308.87	393.14	481.05	421.86	531.13	632.99	19.2
年末营业收入	Operating Revenue (year-end)	907.80	1071.24	1263.74	1462.17	1596.19	1757.39	10.1
实交国家税金	Taxes Paid	20.58	23.62	27.10	28.98	41.54	49.27	18.6
利润总额	Total Profits	75.51	87.56	98.99	106.62	128.30	143.60	11.9
年末职工人数（万人）	Staff and Workers(yearnd) (10000 persons)	190.10	199.38	207.78	216.32	222.60	234.90	5.5
劳动者报酬	Laborers Remuneration	74.93	83.39	91.86	118.53	128.45	142.19	10.7

注:表中资料由省乡镇局提供,增速按可比口径计算。

Note:The data in the table are obtained from provincial Rural Enterprise Administration,the increase rate are calculated at comparable prices.

主要统计指标解释

农林牧渔业总产值　指以货币表现的农、林、牧、渔业全部产品的总量,它反映一定时期内农业生产总规模和总成果。农业总产值的计算方法通常是按农林牧渔业产品及其副产品的产量分别乘以各自单位产品价格求得;然后将四业产品产值相加即为农业总产值。

粮食产量　指全社会的产量。包括国有经济经营的、集体统一经营的和农民家庭经营的粮食产量,还包括工矿企业办的农场和其他生产单位的产量。粮食除包括稻谷、小麦、玉米、高粱、谷子及其他杂粮外,还包括薯类和豆类。其产量计算方法,豆类按去豆荚后的干豆计算;薯类(包括甘薯和马铃薯,不包括芋头和木薯)1963年以前按每4公斤鲜薯折1公斤粮食计算,从1964年开始改为按5公斤鲜薯折1公斤粮食计算。城市郊区作为蔬菜的薯类(如马铃薯等)按鲜品计算,并且不作粮食统计。其他粮食一律按脱粒后的原粮计算。

油料产量　指全部油料作物的生产量。包括花生、油菜籽、芝麻、向日葵籽、胡麻籽(亚麻籽)和其他油料。不包括大豆、木本油料和野生油料。花生以带壳干花生计算。

水产品产量　指人工养殖的水产品和天然生长的水产品的捕捞量。包括海水的鱼类、虾蟹类、贝类和藻类以及内陆水域的鱼类、虾蟹类和贝类,不包括淡水生植物。

猪、牛、羊肉产量　指当年出栏并已屠宰、除去头蹄下水后带骨肉(即胴体重)的重量。

期初(末)畜禽存栏头(只)数　指报告期初(末)农村各种合作经济组织和国营农场、农民个人、机关、团体、学校、工矿企业、部队等单位以及城镇居民饲养的大牲畜、猪、羊、家禽等畜禽的存栏数。

耕地面积　指可以用来种植农作物、经常进行耕锄的田地,包括熟地、当年新开荒地、连续撂荒未满三年的耕地和当年的休闲地(轮歇地),还包括以种植农作物为主并附带种植桑树、茶树、果树和其他林木的土地,以及沿海、沿湖地区已围垦利用的"海涂"、"湖田"等面积。不包括属于专业性的桑园、茶园、果园、果木苗圃、林地、芦苇地、天然或人工草地面积。

农作物播种面积　指实际播种或移植有农作物的面积。凡是实际种植有农作物的面积,不论种植在耕地上还是种植在非耕地上,均包括在农作物播种面积中。在播种季节基本结束后,因遭灾而重新改种和补种的农作物面积,也包括在内。

有效灌溉面积　指具有一定的水源,地块比较平整,灌溉工程或设备已经配套,在一般年景下当年能够进行正常灌溉的耕地面积。

农用化肥施用量　指本年内实际用于农业生产的化肥数量,包括氮肥、磷肥、钾肥和复合肥。化肥施用量要求按折纯量计算数量。折纯量是指把氮肥、磷肥、钾肥分别按含氮、含五氧化二磷、含氧化钾的百分之一百成份进行折算后的数量。复合肥按其所含主要成分折算。

农业机械总动力　指主要用于农、林、牧、渔业的各种动力机械的动力总和。包括耕作机械、排灌机械、收获机械、农用运输机械、植物保护机械、牧业机械、林业机械、渔业机械和其他农业机械〔内燃机按引擎马力折成瓦(特)计算、电动机按功率折成瓦(特)计算〕。不包括专门用于乡、镇、村、组办工业、基本建设、非农业运输、科学试验和教学等非农业生产方面用的动力机械与作业机械。

农林牧渔业劳动力　指全社会直接参加农林牧渔业生产活动的劳动力。

Explanatory Notes on Main Statistical Indicators

Gross Output Value of Farming, Forestry, Animal Husbandry and Fishery refers to the total value of products of farming, forestry, animal husbandry and fishery, which reflects the total scale and result of agricultural production during a given period.Gross output value of agriculture is obtained by first multiplying the output of each product or by product by its price, resulting in the output value of each single item.

Grain Yield refers to the yield in the whole country including grains produced by state farms, collective units, industrial enterprises and mines.Grain includes rice, wheat, corn, sorghum, millet and other miscellaneous grains as well as tubers and beans. Output of beans refers to dry beans without pods. The output of tubers (sweet potatoes and potatoes,not including taros and cassava) was converted into that of grain at the ratio 4:1, i.e. 4 kilograms of fresh tubers was equivalent to 1 kilogram of grain up to 1963.Since 1964 the ratio for conversion has been 5:1. Tubers supplied as vegetables (such as potatoes) in cities and suburbs are calculated as fresh vegetables and their output is not included in the output of grain. Output of all other grains refers to husked grain.

Yield of Oil-bearing Crops refers to the total yield of oil bearing crops of various kinds,including peanuts, (dry, in shell) rapeseeds, sesame, sunflower seeds, flax seeds, and other oil bearing crops.Soybeans,oil-bearing woody plants,and wild oil-bearing crops are not included.

Output of Aquatic Products refers to catches of both artificially cultured and naturally grown aquatic products, including fish,shrimps,crabs and shellfish in sea and inland water as well as seaweed. Freshwater plants are not included.

Output of Pork,Beef,and Mutton refers to the meat of slaughtered hogs,cattle,sheep and goats with head, feet, and offal taken away.

Number of Livestock or Poultry in Stock at Beginning (or End) refers to the total number of large animals,pigs,sheep,fowls,etc.raised by rural cooperative organizations,statefarms,ruralindividuals,governmentagencies, schools,industrial and mining enterprises,army,and urban residents at the beginning (or end) of the reference period.

Cultivated Area(Area under cultivation) refers to farmland which is plowed constantly for growing crops, including cultivated land, newly cultivated land in the current year,farmland left without cultivation for less than three years and fallow land in the current year,rotation land, rotation land of grass and crops, farmland with some fruit trees, mulberry trees and other trees and cultivated seashore land, lake land, and etc. The land of mulberry fields, tea plantations,orchards, nurseries of young plants, forest land, reed land, natural and man-made grassland and other land are not included in cultivated land.

Sown Area of Crops refers to area of land sown or transplanted with crops regardless of being in cultivated area or non cultivated area. Area of land re-sown due to natural disasters is also included.

Irrigated Area refers to areas that are effectively irrigated, i.e. level land which has water source and complete sets of irrigation facilities to lift and move adequate water for irrigation purpose under normal conditions.

Consumption of Chemical Fertilizers in Agriculture refers to the quantity of chemical fertilizers applied in agriculture in the year, including nitrogenous fertilizer, phosphate fertilizer, potash fertilizer, and compound fertilizer. The consumption of chemical fertilizers is required in calculation to convert the gross weight into weight containing 100% effective component (e.g. 100% nitrogen content in nitrogenous fertilizer, 100% phosphorous pentoxide contents in phosphate fertilizer, 100% potassium oxide contents in potash fertilizer). Compound fertilizer is converted with its major component.

Total Power of Farm Machinery refers to total mechanical power of machinery used in farming, forestry, animal husbandry, and fishery, including ploughing, irrigation and drainage, harvesting, transport, plant protection, stock breeding, forestry and fishery. The power of internal combustion engines is required to convert horsepower into watts and the power of electric motors is required to be converted into watts.Machinery employed for non agricultural purposes, such as the machines used in township run and village-run industry,construction,non agricultural transport,scientific experiments and teaching, is excluded.

Labour Force Engaged in Farming,Forestry,Animal Husbandry and Fishery refers to the total laborers who are directly engaged in production of farming, forestry, animal husbandry and fishery.

7

Seven

工 业

Industry

规模以上工业增加值及指数

Value-added of Industry above Designated Size and its Indices

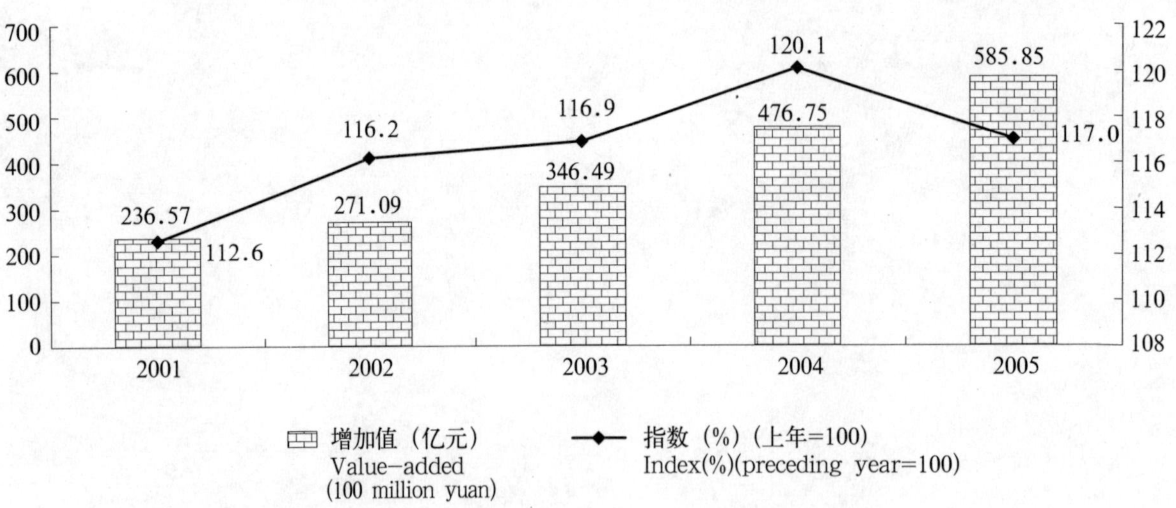

规模以上工业增加值（按轻、重工业分）（亿元）

Value-added of Industry above Lesignated Size

(by Light and Heavy Industry)(100 million yuan)

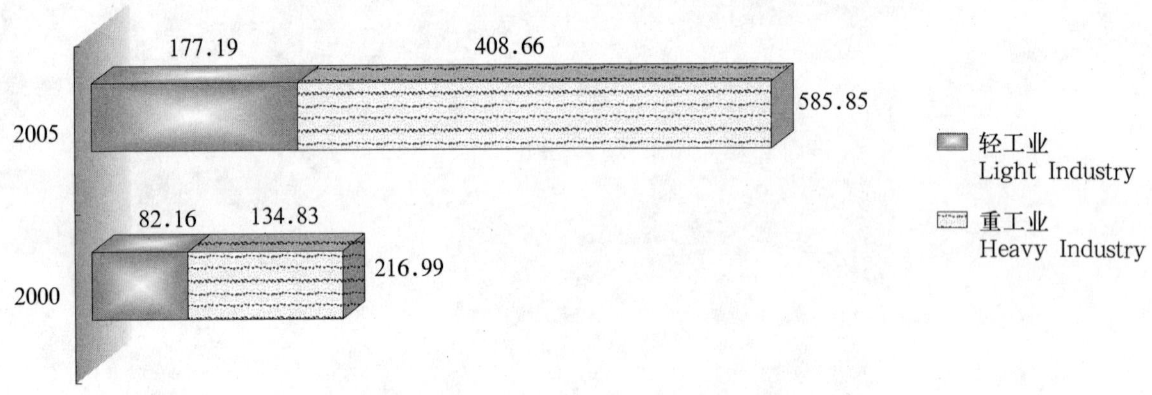

主要工业产品产量

Output of Major Industrial Products

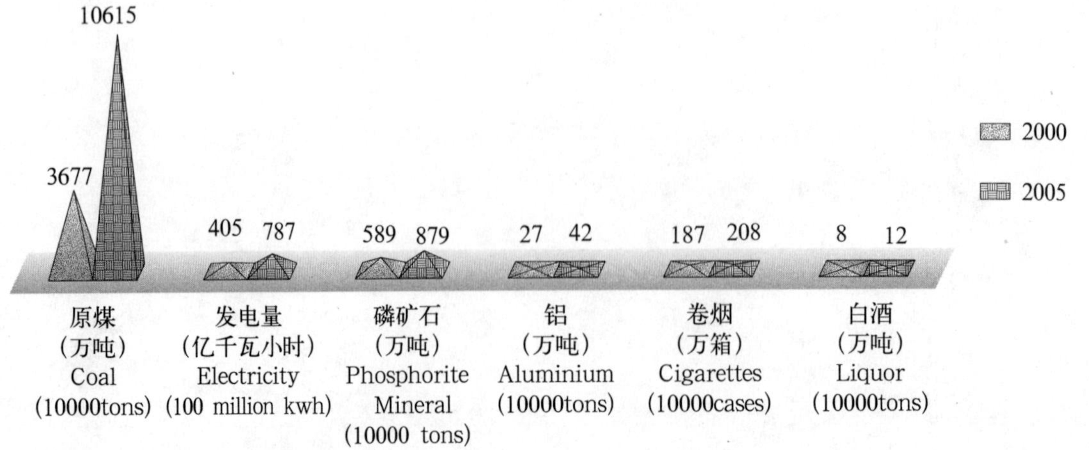

7-1 “十五”时期各年规模以上工业企业单位数

Number of Industrial Enterprises above Designated Size of Each Year in “Tenth Five-year Plan” Period

单位：个(unit)

指　标	Item	2000	2001	2002	2003	2004	2005
总　计	**Total**	**2087**	**2054**	**2067**	**2129**	**2545**	**2585**
按经济类型分:	Grouped by Ownership						
#国有及国有控股企业	State-owned and Statecontrolled Enterprises	1397	1269	1191	1037	1101	927
#港澳台投资企业	Enterprises with Funds from Hong kong, Macao and Taiwan	30	41	36	38	51	48
#外商投资企业	Foreign Funded Enterprises	31	35	37	43	65	58
#农村工业	Rural Industry	95	72	73	64	33	34
按公有非公有分	Grouped by Type of Publicowned or Non-state-owned						
公有经济	Public-owned	1798	1598	1521	1468	1099	912
非公有经济	Non-public-owned	289	456	546	661	1446	1673
按国有非国有分	Grouped by Type of Stateowned orNon-state -owned						
国有经济	State-owned Industry	1397	1269	1191	1037	1101	927
非国有经济	Non-state-owned Industry	690	785	876	1092	1444	1658
按轻重工业分	Grouped by Type of Light and Heavy Industry						
轻工业	Light Industry	810	771	768	710	753	720
重工业	Heavy Industry	1277	1283	1299	1419	1792	1865
按企业规模分	Grouped by Scale of Enterprise						
#大型企业	Large Industry	103	99	98	23	21	23
中型企业	Medium-siaed Industry	119	113	93	201	240	246
小型企业	Small Industry	1865	1842	1876	1905	2284	2316
按主要行业分	Grouped by Main Industrial Sector						
采矿业	Mining and Quarring	202	146	151	180	296	363
制造业	Manufacturing	1638	1663	1672	1700	1980	1949
#农副食品加工业	Processing of Food from Agricultural Products	181	161	158	145	150	138
食品制造业	Manufacture of Foods	52	48	52	52	65	57
饮料制造业	Manufacture of Beverages	85	98	99	82	91	82
烟草制品业	Manufacture of Tobacco	37	35	27	23	15	10
化学原料及化学制品制造业	Manufacture of Raw Chemical Materials and Chemical Products	178	178	185	197	214	222
医药制造业	Manufacture of Medicines	81	82	91	104	108	116
橡胶制品业	Manufacture of Rubber	14	19	16	21	23	19
非金属矿物制品业	Manufacture of Non-metallic Mineral Products	252	259	269	280	282	283
黑色金属冶炼及压延加工业	Smelting and Pressing of Ferrous Metals	91	124	130	157	271	268
有色金属冶炼及压延加工业	Smelting and Pressing of Nonferrous Metals	99	142	125	113	138	132
电气机械及器材制造业	Manufacture of Electrical Equipment and Machinery	31	29	37	39	40	41
电力、燃气及水的生产和供应业	Production and Distribution of Electric Power, Gas and Water	247	245	244	249	269	273

7-2 "十五"时期各年

Value added of Industry above Designated Size of

指 标	Item	2000
总 计	**Total**	**216.99**
按经济类型分：	Grouped by Ownership	
#国有及国有控股企业	State-owned and State-controlled Enterprises	175.83
#港澳台投资企业	Enterprises with Funds from Hong kong,Macao and Taiwan	1.03
#外商投资企业	Foreign Funded Enterprises	3.98
#农村工业	Rural Industry	6.24
按公有非公有分：	Grouped by Type of Public-owned or Non-publi c-owned	
公有经济	Public-owned Industry	194.90
非公有经济	Non-public-owned Industry	22.09
按国有非国有分：	Grouped by Type of State-owned or Non-state-owned	
国有经济	State-owned Industry	175.83
非国有经济	Non-state-owned Industry	41.16
按轻重工业分：	Grouped by Type of Light and Heavy Industry	
轻工业	Light Industry	82.16
重工业	Heavy Industry	134.83
按企业规模分：	Grouped by Scale of Enterprise	
大型企业	Large Industry	105.10
型企业	Medium-siaed Industry	27.78
小型企业	Small Industry	84.10
按主要行业分：	Grouped by Main Industrial Sector	
采矿业	Mining and Quarring	12.59
制造业	Manufacturing	169.85
#农副食品加工业	Processing of Food from Agricultural Products	3.53
食品制造业	Manufacture of Foods	1.24
饮料制造业	Manufacture of Beverages	13.50
烟草制品业	Manufacture of Tobacco	38.87
化学原料及化学制品制造业	Manufacture of Raw Chemical Materials and Chemical Products	16.12
医药制造业	Manufacture of Medicines	12.14
橡胶制品业	Manufacture of Rubber	5.78
非金属矿物制品业	Manufacture of Non-metallic Mineral Products	9.31
黑色金属冶炼及压延加工业	Smelting and Pressing of Ferrous Metals	16.81
有色金属冶炼及压延加工业	Smelting and Pressing of Nonferrous Metals	16.69
电气机械及器材制造业	Manufacture of Electrical Equipment and Machinery	3.88
电力、燃气及水的生产和供应业	Production and Distribution of Electric Power,Gas and Water	34.56

规模以上工业增加值

Each Year in in"Tenth Five-year Plan"Period

单位：亿元(100 million yuan)

2001	2002	2003	2004	2005	2005年比 2000年增长（%） Increase Rate in 2005 over 2000(%)	2005年比 2004年增长（%） Increase Rate in 2005 over 2004(%)
236.57	**271.09**	**346.49**	**476.75**	**585.85**	**123.1**	**17.0**
188.97	217.70	256.35	340.97	420.87	97.8	15.1
1.95	1.67	1.54	3.82	3.58	187.2	-12.6
4.64	1.39	8.68	13.87	9.26	92.3	-37.7
3.43	4.05	3.58	2.20	4.96	-34.3	110.3
197.32	216.60	283.08	325.80	388.73	64.8	11.3
39.25	54.49	63.41	118.74	197.12	637.4	54.8
188.97	217.70	256.35	340.97	420.87	97.8	15.1
47.60	53.39	90.14	135.78	164.98	231.2	13.3
87.66	88.20	116.72	147.79	177.19	78.2	11.8
148.91	182.89	229.77	328.97	408.66	150.4	15.9
122.85	145.26	138.14	202.09	280.61	120.6	29.5
26.70	36.37	121.67	155.79	151.12	349.5	-9.5
87.02	89.45	86.68	118.87	154.13	51.4	20.9
10.90	16.57	22.38	43.99	52.41	244.0	11.1
181.95	195.08	252.53	325.91	388.40	89.0	11.1
3.81	3.81	4.66	4.56	6.27	46.8	28.2
1.87	2.38	3.54	5.15	7.05	369.8	27.7
14.95	21.73	2.63	34.22	39.26	140.3	7.0
42.88	36.37	54.19	66.63	73.22	55.7	2.5
16.79	19.30	25.69	33.39	57.10	192.7	59.5
13.67	12.43	20.67	22.49	32.87	123.7	36.3
6.51	6.80	5.42	6.45	7.02	0.4	1.5
9.64	8.16	11.15	12.59	13.93	23.6	3.2
16.39	20.66	28.93	43.27	40.43	98.7	-12.9
19.19	20.48	28.59	39.25	48.44	139.8	15.1
3.45	3.95	4.57	8.95	8.80	87.4	-8.3
43.72	59.44	71.58	106.85	145.04	246.8	26.6

7-3 "十五"时期各年规模以上工业总产值

Gross Output Value of Industry above Designated Size of Each Year in "Tenth Five-year Plan" Period

单位：亿元(100 million yuan)

指 标	Item	2000	2001	2002	2003	2004	2005
总 计	**Total**	**631.6**	**696.6**	**797.9**	**977.6**	**1394.9**	**1690.4**
按经济类型分:	Grouped by Ownership						
#国有及国有控股企业	State-owned and Statecontrolled Enterprises	500.8	536.0	587.6	667.8	950.8	1154.5
#港澳台投资企业	Enterprises with Funds from Hong kong,Macao and Taiwan	4.8	6.7	7.6	7.1	11.9	13.7
#外商投资企业	Foreign Funded Enterprises	13.8	14.8	17.8	32.4	46.8	38.0
#农村工业	Rural Industry	20.3	12.8	17.5	13.5	10.5	18.1
按公有非公有分	Grouped by Type of Publicowned or Non -publi c-owned						
公有经济	Public-owned Industry	567.3	581.1	637.5	798.7	1018.8	1084.9
非公有经济	Non-public-owned Industry	64.3	115.6	160.4	178.9	376.1	605.5
按国有非国有分	Grouped by Type of State-owned or Non -state-owned						
国有经济	State-owned Industry	500.8	536.0	587.6	667.8	950.8	1154.5
非国有经济	Non-state-owned Industry	130.9	160.7	210.3	309.9	444.2	535.9
按轻重工业分	Grouped by Type of Light and Heavy Industry						
轻工业	Light Industry	206.3	220.1	253.0	279.5	307.8	380.9
重工业	Heavy Industry	425.3	476.5	544.9	698.1	1087.1	1309.6
按企业规模分	Grouped by Scale of Enterprise						
#大型企业	Large Industry	322.6	349.0	373.9	317.6	542.2	716.7
中型企业	Medium-siaed Industry	67.6	66.8	97.9	367.9	451.5	480.9
小型企业	Small Industry	241.4	280.9	326.2	292.1	401.2	492.9
按主要行业分	Grouped by Main Industrial Sector						
采矿业	Mining and Quarring	35.9	41.2	50.8	66.9	110.5	120.4
制造业	Manufacturing	503.7	540.8	615.9	752.3	938.1	1150.9
#农副食品加工业	Processing of Food from Agricultural Products	13.7	16.2	19.1	22.1	24.2	29.9
食品制造业	Manufacture of Foods	3.6	5.2	8.7	11.6	17.2	18.9
饮料制造业	Manufacture of Beverages	24.9	27.6	35.1	41.5	53.8	61.0
烟草制品业	Manufacture of Tobacco	89.8	94.5	101.2	107.0	98.1	114.2
化学原料及化学制品制造业	Manufacture of Raw Chemical Materials and Chemical Products	57.1	62.9	75.6	92.7	115.6	196.4
医药制造业	Manufacture of Medicines	31.3	34.2	42.8	51.4	58.2	84.3
橡胶制品业	Manufacture of Rubber	17.1	20.0	20.9	23.6	29.1	34.1
非金属矿物制品业	Manufacture of Non-metallic Mineral Products	27.2	30.5	31.9	37.3	40.7	47.8
黑色金属冶炼及压延加工业	Smelting and Pressing of Ferrous Metals	58.5	64.7	70.0	103.8	177.3	187.0
有色金属冶炼及压延加工业	Smelting and Pressing of Nonferrous Metal	55.7	55.9	67.0	93.5	124.6	134.2
电气机械及器材制造业	Manufacture of Electrical Equipment and Machinery	16.0	17.4	17.1	20.2	33.8	40.5
电力、燃气及水的生产和供应业	Production and Distribution of Electric Power,Gas and Water	92.1	114.6	131.2	158.5	346.3	419.1

7-4 “十五”时期各年规模以上工业企业主要经济指标

Major Economic Indicators of Industrial Enterprises of Each Year in “Tenth Five-year Plan” Period

指　标	Item	2000	2001	2002	2003	2004	2005
固定资产净值平均余额(亿元)	Average Balance of Net Value of Fixed Assets(100 million yuan)	608.02	672.36	703.16	759.34	969.63	1122.67
流动资产平均余额（亿元）	Average Balance of Circulating Funds(100 million yuan)	650.77	685.41	698.79	752.22	844.71	947.98
产品销售收入（亿元）	Sales Revenue (100 million yuan)	593.80	646.01	752.97	974.30	1325.95	1577.16
利税总额（亿元）	Total Profits and Taxes (100 million yuan)	87.44	94.30	104.74	135.87	201.21	232.49
#利润（亿元）	Total Profits(100 million yuan)	12.56	18.59	21.41	37.52	61.99	70.79
资本保值增值率（%）	Increment Ratio of Capital(%)	114.60	131.93	109.36	112.53	114.60	112.99
总资产贡献率（%）	Ratio of Total Assets to Industrial Output Value(%)	7.70	7.08	6.86	8.80	10.70	10.94
资产负债率（%）	Asset-Liability Ratio(%)	68.60	64.43	62.34	66.56	66.07	64.92
流动资产周转次数（次/年）	Number of Times of Turnover of Circulating Fund(times/year)	0.91	0.89	1.00	1.26	1.47	1.62
成本费用利润率（%）	Ratio of After-tax Profits to Cost and Expenses(%)	2.30	2.91	3.13	3.98	5.90	5.54
全员劳动生产率（元/人、年）	Overall Labor Productivity (yuan/person,year)	31751	35649	41604	41991	65629	89252
产品产销率（%）	Proportion of Industrial Products Sold(%)	95.50	95.10	95.78	96.80	96.20	96.31

7-5 “十五”时期各年大中型企业主要经济指标

Major Economic Indicators of Industrial Enterprises of Each Year in “Tenth Five-year Plan” Period

指 标	Item	2000	2001	2002	2003	2004	2005
固定资产净值平均余额(亿元)	Average Balance of Net Value of Fixed Assets (100 million yuan)	450.87	491.28	509.45	601.79	755.70	902.92
流动资产平均余额(亿元)	Average Balance of Circulating Funds (100 million yuan)	469.67	475.47	483.88	579.85	642.54	735.29
产品销售收入（亿元）	Sales Revenue (100 million yuan)	389.43	415.07	475.94	741.22	962.66	1157.27
利税总额（亿元）	Total Profits and Taxes(100 million yuan)	73.31	79.15	87.25	123.02	165.72	201.40
#利润（亿元）	Total Profits(100 million yuan)	12.67	18.58	21.92	38.47	52.81	66.93
资本保值增值率（%）	Increment Ratio of Capital(%)	110.76	142.49	103.65	120.31	112.83	112.83
总资产贡献率（%）	Ratio of Total Assets to Industrial Output Value(%)	7.98	7.83	8.07	9.30	9.89	10.46
资产负债率（%）	Asset-Liability Ratio(%)	68.29	59.80	60.46	60.10	64.19	64.59
流动资产周转次数(次/年)	Number of Times of Turnover of Circulating Fund(times/year)	0.83	0.87	0.98	1.28	1.50	1.57
成本费用利润率（%）	Ratio of After-tax Profits to Cost and Expenses(%)	3.66	4.98	5.10	5.65	6.15	6.50
全员劳动生产率(元/人、年)	Overall Labor Productivity(yuan/person,year)	32318	38888	53010	69320	91316	105765
产品产销率（%）	Ratio of Industrial Products Sold(%)	99.71	98.64	98.27	97.71	97.11	97.53

7-6 “十五”时期各年主要工业产品产量

Output of Major Industrial Products of Each Year in “Tenth Five-year Plan” Period

产品名称	Item	2000	2001	2002	2003	2004	2005
原煤（万吨）	Coal(10000 tons)	3677.00	3731.39	5001.13	7802.50	9756.62	10615.20
天然气（万立方米）	Natural Gas(10000 cu.m)	7046	6826	4754			
钢（万吨）	Steel(10000 tons)	166.90	146.99	194.65	206.10	208.07	237.83
成品钢材（万吨）	Steel Products(10000 tons)	150.93	138.61	177.79	192.97	203.22	214.85
铁合金（万吨）	Iron Alloy(10000 tons)	61.43	76.12	76.33	99.61	116.54	122.95
铝（万吨）	Aluminium(10000 tons)	27.19	28.39	33.22	41.31	42.29	41.99
氧化铝（万吨）	Aluminum Oxide(10000 tons)	48.16	51.95	67.27	78.45	87.79	97.43
铝材（万吨）	Aluminium Material(10000 tons)	1.05	0.96	0.78	0.93	1.00	1.10
磷矿石（万吨）	Phosphorite Mineral(10000 tons)	588.70	669.91	729.20	783.68	801.98	878.79
生铁（万吨）	Pig Iron(10000 tons)	150.22	149.52	186.42	182.83	200.84	249.56
木材（万立方米）	Timber(10000 cu.m)	19.95	8.28	7.93	11.72		
农用化肥（万吨）	Chemical Fertilizer(10000 tons)	84.05	86.50	158.49	186.89	213.78	268.28
轮胎外胎（万条）	Tires(10000 units)	255.34	279.74	273.52	301.56	355.96	371.66
黄磷（万吨）	Yellow Phosphor(10000 tons)	17.85	19.14	19.16		14.86	
水泥（万吨）	Cement(10000 tons)	783.88	920.01	1121.11	1324.66	1428.80	1557.95
发电量（亿千瓦小时）	Electricity(100 million kwh)	404.70	480.25	547.12	636.60	713.04	786.78
#水电(亿千瓦小时)	Hydro-Power(100 million kwh)	183.44	211.70	221.53	203.87	216.25	217.20
煤气生产量（亿立方米）	Gas Production(100 million cu.m)	1.99	2.32	2.16	2.58	4.22	39.45
自来水生产量（万吨）	Tap Water Production(10000 tons)	38310	42472	40747	42273	740413	
卷烟（万箱）	Cigarettes(10000 cases)	187.35	180.79	177.84	183.19	194.74	208.21
白酒（万吨）	Liquor(10000ton)	8.38	12.11	12.67	15.04	9.22	11.74
饮料酒（万吨）	Beer(10000 tons)		21.59	23.55	27.04	23.14	28.30
食用植物油（万吨）	Edible Vegetable Oil(10000 tons)	8.63	8.78	10.92	10.73	9.13	9.38
中成药（万吨）	Traditional Chinese Medicine(10000 tons)	1.10	1.28	1.56	2.10	2.66	3.61
家用电冰箱（万台）	Household Refrigerators(10000 unit)	25.96	37.21	42.20	50.39	72.20	80.17
彩色电视机(万部)	Color TV Sets(10000 unit)	22.04	23.11	32.25	42.69	62.22	74.10
数字程控交换机（线）	Digital Program-controlled Exchange(unit)	24368	31600	30300	16800	13100	
微型计算机（台）	Microcomputers(unit)	29910	2793	63			
微硬盘（万部）	mini hard disks(10000unit)					76.16	28.18

7-7 规模以上工业企

Main Econornic Indicators of Industrial

指 标	Item	企业单位数 (个) Number of Enterprises (unit)	从业人员年平均人数（万人） Annual Average of All Employees (10000 persons)
总 计	**Total**	**2585**	**68.08**
按登记注册类型分	Gorouped by Status of Registration		
内资企业	Domestic-funded Enterprises	2479	65.68
国有企业	State-owned Industry	675	22.25
中央企业	Central Industry	50	6.04
地方企业	Local Industry	625	16.21
集体企业	Collective-owned Industry	142	2.08
股份合作企业	Cooperative Enterprises	68	0.91
联营企业	Joint Ownership Enterprises	28	0.50
有限责任公司	Limited Liability Corporations	599	22.62
股份有限公司	Share-holding Enterprises	110	6.35
私营企业	Private Enterprises	851	10.90
其他企业	Others Enterprises	6	0.07
港、澳、台商投资企业	Enterprises with Funds from Hong kong,Macao and Taiwan	48	0.75
外商投资企业	Foreign Funded Enterprises	58	1.65
在总计中:	of the Total:		
国有控股企业	State-controlled Enterprises	927	44.23
在总计中:	of the Total:		
农村工业	Rural Industry	34	0.65
按轻重工业分	Grouped by Light and Heavy Industry		
轻工业	Light Industry	720	12.31
重工业	Heavy Industry	1865	55.77
按企业规模分	Grouped by Scale of Enterprise		
大型企业	Large Industry	23	18.38
中型企业	Medium Industry	246	22.44
小型企业	Small Industry	2316	27.26

业主要经济指标(2005)

Enterprises above Designated Size(2005)

单位：亿元(100 million yuan)

工业总产值 Total Output Value of Industry	工业增加值 Value-Added of Industry	资产合计 Total Assets	产品销售收入 Revenue of Products Sales	利税总额 Total Profits and Taxes	利润总额 Total Profits
1690.40	**585.85**	**2734.05**	**1577.16**	**232.49**	**70.79**
1638.72	573.01	2643.02	1530.46	235.62	75.74
633.07	243.03	1025.47	610.96	125.12	30.86
384.96	147.87	524.98	363.22	79.15	9.97
248.11	95.16	500.49	247.74	45.97	20.89
23.91	6.46	17.64	23.68	1.62	0.01
13.71	4.11	16.45	12.17	0.64	0.05
7.37	2.06	7.35	6.37	0.33	0.01
482.72	148.69	820.85	441.59	45.09	17.61
244.50	94.87	583.88	235.46	44.06	23.33
232.63	73.44	170.96	199.65	18.70	3.85
0.81	0.34	0.41	0.58	0.06	0.01
13.71	3.58	21.17	12.65	1.14	0.46
37.97	9.26	69.87	34.05	-4.28	-5.41
1154.51	420.87	2264.10	1114.30	190.10	57.47
18.10	4.96	10.18	15.99	2.46	1.83
380.85	177.19	458.41	338.02	113.49	34.31
1309.55	408.66	2275.64	1239.13	118.99	36.48
716.65	280.61	1457.36	711.55	162.30	53.70
480.89	151.12	741.38	445.72	39.10	13.24
492.86	154.13	535.31	419.88	31.09	3.86

7-8 规模以上工业企业分

Main Economic Indicators of Industrial

指 标	Item	企业单位数(个) Number of Enterprises (unit)	从业人员年平均人数（万人） Annual Average of All Employees (10000 persons)
总 计	**Total**	**2585**	**68.08**
采矿业	Mining and Quarrying	363	13.52
煤炭开采和洗选业	Mining and Washing of Coal	285	11.66
黑色金属矿采选业	Mining and Dressing of Ferrous Metals	18	0.82
有色金属矿采选业	Mining and Dressing of Nonferrous Metals	33	0.52
非金属矿采选业	Mining and Dressing of Nonmetal Minerals	27	0.53
制造业	Manufacturing	1949	47.21
农副食品加工业	Processing of Food from Agricultural Products	138	1.09
食品制造业	Manufacture of Foods	57	0.80
饮料制造业	Manufacture of Beverages	82	1.98
白酒制造	Manufacture of Liquors	48	1.58
烟草加工业	Manufacture of Tobacco	10	1.49
烟叶复烤	Tobacco Leaf Baking	8	0.39
卷烟制造	Cigarettes Production	2	1.10
纺织业	Manufacture of Textile	24	0.59
纺织服装、鞋、帽制造业	Manufacture of Textile Wearing Apparel, Footware,and Caps	8	0.31
皮革、毛皮、羽毛（绒）及其制造业	Manufacture of Leather,Furs,Feather and Related Products	3	0.01
木材加工及木、竹、藤、棕、草制品业	Timber Processing,Manufacture of Wood, Bamboo,Rattan,Palm,and Straw Products	31	0.43
家具制造业	Manufacture of Furniture	8	0.06
造纸及纸制品业	Manufacture of Paper and Paper Products	40	0.43
印刷业、记录媒介的复制	Printing,Reproduction of Recording Media	62	0.64
文教体育用品制造业	Manufacture of Articles For Culture,Education and Sport Activity	4	0.07
石油加工、炼焦及核燃料加工业	Processing of Petroleum,Coking,Processing of Nuclear Fuel	77	0.82

行业主要经济指标(2005)

Enterprises above Designated Size by Sector(2005)

单位：亿元(100 million yuan)

工业总产值 Total Output Value of Industry	工业增加值 Value-Added of Industry	资产合计 Total Assets	产品销售收入 Revenue of Products Sales	利税总额 Total Profits and Taxes	利润总额 Total Profits
1690.40	**585.85**	**2734.05**	**1577.16**	**232.49**	**70.79**
120.37	52.41	227.35	117.70	20.29	6.62
105.97	46.54	196.55	102.68	17.29	5.07
3.33	1.37	15.30	4.03	-0.14	-0.43
4.97	1.93	3.63	4.16	0.65	0.24
6.10	2.57	11.88	6.84	2.48	1.74
1150.91	388.40	1543.14	1071.27	171.42	51.52
29.87	6.27	18.05	27.78	0.58	0.12
18.89	7.05	14.31	18.05	4.82	3.41
61.02	39.26	139.47	54.90	34.50	20.21
54.93	37.01	126.28	49.54	33.37	19.91
114.24	73.22	100.97	115.22	62.37	6.34
2.52	1.82	13.68	3.24	0.58	0.05
111.71	71.40	87.30	111.97	61.79	6.29
3.84	0.90	7.14	3.37	-0.09	-0.24
3.00	0.74	2.70	2.74	0.11	0.07
0.79	0.15	0.62	0.79	0.05	0.05
4.65	1.08	4.02	3.84	…	-0.23
0.19	0.04	0.85	0.23	-0.01	-0.02
5.62	1.96	6.70	4.48	0.10	-0.13
7.05	2.17	11.06	6.24	0.58	0.19
0.41	0.15	0.35	0.30	0.01	-0.02
14.31	4.80	15.68	15.79	1.63	0.08

7-8续表(continued)

指 标	Item	企业单位数(个) Number of Enterprises (unit)	从业人员年平均人数（万人） Annual Average of All Employees (10000 persons)
化学原料及化学制品制造业	Manufacture of Raw Chemical Materials and Chemical Products	222	6.37
医药制造业	Manufacture of Medicines	116	2.22
化学纤维制造业	Manufacture of Chemical Fibers	3	0.03
橡胶制品业	Manufacture of Rubber	19	1.25
塑料制品业	Manufacture of Plastics	53	0.61
非金属矿物制品业	Manufacture of Non-metallic Mineral Products	283	5.54
黑色金属冶炼及压延加工业	Smelting and Pressing of Ferrous Metals	268	7.04
有色金属冶炼及压延加工业	Smelting and Pressing of Non-ferrous Metals	132	3.44
金属制品业	Manufacture of Metal Products	37	1.40
通用设备制造业	Manufacture of General Purpose Machinery	66	1.51
专用设备制造业	Manufacture of Special Purpose Machinery	40	1.13
交通运输设备制造业	Manufacture of Transport Equipment	77	4.89
电气机械及器材制造业	Manufacture of Electrical Equipment and Machinery	41	1.34
通信设备、计算机及其他电子设备制造业	Manufacture of Communication Equipment, Computers and Other Electronic Equipment	22	1.02
仪器仪表及文化、办公用机械制造业	Manufacture of Measuring Instruments and Machinery for Cultural Activity and Office Work	16	0.36
工艺品及其他制造业	Manufacture of Artwork and Other Manufacturing	9	0.33
废弃资源和废旧材料回收加工业	Recycling and Disposal of Waste	1	0.01
电力、燃气及水的生产和供应业	Production and Distribution of Electric Power,Gas and Water	273	7.35
电力、热力的生产和供应业	Production and Distribution of Electric Power and Heat Power	175	6.26
电力生产	Production of Electric Power	102	2.87
电力供应	Distribution of Electric Power	73	3.39
燃气生产和供应业	Production and Distribution of Gas	5	0.28
水的生产和供应业	Production and Distribution of Water	93	0.81

单位：亿元(100 million yuan)

工业总产值 Total Output Value of Industry	工业增加值 Value-Added of Industry	资产合计 Total Assets	产品销售收入 Revenue of Products Sales	利税总额 Total Profits and Taxes	利润总额 Total Profits
196.44	57.10	306.80	185.43	17.66	9.47
84.29	32.87	81.28	55.43	8.98	4.27
0.88	0.16	0.19	0.92	0.02	0.01
34.06	7.02	41.56	36.29	2.85	0.58
9.30	2.08	11.07	8.35	0.18	–0.02
47.78	13.93	94.44	43.27	1.48	–1.72
187.03	40.43	184.48	172.87	6.60	–3.84
134.21	48.44	159.70	128.01	25.16	14.28
18.47	5.15	26.82	18.55	1.08	0.40
13.49	3.75	25.75	12.63	0.41	–0.26
15.60	3.67	30.99	11.70	1.76	1.41
68.29	18.02	130.47	68.30	0.91	–0.70
40.47	8.80	39.98	38.43	1.83	0.91
27.77	6.11	71.91	31.24	–2.43	–3.09
4.02	1.41	5.65	2.60	0.23	…
4.88	1.65	10.10	3.46	0.05	0.01
0.07	0.02	0.03	0.07	…	…
419.12	145.04	963.57	388.18	40.78	12.65
403.40	141.07	912.25	367.75	40.04	12.79
162.02	82.26	631.93	129.15	23.83	8.41
241.38	58.82	280.32	238.61	16.20	4.38
9.89	1.64	15.00	15.78	0.89	0.33
5.82	2.33	36.32	4.65	–0.15	–0.47

7-9 规模以上国有工业

Main Economic Indicators of All State-owned

指 标	Item	企业单位数（个）Number of Enterprises (unit)	从业人员年平均人数（万人）Annual Average of All Employees (10000 persons)
总 计	**Total**	**927**	**44.23**
在总计中:	of the Total		
中央企业	Central Enterprises	104	12.23
地方企业	Local Enterprises	823	32.00
按轻重工业分	Grouped by Type of Light and Heavy Industry		
轻工业	Light Industry	330	6.29
重工业	Heavy Industry	597	37.94
按企业规模分	Grouped by Scale of Enterprise		
大型企业	Large	21	17.96
中型企业	Medium	163	16.87
小型企业	Small	743	9.40
按工业行业分	Grouped by Industrial Sector		
采矿业	Mining and Quarrying	60	9.37
煤炭开采和洗选业	Mining and Washing of Coal	41	8.23
黑色金属矿采选业	Mining and Processing of Ferrous Metal Ores	2	0.67
有色金属矿采选业	Mining and Processing of Nonferrous Metal Ores	10	0.27
非金属矿采选业	Mining and Processing of Nonmetal Ores	7	0.20
制造业	Manufacturing	626	27.74
农副食品加工业	Processing of Food from Agricultural Products	61	0.38
食品制造业	Manufacture of Foods	25	0.30
饮料制造业	Manufacture of Beverages	36	1.34
烟草制品业	Manufacture of Tobacco	10	1.49
纺织业	Manufacture of Textile	15	0.17
纺织服装、鞋、帽制造业	Manufacture of Textile Wearing Apparel, Footware,and Caps	1	0.14
皮革、毛皮、羽毛（绒）及其制造业	Manufacture of Leather,Furs,Feather and Related Products	2	0.01
木材加工及木、竹、藤、棕、草制品业	Processing of Timber,Manufacture of Wood, Bamboo,Rattan,Palm,and Straw Products	9	0.11
家具制造业	Manufacture of Furniture	5	0.04

企业主要经济指标(2005)

above Designated Size Industrial Enterprises(2005)

单位：亿元(100 million yuan)

工业总产值 Total Output Value of Industry	工业增加值 Value-Added of Industry	资产合计 Total Assets	产品销售收入 Revenue of Products Sales	利税总额 Total Profits and Taxes	利润总额 Total Profits
1154.51	**420.87**	**2264.10**	**1114.30**	**190.10**	**57.47**
516.87	196.27	874.52	489.08	101.42	23.27
637.64	224.60	1389.59	625.22	88.68	34.19
216.96	118.80	322.92	215.60	95.29	24.88
937.55	302.07	1941.19	898.70	94.82	32.58
685.48	269.88	1431.43	686.56	159.26	51.81
329.55	104.29	607.08	318.97	26.12	7.10
139.48	46.70	225.60	108.77	4.72	-1.45
77.90	33.91	189.42	77.18	11.19	2.47
72.86	31.68	166.20	70.57	10.67	2.48
0.85	0.26	13.29	1.51	-0.71	-0.76
2.17	0.89	2.27	1.96	0.31	0.10
2.01	1.09	7.67	3.15	0.91	0.64
662.48	245.11	1133.03	653.69	139.41	43.25
7.77	1.46	9.11	7.09	-0.34	-0.43
2.32	0.57	4.46	2.25	0.13	…
43.95	31.41	124.02	45.82	32.14	19.47
114.24	73.22	100.97	115.22	62.37	6.34
0.84	0.14	4.87	0.58	-0.13	-0.19
1.76	0.41	1.41	1.74	0.06	0.06
0.01	-0.02	0.32	0.01	0.05	0.05
1.04	0.11	2.30	0.89	-0.20	-0.28
0.09	0.01	0.65	0.10	-0.02	-0.02

7-9续表(continued)

指 标	Item	企业单位数(个) Number of Enterprises (unit)	从业人员年平均人数（万人） Annual Average of All Employees (10000 persons)
印刷业、记录媒介的复制	Printing,Reproduction of Recording Media	36	0.27
文教体育用品制造业	Manufacture of Articles For Culture, Education and Sport Activity	1	0.01
石油加工、炼焦及核燃料加工业	Processing of Petroleum,Coking,Processing of Nuclear Fuel	5	0.06
化学原料及化学制品制造业	Manufacture of Raw Chemical Materials and Chemical Products	73	4.14
医药制造业	Manufacture of Medicines	6	0.04
橡胶制品业	Manufacture of Rubber	11	1.09
塑料制品业	Manufacture of Plastics	16	0.21
非金属矿物制品业	Manufacture of Non-metallic Mineral Products	74	2.31
黑色金属冶炼及压延加工业	Smelting and Pressing of Ferrous Metals	17	2.90
有色金属冶炼及压延加工业	Smelting and Pressing of Non-ferrous Metals	20	2.28
金属制品业	Manufacture of Metal Products	16	1.23
通用设备制造业	Manufacture of General Purpose Machinery	41	1.26
专用设备制造业	Manufacture of Special Purpose Machinery	30	0.85
交通运输设备制造业	Manufacture of Transport Equipment	52	4.64
电气机械及器材制造业	Manufacture of Electrical Equipment and Machiner	15	0.73
通信设备、计算机及其他电子设备制造业	Manufacture of Communication Equipment, Computers and Other Electronic Equipment	16	0.94
仪器仪表及文化、办公用 机械制造业	Manufacture of Measuring Instruments and Machinery for Cultural Activity and Office.Work	13	0.31
工艺品及其他制造业	Manufacture of Artwork and Other Manufacturing	7	0.29
废弃资源和废旧材料回收加工业	Recycling and Disposal of Waste	1	0.01
电力、燃气及水的生产和供应业	Production and Distribution of Electric Power,Gas and Water	241	7.12
电力、热力的生产和供应业	Production and Distribution of Electric Power and Heat Power	144	6.05
燃气生产和供应业	Production and Distribution of Gas	5	0.28
水的生产和供应业	Production and Distribution of Water	92	0.80

单位：亿元(100 million yusn)

工业总产值 Total Output Value of Industry	工业增加值 Value-Added of Industry	资产合计 Total Assets	产品销售收入 Revenue of Products Sales	利税总额 Total Profits and Taxes	利润总额 Total Profits
1.52	0.50	3.56	1.40	-0.07	-0.18
0.03	0.01	0.13	0.03	…	-0.01
0.85	0.24	1.12	1.15	0.09	-0.01
126.38	35.41	241.03	123.82	13.47	7.00
0.67	0.29	1.44	0.37	0.07	0.02
32.41	6.58	40.54	34.89	2.79	0.60
2.16	0.44	4.56	1.75	-0.01	-0.05
17.46	4.88	48.67	15.31	-0.99	-2.16
70.35	14.71	109.10	69.34	5.01	-0.53
79.06	33.81	130.15	78.08	21.78	14.73
16.22	4.73	24.67	16.28	1.02	0.41
9.83	2.88	21.78	8.88	0.20	-0.34
11.18	2.77	25.69	8.60	2.39	2.08
64.93	17.15	125.41	63.46	1.01	-0.38
26.12	4.97	22.44	24.75	0.66	0.12
21.85	5.34	66.81	25.13	-2.31	-2.96
3.47	1.19	4.62	2.24	0.27	0.06
4.60	1.58	9.91	3.20	0.02	0.01
0.07	0.02	0.03	0.07	…	…
414.13	141.85	941.65	383.43	39.51	11.75
398.67	138.01	891.76	363.25	38.81	11.92
9.89	1.64	15.00	15.78	0.89	0.33
5.56	2.20	34.90	4.39	-0.19	-0.51

7-10 规模以上集体工业

Main Economic Indicators of All Collective-owned

指 标	Item	企业单位数 (个) Number of Enterprises (unit)	从业人员年平均人数（万人） Annual Average of All Employees (10000 persons)
总 计	**Total**	**142**	**20816**
在总计中:	of the Total:		
亏损企业	Loss Making Enterprise	63	10439
在总计中:	of the Total:		
农村工业	Rural Industry	12	1576
按轻、重工业分:	Grouped by Type of Light and Heavy Industry		
轻工业	Light Industry	29	2640
重工业	Heavy Industry	113	18176
按企业规模分:	Grouped by Size of Enterprise		
中型企业	Medium	3	3356
小型企业	Small	139	17460
按工业行业分:	Grouped by Industrial Sector		
采矿业	Mining and Quarrying	11	1693
煤炭开采和洗选业	Mining and Washing of Coal	6	1454
黑色金属矿采选业	Mining and Processing of Ferrous Metal Ores	4	213
有色金属矿采选业	Mining and Processing of Nonferrous Metal Ores	1	26
制造业	Manufacturing	127	18807
农副食品加工业	Processing of Food from Agricultural Products	1	26
食品制造业	Manufacture of Foods	3	115
饮料制造业	Manufacture of Beverages	2	88

企业主要经济指标(2005)

above Designated Size Industrial Enterprises(2005)

单位：万元(10000 yuan)

工业总产值 Total Output Value of Industry	工业增加值 Value-Added of Industry	资产合计 Total Assets	产品销售收入 Revenue of Products Sales	利税总额 Total Profits and Taxes	利润总额 Total Profits
239106	**64604**	**176389**	**236813**	**16206**	**82**
99056	22176	90284	91468	746	
23397	6095	9794	20116	991	288
18077	5045	18876	15196	362	
221030	59559	157513	221617	15845	799
38053	10802	30765	34972	1538	
201054	53801	145625	201840	14669	143
9567	2416	7513	9447	1374	296
5465	901	5119	5470	727	50
3503	1325	2161	3377	590	237
600	190	233	600	57	8
225733	60547	154090	223483	14696	
742	142	463	772	10	
657	159	1198	621		
1926	840	1065	1141	153	57

7-10续表(continued)

指　标	Item	企业单位数(个) Number of Enterprises (unit)	从业人员年平均人数（万人） Annual Average of All Employees (10000 persons)
纺织服装、鞋、帽制造业	Manufacture of Textile Wearing Apparel, Footware,and Caps	2	487
木材加工及木、竹、藤、棕、草制品业	Processing of Timber,Manufacture of Wood, Bamboo,Rattan,Palm,and Straw Products	1	80
家具制造业	Manufacture of Furniture	2	75
造纸及纸制品业	Manufacture of Paper and Paper Products	6	528
印刷业、记录媒介的复制	Printing,Reproduction of Recording Media	5	619
石油加工、炼焦及核燃料加工业	Processing of Petroleum,Coking,Processing of Nuclear Fuel	2	171
化学原料及化学制品制造业	Manufacture of Raw Chemical Materials and Chemical Products	20	2360
医药制造业	Manufacture of Medicines	1	134
橡胶制品业	Manufacture of Rubber	1	1
塑料制品业	Manufacture of Plastics	2	800
非金属矿物制品业	Manufacture of Non-metallic Mineral Products	28	3972
黑色金属冶炼及压延加工业	Smelting and Pressing of Ferrous Metals	18	5814
有色金属冶炼及压延加工业	Smelting and Pressing of Non-ferrous Metals	6	824
金属制品业	Manufacture of Metal Products	10	803
通用设备制造业	Manufacture of General Purpose Machinery	2	254
专用设备制造业	Manufacture of Special Purpose Machinery	1	129
交通运输设备制造业	Manufacture of Transport Equipment	7	830
电气机械及器材制造业	Manufacture of Electrical Equipment and Machinery	6	417
工艺品及其他制造业	Manufacture of Artwork and Other Manufacturing	1	280
电力、燃气及水的生产和供应业	Production and Distribution of Electric Power,Gas and Water	4	316
电力、热力的生产和供应业	Production and Distribution of Electric Power and Heat Power	4	316

单位：万元(10000 yuan)

工业总产值 Total Output Value of Industry	工业增加值 Value-Added of Industry	资产合计 Total Assets	产品销售收入 Revenue of Products Sales	利税总额 Total Profits and Taxes	利润总额 Total Profits
4185	1121	2096	2713	133	
50	24	85	50	22	8
427	98	1191	446	26	
4135	1175	2767	3887	192	
2494	562	5507	2307		
2362	895	1413	2635	55	
47056	14712	30804	37136	1434	
231	41	704	203		
…		1132	67		
4045	1047	2255	3743	470	242
21848	5856	23407	19496	1385	
71005	15694	45444	70230	4067	
34101	10163	5913	30190	4567	364
9881	1628	7767	10728	732	250
2847	727	2307	2958	334	111
1043	324	1804	1228	56	12
9558	3509	12206	26352	996	193
6172	1458	3157	5679	267	70
970	425	1409	903	104	
3807	1641	14786	3883	136	
3807	1641	14786	3883	136	

7-11 规模以上外商投资和港澳台

Major Economic Indicators of all above Designated Size Industrial

指 标	Item	企业单位数（个）Number of Enterprises (unit)	从业人员年平均人数（万人）Annual Average of All Employees (10000 persons)
总 计	**Total**	**2585**	**68.08**
采矿业	Mining and Quarrying	363	13.52
煤炭开采和洗选业	Mining and Washing of Coal	285	11.66
黑色金属矿采选业	Mining and Dressing of Ferrous Metals	18	0.82
有色金属矿采选业	Mining and Dressing of Nonferrous Metals	33	0.52
非金属矿采选业	Mining and Dressing of Nonmetal Minerals	27	0.53
制造业	Manufacturing	1949	47.21
农副食品加工业	Processing of Food from Agricultural Products	138	1.09
食品制造业	Manufacture of Foods	57	0.80
饮料制造业	Manufacture of Beverages	82	1.98
白酒制造	Manufacture of Liquors	48	1.58
烟草加工业	Manufacture of Tobacco	10	1.49
烟叶复烤	Tobacco Leaf Baking	8	0.39
卷烟制造	Cigarettes Production	2	1.10
纺织业	Manufacture of Textile	24	0.59
纺织服装、鞋、帽制造业	Manufacture of Textile Wearing Apparel, Footware,and Caps	8	0.31
皮革、毛皮、羽毛（绒）及其制造业	Manufacture of Leather,Furs,Feather and Related Products	3	0.01
木材加工及木、竹、藤、棕、草制品业	Timber Processing,Manufacture of Wood, Bamboo,Rattan,Palm,and Straw Products	31	0.43
家具制造业	Manufacture of Furniture	8	0.06
造纸及纸制品业	Manufacture of Paper and Paper Products	40	0.43
印刷业、记录媒介的复制	Printing,Reproduction of Recording Media	62	0.64
文教体育用品制造业	Manufacture of Articles For Culture,Education and Sport Activity	4	0.07
石油加工、炼焦及核燃料加工业	Processing of Petroleum,Coking,Processing of Nuclear Fuel	77	0.82

投资工业企业主要经济指标(2005)

Enterprises Funded by Foreigners and Hong kong,Macao and Taiwan(2005)

单位:亿元(100 million yuan)

工业总产值 Total Output Value of Industry	工业增加值 Value-Added of Industry	资产合计 Total Assets	产品销售收入 Revenue of Products Sales	利税总额 Total Profits and Taxes	利润总额 Total Profits
1690.40	**585.85**	**2734.05**	**1577.16**	**232.49**	**70.79**
120.37	52.41	227.35	117.70	20.29	6.62
105.97	46.54	196.55	102.68	17.29	5.07
3.33	1.37	15.30	4.03	-0.14	-0.43
4.97	1.93	3.63	4.16	0.65	0.24
6.10	2.57	11.88	6.84	2.48	1.74
1150.91	388.40	1543.14	1071.27	171.42	51.52
29.87	6.27	18.05	27.78	0.58	0.12
18.89	7.05	14.31	18.05	4.82	3.41
61.02	39.26	139.47	54.90	34.50	20.21
54.93	37.01	126.28	49.54	33.37	19.91
114.24	73.22	100.97	115.22	62.37	6.34
2.52	1.82	13.68	3.24	0.58	0.05
111.71	71.40	87.30	111.97	61.79	6.29
3.84	0.90	7.14	3.37	-0.09	-0.24
3.00	0.74	2.70	2.74	0.11	0.07
0.79	0.15	0.62	0.79	0.05	0.05
4.65	1.08	4.02	3.84	…	-0.23
0.19	0.04	0.85	0.23	-0.01	-0.02
5.62	1.96	6.70	4.48	0.10	-0.13
7.05	2.17	11.06	6.24	0.58	0.19
0.41	0.15	0.35	0.30	0.01	-0.02
14.31	4.80	15.68	15.79	1.63	0.08

7-11续表(continued)

指 标	Item	企业单位数(个) Number of Enterprises (unit)	从业人员年平均人数(人) Annual Average of All Employees (persons)
有色金属矿采选业	Mining and Processing of Nonferrous Metal Ores	1	200
制造业	Manufacturing	102	23197
农副食品加工业	Processing of Food from Agricultural Products	3	279
食品制造业	Manufacture of Foods	2	560
饮料制造业	Manufacture of Beverages	1	182
纺织业	Manufacture of Textile	1	119
纺织服装、鞋、帽制造业	Manufacture of Textile Wearing Apparel, Footware,and Caps	1	200
造纸及纸制品业	Manufacture of Paper and Paper Products	3	304
印刷业、记录媒介的复制	Printing,Reproduction of Recording Media	1	189
文教体育用品制造业	Manufacture of Articles For Culture, Education and Sport Activity	1	422
石油加工、炼焦及核燃料加工业	Processing of Petroleum,Coking,Processing of Nuclear Fuel	1	46
化学原料及化学制品制造业	Manufacture of Raw Chemical Materials and Chemical Products	12	1518
医药制造业	Manufacture of Medicines	12	2195
橡胶制品业	Manufacture of Rubber	1	1283
塑料制品业	Manufacture of Plastics	8	912
非金属矿物制品业	Manufacture of Non-metallic Mineral Products	20	6257
黑色金属冶炼及压延加工业	Smelting and Pressing of Ferrous Metals	6	637
有色金属冶炼及压延加工业	Smelting and Pressing of Non-ferrous Metals	5	937
金属制品业	Manufacture of Metal Products	4	795
通用设备制造业	Manufacture of General Purpose Machinery	4	493
专用设备制造业	Manufacture of Special Purpose Machinery	1	1925
交通运输设备制造业	Manufacture of Transport Equipment	3	670
电气机械及器材制造业	Manufacture of Electrical Equipment and Machinery	3	639
通信设备、计算机及其他电子设备制造业	Manufacture of Communication Equipment, Computers and Other Electronic Equipment	6	2129
仪器仪表及文化、办公用机械制造业	Manufacture of Measuring Instruments and Machinery for Cultural Activity and Office Work	3	506

单位：万元(10000 yuan)

工业总产值 Total Output Value of Industry	工业增加值 Value-Added of Industry	资产合计 Total Assets	产品销售收入 Revenue of Products Sales	利税总额 Total Profits and Taxes	利润总额 Total Profits
693	249	349	391	16	49
51229	12655	90649	46209		
7599	1263	5057	7640	629	691
11657	2616	15814	13676		
15084	6028	10604	14776	5434	6765
308	93	623	279	30	64
1500	368	1326	1396	110	141
8770	2635	6602	7289	925	1294
13600	4285	16115	11538	2645	3524
1222	374	1660	1315		60
534	136	284	503	40	67
51851	10747	73344	50407	3302	5242
99940	39131	92992	55115		
9126	1071	14759	10147	16	629
22642	4614	29642	20370		
91358	35856	184692	78010	6264	12028
11520	2109	21039	11757		
13454	3767	43704	14396	1987	3178
10263	2622	9092	10214		85
5380	934	12017	4413		
19283	1797	34630	14132		
24367	7568	36194	23134	187	1605
15037	37	7484	15804	486	533
73721		281516	91780		
4071	1097	7304	3996		147

7-12 规模以上工业企业主要经济效益指标（2005）

Main Indicators on Economic Efficiency of all above Designated Size Industrial Enterprises(2005)

指 标	Item	产值利税率(%) Ratio of Pre-Tax Profit to Output Value(%)	资金利税率(%) Ratio of Pre-Tax Profit to Assets(%)	销售利税率(%) Ratio of Pre-Tax Profit to Sales(%)	全员劳动生产率(元/人)(按增加值计算) Overall Labor Productivity (yuan/person) (In Term of value added)
总 计	**Total**	**13.75**	**11.23**	**14.74**	**86057**
内资企业	Domestic Enterprise	14.38	11.81	15.40	87249
国有企业	State-owned Industry	19.76	14.50	20.48	109227
中央企业	Central	20.56	17.35	21.79	244804
地方企业	Local	18.53	11.31	18.55	58706
集体企业	Collective-owned Industry	6.78	10.39	6.84	31036
股份合作企业	Cooperation Enterprises	4.66	4.72	5.24	45196
联营企业	Joint-owned Enterprises	4.45	7.13	5.15	41314
有限责任公司	Limited Liability Corporations	9.34	7.74	10.21	65738
股份有限公司	Share Holding Enterprises	18.02	11.63	18.71	149470
私营企业	Private Enterprises	8.04	13.61	9.37	67407
其他企业	Others	7.86	16.78	11.06	47022
港、澳、台商投资企业	Enterprises with Funds from Hong kong,Macao and Taiwan	8.31	6.31	9.01	47533
外商投资企业	Foreign Funded Enterprises	-11.27	-7.49	-12.57	56185
在总计中:	of the Total:				
国有控股企业	State-controlled Enterprises	16.47	11.24	17.06	95160
在总计中:	of the Total:				
农村工业	Rural Industry	13.57	29.43	15.36	76359
按轻重工业分	Grouped by Type of Light and Heavy Industry				
轻工业	Light Industry	29.80	30.38	33.58	143924
重工业	Heavy Industry	9.09	7.01	9.60	73282
在总计中:	of the Total				
大型企业	Large	22.65	15.25	22.81	152643
中型企业	Medium-sized	8.13	6.81	8.77	67353
小型企业	Small	6.31	7.19	7.40	56545
按工业行业分	Grouped by Industrial Sector				
采矿业	Mining and Quarrying	16.86	12.39	17.24	38753
煤炭开采和洗选业	Mining and Washing of Coal	16.32	12.29	16.84	39929
黑色金属矿采选业	Mining and Processing of Ferrous Metal Ores	-4.20	-0.95	-3.47	16703
有色金属矿采选业	Mining and Processing of Nonferrous Metal Ores	13.08	22.34	15.63	37101
非金属矿采选业	Mining and Processing of Nonmetal Ores	40.66	46.10	36.26	48693

7-12续表1(continued)

指　标	Item	产值利税率(%) Ratio of Pre-Tax Profit to Output Value(%)	资金利税率(%) Ratio of Pre-Tax Profit to Assets(%)	销售利税率(%) Ratio of Pre-Tax Profit to Sales(%)	全员劳动生产率(元/人)(按增加值计算) Overall Labor Productivity (yuan/person) (In Term of value added)
制造业	Manufacturing	14.89	14.10	16.00	82276
农副食品加工业	Processing of Food from Agricultural Products	1.94	3.72	2.09	57397
食品制造业	Manufacture of Foods	25.52	44.02	26.70	87589
饮料制造业	Manufacture of Beverages	56.54	33.19	62.84	198423
烟草制品业	Manufacture of Tobacco	54.60	64.25	54.13	491905
纺织业	Manufacture of Textile	-2.34	-1.40	-2.67	15200
纺织服装、鞋、帽制造业	Manufacture of Textile Wearing Apparel,Footware,and Caps	3.67	4.40	4.01	24096
皮革、毛皮、羽毛(绒)及其制造业	Manufacture of Leather,Furs, Feather and Related Products	6.33	11.90	6.33	127119
木材加工及木、竹、藤、棕、草制品业	Processing of Timber,Manufacture of Wood,Bamboo,Rattan,Palm, and Straw Products	…	…	…	24885
家具制造业	Manufacture of Furniture	-5.26	-1.85	-4.35	6932
造纸及纸制品业	Manufacture of Paper and Paper Products	1.78	1.96	2.23	45151
印刷业、记录媒介的复制	Printing,Reproduction of Recording Media	8.23	5.97	9.29	33912
文教体育用品制造业	Manufacture of Articles For Culture, Education and Sport Activity	2.44	4.00	3.33	20353
石油加工、炼焦及核燃料加工业	Processing of Petroleum,Coking, Processing of Nuclear Fuel	11.39	13.43	10.32	58888
化学原料及化学制品制造业	Manufacture of Raw Chemical Materials and Chemical Products	8.99	7.68	9.52	89571
医药制造业	Maufacture of Medicines	10.65	13.83	16.20	148010
化学纤维制造业	Manufacture of Chemical Fibers	2.27	13.33	2.17	52459
橡胶制品业	Manufacture of Rubber	8.37	7.37	7.85	56209
塑料制品业	Manufacture of Plastics	1.94	2.21	2.16	34211
非金属矿物制品业	Manufacture of Non-metallic Mineral Products	3.10	1.84	3.42	25145

7-12续表2(continued)

指 标	Item	产值利税率(%) Ratio of Pre-Tax Profit to Output Value(%)	资金利税率(%) Ratio of Pre-Tax Profit to Assets(%)	销售利税率(%) Ratio of Pre-Tax Profit to Sales(%)	全员劳动生产率(元/人)(按增加值计算) Overall Labor Productivity (yuan/person) (In Term of value added)
黑色金属冶炼及压延加工业	Smelting and Pressing of Ferrous Metals	3.53	4.62	3.82	57437
有色金属冶炼及压延加工业	Smelting and Pressing of Non-ferrous Metals	18.75	20.91	19.65	140851
金属制品业	Manufacture of Metal Products	5.85	4.38	5.82	36862
通用设备制造业	Manufacture of General Purpose Machinery	3.04	1.92	3.25	24915
专用设备制造业	Manufacture of Special Purpose Machinery	11.28	8.14	15.04	32392
交通运输设备制造业	Manufacture of Transport Equipment	1.33	0.88	1.33	36822
电气机械及器材制造业	Manufacture of Electrical Equipment and Machinery	4.52	6.25	4.76	65623
通信设备、计算机及其他电子设备制造业	Manufacture of Communication Equipment Computers and Other Electronic Equipment	-8.75	-4.82	-7.78	60031
仪器仪表及文化、办公用机械制造业	Manufacture of Measuring Instruments and Machinery for Cultural Activity and Office Work	5.72	5.02	8.85	39573
工艺品及其他制造业	Manufacture of Artwork and Other Manufacturing	1.02	0.70	1.45	50551
废弃资源和废旧材料回收加工业	Recycling and Disposal of Waste	…	…	…	34483
电力、燃气及水的生产和供应业	Production and Distribution of Electric Power,Gas and Water	9.73	5.90	10.51	197441
电力、热力的生产和供应业	Production and Distribution of Electric Power and Heat Power	9.93	6.16	10.89	225319
燃气生产和供应业	Production and Distribution of Gas	9.00	7.54	5.64	59636
水的生产和供应业	Production and Distribution of Water	-2.58	-0.51	-3.23	28762

7-13 规模以上国有及国有控股工业企业主要经济效益指标（2005）

Main Indicators on Economic Efficiency of State-owned and State-controlled above Designated Size Industrial Enterprises(2005)

指　标	Item	产值利税率(%) Ratio of Pre-Tax Profit to Output Value(%)	资金利税率(%) Ratio of Pre-Tax Profit to Assets(%)	销售利税率(%) Ratio of Pre-Tax Profit to Sales(%)	全员劳动生产率(元/人)(按增加值计算) Overall Labor Productivity (yuan/person) (In Term of value added)
总　计	**Total**	**16.47**	**11.24**	**17.06**	**95160**
在总计中:	of the Total:				
亏损企业	Loss Making Enterprise	-17.75	-6.75	-17.15	15824
在总计中:	of the Total:				
中央企业	Central	19.62	14.71	20.74	160522
地方企业	Local	13.91	8.86	14.18	70186
按轻、重工业分	Grouped by Type of Light and Heavy Industry				
轻工业	Light Industry	43.92	35.69	44.20	188943
重工业	Heavy Industry	10.11	6.66	10.55	79618
按企业规模分	Grouped by Size of Enterprise				
大型企业	Large	23.23	15.27	23.20	150300
中型企业	Medium	7.93	5.63	8.19	61808
小型企业	Small	3.38	2.56	4.34	49691
按工业行业分	Grouped by Industrial Sector				
采矿业	Mining and Quarrying	14.36	8.25	14.49	36203
煤炭开采和洗选业	Mining and Washing of Coal	14.65	9.08	15.12	38504
黑色金属矿采选业	Mining and Processing of Ferrous Metal Ores	-83.07	-5.31	-47.13	3840
有色金属矿采选业	Mining and Processing of Nonferrous Metal Ores	14.36	16.72	15.96	32767
非金属矿采选业	Mining and Processing of Nonmetal Ores	45.23	32.41	28.91	55419
制造业	Manufacturing	21.04	15.75	21.33	88370
农副食品加工业	Processing of Food from Agricultural Products	-4.32	-4.21	-4.74	38182
食品制造业	Manufacture of Foods	5.62	3.44	5.79	19154
饮料制造业	Manufacture of Beverages	73.12	34.24	70.14	234494
烟草制品业	Manufacture of Tobacco	54.60	64.25	54.14	491934
纺织业	Manufacture of Textile	-15.73	-2.93	-22.87	8414
纺织服装、鞋、帽制造业	Manufacture of Textile Wearing Apparel,Footware,and Caps	3.58	4.65	3.64	28486
皮革、毛皮、羽毛(绒)及其制造业	Manufacture of Leather,Furs, Feather and Related Products	745.23	19.43	570.65	-22657
木材加工及木、竹、藤、棕、草制品业	Processing of Timber,Manufacture of Wood,Bamboo,Rattan,Palm,and Straw Products	-19.02	-10.30	-22.26	10318
家具制造业	Manufacture of Furniture	-17.75	-4.08	-16.24	2277
造纸及纸制品业	Manufacture of Paper and Paper Products	-5.93	-3.43	-6.31	17520

7-13续表(continued)

指 标	Item	产值利税率(%) Ratio of Pre-Tax Profit to Output Value(%)	资金利税率(%) Ratio of Pre-Tax Profit to Assets(%)	销售利税率(%) Ratio of Pre-Tax Profit to Sales(%)	全员劳动生产率(元/人)(按增加值计算) Overall Labor Productivity (yuan/person) (In Term of value added)
印刷业、记录媒介的复制	Printing,Reproduction of Recording Media	-4.29	-1.91	-4.65	18390
文教体育用品制造业	Manufacture of Articles For Culture, Education and Sport Activity	-9.28	-2.84	-8.69	11151
石油加工、炼焦及核燃料加工业	Processing of Petroleum,Coking, Processing of Nuclear Fuel	10.31	8.62	7.62	37136
化学原料及化学制品制造业	Manufacture of Raw Chemical Materials and Chemical Products	10.66	7.52	10.87	85438
医药制造业	Manufacture of Medicines	10.77	8.33	19.50	81191
橡胶制品业	Manufacture of Rubber	8.61	7.42	8.00	60289
塑料制品业	Manufacture of Plastics	-0.37	-0.34	-0.46	21223
非金属矿物制品业	Manufacture of Rubber	-5.64	-2.29	-6.44	21132
黑色金属冶炼及压延加工业	Manufacture of Plastics	7.13	6.29	7.23	50693
有色金属冶炼及压延加工业	Manufacture of Non-metallic Mineral Products	27.55	23.08	27.90	148389
金属制品业	Smelting and Pressing of Ferrous Metals	6.29	4.45	6.27	38502
通用设备制造业	Manufacture of General Purpose Machinery	2.08	1.11	2.30	22800
专用设备制造业	Manufacture of Special Purpose Machinery	21.34	13.90	27.74	32460
交通运输设备制造业	Manufacture of Transport Equipment	1.56	1.01	1.59	36922
电气机械及器材制造业	Manufacture of Electrical Equipment and Machinery	2.53	4.28	2.67	68011
通信设备、计算机及其他电子设备制造业	Manufacture of Communication Equipment,Computers and Other Electronic Equipment	-10.58	-5.07	-9.20	56642
仪器仪表及文化、办公用机械制造业	Manufacture of Measuring Instruments and Machinery for Cultural Activity and Office Work	7.84	7.12	12.12	38686
工艺品及其他制造业	Manufacture of Artwork and Other Manufacturing	0.49	0.32	0.70	54563
废弃资源和废旧材料回收加工业	Recycling and Disposal of Waste	-0.40	-0.85	-0.41	34017
电力、燃气及水的生产和供应业	Production and Distribution of Electric Power,Gas and Water	9.54	5.89	10.30	199099
电力、热力的生产和供应业	Production and Distribution of Electric Power and Heat Power	9.73	6.15	10.68	228248
燃气生产和供应业	Production and Distribution of Gas	9.02	7.57	5.66	59761
水的生产和供应业	Production and Distribution of Water	-3.47	-0.70	-4.39	27338

7-14 规模以上集体工业企业主要经济效益指标（2005）

Main Indicators on Economic Benefit of Collective-owned above Designated Size Industrial Enterprises(2005)

指 标	Item	产值利税率(%) Ratio of Pre-Tax Profit to Output Value(%)	资金利税率(%) Ratio of Pre-Tax Profit to Assets(%)	销售利税率(%) Ratio of Pre-Tax Profit to Sales(%)	全员劳动生产率(元/人)(按增加值计算) Overall Labor Productivity (yuan/person) (In Term of value added)
总 计	**Total**	**6.78**	**10.39**	**6.84**	**31036**
在总计中:	of the Total:				
亏损企业	Loss Making Enterprise	0.75	0.92	0.82	21243
在总计中:	of the Total:				
农村工业	Rural Industry	4.23	10.97	4.93	38671
按轻、重工业分	Grouped by Type of Light and Heavy Industry				
轻工业	Light Industry	2.00	2.11	2.38	19108
重工业	Heavy Industry	7.17	11.42	7.15	32768
按企业规模分	Grouped by Size of Enterprise				
中型企业	Medium	4.04	5.32	4.40	32187
小型企业	Small	7.30	11.55	7.27	30814
按工业行业分	Grouped by Industrial Sector				
采矿业	Mining and Quarrying	14.36	25.82	14.55	14272
煤炭开采和洗选业	Mining and Quarrying	13.30	22.74	13.28	6199
黑色金属矿采选业	Mining and Processing of Ferrous Metal Ores	16.86	30.10	17.48	62183
有色金属矿采选业	Mining and Processing of Nonferrous Metal Ores	9.51	34.46	9.51	73192
制造业	Manufacturing	6.51	10.58	6.58	32194
农副食品加工业	Processing of Food from Agricultural Products	1.32	2.91	1.27	54538
食品制造业	Manufacture of Foods	-0.93	-0.51	-0.98	13783
饮料制造业	Manufacture of Beverages	7.97	17.76	13.45	95398

7-14续表(continued)

指 标	Item	产值利税率(%) Ratio of Pre-Tax Profit to Output Value(%)	资金利税率(%) Ratio of Pre-Tax Profit to Assets(%)	销售利税率(%) Ratio of Pre-Tax Profit to Sales(%)	全员劳动生产率(元/人)(按增加值计算) Overall Labor Productivity (yuan/person) (In Term of value added)
纺织服装、鞋、帽制造业	Manufacture of Textile Wearing Apparel,Footware,and Caps	3.18	6.92	4.90	23010
木材加工及木、竹、藤、棕、草制品业	Processing of Timber,Manufacture of Wood,Bamboo,Rattan,Palm,and Straw Products	44.00	27.03	44.00	3038
家具制造业	Manufacture of Furniture	6.02	2.14	5.76	13107
造纸及纸制品业	Manufacture of Paper and Paper Products	4.65	7.58	4.95	22259
印刷业、记录媒介的复制	Printing,Reproduction of Recording Media	-4.90	-2.64	-5.30	9082
石油加工、炼焦及核燃料加工业	Processing of Petroleum,Coking, Processingof Nuclear Fuel	2.31	3.85	2.07	52316
化学原料及化学制品制造业	Manufacture of Raw Chemical Materials and Chemical Products	3.05	5.40	3.86	62338
医药制造业	Manufacture of Medicines	-54.90	-16.61	-62.48	3030
塑料制品业	Manufacture of Plastics	11.63	35.72	12.56	13093
非金属矿物制品业	Manufacture of Non-metallic Mineral Products	6.34	6.77	7.10	14744
黑色金属冶炼及压延加工业	Smelting and Pressing of Ferrous Metals	5.73	9.41	5.79	26994
有色金属冶炼及压延加工业	Smelting and Pressing of Non-ferrous Metals	13.39	87.67	15.13	123340
金属制品业	Manufacture of Metal Products	7.41	11.90	6.82	20276
通用设备制造业	Manufacture of General Purpose Machinery	11.71	15.97	11.28	28638
专用设备制造业	Manufacture of Special Purpose Machinery	5.37	3.06	4.56	25078
交通运输设备制造业	Manufacture of Transport Equipment	10.42	8.47	3.78	42281
电气机械及器材制造业	Manufacture of Electrical Equipment and Machinery	4.33	8.12	4.71	34959
工艺品及其他制造业	Manufacture of Artwork and Other Manufacturing	10.72	8.06	11.52	15193
电力、燃气及水的生产和供应业	Production and Distribution of Electric Power, Gas and Water	3.58	1.17	3.51	51918
电力、热力的生产和供应业	Production and Distribution of Electric Power and Heat Power	3.58	1.17	3.51	51918

7-15 大中型工业企业主要经济指标及占全省比重（2005）

Main Indicators on Economic of Large and Medium Industrial Enterprises and Its Proportion in Provincial Total(2005)

单位：亿元(100 million yuan)

指标	Item	全省工业 Total Provincial Industry	#大中型 Large-scale and Medium-scale Industrial Enterprises		#国有大中型 State-owned Large-scale and Medium-scale Industrial Enterprises	
			绝对数 Absolute Figure	占全省（%） As Percentage to Provincial Total(%)	绝对数 Absolute Figure	占全省（%） As Percentage to Provincial Total(%)
企业单位数（个）	Number of Industrial Enterprises (unit)	2585	269	10.4	184	7.1
亏损企业个数（个）	Number of Loss Making Industrial Enterprises(unit)	1138	66	5.8	40	3.5
工业总产值	Gross Output Value of Industry	1690.40	1197.54	70.8	1015.03	60.0
工业增加值	Value-added of Industry	585.85	431.73	73.7	374.17	63.9
资产总计	Total Assets	2734.05	2198.74	80.4	2038.51	74.6
#流动资产年平均余额	Average Balance of Circulating Funds	947.98	735.29	77.6	652.74	68.9
固定资产净值年平均余额	Annual Average Balance Net Value of Fixed Assets	1122.67	902.92	80.4	853.90	76.1
负债总计	Total Liabilities	1784.20	1420.22	79.6	1320.36	74.0
产品销售收入	Sales Revenue	1577.16	1157.27	73.4	1005.53	63.8
#产品销售成本	Cost of Sales	1224.83	868.02	70.9	747.68	61.0
产品销售税金及附加	Sales Tax and Extra Charges	64.30	59.04	91.8	58.02	90.2
亏损企业亏损额	Total Deficit of Loss Making Industrial Enterprises	33.20	17.74	53.4	14.62	44.0
利税总额	Total Profits and Taxes	232.49	201.40	86.6	185.38	79.7
从业人员年平均人数（万人）	Annual Average Number of All Employees(10000 persons)	68.08	40.82	60.0	34.83	51.2
资金利税率（%）	Ratio of Pre-Tax Profit and Assets(%)	11.23	12.29	109.5	12.30	109.6
全员劳动生产率(元/人、年)	Overall Labor Productivity (yuan/person,year)	86057	105765	122.9	107428	124.8

7-16 大中型工业企

Main Indicators on Economic of Large and

指 标	Item	企业单位数（个） Number of Enterprises (unit)	从业人员年平均人数（万人） Annual Average of All Employees (10000 persons)
总 计	**Total**	**269**	**40.82**
采矿业	Mining and Quarrying	22	8.71
煤炭开采和洗选业	Mining and Washing of Coal	20	7.99
黑色金属矿采选业	Mining and Processing of Nonferrous Metal Ores	1	0.65
非金属矿采选业	Mining and Processing of Nonmetal Ores	1	0.07
制造业	Manufacturing	209	27.54
农副食品加工业	Processing of Food from Agricultural Products	1	0.12
食品制造业	Manufacture of Foods	5	0.39
饮料制造业	Manufacture of Beverages	7	1.26
烟草制品业	Manufacture of Tobacco	7	1.44
纺织业	Manufacture of Textile	2	0.18
纺织服装、鞋、帽制造业	Manufacture of Textile Wearing Apparel, Footware,and Caps	1	0.14
造纸及纸制品业	Manufacture of Paper and Paper Products	1	0.04
印刷业、记录媒介的复制	Printing, Reproduction of Recording Media	3	0.22
石油加工、炼焦及核燃料 加工业	Processing of Petroleum,Coking,Processing of Nuclear Fuel	2	0.11
化学原料及化学制品制造业	Manufacture of Raw Chemical Materials and Chemical Products	35	4.61
医药制造业	Manufacture of Medicines	19	1.21
橡胶制品业	Manufacture of Rubber	3	0.93
非金属矿物制品业	Manufacture of Non-metallic Mineral Products	15	1.54
黑色金属冶炼及压延 加工业	Smelting and Pressing of Ferrous Metals	22	4.14
有色金属冶炼及压延 加工业	Smelting and Pressing of Non-ferrous Metals	9	2.49
金属制品业	Manufacture of Metal Products	3	0.99
通用设备制造业	Manufacture of General Purpose Machinery	7	0.70
专用设备制造业	Manufacture of Special Purpose Machinery	10	0.71
交通运输设备制造业	Manufacture of Transport Equipment	29	4.16
电气机械及器材制造业	Manufacture of Electrical Equipment and Machinery	13	0.93
通信设备、计算机及其他电子设备制造业	Manufacture of Communication Equipment,Computers and Other Electronic Equipment	9	0.83
仪器仪表及文化、办公用机械制造业	Manufacture of Measuring Instruments and Machinery for Cultural Activity and Office Work	2	0.16
工艺品及其他制造业	Manufacture of Artwork and Other Manufacturing	4	0.24
电力、燃气及水的生产 和供应业	Production and Distribution of Electric Power,Gas and Water	38	4.56
电力、热力的生产和供应业	Production and Distribution of Electric Power and Heat Power	33	4.15
燃气生产和供应业	Production and Distribution of Gas	3	0.25
水的生产和供应业	Production and Distribution of Water	2	0.17

业主要经济指标(2005)

Medium Industrial Enterprises(2005)

单位：亿元(100 million yuan)

工业总产值 Total Output Value of Industry	工业增加值 Value-Added of Industry	资产合计 Total Assets	产品销售收入 Revenue of Products Sales	利税总额 Total Profits and Taxes	利润总额 Total Profits
1197.54	**431.73**	**2198.74**	**1157.27**	**201.40**	**66.93**
73.09	32.37	181.18	71.32	10.68	2.33
71.82	31.93	162.77	69.42	11.23	2.99
0.80	0.21	13.25	1.46	-0.71	-0.75
0.46	0.23	5.16	0.44	0.16	0.09
786.25	287.13	1166.05	751.93	154.49	53.48
1.00	0.32	0.59	0.93	0.14	0.07
11.59	4.69	8.11	11.46	3.56	2.79
43.93	31.68	121.25	45.88	32.45	19.72
114.20	73.35	97.01	115.19	62.61	6.59
1.37	0.40	1.55	1.17	-0.04	-0.06
1.76	0.41	1.41	1.74	0.06	0.06
0.42	0.08	1.33	0.40	-0.06	-0.09
1.84	0.62	2.99	1.52	0.11	-0.01
2.91	0.85	5.80	3.55	0.46	0.08
154.37	45.60	267.59	149.23	15.52	8.80
50.62	19.13	39.66	32.34	5.25	2.27
32.10	6.71	36.07	34.65	2.91	0.74
15.36	4.95	40.18	14.08	-0.18	-1.22
111.25	23.45	134.34	105.09	7.00	0.24
91.59	36.11	133.07	87.22	21.63	14.21
14.46	4.17	21.71	14.70	1.00	0.45
5.89	1.66	14.85	5.10	-0.03	-0.36
11.76	2.71	21.82	8.52	1.83	1.61
61.84	16.19	116.86	60.31	0.90	-0.31
31.38	7.07	25.90	30.29	1.47	0.70
20.75	5.00	62.76	24.14	-2.35	-2.95
1.41	0.50	1.95	1.27	0.15	0.06
4.44	1.51	9.25	3.15	0.10	0.09
338.21	112.23	851.51	334.02	36.23	11.14
326.15	109.86	822.56	317.01	35.52	11.08
9.77	1.61	13.13	15.53	0.88	0.33
2.29	0.76	15.82	1.48	-0.17	-0.27

7-17 工业产品销售产值（2005）

Total Sales Value of Industrial Products (2005)

单位：亿元(100 million yuan)

类 别	Item	销售产值 Sales Value	#出口交货值 Delivery Value of Industry	新产品产值 New Products Value
总 计	**Total**	**1634.46**	**62.29**	**108.65**
按登记注册类型分:	Grouped by Registration			
内资企业	Domestic Enterprises	1584.65	52.72	95.01
国有企业	State-owned Industry	632.32	18.23	36.99
中央企业	Central	390.60	4.24	35.16
地方企业	Local	241.71	13.99	1.83
集体企业	Collective-owned Industry	22.70	0.37	…
股份合作企业	Cooperation Enterprises	13.11	…	…
联营企业	Joint-owned Enterprises	6.34		0.11
有限责任公司	Limited Liability Corporations	455.46	13.06	35.78
股份有限公司	Share Holding Enterprises	235.92	13.00	16.24
私营企业	Private Enterprises	218.14	8.06	5.89
其他企业	Others	0.67		
港、澳、台商投资企业	Enterprises with Funds from Hong kong,Macao and Taiwan	13.01	2.62	0.46
外商投资企业	Foreign Funded Enterprises	36.80	6.95	13.18
在总计中:	of the Total			
国有控股企业	State-controlled Enterprises	1143.70	44.61	80.07
按轻重工业分	Grouped by Type of Light and Heavy Industry			
轻工业	Light Industry	356.17	5.07	60.15
重工业	Heavy Industry	1278.29	57.21	48.50
按企业规模分	Grouped by Scale of Enterprise			
大型企业	Large	712.66	27.91	40.85
中型企业	Medium	455.26	24.08	55.18
小型企业	Small	466.54	10.30	12.62

7-18 主要工业产品销售量和产销率（2005）

Sales Volume of Main Industrial Products and Its Ratio of Products Sold(2005)

产品名称	Item	产量 Output	销售量 Sales Volume	产销率（%）Ratio of Products Sold(%)	2005年比2004年增长(%) Increase Rate in 2005 over 2004(%)	
					产量 Output	销售量 Sales Volume
原煤（万吨）	Coal(10000 tons)	10615.16	9098.78	85.7	10.6	4.1
洗煤（万吨）	Washing Coal(10000 tons)	958.16	963.94	100.6	21.2	20.0
煤气生产量（万立方米）	Volume of Coal Gas Production	394464.87	394464.87	100.0	13.5	持平
发电量（亿千瓦小时）	Electricity(100 million kwh)	786.78	786.78	100.0	10.8	持平
水电（亿千瓦小时）	Hydro-Power	217.20	217.20	100.0	1.8	持平
磷矿石(生产量含P2O530%)（万吨）	Phosphorite Mineral	878.79	541.34	61.6	6.7	19.6
配混合饲料（万吨）	Forage(10000 tons)	30.18	29.97	99.3	9.3	10.5
机制糖（万吨）	Sugar(10000 tons)	1.01	1.01	100.0	-50.4	-50.5
乳制品（吨）	Dairy Products(ton)	2.57	2.48	96.5	1.6	2.5
罐头（吨）	Canned Food(ton)	5061.80	4980.49	98.4	42.5	35.1
白酒(万千升)	Liquor(10000 tons)	11.74	10.16	86.5	26.0	15.8
啤酒(万千升)	Beer(10000 tons)	16.55	16.48	99.6	20.0	22.6
软饮料（万吨）	Soft Drink(10000 tons)	16.06	16.37	101.9	-19.4	-6.9
卷烟（万箱）	Cigarettes(10000 tons)	208.21	209.21	100.5	6.9	5.8
纱（万吨）	Yarn(10000 tons)	1.58	1.15	72.8	-5.8	18.6
布（万米）	Cloth(10000 m)	4425.04	3717.96	84.0	-12.1	3.2
棉布（万米）	Pure Cotton Cloth(10000 m)	108.25	128.37	118.6	-19.1	-39.2
混纺交织布（万米）	Cloth (10000 m)	3448.33	2721.08	78.9	-16.9	2.4
丝（吨）	Silk(ton)	50.94	50.56	99.3	26.4	8.0
服装（万件）	Garment(10000 pieces)	524.68	581.57	110.8	-6.7	13.3
人造板（万立方米）	Artificial Board(10000M3)	22.35	20.74	92.8	5.2	2.3
机制纸（万吨）	Machine-made Paper(10000 tons)	4.12	4.94	119.9	-11.7	4.4

7-18续表1(continued)

产品名称	Item	产量 Output	销售量 Sales Volume	产销率（%）Ratio of Products Sold(%)	2005年比2004年增长(%) Increase Rate in 2005 over 2004(%)	
					产量 Output	销售量 Sales Volume
焦炭（万吨）	Coke(10000 tons)	466.11	365.76	78.5	-5.8	2.8
硫酸（折100%）	Sulfuric Acid	341.10	86.86	25.5	18.0	2.2
氢氧化钠（烧碱 折100%）	Caustic Soda	8.84	8.52	96.4	9.1	8.0
碳化钙(电石 折300 升/千克)	Calcium Carbide	41.27	34.63	83.9	40.7	52.2
合成氨	Synthetic Ammonia	105.95	66.73	63.0	5.6	7.3
农用化学肥料总计(折纯)	Chemical Fertilizer	268.28	261.34	97.4	24.6	21.7
氮肥(折含 N100%)	Nitrogen Fertilizer	111.61	109.08	97.7	24.6	18.4
尿素	Carbamide	49.68	49.25	99.1	4.9	2.8
磷肥(折合 P2O5100%)	Phosphate Fertilizer	156.67	152.26	97.2	24.6	24.2
化学农药（吨）	Chemical Pesticide(ton)	889.90	907.63	102.0	-52.1	-48.2
纯苯（吨）	Pure Benzene	10050.27	10146.01	101.0	8.1	9.9
油漆（吨）	Oil Paint	3259.08	3381.90	103.8	9.6	19.9
合成洗涤剂（万吨）	Synthetic Detergents(10000 tons)	5.71	5.66	99.1	-9.1	-10.0
化学原料药（吨）	Chemical Medicine(ton)	2274.00	2078.65	91.4	174.0	213.0
化学纤维（吨）	Chemical Fiber	6902.35	6613.29	95.8	-10.3	-11.3
合成纤维	Synthetic Fiber	6902.35	6613.29	95.8	-10.3	-11.3
轮胎外胎（万条）	Tires(10000 bar)	371.66	386.90	104.1	4.4	10.9
塑料制品（万吨）	Plastic Products(10000 tons)	4.81	4.78	99.4	13.0	46.2
农用薄膜（吨）	Rural Use Membrane(ton)	8888.90	4468.74	50.3	32.5	109.9
水泥（万吨）	Cement(10000 tons)	1557.97	1529.96	98.2	9.3	7.6
生铁（万吨）	Pig Iron	249.56	75.28	30.2	18.1	57.2
粗钢（万吨）	Steel	237.83	22.84	9.6	11.9	-48.6
钢材（万吨）	Steel Products	214.85	216.66	100.8	3.9	7.2
中小型型钢	Mediun and small Roolled-Steel	7580.00	7080.00	93.4	-84.8	-86.4

7-18续表2(continued)

产品名称	Item	产量 Output	销售量 Sales Volume	产销率（%）Ratio of Products Sold(%)	2005年比2004年增长(%) Increase Rate in 2005 over 2004(%)	
					产量 Output	销售量 Sales Volume
盘条(线材)(万吨)	Wire Rod(10000 tons)	74.84	74.77	99.9	1.3	0.8
无缝钢管（吨）	Seamless Steel Pipe(ton)	17927.39	17897.14	99.8	113.8	109.7
铁合金（万吨）	Iron Alloy(10000 tons)	122.95	115.45	93.9	3.5	7.0
十种有色金属	10 Nonferrous Metal	60.34	59.66	98.9	-2.5	3.1
铅（吨）	Lead(tons)	6759.00	6724.00	99.5	-27.1	-3.5
锌（万吨）	Zinc(10000 tons)	16.35	16.44	100.6	-11.6	13.4
铝	Aluminium	41.99	41.26	98.3	0.7	-1.5
氧化铝	Alumina	97.43	50.49	51.8	11.0	16.7
铝材	Aluminium Material	1.10	1.08	98.2	32.6	4.9
工业锅炉（蒸发量吨）	Boiler Industry Use(vaporize-ton)	21.50	21.50	100.0	355.5	229.8
内燃机(生产量)(万千瓦时)	Internal Combustion Engines (10000 kwh)	10.62	13.40	126.2	-57.3	-22.3
金属切削机床（台）	Metal-cutting Machine Tools(set)	545.00	505.00	92.7	2.1	-8.0
小型拖拉机（辆）	Mini-tractors(set)	3392.00	3543.00	104.5	80.5	119.0
汽车（辆）	Motor Vehicles	1057.00	969.00	91.7	133.3	158.4
公路客车（辆）	Buses	657.00	696.00	105.9	128.1	262.5
轿车（辆）	Cars	32.00	51.00	159.4	-80.6	-72.1
民用钢质船舶（综合吨）	Civil Steel Ships(syn-ton)	213.56	213.56	100.0	-79.2	-79.2
交流电动机（万千瓦）	Alternating Current Motor(10000 kw)	11.48	12.41	108.1	28.7	71.9
家用电冰箱（万台）	Household Refrigerators(10000 sets)	80.17	80.89	100.9	11.0	10.3
半导体集成电路（万块）	Semiconductor Integrated Circui (10000 pcs)	907.73	798.42	88.0	12266.9	-56.1
彩色电视机（万部）	Color TV Sets(10000 sets)	74.10	74.67	100.8	19.1	31.9

7-19 重点企业建立现代企业制度主要经济指标（2005）

Main Economic Indicators on Major Enterprises Set up Modern Enterprises System(2005)

单位：万元(10000 yuan)

分 类	Item	单位数（个）Number of Units (unit)	从业人员年末人数（人）Employment Personnel (year-end) (person)	年末资产总计 Total Assets (year-end)	主营业务收入 Revenue of Main Business	利润总额 Total Profits
总 计	**Total**	**81**	**276125**	**18840134**	**9457854**	**633591**
按重点企业类型分	By Type of Major Enterprises					
520户国家重点企业	520 Major Enterprises of State	8	96074	7512157	3842745	358461
重组为集团公司的原512户国家重点企业	Company Group Rebuilded by 512 Major Enterprises of State	4	31546	3826048	2218586	138231
省级重点企业	Major Enterprises at Province Level	51	169915	9845923	4167323	328355
现企原国家百户试点企业	100 Enterprises Been Made Experiments by State in Modern Enterprises System	3	9255	1108505	361037	32072
现企原省级试点企业	Enterprises Been Made Experiments in Mod ern Enterprises System at Province Level	23	73817	4774927	2075312	243812
试点集团母公司	Parent Company of Enterprises Groups Been Made Experiments	1	10689	417143	173367	3813
按登记注册类型划分	By Registration					
国有企业	State-owned Enterprise	18	51801	4711992	3434525	111304
国有独资公司	State-owned Corporation	9	68509	2788513	1083803	18785
其他有限责任公司	Other Limited Liability Corporations	30	101346	6156159	2812883	297685
股份有限公司	Share-holding Corporations Ltd	17	48706	4964272	1996807	202431
中外合资企业	Enterprises of China and Foreign Countries Joint Venture	5	5151	153163	84881	-11101
按控股情况划分	By Controlling Share					
国有绝对控股	State-owned Absolute Holding	51	232808	14193135	7666948	419308
国有相对控股	State-owned Relatively Holding	5	11082	3160251	673550	49750
其他	Other	23	30346	1470371	1100130	163698
按企业规模划分	By Size of Enterprises					
大型	Large-size	29	230873	16813707	8430261	540462
中型	Medium-size	44	43697	1950260	989241	90090
小型	Small-size	8	1555	76167	38352	3039
按主营行业划分	By Main Business Sector					
采矿业	Mining and Quarrying	3	60010	1329661	523467	10244
制造业	Manufacturing	69	167312	9358108	5658274	511553
电力、燃气及水的生产和供应业	Production and Supply of Electric Power, Gas and Water	4	24805	7245681	2442611	108807
建筑业	Construction	1	20794	828981	822903	6987
交通运输、仓储和邮政业	Transportation,Postal and Telecommunication	1	1290	9108	4229	54
批发和零售业	Wholesale & Retail Trade and Catering Services	3	1914	73855	6370	-4054

7-20 企业集团主要经济指标（2005年）

Main Economic Indicators of Enterprises Groups(2005)

单位：亿元(100 million yuan)

分类	Item	集团个数（个）Number of Enterprises Group (unit)	从业人员年末人数(人) Employment Personnel (year-end) (person)	资产总计 Total Assets	年末负债合计 Total Liabilities (year-end)	主营业务收入 Revenue of Main Business	利润总额 Total Profits
总 计	**Total**	25	242512	1170.6	731.31	520.41	35.43
按审批部门划分	By Department of Approving Enterprise Groups						
国务院主管部门	Departments Managed by the State Council	4	93023	319.12	197.08	190.68	2.69
省级人民政府	Government at Province Level	6	48366	490.11	344.65	180.18	7.32
省级政府主管部门	Departments Managed by Government at Province Level	13	99816	354.81	186.53	146.8	25.22
其他	Others	2	1307	6.56	3.05	2.7	0.19
按母公司登记注册类型划分	By Main Business Sector of Par ent Company						
国有企业	State-owned Enterprise	3	29521	33.33	25.88	24.43	-0.29
国有独资公司	State-owned Corporation	8	108285	382.85	231.16	176.84	4.84
其他有限责任公司	Other Limited Liability Corporations	10	94835	414.26	222.89	249.76	24.17
股份有限公司	Share-holding Corporations Ltd	3	7834	326.69	244.09	62.71	5.52
中外合资企业	Enterprises of China and Foreign Countries Joint Venture	1	2037	13.45	7.28	6.66	1.19
按控股情况划分	By Controlling Share						
国有绝对控股	State-owned Absolute Holding	19	231334	823.89	476.88	448.3	28.53
其他	Other	4	3844	20.87	10.83	9.95	1.38
按企业规模划分	By Size of Enterprises						
大型	Large-size	16	228072	1104.9	688.42	479.03	33.74
中型	Medium-size	7	13264	57.64	40.46	38.81	1.4
小型	Small-size	2	1176	8.04	24.31	2.56	0.29
按主营行业划分	By Main Business Sector						
采矿业	Mining and Quarrying	3	60010	132.96	60.38	52.34	1.02
制造业	Manufacturing	16	124853	595.57	334.62	299.18	28.48
电力、燃气及水的生产和供应业	Production and Supply of Electric Pow er,Gas and Water	2	7620	326.76	243.45	62.58	5.58
建筑业	Construction	2	48396	109.68	87.52	105.67	0.71
批发和零售业	Wholesale & Retail Trade and Catering Se rvices	2	1633	5.61	5.34	0.63	-3.73

主要统计指标解释

工业　指从事自然资源的开采，对采掘品和农产品进行加工和再加工的物质生产部门。具体包括：(1)对自然资源的开采，如采矿、晒盐等(但不包括禽兽捕猎和水产捕捞)；(2)对农副产品的加工、再加工，如粮油加工、食品加工、缫丝、纺织、制革等；(3)对采掘品的加工、再加工，如炼铁、炼钢、化工生产、石油加工、机器制造、木材加工等，以及电力、自来水、煤气的生产和供应等；(4)对工业品的修理、翻新，如机器设备的修理、交通运输工具(包括小卧车)的修理等。

1984年以前农村的村及村以下办工业归属农业，1984年以后划归工业。

工业统计调查单位为独立核算法人工业企业。

独立核算法人工业企业指从事工业生产经营活动的单位。独立核算法人工业企业应同时具备以下条件：①依法成立，有自己的名称、组织机构和场所，能够承担民事责任；②独立拥有和使用资产，承担负债，有权与其他单位签订合同；③独立核算盈亏，并能够编制资产负债表。

本年鉴中涉及的企业登记注册类型：

国有及国有控股企业　指国有企业加上国有控股企业。国有企业(即原全民所有制工业或国营工业)指企业全部资产归国家所有，并按《中华人民共和国企业法人登记管理条例》规定登记注册的非公司制的经济组织。包括国有企业、国有独资公司和国有联营企业。1957年以前的公私合营和私营工业，后均改造为国营工业，1992年改为国有工业，这部分工业的资料不单独分列时，均包括在国有企业内。国有控股企业是对混合所有制经济的企业进行的“国有控股”分类。它是指这些企业的全部资产中国有资产(股份)相对其他所有者中的任何一个所有者占资(股)最多的企业。该分组反映了国有经济控股情况。

集体企业　指企业资产归集体所有，并按《中华人民共和国企业法人登记管理条例》规定登记注册的经济组织。是社会主义公有制经济的组成部分。包括城乡所有使用集体投资举办的企业，以及部分个人通过集资自愿放弃所有权并依法经工商行政管理机关认定为集体所有制的企业。

股份合作企业　指以合作制为基础，由企业职工共同出资入股，吸收一定比例的社会资产投资组建，实行自主经营，自负盈亏，共同劳动，民主管理，按劳分配与按股分红相结合的一种集体经济组织。

联营企业　指两个及两个以上相同或不同所有制性质的企业法人或事业单位法人，按自愿、平等、互利的原则，共同投资组成的经济组织。联营企业包括：

国有联营企业指国有企业与国有企业间的联营；

集体联营企业指集体企业与集体企业间的联营；

国有与集体联营企业指国有企业与集体企业间的联营。

有限责任公司　指根据《中华人民共和国公司登记管理条例》规定登记注册，由两个以上，五十个以下的股东共同出资，每个股东以其所认缴的出资额对公司承担有限责任，公司以其全部资产对其债务承担责任的经济组织。

有限责任公司包括国有独资公司以及其他有限责任公司。

股份有限公司　指根据《中华人民共和国企业法人登记管理条例》规定登记注册，其全部注册资本由等额股份构成并通过发行股票筹集资本，股东以其认购的股份对公司承担有限责任，公司以其全部资产对其债务承担责任的经济组织。

私营企业　指由自然人投资设立或由自然人控股，以雇佣劳动为基础的营利性经济组织。包括按照《公司法》、《合伙企业法》、《私营企业暂行条例》规定登记注册的私营有限责任公司、私营股份有限公司、私营合伙企业和私营独资企业。

港、澳、台商投资企业　指企业注册登记类型中的港、澳、台资合资、合作、独资经营企业和股份有限公司之和。

外商投资企业 指企业注册登记类型中的中外合资、合作经营企业、外资企业和外商投资股份有限公司之和。

“三资”企业系指港、澳、台商投资企业和外资企业的简称。

轻工业 指主要提供生活消费品和制作手工工具的工业。按其所使用的原料不同,可分为两大类: (1)以农产品为原料的轻工业,是指直接或间接以农产品为基本原料的轻工业。主要包括食品制造、饮料制造、烟草加工、纺织、缝纫、皮革和毛皮制作、造纸以及印刷等工业;(2)以非农产品为原料的轻工业,是指以工业品为原料的轻工业。主要包括文教体育用品、化学药品制造、合成纤维制造、日用化学制品、日用玻璃制品、日用金属制品、手工工具制造、医疗器械制造、文化和办公用机械制造等工业。

重工业 指为国民经济各部门提供物质技术基础的主要生产资料的工业。按其生产性质和产品用途,可以分为下列三类:(1)采掘(伐)工业,是指对自然资源的开采,包括石油开采、煤炭开采、金属矿开采、非金属矿开采等工业;(2)原材料工业,指向国民经济各部门提供基本材料、动力和燃料的工业。包括金属冶炼及加工、炼焦及焦炭、化学、化工原料、水泥、人造板以及电力、石油和煤炭加工等工业;(3)加工工业,是指对工业原材料进行再加工制造的工业。包括装备国民经济各部门的机械设备制造工业、金属结构、水泥制品等工业,以及为农业提供的生产资料如化肥、农药等工业。

根据上述划分原则,修理业中以重工业产品为修理作业对象的划为重工业,反之划为轻工业。

工业总产值

(1)定义:工业总产值是以货币形式表现的,工业企业在一定时期内生产的工业最终产品或提供工业性劳务活动的总价值量。它反映一定时间内工业生产的总规模和总水平。

(2)计算原则:

工业生产的原则,即凡是企业在报告期生产的经检验合格的产品,不管是否在报告期销售,均包括在内。

最终产品的原则,即凡是计入工业总产值的产品,必须是本企业生产的经检验合格的,不需要再进行任何加工的最终产品。如果企业有中间产品(半成品)对外销售,则对外销售的中间产品应视为企业的最终产品。

工厂法原则,即工业总产值是以工业企业作为基本计算(核算)单位,即按企业的最终产品计算工业总产值。按这种方法计算的工业总产值,不允许同一产品价值在企业内部重复计算,不能把企业内部各个车间(分厂)生产的成果相加,但允许企业间的重复计算。

(3)内容及计算方法:1995 年全国工业普查对工业总产值(原规定)的内容及计算原则和方法做了某些修订,修订后的工业总产值(新规定)包括三项内容:即本期生产成品价值、对外加工费收入、在制品半成品期末期初差额价值三部分。

本期生产成品价值:指企业本期生产,并在报告期内不再进行加工,经检验、包装入库的全部工业成品(半产品)价值合计,包括企业生产的自制设备及提供给本企业在建工程、其他非工业部门和福利部门等单位使用的成品价值。本期生产成品价值为按自备原材料生产的产品的数量乘以本期不含增值税(销项税额)的产品实际销售平均单价计算;会计核算中按成本价格转帐的自制设备和自产自用的成品,按成本价格计算生产成品价值。生产成品价值中不包括用定货者来料加工的成品(半产品)价值。

对外加工费收入:指企业在报告期内完成的对外承接的工业品加工(包括用定货者来料加工产品)的加工费收入和对外工业修理作业所取得的加工费收入。对外加工费收入按不含增值税(销项税额)的价格计算,可根据会计“产品销售收入”科目的有关资料取得。

对于本企业对内非工业部门提供的加工修理、设备安装的劳务收入,如果企业会计核算基础较好,能取得这部分资料,而且这部分价值所占比重较大,应包括在对外加工费收入中。

自制半成品在制品期末期初差额价值:指企业报告期在制品期末减期初的差额价值,本指标一般可以从会计核算资料中取得。如果会计产品成本核算中不计算半成品、在制品的成本,则总产值中也不包括这部分价值,反之则包括。

(4)工业总产值统计范围变化和计算方法修订情况:

1984 年以前工业总产值不包括村办工业,村办工业总产值划归农业。1984 年以后工业总产值包括村办工业。

1995 年工业普查对工业总产值计算方法做了修订，即从 1995 年始按新修订(新规定)方法计算工业总产值。新规定与原规定的区别如下：

全价与加工费的计算原则不同：新规定为凡自备原材料，不论其生产繁简程度如何，一律按全价计算工业总产值；凡来料加工，允许按加工费计算工业总产值。原规定则视生产加工的繁简程度不同，规定哪些行业按全价，哪些行业按加工费计算工业总产值。

自制半成品、在产品期末期初差额价值的计算原则不同：新规定要求，凡会计产品成本核算时计算了成本的差额价值，总产值中就应包括，否则可不包括；原规定则按生产周期六个月的界限区分，凡生产周期六个月以上的企业，总产值计算中应包括这部分差额价值，否则可不包括。

计算价格不同：新规定按不含增值税(销项税额)的价格计算；原规定则按含增值税(销项税额)的价格计算。

工业增加值 指工业企业在报告期内以货币表现的工业生产活动的最终成果。

工业增加值有两种计算方法：一是生产法，即工业总产出减去工业中间投入加上应交增值税；二是收入法，即从收入的角度出发，根据生产要素在生产过程中应得到的收入份额计算，具体构成项目有固定资产折旧、劳动者报酬、生产税净额、营业盈余，这种方法也称要素分配法。本年鉴中的工业增加值是以生产法计算的。

生产法工业增加值的计算方法为：

工业增加值=工业总产出-工业中间投入+应交增值税

(1)工业总产出：指工业企业在一定时期内工业生产活动的总成果。工业总产出包括：成品生产价值，对外加工费收入，自制半成品、在产品期末期初差额价值。1995 年后用新规定计算的工业总产值代替。

(2)工业中间投入：指工业企业在工业生产活动中消耗的外购物质产品和对外支付的服务费用。服务费用包括支付给物质生产部门(工业、农业、批发零售贸易业、建筑业、运输邮电业)的服务费用和支付给非物质生产部门(如保险、金融、文化教育、科学研究、医疗卫生、行政管理等)的服务费用。工业中间投入的确定须遵循以下原则：必须从外部购入的，并已计入工业总产出的产品和服务价值；必须是本期投入生产，并一次性消耗掉(包括本期摊销的低值易耗品等)的产品和服务价值。

工业中间投入包括直接材料费用、制造费用中的工业中间投入、管理费用中的工业中间投入、销售费用中的工业中间投入和利息支出五部分。

资产总计 指企业拥有或控制的能以货币计量的经济资源，包括各种财产、债权和其他权利。资产按流动性分为流动资产、长期投资、固定资产、无形资产、递延资产和其他资产。该指标根据企业会计“资产负债表”中“资产总计”项目的期末数增列。

流动资产平均余额 指企业在报告期内全部流动资产的平均余额。

固定资产净值年平均余额 指固定资产净值在报告期内余额的平均数。计算公式为：

固定资产净值年平均余额=1 至 12 月各月月初、月末固定资产净值之和/24

该指标根据“资产负债表”中“固定资产原价”、“累计折旧”指标的期初、期末数计算填列。

固定资产净值指固定资产原价减去历年已提折旧额后的净额。计算公式为：

固定资产净值=固定资产原价-累计折旧

产品销售收入 指企业在报告期内生产的成品、自制半成品和工业性劳务取得的收入。

产品销售成本 指企业在报告期内销售本企业生产的成品、自制半成品和工业性劳务等的实际成本。

产品销售税金及附加 指企业在报告期内销售产品、提供的劳务等主要经营业务应负担的城市维护建设税、消费税、资源税和教育费附加等。

利润总额 指企业生产经营活动的最终成果，是企业在一定时期内实现的盈亏相抵后的利润总额(亏损以“-”号表示)，它等于营业利润加上补贴收入加上投资收益加上营业外净收入再加上以前年度损益调整。

本年应交增值税 指企业在报告期内应交纳的增值税额。它等于本年销项税额加上出口退税加上进项税额转出数减去本年进项税额。小规模纳税企业直接按全年计税销售额乘以征收率计算取得。

年末从业人员平均人数 从业人员是指在企业工作并取得劳动报酬的全部人员数。包括在岗职工、再就业的离退休人员、民办教师及在企业工作的外方人员和港澳台方人员、兼职人员、借用的外单位人员和第二职业者。不包括离开本单位但仍保留劳动关系的职工。

总资产贡献率 反映企业全部资产的获利能力，是企业经营业绩和管理水平的集中体现，是评价和考核企业盈利能力的核心指标。计算公式为：

总资产贡献率(%)=利润总额+税金总额+利息支出/平均资金总额×100%

公式中：税金总额为产品销售税金及附加与应交增值税之和；平均资产总额为期初期末资产之和的算术平均值。

资产负债率 该指标既反映企业经营风险的大小，也反映企业利用债权人提供的资金从事经营活动的能力。计算公式为：

资产负债率(%)=负债总额/资产总额×100%

资产与负债均为报告期期末数。

流动资产周转次数 指一定时期内流动资产完成的周转次数，反映投入工业企业流动资金的周转速度。计算公式为：

流动资产周转资转=产品销售收入/全部流动资产平均余额

公式中：全部流动资产平均余额为期初和期末的流动资产之和的算术平均值。

成本费用利润率 反映企业投入的生产成本及费用的经济效益，同时也反映企业降低成本所取得的经济效益。计算公式为：

成本费用利润(%)=利润总额/成本费用总额×100%

公式中：成本费用总额为产品销售成本、销售费用、管理费用、财务费用之和。

Explanatory Notes on Main Statistical Indicators

Industry refers to the material production sector which is engaged in extraction of natural resources and processing and reprocessing of minerals and agricultural products, including (1) extraction of natural resources, such as mining, salt production (but not including hunting and fishing); (2) processing and reprocessing of farm and sideline produces, such as rice husking, flour milling, wine making, oil pressing, silk reeling, spinning and weaving, and leather making; (3) manufacture of industrial products, such as steel making, iron smelting, chemicals manufacturing, petroleum processing, machine building, timber processing; water and gas production and electricity generation and supply; (4)repairing of industrial products such as the repairing of machinery and means of transport (including cars).

Prior to 1984, the rural industry run by villages and cooperative organizations under village was classified into agriculture. Since 1984, it has been grouped into industry.

Units of industrial statistics survey corporate industrial enterprises with independent accounting system.

Corporate industrial enterprises with independent accounting system refer to enterprises engaging in industrial production activities, which meet the following requirements: ①They are established legally, having their own names, organizations, location, able to take civil liability; ②They possess and use their assets independently, assume liabilities, and are entitled to sign contracts with other units; ③They are financially independent and compile their own balance sheets.

Enterprises covered in the industrial statistics in the Yearbook include following categories by their registration:

State-owned and State-Controlled Enterprises refer to state-owned enterprises plus state-holding enterprises. State-owned enterprises (originally known as state-run enterprises with ownership by the whole society) are non-corporate economic entities registered in accordance with the Regulation of the People's Republic of China on the Management of Registration of Legal Enterprises, where all assets are owned by the state. Included in this category are state-owned enterprises, state-funded corporations and state-owned joint-operation enterprises. Joint state-private industries and private industries, which existed before 1957, were transformed into state-run industries since 1957, and into state-owned industries after 1992. Statistics on those enterprises are included in the state-owned industries instead of grouping them separately. State-controlled enterprises is a sub-classification of enterprises with mixed ownership, referring to enterprises where the percentage of state assets (or shares by the state) is larger than any other single share holder of the same enterprise. This sub-classification illustrates the control of the state over a particular industry.

Collective-owned Enterprises refer to economic entities registered in accordance with the Regulation of the People's Republic of China on the Management of Registration of Legal Enterprises, where assets are owned by collectively. Collective enterprises constitute an integral part of the socialist economy with public ownership. They include urban and rural enterprises invested by collectives, and some enterprises registered in industrial and commercial administration agency as collective units where funds are pulled together by individuals who voluntarily give up their right of ownership.

Share-holding Cooperative Enterprises refer to economic units set up on cooperative basis, with funding partly from members of the enterprise and partly from outside investment, where the operation and management is decided by the members who also participate in the production, and the distribution of income is based both on work (labour input) and on shares (capital input).

Joint-operation enterprises refer to economic units that are established by joint investment by two or more corporate enterprises or institutions of the same or different types of ownership on voluntary, equal and mutual-beneficial basis. They include:

a) state-owned joint-operation enterprises (joint operation between state-owned enterprises);

b) collective joint-operation enterprises (joint operation between collective enterprises; and

c) state-collective joint-operation enterprises (joint operation between state and collective enterprises).

Limited Liability Corporations refer to economic units registered in accordance with the Regulation of the People's Republic of China on the Management of Registration of Corporations, with capitals from 2 to 49 investors, each investor bears limited liability to the corporation depending on his/her holding of shares, and the corporation bears liability to its debt to the maximum of its total assets.

Share-holding Corporations Ltd. refer to economic units registered in accordance with the Regulation of the People's Republic of China on the Management of Registration of Corporate Enterprises, with total registered capitals divided into equal shares and raised through issuing stocks. Each investor bears limited liability to the corporation depending on the holding of shares, and the corporation bears liability to its debt to the maximum of its total assets.

Private Enterprises refer to economic units invested or controlled (by holding the majority of the shares) by natural persons who hire labours for profit-making activities. Included in this category are private limited liability corporations, private share-holding corporations Ltd., private partnership enterprises and private sole investment enterprises registered in accordance with the Corporation Law, Partnership Enterprise Law and Tentative Regulation on Private Enterprises.

Enterprises with Funds form Hong Kong, Macao and Taiwan refers to all industrial enterprises registered as the joint-venture, cooperative, sole (exclusive) investment industrial enterprises and limited liability corporations with funds from Hong Kong, Macao and Taiwan.

Foreign Funded Enterprises refers to all industrial enterprises registered as the joint-venture, cooperative, sole (exclusive) investment industrial enterprises and limited liability corporations with foreign funds.

Light Industry refers to the industry that produces consumer goods and hand tools. It consists of two categories, depending on the materials used:

(1) Industries using farm products as raw materials. These are branches of light industry which directly or indirectly use farm products as basic raw materials, including the manufacture of food and beverages, tobacco processing, textile, clothing, fur and leather manufacturing, paper making, printing, etc.

(2) Industries using non farm products as raw materials. These are branches of light industry which use manufactured goods as raw materials, including the manufacture of cultural, educational articles and sports goods, chemicals, synthetic fiber, chemical products for daily use, glass products for daily use, metal products for daily use, hand tools, medical apparatus and instruments, and the manufacture of cultural and clerical machinery.

Heavy Industry refers to the industry which produces capital goods, and provides various sectors of the national economy with necessary material and technical basis. It consists of the following three branches according to the purpose of production or the use of products:

(1) Mining, quarrying and logging industry refers to the industry that extracts natural resources, including extraction of petroleum, coal, metal and non-metal ores.

(2) Raw materials industry refers to the industry that provides various sectors of the national economy with raw materials, fuels and power. It includes smelting and processing of metals, coking and coke chemistry, chemical materials and building materials such as cement, plywood, and power, petroleum refining and coal dressing.

(3) Manufacturing industry refers to the industry that processes raw materials. It includes machine-building industry which equips sectors of the national economy, industries of metal structure and cement products, industries producing means of agricultural production, such as chemical fertilizers and pesticides.

According to the above principle of classification, the repairing trades, which are engaged primarily in repairing products of heavy industry are classified into heavy industry while these engaged in repairing products of light industry are classified into light industry.

Gross Industrial Output Value

(1) Definition: Gross industrial output value is the total volume of final industrial products produced and industrial services provided during a given period. It reflects the total achievements and overall scale of industrial production during a given period.

(2) Principles for calculation:

Statistics on industrial production follow the principle that all products produced by the enterprises and accepted during the reference period are to be included no matter whether they are sold or not during the reference period.

Determination of final products follow the principle that all products that are included in the calculation of grow industrial output value are the final products of the enterprise which have been accepted through quality check and require no further processing. If an enterprise has intermediate (semi-finished) products to sell, these intermediate products are considered as the final products of the enterprise.

Gross industrial output value is calculated following the principle of factory approach, i.e. industrial enterprise is used as the basic accounting unit in calculating the gross industrial output value. By this approach, value of the same product is not to be double counted, and the output value of different workshops (branch factories) should not be added. However, this approach does not exclude the possibility of double counting between enterprises.

(3) Content and calculation method: The old definition of gross industrial output value was modified during the national industrial census in 1995. The revised (new) definition of gross industrial output value consists of 3 components: value of the finished products during the reference period, income from external processing, and value of change in semi-finished products at the end and at the beginning of the reference period.

Value of the finished products during the reference period: refers to the value of all finished (semi-finished) industrial products that are produced during the reference period without the need for further processing, checked for acceptance, packed and put into the warehouse of the enterprise, including the value of own-produced equipment and the value of products provided to the projects under construction of the enterprise, and to other non-industrial or welfare units. Value of finished products during the reference period is calculated by the quantity of products produced using own materials multiplied by the average unit prices at which products are sold (excluding value-added tax). Own-produced equipment and products produced for own use are value at cost prices as in the case of enterprise accounting. Value of finished products does not include the value of finished products (semi-finished products) that are produced using the materials from the clients who make the orders.

Income from external processing: refers to income from contracted external processing of industrial products (including processing of industrial products using materials from the clients), and the income from industrial repairing work provided to other units. Income from external processing is calculated using information from the item "products sales income" in the enterprise accounting at the prices excluding value-added tax.

For income from services such as processing, repairing and installation of equipment provided to non-industrial units within the enterprise, if the accounting work of the enterprise is good enough to separate it from other records, and the share of such services is significant, it should also be included in the income from external processing.

Value of change in semi-finished products at the end and at the beginning of the reference period: refers to the value of change in semi-finished products at the end and at the beginning of the reference period, which generally can be obtained from accounting records of enterprises. If the enterprise accounting excludes the cost of semi-finished products, then it should not be included in the gross industrial output value, and vice versa.

(4) Changes in the coverage and method of calculation of gross industrial output value

Prior to 1984, the value of rural industry run by villages was classified into agriculture instead of industry. Since 1984, it has been included in the gross industrial output value. Method of calculation for the gross industrial output value was modified in the industrial census in 1995. The difference in the new method as compared with the old one is outlined below:

Principle in using full value vs. processing fee: The new method stipulates that all products produced using own materials are to be calculated with full value in reporting the gross industrial output value irrespective of sophistication of production, and for external processing, it allows calculation using processing fee. In the old method, however, the use of full value or processing fee was determined by the degree of sophistication of production in different branches of industries.

Principle in determining the value of change in semi-finished products: The new method requires that value of the change in semi-finished products should be included in the gross industrial output value if it is included in the accounting record of the enterprise, otherwise it should not be included. By the old method, it is determined by the type of enterprises in terms of production cycle. If the production cycle is over 6 months, the value of change in semi-finished products is included in the gross industrial output value, otherwise it is excluded.

Difference in prices: The new method uses prices excluding value-added tax in the calculation of gross industrial output value, while the old method used prices including value-added tax.

Value-added of Industry refers to the final results of industrial production of industrial enterprises in money terms during the reference period.

Industrial value-added can be calculated by two approaches: the production approach, i.e. gross industrial output value minus intermediate input plus value-added tax, and the income approach, i.e. income for various factors used in the course of production, including depreciation of fixed assets, remuneration of labourers, net of production tax, and operating surplus. Value-added of industry in the Yearbook is calculated by production approach as following:

Value-added of industry = gross industrial output industrial intermediate input + value-added tax

(1) Gross industrial output: refers to the total achievements of industrial production during a given period. Gross industrial output includes value of finished products, income from external processing, and value of change in semi-finished products at the end and at the beginning of the reference period. Since 1995, it was substituted by the gross industrial output value by new method.

(2) Industrial intermediate input: refers to purchased goods and paid services consumed during the industrial production of enterprises. Fees paid for services include fees paid for the services provided by material production sectors (industry, agriculture, wholesale and retail trade, construction, transport, post and telecommunications) and by non-material production sectors (insurance, banking, culture, education, scientific research, health and medical care, public administration, etc.). The determination of industrial intermediate input follows the principle that the goods and services must be purchased from outside and included in the gross industrial output, and that the goods and services are inputted into production and consumed (include low-value consumables) during the reference period.

Industrial intermediate input includes 5 components, namely direct consumption of materials, industrial intermediate input in manufacturing cost, industrial intermediate input in management cost, industrial intermediate input in marketing cost and expenditure on interest.

Total Assets refer to all economic resources, in monetary terms, that is owned or controlled by enterprises, including properties, creditors equity and other economic rights of all forms. Classified by the degree of equitability, total assets include circulating assets, long-term investment, fixed assets, intangible assets and deferred assets, and other assets. Data on this indicator can be obtained by the year-end figures of total assets in the Assets and Liability Table of accounting records of enterprises.

Annual Average Value of Working Capitals refers to the average value of all working capitals of the enterprise during the reference period.

Annual Average of Net Value of Fixed Assets refer to average of the net value of fixed assets during the reference period, calculated with the following formula:

Annual Average of Net Value of Fixed Assets = sum of net value of fixed assets at the beginning and at the end of each month from January to December / 24.

Information on this indicator can be obtained from the beginning and ending figures of the original value of fixed assets and cumulative depreciation from the Assets and Liability Table of enterprises.

Net value of fixed assets refers to the original value of fixed assets minus depreciation over the years, i.e.:

Net value of fixed assets = original value of fixed assets cumulative depreciation

Sales Revenue of Industrial Products refers to the revenue from the sales of finished and semi-finished products and from rendering of industrial services by industrial enterprises during the reference period.

Cost of Industrial Products Sold refers to the actual cost of finished and semi-finished products sold and industrial services rendered by industrial enterprises during the reference period.

Tax and Extra Charges on Sales of Products refer to the tax on city maintenance and construction, consumption tax, resources tax and extra charges for education, which should be borne by the enterprises in selling products and providing industrial services during the reference period.

Total Profits refer to the final achievements of production and operation of the enterprises, represented by the total profits after deducting losses (loss is expressed by the negative figure). It is the sum of profits from operation, income from subsidies, investment earnings, net income from activities other than operation, and adjustment of profits and losses of previous years.

Value-added Tax Payable refers to the amount of the value-added tax which should be paid by the enterprises during the reference period. It is the sum of tax on sales, export rebate, and transferred tax on purchases of the current year, minus the tax on purchases of the current year. Value–added tax payable of small–size enterprises is determined by the taxable sales of the year multiplied by the tax rate.

Average Annual Number of Employed Persons Employed persons refer to all those who are employed in enterprises and receive remunerations therefrom, including currently working employees, retirees who are re–employed, teachers of local–run schools, as well as foreigners, staff from Hong Kong, Macao and Taiwan, part–time employees and persons with second job who are employed by the enterprise, and employees of other units temporarily working in the enterprises, but excluding former employees who left the enterprise with their employment records still kept by the enterprises.

Average number of employed persons refers to the number of employees everyday during the reference period, calculated with the following formula:

Monthly average number = sum of actual employees everyday in reference month/number of calendar dates in reference month

Quarterly average number = sum of monthly average number in reference quarter/3

Annual average number = sum of monthly average number in reference year/12

Ratio of Profits, Taxes and Interests to Average Assets reflects the profit–making capability of all assets of the enterprise and is a key indicator manifesting the performance and management and evaluating the profit–making potential of the enterprise. It is calculated as follows:

Ratio of Profits, Taxes and Interests to Average Assets (%) = [(total profits + total taxes + interest payment) / average assets]×100%

In the above formula, total taxes is the sum of tax and extra charges on the sales of products and value–added tax payable; and average assets is the arithmetic mean of the sum of beginning assets and ending assets.

Ratio of Debts to Assets reflect both the operation risk and the capability of the enterprise in making use of the capital from the creditors. It is calculated as follows:

Ratio of Debts to Assets (%) = (total debts / total assets)×100%

Both assets and debts are figures at the end of the reference period.

Turnover of Working Capital refers to the number of times of turnover of working capital in a given period of time, which reflects the speed of the turnover of working capital of industrial enterprises, and is calculated as follows:

Turnover of Working Capital=(sales revenue of products) / (average balance of total working capital)

In the above formula, average balance of total working capital refers to the arithmetic mean of the sum of working capital at the beginning and at the end of the reference period.

Ratio of Profits to Total Industrial Costs refers to the ratio of profits realized in a given period to the total costs in the same period, which reflects the economic efficiency of input cost and is calculated as follows:

Ratio of Profits to Total Industrial Cost(%)=(total profits/ total costs)×100%

Total costs in the above formula is the sum of cost of products sold, marketing cost, management cost and financial cost.

8

Eight

建筑业

Construction

建筑业增加值及指数

Value-added of Construction and Its Indices

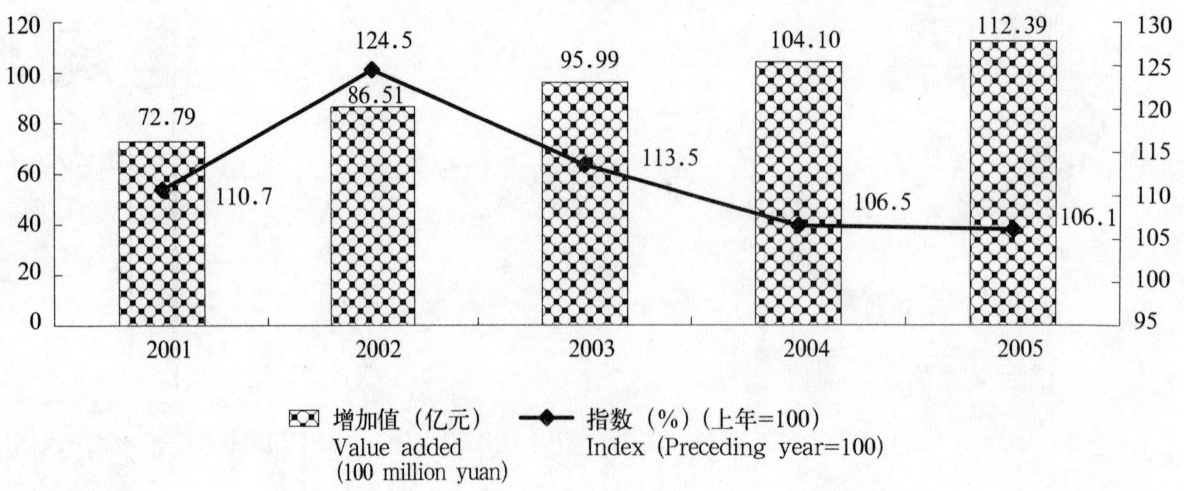

房屋施工面积、竣工面积（万平方米）

Floor Spale of Buildings Under Conseruction and Building Completed (10000 sq.m)

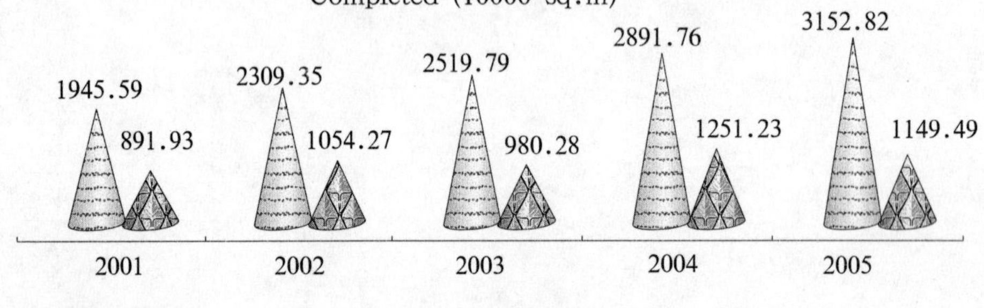

建筑业企业主要效益指标

Main Indicators on Economic Efficiency of Construction Enterprises

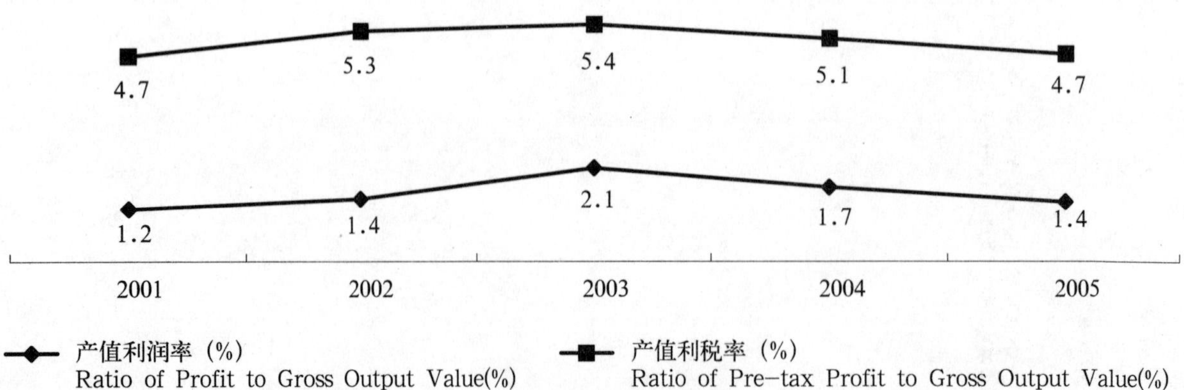

8-1 "十五"时期各年建筑业企业主要经济指标

Main Economic Indicators on Construction Enterprises of Each Year in "Tenth Five-year Plan" Period

指 标	Item	2000	2001	2002	2003	2004	2005
建筑业企业个数（个）	Number of ConstructionEnterprises (unit)	620	633	590	541	641	634
从业人员（万人）	Number of Persons Engaged(10000 persons)	22.3	25.91	27.14	29.33	30.04	30.64
自有固定资产原价（亿元）	Fixed Assets Owned(original value) (100 million yuan)	42.44	52.97	65.77	66.24	71.26	74.06
自有固定资产净价	Fixed Assets Owned(net value)	29.73	38.53	52.37	56.13	49.46	52.14
自有机械设备台数（万台）	Number of Machinery and Equipment Owned (10000 sets)	5.42	5.79	7.15	6.84	7.52	7.30
自有机械设备净值（亿元）	Net Value of Machinery and Equipment Owned (100 million yuan)	11.56	13.64	21.58	22.74	23.97	22.89
自有机械设备总功率(万千瓦)	Total Power of Machinery and Equipment Ownec (10000kw)	88.01	98.08	114.38	117.51	122.56	123.59
建筑业总产值（亿元）	Gross Output Value of Construction (100 million yuan)	109.06	150.2	181.12	212.29	255.45	271.23
建筑业增加值	Value Added of Construction	24.67	33.16	39.97	48.69	55.74	
#本年固定资产折旧	Depreciation of Fixed Assets	2.18	3.08	3.30	3.38	3.90	
应付工资	Main Business Wages Payable	14.31	18.81	22.70	27.46	29.58	
应付福利费	Main Business Welfare Expenses Payable	1.61	2.03	2.63	3.11	2.71	
工程结算税金及附加	Taxes and Extra Charges on Project Settle Accounts	3.46	4.85	6.48	6.51	8.32	
管理费用中的税金	Taxes in Management Expenses	0.26	0.53	0.48	0.46	0.36	
营业利润	Operating Profits	1.7	2.5	2.51	5.93	4.58	
房屋施工面积（万平方米）	Floor Space of Buildings under Construction (10000 sq.m)	1792.5	1945.6	2309.4	2519.8	2891.76	3152.8
竣工面积	Floor Space of Buildings Completed	824.0	891.9	1054.3	980.3	1251.2	1149.5
利润总额（亿元）	Total Profits(100 million yuan)	0.99	1.73	2.60	4.55	4.35	3.71
税金总额	Total Taxes	3.71	5.38	6.95	6.96	8.68	9.17
劳动生产率	Overall Labor Productivity						
按总产值计算（元/人）	In Terms of Gross Output Value(yuan/person)	49713	58942	66747	72152	91658	97411
按增加值计算	In Terms of Value-added	11243	13013	14730	16548	20000	
技术装备率	Value of Machines Per Laborer	5270	5354	7952	7754	7979	7471
动力装备率（千瓦/人）	Power of Machines Per Laborer(kw/person)	4.01	3.85	4.21	4.01	4.08	4.03
房屋建筑面积竣工率（%）	Ratio of Floor Space of Buildings Completed(%)	46.0	45.8	45.7	38.9	43.3	36.5
产值利润率	Ratio of Profit to Gross Output Value	0.9	1.2	1.4	2.1	1.7	1.4
产值利税率	Ratio of Pre-tax Profit to Gross Output Value	4.3	4.7	5.3	5.4	5.1	4.7

8-2 建筑企业生

Main Indicators on

指标	Item	企业个数（个）Number of Constru-stion Enterp-rises (unit)	年末从业人员（万人）Number of Persons Engaged (10000 persons)	签订合同额（万元）Value ofSigned Contract (10000 yuan)	本年新签合同额 New Value of Signed Contract in this year
总计	**Total**	**634**	**30.64**	**5127516**	**2726836**
#国有及国有控股	Enterprises Where State Held The Controlling Share	155	19.23	4143935	2074453
#施工总承包企业	Total Contracted Enterprises of Construction	480	28.97	5003339	2643567
专业承包企业	Special Contracted Enterprises of Construction	154	1.58	124178	83269
按登记注册类型分组	By Registration				
#内资企业	Domestic Funded	630	30.63	5120868	2720508
#国有企业	State-owned	128	17.38	3680324	1816678
集体企业	Collective-owned	138	3.39	237106	144864
股份有限公司	Company Limited with Share Holding	31	0.16	77664	56416
私营企业	Private Enterprises	123	2.44	186031	122491
港、澳、台商投资企业	Funded by Enterprises from Hong Kong,Macao and Taiwan	4	0.01	6648	6328
按国民经济行业分组	By Sector				
房屋和土木工程建筑业	Building and Construction	484	28.17	4744941	2506056
房屋工程建筑	Building Engineering Construction	400	19.16	2235406	1474743
土木工程建筑	Civil Engineering Construction	84	9.01	2509536	1031314
建筑安装业	Construction and Installation	64	1.53	326127	181854
建筑装饰业	Construction and Decoration	63	0.39	24916	17378
其他建筑业	Other Construction	23	0.55	31532	21547

产主要指标(2005)

Construction Enterprises(2005)

建筑业总产值(万元) Total Output Value of Construction(10000 yuan)				房屋建筑施工面积(万平方米) Floor Space of Buildings under Construction (10000 sq.m)			自有机械设备年末净值(万元) Net Value of Machineryand Equipment Owned (10000yuan)	自有机械设备年末总台数(台) Number of Machinery and Equipment Owned (year-end) (unit)	自有机械设备年末总功率(万千瓦) Total Power of Machinery and Equipment Owned (year-end) (10000 kw)
合计Total Output Value	#在省外完成的产值 Value of construction which fulfiued outside of Guizhou Provinle	#建筑工程 Output Value of Construction	#安装工程 Output Value of Instal-lation		#本年新开工面积 Started this year	#实行投标承包面积 Verified Eligible Areaof the First Time			
2712254	**588272**	**2194544**	**467312**	**3152.82**	**1500.32**	**2559.71**	**228935**	**72991**	**123.59**
2078816	585534	1664875	374800	1962.49	818.75	1639.93	151342	31131	75.81
2599626	584852	2127955	424943	3125.43	1484.80	2543.89	218326	67664	117.74
112628	3420	66589	42368	27.38	15.52	15.82	10608	5327	5.85
2711350	588131	2193640	467312	3151.72	1499.22	2558.61	228749	72963	123.43
1835895	502689	1428712	369605	1758.16	729.75	1481.90	128332	28054	66.20
161508	340	144522	14214	393.14	206.11	342.42	21441	13490	12.82
57259		54636	673	68.01	46.41	59.07	6302	4330	4.30
116957	300	102230	12378	281.91	157.83	199.44	16378	9275	7.58
904	141	904		1.10	1.10	1.10	186	28	0.15
2441441	483770	2077878	318636	3068.10	1484.95	2500.00	210728	66899	112.12
1302078	236725	1251764	27822	2908.43	1410.61	2349.12	110260	49632	65.09
1139363	247046	826114	290814	159.67	74.34	150.88	100468	17267	47.03
230833	100456	79671	147955	83.55	15.37	58.55	13855	4342	8.75
19548	4040	18084	721				523	970	0.52
20432	5	18911		1.17		1.17	3828	780	2.19

8-3 建筑企业主

Main Financing Indicators of

指 标	Item	年末资产负债 Assets		
		资产合计 Total Assets	流动资产小 计 Liquid Assets	固定资产小 计 Fixed Assets
总 计	**Total**	**2902824**	**2049423**	**605970**
#国有及国有控股	State-owned Enterprises and Joint-ownership Enterprises Where State Held The Controlling Share	2075412	15292660	379506
#施工总承包企业	Total Contracted Enterprises of Construction	2683930	18967295	567751
专业承包企业	Special Contracted Enterprises of Construction	218894	1526939	38219
按登记注册类型分组	**By Registration**			
#内资企业	Domestic Funded	2892533	20405082	604933
#国有企业	State-owned	1846661	13809044	321039
集体企业	Collective-owned	210658	1258659	67075
股份有限公司	Company Limited with Share Holding	69970	504787	13232
私营企业	Private Enterprises	165344	983868	55949
港、澳、台商投资企业	Funded by Enterprises from Hong Kong,Macao and Taiwan	10291	89152	1036
按国民经济行业分组	**By Sector**			
房屋和土木工程建筑业	Building and Construction	2565782	18033191	553200
房屋工程建筑	Building Engineering Construction	1378452	9304477	318758
土木工程建筑	Civil Engineering Construction	1187330	8728714	234442
建筑安装业	Construction and Installation	255577	1821645	40532
建筑装饰业	Construction and Decoration	39513	332029	3967
其他建筑业	Other Construction	41952	307369	8271

要财务指标(2005)

Construction Enterprises(2005)

单位：万元(10000 yuan)

and Liabilities(year-end)		所有者权益合计 Creditors Equity	损益及分配 Loss-profit and Allocation			
负债合计 Total liabilities	流动负债小计 Liquid Liabilities		工程结算收入 Revenue of Project Settlement Accounts	其他业务收入 Other Revenue from Business	营业利润 Operating Profits	利润总额 Total Profits
1949294	**1803088**	**762285**	**2653271**	**43149**	**35300**	**37149**
1562269	1434529	388322	2028788	32703	13902	14120
1819471	1677277	864459	2547484	39161	33793	34364
129824	125811	89070	105788	3988	1507	2785
1943808	1797602	948725	2652536	43135	35567	37415
1395072	1290440	451589	1769991	23258	6052	7066
114798	109073	95860	139951	2761	692	725
34325	33041	35645	47090	312	3711	3841
69228	66717	96116	108066	750	3105	3730
5487	5487	4804	735	14	-268	-266
1742908	1603160	822874	2398664	35351	28828	29526
848922	820239	529530	1272818	21498	18577	17872
893986	782921	293344	1125846	13853	10251	11655
163549	157417	92028	215402	6338	6418	7441
20440	20336	19072	18789	1175	-444	-460
22397	22175	19556	20416	285	497	641

8-4 建筑企业房屋

Main Indicators of

指标	Item	竣工面积（平方米）Floor Spale of			
		合计 Total	#厂房、仓库 Workshop storehouse	#住宅 Residential Buildings	#教育用房 Educational Buildings
总计	**Total**	**11494851**	**1230628**	**5935809**	**1317346**
#国有及国有控股	State-owned Enterprises and Joint-ownership Enterprises Where State Held The Controlling Share	5905564	1034858	2654361	357048
#施工总承包企业	Total Contracted Enterprises of Construction	11330754	1216228	5851298	1309946
专业承包企业	Special Contracted Enterprises of Construction	164097	14400	84511	7400
按登记注册类型分组	**By Registration**				
#内资企业	Domestic Funded	11494851	1230628	5935809	1317346
#国有企业	State-owned	5240008	853932	2311623	325270
集体企业	Collective-owned	2023381	125060	1152643	368166
股份有限公司	Company Limited with Share Holding	397138	1935	191975	94692
私营企业	Private Enterprises	1117837	22055	703017	157180
按国民经济行业分组	**By Sector**				
房屋和土木工程建筑业	Building and Construction	11233363	1195334	5784733	1280341
房屋工程建筑	Building Engineering Construction	10606478	825210	5556606	1270686
土木工程建筑	Civil Engineering Construction	626885	370124	228127	9655
建筑安装业	Construction and Installation	261488	35294	151076	37005

建筑完成情况(2005)

Construction Enterprises(2005)

Completed(sq.m)		总造价(元/平方米) Value of Buildings Completed (yuans/q.m)					
#卫生医疗用房 Medical Buildings	#科研用房 Scientific and Research Buildings	合计 Total	#厂房、仓库 Workshop storehouse	#住宅 Residential Buildings	#教育用房 Educational Buildings	#卫生医疗用房 Medical Buildings	#科研用房 Scientific and Research Buildings
246937	**23731**	**672**	**1382**	**537**	**501**	**403**	**808**
152357	14673	861	1536	623	677	345	903
241973	23731	674	1390	537	501	399	808
4964		586	713	526	489	580	
246937	23731	672	1382	537	501	403	808
152357	14673	863	1645	600	660	345	903
48798	1899	472	586	471	430	513	465
8387	6126	527	381	516	443	479	705
10474		481	540	466	454	422	
233037	23731	674	1391	541	492	391	808
233037	23731	605	803	540	492	391	808
		1835	2700	567	579		
13900		602	1092	412	813	599	

主要统计指标解释

建筑业统计单位 指从事房屋、构筑物建造和设备安装活动的法人企业。建筑业法人企业应同时具备的条件是:①依法成立,有自己的名称、组织机构和场所,能够承担民事责任;②独立拥有和使用资产,承担负债,有权与其他单位签订合同;③独立核算盈亏,能够编制资产负债表。

建筑业总产值(即自行完成施工产值) 是以货币表现的建筑安装企业在一定时期内生产的建筑业产品的总和。建筑业总产值包括:

(1)建筑工程产值:指列入建筑工程预算内的各种工程价值。

(2)设备安装工程产值:指设备安装工程价值,不包括被安装设备本身价值。

(3)房屋、构筑物修理产值:指房屋、构筑物修理所完成的价值,但不包括被修理房屋、构筑物本身的价值和生产设备的修理价值。

(4)非标准设备制造产值:指加工制造没有定型的、非标准的生产设备的加工费和原材料价值,以及附属加工厂为本企业承建工程制作的非标准设备的价值。

建筑业增加值 指建筑业企业在报告期内以货币表现的建筑业生产经营活动的最终成果。目前建筑业增加值采用分配法(收入法)计算,即从收入的角度出发,根据生产要素在生产过程中应得的收入份额计算。具体计算公式为:

建筑业增加值=本年提取的固定资产折旧+应付工资+应付福利费+管理费用中的劳动待业保险金、税金+工程结算税金及附加+工程结算利润

房屋建筑施工面积 指在报告期内施过工的全部房屋建筑面积,包括本期新开工的房屋面积、上期施工跨入本期继续施工的房屋面积、上期停缓建在本期恢复施工的房屋面积、本期竣工的房屋面积及本期施工后又停缓建的房屋面积。

房屋建筑竣工面积 指在报告期内房屋建筑按照设计要求全部完工,达到了住人和使用条件,经验收鉴定合格,正式移交使用单位的房屋建筑面积。

工程结算收入 指企业承包工程实现的工程价款结算收入,以及向发包单位收取的除工程价款以外的按规定列作营业收入的各种款项,如临时设施费、劳动保险费、施工机械调迁费等以及向发包单位收取的各种索赔款。

工程结算利润 指已结算工程实现的利润,如亏损以"–"号表示。计算公式为:

工程结算利润=工程结算收入–工程结算成本–工程结算税金及附加

企业总收入 指与企业生产经营直接有关的各项收入,包括工程结算收入和其他业务收入。计算公式为:

企业总收入=工程结算收入+其他业务收入

Explanatory Notes on Main Statistical Indicators

Statistical Unit in Construction refers to corporate enterprise engaged in the construction of buildings and structures and in the installation of equipment.A corporate construction enterprise should meet the following 3 requirements: ①being set up in line with relevant legal basis,having its full name,organization and location,and capable of taking civil liabilities; ②independently possessing and using its assets and assuming its liabilities,and entitled to sign contracts with other institutions;and ③ making independent accounts of its profits and losses,and capable of compiling its own balance sheet.

Gross Output Value of Construction (Output Value of Projects Under Construction) refers to total of construction products, expressed in money terms, completed by construction and installation enterprises during a given period of time. It includes:

(1)Output value of construction projects,that is the value of projects covered by the project budgets;

(2)Output value of installation projects,that is the value of the installation of equipment, (excluding the value of the equipment to be installed);

(3)Output value of repair of buildings and structures,that is the value created through the repairs of buildings or structures,but does not include the value of buildings or structures being repaired and the value of the repair of production equipment;

(4)Output value of manufactured non-standard equipment,that is the value of non-standard production equipment (including raw materials and manufacturing cost) made for the construction project,and the equipment manufactured by subsidiary workshops.

Value-added of Construction refers to the final result of the activities of production and management of construction in monetary terms in the reference period. At present, the value-added of construction is calculated with the income approach. In other words, it is the sum of income of various production factors in the production process. The formula is as follows:

Value-added of construction=depreciation of fixed assets in the year+wages payable+welfare expenses payable+insurance premium and tax for waiting for employment in the administrative expenses +taxes and surcharges on project settlement+profit gained from project settlement.

Floor Space of Buildings Under Construction refers to floor space of buildings under construction during the reference period,including newly started buildings,buildings started earlier and continued during the reference period,and buildings suspended earlier but restarted during the reference period, buildings completed during the reference period, and buildings under construction and then suspended during the reference period.

Floor Space of Buildings Completed refers to the floor space of buildings that are completed in the reference period in accordance with the requirements of the design, up to the standard for putting them into use, and have been checked and accepted by concerned departments as qualified ones.

Income from Settlement of Projects refers to the income received by the construction enterprise from the contracted project through settlement procedures, and other charges to the contractoree as operational costs in addition to the value of the project,such as temporary facility fee,labour insurance premium,moving cost of construction equipment,as well as various types of claims to the contractee.

Profit from Settlement of Projects refers to profit realized through settled projects. It is calculated with the following formula:

Profit from Settlement of Projects=Income from Settlement of Projects-Settled Cost-Settled Taxes and Other Cost

Total Revenue of Enterprises refers to the sum of income from production and operation of enterprises, including income from settlement of projects and other operational income, namely:

Total Revenue of Enterprises=Income from Settlement of Projects+Other Operational Income.

9 交通运输、邮电通信

Transportation, Postal and Telecommunication Services

Nine

民用汽车拥有量（万辆）
Number of Civil Motor Vehicles Owned (10000 units)

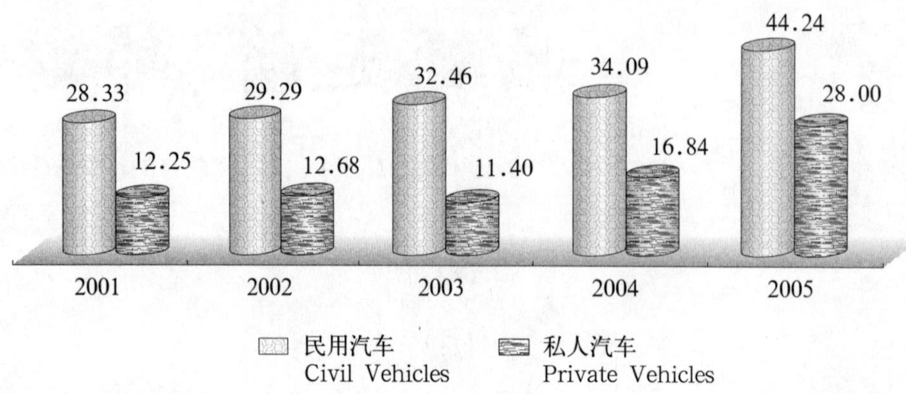

旅客、货物周转量
Passenger-Kilometers and Freight Ton-Kilometers

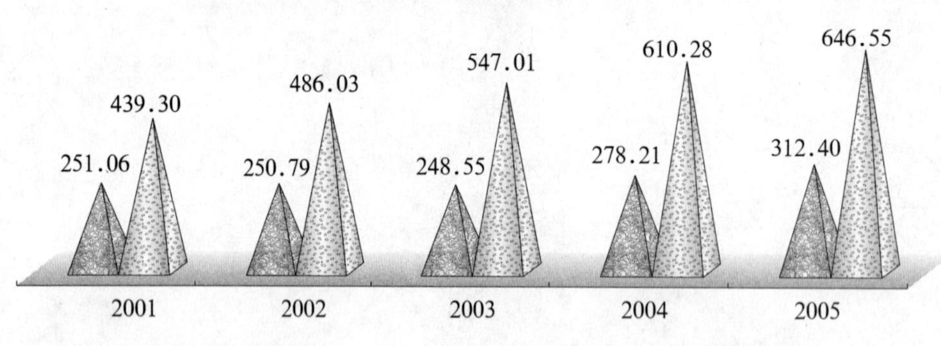

旅客周转量总计(亿人公里)
Passenger-Kilometers
(100 million passenger-km)

货物周转量总计（亿吨公里）
Total Freight Ton-Kilometers
(100 million ton-km)

	2000年	2005年
年末固定电话用户数（万户） Number of Telephone Subscribers at Year-end (10000 subscribers)	157.30	466.49
移动电话用户（万户） Number of Mobile Telephone Subscribers(10000 subscribers)	78.50	509.42
互联网上网人数（万人） Number of Subscribers of Internet Service(10000 persons)	18	109
电话普及率（部/百人） Popularization Rate of Telephone (set/100 persons)	6.36	25.00
国内特快专递（万件） Pieces of Express Mail Services inside Nation (10000 pcs)	151.4	394.0
交换机总容量（万门） Capacity of Telephone Exchanges(10000 line)	385.05	1369.60

9-1 "十五"时期各年境内运输线路长度

Length of Transport Routes of Each Year in "Tenth-Five-Year Plan" Period

单位：公里(km)

指 标	Item	2000	2001	2002	2003	2004	2005	2005年比2004年增长(%) Increase Rate in 2005 over 2004(%)
铁路营业里程	**Length of Railways in Operation**	**1642**	**1644**	**1893**	**1900**	**1891**	**1986**	**5.0**
#复线里程	Double-tracking Length	66	491	493	493	493	493	持平
公路线路里程	**Total Length of Highways**	**34643**	**34617**	**44220**	**45304**	**46128**	**46893**	**1.7**
#等级路	Expressway and Class I to IV Highways	17034	24625	30504	32352	33831	35447	4.8
#高 速	Express-way	258	311	311	323	413	577	39.7
一 级	First Class	26	71	73	87	85	92	8.2
二 级	Second Class	718	1797	2191	2616	2590	2629	1.5
#等外路	Highway Below Class IV	17609	9992	13716	12952	12296	11447	-6.9
内河航道里程	**Length of Navigable Inland Waterways**	**2132**	**2132**	**2132**	**3322**	**3322**	**3322**	**持平**

9-2 "十五"时期各年民用汽车拥有量

Possession of Civil Vehicles of Each Year in "Tenth-Five-Year Plan" Period

单位：万辆(10000 unit)

指 标	Item	2000	2001	2002	2003	2004	2005	2005年比2004年增长(%) Increase Rate in 2005 over 2004(%)
民用汽车合计	**Total**	**26.26**	**28.33**	**29.29**	**32.46**	**34.09**	**44.24**	**29.8**
载客汽车	Passenger Vehicles	11.12	12.58	15.66	17.84	19.27	26.25	36.2
载货汽车	Trucks	14.43	15.04	13.49	14.46	14.57	17.56	20.6
私人汽车合计	Total of Private Vehicles	10.49	12.25	12.68	11.40	16.84	28.00	66.3

9-3 “十五”时期各年旅客运量及周转量

Passenger Traffic and Passenger-Kilometers of Each Year in “Tenth-Five-Year Plan” Period

指　标	Item	2000	2001	2002	2003	2004	2005	2005年比2004年增长(%) Increase Rate in 2005 over 2004(%)
旅客运量总计(万人)	**Total Passenger Traffic (10000 persons)**	**53116**	**54665**	**55980**	**55074**	**58707**	**64450**	**9.8**
铁　路	Railways	2251	2017	1947	1796	1855	2191	18.1
公　路	Highways	50397	52154	53478	52695	56077	61414	9.5
水　运	Waterways	468	494	555	583	775	845	9.0
旅客周转量总计(亿人公里)	**Passenger-Kilometers (100 million passenger-km)**	**238.36**	**251.06**	**250.79**	**248.55**	**278.21**	**312.4**	**12.3**
铁　路	Railways	120.79	124.22	116.10	112.08	125.87	145.71	15.8
公　路	Highways	116.54	125.76	133.60	135.31	150.79	164.91	9.4
水　运	Waterways	1.03	1.08	1.09	1.16	1.55	1.78	14.8
民航旅客吞吐量(万人)	**Volume of Freight Handled in Civil Aviation (10000 persons)**	**138.95**	**152.99**	**174.88**	**197.68**	**278.67**	**307.75**	**10.4**

9-4 “十五”时期各年货物运输量及周转量

Freight Traffic and Ton-Kilometers of Each Year in “Tenth-Five-Year Plan” Period

指　标	Item	2000	2001	2002	2003	2004	2005	2005年比2004年增长(%) Increase Rate in 2005 over 2004(%)
货物运输量总计(万吨)	**Total Freight Traffic (10000 tons)**	**15615**	**16344**	**17399**	**18224**	**19439**	**21771**	**12.0**
铁　路	Railways	3577	3875	4356	4971	5504	6169	12.1
公　路	Highways	11684	12114	12685	12886	13541	15082	11.4
水　运	Waterways	354	355	358	367	394	520	32.0
货物周转量总计(亿吨公里)	**Total Freight Ton-Kilometers (100 million ton-km)**	**404.07**	**439.3**	**486.03**	**547.01**	**610.28**	**646.55**	**5.9**
铁　路	Railways	334.11	364.71	407.26	465.92	520.10	544.31	4.7
公　路	Highways	65.86	70.36	74.25	76.63	84.27	94.15	11.7
水　运	Waterways	4.10	4.23	4.52	4.46	5.91	8.09	36.9
民航货邮吞吐量(万吨)	**Civil Aviation(10000 tons)**	**2.02**	**2.33**	**3.06**	**3.29**	**3.00**	**3.33**	**11.0**

9-5 “十五”时期各年电信主要指标

Major Indicators of Telecommunications of Each Year in “Tenth-Five-Year Plan” Period

指 标	Item	2000	2001	2002	2003	2004	2005	2005年比2004年增长(%) Increase Rate in 2005 over 2004(%)
年末固定电话用户数（万户）	Number of Telephone Subscribers at Year-end(10000 subscribers)	157.3	211.28	274.32	332.4	387.6	466.49	20.4
#农话用户数	Number of Rural Telephone Subscribers	26.62	44.6	70.1	97.5	106.5	138.23	29.8
城市电话用户	Number of Local(urban)Telephone Subscribers	127.1	166.7	204.2	234.8	281	328.26	16.8
#公 用	Number of Public Telephone Subscribers	4.45	5.32	8.98	19.02	27.19	38.4	41.2
#住宅电话	Number of Residential Telephone Subscribers	124.77	168.46	222.82	229.2	299.3	360.69	20.5
净增电话用户	Telephone Users Added	96	148.98	140.04	142.28	164.1	148.31	-9.6
移动电话用户	Number of Mobile Telephone Subscribers	78.5	168.9	246.9	331.1	440	509.42	15.8
数字数据网用户	Digital and Data Users					3261	5830	78.8
互联网上网人数（万人）	Number of Subscribers of Internet Service(10000 persons)	18	20.22	47.3	83.1	98	109	11.2
电话普及率(部/百人)	Popularization Rate of Telephone (set/100 persons)	6.36	11.11	13.90	17.40	21.40	25.00	16.8
住宅电话普及率(部/百户)	Popularization Rate of Household Telephone(set/100 subscribers)	13.4	16.54	21.25	22.39	29.99	31.81	6.1
国内长途电话(万次)	Number of Long Distance Telephone Calls Inside Country (10000 person-time)	25238.9	22623.9	20121.6	15986.4	67325	77609	15.3
国际及港澳长途电话（万次）	Number of Long Distance Telephone Calls outside Country or to Macao、Hong Kong(10000 person-time)	36.0	38.9	46.8	27.34	148.63	155.79	4.8

9-6 “十五”时期各年邮政主要指标

Major Indicators of Postal Routes of Each Year in “Tenth-Five-Year Plan” Period

指 标	Item	2000	2001	2002	2003	2004	2005	2005年比2004年增长(%) Increase Rate in 2005 over 2004(%)
邮电局所总数（处）	Number of Post and Telecommunication Offices(unit)	2515	3407	5871	7491	7860	9138	16.3
邮路总长度（公里）	Number of Postal Routes(km)	63538	67387	64598	67472	65374	64926	-0.7
#汽车邮路	Number of Highway Postal Routes(km)	25546	27642	25773	26693	26463	24541	-7.3
铁路邮路	Number of Railways Postal Routes(km)	6768	6426	6426	6848	6385	6385	持平
交换机总容量（万门）	Capacity of Telephone Exchanges (10000 line)	385.05	586.86	794.30	969.60	1149.10	1369.60	19.2
邮电业务总量（亿元）	Business Volume of Post and Telecommunications(100 million yuan)	40.92	47.57	73.07	101.50	131.23	174.22	32.8
函件（万件）	Number of Letters(100 million pcs)	6943	6221	9021	7852	6956	5728	-17.7
报刊、杂志累计订销数（万份）	Issue of Newspapers and Magazines (10000 copies)	25937	23702	25143	27816	26744	28283	5.8
国内特快专递（万件）	Pieces of Express Mail Servicesinside Nation(10000 pcs)	151.4	115.5	155.0	252.6	326.0	394.0	20.9
国际特快专递	Pieces of Express Mail Servicesoutside Nation(10 000 pcs)	0.6	0.5	0.5	0.6	0.7	0.6	-14.3
邮政储蓄期末余额(亿元)	Post Deposits at the Year-end (100 million yuan)	45.2	59.4	72.0	88.7	109.3	148.4	35.8
集邮业务（万枚）	Stamps for Collection(10000 pcs)	5994	3666	1744	1031	1089	882	-19.1
长话业务电路（2M）	Long Distance Cable Lines(2M)	932	2433	2494	3664	9230	12033	30.4

9-7 “十五”时期各年邮电企业主要财务指标

Major Financial Indicators of Post and Telecommunication Enterprises of Each Year in “Tenth-Five-Year Plan” Period

单位：万元(10000 yuan)

指 标	Item	2000	2001	2002	2003	2004	2005	2005年比2004年增长(%) Increase Rate in 2005 over 2004(%)
全部邮电企业	Total Post and Telecommunication Enterprises							
业务收入	Revenue	351033	406638	502158	566641	678894	832559	22.6
业务支出	Business Expenditure	360113	342202	457069	598077	603424	652481	8.1
营业税金及附加费	Pre-tax and Related Payment	12041	13428	16476	18565	22148	25277	14.1

主要统计指标解释

铁路营业里程 又称营业长度(包括正式营业和临时营业里程),指办理客货运输业务的铁路正线总长度。凡是全线或部分建成双线及以上的线路,以第一线的实际长度计算;复线、站线、段管线、岔线和特殊用途线以及不计算运费的联络线都不计算营业里程。铁路营业里程是反映铁路运输业基础设施发展水平的重要指标,也是计算客货周转量、运输密度和机车车辆运用效率等指标的基础资料。

公路里程 指在一定时期内实际达到《公路工程[WTBZ]技术标准 JTJ01-88》规定的等级公路,并经公路主管部门正式验收交付使用的公路里程数。包括大中城市的郊区公路以及通过小城镇街道部分的公路里程和桥梁、渡口的长度,不包括大中城市的街道、厂矿、林区生产用道和农业生产用道的里程。两条或多条公路共同经由同一路段,只计算一次,不得重复计算里程长度。

内河航道里程 也称内河通航里程,指在一定时期内,能通航运输船舶及排筏的天然河流、湖泊水库、运河及通航渠道的长度。包括全年季节性通航累计三个月以上的航道,不包括仅供零散流放竹、木排的河道。

民用航空航线里程 指民航运输定期班机飞行的航线长度的总和。航线长度按机场之间的距离计算,通常有两种计算方法:一是将每条航线长度相加称为重复计算航线里程;一是将两线或两条以上航线经过同一区段里程,只计算一次航线长度称为不重复计算航线里程,一般常用的是后者。

货(客)运量 指在一定时期内,各种运输工具实际运送的货物(旅客)数量。货运按吨计算,客运按人计算。货物不论运输距离长短、货物类别,均按实际重量统计。旅客不论行程远近或票价多少,均按一人一次客运量统计;半价票、小孩票也按一人统计。

货物(旅客)周转量 指在一定时期内,由各种运输工具运送的货物(旅客)数量与其相应运输距离的乘积之总和。计算货物周转量通常按发出站与到达站之间的最短距离,也就是计费距离计算。计算公式为:

货物(旅客)周转量=∑货物(旅客)运输量×运输距离

邮电业务总量 指以价值量形式表现的邮电通信企业为社会提供各类邮电通信服务的总数量。邮电业务量按专业分类包括函件、包件、汇票、报刊发行、邮政快件、特快专递、邮政储蓄、集邮、公众电报、用户电报、传真、长途电话、出租电路、市话无线寻呼、移动电话、分组交换数据通信、出租代维等。计算方法为各类产品乘以相应的平均单价(不变价)之和,再加上出租电路和设备、代用户维护电话交换机和线路等的服务收入。其计算公式为:

邮电业务总量=∑(各类邮电业务量×不变单价)+出租代维及其他业务收入

无线寻呼电话用户 指携带小型寻呼机,接收市话用户通过无线寻呼中心,在规定范围内向其发出声音、数字或文字显示信息的用户。在寻呼台办理登记手续的无线寻呼用户,每一部寻呼机按一户计算。

移动电话用户 指在移动电话营业部门登记,通过移动电话交换机进入移动电话网、占有移动电话号码的电话用户。用户数量以实际办理登记手续进入邮电部门移动电话网的户数进行计算,一部或一台移动电话统计为一户。

电话用户 指接入国家公众固定电话网,并按固定电话业务进行经营管理的电话用户。

城市电话用户 指直辖市、省辖市、地级市、县级市的市区、市郊区及县城(包括县人民政府所在地的县城关区或行政建制相当于县人民政府所在地的镇)范围内接入局用交换机的电话用户数,包括分布在农村地区的独立工矿区、林区、驻军等电话用户数。

乡村电话用户 指按行政区划属于城市范围内以外的乡镇、村的电话用户数。

住宅电话用户数 指安装在居民住宅或农民家里并按照住宅电话用户登记和收费的电话用户。包括私人付费、单位付费和按规定免费安装的住宅电话用户。

Explanatory Notes on Main Statistical Indicators

Length of Railways in Operation refers to the total length of the trunk line under passenger and freight transportation (including both full operation and temporary operation).The calculation is based on the actual length of the first line even if this line has a full or partial double track or more tracks,excluding double tracks,station sidings, tracks under the charge of stations, branch lines, special-purpose lines and the non-payable connecting lines. The length of railways in operation is an important indicator to show the development of the infrastructure for the railway transport,and also the essential data to calculate volume of passenger freight transport,traffic density and utilization efficiency of the locomotives and carriages.

Length of Highways refers to the length of highways which are built in conformity with the grades specified by the highway engineering standard formulated by the Ministry of Communications, and have been formally checked and accepted by the departments of highways and put into use. The length of highways includes that of the suburb highways at large and medium-sized cities,highways passing through streets at small cities and towns, and also the length of bridges and ferries.It does not include the length of streets in big and medium-sized cities and highways built for the production purpose at factories,mines,forest areas and agricultural areas.If two or more highways go the same section of the way,the length of the section is only calculated for once and no duplication is allowed.

Length of Navigable Inland Waterways an indicator reflecting the size and development of inland water network, it refers to the length of the natural rivers,lakes,reservoirs,canals,and ditches open to navigation during a given period, which enables the transport by ships and rafts. It includes the channels open to navigation for over an accumulative 3 months in a year,yet this does not include the river courses which are only used to float odd logs and bamboo rafts.

Length of Civil Aviation Routes refers to the length of all routes for regular civil aviation flights.There are usually two ways to calculate the distance between airports connected by the route length: One is to put the length of all air routes together, called duplicated calculation of the length of the routes;the other is not to allow the duplication in calculation when two or more routes passing the same section of aviation routes. The latter is usually used,as it can precisely show the size of the civil aviation network and indicate the extent of civil aviation serving the national economy and the people.

Freight(Passenger)Traffic refers to the volume of freight(passenger)transported with various means. Freight transport is calculated in tons and passenger traffic is calculated in the number of persons. Despite the type of freight and travelling distance,the freight transport is calculated in the actual weight of the goods:and despite the travelling distance and ticket price,the passenger traffic is calculated by the principle that one person can be counted only once in one travel. The passenger who travel with a half price ticket or a child ticket is also calculated as one person.

Freight Ton-kilometers (Passenger-kilometers) refer to the sum of the products of the volume of transported cargo (passengers) multiplying by the transport distance,usually using ton-kilometer and passenger-kilometer as units for measurement.Normally, the shortest distance between the departure station and the destination station (i.e., the payable distance) is the basis to calculate the freight ton-kilometers. The formula is as follows:

Freight Ton-kilometers (Passenger-kilometers) = $\sum$ {Freight (Passenger) Traffic × Distance of Transportation}

Measuring unit: ton-kilometer (person-kilometer)

Business Volume of Post and Telecommunications refers to the total amount of post and telecommunications services, expressed in value terms, provided by the post and telecommunications departments for the society.

Post and telecommunication services can be classified as letters, parcels, remittance, issue of newspapers and magazines, fast mail service, express mail service, savings deposits, stamps for collection, public and individual telegraph service, facsimiles, long-distance telephone service, leasing of telephone lines, urban paging service, mobile telephone service, data transfer and transmission, etc. The accounting approach is to multiply the service products of all types with their average unit price (constant price) to get sum of business value, plus income from other services such as leasing of telephone lines and equipment, maintenance of telephone switchboards and lines on behalf of customers.

The formula is as follows:

Business Volume of Post and Telecommunications

$=\sum$ (Transaction of Post and Telecommunication Service × Constant Price) + Income from Leasing, Maintenance and other Services

Subscribers of Paging Services refer to subscribers who carry small-size pagers and receive audio signals, digital signals or character signals sent out by city telephone through wireless paging center within assigned area. Each pager is counted as a subscriber.

Mobile Telephone Subscribers refer to the persons who own mobile telephone number connected with the mobile telephone communication network and have registered in mobile communication enterprises. The number of subscribers is calculated only when the subscribers who have gone through all the register formalities and entered into the mobile telephone network.One mobile telephone is treated as a subscriber.

Telephone Subscribers refer to subscribers that are connected to the public line telephone network provided with telephone services.

Urban Telephone Subscribers refer to number of telephone subscribers, located at municipalities, cities under the jurisdiction of province, cities at prefecture level, downtown and suburb of city at county level town and county towns (including country towns where county government located, and towns of county level according to the administrative organizational system), that are connected to the public line telephone network, including rural mineral area, forest area, military area.

Rural Telephone Subscribers refer to telephone subscribers, located at counties (towns) and villages outside the range of cities according to administrative jurisdiction.

Household Telephone Subscribers refer to telephone sets installed in the dwelling units of urban or rural residents, and registered as residence subscribers for payment, including 3 types of payment for the service: private payment, public payment and free service.

10

Ten

国内商业

Domestic Trade

社会消费品零售总额（亿元）

Total Retail Sales of Consumer Goods (100 million yuan)

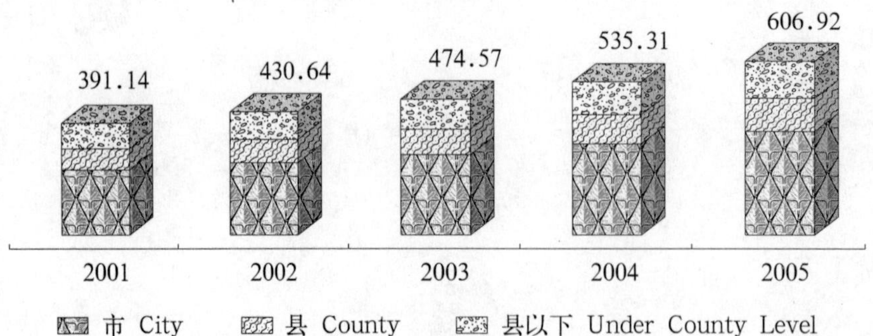

商品交易市场数（个）

Number of Commodity Transaction Markets (unit)

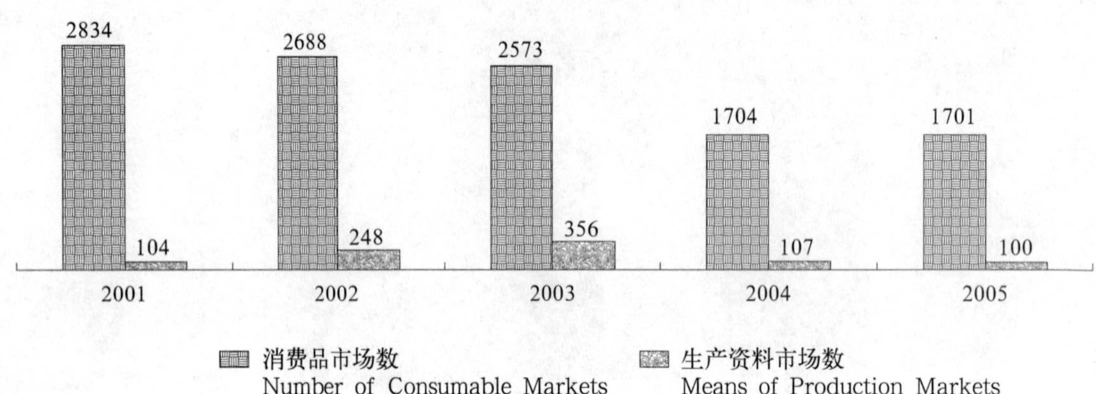

社会消费品零售总额构成（%）

Composition of Retail Sales of Consumer Goods (%)

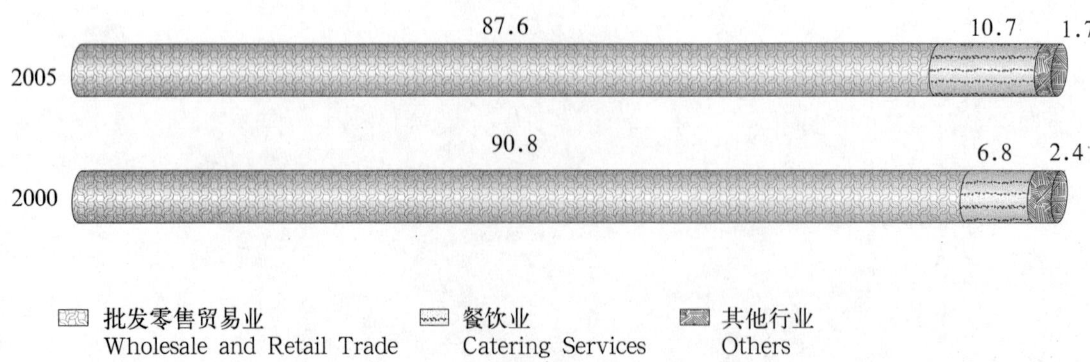

10-1 “十五”时期各年社会消费品零售额

Basic Seatistics on Retail Sales of Consumer Goods of Each Year in “Tenth-Five-year Plan” Period

单位：亿元(100 million yuan)

指　标	Item	2000	2001	2002	2003	2004	2005	2005年比2004年增长(%) Increase Rate in 2005 over 2004(%)
社会消费品零售总额	**Total Retail Sales of Consumer Goods**	**355.58**	**391.14**	**430.64**	**474.57**	**535.31**	**606.92**	**13.4**
按销售单位所在地分	By Location of Establishments							
市	City	204.71	228.25	253.36	281.23	318.63	362.74	13.8
县	County	68.56	74.25	80.71	88.78	102.01	115.80	13.5
县以下	Under County Level	82.31	88.64	96.57	104.56	114.67	128.38	12.0
按行业分	By Sector							
批发零售贸易业	Wholesale and Retail Trade	322.73	352.08	384.66	422.31	467.28	531.86	13.8
餐饮业	Catering Services	24.23	30.04	37.34	43.24	58.64	64.69	10.3
其他行业	Others	8.62	9.02	8.64	9.02	9.39	10.37	10.4

注：本表已按第一次经济普查资料修订。

Note:Data in the table are adjusted on the basis of the statiseics of the first national economic cenus

10-2 “十五”时期各年商品交易市场情况

Number of Commodity Exchange Markets of Each Year in “Tenth-Five-year Plan” Period

单位：个(unit)

指　标	Item	2000	2001	2002	2003	2004	2005
消费品市场数	**Number of Consumable Markets**	**2696**	**2834**	**2688**	**2573**	**1704**	**1701**
消费品综合市场	Consumable Goods Integrative Market	2144	2010	1900	1652	1212	1149
农副产品市场	Agricultural Subproduct Market	413	600	569	778	404	464
农副产品综合市场	Agricultural Subproduct Integrative Market	327	517	491	706	377	430
农副产品专业市场	Agricultural Subproduct Special Market	86	83	78	72	27	34
工业消费品市场	Industrial Consumable Goods Market	111	158	142	97	39	39
工业消费品综合市场	Industrial Consumable Goods Integrative Market	55	101	92	56	26	25
工业消费品专业市场	Industrial Consumer Goods Special Market	56	57	50	41	13	14
其 他	Others	28	66	77	46	49	49
生产资料市场数	**Means of Production Market**	**72**	**104**	**248**	**356**	**107**	**100**
生产资料综合市场	Means of Production Integrative Market	5	25	91	56	28	28
工业生产资料市场	Means of Industrial Production Market	47	56	69	170	40	36
农业生产资料市场	Means of Agricultural Production Market	19	22	74	124	36	36
农业生产资料综合市场	Means of Agricultural Production Integrative Market	2	4	54	123	17	17
农业生产资料专业市场	Means of Agricultural Production Special Market	17	18	20	1	19	19
其 他	Others	1	1	14	6	3	

10-3 限额以上批发零售企业基本情况（2005）

Basic Conditions of Enterprises above Designated Size in Wholesale and Retail Sales（2005）

单位：个、人(unit, person)

指 标	Item	法人企业 Number of Corporation Unit	产业活动单位数 Number of Active Unit	从业人数 Persons Engaged
总 计	**Total**	**248**	**934**	**45199**
批发业	**Wholesale Trade**	**151**	**413**	**27874**
#国有及国有控股	State-owned and Controlling Share Hold by The State	77	271	22972
按登记注册类型分组	**Grouped by Registration**			
内资企业	Domestic-funded Enterprise	145	405	27187
国有企业	State-owned Enterprise	58	216	20382
集体企业	Collective-owned Enterprise	12	72	556
股份合作企业	Copperative Enterprise	1	1	58
有限责任公司	Limited Liability Corporations	45	63	3348
国有独资公司	State-owned Corporation	7	12	538
其他有限责任公司	Other Limited Liability Corporations	38	51	2810
股份有限公司	Share Holding Co.Ltd	10	28	1909
私营企业	Private Enterprise	19	25	934
港、澳、台商投资企业	Enterprises Funded by Hong kong,Macao and Taiwan	3	5	295
外商投资企业	Foreign—funded Enterprises	3	3	392
按国民经济行业分组	**Grouped by National Economic Sector**			
农畜产品批发	Wholesale of Farm Corps and Livestack Products	1	8	279
食品、饮料及烟草制品批发	Wholesale of Food,Beverages and Tobaccos	38	173	17370
#米、面制品及食用油批发	Wholesale of Rice,Flour Articles and Edible Oil	5	16	317
烟草制品批发	Wholesale of Tobaccos and Related Products	23	145	15986
纺织、服装及日用品批发	Wholesale of Textiles,Garments and Daily Consumer Goods	2	2	81
文化、体育用品及器材批发	Wholesale of Culture,Sports Goods and Equipments	5	14	632
医药及医疗器材批发	Wholesale of Medicines and Medical Appliances	19	19	1812
矿产品、建材及化工产品批发	Wholesale of Mininery Products,Building Materials and Chemical Materials	55	101	5337
#煤炭及制品批发	Wholesale of Coal and Related Products	10	17	739
石油及制品批发	Wholesale of Petroleum and Related Products	10	43	3218
金属及金属矿批发	Wholesale of Metal Materials	15	21	545
建材批发	Wholesale of Building Materials	3	3	133
化肥批发	Wholesale of Chemical Fertilizers	9	9	371
机械设备、五金交电及电子产品批发	Wholesale of Machinery,Hardware,Transport, Electric and Electronic Products	24	31	1868
#汽车、摩托车及零配件批发	Wholesale of Motor Vehicles, Motorcycles and Parts	4	4	157
家用电器批发	Wholesale of Household Appliances	4	4	685
计算机、软件及辅助设备批发	Wholesale of Computer,Software and Assistance Appliances	2	4	133
其他批发	Others	7	65	495

10-3续表(continued) 单位：个、人(unit,person)

指 标	Item	法人企业 Number of Corporation Unit	产业活动单位数 Number of Active Unit	从业人数 Persons Engaged
零售业	**Retail Trade**	**97**	**521**	**17325**
#国有及国有控股	State-owned and Controlling Share Hold by the State	19	196	4886
按登记注册类型分组	**Grouped by Registration**			
内资企业	Domestic Funded Enterprises	93	489	15438
国有企业	State-owned Enterprise	14	78	3266
联营企业	Joint Ownership	1	1	118
有限责任公司	Limited Liability Corporations	40	173	5616
国有独资公司	State-owned Corporation	1	38	223
其他有限责任公司	Other Limited Liability Corporations	39	135	5393
股份有限公司	Share Holding Co.Ltd	9	142	2835
私营企业	Private Enterprise	28	94	3514
私营独资企业	Private Enterprise with Sole Investment	3	3	552
私营合伙企业	Private Enterprise with Partnership	4	4	703
私营有限责任公司	Private Limited Liability Corporations	20	86	2220
私营股份有限公司	Private Share Holding Co.Ltd	1	1	39
其他	Others	1	1	89
港、澳、台商投资企业	Enterprise with Funds From Honkong,Macao and Taiwan	2	3	1145
外商投资企业	Enterprise with Foreign Investment	2	29	742
按国民经济行业分组	**Grouped by National Economic Sector**			
综合零售	Polyretail	32	136	9331
#百货零售	Retail of Consumer Goods	12	33	4596
超级市场零售	Retail of Supermarket	19	60	4524
食品、饮料及烟草制品专门零售	Retail of Food,Beverages and Tobaccos	3	51	487
纺织品、服装及日用品专门零售	Retail of Textiles,Garments and Daily Consumer Goods	2	3	255
服装零售业	Retail of Garments	2	2	195
文化、体育用品及器材专门零售	Retail of Culture,Sports Goods and Equipments	4	16	371
图书零售	Retail of Books	4	16	371
医药及医疗器材专门零售	Retail of Medicines and Medical Appliances	9	119	1224
药品零售	Retail of Medicines	9	119	1224
汽车、摩托车、燃料及零配件专门零售	Retail of Motor Vehicles, Motorcycles and Parts	24	167	3217
#汽车零售	Retail of Motor Vehicles	16	21	1241
机动车燃料零售	Retail of Motor Vehicles' Fule	7	145	1915
家用电器及电子产品专门零售	Retail of Household Appliances and Electronic Products	21	27	2290
#家用电器零售	Retail of Household Appliances	13	19	1716
计算机、软件及辅助设备零售	Retail of Computer,Software and Assistance Appliances	2	2	133
通讯设备零售	Retail of Communication Appliances	6	6	441
五金、家具及室内装修材料专门零售	Retail of Hardware,Furniture and Decoration Materials	1	1	86
无店铺及其他零售	Other Retail Trade	1	1	64

10-4 限额以上批发零售业商品购进、销售、库存总额（2005）

Total Purchases,Sales and Inventory of Enterprises above Designated Size in Wholesale and Retail Trade（2005）

单位:万元(10000 yuan)

指 标	Item	购进总额 Total Purchases	销售总额 Total Sales	批发 Wholesale Trade	零售 Retail Trade	年末库存额 Inventory (year-end)
总 计	**Total**	**3803407**	**4793653**	**3592765**	**1200888**	**544654**
批发业	**Wholesale Trade**	**2995104**	**3881528**	**3504412**	**377117**	**425671**
#国有及国有控股	State-owned and Controlling Share Hold by The State	2171961	2990156	2672721	317434	361494
按登记注册类型分组	**Grouped by Registration**					
内资企业	Domestic-funded Enterprise	2928217	3803760	3427908	375852	423203
国有企业	State-owned Enterprise	1870551	2700501	2454817	245684	310454
集体企业	Collective-owned Enterprise	119226	124081	118421	5661	8084
股份合作企业	Copperative Enterprise	3361	3656	3656		533
有限责任公司	Limited Liability Corporations	461953	536526	498327	38199	76252
国有独资公司	State-owned Corporation	84244	105663	105429	234	36699
其他有限责任公司	Other Limited Liability Corporations	377708	430863	392898	37965	39553
股份有限公司	Share Holding Co.Ltd	256240	223334	144336	78999	12438
私营企业	Private Enterprise	216888	215662	208351	7310	15442
私营有限责任公司	Private Limited Liability Corporations	206678	205352	198042	7310	14744
私营股份有限公司	Private Share Holding Co.Ltd	10211	10310	10310		698
港、澳、台商投资企业	Enterprises Funded by Hong kong, Macao and Taiwan	36835	44658	43394	1265	2050
与港澳台商合资经营企业	Joint Venture Enterprise	31641	38336	38336		1734
港澳台商独资	Enterprises with Sole Investment	5195	6322	5058	1265	316
外商投资企业	Foreign Funded Enterprises	30052	33110	33110		418
中外合资经营	Joint-venture Enterprises	24202	26415	26415		165
外资企业	Enterprises with Sole Foreign Investment	5850	6695	6695		253
按国民经济行业分组	**Grouped by National Economic Sector**					
农畜产品批发	Wholesale of Farm Corps and Livestack Products	8229	9576	6536	3040	1194
食品、饮料及烟草制品批发	Wholesale of Food,Beverages and Tobaccos	1483874	2068252	2016375	51876	271389
#米、面制品及食用油批发	Wholesale of Rice,Flour Articles and Edible Oil	23082	24125	23667	458	4559
烟草制品批发	Wholesale of Tobaccos and Related Products	1404318	1699997	1694810	5187	259573
纺织、服装及日用品批发	Wholesale of Textiles,Garments, Shoes and Hats	16144	16309	13484	2825	308
文化、体育用品及器材批发	Wholesale of Culture,Sports Goods and Equipments	81899	83712	81118	2594	2433
医药及医疗器材批发	Wholesale of Medicines and Medical Appliances	255163	253682	224002	29680	28513

10-4续表1(continued)

指 标	Item	购进总额 Total Purchases	销售总额 Total Sales	批发 Wholesale Trade	零售 Retail Trade	年末库存额 Inventory (year-end)
矿产品、建材及化工产品批发	Wholesale of Mininery Products, Building Materials and Chemical Materials	843245	1127410	858190	269220	88831
#煤炭及制品批发	Wholesale of Coal and Related Products	65179	74081	74081		1782
石油及制品批发	Wholesale of Petroleum and Related Products	317136	540283	276949	263334	44899
金属及金属矿批发	Wholesale of Metal Materials	170918	196771	195210	1561	7176
建材批发	Wholesale of Building Materials	51097	54000	49674	4325	2843
化肥批发	Wholesale of Chemical Fertilizers	136348	139895	139895		17469
机械设备、五金交电及电子产品批发	Wholesale of Machinery, Hardware,Transport,Electric and Electronic Products	273942	288221	270917	17304	30139
汽车、摩托车及零配件批发	Wholesale of Motor Vehicles, Motorcycles and Parts	19979	21473	18359	3114	3515
家用电器批发	Wholesale of Household Appliances	87036	88241	88241		2063
计算机、软件及辅助设备批发	Wholesale of Computer,Software and Assistance Appliances	20537	20244	13700	6544	1866
其他批发	Others	32609	34367	33790	578	2864
零售业	**Retail Trade**	**808303**	**912125**	**88354**	**823771**	**118983**
#国有及国有控股	State-owned and Controlling Share Hold by the State	191530	209988	32903	177085	28759
按登记注册类型分组	Grouped by Registration					
内资企业	Domestic Funded Enterprises	762594	811454	88354	723100	112604
国有企业	State-owned Enterprise Joint	101263	99523	23912	75612	8849
联营企业	Ownership	2756	2858		2858	2135
有限责任公司	Limited Liability Corporations	296340	298579	30376	268203	51923
国有独资公司	State-owned Corporation	4410	5150		5150	1027
其他有限责任公司	Other Limited Liability Corporations	291930	293429	30376	263053	50896
股份有限公司	Share Holding Co.Ltd	171303	206129	19082	187047	24641
私营企业	Private Enterprise	189509	202822	14985	187837	24973
私营独资企业	Private Enterprise with Sole Investment	6171	2545		2545	1662
私营合伙企业	Private Enterprise with Partnership	34277	31547		31547	3614

10-4续表2(continued)　　　　单位:万元　(10000 yuan)

指 标	Item	购进总额 Total Purchases	销售总额 Total Sales	批发 Wholesale Trade	零售 Retail Trade	年末库存额 Inventory (year-end)
私营有限责任公司	Private Limited Liability Corporations	146479	165905	14985	150921	19410
私营股份有限公司	Private Share Holding Co.Ltd	2581	2825		2825	287
其他	Others	1423	1543		1543	84
港、澳、台商投资企业	Enterprise with Funds From Honkong,Macao and Taiwan	29701	66246		66246	3077
与港澳台商合资经营	Joint Venture Enterprise	2493	31595		31595	203
与港澳台商合作经营	Cooperation Enterprise	27208	34651		34651	2874
外商投资企业	Enterprise with Foreign Investment	16008	34425		34425	3302
中外合资经营企业	Joint-venture Enterprises	6762	22619		22619	2821
中外合作经营企业	Cooperation Enterprise	9246	11806		11806	481
按国民经济行业分组	**Grouped by National Economic Sector**					
综合零售	Polyretail	202971	242667	3141	239527	54320
#百货零售	Retail of Consumer Goods	101483	135171	2837	132334	35525
超级市场零售	Retail of Supermarket	98479	104168	272	103897	12109
食品、饮料及烟草制品专门零售	Retail of Food,Beverages and Tobaccos	4368	4369	1136	3233	475
纺织品、服装及日用品专门零售	Retail of Textiles,Garments and Daily Consumer Goods	10976	13560		13560	1229
服装零售业	Retail of Garments	1730	1754		1754	748
文化、体育用品及器材专门零售	Retail of Culture,Sports Goods and Equipments	16931	17149	436	16713	1516
图书零售	Retail of Books	16931	17149	436	16713	1516
医药及医疗器材专门零售	Retail of Medicines and Medical Appliances	22280	26118	1074	25044	9580
药品零售	Retail of Medicines	22280	26118	1074	25044	9580
汽车、摩托车、燃料及零配件专门零售	Retail of Motor Vehicles, Motorcycles and Parts	371672	415091	62129	352962	26196
汽车零售	Retail of Motor Vehicles	181914	192836	11322	181514	14075
机动车燃料零售	Retail of Motor Vehicles' Fule	189405	218564	48061	170504	11674
家用电器及电子产品专门零售	Retail of Household Appliances and Electronic Products	174652	188905	20169	168736	23675
#家用电器零售	Retail of Household Appliances	111879	123041	14185	108856	17528
计算机、软件及辅助设备零售	Retail of Computer,Software and Assistance Appliances	5706	7312	1936	5376	619
通讯设备零售	Retail of Communication Appliances	57067	58552	4048	54504	5528
五金、家具及室内装修材料专门零售	Retail of Hardware,Furniture and Decoration Materials	2297	2182		2182	453
无店铺及其他零售	Other Retail Trade	2156	2084	270	1814	1541

10-5 限额以上批发零售贸易业商品分类销售额(2005)

Total Sales of Enterprises above Designated Size in Wholesale and Retail Trade by Category of Main Commodities（2005）

单位：万元(10000 yuan)

项　目	Item	销售合计 Total Sales	批发 Wholesales Trade	零售 Retail Trade
总　计	**Total**	**4384241**	**3300059**	**1084182**
食品、饮料、烟酒类	Food,Beverage and Tobacco and Liquor	1628292	1474773	153520
粮油类	Grain,Edible Vegetable Oil	41002	24572	16430
肉禽蛋类	Meat,Poultry and Eggs	11379	1	11378
其他食品类	Others Food	60114	29143	30972
饮料类	Beverage	14326	2416	11909
烟酒类	Tobacco and Liquor	1501471	1418641	82830
服装鞋帽、针、纺织品类	Garments,Footwear and Hats,Kintwear and Textiles	94720	141	94580
#服装类	Garments	69431	10	69422
鞋帽类	Footwear and Hats	17966	4	17962
针、纺织品类	Kintwear and Textiles	7323	128	7196
化妆品类	Cosmetics	15232	39	15193
金银珠宝类	Gold, Silver and Jewelry	8122		8122
日用品类	Articles for Daily Use	33709	3021	30688
#洗涤用品类	Washing Articles	17752	3000	14752
儿童玩具类	Children's Toy	2448	4	2444
五金、电料类	Hardware and Electrical Materials	15597	14712	886
体育、娱乐用品类	Sports and Recreation Articles	4171	1884	2288
书报杂志类	Newspaper and Magazines	82730	71372	11358
电子出版物及音像制品类	Electric Publication and Sound-video Materials	779	328	450
家用电器和音像器材类	Household Appliances and Video Appliances	204935	98868	106067
中西药品类	Traditional Chinese and Western Medicines	196300	166933	29367
#西　药	Western Medicines	148951	134419	14532
中草药及中成药	Traditional Chinese Medicines	32855	26462	6393
文化办公用品类	Culture and Office Articles	24443	12690	11754
家具类	Furniture	1020	101	919
通讯器材类	Communication Appliances	67710	27440	40270
煤炭及制品类	Coal and Related Products	141128	141128	
木材及制品类	Timber and Related Products	28720	13596	15125
石油及制品类	Petroleum and Related Products	687484	328188	359296
化工材料及制品类	Chemical Materials and Related Products	278984	278983	1
#化肥类	Chemical Fertilizers	89674	89674	
金属材料类	Metal Materials	178334	177390	945
建筑及装潢材料类	Building and Decoration Materials	54020	52757	1263
机电产品及设备类	Mechanical and Electrical Instruments	85043	77000	8043
#农机类	Agricultural Machinery	4277	455	3821
汽车类	Automobile	209347	31643	177703
种子饲料类	Seed and Feedstuff	3620	3620	
其他类	Others	339800	323454	16346

10-6 限额以上批发零售业主要财务指标（2005）

Main Financial Indicators of Enterprises above Designated Size in Wholesale and Retail Trade(2005)

单位：万元(10000 yuan)

指 标	Item	营业收入 Total Sales	主营业务成本 Cost of Products Sold	主营业务税金及附加 Tax and Extra Charges on Sales Products	营业费用 Expenses of Products Sold	营业利润 Total Profits
总 计	**Total**	**4207881**	**3477542**	**11053**	**232103**	**90348**
批发业	**Wholesale Trade**	**3416325**	**2788908**	**9118**	**192356**	**83854**
#国有及国有控股	State-owned and Controlling Share Hold by The State	2584125	2054588	7502	160279	76847
按登记注册类型分组	**Grouped by Registration**					
内资	Domestic-funded Enterprises	3352153	2731520	9097	189768	83746
国有企业	State-owned Enterprises	2254959	1775111	6592	145313	62495
集体企业	Collective-owned Enterprises	124253	115100	242	1757	377
股份合作	Cooperative Enterprises	3656	3505	8	70	5
有限责任公司	Limited Liability Corporations	498354	442182	1214	22347	7237
国有独资公司	State Sole Funded Corporations	99539	81083	192	2602	4525
其他有限责任公司	Other Limited Liability Corporations	398815	361099	1022	19745	2712
股份有限公司	Share Holding Co.Ltd	259918	227913	807	14147	13237
私营企业	Private Enterprises	211013	167709	234	6135	395
私营有限责任公司	Private Limited Liability Corporations	201985	158994	230	5790	454
私营股份有限公司	Private Share Holding Co.Ltd	9027	8716	5	345	-60
港澳台商投资企业	Enterprises Funded by Hong kong, Macao and Taiwan	34097	29597	…	2112	-129
与港澳台商合资经营	Joint Venture Enterprises	34097	29597	…	2112	-129
外商投资企业	Foreign Funded Enterprises	30075	27791	21	476	237
中外合资经营	Cooperative Enterprises	24349	22847	21	5	77
外资企业	Enterprises with Sole Foreign Investment	5726	4943	…	471	160
按国民经济行业分组	**Grouped by National Economic Sector**					
农畜产品批发业	Wholesale of Farm Corps and Livestack Products	5493	5329	…	54	-570
食品、饮料及烟草制品批发业	Wholesale of Food,Beverages and Tobaccos	1706929	1260541	5318	126317	54427
米、面制品及食用油批发业	Wholesale of Rice,Flour and Edible Oil	25289	24024	40	687	-2384
烟草制品批发业	Wholesale of Tobaccos and Related Products	1625124	1191470	5085	121618	54687
纺织、服装及日用品批发业	Wholesale of Textiles,Garments and Daily Consumer Goods	14529	14054	16	120	44
文化、体育用品及器材批发业	Wholesale of Culture,Sports Goods and Equipments	59906	52549	149	3489	-175

10-6续表1(continued)

单位：万元(10000 yuan)

指　标	Item	营业收入 Total Sales	主营业务成本 Cost of Products Sold	主营业务税金及附加 Tax and Extra Charges on Sales Products	营业费用 Expenses of Products Sold	营业利润 Total Profits
医药及医疗器材批发业	Wholesale of Medicines and Medical Appliances	237376	195366	313	3449	2116
矿产品、建材及化工产品批发业	Wholesale of Mininery Products, Building Materials and Chemical Materials	1100038	994120	2830	49404	27709
煤炭及制品批发业	Wholesale of Coal and Related Products	84201	59912	1116	12108	9312
石油及制品批发业	Wholesale of Petroleum and Related Products	527644	482437	640	19034	17511
金属及金属矿批发业	Wholesale of Metal Materials	175392	169445	232	3858	-910
建材批发业	Wholesale of Building Materials	52902	50079	88	957	1035
化肥批发业	Wholesale of Chemical Fertilizers	134747	125104	187	1700	-776
机械设备、五金交电及电子产品批发	Wholesale of Machinery, Hardware,Transport Electric and Electronic Products	262997	240183	440	8993	674
汽车、摩托车及零配件批发业	Wholesale of Motor Vehicles, Motorcycles and Parts	19581	18422	28	363	-2
家用电器批发业	Wholesale of Household Appliances	74906	69285	98	3510	111
计算机、软件及辅助设备批发业	Wholesale of Computer,Software and Assistance Appliances	19745	19113	10	323	31
其他批发业	Others	29057	26766	53	531	-372
零售业	**Retail Trade**	**791556**	**688634**	**1935**	**39747**	**6495**
#国有及国有控股	State-owned and Controlling Share Hold by The State	191595	162469	383	7029	1032
按登记注册类型分组	**Grouped by Registration**					
内资企业	Domestic-funded Enterprises	737617	648421	1836	35511	3479
国有企业	State-owned Enterprises	92999	78434	171	3546	-1832
联营企业	Joint Ownership	2756	1843	3	165	6
其他联营	Others	2756	1843	3	165	6
有限责任公司	Limited Liability Corporations	278329	242859	792	16099	1237
国有独资公司	State Sole Funded Corporations	4536	3633	14	330	-2
其他有限责任公司	Other Limited Liability Corporations	273793	239226	778	15770	1239
股份有限公司	Share Holding Co.Ltd	183664	162973	455	8203	5519
私营企业	Private Enterprises	178326	161484	400	7429	-1441
私营独资	Private-funded Enterprises	2033	1463	9	393	21

10-6续表2(continued) 单位：万元(10000 yuan)

指 标	Item	营业收入 Total Sales	主营业务成本 Cost of Products Sold	主营业务税金及附加 Tax and Extra Charges on Sales Products	营业费用 Expenses of Products Sold	营业利润 Total Profits
私营合伙	Private Enterprisewith Partnership	26040	24819	124	1286	-369
私营有限责任公司	Private Limited Liability Corporations	147429	132521	265	5732	-1111
私营股份有限公司	Private Share Holding Co.Ltd	2825	2681	2	18	18
其他	Other Enterprise	1543	829	16	70	-9
港澳台商投资企业	Enterprises Funded by Hong kong, Macao and Taiwan	33526	23484	59	2603	2557
与港澳台商合资经营	Joint Venture Enterprises	31983	22155	58	2420	2544
与港澳台商合作经营	Coöperative Enterprises	1543	1329	2	183	12
外商投资企业	Enterprise with Foreign Investment	20414	16729	40	1633	460
中外合资经营	Joint Venture Enterprises	20414	16729	40	1633	460
按国民经济行业分组	**Grouped by National Economic Sector**					
综合零售业	Polyretail	197810	155619	1102	17902	1371
百货零售业	Retail of Consumer Goods	128955	98755	767	10745	302
超级市场零售业	Retail of Supermarket	65455	53924	329	6843	1077
食品、饮料及烟草制品专门零售业	Retail of Food,Beverages and Tobaccos	2691	2163	5	195	-189
纺织、服装及日用品专门零售业	Retail of Textiles,Garments and Daily Consumer Goods	1754	475	2	…	-398
服装零售业	Retail of Garments	1754	475	2	…	-398
文化、体育用品及器材专门零售业	Retail of Culture,Sports Goods and Equipments	16044	11326	37	914	327
图书零售业	Retail of Books	16044	11326	37	914	327
医药及医疗器材专门零售业	Retail of Medicines and Medical Appliances	24708	19188	38	2134	13
药品零售业	Retail of Medicines	24708	19188	38	2134	13
汽车、摩托车、燃料及零配件专门零售业	Retail of Motor Vehicles, Motorcycles and Parts	372181	339731	386	11092	5638
汽车零售业	Retail of Motor Vehicles	175329	161977	129	5065	-527
机动车燃料零售业	Retail of Motor Vehicles' Fule	196351	177399	255	5994	6151
家用电器及电子产品专门零售业	Retail of Household Appliances and Electronic Products	172099	157322	355	7232	-313
家用电器零售业	Retail of Household Appliances	113043	103722	163	4667	-1734
计算机、软件及辅助设备零售业	Retail of Computer,Software and Assistance Appliances	8360	5573	16	851	1489
通讯设备零售业	Retail of Communication Appliances	50696	48028	177	1714	-69
五金、家具及室内装修材料专门零售业	Retail of Hardware,Furniture and Decoration Materials	2184	1685	10	275	52
无店铺及其他零售业	Other Retail Trade	2084	1125	1	3	-6

10-7 限额以上餐饮企业主要财务指标(2005)

Main Financial Indicators of Enterprises above Designated Size in Catering Services by Registration(2005)

单位：万元(10000 yuan)

指　标	Item	营业收入 Total Sales	主营业务成本 Cost of Products Sold	主营业务税金及附加 Tax and Extra Charges on Sales Products	营业费用 Expenses of Products Sold	营业利润 Total Profits
总　计	**Total**	**50956**	**25535**	**2782**	**11250**	**46**
#国有及国有控股	State-owned and Controlling Share Hold by The State	1360	743	33	376	-79
按登记注册类型分组	**Grouped by Registration**					
内资企业	Domestic-funded Enterprise	49817	25105	2730	10870	38
国有企业	State-owned Enterprise	870	531	10	173	-35
集体企业	Collective-owned Enterprise	401	59	23	121	156
有限责任公司	Limited Liabilty Corporations	14679	6867	687	3386	337
其他有限责任公司	Other Limited Liability Corporations	14679	6867	687	3386	337
股份有限公司	Share Holding Co.ltd	731	316	41	323	-175
私营企业	Private Enterprise	29140	15301	1695	5971	-11
私营独资	Private-funded Enterprise	9870	4106	600	1579	-54
私营合伙	Private Enterprise with Partnership	1539	546	91	208	38
私营有限责任公司	Private Limited Liabilty Corporations	17732	10649	1004	4184	5
其他企业	Other Enterprise	3997	2033	274	897	-234
港澳台商投资企业	Enterprises Funded by Hong kong, Macao and Taiwan	144	84	2	79	-21
与港澳台商合资经营	Joint Venture Enterprises	144	84	2	79	-21
外商投资企业	Foreign Funded Enterprises	994	346	50	301	29
中外合资经营	Joint Venture Enterprises	994	346	50	301	29
按国民经济行业分组	**Grouped by National Economic Sector**					
正餐服务业	Restaurant Services	46048	24465	2543	10766	…
快餐服务业	Snack Counter Services	4907	1070	239	484	46

主要统计指标解释

社会消费品零售总额 指国民经济各行业直接售给城乡居民和社会集团的消费品总额。它是反映各行业通过多种商品流通渠道向居民和社会集团供应的生活消费品总量，是研究国内零售市场变动情况、反映经济景气程度的重要指标。

社会消费品零售总额包括：⑴售给城乡居民作为生活用的商品和修建房屋用的建筑材料；⑵售给社会集团的各种办公用品和公用消费品；⑶售给机关、团体、学校、部队、企业、事业单位的职工食堂和旅店(招待所)附设专门供本店旅客食用，不对外营业的食堂的各种食品、燃料；企业、单位和国营农场直接售给本单位职工和职工食堂的自己生产的产品；⑷售给部队干部、战士生活用的粮食、副食品、衣着品、日用品、燃料；⑸售给来华的外国人、华侨、港澳台同胞的消费品；⑹居民自费购买的中、西药品、中药材及医疗用品；⑺报社、出版社直接售给居民和社会集团的报纸、图书、杂志，集邮公司出售的新、旧纪念邮票、特种邮票、首日封、集邮册、集邮工具等；⑻旧货寄售商店自购、自销部分的商品；⑼煤气公司、液化石油气站售给居民和社会集团的煤气灶具和罐装液化石油气；⑽农民售给非农业居民和社会集团的商品。不包括售给国民经济各部门企业、事业单位(包括国有经济的农场)生产经营用的各种原材料、燃料、设备、工具等和售给批发零售贸易业、餐饮业作为转卖用的商品，旧货寄售商店受托寄售卖出的商品，服务业的营业收入，邮局出售邮票的收入，自来水、电力、煤气生产(供应)单位的产品供应收入，也不包括农民之间的商品销售。

批发零售贸易业商品购、销、存总额 指各种登记注册类型的批发、零售贸易业(不包括个体)企业（单位）以本企业（单位）为总体的商品购进、销售、库存总额。

商品购进总额 指从本企业(单位)以外的单位和个人购进(包括从境外直接进口)作为转卖或加工后转卖的商品总额。它反映批发零售贸易业从国内、国外市场上购进商品的总量。商品购进总额包括：(1)从工农业生产者购进的商品；(2)从出版社、报社的出版发行部门购进的图书、杂志和报纸；(3)从各种登记注册类型的批发零售贸易企业(单位)购进的商品；(4)从其他单位购进的商品，如从机关、团体、企业等单位购进的剩余物资，从餐饮业、服务业购进的商品，从海关、市场管理部门购进的缉私和没收的商品，从居民手中收购的废旧商品等；(5)从国(境)外直接进口的商品。不包括企业(单位)为自身经营用和未通过买卖行为而收入的商品以及销售退回、商品升溢等。

商品销售总额 指对本企业(单位)以外的单位和个人出售(包括对境外直接出口)的商品总额。它反映批发零售贸易业在国内市场上销售商品以及出口商品的总量。商品销售总额包括：⑴售给城乡居民和社会集团消费用的商品；⑵售给工业、农业、建筑业、运输邮电业、批发零售贸易业、餐饮业、服务业等作为生产、经营使用的商品；⑶售给批发零售贸易业作为转卖或加工后转卖的商品；⑷对国(境)外直接出口的商品。不包括出售本企业(单位)自用的废旧包装用品；未通过买卖行为付出的商品；经本单位介绍，由买卖双方直接结算，本单位只收取手续费的业务；购货退出的商品以及商品损耗和损失等。

批发零售贸易业库存 指报告期末各种登记注册类型的批发零售贸易企业(单位)已取得所有权的商品。它反映批发零售贸易企业(单位)的商品库存情况和对市场商品供应的保证程度。

消费品市场成交额 指从事消费品交易的商品市场的全部商品成交金额。消费品市场包括农副产品市场和工业消费品市场。

Explanatory Notes on Main Statistical Indicators

Total Retail Sales of Consumer Goods refer to the sum of retail sales of consumer goods sold by all sectors of the national economy to urban and rural residents and social groups. This indicator is used to show the supply of consumers goods through various channels to households and institutions, and is very important for the study on changes at the domestic retail market, and on economic cycles.

The retail sales of consumer goods include: (1) commodities sold to urban and rural residents for their daily use and building materials sold to them for the construction or repair of houses; (2) office appliances and supplies sold to institutions; (3) food and fuels sold to canteens of institutions, enterprises ,schools ,military units and to canteens of hotels and hostels that only serve their guests ,and commodities produced by enterprises ,institutions or state farms and sold directly to their employees or their canteens; (4) grain and non–staple food, clothing ,daily articles and fuels sold to military personnel; (5)consumer goods sold to foreigners, overseas Chinese, and Chinese compatriots from Taiwan, Hong Kong and Macao during their stay in the mainland of China; (6) Chinese and western medicines, herbs and medical facilities purchased by residents; (7) newspapers, books and magazines directly sold to residents and social groups by publishers, new and old commemorative stamps, special stamps, first–day covers, stamp albums and other stamp–collection articles sold by stamp companies; (8) consumer goods purchased and then sold by second–hand shops; (9) stoves and other heating facilities and liquefied gas sold by gas companies to households and institutions; and (10) commodities sold by farmers to non–agricultural residents and social groups. Excluded under this heading are:raw materials, fuels, equipment, tools sold to enterprises, institutions and state farms for production purpose; commodities sold to trade establishments for re–selling; commissioned sales at second–hand shops; operational income of urban public utilities; stamps sold at post offices; income of water, power, gas production and supply establishments from the supply of their products; and sales of commodities among farmers.

Purchase,Sales and Stock of Commodities by Wholesale and Retail Trade refer to the purchase, sales and stock of commodities by wholesale and retail establishments of different status of registration (excluding individual sellers).

Total Purchases of Commodities refer to the total value of purchases of commodities by the establishments from other establishments or individuals (including direct import from abroad) for the purpose of re–selling, either with or without further processing of the commodities purchased. This indicator is used to show the total value of purchases of commodities by wholesale and retail establishments from domestic and overseas markets. The total purchases include: (1) agricultural and industrial products purchased from producers; (2) books, magazines and newspapers purchased from distribution departments of the publishers; (3) commodities purchased from wholesale and retail establishments of different status of registration; (4) commodities purchased from other units, such as surplus materials purchased from government agencies, enterprises or institutions, commodities purchased from catering and service establishments, confiscated goods purchased from customs authorities or market management agencies, second–hand goods and wastes purchased from residents; and (5) commodities directly imported from abroad.Excluded are commodities purchased by establishments (units) for use in their own business operation,commodities obtained without buying or selling procedures,rejected commodities,etc.

Total Sales of Commodities refer to value of commodities sold by the establishments to other establishments and individuals (including direct export). This indicator is used to show the total value of sales of commodities at domestic markets and export. The total sales include: (1) commodities sold to urban and rural residents and social groups for their consumption; (2) commodities sold to establishments in industry, agriculture, construction, transportation, post and telecommunications, wholesale and retail trades, catering trade and public utility for their production and operation; (3) commodities sold to wholesale and retail establishments for re selling,with or without further processing; and (4)commodities for direct export to other countries.Excluded are selling of waste packaging materials used by the establishments (units) themselves,commodities transferred without buying or selling procedures,commission income from brokerage in transactions whose settlement is directly handled by buyers and sellers, rejected commodities in the purchase,loss in commodities, etc.

Commodity Stock of Wholesale and Retail Enterprises refers to total commodities possessed by wholesale and retail enterprises (units)of various types of registration status at the end of the reference period,which reflects the commodity stock level of various wholesale and retail enterprises and the potential for market supply.

Volume of Transaction at Free Markets for Consumer Goods refers to the value of transaction of all goods at the free trade markets for consumer goods, where markets include both free markets for farm and sideline products and for manufactured consumer goods.

11 对外经济贸易与合作

Foreign Trade and Economic Cooperation

Eleven

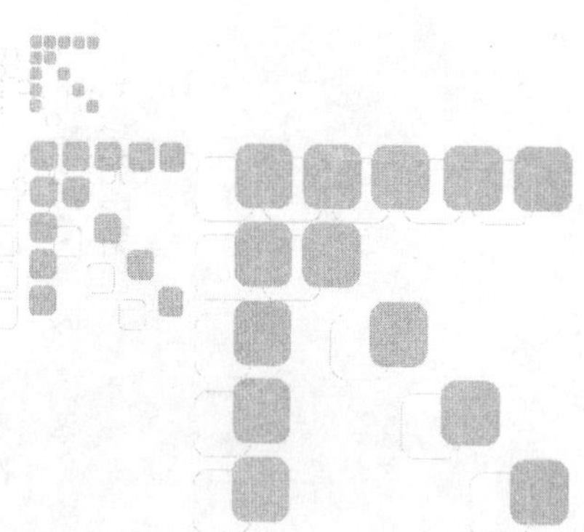

进出口总额（万美元）

Value of Imports and Exports (USD 10000)

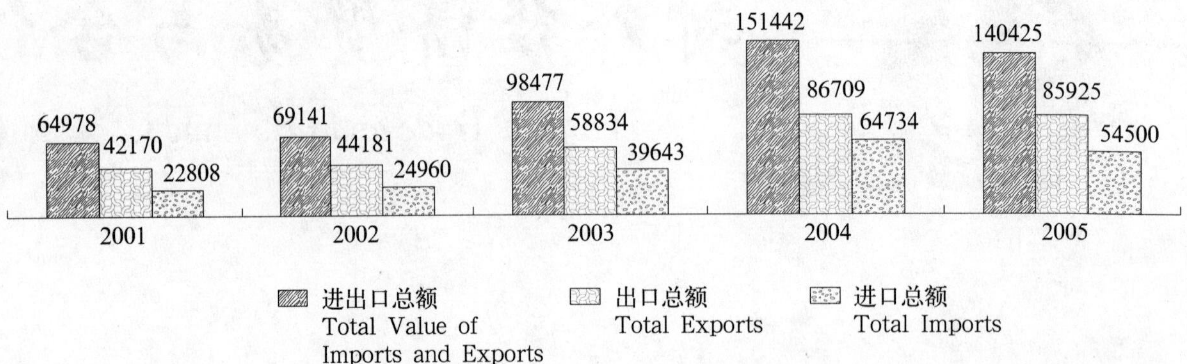

按行业分外商实际直接投资额（万元）

Actually Foreign Direct Investment by Sector (10000 yuan)

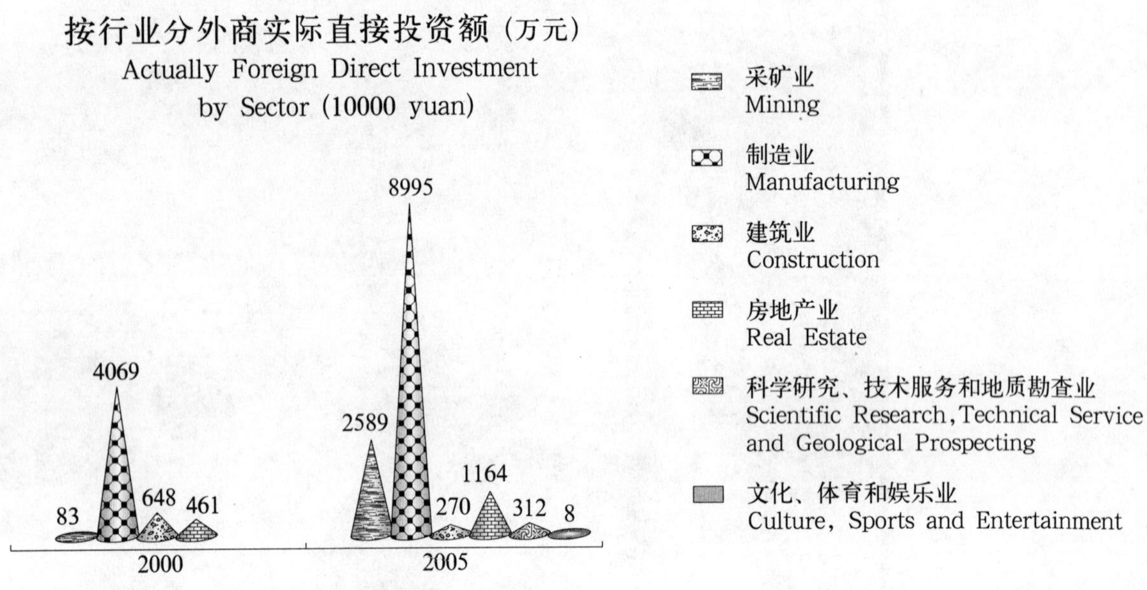

省外经济合作

Economic Cooperation with External Provinces

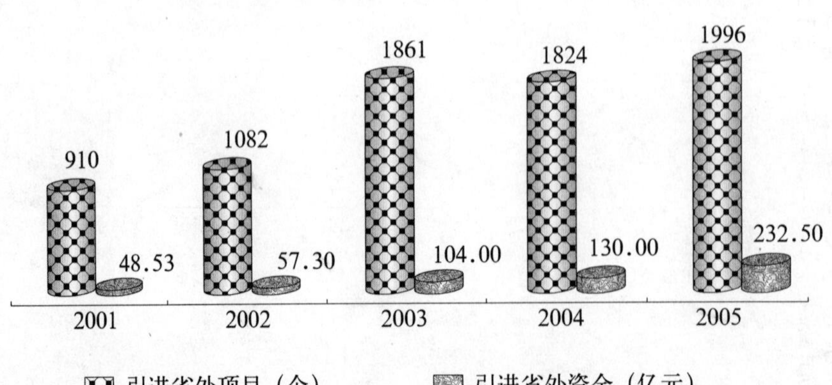

11-1 “十五”时期各年进出口总额

Total Value of Imports and Exports of Each Year in “Tenth-Five-year Plan” Period

指 标	Item	2000	2001	2002	2003	2004	2005	2005年比2004年增长(%) Increase Rate in 2005 over 2004(%)
进出口总额(万元)	**Total Value of Imports and Exports(RMB 10000 yuan)**	**546374**	**537816**	**572287**	**815065**	**1253418**	**1135477**	**-9.4**
出口总额	Total Exports	348179	349037	365691	486952	717647	694790	-3.2
进口总额	Total Imports	198195	188779	206596	328113	535771	440687	-17.7
进出口差额	Balance	149984	160258	159095	158839	181876	254103	39.7
进出口总额(万美元)	**Total Value of Imports and Exports(USD 10000)**	**66002**	**64978**	**69141**	**98477**	**151442**	**140425**	**-7.3**
出口总额	Total Exports	42060	42170	44181	58834	86709	85925	-0.9
进口总额	Total Imports	23942	22808	24960	39643	64734	54500	-15.8
进出口差额	Balance	18118	19362	19221	19191	21975	31425	43.0

11-2 “十五”时期各年按地区分的出口商品总额

Foreign Export Trade with Related Countries(Territories) of Each Year in “Tenth Five-year Plan” Period

单位：万美元(USD 10000)

地区名	Country(Territory)	2000	2001	2002	2003	2004	2005
总 计	**Total**	**42060**	**42170**	**44181**	**58834**	**86709**	**85925**
亚 洲	Asia	28181	27736	29684	41646	59595	55570
非 洲	Africa	850	1286	1004	1120	1928	2586
欧 洲	Europe	5376	5141	5197	6192	10710	11345
南美洲	South America	999	608	760	920	1302	2273
北美洲	North America	4726	4382	5350	6722	9302	10836
大洋洲	Oceania	1928	3017	2186	2234	3871	3315

11-3 “十五”时期各年按地区分的进口商品总额

Foreign Import Trade with Related Countries(Territories) of Each Year in “Tenth-Five-year Plan” Period

单位：万美元(USD 10000)

地区名	Country(Territory)	2000	2001	2002	2003	2004	2005
总 计	**Total**	**23942**	**22808**	**24960**	**39643**	**64734**	**54500**
亚 洲	Asia	12919	9359	15758	25792	41359	29974
非 洲	Africa	600	699	1411	914	1801	916
欧 洲	Europe	4499	5855	3273	4686	9241	7580
南美洲	South America	699	722	1011	243	356	230
北美洲	North America	2677	4522	3085	7410	9389	10941
大洋洲	Oceania	2548	1651	422	598	2587	4859

11-4 “十五”时期各年吸收外资情况

Foreign Capital Absorbed of Each Year in “Tenth Five-year Plan” Period

指 标	Item	2000	2001	2002	2003	2004	2005
签订合同项目（个）	**Number of Signed Contracts(unit)**	**59**	**65**	**55**	**70**	**68**	**61**
#直接利用外资	Direct Foreign Investment	55	59	54	69	61	60
#合资企业	Joint Venture	26	30	20	30	28	19
合作经营企业	Coopratiive Venture	9	8	6	8	7	7
独资企业	Sole-foreign Enterprise	20	21	27	28	26	34
签订合同金额（万美元）	**Contracted Foreign Capital (USD 10000)**	**8098**	**43090**	**19438**	**23747**	**12649**	**19828**
#直接利用外资	Direct Foreign Investment	6738	9111	18943	19947	12649	19488
合资企业	Joint Venture	3058	3689	10284	7576	6331	6420
合作经营企业	Coopratiive Venture	1490	3732	1886	3737	3893	4920
独资企业	Sole-foreign Enterprise	2190	1690	6272	8634	2425	8148
实际吸收外资金额(万美元)	**Foreign Capital Actually Absorbed(USD 10000)**	**19545**	**14010**	**9383**	**13191**	**13932**	**19568**
#直接利用外资	Direct Foreign Investment	2501	2829	3700	5626	6533	10768
#合资企业	Joint Venture	1630	1940	2124	3430	4356	3392
合作经营企业	Coopratiive Venture	121	20	75	42	331	3367
独资企业	Sole-Foreign Enterprise	750	869	1501	2154	1846	4009
外商投资企业基本情况	Registered Foreign-funded Enterprise						
年末实有外商投资企业(个)	Number of Foreign-funded Enterprises at the year-end(unit)	715	714	639	595	641	649
年底登记户数（户）	Number of Registered Enterprises at the year-end(unit)	45	57	54	63	36	52
投资总额（万美元）	Total Investment(USD 10000)	149349	159936	189146	210029	223443	234300
注册资本	Registered Capital	116635	119663	123443	137758	144845	149959
#外 方	Capital from Foreign Partners	75936	78864	81554	93925	99454	103291

11-5 “十五”时期各年外商直接投资按行业分项目个数

Agreement of Foreign Direct Investment by Sector of Each Year in “Tenth Five-year Plan” Period

行 业	Sector	2000	2001	2002	2003	2004	2005
总 计	**Total**	**55**	**59**	**54**	**69**	**61**	**60**
农、林、牧、渔业	Farming,Forestry,Animal Husbandry and Fishery	5	3	3	1	2	5
采矿业	Mining and Quarrying	3	2	6	3	4	4
制造业	Manufacturing	36	41	21	41	35	23
电力、燃气及水的生产和供应业	Electric Power,Gas and Water Production and Supply	1	2	2	1	4	4
建筑业	Construction	2	2	5	1	1	1
交通运输、仓储和邮政业	Transport, Storage and Post			1			3
信息传输、计算机服务和软件业	Information Transmission,Computer Services and Software					1	3
批发和零售业	Wholesale and Retail Trade			1	2	2	4
住宿和餐饮业	Hotel and Restaurants					2	1
房地产业	Real Estate	3	3	6	10	2	6
租赁和商务服务业	Leasing and Business Services		1	2	2	4	1
科学研究、技术服务和地质勘查业	Scientific Research,Technic Serviced and Geological Prospecting				3	2	1
水利、环境和公共设施管理业	Water Conservancy,Envinonment and Public Facilities Services					1	2
居民服务和其他服务业	Services to Households and Other Services	5	5	7	5	1	1
文化、体育和娱乐业	Culture, Sports and Entertainment						1

11-6 “十五”时期各年按行业分外商直接投资协议金额

Agreement of Foreign Direct Investment by Sector of Each Year in “Tenth Five-year Plan” Period

行业	Sector	2000	2001	2002	2003	2004	2005
总计	**Total**	**6738**	**9111**	**18943**	**19947**	**12649**	**19488**
农、林、牧、渔业	Farming,Forestry,Animal Husbandry and Fishery	150	1189	155	810	86	2256
采矿业	Mining and Quarrying	83	46	3824	382	1654	2589
制造业	Manufacturing	4069	7006	4577	12489	9442	8995
电力、燃气及水的生产和供应业	Electric Power,Gas and Water Production and Supply	943	641	5811	362	821	1275
建筑业	Construction	648	368	1468	1200	42	270
交通运输、仓储及邮电通讯业	Transport, Storage and Post			422			34
信息传输、计算机服务和软件业	Information Transmission,Computer Services and Software					3	138
批发和零售业	Wholesale and Retail Trade			24	329	234	475
住宿和餐饮业	Hotel and Restaurants					20	841
房地产业	Real Estate	461	-203	402	2101	453	1164
租赁和商务服务业	Leasing and Business Services		1	1111	749	-575	504
科学研究、技术服务和地质勘查业	Scientific Research,Technic Serviced and Geological Prospecting				1183	4	312
水利、环境和公共设施管理业	Water Conservancy,Envinonment and Public Facilities Services					451	621
居民服务和其他服务业	Services to Households and Other Services	384	63	1149	342	2	6
文化、体育和娱乐业	Culture, Sports and Entertainment					12	8

11-7 “十五”时期各年按行业分外商实际直接投资额

Actually Used Amount of Foreign Direct Investment by Sector of Each Year in “Tenth Five-year Plan” Period

单位：万美元(USD 10000)

指 标	Item	2000	2001	2002	2003	2004	2005
总 计	**Total**	**2501**	**2829**	**3700**	**5626**	**6533**	**10768**
农、林、牧、渔业	Farming, Forestry,Animal usbandry and Fishery	23		36		53	239
采矿业	Mining and Quarrying		4	15	133	238	3749
制造业	Manufacturing	793	2041	2603	4051	4280	5542
电力、燃气及水的生产和供应业	Electric Power,Gas and Water Prod uction and Supply					859	3
建筑业	Construction	20	45	126	71	42	88
交通运输、仓储和邮政业	Transportation,Storage,Postal and Telecommunications Services	24		242		180	2
信息传输、计算机服务和软件业	Information Transmit,Computer Services and Software Trade						13
批发和零售业	Wholesale & Retail Trade and Catering Services	191		24		34	162
住宿和餐饮业	Quarter and Catering Services					41	145
房地产业	Real Estate	1373	450	389	713	457	151
租赁和商务服务业	Leasehold and Commerce Services					108	236
科学研究、技术服务和地质勘查业	Scientific Research,Technic Serviced and Geological Prospecting				335	181	326
水利、环境和公共设施管理业	Water Conservancy,Envinonment and Public Facilities Services						103
居民服务和其他服务业	Recident and other Services	77	289	265	323		
文化、体育和娱乐业	Culture,Sports and Recreational Services					60	9

11-8 “十五”时期各年对外经济合作

Contracted Projects and Labour Cooperation with Foreign Countries or Territories of Each Year in “Tenth Five-year Plan” Period

指　标	Item	2000	2001	2002	2003	2004	2005
境外经济合作	**Economical Cooperation with Foreigh Countries or Territories**						
签订合同项目（个）	Number of Contracted Projects(unit)	40	38	6	3		8
#对外承包工程	#Contracted Projects	4	3	5	3		6
劳务合作	Labour Cooperation	36	35	1			2
签订合同金额（万美元）	Value of Contract(USD 10000)	3357	8558	4412	5606		13783
#对外承包工程	Contracted Projects	3151	8512	4412	5606		13063
劳务合作	Labour Cooperation	206	46				720
实际营业额（万美元）	Actual Turnover(USD 10000)	1948	7461	1943	6435	5433	16396
#对外承包工程	Contracted Projects	1810	7145	1751	6255	5253	16216
劳务合作	Labour Cooperation	138	316	192	180	180	180
年末在外人员（人）	Persons in Abroad(year-end)(person)	345	356	175	103	240	642
#对外承包工程	Contracted Projects	14		24		155	557
劳务合作	Labour Cooperation	331	356	151	103	85	85
省外经济合作	**Economic Cooperation with other province**						
引进省外项目（个）	Number of Contracted Projects(unit)	801	910	1082	1861	1824	1996
引进省外资金（亿元）	Contracted Value(100 million yuan)	33.93	48.53	57.30	104.00	130.00	232.50

11-9 海关出口商品分类情况

Export Commodities in Value by Category(Customs Statistics)

金额：万美元(Value:USD 10000)

指　标	Item	2004	2005	2005年比2004年增长(%) Increase Rate in 2005 over 2004(%)
总　计	**Total**	**86709**	**85925**	**-0.9**
活动物；动物产品	Live Animals & Animal Products	85	60	-29.4
植物产品	Vegetables, Fruits and Cereals	592	395	-33.3
动、植物油、脂及其分解产品；精制的食用油脂；动、植物蜡	Animal and Vegetable Oils,Fats and Wax, Refined Edible Oils and Fats	588	474	-19.4
食品；饮料、酒及醋；烟草及烟草代用品的制品	Food, Beverages, Liquor and Vinegar, Tobacco and Tobacco Substitutes	5667	5882	3.8
矿产品	Minerals	10035	9478	-5.6
化学工业及其相关工业的产品	Chemicals and Related Products	27562	29946	8.6
塑料及其产品；橡胶及其产品	Plastics and Related Products,Rubber and Related Products	5276	7141	35.3
生皮、皮革、毛皮及其制品；鞍具及挽具；旅行用品、手提包及类似物品；动物肠线（蚕胶 丝除外）制品	Raw Hides, Leather, Furs and Related Products, Saddle, Travel Articles,Handbags and Similar Containers	24	31	29.2
木及木制品；木炭；软木及软木制品；稻草、秸秆、针茅或其他编结材料制品；篮筐及柳条编织品	Wood and Wooden Products, Charcoal,Cork and Related Products, Straws,Plaited Products,Baskets and Wickerwork	38	49	28.9
木浆及其他纤维状纤维素浆；回收（废碎）纸或纸板；纸、纸板及其制品	Paper Pulp and Cellulose Pulp,Paper and Waste Paper, Paperboard and Related Products	3	5	66.7
纺织原料及纺织制品	Textile Materials and Products	1275	1390	9.0
鞋、帽、伞、杖、鞭及其零件；已加工的羽毛及其制品；人造花；人发制品	Footwear, Headgear, Umbrellas,Canes, Whips Processed Feather,Artificial,Flowers,Wigs	29	22	-24.1
石料、石膏、水泥、石棉、云母及类似材料的制品；陶瓷产品；玻璃及其制品	Gypsum , Cement, Asbestos,Mica,Ceramic Glass	152	271	78.3
贱金属及其制品	Base Metals and Related Products Machinery,Electric	14147	12285	-13.2
机器、机械器具、电气设备机器零件、录音机及放声机、电视图象、声音的录制和重放设备及其零件、附件	Equipment and Accessories, Recor ders,Videorecorder and Accessories	19464	16281	-16.4
车辆、航空器、船舶及有关运输设备	Locomotives, Vehicles, Aircraft,Ship and Related Transportation Equipment	1068	1616	51.3
光学、照相、电影、计量、检验、医疗或外科用仪器及设备、精密仪器及设备，钟表，乐器及其零附件	Optical,Photographic,Film,Measuring and Checking and Medical Instruments and Equipment, Precision Instruments and Equipment, Clocks, Musical Instruments,Related Parts and Accessories	253	291	15.0
杂项制品	Miscellaneous Products	453	308	-32.0
艺术品、收藏品及古物	Art,Collection and Antique			

11-10 海关进口商品分类情况

Import Commodities in Value by Category (Customs Statistics)

金额：万美元(Value:USD 10000)

指 标	Item	2004	2005	2005年比2004年增长(%) Increase Rate in 2005 over 2004(%)
总 计	**Total**	**64734**	**54500**	**-15.8**
活动物、动物产品	Live Animals & Animal Products	14		
植物产品	Vegetables, Fruits and Cereals	3	7	133.3
食品；饮料、酒及醋；烟草及烟草代用品的制品	Food, Beverages, Liquor and Vinegar, Tobacco and Tobacco Substitutes	347	39	-88.8
矿产品	Minerals	26309	26752	1.7
化学工业及其相关工业的产品	Chemicals and Related Products	2124	1987	-6.5
塑料及其产品；橡胶及其产品	Plastics and Related Products,Rubber and Related Products	4744	5066	6.8
木浆及其他纤维状纤维素浆；回收（废碎）纸或纸板；纸、纸板及其制品	Paper Pulp and Cellulose Pulp, Paper and Waste Paper,Paperboard and Related Products	205	217	5.9
纺织原料及纺织制品	Textile Materials and Products	34	24	-29.4
石料、石膏、水泥、石棉、云母及类似材料的制品；陶瓷产品；玻璃及其制品	Gypsum, Cement, Asbestos, Mica, Ceramic Glass	51	6	-88.2
贱金属及其制品	Base Metals and Related Products	4345	2907	-33.1
机器、机械器具、电气设备 机器零件、录音机及放声机、电视图象、声音的录制和重放设备及其零件、附件	Machinery, Electric Equipment and Accessories, Recorders, Videorecorder and Accessories	23671	15242	-35.6
车辆、航空器、船舶及有关运输设备	Locomotives, Vehicles, Aircraft,Ship and Related Transportation Equipment	535	548	2.4
光学、照相、电影、计量、检验、医疗或外科用仪器及设备、精密仪品及设备，钟表，乐器及其零附件	Optical,Photographic,Film,Measuring and Checking and Medical Instruments and Equipment,Precision Instruments and Equipment, Clocks, Musical Instruments,Related Parts and Accessories	2265	1658	-26.8
杂项制品	Miscellaneous Products	87	45	-48.3

主要统计指标解释

进出口总额 海关进出口总额指实际进出我国国境的货物总金额。包括对外贸易实际进出口货物,来料加工装配进出口货物,国家间、联合国及国际组织无偿援助物资和赠送品,华侨、港澳台同胞和外籍华人捐赠品,租赁期满归承租人所有的租赁货物,进料加工进出口货物,边境地方贸易及边境地区小额贸易进出口货物(边民互市贸易除外),中外合资企业、中外合作经营企业、外商独资经营企业进出口货物和公用物品,到、离岸价格在规定限额以上的进出口货样和广告品(无商业价值、无使用价值和免费提供出口的除外),从保税仓库提取在中国境内销售的进口货物,以及其他进出口货物。进出口总额用以观察一个国家在对外贸易方面的总规模。我国规定出口货物按离岸价格统计,进口货物按到岸价格统计。

利用外资 指我国各级政府、部门、企业和其他经济组织通过对外借款、吸收外商直接投资以及用其他方式筹措的境外现汇、设备、技术等。

对外借款 是我国利用外资的重要部分。指通过对外正式签订借款协议,从境外筹措的资金,包括外国政府贷款、国际金融组织贷款、外国银行商业贷款、出口信贷以及对外发行债券等。1996 年及以前还包括对外发行股票。

外商直接投资 指外国企业和经济组织或个人(包括华侨、港澳台胞以及我国在境外注册的企业)按我国有关政策、法规,用现汇、实物、技术等在我国境内开办外商独资企业、与我国境内的企业或经济组织共同举办中外合资经营企业、合作经营企业或合作开发资源的投资(包括外商投资收益的再投资),以及经政府有关部门批准的项目投资总额内企业从境外借入的资金。

外商其他投资 指除对外借款和外商直接投资以外的各种利用外资的形式。包括企业在境内外股票市场公开发行的以外币计价的股票(目前主要是在香港证券市场发行的 H 股和在境内证券市场发行的 B 股)发行价总额,国际租赁进口设备的应付款,补偿贸易中外商提供的进口设备、技术、物料的价款,加工装配贸易中外商提供的进口设备、物料的价款。

对外承包工程 指各对外承包公司以招标议标承包方式承揽的下列业务:(1)承包国外工程建设项目,(2)承包我国对外经援项目,(3)承包我国驻外机构的工程建设项目,(4)承包我国境内利用外资进行建设的工程项目,(5)与外国承包公司合营或联合承包工程项目时我国公司分包部分,(6)对外承包兼营的房屋开发业务。对外承包工程的营业额是以货币表现的本期内完成的对外承包工程的工作量,包括以前年度签订的合同和本年度新签订的合同在报告期内完成的工作量。

对外劳务合作 指以收取工资的形式向业主或承包商提供技术和劳动服务的活动。我国对外承包公司在境外开办的合营企业,中国公司同时又提供劳务的,其劳务部分也纳入劳务合作统计。劳务合作营业额按报告期内向雇主提交的结算数(包括工资、加班费和奖金等)统计。

对外设计咨询 指以服务成果向业主收费的技术服务项目。包括承担地形地貌测绘,地质资源勘探与普查,建设区域规划,提供设计文件、图纸、生产工艺技术资料和工程技术经济咨询,工程项目的可行性考察、研究和评估,进行技术指导和培训人员等;也包括承担国(境)内利用外资进行建设的工程项目的上述规定的设计咨询项目的收取外币部分。

Explanatory Notes on Main Statistical Indicators

Total Imports and Exports at Customs refer to the value of commodities imported into and exported from the boundary of China. They include the actual imports and exports through foreign trade, imported and exported goods under the processing and assembling trades and materials, supplies and gifts as aid given gratis between governments and by the United Nations and other international organizations, and contributions donated by overseas Chinese, compatriots in Hong Kong and Macao and Chinese with foreign citizenship, leasing commodities owned by tenant at the expiration of leasing period, the imported and exported commodities processed with imported materials, commodities trading in border areas(excluding mutual exchange goods), the imported and exported commodities and articles for public use of the Sino–foreign joint ventures, cooperative enterprises and ventures exclusively with foreign own investment .Also included are import or export of samples and advertising goods for whose CIF or FOB value are beyond the permitted ceiling (excluding goods of no trading or use value and free commodities for export),imported goods sold in China from bonded warehouses and other imported or exported goods.The indicator of the total imports and exports at customs can be used to observe the total size of external trade in a country.In accordance with the stipulation of the Chinese government,imports are calculated at CIF, while exports are calculated at FOB.

Utilization of Foreign Capital refers to remittance, equipment and technology financed from abroad, by loans, foreign direct investment and other forms undertaken by the Chinese governments at all levels, by various departments, enterprises and other economic units.

Foreign Borrowings an important part of China utilization of foreign capital,it refer to funds borrowed from abroad through formal signing of borrowing agreements with foreign institutions, including loans of foreign governments, loans of international financial institutions,commercial loans of foreign banks, export credit, and funds raised by Chinese bonds (and shares before 1996) issued abroad.

Direct Investment by Foreign Entrepreneurs refers to the investments inside China by foreign enterprises and economic organizations or individuals (including overseas Chinese,compatriots from Hong Kong and Macao,and Chinese enterprises registered abroad), following the relevant policies and laws of China, for the establishment of ventures exclusively with foreign own investment, Sino–foreign joint ventures and cooperative enterprises or for cooperative exploration of resources with enterprises or economic organizations in China. It includes the re investment of the foreign entrepreneurs with the profits gained from the investment and the funds that enterprises borrow from abroad in the total investment of projects which are approved by the relevant department of the government.

Other Investment by Foreign Entrepreneurs refers to all forms of utilization of foreign capitals other than foreign borrowings and foreign direct investment. It includes the total value of stock shares in foreign currencies issued by enterprises at domestic or foreign stock exchanges (now mainly consisting of H shares issued at Hong Kong Security Market and B shares issued at domestic security markets), rent payable for the imported equipment through international leasing arrangement, cost of imported equipment, technology and materials provided by foreign counterparts in compensation trade and processing and assembly trade.

Contracted Projects with Foreign Countries refer to projects undertaken by Chinese contractors (project contracting companies)through bidding process.They include: (1)overseas civil engineering construction projects fi–

nanced by foreign investors; (2)overseas projects financed by the Chinese government through its foreign aid programs; (3)construction projects of Chinese diplomatic missions,trade offices and other institutions stationed abroad; (4)construction projects in China financed by foreign investment; (5)sub–contracted projects to be taken by Chinese contractors through a joint umbrella project with foreign contractor (s); (6)housing development projects.The business income from international contracted projects is the work volume of contracted projects completed during the reference period, expressed in monetary terms, including completed work on projects signed in previous years.

Service Cooperation with Foreign Countries refers to the activities of providing technology and labour services to employers or contractors in the forms of receiving salaries and wages. Labour services providing by contractual joint ventures of Chihe statistics of service cooperation with foreign countries.The business income of labour service cooperation is the income in the form of wages and salaries, overtime pay, bonuses and other remuneration received from the employers during the reference period.

Overseas Design and Consultation Service refers to projects with charges for technical services from overseas operators. It includes geographic and topographic mapping, geological resource prospecting and survey, planning of construction areas, provision of design documents, blueprints, materials on production process and techniques, as well as engineering, technical and economic consultation, and feasibility study, research and evaluation of projects. Also included under this category are the above–mentioned services of foreign–financed projects in China that are paid in foreign currencies.

12

Twelve

旅 游

Tourism

境外旅游者人数及国际旅游收入

Namber of International Tourists and Earnings

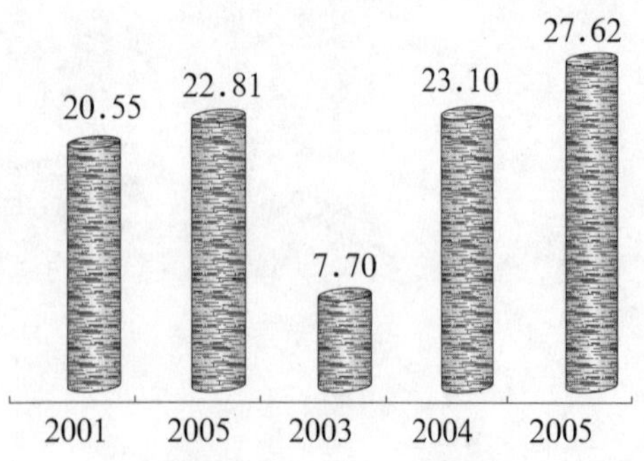

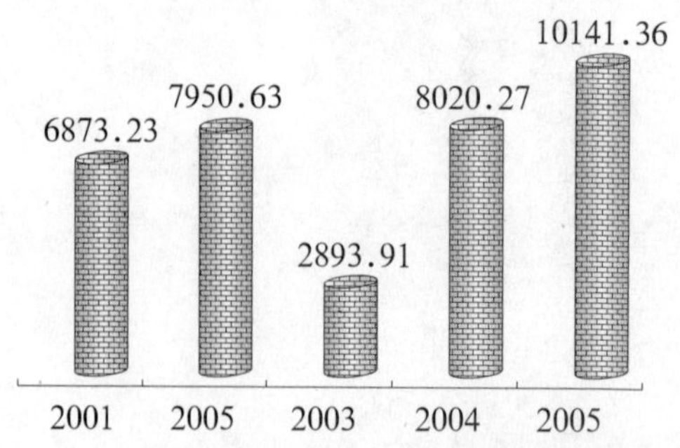

国内旅游人数及旅游收入

Number of Domestic Tourists and Earnings

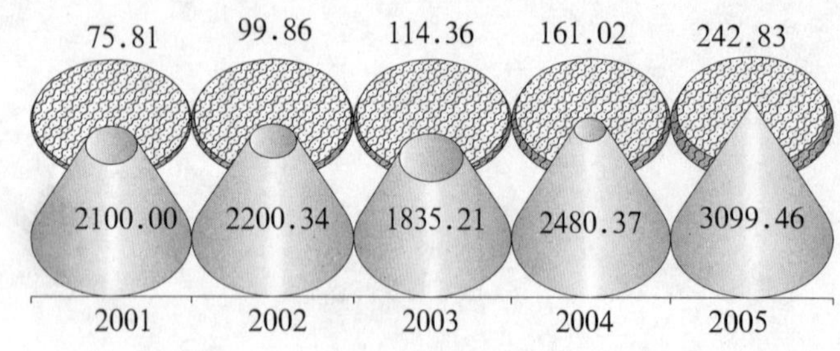

来黔境外旅游人均消费支出及逗留天数

Average per Capita Daily Expentliture and Time Staying of International Tourists

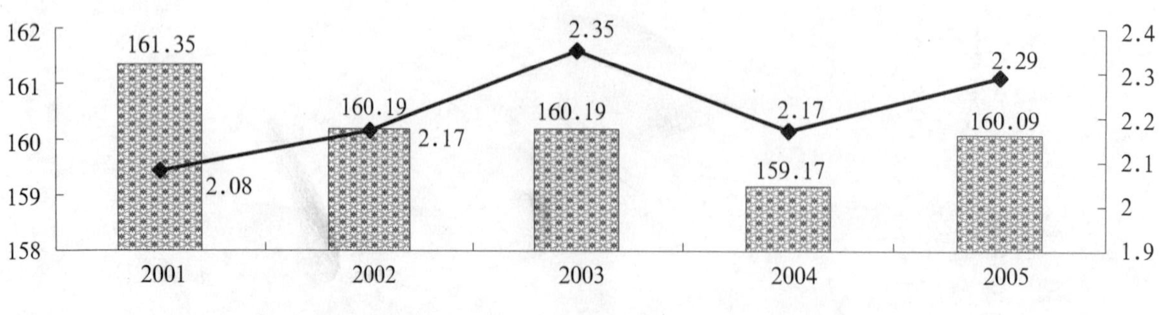

12-1 “十五”时期各年旅游业发展主要指标

Development of Tourism of Each Year in “Tenth Five-year Plan” Period

指 标	Item	2000	2001	2002	2003	2004	2005
旅行社总数（个）	**Total Number of Travel Agencies(unit)**	**107**	**135**	**131**	**142**	**154**	**168**
国际旅行社	International Travel Agencies	13	13	12	12	12	14
国内旅行社	Domestic Travel Agencies	94	122	119	130	142	154
旅行社职工人数（人）	**Number of Staff and Workers of Travel**	**875**	**1154**	**1251**	**1316**	**1819**	**1925**
	Agencies(person)						
国际旅行社	International Travel Agencies	464	510	587	642	715	780
国内旅行社	Domestic Travel Agencies	411	644	664	674	1104	1145
旅行社经营和财务状况	**Management and Financial Status of Travel Agencies**						
营业收入（万元）	Operational Income(10000 yuan)	21232	29041	30205	30859	35487	38257
利润总额	Total Profit	-100.69	-163.98	-189.18	27.38	-50.42	0.09
入境旅游人数(万人次)	**Total Number of International Tourists Inbound (10000 person-times)**	**18.39**	**20.55**	**22.81**	**7.70**	**23.10**	**27.62**
外国人	Foreigners	7.12	7.85	8.45	2.40	7.63	9.26
港澳同胞	Compatriots from Hong Kong and Macao	5.30	5.95	6.53	2.83	6.69	7.82
台湾同胞	Compatriots from Taiwan	5.97	6.75	7.83	2.47	8.77	10.54
三大旅行社接待入境旅游人数(万人)	**Number of International Tourists Received by Three Major Travel Service (10000 persons)**	**2.89**	**5.76**	**6.74**	**2.06**	**2.49**	**3.04**
中国国际旅行社	China International Travel Service	1.6	2.01	2.11	0.51	0.91	0.89
贵州海外旅游总公司	Guizhou Overseas Tourism Corporatior	0.08	2.24	2.4	1.39	1.45	2.05
中国青年旅行社	China Youth Travel Service	1.21	1.51	2.23	0.16	0.13	0.10
国际旅游收入（万美元）	Earnings from International Tourism (USD 10000)	6092.23	6873.23	7950.63	2893.91	8020.27	10141.36
国内旅游人数（万人次）	Total Number of Domestic Tourists (10000 person-times)	1980.00	2100.00	2200.34	1835.21	2480.37	3099.46
国内旅游收入（亿元）	Earnings from Domestic Tourism (100 million yuan)	57.95	75.81	99.86	114.36	161.02	242.83

12-2 “十五”时期各年接待外国旅游人数（按地区分）

Number of Overseas Tourists Visiting Guizhou of Each Year in “Tenth Five-year Plan” Period by Country (Region)

单位：人　(person)

地区名	Country(Territory)	2000	2001	2002	2003	2004	2005	2005年比2004年增长(%) Increase Rate in 2005 over 2004(%)
总　计	**Total**	**71183**	**78514**	**84498**	**23997**	**76335**	**92584**	**21.3**
亚　洲	Asia	45921	52531	56839	16892	54054	45417	-16.0
非　洲	Africa		209	80	39	150	413	175.3
欧　洲	Europe	15849	16595	17617	4354	13497	19219	42.4
拉丁美洲	Latin America	8915	7119	7682	2153	6911	15357	122.2
大洋洲	Oceania						11305	
其　他	Others	498	2060	2280	559	1723	873	-49.3

12-3 “十五”时期各年来黔境外旅游人数及人均消费支出

Number of Overseas Tourists Visiting Guizhou and Average Per Capita Spending of Each Year in “Tenth Five-year Plan” Period

类　别	Item	2000	2001	2002	2003	2004	2005	2005年比2004年增长(%) Increase Rate in 2005 over 2004(%)
来黔境海外旅游者人数（人次）	**Number of Overseas Tourists** Visiting Guizhou(person-times)	**183898**	**205466**	**228091**	**77045**	**231023**	**276194**	**19.6**
外国人	Foreigner	71183	78514	84498	23997	76335	92584	21.3
港澳同胞	Compatriots from Hong Kong and Macao	52997	59461	65255	28359	66952	178032	165.9
台湾同胞	Compatriots from Taiwan	59718	67491	78338	24689	87736	5578	-93.6
平均每人逗留天数（天/人）	Average Time Tourists Staying in Guizhou Per Capita(day/person)	2.13	2.08	2.17	2.35	2.17	2.29	5.5
平均每人每天消费支出（美元/人天）	Average Per Capita Daily Spending(USD/persen-day)	331.70	161.35	160.19	160.19	159.17	160.09	0.6

12-4 “十五”时期各年旅馆业接待经营情况

Operation of Hotels of Each Year in “Tenth Five-year Plan” Period

类 别	Item	2000	2001	2002	2003	2004	2005	2005年比2004年增长(%) Increase Rate in 2005 over 2004(%)
接待能力	**Capacity**							
年末客房数（间）	Guest Rooms (Year-end) (unit)	6082	8658	9061	12043	13280	14464	8.9
年末客房床位数（张）	Guest Beds (Year-end) (bed)	13073	16957	18432	23860	26445	27487	3.9
客房开房率（%）	Room Occupancy Rate(%)	56.1	59.8	61.3	57.5	58.1	60.1	3.4
#星级宾馆	Star-rated Hotels	56.1	59.8	61.3	57.8	60.2	64.7	7.4
实际住宿人次数（万人次）	Actual Number of Guests (10000 person-times)		217.02	231.30	231.40	240.60	366.24	52.2
#海外来黔	Overseas Visitors	18.39	20.55	22.81	7.70	23.10	27.60	19.5
实际住宿人天数（万人天）	Actual Number of Guests and Days of Stay(10000 person-day)		290.41	331.25	314.34	335.71	517.85	54.3
#海外来黔	Overseas Visitors	39.25	42.65	49.53	18.07	50.21	63.37	26.2
经营和财务	**Management and Financial**							
营业收入（万元）	Operational Income(10000 yuan)	39356	46040	53866	97547	105351	140350	33.2

12-5 "十五"时期各年星级饭店情况

Number of Star-rated Hotels of Each Year in "Tenth Five-year Plan" Period

单位：个(unit)

指 标	Item	2000	2001	2002	2003	2004	2005
总 计	**Total**	**62**	**80**	**81**	**123**	**146**	**177**
按经济类型分	Grouped by Ownership						
国有经济	State-owned	57	75	75	103	103	118
集体经济	Collective-owned	1	1	1	15	38	54
外商投资经济	Foreign Funded	4	4	5	5	5	5
按规模分	Grouped by Capacity						
客房总数500间以上	Above 500 Rooms	2	2				
客房总数300-499间	With 300-499 Rooms	3	3	1	1	1	2
客房总数200-299间	With 200-299 Rooms	7	19	7	6	6	7
客房总数100-199间	With 100-199 Rooms	21	25	27	30	33	33
客房总数99间以下	With Less than 100 Rooms	29	31	46	86	106	135

12-6 "十五"时期各年旅游外汇收入

Foreign Exchange Earnings of Each Year in "Tenth Five-year Plan" Period

单位：万美元(USD 10000)

类 别	Item	2000	2001	2002	2003	2004	2005	2005年比2004年增长(%) Increase Rate in 2005 over 2004(%)
总 计	**Total**	**6092.23**	**6873.23**	**7950.63**	**2893.91**	**8020.27**	**10141.36**	**26.4**
长途交通	Long Distance Transportation	1858.13	1928.03	2693.02	879.21	2823.14	3235.09	14.6
游 览	Visiting	158.39	167.48	270.32	104.31	272.69	375.23	37.6
住 宿	Accommodation	816.36	846.37	1351.61	467.39	1363.45	1389.37	1.9
餐 饮	Food and Beverage	584.85	673.66	969.98	405.22	978.47	1186.54	21.3
商品销售	Shopping	1504.78	1495.13	1168.74	486.90	1178.98	2180.39	84.9
娱 乐	Entertainment	85.29	272.09	524.74	162.83	529.33	446.22	-15.7
邮电通讯	Postal and Communication Services	286.33	219.29	254.42	94.52	256.65	283.96	10.6
市内交通	Local Transportation	42.65	18.93	71.55	72.02	72.18	354.95	391.8
其他服务	Other Service	755.45	1252.25	646.25	221.51	545.38	689.61	26.4

12-7 风景名胜区一览表

Schedule of Scenic Spots

名 称	Title	级 别	地 址
红枫湖风景名胜区	Hongfeng Lake Scenic Spot	国家级	贵州省贵阳市清镇
黄果树风景名胜区	Huangguoshu Waterfalls Scenic Spot	国家级	贵州省安顺市镇宁县
龙宫风景名胜区	The Dragon Palace Scenic Spot	国家级	贵州省安顺市
织金洞风景名胜区	Zhijin Cave Scenic Spot	国家级	贵州省毕节地区织金县
九洞天风景名胜区	Jiudongtian Scenic Spot	国家级	贵州省毕节地区
马岭河峡谷风景名胜区	Malinghe Canyon Scenic Spot	国家级	贵州省黔西南州兴义市
㵲阳河风景名胜区	Wuyang Tuorist Area Scenic Spot	国家级	贵州省黔东南州镇远县
黎平侗乡风景名胜区	Liping Dong-Village Scenic Spot	国家级	贵州省黔东南州黎平县
荔波樟江风景名胜区	Libo Zhangjiang Scenic Spot	国家级	贵州省黔南州荔波县
都匀斗篷山——剑江风景名胜区	Duyun Doupeng Mountain--Jianjiang Scenic Spot	国家级	贵州省黔南州
赤水风景名胜区	Chishui Scenic Spot	国家级	贵州省赤水市
九龙洞风景名胜区	Jiulong Cave Scenic Spot	国家级	贵州省铜仁地区铜仁市
紫云格凸河风景名胜区	Ziyun Getu River Scenic Spot	国家级	贵州省安顺市紫云县
百花湖风景名胜区	Baihua Lake Scenic Spot	省级	贵州省贵阳市
花溪风景名胜区	Huaxi Scenic Spot	省级	贵州省贵阳市花溪区
息烽风景名胜区	Xifeng Scenic Spot	省级	贵州省贵阳市息烽县
修文阳明风景名胜区	Xiuwen Yangming Scenic Spot	省级	贵州省贵阳市修文县
香纸沟风景名胜区	Xiangzhigou Scenic Spot	省级	贵州省贵阳市
开阳风景名胜区	Kaiyang Scenic Spot	省级	贵州省贵阳市开阳县
相思河风景名胜区	Xiangsi River Scenic Spot	省级	贵州省贵阳市
清镇暗流河风景名胜区	Qingzhen Undercurrent River Scenic Spot	省级	贵州省贵阳市清镇
普定梭筛风景名胜区	Puding Suoshai Scenic Spot	省级	贵州省安顺市普定县
关岭花江大峡谷风景名胜区	Guanling Huajiang Canyon Scenic Spot	省级	贵州省安顺市关岭县花江镇
平坝天台山——斯拉河风景名胜区	Pingba Tiantai Mountain --Sila River Scenic Spot	省级	贵州省安顺市平坝县
百里杜鹃风景名胜区	One-Hundred-Li Azalea Belt Scenic Spot	省级	毕节地区大方、黔西县
贵州屋脊赫章韭菜坪风景名胜区	Guizhou Fastigium Hezhang Jiucaiping Scenic Spot	省级	贵州省毕节地区赫章县
鲁布革风景名胜区	Lubuge Scenic Spot	省级	贵州省黔西南州兴义市
泥凼石林风景名胜区	Nidang shilin Scenic Spot	省级	贵州省黔西南州兴义市泥凼镇
安龙招堤风景名胜区	Anlong Zhaodi Scenic Spot	省级	贵州省黔西南州安龙县
贞丰三岔河风景名胜区	Zhenfeng Sancha River Scenic Spot	省级	贵州省黔西南州贞丰县
晴隆三望坪风景名胜区	Qinglong Sanwangping Scenic Spot	省级	贵州省黔西南州晴隆县
兴仁放马坪风景名胜区	Xingren Fangmaping Scenic Spot	省级	贵州省黔西南州兴仁县
岑巩龙鳌河风景名胜区	Cengong Longao River Scenic Spot	省级	贵州省黔东南州岑巩县
剑河风景名胜区	Jianhe Scenic Spot	省级	贵州省黔东南州剑河县
麻江下司风景名胜区	Majiang Xiasi Scenic Spot	省级	贵州省黔东南州麻江县

12-7续表(continued)

名　称	Title	级别	地　址
榕江古榕风景名胜区	Rongjiang Gurong Scenic Spot	省级	贵州省黔东南州榕江县
镇远高过河风景名胜区	Zhenyuan Gaoguo River Scenic Spot	省级	贵州省黔东南州镇远县
雷山风景名胜区	Leishan Scenic Spot	省级	贵州省黔东南州雷山县
锦屏三板溪——隆里古城风景名胜区	Jinping Sanbanxi--Longli Scenic Spot	省级	贵州省黔东南州锦屏县
丹寨龙泉山——岔河风景名胜区	Danzhai Longquansan--Chahe Scenic Spot	省级	贵州省黔东南州丹寨县
从江风景名胜区	Congjiang Scenic Spot	省级	贵州省黔东南州从江县
龙里猴子沟风景名胜区	Longli Monkey Fossa Scenic Spot	省级	贵州省黔南州龙里县
福泉洒金谷风景名胜区	Fuquan Sajingu Scenic Spot	省级	贵州省黔南州福泉市
瓮安江界河风景名胜区	Wengan Jiangjie River Scenic Spot	省级	贵州省黔南州瓮安县
惠水涟江——燕子洞风景名胜区	Huishui Lianjiang--Yanzi Cave Scenic Spot	省级	贵州省黔南州惠水县
长顺杜鹃湖——白云山风景名胜区	Changshun Dujuan Lake--Baiyun Mountain Scenic Spot	省级	贵州省黔南州长顺县
平塘风景名胜区	Pingtan Scenic Spot	省级	贵州省黔南州平塘县
三都都柳江风景名胜区	Sandu Duliu River Scenic Spot	省级	贵州省黔南州三都县
贵定洛北河风景名胜区	Guiding Luobei River Scenic Spot	省级	贵州省黔南州贵定县
独山深河桥风景名胜区	Dushan Shenhe Bridge Scenic Spot	省级	贵州省黔南州独山县
遵义娄山风景名胜区	Zunyi Loushan Mountain Scenic Spot	省级	贵州省遵义市遵义县板桥镇
绥阳宽阔水风景名胜区	Suiyang Kuankuoshui Scenic Spot	省级	贵州省遵义市绥阳县
仁怀茅台风景名胜区	Renhuai Moutai Scenic Spot	省级	贵州省遵义仁怀市茅台镇
习水风景名胜区	Xishui Scenic Spot	省级	贵州省遵义市习水县东皇镇
余庆大乌江风景名胜区	Yuqing Wujian River Scenic Spot	省级	贵州省遵义市余庆县白泥镇
湄潭风景名胜区	Meitan Scenic Spot	省级	贵州省遵义市湄潭县
梵净山——太平河风景名胜区	Fanjing Mountain--Taiping River Scenic Spot	省级	贵州省铜仁地区江口县
石阡温泉群风景名胜区	Shiqian Hot Well Flock Scenic Spot	省级	贵州省铜仁地区石阡县
印江木黄风景名胜区	Yinjiang Muhuang Scenic Spot	省级	贵州省铜仁地区印江县
思南乌江白鹭洲风景名胜区	Sinan Wujiang River Bailuzhou Scenic Spo	省级	贵州省铜仁地区思南县
松桃豹子岭——寨英风景名胜区	Songtao Baozi Mountain--Zhaiying Scenic Spot	省级	贵州省铜仁地区松桃县
万山夜郎谷风景名胜区	Wanshan Yelang Canyon Scenic Spot	省级	贵州省铜仁地区万山特区
沿河乌江山峡风景名胜区	Yuanhe Wujiang River Sanxia Scenic Spot	省级	贵州省铜仁地区沿河县
玉屏北洞萧笛之乡风景名胜区	Yuping Beidong Xiaodi-Village Scenic Spot	省级	贵州省铜仁地区玉屏县
六枝牂牁江风景名胜区	Liuzhi Zangke River Scenic Spot	省级	贵州省六盘水市六枝特区
盘县古银杏风景名胜区	Panxian Ancientry Gingko Scenic Spot	省级	贵州省六盘水市盘县石桥镇
盘县大洞竹海风景名胜区	PanXian Dadong Banboo Sea Scenic Spot	省级	贵州省六盘水市盘县珠东乡、老厂镇
盘县坡上草原风景名胜区	PanXian Grassland on Mountain Scenic Spot	省级	贵州省六盘水市盘县四格乡、坪地乡
南开风景名胜区	Nankai Scenic Spot	省级	贵州省六盘水市水城县

12-8 重点文物保护单位

Historical and Cultrual Relics under Key Protection

名 称	Title	地 址
遵义会议会址	The Site of Zunyi Conference	遵义市红花岗区
遵义杨粲墓	Zunyi Yangcan Tomb	遵义市红花岗区
息烽集中营旧址	The Site Concentration Camp Xifeng	贵阳市息烽县
镇远青龙洞	Zhenyuan Qinglong Cave	黔东南州镇远县
毕节大屯彝族土司庄园	Bijie Datun Headman's Castle	毕节地区毕节县
大方奢香夫人墓	The Mausoleum of Lady She Xiang Dafang	毕节地区大方县
从江增冲鼓楼	Congjiang Zengchong Drum-tower	黔东南州从江县
普定穿洞遗址	Puding Chuandong,the Stone Cave	安顺市普定县
盘县大洞遗址	The Site of Dadong Cave PanXian	六盘水市文化局
黔西观音洞遗址	The Site of Kwan-yin Cave Qianxi	毕节地区黔西县
遵义海龙囤	Zunyi Hailongtun	遵义市遵义县
赫章可乐遗址	The Site of Kele Hezhang	毕节地区赫章县
雷山郎德上寨古建筑群	The Ancientry Construction Langdeshangzhai Leishan	黔东南州雷山县
安顺云山屯古建筑群	The Ancientry Construction Yunshantun Anshun	安顺市西秀区七眼桥镇
安顺府文庙	Anshun State Joss House	安顺市西秀区
福泉明城墙	Fuquan Ming Dynasty Wall	黔南州福泉市
石阡万寿宫	Shiqian Wanshou Palace	铜仁地区石阡县文管所
平坝天台山伍龙寺	Pingba Tiantai Wulong Temple	安顺市平坝县天龙镇
黎平地坪风雨桥	Liping Diping Pavilion Bridge	黎平县地坪乡政府办

12-9 星级饭店目录(按星级)

Summary for Tourist Hotels

名 称	Name	星级 Level	评定日期 Date of Assess	客房数 Rooms	床位数 Beds	地 址 Address	电话 Telephone
贵州天怡豪生大酒店	Guizhou Tianyi Haosheng Hotel	5	2005.03	310	439	贵阳市枣山路29号	6518888
贵州圣沣酒店	Guizhou Shengfeng Hotel	5	2005.03	260	366	贵阳市神奇路69号	5568888
贵州饭店	Guizhou Hotel	4	1998.07	382	660	贵阳市北京路66号	6823888
贵阳神奇酒店	Guiyang Shenqi Hotel	4	1999.12	230	339	贵阳市贵开路1号	6771888
贵阳神奇金筑酒店	Guiyang Shenqijinzhu Hotel	4	1991.5	180	230	贵阳市延安东路2号	6825888
贵州鲜花酒店	Guizhou Xuanhua Hotel	4	2001.12	246	403	贵阳市中华南路1号	5867888
贵州柏顿酒店	Guizhou Bodun Hotel	4	2001.5	254	343	贵阳市延安东路18号	5827888
贵州丽豪大酒店	Guizhou Lihao Hotel	4	2005.07	199	355	贵阳市瑞金北路115号	6521888
贵龙饭店	GuiLong Bodun Hotel	4	2001.6	168	316	贵阳市神奇路52号	5593888
能辉酒店	Nenghui Hotel	4	2003.12	125	213	贵阳市瑞金南路38号	5898888
凯里市腾龙凯悦酒店	Kaili Tenglong Kaiyue Hotel	4	2004.5.24	113	191	凯里市宁波东路	8066666
贵州省兴义民航酒店	Guizhou Xingyi Civil Aviaton Hotel	4	2003.7	98	188	贵州省兴义市瑞金南路	3126666
贵州华联酒店	Guizhou Hualian Hotel	3	1999.9	141	261	贵阳市中华中路137号	5810999
贵阳山林大酒店	Guizhou Shanlin Hotel	3	1999.9	158	300	贵阳市山林路118号	6523000
黔灵大酒店	Qianling Hotel	3	2000.4	152	273	贵阳市北京路225号	8271521
金阳宾馆	Jinyang Hotel	3	2000.4	138	266	贵阳市白云区白云公园	4485678
金桥饭店	Jinqiao Hotel	3	2000.12	131	240	贵阳市瑞金中路24号	5829953
黔贵大酒店	Qiangui Hotel	3	2000.12	22	40	贵阳市浣沙路5号	5958888
华城大酒店	Huacheng Hotel	3	2001.12	131	242	贵阳市中华北路67号	6830666
云岩宾馆	Yunyan Hotel	3	2001.12	81	139	贵阳市北京路68号	6822977
贵阳神奇星岛酒店	Guiyang Shenqi Xindao Hotel	3	2002.9	101	180	贵阳市贵开路1号	6751888
黄果树大酒店	Huangguoshu Hotel	3	2002.9	168	339	贵阳市瑞金北路156号	6838888
贵州立云酒店	Guizhou Liyun Hotel	3	2002.12	254	468	贵阳市浣沙路5号	8126666
紫林宾馆	Zilin Hotel	3	2004.2	57	150	贵阳市延安中路110号	5283000
贵橡大酒店	Guixiang Hotel	3	2004.4.5	84	167	贵阳市瑞金北路北段	6871523
燕安大酒店	Yanan Hotel	3	1997.12	81	167	安顺市贵黄路5公里处	3228988
安顺黄果树宾馆	Anshun Huangguoshu Hotel	3	1995.4	158	281	安顺黄果树风景区内	3592110
安顺西秀山宾馆	Anshun Xixiushan Hotel	3	94.4,2002.4	92	153	安顺市南华路48号	3223900
神奇福运大酒店	Shenqi Fuyun Hotel	3	2002.9	90	160	安顺市外环西南路3号	3290000
遵义宾馆	Zunyi Hotel	3	2000.1	181	329	遵义市石龙路3号	8224902
金城大酒店	Jincheng Hotel	3	2000.1	150	256	遵义市香港路中段	8621666
都匀港龙大酒店	Duyun Ganglong Hotel	3	2002.8	126	210	都匀市河滨路134号	8222895

12-9续表1(continued)

名　称	Name	星级 Level	评定日期 Date of Assess	客房数 Rooms	床位数 Beds	地　址 Address	电话 Telephone
兴义宾馆	Xinyi Hotel	3	2000.7	70	130	兴义市瑞金南路	3111101
黔山度假酒店	Qianshan Holiday Hotel	3	2003.7	179	358	兴义市瑞金南路	3116669
贵州清酒醉翁宾馆	Guizhou Qingjiu Zuiwen Hotel	3	2004.5.24	46	92	贵州镇远县	5823238
施秉县三丰迎宾馆	Shibing Sanfeng Hotel	3	2004.5.24	89	190	施秉县平宁桥	4227188
国泰大酒店	Guotai Hotel	3	2004.7	73	135	凯里市北京东路6号	8269888
黔西莲城宾馆	Qianxi Liancheng Hotel	3	2004.10.1	46	88	贵州黔西县	4244666
久远饭店	Jiuyuan Hotel	3	2004.8	169	300	贵阳市瑞金南路36号	5849999
六盘水新华大酒店	Liupangshui Hotel	3	2004.10.1	110	195	六盘水钟山开发区钟山中路	2118888
六盘水红果大酒店	Liupangshui Hongguo Hotel	3	2004.10.1	187	372	盘县红果经济开发区	3631888
茅园宾馆	Maoyuan Hotel	3	2004.10.1	56	110	贵州省仁怀市茅台镇	2386290
贵州腾飞电信酒店	Guizhou Tengfei Telecom Hotel	3	2004.12.08	83	153	贵阳市市南路69号	5529888
修文县珍珠岛度假中心	Xiuwen Zhenzhudao Holiday Hotel	3	2004.11.25	89	220	贵阳修文酒长镇	2436002
贵阳市金品大酒店	Guiyang Jinpin Hotel	3	2004.12.08	112	196	贵阳朝阳洞路建材巷1号	8216666
贵阳南翔酒店	Guiyang Nanxiang Telecom Hotel	3	2004.12.29	63	108	贵阳市延安西路185号	6522888
红阳宾馆	Hongyang Hotel	3	2005.01	73	140	花溪区150号信箱	3853306
贵州宏业宾馆	Guizhou Hongye Hotel	3	2005.02	75	143	贵阳市解放路87号	5566755
金松大酒店	Jinsong Hotel	3	2005.03.21	36	68	铜仁松桃苗族自治县	2839888
铜仁天源大酒店	Tongren Tianyuan Hotel	3	2005.03.21	48	91	铜仁市东太大道	5930555
神泉大酒店	Shengquan Hotel	3	2005.03.21	46	96	罗甸县政府路	7620758
顺庆大酒店	Shunqian Hotel	3	2005.03.21	98	218	荔波樟江北街	3610388
黔中大厦	Qianzhong Hotel	3	2005.07.04	66	113	安顺市南华路68好	3292019
安顺虹山宾馆	Anshun Hongshan Hotel	3	2005.07.04	75	148	安顺市虹湖东路42号	3257999
白马湖山庄	Baimahu Hotel	3	2005.07.04	33	59	安顺市镇宁县白马哨	6791111
兴义市城城大厦	Xingyi Chengcheng Hotel	3	2005.07.04	68	128	兴义市神奇路159号	3112222
盘江宾馆	Panjiang Hotel	3	2005.07.04	123	231	兴义市盘江西路4号	3223456
源丰商务酒店	Yuanfeng Commerce Hotel	3	2005.07.20	62	99	铜仁市锦江南路1号	5222222
雨田酒店	Yutian Hotel	3	2005.07.20	75	126	六盘水市钟山区钟山西路48号	8261888
纪龙酒店	JiLong Hotel	3	2005.09	44	80	龙里县	5620333
锦绣园	Jingxu Hotel	3	2005.09	48	101	龙里县城郊	5669508
贵阳久泰大酒店	Guiyang Juitai Hotel	3	2005.10.9	120	191	贵阳市瑞金北路116号	6685998
聚丰园大酒店	Jufengyuan Hotel	3	2005.10.27	89	121	都匀市剑江中路112号	8756999

12-9续表2(continued)

名称	Name	星级 Level	评定日期 Date of Assess	客房数 Rooms	床位数 Beds	地址 Address	电话 Telephone
遵义港澳大酒店	Zhunyi Gongao Hotel	3	2005.11	81	148	遵义市澳门路8号	8716655
通达饭店	Tongda Hotel	2	1994.4	220	400	贵阳市遵义路86号	8213888
盛安酒店	Shengan Hotel	2	1994.9	50	96	贵阳市中山东路180号	5822898
新联大厦	Xinlian Hotel	2	1997.12	120	200	外环东路227号	6765555
贵阳机场宾馆	Guizhou Airport Hotel	2	2000	168	315	贵阳市龙洞堡机场内	5498585
贵州体育宾馆	Guizhou Sport Hotel	2	1994.9	65	150	遵义路新体育馆内	5798777
丰丰宾馆	Fengfeng Hotel	2	2000.7	81	169	贵阳市体育路5号	5771185
枫叶山庄	Fengye Hotel	2	2000.1	66	129	贵阳市清镇红枫发电总厂内	2554168
溪山酒店	Xishan Hotel	2	2000.11	27	54	贵阳市花溪平桥	3864555
贵州铝厂宾馆	Guizhou Aluminium Processing Manufactory Hotel	2	2004.6	92	152	贵阳市白云区刚玉街	4896111
玉龙宾馆	Yulong Hotel	2	2000.11	35	70	贵阳市花溪	.3863668
白云宾馆	Baiyun Hotel	2	2001.4	38	70	贵阳市白云区白云中路22号	4607856
贵阳明珠饭店	Guiyang Mingzhu Hotel	2	2003.12	65	115	贵阳市四通街8号	5793389
天洋楼大酒店	Tianyanglou Hotel	2	2004.9	42	100	贵阳市民权路5号	5832088
电信宾馆	Dianxin Hotel	2	2001.11	48	90	贵阳市中华南路68号	5868988
安顺民族饭店	Anshun Folk Hotel	2	1995.4	62	127	安顺塔山东路67号	3222500
安顺龙宫水电宾馆	Anshun Longgong Shuidian Hotel	2	1998.11	48	92	安顺龙宫风景区内	3661166
安顺情源宾馆	Anshun Qingyuan Hotel	2	1994.11	86	151	安顺普定县城内	8221999
安顺凤凰山大酒店	Anshun Fenghuangshan Hotel	2	1999.12	41	73	安顺市塔山东路58号	3343413
若飞宾馆	Ruofei Hotel	2	2001.4	41	73	安顺市南华路48号	3225325
龙宫酒店	Longgong Hotel	2	2001.11	34	68	安顺龙宫	3661388
华油宾馆	Huayou Hotel	2	2003.9	56	99	安顺市塔山西路15号	3226020
钟山宾馆	Zhongshan Hotel	2	1994.11	138	330	六盘水市钟山中路52号	8223285
金龙大酒店	Jinlong Hotel	2	2002.5	35	74	六枝特区那平路86号	5322188
六枝工矿迎宾馆	Liuzhi Gongkuang Hotel	2	2002.5	57	114	六枝特区团结路13号	5713548
锦江宾馆	Jinjiang Hotel	2	1996.5	90	130	铜仁市锦江南路8号	5223093
梵宇宾馆	Fanyu Hotel	2	1998	91	211	铜仁市大庆北路85号	5231998
金顶酒店	Jinding Mingzhu Hotel	2	2001.12	48	109	铜仁市北关路80号	5211168
九龙宾馆	Jiulong Hotel	2	2003.9.3	44	90	铜仁市清水路16号	5223659
印江腾龙大酒店	Yinjiang Tenglong Hotel	2	2003.8.23	55	100	印江县城西环开发区	6228888
思南白鹭洲宾馆	Sinan Bailuzhou Hotel	2	2003.6.23	91	230	思南县思塘镇河东	7228118
毕节宾馆	Bijie Hotel	2	1999.6	152	330	毕节桂花路2号	8290008

12-9续表3(continued)

名　称	Name	星级 Level	评定日期 Date of Assess	客房数 Rooms	床位数 Beds	地　址 Address	电话 Telephone
银鹤酒店	Yinhe Hotel	2	2002.1	48	90	毕节市桂花路	8233749
毕节天工大酒店	Bijie Tiangong Hotel	2	1999.6	66	150	毕节洪山路	8292168
洪山宾馆	Hongshan Hotel	2	2004.8.26	208	388	毕节市洪山路1号	8251829
黔西水西宾馆	Qianxi Shuixi Hotel	2	2002.12	35	78	黔西县城内	4242925
黔西新宇大酒店	Qianxi Xinyu Hotel	2	2002.12	38	82	黔西县城内	4241588
洪湾宾馆	Hongwan Hotel	2	2004.6.15	86	148	黔西县洪家渡	7879966
国酒门度假山庄	Guojiumen Holiday Hotel	2	2000.9	27	56	遵义仁怀市中枢镇	2228447
瑞海酒店	Ruihai Hotel	2	2001.12	74	108	遵义市外环路沙坝	8866333
金虹大酒店	Jinhong Hotel	2	1995.1	173	460	遵义市 北京路134号	8822925
正华大酒店	Zhenghua Hotel	2	2002.5	46	105	遵义桐梓县娄山关镇	6657869
民族酒店	Minzu Hotel	2	2004.6	46	86	遵义市海尔大道红花岗武装部	8433888
赤水市电信宾馆	Chishui Telecom Hotel	2	2002.5	56	104	赤水市人民南路43号	2886789
鹏程大酒店	Pengcheng Hotel	2	2003.01	45	89	余庆县香港路	4625868
国酒宾馆	Guojiu Hotel	2	2000.9	69	137	遵义仁怀市国酒中路	2227888
利永宾馆	Liyong Hotel	2	2004.5	83	136	遵义仁怀市国酒中路新车站旁	2250882
凯里市西湖大酒店	Kaili Xihu Hotel	2	2002.12	44	83	凯里市北京西路74号	3826888
国穗大酒店	Guosui Hotel	2	2003.1	28	52	凯里市国税务局大院内	8276888
裕华酒店	Yuhua Hotel	2	2003.1	53	116	凯里市文化北路25号	8515555
酒金大酒店	Jiujin Hotel	2	2001.6	59	135	福泉市酒金北路	2226276
樟江大厦	Zhangjiang Hotel	2	2003.4	34	66	荔波县城内	3618888
荔波宾馆	Libo Hotel	2	2003.4	46	93	荔波县城内县政府大院内	3612169
鲁黔宾馆	Luqian Hotel	2	2003.4	20	52	荔波县樟江中路	3617098
丽人宾馆	Linreng Hotel	2	2003.4	25	50	荔波县城内	3619828
政协宾馆	Zhengxie Hotel	2	2003.4	24	48	荔波县城内	3615573
金穗宾馆	Jinsui Hotel	2	2003.4	28	56	荔波县樟江中路	3611735
溪桥宾馆	Xiqiao Hotel	2	2003.4	38	78	荔波县樟江东路	3618666
锦源宾馆	Jinyuan Hotel	2	2004.1.28	21	47	荔波县广场东路	3618818
鑫光宾馆	Xinguang Hotel	2	2004.1.28	28	55	荔波樟江广场	3619968
水上人间	Shuishang Renjian Hotel	2	2003.12	15	27	荔波县内	8939979
松源宾馆	Songyuan Hotel	2	2003.12	31	56	荔波县内	8967651
东方宾馆	Dongfang Hotel	2	2003.04	20	40	荔波县内	3618968

12-9续表4(continued)

名　称	Name	星级 Level	评定日期 Date of Assess	客房数 Rooms	床位数 Beds	地　址 Address	电话 Telephone
金杏宾馆	Jinxing Hotel	2	2004.06	12	27	荔波县内	3615936
世纪鑫酒店	Shijixin Hotel	2	2003.4	22	56	独山县环城东路	3238688
南方大酒店	Nanfang Hotel	2	2003.12	48	90	独山县内	3238501
天驰宾馆	Tianchi Hotel	2	2003.4	45	90	翁安县城内	2635100
纪龙大酒店	Shijilong Hotel	2	2004.1.28	31	60	龙里县城兴龙路	5620333
永兴山庄	Yongxing Hotel	2	2004.1.28	63	150	龙里县龙山镇	5735010
龙里生态园宾馆	Jinsui Hotel	2	2003.12	40	90	龙里－贵定5公里处	5669506
桥城宾馆	Qiaocheng Hotel	2	1997.11	90	173	都匀市文蜂路10号	8222189
龙潭宾馆	Longtan Hotel	2	1994.12	170	413	都匀市环东路44号	8751900
文峰宾馆	Wenfeng Hotel	2	2000.7	220	346	都匀市剑江中路223号	8223588
南昆宾馆	Nankun Hotel	2	2004.11.9	44	69	黔西南州顶效开发区	2282188
仁达饭店	Renda Hotel	2	2004.9	112	300	中华北路319号	6825301
开阳金都宾馆	Kaiyang Jindu Hotel	2	2004.1	41	87	贵阳市开阳县环城北路	5832088
娄山宾馆	Loushan Hotel	2	2004.9	30	85	桐梓县城河滨南路天门河桥西北侧	6652868
贵阳皇嘉大酒店	Guiyang Huangjia Hotel	2	2004.11	52	86	贵阳市小河区黄河路608号	3808131
贵州民族宾馆	Guizhou Minzu Hotel	2	2004.12	86	170	贵阳市市北路68号	8633666
黑颈鹤大酒店	Heijinghe Hotel	2	1999.6	78	162	威宁建设东路79号	6224426
关岭外事宾馆	Guanling Waishi Hotel	2	2005.03	22	44	关岭县白水镇	3592338
新兴酒楼	Xinxing Hotel	2	2005.06	25	56	安顺市	7223395
腾达酒店	Tengda Hotel	2	2005.06	27	54	安顺市	
瀑布宾馆	Pubu Hotel	2	2005.06	43	86	安顺黄果树风景区内	3592536
京瑞宾馆	Jingrui Hotel	2	2005.06.17	134	300	贵阳市云岩区北京路194号	6891602
石阡宾馆	Shiqian Hotel	2	2005.06	61	115	石阡县汤山镇	7652777
行署会议中心	Xingshu Huiyi Hotel	2	2005.06	40	76	铜仁市花果山路100号	4127888
都匀立都酒店	Duyun Lidu Hotel	2	2005.09	63	97	黔南州地税局培训中心	8318869
石阡临江宾馆	Shiqian Linjiang Hotel	2	2005.09	41	82	石阡县汤山镇河西街	8957399
沿河民族宾馆	Yuanhe Minzhu Hotel	2	2005.09	29	60	沿河县红星路114号	
沿河天龙大酒店	Yuanhe Tianlong Hotel	2	2005.09	96	350	沿河县和平镇城南路23号	

12-9续表5(continued)

名　称	Name	星级 Level	评定日期 Date of Assess	客房数 Rooms	床位数 Beds	地　址 Address	电话 Telephone
织金雅贤宾馆	ZhiJing Yaxian Hotel	2	2005.09	24	45	织金县金中路101号	7638388
赫章汉阳宾馆	Hezhang Hangyang Hotel	2	2005.09	49	93	赫章县城关镇小康东路	3227388
金黔宾馆	Jingqian Hotel	2	2005.09	62	120	贵阳市新华路106号	5500315
怡心宾馆	Yixing Hotel	2	2005.09	15	24	三都三启镇县府路	3927818
六枝宾馆	Liuzhi Hotel	2	2005.10.8	65	160	六枝平寨镇友谊路	5322660
八角岩饭店	Bajiaoyan Hotel	1	1994.9	84	154	北京路64号	6827910
君安宾馆	Junan Hotel	1	1995.11	87	186	黔灵西路62号	6816999
邮电宾馆	Youdian Hotel	1	1995.9	60	128	延安东路1号	5585136
科技宾馆	Keji Hotel	1	2001.6	43	73	贵阳市醒狮路36号	5868906
娄山大酒店	Loushan Hotel	1	2001.12	60	126	遵义桐梓县城	6623442
仁怀宾馆	Renhuai Hotel	1	2000.9	92	218	遵义仁怀市迎宾路	2223182
锦绣宾馆	Jinxiu Hotel	1	2001.1	77	129	赤水市东郊路30号	2821782
金穗宾馆	Jinsui Hotel	1	2001.11	97	255	威宁县城内	6225053
鸿雁宾馆	Hongyan Hotel	1	2004.6.11	39	97	黔西县东路	4225666
黔岭宾馆	Qianling Hotel	1	2002.5	30	60	关岭县城关镇	7224983
金虹宾馆	Jinhong Hotel	1	2003.4	40	76	荔波县樟江东路	8227192
爱得森宾馆	Aidesen Hotel	1	2003.4	16	42	荔波县城	3618858
篮天宾馆	Lantian Hotel	1	2003.4	36	60	荔波县城	3619831
沙梨园宾馆	Shaliyuan Hotel	1	2003.4	18	48	荔波县城	3618258
小七孔饭店	Xiaoqikong Hotel	1	2003.4	43	80	荔波县小七孔景区内	3619053
金都大酒店	Jindu Hotel	1	2003.9.3	36	69	铜仁市东太大道	5930828
思南县电力宾馆	Sinan Dianli Hotel	1	2003.7.28	25	53	思南县中山街55号	7229948
鑫源大酒店	Xingyuan Hotel	1	2005.09	14	26	三都县环城北路	3921729
富康宾馆	Fukamg Hotel	1	2005.09	30	66	三都县三合镇县府路	3924188

主要统计指标解释

旅游者人数

(1)入境国际旅游者人数:指来中国参观、访问、旅行、探亲、访友、休养、考察、参加会议和从事经济、科技、文化、教育、宗教等活动的外国人、华侨、港澳同胞和台湾同胞的人数。不包括外国在我国的常驻机构,如使领馆、通讯社、企业办事处的工作人员;来我国常住的外国专家、留学生以及在岸逗留不过夜人员。

(2)出境居民人数:指大陆居民因公务活动或私人事务短期出境的人数。公务活动出境居民人数包括在国际交通工具上的中国服务员工,因私出境居民人数不包括在国际交通工具上的中国服务员工。

(3)国内旅游者人数:指我国大陆居民和在我国常住 1 年以上的外国人、华侨、港澳台同胞离开常住地在境内其他地方的旅游设施内至少停留一夜,最长不超过 6 个月的人数。

国际旅游(外汇)收入　指入境旅游的外国人、华侨、港澳同胞和台湾同胞在中国大陆旅游过程中发生的一切旅游支出,对于国家来说就是国际旅游(外汇)收入。

国际旅行社　指经营对外招徕并接待外国人、华侨、港澳同胞和台湾同胞来中国、归国或回内地旅游业务的旅行社。

国内旅行社　指负责经营招徕、组团、接待国内旅客的旅游业务,以及不对外招徕,负责经营接待国际旅行社或其它涉外部门组织的外国人、华侨、港澳同胞和台湾同胞来中国、归国或回内地的旅游业务的旅行社。

涉外饭店　指经有关部门批准,允许接待外国人、华侨、港澳同胞和台湾同胞的饭店。

Explanatory Notes on Main Statistical Indicators

Number of Tourists:

(1) International tourists refer to foreigners, overseas Chinese, Chinese compatriots from Hong Kong, Macao and Taiwan coming to China for sightseeing, visits, tours, family reunions, vacations, study tours, conferences and other activities of a business, scientific and technological, cultural, educational and religious nature. It does not include representatives and employees of resident institutions of foreign countries in China such as embassies, consulates, news agencies and offices of foreign companies and organizations, nor does it include long-term foreign experts or students residing in China, or persons in transition without spending a night in China.

(2) Chinese residents going abroad refer to Chinese residents going abroad for short terms for either public business or private purposes. Chinese employees working on international transport carriers are included in those going abroad for public business purpose, not in those for private purpose.

(3) Domestic tourists refer to residents of the mainland of China who stay for one night at least but no more than 6 months at tourist facilities in other places than their permanent residence within the territory of the mainland China, including foreigners, overseas Chinese and Chinese compatriots from Hong Kong, Macao and Taiwan who have resided in China for over one year.

Foreign Exchange Earnings from International Tourism refer to the total expenditures of foreigners, overseas Chinese, Chinese compatriots from Hong Kong, Macao and Taiwan during their stay in the mainland of China, which are earnings of foreign exchange from international tourism from the point of view from China.

International Travel Agencies refer to travel agencies engaged in the promotion, solicitation, organization and reception of tours to the mainland of China by foreigners, overseas Chinese, Chinese compatriots from Hong Kong, Macao and Taiwan.

Domestic Travel Agencies refer to travel agencies engaged in the promotion, solicitation, organization and reception of domestic tourists, and in the reception of foreigners, overseas Chinese, Chinese compatriots from Hong Kong, Macao and Taiwan organized by international travel agencies or other departments concerned, without their own promotion and solicitation programmes.

Tourist Hotels refer to hotels that are able, with the approval of departments concerned, to accommodate foreigners, overseas Chinese, Chinese compatriots from Hong Kong, Macao and Taiwan Province.

13

Thirteen

价格指数

Price Indices

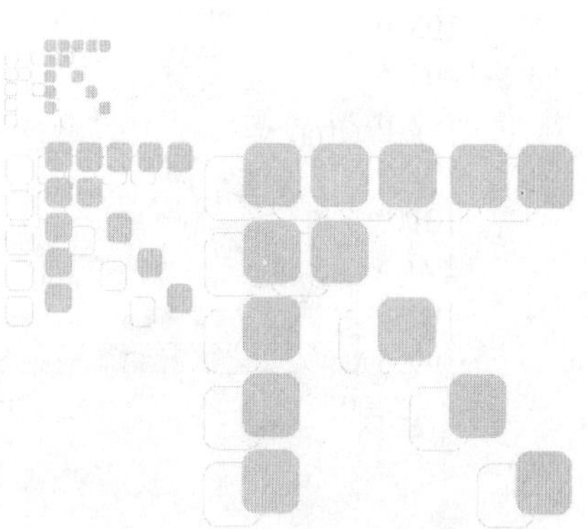

价格指数（上年=100）
Price Indices (preceding year=100)

工业品、原材料、燃料、动力价格指数（上年=100）
Price Indices of Industrial Products,Raw Materials,Fuels and Power (Preceding year=100)

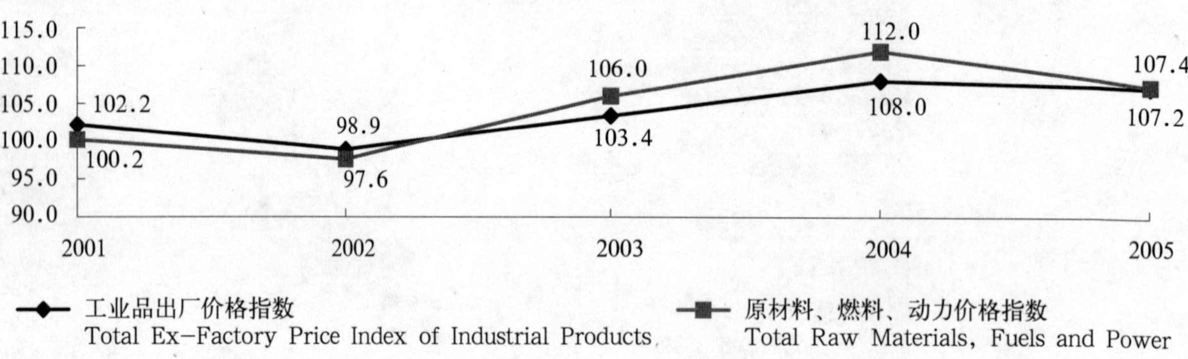

贵阳市房屋销售价格指数（上年=100）
Selling Price Indices of Houses of Guiyang City (preceding year=100)

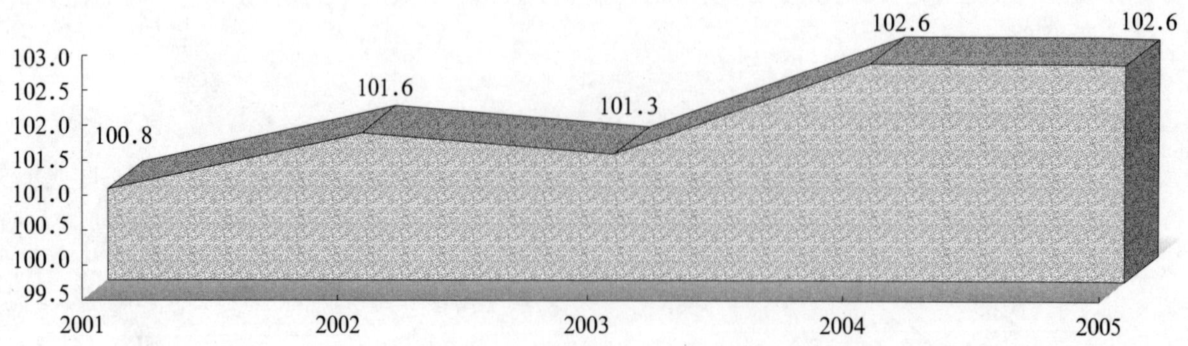

13-1 “十五”时期各年居民消费价格分类指数（上年=100）

Consumer Price Indices by Category of Each Year in “Tenth-Five-year Plan” Period(preceding year=100)

指 标	Item	2000	2001	2002	2003	2004	2005
居民消费价格总指数	**General Consumer Price Index**	**99.5**	**101.8**	**99.0**	**101.2**	**104.0**	**101.0**
非食品价格指数	Non-Food Price Index		103.7	98.6	100.4	100.2	100.9
服务项目价格指数	Services Price Index	117.2	114.0	101.2	103.4	103.0	101.5
扣除鲜菜鲜果总指数	Non-Vegetables and Fresh Fruits Price Index		102.1	99.1	100.7	104.4	101.0
消费品价格指数	**Consumer Price Index**		**98.1**	**98.3**	**100.5**	**104.4**	**100.9**
食品	**Food**	**95.3**	**98.5**	**99.7**	**103.2**	**112.6**	**101.3**
粮食	Grain	92.7	95.6	98.1	103.6	124.7	100.4
淀粉及薯类	Starches and Tubers	95.6	83.4	94.0	106.8	107.3	102.0
干豆类及豆制品	Beans and Its Products	96.1	100.4	95.6	103.7	118.2	101.4
油脂	Oil or Fat	82.1	86.6	100.7	108.9	120.3	88.7
肉禽及其制品	Meat, Poultry and Their Products	94.8	97.8	101.5	102.1	122.8	100.8
食用畜肉及副产品	Livestock for Slaughtering and Sideline Products		98.3	103.1	103.1	128.0	99.2
禽	Poultry		97.2	99.6	99.6	116.0	101.5
肉禽加工制品	Meat,Poultry and Their Products		96.5	97.7	101.0	109.0	108.5
蛋	Eggs	91.7	107.8	104.2	99.8	115.2	102.1
水产品	Aquatic Products	94.2	95.8	98.5	96.5	116.2	106.2
鱼	Fish		96.5	95.2	97.9	118.3	104.6
其他水产品	Other Aquatic Products		92.6	99.6	94.9	110.5	110.1
菜	Vegetables	100.1	99.6	101.1	114.0	98.6	103.7
鲜菜	Fresh Vegetables	102.4	100.3	100.7	116.2	96.7	105.0
调味品	Flavoring	99.8	113.9	100.2	100.5	104.5	99.3
糖	Carbohydrate	103.2	104.9	96.9	99.3	100.5	103.6
茶及饮料	Tea and Beverages		98.9	97.1	98.0	99.6	99.9
干鲜瓜果	Dried and Fresh Melons and Fruits	91.4	99.2	95.7	110.4	101.4	100.1
糕点饼干面包	Cake, Biscuit and Bread	98.1	100.8	99.8	96.2	102.2	104.3
奶及奶制品	Milk and Its Products	101.6	100.4	99.3	100.2	101.8	99.2

13-1续表1(continued)

指标	Item	2000	2001	2002	2003	2004	2005
在外用膳食品	Outward Dinner Food	98.2	100.2	100.3	98.6	106.3	104.1
其他食品及食品加工服务	Other Foods and Manufacturing Services		96.9	97.3	97.2	103.9	107.0
烟酒及用品	**Tobacco, Liquor and Articles**		**100.2**	**99.8**	**99.6**	**99.9**	**100.1**
烟草	Tobacco	94.3	100.2	98.9	100.0	99.1	100.2
酒	Liquor	97.8	99.8	102.9	99.7	101.8	99.4
白酒	Distilled Spirit		101.6	103.7	101.2	102.8	100.2
啤酒	Beer		98.5	101.2	96.9	95.9	98.4
吸烟饮酒用品	Articles for Smoking and Drinking		101.3	98.0	97.0	99.8	100.8
衣着	**Clothing**	**99.6**	**97.8**	**98.0**	**97.6**	**92.2**	**99.3**
服装	Garments	98.9	95.8	98.7	98.7	90.5	99.9
衣着材料	Clothing Materials	96.1	99.2	98.9	102.1	96.6	102.2
鞋袜帽	Footgear and Hats	102.8	101.3	97.4	94.6	94.7	97.9
家庭设备用品及维修服务	**Household Facilities Articles and Repair Services**	**95.9**	**94.6**	**96.3**	**97.2**	**98.6**	**99.4**
耐用消费品	Durable Consumer Goods	94.4	90.4	93.3	96.3	98.8	99.2
家具	Furniture	93.0	93.7	93.4	97.4	98.3	99.5
家庭设备	Household Facilities	95.4	87.4	92.9	95.7	99.1	99.1
室内装饰品	Interior Decorations	97.8	92.8	103.6	99.4	97.6	96.4
床上用品	Bed Articles	99.6	95.8	92.9	93.8	96.9	102.4
家庭日用杂品	Daily Used Household Articles	96.7	98.7	99.3	98.6	98.6	98.7
家庭服务及加工维修服务	Household Service and Manufacturing Upkeep		100.2	99.6	99.8	99.9	104.9
医疗保健和个人用品	**Health Care and Personal Articles**	**98.5**	**102.4**	**98.5**	**104.3**	**105.1**	**100.5**
医疗保健	Health Care		99.0	99.7	107.3	107.2	100.5
医疗器具及用品	Medical Instrument and Articles	100.6	100.0	96.0	96.8	99.5	101.4
中药材及中成药	Traditional Chinese Medicine	98.7	101.1	97.9	100.0	101.4	99.7
西药	Western Medicine	98.2	94.2	98.0	97.6	99.6	98.0
保健器具及用品	Health Care Appliances and Articles	100.6	92.3	103.5	99.4	100.0	98.8
医疗保健服务	Health Care Services	121.0	107.5	105.6	132.9	122.4	104.1

13-1续表2(continued)

指 标	Item	2000	2001	2002	2003	2004	2005
个人用品及服务	Personal Articles and Services		107.7	96.6	100.7	102.6	100.6
化妆美容用品	Cosmetics		99.4	97.8	100.4	102.1	100.0
卫生用品	Sanitation Articles		98.1	96.1	97.1	99.3	102.2
个人饰品	Personal Decorations		107.1	94.5	97.0	100.9	100.8
个人服务	Personal Services	103.1	115.4	98.3	105.8	106.4	99.2
交通和通讯	**Transportation and Communication**	**94.4**	**107.0**	**102.3**	**100.2**	**96.6**	**99.4**
交 通	Transportation		107.0	106.1	105.4	97.1	102.7
交通工具	Transportation Facility	98.2	98.9	96.4	98.2	98.9	99.3
车用燃料及零配件	Fuels and Parts		99.0	97.4	107.8	106.3	109.5
车辆使用及维修	Using and Upkeep Fare		103.4	102.4	102.8	101.0	103.3
市区公共交通	Incity Traffic Fare	104.8	124.6	113.8	102.1	103.7	102.5
城市间交通	Intercity Traffic Fare		96.7	103.5	125.5	90.8	103.1
通 信	Communication		107.0	99.3	94.8	95.4	97.2
通信工具	Communication Facility	91.6	81.4	84.4	91.7	91.2	87.9
通信服务	Communication Service	100.1	113.1	102.3	95.7	97.0	99.1
娱乐教育文化用品及服务	**Recreation,Education and Culture Articles and Services**	**97.2**	**115.0**	**98.3**	**100.7**	**101.0**	**99.0**
文娱用耐用消费品 及服务	Durable Consumer Goods for Cultural and Recreational Use and Services	92.3	91.1	89.2	92.3	93.0	94.2
教 育	Education	106.1	124.9	101.4	102.2	103.2	101.3
文化娱乐用品	Cultural and Recreational Articles	99.5	106.3	97.9	103.6	102.3	100.7
文化娱乐	Recreational and Cultural Articles	98.7	106.9	92.2	98.7	99.5	99.3
书报杂志	Books,Newspapers and Magazines	100.7	104.7	100.8	100.8	100.4	101.0
文娱费	Recreation Fee	121.3	107.1	100.3	110.2	106.0	102.8
旅游及外出	Touring and Outgoing		107.1	89.6	96.5	96.0	91.4
居 住	**Residence**	**104.8**	**99.5**	**98.6**	**101.0**	**104.1**	**106.4**
建房及装修材料	Building and Building Decoration Materials	98.7	99.0	97.8	98.2	101.3	101.7
租 房	Rent	102.3	105.9	105.9	100.0	99.7	110.1
自有住房	Private Housing		100.0	96.9	98.1	100.4	105.6
水、电、燃料	Water, Electricity and Fuels	108.1	99.3	99.3	104.4	107.9	111.0

13-2 "十五"时期各年商品零售价格分类指数（上年=100）

Retail Price Indices by Category of Commodities of Each Year in "Tenth-Five-year Plan" Period(preceding year=100)

指 标	Item	2000	2001	2002	2003	2004	2005
商品零售价格总指数	**Retail Price Index**	**97.3**	**98.4**	**99.3**	**100.0**	**103.2**	**101.3**
食品类	Food	94.4	99.4	100.5	103.5	112.4	101.6
粮食	Grain	93.2	96.9	98.1	103.9	123.8	100.0
油脂	Oil or Fat	81.6	87.6	102.0	108.2	121.2	91.4
肉禽及其制品	Meat,Poultry and Their products	94.6	98.8	103.2	102.6	120.4	101.0
蛋	Eggs				98.9	116.0	105.2
水产品	Aquatic Products	95.2	93.4	98.0	97.0	115.1	106.3
鲜菜	Vegetables	99.4	107.4	95.8	115.7	96.6	105.1
干菜及菜制品	Dried Vegetables and Its Products	92.7	91.8	102.5	103.6	113.6	97.8
鲜果	Fresh Fruits	89.3	99.3	101.6	110.6	94.5	100.7
干（坚）果及瓜果制品	Dried Fruits and Its Products	99.3	96.9	101.7	116.5	116.8	105.7
在外用膳食品	Outward Dinner Food	98.3	100.0	100.2	98.5	103.7	104.0
饮料、烟酒	Beverages,Tobacco and Liquor	96.2	100.1	100.2	99.9	100.6	100.5
服装、鞋帽类	Garments,Shoes and Hats	100.6	98.2	100.3	98.8	91.3	99.7
纺织品类	Textiles	98.4	98.7	97.3	94.6	99.3	103.3
家用电器及音像器材	Household Appliances, Music and Video Equipment	93.8	95.6	96.9	95.4	95.3	96.7
文化办公用品	Cultural and Office Appliances	98.5	96.8	97.9	99.1	99.4	99.8
日用品	Articles for Daily Use	97.2	97.5	98.7	98.9	101.3	100.2
体育娱乐用品	Sports and Recreation Articles	98.9	95.9	95.8	98.6	99.1	101.9
交通、通信用品	Traffic and Communication Appliances				92.4	94.7	94.8
家具	Furniture	95.9	95.4	97.9	95.9	95.6	100.5
化妆品类	Cosmetics	97.6	97.3	96.1	101.0	100.4	102.5
金银珠宝类	Gold,Siluer and Jewelry	95.1	95.2	101.3	106.4	115.7	103.6
中西药品及医疗保健用品类	Traditional Chinese and Western Medicines & Health Cares Articles	98.6	98.6	98.6	98.0	99.7	99.0
书报杂志及电子出版物类	Books, Newspapers, Magazines and Electronic Publications	103.4	100.0	101.1	101.3	101.7	99.9
燃料类	Fuels	113.4	103.2	101.1	107.6	113.4	118.3
建筑材料及五金电料类	Building Materials and Hardware	95.8	99.9	98.3	98.6	101.2	102.8

13-3 “十五”时期各年农业生产资料价格分类指数（上年=100）

Price Indices of Means of Agricultural Production by Category of Each Year in “Tenth-Five-year Plan” Period(preceding year=100)

指 标	Item	2000	2001	2002	2003	2004	2005
农业生产资料价格总指数	**General Price Index of Means of Agricultural Production**	**100.6**	**99.4**	**100.6**	**104.1**	**109.0**	**110.2**
小农具	Small Farm Tools	94.6	101.0	101.7	99.1	106.3	109.5
饲 料	Forage	106.7	101.3	100.1	100.8	116.3	106.9
产品畜	Production Livestocks	102.5	100.0	98.7	107.4	128.5	132.7
役 畜	Labour Livestocks	107.3	107.1	105.2	107.9	119.1	117.5
半机械化农具	Semi-mechanized Farm Tools	99.9	100.0	99.3	95.2	98.9	107.8
机械化农具	Mechanized Farm Machinery	96.3	100.6	93.8	89.3	108.9	104.0
化学肥料	Chemical Fertilizer	104.7	96.8	100.7	107.4	105.7	111.5
农药及农药器械	Pesticide & Its Appliances	98.0	99.0	102.3	104.6	106.6	100.0
化学农药	Chemical Pesticide	95.1	98.6	102.1	100.0	108.4	107.8
农药器械	Appliances for Pesticide	107.8	100.4	102.8	112.9	103.5	87.5
农机用油	Oil for Farm Machinery	116.2	101.2	101.0	114.0	107.2	110.7
其他农业生产资料	Others Means of Agricultural Production	94.1	99.5	105.4	98.4	92.0	103.2

13-4 “十五”时期各年工业品出厂价格分类指数（上年=100）

Ex-Factory Price Indices of Industrial Products by Category of Each Year in “Tenth-Five-year Plan” Period(preceding year=100)

指 标	Item	2000	2001	2002	2003	2004	2005
全部工业品出厂价格指数	**Total Ex-Factory Price Index of Industrial Products**	**100.4**	**102.2**	**98.9**	**103.4**	**108.0**	**107.2**
按轻、重工业分	**Grouped by Industries**						
轻工业	Light Industry	102.6	101.4	101.3	100.5	101.6	101.3
重工业	Heavy Industry	99.3	102.5	97.9	105.2	112.2	110.9
按用途分	**Grouped by Use**						
生产资料	Means of Production	99.2	102.5	97.8	104.3	111.1	109.8
采掘工业	Mining & Quarrying Industry	96.7	105.5	102.6	104.6	111.1	144.0
原材料工业	Raw Materials Industry	99.8	102.8	97.5	105.3	111.1	109.4
加工工业	Manufacturing Industry	98.5	100.5	96.5	103.2	111.2	103.1
生活资料	Consumer Goods	102.9	101.5	101.5	101.1	99.9	100.5
食品类	Food	102.9	102.0	101.9	101.9	100.0	100.8
衣着类	Clothing	96.5	97.6	97.8	98.3	101.2	102.1
一般日用品	Articles for Daily Use	106.2	96.3	99.4	98.0	101.0	99.9
耐用消费品	Durable Consumer Goods	106.3	100.5	102.6	94.0	96.0	97.2
按工业部门分	**Grouped by Sector**						
煤炭开采和洗选业	Mining and Washing of Coal	96.2	106.2	102.2	104.5	116.0	132.3
有色金属矿采选业	Mining and Processing of Non-Ferrous Metal Ores			100.5	114.5	105.4	128.8
非金属矿采选业	Mining and Processing of Nonmetal Ores	100.9	100.5	103.6	104.7	105.1	160.9
农副食品加工业	Processing of Food from Agricultural Products	83.8	98.5	102.1	107.2	110.6	100.3
食品制造业	Manufacture of Foods	115.7	103.8	98.2	101.3	107.0	105.0
饮料制造业	Manufacture of Beverages	101.1	98.2	102.6	101.7	101.7	100.2
烟草制品业	Manufacture of Tobacco	106.3	103.5	101.3	101.3	99.3	100.3
纺织业	Manufacture of Textile	102.2	98.0	96.1	99.7	104.7	107.4
纺织服装、鞋、帽制造业	Manufacture of Textile Wearing Apparel, Footware,and Caps			100.5	97.0	100.7	102.2
皮革、毛皮、羽毛(绒)及其制品业	Manufacture of Leather, Fur, Feather and Related Products			101.2	101.2	99.1	98.1

13-4续表1（Continued)

指 标	Item	2000	2001	2002	2003	2004	2005
木材加工及木、竹、藤、棕、草制品业	Processing of Timber,Manufacture of Wood,Bamboo,Rattan,Palm,and Straw Products	102.2	95.8	99.2	98.2	96.5	103.8
家具制造业	Manufacture of Furniture			98.4	98.9	97.5	100.3
造纸及纸制品业	Manufacture of Paper and Paper Products	100.2	101.5	99.3	98.4	100.6	100.1
印刷业和记录媒介的复制	Printing,Reproduction of Recording Media				97.8	100.5	100.0
文教体育用品制造业	Manufacture of Articles For Culture, Education and Sport Activity	96.1	100.5	101.4	103.7	100.3	100.2
石油加工、炼焦及核燃料加工业	Processing of Petroleum, Coking, Processing of Nuclear Fuel	100.6	94.4	105.7	117.1	131.1	114.7
化学原料及化学制品制造业	Manufacture of Raw Chemical Materials and Chemical Products	93.3	95.6	105.7	105.2	118.1	110.5
医药制造业	Manufacture of Medicines	96.4	99.5	100.0	100.3	94.8	102.0
化学纤维制造业	Manufacture of Chemical Fibers				118.6	110.1	106.5
橡胶制品业	Manufacture of Rubber	96.3	100.8	95.9	97.9	101.5	110.4
塑料制品业	Manufacture of Plastics	126.9	93.6	97.4	96.2	109.7	111.8
非金属矿物制品业	Manufacture of Non-metallic Mineral Products	99.5	97.9	97.8	99.2	105.3	104.7
黑色金属冶炼及压延加工业	Smelting and Pressing of Ferrous Metals	95.1	103.0	96.0	111.3	130.3	95.9
有色金属冶炼及压延加工业	Smelting and Pressing of Non-ferrous Metals	104.8	87.8	95.7	114.0	120.1	114.3
金属制品业	Manufacture of Metal Products	104.3	101.5	96.6	104.0	113.1	99.3
通用设备制造业	Manufacture of General Purpose Machinery	108.4	98.2	97.7	97.0	102.7	101.6
专用设备制造业	Manufacture of Special Purpose Machinery	99.1	101.2	101.8	98.8	98.7	101.8
交通运输设备制造业	Manufacture of Transport Equipment	99.9	102.2	92.0	101.2	101.2	100.7
电气机械及器材制造业	Manufacture of Electrical Machinery and Equipment	94.1	98.0	101.9	98.2	106.9	108.2
通信设备、计算机及其他电子设备制造业	Manufacture of Communication Equipment, Computers and Other Electronic Equipment	110.9	100.7	86.1	94.2	97.3	89.4
仪器仪表及文化、办公用机械制造业	Manufacture of Measuring Instruments and Machinery for Cultural Activity and Office Work	101.3	97.0	97.5	97.1	98.9	102.1
电力、热力的生产的供应业	Production and Distribution of Electric Power and Heat Power	100.0	115.7	99.4	100.3	102.1	108.2
燃气生产和供应业	Production and Distribution of Gas			101.8	100.3	104.1	102.9
水的生产和供应业	Production and Distribution of Water	104.7	106.6	99.7	107.0	115.5	104.9

13-5 “十五”时期各年原材料、燃料、动力购进价格指数(上年=100)

Indices of Purchasing Prices of Raw Materials, Fuels and Power of Each Year in “Tenth-Five-year Plan” Period(preceding year =100)

指 标	Item	2000	2001	2002	2003	2004	2005
全部原材料、燃料、动力购进价格指数	**Total Raw Materials, Fuels and Power**	**102.9**	**100.2**	**97.6**	**106.0**	**112.0**	**107.4**
燃料、动力类	Fuels and Power	105.7	103.5	98.5	104.1	108.9	117.2
黑色金属材料类	Ferrous Metals	99.0	102.6	97.7	112.0	128.9	112.1
#钢 材	Rolled-steel		100.2	98.6	105.1	121.5	114.9
有色金属材料和电线类	Nonferrous Metals and Wire	109.4	88.1	95.2	118.5	117.7	110.8
化工原料类	Raw Chemical Materials	102.3	101.0	96.6	103.6	114.1	107.7
木材及纸浆类	Timber and Paper Pulps	108.6	96.8	95.7	100.8	101.9	105.2
建筑材料及非金属矿类	Building Materials and Nonmetal Minerals Processing	105.0	99.1	100.1	98.5	103.9	102.7
其他工业原材料及半成品类	Other Industrial Raw Materials and Semi-products	95.1	96.2	94.6	102.4	108.7	101.2
农副产品类	Agricultural Products	100.6	99.6	98.9	107.5	112.1	104.9
纺织原料类	Textile Raw Materials	110.8	96.1	91.2	109.1	109.0	96.9

13-6 “十五”时期各年固定资产投资和房地产销售价格指数(上年=100)

Price Indices of Investment in Fixed Assets and Real Estate of Each Year in “Tenth-Five-year Plan” Period(preceding year=100)

指 标	Item	2000	2001	2002	2003	2004	2005
固定资产投资价格指数	**Price Indices of Investment in Fixed Asset**	**102.2**	**100.4**	**100.2**	**102.0**	**104.9**	**101.4**
建筑安装、装饰工程	Construction and Installation,Decoration	102.5	101.2	100.8	103.4	106.4	101.8
设备、工器具购置	Purchase of Equipment,Tools and Instruments	102.7	98.6	98.3	98.8	103.4	100.5
其他费用	Others	100.0	100.0	100.0	100.1	100.5	101.0
贵阳市房屋销售价格指数	**Selling Price Indices of Houses of Guiyang City**	**103.9**	**100.8**	**101.6**	**101.3**	**102.6**	**102.6**
#商品房销售	Commercial Houses	103.8	100.8	101.6	101.0	101.9	102.4
#住 宅	Residential Buildings	104.2	100.9	101.8	101.2	102.2	102.6

13-7 “十五”时期各年建筑业产值价格指数（上年=100）

Price Indices of Construction Output Value of Each Year in “Tenth-Five-year Plan” Period(preceding year=100)

指标	Item	2000	2001	2002	2003	2004	2005
建筑安装工程价格指数	**Price Indices of Construction and Installation**	**102.5**	**101.2**	**100.8**	**103.4**	**106.4**	**101.8**
人工费	Manpower	101.6	102.7	102.1	102.8	103.2	102.9
材料费	Materials	102.2	101.2	100.7	103.9	109.8	101.6
钢 材	Steel Products	102.3	100.5	100.3	106.7	117.3	100.6
木 材	Timber	100.2	100.2	100.8	101.3	104.3	102.4
水 泥	Cement	100.8	101.6	101.2	100.1	103.9	100.9
电 料	Eleetrical Materials	105.0	104.1	100.3	102.0	100.6	103.7
化工材料	Chemical Raw Materials	103.1	98.0	100.2	103.9	104.3	105.8
地方建筑材料	Local Materials	103.4	102.3	103.8	101.9	106.1	102.3
其他材料	Others	100.1	104.2	97.6	102.9	102.5	102.9
机械使用费	Costs for Using Machine	101.6	100.5	101.0	102.1	100.5	101.5

主要统计指标解释

商品零售价格指数 是反映城乡商品零售价格变动趋势的一种经济指数。零售物价的变动直接反映城乡居民的生活支出和国家的财政收入，反映居民购买力和市场供需平衡，反映消费与积累的比例。

居民消费价格指数 是反映一定时期内城乡居民所购买的生活消费品价格和服务项目价格变动趋势和程度的相对数，是对城市居民消费价格指数和农村居民消费价格指数进行综合汇总计算的结果。

农产品收购价格指数 是反映国有商业、集体商业、个体商业、外贸部门、国家机关、社会团体等各种经济类型的商业企业和有关部门收购农产品价格的变动趋势和程度的相对数。

工业品出厂价格指数 是反映全部工业产品出厂价格总水平的变动趋势和程度的相对数，包括工业企业售给本企业以外所有单位的各种产品和直接售给居民用于生活消费的产品。

固定资产投资价格指数 是反映固定资产投资额价格变动趋势和程度的相对数。固定资产投资额是由建筑安装工程投资完成额、设备、工器具购置投资完成额和其他费用投资完成额三部分组成的。编制固定资产投资价格指数应首先分别编制上述三部分投资的价格指数，然后采用加权算术平均法求出固定资产投资价格总指数。

农业生产资料价格指数 是反映一定时期内农业生产资料价格变动趋势和程度的相对数。农业生产资料价格指数分为小农具、饲料、产品畜、役畜、半机械化农具、机械化农具、化学肥料、农药及农具械、农机用油、其他农业生产资料十大类。

原材料、燃料和动力价格指数 是反映工业企业作为生产投入，而从物质交易市场和能源、原材料生产企业购买原材料、燃料和动力产品时，所支付的价格水平变动趋势和程度的统计指标，是扣除工业企业物质消耗成本中的价格变动影响的重要依据。

Explanatory Notes on Main Statistical Indicators

Retail Price Index reflects the general change in retail prices of commodities. The change and adjustment in retail prices directly affect the living expenditure of urban and rural residents, government revenue,purchasing power of residents and the equilibrium of market supply and demand,and the ratio of consumption to accumulation.

Consumer Price Index reflects the trend and degree of changes in prices of consumer goods and services purchased by urban and rural residents,and is a composite index derived from the urban consumer price index and the rural consumer price index.

Index of Purchasing Prices of Farm Products reflects the trend and degree of changes in purchasing prices of farm products purchased by state–owned, collective–owned,and individual commercial enterprises,foreign trade sectors,government agencies,social organizations and other units of various types of ownership. It is used to observe the impact of change in purchasing prices of farm products on the cash income of peasants, and serves as basis for the formulation and supervision of pricing policies for farm products.

Ex–factory Price Index of Industrial Products reflects the trend and degree of changes in general ex–factory prices of all industrial products,including sales of industrial products by an industrial enterprise to all units outside the enterprise, as well as sales of consumer goods to residents.

Price Index of Investment in Fixed Assets reflects the trend and degree of changes in prices of investment in fixed assets. The investment in fixed assets consists of three components, namely the investment in construction and installation,the investment in purchases of equipment and instrument,and the investment in other items. Price index of investment in fixed assets is calculated as the weighted arithmetic mean of the price indices of the three components of investment in fixed assets.

Price Indices of Means of Agricultural Production reflect the trend and degree of changes in prices of means of agricultural production during a given period. Price indices of means of agricultural production are composed of 10 categories including small farm tools, feeds, domestic animals for meat, draught domestic animals, semi–mechanized farm machinery, mechanized farm machinery, chemical fertilizers, pesticides and spraying machinery, fuels for farm machinery and other means of agricultural production.

Indices of Purchasing Prices of Raw Materials, Fuels and Power reflect changes in the level and degree of prices paid by industrial enterprises when they purchase production input such as raw materials, fuels and power from the market or from other energy or raw materials producing enterprises. These indices provide important basis for measuring the material consumption of industrial enterprises after removing influence of price changes.

14 财政、金融、证券、保险

Finance, Banking, Securities and Insurance

Fourteen

财政收支（亿元）
Government Revenue and Expenditure (100 million yuan)

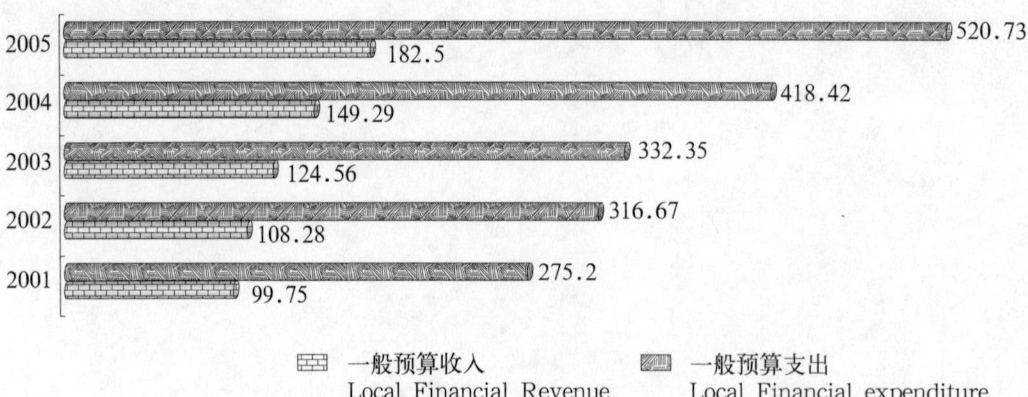

存、贷款余额（亿元）
Balanle of Deposits and Loans (100 million yuan)

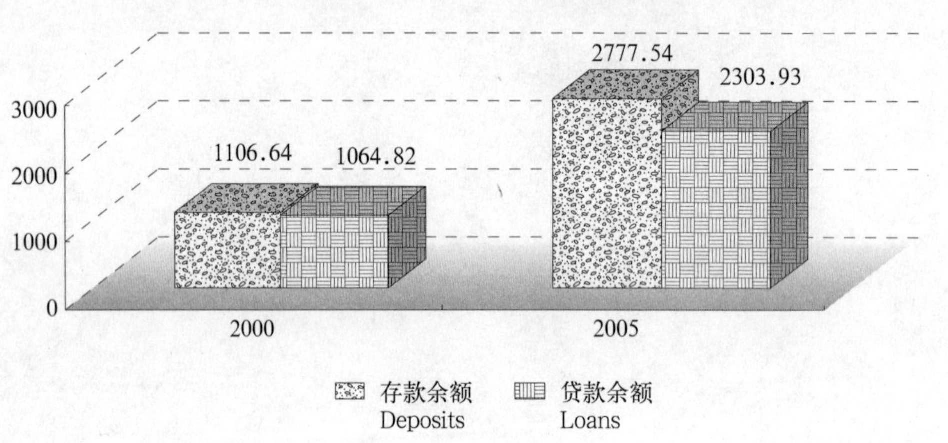

财产保费收入（万元）
Premium (10000 yuan)

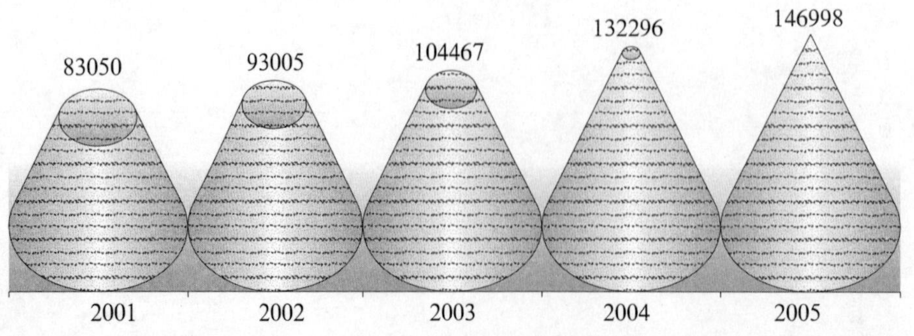

14-1 "十五"时期各年财政收入基本情况

Basic Statistics on Government Revenue of each year in "Tenth-Five-year Plan" Period

单位：亿元(100 million yuan)

指 标	Item	2000	2001	2002	2003	2004	2005
财政总收入	**Total Government Revenue**	**153.04**	**177.04**	**203.03**	**236.64**	**296.48**	**366.16**
#一般预算收入	Local Financial Revenue	85.23	99.75	108.28	124.56	149.29	182.50
#增值税	Value-added Tax	12.18	14.26	17.02	19.43	23.91	31.37
营业税	Business Tax	20.34	22.08	26.95	31.46	37.95	46.31
企业所得税	Enterprises' Income Tax	6.78	12.34	8.77	8.41	12.10	16.08
个人所得税	Individual Income Tax	4.73	6.67	5.56	5.44	7.05	8.90
资源税	Resource Tax	0.74	0.73	0.90	0.97	1.20	1.98
城市维护建设税	Urban Maintenance and Development Tax	5.97	6.33	7.04	8.69	10.49	12.91
农业四税	Agricultural and Related Tax	10.06	9.33	12.35	12.93	13.20	11.92
房产税	Tax on Real Estates	2.73	3.00	3.48	3.67	3.83	4.28
国有资产经营收益	State-owned Assets Profit	2.38	1.99	1.09	1.95	2.95	4.34
征收排污费收入	Fee on Sewage Treatment	0.68	0.95	0.98	1.51	2.00	3.06
罚没收入	Penalty and Confiscatory Income	4.14	4.88	5.76	6.76	8.01	10.10
行政性收费收入	Income from Administrative Fees	4.30	7.68	8.80	11.71	12.99	13.76
专项收入	Expert Project Income	3.21	3.60	3.98	5.24	7.07	10.37
其他收入	Other Revenue	7.67	6.86	6.60	7.90	8.53	10.18

14-2 “十五”时期各年各级财政收入

Basic Statistics on Various Level Financial Revenue of each year in “Tenth-Five-year Plan” Period

单位：亿元（100 million yuan）

指 标	Item	2000	2001	2002	2003	2004	2005
总 计	**Total**	**85.23**	**99.75**	**108.28**	**124.56**	**149.29**	**182.50**
省 级	Provincial Level	15.86	21.61	25.26	28.49	35.50	42.26
地 级	Proefectural Level	20.34	21.73	21.65	25.36	29.50	36.80
县 级	County Level	25.54	31.69	37.30	40.65	48.95	64.77
乡镇级	Township Level	23.49	24.72	24.07	30.06	35.34	38.67

14-3 “十五”时期各年财政一般预算分类别收入

Each Level Local Government Fiscal Revenue by Category of each year in “Tenth-Five-year Plan” Period

单位：亿元(100 million yuan)

指 标	Item	2000	2001	2002	2003	2004	2005
总 计	**Total**	**85.23**	**99.75**	**108.28**	**124.56**	**149.29**	**182.50**
#增值税	Value-added Tax	12.18	14.26	17.02	19.43	23.91	31.37
营业税	Operation Tax	20.34	22.08	26.95	31.46	37.95	46.31
企业所得税	Enterprises' Income Tax	6.78	12.34	8.77	8.41	12.10	16.08
个人所得税	Personal Income Tax	4.73	6.67	5.56	5.44	7.05	8.90
资源税	Resources Tax	0.74	0.73	0.90	0.97	1.20	1.98
城市维护建设税	Tax on Town Maintenance and Construction	5.97	6.33	7.04	8.69	10.49	12.91
房产税	Tax on Real Estates	2.73	3.00	3.48	3.67	3.83	4.28
城镇土地使用税	Tax on the Use of Urban Land	1.28	1.21	1.34	1.46	1.54	1.76
土地增值税	Land Value-added Tax	0.15	0.15	0.19	0.28	0.45	0.87
农业税	Agricultural Tax	3.73	3.03	5.33	5.16	4.11	0.01
农业特产税	Tax on Special Agricultural Products	4.80	4.11	4.66	4.97	5.20	6.68
耕地占用税	Tax on the Occupancy of Cultivated Land	0.85	1.29	1.14	1.04	1.47	1.72
契 税	Contract Tax	0.68	0.90	1.21	1.76	2.43	3.51
国有资产经营收益	State-downed Assets Profit	2.38	1.99	1.09	1.95	2.95	4.34
国有企业计划亏损补贴	Planning Subsidies to Loss-suffering Stated-owned Enterprises	-0.63	-0.52	-0.55	-0.54	-0.38	-0.38
行政性收费收入	Income from Adiministrative Fees	4.30	7.68	8.80	11.71	12.99	13.76
罚没收入	Penalty and Confiscatory Income	4.14	4.88	5.76	6.76	8.01	10.10
专项收入	Expert Project Income	3.21	3.60	3.98	5.24	7.07	10.37

14-4 分部门财政收入（2005）

Local Financial Revenue by Department(2005)

单位:万元(10000 yuan)

指 标	Item	合计 Total	#企业所得税 Income Tax of Enterprises	#国有资产经营收益 State-owned Assets Profit	#国有企业计划亏损补贴 Planning Subsidies to Loss-making State-owned Enterprises	#企业所得税退税 Return for Enterprises Income Tax
总 计	**Total**	**198327**	**160814**	**43352**	**-3761**	**-2078**
工业部门	Industry Department	28697	33446		-3494	-1255
#冶金工业	Metallurgy Industry	47	47			
煤炭工业	Coal Industry	331	364		-33	
电力工业	Electric Power Industry	8176	9379			-1203
建筑材料工业	Construction Materials Industry	-54	19		-73	
烟草企业	Tobacco Industry	22260	22260			
交通邮电部门	Transportation,Postal and Telecommunications Departments	2404	2438		-34	
外贸企业	Foreign Trade Enterprises	50	77		-27	
保险企业	Insurance Enterprises	26	26			
文教企业	Culture and Education Enterprises	1289	1293		-4	
农林水等部门	Agriculture,Forestry and Irrigation Departments	-72	1	3	-76	
罚款和滞纳金收入	Income of Forfeit and Late Fee	764	764			
其他部门	Others Departments	165169	122769	43349	-126	-823

14-5 “十五”时期各年分类别财政支出

Basic Statistics on Financial Expenditure of each year in “Tenth-Five-year Plan” Period

单位：亿元(100 million yuan)

指 标	Item	2000	2001	2002	2003	2004	2005
总 计	**Total**	**201.57**	**275.20**	**316.67**	**332.35**	**418.42**	**520.73**
基本建设支出	Expenditure for Capital Construction	24.82	43.13	36.40	31.64	38.28	41.23
企业挖掘改造资金	Enterprises Innovation Funds	6.41	4.45	7.14	5.49	4.38	5.02
地质勘探费	Geological Prospecting Expenses	1.88	2.69	2.91	3.11	3.54	3.94
科技三项费用	Expense on Science and Technology Promotion	1.34	1.49	1.94	2.31	2.59	3.36
农林水利气象支出	Expenditure for Agriculture,Forest, Irrigation and Meteorology	16.04	19.99	27.99	24.67	52.32	53.28
工业交通部门事业费	Operating Expenses of Industial and Transportation Departments	1.88	2.73	3.80	4.10	5.30	7.03
流通部门事业费	Operating Expenses of Commerce Department	0.53	0.65	0.78	0.82	0.99	1.33
城市维护费	Expenditure for City Maintenance	6.49	7.97	8.47	8.52	10.53	12.93
文教卫生事业费	Operating Expenses for Culture, Education & Health Care	48.62	65.78	80.14	89.01	107.99	137.28
科学事业费	Operating Expenses for Science	1.55	1.74	1.91	1.96	2.64	3.05
抚恤和社会福利救济费	Pensions,Social Welfare and Relief Funds	3.19	4.78	7.10	8.87	10.74	15.23
国防支出	Expenditure for National Defense	0.17	0.20	0.46	0.47	0.47	0.52
行政管理费	Administrative Expenses	24.31	32.19	38.69	43.33	51.10	65.15
武装警察部队支出	Expenditure for Armed Police Troops	0.12	0.19	0.19	0.25	0.28	0.44
公检法司支出	Expenditure for Public Security Agency, Procuratorial Agency and Court of Justice	14.53	18.25	20.57	23.76	28.75	35.83
政策性补贴支出	Expenditure for Price Subsidies	3.85	5.10	2.48	3.00	3.35	3.42
支援不发达地区支出	Expenditure for Supporting Underdeveloped Areas	8.88	9.64	10.16	10.66	11.83	13.14
行政事业单位离退休经费	Expenditure for Retired Pension in Administrative Department	1.29	2.24	2.55	2.76	3.19	3.63
其他支出	Other Expenditures	35.67	51.99	62.99	67.62	80.15	114.92

14-6 财政一般预算分类别支出（2005）

Local Financial Expenditure by Category(2005)

单位：万元(10000 yuan)

指　标	Item	全省合计 Provin -cial Total	省级 Province	地级 Prefec -ture	县级 County	乡镇级 Villages and Towns	2005年比2004年增长(%) Increase Rate in 2005 over 2004(%)
总　计	**Total**	**5207261**	**1626633**	**717942**	**2399339**	**463347**	**24.5**
基本建设支出	Expenditure for Capital Construction	412285	351683	30446	29037	1119	7.7
企业挖掘改造资金	Enterprises Innovation Funds	50171	13166	21192	15335	478	14.5
地质勘探费	Geological Prospecting Expenses	39356	39067		289		11.2
科技三项费用	Expense on Science and Technology Promotion	33615	12879	8285	12100	351	29.8
农林水利气象支出	Expenditure for Agriculture,Forestry, Irrigation and Meteorology	532855	177020	50908	251691	53236	1.8
工业交通部门事业费	Operating Expenses of Industial and Transportation Departments	70315	21480	7432	38795	2608	32.7
流通部门事业费	Operating Expenses of Commercial Department	13263	373	4199	8691		34.0
城市维护费	Expenditure for City Maintenance	129292	585	33693	86877	8137	22.8
文教卫生事业费	Operating Expenses for Culture, Education & Health Care	1372790	221000	159219	905551	87020	27.1
科学事业费	Operating Expenses for Science	30452	21687	5577	3174	14	15.3
抚恤和社会福利救济费	Pensions,Social Welfare and Relief Funds	152226	4614	14514	123986	9112	41.7
国防支出	Expenditure for National Defense	5173	3448	311	1363	51	10.1
行政管理费	Administrative Expenses	651549	54977	102444	282208	211920	27.5
武装警察部队支出	Expenditure for Armed Police Troops	4420	2063	911	1446		57.9
公检法司支出	Expenditure for Public Security Agency, Procuratorial Agency and Court of Justice	358349	126984	71480	158062	1823	24.6
政策性补贴支出	Expenditure for Price Subsidies	34223	28197	1841	4178	7	2.2
支援不发达地区支出	Expenditure for Supporting Underdeveloped Areas	131371	7369	10837	110583	2582	11.0
行政事业单位离退休经费	Expenditure for Retired Pension in Administrative Department	36304	3728	1261	27983	3332	13.8
其他支出	Other Expenditures	1149252	536313	193392	337990	81557	43.4

14-7 "十五"时期各年财政支出

Basic Statistics on Financial Expenditure of each year in "Tenth-Five-year Plan" Period

单位：亿元(100 million yuan)

指　标	Item	2000	2001	2002	2003	2004	2005
财政总支出	**Total Financial Expenditure**	**201.57**	**275.20**	**316.67**	**332.35**	**418.42**	**520.73**
经济建设费	Economic Construction Expense	56.99	79.76	85.73	76.73	113.38	121.61
#基本建设费	Expenditure for Capital Construction	24.82	43.13	36.40	31.64	38.28	41.23
企业挖潜改造资金	Enterprises Innovation Funds	6.41	4.45	7.14	5.49	4.38	5.02
工业交通部门事业费	Operating Expenses of Indusrtial and Transportation Departments	1.88	2.73	3.80	4.10	5.30	7.03
城市维护费	City Maintenance Expense	6.49	7.97	8.47	8.52	10.53	12.93
社会文教费	Expense for Social,Cultural and Educational Development	41.07	56.72	66.65	73.68	91.09	114.51
#通信广播	Communicate Broadcast	1.33	1.51	1.66	1.81	2.06	2.56
国防费	Expenditure for National Defense	0.17	0.20	0.46	0.47	0.47	0.52
行政管理费	Administrative Expenses	24.31	32.19	38.69	43.33	51.10	65.15
抚恤、社会福利费及社会保障支出	Expenditure for Pensions,Social Welfare and Social Security	15.06	21.02	28.11	28.61	33.65	40.57
财政补贴支出	Expense for Finance Subsidies	3.84	5.1	2.48	3.00	3.35	3.42
其 他	Others	60.12	80.21	94.55	106.53	125.38	174.95
国家财政用于教育支出	**Government Expenditure for Education**	**34.74**	**49.35**	**59.32**	**64.38**	**81.45**	**102.00**
教育事业费	Operating Expenses for Education	31.78	44.42	54.51	60.13	73.77	93.37
#高等学校	Higher Education	3.25	3.51	4.06	4.34	5.47	7.84
中等学校	Secondary Schools	9.00	13.84	17.84	20.73	24.62	31.60
小 学	Primary Schools	15.97	23.08	27.45	29.15	35.54	45.59
广播电视教育	Broadcast,TV and Education	0.1	0.11	0.17	0.26	0.28	0.19
教育基建投资	Investment for Education Capital Construction	0.94	2.36	1.92	1.24	4.16	3.92
各部门事业费中用于教育的支出	Education Expenditure from Operating Expenses of all Departments	0.05	0.05		0.18		
城市教育费附加支出	Expenditure from Extracharges for Education of Cities	1.97	2.52	2.89	2.83	3.52	4.71

14–7续表(continued)　　单位：亿元(100 million yuan)

指　标	Item	2000	2001	2002	2003	2004	2005
国家财政用于农业的支出	**Government Financial Expenditure for Agriculture**	**31.90**	**42.50**	**48.56**	**45.31**	**72.31**	**76.59**
支援农村生产支出和各项农业事业费	Expenditure for Supporting Agriculture Production and Agriculture Operating Expenses	14.39	18.12	25.66	24.67	52.32	53.29
基本建设支出	Expenditure for Capital Construction	6.78	12.54	10.10	9.25	7.43	7.40
科技三项费用	Expense on S&T Promotion	0.08	0.13	0.09	0.42	0.14	0.20
农村救济费	Rural Relief Funds	0.12	0.20	0.20	0.27	0.46	2.54
其他	Others	10.53	11.51	12.51	10.70	11.96	13.16
国家财政用于抚恤和社会福利支出	**Government Fiscal Expenditure for Pensions and Social Welfare**	**3.19**	**4.78**	**7.10**	**8.88**	**10.74**	**15.22**
抚恤支出	Pension for Handicapped and Bereaved Families	0.97	1.10	1.31	1.59	1.76	2.68
离退休费	Expenditure on Retires	0.23	0.31	0.42	0.43	0.50	0.59
社会福利救济费	Social Welfare and Relief Funds	0.84	1.51	2.83	4.02	5.28	7.97
自然灾害救济费	Expenses on Disaster Relief	0.67	1.21	1.63	1.58	1.60	1.93
其他	Others	0.48	0.65	0.91	1.26	1.60	2.05
国家财政用于科学研究的支出	**Government Expenditure for Science and Research**	**3.07**	**3.54**	**3.92**	**4.30**	**5.33**	**6.45**
科技三项费	Expense on S&T Promotion	1.34	1.49	1.94	2.31	2.59	3.36
科学事业费	Operating Expenses for Sciences	1.54	1.74	1.91	1.96	2.64	3.05
#自然科学	Natural Science	1.35	1.48	1.64	1.66	2.02	2.35
#社会科学	Social Science	0.10	0.15	0.14	0.14	0.20	0.21
其他科研事业费	Other S&T Operating Expenses	0.09		0.01	0.01	0.02	0.00
科研基建费	Expenses on Capital Construction of S&T Institutes	0.19	0.31	0.06	0.03	0.08	0.04
国家财政用于卫生支出	**Government Financial Expenditure for Sanitation**	**11.06**	**13.55**	**16.67**	**18.33**	**22.50**	**28.59**
#卫生事业费	Operating Expenses for Sanitation Cause	5.44	7.07	7.74	9.72	10.43	15.19
公费医疗	Free Medical Service	5.11	5.75	6.69	6.49	7.77	9.03

注：“支援农村生产支出和各项农业事业费”自2003年后为“农林水利气象支出”之和。

Note：Expenditure for Supporting Agriculture Production and Agriculture Operating Expenses since 2003 included the expenses of Agriculture,Forest,Irrigation and Meteorology.

14-8 “十五”时期各年金融机构存贷款余额

Saving Deposits and Loans of Financial Institutions of each year in “Tenth-Five-year Plan” Period

单位：亿元(100 million yuan)

指 标	Item	2000	2001	2002	2003	2004	2005	2005年比2004年增长(%) Increase Rate in 2005 over 2004(%)
资金来源合计	**All Sources**	**1109.73**	**1278.73**	**1515.56**	**1865.79**	**2185.95**	**3243.07**	**48.4**
各项存款	Deposits	1106.64	1341.11	1553.00	1898.62	2322.27	2777.54	19.6
#企业存款	Deposits of Enterprise	429.58	509.67	547.33	655.52	840.75	895.82	6.6
财政存款	Treasury Deposits	39.61	48.44	41.55	45.98	59.30	61.64	3.9
储蓄存款	Urban and Rural Savings Deposits	539.49	641.67	759.05	912.84	1094.55	1350.90	23.4
农业存款	Agricultural Deposits	23.44	27.55	33.77	41.22	59.88	99.80	66.7
资金运用合计	**All Uses**	**1109.73**	**1278.73**	**1515.56**	**1865.79**	**2185.95**	**3243.07**	**48.4**
各项贷款	Loans	1064.82	1212.23	1403.92	1714.04	2020.04	2303.93	14.1
#短期贷款	Short-term Loans	612.49	587.74	657.76	649.90	708.24	775.45	9.5
#工 业	Industrial Loans	179.62	186.54	195.51	185.82	223.73	200.34	-10.5
商 业	Commercial Loans	226.17	211.06	204.23	186.36	161.97	154.01	-4.9
建筑业	Construction Loans	15.75	23.76	31.77	21.62	27.76	27.57	-0.7
农 业	Agricultural Loans	52.29	65.32	90.44	105.28	140.94	179.05	27.0
乡镇企业	Loans to Township and Village Enterprises	14.46	15.80	15.44	16.35	6.45	5.69	-11.8
私营企业及个体	Loans to Private Enterprises	12.02	8.85	8.76	11.21	13.40	12.56	-6.3
中长期贷款	Medium-term & Long-term Loans	391.84	548.08	654.95	882.00	1128.21	1466.07	29.9

14-9 “十五”时期各年金融机构现金收入

Cash Income of Financial Institutions of each year in "Tenth -Five-year Plan" Period

单位：亿元(100 million yuan)

指　标	Item	2000	2001	2002	2003	2004	2005	2005年比2004年增长(%) Increase Rate in 2005 over 2004(%)
收入总计	**Total Income**	**2283.63**	**2712.10**	**3351.35**	**4318.20**	**5561.10**	**6220.81**	**11.9**
商品销售收入	Income from Commodity Sales	269.10	289.00	341.83	407.41	489.65	560.75	14.5
服务业收入	Income from Service Trade	138.26	171.99	211.80	241.32	312.05	332.77	6.6
税款收入	Income from Taxes	19.23	23.18	28.95	37.52	41.32	47.96	16.1
城乡个体经营收入	Income from Urban and Rural Individual Business	123.46	125.50	131.02	137.62	170.91	164.50	
储蓄存款收入	Income from Savings Deposit	1435.71	1803.57	2289.49	3048.08	3950.73	4561.58	15.5
其他金融机构收入	Income from Other Financial Institutions	38.04	15.15	14.36	17.65	23.44	17.26	-26.4
居民归还贷款收入	Income from Repayment of Loans by Residents	44.49	57.89	79.71	99.21	141.62	163.61	15.5
汇兑收入	Income from Remittances	45.81	48.83	46.76	37.14	39.37	46.79	18.8
有价证券收入	Income from Securities	13.11	12.26	8.72	12.27	9.90	8.08	-18.4
其他收入	Others	156.43	164.72	198.69	280.00	382.16	317.51	-16.9
#兑换外币收入	Income from Exchange of Foreign Currencies	1.89	0.52	2.00	0.21	0.43	1.49	246.5

14-10 “十五”时期各年金融机构现金支出

Cash Expenditures of Financial Institutions of each year in "Tenth -Five-year Plan" Period

单位：亿元 (100 million yuan)

指 标	Item	2000	2001	2002	2003	2004	2005	2005年比2004年增长(%) Increase Rate in 2005 over 2004(%)
支出总计	**Total**	**2325.68**	**2745.70**	**3405.37**	**4359.44**	**5608.15**	**6273.86**	**11.9**
工资性支出	Expenditure for Wages	245.57	278.35	317.40	376.16	420.77	458.17	8.9
农副产品采购支出	Expenditure for Purchases of Agricultural and Sideline Products	56.16	54.44	60.54	67.44	111.85	103.05	-7.9
工矿及其他产品采购支出	Expenditure for Purchases of Industrial and Mineral Products	53.71	56.33	66.90	92.26	138.49	164.12	18.5
行政企业事业管理费支出	Expenditure for Government and Enterprises Overhead	132.04	155.61	184.43	210.12	243.95	285.63	17.1
城乡个体经营支出	Expenditure for Individual Business	141.29	158.29	180.30	201.09	223.09	223.11	0.0
储蓄存款支出	Expenditure for Savings Deposits	1404.27	1750.13	2218.80	2977.09	3899.47	4535.83	16.3
其他金融机构支出	Expenditure for Other Financial Institutions	28.57	11.47	13.28	11.35	20.35	10.43	-48.7
居民提取贷款支出	Expenditure for Loans by Residents	49.59	57.70	92.95	101.44	148.63	139.23	-6.3
汇兑支出	Expenditure for Remittances	29.40	43.17	46.56	54.40	63.99	44.45	-30.5
有价证券支出	Expenditure for Securities	6.74	7.97	8.25	8.85	9.86	7.10	-28.0
其他支出	Other Expenditure	178.34	172.26	215.96	259.24	327.70	302.75	-7.6

14-11 “十五”时期各年保险系统机构数

Number of Institutions in Insurance System of each year in “Tenth-Five-year Plan” Period

单位：个（unit）

项 目	Item	2000	2001	2002	2003	2004	2005	2005年比2004年增长(%) Increase Rate in 2005 over 2004(%)
总 计	**Total**	**239**	**256**	**274**	**276**	**517**	**522**	**1.0**
机构部门按行政区划	By Administrative Areas	239	256	274	276	517	522	1.0
#省级分公司	Provincial Branches	4	5	6	7	8	9	12.5
地市级分公司	Prefecture/City Branches	18	34	38	39	39	41	5.1
县级支公司	County Branches	115	107	132	179	179	180	0.6
办事处或营业部	Business Offices and Departments	102	110	98	51	51	45	-11.8
营销服务部	Vendition Service Deparements					240	247	2.9
机构分布按经济区划	By Economic Level	239	256	274	276	517	522	1.0
#一级分公司	First Level Filiales	4	5	6	7	8	9	12.5
二级分公司	Second Level Filiales	18	34	38	39	39	41	5.1
支公司	Branches	115	107	132	179	179	180	0.6
办事处或营业部	Offices or Business Dempartments	102	110	98	51	51	45	-11.8
营销服务部	Vendition Service Deparements					240	247	2.9

注：根据《保险公司管理规定》，从2004年起营销服务部纳入保险公司分支机构管理，本表2004年起体现营销服务部机构层级。

Note:According to“Insurance Corporations Management Rule”,Vendition Service Deparements regarded as the branches of Insurance Corporations since 2004,Basic statistics on Vendition Service Deparements have been listed since 2004.

14-12 “十五”时期各年保险系统职工人数

Number of Employed Persons in Insurance System of each year in “Tenth-Five-year Plan” Period

单位：人（person）

项　目	Item	2000	2001	2002	2003	2004	2005	2005年比2004年增长(%) Increase Rate in 2005 over 2004(%)
总　计	**Total**	**2880**	**3137**	**3164**	**3382**	**3505**	**3636**	**3.7**
机构部门按行政区划	By Administrative Areas	2880	3137	3164	3382	3505	3636	3.7
#省级分公司	Provincial Branches	682	730	652	749	790	888	12.4
地市级分公司	Prefecture/City Branches	721	968	1321	1447	1494	1486	-0.5
县级支公司	County Branches	757	1127	1122	1165	1011	979	-3.2
办事处或营业部	Business Offices and Departments	720	312	69	21	32	37	15.6
营销服务部	Vendition Service Departments					178	246	38.2
机构分布按经济区划	By Economic Level	2880	3137	3164	3382	3505	3636	3.7
#一级分公司	First Level Filiales	682	730	652	749	790	888	12.4
二级分公司	Second Level Filiales	721	968	1321	1447	1494	1486	-0.5
支公司	Branches	757	1127	1122	1165	1011	979	-3.2
办事处或营业部	Offices or Business Dempartments	720	312	69	21	32	37	15.6
营销服务部	Vendition Service Departments					178	246	38.2

注：本表数据为各保险分公司正式职工人数。

Note:Number of employed persons excludes people engaged in marketing and agency service.

14-13 “十五”时期各年财产保险公司业务情况

Business of Property Insurance Company of each year in “Tenth-Five-year Plan” Period

单位：万元(10000 yuan)

指 标	Item	2000	2001	2002	2003	2004	2005	2005年比2004年增长(%) Increase Rate in 2005 over 2004(%)
保费收入	**Premium**	73608	83050	93005	104467	132296	146998	11.1
企业财产保险	Enterprise Property Insuance	11470	11498	11457	10901	11631	13834	18.9
机动车辆保险	Motor Vehicle Insurance	53721	61585	70705	77551	102907	112658	9.5
货物运输保险	Preight Transport Insurance	4327	4221	4541	4402	4601	4757	3.4
责任保险	Liability Insurance	1625	1875	2591	2254	1868	4159	122.6
信用保证保险	Creclit Guarantee Insurance	303	344	418	1050	83	479	477.1
农业保险	Agriculture Insurance	142	38	57	111	96	97	1.0
其他保险	Other Insurance	2020	3489	3236	8198	11110	11014	-0.9
储 金	Deposits	7310	6115	4729	4752	5342	5091	-4.7
赔案件数（万件）	Cases of Claims(10000 caes)	11	10	12	21	16	18	13.0
赔款支出	Claim and Payment	37856	41277	48391	56723	64105	75133	17.2
企业财产保险	Enterprise Property Insuance	4989	3525	5799	5262	4719	6933	46.9
机动车辆保险	Motor Vehicle Insurance	28864	33630	39356	46365	54288	62914	15.9
货物运输保险	Preight Transport Insurance	1134	1199	744	1028	923	735	-20.4
责任保险	Liability Insurance	1370	955	1080	1876	1085	1126	3.8
信用保证保险	Creclit Guarantee Insurance	438	461	147	255	123	50	-59.3
农业保险	Agriculture Insurance	130	53	19	31	14	28	100.0
其他保险	Other Insurance	931	1454	1246	1906	2953	3346	13.3
未决赔款	Unsettled Claim	9108	12855	13223	14330	21470	29539	37.6

注：1、本表包括人保、太保产险、平安产险、天安保险、安邦保险5家财产保险分公司数据；

2、本表2000年-2004年数据来源于各分公司上报数据，2005年数据来源于各公司上报中国保险统计信息系统业务数据。(14-15表同)

Note:1.data in this table include data from the Branches of PICC,Pacific Property Insurance Company, Pingan Property Insurance Company,Tianan Insurance Company and Anbang Insurance Company;

2.data in 2000-2004 are abtained from the all branches of Insurance Companies´report forms,data in 2005 are abtained from the China Insurance Statistic Information System. (same to 14-15)

14-14 “十五”时期各年财产保险公司主要指标

Major Indicators of Property Insurance Company of each year in “Tenth-Five-year Plan” Period

单位：万元（10000 yuan）

指 标	Item	2000	2001	2002	2003	2004	2005	2005年比2004年增长(%) Increase Rate in 2005 over 2004(%)
保费收入	**Premium**	**97438**	**118606**	**156263**	**194920**	**204318**	**254197**	**24.4**
#新单保费	Premium of New guarantee sup	37482	51439	80014	98449	91452	106642	16.6
个人业务	Personal Business	79540	94356	135917	168451	181102	219725	21.3
人寿保险	Life Insurance	70511	83093	121417	152445	161952	195177	20.5
意外伤害险	Unforeseen Injury Insurance	6458	7581	8975	7123	8610	9689	12.5
健康险	Health Insurance	2571	3682	5525	8883	10540	14859	41.0
团体业务	Group Business	17898	24250	20346	26469	23216	34472	48.5
人寿保险	Life Insurance	13188	20979	15935	17949	13997	17444	24.6
意外伤害险	Unforeseen Injury Insurance	3175	2249	2860	3892	4170	10790	158.8
健康险	Health Insurance	1535	1022	1551	4628	5049	6238	23.6
有效保单件数(万件)	Cases of Virtual guarantee slip(10000cases	133	138	122	146	142	220	54.7
赔款及给付支出	**Claim and payment**	**25170**	**28289**	**28034**	**31736**	**38690**	**41439**	**7.1**
个人业务	Personal Business	17970	17670	20060	23772	28614	29509	3.1
赔款支出	Benefit Paid	3661	5261	5573	5293	6433	6713	4.4
年金给付	Payment for Annuity	8391	4923	5035	8104	9961	7725	-22.4
满期给付	Payment for Exporation	2942	3852	6034	6478	7727	9853	27.5
死伤医疗给付	Payment for Death and Injured person	2976	3634	3418	3897	4493	5218	16.1
团体业务	Group Business	7200	10619	7974	7964	10076	11930	18.4
赔款支出	Benefit Paid	2342	3185	3871	5506	7393	7129	-3.6
年金给付	Payment for Annuity	188	1130	1277	1031	1050	1356	29.1
满期给付	Payment for Exporation	4026	6000	2577	1293	1419	3207	126.0
死伤医疗给付	Payment for Death and Injured person	644	304	249	134	214	238	11.1

注：1、本表数据包含国寿、太保寿险、平安寿险、新华人寿4家人身保险分公司数据；

2、本表2000年-2004年数据来源于各分公司上报数据,2005年数据来源于各公司上报中国保险统计信息系统业务数据.(14-16表同)

Note:1.data in this table include data from the Branches of Guoshou Life Insurance Company,Pacific Life Insurance Company, Pingan Life Insurance Company and Xinhua Life Company;

2.data in 2000-2004 are abtained from the all branches of Insurance Companies'report forms,data in 2005 are abtained from the China Insurance Statistic Information System. (same to 14-16)

14-15 财产保险公司主要指标（2005）

Major Indicators of Property Insurance Company(2005)

单位：万元（10000 yuan)

指 标	Item	合 计 Total	企业财产保险 Enterprise Property Insurance	家庭财产保险 Family Property Insurance	机动车辆保险 Transportation Equipment Insurance	工程保险 Engineering Insurance	责任保险 Responsibility Insurance	保证保险 Pledge Insurance
承保件数（万件）	Amount Insured (10000 cases)	235.15	1.31	40.27	52.66	0.01	3.58	0.76
保险金额或责任限额	Insurance Value or Liability Limit	38476908	12182534	1235650	11063719	973025	1218839	95507
签单保费	Premium of Sign Bill	146998	13834	2168	112658	2602	4159	479
赔付件数（万件）	Amount Claim and Payment (10000 cases)	18.21	0.22	0.15	16.23	0.01	0.14	
已决赔款	Indemnity Expenditure	75132	6933	257	62914	727	1126	50
未决赔款	Indefinite Expenditure	29538	3140	212	22314	526	1658	161

14-15续表(continued)

指 标	Item	船舶保险 Boats and Ships Insurance	货物运输保险 Freight Transport Insurance	特殊风险保险 Special Risk Insurance	农业保险 Agricultural Insurance	健康险 Health Insurance	意外伤害保险 Unforeseen Injury Insurance	其他险 Others
承保件数（万件）	Amount Insured (10000 cases)		7.53			0.04	128.92	0.07
保险金额或责任限额	Insurance Value or Liability Limit	991	2207688		6608	20370	9468038	3939
签单保费	Premium of Sign Bill	30	4757		97	111	6089	14
赔付件数（万件）	Amount Claim and Payment (10000 cases)		0.12		0.01	0.01	1.32	
已决赔款	Indemnity Expenditure	5	735		28	35	2322	
未决赔款	Indefinite Expenditure		384	60	2	5	1076	

14-16 人身保险主要经济指标（2005）

Major Indicators of Life Insurance Company(2005)

单位：万元（10000 yuan)

指标项目	Item	合计 Total	寿险业务 Life Insurance Business	普通寿险 Normal Life Insurance	普通寿险 个人业务 Personal	普通寿险 团体业务 Group	分红寿险 Share out Bonus	分红寿险 个人业务 Personal	分红寿险 团体业务 Group
保费收入	**Premium**	**254197**	**212621**	**87366**	**85378**	**1988**	**109895**	**95830**	**14065**
期末有效保险金额	Virtual Insurance Value at the year-end	24604068	3214695	2632439	2173062	459377	496068	476443	19625
期末有效承保人次(万人)	Virtual Insurance Person-time at the year-end (10000 persons)	1683.25	225.84	189.96	136.51	53.45	32.71	25.74	6.97
期末有效承保保单件数(万件)	Cases of Virtual Guarantee Slip at the year-end (10000 cases)	219.74	165.67	138.92	135.67	3.25	25.34	25.30	0.04
赔款和给付支出	Expenditure for Claim and Payment	41439	27122	21689	19906	1783	2582	2401	181
#赔款支出	Settled Claim	13842							
死伤医疗给付	Payment for Death,Injury or Medical Treatmnet	5455	4982	4470	4281	189	463	450	13
满期给付	Mature Payment	13060	13058	8954	8606	348	1319	1245	74
年金给付	Payment for Annuity	9081	9081	8265	7019	1246	800	706	94
退保金	Insurance withdrawed	27515	26962	9265	7769	1496	16235	15037	1198
在售产品数量(个)	Amount of Products under Selling(unit)	603	260	149	119	30	85	76	9

14-16续表（continued） 单位：万元（10000 yuan）

指标项目	Item	投资连结产品 Life Insurance Product in investment	万能寿险 Omnipotence Life Insurance	健康险业务 Health Insurance	个人业务 Personal	团体业务 Group	意外伤害保险业务 Unforeseen Injury Insurance
保费收入	**Premium**	**2127**	**13233**	**21097**	**14859**	**6238**	**20479**
期末有效保险金额	Virtual Insurance Value at the year-end	40666	45522	8312605	476092	7836513	13076768
期末有效承保人次(万人)	Virtual Insurance Person-time at the year-end(10000 persons)	0.54	2.63	653.52	38.02	615.50	803.89
期末有效承保保单件数(万件)	Cases of Virtual Guarantee Slip at the year-end(10000 cases)	0.47	0.94	31.02	28.85	2.17	23.05
赔款和给付支出	Expenditure for Claim and Payment	45	2806	8362	3852	4510	5955
#赔款支出	Settled Claim			7887	3412	4475	5955
死伤医疗给付	Payment for Death,Injury or Medical Treatmnet	29	20	473	438	35	
满期给付	Mature Payment		2785	2	2		
年金给付	Payment for Annuity	16					
退保金	Insurance withdrawed	526	936	553	487	66	
在售产品数量(个)	Amount of Products under Selling (unit)	3	23	162	111	51	181

14-17 “十五”时期股票交易情况

Basic Statistics on Stocks Exchange of each year in “Tenth-Five-year Plan” Period

指　标	Item	2000	2001	2002	2003	2004	2005
期末上市公司数(家)	**No. of listed Companies at this Year-end(unit)**	**9**	**13**	**13**	**13**	**17**	**17**
本年新增上市公司数	No. of Newly listed Stocks		4			4	1
股票总发行股本(万股)	Total Issued Capital(10000 share)	177162	284749	290249	303269	386501	398462
上市流通股	Negotiable Shares	70585	104373	105986	111423	141975	153668
股票市价总值(亿元)	Total Market Capitalization(100 million yuan)	310.3	415.4	332.6	269.8	355.8	397.6
流通股票市值	Negotiable Market Capitalization	121.6	143.7	115.4	93.9	119.3	134.9
股票成交金额	Total Turnover	444.5	243.59	200.97	194.8	208.56	171.74

14-18 贵州上市公司股票发行情况（A股）（2005）

Summary List of Stocks Publicly Issued by Guizhou Enterprises(A Shares)(2005)

单位：万股(10000 share)

上市公司名称	Listed Companies	上市时间 Listed Time	板块类别	Listed Companies	总股本 Total Capital Stock
世纪中天	CENTURY ZHONGTIAN INVESTMENT JIONT STOCK CO.,LTD.	1994.02.02	房地产	Real Estate	32681.15
黔轮胎	GUI ZHOU TYRE CO., LTD.	1996.03.08	工业	Industry	25432.7
力源液压	GUIZHOU LIYUAN HYDRAULIC COMPONENTS CO.,LTD.	1996.11.06	工业	Industry	11103.2
天创置业	TIANCHUANG PROPERTY CO.,LTD.	1997.01.30	房地产	Real Estate	12870
振华科技	CHINA ZHENHUA(GROUP) SCIENCE & TECHNOLOGY CO.,LTD.	1997.07.03	工业	Industry	35812
长征电器	GUIZHOU CHANGZHENG ELECTRICAL APPARATUS CO.,LTD.	1997.11.27	工业	Industry	17200
高鸿股份	GOHIGH DATA NETWORKS TECHNOLOGY CO.,LTD.	1998.06.09	通讯	communications	22490
南方汇通	SOUTH HUITON CO.,LTD.	1999.06.16	工业	Industry	42200
赤天化	GUIZHOU CHITIANHUA CORP.	2000.02.21	工业	Industry	17000
红星发展	GUIZHOU REDSTAR DEVELOPING CO.,LTD.	2001.03.20	工业	Industry	29120
盘江股份	GUIZHOU PANJIANG REFINED COAL CO.,LTD.	2001.05.31	煤矿开发	Coal Mine Exploiting	37130
贵州茅台	KWEICHOW MOUTAI CO.,LTD.	2001.08.27	酿酒	Vintage	39325
贵航股份	GUIZHOU GUIHANG AUTOMOTIVE COMPONENTS CO.,LTD.	2001.12.27	汽车配件	Automoblile fittings	22000
益佰制药	GUIZHOU YIBAI PHAMACY CO.,LTD.	2004.03.08	医药	Phamacy	6700
贵绳股份	GUIZHOU GUISHENG CO.,LTD.	2004.04.22	工业	Industry	16437
航天电器	GUIZHOU SPACEFLIGHT DIANQI CO.,LTD	2004.07.09	仪电仪表	Measuring Instruments	8000
久联发展	GUIZHOU JIULIAN DEVELOPMENT CO.,LTD.	2004.09.08	工业	Industry	11000
黔源电力	GUIZHOU QIANYUAN ELECTRIC POWER CO.,LTD.	2005.03.03	电力	Electric Power	14025.6

14-18续表(Continued)　　　　单位：万股(10000 share)

上市公司名称	Listed Companies	股本构成 Face Value			募集资金总额(万元) Total Amount Issued (10000 yuan)
		国家股 Government Share	社会法人股 Cooperation Share	流通股 Circulating Share	
世纪中天	CENTURY ZHONGTIAN INVESTMENT JIONT STOCK CO.,LTD.	3624.09	17783.08	11273.98	7354
黔轮胎	GUI ZHOU TYRE CO., LTD.	12970.68		12462.02	52462
力源液压	GUIZHOU LIYUAN HYDRAULIC COMPONENTS CO.,LTD.		7653.2	3450	10344
天创置业	TIANCHUANG PROPERTY CO.,LTD.	2084.41	6495.59	4290	3720
振华科技	CHINA ZHENHUA(GROUP)SCIENCE & TECHNOLOGY CO.,LTD.		18012	17800	140202
长征电器	GUIZHOU CHANGZHENG ELECTRICAL APPARATUS CO.,LTD.	8460.3	3539.7	5200	23419.8
高鸿股份	GOHIGH DATA NETWORKS TECHNOLOGY CO.,LTD.	1474.49	13267.51	7748	15620
南方汇通	SOUTH HUITON CO.,LTD.		24000	18200	59440
赤天化	GUIZHOU CHITIANHUA CORP.		10000	7000	49154
红星发展	GUIZHOU REDSTAR DEVELOPING CO.,LTD.	19976.32	407.68	8736	37980
盘江股份	GUIZHOU PANJIANG REFINED COAL CO.,LTD.		25130	12000	72000
贵州茅台	KWEICHOW MOUTAI CO.,LTD.	27842.1	235.95	11246.95	224438
贵航股份	GUIZHOU GUIHANG AUTOMOTIVE COMPONENTS CO.,LTD.	2157.31	12842.69	7000	34510
益佰制药	GUIZHOU YIBAI PHAMACY CO.,LTD.	4465	235	2000	28800
贵绳股份	GUIZHOU GUISHENG CO.,LTD.	9339	98	7000	51800
航天电器	GUIZHOU SPACEFLIGHT DIANQI CO.,LTD	4880	550	2570	17990
久联发展	GUIZHOU JIULIAN DEVELOPMENT CO.,LTD.	7000		4000	26640
黔源电力	GUIZHOU QIANYUAN ELECTRIC POWER CO.,LTD	6500	2525.6	5000	29850

主要统计指标解释

财政收入 包括地方财政收入和上划中央增值税、消费税两部分。地方财政收入包括营业税、地方企业所得税、个人所得税、城镇土地使用税、固定资产投资方向调节税、城镇维护建设税、房产税、车船使用税、印花税、屠宰税、农牧业税、农业特产税、耕地占用税、契税、增值税25%部分、证券交易税(印花税)的50%部分和除海洋石油资源税以外的其他资源税。

财政支出 国家财政将筹集起来的资金进行分配使用,以满足经济建设和各项事业的需要,主要包括:

基本建设支出,企业挖潜改造资金,地质勘探费用,科技三项费用,支援农村生产支出,农林水利气象等部门的事业费用,工业交通商业等部门的事业费,文教科学卫生事业费,抚恤和社会福利救济费,国防支出,行政管理费,价格补贴支出。

预算外资金收支 预算外资金指国家机关、事业单位和社会团体为履行或代行政府职能,依据国家法律、法规和具有法律效力的规章而收取、提取和安排使用的未纳入国家预算管理的各种财政性资金。

信贷资金 指金融机构以信用方式积聚和分配的货币资金。金融机构信贷资金的来源有各项存款、对国际金融机构负债、流通中货币、银行自有资金及当年结益等;信贷资金的运用有各项贷款、黄金占款、外汇占款、财政借款及在国际金融机构中的资产等。

存款 指企业、机关、团体或居民根据资金必须收回的原则,把货币资金存入银行或其他信用机构保管并取得一定利息的一种信用活动形式。根据存款对象的不同可划分为企业存款、财政存款、机关团体存款、基本建设存款、城镇储蓄存款、农村存款等科目。它是银行信贷资金的主要来源。

贷款 指银行或其他信用机构根据资金必须归还的原则,按一定利率,为企业、个人等提供资金的一种信用活动形式。我国银行贷款分为流动资金贷款、固定资产贷款、城乡个体工商户贷款以及农业贷款等科目。

保险金额 指保险人承担赔偿或者给付保险金责任的最高限额。

保费 指投保人为取得保险人在约定范围内所承担赔偿责任而支付给保险人的费用。

赔款 指保险人根据保险合同的规定,向被保险人支付的赔偿保险责任损失的金额。

给付 包括死伤医疗给付和满期给付。死伤医疗给付是指保险人根据人寿保险及长期健康保险合同的规定,因被保险人在保险期内发生保险责任范围内的保险事故支付给被保险人(或受益人)的金额。满期给付是指被保险人生存期满,保险人按人寿保险合同规定支付给被保险人的满期保险金额。

城乡居民储蓄存款余额 指某一时点城乡居民存入银行及农村信用社的储蓄金额,包括城镇居民储蓄存款和农民个人储蓄存款,不包括居民的手存现金和工矿企业、部队、机关、团体等单位存款。

股票市价总值 指在交易所上市的证券在某一时点按市价与发行数量计算的总金额。计算公式为:

股票市价总值=Σ(市价×发行数量)。

股票流通市值 指在交易所上市的证券在某一时点按市价与上市流通量计算的总金额。计算公式为:

股票流通总值=Σ(市价×可流通量)。

股票成交量 上市公司股票在交易所成交的数量。

股票成交金额 股票成交量乘以成交价格。

Explanatory Notes on Main Statistical Indicators

Government Revenue includes the local government revenue and the consumption tax and value added tax transfered to central government.The revenue of the local government includes business tax,income tax of the enterprises subordinated to the local government,personal income tax,tax on the use of urban land,tax on the adjustment of the investment in fixed assets,tax on town maintenance and construction,tax on real estates,tax on the use of vehicles and ships,stamp tax,slaughter tax,tax on agriculture and animal husbandry,tax on special agricultural products,tax on the occupancy of cultivated land,contract tax,25% of the value added tax,50% of the tax on stock dealing (stamp tax) and tax on resources other than the ocean petroleum resources.

Government Expenditure refers to the distribution and use of the funds the government finance has raised, so as to meet the needs of economic construction and various causes. It includes the following main items:

Expenditure for capital construction, Innovation funds of the enterprises, Geological prospecting expenses, Expenditures for science and technology promotion, Expenditure for supporting rural production, Operating expenses of the departments of farming, forestry, water conservancy and meteorology etc, Operating expenses of the departments of industry, transport and commerce, Operating expenses of the departments of culture, eduation, science and public health, Pension for the disabled or for the families of the bereaved and relief funds for social welfare, Expenditures for national defence, Administrative expenses, Expenditure for price subsidies.

Extra-budgetary Revenue and Expenditure Extra-budgetary fund refers to financial fund of various types not covered by the regular government budgetary management, which is collected, allocated or arranged by government agencies, institutions and social organizations while performing duties delegated to them or on behalf of the government in accordance with laws, rules and regulations.

Credit Funds refer to the funds issued as loans by banking institutions. The sources of credit funds of the banking institutions included deposits, liabilities to international financial institutions, currency in circulation, self-owned funds and current retained profits, etc. The credit funds can be used in forms of loans, gold, foreign exchange, government debt and assets in the international financial institutions.

Deposit is a form of credit by which enterprises, institutions, organizations or households can put money into banks and other credit institutions for safekeeping and interest earning under the principle of free withdrawal. According to different depositors, deposits are divided into enterprise deposits,treasury deposits, deposits of government agencies and organizations,capital construction deposits, urban savings deposits, rural deposits and other deposits. Deposits are major sources of the credit funds of banks.

Loan is a form of credit by which banks and other credit institutions provide funds at certain interest rate to enterprises and individuals in the light of the principle of unconditional repayment. Loans from Chinese banks include circulating capital loans, fixed assets loans, loans to urban and rural individuals engaged in industrial and commercial business and agricultural loans.

Amount Insured refers to the maximum that the insurant will get for the claim of the case insured.

Premium is the fee paid by the insurant to the insurer to obtain the obligation of compensation from the insurance within the agreed terms.

Settled Claim is the compensation paid by the insurer to the insurant in accordance with the insurance contract.

Payment includes payment for death, injury or medical treatment and mature payment. Payment for death, injury or medical treatment refers to the money paid to the insurant (or the beneficiary) in accordance with the life or health insurance contract when the insurant encounters accidents within the insured period covered in the contract. Mature payment refers to the mature payment to the insurant in accordance with the life insurance contract at the end of the insured period.

The Savings Deposits of Urban and Rural Residents refers to the total value of savings deposits of urban and rural households in banks and rural credit cooperatives at a given point of time, including the savings deposit of urban residents and the savings deposit of rural residents. The cash in hand by residents and the deposits of organizations such as enterprises,military units,government agencies, institutions, etc. are not included.

Total Market Capitalization this figure represents the aggregate taken at a given time of the market price the listed volume for each security in the market.

Σ(Marked Price×Negotiable Volume)

Negotiable Market Capitalization this figure represents the aggregate taken at a given time of the market price the negotiable volume for each security in the market.

Σ(Marked Price×Negotiable Volume)

Trading Volume refers to trading volume of shares of listed companies.

Total Turnover refers to the value derived from the current stock price per share times the traded shares.

Fifteen

人民生活

People's Livelihood

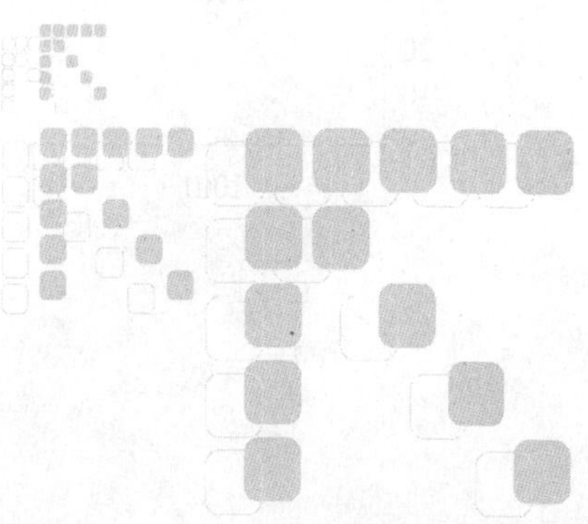

城镇居民人均可支配收入（元）

Per Capita Annual Disposable Income of Urban Households (yuan)

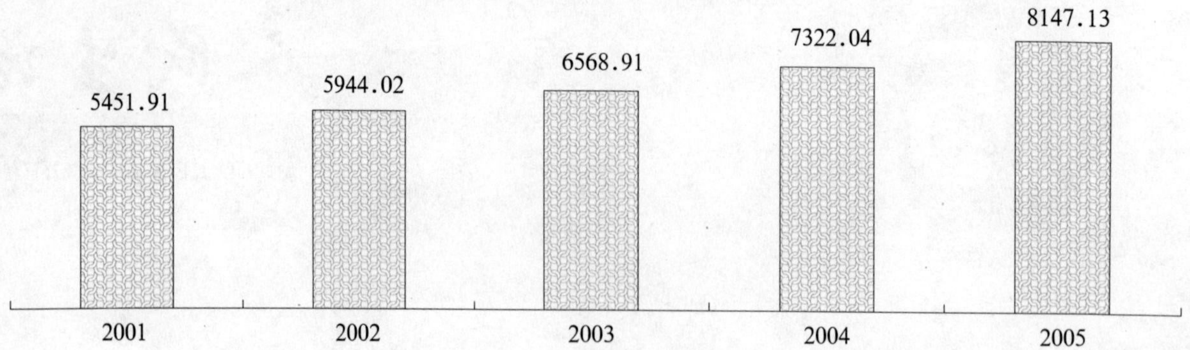

农民人均纯收入（元）

Per Capita Annual Average Net Income Rural Residents (yuan)

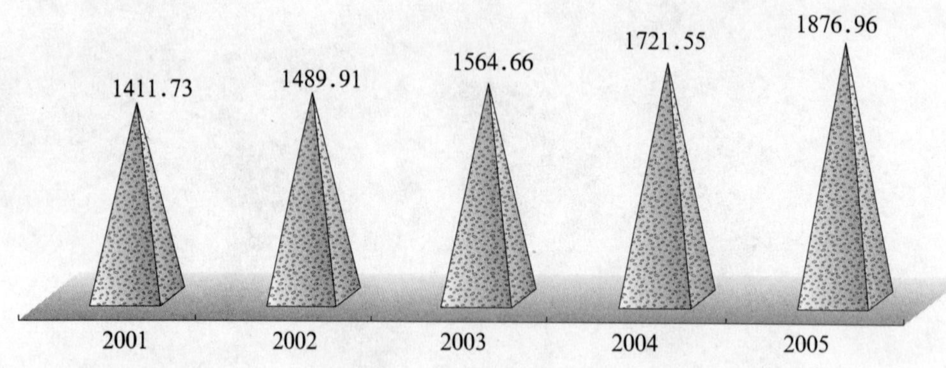

恩格尔系数（%）

Engel Coefficient (%)

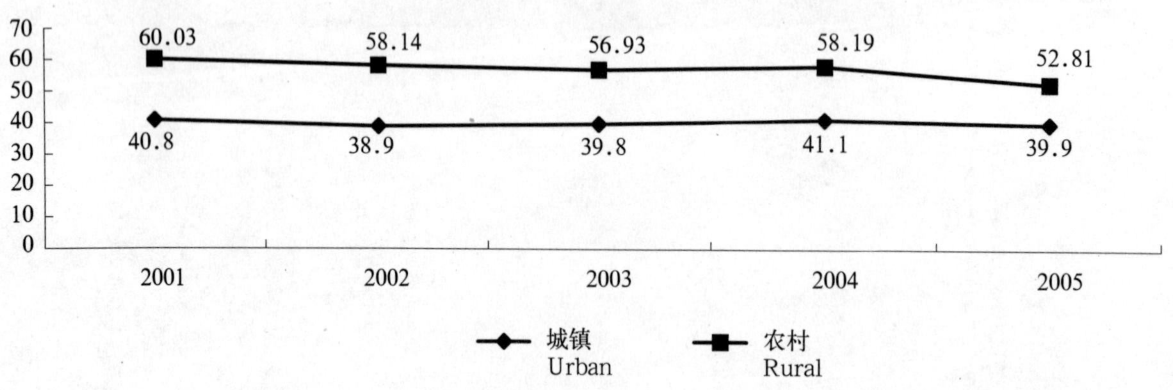

15-1 “十五”时期各年城乡人民生活水平

People's Livelihood in Urban and Rural Areas of Each Year in “Tenth Five-year Plan” Period

指 标	Item	2000	2001	2002	2003	2004	2005
就业状况	**Employment**						
城市居民家庭每户就业人口（人）	Average Number of Employed Personsper Urban Household(person)	1.62	1.66	1.49	1.53	1.51	1.44
城市居民家庭每一就业者赡养人口	Number of Dependents per Employee of Urban Household	1.92	1.88	2.13	2.03	2.03	2.12
城镇平均每户就业面（%）	Proportion of Employment per Urban Household(%)	0.52	0.53	0.47	0.49	0.49	0.47
城镇登记失业人数（万人）	Registered Urban Unemployment Persons (10 000 persons)	10.24	11.15	11.08	11.18	11.61	12.13
城镇登记失业率（%）	Registered Urban Unemployment Rate(%)	3.8	4.0	4.1	4.0	4.1	4.2
农村平均每户劳动力（人）	Average Number of Laborer per Rural Household(person)	2.77	2.74	2.77	2.79	2.85	2.82
农村居民家庭每一劳动力赡养人数	Number of Dependents per Laborer of Rural Household	1.63	1.63	1.61	1.58	1.55	1.56
收入与支出	**Income and Expenditure**						
城镇居民人均可支配收入(元)	Annual Per Capita Disposable Income of Urban Households(yuan)	5122	5452	5944	6569	7322	8147
城镇居民人均消费性支出	Annual Per Capita Consumption Expenditure of Urban Households	4278	4492	4598	4948	5494	6156
在岗职工平均工资	Average Wage of Staff and Workers in their Posts	7468	8991	9810	11027	12431	14344
农民人均纯收入	Annual Per Capita Disposable Income of Rural Households	1374	1412	1490	1565	1722	1877
农村居民人均生活消费支出	Annual Per Capita Living Expenditure of Rural Households	1097	1098	1138	1185	1296	1552
城乡居民平均每人储蓄存款余额	Per Capita Balance of Saving Deposit in Urban and Rural Areas	1445	1699	2082	2359	2816	3448
生活质量	**Life Quality**						
居民家庭恩格尔系数(%)	Household's Engle Coefficient(%)						
城 镇	Urban	43.20	40.80	38.90	39.80	41.14	39.90
农 村	Rural	62.68	60.03	58.14	56.93	58.19	52.81
居住条件(平方米)	Residence Condition(sq.m)						
城镇人均住宅建筑面积	Per Capita Building Space in Urban Areas	17.60	18.40	25.47	25.20	25.50	26.40
农村居民人均住房面积	Per Capita Living Space in Rural Areas	19.75	20.43	21.14	21.62	22.05	23.50

15-1续表1(continued)

指 标	Item	2000	2001	2002	2003	2004	2005
交通条件	**Traffic Condition**						
城镇每万人拥有公共车辆（标台）	Number of Public Transportation per 10 000 Population in City(unit)		3.85	5.58	6.48	5.81	6.05
城市人均拥有道路面积（平方米）	Per Capita Area of Paved Roads in City(sq.m)		2.68	4.37	4.80	5.48	6.05
每百户城镇居民拥有家用汽车(辆)	Number of Family Vehicles Per 100 Urban Households(unit)	0.2	0.4	0.5	0.5	0.4	1.8
每百户农村居民拥有家用摩托车	Number of Motor Cycles Per 100 Rural Households	6.0	7.2	8.7	9.6	11.2	14.0
通信条件	**Communication Condition**						
电话普及率（部/百人）	Telephone Popularization Rate (set/100 persons)	6.36	11.11	13.90	17.40	21.40	25.00
住宅电话普及率（%）	Household Telephone Popularization Rate(%)	13.40	16.54	21.25	22.39	29.99	31.81
每百户拥有移动电话（部）	Per Persons Mobile Telephone(set)						
城 镇	Urban	6.26	29.37	58.20	78.13	96.82	119.22
农 村	Rural	…	1.7	3.7	7.2	12.9	17.0
城市公用设施普及占有率（%）	City Public Utility Rate(%)						
自来水普及率	Rate of Access to Tap Water		48.0	74.6	77.6	84.8	88.4
燃气普及率	Rate of Access to Gas		24.5	46.4	49.5	51.3	54.6
人均公共绿地面积（平方米）	Per Capita Green Area(sq.m)		3.02	4.06	4.40	4.53	5.32
文化、教育和卫生	**Culture,Education and Health**						
文 化	Culture						
广播人口覆盖率（%）	Broadcast Covering Rate of Population(%)	76.2	78.3	79.4	80.0	82.1	83.3
电视人口覆盖率	TV Covering Rate of Population	85.3	87.2	88.2	89.1	89.6	90.5
城镇每百户家用电脑（台）	Computer(set)	5.74	7.86	11.6	16.58	21.02	23.99
每百户彩电拥有量（台/百户）	Number of Computer per 100 Households(set)						
城 镇	Urban	113.78	117.42	121.89	121.25	125.27	124.51
农 村	Rural	21.2	25.9	33.9	39.2	47.2	56.8

15-1续表2(continued)

指 标	Item	2000	2001	2002	2003	2004	2005
居民家庭文化娱乐用品及服务支出（元）	Household Expenditure on Culture, Entertainment and Services(yuan)						
城镇	Urban	490.04	582.74	675.33	713.91	793.39	811.33
农村	Rural	97.26	98.49	108.56	128.13	140.21	160.91
教 育	**Education**						
小学学龄儿童入学率（%）	Enrollment Rate of School-age Children(%)	98.5	98.2	98.2	98.1	97.8	98.3
初中阶段毛入学率	Enrollment Rate of Primary School Graduates Entering into Junior Secondary Schools(%)	73.6	82.0	87.2	94.2	98.7	98.7
高中阶段毛入学率	Enrollment Rate of Junior secondary School Graduates Entering into Senior secondary Schools(%)	21.5	22.9	25.4	24.1	26.4	30.5
高等教育毛入学率	Enrollment Rate of Senior secondary School Graduates Entering into Institution of Higher Learning(%)	5.9	7.3	9.0	10.0	10.0	11.0
每万人口中在校学生(人)	Per 10000 Persons Total Enrollment(person)						
大学生	Students Enrollment of Higher Education	21.26	28.47	34.85	38.62	46.07	52.59
中学生	Students Enrollment of Secondary Schools	418.57	485.98	554.59	608.07	638.73	648.56
小学生	Students Enrollment of Primary Schools	1331.86	1290.42	1262.05	1232.34	1228.09	1205.16
卫 生	**Health**						
每千人拥有医院、卫生院病床(张)	Number of Hospital Beds per 1000 Persons (bed)	14.8	1.48	1.51	1.49	1.49	1.50
每千人拥有医生（人）	Number of Docter per 1000 Persons(person)	1.22	1.23	1.13	1.12	1.22	0.91
社会保障	**Social Security**						
参加基本养老保险职工人数（万人）	Number of Employee Joining Basic Endowment Insurance(10000 person)	165.4	159.0	168.9	168.0	174.9	183.7
参加失业保险职工人数	Number of Person Joining Unemployment Insurance(10000 person)	131.3	136.4	132.2	128.0	129.9	129.3
参加医疗保险职工人数	Number of Person Joining Basic Medical Care System(10000 person)		30.0	94.6	134.1	152.6	180.6
社会保险基金收支（亿元）	Revenue and Expenditure on Social Security (100 million yuan)						
基金收入	Revenue	24.45	32.77	44.08	53.44	60.87	69.85
基金支出	Expenditure	22.07	27.82	35.73	41.13	48.24	52.73

15-2 "十五"时期各年城镇

Basic Conditions of Urban Households of Each

指 标	Item	2000
调查户数	Number of Households Surveyed(household)	850
平均每户常住家庭人口（人）	Average Household Size(person)	3.11
平均每户就业人员	Average Number of Employed Persons Per Household(persons)	1.62
平均每户就业面（%）	Proportion of Employment per Household(%)	0.52
国有经济单位职工人数（人/户）	Number of Staff and Workers in State-owned Units(person/household)	1.32
城镇集体经济单位职工人数	Number of Staff and Workers in Urban Collective-owned Units	0.13
其他各种经济类型单位职工	Number of Staff and Workers in Other Types of Ownership Units	0.01
平均每个就业者赡养人口（人）	Number of Dependents per Employee(person)	1.92
平均每人年可支配收入（元）	**Per Capita Annual Disposable Income (yuan)**	**5122.21**
平均每人年总收入	**Per Capita Annual Income**	**5135.87**
工薪收入	Income of Wages and Salaries	3680.36
#工资及补贴收入	Income of Laborage and Allowance	3521.24
其他劳动收入	Income of other Labor	159.12
经营者净收入	Net Business Income	224.13
财产性收入	Income from Porperties	40.04
转移性收入	Income from Transfer	1191.34
#养老金或离退休金	Annuities or Pension	985.36
出售财物收入	Income of Selling Property and goods	1.32
借贷收入	Income on Loan	1049.30
家庭总支出	**Total Household Expenditure**	**5075.81**
消费支出	Consumption Expenditure	4278.28
购房与建房支出	Expenditure of Purchasing or Building House	69.38
转移性支出	Transfer Expenditure	726.33
财产性支出	Property Expenditure	1.82
社会保障支出	Social Seurity Expenditure	
借贷支出	Expenditure on Loan	912.39

居民家庭生活基本情况

Year in "Tenth-Five-year Plan" Period

2001	2002	2003	2004	2005	2005年比2004年增长(%) Increase Rate in 2005 over 2004(%)
980	1020	1190	1190	1190	
3.12	3.16	3.11	3.05	3.06	
1.66	1.49	1.53	1.51	1.44	
0.53	0.47	0.49	0.49	0.47	
1.29	1.01	1.07	1.01	0.88	
0.14	0.12	0.11	0.10	0.06	
0.02	0.04	0.04	0.04	0.07	
1.88	2.13	2.03	2.03	2.12	
5451.91	**5944.02**	**6568.91**	**7322.04**	**8147.13**	**11.3**
5463.30	**6107.24**	**6745.80**	**7518.71**	**8380.96**	**11.5**
4008.96	4007.40	4664.76	5135.14	5513.48	7.4
3813.80	3853.92	4447.50	4938.56	5322.00	7.8
195.14	153.48	217.26	196.57	191.48	-2.6
285.13	335.02	380.63	576.33	790.46	37.2
18.71	53.01	55.10	54.21	90.20	66.4
1150.52	1711.81	1645.31	1753.03	1986.83	13.3
955.03	1372.78	1293.62	1437.33	1736.52	20.8
3.88	6.06	64.46	19.85	36.69	84.8
896.39	928.42	960.48	1114.83	1398.40	25.4
5331.41	**5573.48**	**6079.39**	**6799.92**	**7640.74**	**12.4**
4492.25	4598.30	4947.62	5494.43	6156.27	12.0
81.54	68.11	131.70	179.93	338.49	88.1
756.52	756.46	840.16	947.08	916.95	-3.2
1.10	4.33	2.37	2.28	16.79	636.4
	146.28	157.54	176.20	212.24	20.5
1143.93	1046.50	1216.80	1496.29	1748.24	16.8

15-3 “十五”时期各年城镇居民家庭人均总收入和可支配收入

Urban Household Per Capita Annual Actural Income and Disposable Income Of Each Year in "Tenth-Tine-year Plan"Perinod

单位：元(yuan)

指 标	Item	2000	2001	2002	2003	2004	2005	2005年比2004年增长(%) Increase Rate in 2005 over 2004(%)
平均每人年总收入	**Annual Actual Income Per Capita**	**5135.87**	**5463.3**	**6107.24**	**6745.80**	**7518.71**	**8380.96**	**11.5**
最低收入户	Lowest Income(First Decile)	2101.59	2081.64	1613.3	1919.47	2504.39	2464.94	-1.6
低收入户	Low Income(Second Decile)	2971.46	3005.13	2792.93	3100.36	3727.01	3820.89	2.5
中等偏下户	Lower Middle Income (Second Quintile)	3963.25	4001.14	3926.51	4324.67	5066.20	5454.44	7.7
中等收入户	Middle Income(Third Quintile)	5066.24	5255.62	5436.48	5908.59	6925.66	7617.41	10.0
中等偏上户	Upper Middle Income (Fourth Quintile)	6251.96	6794.03	7165.54	7786.32	8967.98	10273.12	14.6
高收入户	High Income(Tenth Decile)	7474.32	8424.86	9555.63	10575.50	11580.29	13466.90	16.3
最高收入户	Highest Income(Ninth Decile)	10289.35	11376.42	17249.25	18075.03	17652.48	20222.87	14.6
平均每人年可支配收入	**Annual Disposable Income Per Capita**	**5122.21**	**5451.91**	**5944.02**	**6568.91**	**7322.04**	**8147.13**	**11.3**
最低收入户	Lowest Income(First Decile)	2094.47	2078.49	1441.92	1798.72	2438.99	2370.17	-2.8
低收入户	Low Income(Second Decile)	2957.48	2983.41	2698.96	3006.20	3664.00	3756.21	2.5
中等偏下户	Lower Middle Income (Second Quintile)	3952.32	3990.24	3826.98	4221.85	4961.66	5310.65	7.0
中等收入户	Middle Income(Third Quintile)	5049.42	5249.83	5282.84	5748.09	6740.03	7356.43	9.1
中等偏上户	Upper Middle Income (Fourth Quintile)	6236.86	6778.67	6991.29	7573.24	8719.08	10022.34	14.9
高收入户	High Income(Tenth Decile)	7452.75	8407.75	9340.88	10294.50	11226.46	13049.13	16.2
最高收入户	Highest Income(Ninth Decile)	10279.98	11370.74	16905.04	17708.59	17168.78	19683.63	14.6

15-4 “十五”时期各年城镇居民家庭人均现金收支情况

Per Capita Annual Cash Inlome and Expenditure of Urban Households of Each Year in “Tenth-Five-year Plan” Period

单位:元(yuan)

指 标	Item	2000	2001	2002	2003	2004	2005	2005年比2004年增长(%) Increase Rate in 2005 over 2004(%)
家庭总收入	**Total Households Income**	**5135.87**	**5463.30**	**6107.24**	**6745.80**	**7518.71**	**8380.96**	**11.5**
#可支配收入	Disposable Income	5122.21	5451.91	5944.02	6568.91	7322.04	8147.13	11.3
工薪收入	Income of Wages and Salaries	3680.36	4008.96	4007.40	4664.76	5135.14	5513.48	7.4
#工资及补贴收入	Income of Laborage and Allowance	3521.24	3813.80	3853.92	4447.50	4933.56	5322.00	7.9
其他劳动收入	Income of other Labor	159.12	195.14	153.48	217.26	196.57	191.48	-2.6
经营净收入	Net Business Income	224.13	285.13	335.02	380.63	576.33	790.46	37.2
财产性收入	Income from Porperties	40.04	18.71	53.01	55.10	54.21	90.20	66.4
#利息收入	Interest Income	6.32	4.58	3.21	6.40	1.75	1.22	-30.3
股息与红利收入	Dividends and Bonus Income	4.73	5.73	4.73	9.83	6.34	3.62	-42.9
转移性收入	Income from Transfer	1191.34	1150.52	1711.81	1645.31	1753.03	1986.83	13.3
#养老金或离退休金	Annuities or pension	985.36	955.03	1372.78	1293.62	1437.33	1736.52	20.8
出售财物收入	Income of Selling Property and goods	1.32	3.88	6.06	64.46	19.85	36.69	84.8
借贷收入	Income on Loan	1049.30	896.39	928.42	960.48	1114.83	1398.40	25.4
#提取储蓄存款	Drawing Money from Banks	913.45	781.85	693.17	809.79	1024.16	1200.61	17.2
其他借贷收入	Others	20.93	39.40	74.18	21.69	1.05	1.00	-4.8
家庭总支出	**Total Households Expenditure**	**5075.81**	**5331.41**	**5573.48**	**6079.39**	**6799.92**	**7640.74**	**12.4**
消费支出	Consumption Expenditure	4278.28	4492.25	4598.30	4947.62	5494.43	6156.27	12.0
#服务性消费支出	Services	980.75	1095.10	1324.71	1358.64	1538.96	1663.85	8.1
购房与建房支出	Expenditure of Purchasing or Building House	69.38	81.54	68.11	131.70	179.93	338.49	88.1
转移性支出	Transfer Expenditure	726.33	756.52	756.46	840.16	947.08	916.95	-3.2
#交纳的个人收入税	Individual Income Tax	2.67	1.55	4.01	3.50	5.87	4.81	-18.1
各种非储蓄性保险支出	Various Nonsaving Insurance Expenditure	2.73	5.46	8.32	5.21	3.10	1.39	-55.2
其他转移性支出	Others	37.48	37.88	40.29	35.94	36.95	30.75	-16.8
财产性支出	Property Expenditure	1.82	1.10	4.33	2.37	2.28	16.79	636.4
社会保障支出	Social Seurity Expenditure			146.28	157.54	176.20	212.24	20.5
借贷支出	Expenditure on Loan	912.39	1143.93	1046.50	1216.80	1496.29	1748.24	16.8
#存入储蓄款	Saving Deposits	647.26	850.08	883.41	1008.62	1237.74	1490.77	20.4
购置有价证券	Purchasing Seurities	4.30	12.76	1.09	3.69	3.81	4.14	8.7
其他借贷支出	Others	57.13	57.75	6.65	4.51	6.81	4.35	-36.1

15-5 “十五”时期各年城镇居民家庭人均消费性支出

Per Capita Annual Consumption Expenditure of Urban Household of Each Year in “Tenth-Five-year Plan” Period

单位：元 (yuan)

指 标	Item	2000	2001	2002	2003	2004	2005	2005年比2004年增长(%) Increase Rate in 2005 ove 2004(%)
恩格尔系数(%)	**Engel Coefficient(%)**	**43.2**	**40.8**	**38.9**	**39.8**	**41.1**	**39.9**	
消费性支出	**Consumption Expenditure**	**4278.28**	**4492.25**	**4598.30**	**4947.62**	**5494.43**	**6156.27**	**12.0**
食品	**Food**	**1847.63**	**1832.26**	**1788.61**	**1967.67**	**2260.46**	**2457.09**	**8.7**
#粮食	Grain	185.68	171.89	145.24	157.24	204.02	219.89	7.8
糖、烟、酒、饮料类	Sugar, Cigarette, Liquor and Beverage	300.67	297.17	257.99	262.47	289.28	338.25	16.9
在外饮食	Dining Out	262.06	279.35	276.84	331.60	391.95	436.97	11.5
衣着	**Clothing**	**453.10**	**506.17**	**483.88**	**524.81**	**585.18**	**702.56**	**20.1**
家庭设备、用品及服务	Household Appliances and Services	316.69	348.42	280.90	286.63	286.56	335.52	17.1
#耐用消费品	Durable Consumer Goods	147.00	158.79	110.62	100.66	89.31	113.41	27.0
医疗保健	Health Care and Medical Services	233.28	268.42	265.29	291.75	301.26	403.23	33.8
交通和通信	**Transport and Communications**	**369.02**	**417.97**	**460.92**	**561.03**	**601.08**	**625.14**	**4.0**
#交通	Transport	169.36	171.94	174.11	212.93	219.09	219.40	0.1
通信	Communications	199.66	246.03	286.81	348.10	381.98	405.73	6.2
娱乐、教育、文化服务	Recreation,Education and Culture Services	490.04	582.74	675.33	713.91	793.39	811.33	2.3
#文化娱乐用品	Recreation Articles	155.13	156.19	160.29	199.04	188.12	204.72	8.8
文化娱乐服务	Recreation Services	82.40	87.68	143.72	136.74	205.93	223.78	8.7
学杂费	Tuition Fee	161.70	244.72	220.53	202.89	190.02	183.97	-3.2
托幼费	Child-care Fee	22.46	24.33	25.90	33.48	28.31	39.96	41.2
书报杂志	Books,Newspaper and Magazines	21.99	22.26	26.22	25.54	29.21	27.69	-5.2
居住	**Houseing**	**423.65**	**397.07**	**476.10**	**422.01**	**468.21**	**583.17**	**24.6**
#房租	Rent	15.76	11.33	15.95	14.83	18.41	14.58	-20.8
水费	Water	30.90	32.91	37.24	39.30	43.88	55.77	27.1
电费	Electricity	115.89	127.92	141.71	167.86	202.91	248.76	22.6
燃料费	Fuels	72.10	69.79	92.06	100.34	110.41	146.46	32.7
杂项商品和服务	Miscellaneous Goods and Services	144.86	139.21	167.27	179.81	198.30	238.23	20.1

15-6 "十五"时期各年城镇居民家庭人均购买主要商品数量

Per Capita Annual Purchases of Major Commodities of Urban Households of Each Year in "Tenth-Five-year Plan" Period

单位：公斤 (kg)

指 标	Item	2000	2001	2002	2003	2004	2005	2005年比2004年增长(%) Increase Rate in 2005 over 2004(%)
粮 食	Crain	85.37	81.82	67.23	71.66	72.16	75.79	5.0
食用植物油	Edible Vegetable Oil	6.76	6.07	6.90	7.73	8.18	8.89	8.7
猪 肉	Pork	25.19	24.00	26.68	27.69	26.46	26.52	0.2
牛、羊肉	Beef and Mutton	1.47	1.30	1.47	1.18	1.48	1.65	11.5
禽 类	Poultry	6.85	7.33	7.76	8.61	7.93	9.66	21.8
蛋 类	Eggs	6.91	6.50	4.70	5.14	5.07	5.23	3.2
水产品类(元)	Aquatic Products(yuan)	38.58	39.11	41.67	43.50	45.89	49.87	8.7
鲜 菜	Fresh Vegetables	105.49	101.90	87.37	92.04	93.74	92.10	-1.7
糖类(元)	Sugar(yuan)	35.28	36.75	31.63	31.74	31.54	33.88	7.4
烟草类(元)	Cigarettes(pack)(yuan)	159.93	153.19	137.77	134.86	157.95	194.18	22.9
酒 类	Liquor	7.99	7.70	5.28	5.26	5.20	6.10	17.3
糕点类	Cake	3.10	3.04	2.70	2.97	3.03	2.88	-5.0
干鲜瓜果类	Dried and Fresh Melons and Fruits	46.89	49.97	40.11	44.01	43.79	46.89	7.1
奶类及制品（元）	Milk and Its Products(yuan)	47.79	60.24	66.16	82.46	86.59	96.35	11.3

15-7 "十五"时期各年末每百户城镇居民家庭耐用消费品拥有量

Number of Major Durable Consumer Goods Owned Per 100 Urban Households at the every Year-end in "Tenth-Five-year Plan" Period

指 标	Item	2000	2001	2002	2003	2004	2005	2005年比2004年增长(%) Increase Rate in 2005 over 2004(%)
摩托车（辆）	Motorcycle(unit)	8.92	9.21	6.84	7.67	8.61	7.29	-15.3
自行车	Bicycle	24.82	25.79	20.09	20.56	22.91	17.08	-25.4
家用汽车	Automobile	0.19	0.40	0.52	0.54	0.38	1.81	376.3
洗衣机（台）	Washing Machine(set)	96.08	98.62	94.46	94.72	98.05	97.10	-1.0
电风扇	Electric Fan	98.17	99.13	97.86	97.44	103.42	93.50	-9.6
电冰箱	Refrigerator	82.82	84.42	85.38	84.43	86.43	86.13	-0.3
冰 柜	Glacial Cabinet	2.98	4.32	5.30	4.56	5.79	5.96	2.9
彩色电视机	Color TV Sets	113.78	117.42	121.89	121.25	125.27	124.51	-0.6
影碟机	Video-recorder	50.44	60.93	63.86	69.35	78.71	79.24	0.7
家用电脑	Household Computer	5.74	7.86	11.60	16.58	21.02	23.99	14.1
组合音响（套）	Hi-Fi Stereo Component Players(unit)	31.29	34.80	33.90	38.30	39.34	38.71	-1.6
照相机（架）	Cameras(unit)	30.19	27.79	27.23	30.20	33.83	33.73	-0.3
钢琴	Piano	0.66	1.13	1.43	1.89	2.07	1.72	-16.9
微波炉（台）	Microwave Oven(set)	13.16	15.39	22.95	26.98	32.70	35.18	7.6
空调器	Air Conditioners	3.30	3.41	3.22	4.04	6.38	10.66	67.1
取暖器	Heating Apparatus			39.50	52.73	59.81	59.68	-0.2
电炊具（个）	Electrical Cooker(unit)	112.92	113.71	103.35	104.32	108.61	98.12	-9.7
淋浴热水器(台)	Water Heater(set)	34.84	36.30	40.04	45.11	50.72	55.37	9.2
健身器材（套）	Healthy Equipment(unit)	2.04	1.00	2.23	2.05	1.99	2.75	38.2
普通电话（部）	Telephone(unit)			91.42	91.24	94.07	89.42	-4.9
移动电话	Mobile Phone	6.26	29.37	58.20	78.13	96.82	119.22	23.1

15-8 “十五”时期各年农村居民家庭生活基本情况

Basic Conditions of Rural Households of Each Year in “Tenth Five-year Plan” Period

指 标	Item	2000	2001	2002	2003	2004	2005	2005年比2004年增长(%) Increase Rate in 2005 over 2004(%)
调查户数（户）	Households Surveyed(household)	2240	2240	2240	2240	2240	2240	持平
平均每户人口（人）	Average Number of Persons Per Household(person)	4.52	4.47	4.45	4.42	4.41	4.40	-0.2
平均每户劳动力	Average Number of Laborers Per Household	2.77	2.74	2.77	2.79	2.85	2.82	-1.1
平均每一劳动力赡养人口	Average Number Persons Supported by a Laborer	1.63	1.63	1.61	1.58	1.55	1.56	0.6
平均每百个劳动力中	In Per 100 Laborers							
文盲或半文盲	Illiterate or Semi-Illiterate	21.42	20.17	19.67	18.63	17.35	14.48	-16.5
小学程度	Elementary School	39.77	39.84	39.42	39.20	38.95	38.29	-1.7
初中程度	Junior High School	33.95	34.48	35.33	36.70	37.80	41.14	8.8
高中程度	Senior High School	3.27	3.62	3.66	3.71	4.02	3.92	-2.5
中专程度	Technical Secondary School	1.37	1.58	1.66	1.55	1.39	1.68	20.9
大专以上	Junior College	0.21	0.31	0.26	0.24	0.48	0.49	2.1
劳动力平均受教育年限(年)	Average Fixed Number of Year of Receiving Education of the Laborers(year)	6.03	6.17	6.22	6.32	6.47	6.75	4.3
平均每人年总收入（元）	**Annual Average Income Per Capita(yuan)**	**1947.5**	**1987.5**	**2072.1**	**2147.3**	**2410.6**	**2660.6**	**10.4**
平均每人年纯收入	**Annual Average Net Income Per Capita**	**1374.2**	**1411.7**	**1489.9**	**1564.7**	**1721.6**	**1877.0**	**9.0**
劳动者的报酬收入	Payment for Labour	274.9	317.5	386.9	458.8	505.2	583.3	15.5
家庭经营纯收入	Household Business Income	1029.5	1013.9	988.9	988.5	1115.9	1153.4	3.4
转移性和财产性收入	Property and Transfer Income	69.8	80.3	114.1	117.4	100.4	140.3	39.7
平均每人年总支出(元)	Annual Average Expenditure Per Capita(yuan)	1717.5	1709.9	1777.1	1840.5	2093.7	2490.7	19.0
生活消费支出	Living Expenditure	1096.6	1098.4	1137.6	1185.2	1296.3	1552.4	19.8
恩格尔系数（%）	Engel Coefficient(%)	62.7	60.0	58.1	56.9	58.2	52.8	-5.4 (百分点)
平均每人年末居住房屋面积(平方米)	Average Per Capita Living Space at the Year-end(sq.m)	19.8	20.4	21.1	21.6	22.1	23.5	6.6

15-9 "十五"时期各年农民家庭人均纯收入

Per Capita Annual Net Income of Rural Households of Each Year in "Tenth Five-year Plan" Period

单位:(元)

指 标	Item	2000	2001	2002	2003	2004	2005	2005年比2004年增长(%) Increase Rate in 2005 over 2004(%)
全年纯收入	**Annual Net Income**	**1374.16**	**1411.73**	**1489.91**	**1564.66**	**1721.55**	**1876.96**	**9.0**
基本收入	Basic Income	1304.35	1331.45	1375.78	1447.32	1621.11	1736.64	7.1
劳动者报酬	Laborers Remuneration	274.90	317.54	386.86	458.84	505.24	583.28	15.5
#乡村企业劳动报酬	From Township Enterprises	21.93	21.19	19.23	13.47	7.84	10.84	38.3
家庭经营收入	Income from Household Business Operation	1029.45	1013.91	988.92	988.48	1115.87	1153.36	3.4
第一产业	Primary Industry	878.20	855.45	815.19	827.53	947.51	960.65	1.4
农业收入	Agriculture	674.30	648.49	588.12	621.11	730.32	717.62	-1.7
林业收入	Forestry	14.36	18.67	14.89	25.19	21.50	24.80	15.3
牧业收入	Animal Husbandry	187.82	186.93	210.56	178.87	193.33	216.53	12.0
渔业收入	Fishery	1.72	1.36	1.62	2.37	2.36	1.70	-28.0
第二产业	Secondary Industry	41.92	46.99	46.82	38.00	42.28	36.76	-13.1
工业收入	Industry	22.20	21.55	22.56	13.10	11.21	15.44	37.7
建筑业收入	Construction	19.72	25.44	24.26	24.90	31.07	21.32	-31.4
第三产业	Tertiary Industry	109.33	111.41	126.91	122.95	126.08	155.95	23.7
交通运输邮电业收入	Transport & Post	26.83	24.08	30.21	29.85	37.11	32.04	-13.7
批发贸易餐饮业收入	Wholesale and Retail Trade & Catering Services	35.33	46.29	54.05	58.26	55.72	77.55	39.2
社会服务业收入	Social Services	8.76	9.46	9.10	7.96	9.37	19.09	103.7
其他家庭经营收入	Others	38.41	31.64	33.55	26.88	23.87	27.27	14.2
转移性收入	Transfer Income	62.84	67.72	84.58	80.59	81.89	104.81	28.0
财产性收入	Property Income	6.97	12.55	29.55	36.77	18.55	35.51	91.4

15-10 “十五”时期各

Per Capita Annual Gross Expenditures of Rural

指 标	Item	2000
全年总支出	**Gross Expenditure**	**1717.47**
生活消费支出	Living Expenditure for Consumption	1096.59
食 品	Food	687.31
衣 着	Clothing	53.03
居 住	Residence	138.90
家庭设备、用品及服务	Household Facilities,Articles and Services	38.23
医疗保健	Medicines and Medical Services	27.68
交通和通信	Transport and Telecommunications	26.92
文教娱乐用品及服务	Cultural,Education and Recreation Article and Services	97.26
其他商品和服务	Other Commodities and Services	27.25
家庭经营费用支出	Expenditure for Household Business	447.10
#种植业生产支出	Farming Production Costs	169.23
牧业生产支出	Animal Husbandry Costs	232.64
购置生产用固定资产支出	Expenditure for Purchasing Productive Fixed Assets	45.07
税费支出	Taxes	36.09
转移性支出	Transfer Expenditures	89.03
寄给和带给在外人口	Posting or Taking to Outside City	6.91
财产性支出	Property Expenditures	3.59

年农民家庭人均总支出

Households of Each Year in "Tenth Five-year Plan" Period

2001	2002	2003	2004	2005	2005年比2004年增长(%) Increase Rate in 2005 over 2004(%)
1709.92	**1777.14**	**1840.51**	**2093.66**	**2490.70**	**19.0**
1098.39	1137.57	1185.17	1296.34	1552.39	19.8
659.37	661.35	674.71	754.39	819.87	8.7
50.54	55.16	54.46	55.63	79.59	43.1
146.77	149.69	170.56	165.95	235.50	41.9
45.19	49.04	41.51	41.48	61.69	48.7
30.86	32.36	46.62	47.19	71.79	52.1
35.38	48.69	49.59	70.41	99.22	40.9
98.49	108.56	128.13	140.21	160.91	14.8
31.80	32.71	19.59	21.07	23.82	13.1
442.15	449.50	473.30	585.90	675.68	15.3
160.28	153.60	156.60	201.87	223.03	10.5
241.47	252.24	270.79	343.94	382.59	11.2
42.09	52.57	56.29	80.69	84.15	4.3
22.07	23.86	26.40	22.24	2.19	-90.2
86.81	108.09	97.96	105.26	172.08	63.5
9.22	13.85	14.89	25.62	20.85	-18.6
5.71	3.28	1.38	2.96	2.33	-21.3

15-11 “十五”时期各

Per Capita Annual Cash Income of Rural Households

指　标	Item	2000
年内现金收入合计	**Total Annual Cash Income**	**1496.38**
基本现金收入	Basic Cash Income	1136.38
劳动者报酬	Laborers Remuneration	273.55
#乡镇企业报酬	From Township and Village Enterprises	21.89
家庭经营现金收入	Income from Household Business Operation	748.51
出售产品收入	Income from Selling Product	568.41
工业服务性收入	Industry Processing Fee	19.83
建筑业收入	Construction	25.74
交通运输邮电业收入	Transport & Post	40.62
批发和零售贸易餐饮业收入	Wholesale and Retail, Trade & Catering Services	41.53
社会服务业收入	Social Service	10.93
文教卫生业收入	Culture, Education and Health Care	3.58
其他家庭经营现金收入	Others	34.27
转移性现金收入	Transfer Cash Income	107.35
#在外人口寄回和带回	Income from Outside City	27.91
亲友赠送	Income from Friends and Relativesas Presents	45.39
抚恤金	Pension	…
财产性现金收入	Property Cash Income	6.97
#租金收入	Rental Income	2.51
非收入所得	Reward From Other Way	245.68
银行、信用社贷款	Loans of Bank and Credit Union	63.25
借入款	Borrowed Money	107.40
收回借出款	Drawing Back Loan	23.18
从银行、信用社取回存款	Drawing Money from Banks and Credit Union	27.64
收回投资款	Disinvestment	0.07

年农民人均现金收入

of Each Year in "Tenth Five-year Plan" Period

单位:元 (yuan)

2001	2002	2003	2004	2005	2005年比2004年增长(%) Increase Rate in 2005 over 2004(%)
1421.19	**1589.91**	**1759.08**	**1925.79**	**2380.10**	**23.6**
1084.46	1204.69	1323.77	1501.74	1773.16	18.1
317.07	386.59	458.47	505.07	583.09	15.4
22.51	19.23	13.40	7.84	10.87	38.6
767.39	818.10	865.30	996.67	1190.07	19.4
578.25	614.43	655.19	779.51	922.03	18.3
21.86	20.80	9.52	9.72	14.28	46.9
30.99	26.59	27.92	33.90	24.40	-28.0
34.09	46.09	50.69	54.93	56.62	3.1
57.38	61.71	69.90	63.03	106.56	69.1
11.33	12.20	9.58	12.53	20.96	67.3
4.38	6.55	8.60	7.47	10.86	45.4
27.27	27.91	23.39	25.05	22.35	-10.8
119.26	137.68	107.32	104.00	145.92	40.3
27.72	33.37	24.48	15.65	18.11	15.7
49.76	58.30	40.46	34.43	44.79	30.1
1.66	0.88	4.44	0.96	1.96	104.2
12.73	29.25	32.55	16.78	34.44	105.2
2.89	4.22	6.32	3.96	22.51	468.4
204.74	218.29	295.44	303.27	426.58	40.7
41.74	49.39	58.18	47.25	64.22	35.9
90.90	92.86	106.36	105.29	123.60	17.4
17.99	13.00	12.47	21.28	27.90	31.1
25.45	17.43	23.91	24.86	78.41	215.4
0.18	2.90	0.10	0.02		

15-12 “十五”时期各年农民人均现金支出

Per Capita Annual Cash Expenditures of Rural Households of Each Year in “Tenth Five-year Plan” Period

单位:(元)

指 标	Item	2000	2001	2002	2003	2004	2005	2005年比2004年增长(%) Increase Rate in 2005 over 2004(%)
支出合计	**Total Expenditure**	**1063.25**	**1096.59**	**1183.98**	**1213.30**	**1396.83**	**1823.06**	**30.5**
#生产费用支出	Expenditure for Operating Costs	317.36	316.99	342.98	344.85	447.79	551.60	23.2
缴纳税金	Taxes	18.50	20.30	23.42	25.36	21.07	2.19	-89.6
生活消费支出	Living Expenditure for Consumption	622.51	656.26	705.78	745.20	821.69	1095.55	33.3
转移性支出	Transfer Expenditures	88.45	84.94	106.44	96.50	103.33	171.39	65.9
#寄给在外人口	Posting to Outside City	6.89	9.06	13.72	14.77	25.51	20.85	-18.3
赠送亲友	Present to Relatives and Friends	76.61	69.42	82.76	74.95	73.43	137.75	87.6
非消费性现金支出	Nonconsumptive Expenditure	129.08	140.48	181.96	204.43	266.31	242.66	-8.9
#归还银行、信用社存款	Deposits of Bank and Credit Union Recession	23.23	24.10	38.97	31.36	36.03	38.17	5.9
借出款	Loan	13.71	13.22	18.54	10.73	22.11	11.59	-47.6
归还借款	Loan Recession	81.26	74.18	72.63	62.19	64.56	74.02	14.7
存入银行、信用社	Deposit	18.74	27.97	49.37	68.80	120.10	84.50	-29.6

注：现金支出合计不包括非消费性现金支出数据在内。

Note:Data of Total Expenditure in cash didn't included the date of non-Consumption paid in cash.

15-13 "十五"时期各年农村住户家庭经营情况

Indicators of Household Business in Rural Households of Each Year in "Tenth Five-year Plan" Period

指 标	Item	2000	2001	2002	2003	2004	2005	2005年比2004年增长(%) Increase Rate in 2005 over 2004(%)
经营耕地面积（亩/人）	Management Cultivated Area (mu/person)	1.06	1.08	1.07	1.06	1.09	1.02	-6.4
年内出售肥猪头数（头/户）	Number of Selling Fattened Hogs in the Year(head/household)	1.21	1.34	1.29	1.36	1.23	1.32	7.3
年内自宰肥猪头数	Number of Fattened Hogs Slaughtered by Peasants Themselves	0.86	0.89	0.94	0.98	0.92	0.95	3.3
出售、自宰肥猪肉产量（公斤/户）	Output of Pork Slaughtered by Peasants Themselves and Sold (kg/household)	219.65	227.59	232.48	209.09	190.15	212.86	11.9
每头猪肉产量（公斤/头）	Output of Per Slaughtered Hog (kg/head)	106.12	102.06	103.94	89.44	88.36	93.77	6.1
年内出售菜羊只数（只/户）	Number of Sold Mutton Sheep and Goat in the Year (head/household)	0.15	0.07	0.11	0.12	0.14	0.13	-7.1
出售、自宰羊的肉产量（公斤/户）	Output of Mutton Slaught ered by Peasants Themselves and Sold (kg/household)	3.71	1.77	2.89	2.95	3.27	2.99	-8.6
年内出售肉牛数（头/百户）	Number of Sold Fattened Cattle in the Year(head/100household)	5.54	7.05	5.85	3.57	4.11	3.44	-16.3

15-14 按劳动力文化程度分组的农村住户家庭基本情况（2005）

Basic Conditions of Rural Households Grouped by Education Level of Laborers(2005)

指 标	Item	文盲 Illite -rate	小学 Elementary School	初中 Junior High School	高中 Senior High School	中专 Technical Secondary School	大学 College
调查户数（户）	Number of Households Surveyed(Household)	52	556	1299	202	89	27
常住人口（人）	Number of Permanent Residents(person)	209	2301	5887	934	393	110
整半劳动力（个）	Number of Able-bodied and Semi-able-bodied Laborers Per Household(person)	105	1412	3821	620	267	82
平均每一劳动力负担人口(人)	Average Number of Persons Supported by a Laborer (person)	1.99	1.63	1.54	1.51	1.47	1.34
人均家庭经营耕地面积(亩)	Per Capita Management Cultivated Areas(mu)	1.00	1.13	1.00	0.98	0.80	0.72
人均生产性固定资 产原值(元)	Per Capita Original Value of Productive Fixed Assets(yuan)	817.68	954.07	920.63	1042.16	1113.26	1129.32
人均使用房屋面积(平方米)	Per Capita Floor Space for use (sq.m)	15.98	21.11	23.81	26.03	28.41	30.25
人均使用房屋价值(元)	Per Capita Houses Value for use(yuan)	1860.77	2830.86	3301.92	3988.24	4715.01	7542.73
人均总收入	Per Capita Annual Income	2004.92	2332.42	2617.40	3279.41	3719.73	3753.90
现金收入	Cash Income	1345.27	1589.27	1909.50	2608.74	3066.65	3299.68
人均纯收入	Per Capita Net Income	1292.82	1616.83	1834.38	2301.31	2894.96	3170.27
人均生活费支出	Per Capita Living Expenditures	1101.69	1299.48	1552.97	1801.79	2378.14	2171.55
常住人口外出劳动人数(人)	Laborers Outside between Permanent Residents(person)	8	241	953	142	41	10

15-15 "十五"时期各年农民家庭人均经营费用和生产性固定资产购置

Per Capita Expenditure for Household Business Operation and Expenditure for Purchasing Productive Fixed Assets of Rural Households of Each Year in "Tenth Five-year Plan" Period

单位:元(yuan)

指 标	Item	2000	2001	2002	2003	2004	2005	2005年比2004年增长(%) Increase Rate in 2005 over 2004(%)
家庭经营费用支出	**Expenditure for Household Business Operation**	**447.10**	**442.15**	**449.50**	**473.30**	**585.90**	**675.68**	**15.3**
农业生产支出	Expenditure for Agricultural Production	172.40	160.28	153.60	156.60	201.87	223.03	10.5
林业生产支出	Forestry	3.77	1.37	2.57	3.82	3.34	1.33	-60.2
牧业生产支出	Animal Husbandry	232.64	241.47	252.24	270.79	343.94	382.59	11.2
渔业生产支出	Fishery	0.86	0.35	0.28	0.65	0.52	0.13	-75.0
工业生产支出	Industry	6.24	9.41	11.44	7.90	4.61	12.16	163.8
建筑业支出	Construction	5.28	4.84	2.07	2.08	1.86	2.71	45.7
交通运输邮电业支出	Transport & Post	11.82	8.72	14.02	15.59	12.59	18.54	47.3
批发和零售贸易、餐饮业支出	Wholesale and Retail, Trade & Catering Services	6.17	9.66	6.76	10.38	5.74	27.54	379.8
社会服务业支出	Social Services	1.86	1.63	2.73	1.24	2.89	1.51	-47.8
文教卫生支出	Culture, Education and Health Care	0.37	0.27	0.40	1.43	2.18	3.59	64.7
其他经营支出	Others	5.69	4.14	3.39	2.82	6.36	2.55	-59.9
购置生产用固定资产支出	Expenditure for Purchasing Productive Fixed Assets	45.07	42.09	52.57	54.95	80.69	84.15	4.3
农林牧渔业机械	Machinery of Farming, Forestry, Animal Husbandry and Fishery	2.24	4.26	2.16	4.05	8.54	10.37	21.4
工业机械	Industrial Machinery	3.77	2.83	4.61	3.95	1.17	2.45	109.4
运输机械	Transportation Machinery	13.18	11.34	14.14	8.25	27.08	30.65	13.2
役畜、产品畜	Draught Animals and Commodity Animals	23.29	22.08	29.60	30.40	37.24	25.62	-31.2

15-16 “十五”时期各年农村住户人均主要产品商品率

Per Capita Output of Major Agricultural Products and Commodity Rate of Rural Household of Each Year in “Tenth Five-year Plan” Period

单位：%

指 标	Item	2000	2001	2002	2003	2004	2005
粮 食	Grain	18.2	18.55	18.0	15.80	15.8	17.7
油 料	Oil-bearing Crops	61.7	56.63	59.0	61.6	61.6	55.6
糖 料	Sugar Crops	10.9	58.27	45.6	55.1	55.1	55.4
烟 叶	Tobacco	80.3	82.16	88.0	90.1	90.1	89.7
蔬 菜	Vagetable	18.7	20.28	18.7	28.6	28.6	30.7
果用瓜	Melon	26.9	86.47	72.0	57.0	57.0	82.2
水 果	Fruits	43.2	56.84	54.9	66.0	66.0	62.1
茶 叶	Tea	90.9	26.56	15.9	18.5	18.5	25.0
油桐籽	Tung-oil Seeds	91.2	80.79	86.9	86.1	86.1	55.8
油茶籽	Tea-oil Seeds	80.0	20.00	25.0		持平	持平
核 桃	Walnuts	43.8	40.00	23.5	64.7	64.7	47.1
出售、自宰猪肉	Pork Slaughtered by Peasants Themselves & Sold	53.5	56.26	52.4	56.2	56.2	60.6
出售、自宰羊肉	Mutton Slaughtered by Peasants Themselves & Sold	82.8	78.00	76.9	85.1	85.1	77.9
出售、自宰家禽	Poultry Slaughtered by Peasants Themselves & Sold	92.1	30.11	31.3	69.6	69.6	60.8
禽 蛋	Poultry and Eggs	53.1	47.37	44.1	40.8	40.8	39.9

15-17 “十五”时期各年农民人均粮食收支存

Per Capita Grain Income,Expense and Stock of Rural Households of Each Year in “Tenth Five-year Plan” Period

单位：公斤(kg)

指　标	Item	2000	2001	2002	2003	2004	2005	2005年比2004年增长(%) Increase Rate in 2005 over 2004(%)
年内粮食收入合计	**Grain Income within Current Year**	**495.37**	**461.78**	**408.52**	**457.43**	**490.47**	**440.16**	**-10.3**
家庭经营生产的	From Household Operation	423.19	403.80	347.76	397.80	432.88	373.84	-13.6
购　入	Bought Grain	70.65	55.53	54.80	53.17	46.62	64.04	37.4
借　入	Borrowed Grain	0.89	0.78	0.50	0.69	0.17	0.10	-41.2
收回借出粮	Recall of Loaned Grain	0.25	1.25	2.66	2.14	8.29	1.26	-84.8
其它粮食收入	Other Grain Income	0.38	0.42	2.80	3.64	2.51	0.92	-63.3
年内粮食支出合计	**Grain Expense within Current Year**	**459.40**	**423.28**	**404.14**	**402.05**	**432.72**	**443.47**	**2.5**
主食用粮	Staple Food Grain	227.44	212.66	207.92	203.84	197.61	188.69	-4.5
出　售	Sold Grain	77.12	74.92	62.55	64.02	68.26	66.24	-3.0
种　籽	Seed	13.58	12.41	11.89	13.05	18.59	18.48	-0.6
饲　料	Forage	133.69	116.77	114.56	118.88	143.93	169.41	17.7
借　出	Loaned Grain	0.30	0.39	2.13	0.01	1.14		
其它粮食支出	Other Grain Expenses	3.12	3.68	2.31	2.24	2.71	0.59	-78.2
年末结存	Stock of Grain at the Year-end	296.14	327.11	314.26	408.49	353.33	346.72	-1.9
#口　粮	Grain Ration	210.26	215.40	194.99	197.28	169.42	167.14	-1.3
种　籽	Seed	13.10	9.80	13.51	12.03	14.13	11.65	-17.6
饲　料	Forage	67.67	76.88	78.67	110.00	100.99	105.05	4.0

15-18 “十五”时期各年农村居民家庭每人主要消费品消费量

Per Capita Annual Consumption of Major Consumer Goods in Rural Households of Each Year in “Tenth Five-year Plan” Period

单位：公斤(kg)

指 标	Item	2000	2001	2002	2003	2004	2005	2005年比2004年增长(%) Increase Rate in 2005 over 2004(%)
粮 食	Grain	227.15	211.54	206.08	203.84	197.61	188.69	-4.5
#大 米	Rice	153.55	148.36	145.05	150.90	146.96	140.39	-4.5
食 油	Edible Oil	4.97	4.64	4.67	3.85	3.09	4.01	29.8
肉禽及其制品	Meat,Poultry and Related Product	25.44	26.55	29.27	29.36	29.32	32.46	10.7
#猪 肉	Pork	23.83	24.80	27.23	27.37	27.38	30.21	10.3
家 禽	Poultry	1.00	1.16	1.14	1.18	1.36	1.69	24.3
蛋类及蛋制品	Eggs and Their Products	1.25	1.27	1.22	1.20	1.22	1.28	4.9
水产品	Aquatic Products	0.36	0.32	0.32	0.33	0.35	0.36	2.9
#鱼 类	Fish	0.25	0.22	0.25	0.27	0.29	0.31	6.9
蔬 菜	Vegetables	139.14	131.18	126.01	130.67	136.27	135.51	-0.6
瓜 果	Melon and Fruits	5.41	6.18	6.30	6.33	6.38	7.54	18.2
食 糖	Sugar	0.91	0.92	0.94	0.84	0.87	0.85	-2.3
卷 烟（盒）	Cigarette(pack)	25.62	24.93	24.52	22.47	21.52	23.79	10.5
酒	Liquor	5.77	6.03	5.54	5.18	5.49	6.26	14.0

15-19 “十五”时期各年每百户农村居民家庭年末耐用消费品拥有量

Average Possession of Durable Consumer Goods Per 100 Rural Households at each Year-end in “Tenth Five-year Plan” Period

单位：台(unit)

指 标	Item	2000	2001	2002	2003	2004	2005	2005年比2004年增长(%) Increase Rate in 2005 over 2004(%)
自行车(辆)	Bicycle(unit)	8.2	7.2	6.6	7.6	10.1	7.5	-25.7
黑白电视机(台)	Black/White TV Set(unit)	40.3	37.4	34.3	32.9	27.8	13.0	-53.2
彩色电视机	Color TV Set	21.2	25.9	33.9	39.2	47.2	56.8	20.3
电风扇	Electric Fan	22.0	26.2	28.6	30.4	32.9	44.7	35.9
电冰箱	Refrigerator	2.4	3.0	3.8	3.5	3.9	5.8	48.7
洗衣机	Washing Machine	12.1	12.7	15.0	17.4	19.7	24.8	25.9
收录机	Recorder	12.2	12.6	11.4	9.8	7.8	2.4	-69.2
录像机	Video-recorder	1.0	1.3	1.2	1.2	1.0	0.6	-40.0
照相机（架）	Camera（unit)	0.8	0.9	1.1	1.2	1.2	0.6	-50.0
影碟机	Video Disc Player	7.7	10.6	15.7	19.3	25.5	39.1	53.3
摩托车（辆）	Motorcycles(set)	6.0	7.2	8.7	9.6	11.2	14.0	25.0
热水器	Water Heater	…	0.7	0.9	1.2	1.7	2.9	70.6
电话机（部）	Telephone(unit)	3.0	6.6	10.8	17.1	21.5	26.6	23.7
移动电话	Mobile Telephone	…	1.7	3.7	7.2	12.9	17.0	31.8

主要统计指标解释

一、城镇住户

城镇家庭人口 指居住在一起,经济上合在一起共同生活的家庭成员。凡计算为家庭人口的成员其全部收支都包括在本家庭中。

城镇就业面 指就业人口占家庭人口的百分比。

城镇就业者负担人数 指家庭人口与就业人口之比。

城镇家庭总收入 指家庭成员得到的工薪收入、经营净收入、财产性收入、转移性收入之和,不包括出售财物收入和借贷收入。

城镇家庭可支配收入 指家庭成员得到可用于最终消费支出和其它非义务性支出以及储蓄的总和,即居民家庭可以用来自由支配的收入。它是家庭总收入扣除交纳的所得税、个人交纳的社会保障支出以及记账补贴后的收入。计算公式为:

可支配收入=家庭总收入-交纳所得税-个人交纳的社会保障支出-记帐补贴

城镇家庭总支出 指除借贷支出以外的全部家庭支出。包括消费性支出、购房建房支出、转移性支出、财产性支出、社会保障支出。

城镇家庭消费性支出 指家庭用于日常生活的支出,包括食品、衣着、家庭设备用品及服务、医疗保健、交通和通信、娱乐教育文化服务、居住、杂项商品和服务等八大类支出。

城镇家庭服务性消费支出 指家庭用于支付社会提供的各种非商品性服务费用。

城镇家庭收入分组方法 将所有调查户依户人均可支配收入由低到高排队，按10%,10%,20%,20%,20%,10%,10%的比例依次分成:最低收入户、低收入户、中等偏下收入户、中等收入户、中等偏上收入户、高收入户、最高收入户等七组。总体中最低5%的户为困难户。

恩格尔系数 指食物支出金额在生活消费总支出金额中所占的比例。计算公式为:

恩格尔系数=食品支出金额/生活消费总支出金额×100%

二、农村住户

农村住户 指农村常住户。农村常住户指长期(一年以上)居住在乡镇(不包括城关镇)行政管理区域内的住户,以及长期居住在城关镇所辖行政村范围内的农村住户。户口不在本地而在本地居住一年及以上的住户也包括在本地农村常住户范围内;有本地户口,但举家外出谋生一年以上的住户,无论是否保留承包耕地都不包括在本地农村住户范围内。

常住人口 指全年经常在家或在家居住6个月以上,而且经济和生活与本户连成一体的人口。外出从业人员在外居住时间虽然在6个月以上,但收入主要带回家中,经济与本户连为一体,仍视为家庭常住人口;在家居住,生活和本户连成一体的国家职工、退休人员也为家庭常住人口。但是现役军人、中专及以上(走读生除外)的在校学生、以及常年在外(不包括探亲、看病等)且已有稳定的职业与居住场所的外出从业人员,不算家庭常住人口。家庭常住人口主要作为计算农村住户平均每人收入、消费和积累水平及分析家庭人口状况的依据。

整、半劳动力 整劳动力指男子18周岁到50周岁,女子18周岁到45周岁;半劳动力指男子16周岁到17周岁,51周岁到60周岁;女子16周岁到17周岁,46周岁到55周岁,同时具有劳动能力的人。虽然在劳动年龄之内,但已丧失劳动能力的人,不应算为劳动力;超过劳动年龄,但能经常参加劳动,计入半劳动力数内。常住人口中的职工,若这些职工为劳动力,就包括在本户的整半劳动力中。

总收入 指调查期内农村住户和住户成员从各种来源渠道得到的收入总和。按收入的性质划分为工资性收入、家庭经营收入、财产性收入和转移性收入。

工资性收入 指农村住户成员受雇于单位或个人,靠出卖劳动而获得的收入。

家庭经营收入 指农村住户以家庭为生产经营单位进行生产筹划和管理而获得的收入。农村住户家庭经营活动按行业划分为农业、林业、牧业、渔业、工业、建筑业、交通运输业邮电业、批发和零售贸易餐饮业、社会服务业、文教卫生业和其他家庭经营。

财产性收入 指金融资产或有形非生产性资产的所有者向其他机构单位提供资金或将有形非生产性资产供其支配,作为回报而从中获得的收入。

转移性收入 指农村住户和住户成员无须付出任何对应物而获得的货物、服务、资金或资产所有权等,不包括无偿提供的用于固定资本形成的资金。一般情况下,是指农村住户在二次分配中的所有收入。

现金收入 指农村住户和住户成员在调查期内得到以现金形态表现的收入。按来源分成工资性收入、家庭经营现金收入、财产性收入、转移性收入。

纯收入 指农村住户当年从各个来源得到的总收入相应地扣除所发生的费用后的收入总和。计算方法:

纯收入=总收入-税费支出-家庭经营费用支出-税费支出-生产性固定资产折旧-调查补贴-赠送农村外部亲友支出

纯收入主要用于再生产投入和当年生活消费支出,也可用于储蓄和各种非义务性支出。“农民人均纯收入”按人口平均的纯收入水平,反映的是一个地区或一个农户农村居民的平均收入水平。

总支出 指农村住户用于生产、生活和再分配的全部支出。家庭经营费用支出、购置生产性固定资产支出、生产性固定资产折旧、税费支出、生活消费支出、财产性支出和转移性支出。

Explanatory Notes on Main Statistical Indicators

I. Urban Households

Population of urban households refer to members of the household living and sharing economically together. All income and expenditure of the population of the household are included in the income and expenditure of the household.

Proportion of urban employment refer to the proportion of employed population to the population of urban households.

Number of dependents per urban employee refers to the ratio between number of persons in urban households and the number of dependents.

Total Income of Urban Households refers to the sum of wage and salary, net business income, income from properties, and income from transfers of members of the households, excluding income from selling of properties and income from borrowings.

Disposable Income of Urban Households refers to the actual income at the disposal of members of the households which can be used for final consumption, other non-compulsory expenditure and savings. This equals to total income minus income tax, personal contribution to social security and sample household subsidy for keeping diaries. Following formula is used:

Disposable income = total household income – income tax – personal contribution to social security – sample household subsidy for keeping diaries

Total expenditure of Urban Households refer to all expenditure of the households except expenditure on leading. It includes expenditure on consumption, on purchasing or building houses, on transfers, on properties and on social security.

Consumption Expenditure of Urban Households refers to total expenditure of the sample households for consumption in daily life, including expenditure on eight categories such as food, clothing, household appliances and services, health care and medical services, transport and communications, recreation, education and cultural services, housing, miscellaneous goods and services.

Expenditure of Urban Households on Consumption of Services refers to expenditure of households on services of various kinds provided by the society.

Urban Households by Income Group All households in the sample are grouped, by per capita disposable income of the household, into groups of lowest income, low income, lower middle income, middle income, upper middle income, high income and highest income, each group consisting of 10%, 10%, 20%, 20%, 20%, 10% and 10% of all households respectively. The lowest 5% of households are also referred to as poor households.

Engel Coefficient refers to the percentage of expenditure on food in the total consumption expenditure, using the following formula:

Engel Coefficient = (expenditure on food / total consumption expenditure) × 100%

II. Rural Households

Rural Households refer to resident households in rural areas. Resident households in rural areas are the households residing for more than one year in the areas under the jurisdiction of administration of township governments(excluding county towns), and in the areas under the jurisdiction of administration of villages in county towns. Migrated households residing in the current addresses for over one year with their household registration in other places are included in the resident households of their current addresses. For households with their household registration in one place but all members of the households moving away for living in another place for over one year, they will not be included in the rural households of the area where they are registered, irrespective of whether they still keep their contracted land.

Resident Population refers to population staying at home permanently or for over 6 months during a year and sharing life economically with the household. Members of the household staying away from the household for over 6 months but keeping a close economic relation with the household by sending the majority of income to the household are regarded as resident population of the household. Government staff and workers or retirees living as close members of the household are also considered as resident population. However, servicemen, students of secondary technical schools or schools of higher education and persons with stable jobs and residence outside the household (excluding those visiting relatives or seeking medical service) are not included as resident population of the household. Resident population is used in calculating income, consumption, accumulation on per capita basis of rural households and in analyzing composition of rural households.

Full/Semi Labour Force Full labour force refers to persons capable of work, aged 18–50 for males and 18–45 for females. Semi labour force refers to persons capable of work, aged 16–17 and 51–60 for males and 16–17 and 46–55 for females. Persons at their working ages but not capable of work are not to be included as labour force. Persons not at working ages but participating regularly in work are included in semi labour force. For staff and workers as resident population of the household, they are included as full or semi labour force of the household if they are in the labour force.

Total Income refers to the sum of income earned from various sources by the rural households and their members during the reference period, and is classified as income from wages and salaries, income from household operations, income from properties and income from transfers.

Income from Wages and Salaries refers to income from labour earned by the members of rural households employed by other units or individuals.

Income from Household Operations refers to income by the rural households as units of production and operations. Operations by rural households are classified by economic activities as agriculture, forestry, animal husbandry, fishery, manufacturing, construction, transportation, post and telecommunications, wholesale, retail and catering, social service, culture, education, health, and other household operations.

Income from Properties refers to the income received as returns by owners of financial assets or tangible non–productive assets by providing capitals or tangible non–productive assets to other institutional units.

Income from Transfers refers to the receipt by rural households and their members of goods, services, capitals or rights of assets without giving or repaying accordingly, excluding capitals provided to them for the formation of fixed assets. In general, it refers to all income received by rural households through redistribution.

Cash Income refers to income received by rural households and their members in the form of cash during the reference period. It is classified, by source of income, into income from wages and salaries, cash income from household operations, income from properties and income from transfers.

Net Income refers to the total income of rural households from all sources minus all corresponding expenses. The formula for calculation is as follows:

Net income = total income – taxes and fees paid – household operation expenses – taxes and fees – depreciation of fixed assets for production – subsidy for participating in household survey – gifts to non–rural relatives

Net income is mainly used as input for reproduction and as consumption expenditure of the year, and also used for savings and non–compulsory expenses of various forms. ?°Per capita net income of farmers?± is the level of net income averaged by population which reflects the average income level of rural households in a given area.

Total Expenditure refers to total expenses of rural households on production, consumption and redistribution, including expenditure on household operations, on purchase of productive fixed assets, depreciation of productive fixed assets, taxes and fees, expenses on household consumption, expenses on properties and expenses on transfers.

16

科技、教育和文化

Science & Tethnology, Education and Culture

Sixteen

科技活动情况
Science and Tethnology

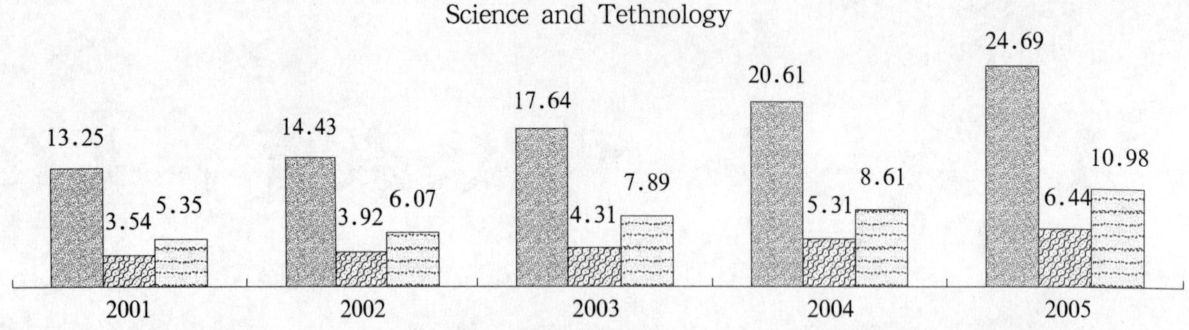

申请、授权专利情况
Patent Applications and Authorizations

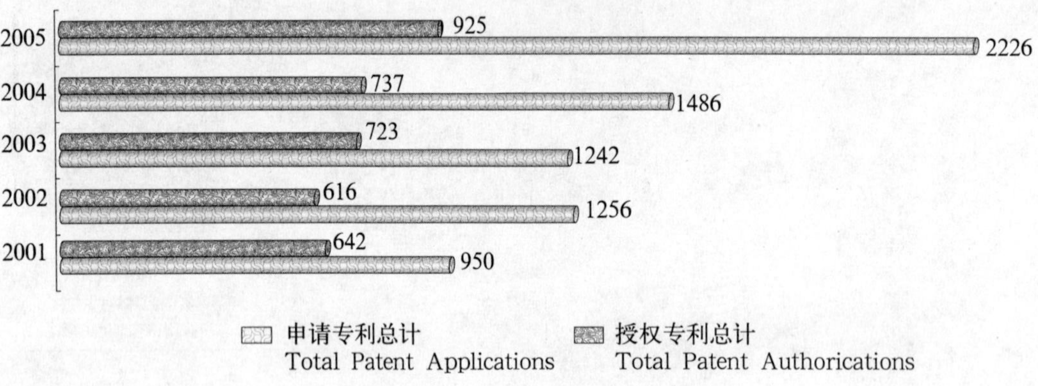

入学率
Enrollment Rate

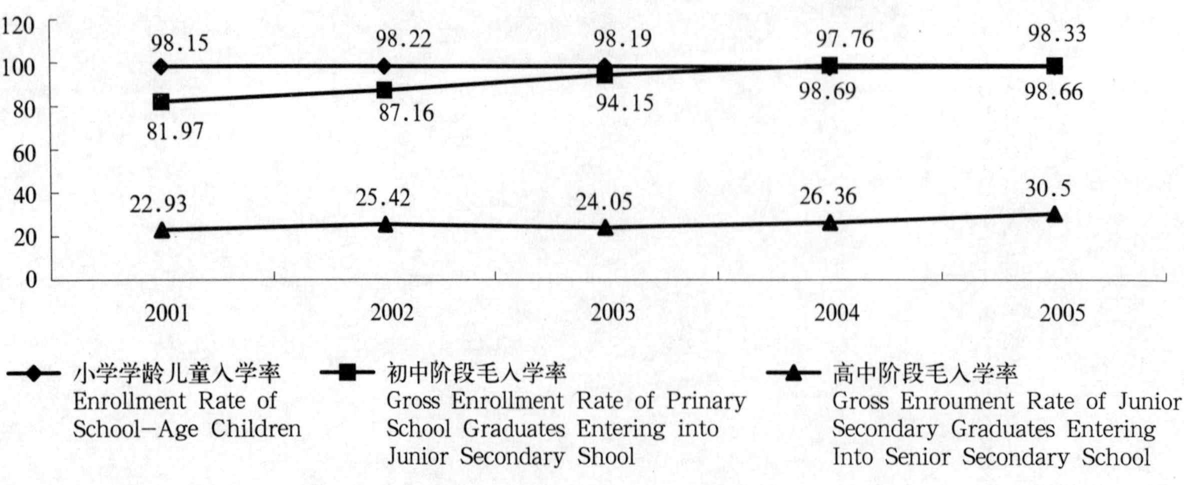

16-1 “十五”时期各年科技活动情况

Basic Statistics on Scientific and Technological Activities of Each Year in “Tenth Five-year Plan” Period

指 标	Item	2000	2001	2002	2003	2004	2005	2005年比2004年增长(%) Increase Rate in 2005 over 2004(%)
科技机构数（个）	**Number of Scientific Technological Research Institutions(unit)**	**310**	**266**	**230**	**210**	**296**	**283**	**-4.4**
科研单位	Scientific Reseach Unit	135	116	109	105	98	98	0.0
大中型工业企业	In Large and Medium Industrial Enterprises	98	87	79	60	100	95	-5.0
高等院校	Institutions of Higher Education	33	33	17	20	69	76	10.1
其 他	Others	44	30	25	25	29	14	-51.7
科技活动人员数(人)	Number of Persons Engaged in Scientific and Technological Activities(person)	34041	33989	32897	30153	29430	31094	5.7
科研单位	Scientific Reseach Unit	5555	4887	3873	3878	3961	3985	0.6
大中型工业企业	In Large and Medium Industrial Enterprises	19554	19390	18791	15666	15425	16116	4.5
高等院校	Institutions of Higher Education	2356	3030	3130	3530	2841	3173	11.7
其 他	Others	6576	6682	7103	7079	7203	7820	8.6
#科学家、工程师	Scientists and Engineers	18659	19452	19048	19069	17841	18796	5.4
#研究与试验发展人员(人年)	Personnel Engaged in Activities of Research and Experiment(person.year)	8131	9488	8960	8623	7119	9638	35.4
科技活动经费筹集总额(亿元)	Sum of Funds for Scientific and Technological Activities (100 million yuan)	11.70	13.25	14.43	17.64	20.61	24.69	19.8
政府资金	From Government	3.38	3.71	4.63	4.84	4.63	5.50	18.9
企业资金	From Corporation	6.48	7.28	8.09	10.10	13.45	16.17	20.3
事业单位资金	From Institution	0.93	0.69	0.47	0.85	0.82	0.79	-3.7
金融机构贷款	Loans of Financial Institutions	0.66	0.71	0.61	1.13	1.06	1.64	54.8
国外资金	From Abroad	0.01	0.01	0.02	0.01	0.03	0.02	-31.9
其 他	Others	0.25	0.85	0.61	0.70	0.63	0.57	-10.4
科技活动经费支出总额(亿元)	Expenditures for Scientific and Technological Activities (100 million yuan)	10.87	13.31	15.30	15.48	21.80	24.73	13.4
#内部支出	Inner Expenditure	10.11	12.42	14.31	14.80	20.28	23.52	15.9
#劳务费	Service Fee	2.98	11.22	4.53	4.59	5.77	5.17	-10.4
固定资产购建支出	Purchases for Fixed Assets	3.19	3.54	4.54	3.04	6.68	8.22	23.2
财政对科技拨款(亿元)	Government Expenditure for Scientific Research(100 million yuan)	3.08	3.54	3.92	4.31	5.31	6.44	21.3
科技拨款占财政支出的比重(%)	Expenditure for Scientific Research as Percentage in Financial Expenditure(%)	1.53	1.29	1.2	1.3	1.27	1.24	0.03 (百分点)
研究与发展经费(R&D)支出(亿元)	Expenditures on Research and Development(100 million yuan)	4.18	5.35	6.07	7.89	8.61	10.98	27.5
R&D经费支出占 生产总值的比重(%)	Proportion of Expenditure on R&D to GDP	0.41	0.47	0.49	0.55	0.51	0.57	0.06 (百分点)

注：R&D经费支出占生产总值的比重已按经济普查数据调整。

Note:Change is made in the table on R&D expense as percentage to GDP due to the data of economic census.

16-2 "十五"时期各年政府属独立研

Basic Statistics on Scientific Research and Development Institution

指 标	Item
科技机构数(个)	**Number of S&T Institutions(unit)**
县级以上研究与开发机构	Scientific Research and Development Institution at County and Higher Levels
县级以上部门属科技情报与文献机构	Department of S&T Informations and Literature Institutions at County and Higher Levels
县级政府部门属研究与开发机构	Scientific Research and Development Institutions at County Level
社会、人文科学研究机构	Research Institutions of Social and Human Studies
科技活动人员数(人)	**Personnel Engaged in S&T Activities(person)**
县级以上研究与开发机构	Scientific Research and Development Institution at County and Higher Levels
县级以上部门属科技情报与文献机构	Department of S&T Informations and Literature Institutions at County and Higher Levels
县级政府部门属研究与开发机构	Scientific Research and Development Institutions at County Level
社会、人文科学研究机构	Research Institutions of Social and Human Studies
科学家、工程师	**Scientists and Engineers**
县级以上研究与开发机构	Scientific Research and Development Institution at County and Higher Levels
县级以上部门属科技情报与文献机构	Department of S&T Informations and Literature Institutions at County and Higher Levels
县级政府部门属研究与开发机构	Scientific Research and Development Institutions at County Level
社会、人文科学研究机构	Research Institutions of Social and Human Studies
经费收入总额(万元)	**Funding for S&T Activities(10000 yuan)**
县级以上研究与开发机构	Scientific Research and Development Institution at County and Higher Levels
县级以上部门属科技情报与文献机构	Department of S&T Informations and Literature Institutions at County and Higher Levels
县级政府部门属研究与开发机构	Scientific Research and Development Institutions at County Level
社会、人文科学研究机构	Research Institutions of Social and Human Studies
经费支出总额(万元)	**Expenditures on S&T Activities(10000 yuan)**
县级以上研究与开发机构	Scientific Research and Development Institution at County and Higher Levels
县级以上部门属科技情报与文献机构	Department of S&T Informations and Literature Institutions at County and Higher Levels
县级政府部门属研究与开发机构	Scientific Research and Development Institutions at County Level
社会、人文科学研究机构	Research Institutions of Social and Human Studies
研究与试验发展经费支出(R&D经费支出)(万元)	**Expenditure on R&D(10000 yuan)**
县级以上研究与开发机构	Scientific Research and Development Institution at County and Higher Levels
县级以上部门属科技情报与文献机构	Department of S&T Informations and Literature Institutions at County and Higher Levels
县级政府部门属研究与开发机构	Scientific Research and Development Institutions at County Level
社会、人文科学研究机构	Research Institutions of Social and Human Studies

注:1、县级以上研究与开发机构 2001 年至 2005 年的数据不含转制机构,机构减少主要是科研机构体制改革。2、数据来源于《贵州

Note:1.The data on Scientific Research and Development Institution at County and Higher Levels Research in 2001 –2005 excluded the Development Institution. 2.The data in the table are obtained from the "Guizhou S&T Statistical Yearbook".

究与开发机构科技活动基本情况

with Independent System of Each Year in"Tenth Five-year Plan" Period

2000	2001	2002	2003	2004	2005	2005年比2004年增长(%) Increase Rate in 2005 over 2004(%)
135	**116**	**109**	**105**	**98**	**98**	**持平**
103	84	78	76	73	74	1.4
10	10	9	8	6	6	持平
21	20	19	18	16	15	-6.3
1	2	3	3	3	3	持平
5555	**4887**	**3873**	**3878**	**3961**	**3985**	**0.6**
5089	4374	3378	3402	3514	3555	1.2
138	139	131	129	105	101	-3.8
203	202	180	155	140	142	1.4
125	172	184	192	202	187	-7.4
3278	**2820**	**2402**	**2341**	**2292**	**2434**	**6.2**
3051	2557	2134	2073	2018	2218	9.9
84	84	85	83	83	73	-12.0
36	34	37	35	29	23	-20.7
107	145	146	150	162	120	-25.9
35025	**39581**	**33991**	**36598**	**43481**	**50439**	**16.0**
33548	37739	31911	34391	40852	46536	13.9
639	668	858	862	762	1033	35.6
342	447	403	357	352	449	27.6
495	728	819	988	1515	2421	59.8
30560	**36994**	**31005**	**34436**	**43131**	**49848**	**15.6**
29205	35150	28972	32266	40633	46486	14.4
529	650	800	798	741	923	24.6
316	449	399	374	351	468	33.3
510	746	834	998	1406	1971	40.2
4729	**7468**	**8603**	**12172**	**11893**	**13490**	**13.4**
4702	7455	8551	12064	11634	12598	8.3
		6	6		3	
27	13	16	19	19	12	-36.8
		30	82	240	877	265.4

科技统计年鉴》

research institutions which system are transfering,institutions decreaseddue to the system reformation of Scientific Research and

16-3 "十五"时期各年事业、企业单位各类专业人员情况

Number of Scientific and Technological Personnel of National Economy Units by Category of Each Year in "Tenth Five-year Plan" Period

单位：万人 (10000 person)

指 标	Item	2000	2001	2002	2003	2004	2005	2005年比2004年增长(%) Increase Rate in 2005 over 2004(%)
总 计	**Total**	**53.07**	**54.07**	**54.47**	**55.29**	**57.10**	**57.63**	**9.3**
#女 性	Female	19.81	20.36	20.70	21.36		22.55	
按专业分	By Specialized Subject							
#工程技术人员	Engineering Technical Personnel	6.73	6.65	6.44	6.37		6.18	
农业技术人员	Agricultural Technical Personnel	2.58	2.65	2.67	2.72		2.75	
卫生技术人员	Medical Technical Persomnel	7.07	7.12	7.03	7.13		7.40	
科学研究人员	Scientific Research Personnel	0.17	0.17	0.16	0.16		0.16	
教学人员	Teaching Personnel	29.43	30.70	31.78	32.88	33.80	34.75	2.8
按专业技术职务分	By Professional Titles							
#高 级	Senior	1.52	1.61	1.77	1.97	2.20	2.41	9.5
中 级	Medium	10.19	10.52	10.95	11.78	12.90	13.56	5.1
初 级	Junior	41.36	37.23	37.28	37.06	37.30	36.98	-0.9
按学历分	By Education Background							
#大学本科以上	Higher Education and above	6.37	6.64	7.00	7.84		10.40	
大学专科	Specialized Secondary School	13.65	14.64	16.06	18.00		15.86	
中专以下	Senior Middle School and the Level below	33.04	32.78	31.41	29.45		23.49	

16-4 "十五"时期各年民营科技企业情况

Basic Statistics on Scientific and Technological Research Institutions Running by Local People Enterprises of Each Year in "Tenth Five-year Plan" Period

指 标	Item	2000	2001	2002	2003	2004	2005
机构数(个)	Number of Scientific and Technological Institutions(unit)	353	328	353	295	308	326
#集体经济单位	Collective-owned Institutions	74	64	45	23	17	14
从业人员(人)	Personnel Engaged in S&T Activities(person)	21821	24409	28511	25800	25345	27528
#从事科技活动的中高级职称人数	Professors and Associate Professors Engaged in S&T Activities	3632	3290	3457	2566	2561	2702
技工贸收入(万元)	Income on S&T Activities(10000 yuan)	280000	300000	390000	348074	434800	665248
研究开发支出(万元)	Expenditure on R&D(10000 yuan)	10000	10000	9246	6594	11800	7916

注：本资料由省科技厅提供。

Note:Data in this table are obtained from Department of Ecience and Techenology.

16-5 “十五”时期各年高等院校科技活动基本情况

Basic Statistics on Higher Education for Scientific and Technological Activities of Each Year in “Tenth Five-year Plan” Period

指 标	Item	2000	2001	2002	2003	2004	2005	2005年比2004年增长(%) Increase Rate in 2005 over 2004(%)
从事科技活动人数(人)	**Personnel Engaged in S&T Activities(person)**	**2356**	**3030**	**3130**	**3530**	**2841**	**3173**	**11.7**
#教 师	Teacher	2100	2393	2135	2625	2143	2485	16.0
其他技术人员	Other Technical Personnel	240	577	711	890	660	635	-3.8
辅助人员	Assistant	16	60	284	15	38	53	39.5
从事研究与发展活动人员(人年)	Personnel Engaged in Activities of Research and Development(person.year)	752	1069	1081	1377	1525	1521	-0.3
#正高职称	Professor	151	124	165	179	248	285	14.9
副高职称	Associate Professor	257	353	355	519	499	554	11.0
中级职称	Lecturer	258	134	335	506	548	523	-4.6
初级职称	Assistant	86	458	226	129	187	135	-27.8
科技活动机构(个)	Institution of Scientific and Technological Activities Institution(unit)	33	33	17	20	69	76	10.1
机构中科技活动人员(人)	Number of Persons Engaged in Scientific and Technological Activities Institutions(person)	336	197	446	591	618	746	20.7
当年科技经费收入(万元)	Income of Scientific and Technological Activities(10000 yuan)	3252	4604	5474	6888	6647	10977	65.1
#科研事业费	Expenses for Scientific Research	706	1235	2123	2546	1422	1713	20.5
研究与发展课题(项)	**Project on Research and Development(unit)**	**555**	**912**	**1342**	**1507**	**1593**	**1824**	**14.5**
#基础研究	Basic Research	169	332	511	614	550	709	28.9
应用研究	Applied Research	274	291	530	598	763	906	18.7
试验发展	Activities of Experiment	112	289	228	295	280	209	-25.4
研究与发展成果	**Achievement of Research and Development**							
出版科学著作(部)	Scientific Work Published(unit)	100	94	184	201	117	166	41.9
发表学术论文(篇)	Research Paper Issued(unit)	4499	4503	3956	4196	4308	4899	13.7
科技成果获奖(项)	Scientific Achievement Rewarded(unit)	92	42	75	29	38	105	176.3

16-6 大中型工业企业科技活动人员情况（2005）

Basic Statistics on Persons Engaged in Scientific and Technological Activities in Large and Medium Industrial Enterprises(2005)

单位：人(person)

指 标	Item	科技活动人员 Persons Engaged in Scientific and Technological Activities	全时人员 Full-time Personnel	非全时人员 Part-time Personnel	#科学家和工程师 Scientists and Engineers	#研究与试验人员 Research and Experiment Personnel
总 计	**Total**	**16116**	**6576**	**9540**	**9128**	**6688**
#国有控股企业	Of the Total:Stated-controlled Enterprises	14831	6132	8699	8367	6035
按企业规模分组	**Grouped by Size**					
大型企业	Large Enterprises	5173	1792	3381	3309	1738
中型企业	Medium Enterprises	10943	4784	6159	5819	4950
按登记注册类型分组	**Grouped by Registration Categories**					
内资企业	Domestic Investment Enterprises	15916	6498	9418	9013	6512
国有企业	State-owned Enterprises	6821	2824	3997	3792	3279
集体企业	Collective-owned Enterprises	30	15	15	18	12
有限责任公司	Companies with Limited Liabilities	5322	2110	3212	3026	1810
国有独资公司	Sole State-owned Companies with Limited Liabilities	2954	1023	1931	1671	828
其他有限责任公司	Other Companies with Limited Liabilities	2368	1087	1281	1355	982
股份有限公司	Share-holding Companies with Limited Liabilities	3529	1512	2017	2039	1287
私营企业	Private Enterprises	214	37	177	138	124
私营合伙企业	Private Cooperative Enterprises	92	6	86	37	92
私营有限责任公司	Private Companies with Limited Liabilities	122	31	91	101	32
港、澳、台商投资企业	Enterprises with Funds from Hong Kong,Macao and Taiwan	11	8	3	5	10
外商投资企业	Foreign Funded Enterprises	189	70	119	110	166
按工业行业大类分组	**Grouped by Industrial Sector**					
采矿业	Mining and Quarrying	280	75	205	268	134
煤炭开采和洗选业	Mining and Washing of Coal	250	60	190	250	122
非金属矿采选业	Mining and Processing of Nonmetal Ores	30	15	15	18	12
制造业	Manufacturing	15600	6465	9135	8733	6553
食品制造业	Manufacture of Foods	143	71	72	93	
饮料制造业	Manufacture of Beverages	465	235	230	337	422
烟草制品业	Manufacture of Tobacco	127	40	87	75	16
纺织业	Manufacture of Textile	80	10	70	34	

16-6续表（continued）

指　标	Item	科技活动人员 Persons Engaged in Scientific and Technological Activities	全时人员 Full-time Personnel	非全时人员 Part-time Personnel	#科学家和工程师 Scientists and Engineers	#研究与试验人员 Research and Experiment Personnel
印刷业和记录媒介的复制	Printing,Reproduction of Recording Media	8	4	4	5	6
化学原料及化学制品制造业	Manufacture of Raw Chemical Materials and Chemical Products	1376	423	953	573	445
医药制造业	Manufacture of Medicines	442	181	261	369	206
橡胶制品业	Manufacture of Rubber	704	212	492	413	197
非金属矿物制品业	Manufacture of Non-metallic Mineral Products	137	80	57	83	70
黑色金属冶炼及压延加工业	Smelting and Pressing of Ferrous Metals	641	198	443	500	85
有色金属冶炼及压延加工业	Smelting and Pressing of Non-ferrous Metals	1077	471	606	554	296
金属制品业	Manufacture of Metal Products	566	249	317	446	86
通用设备制造业	Manufacture of General Purpose Machinery	648	234	414	425	329
专用设备制造业	Manufacture of Special Purpose Machinery	1707	690	1017	727	1040
交通运输设备制造业	Manufacture of Transport Equipment	5082	1968	3114	2812	2386
电气机械及器材制造业	Manufacture of Electrical Machinery and Equipment	266	91	175	150	197
工艺品及其他制造业	Manufacture of Artwork and Other Manufacturing	566	435	131	330	95
其他未列明的制造业	Other Manufacture	566	435	131	330	95
电力、燃气及水的生产和供应业	Production and Distribution of Electric Power,Gas and Water	236	36	200	127	1
电力、热力的生产和供应业	Production and Distribution of Electric Power and Heat Power	84		84	71	1
燃气生产和供应业	Production and Distribution of Gas	152	36	116	56	
按隶属关系分组	**Grouped by Administrative Relationship**					
中央	Central	8603	3700	4903	4588	3930
省	Province	4144	1669	2475	2478	1390
地	Prefecture	2120	697	1423	1296	838
县	County	455	154	301	274	172
其他	Other	794	356	438	492	358

16-7 大中型工业企业科技活动经费筹集情况（2005）

Basic Statistics on Sum of Funds for Scientific and Technological Activities in Large and Medium Industrial Enterprises(2005)

单位：万元 (10000 yuan)

指 标	Item	科技活动经费筹集总额 Sum of Funds for Scientific and Technological Activities	企业资金 From Corporation	金融机构贷款 Loans of Financial Institutions	政府资金 From Gover-nment	事业单位资金 From Institution	其他 Others
总 计	**Total**	**165991**	**136682**	**13407**	**13809**	**7**	**2087**
#国有控股企业	Of the Total:Stated-controlled Enterprises	153085	126747	11682	12568	1	2087
按企业规模分组	**Grouped by Size**						
大型企业	Large Enterprises	83195	80163	1857	1175		
中型企业	Medium Enterprises	82796	56519	11550	12634	7	2087
按登记注册类型分组	**Grouped by Registration Categories**						
内资企业	Domestic Investment Enterprises	165221	135912	13407	13809	7	2087
国有企业	State-owned Enterprises	80882	63849	10050	6983		
集体企业	Collective-owned Enterprises	11	5	5	1		
有限责任公司	Companies with Limited Liabilities	45457	35715	2692	5504	1	1545
国有独资公司	Sole State-owned Companies with Limited Liabilities	22789	17449		4109	1	1229
其他有限责任公司	Other Companies with Limited Liabilities	22668	18266	2692	1395		316
股份有限公司	Share-holding Companies with Limited Liabilities	37868	35470	660	1195		542
私营企业	Private Enterprises	1004	873		125	6	
私营合伙企业	Private Cooperative Enterprises	120	112		8		
私营有限责任公司	Private Companies with Limited Liabilities	884	761		117	6	
港、澳、台商投资企业	Enterprises with Funds from Hong Kong, Macao and Taiwan	40	40				
外商投资企业	Foreign Funded Enterprises	730	730				
按工业行业大类分组	**Grouped by Industrial Sector**						
采矿业	Mining and Quarrying	7487	7481	5	1		
煤炭开采和洗选业	Mining and Washing of Coal	7476	7476				
非金属矿采选业	Mining and Processing of Nonmetal Ores	11	5	5	1		
制造业	Manufacturing	156069	127195	13402	13378	7	2087
食品制造业	Manufacture of Foods	951	876		75		
饮料制造业	Manufacture of Beverages	21901	21871		30		
烟草制品业	Manufacture of Tobacco	5333	5333				
纺织业	Manufacture of Textile	19	19				

16-7续表(continued)

指 标	Item	科技活动经费筹集总额 Sum of Funds for Scientific and Technological Activities	企业资金 From Corporation	金融机构贷款 Loans of Financial Institutions	政府资金 From Gover-nment	事业单位资金 From Institution	其他 Others
印刷业和记录媒介的复制	Printing,Reproduction of Recording Media	21	21				
化学原料及化学制品制造业	Manufacture of Raw Chemical Materials and Chemical Products	20807	18210	1857	734	6	
医药制造业	Manufacture of Medicines	5133	3478	720	935		
橡胶制品业	Manufacture of Rubber	14273	14253		20		
非金属矿物制品业	Manufacture of Non-metallic Mineral Products	287	287				
黑色金属冶炼及压延加工业	Smelting and Pressing of Ferrous Metals	1588	1500		88		
有色金属冶炼及压延加工业	Smelting and Pressing of Non-ferrous Metals	8174	8174				
金属制品业	Manufacture of Metal Products	5229	4871		358		
通用设备制造业	Manufacture of General Purpose Machinery	3652	3459		189	1	3
专用设备制造业	Manufacture of Special Purpose Machinery	8194	3231	2082	2566		316
交通运输设备制造业	Manufacture of Transport Equipment	40028	24868	7743	6191		1226
电气机械及器材制造业	Manufacture of Electrical Machinery and Equipment	9178	7950	1000	228		
工艺品及其他制造业	Manufacture of Artwork and Other Manufacturing	3462	2796		665		
其他未列明的制造业	Other Manufacture	3462	2796		665		
电力、燃气及水的生产和供应业	Production and Distribution of Electric Power,Gas and Water	2436	2006		430		
电力、热力的生产和供应业	Production and Distribution of Electric Power and Heat Power	560	560				
燃气生产和供应业	Production and Distribution of Gas	1876	1446		430		
按隶属关系分组	Grouped by Administrative Relationship						
中央	Central	64660	43466	9725	9927		1541
省	Province	61364	56771	1857	2194		542
地	Prefecture	23038	22147	60	827	1	3
县	County	2750	2501	105	144		
其他	Other	14179	11797	1660	716	6	

16-8 大中型工业企业科技

Expenditures for Scientific and Technological Activities

指 标	Item	科技活动经费支出总额 Expenditures for Scientific and Technological Activities
总 计	**Total**	**168793**
总计中:国有控股企业	Of the Total:Stated-controlled Enterprises	159234
按企业规模分组	**Grouped by Size**	
大型企业	Large Enterprises	93724
中型企业	Medium Enterprises	75069
按登记注册类型分组	**Grouped by Registration Categories**	
内资企业	Domestic Investment Enterprises	168023
国有企业	State-owned Enterprises	86698
集体企业	Collective-owned Enterprises	16
有限责任公司	Companies with Limited Liabilities	42090
国有独资公司	Sole State-owned Companies with Limited Liabilities	22367
其他有限责任公司	Other Companies with Limited Liabilities	19723
股份有限公司	Share-holding Companies with Limited Liabilities	38025
私营企业	Private Enterprises	1195
私营合伙企业	Private Cooperative Enterprises	120
私营有限责任公司	Private Companies with Limited Liabilities	1075
港、澳、台商投资企业	Enterprises with Funds from Hong Kong, Macao and Taiwan	40
外商投资企业	Foreign Funded Enterprises	730
按工业行业大类分组	**Grouped by Industrial Sector**	
采矿业	Mining and Quarrying	6934
煤炭开采和洗选业	Mining and Washing of Coal	6918
非金属矿采选业	Mining and Processing of Nonmetal Ores	16
制造业	Manufacturing	159455
食品制造业	Manufacture of Foods	296
饮料制造业	Manufacture of Beverages	28892
烟草制品业	Manufacture of Tobacco	5350
纺织业	Manufacture of Textile	19

活动经费支出情况(2005)

in Large and Medium-sized Enterprise(2005)

单位：万元(10000 yuan)

内部支出 Inner Expenditure	#劳务费 Service Fee	#原材料费 Raw Material Fee	#其他 Other	#内部支出中研究与试验发展支出 Expenditure for Development of Research and Experiment in Inner Expenditure	#内部支出中新产品开发支出 Expenditure for New product in Inner Expenditure	科技经费外部支出 Extenior Expenditure of Science and Technology Outlay
159004	**30219**	**55262**	**73524**	**97986**	**80818**	**9789**
150231	28562	52388	69281	92420	76291	9003
87698	12074	33941	41684	50651	47936	6026
71306	18146	21321	31839	47336	32882	3763
158234	29939	54944	73351	97476	80048	9789
83404	14098	32449	36857	54436	49833	3294
16	5	3	8	11	11	
37775	8159	11434	18182	24859	12743	4315
18798	5264	5753	7781	12225	6534	3569
18977	2895	5681	10402	12634	6209	746
36151	7392	10835	17924	17783	17245	1874
889	285	224	380	388	216	306
120	55	16	49	86	115	
769	231	208	331	301	102	306
40	22	4	14	38	40	
730	258	314	159	473	730	
4659	871	1270	2518	793	566	2275
4643	866	1268	2509	782	555	2275
16	5	3	8	11	11	
151942	29094	53098	69750	97194	80232	7514
282	114	32	136	196		15
26841	2735	14569	9537	18821	19622	2051
5309	465	2067	2777	2236	2017	41
19	15	4		19		

16-8续表（continued）

指　标	Item	科技活动经费支出总额 Expenditures for Scientific and Technological Activities
印刷业和记录媒介的复制	Printing,Reproduction of Recording Media	21
化学原料及化学制品制造业	Manufacture of Raw Chemical Materials and Chemical Products	24811
医药制造业	Manufacture of Medicines	3786
橡胶制品业	Manufacture of Rubber	15520
非金属矿物制品业	Manufacture of Non-metallic Mineral Products	287
黑色金属冶炼及压延加工业	Smelting and Pressing of Ferrous Metals	1168
有色金属冶炼及压延加工业	Smelting and Pressing of Non-ferrous Metals	7778
金属制品业	Manufacture of Metal Products	5332
通用设备制造业	Manufacture of General Purpose Machinery	3650
专用设备制造业	Manufacture of Special Purpose Machinery	7271
交通运输设备制造业	Manufacture of Transport Equipment	36152
电气机械及器材制造业	Manufacture of Electrical Machinery and Equipment	6711
仪器仪表及文化、办公用机械制造业	Manufacture of Measuring Instruments and Machinery for Cultural Activity and Office Work	313
工艺品及其他制造业	Manufacture of Artwork and Other Manufacturing	4168
其他未列明的制造业	Other Manufacture	4168
电力、燃气及水的生产和供应业	Production and Distribution of Electric Power,Gas and Water	2404
电力、热力的生产和供应业	Production and Distribution of Electric Power and Heat Power	560
燃气生产和供应业	Production and Distribution of Gas	1844
按隶属关系分组	**Grouped by Administrative Relationship**	
中央	Central	60568
省	Province	70629
地	Prefecture	23601
县	County	2887
其他	Other	11107

单位：万元(10000 yuan)

内部支出 Inner Expenditure	#劳务费 Service Fee	#原材料费 Raw Material Fee	#其他 Other	#内部支出中研究与试验发展支出 Expenditure for Development of Research and Experiment in Inner Expenditure	#内部支出中新产品开发支出 Expenditure for New product in Inner Expenditure	科技经费外部支出 Extenior Expenditure of Science and Technology Outlay
21	11	10		21	21	
24042	1610	5982	16450	13852	14567	769
3010	580	779	1652	2477	1671	776
15220	2375	5449	7396	6314	8064	300
287	62	99	126	53	69	
1164	415	397	352	852	79	5
7301	2210	1035	4056	1166	2943	478
5101	846	2241	2014	4570	531	231
3624	570	2332	723	3076	2069	26
6776	2430	1526	2819	5422	4655	495
34640	10318	12193	12130	26031	16936	1512
6701	673	1478	4550	2771	1784	10
313	212	66	35	271	313	
4056	1325	1234	1497	3088	516	112
4056	1325	1234	1497	3088	516	112
2404	255	894	1256		20	
560	148	217	195		20	
1844	107	677	1060			
57895	17034	17044	23817	36981	28244	2673
64516	7779	25007	31730	42417	37633	6114
23213	3795	9928	9490	11417	11878	389
2887	373	591	1922	1791	1230	
10494	1239	2691	6564	5380	1833	613

16-9 “十五”时期各年专利申请及授权情况

Basic Statistics on Patent Applications and Authorigations of Each Year in “Tenth Five-year Plan” Period

单位：件(item)

指　标	Item	2000	2001	2002	2003	2004	2005	2005年比2004年增长(%) Increase Rate in 2005 over 2004(%)
申请专利总计	**Total Patent Applications**	**986**	**950**	**1256**	**1242**	**1486**	**2226**	**49.8**
按种类分	**Grouped by Sort**							
发　明	Creations and Inventions	173	178	350	385	450	782	73.8
实用新型	Utility Models	503	513	544	566	765	1065	39.2
外观设计	Designs	310	259	362	291	271	379	39.9
按对象分	**Grouped by Applicant**							
非职务发明创造	Non-service Creations and Inventions	708	684	818	776	768	1028	33.9
职务发明创造	Service Creations and Inventions	278	266	438	466	718	1198	66.9
#大专院校	Universities and Colleges	3	2	9	34	16	19	18.8
科研单位	Research Institutions	20	26	12	16	184	380	106.5
工矿企业	Industrial and Mineral Enterprises	250	234	403	404	511	796	55.8
机关团体	Government Agencies and Organizations	5	4	14	12	7	3	-57.1
授权专利总计	**Total Patent Authorigation**	**710**	**642**	**616**	**723**	**737**	**925**	**25.5**
按种类分	Grouped by Sort							
发　明	Creations and Inventions	65	42	47	79	179	162	-9.5
实用新型	Utility Models	377	357	335	355	364	533	46.4
外观设计	Designs	268	243	234	289	194	230	18.6
按对象分	**Grouped by Applicant**							
非职务发明创造	Non-service Creations and Inventions	449	443	427	446	433	464	7.2
职务发明创造	Service Creations and Inventions	261	199	189	277	304	461	51.6
#大专院校	Universities and Colleges	2	4		7	7	11	57.1
科研单位	Research Institutions	11	16	11	10	16	107	568.8
工矿企业	Industrial and Mineral Enterprises	244	177	174	258	275	332	20.7
机关团体	Government Agencies and Organizations	4	2	4	2	6	11	83.3

16-10 “十五”时期各年各级各类学校数

Number of Schools by Level and Type of School of Each Year in “Tenth Five-year Plan” Period

指　标	Item	2000	2001	2002	2003	2004	2005	2005年比2004年增长(%) Increase Rate in 2005 over 2004(%)
学校数（所）	**Number of Schools(unit)**							
研究生培养机构	Postgraduates Education	7	7	7	7	7	7	持平
普通高等学校	Regular Institutions of Higher Education	24	30	32	34	34	34	持平
成人高等教育	Higher Education Inst. For Adult							
#成人高等学校	Higher Education Inst.Schools For Adult	10	7	7	7	7	6	-14.3
中等职业教育	Reg.Secondary Schools	302	253	241	223	221	217	-1.8
调整后中等职业教育	Regulated Middling Vocational Education				20	20	17	-15.0
普通中等专业教育	General Middling Speciality Education	104	89	79	77	69	68	-1.4
职业高中	Vocational Senior High Schools	164	131	131	105	111	111	持平
成人中等专业教育	Specialized Sec.Educaiton for Adults							
#成人中等专业学校	Specialized Sec.Schools for Adults	34	33	31	21	21	21	持平
普通中学	General Sec. Schools	1953	2222	2291	2488	2635	2666	1.2
高　中	Senior Sec. Schools	305	328	368	420	452	473	4.6
初　中	Junior Sec. Schools	1648	1523	1513	1622	1720	1698	-1.3
九年一贯制学校	Schools of Nine-year Consistent System		371	410	446	463	495	6.9
职业初中	Vocational sec. Schools	94	86	82	84	78	69	-11.5
小　学	Primary Schools	17985	15339	14822	14504	14257	14258	…
幼儿园	Kindergartens	1435	1006	1179	1319	1484	1587	6.9
特殊教育	Special Education	28	35	38	38	38	39	2.6
工读学校	Correctional Work-study Schools	3	3	3	3	3	4	33.3
成人中学	General Sec.Schools for Adults	27	7	7	39	53	43	-18.9
成人技术培训学校	Technical Schools for Adults	15235	14153	15923	12511	11208	12108	8.0
成人小学	Adult Primary Schools	4387	6586	7473	9820	7600	8224	8.2

16-11 “十五”时期各年各级各类学校专任教师数

Number of Full-time Teachers by Level and Type of School of Each Year in “Tenth Five-year Plan” Period

指　标	Item	2000	2001	2002	2003	2004	2005	2005年比2004年增长(%) Increase Rate in 2005 over 2004(%)
专任教师（人）	**Number of Full-time Teachers(person)**							
培养研究生的单位	Postgraduates	614	694	912	1154	1549	1688	9.0
普通高等学校	Reg. Inst. of Higher Education	7240	9007	11079	11775	13792	14353	4.1
成人高等教育	Higher Education Inst.For Adult							
#成人高等学校	Higher Education Inst.Schools For Adult	1109	856	953	973	1139	1102	-3.2
中等职业教育	Reg.Secondary Schools	11504	9959	8915	8008	7612	8012	5.3
调整后中等职业教育	Regulated Middling Vocational Education				523	513	455	-11.3
普通中等专业教育	General Middling Speciality Education	6628	5748	4864	4522	3905	3905	持平
职业高中	Vocational Senior High Schools	3056	2731	2635	1875	2175	2485	14.3
成人中等专业教育	Specialized Sec.Educaiton for Adults							
#成人中等专业学校	Specialized Sec.Schools for Adults	1820	1480	1416	818	1280	747	-41.6
其它机构	Other Institutions				270	254	420	65.4
普通中学	General Sec. Schools	81156	88079	97641	107312	115616	122721	6.1
高　中	Senior Sec. Schools	11658	13613	16230	19413	22488	25638	14.0
初　中	Junior Sec. Schools	69498	74466	81411	87899	93128	97083	4.2
职业初中	Vocational sec. Schools	2312	2270	2277	2078	2000	1947	-2.7
小　学	Primary Schools	174822	173238	177920	179367	180793	183679	1.6
幼儿园	Kindergartens	14204	6991	7920	8751	9514	10025	5.4
特殊教育	Special Education	1482	485	518	517	548	603	10.0
工读学校	Correctional Work-study Schools	34	34	33	38	31	41	32.3
成人中学	General Sec.Schools for Adults	61	67	38	75	60	129	115.0
成人技术培训学校	Technical Schools for Adults	3530	1514	793	2402	2588	5169	99.7
成人小学	Adult Primary Schools	2177	2985	852	2760	2481	4708	89.8

16-12 “十五”时期各年各级各类学校招生数

Number of New Students Enrollment by Level and Type of School of Each Year in “Tenth Five-year Plan” Period

指　标	Item	2000	2001	2002	2003	2004	2005	2005年比2004年增长(%) Increase Rate in 2005 over 2004(%)
招生数（人）	**Entrants(person)**							
研究生	Postgraduates	458	659	875	1458	2165	2584	19.4
普通高等教育	Reg. Inst. of Higher Education	33718	44597	41565	53318	60578	68586	13.2
成人高等教育	Higher Education Inst.For Adult	35109	38298	51420	78075	76929	38168	-50.4
#成人高等学校	Higher Education Inst.Schools For Adult	18148	13735	12557	16974	15806	9396	-40.6
中等职业教育	Reg.Secondary Schools	65419	53318	59981	59000	61662	99706	61.7
调整后中等职业教育	Regulated Middling Vocational Education				3284	3211	8243	156.7
普通中等专业教育	General Middling Speciality Education	38447	31159	37620	38364	39076	53931	38.0
职业高中	Vocational Senior High Schools	12801	12076	13891	12109	14142	30268	114.0
成人中等专业教育	Specialized Sec.Educaiton for Adults	14171	10083	8470	5243	5233	7265	38.8
#成人中等专业学校	Specialized Sec.Schools for Adults	8256	7077	5489	5220	5144	6975	35.6
普通中学	General Sec. Schools	641860	747907	838530	885474	895228	904671	1.1
高　中	Senior Sec. Schools	84393	109691	135425	156515	173638	193814	11.6
初　中	Junior Sec. Schools	557466	638216	703105	728959	721590	710857	-1.5
职业初中	Vocational sec. Schools	19023	18820	16816	15855	13910	11921	-14.3
小　学	Primary Schools	810492	830232	848378	827264	836431	772201	-7.7
幼儿园	Kindergartens	444311	429725	488329	536093	565322	583944	3.3
特殊教育	Special Education	2225	2690	2453	2051	1735	2096	20.8
工读学校	Correctional Work-study Schools	901	813	806	45	8	138	1625.0

16-13 “十五”时期各年各级各类学校在校生数

Number of Students Enrollment by Level and Type of School of Each Year in “Tenth Five-year Plan” Period

指 标	Item	2000	2001	2002	2003	2004	2005	2005年比2004年增长(%) Increase Rate in 2005 over 2004(%)
在校学生（人）	**Enrollment(person)**							
研究生	Postgraduates	1002	1418	1973	2966	4457	6168	38.4
普通高等教育	Reg. Inst. of Higher Education	79833	108159	122742	149444	179852	206754	15.0
成人高等教育	Higher Education Inst.For Adult	57627	82648	109470	148117	104089	114055	9.6
#成人高等学校	Higher Education Inst.Schools For Adult	30909	31337	32566	35398	20718	22731	9.7
中等职业教育	Reg.Secondary Schools	194290	180250	184439	160616	158768	201373	26.8
调整后中等职业教育	Regulated Middling Vocational Education				5796	6841	13227	93.3
普通中等专业教育	General Middling Speciality Education	119991	114765	117970	114895	109744	126440	15.2
职业高中	Vocational Senior High Schools	34029	28835	29139	22817	28144	47533	68.9
成人中等专业教育	Specialized Sec.Educaiton for Adults	40270	36650	37330	17108	14039	14173	1.0
#成人中等专业学校	Specialized Sec.Schools for Adults	26219	23061	27804	15414	13485	13630	1.1
普通中学	General Sec. Schools	1572025	1846015	2128111	2353007	2493395	2549575	2.3
高 中	Senior Sec. Schools	191059	244571	314077	383052	444031	495193	11.5
初 中	Junior Sec. Schools	1380966	1601444	1814034	1969955	2049364	2054382	0.2
职业初中	Vocational sec. Schools	45908	45592	44443	43493	37787	36538	-3.3
小 学	Primary Schools	5002082	4901665	4842831	4768740	4794083	4737645	-1.2
幼儿园	Kindergartens	496044	493770	564782	620089	657060	691428	5.2
特殊教育	Special Education	15845	16007	15664	13812	13397	14676	9.5
工读学校	Correctional Work-study Schools	918	837	123	57	31	82	164.5
成人中学	General Sec.Schools for Adults	3699	3316	1304	111141	99840	2594	-97.4
成人技术培训学校	Technical Schools for Adults	3158125	3425939	2732961	2152480	2462777	2755638	11.9
成人小学	Adult Primary Schools	319027	342411	284593	334479	431954	348425	-19.3

16-14 "十五"时期各年各级各类学校毕业生数

Number of Graduates by Level and Type of School of Each Year in "Tenth Five-year Plan" Period

指　标	Item	2000	2001	2002	2003	2004	2005	2005年比2004年增长(%) Increase Rate in 2005 over 2004(%)
毕业生数（人）	**Graduates(person)**							
研究生	Postgraduates	218	231	303	444	640	834	30.3
普通高等教育	Reg. Inst. of Higher Education	13739	15092	17874	25362	31059	38681	24.5
成人高等教育	Higher Education Inst.For Adult	12977	14507	22980	39186	39618	25180	-36.4
#成人高等学校	Higher Education Inst.Schools For Adult	8376	6208	9832	16458	13589	5719	-57.9
中等职业教育	Reg.Secondary Schools	60910	47578	59910	56261	48252	43770	-9.3
调整后中等职业教育	Regulated Middling Vocational Education				1217	1366	1812	32.7
普通中等专业教育	General Middling Speciality Education	35003	34361	36664	42031	35929	30124	-16.2
职业高中	Vocational Senior High Schools	13792		10301	7884	7157	8255	15.3
成人中等专业教育	Specialized Sec.Educaiton for Adults	12115	13217	12945	5129	3800	3579	-5.8
#成人中等专业学校	Specialized Sec.Schools for Adults	9329	7550	7310	3218	2601	3140	20.7
普通中学	General Sec.Schools	377175	409768	490753	577392	668234	746415	11.7
高　中	Senior Sec. Schools	45846	47121	55820	75141	94939	119161	25.5
初　中	Junior Sec. Schools	331329	362647	434933	502251	573295	627254	9.4
职业初中	Vocational sec. Schools	10646		11091	11883	11986	11445	-4.5
小　学	Primary Schools	732301	778446	816123	805694	766334	742112	-3.2
幼儿园	Kindergartens		277319	300768	326514	363897	372637	2.4
特殊教育	Special Education	960	1414	1261	1237	952	929	-2.4
工读学校	Correctional Work-study Schools	854	616	715	27	49	98	100.0
成人中学	General Sec.Schools for Adults	1081	281	527	110066	98350	1978	-98.0
成人技术培训学校	Technical Schools for Adults	3144644	3378679	2550000	2248044	2235237	2586591	15.7
成人小学	Adult Primary Schools	285360	298330	257759	293015	336488	299422	-11.0

16-15 “十五”时期各年各级学校女学生和女教师情况

Statistics on Female Students and Teachers of Each Year in “Tenth Five-year Plan” Period

单位：人(person)

指 标	Item	2000	2001	2002	2003	2004	2005	2005年比2004年增长(%) Increase Rate in 2005 over 2004(%)
女学生在校生数	**Number of Female Students**							
普通高等教育	Institutions of Higher Education	27497	41982	48431	59936	79646	94546	18.7
成人高等教育	Adult Higher Education Institutions	26275	39434	50400	59309	44466	46913	5.5
中等职业教育	Specialized Secondary Schools				76595	77990	98340	26.1
普通中学	Regular Secondary Schools	663294	792994	923857	1033070	1105806	1137709	2.9
#高 中	Senior Secondary Schools	593378	700892	802017	152596	182621	207793	13.8
初 中	Junior Secondary Schools	69916	92102	121840	880474	923185	929916	0.7
职业初中	Vocational Secondary Schools	19538	19718	19198	18997	16722	16311	-2.5
小 学	Primary Schools	2319257	2276008	2258597	2238724	2264253	2251308	-0.6
女教师数	**Number of Female Full-time Teachers**							
普通高等学校	Institutions of Higher Education	2993	3811	4702	5222	6184	6571	6.3
成人高等学校	Higher Education Inst.Schools for Adult	411	361	406	443	528	512	-3.0
中等职业学校	Specialized Secondary Schools	4611	4224	3731	3289	3159	3340	5.7
普通中学	Regular Secondary Schools	24631	27324	30517	34201	37400	40684	8.8
#高 中	Senior Secondary Schools	3265	4081	5045	6265	7529	8914	18.4
初 中	Junior Secondary Schools	21366	23243	25472	27936	29871	31770	6.4
职业初中	Vocational Secondary Schools	574	645	662	559	563	585	3.9
小 学	Primary Schools	66103	68944	72666	74594	76365	78430	2.7

16-16 “十五”时期各年研究生数

Number of Postgraduates of Each Year in “Tenth Five-year Plan” Period

单位：人(person)

指　标	Item	2000	2001	2002	2003	2004	2005	2005年比2004年增长(%) Increase Rate in 2005 over 2004(%)
招研究生数	Number of Entrants of Postgraduate	458	659	875	1458	2165	2584	19.4
#女性	Female	165	219	347	587	834	1064	27.6
在校研究生数	Number of Enrollment of Postgraduate	1002	1418	1973	2966	4457	6168	38.4
#女性	Female	356	497	762	1185	1825	2493	36.6
毕业研究生数	Number of Graduates of Postgraduate	218	231	303	444	640	834	30.3
#女性	Female	75	85	97	160	250	358	43.2

16-17 普通高等学校基本情况（2005）

Basic Statistics for Institution of Higher Education(2005)

单位：人(person)

类　别	Sort	学校数（所）Schools (unit)	毕业生数 Grad-uates	招生数 Entr-ants	在校学生人数 Enro-llment	教职员工 Teachers, Staff & Workers	#专任教师 Full-time Teachers	#正、副教授 Senior and Sub-senior
总　计	**Total**	**34**	**37126**	**66636**	**201777**	**23664**	**14353**	**4958**
综合大学	Comprehensive Universities	11	12782	23128	68558	9785	5506	1904
理工院校	Natural Sciences & Technology	7	1259	6805	14038	1498	948	223
医药院校	Medicine & Pharmacy	4	5521	8179	30271	3828	2340	1011
师范院校	Teacher Training	8	10556	16946	52572	5233	3358	1070
财经院校	Finance & Economics	2	3866	5770	18914	1678	1199	362
政法院校	Politics and Law	1	1083	1971	5467	507	316	103
民族院校	Ethnic Minortities	1	2059	3837	11957	1135	686	285
#高等职业技术学院	Non-university Tertiry	16	4638	13735	30489	4739	2867	638

16-18 普通高等学校分科专任教师数和学生数（2005）

Number of Full-time Teachers and Students in Institutions of Higher Education by Field of Study(2005)

单位：人(person)

类 别	Sort	专任教师数 Full-time Teachers	正高级 Senior	副高级 Sub-senior	中级 Middle	初级 Junior	无职称 No Rank	毕业生人数 Graduates	招生数 Entrants	在校学生数 Enrollment
总 计	**Total**	**14353**	**949**	**4009**	**5005**	**3385**	**1005**	**37126**	**66636**	**201777**
哲 学	Philosophy	715	42	201	272	158	42	60	46	191
经济学	Economics	850	42	199	326	212	71	1189	1814	7458
法 学	Law	736	44	221	229	188	54	3163	4435	15555
教育学	Education	1066	33	270	397	299	67	5210	11712	28066
文 学	Literature	2596	117	559	950	731	239	4851	7668	26237
历史学	History	238	21	76	83	44	14	219	364	1083
理 学	Science	1844	90	589	649	406	110	2545	3542	13164
工 学	Engineering	3105	202	942	1040	697	224	7369	14825	42632
农 学	Agriculture	595	55	159	217	126	38	1020	1034	3349
医 学	Medicine	1971	279	648	618	353	73	6327	10387	34269
管理学	Management	637	24	145	224	171	73	5173	10809	29773

16-19 中等职业学校基本情况（2005）

Basic Statistics on Specialized Secondary Schools(2005)

单位：人(person)

类别	Sort	学校数（所）Schools (unit)	毕业生数 Graduates	招生数 New Student Enrollment	在校学生数 Student Enrolment	教职员工 Teachers, Staff & Workers	#专任教师 Full-time Teachers
中等职业学校	**Middling Vocational Schools**	**217**	**43770**	**99706**	**201373**	**12617**	**8012**
调整后中等职业学校	Regulated Middling Vocational Schools	17	1812	8243	13227	604	455
普通中等专业学校	General Middling Speciality Schools	68	30124	53931	126440	6354	3905
成人中等专业学校	Middling Speciality Schools for Adult	21	3579	7264	14173	1448	747
职业高中	Vocational Senior High Schools	111	8255	30268	47533	3545	2485
其它机构（教学点）	Others Institutions	35				666	420

注：其它机构（教学点）不计入学校数。

Note:Total of schools don't include the others Institutions for education

16-20 初中毕业生和小学毕业生升学率及小学学龄儿童入学率

Proportion of Graduates of Junior Secondary Schools and Primary Schools Entering into Schools of Higher Grade and Enrollment Rate of School-age Children

单位:%

指标	Item	2000	2001	2002	2003	2004	2005	2005年比2004年增减百分点 Up(down) Percentege points in 2005 over 2004
小学学龄儿童入学率	Enrollment Rate of School-Age Children	98.45	98.15	98.22	98.19	97.76	98.33	0.57
初中阶段毛入学率	Rate of Primary School Graduates Entering into Junior Secondary Schools	73.63	81.97	87.16	94.15	98.69	98.66	-0.03
高中阶段毛入学率	Rate of Junior Secondary School Graduates Entering into Senior Secondary Schools	21.5	22.93	25.42	24.05	26.36	30.50	4.14
高等教育毛入学率	Rate of Senior Secondary School Graduates Entering into Institution of Higher Learning	5.85	7.3	9.0	10.0	10.0	11.0	1.00

16-21 “十五”时期各年民族教育情况

Basic Statistics on Nationality Education of Each Year in “Tenth Five-year Plan” Period

类　别	Item	2000	2001	2002	2003	2004	2005
学校数（所）	**Number of Schools(unit)**						
普通高校	Regular Institutions of Higher Education	1	1	1	1	1	1
普通中学	Regular Secondary Schools	114	82	86	94	88	109
职业初中	Vocational Junior Secondary Schools				3	5	4
小　学	Primary Schools	229	150	145	134	137	159
专任教师数(人)	**Full-time Teachers(person)**						
普通高校	Regular Institutions of Higher Education	1275	1315	2178	2376	2717	2395
成人高校	Adult Institutions of Higher Education	140	109	132	116	146	197
普通中学	Regular Secondary Schools	27109	31813	35924	40597	44881	48605
#高　中	Senior Secondary Schools		4502	5504	7004	8174	9440
中等职业学校	Vocational Secondary Schools		2121	2506	1803	1514	1686
职业初中	Vocational Junior Secondary Schools		859	860	810	765	608
小　学	Primary Schools	73116	70188	72670	73560	74880	77220
在校生数（人）	**Number of Students Enrollment (person)**						
普通高等教育	Regular Higher Education	27330	35798	46189	53587	57455	73551
成人高等教育	Adult Institutions of Higher Education	6632	6381	23158	37398	26723	26467
普通中学	Regular Secondary Schools	515944	675415	785005	879101	952658	993281
#高　中	Senior Secondary Schools		96097	122503	148874	173338	193922
中等职业学校	Vocational Secondary Schools				51920	46779	61302
职业初中	Vocational Junior Secondary Schools		17734	18050	17348	13963	12630
小　学	Primary Schools	1829691	1896676	1884724	1870385	1900618	1884252
毕业生数（人）	Number of Graduates						
普通中学	Regular Secondary Schools	126995	145059	174574	213544	248916	279009
#高　中	Senior Secondary Schools		16804	20285	29226	37674	45591
职业初中	Vocational Junior Secondary Schools		3818	4318	4892	4627	3975
小　学	Primary Schools	256927	284719	307220	308029	291915	288775

16-22 “十五”时期各年民办教育情况

Basic Statistics on Education run by Non-public of Each Year in “Tenth Five-year Plan” Period

类 别	Item	2000	2001	2002	2003	2004	2005
学校数（所）	**Number of Schools(unit)**						
普通高等学校	Regular Institutions of Higher Education		1	1	1	1	1
中等职业教育学校	Regular Secondary Schools	35	26	28	26	26	25
普通中学	Vocational Junior Secondary Schools	98	163	208	279	348	360
#高 中	Primary Schools	16	37	58	89	158	119
职业初中	Full-time Teachers(person)	5	6	6	3	4	4
小 学	Regular Institutions of Higher Education	453	408	405	388	419	444
在校学生数（人）	**Adult Institutions of Higher Education**						
普通高等学校	Regular Secondary Schools			43	201	17898	24008
中等职业教育学校	Senior Secondary Schools	5480	5242	4969	4391	5862	7364
普通中学	Vocational Secondary Schools	27273	43233	58848	76989	111203	117107
#高 中	Vocational Junior Secondary Schools	3510	7827	13853	19565	32328	36982
职业初中	Primary Schools	931	1024	978	602	304	340
小 学	Number of Students Enrollment(person)	164901	119854	138132	140905	150625	163211
教职员工数（人）	**Regular Higher Education**						
普通高等学校	Adult Institutions of Higher Education		76	107	107	1341	1681
中等职业教育学校	Regular Secondary Schools				530	555	673
普通中学	Senior Secondary Schools	1634	3263	4540	5905	7657	8480
职业初中	Vocational Secondary Schools				32	21	22
小 学	Vocational Junior Secondary Schools	4179	4449	5468	5788	6687	7145
专任教师数（人）	**Primary Schools**						
普通高等学校	Number of Graduates		58	86	86	1118	1366
中等职业教育学校	Regular Secondary Schools				290	296	376
普通中学	Senior Secondary Schools	1231	2163	2989	3971	5224	5775
职业初中	Vocational Junior Secondary Schools				29	18	18
小 学	Primary Schools	3705	3611	4449	4726	5412	5903

16-23 “十五”时期各年成人教育情况

Basic Statistics on Adult Education of Each Year in “Tenth Five-year Plan” Period

类 别	Item	2000	2001	2002	2003	2004	2005
学校数（所）	**Number of Schools(unit)**						
成人高等教育学校	Adult Institutions of Higher Education	10	7	7	7	7	6
成人中等专业教育学校	Adult Vocational Secondary Schools	34	33	31	21	21	21
成人中学	Adult Secondary Schools	27	7	7	39	53	43
成人技术培训学校	Adult Vocational/Technical Training Schools	15235	14153	15923	12511	11208	12108
成人小学	Adult Primary Schools	4387	6586	7473	9820	7600	8224
在校生数（万人）	**Number of Students Enrollment(10000 person)**						
成人高等教育	Adult Higher Education	5.76	8.26	10.95	14.81	10.41	11.41
成人中等专业教育	Adult Vocational Secondary Education	4.03	3.67	3.73	1.71	1.40	1.42
成人中学	Adult Secondary Schools	0.37	0.33	0.13	11.11	9.98	0.26
成人技术培训学校	Adult Vocational Technical Training Schools	315.81	342.59	273.30	215.25	246.28	275.57
成人小学	Adult Primary Schools	31.90	34.24	28.46	33.45	43.20	34.84
毕业生数（万人）	**Number of Graduates (10000 person)**						
成人高等教育	Adult Higher Education	1.30	1.45	2.30	3.92	3.96	2.52
成人中等专业教育	Adult Vocational Secondary Education	1.21	1.32	1.29	0.51	0.38	0.36
成人中学	Adult Secondary Schools	0.11	0.03	0.05	11.01	9.84	0.20
成人技术培训学校	Adult Vocational/Technical Training Schools	314.46	337.87	255.00	224.80	223.52	258.66
成人小学	Adult Primary Schools	28.54	29.83	25.78	29.30	33.65	29.94

16-24 “十五”时期各年教师队伍职称情况

Basic Statistics on the title of technical post of Teachers of Each Year in “Tenth Five-year Plan” Period

单位：(人)

类 别	Item	2000	2001	2002	2003	2004	2005
高等学校	**Regular Institutions of Higher Education**	**8349**	**9863**	**12032**	**12748**	**14931**	**15455**
正高级	Professor	427	529	631	713	957	964
副高级	Associate Professor	2106	2403	2924	3292	4125	4224
中 级	Lecturer	3183	3800	4643	4697	5311	5550
初 级	Assistant	1901	2387	2907	3057	3455	3643
无职称	No Rank	732	744	927	989	1083	1074
中等职业学校	**Vocational Secondary Schools**				**8008**	**7612**	**8012**
正高级	Professor						48
副高级	Associate Professor				1278	1265	1390
中 级	Lecturer				3458	3225	3334
初 级	Assistant				2908	2725	2773
无职称	No Rank				364	397	467
普通中学	**Regular Secondary Schools**	**81156**	**88079**	**97641**	**107312**	**115616**	**122721**
中学高级	Senior-Grade of Secondary Teacher	3473	4046	5056	6230	7429	8662
中学一级	First-Grade of Secondary Teacher	17208	18533	20097	22204	25055	28429
中学二级	Second-Grade of Secondary Teacher	38330	41486	45185	47499	50425	52617
中学三级	Third-Grade of Secondary Teacher	13410	14055	15260	17123	17463	18254
未评职称	No Grade of Secondary Teacher	8735	9959	12043	14256	15244	14759
职业初中	**Vocational Junior Secondary Schools**	**2312**	**2270**	**2277**	**2078**	**2000**	**1947**
中学高级	Senior-Grade of Secondary Teacher	16	19	25	15	22	29
中学一级	First-Grade of Secondary Teacher	256	306	340	312	323	341
中学二级	Second-Grade of Secondary Teacher	1264	1307	1249	1115	984	934
中学三级	Third-Grade of Secondary Teacher	499	396	358	344	382	369
未评职称	N0 Grade of Secondary Teacher	277	242	305	292	289	274
小 学	**Regular Primary Schools**	**174822**	**173238**	**177920**	**179367**	**180793**	**183679**
中学高级	Senior-Grade of Secondary Teacher	53	98	162	153	132	111
小学高级	Senior-Grade of Primary Teacher	21471	22721	25691	30409	36496	42097
小学一级	First-Grade of Primary Teacher	91294	91134	92867	92641	92871	86086
小学二级	Second-Grade of Primary Teacher	37476	36791	36774	35787	32886	35359
小学三级	Third-Grade of Primary Teacher	4419	3557	3018	3408	2497	4605
未评职称	No Grade of Primary Teacher	20109	18937	19408	16969	15911	15421

16-25 “十五”时期各年教师负担学生情况

Student-Teacher Ratio by Level of Regular School of Each Year in “Tenth Five-year Plan” Period

单位：学生/教师 (Student/Teacher)

类 别	Item	2000	2001	2002	2003	2004	2005
普通高中	Regular Senior Secondary Schools	16.36	17.97	19.35	19.73	19.75	19.31
普通初中	Regular Junior Secondary Schools	19.87	21.51	22.28	22.41	22.01	21.16
职业初中	Junior Secondary Vocational Schools	19.86	20.08	19.52	20.93	18.89	18.77
小学	Primary Schools	28.61	28.29	27.22	26.59	26.52	25.79

16-26 “十五”时期各年文化事业机构和人员

Number of Institutions and Personnel in Culture of Each Year in “Tenth Five-year Plan” Period

指 标	Item	2000	2001	2002	2003	2004	2005	2005年比2004年增长(%) Increase Rate in 2005 over 2004(%)
机构数总计（个）	**Number of Institutions(unit)**	**1295**	**1364**	**1439**	**1573**	**1653**	**1670**	**1.0**
#艺术事业	Art Institntions	63	61	60	58	57	57	持平
文物事业	Cultural Relics	95	97	101	103	103	104	1.0
图书馆事业	Libraries	89	90	90	90	90	91	1.0
群众文化事业	Mass Culture	1030	1097	1169	1303	1384	1401	1.2
文艺科研	Cultural and Art Research Institutions	4	4	4	4	4	4	持平
其他文化事业	Other Culture Units	14	10	9	8	9	7	-22.2
人员数总计（人）	**Number of Persons Engaged(person)**	**6824**	**6754**	**6894**	**7681**	**7745**	**8207**	**6.0**
#艺术事业	Art Institntions	2688	2636	2556	2487	2507	2493	0.6
文物事业	Cultural Relics	606	589	586	644	698	815	16.8
图书馆事业	Libraries	876	887	880	878	881	905	2.7
群众文化事业	Mass Culture	2142	2229	2389	3168	3170	3577	12.8
文艺科研	Cultural and Art Research Institutions	28	33	24	24	24	27	12.5
其他文化事业	Other Culture Units	484	309	354	368	399	341	-14.5

16-27 文化部门艺术剧团情况（2005）

Basic Statistics on Art Troupes of Culture Department(2005)

指 标	Item	剧团数（个）Number of Troupes (unit)	从业人员（人）Number of Staff and Workers (person)	国内演出(场) Times of Domestic Performance (show)	#在农村演出 Shows in Rural Areas	国内观众人数(万人次) Number of Domestic Spectators (10000 person-times)	国外出访演出(场) Number of Performances Outbound (show)
总 计	**Total**	**26**	**1921**	**2391**	**785**	**270.19**	**300**
按隶属关系分	Grouped by Ownership						
#国有剧团	State-owned Troupes	26	1921	2391	785	270.19	300
按剧种分	Grouped by Drama						
#话剧、儿童剧、滑稽剧团	Drama, Children, Plays and Comedy Troupes	1	69	118	80	11.8	
歌剧、舞剧、歌舞剧团	Opera, Ballet and Dance Troupes	1	155	151	30	16.0	
乐团、歌舞团、轻音乐团	Song and Dance Troupe, Light Music Troupes	8	620	1059	250	114.1	
戏曲剧团	Local Opera Troupes	10	706	596	209	71.1	
曲艺、杂技、木偶、皮影团	Recitation and Ballad Troupes, Acrobatics and Circus Troupes, Puppet Show Troupes and Shadow Play Troupes	3	242	277	116	31.4	300
文工团	Cultural and Performance Troupes	3	129	190	100	25.8	

16-28 文化娱乐业基本情况（2005）

Basic Statistics on Culture and Entertainment(2005)

类别	Sort	机构数（个）Institution (unit)	从业人员（人）Number of Employment (person)	营业收入（万元）Primary Business Income (10000 yuan)	主营业务利润（万元）Primary Business Profit (10000 yuan)
总计	**Total**	**3345**	**13910**	**56184.8**	**14285.7**
歌舞娱乐场所	Song and Dance Centers	965	6752	23561.1	6157.8
游戏电子游艺经营场所	Computer Game Management Centers	682	1484	4029.3	1233.2
其他娱乐场所	Other Entertainment Centers	244	513	2128.3	435.4
网吧	Internet Bar	1442	5123	26370.2	6432.8
经营性互联网单位	Internet Management institution	5	14	19.5	5.4

16-29 艺术表演场所情况（2005）

Basic Statistics on Art Preformances Place(2005)

类别	Sort	机构数（个）Number of Instit-utions (unit)	从业人员（人）Number of Staff and Workers (person)	座席数（个）Seats (unit)	演（映）出场次（场）Number of Perfo-rmances (show)	#艺术演出场次 Art Perfo-rmance	观众人次(万人次) Number of Spectators (10000 person -times)	#艺术演出人次 Art Perfo-rmances
总计	**Toatl**	**12**	**290**	**6493**	**12993**	**339**	**56.4**	**21.1**
按隶属关系分	Grouped by Administrative Relationship							
#省级	Province Level	4	128	1465	1804	165	16.6	14.9
地级	Prefectural Level	6	110	3262	10828	40	29.2	1.7
县级	County Level	2	52	1766	361	134	10.6	4.5
按系统分	Grouped by Administration Relationship							
#文化系统	Cultural Organizations and Institutions	12	290	6493	12993	339	56.4	21.1

16-30 群众艺术馆和文化馆（站）情况（2005）

Basic Statistics on Mass Art Centers and Culture Centers(Stations)(2005)

指标	Item	合计 Total	群众艺术馆 Mass Art Centers	文化馆 Culture Centers	文化站 Culture Stations
馆（站）个数（个）	**Number of Centers(unit)**	**1401**	**8**	**87**	**1306**
下基层服务次数（次）	Number of go to the foundation (time)	5889	164	1670	4055
组织各类讲座次数（次）	Organizing Lectures(time)	102	39	63	
组织文艺活动次数（次）	Organizing Art Performances(time)	5759	258	2240	3261
举办业余文艺训练班(班次)	Conducting Amateur Art Training Courses(class)	1089	174	477	438
#结业人数（万人次）	Number of Persons Completed(10000 person-times)	3.2	0.4	1.6	1.2
举办展览次数（次）	Number of Exhibitions(unit)	934	28	200	706

16-31 “十五”时期各年电视台、广播电台情况

Basic Statistics on Broadcasting and Television Stations of Each Year in “Tenth Five-year Plan” Period

<table>
<tr><th>指 标</th><th>Item</th><th>2000</th><th>2001</th><th>2002</th><th>2003</th><th>2004</th><th>2005</th></tr>
<tr><td>电视台</td><td>Television Stations</td><td></td><td></td><td></td><td></td><td></td><td></td></tr>
<tr><td>无线电视台（座）</td><td>No-wire Television Stations(unit)</td><td>10</td><td>10</td><td>10</td><td>10</td><td>5</td><td>5</td></tr>
<tr><td>自办节目（套）</td><td>Self-Produced Programs(set)</td><td>16</td><td>31</td><td>31</td><td>31</td><td>40</td><td>91</td></tr>
<tr><td>全年节目播出时间（万小时）</td><td>Program Hours Per Week(hour)</td><td>7.72</td><td>12.27</td><td>13.28</td><td>16.99</td><td>20.53</td><td>21.90</td></tr>
<tr><td>有线电视用户(万户)</td><td>User of Community Antenna Television</td><td>209.94</td><td>228.10</td><td>232.07</td><td>273.33</td><td>277.28</td><td>280.33</td></tr>
<tr><td>有线电视入户率(%)</td><td>Viewer Rating of Community Antenna Television(%)</td><td></td><td></td><td></td><td>24.2</td><td>27.2</td><td>29.00</td></tr>
<tr><td>电视人口覆盖率（%）</td><td>Viewer Rating(%)</td><td>85.3</td><td>87.2</td><td>88.2</td><td>89.1</td><td>89.6</td><td>90.5</td></tr>
<tr><td>广播电台</td><td>Broadcasting Stations</td><td></td><td></td><td></td><td></td><td></td><td></td></tr>
<tr><td>无线电台（座）</td><td>No-wire Broadcasting Stations(unit)</td><td>4</td><td>4</td><td>4</td><td>4</td><td>4</td><td>4</td></tr>
<tr><td>自办节目（套）</td><td>Self-produced Programs(set)</td><td>14</td><td>14</td><td>14</td><td>15</td><td>16</td><td>22</td></tr>
<tr><td>全年节目播出时间（万小时）</td><td>Program Hours Per Year(hour)</td><td>6.90</td><td>6.90</td><td>7.30</td><td>8.87</td><td>12.50</td><td>10.65</td></tr>
<tr><td>广播人口覆盖率（%）</td><td>Listener Rating(%)</td><td>76.2</td><td>78.3</td><td>79.4</td><td>80.0</td><td>82.1</td><td>83.3</td></tr>
<tr><td>乡镇广播电视站(座)</td><td>Number of Broadcasting and TV Stations in Township and Town(unit)</td><td>1281</td><td>1289</td><td>1300</td><td>1320</td><td>1342</td><td>1375</td></tr>
<tr><td>通广播的乡镇(个)</td><td>Number of Towship and Town with Broadcasting(unit)</td><td>1434</td><td>1402</td><td>1448</td><td>1453</td><td rowspan="2">1482</td><td rowspan="2">1481</td></tr>
<tr><td>通电视的乡镇(个)</td><td>Number of Towship and Town with TV(unit)</td><td>1482</td><td>1453</td><td>1486</td><td>1488</td></tr>
<tr><td>通广播的村(个)</td><td>Number of Village with Broadcating(unit)</td><td>20055</td><td>22140</td><td>22586</td><td>21610</td><td rowspan="2">21293</td><td rowspan="2">20240</td></tr>
<tr><td>通电视的村(个)</td><td>Number of Village with TV(unit)</td><td>23642</td><td>24494</td><td>24542</td><td>23340</td></tr>
</table>

注：表中数据由省广播电视局提供。
Note:Rata in this table are abtained from the provincial Radio and TV Administration.

16-32 电视台、广播电台情况（2005）

Basic Statistics on Broadcasting and Television Stations(2005)

指 标	Item	全年公共节目播出时间（小时）Program Hours Per Year(hour)	新闻咨询类节目 News	专题服务类节目 Special Subject	综合益智类节目 General Entertainment
电视台	**No-wire Television Stations**	**219049**	**35375**	**16032**	**14524**
省 级	Province Level	45735	948	2131	3846
地 级	Prefectural Level	118241	12070	5282	6180
县 级	Connty Level	55073	22357	8619	4498
广播电台	**No-wire Broadcasting Stations**	**106467**	**23578**	**24199**	**40584**
省 级	Province Level	41623	5349	11367	16957
地 级	Prefectural Level	56943	13522	12276	22107
县 级	Connty Level	7901	4707	556	1520

16-33 “十五”时期各年文化设施

Basic Statistics on Culture Establishment of Each Year in “Tenth Five-year Plan” Period

类 别	Sort	2000	2001	2002	2003	2004	2005
艺术表演场所	**Arts Centers**	**14**	**13**	**13**	**13**	**12**	**12**
公共图书馆	Public Libraries	89	90	90	90	90	91
博物馆、纪念馆	Museums and Memorials	8	9	10	10	10	11
群众艺术馆、文化馆	Mass Art Centers and Cultural Centers	93	94	94	95	95	95
档案馆	Archives	96	97	97	98	98	98

16-34 “十五”时期各年图书出版情况

Number of Books Published of Each Year in “Tenth Five-year Plan” Period

类 别	Sort	2000	2001	2002	2003	2004	2005
种 数（种）	**Number of Publications(kind)**	**825**	**961**	**1022**	**840**	**869**	**1554**
#新出版	New-Publications	348	486	538	499	460	530
总印数（万册）	Printed Copies(10000 copies)	10288	12767	15030	12364	8890	9993
总印张数（万印张）	Printed Sheets(10000 sheets)	44109	56754	68681	58625	48611	55368

16-35 图书分类出版数量（2005）

Number of Books Published by Category(2005)

类 别	Sort	种数（种） Number of Publications (kind)	#新出版 New-Published	总印数（万册、张） Total Printed (10000 copies)	总印张数（千印张） Total Printed Sheets (1000 sheets)
总 计	**Total**	**1554**	**530**	**9993**	**553679**
#书籍	Books				
#哲学、社会科学	Philosophy and Social Sciences	21	19	5	722
文化教育	Culture and Education	584	181	7505	422209
文学艺术	Literature and Arts	86	72	699	18560
少年儿童读物	Juvenile and Children's books	11		38	573
#课本	Textbooks				
#大专课本	For Colleges and Universities	16	8	5	599
中学课本	For Secondary Schools	166	20	2005	204601
小学课本	For Primary Schools	164	18	307	123236
教学用书	For Teaching References	52		22	1830

16-36 “十五”时期各年杂志出版情况

Number of Magazines Published of Each Year in “Tenth Five-year Plan” Period

类 别	Sort	2000	2001	2002	2003	2004	2005
种 数（种）	**Number of Publications(kind)**	**98**	**97**	**98**	**88**	**89**	**87**
每期平均印数(万册、份)	Average Printed Copies Per Issue(10000 copies)	92	95	107	85	91	95
总印数（万册、份）	Printed Copies(10000 copies)	994	1210	1339	1039	1281	1349
总印张数（万印张）	Printed Sheets(10000 sheets)	3615	4039	5345	5339	6802	7401

16-37 杂志分类出版数量（2005）

Number of Magazines Published by Category(2005)

类　别	Sortr	种数（种）Number of Publications (kind)	每期平均印数（万册）Average Publication Per Issue (10000 copies)	总印数(万册、份) Total Printed (10000 copies)	总印张数（千印张）Total Printed Sheets (1000 sheets)
总　计	**Total**	**87**	**95**	**1349**	**74002**
#综合	Comprehensive	19	25	407	16805
哲学、社会科学	Philosophy and Social Sciences	14	6	54	2527
自然科学技术	Natural Sciences and Technology	33	12	131	7367
文化教育	Culture and Education	11	23	353	19775
文学艺术	Literature and Arts	8	26	361	25046
少年儿童读物	Juvenile and Children's books	1	3	40	2376

16-38 “十五”时期各年报纸出版情况

Number of Newspaper Pulished of Each Year in “Tenth Five-year Plan” Period

类　别	Sort	2000	2001	2002	2003	2004	2005
种 数（种）	**Number of Publications(kind)**	**50**	**39**	**41**	**31**	**31**	**45**
每期平均印数（万册、份）	Average Printed Copies Per Issue (10000 copies)	131	136	128	131	134	81
总印数（万册、份）	Printed Copies(10000 copies)	28887	31677	31507	34148	33689	35172
总印张数（万印张）	Printed Sheets(10000 sheets)	58421	73423	66946	93476	103734	198381

16-39 报纸分类出版数量（2005）

Number of Newspaper Published by Category(2005)

类别	Sortr	种数（种）Number of Public-ations (kind)	每期平均印数（万份）Average Publication Per Issue (10000 copies)	总印数（万份）Total Printed (10000 copies)	总印张数（千印张）Total Printed Sheets (1000 sheets)
总　计	**Total**	**45**	**81**	**35172**	**1983807**
综合报	Comprehensive	17	52	1840	663353
专业报	Specialized	15	24	1869	83758
在总计中	of the Total				
#贵州日报	Guizhou Daily	1	13	4884	97687
贵州都市报	Guizhou Urban Newspaper	1	22	7884	394219
贵阳晚报	Guiyang Evening Newspaper	1	21	7455	447299
文摘	Press Digest	1	2	102	2040
每周广播电视报	Broadcasting and Television Newspaper Every Week	1	2	479	14846

16-40 “十五”时期各年境外来黔专家基本情况

Basic Statistics on Foreign Specialist of Giving Service to GuiZhou of each year in “Tenth-Five-year Plan” Period

单位:人次(person-time)

类别	Sort	2000	2001	2002	2003	2004	2005
合 计	**Total**	**1222**	**2459**	**1701**	**2027**	**922**	**1072**
按专家身份分组	by Country(Region)						
外国专家	Foreign Specialist	1188	1759	1071	1277	777	933
港澳台专家	Specialist from Hong Kong,Macao and Taiwan	34	700	630	750	145	139
按专家类别分组	by Sort						
经济技术管理类	Economic, Tethnology and Management	1222	1869	801	724	495	657
文教科卫类	Culture,Education,Science and Public Health		590	900	1303	427	415
按专家来黔时间分组	by Time						
长期专家	Long-term	64	495	1114	1565	310	329
短期专家	Short-term	1158	1964	587	462	612	743
按专家的性别分组	by Sex						
男	Male	1147	2256	1386	1624	769	914
女	Female	75	203	315	403	153	158

注：表中2000年数据仅为经济技术管理专家。（以下各表同）

note:The data in 2000 included the Specialist of Economic,Tethnology and Management Only.(Same to next)

16-41 “十五”时期各年境外来黔专家人员结构

Composition of Foreign Specialist of Giving Service to GuiZhou of each year in “Tenth-Five-year Plan” Period

单位:%

类　别	Sort	2000	2001	2002	2003	2004	2005
按专家身份分组	**by Country(Region)**	**100.0**	**100.0**	**100.0**	**100.0**	**100.0**	**100.0**
外国专家	Foreign Specialists	97.2	71.5	63.0	63.0	84.3	87.0
港澳台专家	Specialists from Hong Kong,Macao and Taiwan	2.8	28.5	37.0	37.0	15.7	13.0
按专家类别分组	by Sort	100.0	100.0	100.0	100.0	100.0	100.0
经济技术管理类	Economic, Tethnology and Management	100.0	76.0	47.1	35.7	53.7	61.3
文教科卫类	Culture,Education,Science and Public Health		24.0	52.9	64.3	46.3	38.7
按专家来黔时间分组	by Time	100.0	100.0	100.0	100.0	100.0	100.0
长期专家	Long-term	5.2	20.1	65.5	77.2	33.6	30.7
短期专家	Short-term	94.8	79.9	34.5	22.8	66.4	69.3
按专家的性别分组	by Sex	100.0	100.0	100.0	100.0	100.0	100.0
男	Male	93.9	91.7	81.5	80.1	83.4	85.3
女	Female	6.1	8.3	18.5	19.9	16.6	14.7

16-42 “十五”时期各年境外来黔专家在三次产业中的分布

Foreign Specialist of Giving Service to GuiZhou by Three Industries of each year in “Tenth-Five-year Plan” Period

类　别	Sort	2000	2001	2002	2003	2004	2005
合计（人次）	**Tetal(person-time)**	**1222**	**2459**	**1701**	**2027**	**922**	**1072**
第一产业	Primary Industry	76	431	42	34	57	58
第二产业	Secondary Industry	929	1042	570	481	232	243
第三产业	Tertiary Industry	217	986	1089	1512	633	771
合计（%）	**Tetal(%)**	**100.0**	**100.0**	**100.0**	**100.0**	**100.0**	**100.0**
第一产业	Primary Industry	6.2	17.5	2.5	1.7	6.2	5.4
第二产业	Secondary Industry	76.0	42.4	33.5	23.7	25.2	22.7
第三产业	Tertiary Industry	17.8	40.1	64.0	74.6	68.7	71.9

16-43 “十五”时期各年境内各种类型单位聘请境外专家情况

Basic Statistics on Foreign Specialist of Giving Service to GuiZhou by Sector of each year in “Tenth-Five-year Plan” Period

单位:人次

类 别	Sort	2000	2001	2002	2003	2004	2005
合 计	**Total**	**1222**	**2459**	**1701**	**2027**	**922**	**1072**
企、事业单位聘用	Enterprises and Institutions	1061	2456	1604	1922	820	920
内资企、事业单位	Inner Country Units	970	1318	559	513	654	719
#国有企业	State-owned Enterprises	861	460	268	257	377	420
各类学校	Educational Institution		47	135	167	170	171
港澳台商投资企、事业单位	Units with Funds from Hong Kong, Macao & Taiwan	47	662	520	760	48	48
外商投资企、事业单位	Foreign Funded Units	44	476	525	649	118	153
机关、社会团体聘用	Agencies & Organizations and Social Organizations	161	3	97	102	102	150
重点建设项目聘用	Emphases Construction Project				3		2
长期专家合计	**Total Long-term Specialists**	64	495	1114	1565	310	329
企、事业单位聘用	Enterprises and Institutions	60	495	1109	1555	304	324
内资企、事业单位	Inner Country Units	26	167	164	260	172	181
#国有企业	State-owned Enterprises	21	66	70	124	106	107
各类学校	Educational Institution		44	101	129	52	50
港澳台商投资企、事业单位	Units with Funds from Hong Kong, Macao & Taiwan	6	208	420	646	42	41
外商投资企、事业单位	Foreign Funded Units	28	120	525	649	90	102
机关、社会团体聘用	Agencies & Organizations and Social Organizations	4		5	10	6	5
短期专家合计	**Total Short-term Specialists**	1158	1964	587	462	612	743
企、事业单位聘用	Enterprises and Institutions	1001	1961	495	367	516	596
内资企、事业单位	Inner Country Units	944	1151	395	253	482	538
#国有企业	State-owned Enterprises	840	394	198	133	271	313
各类学校	Educational Institution		3	34	38	118	121
港澳台商投资企、事业单位	Units with Funds from Hong Kong, Macao & Taiwan	41	454	100	114	6	7
外商投资企、事业单位	Foreign Funded Units	16	356			28	51
机关、社会团体聘用	Agencies & Organizations and Social Organizations	157	3	92	92	96	145
重点建设项目聘用	Emphases Construction Project				3		2

16-44 “十五”时期各年境外来黔专家国别(地区)情况

Basic Statistics on Foreign Specialist of Giving Service to GuiZhou by Country (Region) of each year in “Tenth-Five-year Plan” Period

单位：人次(person-time)

国别（地区）	Country(Region)	2000	2001	2002	2003	2004	2005
合　计	**Total**	**1222**	**2459**	**1701**	**2027**	**922**	**1072**
港澳台	Hong Kong,Macao and Taiwan	34	700	630	750	145	139
以色列	Israel	262	3	3		7	10
日本	Japan	242	205	287	294	106	133
新加坡	Singapore	23	166	23	51	20	14
韩国	Korea Rep.	5	35	43	53	20	28
英国	United Kingdom	52	82	67	60	62	68
德国	Germany	82	99	26	149	50	82
法国	France	40	84	46	45	33	50
意大利	Italy	33	33	6	16	10	25
荷兰	Netherlands	41	76	11	10	2	
奥地利	Austria	4	8	11	2	7	14
俄罗斯	Russia	5		1		8	11
乌克兰	Ukraine	1				10	10
加拿大	Canada	61	77	34	35	64	33
美国	United States	117	268	276	267	185	232
澳大利亚	Australia	108	146	56	85	26	59
新西兰	New Zealand	51	215	27	56	13	18
其他	Others	61	262	154	154	154	146

16-45 “十五”时期各年境外来黔长期专家情况

Basic Statistics on Long-term Foreign Specialist of Giving Service to GuiZhou by Country(Region) of each year in “Tenth-Five-year Plan” Period

单位：人次(person-time)

国别（地区）	Country(Region)	2000	2001	2002	2003	2004	2005
合　计	**Total**	**64**	**495**	**1114**	**1565**	**310**	**329**
港澳台	Hong Kong,Macao and Taiwan	7	174	508	636	52	66
日本	Japan	10	44	160	220	20	31
新加坡	Singapore	7	26		27	15	9
韩国	Korea Rep.		17	35	41	6	11
英国	United Kingdom	7	42	46	41	36	39
德国	Germany	7	8	1	125	3	4
法国	France	1	8	18	25	8	6
意大利	Italy					1	1
荷兰	Netherlands			1	1		
奥地利	Austria			3		1	4
乌克兰	Ukraine					10	9
加拿大	Canada	14	12	26	32	6	11
美国	United States	6	70	188	198	95	100
澳大利亚	Australia	4	42	48	69	12	21
新西兰	New Zealand			14	45	3	3
其他	Others	1	52	66	105	42	14

16-46 “十五”时期各年境外来黔短期专家情况

Basic Statistics on Short-term Foreign Specialist of Giving Service to GuiZhou by Country(Region) of each year in “Tenth-Five-year Plan” Period

单位：人次(person-time)

国别（地区）	Country(Region)	2000	2001	2002	2003	2004	2005
合　计	**Total**	**1158**	**1964**	**587**	**462**	**608**	**743**
港澳台	Hong Kong,Macao and Taiwan	27	526	122	114	89	73
以色列	Israel	262	3	3		7	10
日本	Japan	232	161	127	74	86	102
新加坡	Singapore	16	140	23	24	5	5
韩国	Korea Rep.	5	18	8	12	14	17
英国	United Kingdom	45	40	21	19	26	29
德国	Germany	75	91	25	24	47	78
法国	France	39	76	28	20	25	44
意大利	Italy	33	33	6	16	9	24
荷兰	Netherlands	41	76	10	9	2	
奥地利	Austria	4	8	8	2	6	10
俄罗斯	Russia	5		1		8	11
乌克兰	Ukraine	1					1
加拿大	Canada	47	65	8	3	58	22
美国	United States	111	198	88	69	90	132
澳大利亚	Australia	104	104	8	16	14	38
新西兰	New Zealand	51	215	13	11	10	15
其他	Others	60	210	88	49	112	132

主要统计指标解释

普通高等学校 指按照国家规定的设置标准和审批程序批准举办，通过国家统一招生考试，招收高中毕业生为主要培养对象，实施高等教育的全日制大学、独立设置的学院和高等专科学校、短期职业大学。

成人高等学校 指按照国家有关规定审批，招收通过全国成人高教统一招生考试的具有高中毕业或同等学历的在职从业人员，利用脱产、半脱产、业余或函授等多种形式对其实施高等学历教育，培养高等教育专科或本科毕业水平的专门人才，修业年限、课程设置和总学时数均按高等学历教育要求付诸实施的学校。包括广播电视大学、职工高等学校、农民高等学校、管理干部学院、教育学院、独立设置的函授学院等。

小学学龄儿童入学率 指调查范围内已入小学学习的学龄儿童占校内外学龄儿童总数（包括弱智儿童，不包括盲聋哑儿童)的比重。计算公式为：

小学学龄儿童入学率=已入学的小学学龄儿童数/校内外小学学龄儿童总数×100%

科技活动 指在自然科学、农业科学、医药科学、工程与技术科学、人文与社会科学领域(简称科学技术领域)中，与科技知识的产生、发展、传播和应用密切相关的有组织的活动。可分为研究与试验发展(R&D)、研究与试验发展成果应用及相关的科技服务三类活动。该定义是联合国教科文组织考虑成员国特别是发展中国家开展科技统计工作的需要，而对科技活动所作的统计界定。

科技活动人员 指直接从事科技活动、以及专门从事科技活动管理和为科技活动提供直接服务，累计的实际工作时间占全年制度工作时间10%及以上的人员。(1)直接从事科技活动的人员包括：在独立核算的科学研究与技术开发机构、高等学校、各类企业及其他事业单位内设的研究室、实验室、技术开发中心及中试车间(基地)等机构中从事科技活动的研究人员、工程技术人员、技术工人及其它人员；虽不在上述机构工作，但编入科技活动项目(课题)组的人员；科技信息与文献机构中的专业技术人员；从事论文设计的研究生等。(2)专门从事科技活动管理和为科技活动提供直接服务的人员，包括：独立核算的科学研究与技术开发机构、科技信息与文献机构、高等学校、各类企业及其他事业单位主管科技工作的负责人，专门从事科技活动的计划、行政、人事、财务、物资供应、设备维护、图书资料管理等工作的各类人员，但不包括保卫、医疗保健人员、司机、食堂人员、茶炉工、水暖工、清洁工等为科技活动提供间接服务的人员。该指标用来反映投入科技活动人力的规模。

科学家与工程师 指科技活动人员中具有高、中级技术职称(职务)的人员和不具有高、中级技术职称(职务)的大学本科及以上学历人员。该指标用来反映投入科技活动人力的素质。

研究与试验发展(R&D) 指在科学技术领域，为增加知识总量、以及运用这些知识去创造新的应用进行的系统的创造性的活动，包括基础研究、应用研究、试验发展三类活动。国际上通常采用R&D活动的规模和强度指标反映一国的科技实力和核心竞争力。

基础研究 指为了获得关于现象和可观察事实的基本原理的新知识(揭示客观事物的本质、运动规律，获得新发现、新学说)而进行的实验性或理论性研究，它不以任何专门或特定的应用或使用为目的。其成果以科学论文和科学著作为主要形式。用来反映知识的原始创新能力。

应用研究 指为获得新知识而进行的创造性研究，主要针对某一特定的目的或目标。应用研究是为了确定基础研究成果可能的用途，或是为达到预定的目标探索应采取的新方法(原理性)或新途径。其成果形式以科学论文、专著、原理性模型或发明专利为主。用来反映对基础研究成果应用途径的探索。

试验发展 指利用从基础研究、应用研究和实际经验所获得的现有知识，为产生新的产品、材料和装置，建立新的工艺、系统和服务，以及对已产生和建立的上述各项作实质性的改进而进行的系统性工作。其成果形式主要是专利、专有技术、具有新产品基本特征的产品原型或具有新装置基本特征的原始样机等。在社会科学领域,试验发展是指把通过基础研究、应用研究获得的知识转变成可以实施的计划(包括为进行检验和评估实施示范项目)的过程。人文科学领域没有对应的试验发展活动。主要反映将科研成果转化为技术和产品的能力,是科技推动经济社会发展的物化成果。

研究与试验发展人员 指参与研究与试验发展项目研究、管理和辅助工作的人员, 包括项目(课题)组人员,企业科技行政管理人员和直接为项目(课题)活动提供服务的辅助人员。反映投入从事拥有自主知识产权的研究开发活动的人力规模。

研究与试验发展人员全时当量 指全时人员数加非全时人员按工作量折算为全时人员数的总和。例如:有两个全时人员和三个非全时人员(工作时间分别为20%、30%和70%),则全时当量为2+0.2+0.3+0.7=3.2人年。为国际上比较科技人力投入而制定的可比指标。

专业技术人员 指从事专业技术工作和专业技术管理工作的人员,即企事业单位中已经聘任专业技术职务从事专业技术工作和专业技术管理工作的人员,以及未聘任专业技术职务,现在专业技术岗位上工作的人员。包括工程技术人员,农业技术人员,科学研究人员,卫生技术人员,教学人员,经济人员,会计人员,统计人员,翻译人员,图书资料、档案、文博人员,新闻出版人员,律师、公证人员,广播电视播音人员,工艺美术人员,体育人员,艺术人员及企业政治思想工作人员,共十七个专业技术职务类别。用来反映科技人力资源情况。

科技活动经费筹集 指从各种渠道筹集到的计划用于科技活动的经费,包括政府资金、企业资金、事业单位资金、金融机构贷款、国外资金和其他资金等。反映各社会经济主体对促进科技进步所做的努力。

政府资金 指从各级政府部门获得的计划用于科技活动的经费,包括科学事业费、科技三项费、科研基建费、科学基金、教育等部门事业费中计划用于科技活动的经费以及政府部门预算外资金中计划用于科技活动的经费等。

企业资金 指从自有资金中提取或接受其他企业委托的、科研院所和高校等事业单位接受企业委托获得的,计划用于科研和技术开发的经费。不包括来自政府、金融机构及国外的计划用于科技活动的资金。

金融机构贷款 指从各类金融机构获得的用于科技活动的贷款。

科技活动经费内部支出 指报告年内用于科技活动的实际支出,包括劳务费、科研业务费、科研管理费,非基建投资购建的固定资产、科研基建支出以及其他用于科技活动的支出。不包括生产性活动支出、归还贷款支出及转拨外单位支出。反映科技投入实际完成情况。

劳务费 指以货币或实物形式直接或间接支付给从事科技活动人员的劳动报酬及各种费用。包括各种形式的工资、津贴、奖金、福利、离退休人员费用、人民助学金等。反映改善科技人员待遇情况。

固定资产购建费 指报告年内使用非基建投资购建的固定资产和用于科研基建投资的实际支出额,即固定资产实际支出和科研基建投资实际完成额之和。固定资产是指长期使用而不改变原有实物形态的主要物资设备、图书资料、实验材料和标本以及其他设备和家具、房屋、建筑物。反映用于改善科研条件和科研手段方面的投入情况。

新产品 指采用新技术原理、新设计构思研制、生产的全新产品,或在结构、材质、工艺等某一方面比原有产品有明显改进,从而显著提高了产品性能或扩大了使用功能的产品。既包括政府有关部门认定并在有效期内的新产品,也包括企业自行研制开发,未经政府有关部门认定,从投产之日起一年之内的新产品。用来反映科技产出及对经济增长的直接贡献。

专利 是专利权的简称,是对发明人的发明创造经审查合格后,由专利局依据专利法授予发明人和设计人对该项发明创造享有的专有权。包括发明、实用新型和外观设计。反映拥有自主知识产权的科技和设计成果情况。

发明 是专利法及其实施细则所称的发明,指对有关产品、方法或其改进所提出的新的技术方案。

实用新型 是专利法及其实施细则所称的实用新型，指对产品的形状、构造或者其结合所提出的适于实用的新的技术方案。

外观设计 专利法及其实施细则所称的外观设计，指对产品的形状、图案、色彩或者其结合所作出的富有美感并适于工业上应用的新设计。

文化事业机构 指从事专业文化工作和为专业文化工作服务的独立建制的单位。不包括这些单位另外举办独立核算的其他机构和各部门的业余文化组织。

艺术表演团体 指从事戏曲、音乐、舞蹈、杂技等专业艺术表演，有独立帐户的单位，不包括半工半艺、半农半艺和民间职业剧团。

电影放映单位 指具有放映机器设备、固定或不固定的放映场所与专职或兼职的放映技术人员，经有关部门登记批准，经常为一定的观众对象放映电影的机构。包括经批准对外开放进行营业，并与电影发行放映管理机构分帐的专用放映单位和军委系统租片单位。

艺术表演观众人数(人次) 指售票、包场演出或民族地区免费演出的艺术表演观众人次数，不包括彩排审查和内部观摩演出的观看人次数。

Explanatory Notes on Main Statistical Indicators

Regular Institutions of Higher Learning refer to educational establishments set up according to the government evaluation and approval procedures, enrolling graduates from senior secondary schools and providing higher education courses and training for senior professionals.They include full-time universities, colleges, high professional schools and short-term professional universities.

Institutions of Higher Learning for Adults refer to educational establishments, set up in line with relevant rules approved by the government, enrolling staff and workers with senior secondary school or equivalent education ,and providing higher education courses in many forms of full time, part time, spare time, or correspondence for adults. Professionals thus trained receive a qualification equivalent to graduates studying regular courses at regular universities, colleges and professional colleges. Institutions of higher learning for adults include Radio and TV universities, schools of high education for staff and workers and peasants, colleges for management cadres, pedagogical colleges, independent correspondence colleges.

Enrollment Rate of Primary School Age Children refers to the proportion of school age children enrolled at schools to the total number of school age children both in and outside schools (including retarded children ,but excluding blind, deaf and mute children). The formula is:

Enrollment Rate of Primary School age Children=(Total Primary School age Children at Schools)÷ (Total Primary School age Children Both at and Outside Schools) ×100%

Scientific and Technological Activities (S&T Activities) refer to organized activities which are closely related with the creation, development, dissemination and application of the scientific and technical knowledge in the fields of natural sciences, agricultural science, medical science, engineering and technological science, humanities and social sciences (referred to as scientific and technological fields). S&T activities can be classified in to 3 categories: research and development (R&D) activities, application of R&D results, and related S&T services. This statistical definition is made by UNICHIEF for scientific and technological activities to meet the need of carrying out statistical work in this field for its member countries in particular those developing countries.

Personnel Engaged in S&T Activities refer to personnel directly engaged in S&T activities, in the management of S&T activities, and in providing direct service to S&T activities, who spend over 10% of the total working hours in a year in S&T activities. (1) Personnel directly engaged in S&T activities include researchers, engineers, technicians and other related personnel engaged in S&T activities in independent-accounting R&D institutions, institutions of higher learning, and in research institutes, laboratories, technology development centers and central experiment workshops under enterprises and institutions. Also included are people working in S&T research project teams, professional and technical personnel working in S&T information archiving institutes, and graduate students working on the design of their thesis. (2) Personnel engaged in the management of S&T activities and in providing direct service to S&T activities include senior management people responsible for S&T activities in independent-accounting R&D institutions, S&T information archiving institutes, institutions of higher learning, and in enterprises and institutions where S&T activities are undertaken. Also included are people responsible for the planning, administration, personnel management, financial management, logistics supply, equipment maintenance, information and library management that are related with S&T activities. People providing indirect services are excluded, such as security, medical service, drivers, plumbers, cleaners and those providing catering and related service. This indicator reflects the size of personnel engaged in S&T activities.

Scientists and Engineers refer to persons engaged in S&T activities who have obtained titles of senior and middle level professional positions, and those without such position but have completed university or higher education. This indicator reflects the quality of personnel engaged in S&T activities.

Research and Development (R&D) refers to systematic and creative activities in the field of science and technology aiming at increasing the knowledge and using the knowledge for new application. R&D includes 3 categories of activities: basic research, applied research and experiments and development. The scale and intensity of R&D are widely used internationally to reflect the strength of S&T and the core competitiveness of a country in the world.

Basic Research refers to empirical or theoretical research aiming at obtaining new knowledge on the fundamental principles of phenomena of observable facts to reveal the nature and law of movement of objects and to acquire new discoveries or new theories. Basic research takes no specific or designated application as the aim of the research. Results of basic research are mainly released or disseminated in the form of scientific papers or monographs. This indicator reflects the original innovation capacity of knowledge.

Applied Research refers to creative research aiming at obtaining new knowledge on a specific objective or target. Purpose of the applied research is to identify the possible use of results from basic research, or to explore new (fundamental) methods or new approaches. Results of applied research are expressed in the form of scientific papers, monographs, fundamental models or invention patents. This indicator reflects the exploration of ways to apply the results of basic research.

Experiments and Development refer to systematic activities aiming at using the knowledge from basic and applied researches or from practical experience to develop new products, materials and equipment, to establish new production process, systems and services, or to make substantial improvement on the existing products, process or services. Results of experiment and development activities are embodied in patents, exclusive technology, and monotype of new products or equipment. In social sciences, experiment and development activities refer to the process of converting the knowledge from basic or applied researches into feasible programmes (including conduct of demonstration projects for assessment and evaluation). There are no experiment and development activities in the science of humanities. This indicator reflects the capability of transferring the results of S&T into technique and products, which is the materialized measurement of S&T pushing forward the economic and social development.

R&D Personnel refer to persons engaged in research, management and supporting activities of R&D, including persons in the project teams, persons engaged in the management of S&T activities of enterprises and supporting staff providing direct service to the research projects. This indicator reflects the size of personnel engaged in R&D activities with independent intellectual property.

Full-time Equivalent of R&D Personnel refers to the sum of the full-time persons and the full-time equivalent of part-time persons converted by workload. For instance, if there are 2 full-time persons and 3 part-time workers (20%, 30% and 70% of working hours respectively on R&D activities), the full-time equivalent is 2+0.2+0.3+0.7=3.2 person-years. This is an internationally comparable indicator of input of personnel in S&T activities.

Professional and Technical Personnel refer to persons engaged in professional and technical work or in the management of professional and technical activities, i.e., people with professional or technical positions who are engaged in professional and technical work or in the management of professional and technical activities, and people without professional or technical positions but are working on professional or technical posts. They include professionals and technicians working in 17 categories of technical occupations including engineering, agriculture, scientific researches, medical service, teaching, economic research and application, accounting, statistics, translation, libraries, archives, cultural and museum service, journalism and publication, lawyers, notarization service, radio and television broadcasting, handicraft and fine arts, sports, performing art, and political workers in enterprises. This indicator reflects the condition of human resources in S&T.

Government Funds refer to funds obtained from government agencies at all levels to be used for S&T activities, including fund for scientific undertakings, 3 kinds of fund for S&T activities, fund for capital construction for scientific researches, science fund, funds from education expenditures by education departments for S&T activities, and extra-budget fund from government agencies for S&T activities.

Self-raised Funds by Enterprises refers to self-raised funds by enterprises from their own expenditure or from other enterprises and funds received by universities or research institutions from enterprises for scientific research or technical development projects. Excluded in this category are funds from government agencies, financial institutions or from foreign institutions.

Loans from Financial Institutions refer to loans from various financial institutions for S&T activities.

Internal Expenditures on S&T activities refer to the actual expenditures on S&T activities during the reference year, including service fees, expenditure on research activities, expenditure on research management, purchase or construction of fixed assets not included in the investment for capital construction, expenditure on capital construction for scientific researches, and other expenditures on S&T activities. Not included are expenditure on production activities, repayment of loans and transfer expenditure. This indicator reflects the real accomplishment of input in S&T.

Service Fees refer to direct or indirect payment, in cash or in kind, made to personnel engaged in S&T activities as remuneration and other fees. They include, in various forms, salaries, subsidies, bonus, benefits, retirement pension, stipend, etc. This indicator reflects the improvement of treatment toward S&T personnel.

Purchase or Construction of Fixed Assets refers to the fixed assets purchased or constructed using funds other than the investment in capital construction, and the actual expenditure on capital construction for scientific researches. In other words, it is the sum of the actual expenditure on fixed assets and the accomplished investment in capital construction for scientific researches. Fixed assets refer to main materials and equipment, literatures and documents in libraries, materials for experiments, specimen, instruments, furniture, buildings and constructions that can be used for a long time without changing the form and shape of those articles or constructions. This indictor reflects the input in improving the condition of S&T and the means of scientific research.

New Products refer to new products produced with new technology and new design, or products that represent noticeable improvement in terms of structure, material, or production process so as to improve significantly the character or function of the older versions. They include new products certified by relevant government agencies within the period of certification, as well as new products designed and produced by enterprises within a year without certification by government agencies. This indictor reflects the direct contribution of S&T output to economic growth.

Patent is an abbreviation for the patent right and refers to the exclusive right of ownership by the inventors or designers for the creation or inventions, given from the patent offices after due process of assessment and approval in accordance with the Patent Law. Patents are granted for inventions, utility models and designs. This indicator reflects the achievements of S&T and design with independent intellectual property.

Inventions refer to the inventions as specified by the patent law and its detailed rules and regulations for implementation. They refer to the new technical proposals to the products or methods or their modifications.

Utility Models refer to the utility models as specified by the patent law and its detailed rules and regulations for implementation. They refer to the practical and new technical proposals on the shape and structure of the product or the combination of both.

Designs refer to the designs as specified by the patent law and its detailed rules and regulation for implementation. They refer to the aesthetics and industry applicable new designs for the shape, pattern and color of the product, or their combinations.

Cultural Institutions refer to units which have their own organizational system and independent accounting system and specialize in or serve cultural development. They exclude other establishments run by these cultural institutions and amateur cultural groups established by various departments.

Art Troupe refers to the troupe which is engaged in drama, opera, music, dance, acrobatics or other art performance, opens independent accounts with banks and has self-supporting accounting system; excluding the troupes which are engaged partly in industrial or agricultural activities, partly in art performance and the professional troupes organized by the people.

Film Projection Units refer to units with film projection equipment, full or part time projectionists, permanent or non permanent places,approved by related administrative departments to show films regularly for certain groups of audience, including those film projection units which have been approved to give commercial shows and run business with independent accounting system as well as those filmrenting units of the military system.

Number of Spectators at Art Performance refers to the number of attendants at commercial shows, completely booked shows or free shows given in minority national areas,and does not include the number of spectators at rehearsals for examination and internal shows for study.

资源、环境

Natural Resources and Environment

Seventeen

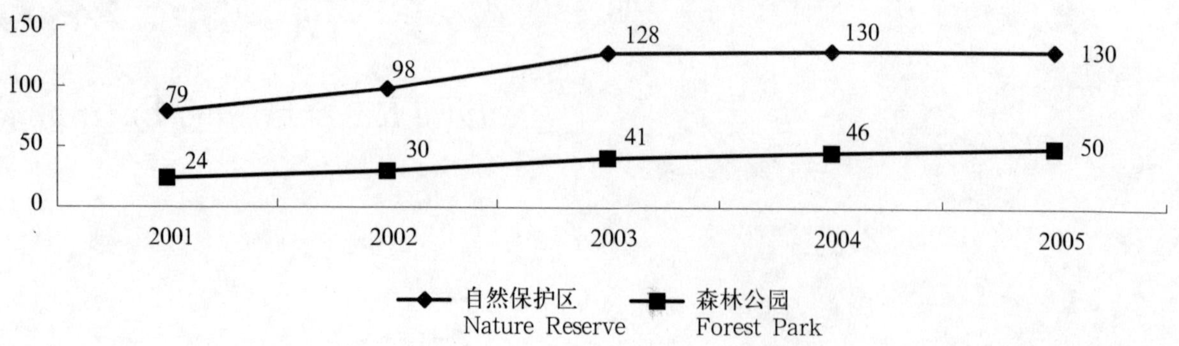
自然保护区、森林公园数（个）
Number of Nature Reserves and Forest Parks (unit)
150
100
50
0
79
98
128
130
130
24
30
41
46
50
2001
2002
2003
2004
2005
自然保护区
Nature Reserve
森林公园
Forest Park

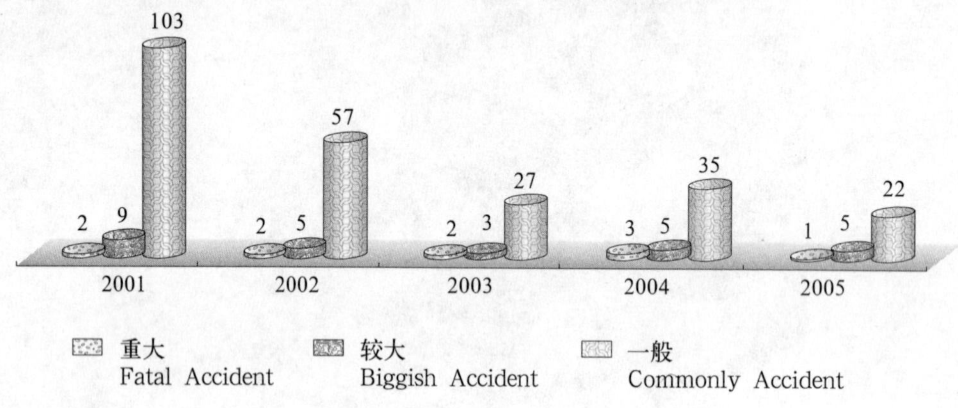
环境污染事故情况（起）
Environment Pollution Accidents (unit)
2
9
103
2
5
57
2
3
27
3
5
35
1
5
22
2001
2002
2003
2004
2005
重大
Fatal Accident
较大
Biggish Accident
一般
Commonly Accident

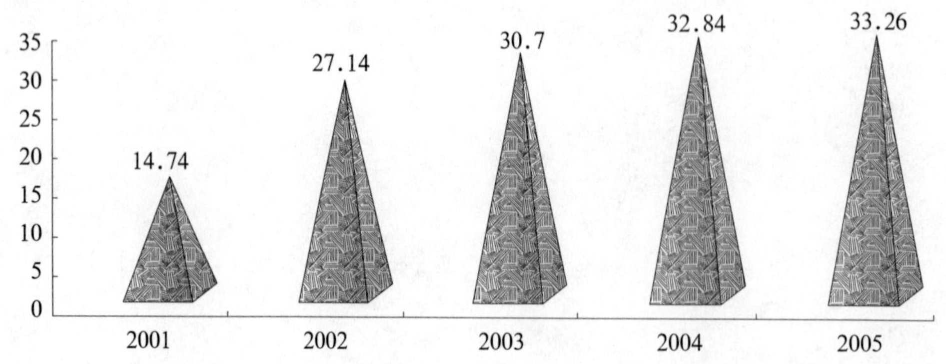
环保资金投入（亿元）
Environment Protection Investment (100 million yuan)
35
30
25
20
15
10
5
0
14.74
27.14
30.7
32.84
33.26
2001
2002
2003
2004
2005

17-1 主要河流（省内部分）主要特征值(2005)

Major Feature of Some Part of The Main River(2005)

水　系	Water System	流域面积（平方公里）Drainage Area(sq.km)	河长（千米）Length of River (1000 m)	平均坡降（‰）Average Slope Falling
长江流域	**Changjiang River Drainage**			
金沙江	Jinshajiang	4888	199	1.2
赤水河	Chishuihe	11412	299	2.3
乌江	Wujiang	66807	889	3.3
清水江	Qingshuijiang	17145	459	3.4
洪州河	Hongzhouhe	975	81	1.2
㵲阳河	Wuyanghe	6474	258	1.1
锦江	Jinjiang	4017	168	2.0
松桃河	Songtaohe	1536	88	2.3
珠江流域	**Zhujiang River Drainage**			
南盘江	Nanpanjiang	7651	264	1.6
北盘江	Beipanjiang	20982	318	3.1
红水河	Hongshuihe	15978	106	2.2
都柳江	Duliujiang	11586	330	3.8

17-2 主要矿产资源（2005）

Major Mineral Resources(2005)

名称	Item	计量单位	Unit	保有资源储量 Ensuned Reserves	累计查明资源储量 Basic Reserves (accumulative total)
矿产资源(保有储量)	**Mineral Resources (Ensured Reserves)**				
煤炭	Coal	亿吨	100 million tons	504.3	512.5
铁矿	Iron	矿石 亿吨	100 million tons	7.4	7.6
锰	Manganese	矿石万吨	10000 tons	7644.90	8799.40
钒矿	Vanadium	V205万吨	10000 tons	17.78	17.78
铜矿	Copper	铜万吨	10000 tons	7.94	8.18
铅	Plumbum	铅万吨	10000 tons	34.98	51.76
锌	Zincum	锌万吨	10000 tons	82.68	126.43
铝土矿	Bauxite Ore	矿石亿吨	100 million tons	4.2	4.5
镁(炼镁白云岩)	Magnesium	矿石万吨	10000 tons	3213.10	3213.30
汞	Hydrargyrum	汞万吨	10000 tons	3.30	9.37
锑	Antimony	锑万吨	10000 tons	23.29	50.54
金矿（岩金）	Gold mine	岩金金千克	kg	230248	253059
冶金用砂岩	Gritstone for Metallurgy	矿石万吨	10000 tons	8238.0	8264.7
硫铁矿	Pyrites Ore	矿石亿吨	100 million tons	6.1	6.2
重晶石	Barite Ore	矿石亿吨	100 million tons	1.1	1.2
磷矿	Phosphorus Ore	矿石亿吨	100 million tons	26.7	28.4
水泥用灰岩	Limestone for Cement	亿吨	100 million tons	16.4	17.1
玻璃用砂岩	Gritstone for Glass	矿石万吨	10000 tons	5124.0	5153.0

注：资料来源：省国土资源厅。

Note:Data in this table are obtained from land Department.

17-3 城市气象(2005)

Climate of Major Cities(2005)

城市名称	Name of City	年平均气温(℃) Annual Average Temperature(℃)	年降水量(毫米) Annual Precipitation(mm)	年日照时数(小时) Annual Sunshine Hours(hour)	相对湿度（%） Relative Temperature（%）
贵 阳 市	Guiyang	14.1	1067.5	1004.1	85
六盘水市	Liupanshui	12.8	1236.1	1260.5	78
遵 义 市	Zunyi	15.8	903.7	954.8	80
安 顺 市	Anshun	13.9	1172	1077.7	88
铜 仁 市	Tongren	17.5	898.8	1002.9	79
兴 义 市	Xingyi	16.6	1241.8	1448.8	82
毕 节 市	Bijie	13.2	766.4	1104.9	80
凯 里 市	Kaili	16	776.1	1033.1	82
都 匀 市	Duyun	16.3	973.8	974.3	82
赤 水 市	Chishui	17.8	1361.9	1045	89
清 镇 市	Qingzhen	14.4	1073.3	859.2	83
仁 怀 市	Renhuai	15.8	956.0	1002.9	81
福 泉 市	Fuquan	15.1	984.3	969.4	83

17-4 主要城市平均气温(2005)

Monthly Average Temperature of Major Cities(2005)

单位：℃

城市名称	Name of City	1月 Jan.	2月 Feb.	3月 Mar.	4月 Apr.	5月 May.	6月 June.	7月 July.	8月 Aug.	9月 Sept.	10月 Oct.	11月 Nov.	12月 Dec.
贵阳市	Guiyang	1.8	3.4	8.0	16.1	20.1	22.1	23.3	22.1	21.2	14.9	12.0	4.5
六盘水市	Liupanshui	2.7	6.4	8.4	14.4	18.9	19.5	20.6	19.3	18.0	13.1	9.9	2.7
遵义市	Zunyi	3.3	3.9	10.3	17.6	20.7	24.3	26.1	24.4	23.2	16.3	12.7	6.3
安顺市	Anshun	2.7	5.3	9.1	15.5	19.7	21.2	21.9	21.0	20.0	14.4	11.8	4.2
铜仁市	Tongren	3.7	4.4	11.2	19.9	22.2	26.7	29.0	26.4	25.5	18.4	14.6	8.0
兴义市	Xingyi	6.4	10.3	12.6	18.7	23.7	22.5	22.8	21.8	21.5	17.0	14.3	7.5
毕节市	Bijie	2.1	4.4	8.1	14.7	18.1	20.7	22.8	20.9	19.5	13.4	10.1	3.0
凯里市	Kaili	2.7	3.3	10.3	18.1	21.8	24.6	26.7	24.4	23.2	17.2	13.5	6.2
都匀市	Duyun	3.7	5.0	10.9	18.1	21.9	24.2	25.6	24.4	23.3	17.7	14.4	6.9
赤水市	Chishui	7.4	9.1	13.1	19.7	22.2	25.5	27.6	24.8	24.9	17.1	14.0	8.4
清镇市	Qingzhen	2.8	4.7	9.3	16.0	20.3	22.0	23.1	22.0	21.0	15.0	12.4	4.7
仁怀市	Renhuai	3.9	5.0	10.8	17.6	20.6	23.8	26.5	24.4	23.7	15.8	12.1	5.7
福泉市	Fuquan	2.4	3.0	9.7	16.8	20.9	23.5	24.9	23.4	21.9	16.0	12.7	5.5

17-5 “十五”时期各年森林资源基本情况

Basic Statistics on Forest Resource of Each Year in “Tenth Five-year Plan” Period

指 标	Item	2000	2001	2002	2003	2004	2005	2005年比2004年增长(%) Increase Rate in 2005 over 2004(%)
森林面积(含灌丛)(万公顷)	**Area of Forest (10000 hektare)**	543.00	543.00	543.00	613.00	613.00	613.00	持平
森林覆盖率(%)	Rate of Forest Covered (%)	30.83	30.83	30.83	34.90	34.90	34.90	持平
有林地覆盖率	Rate of Woodland Covered	25.66	25.66	25.66	29.73	29.73	29.73	持平
活立木总蓄积量(亿立方米)	Total Standing Fovest Stock (100 million stere)	2.10	2.10	2.10	2.11	2.11	2.11	持平
完成造林面积(万公顷)	Area of Fulfilled Forestation (10000 Ha.)	29.37	24.07	37.43	37.79	17.71	13.56	-23.4
封山育林面积	Area of Seal Mountain Pass for Forestation	30.23	21.47	13.25	8.03	11.13	13.19	18.5
实施退耕还林工程中:	**In Implement Cancel Infield for Forest Project**							
完成退耕地造林种草(万公顷)	Fulfilled Canael Infield Forestation and Grow Grass (10000 ha.)	1.33	0.75	15.35	17.34	3.33	4.66	39.9
宜林荒山造林	Forestation for Feasible deserted Mountain	0.47	1.30	15.35	17.35	11.03	6.66	-39.6
天然林保护工程中:	**In Savageness Forest Protect Project**							
完成飞播造林(万公顷)	Fulfilled Forestation by Airplane Planting (10000 ha.)		1.33	2.33	1.77	0.70	0.34	-51.4
封山育林(万公顷)	Seal Mountain Pass for Forestation (10000 Ha.)	10.75	2.42	4.63	5.92	4.85	4.95	2.1
森林火灾(起)	Forest Fire (unit)	648	817	1803	2154	1249	1148	-8.1
森林火灾受害率(‰)	Rate of Fall Victim for Forest Fire (‰)	0.32	0.32	0.60	0.53	0.31	0.33	7.5
森林病虫鼠害面积(万公顷)	Area of Fall Victim for Insect Pest(10000 ha.)			23.45	22.19	27.02	27.18	0.6
森林病虫鼠害防治面积	Prevention Area of Forest Insect Pest			18.20	17.57	22.74	22.79	0.2
森林病虫鼠害防治率(%)	Prevention Rate of Forest Insect Pest (%)			77.75	80.43	84.17	83.80	-0.4

17-6 “十五”时期各年自然保护区基本情况

Basic Statistics on Natural Reserves of Each Year in “Tenth Five-year Plan” Period

指 标 Item	2000	2001	2002	2003	2004	2005	2005年比2004年增长(%) Increase Rate in 2005 over 2004(%)
自然保护区个数(个) Number of Nature Reserves (unit)	**72**	**79**	**98**	**128**	**130**	**130**	**持平**
#国家级自然保护区 Nature Reserves of National-level	5	6	6	7	7	7	持平
省级自然保护区 Nature Reserves of Guizhou Province	3	3	3	3	3	4	33.3
地市级自然保护区 Nature Reserves of Region	11	11	12	22	22	22	持平
县级自然保护区 Nature Reserves of County	53	59	77	96	98	97	…
自然保护区面积(万公顷) Area of Nature Reserves (10000 hectare)	45.89	46.38	61.60	94.64	96.10	96.10	持平
自然保护区面积约占全省国土面积(%) Percentage of Nature Reserves in Guizhou Province Land(%)	2.6	2.6	3.5	5.4	5.5	5.5	持平
自然保护区中: In Nature Reserves							
森林生态系统、野生动、植物类型(个) Forest Biogeocenose,Wildness Animal and Plant(unit)	63	69	106	118	120	121	0.8
内陆湿地类型 Wetlands inside Land	8	8	8	8	8	8	持平
古生物遗迹类型 Ancient Biology Relic	1	1	1	1	1	1	持平

17-7 “十五”时期各年生态示范区、森林公园基本情况

Basic Statistics on the Section of Ecological Demonstration and Forest Park of Each Year in “Tenth Five-year Plan” Period

指 标 Item	2000	2001	2002	2003	2004	2005	2005年比2004年增长(%) Increase Rate in 2005 over 2004(%)
生态示范区 **The Section of Ecological Demonstration**							
国家级生态示范区(个) The Section of Ecological Demonstration of National-level(unit)	3	3	3	12	12	12	持平
省级生态示范乡镇 The Section of Ecological Demonstration of Guizhou Province-level			3	13	13	13	持平
当年推广省柴节煤灶(万户) The Scanty Kitchen Range Extended in This Year((10000 unit)				15.00	41.90		
新建沼气池(万口) The New Marsh Gas Pool in This Year (10000 unit)	2.63	3.61	21.82	10.74	12.20	21.24	74.1
森林公园 **Forest Park**							
森林公园(个) Forest Park (unit)	8	24	30	41	46	50	8.7
国家级森林公园(个) Forest Park of National-level	2	7	9	11	15	19	26.7
省级森林公园 Forest Park of Guizhou Province-level	6	14	18	22	21	23	9.5
森林公园面积(公顷) Area of Forest Park (hectare)	3.50	8.40		15.86	20.41	21.00	2.9
森林公园面积约占全省国土面积(%) Percentage of Forest Park in the Guizhou Province Land Area(%)	0.2	0.5		0.9	1.2	1.2	持平

17-8 “十五”时期各年水资源和水质监测情况

Basic Statistics on Water Resource and Inspeeting of Water Quality of Each Year in “Tenth Five-year Plan” Period

指 标 Item	2000	2001	2002	2003	2004	2005	2005年比2004年增长(%) Increase Rate in 2005 over 2004(%)
水资源总量（亿立方米） Total Water Resources(100 million cu.m)	**1217.5**	**972.5**	**1117.5**	**916.07**	**990.90**	**834.60**	**-15.8**
#地表水 Surface Water Resources	1217.5	972.5	1117.5	916.07	990.90	834.60	-15.8
人均水资源量（立方米） Per Capita Water Resources(cu.m/person)	3242	2560	1912	2367	2555	2123	-16.9
供水总量（亿立方米） Water Supply(100 million cu.m)	85.58	87.16	89.90	93.70	94.32	97.22	3.1
#地表水 Surface Water Supply	77.50	71.47	73.22	85.47	85.86	91.24	6.3
用水总量（亿立方米） Water Use(100 million cu.m)	84.18	87.16	89.90	93.70	94.32	97.22	3.1
河流水质 Water Quality of River							
监测河流(条) Inspected River (unit)	29	32	33	33	33	33	持平
监测河段断面(个) Inspected Section of River (unit)	64	73	73	74	74	74	持平
满足规定水质类别的断面占总监测断面百分比(%) Section of River of Satisfy I-III Genus Water Quality (%)	54.7	61.6		62.2	62.2	63.5	1.3 (百分点)
出境断面水质良好的断面(个) Favorable Water Quality Section of River of(unit)				12	12	12	持平
湖泊水质 Water Quality of Lake							
监测湖库(个) Inspect lake (unit)	5	7	7	7	8	8	持平
监测点 Inspect Point	20	23	23	23	25	25	持平
满足规定水质类别的测点占总监测点百分比(%) Section of River of Satisfy I-III Genus Water Quality(%)	10	26.1		43.5	32	12	-20.0 (百分点)

17-9 "十五"时期各年环保系统机构、人员数

Enviornmental Protection Agencies and Persons Engaged of Each Year in "Tenth Five-year Plan" Period

指 标	Item	2000	2001	2002	2003	2004	2005	2005年比2004年增长(%) Increase Rate in 2005 over 2004(%)
机构总数(个)	**Number of Agencies(unit)**	**272**	**261**	**259**	**276**	**310**	**284**	**-8.4**
#省	Province	5	4	4	12	12	4	-66.7
地	Prefecture	27	27	29	35	43	30	-30.2
县	County	205	211	207	226	231	227	-1.7
年末人员总数(人)	**Number of Staff and Workers(person)**	**1790**	**1930**	**1928**	**2074**	**2279**	**2277**	**-0.1**
#省	Province	251	236	236	334	329	253	-23.1
地	Prefecture	492	517	513	523	612	588	-3.9
县	County	903	1073	1076	1208	1265	1353	7.0
#科研人员	Scientific and Technical Personnel	95	91	94	112	106	107	0.9
监测人员	Monitoring Personal	577	585	568	586	602	613	1.8
监理人员	Supervising and Administrative Personnel	438	496	484	565	673	706	4.9

17-10 “十五”时期各年废水治理基本情况

Basic Statistics on Treatment of Waste Water of Each Year in “Tenth Five-year Plan” Period

指 标 Item	2000	2001	2002	2003	2004	2005	2005年比2004年增长(%) Increase Rate in 2005 over 2004(%)
废 水 **Waste Water**							
排放总量(亿吨) Total Waste Water Discharged (100 million tons)	5.54	5.57	5.33	5.55	5.57	5.57	持平
工业废水 Volume of Industrial Waste Water Discharged	2.06	2.08	1.72	1.68	1.61	1.49	-7.5
生活废水 Volume of Residential Waste Water Discharged	3.48	3.49	3.61	3.87	3.96	4.08	3.0
废水中化学需氧排放量(万吨) Totel Emission of Oxygen Needed by Chemistry(10000 tons)	22.79	20.69	20.52	22.03	22.33	22.56	1.0
工业废水 Industrial Sector	5.15	3.01	2.70	2.54	2.31	2.25	-2.6
生活污水 Residential Sector	17.64	17.68	17.82	19.49	20.02	20.31	1.4
水污染防治 **Prevention of Water Pollution**							
工业废水排放达标率(%) Up-to-standard Rate of Industrial Sewage Discharge(%)	47.41	58.21	56.79	55.97	58.20	67.70	16.3 (百分点)
当年完成工业废水治理项目(个) Father Item of Industry Waste Water in This Year(unit)	100	92	92	75	108	175	62.0
新增废水治理能力(万吨/日) Newly Desinged Treatment and Utilization Capacity of Waste Water (10000 tons/day)	8.80	11.60	10.66	25.13	21.94	34.90	59.1
城市污水处理率(%) Rate of Treatment of City Waste Water (%)		3.3	2.4	2.8	10.3	21.1	10.8 (百分点)

17-11 "十五"时期各年空气质量及空气污染治理情况

Atmosphere Quality and Treatment of Industrial Waste Gas of Each Year in "Tenth Five-year Plan" Period

指 标 Item	2000	2001	2002	2003	2004	2005	2005年比2004年增长(%) Increase Rate in 2005 over 2004(%)
城市空气质量 **Atmosphere Quality of City**							
达到国家环境空气质量二级标准城市(个) Reach the Second National-Level Standard of Atmosphere Quality of City (unit)		2	2	5	4	7	75.0
占统计城市数(%) Percentage in Total (%)		16.7	16.7	41.7	33.3	58.3	25.0 (百分点)
城市空气污染物 **Contamination in City Atmosphere**							
二氧化硫年均浓度值(毫克/立方米) Annud Average So2 Concentration in Downtown(mg/cu.m)	0.11	0.08	0.08	0.07	0.07	0.06	-7.7
达到国家空气质量二级标准城市(个) Reach the Second National-Level Standard of Atmosphere Quality of City (unit)	3	3	3	5	4	7	75.0
二氧化氮年均浓度值(毫克/立方米) Annual Average NO2 Concentration in Downtown(mg/cu.m)	0.03	0.02	0.02	0.02	0.02	0.02	-5.0
达到国家空气质量一级标准城市(个) Reach National-Level Standard of Atmosphere Quality of City(unit)	10	11	12	12	12	12	持平
城市总悬浮颗粒物年均浓度值(毫克/立方米) Average Chroma of City Suspend Grain(mg./stere)	0.23	0.19	0.19	0.16	0.15	0.13	-11.6
达到国家空气质量二级标准城市(个) Reach The Second National-Level Standard of Atmosphere Quality of City (unit)	5	7	7	10	12	12	持平
废气中污染物排放 **Contamination Discharged of Exhaust Gas**							
二氧化硫排放总量(万吨) Discharged Volume of SO2(10000 tons)	145.01	138.12	134.11	132.29	131.50	135.80	3.3
#工业 Industrial	64.25	57.14	57.71	57.03	59.98	65.94	9.9

17-11续表（continued）

指 标 Item	2000	2001	2002	2003	2004	2005	2005年比2004年增长(%) Increase Rate in 2005 over 2004(%)
生活及其它废气中二氧化硫排放量 Discharged Volume of SO2 from Living and Other Exhaust	80.76	80.98	76.40	75.26	71.52	69.86	-2.3
烟尘排放总量 Total Volume of Dust Emission	50.57	49.52	45.79	39.13	32.14	36.38	13.2
#工业 Industrial	34.24	28.17	26.27	22.21	18.48	20.51	11.0
生活及其它废气中烟尘排放量 Discharged Volume of Dusts from Living	16.33	21.35	19.52	16.92	13.65	15.87	16.3
工业粉尘排放量 Volume of Industrial Dust Emission	40.62	24.99	24.08	25.34	24.91	19.12	-23.2
空气污染治理 **Discharged Volume of Industrial Dust Emission**							
工业废气中： In Industrial Exhaust Gas							
二氧化硫去除率(%) Wipe off Rate of SO2 (%)	11.7	16.3	16.1	17.5	22.0	21.3	-0.7 (百分点)
烟尘去除率(%) Wipe off Rate of Soot	89.0	91.9	93.9	94.7	96.1	96.0	-0.1 (百分点)
工业粉尘去除率(%) Wipe off Rate of Industrial Dust Emission（%）	54.2	74.4	81.6	82.0	80.4	86.1	5.7 (百分点)
当年完成废气治理项目(个) Exhaust Gas Treatment Item of Fulfilled in This Year (unit)	229	77	104	95	111	142	27.9
新增废气治理能力(万标立方米/小时) New Exhaust Gas Treatment Capacity in This Year (10000 stere/hour)	388.20	350.04	199.57	210.96	365.34	1093.38	199.3
各城市建成烟尘控制区(个) Soot Cortral Section of City (unit)	59	57	58	79	82	54	-34.1
各城市建成烟尘控制区面积(平方公里) Area of Soot Cortral Section in City (sq.km)	201.5	203.4	211.0	267.4	319.9	344.6	7.7
城市燃气普及率(%) Popularization Rate of City Coal Gas (%)		24.5	46.4	49.5	51.3	54.5	3.2 (百分点)

17-12 “十五”时期各年固体废物产生及处理情况

Production and Treatment of Industrial Solid Wastes of Each Year in “Tenth Five-year Plan” Period

指 标 Item	2000	2001	2002	2003	2004	2005	2005年比2004年增长(%) Increase Rate in 2005 over 2004(%)
工业固体废物产生量(万吨) Produced Volume of Industrial Solid Wastes(10000 tons)	**2271.80**	**2367.43**	**2878.68**	**3771.59**	**4560.09**	**4854.38**	**6.5**
工业固体废物排放量 Discharged Volume of Industrial Solid Wastes	410.70	342.03	238.43	318.48	216.62	131.28	-39.4
生活垃圾清运总量 Produced Volume of Subsistence Wastes			397	434	440	383	-13.0
工业固体废物治理 Treatment of Industrial Solid Wastes							
工业固体废物综合利用量(万吨) Colligate Using Volume of Industrial Solid Wastes (10000 tons)	689.00	860.29	839.85	1104.56	1838.47	1658.39	-9.8
工业固体废物处置量 Treatment Volume of Industrial Solid Wastes	362.79	437.07	893.14	1324.94	1266.64	1936.98	52.9
工业固体废物综合利用率(%) Rate of Treatment of Industrial Solid Wastes	30.3	36.3	29.0	29.2	40.3	34.1	-6.2(百分点)
当年完成工业固体废物治理项目(个) Item of Industrial Solid Wastes had been Fulfilled in This Year (unit)	9	17	20	11	22	29	31.8
新增固体废物治理能力(万吨/日) Newly Desinged Treatment and Utilization Capacity of Solid Wastes(10000 tons/day)	0.18	1.86	2.15	0.48	3.83	32.80	756.4
生活垃圾处理总量(万吨) Produced Volume of Industrial Solid Wastes (10000 tons)		236.00	234.00	273.69	319.07	299.51	-6.1
#无害化处理量 Volume of Wastes Disposed		45.00	43.74	48.80	80.50	102.10	26.8
城市生活垃圾无害化处理率(%) Treatment Rate of Consumption Wastes in Cities(%)		3.2	10.9	11.3	18.3	26.7	8.4(百分点)

17-13 "十五"时期各年环境污染事故情况

Accident of Environment Pollution of Each Year in "Tenth Five-year Plan" Period

指 标 Item	2000	2001	2002	2003	2004	2005	2005年比2004年增长(%) Increase Rate in 2005 over 2004(%)
环境污染事故(起) Namber of Environment Pollution Accidents(unit)	**54**	**114**	**64**	**32**	**43**	**28**	**-34.9**
#重大事故 Fatal Accident		2	2	2	3	1	-66.7
较大事故 Biggish Accident	5	9	5	3	5	5	持平
一般事故 Commonly Accident	49	103	57	27	35	22	-37.1
#水污染事故 Water Pollution Accident	26	40	16	18	30	17	-43.3
空气污染事故 Air Pollution Accident	27	55	42	12	9	10	11.1
污染事故直接经济损失(万元) Direct Economy Losses on Pollute Accident (10000 yuan)	**39.83**	**151.80**	**143.30**	**43.30**	**38.20**	**57.90**	**51.6**

17-14 "十五"时期各年自然灾害基本情况

Basic Statistics on Natural Disasters of Each Year in "Tenth Five-year Plan" Period

指 标	Item	2000	2001	2002	2003	2004	2005	2005年比2004年增长(%) Increase Rate in 2005 over 2004(%)
遭受自然灾害县个数(个)	County of Suffer from Natural Disasters(unit)	86	86	86	87	86	88	2.3
受灾人口(万人)	The Population of be hit by Natural Disasters (10000 person)	2285.33	2303.73	2184.16	2469.8	1744.42	2326.49	33.4
农作物受灾面积(万公顷)	Area of Crop had been hit by Nature Disasters(10000 ha)	137.35	174.53	187.52	159.2	93.90	129.04	37.4
#绝收面积	The Gainless Area of Crop for Nature Disasters	19.77	34.27	34.29	26.9	14.19	23.81	67.6
因自然灾害造成直接经济损失(亿元)	The Direct Economy Losing for Nature Disasters (100 million yuan)	52.78	46.22	78.72	55.0	24.0	34.2	42.5

17-15 “十五”时期各年环境保护资金投入情况

Investment in Environment Protection of Each Year in “Tenth Five-year Plan” Period

单位:亿元(100 million yuan)

指 标 Item	2000	2001	2002	2003	2004	2005	2005年比2004年增长(%) Increase Rate in 2005 over 2004(%)
环保资金投入 Investment in Environment Protection	**10.98**	**14.74**	**27.14**	**30.70**	**32.84**	**33.26**	**1.3**
环保资金投入占生产总值(%) Investment in Environment Protection as Percent of GDP(%)	1.1	1.4	2.3	2.3	2.1	1.7	-0.4(百分点)
环保资金投入中: In Investment of Environment Protection							
#老工业污染源治理 Old Industry Pollute Fountain Treatment	2.37	1.63	2.13	2.63	4.56	7.79	70.8
建设项目“三同时”污染防治 Santongshi Pollution Prevention of Constructive Item	1.60	1.23	0.91	1.94	1.42	1.80	26.8
城市环境基础设施建设 Foundation Establishment Construct of City Environment	4.11	8.01	19.93	21.80	22.13	18.01	-18.6
环境管理能力建设 Capacity Construct of Environment Management	0.07	0.08	0.14	0.20	0.24	0.33	37.5
工业污染治理设施运行费用 Function Expense of Industry Pollution Treatment	2.84	3.78	4.03	4.13	4.48	5.33	19.0
全省征收排污费总额 Totel Expense of Collection Discharged Wastes	0.78	0.85	1.14	1.39	2.22	3.40	53.2

主要统计指标解释

国土 指中华人民共和国国家管辖下的领土、领海和领空。

气候 指地球与大气之间长期能量交换与质量交换所形成的一种自然环境状态，它是多种因素综合作用的结果。气候既是人类生活和生产的环境要素之一，又是供给人类生活和生产的重要资源。气温、降水、湿度等气象要素的多年平均值是用来描述一个地区气候状况的主要参数，而各种气象要素某年、某月的平均值(或总量)则可以反映出该时期天气气候状况的重要特征。

自然资源 指人类可以直接从自然界获得，并用于生产和生活的物质资源。自然资源一般可以分成可再生资源和非再生资源两大类。可再生资源指在较短时间内可以再生、可以循环利用的资源，包括土地资源、水资源、气候资源、生物资源和海洋资源等。非再生资源指在使用后不能再生的资源，包括矿产资源和地热能源。

土地资源 土地指陆地的表层部分，它主要由岩石、岩石的风化物和土壤构成。土地资源按利用类型可以分为农用地、建筑用地和未利用地。农用地包括耕地、园地、林地、牧草地和水面。建筑用地包括居民点及工矿用地、交通用地和水利设施用地。未利用地指农用地和建筑用地以外的土地，包括滩涂、荒漠、戈壁、冰川和石山等。

耕地面积 指经过开垦用以种植农作物并经常进行耕耘的土地面积。包括种有作物的土地面积、休闲地、新开荒地和抛荒未满三年的土地面积。

森林资源 指森林、林木、林地以及依托森林、林木、林地生存的野生动物、植物和微生物。林木指树木和竹子。森林指以乔木为主体的植物群落，是集生的乔木及与共同作用的植物、动物、微生物和土壤、气候等的总体。

活立木总蓄积量 指一定范围内土地上全部树木蓄积的总量，包括森林蓄积、疏林蓄积、散生木蓄积和四旁树蓄积。

森林面积 指由乔木树种构成，郁闭度 0.2 以上(含 0.2)的林地或冠幅宽度 10 米以上的林带的面积，即有林地面积。森林面积包括天然起源和人工起源的针叶林面积、阔叶林面积、针阔混交林面积和竹林面积，不包括灌木林地面积和疏林地面积。

森林蓄积量 指一定森林面积上存在着的林木树干部分的总材积。它是反映一个国家或地区森林资源总规模和水平的基本指标之一，也是反映森林资源的丰富程度、衡量森林生态环境优劣的重要依据。

森林覆盖率 指一个国家或地区森林面积占土地总面积的百分比。森林覆盖率是反映森林资源的丰富程度和生态平衡状况的重要指标。在计算森林覆盖率时，森林面积包括郁闭度 0.2 以上的乔木林地面积和竹林地面积，国家特别规定的灌木林地面积、农田林网以及四旁(村旁、路旁、水旁、宅旁)林木的覆盖面积。计算公式为：

森林覆盖率(%)=森林面积/土地总面积×100%

水资源 水在自然界中以固体、液体和气态三种聚集状态存在，分布于海洋、陆地(包括土壤)以及大气之中，通过水循环形成水资源。水资源包括经人类控制并直接可供灌溉、发电、给水、航运、养殖等用途的地表水和地下水，以及江河、湖泊、井、泉、潮汐、港湾和养殖水域等。水资源是发展国民经济不可缺少的重要自然资源。

地表水和地下水 陆地上的水因空间分布不同，分为地表水和地下水。地表水指分别存在于河流、湖泊、沼泽、冰川和冰盖等水体中水分的总称，又称陆地水。地下水指储存在地面以下饱和岩土孔隙、裂隙及溶洞中的水。

矿产资源 矿产指由地质作用形成,富集于地壳中或出露于地表达到工农业利用要求的有用矿物。矿产是一种重要的自然资源,是社会发展的重要物质基础。

流域 每条河流都有自己的干流和支流,干支流共同组成这条河流的水系。每条河流都有自己的集水区域,这个集水区域就称为该河流的流域。

气温 指空气的温度,我国一般以摄氏度(℃)为单位表示。气象观测的温度表是放在离地面约 1.5 米处通风良好的百叶箱里测量的,因此,通常说的气温指的是离地面 1.5 米处百叶箱中的温度。其统计计算方法为:

月平均气温是将全月各日的平均气温相加,除以该月的天数而得。

年平均气温是将 12 个月的月平均气温累加后除以 12 而得。

相对湿度 指空气中实际所含水蒸气密度和同温度下饱和水蒸气密度的百分比值。其统计方法与气温相同。

降水量 指从天空降落到地面的液态或固态(经融化后)水,未经蒸发、渗透、流失而在地面上积聚的深度。其统计计算方法为:

月降水量是将全月各日的降水量累加而得。

年降水量是将 12 个月的月降水量累加而得。

日照时数 指太阳实际照射地面的时间。其统计方法与降水量相同

水资源总量 一定区域内的水资源总量指当地降水形成的地表和地下产水量，即地表径流量与降水入渗补给量之和,不包括过境水量。

用水总量 指分配给用户的包括输水损失在内的毛用水量。按用户特性分为农业、工业、生活和生态用水四大类。

农业用水 包括农田灌溉和林牧渔业用水。林牧渔业用水指林果地灌溉、草地灌溉和鱼塘补水。

工业用水 按新水取用量计,不包括企业内部的重复利用水量。

生活用水 包括城镇生活用水和农村生活用水。城镇生活用水由居民用水和公共用水(含服务业、商饮业、货运邮电业及建筑业等用水)组成;农村生活用水除居民生活用水外,还包括畜用水在内。

工业废水排放量 指经过企业厂区所有排放口排到企业外部的工业废水量。包括生产废水、外排的直接冷却水、超标排放的矿井地下水和与工业废水混排的厂区生活污水,不包括外排的间接冷却水(清污不分流的间接冷却水应计算在内)。

工业废水排放达标量 指报告期内废水中各项污染物指标都达到国家或地方排放标准的外排工业废水量,包括未经处理外排达标的,经废水处理设施处理后达标排放的,以及经污水处理厂处理后达标排放的。

工业废水排放达标率 指工业废水排放达标量占工业废水排放量的百分率,计算公式为:

工业废水排放达标率=工业废水排放达标量/工业废水排放量×100%

城镇生活污水排放量 指城镇居民每年排放的生活污水。用人均系数法测算。测算公式为:

城镇生活污水排放量=城镇生活污水排放系数×市镇非农业人口×365

城镇生活污水中化学需氧量(COD)产生量 指城镇居民每年排放的生活污水中的 COD 的产生量。用人均系数法测算。测算公式为:

城镇生活污水中 COD 产生量=城镇生活污水中 COD 产生系数×市镇非农业人口×365

化学需氧量(COD) 测量有机和无机物质化学所消耗氧的质量浓度的水污染指数。

工业废气排放量 指报告期内企业厂区内燃料燃烧和生产工艺过程中产生的各种排入大气的含有污染物的气体的总量,以标准状态(273K,101325Pa)计算。测算公式为:

工业废气排放量=燃料燃烧过程中废气排放量+生产工艺过程中废气排放量

生活及其他 SO_2 排放量 以生活及其他煤炭消费量和其含硫量为基础,根据以下公式计算:

生活及其他 SO_2 排放量=生活及其他煤炭消费量×含硫量×0.8×2

工业 SO_2 排放量 指报告期内企业在燃料燃烧和生产工艺过程中排入大气的 SO_2 总量,计算公式为:

工业 SO_2 排放量=燃料燃烧过程中 SO_2 排放量+生产工艺过程中 SO_2 排放量

工业烟尘排放量 指企业厂区内燃料燃烧过程中产生的烟气中夹带的颗粒物排放量。

生活及其他烟尘排放量 指除工业生产活动以外的所有社会、经济活动及公共设施的经营活动中燃烧所排放的烟尘纯重量。以生活及其他煤炭消费量为基础进行测算。

工业粉尘排放量 指企业在生产工艺过程中排放的能在空气中悬浮一定时间的固体颗粒物排放量。如钢铁企业的耐火材料粉尘、焦化企业的筛焦系统粉尘、烧结机的粉尘、石灰窑的粉尘、建材企业的水泥粉尘等。不包括电厂排入大气的烟尘。

工业固体废物产生量 指报告期内企业在生产过程中产生的固体状、半固体状和高浓度液体状废弃物的总量,包括危险废物、冶炼废渣、粉煤灰、炉渣、煤矸石、尾矿、放射性废物和其他废物等;不包括矿山开采的剥离废石和掘进废石(煤矸石和呈酸性或碱性的废石除外)。酸性或碱性废石指采掘的废石其流经水、雨淋水的 pH 值小于 4 或 pH 值大于 10.5 者。

危险废物 指列入国家危险废物名录或根据国家规定的危险废物鉴别标准和鉴别方法认定的,具有爆炸性、易燃性、易氧化性、毒性、腐蚀性、易传染疾病等危险特性之一的废物。

工业固体废物综合利用量 指报告期内企业通过回收、加工、循环、交换等方式,从固体废物中提取或者使其转化为可以利用的资源、能源和其他原材料的固体废物量(包括当年利用往年的工业固体废物贮存量),如用作农业肥料、生产建筑材料、筑路等。综合利用量由原产生固体废物的单位统计。

工业固体废物综合利用率 指工业固体废物综合利用量占工业固体废物产生量(包括综合利用往年贮存量)的百分率。计算公式为:

工业固体废物综合利用率=工业固体废物综合利用量/工业固体废物产生量+综合利用往年贮存量×100%

工业固体废物贮存量 指报告期内企业以综合利用或处置为目的,将固体废物暂时贮存或堆存在专设的贮存设施或专设的集中堆存场所内的数量。专设的固体废物贮存场所或贮存设施必须有防扩散、防流失、防渗漏、防止污染大气、水体的措施。

工业固体废物处置量 指报告期内企业将固体废物焚烧或者最终置于符合环境保护规定要求的场所,并不再回取的工业固体废物量(包括当年处置往年的工业固体废物贮存量)。处置方式有填埋(其中危险废物应安全填埋)、焚烧、专业贮存场(库)封场处理、深层灌注、回填矿井及海洋处置(经海洋管理部门同意投海处置)等。

工业固体废物排放量 指报告期内企业将所产生的固体废物排到固体废物污染防治设施、场所以外的数量,不包括矿山开采的剥离废石和掘进废石(煤矸石和呈酸性或碱性的废石除外)。

"三废"综合利用产品产值 指报告期内利用"三废"作为主要原料生产的产品价值(现行价);已经销售或准备销售的应计算产品价值,留作生产自用的不应计算产品价值。

生活垃圾清运量 指报告期内收集和运送到垃圾处理厂(场)的生活垃圾数量。生活垃圾指城市日常生活或为城市日常生活提供服务的活动中产生的固体废物以及法律行政规定的视为城市生活垃圾的固体废物。包括:居民生活垃圾、商业垃圾、集市贸易市场垃圾、街道清扫垃圾、公共场所垃圾和机关、学校、厂矿等单位的生活垃圾。

生活垃圾无害化处理率 指报告期生活垃圾无害化处理量与生活垃圾产生量比率。在统计上,由于生活垃圾产生量不易取得,可用清运量代替。计算公式为:

生活垃圾无害化处理率=生活垃圾无害化处理量/生活垃圾产生量×100%

造林总面积 指报告期内在荒山、荒地、沙丘、退耕地等一切可以造林的土地上,采用人工播种、飞机播种、植苗造林、分植造林等方法新植成片乔木林和灌木林,经过检查验收符合《造林技术规程》要求的单位面积株数,并按《中华人民共和国森林法实施条例》规定,成活率达 85%以上(含 85%,年降雨量在 400 毫米以下且无浇灌条件的地区造林成活率达70%以上)的总面积。四旁植树如一侧在四行以上,连片面积0.066公顷(一亩)以上,应统计在造林面积内。造林面积,通常按所有制(国有、国有集体合作、集体和个人)、造林方式(人工、飞机播种)、主要林种用途(用材林、经济林、防护林、薪炭林、特种用途林)分组进行统计。

退耕还林还草工程 是我国林业建设上涉及面最广、政策性最强、工序最复杂、群众参与度最高的生态建设工程。主要解决重点地区的水土流失问题。

自然保护区 指对有代表性的自然生态系统、珍稀濒危野生动植物物种的天然分布区、水源涵养区、有特殊意义的自然历史遗迹等保护对象所在的陆地、陆地水体或海域,依法划出一定面积进行特殊保护和管理的区域。以县及县以上各级人民政府正式批准建立的自然保护区为准(包括"六五"以前由部门或"革委会"批准且现仍存在的自然保护区)。风景名胜区、文物保护区不计在内。

生态示范区 指省级以上环境保护行政主管部门批准,以省、地、县政府为主按批准的生态示范区建设规划实施的行政区域。包括已经过国家或省级环境保护行政主管部门验收的和正在开展试点工作的。

环境污染与破坏事故 指由于违反环境保护法规的经济、社会活动与行为,以及意外因素的影响或不可抗拒的自然灾害等原因,致使环境受到污染,国家重点保护的野生动植物、自然保护区受到破坏,人体健康受到危害,社会经济和人民财产受到损失,造成不良社会影响的突发性事件。

环境污染治理投资 指在工业污染源治理和城市环境基础设施建设的资金投入中,用于形成固定资产的资金。包括工业新老污染源治理工程投资、建设项目"三同时"环保投资,以及城市环境基础设施建设所投入的资金。

Explanatory Notes on Main Statistical Indicators

Territory refers to territorial land, sea and air space under the administration of the People′s Republic of China.

Climate refers to the natural environmental status formed by the long–term exchange of energy and mass between the earth and the air, and is the results of interaction of many factors. Climate is both one of the environment factors and the important resources for the living and production activities of the human being. The average values across several years of meteorological factors such as temperature, rainfall and humidity are used as important parameters to describe the climate of a region, while the average values (or total values) of a given year or month of meteorological factors reflect the key characteristics of climate for that period of time.

Natural Resources refer to material resources that could be obtained from the nature by human being and used for production and living. Natural resources in general can be classified as renewable resources and non–renewable resources. Renewable resources refer to resources that could be renewed and recycled during a relatively short period of time, including land resource, water resource, climate resource, biology resource and marine resource. Non–renewable resources include resources that could not be renewed, such as minerals and geothermal resource.

Land Resource Land refers to the surface of the earth, consisting of mainly rocks and its weathering and earth. Land resource can be classified, by its utilization, as land for agriculture, land for construction and unused land. Land for agriculture includes cultivated land, plantation land, forestland, grassland and waters. Land for construction includes land for residential purpose, for manufacturing and mining, for transportation and for water–conservancy projects. Unused land refers to land other than land for agriculture and construction, including beaches, deserts, Gobi, glaciers and rock mountains.

Area of Cultivated Land refers to area of land reclaimed for the regular cultivation of various farm crops, including crop–cover land, fallow, newly reclaimed land and land laid idle for less than 3 years.

Forest Resource refers to forests, trees, forestland and wild animals, plants and microorganism that live on forest and trees. Trees include trees and bamboo. Forest refers to the population of clusters of trees and other plants, animals and microorganism as well as the earth and climate that have interactions with the trees.

Forest Area refers to the area of forest where trees and bamboo grow with canopy density above 0.2, including land of natural woods and planted woods, but excluding bush land and thin forest land. It reflects the total areas of afforestation.

Stock Volume of Forest refers to total stock volume of wood growing in forest area, which shows the total size and level of forest resources of a country or a region. It is also an important indicator illustrating the richness of forest resource and the status of forest ecological environment.

Forest Coverage Rate refers to the ratio of area of afforested land to total land area. It is a very important indicator that reflects the status of abundance of forest resource and ecosystem balance. Forest area includes the area of trees and bamboo grow with canopy density above 0.2, the area of shrubby tree according to regulations of the government, the area of forest land inside farm land and the area of trees planted by the side of villages, farm houses and along roads and rivers. The formula for calculating forest coverage rate is as follows:

Forestry coverage rate (%)= (Area of Afforested Land/Area of Total Land) x 100%

Water Resource Water exists in the nature in solid, liquid and gaseous states, is distributed in the ocean, land (including earth) and air, and constitutes the water resource through the circulation of water. Water resource includes the surface water and underground water that is controlled by the human being for irrigation, power-generation, water supply, navigation and cultivation. It also includes rivers, lakes, wells, springs, tides, gulf and water area for cultivation. Water resource as an important natural resource is indispensable for the development of the national economy.

Surface Water and Underground Water Water on earth can be divided into surface water and underground water according to its distribution. Surface water refers to moisture exists in rivers, lakes, swamps, glaciers, icecaps and so on. It is also called land water. The underground water refers to water deposited underground in the cranny and the hole of saturated rock soil and in the water-eroded cave.

Mineral Resources refer to useful minerals that can be used for industrial or agricultural purposes enriched in lithosphere or on earth due to the geological process. Minerals are important natural resources, and important material base for social development.

Drainage Area Each river has its own main stream and branches to form the water system of the river. Each river has its own catchment′s area, which is also called as the drainage area of the river.

Temperature refers to the air temperature. China uses centigrade as the unit. The thermometry used for weather observation is put in a breezy shutter, which is 1.5 meters high from the ground. Therefore, the commonly used temperature refers to the temperature in the breezy shutter 1.5 meters away from the ground. The calculation method is as follows:

Monthly average temperature is the summation of average daily temperature of one month divided by the actual days of that particular month.

Annual average temperature is the summation of monthly average of a year divided by 12 months.

Relative Humidity refers to the ratio of actual water vapor pressure to the saturation water vapor density under the current temperature. The statistical method is the same as that of temperature.

Volume of Precipitation refers to the deepness of liquid state or solid state (thawed) water falling from the sky to the ground that has not been evaporated, infiltrated or run off. The calculation method is as follows:

Monthly precipitation is the summation of daily precipitation of a month.

Annual precipitation is the summation of 12 months precipitation of a year.

Sunshine Hours refer to the actual hours of sun irradiating the earth. The calculation method is the same as that of the precipitation.

Total Water Resources refers to total volume of water resources measured as run-off for surface water from rainfall and recharge for groundwater in a given area, excluding transit water.

Water Use refers to gross water use distributed to users, including loss during transportation, broken down with use by agriculture, industry, living consumption and biological protection.

Water Use by Agriculture includes uses of water by irrigation of farming fields and by forestry, animal husbandry and fishing. Water use by forestry, animal husbandry and fishing includes irrigation of forestry and orchards, irrigation of grassland and replenishment of fishing pools.

Water Use by Industry refers to new withdrawals of water, excluding reuse of water within enterprises.

Water Use by Living Consumption includes use of water for living consumption in both urban and rural areas. Urban water use by living consumption is composed of household use and public use (including services, commerce, restaurants, cargo transportation, posts, telecommunication and construction). Rural water use by living consumption includes both households and animals.

Waste Water Discharged by Industry refers to the volume of waste water discharged by industrial enterprises through all their outlets, including waste water from production process, directly cooled water, groundwater from mining wells which does not meet discharge standards and sewage from households mixed with waste water produced by industrial activities, but excluding indirectly cooled water discharged (It should be included if the discharge is not separated with waste water).

Industrial Waste Water Meeting Discharge Standards refers to volume of industrial waste water discharge which, with or without treatment, reaches national or local standards with regard to all pollutants.

Ratio of Industrial Waste Water Meeting Discharge Standards refers to percentage of industrial waste water meeting discharge standards over total industrial waste water discharge. It is calculated as:

Ratio of industrial waste water meeting discharge standards = industrial waste water meeting discharge standards / total industrial waste water discharge

Urban Non–industrial Waste Water Discharge refers to annual discharge of non–industrial waste water by urban households. It is estimated by per capita coefficient using the formula:

Urban non–industrial waste water discharge = urban non–industrial waste water discharge coefficient urban non–agricultural population 365

Volume of Chemical Oxygen Demand(COD) Generated by Urban Non–industrial Waster Water refers to chemical oxygen demand generated through the annual discharge of non–industrial waste water by urban households. It is estimated as:

Volume of chemical oxygen demand (cod) generated by urban non–industrial waster water = Coefficient of COD generated through urban non–industrial waste water urban non–agricultural population 365

Chemical Oxygen Demand (COD) refers to index of water pollution measuring the mass concentration of oxygen consumed by the chemical breakdown of organic and inorganic matter.

Industrial Waste Air Emission refers to discharge into atmosphere of waste air containing pollutants generated from fuel burning and production process in enterprises within a given period of time. It is calculated at standard status (273K, 101325Pa) as:

Industrial waste air emission = emission through fuel burning + emission through production process

SO_2 Emission through Non–industrial and Other Activities is calculated on the basis of consumption of coal by households and other activities and the sulphur content of coal with the following formula:

SO_2 emission through non–industrial and other activities = consumption of coal by households and other activities sulphur content 0.8 2

SO_2 Emission through Industrial Activities refers to volume of sulphur dioxide emission from fuel burning and production process by enterprises during a given period of time. It is calculated as:

SO_2 emission through industrial activities = SO2 emission from fuel burning + SO2 emission from production process

Industrial Soot Emission refers to volume of soot in smoke emitted in process of fuel burning in premises of enterprises.

Soot Emission by Consumption and Others refers to net volume of soot emitted by fuel burning from all social and economic activities and operation of public facilities other than industrial activities. It is calculated on the basis of coal consumption by households and others.

Industrial Dust Emission refers to volume of dust emitted by production process of enterprises and suspended in the air for a given period of time, including dust from refractory material of iron and steel works, dust from coke-screening systems and sintering machines of coke plants, dust from lime kilns and dust from cement production in building material enterprises, but excluding soot and dust emitted from power plants.

Industrial Solid Wastes Produced refers to total volume of solid, semi-solid and high concentration liquid residues produced by industrial enterprises from production process in a given period of time, including hazardous wastes, slag, coal ash, gangue, tailings, radioactive residues and other wastes, but excluding stones stripped or dug out in mining (gangue and acid or alkaline stones not included). A stone is acid or alkaline depending on the pH value of the water below 4 or above 10.5 when the stone is in, or soaked by, the water.

Hazardous Wastes refers to those included in the national hazardous wastes catalogue or specified as any one of the following properties in the national hazardous wastes identification standards: explosive, ignitable, oxidizable, toxic, corrosive or liable to cause infectious diseases or lead to other dangers.

Industrial Solid Wastes Utilized refers to volume of solid wastes from which useful materials can be extracted or which can be converted into usable resources, energy or other materials by means of reclamation, processing, recycling and exchange (including utilizing in the year the stocks of industrial solid wastes of the previous year). Examples of such utilizations include fertilizers, building materials and road materials. The information shall be collected by the producing units of the wastes.

Ratio of Industrial Solid Wastes Utilized refers to the percentage of industrial solid wastes utilized over industrial solid wastes produced (including stocks of the previous years). It is calculated as:

Ratio of industrial solid wastes utilized = volume of industrial solid wastes utilized / (industrial solid wastes produced + stock of previous years) 100%

Stocks of Industrial Solid Wastes refers to volume of solid wastes placed in special facilities or special sites for purposes of utilization or disposal. The sites or facilities should take measures against dispersion, loss, seepage, and air and water contamination.

Industrial Solid Wastes Disposed refers to quantity of industrial solid wastes which are burnt or placed ultimately in the sites meeting the requirements for environmental protection and not salvaged or recycled (including disposition in the year of those wastes of previous years). The disposition includes landfill (Safe landfills should be conducted for hazardous wastes), incineration, containment spaces, deep underground disposal, backfill in mining pits and disposal at sea.

Industrial Solid Wastes Discharged refers to volume of industrial solid wastes discharged by producing enterprises to disposal facilities or to other sites. The wastes exclude stones stripped or dug from mining (gangue and acid or alkaline waste stones not included).

Output Value of Products Made from Waste Gas, Waste Water and Solid Wastes refers current value of products with waste gas, waste water and solid wastes as main materials of production. Products sold and ready to sell shall be included while those produced for own use shall not be included.

Consumption Wastes Transported refers to volume of consumption wastes collected and transported to disposal factories or sites. Consumption wastes are solid wastes produced from urban households or from service activities for urban households, and solid wastes regarded by laws and regulations as urban consumption wastes, including those from households, commercial activities, markets, cleaning of streets, public sites, offices, schools, factories, mining units and other sources.

Ratio of Consumption Wastes Treated refers to consumption wastes treated over that produced. In practical statistics, as it is difficult to estimate, the volume of consumption wastes produced is replaced with that transported. It is calculated as:

Ratio of consumption wastes treated = consumption wastes treated / consumption wastes produced ×100%

Total Area of Afforestation refers to the total area of land suitable for afforestation, including barren hills, idle land, sand dunes, rain for green land, on which acres of arbores or bushes are planted through manual planting, airplane planting, plant seedlings, etc. in accordance with the required density standards of the Technical Procedures of Afforestation, and with a survival rate of over 85% in line with the Implementing Rules of the Forest Law of the People's Republic of China (or a survival rate of 75% in areas with less that 400 mm of annual rainfall and without irrigation facilities). Included in the this category are trees planted alone the roadsides, riversides, or next to houses that occupy an area over 0.066 hectares, or where more than 4 lines of trees are planted. Total area of afforestation is further classified by ownership (state-owned, state-collective, collective or private), by approach of planting (manual, airplane), and by type of forests (timber, by-products, protection, fuel, special use, etc.).

Projects on Converting Cultivated Land to Forests and Grassland (Grain for Green Projects) aiming at preventing soil erosion in key regions, these projects are ecological construction projects in the development of forest industry that have the widest coverage and most sophisticated procedures, with strong policy implications and most active participation of the people.

Nature Reserves refer to certain areas of land, waters or sea that are representative in natural ecological systems, or are natural habitats for rare or endangered wild animals or plants, or water conservation zones, or the location of important natural or historic relics, which are demarked by law and put under special protection and management. Nature reserves are designated by the formal approval of governments at and above county level (including those approved by relevant departments or "revolutionary committees" before 1980). Scenic spots and cultural preservation zones are not included.

Ecological Demonstration Zones refer to administrative areas approved by the environment protection agencies of central and provincial governments and established by provincial, prefecture or county governments in line with the approved programme for ecological demonstration zones. They include those evaluated and accepted by the environment protection agencies of central and provincial governments and those under pilot development stage.

Environment Pollution and Destruction Accidents refer to sudden accidents, due to economic or social activities that are in contrast to environment protection laws or due to unforeseen factors or natural disasters, that lead to the environment pollution, the destruction of protected wild animals, plants or nature reserves, the damage to human health, the economic and property losses, and the negative impact on the society.

Investment in Environment Pollution Harnessing Projects refers to the proportion of investment in fixed assets in the total investment in harnessing industrial pollution and in the construction of urban environment infrastructure facilities. It includes investment in harnessing sources of industrial pollution, investment in environment protection facilities designed concurrently with construction projects, and investment in urban environment infrastructure facilities.

18

体育、卫生及其他

Sports, Public Health and Others

Eighteen

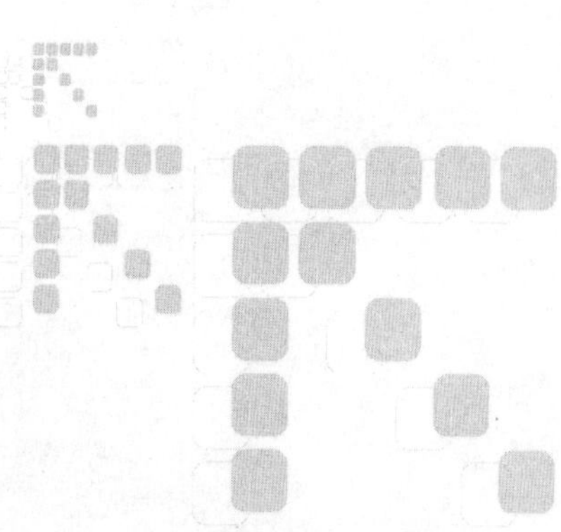

体育运动员情况（人）
Number of Athletes (person)

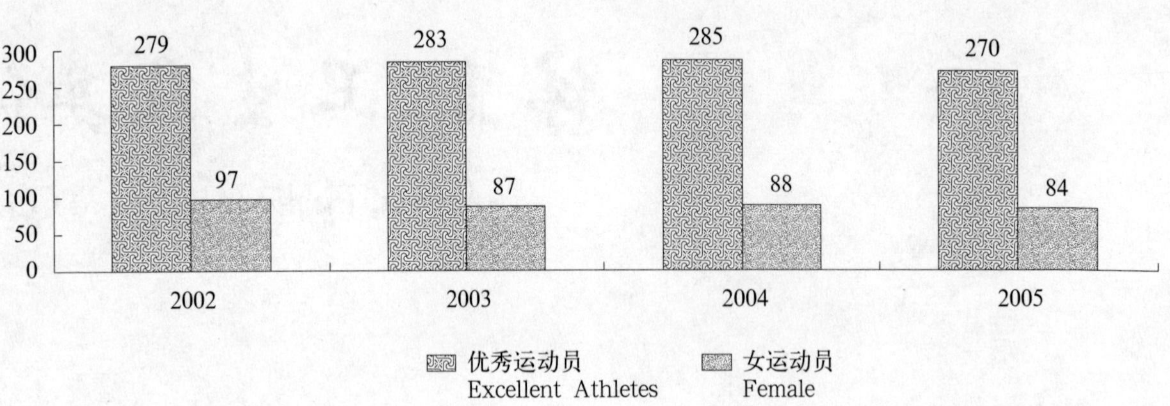

聘请常年法律顾问（个）
Number of Permanent Legal Advisors (person)

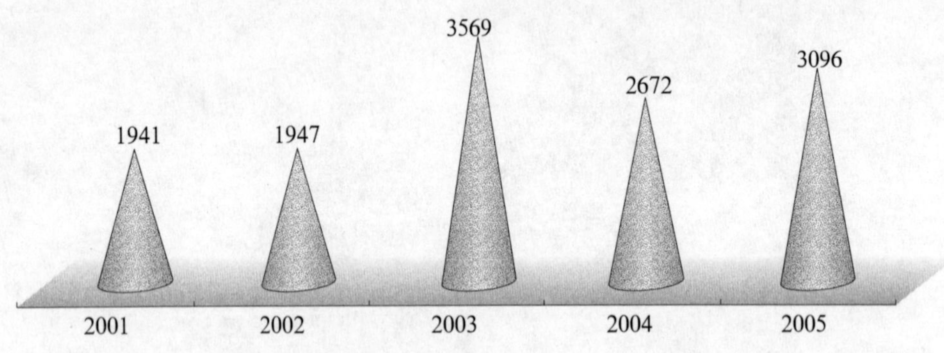

消费者协会受理投诉情况（件）
Cases Accepted by Consumers Association (unit)

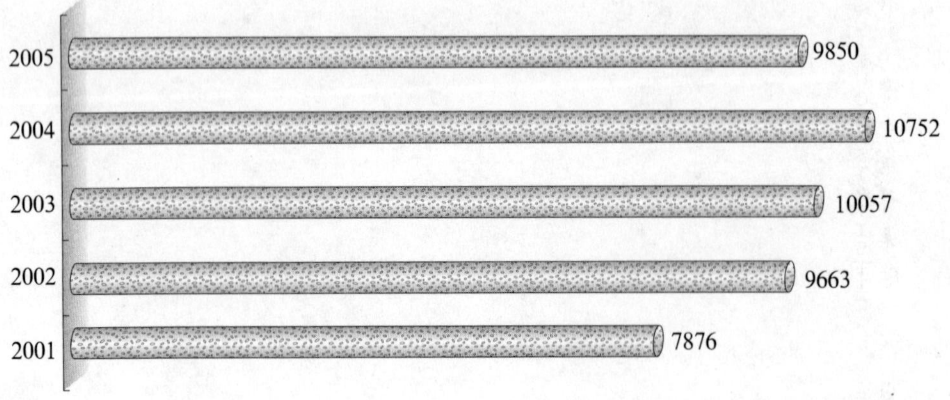

18-1 "十五"时期各年体育运动员情况

Sports Athletes of Each Year in "Tenth Five-year Plan" Period

单位：人(person)

指 标	Item	2000	2001	2002	2003	2004	2005
优秀运动员	**Excellent Athletes**	**142**	**137**	**279**	**283**	**285**	**270**
#女运动员	Female	54	50	97	87	88	84
专职教练员	Full-time Coaches	85	87	166	228	249	217
#女专职教练员	Female	20	20	44	61	63	53
等级运动员发展人数	**Number of Certified Athletes**	**597**	**622**	**711**	**323**	**172**	**213**
#国际运动健将	International Master Athletes					1	
运动健将	Master Athletes	10	2	2		17	13
等级裁判员发展人数	**Number of Certified Referees**	**808**	**1905**	**2037**	**207**	**158**	**66**
#国家级	National Referees	2	5	5		6	2

18-2 "十五"时期各年体育运动获奖情况

Basic Statistics on Medals Won by Guizhou Sports Athletes in domestic and international competitions of Each Year in "Tenth Five-year Plan" Period

单位：项(unit)

指 标	Item	2000	2001	2002	2003	2004	2005
国内外大赛第一名	Number of the First-Order	21	16	13	13	4	20
国内外大赛第二名	Number of the Second-Order	16	21	17	12	8	8
国内外大赛第三名	Number of the Third-Order	15	14	14	16	20	22
国内外大赛第四至八名	Number of the Fourth-Order to Eighth-Order	7	3	49	46		

18-3 “十五”时期各年公共体育场地

Number of Public Stadiums and Gymnasiums of Each Year in “Tenth Five-year Plan” Period

单位：个(unit)

指 标	Item	2000	2001	2002	2003	2004	2005
总 计	**Total**	**11965**	**11987**	**11997**	**12007**	**12012**	**12014**
#体育场	Stadiums	33	42	44	46	49	49
体育馆	Gymnasiums	14	16	16	17	19	21
游泳池	Swimming Pools	84	84	87	88	88	88
有固定看台的灯光球场	Illuminated Fields with Fixed Seating	164	168	171	172	172	172

注：本表数据为体育系统数据。

Note:Data in the table refers to the data in sports commissions.

18-4 “十五”时期各年群众体育活动情况

Activities of Mass Sports of Each Year in “Tenth Five-year Plan” Period

单位：万人(10000 persons)

指 标	Item	2000	2001	2002	2003	2004	2005
举办县级以上运动会(万次)	**Number of Sports Meeting at and above County Level(10000 times)**	**0.11**	**0.10**	**0.06**	**0.08**	**0.11**	**0.09**
参加运动会的运动员(万人次)	Number of Athletes Attending Sports Meets (10000 person-times)	52.35	48.2	137.6	200.50	269.44	247.55
青少年体育俱乐部(个)	Athletic Club for Youngsters at This Year(unit)	11	11	7	9	5	5
青少年体育俱乐部(个)(累计数)	Athletic Club for Youngsters(unit) (accumulative total)	11	22	29	38	43	48
全民健身工程(条)	Body-building Activities of The Whole Nation (unit)	54	69	61	125	128	99

18-5 “十五”时期各年卫生事业基本情况

Basic Statistics on Health Care of Each Year in “Tenth Five-year Plan” Period

指　标	Item	2000	2001	2002	2003	2004	2005	2005年比2004年增长(%) Increase Rate in 2005 over 2004(%)
卫生机构（个）	**Number of Health Institutions (unit)**	**8992**	**8791**	**7027**	**6499**	**6664**	**6571**	**-1.4**
#医院、卫生院	Hospitals and Township Hospitals	1878	1872	1857	1866	1850	1843	-0.4
床位数（万张）	**Number of Beds(10000 beds)**	**5.8**	**5.91**	**5.99**	**5.93**	**6.13**	**6.18**	**0.8**
#医院、卫生院床位	Number of Hospital and Township Hospitals Beds	5.51	5.59	5.76	5.64	5.81	5.84	0.5
卫生人员合计（万人）	**Number of Medical Technical Personnel(10000 persons)**	**10.16**	**10.24**	**9.38**	**9.11**	**9.02**	**9.21**	**2.1**
#卫生技术人员	Medical Technical Personnels	8.54	8.61	7.97	7.76	7.67	7.78	1.4
#执业医生	Doctors	4.57	4.64	3.15	3.69	3.69	3.55	-3.8
医疗机构病床使用率(%)	**Utilization Rate in Medical Institutions(%)**	**55.00**	**58.80**	**64.1**	**65.32**	**63.40**	**67.70**	**4.3 (百分点)**
人均卫生费（元）	Expenditure for Health of each Person (yuan)	15.87	19.45	20.27	22.84	26.59	36.71	38.0
平均每千人拥有:	**Per 1000 Person:**							
#医院、卫生院床位(张)	Number of Hospital Beds(bed)	1.48	1.48	1.51	1.49	1.49	1.50	0.8
卫生人员（人）	Number of Medical Technical Personnels(person)	2.72	2.72	2.46	2.36	2.31	2.34	1.3
#卫生技术人员	Medical Technical Personnels	2.29	2.28	2.09	2.01	1.96	1.98	0.8
#医生	Doctors	1.22	1.23	1.13	1.12	1.22	0.91	-25.4

18-6 “十五”时期各年卫生防疫防治和妇幼卫生事业情况

Basic Statistics on Sanitation and Epidemic Prevention,Maternity and Child Care of Each Year in “Tenth Five-year Plan” Period

类　别	Sort	2000	2001	2002	2003	2004	2005
防治所、站机构数（个）	**Prevention and Treatment Centers or Stations(unit)**	**62**	**61**	**23**	**12**	**7**	**6**
人员总数（人）	Number of Personnels(person)	848	802	487	235	157	142
卫生技术人员数（人）	Medical Technical Personnels(person)	649	603	353	179	117	112
床位数（张）	Hospital Beds(bed)	113	120	472	205	276	175
卫生防疫机构数（个）	**Institutions of Sanitation and Antiepidemic Agencies(unit)**	**113**	**113**	**100**	**100**	**106**	**103**
人员总数（人）	Number of Personnels(person)	4909	4946	4837	4599	4479	4575
卫生技术人员数（人）	Medical Technical Personnels(person)	3984	3986	3852	3671	3630	3710
妇幼保健机构合计（个）	**Maternity and Child Care Centers(unit)**	**98**	**99**	**88**	**93**	**82**	**84**
人员总数（人）	Number of Personnels(person)	3073	3166	2123	3069	2702	2814
卫生技术人员数（人）	Medical Technical Personnels(person)	2585	2648	1785	2653	2290	2405
床位数（张）	Hospital Beds(bed)	1613	1691	1238	1846	1720	1797

18-7 卫生机构、床位、人员数(2005)

Number of Health Institutions,Beds and Personnels(2005)

类 别	Item	机构数（个）Institutions (unit)	床位数(张) Hospital Beds (Bed)	人员数（人）Number of Personels (person)	#卫生技术人员数 Medical Technical Personels
合 计	**Total Number of Institutions**	**6571**	**61784**	**92121**	**77805**
医 院	Hospitals	383	44165	53676	44616
市	City	229	29310	37089	30553
县	County	154	14855	16587	14063
#综合医院	Genaral Hospital	269	36771	44418	36903
#县医院	Hospitals at County Level	71	9818	11081	9435
中医医院	Hospital TCM	64	4724	5590	4792
中西医结合医院	Combine Hospitals of Chinese and Western Medicine	7	375	612	524
其他专科医院	Other Specialized Hospitals	40	2199	2972	2330
疗养院（所）	Sanitariums	2	540	276	172
社区卫生服务中心(站)	Total Health Service Centers for Community	202	401	2033	1938
#社区卫生服务中心	Health Service Centers for Community	37	401	604	509
社区卫生服务站	Health Service stations for Community	165		1429	1429
卫生院	Health Centers	1460	14233	19141	17393
#农村乡镇卫生院	Health Centers of Villages and Towns in Country	1449	14177	19031	17294
#中心乡镇卫生院	Health Centers Focus Villages and Towns	467	7488	9456	8587
一般乡镇卫生院	Health Centers of Commonly Villages and Towns	982	6689	9566	8716
门诊部、所、医务室	Outpatient Department Clinic and Infirmary	4171	289	6849	5590
#私人办诊所	Personal Clinique	3719		3863	3863
专科防治所(站)	Specialized Prevention and Cure Centers	6	175	142	112
疾控中心(卫生防疫站)	CDC(Epidemic Prevention Station)	103	105	4575	3710
#县疾控中心	CDC at County Level	72	20	2577	2194
卫生监督所	Sanitation Supervise Centers	91		1488	1149
#县卫生监督所	Sanitation Supervise Centers of County Level	69		960	741
妇幼保健所、站	MCH Center	84	1797	2814	2405
#县妇幼保健所站	MCH Centers at County level	65	1003	1502	1299
医学科学研究机构	Research Institution of Medicine Science	2	20	11	10
其他卫生事业机构	Other Health Project Institution	67	59	1116	710

18-8 卫生机构、床位、人员数(2005)

Number of Health Institutions,Beds and Personnels(2005)

类别	Sort	总计 Total	卫生部门 Health Department	工业及其他部门 Industrial and Other Department	集体所有制 Collective-owned	私人办 Private Practice
机构数（个）	**Number of Institutions (unit)**	**6571**	**2018**	**572**	**169**	**3812**
构成(%)	Composition(%)	100.0	30.7	8.7	2.6	58.0
床位数（张）	**Number of Beds(bed)**	**61784**	**49012**	**10583**	**766**	**1423**
构成(%)	Composition(%)	100.0	79.3	17.1	1.2	2.3
人员数（人）	**Number of Personnels(person)**	**94854**	**67016**	**15317**	**1381**	**11140**
构成(%)	Composition(%)	100.0	70.7	16.1	1.5	11.7
#卫生技术人员数(人)	Medical Technical Personnels(person)	81723	56802	13058	1140	10723
构成(%)	Composition	100.0	69.5	16.0	1.4	13.1

18-9 县及县以上医院、卫生院医疗工作情况（2005）

Status of Hospitals and Rural Township Hospitals at and above County Level(2005)

类 别	Sort	机构合计(个) Insti-tutions (unit)	诊疗人次数(人次) Total Patients Treated (person-times)	#门诊人次数 Out-Patients	入院人数（人次）Hospital Admi-ssions (person-times)	出院人数（人次）Leave Hospital (person-times)	出院病人治愈率% Recovering Rate(%)
县及县以上医院合计	**Hospitals at and above County Level**	**383**	**42066261**	**27506748**	**925172**	**923156**	**68.39**
#综合医院	Comprehensive Hospitals	269	12228333	10701948	800229	798750	68.27
#中医医院	Hospital of Chinese Medicine	64	3751268	2291982	87526	87673	68.61
妇幼保健院	Maternity and Child Care Hospital	19	634941	559914	29115	28995	79.65
卫生院合计	Township Hospitals	1460	23814453	12528542	415427	421232	87.01
#农村乡镇卫生院	Rural Township Hospitals	1449	23749774	12468611	414098	419903	87.00
#中心乡镇卫生院	Central Township Hospitals	467	6704264	6314870	259078	259971	86.91
一般乡镇卫生院	Ecumenic Township Hospitals	982	17045510	6153741	155020	159932	87.16

18-9 续表(continued)

类 别	Sort	平均开放病床数(张) Sickbeds Setup (bed)	病床周转次数（次/年）Turnover of Beds (time/year)	病床工作日(日) Number of Days Per Bed in Use (day)	病床使用率（%）Utili-zation Rate of Beds(%)	出院者平均住院日(天) Average Hospit-alization Period(day)	每100次门(急)诊入院人数(人) Hospital Admissions Per 100 Out-Patient Times and Emergency Patient-Times (person)
县及县以上医院合计	**Hospitals at and above County Level**	**37580**	**24.57**	**247.13**	**67.7**	**9.07**	**6.28**
#综合医院	Comprehensive Hospitals	31179	25.62	250.40	68.60	8.85	6.88
#中医医院	Hospital of Chinese Medicine	4291	20.43	225.95	61.90	10.24	3.66
妇幼保健院	Maternity and Child Care Hospital	824	35.18	243.14	66.61	6.75	4.72
卫生院合计	Township Hospitals	11951	35.25	124.40	34.08	2.86	3.28
#农村乡镇卫生院	Rural Township Hospitals	11896	35.30	124.48	34.10	2.85	3.28
#中心乡镇卫生院	Central Township Hospitals	6521	39.87	137.29	37.61	2.98	4.06
一般乡镇卫生院	Ecumenic Township Hospitals	5376	29.75	108.94	29.85	2.66	2.49

18-10 卫生部门城市医院住院病人前十位疾病构成与全国比较(2005)

Composition of 10 Major diseases of Impatient in Urban Areas Compared with Na tional Total(2005)

疾病种类 Kind of Disease	贵州省 Guizhou Province	疾病构成（%） Composition(%)	位次 Order
十种疾病构成比合计	**Total of the Composition Ratio**	**74.98**	
呼吸系病	Respiratory Disease	13.55	1
消化系病	Digestive Disease	12.84	2
损伤、中毒和外因	Injury,Poisoning & External Causes	10.29	3
传染病和寄生虫病	Certain Infestious and Parasitic Diseases	8.93	4
恶性肿瘤	Malignant Neoplasms	6.15	5
脑血管病	Cerebrovascular Disease	6.06	6
妊娠、分娩和产褥期病	Pregnancy,childbirth & the Puerperium	5.75	7
泌尿生殖系病	Diseases of the Genitourinary System	5.11	8
肌肉骨骼系统和结缔组织病	Diseases of the Muscle and Skeleton System & Connective tissue Disease	3.17	9
缺血性心脏病	Ischaemic Heart Disease	3.13	10

疾病种类 Kind of Disease	全 国 National Total	疾病构成（%） Composition(%)	位次 Order
十种疾病构成比合计	**Total of the Composition Ratio**	**71.00**	
呼吸系病	Respiratory Disease	12.77	1
消化系病	Digestive Disease	11.60	2
损伤、中毒和外因	Injury,Poisoning & External Causes	11.10	3
妊娠、分娩和产褥期病	Pregnancy,childbirth & the Puerperium	9.50	4
泌尿生殖系病	Diseases of the Genitourinary System	6.14	5
恶性肿瘤	Malignant Neoplasms	6.05	6
脑血管病	Cerebrovascular Disease	4.35	7
传染病和寄生虫病	Certain Infestious and Parasitic Diseases	3.35	8
缺血性心脏病	Ischaemic Heart Disease	3.17	9
肌肉骨骼系统和结缔组织病	Diseases of the Muscle and Skeleton System & Connective tissue Disease	2.97	10

18-11 "十五"时期各年农村三级医疗、预防、保健网情况

Basic Statistics on Health Organization at County,Town and Village Level of Each Year in "Tenth Five-year Plan" Period

指 标	Item	2000	2001	2002	2003	2004	2005	2005年比2004年增长(%) Increase Rate in 2005 over 2004(%)
县医院个数（个）	**Number of Hospitals at County Level(unit)**	**69**	**69**	**69**	**69**	**71**	**71**	**持平**
平均每院病床数(张)	Number of Beds Per Hospital(bed)	126.87	126.55	126.67	126.54	132.85	139.69	5.1
平均每院人员数(人)	Personnels Per Hospital(person)	147.04	149.42	149.94	148.86	152.66	157.48	3.2
#平均每院卫生技 术人员数(人)	Medical Technical Personnels Per Hospital(person)	121.41	123.97	122.41	121.82	129.54	134.01	3.5
县妇幼保健所、站机构数(个)	**Maternity and Child Care Centers at County Level (unit)**	**62**	**62**	**62**	**62**	**67**	**65**	**-3.0**
平均每所站床位数(张)	Number of Beds Per Station(bed)	12.44	12.5	12.53	12.64	15.22	15.43	1.4
平均每所站人员数 (人)	Personnels Per Station(person)	21.4	21.52	21.7	21.58	23.51	23.11	-1.7
#每所站卫生技术人员数(人)	Medical Technical Personnels Per Stati on(person)	18.65	18.52	19.35	19.34	19.96	19.98	0.1
县卫生防疫站机构数(个)	**Institutions of Epidemic Prevention Station at County Level(unit)**	**67**	**67**	**67**	**67**	**78**	**72**	**-7.7**
平均每所站人员数(人)	Personnels Per Station(person)	35.88	36.06	37.08	35.42	34.09	35.79	5.0
#平均每站卫生技术人员数(人)	Medical Technical Personnels Per Station(person)	30.54	30.34	31.25	30.64	28.47	30.47	7.0
农村乡镇卫生院机构数(个)	**Institutions of Rural Township Hospitals(unit)**	**1457**	**1456**	**1452**	**1451**	**1449**	**1449**	**持平**
农村乡镇卫生院床位数 (张)	**Number of Beds of Rural Township Hospitals(bed)**	**14307**	**14427**	**14081**	**14142**	**14236**	**14177**	**-0.4**
平均每院床位数(张)	Average Number of Beds Per Hospital(bed)	9.82	9.91	9.7	9.75	9.82	9.78	-0.5

18-11续表（continued）

指 标	Item	2000	2001	2002	2003	2004	2005	2005年比2004年增长(%) Increase Rate in 2005 over 2004(%)
平均每千农业人口乡镇卫生院床位数(张)	Average Number o f Beds of Rural Township Hospitals Per 1000 Rural Personnels(bed)	0.45	0.44	0.44	0.43	0.43	0.44	0.7
农村乡镇卫生院人员数(人)	Personnels of Rural Township Hospitals (person)	23008	22874	22523	21807	19326	19031	-1.5
平均每院人员数(人)	Personnels Per Hospital(person)	15.79	15.71	15.51	15.03	13.34	13.13	-1.6
平均每千农业人口乡镇卫生院人员数(人)	Medical Technical Personnels Per Hospital(person)	0.72	0.7	0.7	0.66	0.59	0.58	-0.4
设置医疗点的村数(个)	Villages Set up Medical Treatment Sations (unit)	21374	21258	21244	21322	18551	18805	1.4
无医疗点的的村数(个)	Villages without Medical Treatment Sations(unit)	4481	4234	4222	4179	3468	1053	-69.6
村卫生室覆盖率(%)	Coverage Rate of Township Hospitals(%)	82.67	83.4	83.4	83.6	84.3	94.7	10.4 (百分点)
开展合作医疗的村数(个)	Villages of Pushing Cooperative Medical Treatment(unit)	2034	2321	2547	2490	2814	1905	-32.3
开展合作医疗的村覆盖率(%)	Coverage Rate of Villages Pushed Coopera tive Medical Treatment(%)	7.87	9.1	10	9.8	12.78	9.49	-3.3 (百分点)
平均每村设置的医疗点数(个)	Average Number of Medical Treatment Stations Run by Village Per Village(unit)	0.85	0.87	0.83	0.85	0.84	0.95	13.1
乡村医生和卫生员数(人)	Doctors and Health Workers(person)	38567	37976	34599	35081	29297	25710	-12.2
#乡村医生所占比例%	Proportion of Rural Doctors(%)	55.93	53.9	65.1	64.2	71.1	81.7	10.6 (百分点)
平均每村乡村医生和卫生员数（人）	Average Number of Doctors and Health Workers Per Village(person)	1.49	1.49	1.36	1.38	1.33	1.3	-2.3
平均每千农业人口乡村医生和卫生员数(人)	Ave rage Number of Doctors and Health Workers Per 1000 Rural Personnels (person)	1.2	1.17	1.07	1.06	0.89	0.79	-11.3

18-12 “十五”时期各年人民法院刑事一审案件收案情况

First Trail Criminal Cases Accepted by Courts of Each Year in “Tenth Five-year Plan” Period

单位：件(case)

类 别	Sort	2000	2001	2002	2003	2004	2005	2005年比2004年增长(%) Increase Rate in 2005 over 2004(%)
总 计	**Total**	**18792**	**22361**	**22068**	**21257**	**19442**	**19533**	**0.5**
#危害国家安全罪	Offences Against State Security	1	3	1	2	2	3	50.0
危害公共安全罪	Offences Against Public Security	903	1450	1645	1821	1794	1744	-2.8
破坏社会主义市场经济秩序罪	Offences Against Socialist Economic Order	257	242	218	228	198	168	-15.2
侵犯公民人身权利民主权利罪	Offences Against Citizens' Personal and Democratic Rights	6510	6954	6232	6182	5158	5231	1.4
侵犯财产罪	Offences Against Properties	7078	8718	9179	9189	8629	8401	-2.6
妨害社会管理秩序罪	Offences Against Social Management of Order	3441	4318	4142	3097	2699	2969	10.0
危害国防利益罪	Offences Against National Defense		2	1	2	1	4	300.0
贪污贿赂罪	Offences on Corruption and Bribery	555	614	555	676	855	899	5.2
渎职罪	Offences on Dereliction of Duty	47	60	59	59	106	109	2.8

18-13 “十五”时期各年人民法院刑事一审案件结案情况

First Trail Criminal Cases Settled by Courts of Each Year in “Tenth Five-year Plan” Period

单位：件(case)

指 标	Item	2000	2001	2002	2003	2004	2005	2005年比2004年增长(%) Increase Rate in 2005 over 2004(%)
总 计	**Total**	**18507**	**21992**	**21626**	**20916**	**19176**	**19269**	**0.5**
#危害国家安全罪	Offences Against National Security	1	3	1	2	2	3	50.0
危害公共安全罪	Offences Against Public Security	898	1437	1628	1811	1784	1724	3.4
破坏社会主义市场经济秩序罪	Offences Against Socialist Economic Order	252	235	208	220	193	163	-15.5
侵犯公民人身权利民主权利罪	Offences Against Citizens'Personal and Democratic Rights	6348	6758	6020	6041	5024	5082	1.2
侵犯财产罪	Offences Against Properties	7017	8627	9045	9070	8576	8373	2.4
妨害社会管理秩序罪	Offences Against Social Management of Order	3404	4273	4090	3058	2662	2935	10.3
危害国防利益罪	Offences Against National Defense		2	1	2	1	4	300.0
贪污贿赂罪	Offences on Corruption and Bribery	543	598	540	658	830	877	5.7
渎职罪	Offences on Dereliction of Duty	44	59	57	53	104	103	1.0

18-14 “十五”时期各年人民法院刑事案件中青少年犯罪情况

Juvenile Delinquency Among Criminal Cases of Each Year in “Tenth Five-year Plan” Period

单位：人(person)

指 标	Item	2000	2001	2002	2003	2004	2005	2005年比2004年增长(%) Increase Rate in 2005 over 2004(%)
刑事罪犯总数	Offenders	19915	24081	19238	22677	22218	21971	-1.1
#青少年罪犯	Young Offenders	6476	7395	4937	6790	7580	7905	4.3
#不满18岁	Less Than 18	1226	1587	1230	2107	2702	2946	9.0
18-25岁	Between 18 to 25	5250	5808	3707	4683	4878	4959	1.7
青少年罪犯占刑事罪犯（%）	Proportion to Total(%)	32.5	30.7	25.7	29.9	34.1	36.0	1.9 (百分点)

18-15 “十五”时期各年律师、公证、调解工作基本情况

Basic Statistics on Lawyers ,Notarization and Mediation of Each Year in “Tenth Five-year Plan” Period

指 标	Item	2000	2001	2002	2003	2004	2005	2005年比2004年增长(%) Increase Rate in 2005 over 2004(%)
律师工作	**Lawyers**							
法律律师事务所(个)	Number of Law Offices(unit)	153	169	169	177	190	185	-2.63
专职律师（人）	Full-time Lawyers(person)	790	865	865	989	1058	1129	6.71
辅助工作人员(人)	Assistant(person)	358	310	310	436	466	438	-6.01
聘请常年法律顾问(个)	Number of Permanent Legal Advisors (person)	1728	1941	1947	3569	2672	3096	15.87
全年办理（件）	Number of Cases in Whole Year(case)	110471	85337	85517	114965	73541	112249	52.63
#民事诉讼代理	Agent of Civil Cases	9746	10630	10630	12026	10179	15604	53.30
刑事案件诉讼代理	Defender of Criminal Cases	6388	7032	7032	6616	4668	6835	46.42
经济案件诉讼代理	Agent of Economic Cases	3254	2921	2921	1906	1618	1727	6.74
非诉讼法律事务	Agent of Non-litigious Legal Affairs	2571	4104	4104	3464	2404	2847	18.43
解答法律询问	Agent of Legal Advisory Services	67505	46231	46231	73050	45269	74346	64.23
代写法律事务文书	Agent of Legal Document Written on Behalf of Clie nts	20152	13571	13751	13343	8837	9978	12.91
行政诉讼代理	Agent of Administrative Action	855	848	848	793	566	912	61.13
公证工作	**Notarization**							
公证处（个）	Number of Notarial Offices(unit)	96	96	97	97	97	97	持平
公证员（人）	Notaries(person)	117	229	205	347	347	187	-46.11
公证辅助人员(人)	Notarial Assistant(person)	229	119	122	147	147	148	0.68
办理公证文书(件)	Number of Notarized Documents(case)	215518	164205	163302	147717	100637	104778	4.11
#经济合同公证	Notarized Documents on Economic Affairs	122251	54278	53297	44731	53976	29651	-45.07

18-15续表(continued)

指 标	Item	2000	2001	2002	2003	2004	2005	2005年比2004年增长(%) Increase Rate in 2005 over 2004(%)
#涉外公证	Notarization of Foreignrelated		6939	6132	5993	10193	8708	-14.57
国内公证	Domestic Notarization	5738	102988	103873	140506	88011	66419	-24.53
公证费收入(万元)	Income of Notarization(10000 yuan)	703.81	663.49	690.45	771.07	1114.2	778.91	-30.09
人民调解工作	**People's Mediation**							
人民调解委员会(个)	Number of People's Mediation Committees(unit)	21636	30678	30548	29534	24370	25267	3.7
人民调解人员(人)	Number of Mediators(person)	117001	111929	89582	120659	122487	119622	-2.3
调解民间纠纷(件)	Number of Civil Disputes Mediated (case)	15245	168293	159104	101642	103716	114534	10.4
调解成功率(%)	The Rate of Success of Mediation(%)	99.7	93	94	96	96	96	持平
基层法律服务工作	**Law Service at Basic Level(unit)**							
法律服务所(个)	Offices for Law Service(unit)	652	617	574	586	586	579	-1.2
法律工作者(人)	Law Staffs(person)	2167	2074	1927	1931	1948	1780	-8.6
代理案件(件)	Cases Deputed(case)	14949	12113	12812	11226	11309	12727	12.5
避免经济损失(万元)	Number of Avoided Economical Loss (10000 yuan)	10973	6625	458606	3958	4037	13461	233.4
刑释解教人员安置帮教工作	**Settling and Assisting and Teaching Work for People That Been Released After Serving a Sentence**							
设立工作机构(个)	Institutions Established(unit)	97	97	97	97	97	97	持平
工作人员(人)	Staffs(person)	1166	1376	1261	1296	1633	1596	-2.3
安置人数	Number of Persons Been Helped Settle Down	8002	10901	6015	6762	10113	7382	-27.0
帮教人数	Number of Persons Been Assisted and Teached	6414	10208	7849	9225	10026	8753	-12.7

18-16 “十五”时期各年国内公证文书分类情况

Domestic Notarial Documents by Type of Each Year in “Tenth Five-year Plan” Period

单位：件(unit)

指 标	Item	2000	2001	2002	2003	2004	2005	2005年比2004年增长(%) Increase Rate in 2005 over 2004(%)
总 计	**Total**	**35365**	**34230**	**59394**	**140506**	**88011**	**46017**	**-47.7**
经济合同公证合计	**Notarized Documents on Economic Affairs**	**19561**	**19131**	**43571**	**44731**	**53976**	**23237**	**-56.9**
#购销	Purchases and Sales of Products	372	402	14851	345	467	420	-10.1
联营	Joint Business	113	60	47	92	43	128	197.7
贷款	Loans	16491	16913	24186	27255	33321	21542	-35.4
招标、投标	Bidding and Invite Public Bidding	346	217	267	242	362	232	-35.9
劳务合同	Labor Contracts	643	521	2891	389	384	398	3.6
建筑工程承包	Construction Project Countracts	201	130	169	93	50	18	-64.0
农、林、牧、副、渔业承包	Farming,Forestry, Animal Husbandry , Sideline Production and Fishery Contracts	1251	614	725	457	540	384	-28.9
财产租赁	Property Leases	89	137	233	376	22	20	-9.1
法人（代表）资格	Legal Person(Agent)Identification	9	40	157	230	16		
委托书	Legal Person Trust Deeds	46	97	45	107	44	95	115.9
民事法律关系公证合计	**Notarized Documents on Civil Legal Relations**	**15804**	**15099**	**15823**	**95775**	**34035**	**22780**	**-33.1**
#收 养	Child Adoption	617	188	174	146	126	96	-23.8
解除收养	Adoption Renouncement	17	10	10	2	119	18	-84.9
继承权	Right of Inheritance	845	1009	1182	1377	1721	2440	41.8
遗嘱	Testaments	656	705	625	520	501	644	28.5
产权	Property Right	165	128	165	163	194	140	-27.8
亲属关系	Relatives	885	841	540	487	578	1090	88.6
房屋买卖	Purchases and Sales of Houses	2613	3445	3287	2764	2721	2954	8.6
房屋租赁	House Leases	150	152	218	124	132	66	-50.0
留学协议	Foreign Study Contracts	172	144	112	228	172	78	-54.7
遗赠抚养协议	Donations and Family Fostering	97	155	82	215	181	64	-64.6
其他民事协议	Other Civil Agreements	5491	3689	5458	8891	8060	3806	-52.8
委托书	Trust Deeds	620	816	995	1458	2323	4132	77.9
赠与书	Presentation Documents	2599	2566	1733	1687	2007	3716	85.2
声明书	Declarations	776	1006	910	1326	2496	3418	36.9
建房宅基使用协议	Right to Housing Site	101	245	332	129	137	118	-13.9

18-16续表(continued)

指　标	Item	2000	2001	2002	2003	2004	2005	2005年比2004年增长(%) Increase Rate in 2005 over 2004(%)
#涉外公证	Notarization of Foreignrelated		6939	6132	5993	10193	8708	-14.57
国内公证	Domestic Notarization	5738	102988	103873	140506	88011	66419	-24.53
公证费收入(万元)	Income of Notarization(10000 yuan)	20.866	663.49	6904.5	771.07	1114.2	778.91	-30.09
人民调解工作	**People's Mediation**							
人民调解委员会(个)	Number of People's Mediation Committees(unit)	21636	30678	30548	29534	24370	25267	3.7
人民调解人员(人)	Number of Mediators(person)	117001	111929	89582	120659	122487	119622	-2.3
调解民间纠纷(件)	Number of Civil Disputes Mediated(case)	15245	168293	159104	101642	103716	114534	10.4
调解成功率(%)	The Rate of Success of Mediation(%)	99.7	93	94	96	96	96	持平
基层法律服务工作	Law Service at Basic Level(unit)							
法律服务所(个)	Offices for Law Service(unit)	652	617	574	586	586	579	-1.2
法律工作者(人)	Law Staffs(person)	2167	2074	1927	1931	1948	1780	-8.6
代理案件(件)	Cases Deputed(case)	14949	12113	12812	11226	11309	12727	12.5
避免经济损失(万元)	Number of Avoided Economical Loss (10000 yuan)	10973	6625	458606	3958	4037	13461	233.4
刑释解教人员安置帮教工作	Settling and Assisting and Teaching Work for People That Been Released After Serving a Sentence							
设立工作机构(个)	Institutions Established(unit)	97	97	97	97	97	97	持平
工作人员(人)	Staffs(person)	1166	1376	1261	1296	1633	1596	-2.3
安置人数	Number of Persons Been Helped Settle Down	8002	10901	6015	6762	10113	7382	-27.0
帮教人数	Number of Persons Been Assisted and Teached	6414	10208	7849	9225	10026	8753	-12.7

18-17 “十五”时期各年消费者协会受理投诉情况

Basic Statistics on Cases Accepted and Heard by Consumer Association of Each Year in “Tenth Five-year Plan” Period

单位：件(piece)

指 标	Item	2000	2001	2002	2003	2004	2005	2005年比2004年增长(%) Increase Rate in 2005 over 2004(%)
总 计	**Total**	**8511**	**7876**	**9663**	**10057**	**10752**	**9850**	**-8.4**
家用电器类	Household Appliances	1238	1361	2733	3057	2878	2896	0.6
#电视机	Televison	489	575	727	534	535	512	-4.3
电冰箱	Refrigerators	114	107	132	202	146	136	-6.9
洗衣机	Washing Machines	79	109	172	207	142	142	0.0
空调器	Air-Conditioner	17	37	98	158	132	92	-30.3
家用机械类	Household Machinery	611	514	550	622	598	424	-29.1
#摩托车	Motorcycles	134	132	128	139	145	89	-38.6
百货类	Daily Use Goods	1709	1631	3209	3398	3600	2893	-19.6
#药品	Materia Medica			132	135	53	51	-3.8
医疗辅助用品	Assistant Things of Medical Treatment			9	19	14	7	-50.0
服装鞋帽	Dress Shoes and Caps			932	956	830	1190	43.4
家具	Furniture	138	146	135	227	180	101	0.3
食品	Foods			818	627	594	640	7.8
房屋及装修建材	Houses and Fitment Material			695	600	566	575	1.6
#房屋	Houses			375	247	266	289	8.7
装饰材料	Fitment Material			241	215	197	186	-5.6
服务类	Services	1620	1353	1410	1415	1773	1878	5.9
#电信	Telecome			98	110	155	259	67.1
邮政	Mail			38	18	54	40	-25.9
农用生产资料类	Agricultural Production Materials	378	414	384	375	471	419	-11.0
其他类	Others	785	698	682	590	866	765	-11.7

18-18 “十五”时期各年生产安全事故情况

Basic Statistics on Production Security Accidents of Each Year in “Tenth Five-year Plan” Period

项　目	Item	2000	2001	2002	2003	2004	2005
各类事故死亡人数合计（人）	**Number of Deaths(person)**	**2445**	**2723**	**3089**	**3440**	**3313**	**3239**
工矿商贸企业	Production Security Accidents of Enterprises of Industry,Mining,Commerce and Trade	930	867	1093	1248	1218	1192
煤矿	Coal Mine	777	673	891	972	930	837
金属与非金属矿	Metallic and Non-metallic Mine		97	46	65	105	120
建筑业	Construction		54	93	97	85	127
其他	Other		43	63	114	98	108
火灾	Fire Accidents	68	95	98	77	63	97
道路交通	Roadway Traffic Accidents	1251	1655	1759	1976	1831	1647
铁路交通	Railway Traffic Accidents	125	91	96	98	161	303
其他	Others	71	15	43	41	40	
亿元生产总值生产安全事故死亡人数(人/亿元)	Number of Deaths/GDP (person/per 100 million yuan)	2.37	2.4	2.48	2.41	1.97	1.67
工矿商贸企业从业人员10万人死亡率(人/10万人)	Number of Deaths/Employed Personels of Enterprises of Industry,Mining,Commerce and Trade(person/per 100000 persons)	16.58	23.06	26.79	26.38	23.7	23.19
煤矿百万吨死亡人数(人/百万吨)	Number of Deaths/Yields of Coal Mine (person/per million tons)	21.13	18.04	17.82	12.46	9.53	7.88
道路交通万车死亡人数(人/万车)	Number of Deaths/Number of Vehicles (person/per 10000 sets)	24.07	30.17	28.46	26.67	21.67	15.39

18-19 火灾情况（2005）

Basic Statistics on Fires（2005）

指　标	Item	合计 Total	特大 Extraordinarily Serious	重大 Serious	一般 Ordinary
实际发生数（起）	**Number of Fires(case)**	**778**	**1**	**6**	**771**
按火灾原因分	Grouped by Cause(unit)				
#放 火	Setting on Fire	43			43
违反电器安装规定	Violate Install Regulation of Electric Equipment	250		2	248
违反安全制度	Violate Safety Regulation	41			41
吸 烟	Smoking	16	1		15
生活用火不慎	Not Careful with Cooking Fire	233		3	230
玩 火	Playing with Fire	47			47
自 燃	Natural Fire	19			19
其 他	Others	62		1	61
不 明	Uncertain	67			67
死亡人数（人）	Number of Deaths(person)	97	3	13	81
伤残人数（人）	Number of Injuries(person)	62		3	59
损失折款（万元）	Losses Converted into Cash(10000 yuan)	1671.21	68.00	191.11	1412.10
平均每起事故损失（万元）	Average Loss Per Fire(10000 yuan)	2.15	68.00	31.85	1.83

18-20 交通事故情况（2005）

Basic Statistics on Traffic Accidents(2005)

指　标	Item	发生数（起） Number of Traffic Accidents(case)	死亡人数(人) Number of Deaths (person)	受伤人数（人） Number of Injuries (person)	损失折款（万元） Losses Convertedinto Cash(10000 yuan)
总　计	**Total**	**3315**	**1647**	**3984**	**2507.01**
#重大事故	Extraordinarily Serious	1163	1278	2666	1130.33
特大事故	Serious	82	369	318	376.68
机动车	Motor Vehicles	3137	1551	3893	2462.80
#汽车	Automobiles	2476	1256	3071	2314.83
摩托车	Motorcycles	589	254	743	126.57
拖拉机	Tractors	68	38	78	21.40
非机动车	Non-motor-driven Vehicles	22	6	19	7.00
#自行车	Bicycles	17	3	16	1.38
行人乘车人	Pedestrians and Passengers	156	90	72	37.31

主要统计指标解释

等级运动员人数 指经考核正式批准授予等级运动员称号的人数。运动员等级分为国际级运动健将、运动健将、一级运动员、二级运动员、三级运动员、少年级运动员。

等级裁判员人数 指经考核正式批准授予等级裁判员称号的人数。裁判员等级分为国际裁判、国家级裁判、一级裁判、二级裁判、三级裁判。

体育场 指有400米跑道(中心含足球场),有固定道牙,跑道6条以上,并有固定看台的室外田径场地。体育场按看台容纳观众人数分为:甲级25000人以上,乙级15000-25000人,丙级5000-15000人,丁级5000人以下。

体育馆 指有固定看台,可供篮球、排球、羽毛球、乒乓球、体操等项目训练比赛活动用的室内运动场地。体育馆按看台容纳观众人数分为:甲级6000人以上,乙级4000-6000人,丙级2000-4000人,丁级2000人以下。

卫生机构 包括医疗机构、疾病预防控制中心(防疫站)、采供血机构、卫生监督及监测(检验)机构、医学科研和在职培训机构、健康教育所等。

医疗机构 包括医院、社区卫生服务中心(站)、疗养院、卫生院、门诊部、诊所(卫生所、医务室)、妇幼保健院(所、站)、专科疾病防治院(所、站)、急救中心(站)和临床检验中心。医疗机构分为非赢利性医疗机构和赢利性医疗机构。

医院 包括综合医院、中医医院、中西医结合医院、民族医院、各类专科医院和护理院。

卫生技术人员 指卫生机构中医生、护理人员、药剂人员、检验人员等卫生技术人员。

医生 指在医疗、预防保健机构工作且取得《执业医师证书》的执业医师和执业助理医师。

公证人员 指在国家公证机关依法办理公证事务的司法人员,包括公证员、助理公证员和在公证处工作的其他人员。

办理公证文书 指公证处在一定时期内办结的公证文书件数。公证文书按司法部规定或批准的格式制作,包括国内公证和涉外公证两部分。国内公证分为经济合同公证和民事法律关系公证两大类。

调解人员 指在人民调解委员会担负调解民间一般民事纠纷和轻微违法行为引起纠纷的工作人员,包括调解委员会的委员和调解小组的调解员。

调解民间纠纷 指调解委员会依照法律规定,根据自愿原则,用说服教育的方法调解民间发生的有关民事权利和义务的争执,促成当事双方达到协议和谅解,解决纠纷。包括婚姻家庭纠纷,财产权益纠纷等,不包括法院受理调解的民事案件数。

离休、退休、退职人员 指正式办理了离休、退休、退职手续,并享受相应的离休、退休、退职待遇的人员。

保险福利费用 指企业、事业、机关单位在工资以外实际支付给职工和离休、退休、退职人员个人以及用于集体的

(1)职工保险福利费用包括:医疗卫生费;文体宣传费;集体福利事业补贴费;集体福利设施费;其他。

(2)离休、退休、退职人员保险福利费用包括:离休金;退休金;退职生活费;其他。

Explanatory Notes on Main Statistical Indicators

Number of Athletes in Grades refers to the number of athletes who have been given titles through examination. The titles of athletes include international masters of sports, masters of sports, first-grade, second-grade and third-grade sportsmen and young athletes.

Number of Referees in Grades refers to the number of referees who have been given titles after examination. They are classified as international referees, national referees and referees of the first, second and third grades.

Stadiums refer to stadiums for track and field events with six lane 400-meter tracks around soccer fields, permanent track marks and permanent bleachers. Stadiums are classified according to seating capacity. They include: Class A stadiums seating 25000 people each. Class B stadiums seating 15000 to 25000 people each. Class C stadiums seating 5000 to 15000 people each, and Class D stadiums seating fewer than 5000 people.

Gymnasiums refer to indoor sports grounds with permanent seats in which basketball, volleyball. badminton, table tennis and gymnastics competitions can be held. Gymnasiums are classified according to seating capacity. They include Class A gymnasiums seating over 6000 people. Class B gymnasiums seating 4000 to 6000 people. Class C gymnasiums seating 2000 to 4000 people, and Class D gymnasiums seating fewer than 2000 people.

Health Care Institutions include: medical institutions, disease prevention and control centers (epidemic prevention stations), blood gathering and supplying institutions, health supervision and inspection (check up) institutions, medicinal scientific research and on-job training institutions, health education and so on.

Medical Organizations include: hospitals, health service centers (stations) of communities, nursing homes, health centers, clinics, clinics (health stations and infirmaries), maternity and child care agencies (centers and stations), special disease prevention and curing agencies (centers and stations), first aid centers (stations) and clinical inspection centers. Medical organizations are grouped by two types: profit-making and non-profit-making medical organizations.

Hospitals include: polyclinics, traditional Chinese medical hospitals, hospitals integrated with traditional Chinese therapeutics and western therapeutics, ethical hospitals, various specialties hospitals and nursing hospitals.

Medical Technical Personnel refers to doctors, assistant nurses, pharmacists, and laboratory technicians working in medical institutions.

Doctors refer to certified physicians and certified assistant physicians with certifications working in medical and health care and prevention agencies.

Notary Personnel refers to judicial workers of the state notary offices handling notarization work according to law. They include notaries, assistant notaries, and other people working for notary offices.

Notarized Documents refer to the documents settled by notary offices in a year. The notary documents are drawn up in accordance with the regulations of the Ministry of Justice, including domestic documents and foreign-related documents. Domestic documents are divided into two major categories, documents on economic contracts and documents on civil legal relations.

Mediators refer to workers on peoples mediation committees responsible for mediating in civil disputes and cases of slight infraction of the law. They include members of the mediation committees and mediators of mediation groups.

Mediation of Civil Disputes refers to mediation committeeswork in mediating in civil disputes concerning civil rights and duties through persuasion and education in accordance with the provisions of law on a voluntary basis, so as to solve disputes by helping the parties involved come to an agreement and understanding. These disputes include divorce cases and disputes over property ownership, but exclude the civil cases to be handled by the court.

Retired or Resigned Personnel refers to the persons who have formally gone through the formalities for their retirement or quitting work and enjoy the corresponding treatments.

Insurance and Welfare Funds refers to labour insurance and welfare fund paid by enterprises, organizations and institutions to their staff and workers as well as retired and resigned persons in addition to their wages and salaries.

(1) Insurance and Welfare Funds for Staff and Workers include: Medical Care Allowance; Expenses for Recreational, Sports and Publicity Activities; Subsidies to Collective Welfare Undertakings: Expenses for Collective Welfare Facilities, Others

(2)Insurance and Welfare Funds for Retired and Resigned Staff and Workers: Pensions for retired veteran cadres, Pensions for Retirement, Resignation Allowances for Living Expenses, Others.

19

非公有制经济

Non-public-owned Economy

Nineteen

19-1 非公有制工

Main Economic Indicators Non-public-

指 标	Item	单位个数（个） Number of Enterprises(unit)		固定资产原价 Net Value of Fixed Assets(100 million yuan)	
		2004	2005	2004	2005
绝对数	**Absolute Figure**				
全省总计	Total	99434	106901	1655.39	1882.26
#非公有经济	Non-public-owned Economic Unit	97179	105107	406.30	580.35
#非公有企业	Non-public-owned Enterprises	9597	7891	384.57	537.41
个体经营户	Individual Proprietor	87582	97216	21.73	42.94
规模以上合计	Total(Above Designated Size)	2545	2585	1509.18	1711.11
#非公有企业	Non-public-owned Enterprises	1446	1673	282.05	425.12
规模以下合计	Total(Under Designated Size)	96889	104316	146.21	171.15
#非公有企业	Non-public-owned Enterprises	8151	6218	102.52	112.28
个体经营户	Individual Proprietor	87582	97216	21.73	42.94
构成（%）	**Composition(%)**				
以全省总计为100	Total(=100)	100.0	100.0	100.0	100.0
#非公有经济	Non-public-owned Economic Unit	97.7	98.3	24.5	30.8
#非公有企业	Non-public-owned Enterprises	9.7	7.4	23.2	28.6
个体经营户	Individual Proprietor	88.1	90.9	1.3	2.3
规模以上	Total(Above Designated Size)(=100)	100.0	100.0	100.0	100.0
#非公有企业	Non-public-owned Enterprises	56.8	64.7	18.7	24.8
规模以下	Total(Under Designated Size)(=100)	100.0	100.0	100.0	100.0
#非公有企业	Non-public-owned Enterprises	8.4	6.0	70.1	65.6
个体经营户	Individual Proprietor	90.4	93.2	14.9	25.1

注： 1. 个体经营户只有营业收入。2. 非公有单位个数，指单位实收资本中拥有非公有投资成份的单位数。

Note: 1. Data of individual proprietor revenue refers to the data of operating revenue in this table.

2. In accordance with the Statistic Regulation of Guizhou Non-public-owned Economic Unit,number of non-public-owned Enterprises

业主要经济指标

owned Industrial Enterprises

工业总产值（亿元）Gross Industrial Output (100 million yuan)		主营业务收入（亿元）Prime Operating Revenue (100 million yuan)		利润总额（亿元）Total Profits (100 million yuan)		从业人员（万人）Annual Average Number of Employed Persons(10000 persons)	
2004	2005	2004	2005	2004	2005	2004	2005
1643.53	1846.18	1564.64	1826.08	98.89	108.79	118.00	131.21
505.41	741.96	562.40	771.85	55.39	54.51	64.39	82.53
505.41	741.96	465.03	671.57	33.17	31.62	40.28	46.41
		97.37	100.28	22.22	22.88	24.11	36.12
1394.91	1690.40	1325.95	1577.16	61.99	70.79	66.87	68.08
376.10	605.52	342.69	541.39	20.11	18.38	17.36	23.59
151.25	155.78	241.70	248.93	36.90	38.00	51.13	63.13
129.31	136.43	122.35	130.18	13.06	13.24	22.82	22.82
		97.37	100.28	22.22	22.88	24.11	36.12
100.0	100.0	100.0	100.0	100.0	100.0	100.0	100.0
30.8	40.2	35.9	42.3	56.0	50.1	54.6	62.9
30.8	40.2	29.7	36.8	33.5	29.1	34.1	35.4
		6.2	5.5	22.5	21.0	20.4	27.5
100.0	100.0	100.0	100.0	100.0	100.0	100.0	100.0
27.0	35.8	25.8	34.3	32.4	26.0	26.0	34.7
100.0	100.0	100.0	100.0	100.0	100.0	100.0	100.0
85.5	87.6	50.6	52.3	35.4	34.8	44.8	36.1
		40.3	40.3	60.2	60.2	47.2	57.2

refers to number of Enterprises which paicl-up capital included investment of non-public-owned economic unit.

19-2 非公有制建筑

Main Economic Indicators Non-

指 标	Item	单位个数（个） Number of Enterprises(unit)		固定资产原价（亿元） Net Value of Fixed Assets (100 million yuan)	
		2004	2005	2004	2005
绝对数	**Absolute Figure**				
全省总计	Total	7225	7081	75.25	78.34
#非公经济	Non-public-owned Economic Unit	6898	6773	13.48	18.97
非公有企业	Non-public-owned Enterprises	732	681	11.91	17.10
个体经营户	Individual Proprietor	6166	6092	1.57	1.87
资质以上合计	Total(Above Designated Size)(=100)	641	580	71.26	74.06
#非公有企业	Non-public-owned Enterprises	314	272	11.16	16.35
资质以下合计	Total(Under Designated Size)(=100)	6584	6501	3.99	4.28
#非公有企业	Non-public-owned Enterprises	418	409	0.75	0.75
个体经营户	Individual Proprietor	6166	6092	1.57	1.87
构成（%）	**Composition(%)**				
以全省总计为100	Total(=100)	100.0	100.0	100.0	100.0
#非公经济	Non-public-owned Economic Unit	95.5	95.7	17.9	24.2
非公有企业	Non-public-owned Enterprises	10.1	9.6	15.8	21.8
个体经营户	Individual Proprietor	85.3	86.0	2.1	2.4
资质以上合计	Total(Above Designated Size)(=100)	100.0	100.0	100.0	100.0
#非公有企业	Non-public-owned Enterprises	49.0	46.9	15.7	22.1
资质以下合计	Total(Under Designated Size)(=100)	100.0	100.0	100.0	100.0
#非公有企业	Non-public-owned Enterprises	6.3	6.3	18.9	17.6
个体经营户	Individual Proprietor	93.7	93.7	39.4	43.6

业主要经济指标

public-owned Construction Enterprises

建筑业总产值（亿元） Gross Output Value of Construction (100 million yuan)		工程结算收入（亿元） Prime Operating Revenue (100 million yuan)		利润总额（亿元） Total Profits (100 million yuan)		从业人员（万人） Annual Average Number of Employed Persons (10000 persons)	
2004	2005	2004	2005	2004	2005	2004	2005
260.65	276.69	271.92	281.65	6.73	6.32	31.84	31.69
32.85	56.23	40.21	67.22	3.28	4.90	8.77	10.46
32.85	56.23	30.50	56.69	1.08	2.49	5.83	7.56
		9.71	10.53	2.20	2.41	2.94	2.90
255.45	271.23	256.59	265.33	4.35	3.71	27.87	27.84
30.78	54.06	28.27	54.39	1.09	2.50	5.35	7.12
5.20	5.46	15.33	16.32	2.38	2.60	3.96	3.85
2.06	2.17	2.23	2.30			0.49	0.44
		9.71	10.53	2.20	2.41	2.94	2.90
100.0	100.0	100.0	100.0	100.0	100.0	100.0	100.0
12.6	20.3	14.8	23.9	48.7	77.6	27.5	33.0
12.6	20.3	11.2	20.1	16.1	39.5	18.3	23.9
		3.6	3.7	32.6	38.1	9.2	9.2
100.0	100.0	100.0	100.0	100.0	100.0	100.0	100.0
12.0	19.9	11.0	20.5	25.0	67.2	19.2	25.6
100.0	100.0	100.0	100.0	100.0	100.0	100.0	100.0
39.7	39.7	14.6	14.1			12.3	11.5
		63.3	64.5	92.1	92.4	74.1	75.3

19-3 非公有制批发零售

Main Economic Indicators Non-public-owned Enterprises

指 标	Item	单位个数（个） Number of Enterprises(unit)		固定资产原价（亿元） Net Value of Fixed Assets(100 million yuan)	
		2004	2005	2004	2005
绝对数	**Absolute Figure**				
全省总计	Total	430175	432896	212.72	230.92
非公有制经济	Non-public-owned Economic Unit	427417	429567	88.07	91.54
限额以上非公	Above Designated Size of Chain	255	283	15.70	24.88
限额以下非公	Under Designated Size of Chain	5330	5344	22.08	16.11
个体经营户	Individual Proprietor	421832	423940	50.29	50.54
批发业合计	Total Wholesale Trade	23845	24183	75.22	84.56
限额以上非公	Above Designated Size of Chain	67	71	2.19	5.15
限额以下非公	Under Designated Size of Chain	2485	2697	5.06	5.76
个体经营批发业	Individual Proprietor	20008	20108	2.70	2.71
零售业合计	Total Retail Trade	344304	346293	74.46	77.95
限额以上非公	Above Designated Size of Chain	73	79	6.03	7.01
限额以下非公	Under Designated Size of Chain	2352	2647	9.54	10.36
个体经营零售业	Individual Proprietor	340749	342453	31.01	31.16
餐饮业合计	Total Catering Services	57779	57939	21.22	21.86
限额以上非公	Above Designated Size of Chain	57	54	1.42	1.44
限额以下非公	Under Designated Size of Chain	264	290	2.98	3.31
个体经营餐饮业	Individual Proprietor	57226	57512	12.65	12.71
住宿业合计	Total Quartering Services	4247	4481	41.81	46.56
限额以上非公	Above Designated Size of Chain	58	79	6.07	11.29
限额以下非公	Under Designated Size of Chain	229	249	4.51	4.15
个体经营住宿业	Individual Proprietor	3849	3868	3.93	3.95
构成（%）	**Composition(%)**				
全省总计为100	Total(=100)	100.0	100.0	100.0	100.0
非公有经济	Non-public-owned Economic Unit	99.4	99.2	41.4	39.6
限额以上非公	Above Designated Size of Chain	0.1	0.1	7.4	10.8
限额以下非公	Under Designated Size of Chain	1.2	1.2	10.4	7.0
个体经营户	Individual Proprietor	98.1	97.9	23.6	21.9

注：非公有单位个数，指单位实收资本中拥有非公有投资成份的单位数

Note: Number of non-public-owned Enterprises refers to number of Enterprises which paicl-up capital included investment of non-

贸易餐饮业主要经济指标

of Wholesale&Retail Trade and Catering & Quartering Services

主营业务收入（亿元） Prime Operating Revenue (100 million yuan)		利润总额（亿元） Total Profits (100 million yuan)		从业人员（万人） Annual Average Number of Employed Persons(10000 persons)	
2004	2005	2004	2005	2004	2005
1029.71	1161.12	92.13	93.57	84.24	86.63
572.50	681.82	82.19	84.62	73.79	71.07
88.23	143.83	0.07	1.82	2.29	2.16
145.78	156.41	-0.05	0.22	7.55	4.64
379.68	381.58	82.17	82.58	63.95	64.27
585.14	653.10	26.46	27.04	12.81	14.18
43.28	83.87	0.48	1.62	0.33	0.51
93.77	102.00	0.10	0.18	3.02	2.31
77.58	77.97	14.53	14.60	3.87	3.89
419.00	438.05	53.05	53.70	52.34	52.83
40.21	52.13	-0.09	0.41	1.11	1.04
48.52	54.42	-0.04	0.04	3.01	2.34
253.96	255.23	53.77	54.03	45.42	45.65
11.82	53.84	12.84	12.94	15.54	15.78
2.88	4.08	-0.04	0.02	0.46	0.61
1.59	1.75	-0.04	-0.04	0.79	0.67
45.77	46.00	12.92	12.98	13.75	13.82
13.75	16.13	-0.23	-0.11	3.55	3.73
1.85	3.75	-0.28	-0.22	0.39	0.59
1.90	1.85	-0.07	-0.05	0.73	0.45
2.37	2.38	0.96	0.96	0.90	0.90
100.0	100.0	100.0	100.0	100.0	100.0
55.6	58.7	89.2	90.4	87.6	82.0
8.6	12.4	0.1	1.9	2.7	2.5
14.2	13.5		0.2	9.0	5.4
36.9	32.9	89.2	88.3	75.9	74.2

public-owned economic unit.

19-4 规模以上非公有制工业

Main Economic Indicators of Non-public-owned

指 标	Item	企业单位数（个）Number of Enterprises (unit)
总 计	**Total**	**1673**
按登记注册类型分组:	Grouped by Registration Categories	
内资企业	Domestic Investment Enterprises	1568
国有企业	State-owned Enterprises	18
集体企业	Collective-owned Enterprises	55
股份合作企业	Share-holding Cooperative Enterprises	57
联营企业	Joint Owned Enterprises	25
国有联营企业	Joint Owned Enterprises of State-owned	4
集体联营企业	Joint Owned Enterprises of Collective-owned	3
国有与集体联营企业	Joint Owned Enterprises of State-owned and Collective-owned	4
其他联营企业	Others	14
有限责任公司	Companies with Limited Liabilities	489
国有独资公司	Sole State-owned	1
其他有限责任公司	Others	488
股份有限公司	Share-holding Companies with Limited Liabilities	92
私营企业	Private Enterprises	826
私营独资企业	Enterprises Investments with Sole Private	303
私营合作企业	Cooperative Enterprises	93
私营有限责任公司	Companies with Limited Liabilities	371
私营股份有限公司	Share-holding Companies with Limited Liabilities	59
其他企业	Others	6
港、澳、台商投资企业	Enterprises with Funds from Hong Kong, Macao and Taiwan	48
合资经营企业(港或澳、台资)	Joint-venture Enterprises(with Funds from Hong Kong,Macao and Taiwan)	26
港澳台商独资经营企业	Enterprises with Sole Funds from Hong Kong, Macao and Taiwan	21
港澳台商投资股份有限公司	Share-holding Companies with Funds from Hong Kong,Macao and Taiwan	1
外商投资企业	Foreign Funded Enterprises	57
中外合资经营企业	Joint-venture Enterprises	43
中外合作经营企业	Cooperative Enterprises	1
外资企业	Enterprises with Sole Foreigner	10
外商投资股份有限公司	Share-holding Companies with Funds from Foreigner	3
在总计中:亏损企业	Of the Total:Loss Making Industry	720
在总计中：轻工业	Of the Total:Light Industry	386
重工业	Heavy Industry	1287
在总计中：大型企业	Of the Total:Large Industry	11
中型企业	Medium	120
小型企业	Small	1542

企业主要经济指标(一)(2005)

above Designated Size Industrial Enterprises(2005)

单位：万元(10000 yuan)

工业总产值（当年价）Gross IndustialOutput Value(current price)	固定资产原价 Net Value of Fixed Assets	主营业务收入 Prime Operating Revenue	利润总额 Total Profits	从业人员平均人数（人）Annual Average Number of Employed Persons (person)
6055248	**4251234**	**5413883**	**183835**	**235943**
5623681	3892908	5023780	219023	217213
21030	10585	19114	3999	1031
30333	10646	31954	444	2492
109093	88309	98178	1572	6528
37891	9891	34069	614	2090
1234	1039	1205	-115	136
1396	705	1212	49	93
801	785	699	-145	210
34460	7361	30953	824	1650
1698572	820468	1521345	65098	64994
413	286	723	101	37
1698158	820182	1520623	64997	64956
1493168	2179245	1407802	109850	35070
2225492	772290	1905558	37300	104282
469731	224275	404965	14759	35933
112204	51230	106376	2802	10598
1378038	412756	1179483	18766	49625
265519	84028	214734	974	8126
8102	1475	5758	148	726
118488	122214	109626	6109	6524
67486	90672	64047	5476	3451
50067	26366	44898	1037	3023
935	5176	681	-404	50
313080	236112	280478	-41298	12207
253478	191503	225491	-43933	10723
2990	4560	3283	-116	206
34230	36636	36873	2360	793
22382	3413	14831	391	485
1698672	917945	1428242	-171767	81316
1557720	468760	1189590	88926	51297
4497528	3782474	4224294	94909	184646
1208184	1939226	1173804	62197	23127
1820377	946337	1583188	74844	63538
3026687	1365671	2656891	46794	149278

19-5 规模以上非公有制工业企

Main Economic Indicators of Non-public-owned

指 标	Item	企业单位数（个）Number of Enterprises (unit)
采掘业	**Mining and Quarrying**	**294**
煤炭开采和洗选业	Mining and Washing of Coal	235
石油和天然气开采业	Extraction of Petroleum and Natural Gas	
黑色金属矿采选业	Mining and Processing of Ferrous Metal Ores	14
有色金属矿采选业	Mining and Processing of Non-Ferrous Metal Ores	24
非金属矿采选业	Mining and Processing of Nonmetal Ores	21
其他采矿业	Mining of Other Ores	
制造业	**Manufacturing**	**1345**
农副食品加工业	Processing of Food from Agricultural Products	81
食品制造业	Manufacture of Foods	34
饮料制造业	Manufacture of Beverages	48
烟草制品业	Manufacture of Tobacco	
纺织业	Manufacture of Textile	9
纺织服装、鞋、帽制造业	Manufacture of Textile Wearing Apparel,Footware, and Caps	5
皮革、毛皮、羽毛(绒)及其制品业	Manufacture of Leather, Fur, Feather and Related Products	1
木材加工及木竹藤棕草制品业	Processing of Timber, Manufacture of Wood,Bamboo,Rattan, Palm,	23
家具制造业	Manufacture of Furniture	2
造纸及纸制品业	Manufacture of Paper and Paper Products	25
印刷业和记录媒介的复制	Printing,Reproduction of Recording Media	21
文教体育用品制造业	Manufacture of Articles For Culture, Education and Sport Activity	3
石油加工、炼焦及核燃料加工业	Processing of Petroleum, Coking, Processing of Nuclear Fuel	69
化学原料及化学制品制造业	Manufacture of Raw Chemical Materials and Chemical Products	157
医药制造业	Manufacture of Medicines	105
化学纤维制造业	Manufacture of Chemical Fibers	3
橡胶制品业	Manufacture of Rubber	10
塑料制品业	Manufacture of Plastics	33
非金属矿物制品业	Manufacture of Non-metallic Mineral Products	207
黑色金属冶炼及压延加工业	Smelting and Pressing of Ferrous Metals	242
有色金属冶炼及压延加工业	Smelting and Pressing of Non-ferrous Metals	115
金属制品业	Manufacture of Metal Products	21
通用设备制造业	Manufacture of General Purpose Machinery	36
专用设备制造业	Manufacture of Special Purpose Machinery	14
交通运输设备制造业	Manufacture of Transport Equipment	29
电气机械及器材制造业	Manufacture of Electrical Machinery and Equipment	25
通信设备、计算机及其他电子设备制造业	Manufacture of Communication Equipment, Computers and Other Electronic Equipment	16
仪器仪表及文化、办公用机械制造业	Manufacture of Measuring Instruments and Machinery for Cultural Activity and Office Work	8
工艺品及其他制造业	Manufacture of Artwork and Other Manufacturing	3
废弃资源和废旧材料回收加工业	Recycling and Disposal of Waste	
电力、煤气、水的生产和供应业	**Production and Distribution of Electric Power, Gasand Water**	**34**
电力、热力的生产和供应业	Production and Distribution of Electric Power and Heat Power	30
燃气生产和供应业	Production and Distribution of Gas	1
水的生产和供应业	Production and Distribution of Water	3

企业主要经济指标(二)(2005)

above Designated Size Industrial Enterprises(2005)

单位：万元(10000 yuan)

工业总产值（当年价）Gross IndustialOutput Value(current price)	固定资产原价 Net Value of Fixed Assets	主营业务收入 Prime Operating Revenue	利润总额 Total Profits	从业人员平均人数（人）Annual Average Number of Employed Persons (person)
374004	**207988**	**352011**	**34243**	**39358**
293124	188919	280844	23448	32945
16807	3167	17124	1514	1124
29031	8038	22672	1125	2534
35043	7864	31372	8156	2755
4990990	**2278300**	**4376186**	**86287**	**188280**
196395	32566	185527	5257	6190
157427	37892	149886	33393	4555
161285	65707	86481	10890	5450
21872	8600	18558	-410	2904
7763	4366	6959	112	1089
7819	83	7819	24	48
33969	5950	27515	435	3093
549	826	884	16	57
30198	11462	24427	409	1536
40793	45878	36276	3179	2258
3716	546	2718	-100	646
107283	40612	118291	2662	6260
699144	414988	628734	30816	22488
717099	217206	465638	32071	18291
8750	206	9185	96	304
145793	108153	155966	2641	4633
46650	25877	43424	870	2261
308171	328483	280709	4609	30859
930778	203795	831092	-26140	29926
634246	266635	586096	33067	12527
89779	55052	90086	1862	6153
61519	31424	60010	1486	3923
50432	20333	31568	-2736	2883
165583	154458	171871	-20998	7933
179080	50073	160921	6701	5429
160625	139622	182308	-33501	5283
13317	3028	6627	-488	797
10956	4479	6611	64	502
690255	**1764946**	**685686**	**63304**	**8305**
656592	1743890	653166	62299	7640
32311	15628	31217	814	590
1352	5428	1303	191	75

19-6 资质以上非公有制建

Main Economic Indicators of Non-public-owned

指 标	Item	有工作量企业数(个) Number of Enterprises (unit)
总 计	**Total**	**272**
按登记注册类型分组	**Grouped by Registration Categories**	
内资企业	Domestic Investment Enterprises	269
联营企业	Joint Owned Enterprises	2
其他联营企业	Others	2
有限责任公司	Companies with Limited Liabilities	143
其他有限责任公司	Others	143
股份有限公司	Share-holding Companies with Limited Liabilities	31
私营企业	Private Enterprises	93
私营独资企业	Enterprises Investments with Sole Private	3
私营合伙企业	Cooperative Enterprises	1
私营有限责任公司	Companies with Limited Liabilities	81
私营股份有限公司	Share-holding Companies with Limited Liabilities	8
港、澳、台商投资企业	Enterprises with Funds from Hong Kong, Macao and Taiwan	3
合资经营企业(港或澳、台资)	Joint-venture Enterprises(with Funds from Hong Kong, Macao and Taiwan)	3
按建筑业行业中类分组	**By Sector**	
建筑业	Construction	272
房屋和土木工程建筑业	Housing Construction and Civil Engineering Industry	183
建筑安装业	Construction and Installation Industry	38
建筑装饰业	Construction and Descoration Industry	40
其他建筑业	Other Construction Industries	11
按企业资质等级分组	**By Qualification Standard**	
施工总承包	Chief Construction Contract	181
一级	First Grade	4
二级	Second Grade	28
三级及以下	Third and Lower Grade	149
专业承包	Professional Contract	91
一级	First Grade	1
二级	Second Grade	49
三级及以下	Third and Lower Grade	41

筑企业主要经济指标(2005)

above Designated Size Construction Enterprises(2005)

单位：万元(10000 yuan)

固定资产原价 Net Value of Fixed Assets	建筑业总产值 Gross Output Value of Construction	工程结算收入 Prime Operating Revenue	利润总额 Total Profits	平均人数（人） Annual Average Number of Employed Persons(person)
163400	**540555**	**543861**	**24981**	**71192**
161796	539668	543139	25243	71121
709	631	631	7	191
709	631	631	7	191
99777	385746	407825	18015	46295
99777	385746	407825	18015	46295
16442	55400	45228	3699	7047
44868	97891	89455	3523	17588
1604	2123	2123	231	489
450	529	529	47	213
38761	87419	79819	2981	15382
4053	7821	6984	264	1504
1604	887	722	-263	71
1604	887	722	-263	71
163400	540555	543861	24981	71192
142152	453817	457732	19265	63017
11779	60583	60519	5467	3690
4194	11672	10856	-371	2215
5385	14484	14753	619	2271
138814	481533	486454	22244	63097
19479	124495	148070	5703	9624
52085	179142	173720	13451	20376
67250	177895	164664	3090	33097
24587	59022	57407	2737	8095
126	925	925	97	391
9666	28083	26769	168	3751
14795	30014	29713	2472	3953

19-7 限额以上非公有制批发零

Main Economic Indicators of Non-public-owned Enterprises

指 标	Item
总 计	**Total**
批发业	Wholesale Trade
按登记注册类型分组	**Grouped by Registration Categories**
内资企业	Domestic Investment Enterprises
国有企业	State-owned Enterprises
集体企业	Collective-owned Enterprises
股份合作企业	Share-holding Cooperative Enterprises
有限责任公司	Companies with Limited Liabilities
国有独资公司	Sole State-owned
其他有限责任公司	Others
股份有限公司	Share-holding Companies with Limited Liabilities
私营企业	Private Enterprises
私营有限责任公司	Companies with Limited Liabilities
私营股份有限公司	Share-holding Companies with Limited Liabilities
港、澳、台商投资企业	Enterprises with Funds from Hong Kong, Macao and Taiwan
合资经营企业(港或澳、台资)	Joint-venture Enterprises(with Funds from Hong Kong, Macao and Taiwan)
外商投资企业	Foreign Funded Enterprises
中外合资经营企业	Joint-venture Enterprises
外资企业	Enterprises with Sole Foreigner
按批发行业分组	**Grouped by Wholesale Trade Sector**
食品、饮料及烟草制品批发	Food, Beverages, Tobacco
纺织、服装及日用品批发	Textiles Products,Gaments and Commodity
文化、体育用品及器材批发	Culture&Sports Articles and Equipments
医药及医疗器材批发	Medicines and Special Appliances of Medicines
矿产品、建材及化工产品批发	Mineral Products,Materials of Construction and Chemical Products
机械设备、五金交电及电子产品批发	Mechinery Equipments,Hardwares,Electric Appliances and Eletronic Products
其他批发	Others

售企业主要经济指标(2005)

above Designated Size of Chain Wholesale and Retail Trade(2005)

单位：万元(10000 yuan)

企业个数（个） Number of Enterprises(unit)	固定资产原价 Net Value of Fixed Assets	主营业务收入 Prime Operating Revenue	利润总额 Total Profits	从业人员平均人数（人） Annual Average Number of Employed Persons(person)
150	**121572**	**1359970**	**20225**	**15473**
71	51481	838705	16157	5089
65	48239	794223	16092	4656
1	25	98	2	22
1	131	2158	5	18
1	254	3656	5	58
36	12724	369557	1719	2166
1	133	223		7
35	12591	369333	1719	2159
8	32270	228150	14083	1552
18	2835	190603	279	841
17	2618	181576	338	820
1	215	9027	-60	21
3	1222	14410	-2	93
3	1222	14410	-2	93
3	2023	30072	67	340
2	1959	24349	82	237
1	63	5723	-16	103
5	2695	39459	-43	110
1	1	361	1	2
1	8545	48590	1621	206
14	4838	161606	268	896
30	9821	345227	2065	2030
17	7798	116327	5721	929
3	17784	127134	6526	916

19-7续表(continued)

指标	Item
零售业	**Retail Trade**
按登记注册类型分组	**Grouped by Registration Categories**
内资企业	Domestic Investment Enterprises
国有企业	State-owned Enterprises
股份合作企业	Share-holding Cooperative Enterprises
其他联营企业	Other Joint Owned Enterprises
有限责任公司	Companies with Limited Liabilities
其他有限责任公司	Others
股份有限公司	Share-holding Companies with Limited Liabilities
私营企业	Private Enterprises
私营独资企业	Enterprises Investments with Sole Private
私营合伙企业	Cooperative Enterprises
私营有限责任公司	Companies with Limited Liabilities
私营股份有限公司	Share-holding Companies with Limited Liabilities
其他	Others
港、澳、台商投资企业	Enterprises with Funds from Hong Kong, Macao and Taiwan
与港澳台商合资经营	Joint-venture Enterprises(with Funds from Hong Kong,Macao and Taiwan)
与港澳台商合作经营	Cooperative Enterprises(with Funds from Hong Kong, Macao and Taiwan)
外商投资企业	Foreign Funded Enterprises
中外合资经营企业	Joint-venture Enterprises
按零售行业小类分组	**Grouped by Retail Trade Sector**
综合零售	Comprehensive Retail Sale
食品、饮料及烟草制品专门零售	Food, Beverages, Tobacco
纺织、服装及日用品专门零售	Textiles Products,Gaments and Commodity
医药及医疗器材专门零售	Medicines and Special Appliances of Medicines
汽车、摩托车、燃料及零配件专门零售	Automobiles,Motocycles,Fuels and Their Parts
家用电器及电子产品专门零售	Household Electrical Appliances and Electronic Products
五金、家具及室内装修材料专门零售	Hardwares,Furnitures and Materials of Decoration

企业个数（个） Number of Enterprises(unit)	固定资产原价 Net Value of Fixed Assets	主营业务收入 Prime Operating Revenue	利润总额 Total Profits	从业人员平均人数（人） Annual Average Number of Employed Persons(person)
79	**70091**	**521266**	**4068**	**10384**
75	62243	472310	1026	9234
2	28	21		5
1	58	2756	6	120
1	58	2756	6	120
38	31223	256150	1815	4774
38	31223	256150	1815	4774
5	14984	33667	750	980
28	15861	178171	-1535	3261
3	1487	2033	22	398
4	2408	26040	-371	561
20	11894	147274	-1187	2263
1	71	2825		39
1	88	1543	-9	94
2	1265	28547	2589	480
1	912	27004	2573	420
1	354	1543	16	60
2	6583	20410	453	670
2	6583	20410	453	670
30	35710	167847	4766	6013
2	432	341	5	45
1	2	619	6	67
7	933	18830	-22	841
20	17000	193729	-641	1329
18	15380	137716	-59	2017
1	635	2184	14	72

19-8 限额以上非公有制餐饮住

Main Economic Indicators of Non-public-owned Enterprises above

指 标	Item
总 计	**Total**
住宿业	**Quartering Services**
按登记注册类型分组	**Grouped by Registration Categories**
内资企业	Domestic Investment Enterprises
国有企业	State-owned Enterprises
集体企业	Collective-owned Enterprises
股份合作企业	Share-holding Cooperative Enterprises
有限责任公司	Companies with Limited Liabilities
国有独资公司	Sole State-owned
其他有限责任公司	Others
股份有限公司	Share-holding Companies with Limited Liabilities
私营企业	Private Enterprises
私营独资企业	Enterprises Investments with Sole Private
私营合伙企业	Cooperative Enterprises
私营有限责任公司	Companies with Limited Liabilities
私营股份有限公司	Share-holding Companies with Limited Liabilities
其他企业	Others
港、澳、台商投资企业	Enterprises with Funds from Hong Kong, Macao and Taiwan
合资经营企业(港或澳、台资)	Joint-venture Enterprises(with Funds from Hong Kong, Macao and Taiwan)
外商投资企业	Cooperative Enterprises(with Funds from Hong Kong, Macao and Taiwan)
中外合资经营企业	Foreign Funded Enterprises
中外合作经营企业	Joint-venture Enterprises
外资企业	Enterprises with Sole Foreigner
按住宿行业分组	**Grouped by Quartering Services Sector**
旅游饭店	Tourism Hotels
一般旅馆	General Hotels
其他住宿服务	Others
餐饮业	**Catering Services**
按登记注册类型分组	**Grouped by Registration Categories**
内资企业	Domestic Investment Enterprises
集体企业	Collective-owned Enterprises
有限责任公司	Companies with Limited Liabilities
其他有限责任公司	Others
股份有限公司	Share-holding Companies with Limited Liabilities
私营企业	Private Enterprises
私营独资企业	Enterprises Investments with Sole Private
私营合伙企业	Cooperative Enterprises
私营有限责任公司	Companies with Limited Liabilities
其他企业	Others
港、澳、台商投资企业	Enterprises with Funds from Hong Kong, Macao and Taiwan
合资经营企业(港或澳、台资)	Joint-venture Enterprises(with Funds from Hong Kong, Macao and Taiwan)
外商投资企业	Foreign Funded Enterprises
中外合资经营企业	Joint-venture Enterprises
按餐饮行业分组	**Grouped by Catering Services Sector**
正餐服务	Restaurant
快餐服务	Snack Counter

宿企业主要经济指标(2005)

Designated Size of Chain Catering and Quartering Services(2005)

单位：万元(10000 yuan)

企业个数（个） Number of Enterprises(unit)	固定资产原价 Net Value of Fixed Assets	主营业务收入 Prime Operating Revenue	利润总额 Total Profits	从业人员平均人数（人） Annual Average Number of Employed Persons(person)
133	**127272**	**78309**	**-2074**	**12018**
79	**112874**	**37496**	**-2227**	**5873**
70	65973	26746	-517	4299
8	9506	1490	-517	442
1		58	-28	
2	592	502	27	133
16	28572	8819	540	1383
1	377	279	1	73
15	28195	8540	539	1310
7	2556	1056	114	105
33	24109	14426	-740	2093
18	9196	7366	-122	958
1	700	344	5	60
13	14213	6632	-626	1045
1		83	3	30
3	638	396	87	143
3	11670	4089	-312	496
3	11670	4089	-312	496
6	35231	6661	-1399	1078
4	15905	3274	-1053	584
1	2434	396	-17	55
1	16893	2991	-329	439
72	107204	35527	-2337	5405
5	5360	1812	99	428
2	309	158	10	40
54	**14399**	**40813**	**153**	**6145**
52	14202	39675	128	5989
1	127	401	156	87
16	2672	6710	111	988
16	2672	6710	111	988
2	203	731	-1	196
26	10777	27835	121	4014
13	2408	8933	39	1438
3	164	1539	38	211
10	8205	17363	44	2365
7	424	3997	-241	704
1	62	144	-21	98
1	62	144	-21	98
1	135	994	29	58
1	135	994	29	58
50	13766	36033	108	5780
4	633	4780	45	364

19-9 全社会非公有制经济完成投资额（2005）

Investment of Non-public-owned Economic Unit(2005)

单位：万元(10000 yuan)

指标	Item	非公有 Non-public-owned	非公有投资占全省比重（%） Proportion of Investments of Non-public-owned Economic Units to Total Investments(%)
完成投资额合计	**Total**	**4377787**	**43.1**
农、林、牧、渔业	Agriculture,Forestry,Animal Husbandry and Fishing	164774	66.9
采矿业	Mining	149109	35.9
制造业	Manufacturing	848717	63.8
电力、燃气及水的生产和供应业	Production and Distribution of Electricity,Gas and Water	753800	31.4
建筑业	Construction	4374	23.1
交通运输、仓储和邮政业	Transport,Storage and Post	131709	9.1
信息传输、计算机服务和软件业	Information Transmission,Computer Service and Software	36697	12.3
批发和零售业	Wholesale and Retail Trade	77828	58.7
住宿和餐饮业	Hotel and Restaurants	57282	49.3
金融业	Financial Intermediation	3019	16.4
房地产业	Real Estate	2009359	92.6
租赁和商务服务业	Leasing and Business Services	9470	24.0
科学研究、技术服务和地质勘查	Scientific Research, Technical Services, and Geological Prospecting	3014	7.3
水利、环境和公共设施管理业	Management of Water Conservancy, Environment and Public Facilities	66448	10.6
居民服务和其他服务业	Services to Households and Other Services	13459	71.4
教育	Education	24257	8.2
卫生、社会保障和社会福利业	Health, Social Securities and Social Welfare	8678	9.7
文化、体育和娱乐业	Culture, Sports and Entertainment	14618	17.1
公共管理和社会组织	Public Management and Social Organization	1175	0.3

注:本表数据根据投资单位登记注册类型汇总。

Note:Data in the table are calculated by investment unit's registration status.

民族自治地区

Minority Nationality Autonomous Areas

Twenty

20-1 少数民族自治地方行政区划（2005）

Administrative Division of Minority Nationality Autonomous Areas(2005)

单位：个(unit)

民族自治州(县)名称	Autonomous State(County)	地级 Prefectural Level	县级 County Level	#县级市 City at Cou nty Level
黔东南苗族侗族自治州	Qiandongnan(Miao & Dong)Autonomous State	1	16	1
黔南州布依族苗族自治州	Qiannan(Bouyei & Miao)Autonomous State	1	12	2
黔西南布依族苗族自治州	Qianxinan(Bouyei & Miao)Autonomous State	1	8	1
道真仡佬族、苗族自治县	Daozhen(Gelo & Miao)Autonomous County		1	
务川仡佬族、苗族自治县	Wuchuan(Gelo & Miao)Autonomous County		1	
玉屏侗族自治县	Yuping(Dong)Autonomous County		1	
印江土家族、苗族自治县	Yinjiang(Tujia & Miao)Autonomous County		1	
沿河土家族自治县	Yanhe(Tujia)Autonomous County		1	
松桃苗族自治县	Songtao(Miao)Autonomous County		1	
关岭布依族苗族自治县	Guanling(Bouyei & Miao)Autonomous County		1	
镇宁布依族苗族自治县	Zhenning(Bouyei & Miao)Autonomous County		1	
紫云苗族布依族自治县	Ziyun(Miao & Bouyei)Autonomous County		1	
威宁彝族、回族、苗族自治县	Weining(Yi,Hui & Miao)Autonomous County		1	
三都水族自治县	Sandu(Shui)Autonomous County		1	

20-2 少数民族分布情况

Geographic Distribution of Minority Nationalities

民 族	Nationality	分布的主要地区	Main Geographic Distribution
苗 族	Miao	黔东南州、松桃县、威宁县	Qiandongnan,Songtao,Weining
布依族	Bouyei	黔南州、黔西南州	Qiannan,Qianxinan
侗 族	Dong	黔东南州、玉屏县	Qiandongnan,Yuping
土家族	Tujia	铜仁地区	Tongren
彝 族	Yi	毕节地区、六盘水市	Bijie,Liupanshui
仡佬族	Gelo	遵义市、安顺市	Zunyi,Anshun
水 族	Shui	三都县	Sandu
回 族	Hui	威宁县、兴仁县、平坝县	Weining,Xingren,Pingba
白 族	Bai	毕节地区	Bijie
瑶 族	Yao	黔东南州、三都县	Qiandongnan,Sandu
壮 族	Zhuang	从江县、黎平县、独山县、荔波县	Congjiang,Liping,Dushan,Libo
畲 族	She	凯里市、麻江县、都匀市、福泉市	Kaili,Majiang,Duyun,Fuquan
毛南族	Maonan	平塘县、独山县、惠水县	Pingtang,Dushan,Huishui
蒙古族	Mongolian	毕节地区、石阡县	Bijie,Shiqian
仫佬族	Mulam	凯里市、麻江县、黄平县	Kaili,Majiang,Huangping
满 族	Man	黔西县、大方县、金沙县	Qianxi,Dafang,Jinsha
羌 族	Qiang	石阡县、江口县	Shiqian,Jiangkou

20-3 少数民族自治地方基本情况（2005）

Basic Conditions of Minority Nationality Autonomous Areas(2005)

民族自治州(县)名称	Autonomous State(County)	成立时间 Time of Comeinto Existence	土地面积(平方公里) Total Land Area(sq.km)	年末常住人口(万人) Total Population at The Year-end (10000 persons)	#少数民族 Minority Nationalities
黔东南苗族侗族自治州	Qiandongnan(Miao & Dong) Autonomous State	1956.07.23	30334.7	441.72	334.40
黔南州布依族苗族自治州	Qiannan(Bouyei & Miao) Autonomous State	1956.08.08	26197.0	396.39	215.02
黔西南布依族苗族自治州	Qianxinan(Bouyei & Miao) Autonomous State	1982.05.01	16804.1	311.73	133.88
道真仡佬族、苗族自治县	Daozhen(Gelo & Miao) Autonomous County	1987.11.29	2156.2	34.27	26.71
务川仡佬族、苗族自治县	Wuchuan(Gelo & Miao) Autonomous County	1987.11.26	2772.8	42.77	41.07
玉屏侗族自治县	Yuping(Dong)Autonomous County	1984.11.07	515.9	14.35	11.84
印江土家族、苗族自治县	Yinjiang(Tujia & Miao) Autonomous County	1987.11.20	1961.1	42.23	29.07
沿河土家族自治县	Yanhe(Tujia)Autonomous County	1987.11.23	2468.8	57.13	31.89
松桃苗族自治县	Songtao(Miao)Autonomous County	1956.12.31	2861.2	65.31	30.80
关岭布依族苗族自治县	Guanling(Bouyei & Miao) Autonomous County	1981.12.31	1468.0	33.10	19.24
镇宁布依族苗族自治县	Zhenning(Bouyei & Miao) Autonomous County	1963.09.11	1702.6	35.33	20.14
紫云苗族布依族自治县	Ziyun(Miao & Bouyei) Autonomous County	1966.02.11	2283.7	34.76	22.84
威宁彝族、回族、苗族自治县	Weining(Yi,Hui & Miao) Autonomous County	1954.11.11	6296.3	112.01	28.90
三都水族自治县	Sandu(Shui)Autonomous County	1957.01.02	2383.7	33.22	30.73

20-3续表(continued) 单位：亿元（100 million yuan ）

民族自治州(县)名称	Autonomous State(County)	生产总值 Gross Domestic Product	财政一般预算收入 Local Financial Revenue	财政一般预算支出 Expenditures of Governments
黔东南苗族侗族自治州	Qiandongnan(Miao & Dong)Autonomous State	145.40	7.73	39.74
黔南州布依族苗族自治州	Qiannan(Bouyei & Miao)Autonomous State	167.96	9.55	37.18
黔西南布依族苗族自治州	Qianxinan(Bouyei & Miao)Autonomous State	119.93	8.28	24.94
道真仡佬族、苗族自治县	Daozhen(Gelo & Miao)Autonomous County	10.04	0.42	2.47
务川仡佬族、苗族自治县	Wuchuan(Gelo & Miao)Autonomous County	10.36	0.46	2.85
玉屏侗族自治县	Yuping(Dong)Autonomous County	11.05	0.72	1.72
印江土家族、苗族自治县	Yinjiang(Tujia & Miao)Autonomous County	11.01	0.49	2.80
沿河土家族自治县	Yanhe(Tujia)Autonomous County	13.62	0.59	3.65
松桃苗族自治县	Songtao(Miao)Autonomous County	17.71	0.62	3.88
关岭布依族苗族自治县	Guanling(Bouyei & Miao)Autonomous County	10.17	0.50	2.39
镇宁布依族苗族自治县	Zhenning(Bouyei & Miao)Autonomous County	11.25	0.57	2.46
紫云苗族布依族自治县	Ziyun(Miao & Bouyei)Autonomous County	6.76	0.30	2.30
威宁彝族、回族、苗族自治县	Weining(Yi,Hui & Miao)Autonomous County	26.63	1.46	5.35
三都水族自治县	Sandu(Shui)Autonomous County	7.40	0.26	2.51

20-4 "十五"时期各年民族

Major Social and Economic Indicators of Minority Nationality

指　标	Item	2000
年末常住人口（万人）	**Number of Permanent Population at The Year-end(10000 persons)**	**1547.50**
#少数民族人口	Minority Population	882.44
生产总值（亿元）	**Gross Domestic Product(100 million yuan)**	**309.30**
第一产业	Primary Industry	130.13
第二产业	Secondary Industry	98.50
第三产业	Tertiary Industry	80.67
固定资产投资（亿元）	**Investment in Fixed Assets(100 million yuan)**	
固定资产投资总额	Total Investment in Fixed Assets	57.99
#基本建设	Capital Construction	29.56
更新改造	Innovation	20.89
房地产开发	Real Estate Development	2.59
财政、金融（亿元）	**Government Finance and Banking(100 million yuan)**	
财政一般预算收入	Local Financial Revenue	18.27
财政一般预算支出	Financial Expenditure	46.47
金融机构年末存款余额	Total Savins Deposit Balance at The Year-end	214.14
金融机构年末贷款余额	Total Loan Balance at The Year-end	231.39
城乡居民储蓄余额	Urban and Rural Resident Savings Deposit Balance	137.33
农　业	**Agriculture**	
耕地面积（千公顷）	Cultivated Area for Freguently Use(1000 hectares)	799.72
农业总产值（亿元）	Gross Agricultural Output Value(100 million yuan)	205.38
粮食产量（万吨）	Output of Grain(10000 tons)	512.47
油料产量	Output of Oil-bearing Crops	26.10
烟叶产量	Output of Flue-cured Tobacco	11.17
大牲畜年底头数（万头）	Large Animals(year-end)(10000 heads)	458.89
猪年底头数	Hogs(year-end)	826.21
羊年底头数（万只）	Sheep and Goats(year-end)(10000 heads)	200.95
工　业	**Industry**	
原煤产量(万吨)	Output of Coal(10000 tons)	694.24
发电量（亿千瓦小时）	Output of Electricity(100 million kwh)	146.17
生铁产量（万吨）	Pig Iron(10000 tons)	
运输邮电	**Transportation and Post**	
公路里程(公里)	Length of Highways(km)	25848
邮路总长度	Length of Postal Routes	10273
商　业	**Trade**	
社会消费品零售总额(亿元)	Total Retail Sales of Consumer Goods(100 million yuan)	80.58
教　育	**Education**	
在校学生数（万人）	Students Enrollment(10000 persons)	
高等学校	Institutions of Higher Education	0.86
中等学校	Secondary Schools	63.53
小学	Primary Schools	210.05
专任教师	Full-time Teachers	
高等学校	Institutions of Higher Education	0.07
中等学校	Secondary Schools	3.28
小　学	Primary Schools	7.39
人均水平	**Per Capita Standard of Living**	
人均生产总值（元）	Per Capita Gross Domestic Product(yuan)	2039
人均地方财政收入	Per Capita Local Financial Revenue	119
城乡居民人均储蓄	Per Capita Urban and Rural Resident Savings	902

自治地方经济社会主要指标

Autonomous Areas of Each Year in "Tenth-Five-Year Plan" Period

2001	2002	2003	2004	2005	2005年比2004年增长(%) Increase Rate in 2005 over 2004(%)
1565.13	**1580.33**	**1593.86**	**1608.24**	**1621.10**	**0.8**
869.08	901.53	915.87	934.01	945.79	1.3
333.83	**365.62**	**407.97**	**470.28**	**561.89**	**12.0**
135.04	136.77	147.64	167.51	186.39	6.5
103.89	120.22	136.17	164.06	176.96	14.9
94.90	108.62	124.16	138.70	198.54	14.6
77.90	101.31	128.13	157.59	206.11	30.8
38.70	58.01	71.98	92.90	126.22	35.9
24.81	25.40	29.79	32.70	49.07	50.1
7.07	10.26	14.91	17.50	20.70	18.3
19.73	20.42	22.61	26.63	31.67	18.9
63.11	76.14	85.04	101.95	131.74	29.2
257.45	296.23	358.83	455.64	560.43	23.0
243.52	273.03	279.04	312.88	365.04	16.7
161.08	185.92	222.49	271.83	337.42	24.1
794.97	769.58	761.50	762.19	761.65	-0.1
212.33	218.33	241.22	275.80	298.85	6.6
506.46	433.02	505.70	526.19	523.79	-0.5
25.29	25.62	25.80	28.29	29.42	4.0
10.91	12.12	11.22	11.89	13.54	13.9
469.73	477.31	491.09	510.56	527.28	3.3
851.34	878.32	911.45	958.61	1010.65	5.4
206.30	206.26	220.79	237.98	254.55	7.0
959.49	1113.22	1624.19	1999.87	2039.02	23.1
181.79	190.31	178.28	172.64	167.55	-3.2
		8.83	11.33	14.89	28.3
26553	27651	29278	35248	62021	20.4
10538	10427	14536	14706	14948	1.2
87.13	96.47	109.74	127.36	151.41	16.1
1.05	1.82	2.00	2.49	3.32	24.6
72.22	85.52	94.62	104.84	108.70	10.8
197.97	202.02	199.94	199.99	194.05	…
0.15	0.12	0.17	0.19	0.20	12.9
3.39	3.83	4.27	4.78	5.10	11.9
7.51	7.60	7.55	7.57	7.84	0.3
2145	2325	2571	2937	3480	14.3
127	130	142	166	196	16.9
1035	1182	1402	1698	2081	21.1

20-5 少数民族自治地方经济发展主要指标（2005）

Major Economic Indicators of Minority Nationality Autonomous Areas(2005)

指 标	Item	民族自治地方 Minority Nationality Autonomous Areas	民族自治州 Minority Nationality Autonomous State	民族自治县 Minority Nationality Autonomous County
生产总值（亿元）	**Gross Domestic Product(100 million yuan)**	**561.89**	**433.29**	**135.99**
第一产业	Primary Industry	186.39	130.91	59.21
第二产业	Secondary Industry	176.96	146.20	31.29
第三产业	Tertiary Industry	198.54	156.18	45.50
农 业	**Agriculture**			
乡村人口（万人）	Rural Population(10000 persons)	1439.61	1001.02	469.53
年末实有耕地面积(千公顷)	Cultivated Areas(year-end)(1000 hectares)	761.65	516.33	258.87
农用机械总动力（万千瓦）	Total Agricultural Machinery Power(10000 kw)	438.77	334.06	112.48
农村用电量（万千瓦小时）	Electricity Consumed in Rural Areas(10000 kwh)	62113.88	46650.12	16959.13
化肥使用量(折纯量)(万吨)	Consumption of Chemical Fertilizers(10000 tons)	45.61	35.12	10.79
有效灌溉面积（千公顷）	Effective Irrigated Areas(1000 hectares)	330.75	257.82	80.02
农作物播种面积	Sown Areas of Farm Crops	1989.70	1359.14	663.90
#粮 食	Grain Crops	1235.41	842.50	415.15
油 料	Oil-bearing Crops	231.69	176.54	61.73
粮食总产量（万吨）	Total Grain Yield(10000 ton)	523.79	367.29	165.91
油料产量	Oil-bearing Crops Yield	29.42	20.16	9.92
烟叶产量	Tobacco Yield	13.54	7.73	5.81
茶叶产量	Tea Yield	1.02	0.75	0.28
当年造林面积（千公顷）	Afforested Areas in 2004(1000 hectares)	83.00	57.51	27.07
牲畜当年出栏数	Number of Slaughtered Animals			
大牲畜（万头）	Large Animals(10000 heads)	100.30	74.88	28.04
猪	Hogs	892.51	646.35	264.17
羊（万只）	Sheep and Goats(10000 heads)	175.51	72.86	103.14
牲畜当年存栏数	Animals in Hand			
大牲畜（万头）	Large Animals(10000 heads)	527.28	389.54	154.25
猪	Hogs	1010.65	706.04	322.57
羊（万只）	Sheep and Goats(10000 heads)	254.55	119.20	136.05
肉类总产量（万吨）	Output of Meat(10000 tons)	91.18	62.65	30.09
水产品产量(吨)	Aquatic Products(ton)	49503	41530	9073
农林牧渔业总产值（亿元）	Gross Output Value of Farming,Forestry,Animal Husbandry and Fishery(100 million yuan)	298.85	212.26	92.31
#农 业	Farming	159.06	108.94	53.07

20-5续表(continued)

指　标	Item	民族自治地方 Minority Nationality Autonomous Areas	民族自治州 Minority Nationality Autonomous State	民族自治县 Minority Nationality Autonomous County
林　业	Forestry	16.54	14.13	2.74
牧　业	Animal Husbandry	112.49	80.41	34.28
渔　业	Fishery	4.82	4.10	0.84
农林牧渔业增加值	Value-added of Farming,Forestry,Animal Husbandry and Fishery	185.83	130.91	58.65
工业（规模以上）	**Industry(above designated size)**			
企业单位数（个）	Number of Industrial Enterprises(unit)	993.00	819.00	187.00
工业总产值（亿元）	Total Gross Industrial Output Value above Designated Size(100 million yuan)	328.61	275.72	54.20
工业销售产值	Sales Output Value of Industry	291.92	241.52	51.61
工业增加值	Value-added of Industry	106.02	92.72	13.67
利润总额	Total Profits and Taxes	3.76	2.80	0.90
主要工业产品产量	Output of Major Industrial Products			
原　煤（万吨）	Coal(10000 tons)	2039.02	1833.75	205.27
生　铁（万吨）	Pig Iron(10000 tons)	14.89	5.80	9.09
卷　烟（万支）	Cigarettes(10000 cases)	20.00	20.00	
水　泥（万吨）	Cement(10000 tons)	470.64	404.46	73.41
发电量（亿千瓦小时）	Electricity(100 million kwh)	167.55	159.18	8.41
固定资产投资	**Investment in Fixed Assets**			
全社会固定资产投资完成额(亿元)	Total Investment in Fixed Assets(100 million yuan)	248.44	190.94	59.31
国有经济	State-owned Units	104.81	67.85	37.74
集体经济	Collective_owened Units	2.06	1.04	1.02
外商港澳台经济	Units with Funds from Foreign,Hong Kong, Macao and Taiwan	4.60	3.91	0.69
其他投资	Others	136.97	118.15	19.85
商　业	**Trade**			
社会消费品零售总额	Total Retail Sales of Consumer Goods	151.41	123.64	30.05
财政、金融	**Government Finance and Banking**			
财政一般预算收入(亿元)	Local Financial Revenue(100 million yuan)	31.67	25.57	6.37
财政一般预算支出	Financial Expenditure	131.74	101.87	32.39
存款余额	Deposits	560.43	461.50	105.10
贷款余额	Loans	365.04	288.11	79.52
城乡居民储蓄余额	Urban and Rural Resident Savings Deposit Balance	337.42	274.98	66.39

20-6 少数民族自治地方社会发展主要指标（2005）

Major Indicators on Social Development of Minority Nationality Autonomous Areas(2005)

指 标	Item	民族自治地方 Minority Nationality Autonomous Areas	民族自治州 Minority Nationality Autonomous State	民族自治县 Minority Nationality Autonomous County
人 口	**Population**			
年末人口（万人）	Number of Population at The Year-end(10000 persons)	1621.10	1149.84	504.48
#少数民族人口	Minority Population	945.79	683.30	293.22
人口密度(人/平方公里)	Population Density(person/sq.km)	166.05	156.88	188.87
交通运输	**Traffic**			
民用汽车拥有量（辆）	Number of Civil Motor Vehicles Owned(unit)	94256	73181	21674
公路线路里程（公里）	Length of Highways(km)	62021	49717	13294
内河航道里程	Length of Navigable Inland Waterways	2086	1815	271
邮电、通讯	**Post and Telecommunications**			
邮政所总数（处）	Number of Post Offices(unit)	522	386	150
邮路总长度（公里）	Length of Postal Routes(km)	14948	8265	6788
农村投递线路总长度	Length of Rural Delivery Routes	34498	25163	10793
本地电话年末用户(万户)	Number of Telephone Sets at the Year-end(10000 unit)	142.15	122.65	21.72
#住宅电话用户	Residence Telephone	66.07	56.71	9.36
教 育	**Education**			
普通高等学校	Regular Institutions of Higher Education			
学校数（所）	Number of Schools(unit)	8	8	
在校学生数（人）	Students Enrollment(person)	33225	33225	
招生数	New Student Enrollment	11878	11878	
毕业生数	Graduates	6570	6570	
专任教师数	Full-time Teachers	2017	2017	
中等专业学校	Specialized Secondary Schools			
学校数（所）	Number of Schools(unit)	36	33	4
在校学生数（人）	Students Enrollment(person)	40649	38217	3767
招生数	New Student Enrollment	20335	19315	1865
毕业生数	Graduates	8504	8161	584
专任教师数	Full-time Teachers	1197	1001	286
普通中学	Regular Secondary Schools			
学校数（所）	Number of Schools(unit)	1019	762	276
在校学生数（万人）	Students Enrollment(10000 person)	102.46	74.43	30.03
招生数	New Student Enrollment	36.45	25.92	11.23
毕业生数	Graduates	29.20	22.18	7.59
专任教师数	Full-time Teachers	4.87	3.59	1.35
小 学	Primary Schools			
学校数（所）	Number of Schools(unit)	7025	5150	2015
在校学生数（万人）	Students Enrollment(10000 person)	194.05	130.43	67.68
招生数	New Student Enrollment	30.00	19.74	10.89
毕业生数	Graduates	31.28	21.73	10.20
专任教师数	Full-time Teachers	7.84	5.63	2.37

20-7 少数民族教育基本情况（2005）

Basic Statistics on Minority Nationality Education(2005)

单位:人(person)

类 别	Sort	毕业生 Graduates	招生 New Students Enrollment	在校生 Students Enrollment	毕业班学生 Students in Graduated Class	专任教师 Full-time Teachers	独立设置的少数民族学校 Minority Nationality Schools	
							学校数 Number of Schools	在校学生 Students Enrollment
普通中学	Regular Secondary Schools	279009	355001	993281	305599	48605	109	133403
#高 中	Senior	45591	75770	193922	55399	9440		55008
初 中	Junior	233418	279231	799359	250200	39165		78395
职业初中	Vocational JSSs	3975	4332	12630	4123	608	4	1096
小 学	Primary Schools	288775	303601	1884252	283813	77220	159	
特殊教育学校	Special Education Schools							
幼儿园	Kindergartens	21790	39270	68144		3086	11	

20-8 少数民族自治地方财政一般预算收入（2005）

Total Financial Revenue of Minority Nationality Autonomous Areas(2005)

单位:万元(10000 yuan)

指 标	Item	民族自治地方合计 Miniority Nationality Áutonomous Area	民族自治州合计 Nationality Minority Autonomous State	民族自治县合计 Minority Nationality Autonomous County
总 计	**Total**	**316746**	**255654**	**61092**
#农业四税	Agricultural Taxes and Related	37969	26790	11179
企业所得税类	Income Tax of Enterprises	11580	8800	2780
国有资产经营收益	Business Revenue of State-owned Properties	9223	6616	2607
国有企业计划亏损补贴类	Planning Subsidies to Loss-suffering Stated-owned Enterprises	-36	-15	-21
其他收入类	Other Revenue	20502	15399	5103
专项收入类	Revenue of Special Item	12831	10494	2337
罚没收入行政性收费收入类	Fine,Administrative Collecting Fees	41965	33857	8108

20-9 少数民族自治地方财政一般预算支出（2005）

Total Financial Expenditure of Minority Nationality Autonomous Areas (2005)

单位:万元(10000 yuan)

指　标	Item	民族自治地方合计 Miniority Nationality Autonomous Area	民族自治州合计 Minority Nationality Autonomous State	民族自治县合计 Minority Nationality Autonomous County
总　计	**Total**	1317414	1018662	298752
基本建设支出	Expenditure for Capital Construction	17003	15808	1195
企业挖掘改造资金	Enterprises Innovation Funds	6281	5767	514
科技三项费用	Expense on Science and Technology Promotion	3187	2918	269
农林水利气象支出	Expenditure for Agriculture,Forest,Irrigation and Meteorology	151669	118691	32978
工业交通部门事业费	Operating Expenses of Industial and Transportation Departments	23861	20942	2919
城市维护费	City Maintenance Expenditure	34426	27804	6622
文教卫生事业费	Operating Expenses for Culture, Education and Health Care	471217	353947	117270
科学事业费	Operating Expenses of Department of Science	2543	2090	453
其他部门事业费	Operating Expenses of Other Department	29406	24149	5257
抚恤和社会福利救济费	Pensions,Social Welfare and Relief Funds	49337	35573	13764
行政管理费	Administrative Expenses	233121	177368	55753
公检法支出	Agencies of Public Security,Procuratorial and Court of Justice	69861	54720	15141
支援不发达地区支出	Expenditure for Supporting Underdeveloped Areas	61414	44055	17359
其他支出	Others	164088	134830	29258

20-10 各少数民族自治州经济发展主要指标（2005）

Major Indicators on Economic Development of Minority Nationality Autonomous States(2005)

指标名称	Item	黔西南州 Qianxinan	黔东南州 Qiandongnan	黔南州 Qiannan
生产总值（亿元）	**Gross Domestic Product(100 million yuan)**	119.93	145.40	167.96
第一产业	Primary Industry	35.18	46.78	48.95
第二产业	Secondary Industry	43.48	38.97	63.75
第三产业	Tertiary Industry	41.28	59.64	55.26
农 业	**Agriculture**			
乡村人口（万人）	Rural Population(10000 persons)	280.47	382.82	337.73
年末实有耕地面积(千公顷)	Cultivated Areas(year-end)(1000 hectares)	161.52	178.58	176.23
农用机械总动力（万千瓦）	Total Agricultural Machinery Power (10000 kw)	98.34	121.06	114.66
农村用电量（万千瓦小时）	Electricity Consumed in Rural Areas(10000 kwh)	11358.93	17345.00	17946.19
化肥使用量(折纯量)(万吨)	Consumption of Chemical Fertilizers(10000 tons)	6.93	20.91	7.28
有效灌溉面积（千公顷）	Effective Irrigated Areas(1000 hectares)	54.43	113.29	90.10
农作物播种面积	Sown Areas of Farm Crops	379.61	518.97	460.56
#粮 食	Grain Crops	247.99	302.70	291.81
油 料	Oil-bearing Crops	29.14	57.96	89.44
粮食总产量（万吨）	Total Grain Yield(10000 ton)	104.33	134.36	128.60
油料产量	Oil-bearing Crops Yield	3.48	7.73	8.94
烟叶产量	Tobacco Yield	2.84	1.67	3.22
茶叶产量	Tea Yield	0.25	0.25	0.24
当年造林面积（千公顷）	Afforested Areas in 2004(1000 hectares)	23.06	19.43	15.02
牲畜当年存栏数	Animals in Hand			
大牲畜（万头）	Large Animals(10000 heads)	107.58	141.33	140.63
猪	Hogs	184.26	275.13	246.65
羊（万只）	Sheep and Goats(10000 heads)	35.51	61.59	22.10
牲畜当年出栏数	Number of Slaughtered Animals			
大牲畜（万头）	Large Animals(10000 heads)	22.34	29.52	23.02
猪	Hogs	187.66	229.95	228.74
羊（万只）	Sheep and Goats(10000 heads)	20.18	38.27	14.41
肉类总产量（万吨）	Output of Meat(10000 tons)	19.46	21.53	21.67
水产品产量(吨)	Aquatic Products(ton)	14092	20652	6786
农林牧渔业总产值（亿元）	Gross Output Value of Farming,Forestry,Animal Husb andry and Fishery(100 million yuan)	57.94	74.84	79.48
#农 业	Farming	28.83	38.94	41.17

20-10续表(continued)

指标名称	Item	黔西南州 Qianxinan	黔东南州 Qiandongnan	黔南州 Qiannan
林 业	Forestry	3.32	7.10	3.70
牧 业	Animal Husbandry	23.95	25.30	31.16
渔 业	Fishery	1.04	2.37	0.69
农林牧渔业增加值	Value-added of Farming,Forestry,Animal Husbandry and Fishery	35.18	46.78	48.95
工业（规模以上）	**Industry(above designated size)**			
企业单位数（个）	Number of Industrial Enterprises(unit)	266	247	306
工业总产值（亿元）	Total Gross Industrial Output Valueabove Designated Size(100 million yuan)	75.99	76.49	123.25
工业销售产值	Sales Output Value of Industry	73.94	55.35	112.24
工业增加值	Value-added of Industry	33.66	22.28	36.78
利润总额	Total Profits	1.08	-0.14	1.86
主要工业产品产量	Output of Major Industrial Products			
原煤（万吨）	Coal(10000 tons)	1041.33	232.43	559.99
生铁（万吨）	Pig Iron(10000 cu.m)			5.80
卷烟（万支）	Cigarettes(10000 cases)	20.00		
水泥（万吨）	Cement(10000 tons)	140.21	107.42	156.83
发电量（亿千瓦小时）	Electricity(100 million kwh)	114.30	38.71	6.17
固定资产投资	**Investment in Fixed Assets**			
全社会固定资产投资完成额(亿元)	Total Investment in Fixed Assets(100 million yuan)	53.31	85.54	52.10
国有经济	State-owned Units	12.03	38.47	17.34
集体经济	Collective_owened Units	0.10	0.52	0.42
外商港澳台经济	Units with Funds from Foreign,Hong Kong,Macao and Taiwan	2.73	0.03	1.14
其他投资	Others	38.45	46.51	33.19
商 业	**Trade**			
社会消费品零售总额(亿元)	Total Retail Sales of Consumer Goods(100 million yuan)	36.78	48.25	38.61
财政、金融	**Treasury and Finance**			
财政一般预算收入(亿元)	General Budgetary Fiscal Revenue(100 million yuan)	8.28	7.73	9.55
财政一般预算支出	General Budgetary Fiscal Expenditure	24.94	39.74	37.18
存款余额	Deposits	130.26	164.02	167.22
贷款余额	Loans	77.36	120.25	90.50
城乡居民储蓄余额	Urban and Rural Resident Savings Deposit Balance	68.82	106.40	99.75

20-11 各少数民族自治州社会发展主要指标（2005）

Major Indicators on Social Development of Minority Nationality Autonomous State(2005)

指标名称	Item	黔西南州 Qianxinan	黔东南州 Qiandongnan	黔南州 Qiannan
人 口	**Population**			
年末人口（万人）	Number of Population at The Year-end(10000 persons)	311.73	441.72	396.39
#少数民族人口	Minority Population	133.88	334.40	215.02
人口密度(人/平方公里)	Population Density(persons/sq.km)	185.51	145.62	151.31
交通运输	**Traffic**			
民用汽车拥有量（万辆）	Number of Civil Motor Vehicles Owned(unit)	3.05	2.85	1.42
公路线路里程（公里）	Length of Highways(km)	7925	6766	35026
内河航道里程	Length of Navigable Inland Waterways	515	1300	
邮电、通讯	**Post and Telecommunications**			
邮政所总数（处）	Number of Post Offices(unit)	95	159	132
邮路总长度（公里）	Length of Postal Routes(km)	1894	4494	1877
农村投递线路总长度	Length of Rural Delivery Routes	4759	10569	9835
本地电话年末用户(万户)	Number of Telephone Sets at the Year-end (10000 units)	31.34	50.05	41.26
#住宅电话用户	Residence Telephone	16.47	29.47	10.77
教 育	**Education**			
普通高等学校	Regular Institutions of Higher Education			
学校数（所）	Number of Schools(unit)	2	3	3
在校学生数（人）	Students Enrollment(person)	3309	11982	17934
招生数	New Student Enrollment	1458	4562	5858
毕业生数	Graduates	654	2745	3171
专任教师数	Full-time Teachers	334	788	895
中等专业学校	Specialized Secondary Schools			
学校数（所）	Number of Schools(unit)	3	27	3
在校学生数（人）	Students Enrollment(person)	4288	26816	7113
招生数	New Student Enrollment	1927	14367	3021
毕业生数	Graduates	1661	5013	1487
专任教师数	Full-time Teachers	208	579	214
普通中学	Regular Secondary Schools			
学校数（所）	Number of Schools(unit)	217	285	260
在校学生数（人）	Students Enrollment(person)	212782	283820	247691
招生数	New Student Enrollment	74669	97939	86628
毕业生数	Graduates	62842	85224	73703
专任教师数	Full-time Teachers	9876	14280	11780
小 学	Primary Schools			
学校数（所）	Number of Schools(unit)	1695	1913	1542
在校学生数(人)	Students Enrollment(person)	399697	465541	439085
招生数	New Student Enrollment	61867	72161	63420
毕业生数	Graduates	67508	78623	71169
专任教师数	Full-time Teachers	15520	21164	19593

20-12 各少数民族自治县

Major Indicators on Economic Development of

指 标	Item	道真县 Daozhen	务川县 Wuchuan
生产总值（万元）	**Gross Domestic Product(10000 yuan)**	**100351**	**103605**
第一产业	Primary Industry	47996	52795
第二产业	Secondary Industry	15382	11736
第三产业	Tertiary Industry	36973	39074
农 业	**Agriculture**		
乡村人口（万人）	Rural Population(10000 persons)	30.60	39.96
年末实有耕地面积（千公顷）	Cultivated Areas(year-end)(1000 hectares)	23.47	28.37
农用机械总动力（万千瓦）	Total Agricultural Machinery Power (10000 kw)	8.20	12.28
农村用电量（万千瓦小时）	Electricity Consumed in Rural Area s(10000 kwh)	1981.00	1842.00
化肥使用量（折纯量）（万吨）	Consumption of Chemical Fertilizers(10000 tons)	0.93	0.86
有效灌溉面积（千公顷）	Effective Irrigated Areas(1000 hectares)	7.92	9.68
农作物播种面积	Sown Areas of Farm Crops	69.08	87.33
#粮食	Grain Crops	43.13	56.87
油料	Oil-bearing Crops	8.15	11.57
粮食总产量（吨）	Total Grain Yield(ton)	133720	170394
油料产量	Oil-bearing Crops Yield	8034	15806
烟叶产量	Tobacco Yield	9183	13699
茶叶产量	Tea Yield	618	157
当年造林面积（千公顷）	Afforested Areas in 2004(1000 hectares)	1.67	3.73
牲畜当年存栏数	Animals in Hand		
大牲畜（万头）	Large Animals(10000 heads)	9.39	14.81
猪	Hogs	38.13	28.64
羊（万只）	Sheep and Goats(10000 heads)	10.60	17.74
牲畜当年出栏数	Number of Slaughtered Animals		
大牲畜（万头）	Large Animals(10000 heads)	2.30	2.66
猪	Hogs	32.37	21.80
羊（万只）	Sheep and Goats(10000 heads)	6.33	13.48
肉类总产量（吨）	Output of Meat(10000 tons)	32420	25656
水产品产量(吨)	Aquatic Products(ton)	327	313
农林牧渔业总产值（万元）	Gross Output Value of Farming,Forestry,Animal Husb andry and Fishery(10000 yuan)	78567	85235
农 业	Farming	40714	53654

经济发展主要指标(2005)

Minority Nationality Aut onomous Countys(2005)

玉屏县 Yuping	松桃县 Songtao	印江县 Yinjiang	沿河县 Yanhe	威宁县 Weining	镇宁县 Zhenning	紫云县 Ziyun	关岭县 Guanling	三都县 Sandu
110460	**177135**	**110140**	**136193**	**266266**	**112504**	**67602**	**101669**	**73968**
25079	80434	61623	71084	114035	26760	36127	38837	37288
48384	46693	13291	19377	74434	38752	8254	31270	5305
36997	50008	35226	45732	77797	46992	23221	31562	31375
11.73	62.38	39.01	54.43	103.49	32.33	33.29	31.37	30.94
5.63	26.34	18.42	26.41	71.93	13.84	15.91	15.00	13.55
6.20	11.70	7.50	16.60	18.92	7.51	8.60	7.20	7.77
396.20	1864.00	1941.50	940.10	3928.00	561.33	779.63	1230.00	1495.37
0.16	1.24	0.68	1.32	2.40	0.68	0.62	1.60	0.30
4.10	13.00	8.00	7.30	5.18	5.62	6.63	5.50	7.09
19.35	68.42	53.62	71.72	151.62	32.24	42.68	34.50	33.35
9.25	47.01	36.24	51.71	75.81	21.82	27.13	23.95	22.23
3.82	10.49	7.59	7.35	0.74	0.57		4.87	6.58
43150	230562	137436	158292	354686	109598	115895	111282	94048
5391	16827	13006	10297	724	10903	6171	5504	6577
14	3152	6225	6306	16968	192	2084	234	45
26	1122	537	122	51.65	41.37	74	31	42
0.74	4.33	1.45	3.05	3.13	2.67	4.42	0.30	1.58
3.62	12.79	14.65	15.99	24.43	13.24	13.56	15.26	16.51
9.58	41.34	28.95	35.14	72.23	13.15	23.28	14.17	17.96
3.08	13.95	14.26	37.75	31.80	0.81	3.02	2.34	0.70
1.41	2.86	3.34	1.84	4.79	2.24	1.76	2.22	2.62
11.66	36.68	31.56	29.21	42.12	10.47	17.51	12.78	18.01
2.40	13.66	14.16	34.63	14.69	0.34	1.66	1.29	0.50
11831	38378	37260	37277	55428	12177	19927	15000	15580
895	1894	1482	1401	76	742	503	340	1100
39108	129053	97598	112137	167321	41489	55160	60211	57201
22800	81201	54046	68069	93361	25957	24706	36665	29481

20-12续表1(continued)

指 标	Item	道真县 Daozhen	务川县 Wuchuan
林 业	Forestry	3409	3438
牧 业	Animal Husbandry	33354	26543
渔 业	Fishery	392	275
农林牧渔业增加值（万元）	Value-added of Farming,Forestry,Animal Husbandry and Fishery	49128	52147
工业（规模以上）	**Industry(above designated size)**		
企业单位数（个）	Number of Industrial Enterprises(unit)	7	6
工业总产值（万元）	Total Gross Industrial Output Value(10000 yuan)	13184	7525
工业销售产值	Sales Output Value of Industry	12314	7205.7
工业增加值	Value-added of Industry	3726	2150
利润总额	Total Profits	358	-20
主要工业产品产量	Output of Major Industrial Products		
原煤（万吨）	Coal(10000 tons)	16	13.5
生铁（万吨）	Pig Iron(10000 cu.m)	0.215	
水泥（万吨）	Cement(10000 tons)	5.415	6.18
发电量（亿千瓦小时）	Electricity(100 million kwh)	1.5619	0.2631
固定资产投资	**Investment in Fixed Assets**		
全社会固定资产投资完成额(万元)	Total Investment in Fixed Assets(10000 yuan)	64312	66585
国有经济	State-owned Units	53791	45175
集体经济	Collective_owened Units	200	1000
外商港澳台经济	Units with Funds from Foreign,Hong Kong,Macao and Taiwan		
其他投资	Others	10321	20410
商 业	**Trade**		
社会消费品零售总额	Total Retail Sales of Consumer Goods	18518	28154
财政、金融	**Treasiury and Finance**		
财政一般预算收入(万元)	Budgetary Fiscal Revenue(10000 yuan)	4150	4558
财政一般预算支出	Budgetary Fiscal Expenditure	24735	28526
存款余额	Deposits	105035	83345
贷款余额	Loans	49160	38053
城乡居民储蓄余额	Urban and Rural Resident Savings Deposit Balance	75673	54058

玉屏县 Yuping	松桃县 Songtao	印江县 Yinjiang	沿河县 Yanhe	威宁县 Weining	镇宁县 Zhenning	紫云县 Ziyun	关岭县 Guanling	三都县 Sandu
463	2973	1282	2196	1140	1865	4519	2818	3279
13746	41725	39758	38440	69649	12782	24396	20317	22042
722	1544	1479	1156	78	714	570	326	1152
25079	80314	61623	71084	108900	28448	36127	36367	37288
37	27	14	10	35	15	9	14	13
133239	120118	14511	12288	117108	56275.2	19312	35278	13120
120949	117219	13407	11958	115930	53950.9	18485	32496.6	12149.2
25456	27898	4108	3076	35133.4	21094.9	4008	6288	3755
655	–757	–427	–139	1869	8156.3	–948	885.1	–584
		6.0486	28.56	134.26	4.3		2.6	
				8.8707				
10.3826	1.5	4.01	14.8109	3.9312	3.47	5.78	10.7	7.23
0.72882	0.5336	0.2869	0.2231	0.14749	1.1191	0.673	2.8377	0.035
140020	50426	44118	60782	68000	30132	28876	21700	18141
126530	26296	29129	29316	36878	3899	8120	10523	7792
147		488					8354	60
	2325		4495			55		
13343	21805	14501	26971	31122	26233	20701	2823	10289
18883	37897	22322	30551	44558	26434	23649	26740	22775
7242	6179	4870	5866	14648	5660	2955	4966	2639
17157	38776	28043	36543	53513	24649	22952	23858	25136
76592	136755	95624	110176	140094	91336	55032	95263	61747
214497	60744	52144	55006	40072	59990	49247	150383	25924
47486	83459	75981	73950	87373	47929	27391	51134	39424

20-13 各少数民族自治县

Major Indicators on Social Development of

指 标	Item	道真县 Daozhen	务川县 Wuchuan
人 口	**Population**		
年末人口（万人）	Number of Population at The Year-end(10000 persons)	34.27	42.77
#少数民族人口	Minority Population	26.71	41.07
人口密度(人/平方公里)	Population Density(persons/sq.km)	158.95	154.25
交通运输	**Traffic**		
民用汽车拥有量（辆）	Number of Civil Motor Vehicles Owned(unit)	2525	2851
公路线路里程（公里）	Length of Highways(km)	1344	1650
内河航道里程	Length of Navigable Inland Waterways		
邮电、通讯	**Post and Telecommunications**		
邮政所总数（处）	Number of Post Offices(unit)	24	15
邮路总长度（公里）	Length of Postal Routes(km)	347	511
农村投递线路总长度	Length of Rural Delivery Routes	882	1205
本地电话年末用户（万户）	Number of Telephone Sets(10000 units)	1.75	1.72
#住宅电话用户	Residence Telephone		1.34
教 育	**Education**		
普通中学	Regular Secondary Schools		
学校数（所）	Number of Schools(unit)	25	28
在校学生数（人）	Students Enrollment(person)	20020	27372
招生数	New Student Enrollment	6354	8263
毕业生数	Graduates	6717	5893
专任教师数	Full-time Teachers	1085	1249
小 学	Primary Schools		
学校数（所）	Number of Schools(unit)	142	222
在校学生数（人）	Students Enrollment(person)	28769	57924
招生数	New Student Enrollment	5364	9951
毕业生数	Graduates	4829	8530
专任教师数	Full-time Teachers	1541	2258

社会发展主要指标(2005)

Minority Nationality Autonomous Countys(2005)

玉屏县 Yuping	松桃县 Songtao	印江县 Yinjiang	沿河县 Yanhe	威宁县 Weining	镇宁县 Zhenning	紫云县 Ziyun	关岭县 Guanling	三都县 Sandu
14.35	65.31	42.23	57.13	112.01	35.33	34.76	33.10	33.22
11.84	30.80	29.07	31.89	28.90	20.14	22.84	19.24	30.73
278.15	228.26	215.34	231.41	177.90	207.51	152.21	225.48	139.36
3537	1950	1216	1826	2418	2056	1002	1694	599
337	1601	1526	1399	2005	901	850	692	989
11	48		132				80	
9	14	13	21	14	7	11	8	14
2	1383	228	421	2950	425	336	80	105
583	547	848	1050	2412	316	532	960	1458
1.48	2.20	2.19	1.82	2.10	2.96	1.73	1.55	2.22
1.00	0.61	0.58	0.75	0.55	1.06	1.58	1.13	0.76
10	37	22	27	51	19	20	18	19
9037	42220	27041	35770	57984	20589	18079	22195	20035
2904	16019	9498	13504	25351	7025	8527	7801	7058
2937	9629	8322	8481	13367	5110	3532	6218	5703
532	2158	1438	1683	2061	937	731	851	818
71	314	133	213	346	137	143	154	140
12082	89394	45298	84167	172168	45647	55762	44964	40628
2408	9552	7538	12150	33305	6339	10019	5960	6289
2000	14692	7250	16131	21062	6475	6838	7690	6457
554	3449	2219	3006	3785	1742	1881	1679	1604

21

Twenty-One

经济强县

Strongly Economic County

21-1 经济强县主要指标（一）（2005）

Major Indicators of Strongly Economic County(1)(2005)

单位：万元 (10000 yuan)

县(市、区)名 称	County (City,Section)	生产总值 Gross Domestic Product	第一产业 Primary Industry	第二产业 Secondary Industry	第三产业 Tertiary Industry	2005年比2004年增长（%）、Increase Rate in 2005 over 2004(%)
云岩区	Yunyan	1565262	1262	717528	846472	14.1
南明区	Nanming	965077	4550	298641	661886	14.1
白云区	Baiyun	475781	17248	342748	115785	14.1
红花岗区	Honghuagang	868478	45739	307693	515046	16.8
乌当区	Wudang	531830	61734	279381	190715	19.5
盘 县	Panxian	786726	76377	509297	201052	17.3
仁怀市	Renhuai	598442	83733	409682	105027	16.4
钟山区	Zhongshan	781294	15012	440021	326261	17.6
兴义市	Xingyi	606736	106393	274498	225845	19.4
清镇市	Qingzhen	447564	58985	221239	167340	15.1
遵义县	Zunyi	656535	209000	232919	214616	14.1
花溪区	Huaxi	371238	54760	138875	177603	14.8
开阳县	Kaiyang	303022	64272	160095	78655	16.5
都匀市	Duyun	336657	45387	132740	158530	15.0
西秀区	Xixiu	438484	74777	139533	224174	13.0
金沙县	Jinsha	321720	79798	178504	63418	17.4
毕节市	Bijie	528329	134119	207289	186921	13.7
赤水市	Chishui	189257	55248	81478	52531	14.3
铜仁市	Tongren	238436	46948	90151	101337	12.0
凯里市	Kaili	382020	46528	152004	183488	11.5

21-2 经济强县主要指标（二）（2005）

Major Indicators of Strongly Economic County(2)(2005)

县(市、区)名称	County (City,Section)	人均生产总值(元) Per Capita Gross Domestic Product (yuan)	2005年比2004年增长（%） Increase Rate in 2005 over 2004(%)	财政总收入（万元） Total Fiscal Revenue (10000 yuan)	2005年比2004年增长（%） Increase Rate in 2005 over 2004(%)	人均财政总收入（元） Per Total Fiscal Revenue (yuan)	2005年比2004年增长（%） Increase Rate in 2005 over 2004(%)
云岩区	Yunyan	28274	13.6	103005	20.5	1861	19.9
南明区	Nanming	19009	13.4	93075	19.5	1833	18.8
白云区	Baiyun	27203	13.0	84950	19.3	4860	18.2
红花岗区	Honghuagang	16131	15.8	51778	27.9	962	26.9
乌当区	Wudang	17239	18.6	59388	28.9	1925	28.0
盘　县	Panxian	6673	16.3	122594	47.2	1040	46.1
仁怀市	Renhuai	9815	15.6	150684	34.1	2471	33.2
钟山区	Zhongshan	18019	16.5	40870	70.8	943	69.2
兴义市	Xingyi	8088	18.4	62308	23.4	831	22.6
清镇市	Qingzhen	8582	14.4	49686	23.6	953	22.8
遵义县	Zunyi	5663	13.6	56812	35.2	490	34.6
花溪区	Huaxi	11440	14.1	33706	17.6	1039	16.9
开阳县	Kaiyang	6895	15.8	38954	34.5	886	33.6
都匀市	Duyun	6847	14.3	33167	20.3	675	19.7
西秀区	Xixiu	5257	12.1	52219	16.0	626	15.1
金沙县	Jinsha	5403	16.8	64322	42.4	1080	41.6
毕节市	Bijie	4051	12.5	31239	15.7	240	14.8
赤水市	Chishui	6010	13.7	16088	17.2	511	16.7
铜仁市	Tongren	6911	11.2	16963	18.8	492	18.0
凯里市	Kaili	8307	10.7	35021	16.3	761	15.3

21-3 经济强县主要指标（三）（2005）

Major Indicators of Strongly Economic County(3)(2005)

县(市、区) 名 称	County (City,Section)	财政一般预算收入（万元） Local Financial Revenue (10000 yuan)	2005年比2004年增长（%） Increase Rate in 2005 over 2004(%)	城镇居民人均可支配收入（元） Per Capita Annual Net Income of Urban Households (yuan)	2005年比2004年增长（%） Increase Rate in 2005 over 2004(%)	农民人均纯收入（元） Per Capita Net Income of Rural Residents (yuan)	2005年比2004年增长（%） Increase Rate in 2005 over 2004(%)	招商引资到位资金（亿元） Actually Utilized Outside Capital of Guizhou Province (100 million yuan)	2005年比2004年增长（%） Increase Rate in 2005 over 2004(%)
云岩区	Yunyan	53471	19.0	10074	9.8			21.60	43.9
南明区	Nanming	52542	24.5	9765	9.4			26.06	20.2
白云区	Baiyun	30887	19.6	9450	12.1			22.70	20.4
红花岗区	Honghuagang	30115	20.0	8453	15.2			14.88	37.3
乌当区	Wudang	32280	31.0	9285	12.1			15.79	27.5
盘　县	Panxian	45004	45.2			1923	6.9	9.19	45.6
仁怀市	Renhuai	33875	25.4			2496	6.5	4.61	79.7
钟山区	Zhongshan	23591	57.3	8032	11.8			4.07	21.1
兴义市	Xingyi	30598	22.5			2568	7.4	5.00	101.9
清镇市	Qingzhen	22317	26.0			2858	8.7	13.95	44.7
遵义县	Zunyi	26601	23.6			2907	6.9	9.33	55.1
花溪区	Huaxi	18548	20.8	9264	12.4			7.10	41.9
开阳县	Kaiyang	18933	15.8			2900	6.5	9.50	110.7
都匀市	Duyun	18902	20.5			2482	6.4	4.46	49.6
西秀区	Xixiu	31289	29.4	7337	7.5			2.40	108.5
金沙县	Jinsha	24759	30.5			2306	5.0	1.98	19.8
毕节市	Bijie	24419	13.9			2141	5.0	0.75	22.4
赤水市	Chishui	9450	13.3			2512	5.0	2.08	59.8
铜仁市	Tongren	13322	15.0			2356	5.8	2.85	24.7
凯里市	Kaili	18086	14.7			2177	5.2	3.36	14.6

21-4 经济强县主要指标（四）（2005）

Major Indicators of Strongly Economic County(4)(2005)

县(市、区)名 称	County (City,Section)	城镇化率（%）Proportion of Urban Populations to Total Populations (%)	2005年比2004年增减百分点 Up（Down）Percentage Points in 2005 over 2004	科技三项费占财政支出比重（%）Proportion of Expense on S&T Promotion to Total Financial Expenditure (%)	高中阶段毛入学率（%）Enrollment Rate of Junior secondary School Graduates Entering into Senior secondary Schools(%)	2005年比2004年增减百分点 Up（Down）Percentage Points in 2005 over 2004(%)	生育政策符合率（%）Family Planning Rate (%)
云岩区	Yunyan	97.7	1.0	1.83	78.30	0.4	99.89
南明区	Nanming	97.7	1.6	2.03	78.20	16.0	99.72
白云区	Baiyun	65.5	0.2	1.20	70.63	2.1	99.48
红花岗区	Honghuagang	60.2	1.3	1.45	55.50	3.8	97.35
乌当区	Wudang	35.0	2.2	1.67	46.96	3.8	97.89
盘 县	Panxian	21.5	1.5	0.51	29.59	4.1	97.13
仁怀市	Renhuai	30.4	2.3	0.64	30.51	3.7	93.53
钟山区	Zhongshan	66.0	0.2	0.73	49.31	8.2	97.10
兴义市	Xingyi	32.0	1.0	1.03	38.28	5.3	93.31
清镇市	Qingzhen	27.8	3.8	2.03	24.20	3.6	94.30
遵义县	Zunyi	34.5	1.6	0.71	38.89	3.6	92.68
花溪区	Huaxi	38.8	1.6	1.36	44.16	5.3	96.94
开阳县	Kaiyang	28.1	1.2	1.37	44.80	5.2	95.75
都匀市	Duyun	46.2	1.1	1.59	39.28	8.5	96.89
西秀区	Xixiu	45.7	1.5	1.26	35.61	6.5	94.83
金沙县	Jinsha	28.0	1.0	1.25	23.46	3.9	96.15
毕节市	Bijie	12.0	1.7	0.71	26.12	4.1	91.43
赤水市	Chishui	37.7	1.0	0.85	32.00	3.7	96.58
铜仁市	Tongren	42.4	1.0	0.73	42.00	7.0	95.08
凯里市	Kaili	39.7	1.6	1.00	51.90	2.7	95.46

21-5 经济强县主要指标（五）（2005）

Major Indicators of Strongly Economic County(5)(2005)

单位：万元(10000 yuan)

县(市、区)名　称	County (City,Section)	城镇登记失业率（%）Registered Unemployment Rate in Urban Areas（%）	环境保护和建设 Environment Protection and Construction	年末常住人口(万人) Number of Permanent Total Population (year-end) (10000 persons)	农林牧渔业总产值 Gross Output Value of Farming, Forestry, Animal Husbandry and Fishery	2005年比2004年增长（%）Increase Rate in 2005 over 2004(%)	固定资产投资 Investment in Fixed Assets
云岩区	Yunyan	3.98	优	55.49	4215	-0.4	544642
南明区	Nanming	4.17	优	50.95	6978	-10.8	547186
白云区	Baiyun	3.30	良	17.59	27352	5.9	187497
红花岗区	Honghuagang	4.50	良	53.93	71115	6.7	276756
乌当区	Wudang	3.75	良	30.97	94593	9.6	216331
盘　县	Panxian	4.27	良	118.29	120773	9.6	367852
仁怀市	Renhuai	4.67	良	61.11	128378	4.4	111010
钟山区	Zhongshan	4.00	良	43.48	25459	15.7	448455
兴义市	Xingyi	3.47	良	75.3	186939	11.2	199015
清镇市	Qingzhen	4.00	良	52.33	89713	9.2	167655
遵义县	Zunyi	3.90	良	116.24	324791	8.4	308536
花溪区	Huaxi	3.79	良	32.54	80257	7.9	148384
开阳县	Kaiyang	3.44	良	44.06	107459	7.6	148296
都匀市	Duyun	3.90	良	49.29	77983	9.0	116283
西秀区	Xixiu	4.41	良	83.67	112702	9.5	111978
金沙县	Jinsha	3.66	良	59.66	127577	4.5	41060
毕节市	Bijie	4.10	良	131.09	203064	6.2	73061
赤水市	Chishui	4.12	良	31.56	89636	9.1	128588
铜仁市	Tongren	4.10	良	34.59	80408	6.4	135958
凯里市	Kaili	4.49	良	46.15	71644	5.0	155397

21-6 经济强县主要指标（六）（2005）

Major Indicators of Strongly Economic County(6)(2005)

单位：万元 (10000 yuan)

县(市、区)名称	County (City,Section)	规模以上工业总产值 Total Gross Industrial Output Value above Designated Size	社会消费品零售总额 Total Retail Sales of Consumer Goods	城乡居民储蓄余额 Urban and Rural Resident Savings Deposit Balance	2005年比2004年增长（%） Increase Rate in 2005 over 2004(%)
云岩区	Yunyan	1545879	829947		
南明区	Nanming	712667	645324		
白云区	Baiyun	882806	69053		
红花岗区	Honghuagang	682582	402002	979875	61.0
乌当区	Wudang	609460	42379	169854	28.1
盘　县	Panxian	566235	159313	284384	25.2
仁怀市	Renhuai	500496	117316	121683	26.1
钟山区	Zhongshan	1035472	309875	530317	29.5
兴义市	Xingyi	522054	237653	352704	18.7
清镇市	Qingzhen	489751	73101	163622	17.9
遵义县	Zunyi	423855	144963	269454	11.0
花溪区	Huaxi	244836	72011	209637	27.9
开阳县	Kaiyang	321740	71752	102999	27.6
都匀市	Duyun	190266	117058	351480	20.0
西秀区	Xixiu	264023	149624	443921	21.0
金沙县	Jinsha	339541	47251	119232	34.6
毕节市	Bijie	120234	78164	293935	21.8
赤水市	Chishui	172106	38756	148060	18.5
铜仁市	Tongren	147438	89961	196812	19.7
凯里市	Kaili	348401	165465	347421	25.7

经济强县 STRONG ECONOMIC COUNTY

2006

云岩区简介

云岩区是贵州省的省会城市贵阳市的中心城区之一，位于贵阳市北半城，现辖15个街道办事处、1个镇，总面积67.5平方公里，总人口59.05万。云岩区是全省重要的政治、经济、文化中心，位于贵阳市繁华区域，地理位置优越，自然环境优美、交通便利、通讯发达、高校众多，科教先进，市场广阔、商贸繁荣，人流、物流、信息流、资金流等资源要素集聚。辖区内横贯贵遵(贵阳至遵义)、贵黄(贵阳至黄果树)、贵新(贵阳至新寨)高速公路，中心区到贵阳火车站、贵阳龙洞堡机场的车程分别约为10分钟和15分钟，是贵州对外开放的前沿。

改革寨开放以来，云岩区紧紧围绕“市场带动”、“科教兴区”、“开放带动”、“可持续发展”四大战略，开拓创新，扎实工作，不断调整和优化产业结构，形成了以第三产业为龙头，区街工业和乡镇企业为两翼的“三、二、一”产业格局。“十五”期间(2004年数据)，全区生产总值达到126.09亿元，财政总收入达到8.48亿元，地方财政收入达到5.63亿元，城镇居民人均可支配收入达到9113元，农民人均纯收入达到4293元。在全省第二轮建设经济强县考核中名列第一，获得了中科院颁发的“中国·西部开发贡献奖——西部区域经济增长最快区、县、市奖”和“全国创建文明城市工作先进城区、全国科技工作先进区”等荣誉称号，全区经济社会实现了跨越式发展，成为西部地区的一个发展重镇。

“三圈”发展示意图
The sketch map of "three circles" development

行政中心
The administrative center

经济强县 STRONG ECONOMIC COUNTY

2006

云岩区简介

云岩区是贵州省的省会城市贵阳市的中心城区之一，位于贵阳市北半城，现辖15个街道办事处、1个镇，总面积67.5平方公里，总人口59.05万。云岩区是全省重要的政治、经济、文化中心，位于贵阳市繁华区域，地理位置优越，自然环境优美、交通便利、通讯发达、高校众多，科教先进，市场广阔、商贸繁荣，人流、物流、信息流、资金流等资源要素集聚。辖区内横贯贵遵(贵阳至遵义)、贵黄(贵阳至黄果树)、贵新(贵阳至新寨)高速公路，中心区到贵阳火车站、贵阳龙洞堡机场的车程分别约为10分钟和15分钟，是贵州对外开放的前沿。

改革寨开放以来，云岩区紧紧围绕“市场带动”、“科教兴区”、“开放带动”、“可持续发展”四大战略，开拓创新，扎实工作，不断调整和优化产业结构，形成了以第三产业为龙头，区街工业和乡镇企业为两翼的“三、二、一”产业格局。“十五”期间(2004年数据)，全区生产总值达到126.09亿元，财政总收入达到8.48亿元，地方财政收入达到5.63亿元，城镇居民人均可支配收入达到9113元，农民人均纯收入达到4293元。在全省第二轮建设经济强县考核中名列第一，获得了中科院颁发的“中国·西部开发贡献奖——西部区域经济增长最快区、县、市奖”和“全国创建文明城市工作先进城区、全国科技工作先进区”等荣誉称号，全区经济社会实现了跨越式发展，成为西部地区的一个发展重镇。

“三圈”发展示意图
The sketch map of "three circles" development

行政中心
The administrative center

The Introduction of Yunyan District

Yunyan district is the one of the central urban district of Guiyang city which is the provincial capital city of Guizhou province, is located in the north half of Guiyang city. It currently governs 15 neighborhood offices, 1 town, with a total area of 67.5 square kilometers and a total population of 590,500. Yunyan district is a provincial major political, economic and cultural center, and is located in bustling region of Guiyang city, it has superior geography location, beautiful natural environment, convenient transportation, developed communication, numerous colleges and universities, advanced science and education, vast market, and flourishing trade, the flow of people, goods, information, capital and other resources gather together. Guizun (Guiyang to Zunyi), Guihuang (Guiyang to Huangguoshu), Guixin (Guiyang to Xinzhai) expressways traverse the district, the vehicle distance of district's central area to Guiyang Railway Station, Guiyang Longdongbao Airport is respectively about 10 minutes and 15 minutes, it is the forefront of opening up of Guizhou.

Since the beginning of reform and opening up, Yunyan district closely surrounding four major strategies of "market leading", "science and education thriving the district", "opening up leading" and "sustainable development", explored and innovated, solidly worked, and continued to adjust and optimize the industrial structure, formed the "three, two, one" industrial pattern taking the tertiary industry as the leading, the district's street industries and township enterprises as two flanks. During the period of "Tenth Five" (data of 2004), the GDP of the district reached 12.609 billion yuan, total financial revenue reached 848 million yuan, local financial revenue reached 563 million yuan, the per capita disposable income of urban residents reached 9,113 yuan, and per capita net income of farmers reached 4,293 yuan. The district ranked the first in the assessment of provincial second round construction economic strong county, was awarded "China · the West Development Contributions Prize --- the prize of the fastest economic growth district, county, and city of the western region" which issued by the CAS, and was awarded honorary titles of "the national creation civilized city work advanced district, the national science and technology work advanced district". The district achieved the economic and social leap development to become an important development region of the West.

市西商业步行街
Shixi commercial pedestrian street

贵州益佰制药股份有限公司
Guizhou Yibai Pharmaceutical Stock Co., Ltd.

大十字街景
The street landscape of Grand Cross

绿色家园——欣歆园
The green home — Xinxin Garden

贵州西牛王印务有限责任公司
Guizhou Xiniuwang Printing Limited Liability Company

南明区

南明区地处云贵高原东北部，是贵州省会贵阳市的中心城区之一，是省委办公所在地，是全省、全市的政治、经济、文化、科技和教育中心，是全省首批建设的经济十强县之一，是西南重要的交通枢纽和旅游胜地。全区总面积89.1平方千米，辖两个乡和15个街道办事处。总人口53.17万，城镇化率达99.28%。

2005年，在市委、市政府的正确领导下，南明区坚持把发展作为执政兴区的第一要务，以树立科学的发展观统揽工作全局，以构建和谐社会为目标，深入推进“三产兴区、工业强区、环境立区”发展战略。全年生产总值达到96.51亿元，比上一年增长14.10%，全社会固定资产投资完成65.73亿元，增长11.70%。财政总收入完成9.51亿元，增长22.36%，地方财政收入完成6.84亿元，增长24.06%。实现利用外资906万美元，引进内资26.06亿元，分别增长7.86%和20.15%。城镇居民人均可支配收入达到9765元，农民人均纯收入达到4653元。全区经济社会发展质量、效益跃上新台阶，为完成“十五”计划画上了圆满的句号，也为顺利实施“十一五”规划奠定了坚实的基础。

2005年，全区三次产业占生产总值的比重为0.47:30.94:68.59，标志着全区经济社会发展开始进入以服务业为主的工业化中期阶段。第三产业发展领域不断扩大，整体水平继续提升。初步构建起大市场、大贸易的格局和辐射全市乃至全省的服务体系。以贵阳浙江商城、贵州茶城、海港大酒楼、富源美家居、荔星百货等重点项目的建成开业为契机，带动区域经济发展，优化产业结构；积极参与国有企业改制，发展壮大贵钢再就业基地、五里冲农副产品批发市场、谷丰粮油食品交易市场；大力发展社区服务业、楼宇经济、总部经济等新型服务业，积极促进现代物流业的发展；消费市场繁荣活跃，沃尔玛超市等运转良好。居民教育、住房、旅游、保健等消费支出明显增加，全年完成社会消费品零售总额63.75亿元，增长15.3%。积极推进龙洞堡新区、上下坝科技工业基地、笋子林工业基地的开发建设，加快形成大基地、大企业、大项目、名品牌的工业发展战略步伐。全年区属规模以上企业实现工业总产值22.65亿元，同比增长23.32%；区属工业销售收入实现43.29亿元，同比增长27.91%；利税总额实现9.14亿元，同比增长49.3%。国民经济持续快速健康发展。

积极开展“为民办实事，满意到万家”活动，按照市委、市政府提出“一排、二降、三畅、四增”的要求，大力开展交通、卫生、秩序等整治工作。全年新增绿地3.5万平方米。获得了贵阳市文明区(县)创建活动第一名的优异成绩。10所中学的下划，极大的扩充了全区优质教育资源总量。顺利通过省级“四五”普法验收工作，获得了全国司法行政基层建设工作先进单位的荣誉称号。做好了高致病性禽流感的防治工作。成功举办了区第六届运动会等大型文体活动，积极组队参加“多彩贵州”歌唱大赛、“四月八”民族团结周系列活动暨第七届少数民族传统体育运动会等活动。社会事业蓬勃发展，群众生活水平不断提高。

招商引资硕果累累
Making excellent results in introducing business and attracting investment

Nanming district is located in the northeast of Yunnan-Guizhou Plateau, is the one of the center city of the Guizhou provincial capital Guiyang city, is the seat of the Provincial Party Committee, is the provincial and the city's political, economic, cultural, scientific and technological, educational center, is the one of economy ten strong counties of first building of the province, is an important traffic hub and a tourist resort in southwest. The total area of the district is 89.1 sq km, governs 2 townships and 15 neighborhood offices. Total population is 531,700, the rate of urban and town is up to 99.28%.

In 2005, under the correct leadership of the city Party committee, the city government, Nanming district insisted on taking development as the top priority to administrative, took establishment scientific development concept to unite overall work, took building a harmonious society as the goal, in-depth improved the development strategy of "three industries thriving the district, industry enhancing the district, environmental building the district". Annual GDP reached 9.651 billion yuan, 14.10% growth than the previous year, fixed-assets investment completed 6.573 billion yuan, an increase of 11.70%. Financial revenue completed

不断发展中的南明区正奋力向“西部生态经济强区”迈进
The constant developing Nanming district is struggling to step "the

Nanming District

951 million yuan, an increase of 22.36%, the local revenue completed 684 million yuan, an increase of 24.06%. Actually foreign investment achieved 9.06 million USD, introduced domestic investment of 2.606 billion yuan, growth of 7.86% and 20.15% respectively. Per capita disposable income of urban residents reached 9,765 yuan and the per capita net income of farmers reached 4,653 yuan. The quality and efficiency of economic and social development in the district jumped to a higher level, and painted a satisfactory conclusion for the completion of the "Tenth Five-Year Plan", but also laid a solid foundation for the successful implementation the "Eleventh Five-Year Plan".

In 2005, the proportion of three industries accounting for the GDP of the district was 0.47: 30.94: 68.59, that marked the economic and social development of the district having begun to enter a industrialization interim stage taking service as the main. The development field of the third industry has been expanding, continuously enhancing the overall level. Initially built up the pattern of big market, trade, and the service system which covered all the city and the province. Took Zhejiang Mall of Guiyang, Guizhou Tea City, Haigang Restaurant, Fuyuanmei Home, Lixing General Store, and other key projects building and business as an opportunity to promote regional economic development and optimize the industrial structure; active participation in state-owned enterprises reform, developed and strengthened Gui Steel Reemployment Base, Wulichong Agricultural and Sideline Products Wholesale Market, Gufeng Foodstuffs Trade Market; vigorously developed the new service industry such as community service, building economy, headquarters economy, and actively promoted the development of the modern logistics industry; consumer markets were prosperous, and well-functioning of Wal-Mart Supermarket. The consumption expenditures as resident education, housing, tourism, health care increased markedly, complete retail sales of consumer goods annual totaled 6.375 billion yuan, growth 15.3%. Actively promoted the development and construction of Longdongbao new district, Shangxiaba scientific and technological industrial base, Sunzilin industrial base, and speeded up formation the pace of industrial development strategies of big base, large corporations, great projects and famous brand. Annual the total output value of enterprises above designated size of the district realized 2.265 billion yuan, up 23.32% than the same time of the last year; the industrial sales income of the district realized 4.329 billion yuan, up 27.91%; total profits and taxes were up to 914 million yuan, up 49.3%. The national economy maintained sustained, rapid and healthy development.

Actively carried out the activity of "doing real things for people, satisfying to ten thousand families", in accordance with the requirements of "one draining, two drops, three cleans, four additions" advanced by city Party committee and government, vigorously conducting the rectification work as traffic, health, order. 35,000 square meters green were annually newly increased. The district awarded the first excellence result in Guiyang city civilized district (county) building activity. The inducement of 10 secondary schools, which greatly expanded the total of quality education resources of the district. Successfully passed the provincial "45" public law acceptance work, and awarded the title of national administration of justice grass-roots building work advanced unit. The H5N1 avian flu prevention and control work was made a good job. The district successfully held the sixth district's games and other large cultural and sports activities, actively organized team to participate "Colorful Guizhou" singing contest, "the eighth of April" nationality unity Week series activities cum the seventh minority traditional sports games and other activities. Social undertakings were flourishing, the people's living standards constantly improved.

Ecological and Economic Strength District of the West."

多彩多姿的少数民族歌舞
Colorful minority nationality song and dance

南明夜景
Night scene of Nanming

白云区 Baiyun District

四大班子领导出席“两会”
Four leader groups attended the "two congresses"

贵州花卉新宠——白云蝴蝶兰
The favor flowers and plants of Guizhou — butterfly-orchid of Baiyun

“十五”以来，在市委、市政府的正确领导下，我区抓住实施西部大开发、省建设经济强县和贵阳市建设金阳新区三大机遇，面对各种困难和挑战，坚持创新发展思路，强力推进各项工作，经济社会持续快速健康发展。“十五”时期是白云区经济发展最快、城市面貌变化最大、全区人民得到实惠最多的时期。

经济综合实力快速提升。预计2005年全区生产总值达61.25亿元，5年年均增长13.1%；区属固定资产投资达19.65亿元，年均增长51.04%；社会消费品零售总额达到6.82亿元，年均增长13.5%；财政总收入达9.25亿元，年均增长17.22%；地方财政收入达3.59亿元，年均增长23.89%；城镇居民可支配收入达9450元，年均增长12.1%；农民人均纯收入达3945元，年均增长8.3%。主要指标均达到或超过“十五”计划的预期目标，其中，地区生产总值和财政总收入五年翻一番，地方财政收入比“十五”期末增长近3倍，提前两年实现了“一小步、三大步”战略的第一大步目标。

城市功能明显增强。完成了南湖新区道路主骨架建设，实现了区级行政中心整体搬迁；基本完成了旧城改造和白云南路、中路等城市主干道的改造，城市面貌日新月异，人居环境极大改善；集镇建设步伐加快，各具特色，各集镇成为具有一定规模，基本具备基础设施和城市功能的生产生活中心；交通、供水、供电、市政、生态环保等基础设施取得重大成效。

社会各项事业全面进步。全省率先在农村实现水电路等“七通”基础上，又率先在全省取消农业税和消灭了茅草房，科技进步继续推进，教育事业不断提高，文化体育事业进一步繁荣，各项改革不断深化；困难群众生产生活问题得到较好解决，城乡人民生活水平显著提高；党的建设、精神文明和民主法制建设全面加强。

“十五”期间我区先后被命名为中国西部投资环境最佳县（区）、西部风筝放飞之乡、全国科普示范城区、国家科技工作先进县、全国食品工业强县、全国“两基”教育工作先进县、全国初保先进县、国家残疾人康复先进区等，被省政府授予贵州省卫生县城、发展乡镇企业明星县、“双拥”模范县。2003年，在全省第一轮建设的20个经济强县考核中综合排名第三，获“全省经济十强县”称号。

中铝贵州分公司厂区 The factory area of Chinese Aluminum Industry Guizhou Branch

天津塑力生产现场
Production site of Tianjin Suli

西南家居城建设现场
The construction site of Southwest Home City

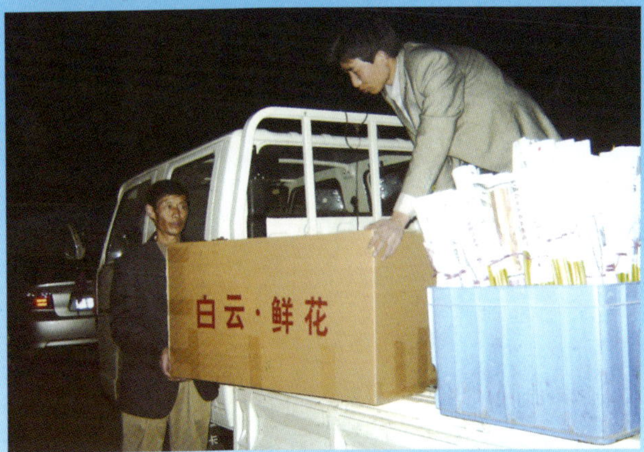

白云花卉远销全国
The flowers and plants of Baiyun are sold to the country

原生态乡村旅游布依村寨景色
The landscape of Buyi village of the original ecological rural tourism

Since "Tenth Five", under the correct leadership of the city Party committee and government, our district seized the three opportunities of implementation western development, provincial construction economic strong county and building Jinyang new area of Guiyang city, faced various kinds of difficulties and challenges, insisted on the innovation development thought, vigorously pushed various works, made economic and social sustained, rapid and healthy development. In "10th Five-Year Plan" period, the economy of Baiyun district was the fastest-growing, the appearance of the city was the biggest change, and the people of the district gained the most benefits.

Comprehensive economic strength has improved rapidly. The district's estimated GDP reached 6.125 billion yuan in 2005, an average annual increase of 13.1% in five years; the investment in fixed assets reached 1.965 billion yuan, with an average annual growth 51.04%; the total retail sales of consumer goods reached 682 million yuan, an average annual increase of 13.5%; the financial revenue reached 925 million yuan, an average annual increase of 17.22%; the local financial revenue reached 359 million yuan, an average annual increase of 23.89%; the disposable income of urban residents reached 9,450 yuan, an average annual increase of 12.1%; the per capita net income of farmers reached 3,945 yuan, with an average annual increase of 8.3%. Major indexes have all reached or surpassed the expected targets of "10th Five-Year" Plan, including regional GDP and financial revenue were doubled in five years, the local financial revenue increased nearly three times than the end of the "Tenth Five Year Plan", achieved the first goal of "one measured step, three strides" strategy two years ahead of time.

The city function obviously increased. Completed road main backbone construction of Nanhu New-district, realized the integral moving of the district's administrative center; basically completed a transformation of the old city and the transformation of Baiyunnan road and Baiyunzhong road and other main roads, the appearance of the city changed for the better day by day, the living environment greatly improved; accelerated the pace of building unique feature towns, each town became the production and livelihood center having certain scale, basic infrastructure and city function; transport, water and electricity supply, municipal administration, ecological environment protection and other infrastructure achieved significant results.

The various social undertakings comprehensively progressed. On the basis of taking the lead in achieving rural water and electricity supply and other "seven openings" in the province, has taken the lead in abolishing agricultural tax and eliminating from twitch-grass cottages again in the province, continued to push forward scientific and technological progress, constantly improved education cause, culture and sports causes furthered prosperity, continuously deepened the various reforms; better solved the masses with difficulties in production and daily life problems, urban and rural people's living standards have markedly improved; comprehensively strengthened Party building and the construction of spiritual civilization, democracy and legality.

"10th Five-Year Plan" period, our district has been named as the best investment environment counties (districts) of China western, the kite-flying township of the western, the national popularization of science demonstration district, the state scientific and technological work advanced county, the national food industry strong county, the national "two basics" education work advanced county, the national primary care advanced county, the state rehabilitation advanced district for the handicapped. The district has been granted the health county of Guizhou province, the development township enterprise star county, and the "double supports" model county by provincial government. In 2003, the district ranked the third in the provincial first round building 20 economic strong counties overall assessment, and awarded the title of "the provincial economy ten strong county".

遵义市

Honghuagang

凤凰山广场
Phoenix Mountain Place

火树银花不夜天——城区夜景
Fiery trees and silver flowers on night — the night view of the city

红花岗区是遵义市的中心城区之一，辖8个镇，8个街道办事处，53个村委会，63个居委会，总人口53.93万。

2005年，全区生产总值达86.74亿元，增长16.8%，人均生产总值达1.61万元，增长15.8%以上。三次产业比重为5.27: 35.47: 59.26。财政总收入达52052万元，增长29.4%。全社会消费品零售总额达40.2亿元，增长12.82%。

工业经济持续发展。遵义高新技术产业园、遵义国家新材料产业化坪桥基地入驻企业分别达到20户和25户，投资规模分别达到4.5亿元和4.7亿元，产值达13.45亿元；辖区规模以上工业增加值达25.48亿元，增长37.4%，其中区级规模以上工业增加值达8.7亿元，增长37.7%。

农村经济稳步增长。生产粮食9.07万吨，蔬菜12.48万吨；养殖大户发展到3445户，肉类总产量达2.4万吨，农业总产值达7.11亿元，增长6.66%。

基础设施建设进一步完善。完成“中国优秀旅游城市”、“国家园林城市”创建任务，南部新城道路骨架网络基本形成，改造小街小巷138条，拆除违法违章建筑4.92万平方米，城区绿化覆盖率达41.7%，城镇化率达60.23%以上。改建通村通组公路207.5公里，改建通乡油路46.30公里，在全市率先实现村村通公路。

社会事业全面进步。建成六所中（小）学教学楼，办学条件进一步改善，实行义务教育“一费制”，兑现“两免一补”政策，适龄儿童入学率达99.9%以上，初、高中阶段毛入学率分别达到116.9%、55.5%。“全国计划生育先进区”顺利通过复核验收，扎实推进计划生育优质服务和“少生快富”工程，全区符合政策生育率提高到97.35%，人口出生率控制在9.36‰以内。加强疾病预防控制、医疗卫生保健和卫生监督体系建设，建立农村、城市医疗救助制度，第一轮农村初级卫生保健顺利通过验收，完成8镇卫生院改扩建主体工程建设。大力发展文化、体育事业，成功承办了“首届航模节暨全国海模对抗赛”、“遵义市首届农民科技文化体育活动周”、“遵义市龙舟大赛”等文体活动。

人民生活水平不断提高。积极拓宽就业渠道，大力推进再就业工作，建立健全社会保障体系，着力抓好社区就业和劳动保障平台的建设。继续加强“两个确保”和城市低保工作，认真做好“三条保障线”的衔接，做到分类救助，实现应保尽保。城镇居民人均可支配收入达8453元，增长13.34%；建成10个“阳光工程”农村劳动力培训基地，培训农村劳动力3204人，转移农村富余劳动力7156人；全面取消农业税，减免税额达462万元，兑现农民种粮补贴36万元，兑现灾欠减免53万元，农村茅草房全面消除，农民人均纯收入达3141元，增长9.55%。

环保型工厂——新蒲瑞安水泥
The environment-type factory -- Ruian Cement of Xinpu

南部新城一角
A corner of new -- city of the south

红花岗区

District of Zunyi City

Honghuagang district is the one of the central district of Zunyi city, governs 8 towns, 8 neighborhood offices, 53 village committees, 63 neighborhood committees, has a total population of 539,300.

In 2005, the district's GDP reached 8.674 billion yuan, an increase of 16.8%, the per capita GDP reached 16,100 yuan, an increase of 15.8% above. The proportion of three industries was 5.27:35.47:59.26. The financial revenue reached 520.52 million yuan, an increase of 29.4%. The total retail sales of consumer goods in the whole society reached 4.02 billion yuan, an increase of 12.82%.

Industrial economy continuously developed. Respectively 20 and 25 enterprises were stationed in Zunyi High-tech Industrial Park and Zunyi National New-material Industry Pingqiao Base, and the scale of investment respectively reached 450 million yuan and 470 million yuan, the total output value reached 1.345 billion yuan; The added value of industry above designated size of the area under Honghuagang's jurisdiction reached 2.548 billion yuan, an increase of 37.4%, of which the district's added value of industry above designated size reached 870 million yuan, growth 37.7%.

Rural economy continued to grow steadily. The district produced 90,700 tons of grain, 124,800 tons of vegetables; the district had 3,445 livestock breeding households, the yield of meat reached 24,000 tons, total agricultural output value reached 711 million yuan, an increase of 6.66%.

The infrastructure construction further improved. Completed "China Excellent Tourism City", "National Garden City" creation tasks, road skeleton network of southern new-city has basically taken shape, transformed 138 side streets and alleys, removed 49,200 square meters of illegal buildings, urban green coverage rate reached 41.7%, urbanization rate reached 60.23% over. Respectively rebuilt 207.5 and 46.30 kilometers pitch roads going to villages and townships, took the lead in realizing roads going to all villages in the city.

The social causes made overall progresses. Completed 6 teaching buildings of middle (primary) school, further improved teaching conditions, realized compulsory education the "system of one fee", carried out the "two exemptions and one premium" policy, the enrollment rate of school-age children reached over 99.9%, the gross enrollment rates of junior and senior school were 116.9% and 55.5% respectively. "National Family Planning Advanced District" smoothly passed check and test, solidly promoted quality service for family planning and "less population rapid wealth" project, the district's family planning rate increased to 97.35%, the birth rate controlled within 9.36‰. Enhanced the constructions of disease prevention and control, medical and health care and health monitoring system, built rural and urban medical assistance system, the first round of rural primary health care smoothly passed acceptance, completed rebuilding main projects for 8 town public health centers. Vigorously developed cultural, sports undertakings, successfully held the "First Model Airplane Festival cum National Model Sea Tournament", the "first week of farmer science and technology, culture, sports activity of Zunyi city", "Dragon Boat Race of Zunyi City" and other cultural activities.

国家级森林公园——大板水独特地貌
The national-level forest park – Dabanshui unique landscape

People's lives have been constantly improved. Actively expanded employment channels, vigorously promoted the re-employment work and created a sound social security system, paid attention to the building of community employment and labor security platform. Continued to strengthen the "two guarantees" and the work for urban subsistence allowance, and seriously did a good connection job of "three guarantee lines", accomplished relief classification and achieved the guarantee. The per capita disposable income of urban residents reached 8,453 yuan, an increase of 13.34%; Built 10 "Sunshine Project" rural labor force training bases, trained rural laborer of 3204 persons, and transferred rural surplus laborer of 7,156 persons; Totally canceled the agricultural tax, and reduced tax of 4.62 million yuan, subsidized grain allowance of 360 thousand yuan to farmers and disaster remission of 530 thousand yuan, totally eliminated from rural thatched cottages, the per capita net income of farmers reached 3,141 yuan, an increase of 9.55%.

遵义会议会址
The site of the Zunyi Conference

农业产业化奶牛基地
The dairy cattle base of agriculture industrialization

国家级文物杨粲墓
The national-level cultural relic Yang Can Tomb

乌当区

Wudang District

区委书记郭文忠、区长刘崇荣陪同省委副书记黄瑶视察新农村建设
The secretary of the district Party committee Guo Wenzhong, the governor of the district Liu Chongrong accompanied the deputy secretary of the provincial Party committee Huang Yao inspecting new rural building

乌当，一颗镶嵌在贵州省省会城市——贵阳市东北部的璀璨明珠，是贵州省首批建设的20个经济强县（市、区）之一，是贵阳市新城区规划的9个城市组团之一，是西部大开发国家重点建设南（宁）贵（阳）昆（明）经济带上的一个中心城区，全省唯一的国家级高新技术产业开发区和国家级农业科技园区（试点）坐落其中。

今日乌当，经过历届区委、区政府和广大人民群众的奋力拼搏，国民经济持续、快速、健康发展，国内生产总值和财政总收入保持两位数以上的速度高速增长，区域综合实力显著增强，三次产业结构实现了由“二一三”向“二三一”的转变；高新技术产业和医药工业发展迅速，98家高新技术产业、20余家生物制药业和南方汇通、振华科技等7家上市公司及世界500强企业——日本京瓷株式会社入驻园区，为乌当区的发展注入新的活力。2005年，在全省第一轮建设的20个经济强县（市、区）中，综合评定排名第4位。

新时期，新机遇，乌当区将始终抓住发展这个第一要务，大力弘扬“团结拼搏、负重前进、开拓创新、富民强区”的乌当精神，围绕建设“经济强区、高新技术区和生态区”目标，积极实施开放带动、高新技术带动和城镇化战略，不断扩大对外开放水平，加大招商引资力度，大力发展高新技术产业，推进新型工业化进程；进一步转变政府职能，加强法制建设，强化服务意识，努力营造公平、公开和公正的环境；不断加快城市化建设步伐，推进城乡一体化进程，为建设“大贵阳”作出积极贡献，推动区域经济超常规、跨越式发展，率先在全市实现全面建设小康社会目标。

开放的乌当，向您郑重承诺：您投资，我服务；您发展，我开路；您困难，我帮助；您受益，我保护。26万乌当人民竭诚欢迎海内外有识之士投资乌当，建设乌当，共同开发乌当这片热土，共同创造“黔中秘境、林中泉城”！

行政中心
The administrative center

南方汇通微硬盘生产基地
South Huitong micro hard disk production base

仁恒商业街
Renheng commercial street

Wudang, a bright pearl of the northeast of Guiyang city -- capital city of Guizhou province, is the one of first building 20 economic strong counties (cities and districts) of Guizhou province, is the one of nine city groups of Guiyang city new urban planning, is a central city of the West Developing state key construction Nan(ning) Gui(yang) Kun(ming) economic region. The only state-level high-tech industrial development zone and state-level agricultural technology park (pilot) are located in Wudang.

Today Wudang, hard working by successive district Party committee, the district government and the broad masses of people, the national economy maintained sustained, rapid and healthy development. The GDP and financial revenue maintained rapid growth with over double-digit. The region overall strength remarkably increased and three industrial structure achieved the change from "213" to "231" ; The rapid development of high-tech industries and the pharmaceutical industry, 98-high-tech industrial, over 20 biological pharmaceutical industry enterprises and seven listed companies such as South Huitong, Zhenhua Technology, and the one of the world's 500 strong enterprises -- Japanese Jingci Company were settled down the district, injected new vitality for Wudang district. In 2005, in the first round of the construction 20 economic strong counties (cities and districts), Wudang district was ranked the fourth in comprehensive assessment.

Face the new era, new opportunities, Wudang district will always seize the top priority of development, vigorously expand the Wudang spirit "unit and work hard, carrying forward, exploration and innovation, people enrichment and strong district", surrounding construction the goal "economy strong district and high-tech district and ecological district", actively promote the implementation of open lead, high-tech driven and urbanization strategy, continuously expand the level of opening up, intensify efforts to attract foreign investment and vigorously develop hi-tech industrial, promote the new industrialization proceeding; Further transform government functions and strengthen the legal system construction, strengthen the concept of service, and strive to create a fair, open and fair environment; Accelerating urbanization construction, and promote the integration process of urban and rural to make a positive contribution for building "Great Guiyang", improve regional economic super-convention, leap development, take the lead in realizing the goal of comprehensive building a well-off society in the city.

Open Wudang solemnly promises to you: You invest, we service; You develop, we open a way; You have difficulties, we help; You are benefited, we protect. 260,000 Wudang people wholeheartedly welcome persons with breadth of vision at home and abroad to invest Wudang and build Wudang, jointly develop the warm land Wudang, jointly create "whistler in the middle of Guizhou, spring city in the middle of forest"!

振华广场
Zhenhua plaza

花卉基地
Flower base

森普管材
Senpu Pipe Co., Ltd.

京资手机生产线
Jingci mobile phone production line

盘县 Pan County

中共六盘水市委常委、盘县县委书记徐毓贤
The member of standing committee of the CPC Liupanshui city, the secretary of Pan county, Xu Yuxian

盘县人民政府县长刘剑
The governor of Pan county, Liu Jian

盘县位于贵州西部，六盘水市西南部，素有“滇黔咽喉”、“滇黔锁钥”之称，是贵州的“西大门”。全县国土面积4056平方公里，辖37个乡镇、450个行政村、27个居委会、18个社区，总人口118万，国土面积和人口均占六盘水市的40%，是贵州省百万人口大县。在2005年第五届中国西部百强县（市）的评价中，列第39位。

2005年全县生产总值完成80.01亿元，同比增长19.2%。财政总收入完成13.01亿元，同比增长49.77%，增收4.3亿元。本级财政收入完成4.5亿元，同比增长45.27%，增收1.4亿元。固定资产投资44.79亿元，增长39.33%。主要特点是：

——经济快速增长，质量和效益明显提高。“十五”期间全县生产总值持续保持两位数增长，五年年均增幅达15.8%；财政总收入和本级财政收入快速增加，年均增收1亿元以上。县域经济综合实力和活力明显提高，经济强县建设位居全省第七。

——西部大开发各项战略重点扎实推进。以“西电东送”为重点的“中国煤电大县”建设取得重大突破，贵州首座百万千瓦级的盘县发电厂建成发电，装机360万千瓦的盘南电厂首台机组2006年3月并网发电。原煤产量由“九五”期末的560万吨增加到2005年的2160万吨，占全省原煤产量的1/5强，占全市的1/2强；以退耕还林为重点的生态建设和环境保护取得明显成效。“十五”期间全县累计完成造林63.7万亩（其中退耕还林39.6万亩），2005年全县森林覆盖率达31%。

——重要领域、重点工作和关键环节取得重要进展，经济社会发展的基础条件逐年改善。困扰盘县经济社会发展的安全生产和计划生育两大难题取得重大突破。煤炭安全生产走出重灾区阴影，百万吨死亡率逐年下降，由2000年的47.07下降到2005年的1.54，成为全省先进；计划生育工作扭转了多年的被动局面，人口自然增长率、符合政策生育率均创历史最好水平，获得了全省计生工作先进县和百万人口大县突出进步奖；禁毒工作扎实有效开展，有力地促进了社会治安明显好转，得到了省市的充分肯定，迎来了全省禁毒工作盘县现场会的召开；制约盘县加快发展的交通瓶颈现状得到实质性的突破，境内高速公路、主要经济干线、公路网建设步伐加快；城市建设日新月异，红果新城建设速度加快，古城改造力度加大，重点小城镇建设扎实推进，城镇化率达21.5%。

——社会主义新农村建设力度加大，人民生活水平显著提高。全力打好“三农”攻坚，组织实施了“万户温饱、千户安居、百村文明”等工程。县财政投入700万元实施“万户温饱”工程，解决6.78万农村贫困人口的生产生活困难；各界人士捐款372万元，启动实施“千户安居”工程，共解决1063户农村无房户和基本无房户的住房困难；县级财政投资350万元，带动全县社会各界捐款投资3000余万元，实施“百村文明”工程，209个村寨、3.5万户、13.3万人直接受益。2005年全县共免农业税1702.91万元，农民人均纯收入由2000年的1363元上升到2005年的1923元，年均增长7.1%。社会主义新农村建设扎实推进，人民生活明显提高。

Pan county is located in the west of Guizhou, the southwest of Liupanshui city, known as "the throat of Yunnan & Guizhou", "the key of Yunnan & Guizhou", and it is "the west gate" of Guizhou. The county has 4056 square kilometres area of land, governs 37 townships and 450 administrative villages, 27 neighborhood committees,

盘县红果新城夜景
Night scene of Honggauo New City of Pan county

18 communities with a total population of 1.18 million, land area and population accounting for 40% of Liupanshui city. It is a large county with millions population in Guizhou province. In the evaluation of the fifth China's western 100 strong counties (cities) of 2005, the county was placed the No.39.

The year of 2005, the GDP of the county completed 8.001 billion yuan, up 19.2% than that of the same period of last year. The financial revenues completed 1.301 billion yuan, up 49.77%, increasing 430 million yuan. The revenues of central level finance finished 450 million yuan, up 45.27%, increasing 140 million yuan. The fixed assets investment was 4.479 billion yuan, an increase of 39.33%. Main features were:

--Rapid economic growth, quality and efficiency improved markedly. During the period of "Tenth Five", the GDP of the county sustained double-digit growth, average annual increase 15.8% over five years; the financial revenue and the revenue of central level finance rapidly increased, the average annual increase income of 100 million yuan above. The economic comprehensive strength and vitality of the county markedly improved, the building of economy strong county was occupied the seventh among the province.

--The West Development strategy focus solidly improved. The construction of "China coal major county" taking "electric transferred from the west to the east" as the point, gained a major breakthrough. Pan county power station, the first 1 million thousand kilowatt power station of Guizhou was built and generated electricity. The first generating unit of Pannan power station with installed 3.6 million thousand kilowatts was merged into electrified wire and generated electricity in March 2006. The production of raw coal of 5.6 million tons from the end of "Ninth Five" increased to 21.6 million tons of 2005, accounting for 1/5 above of raw coal production in the province, and 1/2 above in the city; Focusing on returning the grain plots to forest, ecological construction and environmental protection achieved remarkable results. During the period of "Tenth Five", the county accumulated afforestation of 637 thousand mu (396 thousand mu of returning the grain plots to forest). The forest coverage rate of the county reached 31% in the year of 2005.

红果新城街景

The street scene of Hongguo New City

红二、六军团“盘县会议”会址

The site of "Pan county conference" Red Army 2, 6 army group

--Important field, main work and key link made important progress, the basic condition for economic and social development has improved year after year. Two problems of safety production and Family Planning, were puzzled by economic and social development of Pan county, that achieved significant breakthrough. Coal production safety went out of the shadow of disaster, millions tons of mortality dropped year by year from 47.07 in 2000 to 1.54 in 2005, became the advanced in the province; Family planning work reversed years of a passive situation, the natural growth rate and birth rate in legality achieved a record level, was awarded the prize of the provincial Family Planning work advanced county and the outstanding progress county with millions population; The solid and effective anti-narcotics work was carried out to promote social public order taking a turn for the better, that was gained the full approval of the province and the city, and held the Pan county site meeting of the provincial anti-drug work; The status of traffic bottleneck, restricting Pan county acceleration developing, got substantive breakthrough. The construction of highway, main economic lines and road network accelerated; the city construction has changed rapidly, accelerated construction of Hongguo New City, increased reconstruction of ancient city, solidly improved construction of key small towns, the rate of urban and towns reached 21.5%.

--The construction of socialist new rural areas has been intensified. People's living standards have markedly improved. Supporting doing well "three agricultures", organized implementation some projects of "enough food and clothing for millions households, peace housing for thousands households, civilization for hundreds villages". County finance inputted 7 million yuan to implement the "enough food and clothing for millions households" projects to solve the 67,800 rural poor production life difficulty; People of all circles contributed 3.72 million yuan to start implementing the "peace housing for thousands households" project, solved housing difficulty of a total of 1063 households without housing and basic without housing in rural areas; County finance invested 3.5 million yuan to bring along more than 30 million yuan contributed by people of all circles in the county, implemented the "civilization for hundreds villages" project, 209 villages, 35,000 households, 133,000 persons have directly benefited. In 2005, the agricultural tax of the county was exempted a total of 17.0291 million yuan. The per capita net income of peasants from 1,363 yuan in 2000 rose to 1,923 yuan in 2005, an average annual increase of 7.1%. The construction of socialist new rural areas has been intensified.People's living standards have markedly improved.

市长房国兴会见泰国公主
The mayor Fang Guoxing was meeting with the princess of the Kingdom of Thailand

“十五”期间，仁怀市按照“培植特色产业，发展特色经济，建设特色城市”的发展思路，聚精会神搞建设，一心一意谋发展，强力推进农业产业化、工业化、城镇化进程，把发展作为第一要务，把酒业作为主要经济支柱来培育，带动了经济链条的整体良性互动，市域经济快速发展，取得了辉煌成就。表现在经济总量跃上新台阶，“三化”建设迈出新步伐，基础设施得到新加强，改革开放谱写新篇章，社会事业取得新进步，人民生活又有新改善。

2005年实现地区生产总值59.84亿元，比2000年的20.62亿元，净增39.22亿元，增长190.2%；地方财政收入2005年达到3.39亿元，比2000年的1.3亿元，净增2.09亿元，增长160.77%；社会固定资产投资2005年完成15.39亿元，比2000年的全市投资6.26亿元，净增9.13亿元，增长145.85%；农民人均纯收入2005年达到2496元，比2000年的1181元，增长111.35%；城镇居民可支配收入2005年达到7500元，比2000年的5376元，增长39.50%；高中阶段毛入学率，2005年达到30.7%，比2000年的25.2%增长了5.5个百分点。名列贵州省“经济十强县（市）”第6位，西部百强县（市）第48位。

仁怀市政大楼
Renhuai municipal building

盐津河生态旅游区
Yanjin River eco-tourism zone

茅台酒之源——红高粱
The resource of Moutai — red sorghum

的“十五”

Five" of Renhuai

市领导接过中国酒都牌匾
The leaders of the city accepted the plate of China Wine--city

During the period of "Tenth Five", Renhuai city in accordance with the development ideas of "nurturing particular industries, developing specialized economy, building characteristics city", constructed with great attention, wholeheartedly for the development, strongly promoted the process in industrialization of agriculture, industrialization, urbanization, and took the development as a top priority, took winemaking industry as a main economic pillar cultivation to lead economy overall good development, the economy of the city rapidly developed to make splendid achievements. That showed the economic amount stepped to a higher level, the building "three industrializations" took new strides, new infrastructure has been strengthened, wrote a new chapter of reform and opening up, social undertakings made new progresses, the people's life had the new improvements

In 2005 the GDP of the city realized 5.984 billion yuan, net increase of 3.922 billion yuan than 2.062 billion yuan of 2000, an increase of 190.2%; local revenue of 2005 reached 339 million yuan, net increase of 209 million yuan than 130 million yuan of 2000, an increase of 160.77%; Social investment in fixed assets in 2005 completed 1.539 billion yuan, net increase of 913 million yuan than the investment of 626 million yuan in 2000, an increase of 145.85%; Per capita net income of farmers reached 2,496 yuan of 2005, increase of 111.35% than 1,181 yuan of 2000; Disposable income of urban residents reached 7,500 yuan of 2005, increase of 39.50% than 5,376 yuan of 2000; Senior high school gross enrollment rate in 2005 reached 30.7%, grew by 5.5 percentage points than the 25.2% in 2000. The city was ranked the sixth place in "Ten Economic Strongest Counties (cities)" of Guizhou province, the 48th place in the 100 Strongest Counties (cities) of the West.

国酒大道一瞥
A glimpse of the state--wine avenue

茅台镇一瞥
A glimpse of Maotai town

钟山区行政办公楼
The administrative building of Zhongshan district

钟山区是"中国凉都·六盘水"的政治、经济、文化、交通中心，总面积478.84平方公里，总人口43.18万；是"攀西——六盘水地区资源综合开发区"和"毕水兴"经济带的重要组成部分；境内有贵昆、内昆、水红、株六、水大支线铁路交汇形成西南地区重要的铁路交通枢纽，有"四省立交桥"之称；资源丰富，蕴藏着煤、铅、锌、铁、铜、白云石、重晶石、石灰石等多种矿产；自然风光绚丽多彩，奇山秀水、怪石、异洞与人文景观浑然一体，属湿润季风性气候区，冬无严寒，夏无酷暑，是难得的避暑胜地。

按照"城市兴区、工业强区、生态立区"的发展战略，建设大城市、服务大企业、统筹城乡发展、构建和谐社会。牢牢抓住西部大开发、经济强区建设等重大战略机遇，抢抓发展机遇，充分利用区内外两个市场、两种资源，大力引导、扶持电力、冶金、建材等传统产业做大做强，积极发展煤电化、煤气化等煤化工新兴产业，做大做强城市经济，逐步建成一批投资大、质量高、效益好的重大项目，为经济社会各项事业又快又好发展打牢基础。

2005年，区域经济社会稳步发展，城市建设日新月异，农村整体脱贫、安全生产"双升双降"、计划生育再上台阶。完成地区生产总值78.3亿元，同比增长17.8%；固定资产47.1亿元，同比增长47.37%；社会消费品零售总额18.46亿元，同比增长18.01%，财政总收入4.088亿元，同比增长70.75%，其中地方财政收入2.36亿元，增长57.3%；城镇居民可支配收入8032元，增长11.2%；农民人均纯收入2246元，增长13.4%。

围绕打造"中国凉都·六盘水"品牌，以创建全国文明卫生城市、全国优秀旅游城市和建设贵州西部中心城市为目标，加快城市新区和城市基础设施建设，不断完善城市功能，加大城市管理力度，强化市容环境管理，丰富城市文化内涵，进一步提升城市影响力、竞争力。

围绕"基本建成重要能源、原材料和煤化工基地，基本实现小康、步入社会主义新农村，基本建成和谐文明、现代开放的中心城市"的发展目标，加快发展区域经济，大力构筑城中品牌商业经济，城边市场物流经济、城郊工业园区经济，城外都市农业经济四大支柱产业，努力实现经济社会又快又好发展和人民生活的稳步提高，加快实现强区升位的步伐。

开放的钟山区热忱欢迎各方、各界人士到钟山区考察、度假、投资和发展。

人民广场
The People's Square

Zhongshan district is the political, economic, cultural, transportation center of "China Cool City · Liupanshui", with a total area of 478.84 square kilometers, and a total population of 431,800; is an important component part of "Panxi -- Liupanshui regional resource comprehensive development zone" and "Bijie Shuicheng Xingyi" economic belt; It has Guikun Neikun, Shuihong, Zhuliu, and Shuida feeder railway, that gather forming the important railway hub in southwest region, so it has the name of "the overpass of four provinces"; there has rich resources such as coal, lead, zinc, iron, copper, dolomite, barytes, limestone and other minerals; Here has

六盘水凤池园
Fengchi Park of Liupanshui

钟山区
Liupanshui City

六盘水南编组站
The south yard of Liupanshui

野马寨发电厂
Yemazhai Power Plant

glorious and colorful scenery, and rare mountain and beautiful water, queer stone, strange hole with cultural landscape all blend into one whole. It belongs to humid monsoon climate. There's no bitter cold in winter or intense hot in summer, and is a rare summer resort.

According to the development strategy of "urban thriving the district, industry strong the district, ecology establishment the district", the district constructed large city, serviced large enterprises, commanded urban and rural development, and built a harmonious society. Firmly grasped the major strategic opportunity of the West Developing and economy strong district construction, seized development opportunity, made full use of two markets and two resources in district or outside, and vigorously guided and supported electricity, metallurgy, building material, and other traditional industries to grow in size and strength, positively developed coal chemical emerging industries such as coal electricity, coal gas, made the city economy to grow in size and strength, and gradually built a lot of major projects with large investment, high quality and good benefits, laid a solid foundation for rapid and good development of all the economic social undertakings.

In 2005, the regional economic society steadily developed, the urban construction changed rapidly, the rural areas totally got out of poverty and safe production was of "double rising or double falling", the work of Family Planning stepped again. The regional GDP completed 7.83 billion yuan, more 17.8% than period time of last year; The investment in fixed assets was 4.71 billion yuan, an increase of 47.37%; Total retail sales of consumer goods was 1.846 billion yuan, up 18.01%, the financial revenue was 408.8 million yuan, up 70.75%, including the local revenue of 236 million yuan, an increase of 57.3%; The disposable income of urban residents was 8,032 yuan, an increase of 11.2%; The per capita net income of farmers was 2,246 yuan, growth of 13.4%.

Focusing on building the brand of "China Cool city · Liupanshui", taking creation the National Civilized Health City, the National Excellent Tourist City and building the central city in the west of Guizhou as the aim, accelerated the infrastructure construction in city's new district and urban, and constantly improved the functions of city, enlarged urban management, strengthened the city environmental management, enriched urban cultural connotation, and further enhanced the influence and competitiveness of the city.

Surrounding the development goal of "basic completion important energy and raw material and coal chemical base, basic achievement well-off, stepping into socialist new rural areas, basic building the central city with harmonious civilization, modern and open", accelerated development regional economy, vigorously built four pillar industries of the brand commercial economy inner city, the market logistics economy in side of city, the industrial park economy in suburb, the urban agriculture economy outside the city, and strived to achieve the rapid and good development of economic society and the steady improvement of people's living, accelerated to achieve the pace of the strong district promotion place.

Open Zhongshan district warmly welcomes people from all circles to Zhongshan district investigation, vacation, investment and development.

兴义市

Xingyi City

——黔滇桂三省（区）结合部一座正在崛起的新兴城市

—A new city in the integration of Guizhou, Yunnan and Guangxi provinces (autonomous regions) in rising

南昆线上最大的货运编组站——威舍火车站

The largest freight yard of Nanning - Kunming line -- Weishe Railway Station

机场

The airport

国家级风景名胜区马岭河峡谷

The state level scenic spot Maling River Valley

兴义市地处黔、滇、桂三省（区）结合部，素有“三省通衢”之称。辖区国土面积2915平方公里，总人口75万人。拥有金、煤等多种矿产资源，其中煤的储量极为丰富，储量达3亿吨；拥有充足水能资源，理论储量达261万千瓦，已建成天生桥、鲁布革等大中型水电站；拥有国家首批自然遗产、国家重点风景名胜区马岭河峡谷——万峰湖，中国最美的地方之一的万峰林，国家非物质文化遗产“布依八音坐唱”和贵州兴义国家地质公园、省级文物保护单位何应钦故居等独具特色的旅游资源；拥有烤烟、芭蕉芋、生姜等多种农特产品。这里交通便捷。形成了集铁路、公路、航空、航运四位一体的立体交通运输网络，成为西南出海的重要交通枢纽。

“十五”以来，兴义市经济建设和社会发展取得了显著成绩，综合经济实力进入全省十强和西部百强县市。

兴义市今后的发展战略定位是：黔西南州政治、经济、文化中心和信息中心；黔、滇、桂三省区结合部的中心市场和物流中心；“西电东送”的电源基地和电力枢纽；大西南出海通道和南贵昆经济圈的工业重镇；珠江上游重要的生态屏障和绿色走廊；中国优秀旅游城市和最佳人居环境城市。

Xingyi city is located in the integration of Guizhou, Yunnan and Guangxi provinces (autonomous regions), is known as the name of "the hub of three provinces". The land area of the city is 2,915 square kilometers, has a total population of 750,000 people. The city has gold, coal and other mineral resources, of which the reserves of coal is abundant, with 300 million tons of reserves; has sufficient water resources with theory reserves reaching 2.61 million kilowatts, has built Tiansheng Bridge, Lubuge and other large and medium-sized hydropower stations; possesses the first batch of national natural heritage, the national key point scenic spot Maling River Valley--Wanfeng Lake, Wanfeng Forest, the one of China's most beautiful places, national non-material cultural heritage "Buyi music sitting singing" and the National Geological Park of Guizhou Xingyi, the provincial cultural relics conservation unit, the former home of He Yingqin and other unique tourism resources; possesses the flue-cured tobacco, plantain- taro, ginger and other agro-products. The city has convenient traffic, and forms the three-dimensional transportation network integration railway, highway, aviation and shipping, has become a major transport hub access to the sea in the southwest.

Since "Tenth Five", Xingyi city's economic construction and social development achieved remarkable results, the overall economic strength entered into the provincial ten strongest and the top 100 counties, cities of the western.

The future development strategy of Xingyi city is : the political, economic, cultural and information centers of Qianxinan prefecture; the central market and logistics center of the integration of Guizhou, Yunnan and Guangxi, the electricity supply base and electricity hub for "transfer electricity from west to east"; the access to the sea in the southwest and the industrial important city of Nanning Guiyang Kunming economic circle; the important ecological barrier and the green corridor of the upstream of Pearl River; the China's excellent tourism city and the best living environment city.

桔山城市中心区 The city central district of Jushan

清镇市概况

The Summary of Qingzhen City

钱运录同志到清镇调研农业农村工作
Comrade Qian Yunlu studied agricultural rural work in Qingzhen

清镇市地处贵州省中部，省会贵阳市西部，距贵阳市城区22公里，是省会贵阳重要的卫星城市。全市总面积1492平方公里，其中耕地1.8万公顷，林地2.93万公顷。全市辖6个乡（其中3个民族乡）、4个镇、1个街道办事处，299个村、30个居委会（社区），总人口50万人，其中农业人口38.5万人，少数民族人口12.2万人。

清镇市区位优势、交通便利、资源丰富、山川秀美。市境内有10余家省、贵阳市属国有大中型企业，是贵州省重要的电力、化工、磨料等工业基地。已探明的主要矿藏有铝土矿、铁矿、煤矿、磷矿、硅石、重晶石等30多种，其中铝土矿已探明储量3.6亿吨，远景储量在1.2亿吨以上，在全省位居第一，境内猫场矿区是全国已探明的铝土矿储量最大、品位最高的整体连片矿区。煤炭储量41.9亿吨。全市水域面积78.5平方公里，水能蕴藏量36万千瓦，蓄水量达18亿立方米，是贵阳市的主要饮用水源地。境内4A级风景名胜区红枫湖享誉国内外。道路交通发达，已经实现村村通公路、乡乡通油路。

2005年，全市地方生产总值完成447564万元，比上年增长15.1%。三次产业比重为13.18：49.43：37.39。非公有制经济增加值完成187261万元，比上年增长23.2%，在国民经济中所占比重为41.8%，比上年上升了4.6个百分点。全市工业总产值完成628931万元，比上年增长17.3%。全市财政总收入完成57008万元，同比增长20.17%。城镇居民人均可支配收入达到8871.82元，同比增长14.8%；农民人均纯收入达到2858.04元，同比增长12.6%。全社会固定资产投资总额完成22.82亿元，同比增长36.3%。全年共引进内资项目104个，实际到位资金139488万元，同比增长44.7%；引进外资项目4个，实际到位资金246万美元。社会各项事业全面进步，构建社会主义和谐社会深入推进。

Qingzhen city is located in the middle of Guizhou Province, the western of provincial capital of Guiyang city, 22 km away from Guiyang city, is the important satellite city of provincial capital of Guiyang. The total area of the city is 1,492 square kilometres, of which 18 thousand hectares of arable land, 29.3 thousand hectares of woodland. The city governs 6 townships (including 3 national townships), 4 towns, 1 neighborhood office, 299 villages and 30 resident committees (community), total population of 500,000 persons, of whom 385,000 persons of agricultural population, the minority population of 122,000 persons.

Qingzhen city has advantage position, convenient transport, rich natural resources and beautiful mountains. There are over 10 provincial, Guiyang municipal large and medium-sized state-owned enterprises, and it is an important power, chemical industry, abrasive, and other industrial base. The county has proved 30 major mineral such as bauxite, iron ore, coal, phosphate, silica, barite, of which bauxite proved reserves of 360 million tons, vision reserves in above of 120 million tons, ranking the first in the province, and the Maochang Mine is the overall mine area which is the largest and highest grade proven bauxite reserves in the country. The coal reserves are 4.19 billion tons. The waters area of the city are 78.5 square kilometres, hydropower potential of 360 thousand kilowatts, the amount of store water reaching to 1.8 billion cubic meters, is the main source of drinking water in Guiyang city. 4A-class scenic areas Hongfeng Lake in the city is famed the country and the word. The county has convenient road traffic, has achieved all villages and townships access roads.

In 2005, the GDP of the city completed 4475.64 million yuan, 15.1% higher than the previous year. The proporation of three industries was 13.18:49.43:37.39. Non-public economic completed 1872.61 million yuan in added value, increase 23.2% than the previous year, accounting for 41.8% in the national economy, increased by 4.6 percentage points over the previous year. The industrial output value of the city completed 6289.31 million yuan, 17.3% higher than the previous year. The government revenue completed 570.08 million yuan, 20.17% more than the same of last year. Per capita disposable income of urban residents reached 8871.82 yuan, an increase 14.8%; per capita net income of peasants reached 2858.04 yuan, an increase of 12.6%. Total fixed asset investment accomplished 2.282 billion yuan, up 36.3%.Annual totally 104 domestic projects were introduced, the actual capital of 1394.88 million yuan, increased 44.7% than the same of last year; 4 foreign investment projects were introduced with actual available funds of 2.46 million USD. Social all the causes made overall progresses and built a socialist harmonious society in advancement.

百花湖美景
Beautiful Baihua Lake

高原湖城
Lake City of plateau

清镇高速公路上的红枫湖大桥
Hongfeng Lake Bridge of Qingzhen Highway

奋进中的

Zunyi County in

遵义县地处贵州省北部，县域环绕历史文化名城遵义，210、326国道和川黔电气化铁路、贵遵高等级公路贯穿全境，县城南白镇距贵阳市130公里、重庆市270公里。辖29个镇2个民族乡，国土面积4092平方公里，总人口115.7万。境内山川秀丽，气候宜人，物产丰富，交通便捷，年平均气温14℃。

遵义县是全省经济强县之一。“十五”以来，全县人民紧紧抓住西部大开发机遇，求真务实，开拓进取，经济社会取得长足发展。先后荣获全国文化先进县、全国民政工作先进县、全国基础教育先进县、全国乡村城市化示范县、全国农村公路建设工程示范县、全国辣椒产业十强县、中国辣椒之都等称号，是全国瘦肉型商品猪生产基地县、全国无公害农产品示范基地县、国家优质烤烟生产基地县、中国“双低”油菜生产大县、粮食生产大县。2005年，全县生产总值65.65亿元，比上年增长（下同）14.1%；人均生产总值5663元，增长13.6%。粮食总产量60.97万吨，增长8.0%；油菜籽产量6.91万吨，增长7.2%。工业总产值53.64亿元，增长40.1%，其中规模以上工业产值42.39亿元，增长50.3%。固定资产投资29.44亿元，增长3.8%。社会消费品零售总额14.51亿元，增长13.0%。财政总收入5.88亿元，增长36.2%；地方财政收入2.66亿元，增长23.7%。农民人均纯收入2906元，增长6.9%，城镇居民人均可支配收入8208元，增长12.8%。同时，以富、学、乐、美“四在农家”和安、康、乐、便“四民社区”创建活动为载体，积极推进社会主义新农村建设，城乡精神文明建设水平得到整体提升，并受到中央、省委的充分肯定和高度重视。

“十一五”期间，遵义县将以科学发展为统领，紧紧围绕全面建设小康社会目标，坚持发展第一要务，加快转变经济增长方式，突出工业强县战略，以工业化引领“三化一业一强”建设，努力促进经济社会快速健康协调发展和人的全面进步！

贵州省中型企业遵义铝业股份有限公司
Zunyi Aluminium Stock Corporation Ltd, Guizhou province medium-sized company

县城万寿广场夜景
Night scene of Wanshou Plaza of the county

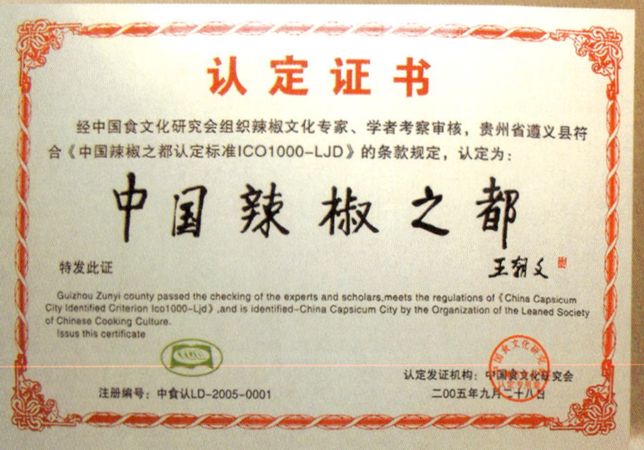

认定证书

经中国食文化研究会组织辣椒文化专家、学者考察审核，贵州省遵义县符合《中国辣椒之都认定标准ICO1000-LJD》的条款规定，认定为：

中国辣椒之都

特发此证

王朝文

Guizhou Zunyi county passed the checking of the experts and scholars,meets the regulations of《China Capsicum City Identified Criterion Ico1000-Ljd》,and is identified-China Capsicum City by the Organization of the Leaned Society of Chinese Cooking Culture.

Issus this certificate

认定发证机构：中国食文化研究会

注册编号：中食认LD-2005-0001

二00五年九月二十八日

中国辣椒之都认定证书
The certificate of China Capsicum City

Zunyi county is located in the north of Guizhou province, going in a ring of historical and cultural city Zunyi, 210, 326 Nation Road and Chuanqian electrified railway, Guizun high-grade highway running through the county, Nanbai town of the county is 130 km away from Guiyang city and 270 km from Chongqing city. The county governs 29 towns 2 nationalities towns, which has an area of 4,092 square kilometres, with a total population of 1.157 million. The county has beautiful mountains and rivers, mild and delightful climate, abundant products, convenient transportation, an average temperature of 14 degrees.

Zunyi county is the one of the economic strong county in the province. Since "Tenth Five" the people of the county seized opportunities of developing the western region, seeking the truth and open and advancing, achieved significant economic and social development. The county has won the title of National Cultural Advanced County, National Civil Work Advanced County, National Basic Education Advanced County, and National Rural Urbanization Model County, National Rural Road Construction Model County, National Capsicum Industry Ten-strong County, China Capsicum City and is the national lean meat commodity pig production base county, national free-pollution agricultural products model base county, national quality flue-cured tobacco production base county, China "double low" cole production great county, grain production great county. In 2005, the GDP of the county was 6.565 billion yuan, more 14.1% than the previous year (the same below); 5,663 yuan per capita GDP growth 13.6%. Output yield of grain was 609,700 tons, an increase of 8.0%; 69,100 tons of

遵义县
Advancement

遵义县云门囤风光
Yunmentu scenery of Zunyi county

rapeseed output, growth 7.2%. Output value of industry was 5.364 billion yuan, an increase of 40.1%, of which 4.239 billion yuan of output value of industry above designated size, growth 50.3%. Investment in fixed assets was 2.944 billion yuan, an increase of 3.8%. Retail sales of consumer goods were 1.451 billion yuan, an increase of 13.0%. Financial revenue totaled 588 million yuan, an increase of 36.2%; 266 million yuan of local revenue, growth 23.7%. Per capita net income of peasants was 2,906 yuan, an increase of 6.9%, average disposable income of urban residents of 8,208 yuan, an increase of 12.8%. At the same time, taking the building activities rich, study, happy, beauty "Four Things in Farmer Family" and peace, health, happy, convenient "Four convenient in community" as the carrier, actively promoted the construction of a new socialist rural area, construction level of urban and rural spiritual civilization was overall upgrading, and fully affirmed and highly valued by the central and provincial Party committee.

The period of "Eleventh Five", Zunyi county will take the development of science as the guide, closing centering on the objective of overall building a moderate prosperous society, insist on taking development as the top priority, speed up the transformation of the mode of economic growth, stress the strategy of industry strong county, take industrializations lead construction "three industrialization one industry one strong", in an effort to promote economic and social rapid and healthy coor-dination development and overall progress of human!

遵义县一中校园一角
A corner of the No.1 middle school of Zunyi county

四在农家新气象
Four Things in Farmer Family in the new atmosphere

摄影 江伦生
Photographer Jiang Lunsheng

居危奋进　务实苦干

Advancement in crisis time · Work hard with Practicality

2005年，都匀市在省委、省政府和州委、州政府的正确领导下，在省、州建强办的关心和指导下，积极贯彻落实《中共贵州省委、贵州省人民政府关于进一步推进经济强县建设的意见》(黔党发[2004]6号)文件精神和全省经济强县建设经验交流会议精神，全面安排部署经济强县建设工作，较好地完成了2005年度建强各项指标任务，推动了全市经济社会的持续快速协调发展。

认真解决问题背后的问题。市委八届九次全委（扩大）会议要求各级各部门要做到主动求人、把人求好，工作作风才能改变，服务态度才能改善，投资环境才能变优，建强工作才能做好。都匀经济社会才能快速发展，才能做大总量，提升质量，实现更快更好发展。

优化环境，全面推进经济社会发展的历史性跨越。市委、市政府把“环境立市”作为经济社会发展的重要战略，明确“抓环境就是抓机遇，抓环境就是抓发展”的理念，将改善环境作为全市经济发展的重点工作来抓。成立了投资环境综合整治领导小组，出台了《都匀市投资环境考评办法》及相关制度。围绕“三纵九横五出口六连线”的路网建设目标，加强城市基础设施建设。按照“山水桥城、魅力都匀”的城市定位，继续抓好旅游基础设施建设。“省级园林城市”已通过评审，并获得“全国园林绿化先进市”、“贵州省绿化模范市”称号。

以招商引资为主抓手，全力发展工业经济，做大经济总量。进一步优化投资环境，改善服务，把招商引资作为加快城市经济社会快速协调发展的主抓手。实施招商引资奖励政策，不断拓宽招商引资渠道。2005年共引进项目94个，实际到位资金58604.8万元，同比增长65.16%。

突出结构调整和“文明生态小康村”建设，抓实“三农”工作。围绕中央提出的“生产发展、生活宽裕、乡风文明、村容整洁、管理民主”的目标要求，在18个村深入开展文明生态小康村建设。坚持“稳粮、强牧、扩经、增效”的八字方针，发展生态效益型农业和立体农业，2005年，粮食生产喜获丰收，总产量达98901吨，增长3.5%；烤烟收购30080担，增长27.84%；畜牧水产业总产值完成35100万元，增长7.79%。目前，一批种养基地、示范村、示范点以及农村经济合作组织初步形成。农村基础设施建设得到进一步加强。

以旅游为龙头，带动第三产业迅速发展。围绕三个黄金周和节庆活动，加快旅游市场的培育。2005年，全市接待游客147万人次，旅游综合收入达24200万元，同比增长35.2%。

推进各项事业全面发展，努力构建和谐社会。加强教育基础设施建设，发展现代远程教育，加强科技成果和先进适用技术的引进、转化和推广。全国文化先进市创建成功。计生“创优”成效明显，生育政策符合率稳步提高。加强城市基础设施建设，加快城市化发展步伐，保持城镇化率每年提高1个百分点以上。建立并逐步完善低保发放、帮扶困难企业和困难职工、特困职工和农村困难农户子女教育救助、医疗保障、廉租房、社会捐赠、走访帮扶四级责任制等七大救助机制，实施农村贫困学生“鸡蛋工程”。进一步加强新形势下安全生产工作，努力构建社会主义和谐社会。

州委常委、市委书记周建琨深入联系点上党课
The standing member of the state Party committee, the secretary of the city Party committee Zhou Jiankun gave the Party lecture in contact point

中共都匀市委副书记、市长胡晓剑深入联系点检查指导工作
The deputy secretary of the Duyun city Party committee, the mayor Hu Xiaojian inspected and guided work in contact point

文明生态小康村是社会主义新农村的科学实践。图为都匀市党建导富暨文明生态小康村建设现场会
The civilized well-off eco-village is the scientific practice of socialist new rural. Photograph shows the site meeting of Duyun city Party building guidance rich cum civilized well-off eco-village building

谱写都匀发展新篇章

Write a new chapter in the development of Duyun

实施“鸡蛋工程”，惠及全市1.3万寄宿制贫困中小学生
Implementation "egg project", 13,000 boarding poverty students were benefited

In 2005, under the correct leadership of the provincial Party committee, provincial government and the state Party commission, state government, under the concern and guidance of the province, state building-strong office, Duyun city actively implemented the document spirit "opinion on further promoting economic strong county building of CPC Guizhou provincial Party committee, Guizhou province government"(Qian Party sending [2004]No.6) and the conference spirit of provincial economic strong county building experience exchange, comprehensively arranged economic strong county construction work, and completed 2001-2005 all indicators of building-strong, promoted the sustained, rapid and coordinated economic and social development.

The underlying problem has been seriously settled. The Ninth (expansion) Conference of the Eighth Session City's Party Committee required departments at all levels should take the initiative to ask for, the people must be done well, can change the style of work, service attitude can be improved, the investment environment can be changed finely, the building-strong work can be done well. So, the economy and society of Duyun can be rapidly developed, can grow the amount, enhance the quality, achieve faster and better development.

To optimize the environment and promote economic and social development of historic leap. Municipal Party committee and government took the "environment building the city" as an important economic and social development strategy, defined the concept "grasping the environment means grasping chance, grasping the environment means grasping development", took improvement the environment as the city's economic development focus. Set up a investment environment comprehensive renovation leading group, introduced the "Duyun city investment environment appraisal method" and related systems. Surrounding the road network building objective "three vertical nine horizontal five exports six lines", urban infrastructure was strengthened. According to the urban location "nature Bridge City, charm Duyun", continued to do a good job in the tourism infrastructure. "Provincial Garden City" has been passed accreditation and awarded the title "National Garden Green Advanced City", "Guizhou Province Green Model City".

Taking attracting foreign investment as focus, the industrial economy has been fully developed, and economy amount was enhanced. Further optimized the investment environment, improved service, took attracting foreign investment as the main in acceleration city's economic and social coordinate development. Implementation incentive policy of attracting foreign investment, and the attracting foreign investment channel was continually expanded. A total of 94 introduced projects in 2005, actual capital of 586.048 million yuan, increased 65.16% than last year.

By prominent structural adjustment and "civilized eco-village" building, the work of "three agricultures" was solidly grasped. Around objective of the Central "production development, living well-off, township civilization, clean village, democratic management", in-depth developed the civilization well-off eco-village building in 18 villages. Insisted on the eight-character principle "stable grain, strong livestock, expansion economy, increase efficiency" to develop the ecological efficiency agriculture and the stereoscopic agriculture. In 2005, a good harvest was of grain, total yield reached 98,901 tons, an increase of 3.5%; purchased flue-cured tobacco 30,080 dans, growth 27.84%; out put value of livestock and aquaculture industry completed 351 million yuan, an increase of 7.79%. Currently, a number of breeding bases, model villages, model points and rural economic cooperation organizations initially shaped. Rural infrastructure construction has been further strengthened.

Taking the tourism as dragon head, the third industry has developed rapidly. Surrounding three Golden Week and festivals activities accelerated development the tourist market. In 2005, the city received visitors of 1.47 million person times, tourism comprehensive income amounted to 242 million yuan, more 35.2% than last year.

The various undertakings have been promoted the comprehensive development, built up a harmonious society. Strengthened the educational infrastructure construction and developed modern distance education and strengthened scientific and technological results and the introduction of advanced technologies, conversion and extension. National Cultural Advanced City was successfully built. Family Planning "Creation the Best" was made obvious result, the rate of Family Planning steadily increased. Strengthened urban infrastructure construction, and speed up the pace of urbanization, maintained increase 1 percentage above each year. Established and gradually improved the seven relief assistance systems such as low assurance issuance, helping difficulty enterprises and workers, especially difficulty and hardship workers and rural poverty students education rescue, medical support, and low-cost housing, community donations, visited support four-level responsibility mechanisms, implemented rural poverty students "egg project". Further strengthened safety work under the new situation, and strived to build a socialist harmonious society.

采取有效措施促农增收。图为水族妇女在新引进的棒球厂做工
Taking effective measures to promote agricultural growth. The Photograph shows women are working in the baseball factory which was newly introduced

花溪区
Huaxi District

省长石秀诗在镇山调研
The governor Shi Xiushi was investing in Zhenshan

花溪是贵阳市著名的生态区、旅游区、文化区，是贵州省和贵阳市的重要窗口，素有贵州高原明珠的美誉。全区区域面积976.8平方公里，现辖3个办事处、2个镇、10个乡，165个行政村，22个社区，总人口32.87万人。

2005年，花溪区生产总值完成371238万元，比上年增长14.8%，一、二、三次产业结构比为14.75：37.41：47.84，产业结构进一步优化。人均生产总值11440元，比上年增长14.1%。财政总收入完成34081.4万元，比上年增长16.26%；地方财政收入完成22291.7万元，比上年增长20.88%。社会消费品零售总额完成72011万元，比上年增长18.3%。城镇居民人均可支配收入达9265元，比上年增长13.2%；农民人均纯收入达3220元，比上年增长10.8%。

实施“十五”计划的五年，是花溪城乡基础设施发生历史性变化，经济发展实现转折性增长，社会事业的一些领域取得重要突破的五年，成为改革开放以来综合经济实力提高最快、城乡面貌变化最大、人民群众得到实惠最多、社会事业得到全面发展的时期。

全社会固定资产投资完成17.19亿元，同比增长47.5%，是2000年的9.17倍。全年共签订招商引资项目122个，协议利用资金60多亿元，实际到位资金9.94亿元。森林覆盖率比2004年提高2个百分点。2005年10月被省政府命名为贵州省农产品加工业示范基地。同年被农业部确定为第二批全国（贵州省唯一）农产品加工业示范基地。青岩镇被建设部、国家文物局命名为“中国历史文化名镇”，并在CCTV·2005“魅力名镇”评选活动中进入20强。全年共接待中外游客490.1万人次，比2000年增长109.4%，年均增长15.9%；旅游总收入3.9亿元，比2000年增长197.7%，年均增长24.4%。全区适龄儿童入学率达99.3%。被教育部授予“师资培训示范区”称号。荣获全国计划生育信息化先进区、全省优质服务先进区等称号。

Huaxi is a famous ecological zone, tourist area, and cultural area of Guiyang city, is an important window of Guizhou province and Guiyang city, is known as the reputation of A Pearl of Guizhou Plateau. The region area is 976.8 square kilometers. The district now governs 3 offices, 2 towns, 10 townships and 165 administrative villages, 22 communities with a total population of 328,700 people.

In 2005, the GDP of HUaxi district completed 3.71238 billion yuan, an increase of 14.8% over the last year, and the proporation of the first, second, third industrial was 14.75:37.41:47.84 and further optimized the industrial structure. Per capita GDP was 11,440 yuan, growth of 14.1% over the previous year. Financial revenue completed 340.814 million yuan, increased 16.26% than last year; local revenue completed 222.917 million yuan, 20.88% higher than the previous year. Total retail sales of consumer goods completed 720.11 million yuan, 18.3% higher than the previous year. Per capita disposable income of urban residents reached 9,265 yuan, increased 13.2%; per capita net income of farmers reached 3,220 yuan, increased 10.8%.

The five years of implementation "Tenth Five-Year Plan", that Huaxi happened a historic change in urban and rural infrastructure, achieved turning growth in economic development, made important breakthroughs in some areas of social undertakings, and became the period that the fastest growth in comprehensive economic strength, the biggest changes in the urban and rural landscape, the people obtaining the largest benefit, and comprehensive development in social undertakings since the reform and opening up.

Total fixed asset investment accomplished 1.719 billion yuan, up 47.5% than the same time of last year, was 9.17 times of the year of 2000. Signed investment projects for a total of 122, agreed to use funds more than 6 billion yuan, 994 million yuan of funds actually in place. The rate of forest covering increased 2 percentage points than in 2004. In October of 2005, Huaxi was named Guizhou Province Agricultural Product Processing Industry Demo Base by the provincial government, at the same year, was identified as the second National (the only one in Guizhou province) Agricultural Product Processing Industry Demo Base by the Ministry of Agriculture. Qingyan town was named "Chinese historic and cultural famous town" by the Ministry of Construction, the State Administration of Cultural Heritage, and ranked 20 strong in the selection activity of CCTV · 2005 "charm of famous town". Chinese and foreign tourists were annual received 4.901 million person times, growth 109.4% than in 2000, an average annual increase of 15.9%; 390 million yuan of total tourism income, growth 197.7% than in 2000, an average annual increase of 24.4%. The rate of all school-age children enrolment was up to 99.3%. Huaxi was awarded the title of "Teacher Resource Training Demonstration District" by the Ministry of Education. Won the title of national family planning information advanced district, high quality service advanced district of the province.

花溪公园放鸽桥
Pigeons bridge of Huaxi Park

西秀区
Xixiu District

西秀白塔已成为安顺经济、社会、文化发展的见证
Bai Tower of Xixiu has become economic, social and cultural development witness of Anshun

西秀区是安顺市的政治、经济、科技、文化中心。全区行政区域总面积1710平方公里，耕地面积27727公顷。辖7个乡（其中5个民族乡），10个镇，6个街道办事处，498个村民委员会，54个居民委员会。年末，西秀区共有人口836700人。其中非农业人口228483人，占人口总数的27.3%。人口较多的少数民族有苗族、布依族等。人口出生率14.39‰，自然增长率7.48‰，计划生育率95.56%。

2005年，全区生产总值438484万元，比上年增长13.0%；农林牧渔业总产值112702万元，增长9.48%；规模以上工业总产值264023万元，全年实现乡镇企业总产值185966万元；财政总收入48000万元，较2004年增长14.01%，其中，地方财政收入27884万元，增长28.17%；全年累计完成全社会固定资产投资155633万元，增长15.82%；社会消费品零售总额149624万元，较上年增长15.79%；城镇居民人均可支配性收入为7337元，较2004年增长8.66%，农民人均纯收入为2466元，较2004年增长9.12%。全年接待海内外游客125.24万人次，较2004年增长45%，旅游总收入47200万元，较2004年增长117%。

古老的民居，蕴涵的是数百年前的江南遗风
The old residences, meant that Jiangnan style with a few hundred years ago

Xixiu district is the political, economic, scientific and technological, and cultural center of Anshun city. The total area of administrative region is 1,710 square kilometers, 27727 hectares of arable land. It governs 7 townships (including 5 nationalities townships), 10 towns, 6 neighborhood offices, 498 village committees, 54 resident committees. A total population of the end of the year of Xixiu district was 836,700 people, including non-agricultural population of 228483, accounting for 27.3% of the total population. The minority nationalities with more population are Miao and Buyi minority. Birth rate is 14.39‰, 7.48‰ of natural growth rate, family planning rate of 95.56%.

In 2005, the GDP of the district was 4.38484 billion yuan, increased 13.0%; the gross output value of farming, forestry, animal husbandry and fishery was 1.12702 billion yuan, an increase of 9.48%; the gross output value of industry above designated size was 2.64023 billion yuan, the annual output value of township enterprises realized 1.85966 billion yuan; the financial revenue was 480 million yuan, more 14.01% than 2004, among which, the local revenue of 278.84 million yuan, growth 28.17%; the fixed-assets investment annual cumulatively completed 1.55633 billion yuan, an increase of 15.82%; total retail sales of consumer goods were 1.49624 billion yuan, growth 15.79% than last year; per capita disposable income of urban residents was up to 7,337 yuan, 8.66% growth over 2004, per capita net income of peasants was 2,466 yuan, 9.12% growth over 2004. The reception number of tourists at home and abroad annually was 1.2524 million person times, increase 45% than 2004, and total tourism income was 472 million yuan, growth 117% than 2004.

西秀新区已经成为西秀区新的经济增长点。图为若飞东路延伸段
Xiziu new district has become new economic growth point of Xixiu district. Photograph shows Ruofeidong Road extension session

漫山遍野的油菜花昭示着丰收的到来 The rape flower over hill and dale beckoned the harvest arrival

开放的毕节欢迎您

The open Bijie welcomes you

毕节学院艺术楼
The art building of Bijie College

人民公园
People Park

城市道路改造工程
The reform project of city roc

中共中央政治局“鸡鸣三省会会址
The site of "Jiming three prov meeting of the CPC Central Committee Political Bureau

毕节市是黔西北区域性中心城市，全国第七批国家级生态示范县之一。毕节市位于川、滇、黔三省结合部，冬无严寒，夏无酷暑，境内峰峦叠嶂，溪流纵横，河流总长695公里，水能蕴藏量20.83万千瓦，可开发量11.56万千瓦。现已探明矿产资源有煤、硫，铁、锌、大理石等20余种，其中煤炭储量达54亿吨以上。

毕节市旅游资源丰富，风景名胜颇多。有全国重点文物保护单位大屯彝族土司庄园、拱拢坪国家级森林公园、七星关古遗址等人文景观和自然景观。贵州省中共组织发源地、中共中央政治局“鸡鸣三省”会议会址、川滇黔苏维埃革命政权旧址、长征“扩红”和建立的唯一省级抗日武装都在毕节，具备红色旅游经典景区开发建设的优越条件。

毕节市投资环境明显优化，对外开放日益扩大。硬环境建设方面，旧城改造与新区开发并举，城区面积从建市初期的9.7平方公里扩展到现在的15平方公里。软环境建设方面，全面推行“一站式”办公和“一条龙”服务。成立市政务服务中心、行政投诉中心、外来投资者投诉中心，为外来投资者提供安全、稳定和良好的投资环境。

希望有更多的有识之士了解和认识毕节，有更多的投资者关注和走向毕节。

Bijie city is a regional center city of northwest of Guizhou, is the one of the seventh state-level ecological demonstration counties. Bijie city is located in the joint of Sichuan, Yunnan, Guizhou provinces. There's no bitter cold in winter or intense heart in summer. There is ridges and peaks rising one higher than another, and ravine streams with great ease in the territory. The total length of rivers is 695 km, the water reserve is 208.3 thousand kilowatts, 115.6 thousand kilowatts of capacity can be developed. Coal, sulfur, iron, zinc, marble and more than 20 kinds of mineral resources have been proven, which coal reserve reached 5.4 billion tons above.

Bijie city is rich in tourism resources, with many scenic spots. There has national key preservation cultural relics unit of Yi nationality Chieftain Manor of Datun, Gonglongping national-level forest park, Qixing Gorge Ancient Ruin and other cultural landscape and natural scenery. The birthplace of the CPC Guizhou Provincial Committee Organization, the site of "Jiming three provinces" meeting of the CPC Central Committee Political Bureau , the former site of Sichuan, Yunnan, Guizhou Soviet revolutionary regime, the Long March "expansion Red Army" and the only one the provincial anti-Japanese armed forces are all in Bijie, so it is provided with the advantage conditions to develop building red tourism classic scenery areas.

Bijie city was of optimization investment environment, opened-up was getting stronger day by day. In tough environment building respect, old city renewal and new district development promoted simultaneously, the area of the city expanded from the initial foundation city of 9.7 square kilometers to the current 15 square kilometers. In soft environment building respect, fully implemented "one-stop" office and "one continuous line" service. Established municipal service center, administrative complaint center, foreign investors complaint center to provide security, stability and good investment environment for foreign investors.

We hope more people with breadth of vision to understand and know Bijie, and more investors to give attention to Bijie, go to Bijie.

市行政办公中心大楼
The city administrative office center building

铜仁简介

The Synopsis of Tongren

南岳飞瀑
The flying waterfall of Nanyue

铜仁市位于贵州东北部，地处湘、渝、鄂、黔四省（市）交界处，素有“黔东门户”之称。全市辖17个乡、镇、办事处，总面积1513平方公里，是铜仁地区政治、经济、文化中心。铜仁自古就有“黔中各郡邑，独美于铜仁”之美誉。清澈秀美的十里锦江绕城而过，两岸人文景观星罗棋布：“锦江十二景”交相辉映、国家级风景名胜区九龙洞神奇险绝、中国红色旅游景点“周逸群故居”肃穆凝重、中南门古城区见证了铜仁历史的悠长久远。更有被称之为“戏剧活化石”的傩戏及傩戏博物馆，还有花灯、龙灯、踩高跷、赛龙舟等独特民风名俗。2003年，在央视西部频道举办的“我最喜爱的西部名城”网上评选中，铜仁市名列榜首，获得“中国西部名城”称号。

2005年全市国民生产总值达23.84亿元，同比增长12%。产业结构发生积极变化，三次产业结构由上年22.2:33.7:44.1调整为19.7:37.7:42.6。财政总收入完成1.71亿元，同比增长19.16%。目前，铜仁市围绕打造集轻工、商贸、旅游为一体的山水园林城市的发展思路，正着手开发灯塔和谢桥两大工业区及谢桥新区，争创文明卫生城市，营造良好的人居环境。同时，积极发展“通道经济”和观光农业，大力开发旅游资源，倾力打造十里锦江旅游观光带，力争短期内使铜仁发展商贸业，抓紧建设西南最大的金滩批发城、铜仁商贸城和融入张家界——湘西——重庆旅游沿线，并成为旅游热点。此外，正集中大型农产品批发市场，争取把铜仁打造成为湘、鄂、渝、黔边区的物流集散地。

Tongren city is located in the northeast of Guizhou, in the junction of Hunanan, Chongqing, Hubei, Guizhou four provinces (municipalities), is known as "the gateway of Qiandong". The city governs 17 townships, towns, offices, a total area of 1,513 square kilometers, and is the political, economic and cultural center of Tongren region. Tongren had the reputation of "each city in the middle of Guizhou, the best beautiful city is Tongren " since ancient times. Clear and beautiful ten li Jin River going around the city, and humanity landscapes spread out all over two sides : "12 scenes of Jing River" enhance each other's beauty, national level scenic area Nine-dragon Hole is miraculous and precipitous, China Red tourist scenic spot "former residence of Zhou Yiqun" is solemn and sober, ancient area of Zhongnan Gate witnessed the long history of Tongren. And there have Nuo drama known as "living fossil theatre" and museum of Nuo drama, and flower lantern and dragon lantern, walking on stilts, the dragon-boat race, and other unique folk customs. In 2003, in the selection online "the fondest famous cities of the West" organized by the western channel of CCTV, Tongren city ranked the first and awarded the title of "famous city of the West of China".

In 2005, the GDP of the city amounted to 2.384 billion yuan, more 12% than previous year. Positive changes in the industrial structure, the structure proportion of three industries adjusted from 22.2:33.7:44.1 of the previous year to 19.7:37.7:42.6. Financial revenues completed 171 million yuan, up 19.16%. Currently, surrounding the development idea of building the landscape garden city with light industry, commerce and tourism, Tongren city is developing Dengta and Xieqiao two industrial zones and Xieqiao new district, and creating civilized health city and building a good living environment. At the same time, Tongren city is positively developing "economic corridor" and tourism agriculture, vigorously developing tourism resources, building ten li Jing River tourism belt, to shortly go to the development of commerce industry, to build the largest Jintan Wholesale City, Tongren Commerce City of the southwest, and will go into Zhangjiajie -- Xiangxi -- Chongqing tourism line to become a tourist attraction spot. In addition, large agricultural products wholesale markets are being concentrated, Tongren is being strive for building the logistics center in border of Hunan, Hubei, Chongqing, Guizhou.

铜仁锦江风光
The scenery of Jing River of Tongren

美丽的铜仁城
Beautiful Tongren city

凯里市 Kaili City

全市行政区域面积1306平方公里，城区规划面积88平方公里，辖2乡8镇，5个街道办事处，201个村民委员会，16个社区居民委员会，2005年年末总人口46.15万人，其中少数民族占75.78%，是一个以苗族为主体，多民族聚居的城市，被誉为“苗岭明珠”。该市资源丰富，主要矿藏有煤、铁、铅、锌、重晶石、铝矾土、石英石、硅石岩等，其中硅石中二氧化硅含量高达98%，名列西南之冠。

2005年该市生产总值为382020万元，比上年增长11.5%，人均生产总值达到8312元，比上年增长10.65%。全市财政总收入完成35018万元，比上年增长16.54%。全社会固定资产投资达166387万元，比上年增长16.3%。城镇居民人均可支配收入达到7707元，比上年增长9.1%。农民人均纯收入达2177元，比上年增长9%。全社会消费品零售总额达165465万元，比上年增长14.7%，城镇登记失业率控制在4.3%，低于全省平均水平。全市城镇化水平达39.7%，比“九五”末提高3个百分点。共完成招商引资签约项目47个，比上年增长11%；合同引资61699万元，实际到位资金33552万元，比上年增长14.6%。

农村经济稳步发展，农业结构调整力度加大。2005年全市完成农业总产值71644万元，比上年增长4.97%。城郊型农业初步形成，烤烟、生姜、大蒜、辣椒、反季节蔬菜、葡萄种植初具规模。

工业经济规模不断扩大，效益有所提高。辖区工业增加值完成125270万元，比上年增长7.3%。

经济社会协调发展，建设和谐社会取得新成绩。城市功能进一步完善，相继建成了水厂、体育运动中心，公园等公益性基础设施；在旧城改造中，逐步完善了城市功能；加大了新区开发，城区建成面积从2004年的23平方公里增加到23.8平方公里。

以“两基”巩固提高和基本普及高中教育为重点，全面推行素质教育，深化教育改革，促进各项教育协调发展。搞好“普九”工作，小学适龄儿童入学率为98.8%。

城乡医疗卫生条件不断改善。新型农村合作医疗试点工作进展顺利，覆盖率达70%。成为黔东南州唯一的新一轮初级卫生保健工作首轮达标县。人口自然增长率控制在9.06‰以内。

优化服务，打造投资佳境。对项目审批、登记办证等依法简化程序，相继建立和完善咨询、审批、投诉等服务机制，加强与投资者的联系渠道。

创建“文明城市”，建设“和谐”凯里。以创建“文明城市”为突破口，努力改善城市环境卫生与秩序，提高市民综合素质，致力将凯里打造为黔东地区经济和文化、旅游中心。凯里文明创建已成为全省的样板和示范。

2005年凯里成功举办了第六届中国凯里国际芦笙节。该市位列“2005年度全国中小城市综合实力100强”排名第98位，“2005年度全国最具投资潜力中小城市50强”排名第33位。2005年该市还荣获全省维稳工作先进市、全省流动人口工作先进市等称号。

凯里市行政中心
The administrative center of Kaili city

铝锭产品
Aluminum products

平良古峡
Pingliang ancient gap

The regional administrative area of the city is 1,306 square kilometres, 88 square kilometres of urban planning area. The city governs 2 townships 8 towns, 5 neighborhood offices, 201 village committees, 16 community residents. The total population of the end of 2005 was 461,500 people, of which minorities account for 75.78%. Kaili is the city with many nationalities, the Miao nationality in main, named as "A Pearl of Miao Mountain". The city is rich in resources, major deposits of coal, iron ore, lead, zinc, barite, bauxite, quartz rock, silicon and others, including the content of silicon dioxide in silica reaching to 98%, ranking the highest of the southwest.

In 2005, the GDP of the city was 3820.20 million yuan, 11.5% higher than the previous year, and per capita GDP reaching 8,312 yuan, 10.65% higher than the previous year. The city's financial revenue completed 350.18 million yuan, increased 16.54% than last year. Total fixed asset investment reached 1663.87 million yuan, 16.3% higher than the previous year. Per capita disposable income of urban residents reached 7,707 yuan, 9.1% higher than the previous year. Per capita net income of farmers reached 2,177 yuan, an increase of 9% over the previous year. Total retail sales of consumer goods amounted to 1654.65 million yuan, 14.7% higher than the previous year, the rate of registered unemployment controlled within 4.3%, lower than the provincial average. The rate of urbanization reached 39.7%, increased three percentage points than the end of "Ninth Five". A total of introduced business and attracted investment completed 47 agreement projects, increased 11% than the previous year; 616.99 million yuan of contract attracting investment, but the actual fund of 335.52 million yuan, 14.6% higher than the previous year.

Steady economic development in rural, agricultural restructuring would be intensified. In 2005, the agricultural total output value completed 716.44 million yuan, 4.97% higher than the previous year. The urban agriculture has begun to take shape, flue-cured tobacco, ginger, garlic, hot peppers, anti-season vegetables, grape cultivation begun to take shape.

The scale of industrial economy continued to expand, the efficiency has improved. The industrial added value in the city completed 1252.7 million yuan in, increased 7.3% than last year.

Coordinated economic and social development, achieved new results in building social harmony. Further improved the urban functions, successively established water works, sports centre, parks and other public welfare infrastructure; in the transformation of old city, gradually improved the city function; increased development of new districts, the built area of the city increased from 23 square kilometres of 2004 to 23.8 square kilometres.

Took the "two basics" solid improvement and spread secondary education as focus, fully implemented quality education, deepening reform and promoting the coordinated development of education. The work of "universal nine years education" was done well, and the rate of primary school enrolment was 98.8% among the school age children.

Urban and rural medical and health conditions continued to improve. New rural cooperative medical experimental work carried out smoothly, covering rate was up to 70%. The county became the only first round reached-standard county of Qiandongnan prefecture in the new round primary health care work. The rate of natural population growth controlled within 9.06‰.

Optimized service and built investment prospect. Simplified procedures according to law to project approval, registration processing, and successively established and improved advice, examination and approval, complaint and other service mechanisms, and strengthened the contact channel with investors.

Established "civilization city" and built a "harmonious" Kaili. Taking establishment "civilization city" as a breakthrough, in efforts to improve urban environmental health and order, and improvement the overall quality of the people, Kaili would be devoted to build an economic, cultural and tourist center in Qiandong area. The civilized creation of Kaili has become the provincial model and sample.

In 2005 Kaili successfully held the sixth China Kaili International Lusheng Festival. The city was ranked the 98th place in "2005 annual national medium and small cities comprehensive strength 100 strong", the 33th place in "2005 annual national the most investment potential medium and small cities 50 strong". In 2005, the city also awarded the title of the provincial sustaining stability advanced city, the provincial mobile population advanced city.

花园工厂
Garden factory

文明创建大会
The civilization creation meeting

凯里新貌 The new performance of Kaili

小河区农村信用合作联社

Rural Credit Cooperative of China Xiaohe District United

理事长 雷成元
The head of council Lei Chengyuan

贵阳市小河区农村信用合作联社是2005年4月21日在小河区原有农村信用社基础上改制后，经中国银行业监督管理委员会贵州监管局批准成立的小河区唯一的农村合作金融机构。

便民利民，小河区农村信用合作联社在小河境内长江路、蒲江路、中曹司等处设置十个营业网点。所有网点均实现门柜微机综合化服务，储蓄业务全省通存通兑，存取便捷。贵州省农村信用社信合卡业务的开办，对农信社各项业务的发展取到了推波助澜的作用。2002年，小河区农村信用合作联社率先在全省农村信用社系统开办代扣代缴国税税款业务及代发代收工资业务；2003年，率先在全省农村信用社系统与政府合作探索中小型企业贷款担保模式，并开通了全国大额支付结算系统。目前业务经营范围主要有储蓄、存款、贷款（含住房按揭贷款、小额农户贷款等）票据贴现、国内结算、中间业务（含代缴代扣国税、代理保险、代发企事业单位工资等）及经中国银行监督管理机构批准的其他业务。

小河区农村信用合作联社新办公大楼
The new office building of Rural Credit Cooperative of China Xiaohe District United

Rural Credit Cooperative of China Guiyang City Xiaohe District United, after restructuring on the base of the original Xiaohe District Rural Credit Cooperatives, is the only rural cooperative financial institution in Xiaohe district approved by the China Banking Regulatory Commission Guizhou EAA, was founded on April 21, 2005.

For convenience people, Rural Credit Cooperative of China Xiaohe District United set up 10 business points in Changjinag Road, Pujiang Road, Zhongcaosi and other places of Xiaohe district. All points are achieved door cabinets computer integrated services, the savings business are unobstructed in deposit and exchange, and convenient in the province. The opening of credit card business of Guizhou province rural credit cooperatives, that made an add role to the development of rural credit cooperatives. In 2002, Rural Credit Cooperative of China Xiaohe District United in the first set up acting deduction and acting payment national tax business and acting dispatch and acting receipt wage operation in the provincial rural credit cooperatives system; in 2003, in the first explored SME Loan Guarantee model in cooperation with the government and launched large national payment settlement system in the provincial rural credit cooperatives system. There are currently operating mainly savings, deposits, loans (including housing mortgages, small farmers loans) bills discounting, domestic accounting, intermediate business (including acting deduction and acting payment national tax, insurance agent, acting dispatch enterprises and institutions wages) and other businesses approved by the China banking regulatory organ.

宽敞明亮的营业大厅
The spacious and bright business hall

反假币宣传
The propaganda of anti-counterfeit money

崛起的贞丰
Zhenfeng in Rising

省委书记钱运录在贞丰视察黄金产业工作
The secretary of the provincial Party committee Qian Yunlu inspected the gold industry work in Zhenfeng

石秀诗省长到水银洞金矿考察
The governor of the province Shi Xiushi inspected Shuiyin Hole Gold Ore

省委副书记王富玉参加贞丰布依族风情节
The deputy secretary of the provincial Party committee Wang Fuyu participated in Buyi Nationality festival of Zhenfeng

贞丰县2005年完成生产总值11亿元，五年内年均增长21.64%。财政总收入1.18亿元，年均增长33.32%。“十五”期间，全社会固定资产累计投资23.36亿元。县城面积从“九五”末的2平方公里增加到“十五”末的5平方公里；建成了通水银洞金矿、烂泥沟金矿和通马马岩电站、董箐电站公路；关兴公路的建成结束了我县没有高等级公路的历史。

煤炭、黄金、电力实现突破，六大产业逐步健康发展。狠抓煤矿的技改和整合工作，努力提高单产，使其成为县域经济中最大的支柱产业；以烂泥沟特大型金矿的建设为标志，全面拉开了“中国金州”的黄金中心生产基地建设的序幕；引资建成了大田河电站和丰发电站；成功举办了四届“六月六”布依风情节，掀起了推介贞丰秀丽山川、民族风情的高潮。

城乡居民收入水平显著提高，农村生产、生活条件得到明显改善。2005年城镇居民人均可支配收入5600元，比2000年增加2680元；农民人均纯收入达1805元，比2000年增加507元。实现了村村通电话、通广播电视。积极推进农村扶贫开发，使19785人越过温饱线。改革开放稳步推进，招商引资成效突出。“十五”期间累计招商引资28亿元，为全县经济的发展注入了新的活力。社会事业全面进步，经济社会协调发展。“十五”期间共投入教育基础设施建设经费4105.4万元。“两基”攻坚通过省人民政府评估验收。2005年，《布依铜鼓十二则》、《小屯白绵造纸工艺》被省政府列为首批省级非物质文化遗产代表作。

贞丰县水银洞金矿
Shuiyin Hole Gold Ore of Zhenfeng county

The GDP of Zhenfeng of 2005 completed 1.1 billion yuan, average annual growth 21.64% within five years. Financial revenue totaled 118 million yuan, average annual increase of 33.32%. "10th Five-Year Plan" period, investment in fixed assets totaled 2.336 billion yuan. The area of the county increased from 2 square kilometers of the end of "Ninth Five-Year Plan" to 5 square kilometers of the end of the "10th Five-Year Plan"; roads of Shuiyin Hole Gold Ore, Lannigou Gold Ore and Mamayan Power Station, Dongjing Power Station were built and opened; the completion of Guanxing Road finished the history of our county having no high-grade road.

The industries of coal, gold, power achieved a breakthrough, six major industries steadily healthy developed. Firmly grasped the technical transformation and integration work of coal mine, and strived to improve the yield, made it becoming the largest pillar industry of county's economy; Took the building of Lannigou Super-huge Gold Ore as the sign to comprehensively open the beginning of gold center production base building of "China Golden State"; Attracted investment to build Datian River Power Station and Fengfa Power Station; Successfully held four times "6th of June" Buyi Festival to raise a climax for propaganda Zhenfeng beautiful mountains and ethnic customs.

The income of urban and rural residents significantly increased, rural production and living conditions have been improved markedly. In 2005 the per capita disposable income of urban residents was 5,600 yuan, increase 2,680 yuan than in 2000; the per capita net income of farmers reached 1,805 yuan, increase 507 yuan than in 2000. Every village realized the opening of telephone, radio and television. Actively promoted the development of rural help-the-poor, 19,785 people crossed the line of food and clothing. The reform and opening up steadily improved, attracting investment made outstanding results. "10th Five-Year Plan" period totaled 2.8 billion yuan on attracting investment to injecte the new vitality for the county's economic development. Social undertakings made overall progressed and economic and social were coordinate development. "10th Five-Year Plan" period put into 41.054 million yuan on education infrastructure construction. "Two basics" storm was passed the provincial government acceptance. In 2005, "12 Standards of Buyi Bronze Drum", "Papermaking Craft of Xiaotun Baimian" were placed the first provincial level non-material cultural heritage representative work by provincial government.

雄奇壮丽的北盘江大峡谷
The magnificent Beipan River Grand Canyon

三岔河之秋
The autumn of Sancha River

贵州省农办(省扶贫办、省综开办)

Guizhou Provincial Agriculture Office (Provincial Office for assisting the poor, Provincial Agriculture Comprehensive Development Office)

省农办保持共产党员先进性教育活动动员大会
The mobilization meeting of maintaining Party members advanced educational activities of provincial agricultural office

考察册亨县种草养畜项目
Inspection the project of cultivating grass and breeding cattle in Ceheng county

兴仁县坡改梯烤烟种植项目
The flue-cured tobacco cultivation project after changing slope to terraced field in Xingren county

兴义市纳灰村秋收景象
The Autumn Harvest scene in Nahui village Xingyi city

2005年，我省粮食继续丰收，农民收入持续增长，农业结构调整取得新的进展，扶贫开发深入开展，农业综合开发稳步推进，全省农业和农村经济保持良好的发展态势。

一、农业和农村经济持续健康发展

1、粮食综合生产能力稳定提高。完成以坡改梯为主要内容的基本农田建设51.84万亩，超计划1.04%；改造中低产田土51.45万亩，建成灌排渠系工程1026.35公里；粮食总产量达到1152.06万吨，比上年增产0.22%，油菜籽产量76.5万吨，增长3.47%，烟叶收购671万担，比上年增加103.5万担；全年农业增加值365亿元，比上年增长5.1%。

2、农民收入持续增长。由于农业结构调整步伐加快，农民收入持续、稳定增长。全年农民人均纯收入1877元，比上年多收入约155.5元，扣除物价因素实际增长5.2%。

3、农业和农村经济结构调整力度加大。生态畜牧业持续发展，畜牧业产值达188亿元，增长11.24%。全省优质稻、特用玉米、双低油菜、中药材、夏秋反季节蔬菜、辣椒、投产茶园、果园、花卉等种植面积均比上年有所增加。

二、扶贫开发深入开展

投入财政扶贫资金71398万元、以工代赈资金26500万元、信贷扶贫资金72685.25万元、社会帮扶资金20724.5228万元，继续加大对100个一类乡镇的扶持力度，对1100个重点村实施整村推进，有组织培训转移贫困地区农业劳动力8万人，全年解决31.7万农村贫困人口的温饱问题，净减少绝对贫困人口11万人、低收入贫困人口12万人，易地扶贫搬迁4万人。

三、农业综合开发工作稳步推进

改造中低产田土51.45万亩，维修改造灌排渠系工程1026.35公里，技术培训14.76万人(次)。

In 2005, the province's grain reaped harvest continuously, sustained growth of the income of farmers, agricultural restructuring has made new progress in efforts to help the poor in-depth, comprehensive agricultural development steady, the province's agriculture and rural economy maintained a good development trend.

First, agriculture and rural economy maintained sustained and healthy development.

A, Grain comprehensive production capability increased steadily. Finished the construction of basic farmland of 518.4 thousand mu taking changing slope to terraced field as the main, surpassed plan 1.04%; Transformed middle and low-yielding land of 514.5 thousand mu, built diversion canals engineering of 1026.35 km; Total yield of grain reached 11.5206 million tons, 0.22% increase over the previous year, yield of rapeseed of 765,000 tons, an increase of 3.47%, 6.71 million dans tobacco leaf purchase, increased 1.035 million dans over the previous year; The annual added value of agriculture reached 36.5 billion yuan, increased 5.1%.

B, The incomes of peasant sustained growth. Because of the accelerating pace of agricultural restructuring, and peasants' income was sustained and stable growth. The annual net income of per peasant was 1,877 yuan, more than about 155.5 yuan of the previous year, actual growth of 5.2% after deducting the prices factor.

C, Agricultural and rural economic restructuring have been enlarged. Ecological animal husbandry developed continually, animal husbandry output value reached 18.8 billion yuan, an increase of 11.24%. The cultivation area of high quality rice, special-use maize, double low cole, Chinese medicines materials, anti-season vegetables, chili, tea production, orchards, flowers increased.

Second, developed the supporting the poor in-depth.

Invested 713.98 million yuan in financial aid funds, 265 million yuan of funds work relief, credit poverty funds 726.8525 million yuan, social relief funds of 207.245228 million yuan, and continued to enlarge the support of 100 townships category I and implement 1,100 villages improvement on the whole village, organized train and transfer the agricultural labor force 80,000 people in poor areas, annual resolved the problem of food and clothing of the rural poor population of 317,000, with a net reduction of 110 thousand people living in absolute poverty, the poverty of low-income population of 120 thousand people, and relocated 40,000 people through help the poor relocation .

Third, the agriculture comprehensive development work steadily improved

Transformed the middle and low-yielding land of 514.5 thousand mu and the maintenance of diversion canals engineering 1026.35km. Held the technical train 147,600 person (times).

Twenty-Two

扶贫与开发

Anti-poverty and Development

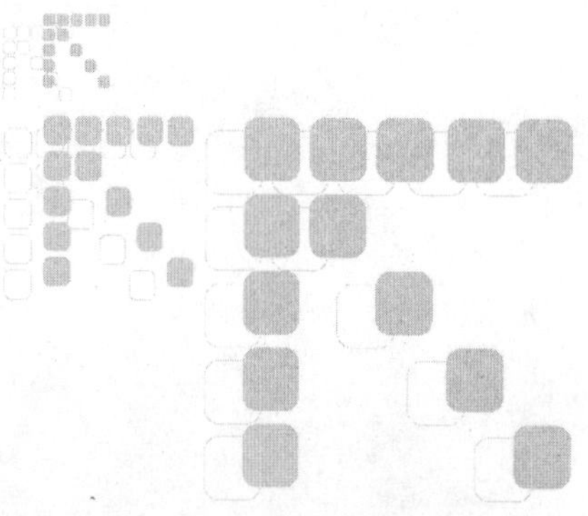

22-1 贫困人口及发生率(2005)

Number of Poverty Population and it's Arisen Rate(2005)

县(市、区) 名　称	County (City,Section)	年末总人口 （万人） Total Population at the Year-end (10000 persons)	农村贫困人口 （万人） Poverty Population (10000 persons)	农村贫困 发生率（%） Arisen Rate of Poverty (%)
全省合计	**National Total**	**3931.12**	**265.74**	**7.9**
扶贫开发重点县小计	**Basilic Counties of Anti-poverty and Development**	**2180.83**	**199.69**	**9.8**
贵阳市	**Guiyang**	**353.09**	**7.06**	**3.7**
南明区	Nanming	50.95	0.01	0.4
云岩区	Yunyan	55.49	0.01	0.3
花溪区	Huaxi	32.54	0.78	3.2
乌当区	Wudang	30.97	0.51	2.30
白云区	Baiyun	17.59	0.08	1.1
开阳县	Kaiyang	44.06	1.30	3.3
息烽县	Xifeng	26.18	1.45	6.2
修文县	Xiuwen	30.96	1.28	4.7
清镇市	Qingzhen	52.33	1.64	4.0
六盘水市	**Liupanshui**	**302.70**	**22.68**	**9.3**
钟山区	Zhongshan	43.48	1.17	6.6
△六枝特区	Liuzhi	64.57	3.71	7.2
△水城县	Shuicheng	76.36	8.44	11.3
△盘 县	Panxian	118.29	9.36	9.3
遵义市	**Zunyi**	**743.28**	**31.78**	**4.9**
红花岗区	Honghuagang	53.93	0.39	1.4
汇川区	huichuan	33.91	0.41	2.1
遵义县	Zunyi	116.24	4.26	3.8
桐梓县	Tongzi	66.77	2.27	4.1
绥阳县	Suiyang	51.60	1.51	3.1
△正安县	Zhengan	61.18	4.19	7.2
△道真县	Daozhen	34.27	2.65	8.4
△务川县	Wuchuan	42.77	3.15	7.9
凤冈县	Fenggang	41.91	1.88	4.8
湄潭县	Meitan	48.15	1.55	3.6
余庆县	Yuqing	29.68	0.94	3.5
△习水县	Xishui	70.20	5.30	8.2
赤水市	Chishui	31.56	0.97	3.9
仁怀市	Renhuai	61.11	2.31	4.1
安顺市	**Anshun**	**264.25**	**17.52**	**7.8**
西秀区	Xixiu	83.67	2.06	3.4
平坝县	Pingba	35.62	1.94	6.7

22-1续表1(continued)

县(市、区)名 称	County (City,Section)	年末总人口（万人）Total Population at the Year-end (10000 persons)	农村贫困人口（万人）Poverty Population (10000 persons)	农村贫困发生率（%）Arisen Rate of Poverty (%)
△普定县	Puding	41.77	3.39	8.6
△镇宁县	Zhenning	35.33	3.23	10.0
△关岭县	Guanling	33.10	3.35	10.9
△紫云县	Ziyun	34.76	3.55	10.9
铜仁地区	**Tongren**	**392.84**	**33.61**	**9.4**
铜仁市	Tongren	34.59	1.90	7.4
△江口县	Jiangkou	22.82	1.86	8.9
玉屏县	Yuping	14.35	0.74	6.2
△石阡县	Shiqian	39.08	3.59	9.8
△思南县	Sinan	64.70	5.56	9.1
△印江县	Yinjiang	42.23	3.76	9.5
△德江县	Dejiang	45.93	4.14	9.7
△沿河县	Yanhe	57.13	5.52	10.3
△松桃县	Songtao	65.31	6.06	9.8
万山特区	Wanshan	6.70	0.48	9.5
黔西南州	**Qianxinan**	**311.73**	**23.42**	**8.3**
兴义市	Xingyi	75.30	2.49	3.9
△兴仁县	Xingren	47.04	3.45	7.9
△普安县	Puan	29.30	2.60	9.5
△晴隆县	Qinglong	29.26	3.22	11.9
△贞丰县	Zhenfeng	35.64	3.28	10.0
△望漠县	Wangmo	28.91	3.11	11.3
△册亨县	Ceheng	22.45	2.37	11.0
△安龙县	Anlong	43.83	2.90	7.1
毕节地区	**Bijie**	**725.12**	**61.61**	**9.0**
毕节市	Bijie	131.09	7.85	6.6
△大方县	Dafang	99.27	9.43	9.9
黔西县	Qianxi	84.30	5.71	7.2
金沙县	Jinsha	59.66	2.46	4.5
△织金县	Zhijin	94.90	9.73	10.8
△纳雍县	Nayong	78.03	9.40	12.6
△威宁县	Weining	112.01	10.39	9.7

22-1续表2(continued)

县(市、区)名称	County (City,Section)	年末总人口（万人）Total Population at the Year-end (10000 persons)	农村贫困人口（万人）Poverty Population (10000 persons)	农村贫困发生率（%）Arisen Rate of Poverty (%)
△赫章县	Hezhang	65.86	6.64	10.7
黔东南州	**Qiandongnan**	**441.72**	**37.15**	**9.4**
凯里市	Kaili	46.15	1.86	6.3
△黄平县	Huangping	35.55	3.38	10.1
△施秉县	Shibing	15.79	1.22	8.4
△三穗县	Sansui	21.08	1.84	9.4
镇远县	Zhenyuan	26.14	1.56	6.8
△岑巩县	Cengong	22.49	1.95	9.3
△天柱县	Tianzhu	41.51	2.82	7.3
△锦屏县	Jinping	22.68	2.01	9.8
△剑河县	Jianhe	24.48	2.23	9.8
△台江县	Taijiang	14.72	1.51	11.3
△黎平县	Liping	51.13	3.99	8.2
△榕江县	Rongjiang	33.44	2.95	9.5
△从江县	Congjiang	32.42	3.41	11.1
△雷山县	Leishan	15.19	1.97	13.9
△麻江县	Majiang	22.35	2.64	12.6
△丹寨县	Danzhai	16.59	1.81	11.8
黔南州	**Qiannan**	**396.39**	**30.91**	**8.9**
都匀市	Duyun	49.29	1.50	4.6
福泉市	Fuquan	31.36	2.12	8.1
△荔波县	Libo	17.10	2.06	13.1
贵定县	Guiding	29.30	1.69	6.8
瓮安县	Wengan	46.61	3.15	7.5
△独山县	Dushan	35.44	2.65	8.3
△平塘县	Pingtang	30.87	3.54	12.0
△罗甸县	Luodian	33.41	3.61	11.5
△长顺县	Changshun	25.07	3.24	13.9
龙里县	Longli	20.85	1.57	8.2
惠水县	Huishui	43.87	2.25	5.6
△三都县	Sandu	33.22	3.53	11.2

注：△为新阶段扶贫开发工作重点县。（22-5 表同）

Note: The county is Labeled by "△" is the inportant Point of work about anti-poverty and development in new phase.(same as in 22-5)

22-2 扶贫开发重点县

Major Economic Indicators on Basilic county

扶贫开发重点县名称	County	生产总值 Gross Domestic Product	财政一般预算收入 Local Financial Revenue	财政一般预算支出 Financial Expenditure	常用耕地面积(公顷) Cultivated Area for Frequently Use (hectare)	农林牧渔业总产值 Gross Output Value of Farming, Forestry, Animal Husbandry and Fishery
扶贫开发重点县合计	**Total**	**6524428**	**346767**	**1472754**	**1038717**	**3639028**
六盘水市	**Liupanshui**					
六枝特区	Liuzhi	228400	12123	44385	25776	59751
水城县	Shuicheng	273225	16505	46968	33201	86773
盘　县	Panxian	786726	45004	80759	44197	120773
遵义市	**Zunyi**					
正安县	Zhengan	141564	5109	32320	31157	131083
※道真县	Daozhen	100351	4150	24735	23470	78567
※务川县	Wuchuan	103605	4558	28526	28375	85235
习水县	Xishui	238363	9043	41808	40671	112489
安顺市	**Anshun**					
普定县	Puding	149205	9097	25257	16475	51370
※镇宁县	Zhenning	112504	5660	24649	13841	41489
※关岭县	Guanling	101669	4966	23858	14991	60211
※紫云县	Ziyun	67602	2955	22952	15906	55160
铜仁地区	**Tongren**					
江口县	Jiangkou	69152	3002	18528	11014	50156
石阡县	Shiqian	101336	5380	28831	20805	91508
思南县	Sinan	178795	8005	40186	28823	138814
※印江县	Yinjiang	110140	4870	28043	18424	97598
德江县	Dejiang	142064	5952	29152	21606	115393
※沿河县	Yanhe	136193	5866	36543	26412	112137
※松桃县	Songtao	177135	6179	38776	26335	129053
黔西南州	**Qianxinan**					
兴仁县	Xingren	150190	11907	31497	20713	77619
普安县	Puan	85707	10209	23382	16507	41890
晴隆县	Qinglong	68048	5119	21187	14013	38315
贞丰县	Zhenfeng	107055	7005	23451	20353	62255
望谟县	Wangmo	52000	2782	22047	26637	47722

主要经济指标(2005)

of Anti-poverty and Development(2005)

单位：万元 (10000 yuan)

粮食产量 (万吨) Output of Grain (10000 tons)	规模以上工业总产值 Total Gross Industrial Output Value above Designated Size	金融机构 存款余额 Total Savings Deposit Balance	金融机构 贷款余额 Total Loan Balance	城乡居民储蓄额 Urban and l Rura Resident Savings Deposit Balance	固定资产 投 资 Investment in Fixed Assets	社会消费品 零售总额 Total Retail Sales of Consumer Goods
723.64	**2881346**	**5046870**	**3158624**	**3089302**	**2509669**	**1492820**
18.31	110336	195628	94416	128292	29414	74072
24.29	222592	27519	23949	13371	218374	37366
32.84	566235	588555	305096	284384	367852	159313
25.76	19402	121273	61845	90144	32730	30324
13.37	13184	105035	49160	75673	57494	18518
17.04	7525	83345	38053	54058	54548	28154
28.61	190367	180854	147175	115652	85061	78034
11.79	174850	74184	209124	41561	23469	21817
10.96	56275	91336	59990	47929	16107	26434
11.13	35278	95263	150383	51134	8668	26740
11.59	19313	52329	49247	27391	18238	23649
9.01	11137	63561	28511	46197	29643	18027
17.29	9125	66135	38530	48145	29632	20906
22.40	14908	117032	83840	89368	103985	44260
13.74	14511	95624	52144	75981	34508	22322
16.02	18592	62750	46030	51201	33837	28322
15.83	12288	110176	55006	73950	53458	30551
23.06	120118	136755	60744	83459	44204	37897
17.50	50126	107763	53005	66370	41831	39895
8.72	45441	82133	26622	47961	24174	14157
8.88	19368	95275	39304	42259	16035	14685
11.52	53558	100358	49398	34466	83415	19292
8.55	5267	60390	21822	22857	5875	10091

22-2续表(continued)

扶贫开发重点县名称	County	生产总值 Gross Domestic Product	财政一般预算收入 Local Financial Revenue	财政一般预算支出 Financial Expenditure	常用耕地面积(公顷) Cultivated Area for Frequently Use (hectare)	农林牧渔业总产值 Gross Output Value of Farming, Forestry, Animal Husbandry and Fishery
册亨县	Ceheng	50265	2161	19215	13467	44483
安龙县	Anlong	144650	8297	26370	20472	80160
毕节地区	**Bijie**					
大方县	Dafang	233515	15409	49743	50100	138685
织金县	Zhijin	219485	18865	54709	40890	138799
纳雍县	Nayong	331039	15037	41855	30761	120075
※威宁县	Weining	266266	14648	53513	71933	167321
赫章县	Hezhang	159544	7189	38388	37838	95377
黔东南州	**Qiandongnan**					
黄平县	Huangping	69066	3436	22889	15218	51613
施秉县	Shibing	56817	5688	17532	8126	29637
三穗县	Sansui	60720	2669	18462	7691	31333
岑巩县	Cengong	63739	2603	18889	11708	37114
天柱县	Tianzhu	111147	4931	28765	15935	64429
锦屏县	Jinping	63035	3283	23130	8570	33375
剑河县	Jianhe	62810	2520	26568	9031	43130
台江县	Taijiang	42032	2172	15399	6239	23213
黎平县	Liping	113179	3462	32888	18587	89203
榕江县	Rongjiang	77719	2783	26105	12702	61364
从江县	Congjiang	75487	3087	26558	13896	69155
雷山县	Leishan	34923	1782	16056	6847	20393
麻江县	Majiang	58351	3002	18246	10961	35196
丹寨县	Danzhai	42439	1625	16094	7330	26772
黔南州	**Qiannan**					
荔波县	Libo	67645	5556	18595	7996	37606
独山县	Dushan	108323	5515	29201	15203	88299
平塘县	Pingtang	72391	3709	24936	14343	50121
罗甸县	Luodian	110893	4762	25444	16820	72106
长顺县	Changshun	73951	4491	20228	12802	47507
※三都县	Sandu	73968	2639	25136	13549	57201

单位：万元　(10000 yuan)

粮食产量 (万吨) Output of Grain (10000 tons)	规模以上工业总产值 Total Gross Industrial Output Value above Designated Size	金融机构存款余额 Total Savings Deposit Balance	金融机构贷款余额 Total Loan Balance	城乡居民储蓄额 Urban and l Rura Resident Savings Deposit Balance	固定资产投资 Investment in Fixed Assets	社会消费品零售总额 Total Retail Sales of Consumer Goods
6.42	6900	52861	15403	24699	15500	7509
17.52	57177	116922	77566	70053	72110	24513
31.82	24919	195513	155979	117209	146077	57162
32.77	26463	165645	50759	92487	20222	49902
28.11	254830	142183	140092	73115	185337	37881
35.47	117108	140094	40072	87373	14273	44558
20.50	57857	118708	44257	80850	11202	30550
10.43	6769	89855	42897	66159	10157	19724
6.13	66738	43784	27374	30863	5534	15462
5.83	15723	64661	30949	47601	53589	25518
7.12	44203	53468	52423	35433	18587	20776
13.50	21410	117366	50096	93188	55610	35947
6.69	10332	91485	30606	60864	178237	24697
6.79	2709	101387	36601	57981	67186	17282
4.61	18012	62984	168712	34345	40528	11001
15.68	33348	101307	70492	75927	41346	39561
9.77	14114	73405	57381	47918	8443	23197
11.81	13300	43999	33508	28230	21443	21188
5.07	17501	36707	25443	25403	11848	10982
7.17	49667	45141	29159	32627	6901	14693
5.33	17214	37077	21351	26043	13341	11232
5.58	26597	73611	35676	45393	22580	19113
11.18	67136	130880	39119	85530	11303	29880
10.20	17105	60957	27375	39949	10679	14504
10.62	50149	67412	68441	33972	28860	19440
9.91	41149	44439	17575	24863	14358	18947
9.40	13120	61747	25924	39424	11866	22775

22-3 扶贫开发重点县主要经

Major Per Capita Economic Indicators and Their Orders on

扶贫开发重点县名称	County	人均生产总值 Per Capita Gross Domestic Product	位次 Order	人均粮食(公斤) Per Capita Output of Grain(kg)	位次 Order
六盘水市	**Liupanshui**				
六枝特区	Liuzhi	3548	7	358	11
水城县	Shuicheng	3590	5	340	16
盘　县	Panxian	6673	1	327	19
遵义市	**Zunyi**				
正安县	Zhengan	2320	42	466	2
※道真县	Daozhen	2936	20	437	5
※务川县	Wuchuan	2428	34	426	6
习水县	Xishui	3400	8	464	3
安顺市	**Anshun**				
普定县	Puding	3584	6	306	22
※镇宁县	Zhenning	3195	12	339	17
※关岭县	Guanling	3082	14	355	12
※紫云县	Ziyun	1952	48	348	14
铜仁地区	**Tongren**				
江口县	Jiangkou	3037	17	444	4
石阡县	Shiqian	2602	30	471	1
思南县	Sinan	2774	25	383	9
※印江县	Yinjiang	2619	29	352	13
德江县	Dejiang	3104	13	389	8
※沿河县	Yanhe	2393	36	291	23
※松桃县	Songtao	2723	26	370	10
黔西南州	**Qianxinan**				
兴仁县	Xingren	3206	11	413	7
普安县	Puan	2937	19	319	20
晴隆县	Qinglong	2331	41	337	18
贞丰县	Zhenfeng	3041	16	343	15
望谟县	Wangmo	1809	50	310	21

济指标人均水平及位次(2005)

Basilic County of Anti-poverty and Development(2005)

单位:元(yuan)

人均财政一般预算收入 Per Capita Local Financial Revenue	位次 Order	人均财政一般预算支出 Per Capita Financial Expenditure	位次 Order	农民人均纯收入 Per Capita Annual Net Income of Rural Househo lds	位次 Order	城乡居民人均储蓄 Per Capita Urban and Rural Resident Savings Deposit	位次 Order
188.33	7	689.52	9	1749	6	1993	4
216.88	5	617.16	19	1730	7	176	23
381.73	1	685.00	10	1923	1	2412	1
83.71	23	529.55	23	1765	4	1477	9
121.42	16	723.70	6	1680	10	2214	2
106.90	18	669.02	12	1598	15	1268	16
129.17	14	597.20	21	1760	5	1652	6
218.50	4	606.64	20	1630	13	998	19
160.73	9	699.99	8	1521	21	1361	13
150.52	10	723.13	7	1590	16	1550	8
85.34	22	662.84	15	1550	17	791	22
131.83	12	813.65	1	1670	11	2029	3
138.16	11	740.41	4	1633	12	1236	17
124.18	15	623.39	18	1506	23	1386	12
115.83	17	666.96	13	1695	9	1807	5
130.04	13	636.91	17	1538	18	1119	18
103.08	19	642.16	16	1531	19	1300	14
94.99	21	596.13	22	1617	14	1283	15
254.17	3	672.35	11	1902	2	1417	11
349.86	2	801.28	2	1706	8	1644	7
175.41	8	726.01	5	1527	20	1448	10
199.01	6	666.25	14	1805	3	979	20
96.79	20	767.01	3	1508	22	795	21

22-3续表(continued)

扶贫开发重点县名称	County	人均生产总值 Per Capita Gross Domestic Product	位次 Order	人均粮食(公斤) Per Capita Output of Grain (kg)	位次 Order
册亨县	Ceheng	2232	46	305	26
安龙县	Anlong	3311	10	438	1
毕节地区	**Bijie**				
大方县	Dafang	2384	37	352	16
织金县	Zhijin	2312	43	375	6
纳雍县	Nayong	4252	2	383	5
※威宁县	Weining	2397	35	343	18
赫章县	Hezhang	2433	33	327	21
黔东南州	**Qiandongnan**				
黄平县	Huangping	1949	49	321	22
施秉县	Shibing	3612	4	438	1
三穗县	Sansui	2891	21	308	24
岑巩县	Cengong	2845	23	356	15
天柱县	Tianzhu	2687	27	372	7
锦屏县	Jinping	2789	24	338	19
剑河县	Jianhe	2574	31	306	25
台江县	Taijiang	2865	22	357	14
黎平县	Liping	2222	47	334	20
榕江县	Rongjiang	2333	40	321	22
从江县	Congjiang	2337	39	385	4
雷山县	Leishan	2308	44	364	10
麻江县	Majiang	2621	28	361	12
丹寨县	Danzhai	2564	32	368	8
黔南州	**Qiannan**				
荔波县	Libo	3972	3	362	11
独山县	Dushan	3070	15	366	9
平塘县	Pingtang	2355	38	345	17
罗甸县	Luodian	3333	9	358	13
长顺县	Changshun	2962	18	427	3
※三都县	Sandu	2237	45	304	27

单位:元(yuan)

人均财政一般预算收入 Per Capita Local Financial Revenue	位次 Order	人均财政一般预算支出 Per Capita Financial Expenditure	位次 Order	农民人均纯收入 Per Capita Annual Net Income of Rural Households	位次 Order	城乡居民人均储蓄 Per Capita Urban and Rural Resident Savings Deposit	位次 Order
95.98	23	853.46	9	1450	27	1097	21
189.90	5	603.54	22	1852	2	1603	11
155.95	8	503.42	26	1605	24	1186	20
199.43	3	578.34	24	1707	10	978	24
193.38	4	538.25	25	1656	15	940	25
131.66	13	480.98	27	1642	21	785	27
109.65	19	585.49	23	1656	15	1233	18
96.93	22	645.73	21	1633	22	1866	9
361.62	1	1114.62	1	1882	1	1962	8
127.09	14	879.14	8	1733	6	2267	6
116.20	18	843.25	10	1739	5	1582	12
119.23	16	695.52	19	1776	3	2253	7
145.27	10	1023.50	6	1584	26	2693	1
103.28	20	1088.85	3	1711	9	2376	4
148.11	9	1050.05	5	1662	14	2342	5
67.98	27	645.81	20	1702	12	1491	14
83.54	25	783.64	16	1613	23	1438	16
95.57	24	822.17	12	1705	11	874	26
117.79	17	1061.33	4	1600	25	1679	10
134.83	12	819.50	13	1676	13	1465	15
98.22	21	972.75	7	1712	7	1574	13
326.26	2	1091.93	2	1655	17	2666	2
156.27	7	827.44	11	1761	4	2424	3
120.66	15	811.23	14	1651	18	1300	17
143.14	11	764.84	17	1648	20	1021	22
179.87	6	810.13	15	1712	8	996	23
79.80	26	760.05	18	1651	18	1192	19

22-4扶贫开发重点县主要经济指标占全省比重（2005）

Major Economic Indicators of Basilic County of Anti-poverty and Development and Its Percentage to Provincial Total(2005)

指 标	Item	全省合计 Provincial Total	贫困县合计 Poverty Counties Total	贫困县占全省的比重(%) As Percentage to Provincial Total(%)
国土面积（万平方公里）	Area of Territory(10000 sq.km)	17.62	11.63	66.0
常用耕地面积（千公顷）	Cultivated Area for Frequently Use (1000 hectares)	1753.50	1038.72	59.2
年末总人口（万人）	Total Population at the Year-end (10000 persons)	3931.12	2180.83	55.5
生产总值（亿元）	Gross Domestic Product(100 million yuan)	1979.06	652.44	33.0
财政一般预算收入	Local Financial Revenue	182.50	34.68	19.0
财政一般预算支出	Financial Expenditure	520.73	147.28	28.3
农林牧渔业总产值	Gross Output Value of Farming,Forestry, Animal Husban dry and Fishery	571.84	363.90	63.6
粮食产量（万吨）	Output of Grain(10000 tons)	1152.06	723.64	62.8
规模以上工业总产值（亿元）	Total Gross Industrial Output Value above Designated Size(100 million yuan)	585.85	288.13	49.2
社会消费品零售总额	Total Retail Sales of Consumer Goods	606.92	149.28	24.6
金融机构存款余额	Total Savings Deposit Balance	2777.54	504.69	18.2
金融机构贷款余额	Total Loan Balance	2303.93	315.86	13.7
城乡居民储蓄余额	Urban and Rural Resident Savings Deposit Balance	1350.90	308.93	22.9

22-5 扶贫开发效益及成果(2005)

Benefits and Achievements of Anti-poverty and Development(2005)

县(市、区)名 称	County (City,Section)	当年新增基本农田(亩) Farmland Newly Increased in 2005(mu)	当年新增及改扩建公路里程(公里) Length of Highways Newly Increased in 2005(km)	当年新增经济林(亩) Area of Orchards Newly Increased in 2005(mu)	向其他地区输出劳动力(人) Output Labour to other area (person)	#向省外 to other Provinces (person)
全省合计	**National Total**	**307665**	**10355**	**276840**	**250153**	**160341**
扶贫开发重点县小计	**Basilic Counties of Antipoverty and Development**	**185760**	**7613**	**221880**	**157073**	**105379**
贵阳市	**Guiyang**	**33135**	**349**	**6255**	**27144**	**15031**
南明区	Nanming					
云岩区	Yunyan					
花溪区	Huaxi		4		400	400
乌当区	Wudang					
白云区	Baiyun					
开阳县	Kaiyang	3000	25		6300	5310
息烽县	Xifeng	135	121	3405	9003	5196
修文县	Xiuwen		92	855	4000	3000
清镇市	Qingzhen	30000	107	1995	7441	1125
六盘水市	**Liupanshui**	**17400**	**773**	**1140**	**13733**	**1824**
钟山区	Zhongshan		6	1095	5673	
△六枝特区	Liuzhi	405	23	15	2730	229
△水城县	Shuicheng	10995	579	30	3140	1099
△盘　县	Panxian	6000	165		2190	496
遵义市	**Zunyi**	**26220**	**1358**	**30030**	**47238**	**32895**
红花岗区	Honghuagang		2	195	712	383
汇川区	Huichuan	930	71	4800	200	200
遵义县	Zunyi	5850	156	15000	5100	3500
桐梓县	Tongzi		116	600	800	800
绥阳县	Suiyang	495	171		1600	1600
△正安县	Zhengan	495	83	795	1350	1350
△道真县	Daozhen	5295	186		2300	1150
△务川县	Wuchuan	300	118	975	8500	8500
凤冈县	Fenggang		160		1540	1230
湄潭县	Meitan	195	17	1275	1050	850
余庆县	Yuqing	4650	20	90	15843	9600
△习水县	Xishui	4005	80		954	725
赤水市	Chishui		50		5039	757
仁怀市	Renhuai	4005	128	6300	2250	2250
安顺市	**Anshun**	**12900**	**514**	**15345**	**21287**	**12591**
西秀区	Xixiu		30		1074	412

22-5续表1(continued)

县(市、区)名称	County (City,Section)	当年新增基本农田(亩) Farmland Newly Increased in 2005(mu)	当年新增及改扩建公路里程(公里) Length of Highways Newly Increased in 2005(km)	当年新增经济林(亩) Area of Orchards Newly Increased in 2005(mu)	向其他地区输出劳动力(人) Output Labour to other area (person)	#向省外 to other Provinces (person)
平坝县	Pingba		61	8550	4211	3453
△普定县	Puding	4500	115	795	5097	3568
△镇宁县	Zhenning	7905	133	600	5668	1198
△关岭县	Guanling	150	155	5400	1237	960
△紫云县	Ziyun	345	20		4000	3000
铜仁地区	**Tongren**	**27900**	**1407**	**25695**	**14138**	**11464**
铜仁市	Tongren		82	195	1670	1210
△江口县	Jiangkou	10845	111	1050	476	476
玉屏县	Yuping	1395	10	105	112	73
△石阡县	Shiqian	1605	185	13995	450	450
△思南县	Sinan	105	143	840	1900	1900
△印江县	Yinjiang	3900	220	3000	1672	1205
△德江县	Dejiang	2400	119	2880	4573	4000
△沿河县	Yanhe	7200	250	3000	1200	1000
△松桃县	Songtao	450	206	570	1035	350
万山特区	Wanshan		81	60	1050	800
黔西南州	**Qianxinan**	**29235**	**1184**	**122820**	**27528**	**21117**
兴义市	Xingyi	1725	132	3900	2700	1500
△兴仁县	Xingren	645	109		1671	1671
△普安县	Puan	270	205	100005	1472	1472
△晴隆县	Qinglong	7800	180	450	5614	4056
△贞丰县	Zhenfeng	9105	176	4905	1583	1434
△望谟县	Wangmo	7995	165	6825	8319	5840
△册亨县	Ceheng	600	181	5895	3125	2100
△安龙县	Anlong	1095	36	840	3044	3044
毕节地区	**Bijie**	**27525**	**1672**	**14400**	**35727**	**16393**
毕节市	Bijie	2895	352	1155	2100	1650
△大方县	Dafang	1005	139		24830	8750
黔西县	Qianxi	1500	105	135	1654	1654
金沙县	Jinsha	2910	48	480	1500	274
△织金县	Zhijin	630	172		1061	1061
△纳雍县	Nayong	1245	322	4380	1595	1324
△威宁县	Weining	13590	315	7995	1867	560

22-5续表2(continued)

县(市、区)名称	County (City,Section)	当年新增基本农田(亩) Farmland Newly Increased in 2005(mu)	当年新增及改扩建公路里程(公里) Length of Highways Newly Increased in 2005(km)	当年新增经济林(亩) Area of Orchards Newly Increased in 2005(mu)	向其他地区输出劳动力(人) Output Labour to other area (person)	#向省外 to other Provinces (person)
△赫章县	Hezhang	3750	219	255	1120	1120
黔东南州	**Qiandongnan**	**61950**	**1974**	**29595**	**23369**	**17352**
凯里市	Kaili	31935	45		2200	2000
△黄平县	Huangping	960	27	330	547	547
△施秉县	Shibing	2520	128		344	144
△三穗县	Sansui	495	257	1995	1890	1780
镇远县	Zhenyuan		68	495	500	100
△岑巩县	Cengong	180	28	225	1800	1800
△天柱县	Tianzhu	1980	138		1944	1338
△锦屏县	Jinping	3525	151	375	2600	425
△剑河县	Jianhe	3795	120		453	427
△台江县	Taijiang	1815	120	10005	1402	1402
△黎平县	Liping	2295	204	30	1087	1087
△榕江县	Rongjiang	255	160	240	4315	2015
△从江县	Congjiang	6390	190	525	350	350
△雷山县	Leishan	3150	32	5550	1600	1600
△麻江县	Majiang		120	1650	1510	1510
△丹寨县	Danzhai	2655	186	8175	827	827
黔南州	**Qiannan**	**71400**	**1124**	**31560**	**39989**	**31674**
都匀市	Duyun	13605	225		3202	3202
福泉市	Fuquan	4500	10	375	400	201
△荔波县	Libo	4950	70	3990	3400	1200
贵定县	Guiding	1380	8		420	344
瓮安县	Wengan	3000	22		1754	1146
△独山县	Dushan	3510	185	4305	2247	2247
△平塘县	Pingtang	11070	86	4770	521	123
△罗甸县	Luodian	12315	93	12990	22680	19756
△长顺县	Changshun	8100	92		1416	746
龙里县	Longli	1005	64		582	382
惠水县	Huishui	6795	153	3900	1000	360
△三都县	Sandu	1170	116	1230	2367	1967

23 地县社会经济发展概况

Prefecture (County) Social and Economic Summary

Twenty-Three

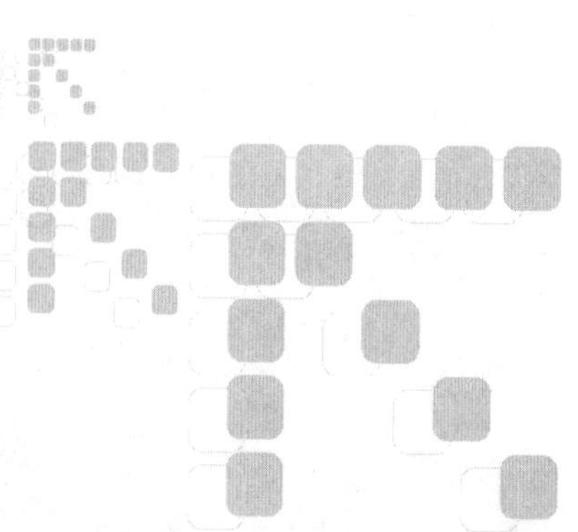

23-1 各州（市、地）生产总值及构成（2005）

Gross Domestic Product and Its Composition by Region(2005)

州(市、地)名称	State(City,Prefecture)	生产总值 Gross Domestic Product	第一产业 Primary Industry	第二产业 Secondary Industry	第三产业 Tertiary Industry	2005年比2004年增长(%) Increase Rate in 2004 ove 2003(%)	人均生产总值（元）Per Capita Gross Domestic Product (yuan)	位次 Order
绝对数(万元)	**Absolute Figure (10000 yuan)**							
贵阳市	Guiyang	5256159	350217	2493874	2412068	14.6	14934	1
六盘水市	Liupanshui	2075506	186880	1180813	707814	17.5	6879	2
遵义市	Zunyi	4075747	1033279	1607998	1434470	14.3	5497	3
安顺市	Anshun	1060334	240769	394629	424936	12.7	4026	5
铜仁地区	Tongren	1280516	559957	290376	430183	12.1	3271	8
黔西南州	Qianxinan	1199349	351785	434771	412793	13.4	3864	6
毕节地区	Bijie	2310243	743119	866572	700551	16.6	3200	9
黔东南州	Qiandongnan	1454010	467836	389725	596449	11.7	3304	7
黔南州	Qiannan	1679567	489461	637549	552557	11.8	4256	4
构成(%)	**Composition(%)**							
贵阳市	Guiyang	100.0	6.7	47.4	45.9			
六盘水市	Liupanshui	100.0	9.0	56.9	34.1			
遵义市	Zunyi	100.0	25.4	39.5	35.1			
安顺市	Anshun	100.0	22.7	37.2	40.1			
铜仁地区	Tongren	100.0	43.7	22.7	33.6			
黔西南州	Qianxinan	100.0	29.3	36.3	34.4			
毕节地区	Bijie	100.0	32.2	37.5	30.3			
黔东南州	Qiandongnan	100.0	32.2	26.8	41.0			
黔南州	Qiannan	100.0	29.1	38.0	32.9			

注:本表绝对数按当年价格计算,增长速度按可比价格计算。

Note:Absolute figures in this table are calculated at current prices, while increase rate are calculated at comparable prices.

23-2 各州(市、地）常住人口

Permanent Residents by Region

州（市、地）名 称	State (City,Prefecture)	总户数（万户）Total Number of Household (10000 households)		平均每户人数（人）Population of Per Household(person)		年末人口数（万人）Total Population at The Year-end(10000 persons)	
		2004	2005	2004	2005	2004	2005
贵阳市	Guiyang	103.53	110.69	3.39	3.19	350.86	353.09
六盘水市	Liupanshui	82.81	86.24	3.63	3.51	300.76	302.70
遵义市	Zunyi	209.36	225.92	3.53	3.29	739.68	743.28
安顺市	Anshun	70.19	74.65	3.74	3.54	262.48	264.25
铜仁地区	Tongren	106.15	113.54	3.67	3.46	390.05	392.84
黔西南州	Qianxinan	78.02	84.71	3.96	3.68	309.02	311.73
毕节地区	Bijie	184.24	196.51	3.90	3.69	718.83	725.12
黔东南州	Qiandongnan	113.33	130.30	3.87	3.39	438.50	441.72
黔南州	Qiannan	104.62	111.97	3.76	3.54	393.54	396.39

23-3 各州(市、地）户籍人口

Permanent Residents by Region

州（市、地）名 称	State (City,Prefecture)	按农业与非农业分（万人）By Agricultural and Non-Agricultural(10000 persons)				按性别分(万人) Grouped by sex(10000 persons)			
		农业 Agricultural		非农业 Non-Agricultural		男 Male		女 Female	
		2004	2005	2004	2005	2004	2005	2004	2005
贵阳市	Guiyang	178.58	178.87	169.23	171.79	179.01	180.27	168.80	170.39
六盘水市	Liupanshui	230.37	231.88	65.14	65.29	154.86	155.75	140.64	141.42
遵义市	Zunyi	611.05	616.76	111.96	108.78	374.17	375.70	348.84	349.84
安顺市	Anshun	216.36	217.13	39.81	39.75	132.65	132.80	123.52	124.08
铜仁地区	Tongren	344.02	345.91	40.24	42.31	202.00	203.88	182.26	184.34
黔西南州	Qianxinan	274.51	280.89	29.66	29.24	156.76	160.12	147.41	150.01
毕节地区	Bijie	663.39	675.26	50.95	51.69	371.42	379.80	342.92	347.15
黔东南州	Qiandongnan	376.16	380.29	48.10	49.13	224.68	227.02	199.58	202.4
黔南州	Qiannan	330.17	331.05	51.49	51.72	197.65	197.94	184.02	184.83

23-4 各州（市、地）在岗职工人数、年平均工资（2005）

Number of Staff and Workers and Their Annual Average Wages by Region (2005)

州（市、地）名 称	State (City,Prefecture)	合 计 Total	国有经济 State -owned units	城镇集体经济 Urban Collective-owned Units	其他经济类型 Units of Other Types of Ownership	2005年比2004年增长（%）Increase Rate in 2005 over 2004(%)
在岗职工人数（万人）	**Number of Staff and Workers(10000 persons)**					
贵 阳 市	Guiyang	60.59	36.73	4.13	19.73	5.7
六盘水市	Liupanshui	17.19	7.17	0.28	9.74	3.9
遵 义 市	Zunyi	26.78	20.49	0.97	5.32	11.4
安 顺 市	Anshun	11.52	8.41	0.69	2.42	-3.1
铜仁地区	Tongren	13.21	11.36	0.73	1.12	3.6
黔西南州	Qianxinan	11.23	8.47	0.52	2.30	1.2
毕节地区	Bijie	19.34	14.98	0.89	3.47	8.5
黔东南州	Qiandongnan	15.46	11.98	0.78	2.70	4.2
黔 南 州	Qiannan	15.67	11.99	0.83	2.85	2.1
平均工资（元）	**Annual Average Wages(yuan)**					
贵 阳 市	Guiyang	16553	18180	10413	14862	17.4
六盘水市	Liupanshui	16747	15117	10026	18132	22.5
遵 义 市	Zunyi	16183	17050	13262	13268	20.7
安 顺 市	Anshun	13952	15084	10001	11146	18.0
铜仁地区	Tongren	13933	14157	11488	11708	17.7
黔西南州	Qianxinan	13496	14272	8625	11637	20.5
毕节地区	Bijie	12937	13612	7859	11317	21.2
黔东南州	Qiandongnan	14158	15337	12650	9606	21.4
黔 南 州	Qiannan	14054	15346	9515	9996	19.6

23-5 各州（市、地）固定资产投资（一）（2005）

Investment in Fixed Assets by Region(1)(2005)

单位：万元 (10000 yuan)

州(市、地)名称	State (City,Prefecture)	固定资产投资总额 Total Investment in Fixed Assets	基本建设 Capital Construction	更新改造 Investment in Innovation	其他投资 Other Investment	房地产开发 Real Estate Development	2005年比2004年增长(%) Increase Rate in 2005 over 2004(%)
绝对数(万元)	**Absolute Figure (10000 yuan)**						
贵阳市	Guiyang	3273032	1412345	753697	362523	911166	16.4
六盘水市	Liupanshui	1064095	596675	274635	126769	66016	43.1
遵义市	Zunyi	1691905	1030093	398009	26172	237631	19.4
安顺市	Anshun	205806	94189	51946	2397	57274	6.3
铜仁地区	Tongren	617323	376531	126929	45161	68702	30.2
黔西南州	Qianxinan	457955	268670	128406	41665	19214	42.7
毕节地区	Bijie	658332	589133	38155	5046	25998	-21.2
黔东南州	Qiandongnan	774914	615670	49158	25248	84838	64.9
黔南州	Qiannan	388843	149002	158423	4670	76748	10.1
构成(%)	**Composition(%)**						
贵阳市	Guiyang	100.0	43.2	23.0	11.1	22.7	
六盘水市	Liupanshui	100.0	56.1	25.8	11.9	6.2	
遵义市	Zunyi	100.0	60.9	23.5	1.5	14.0	
安顺市	Anshun	100.0	45.8	25.2	1.2	27.8	
铜仁地区	Tongren	100.0	61.0	20.6	7.3	11.1	
黔西南州	Qianxinan	100.0	58.7	28.0	9.1	4.2	
毕节地区	Bijie	100.0	89.5	5.8	0.8	3.9	
黔东南州	Qiandongnan	100.0	79.5	6.3	3.3	10.9	
黔南州	Qiannan	100.0	38.3	40.7	1.2	19.7	

23-6 各州（市、地）固定资产投资(二)（2005）

Investment in Fixed Assets by Region(2)(2005)

单位：万元 (10000 yuan)

州(市、地)名 称	State(City,Prefecture)	固定资产投资总额 Total Investment in Fixed Assets	按国有非国有分 Grouped by State-owned and Non-state-owned	
			国有经济 State-owned	非国有经济 Non-state-owned
贵阳市	Guiyang	3273032	1484828	1954903
六盘水市	Liupanshui	1064095	821046	243049
遵义市	Zunyi	1691905	1086478	605427
安顺市	Anshun	205806	69116	136690
铜仁地区	Tongren	617323	432284	185039
黔西南州	Qianxinan	457955	120300	337655
毕节地区	Bijie	658332	572280	86052
黔东南州	Qiandongnan	774914	488516	286398
黔南州	Qiannan	388843	170540	218303

23-7 各市（州、地）农业常用耕地面积（2005）

Cultivated Area for Frequently Use by Region(2005)

单位:千公顷(1000 hectares)

市(州、地)名 称	City(State、Prefecture)	常用耕地面积 Cultivated Area	#水田 Paddy Fields	#水浇地 Fields Irrgated by Water
贵阳市	Guiyang	93.92	41.98	16.07
六盘水市	Liupanshui	106.66	21.14	
遵义市	Zunyi	391.25	193.34	106.50
安顺市	Anshun	106.29	55.24	1.23
铜仁地区	Tongren	173.76	104.08	16.77
黔西南州	Qianxinan	161.52	53.49	13.47
毕节地区	Bijie	365.28	47.09	2.05
黔东南州	Qiandongnan	178.58	134.55	
黔南州	Qiannan	176.23	105.74	11.83

23-8 各市（州、地）乡村从业人员数（2005）

Rural Employment by Region(2005)

单位:万人(10000 persons)

市(州、地)名称	City(State、Prefecture)	合计 Total	农业 Agric-ulture	工业 Indu-stry	建筑业 Constru-ction	交运仓储和邮政业 Trans-port, Storage and Post	信息传输、计算机服务和软件业 Information Transmission, Computer Services and Software	批发与零售业 Whole-sale and Retail Trade	住宿和餐饮业 Hotel and Resta-urants	其他行业 Others Sectors
贵阳市	Guiyang	111.08	71.61	7.34	3.82	2.56	0.19	3.35	2.15	20.05
六盘水市	Liupanshui	126.81	89.23	6.95	2.38	2.68	0.03	2.39	0.65	22.51
遵义市	Zunyi	371.41	229.64	11.12	10.35	4.47	0.31	8.89	2.15	104.47
安顺市	Anshun	132.66	93.47	5.87	4.45	1.99	0.15	3.04	1.12	22.55
铜仁地区	Tongren	216.55	133.89	7.34	6.15	2.59	0.06	4.80	1.01	60.71
黔西南州	Qianxinan	162.92	117.95	5.16	4.15	2.29	0.22	3.37	1.08	28.70
毕节地区	Bijie	389.68	249.84	25.75	8.40	4.71	0.58	8.72	3.09	88.58
黔东南州	Qiandongnan	221.60	148.99	5.46	5.39	2.29	0.24	4.39	1.44	53.41
黔南州	Qiannan	201.45	133.48	6.80	5.19	2.15	0.14	3.96	1.77	47.96

23-9 各市（州、地）农、林、牧、渔业总产值（2005）

Gross Output Value and Its Composition of Farming,Forestry, Animal Husban dary, Fishery by Region(2005)

单位：万元 (10000 yuan)

市（州、地）名称	City (State、Prefecture)	农林牧渔业总产值 Gross Output Value of Farming, Forestry,Animal Husbandary, Fishery	农业 Farming	林业 Forestry	牧业 Animal Husbandary	渔业 Fishery	服务业 Services	2005年比2004年增长(%) Increase Rate in 2005 over 2004(%)
贵阳市	Guiyang	547663	313678	4514	215686	10646	3139	8.6
六盘水市	Liupanshui	292756	170221	8725	105740	488	7582	9.1
遵义市	Zunyi	1671405	931645	64100	637999	17278	20383	6.1
安顺市	Anshun	371640	216758	11219	136571	4596	2496	10.0
铜仁地区	Tongren	865845	519049	14717	309193	11005	11881	5.8
黔西南州	Qianxinan	579383	288258	33230	239539	10424	7932	7.9
毕节地区	Bijie	1142210	658109	11519	451699	2075	18808	7.0
黔东南州	Qiandongnan	748439	389420	71049	252964	23661	11345	6.6
黔南州	Qiannan	794819	411700	37016	311645	6870	27588	6.6

注:本表绝对数按当年价格计算,增长速度按可比价格计算。

Note: Absolute figure in this table are calculated at current prices,while the increase rate are calculated at comparable prices.

23-10 各市（州、地）农民人均纯收入（2005）

Per Capita Net Income of Rural Households by Region(2005)

单位：元 (yuan)

市（州、地）名称	City (State、Prefecture)	农村居民人均纯收入 Per Capita Net Income of Rural Households	位次 Order	农村居民人均年现金收入 Annual Per Capita Cash Income of Rural Households	位次 Order	农村居民人均年消费性支出 Annual Per Capita Living Expenditures of Rural Households	位次 Order
贵阳市	Guiyang	3135	1	3235	1	2296	1
六盘水市	Liupanshui	1863	3	1829	5	1340	8
遵义市	Zunyi	2319	2	2203	2	1684	2
安顺市	Anshun	1828	5	1732	6	1391	6
铜仁地区	Tongren	1700	9	1615	8	1430	5
黔西南州	Qianxinan	1785	7	1954	3	1500	4
毕节地区	Bijie	1795	6	1727	7	1264	9
黔东南州	Qiandongnan	1728	8	1580	9	1353	7
黔南州	Qiannan	1846	4	1941	4	1556	3

23-11 各市（州、地）农业机械总动力及拥有量（2005）

Total Power and Possession of Agricultural Machinery by Region(2005)

市（州、地）名称	City (State、Profecture)	农业机械总动力（万千瓦）Total Power of Agricultural Machinery (10000 kw)	大中型农用拖拉机(万台) Large and Medium Agricultural Tractors	小型拖拉机(万台) Mini Agricultural Tractors	农用运输车(万台) Transpotr Trucks for Agricultural Use	农用水泵(万台) Agricultural Water Pump
贵阳市	Guiyang	73.00	0.17	0.28	1.12	1.23
六盘水市	Liupanshui	93.95	0.09	0.47	1.44	0.38
遵义市	Zunyi	209.75	0.85	0.89	1.38	4.42
安顺市	Anshun	69.23	0.26	0.33	0.50	0.52
铜仁地区	Tongren	91.58	0.38	0.23	0.56	2.26
黔西南州	Qianxinan	98.35	0.45	0.33	0.53	1.13
毕节地区	Bijie	139.95	1.14	1.36	1.01	2.18
黔东南州	Qiandongnan	121.06	0.34	0.41	0.43	0.87
黔南州	Qiannan	114.66	0.47	0.53	0.65	1.64

注：本表资料由省农机局提供。

Note:Data in this table are obtained from the agricultural machinery department.

23-12 各市（州、地）农用化肥施用量（2005）

Consumption of Chemical Fertilizers for Agricultural Use by Region (2005)

单位:吨 (ton)

市（州、地）名称	City (State、Profecture)	合计 Total	氮肥 Nitrogenous Fertilizer	磷肥 Phosphate Fertilizer	钾肥 Potash Fertilizer	复合肥 Compound Fertilizer	2005年比2004年增长(%) Increase Rate in 2005 over 2004(%)
贵阳市	Guiyang	63482	32693	7902	7532	15355	0.7
六盘水市	Liupanshui	56144	38320	5847	3956	8021	2.1
遵义市	Zunyi	171056	98618	21591	16872	33975	18.7
安顺市	Anshun	55936	29288	11483	2594	12571	1.0
铜仁地区	Tongren	41140	20495	6519	3360	10766	-17.0
黔西南州	Qianxinan	69278	48197	9751	6931	4399	4.2
毕节地区	Bijie	181796	105653	19329	8487	48327	3.0
黔东南州	Qiandongnan	62453	25943	9066	5568	21876	-0.4
黔南州	Qiannan	72810	46381	9294	3847	13288	3.4

注:本表按折纯法计算。

Note:Consumption of chemical fertilizers is required in calculation to convert the gross weight into weight containing 100% effective component.

23-13 各市（州、地）主要农作物播种面积（2005）

Sown Areas of Major Farm Crops by Region(2005)

单位:千公顷 (1000 hectares)

市（州、地）名称	City (State、Profecture)	总计 Total	粮食作物 Sown Areas of Grain Arops	#夏粮 Summer Grain Crops	按品种分 #小麦 Wheat	#稻谷 Rice	#玉米 Corn	#大豆 Soybeans	油菜籽 Rapeseed	烤烟 Fluecured Tobacco
贵阳市	Guiyang	235.66	131.40	41.27	13.03	39.18	38.13	6.36	37.34	11.67
六盘水市	Liupanshui	239.54	187.45	81.49	38.80	19.21	67.96	8.29	6.42	4.82
遵义市	Zunyi	1181.30	780.21	279.70	81.90	170.56	141.51	30.46	142.96	59.66
安顺市	Anshun	249.55	153.80	42.60	20.87	54.85	44.06	5.05	55.66	6.84
铜仁地区	Tongren	515.97	347.65	102.47	38.94	100.29	65.46	17.23	58.54	24.19
黔西南州	Qianxinan	379.61	247.99	80.26	62.19	53.22	89.38	6.00	24.44	15.23
毕节地区	Bijie	1022.95	630.74	273.61	102.49	47.12	162.58	36.47	60.97	55.38
黔东南州	Qiandongnan	518.97	302.70	77.76	10.37	131.85	39.94	10.06	51.66	9.23
黔南州	Qiannan	460.56	291.81	80.23	42.05	105.41	70.52	10.74	66.78	19.55

23-14 各市（州、地）主要农产品产量（2005）

Output of Major Farm Crops by Region(2005)

单位：万吨 (10000 tons)

市（州、地）名称	City (State、Profecture)	粮食 Grain	#夏粮 Summer Grain Crops	2005年比2004年增长（%）Increase Rate in 2005 over 2004(%)	油菜籽 Rapeseeds	烤烟 Fluecured Tobacco	茶叶 Tea	水果 Fruits
贵阳市	Guiyang	61.21	10.76	2.6	6.12	2.06	0.15	9.18
六盘水市	Liupanshui	77.86	16.38	2.7	0.63	0.96	0.03	1.90
遵义市	Zunyi	321.65	78.32	0.3	26.47	8.99	0.97	17.74
安顺市	Anshun	77.10	8.79	1.9	7.08	1.07	0.08	6.58
铜仁地区	Tongren	135.67	27.47	-7.4	8.65	3.71	0.28	7.30
黔西南州	Qianxinan	104.33	14.99	2.0	2.61	2.80	0.25	10.40
毕节地区	Bijie	247.22	61.90	3.8	10.16	10.43	0.07	6.69
黔东南州	Qiandongnan	134.36	17.44	-0.3	6.41	1.33	0.21	25.34
黔南州	Qiannan	128.60	17.70	3.1	8.38	3.11	0.24	10.84

23-15 各市（州、地）牲畜出存栏量(2005)

Amount of Livestocks in Hand and Slaughtered by Region(2005)

单位：万头、万只(10000 heads)

市（州、地）名称	City (State、Profecture)	出栏 Amount of Slaughtered Livestocks			存栏 Amount of Livestock in Hand		
		猪 Hogs	牛 Cattle and Buffalo	羊 Sheep and Goats	猪 Hogs	牛 Cattle and Buffalo	羊 Sheep and Goats
贵阳市	Guiyang	170.50	7.03	4.86	133.64	41.19	5.30
六盘水市	Liupanshui	89.77	9.20	14.19	118.47	43.05	31.57
遵义市	Zunyi	602.27	31.17	93.88	586.03	150.64	130.20
安顺市	Anshun	99.07	10.44	4.00	107.77	66.56	7.32
铜仁地区	Tongren	258.91	21.03	119.62	281.55	95.66	126.47
黔西南州	Qianxinan	187.66	20.35	20.18	184.26	93.36	35.51
毕节地区	Bijie	303.39	20.88	43.24	399.95	132.01	84.23
黔东南州	Qiandongnan	229.95	29.13	38.27	275.13	136.38	61.59
黔南州	Qiannan	228.74	20.34	14.41	246.65	118.58	22.10

23-16 各市（州、地）主要畜产品及水产品产量（2005）

Output of Major Livestock Products and Aquatic Products by Region (2005)

单位:万吨 (10000 tons)

市（州、地）名 称	City (State、Profecture)	肉类总产量 Total Output of Meat	#猪肉 Pork	#牛肉 Beef	2005年比2004年增长(%) Increase Rate in 2005 over 2004(%)	禽蛋 Poulty and Eggs	水产品 Aquatic Products
贵 阳 市	Guiyang	18.06	15.26	0.94	9.2	1.40	1.01
六盘水市	Liupanshui	10.24	8.57	0.78	13.8	0.51	0.10
遵 义 市	Zunyi	60.41	51.71	3.24	13.1	3.71	1.85
安 顺 市	Anshun	11.40	8.80	1.09	16.6	1.08	0.50
铜仁地区	Tongren	28.52	23.08	2.17	16.7	1.81	1.30
黔西南州	Qianxinan	19.46	15.84	1.90	7.9	1.67	1.24
毕节地区	Bijie	35.08	29.98	2.51	8.6	2.00	0.60
黔东南州	Qiandongnan	21.53	16.68	2.67	10.1	0.75	2.15
黔 南 州	Qiannan	21.67	18.31	1.85	15.8	0.88	0.72

注：表中水产品产量为部门数。

Note:Output of aquatic products in this table are obtained from the fishery department.

23-17 各市（州、地）主要林产品产量（2005）

Output of Major Forestry Products by Region(2005)

单位：吨 (ton)

市（州、地）名 称	City (State、Profecture)	生漆 Lacquer	油桐籽 Tung-Oil Seed	油茶籽 Tea-Oil Seed	乌桕籽 Tallow-seeds	五倍籽 Nutgall	棕片 Palm-flake	核桃 Walnuts	板栗 Chestnut
贵 阳 市	Guiyang	30	234	112	15	27	82	149	287
六盘水市	Liupanshui	121	140	6			149	1458	388
遵 义 市	Zunyi	339	4355	215	1147	875	1308	760	968
安 顺 市	Anshun	12	8385	240	87	9	151	186	278
铜仁地区	Tongren	87	10269	1398	1324	322	627	246	859
黔西南州	Qianxinan	156	34860	2718	35	112	1610	951	5151
毕节地区	Bijie	436	74	250	14	29	201	2328	656
黔东南州	Qiandongnan	42	9252	5220	208	234	304	93	1417
黔 南 州	Qiannan	105	14100	399	118	335	301	669	2282

23-18 各州（市、地）规模以上轻重工业总产值（2005）

Total Gross Industrial Output Value above Designated Size of Light Industry and Heavy Industry by Region(2005)

单位：万元 (10000 yuan)

市(州、地)名称	City (State、Profecture)	合计 Total	轻工业 Light Industry	重工业 Heavy Industry
贵阳市	Guiyang	5740645	1783270	3957375
六盘水市	Liupanshui	1934635	18859	1915775
遵义市	Zunyi	2361441	845893	1515548
安顺市	Anshun	630738	93348	537390
铜仁地区	Tongren	525504	43144	482360
黔西南州	Qianxinan	759891	73752	686139
毕节地区	Bijie	1006810	38118	968692
黔东南州	Qiandongnan	764894	44093	720801
黔南州	Qiannan	1232454	196671	1035784

23-19 各州（市、地）规模以上工业企业主要工业产品产量（2005）

Ouput of Major Industrial Products above Designated Size by Region(2005)

市(州、地)名称	City (State、Profecture)	原煤（万吨）Coal (10000 tons)	发电量（万千瓦小时）Electricity (10000 kwh)	化肥（万吨）Chemical Fertilizer (10000 tons)	水泥（万吨）Cement (10000 tons)
贵阳市	Guiyang	584.75	936982	103.73	333.15
六盘水市	Liupanshui	2763.27	991995	1.75	166.34
遵义市	Zunyi	1149.42	1273913	33.44	363.53
安顺市	Anshun	787.65	867405	7.80	95.00
铜仁地区	Tongren	58.89	39669	0.33	96.18
黔西南州	Qianxinan	1041.33	1142983	140.21	140.21
毕节地区	Bijie	2573.70	2171528	8.87	97.84
黔东南州	Qiandongnan	232.43	387105		107.42
黔南州	Qiannan	559.99	61679	98.87	156.83

23-20 各州（市、地）社会消费品零售总额（2005）

Total Retail Sales of Consumer Goods by Region(2005)

单位：万元 (10000 yuan)

市(州、地)名称	City (State、Profecture)	社会消费品零售总额 Total Retail Sales of Consumer Goods	按销售地区分 Grouped by Distribution Area 市 City	县 County	县以下 Below County Level
贵阳市	Guiyang	2043210	1867646	88207	87357
六盘水市	Liupanshui	580626	316315	148655	115656
遵义市	Zunyi	1222403	644792	250416	327195
安顺市	Anshun	280210	96874	60634	122702
铜仁地区	Tongren	317029	68323	123534	125172
黔西南州	Qianxinan	367795	163981	76892	126922
毕节地区	Bijie	389345	62333	146749	180263
黔东南州	Qiandongnan	482483	129951	180324	172208
黔南州	Qiannan	386079	124165	129647	132267

23-21 各州（市、地）财政一般预算收入（2005）

Local Financial Revenue by Region(2005)

市(州、地)名称	City (State, Prefecture)	合计(万元) Total (10000 yuan)	#增值税 Value-added Tax	#营业税 Operation Tax	#企业所得税 Enterprises' Income Tax	#个人所得税 Individual Income Tax	2005年比2004年增长(%) Increase Rate in 2005 over 2004(%)	人均财政一般预算收入(元) Per Capita Local Financial Revenue(yuan)
贵阳市	Guiyang	498016	63040	152509	49148	35424	22.2	1414.92
六盘水市	Liupanshui	132340	24795	36804	4668	8709	36.4	438.60
遵义市	Zunyi	221561	32342	58307	10775	10701	22.9	298.81
安顺市	Anshun	74415	8922	20982	2152	1435	27.6	282.55
铜仁地区	Tongren	71918	5770	19622	500	932	13.1	183.72
黔西南州	Qianxinan	82839	10588	26244	4725	3241	24.0	266.90
毕节地区	Bijie	148448	21122	28199	1941	8561	24.6	205.61
黔东南州	Qiandongnan	77347	7730	27944	751	3109	17.4	175.74
黔南州	Qiannan	95468	13910	26425	3324	5108	20.4	241.71

23-22 各州（市、地）财政支出（2005）

Financial Expenditure by Region(2005)

州(市、地)名称	State (City, Prefecture)	合计(万元) Total (10000 yuan)	#基本建设支出 Expenditure for Capital Construction	#农业支出 Expenditure for Agriculture	#教育支出 Operating Expenses for Education	#社会保障补助支出 Expenditure on Subsidies to Social Security Programs	2005年比2004年增长(%) Increase Rate in 2005over 2004(%)	人均财政支出(元) Per Capita Financial Expenditure (yuan)
贵阳市	Guiyang	725719	28992	30408	96566	60898	21.1	2061.85
六盘水市	Liupanshui	275999	2802	16472	53644	7638	26.6	914.72
遵义市	Zunyi	584724	4353	37025	151279	17319	27.6	788.59
安顺市	Anshun	221251	2322	13060	48754	10597	27.9	840.09
铜仁地区	Tongren	314085	450	24715	83165	7496	29.1	802.37
黔西南州	Qianxinan	249445	9168	16612	61638	4622	24.7	1280.51
毕节地区	Bijie	440188	5875	28411	121088	7356	27.5	609.70
黔东南州	Qiandongnan	397438	260	25792	106722	11836	30.7	566.78
黔南州	Qiannan	371779	6380	26009	91823	11682	30.1	941.30

23-23 各州（市、地）所在地城市居民消费价格指数(上年=100）（2005）

Residents Consumer Price Indices of Major Cities by Region（preceding year=100)(2005)

城市名称	City	居民消费价格指数 Residents Consum er Price Index		商品零售价格指数 Retail Price Index of Commodities	
		2004	2005	2004	2005
贵阳市	Guiyang	102.1	100.7	100.4	100.2
六盘水市	Liupanshui	106.9	100.1	106.0	99.3
遵义市	Zunyi	104.4	100.2	104.1	101.9
安顺市	Anshun	104.3	101.1	103.6	101.6
铜仁市	Tongren	105.9	102.1	105.4	101.8
兴义市	Xingyi	105.2	102.0	104.6	102.4
毕节市	Bijie	104.1	102.0	103.7	102.1
凯里市	Kaili	103.9	100.4	102.3	100.0
都匀市	Duyun	104.9	101.6	104.6	102.1

23-24 各州（市、地）所在地城市城镇居民家庭人均收支(2005)

Per Capital Annual Income and Expenditure of Urban Household by Region(2005)

单位：元 (yuan)

城市名称	City	城镇居民家庭人均可支配收入 Per Capita Annual Disposal Income of Urban Household	位次 Order	2005年比2004年增长(%) Increase Rate in 2005 over 2004(%)	城镇居民家庭人均消费性支出 Per Capita Annual Consumption Expenditnre of Urban Household	位次 Order	2005年比2004年增长(%) Increase Rate in 2005 over 2004(%)
贵 阳 市	Guiyang	9927.97	1	10.5	7692.62	1	11.3
六盘水市	Liupanshui	8032.22	3	11.9	5629.12	5	15.1
遵 义 市	Zunyi	8205.65	2	13.1	6094.32	2	13.0
安 顺 市	Anshun	7336.99	7	8.7	5266.98	9	10.6
铜 仁 市	Tongren	6718.75	9	12.9	5385.81	8	11.1
兴 义 市	Xingyi	8022.12	4	9.1	6048.34	3	17.8
毕 节 市	Bijie	7215.03	8	23.8	5791.42	4	15.0
凯 里 市	Kaili	7709.97	5	9.2	5738.71	5	11.7
都 匀 市	Duyun	7393.39	6	12.6	5520.68	7	8.2

23-25 各州（市、地）大中型工业企业科技活动人员情况（2005）

Basic Statistics on Persons Engaged in Scientific and Technological Activities in Large and Medium Industrial Enterprises(2005)

单位：人(person)

市(州、地)名称	City (State,Prefecture)	科技活动人员 Persons Engaged in Scientific and Technological Activities	全时人员 Full-time Personnel	非全时人员 Part-time Personnel	#科学家和工程师 Scientists and Engineers	#研究与试验人员 Research and Experiment Personnel
贵 阳 市	Guiyang	7195	2935	4260	3878	2623
六盘水市	Liupanshui	652	178	474	550	211
遵 义 市	Zunyi	4244	2036	2208	2493	1635
安 顺 市	Anshun	2951	1117	1834	1731	1805
毕节地区	Bijie	10		10	10	
黔东南州	Qiandongnan	109	32	77	59	
黔 南 州	Qiannan	955	278	677	407	414

23-26 各州（市、地）大中型工业企业科技活动经费筹集情况（2005）

Basic Statistics on Sum of Funds for Scientific and Technological Activi ties in Large and Medium Industrial Enterprises by Region（2005）

单位：万元(10000 yuan)

市(州、地)名 称	City (State,Prefecture)	科技活动经费筹集总额 Sum of Funds for Scientific and Technological Activities	企业资金 From Corporation	金融机构贷款 Loans of Financial Institutions	政府资金 From Government	事业单位资金 From Institution	其他 Others
贵 阳 市	Guiyang	66528	57883	1665	5484		1497
六盘水市	Liupanshui	8380	8319		61		
遵 义 市	Zunyi	53780	43556	5289	4614	6	316
安 顺 市	Anshun	19929	10662	6243	2748	1	274
毕节地区	Bijie	419	419				
黔东南州	Qiandongnan	384	119		265		
黔 南 州	Qiannan	16572	15725	210	637		

23-27 各州（市、地）大中型工业企业科技活动经费支出情况（2005）

Expenditures for Scientific and Technological Activities in Large and Medium-sized Enterprise by Region(2005)

单位：万元(10000 yuan)

市(州、地)名 称	City (State, Prefecture)	科技活动经 费支出总额 Expen-ditures for Scientific and Techno-logical Activities	内部支出 Inner Expen-diture	#劳务费 Service Fee	#原材料费 Raw Material Fee	#其他 Other	#内部支出中研究与试验发展支出 Expenditure for Development of Research and Exper-iment in Inner Expenditure	#内部支出中新产品开发支出 Expen-diture for Newp-roduct in Inner Expen-diture	科技经费外部支出 Extenior Expenditure of Science and Technology Outlay
贵 阳 市	Guiyang	63854	60698	12861	20146	27692	34433	28149	3155
六盘水市	Liupanshui	7393	5118	1197	1443	2478	1049	662	2275
遵 义 市	Zunyi	57257	53867	10157	21578	22132	37869	26929	3390
安 顺 市	Anshun	20293	19515	5339	7168	7008	12788	11569	778
毕节地区	Bijie	418	418	21		397			
黔东南州	Qiandongnan	384	384	218	58	109	384		
黔 南 州	Qiannan	19194	19004	427	4869	13708	11465	13509	190

23-28 各州（市、地）教育事业主要指标（2005）

Major Indicators of Education by Region(2005)

市(州、地)名称	City (State,Prefecture)	高等学校（所） Institutions of Higher Education (unit)	在校学生（人） Students Enrollment (person)	普通中学（所） Secondary Schools (unit)	在校学生（人） Students Enrollment (person)	小学（所） Primary Schools (unit)	在校学生（万人） Students Enrollment (10000 persons)
贵阳市	Guiyang	14	140690	306	218994	957	37.53
六盘水市	Liupanshui	2	4242	238	210075	1085	41.41
遵义市	Zunyi	2	13573	548	498081	2452	82.86
安顺市	Anshun	2	7590	153	165916	1044	33.95
铜仁地区	Tongren	2	4576	239	267379	1626	48.84
黔西南州	Qianxinan	2	3309	217	212782	1136	39.97
毕节地区	Bijie	1	4894	422	444909	2521	98.75
黔东南州	Qiandongnan	3	11982	285	283820	1913	46.55
黔南州	Qiannan	3	17934	260	247691	1542	43.91

23-29 各州（市、地）城乡居民年末储蓄余额（2005）

Urban and Rural Resident Savings Deposit Balance at The Year-end by Region(2005)

单位：亿元 (100 million yuan)

市(州、地)名称	City (State,Prefecture)	金融机构存款余额 Total Savings Deposit Balance	#城乡居民储蓄余额 Urban and Rural Resident Savings Deposit Balance	2005年比2004增长(%) Increase Rate in 2005 over 2004(%)	金融机构贷款余额 Total Loans Balance	2005年比2004增长(%) Increase Rate in 2005 over 2004(%)
贵阳市	Guiyang	1260.43	497.74	18.0	1038.18	14.0
六盘水市	Liupanshui	196.39	95.64	16.5	139.55	24.2
遵义市	Zunyi	424.14	234.87	19.6	238.27	8.0
安顺市	Anshun	138.57	77.34	18.9	122.63	…
铜仁地区	Tongren	112.29	73.08	20.2	94.93	25.0
黔西南州	Qianxinan	130.26	68.82	26.2	77.36	28.0
毕节地区	Bijie	170.63	97.25	27.7	115.17	12.4
黔东南州	Qiandongnan	164.02	106.40	15.6	120.25	13.2
黔南州	Qiannan	167.22	99.75	26.7	90.50	1.9

23-30 各县(市、区)生产总值（2005）

Gross Domestic Product by County(City,Section)(2005)

单位：万元 (10000 yuan)

县(市、区)名称	County (City,Section)	生产总值 Gross Domestic Product	第一产业 Primary Industry	第二产业 Secondary Industry	第三产业 Tertiary Industry	位次 Order	2005年比2004年增长(%) Increase Rate in 2005 over 2004(%)
南明区	Nanming	965077	4550	298641	661886	2	14.1
云岩区	Yunyan	1565262	1262	717528	846472	1	14.1
花溪区	Huaxi	371238	54760	138875	177603	16	14.8
乌当区	Wudang	531830	61734	279381	190715	9	19.5
白云区	Baiyun	475781	17248	342748	115785	12	14.1
小河区	Xiaohe	240558	6005	134706	99847	25	19.5
开阳县	Kaiyang	303022	64272	160095	78655	20	16.5
息烽县	Xifeng	237452	33792	151367	52293	28	20.1
修文县	Xiuwen	200071	49000	76609	74462	33	22.8
清镇市	Qingzhen	447564	58985	221239	167340	13	15.1
钟山区	Zhongshan	781294	15012	440021	326261	5	17.6
六枝特区	Liuzhi	228400	43268	86989	98143	31	13.8
水城县	Shuicheng	273225	54252	138886	80087	21	16.5
盘 县	Panxian	786726	76377	509297	201052	4	17.3
红花岗区	Honghuagang	868478	45739	307693	515046	3	16.8
汇川区	Huicuan	501905	33008	271623	197274	11	15.3
遵义县	Zunyi	656535	209000	232919	214616	6	14.1
桐梓县	Tongzi	231431	86982	56640	87809	30	12.1
绥阳县	Suiyang	178398	93166	30826	54406	37	13.0
正安县	Zhengan	141564	79674	14699	47191	49	10.8
※道真县	Daozhen	100351	47996	15382	36973	65	11.7
※务川县	Wuchuan	103605	52795	11736	39074	62	9.5
凤冈县	Fenggang	118204	58054	13484	46666	52	12.0
湄潭县	Meitan	143858	61200	25252	57406	47	12.2
余庆县	Yuqing	147314	65601	30085	51628	45	12.4
习水县	Xishui	238363	69115	85054	84194	27	12.4
赤水市	Chishui	189257	55248	81478	52531	35	14.3
仁怀市	Renhuai	598442	83733	409682	105027	8	16.4
西秀区	Xixiu	438484	74777	139533	224174	14	13.0
平坝县	Pingba	197653	32270	116684	48699	34	11.1

23-30续表1(continued)

单位：万元(10000 yuan)

县(市、区)名称	County (City,Section)	生产总值 Gross Domestic Product	第一产业 Primary Industry	第二产业 Secondary Industry	第三产业 Tertiary Industry	位次 Order	2005年比2004年增长(%) Increase Rate in 2005 over 2004(%)
普定县	Puding	149205	32507	80732	35966	43	6.3
※镇宁县	Zhenning	112504	26760	38752	46992	55	10.2
※关岭县	Guanling	101669	38837	31270	31562	63	13.5
※紫云县	Ziyun	67602	36127	8254	23221	76	11.1
铜仁市	Tongren	238436	46948	90151	101337	26	12.0
江口县	Jiangkou	69152	34291	9904	24957	72	11.7
※玉屏县	Yuping	110460	25079	48384	36997	58	8.6
石阡县	Shiqian	101336	55322	11232	34782	64	10.7
思南县	Sinan	178795	97195	39801	41799	36	16.3
※印江县	Yinjiang	110140	61623	13291	35226	59	11.6
德江县	Dejiang	142064	78922	19978	43164	48	11.6
※沿河县	Yanhe	136193	71084	19377	45732	50	13.3
※松桃县	Songtao	177135	80434	46693	50008	38	13.3
万山特区	Wanshan	28915	6760	14499	7656	88	18.0
兴义市	Xingyi	606736	106393	274498	225845	7	19.4
兴仁县	Xingren	150190	48022	52038	50130	42	18.1
普安县	Puan	85707	26274	34558	24875	66	20.1
晴隆县	Qinglong	68048	23620	21482	22946	74	16.0
贞丰县	Zhenfeng	107055	40499	42100	24456	61	9.0
望谟县	Wangmo	52000	28860	6240	16900	83	8.3
册亨县	Ceheng	50265	27910	9080	13275	84	10.1
安龙县	Anlong	144650	48100	43729	52821	46	18.4
毕节市	Bijie	528329	134119	207289	186921	10	13.7
大方县	Dafang	233515	88865	71992	72658	29	16.9
黔西县	Qianxi	264815	98434	87415	78966	23	20.9
金沙县	Jinsha	321720	79798	178504	63418	19	17.4
织金县	Zhijin	219485	93641	52298	73546	32	10.7
纳雍县	Nayong	331039	76112	186761	68167	18	24.1
※威宁县	Weining	266266	114035	74434	77797	22	9.6

23-30续表2(continued)

单位：万元(10000 yuan)

县(市、区)名称	County (City,Section)	生产总值 Gross Domestic Product	第一产业 Primary Industry	第二产业 Secondary Industry	第三产业 Tertiary Industry	位次 Order	2005年比2004年增长(%) Increase Rate in 2005 over 2004(%)
赫章县	Hezhang	159544	65400	42681	51463	41	14.0
凯里市	Kaili	382020	46528	152004	183488	15	11.5
黄平县	Huangping	69066	31651	5273	32142	73	10.6
施秉县	Shibing	56817	18530	18064	20223	82	7.9
三穗县	Sansui	60720	18533	14387	27800	80	10.5
镇远县	Zhenyuan	113754	40475	37349	35930	53	9.3
岑巩县	Cengong	63739	23279	17313	23147	77	11.9
天柱县	Tianzhu	111147	40076	27940	43131	56	15.4
锦屏县	Jinping	63035	18157	15934	28944	78	12.2
剑河县	Jianhe	62810	26621	11312	24877	79	11.3
台江县	Taijiang	42032	16035	10184	15813	86	12.3
黎平县	Liping	113179	49348	19648	44183	54	11.1
榕江县	Rongjiang	77719	40774	9309	27636	67	9.8
从江县	Congjiang	75487	39026	12017	24444	68	11.0
雷山县	Leishan	34923	12658	6749	15516	87	11.5
麻江县	Majiang	58351	21802	17799	18750	81	10.5
丹寨县	Danzhai	42439	16693	9752	15994	85	12.6
都匀市	Duyun	336657	45387	132740	158530	17	15.0
福泉市	Fuquan	246123	57440	121120	67563	24	12.1
荔波县	Libo	67645	20222	22489	24934	75	13.5
贵定县	Guiding	170543	34890	83789	51864	39	10.5
瓮安县	Wengan	162122	58149	53252	50721	40	11.8
独山县	Dushan	108323	50860	15621	41842	60	5.4
平塘县	Pingtang	72391	32448	11863	28080	71	13.5
罗甸县	Luodian	110893	43985	33808	33100	57	11.0
长顺县	Changshun	73951	26700	16349	30902	70	12.1
龙里县	Longli	147668	20024	100675	26969	44	24.4
惠水县	Huishui	135186	58806	35975	40405	51	10.1
※三都县	Sandu	73968	37288	5305	31375	69	11.2

注:表中绝对数按当年价格计算，增长速度按可比价格计算。

Note: Absolute figures in this table are calculated at current prices while increase rate are calculated at comparable prices.

23-31 各县(市、区)人均生产总值及位次(2005)

Per Capita Gross Domestic Product and Its Order by County(City,Section) (2005)

单位：元(yuan)

县(市、区)	County	人均生产总值 Per Capita Gross Domestic Product(yuan)	位次 Order	县(市、区)	County	人均生产总值 Per Capita Gross Domestic Product(yuan)	位次 Order
南明区	Nanming	19009	4	湄潭县	Meitan	2996	54
云岩区	Yunyan	28274	1	余庆县	Yuqing	4997	29
花溪区	Huaxi	11440	9	习水县	Xishui	3400	42
乌当区	Wudang	17239	6	赤水市	Chishui	6010	23
白云区	Baiyun	27203	2	仁怀市	Renhuai	9815	10
小河区	Xiaohe	20079	3	西秀区	Xixiu	5257	28
开阳县	Kaiyang	6895	19	平坝县	Pingba	5568	26
息烽县	Xifeng	9090	11	普定县	Puding	3584	37
修文县	Xiuwen	6481	22	※镇宁县	Zhenning	3195	46
清镇市	Qingzhen	8582	12	※关岭县	Guanling	3082	50
钟山区	Zhongshan	18019	5	※紫云县	Ziyun	1952	86
六枝特区	Liuzhi	3548	38	铜仁市	Tongren	6911	18
水城县	Shuicheng	3590	36	江口县	Jiangkou	3037	53
盘 县	Panxian	6673	21	※玉屏县	Yuping	7719	16
红花岗区	Honghuagang	16131	7	石阡县	Shiqian	2602	68
汇川区	Huichuan	15888	8	思南县	Sinan	2774	63
遵义县	Zunyi	5663	25	※印江县	Yinjiang	2619	67
桐梓县	Tongzi	3472	40	德江县	Dejiang	3104	48
绥阳县	Suiyang	3465	41	※沿河县	Yanhe	2393	74
正安县	Zhengan	2320	80	※松桃县	Songtao	2723	64
※道真县	Daozhen	2936	57	万山特区	Wanshan	4322	31
※务川县	Wuchuan	2428	72	兴义市	Xingyi	8088	14
凤冈县	Fenggang	2829	61	兴仁县	Xingren	3206	45

23-31续表(continued)

单位:元(yuan)

县(市、区)名称	County (City,Section)	人均生产总值 Per Capita Gross Domestic Product(yuan)	位次 Order	县(市、区)名称	County (City,Section)	人均生产总值 Per Capita Gross Domestic Product(yuan)	位次 Order
普安县	Puan	2937	56	锦屏县	Jinping	2789	62
晴隆县	Qinglong	2331	79	剑河县	Jianhe	2574	69
贞丰县	Zhenfeng	3041	52	台江县	Taijiang	2865	59
望谟县	Wangmo	1809	88	黎平县	Liping	2222	85
册亨县	Ceheng	2232	84	榕江县	Rongjiang	2333	78
安龙县	Anlong	3311	44	从江县	Congjiang	2337	77
毕节市	Bijie	4051	33	雷山县	Leishan	2308	82
大方县	Dafang	2384	75	麻江县	Majiang	2621	66
黔西县	Qianxi	3151	47	丹寨县	Danzhai	2564	70
金沙县	Jinsha	5403	27	都匀市	Duyun	6847	20
织金县	Zhijin	2312	81	福泉市	Fuquan	7848	15
纳雍县	Nayong	4252	32	荔波县	Libo	3972	34
※威宁县	Weining	2397	73	贵定县	Guiding	5845	24
赫章县	Hezhang	2433	71	瓮安县	Wengan	3473	39
凯里市	Kaili	8307	13	独山县	Dushan	3070	51
黄平县	Huangping	1949	87	平塘县	Pingtang	2355	76
施秉县	Shibing	3612	35	罗甸县	Luodian	3333	43
三穗县	Sansui	2891	58	长顺县	Changshun	2962	55
镇远县	Zhenyuan	4368	30	龙里县	Longli	7106	17
岑巩县	Cengong	2845	60	惠水县	Huishui	3093	49
天柱县	Tianzhu	2687	65	※三都县	Sandu	2237	83

23-32 各县（市、区）年末常住人口主要指标（2005）

Major Indicators of Permanent Residents at The Year-end by County(City,Section)(2005)

单位：万人（10000 persons）

县（市、区）名称	County (City,Section)	总人口 Total Population	位次 Order	县（市、区）名称	County (City,Section)	总人口 Total Population	位次 Order
南明区	Nanming	50.95	27	湄潭县	Meitan	48.15	29
云岩区	Yunyan	55.49	22	余庆县	Yuqing	29.68	64
花溪区	Huaxi	32.54	57	习水县	Xishui	70.20	12
乌当区	Wudang	30.97	61	赤水市	Chishui	31.56	59
白云区	Baiyun	17.59	80	仁怀市	Renhuai	61.11	19
小河区	Xiaohe	12.02	87	西秀区	Xixiu	83.67	8
开阳县	Kaiyang	44.06	34	平坝县	Pingba	35.62	45
息烽县	Xifeng	26.18	69	普定县	Puding	41.77	41
修文县	Xiuwen	30.96	62	※镇宁县	Zhenning	35.33	48
清镇市	Qingzhen	52.33	24	※关岭县	Guanling	33.1	56
钟山区	Zhongshan	43.48	37	※紫云县	Ziyun	34.76	49
六枝特区	Liuzhi	64.57	17	铜仁市	Tongren	34.59	50
水城县	Shuicheng	76.36	10	江口县	Jiangkou	22.82	73
盘 县	Panxian	118.29	2	※玉屏县	Yuping	14.35	86
红花岗区	Honghuagang	53.93	23	石阡县	Shiqian	39.08	43
汇川区	Huichuan	33.91	52	思南县	Sinan	64.70	16
遵义县	Zunyi	116.24	3	※印江县	Yinjiang	42.23	39
桐梓县	Tongzi	66.77	13	德江县	Dejiang	45.93	33
绥阳县	Suiyang	51.60	25	※沿河县	Yanhe	57.13	21
正安县	Zhengan	61.18	18	※松桃县	Songtao	65.31	15
※道真县	Daozhen	34.27	51	万山特区	Wanshan	6.70	88
※务川县	Wuchuan	42.77	38	兴义市	Xingyi	75.30	11
凤冈县	Fenggang	41.91	40	兴仁县	Xingren	47.04	30

23-32续表(continued)

县（市、区）名称	County (City,Section)	总人口 Total Population	位次 Order	县（市、区）名称	County (City,Section)	总人口 Total Population	位次 Order
普安县	Puan	29.30	65	锦屏县	Jinping	22.68	74
晴隆县	Qinglong	29.26	67	剑河县	Jianhe	24.48	72
贞丰县	Zhenfeng	35.64	44	台江县	Taijiang	14.72	85
望谟县	Wangmo	28.91	68	黎平县	Liping	51.13	26
册亨县	Ceheng	22.45	76	榕江县	Rongjiang	33.44	53
安龙县	Anlong	43.83	36	从江县	Congjiang	32.42	58
毕节市	Bijie	131.09	1	雷山县	Leishan	15.19	84
大方县	Dafang	99.27	5	麻江县	Majiang	22.35	77
黔西县	Qianxi	84.3	7	丹寨县	Danzhai	16.59	82
金沙县	Jinsha	59.66	20	都匀市	Duyun	49.29	28
织金县	Zhijin	94.9	6	福泉市	Fuquan	31.36	60
纳雍县	Nayong	78.03	9	荔波县	Libo	17.10	81
※威宁县	Weining	112.01	4	贵定县	Guiding	29.30	65
赫章县	Hezhang	65.86	14	瓮安县	Wengan	46.61	31
凯里市	Kaili	46.15	32	独山县	Dushan	35.44	47
黄平县	Huangping	35.55	46	平塘县	Pingtang	30.87	63
施秉县	Shibing	15.79	83	罗甸县	Luodian	33.41	54
三穗县	Sansui	21.08	78	长顺县	Changshun	25.07	71
镇远县	Zhenyuan	26.14	70	龙里县	Longli	20.85	79
岑巩县	Cengong	22.49	75	惠水县	Huishui	43.87	35
天柱县	Tianzhu	41.51	42	※三都县	Sandu	33.22	55

23-33 各县(市、区)固定资产投资（2005）

Investment in Fixed Assets by County(City,Section)(2005)

单位:万元 (10000 yuan)

县(市、区)名称	County (City,Section)	固定资产投资 Total Investment in Fixed Assets	基本建设 Capital Construction	更新改造 Innovation	其他投资 Other Investment	房地产投资 Real Estate
南明区	Nanming	547186	81677	104911	92467	268131
云岩区	Yunyan	544642	63882	71312	34393	375055
花溪区	Huaxi	148384	95812	20739	4867	26966
乌当区	Wudang	216331	57373	52642	22290	84026
白云区	Baiyun	187497	79602	54787	15127	37981
小河区	Xiaohe	240664	109268	29496	18879	83021
开阳县	Kaiyang	148296	38395	59698	37556	12647
息烽县	Xifeng	96200	23746	54775	11144	6535
修文县	Xiuwen	79101	24447	39556	12736	2362
清镇市	Qingzhen	167655	58430	85368	5448	18409
钟山区	Zhongshan	448455	79844	225602	88976	54033
六枝特区	Liuzhi	29414	22894	2889	511	3120
水城县	Shuicheng	218374	169653	22918	22262	3541
盘 县	Panxian	367852	324284	23226	15020	5322
红花岗区	Honghuagang	276756	97521	77620	400	101215
汇川区	Huicuan	244426	113255	54131		77040
遵义县	Zunyi	308536	230071	66606	531	11328
桐梓县	Tongzi	131037	111840	8865	3450	6882
绥阳县	Suiyang	31080	20167	7401	1786	1726
正安县	Zhengan	32730	19846	12684	200	
※道真县	Daozhen	57494	33888	17000	6606	
※务川县	Wuchuan	54548	27466	22373	1507	3202
凤冈县	Fenggang	26916	15438	7705	250	3523
湄潭县	Meitan	37050	17487	14258	1467	3838
余庆县	Yuqing	166673	154991	8250	1010	2422
习水县	Xishui	85061	46078	37233	750	1000
赤水市	Chishui	128588	99654	9762	8215	10957
仁怀市	Renhuai	111010	42391	54121		14498
西秀区	Xixiu	111978	41096	28218	871	41793
平坝县	Pingba	13622	6317	2894		4411

23-33续表1(continued)　　单位:万元(10000 yuan)

县(市、区)名 称	County (City,Section)	固定资产投资 Total Investment in Fixed Assets	基本建设 Capital Construction	更新改造 Innovation	其他投资 Other Investment	房地产投资 Real Estate
普定县	Puding	23469	7409	7800	394	7866
※镇宁县	Zhenning	16107	13091	1969	742	305
※关岭县	Guanling	8668	4711	3529		428
※紫云县	Ziyun	18238	8164	7321	353	2400
铜仁市	Tongren	135958	74796	11115	11124	38923
江口县	Jiangkou	29643	23624	2000	100	3919
※玉屏县	Yuping	137912	36702	97995	1565	1650
石阡县	Shiqian	29632	22493	1118	3071	2950
思南县	Sinan	103985	90993	1624	8336	3032
※印江县	Yinjiang	34508	26945	966	6597	
德江县	Dejiang	33837	29317	3720	800	
※沿河县	Yanhe	53458	29295	470	8775	14918
※松桃县	Songtao	44204	34274	3041	3579	3310
万山特区	Wanshan	9306	8092		1214	
兴义市	Xingyi	199015	81819	88890	9092	19214
兴仁县	Xingren	41831	17352	2884	21595	
普安县	Puan	24174	16530	7330	314	
晴隆县	Qinglong	16035	6358	873	8804	
贞丰县	Zhenfeng	83415	57688	25143	584	
望谟县	Wangmo	5875	4742	405	728	
册亨县	Ceheng	15500	15500			
安龙县	Anlong	72110	68681	2881	548	
毕节市	Bijie	73061	30085	24337	3409	15230
大方县	Dafang	146077	144086	308	1224	459
黔西县	Qianxi	167100	157810	6040		3250
金沙县	Jinsha	41060	34891	5550	289	330
织金县	Zhijin	20222	13369		124	6729
纳雍县	Nayong	185337	183417	1920		
※威宁县	Weining	14273	14273			

23-33续表2(continued)

单位:万元(10000 yuan)

县(市、区)名称	County (City,Section)	固定资产投资 Total Investment in Fixed Assets	基本建设 Capital Construction	更新改造 Innovation	其他投资 Other Investment	房地产投资 Real Estate
赫章县	Hezhang	11202	11202			
凯里市	Kaili	155397	46329	40838	13097	55133
黄平县	Huangping	10157	8299	768	375	715
施秉县	Shibing	5534	3732	200		1602
三穗县	Sansui	53589	51409			2180
镇远县	Zhenyuan	86767	83448	31	2610	678
岑巩县	Cengong	18587	13117	1251	3732	487
天柱县	Tianzhu	55610	52912	1900		798
锦屏县	Jinping	178237	173414	302		4521
剑河县	Jianhe	67186	67186			
台江县	Taijiang	40528	37564	720		2244
黎平县	Liping	41346	32713			8633
榕江县	Rongjiang	8443	6530	615	1005	293
从江县	Congjiang	21443	18054	254	55	3080
雷山县	Leishan	11848	4840	196	2938	3874
麻江县	Majiang	6901	4635	1090	576	600
丹寨县	Danzhai	13341	11488	993	860	
都匀市	Duyun	116283	39952	23554	1955	50822
福泉市	Fuquan	61151	3706	52360	118	4967
荔波县	Libo	22580	19850	30		2700
贵定县	Guiding	17352	5105	10119		2128
瓮安县	Wengan	19699	5349	9468		4882
独山县	Dushan	11303	8727	2271		305
平塘县	Pingtang	10679	8059	750	238	1632
罗甸县	Luodian	28860	9858	14216	891	3895
长顺县	Changshun	14358	12288	2070		
龙里县	Longli	34047	8437	23100		2510
惠水县	Huishui	40665	21560	16676		2429
※三都县	Sandu	11866	6111	3809	1468	478

23-34各县(市、区)乡村从业人员（2005）

Number of Rural Employment by County (City,Section)(2005)

单位:万人(10000 persons)

县(市、区)名　称	County (City,Section)	乡村从业人员 Rural Employment	第一产业 Primary Industry	第二产业 Secondary Industry	第三产业 Tertiary Industry	2005年比2004年增长(%) Increase Rate in 2005 over2004(%)
南明区	Nanming	1.92	0.82	0.36	0.74	5.5
云岩区	Yunyan	2.24	1.22	0.19	0.83	53.4
花溪区	Huaxi	13.67	9.16	1.34	3.18	0.8
乌当区	Wudang	13.57	7.66	2.43	3.48	2.0
白云区	Baiyun	4.49	2.54	0.88	1.07	-4.7
小河区	Xiaohe	1.85	0.88	0.34	0.63	0.5
开阳县	Kaiyang	20.75	13.77	1.36	5.62	-1.2
息烽县	Xifeng	12.38	7.74	0.97	3.68	1.0
修文县	Xiuwen	15.61	10.56	1.30	3.75	1.4
清镇市	Qingzhen	24.60	17.27	2.01	5.33	-1.0
钟山区	Zhongshan	8.09	5.63	1.14	1.32	0.2
六枝特区	Liuzhi	29.10	17.22	2.64	9.23	2.8
水城县	Shuicheng	37.00	26.85	2.30	7.85	3.1
盘　县	Panxian	52.62	39.53	3.24	9.84	1.2
红花岗区	Honghuagang	12.19	7.57	1.47	3.15	1.1
汇川区	Huicuan	11.78	6.82	1.41	3.56	-2.6
遵义县	Zunyi	63.76	41.47	4.34	17.94	0.6
桐梓县	Tongzi	31.52	19.20	2.18	10.14	1.5
绥阳县	Suiyang	28.93	19.08	1.19	8.66	1.4
正安县	Zhengan	33.02	17.50	1.57	13.95	-3.6
※道真县	Daozhen	18.57	9.58	0.64	8.35	10.5
※务川县	Wuchuan	24.39	16.58	0.51	7.29	0.5
凤冈县	Fenggang	24.28	14.82	1.18	8.29	-1.1
湄潭县	Meitan	26.59	16.57	1.18	8.84	-1.0
余庆县	Yuqing	16.86	10.40	0.98	5.48	3.9
习水县	Xishui	33.65	20.57	2.11	10.97	7.6
赤水市	Chishui	13.19	7.83	0.95	4.41	-0.1
仁怀市	Renhuai	32.68	21.65	1.77	9.27	-1.9
西秀区	Xixiu	35.38	22.80	4.31	8.28	1.8
平坝县	Pingba	17.10	13.56	0.98	2.56	1.2

23-34续表1(continued)

单位:万人(10000 persons)

县(市、区)名 称	County (City,Section)	乡村从业人员 Rural Employment	第一产业 Primary Industry	第二产业 Secondary Industry	第三产业 Tertiary Industry	2005年比2004年增长(%) Increase Rate in 2005 over2004(%)
普定县	Puding	22.99	15.00	1.25	6.74	7.8
※镇宁县	Zhenning	19.16	15.64	1.09	2.43	0.4
※关岭县	Guanling	17.99	12.63	0.99	4.37	0.8
※紫云县	Ziyun	20.04	13.85	1.71	4.48	-0.1
铜仁市	Tongren	15.63	8.21	1.58	5.85	1.0
江口县	Jiangkou	11.83	7.75	0.71	3.37	-9.5
※玉屏县	Yuping	7.35	4.12	0.98	2.26	0.4
石阡县	Shiqian	23.31	14.36	1.31	7.64	0.1
思南县	Sinan	36.22	22.23	1.83	12.17	2.0
※印江县	Yinjiang	23.82	13.13	2.52	8.17	4.7
德江县	Dejiang	26.90	18.76	1.32	6.81	0.6
※沿河县	Yanhe	30.02	20.14	0.85	9.03	2.3
※松桃县	Songtao	38.64	23.79	2.23	12.61	1.4
万山特区	Wanshan	2.83	1.40	0.17	1.26	1.1
兴义市	Xingyi	37.56	27.08	3.34	7.15	3.6
兴仁县	Xingren	24.81	17.23	1.89	5.70	0.3
普安县	Puan	14.35	10.23	0.60	3.53	3.6
晴隆县	Qinglong	15.52	12.06	0.36	3.10	1.0
贞丰县	Zhenfeng	20.12	13.63	1.16	5.33	3.8
望谟县	Wangmo	14.89	12.10	0.66	2.13	1.1
册亨县	Ceheng	11.67	9.29	0.18	2.20	0.4
安龙县	Anlong	23.99	16.34	1.12	6.52	-0.1
毕节市	Bijie	65.84	36.58	5.13	24.13	1.9
大方县	Dafang	58.61	39.35	4.33	14.93	2.1
黔西县	Qianxi	45.85	28.91	4.09	12.85	7.9
金沙县	Jinsha	33.19	19.92	4.17	9.10	7.5
织金县	Zhijin	49.25	29.00	6.04	14.22	2.1
纳雍县	Nayong	42.23	25.01	3.84	13.38	0.5
※威宁县	Weining	61.68	48.86	3.49	9.33	2.1

23-34续表2(continued)

单位:万人(10000 persons)

县(市、区)名称	County (City,Section)	乡村从业人员 Rural Employment	第一产业 Primary Industry	第二产业 Secondary Industry	第三产业 Tertiary Industry	2005年比2004年增长(%) Increase Rate in 2005 over2004(%)
赫章县	Hezhang	33.04	22.21	3.06	7.76	2.3
凯里市	Kaili	15.98	10.38	1.43	4.16	4.3
黄平县	Huangping	18.23	11.66	1.34	5.23	2.6
施秉县	Shibing	8.34	6.45	0.27	1.62	1.2
三穗县	Sansui	11.17	7.20	0.69	3.28	0.9
镇远县	Zhenyuan	11.91	7.57	1.13	3.21	-2.9
岑巩县	Cengong	11.26	7.75	0.31	3.19	0.3
天柱县	Tianzhu	22.55	15.06	1.10	6.39	0.5
锦屏县	Jinping	11.02	6.30	0.38	4.33	0.1
剑河县	Jianhe	13.36	9.12	0.43	3.80	1.3
台江县	Taijiang	6.96	3.78	0.69	2.48	-0.6
黎平县	Liping	26.48	17.55	0.71	8.22	-0.1
榕江县	Rongjiang	17.70	13.14	0.59	3.97	2.0
从江县	Congjiang	18.39	14.61	0.32	3.45	-0.8
雷山县	Leishan	7.91	4.99	0.29	2.63	0.5
麻江县	Majiang	11.59	8.32	0.61	2.66	0.5
丹寨县	Danzhai	8.75	5.09	0.53	3.13	4.3
都匀市	Duyun	18.20	11.12	1.35	5.73	2.6
福泉市	Fuquan	15.78	10.20	1.74	3.83	2.5
荔波县	Libo	9.04	6.50	0.35	2.19	0.3
贵定县	Guiding	13.56	9.17	0.70	3.70	1.3
瓮安县	Wengan	24.58	14.85	1.24	8.50	6.4
独山县	Dushan	18.53	12.05	1.12	5.35	-0.9
平塘县	Pingtang	18.49	13.36	0.89	4.25	1.3
罗甸县	Luodian	16.65	11.07	0.76	4.83	1.2
长顺县	Changshun	13.03	9.04	0.63	3.35	-4.9
龙里县	Longli	11.08	8.35	0.53	2.19	1.5
惠水县	Huishui	24.85	15.35	2.05	7.44	2.7
※三都县	Sandu	17.66	12.42	0.62	4.63	1.6

23-35 各县(市、区)常用耕地面积(2005)

Cultivated Areas for Frequently Use by County(City,Section)(2005)

单位:公顷 (hectare)

县(市、区)名称	County (City,Section)	常用耕地面积 Cultivated Area for Frequently Use	#水田 Paddy Fields	#水浇地 Fields Irrigated by Water
南明区	Nanming	205		205
云岩区	Yunyan	238	2	25
花溪区	Huaxi	11868	6568	1438
乌当区	Wudang	9638	6810	1108
白云区	Baiyun	2694	1512	1053
小河区	Xiaohe	300	125	55
开阳县	Kaiyang	22693	9272	2761
息烽县	Xifeng	13243	5166	
修文县	Xiuwen	15790	6287	190
清镇市	Qingzhen	17251	6238	9239
钟山区	Zhongshan	3483	111	
六枝特区	Liuzhi	25776	10029	
水城县	Shuicheng	33201	4261	
盘县	Panxian	44197	6741	
红花岗区	Honghuagang	9207	5525	3681
汇川区	Huicuan	10368	5951	442
遵义县	Zunyi	66064	33141	6282
桐梓县	Tongzi	36410	12469	20752
绥阳县	Suiyang	27493	14151	12342
正安县	Zhengan	31157	15796	14568
※道真县	Daozhen	23470	14830	7859
※务川县	Wuchuan	28375	11274	16231
凤冈县	Fenggang	26517	14525	11232
湄潭县	Meitan	31026	19195	6656
余庆县	Yuqing	19162	11425	2335
习水县	Xishui	40671	14397	21
赤水市	Chishui	13566	10806	1139
仁怀市	Renhuai	27768	9855	2956
西秀区	Xixiu	27727	18510	713
平坝县	Pingba	17350	9444	30

23-35续表1(continued) 单位:公顷 (hectare)

县(市、区)名 称	County (City,Section)	常用耕地面积 Cultivated Area for Frequently Use	#水田 Paddy Fields	#水浇地 Fields Irrigated by Water
普定县	Puding	16475	7197	205
※镇宁县	Zhenning	13841	8018	133
※关岭县	Guanling	14991	5434	
※紫云县	Ziyun	15906	6634	149
铜仁市	Tongren	12451	7788	1477
江口县	Jiangkou	11014	7164	
※玉屏县	Yuping	5631	3920	
石阡县	Shiqian	20805	12560	
思南县	Sinan	28823	17712	
※印江县	Yinjiang	18424	11867	
德江县	Dejiang	21606	13412	
※沿河县	Yanhe	26412	11119	15292
※松桃县	Songtao	26335	16981	
万山特区	Wanshan	2255	1552	
兴义市	Xingyi	29353	9083	358
兴仁县	Xingren	20713	8391	1172
普安县	Puan	16507	5008	
晴隆县	Qinglong	14013	4615	20
贞丰县	Zhenfeng	20353	6845	
望谟县	Wangmo	26637	5450	
册亨县	Ceheng	13467	4292	9175
安龙县	Anlong	20472	9802	2745
毕节市	Bijie	59162	6421	1129
大方县	Dafang	50100	4875	254
黔西县	Qianxi	40408	8705	3
金沙县	Jinsha	34187	10828	
织金县	Zhijin	40890	10275	39
纳雍县	Nayong	30761	4154	
※威宁县	Weining	71933	613	401

23-35续表2(continued)　　单位:公顷　(hectare)

县(市、区)名　称	County (City,Section)	常用耕地面积 Cultivated Area for Frequently Use	#水田 Paddy Fields	#水浇地 Fields Irrigated by Water
赫章县	Hezhang	37838	1214	227
凯里市	Kaili	13432	9331	
黄平县	Huangping	15218	10987	
施秉县	Shibing	8126	4699	
三穗县	Sansui	7691	5419	
镇远县	Zhenyuan	12309	7415	
岑巩县	Cengong	11708	7373	
天柱县	Tianzhu	15935	11606	
锦屏县	Jinping	8570	6735	
剑河县	Jianhe	9031	7567	
台江县	Taijiang	6239	4966	
黎平县	Liping	18587	17644	
榕江县	Rongjiang	12702	10408	
从江县	Congjiang	13896	11892	
雷山县	Leishan	6847	5571	
麻江县	Majiang	10961	7018	
丹寨县	Danzhai	7330	5917	
都匀市	Duyun	13615	10429	2000
福泉市	Fuquan	15467	7925	4542
荔波县	Libo	7996	6356	1040
贵定县	Guiding	11928	6894	500
瓮安县	Wengan	25792	11672	
独山县	Dushan	15203	12638	
平塘县	Pingtang	14343	8592	3751
罗甸县	Luodian	16820	7149	
长顺县	Changshun	12802	6067	
龙里县	Longli	10860	6622	
惠水县	Huishui	17851	11515	
※三都县	Sandu	13549	9878	

23-36 各县(市、区)农林牧渔业总产值及位次（2005）

Gross Output Value of Farming,Forestry,Animal Husbandry and Fishery and Its Order by County(City,Section)(2005)

单位:万元 (10000 yuan)

县(市、区)名称	County (City,Section)	农林牧渔业总产值 Gross Output Value of Farming, Forestry,Animal Husbandry and Fishery	农业 Farming	林业 Forestry	牧业 Animal Husbandry	渔业 Fishery	服务业 Services	位次 Order	2005年比2004年增长(%) Increase Rate in 2005 over 2004(%)
南明区	Nanming	6978	3441	1	3377	114	45	87	-10.8
云岩区	Yunyan	4215	2359	1	1798	5	52	88	-0.4
花溪区	Huaxi	80257	50558	644	28545	380	130	39	7.9
乌当区	Wudang	94593	63400	569	29086	808	730	28	9.6
白云区	Baiyun	27352	14975	363	11412	202	400	80	5.9
小河区	Xiaohe	9098	6742	10	2002	298	46	86	7.8
开阳县	Kaiyang	107459	50020	763	55333	553	790	21	7.6
息烽县	Xifeng	51734	30126	406	18987	1872	343	58	10.7
修文县	Xiuwen	76264	41951	943	32337	832	201	44	11.2
清镇市	Qingzhen	89713	50106	814	32809	5582	402	30	9.2
钟山区	Zhongshan	25459	10380	219	13770	70	1020	82	15.7
六枝特区	Liuzhi	59751	38071	1441	16872	150	3217	54	5.9
水城县	Shuicheng	86773	55037	2576	27745	15	1400	35	9.1
盘 县	Panxian	120773	66733	4489	47353	253	1945	15	9.6
红花岗区	Honghuagang	71115	41113	811	27403	485	1303	47	6.7
汇川区	Huicuan	56090	27544	454	25415	239	2438	56	6.6
遵义县	Zunyi	324791	183308	3787	123949	9551	4196	1	8.4
桐梓县	Tongzi	138661	78234	10077	49099	880	371	10	5.3
绥阳县	Suiyang	147124	98124	2548	43978	934	1540	6	6.7
正安县	Zhengan	131083	71265	5919	52512	427	960	11	4.8
※道真县	Daozhen	78567	40714	3409	33354	392	698	41	2.0
※务川县	Wuchuan	85235	53654	3438	26543	275	1325	36	3.7
凤冈县	Fenggang	98911	51649	10533	35807	302	620	25	3.8
湄潭县	Meitan	105596	63978	1285	37283	973	2077	22	5.2
余庆县	Yuqing	103729	58823	1111	42359	584	852	23	6.7
习水县	Xishui	112489	58280	3537	49522	384	766	19	8.1
赤水市	Chishui	89636	40189	11244	35998	1003	1202	31	9.1
仁怀市	Renhuai	128378	64770	5947	54777	849	2035	13	4.4
西秀区	Xixiu	112702	70712	889	39974	722	405	18	9.5
平坝县	Pingba	50708	30389	581	18434	1016	288	61	10.6

23-36续表1(continued) 单位:万元 (10000 yuan)

县(市、区)名称	County (City,Section)	农林牧渔业总产值 Gross Output Value of Farming, Forestry,Animal Husbandry and Fishery	农业 Farming	林业 Forestry	牧业 Animal Husbandry	渔业 Fishery	服务业 Services	位次 Order	2005年比2004年增长(%) Increase Rate in 2005 over 2004(%)
普定县	Puding	51370	28329	547	20668	1248	578	60	10.7
※镇宁县	Zhenning	41489	25957	1865	12782	714	171	71	8.4
※关岭县	Guanling	60211	36665	2818	20317	326	85	53	9.8
※紫云县	Ziyun	55160	24706	4519	24396	570	969	57	11.5
铜仁市	Tongren	80408	52368	1100	23990	1492	1458	38	6.4
江口县	Jiangkou	50156	28549	959	18799	926	923	63	7.7
※玉屏县	Yuping	39108	22800	463	13746	722	1377	72	8.5
石阡县	Shiqian	91508	53895	938	35154	857	664	29	6.2
思南县	Sinan	138814	81087	887	53559	1655	1626	7	5.7
※印江县	Yinjiang	97598	54046	1282	39758	1479	1033	26	4.9
德江县	Dejiang	115393	70379	3595	39687	937	795	17	7.0
※沿河县	Yanhe	112137	68069	2196	38440	1156	2276	20	4.7
※松桃县	Songtao	129053	81201	2973	41725	1544	1610	12	4.3
万山特区	Wanshan	11670	6655	324	4335	237	119	85	6.4
兴义市	Xingyi	186939	83471	5214	90886	3979	3389	3	11.2
兴仁县	Xingren	77619	41484	2468	33417	67	183	43	7.7
普安县	Puan	41890	24104	3592	13569	67	558	69	8.3
晴隆县	Qinglong	38315	20754	2097	14945	21	498	73	6.2
贞丰县	Zhenfeng	62255	32699	4319	24603	108	526	50	5.1
望谟县	Wangmo	47722	24167	7754	14998	134	669	65	4.4
册亨县	Ceheng	44483	19739	5020	18699	73	952	67	7.2
安龙县	Anlong	80160	41840	2766	28422	5975	1157	40	7.0
毕节市	Bijie	203064	114304	2350	82262	408	3740	2	6.2
大方县	Dafang	138685	87686	1236	47735	240	1788	9	6.6
黔西县	Qianxi	148870	90467	2136	54429	149	1689	5	8.0
金沙县	Jinsha	127577	72102	645	52455	486	1889	14	4.5
织金县	Zhijin	138799	71580	982	63995	229	2013	8	7.3
纳雍县	Nayong	120075	68697	973	49151	289	965	16	5.8
※威宁县	Weining	167321	93361	1140	69649	78	3093	4	8.0

23-36续表2(continued)　　单位:万元　(10000 yuan)

县(市、区)名称	County (City,Section)	农林牧渔业总产值 Gross Output Value of Farming, Forestry,Animal Husbandry and Fishery	农业 Farming	林业 Forestry	牧业 Animal Husbandry	渔业 Fishery	服务业 Services	位次 Order	2005年比2004年增长(%) Increase Rate in 2005 over 2004(%)
赫章县	Hezhang	95377	59912	2057	32023	196	1189	27	10.2
凯里市	Kaili	71644	41527	3599	23868	1868	782	46	5.0
黄平县	Huangping	51613	29081	6161	14147	798	1426	59	7.7
施秉县	Shibing	29637	18290	1620	8432	585	710	79	4.2
三穗县	Sansui	31333	14703	2551	12853	245	981	78	3.2
镇远县	Zhenyuan	60868	35926	7122	17157	432	231	52	5.2
岑巩县	Cengong	37114	21209	1440	13275	266	924	75	6.4
天柱县	Tianzhu	64429	36982	4722	21703	612	410	49	10.7
锦屏县	Jinping	33375	14576	6502	10019	1607	671	77	6.0
剑河县	Jianhe	43130	17562	6074	17237	1807	450	68	4.8
台江县	Taijiang	23213	10125	5057	6314	1173	544	83	5.3
黎平县	Liping	89203	38880	8744	36587	3927	1065	32	7.1
榕江县	Rongjiang	61364	31446	7680	16600	5295	343	51	7.4
从江县	Congjiang	69155	34678	4866	26085	2700	826	48	6.3
雷山县	Leishan	20393	10445	1136	6867	919	1026	84	7.1
麻江县	Majiang	35196	20302	1713	12453	478	250	76	9.1
丹寨县	Danzhai	26772	13688	2062	9367	949	706	81	8.1
都匀市	Duyun	77983	32556	2160	37712	1055	4500	42	9.0
福泉市	Fuquan	81578	46763	710	33456	504	145	37	4.5
荔波县	Libo	37606	14688	5543	13380	1175	2820	74	5.4
贵定县	Guiding	50476	26022	1903	16877	120	5554	62	4.6
瓮安县	Wengan	87638	45415	3122	37226	495	1380	34	4.4
独山县	Dushan	88299	52011	2804	31755	973	756	33	9.3
平塘县	Pingtang	50121	27241	3250	18590	156	884	64	8.4
罗甸县	Luodian	72106	36402	6054	28435	309	906	45	5.8
长顺县	Changshun	47507	25763	1256	17559	204	2725	66	4.1
龙里县	Longli	41546	25450	620	15041	209	226	70	7.3
惠水县	Huishui	102758	49908	6315	39572	518	6445	24	7.4
※三都县	Sandu	57201	29481	3279	22042	1152	1247	55	7.9

23-37 各县(市、区)农民人均纯收入及位次（2005）

Per Capita Net Income of Rural Households and Its Order by County(City,Section)(2005)

县(市、区)名称	County (City,Section)	纯收入(元) Net Income (yuan)	位次 Order	县(市、区)名称	County (City,Section)	纯收入(元) Net Income (yuan)	位次 Order
南明区	Nanming	4653	2	湄潭县	Meitan	2604	14
云岩区	Yunyan	4669	1	余庆县	Yuqing	2829	12
花溪区	Huaxi	3220	6	习水县	Xishui	1760	45
乌当区	Wudang	3553	5	赤水市	Chishui	2512	17
白云区	Baiyun	3945	4	仁怀市	Renhuai	2496	18
小河区	Xiaohe	4079	3	西秀区	Xixiu	2466	20
开阳县	Kaiyang	2900	10	平坝县	Pingba	1976	32
息烽县	Xifeng	2372	21	普定县	Puding	1630	72
修文县	Xiuwen	2702	13	※镇宁县	※Zhenning	1521	84
清镇市	Qingzhen	2858	11	※关岭县	※Guanling	1590	78
钟山区	Zhongshan	2246	26	※紫云县	※Ziyun	1550	80
六枝特区	Liuzhi	1749	46	铜仁市	Tongren	2356	22
水城县	Shuicheng	1730	50	江口县	Jiangkou	1670	61
盘 县	Panxian	1923	34	※玉屏县	※Yuping	2302	24
红花岗区	Honghuagang	3141	8	石阡县	Shiqian	1633	70
汇川区	Huichuan	3220	6	思南县	Sinan	1506	86
遵义县	Zunyi	2907	9	※印江县	※Yinjiang	1695	58
桐梓县	Tongzi	2294	25	德江县	Dejiang	1538	81
绥阳县	Suiyang	2539	16	※沿河县	※Yanhe	1531	82
正安县	Zhengan	1765	43	※松桃县	※Songtao	1617	73
※道真县	※Daozhen	1680	59	万山特区	Wanshan	1482	87
※务川县	※Wuchuan	1598	77	兴义市	Xingyi	2568	15
凤冈县	Fenggang	2016	30	兴仁县	Xingren	1902	35

23-37续表(continude)

县(市、区) 名 称	County (City,Section)	纯收入(元) Net Income (yuan)	位次 Order	县(市、区) 名 称	County (City,Section)	纯收入(元) Net Income (yuan)	位次 Order
普安县	Puan	1706	55	锦屏县	Jinping	1584	79
晴隆县	Qinglong	1527	83	剑河县	Jianhe	1711	53
贞丰县	Zhenfeng	1805	41	台江县	Taijiang	1662	62
望谟县	Wangmo	1508	85	黎平县	Liping	1702	57
册亨县	Ceheng	1450	88	榕江县	Rongjiang	1613	74
安龙县	Anlong	1852	39	从江县	Congjiang	1705	56
毕节市	Bijie	2141	28	雷山县	Leishan	1600	76
大方县	Dafang	1605	75	麻江县	Majiang	1676	60
黔西县	Qianxi	1745	47	丹寨县	Danzhai	1712	51
金沙县	Jinsha	2306	23	都匀市	Duyun	2482	19
织金县	Zhijin	1707	54	福泉市	Fuquan	1902	35
纳雍县	Nayong	1656	63	荔波县	Libo	1655	65
※威宁县	※Weining	1642	69	贵定县	Guiding	1872	38
赫章县	Hezhang	1656	63	瓮安县	Wengan	2007	31
凯里市	Kaili	2177	27	独山县	Dushan	1761	44
黄平县	Huangping	1633	70	平塘县	Pingtang	1651	66
施秉县	Shibing	1882	37	罗甸县	Luodian	1648	68
三穗县	Sansui	1733	49	长顺县	Changshun	1712	51
镇远县	Zhenyuan	1840	40	龙里县	Longli	2028	29
岑巩县	Cengong	1739	48	惠水县	Huishui	1939	33
天柱县	Tianzhu	1776	42	※三都县	※Sandu	1651	66

23-38 各县(市、区)粮食、肉类产量及位次(2005)

Output of Grain, Meat and Its Order by County(City,Section)(2005)

县(市、区)名 称	County (City,Section)	粮食产量(万吨) Output of Grain (10000 tons)	位次 Order	2005年比2004年增长(%) Increase Rate in 2005 over 2004(%)	人均粮食产 量(公斤) Per Capita Output of Grain (kg)	位次 Order	肉类产量(吨) Output Meat (ton)	位次 Order	2005年比2004年增长(%) Increase Rate in 2005 over 2004(%)
南明区	Nanming						2932	86	-16.0
云岩区	Yunyan						1309	88	-20.6
花溪区	Huaxi	8.61	65	1.2	365	44	22414	40	8.4
乌当区	Wudang	6.52	74	0.5	300	83	20277	46	12.3
白云区	Baiyun	2.12	84	1.4	310	76	8319	80	7.8
小河区	Xiaohe	0.16	86	14.3	60	86	1556	87	0.3
开阳县	Kaiyang	13.19	38	-0.1	351	57	52621	6	11.2
息烽县	Xifeng	7.72	69	持平	363	46	15169	61	16.2
修文县	Xiuwen	9.77	55	7.1	382	36	30354	30	10.7
清镇市	Qingzhen	13.12	39	5.9	315	75	25639	34	4.6
钟山区	Zhongshan	2.43	83	5.7	171	85	11125	74	17.9
六枝特区	Liuzhi	18.31	23	3.1	358	50	19415	50	12.2
水城县	Shuicheng	24.29	17	3.2	340	63	27051	32	14.6
盘 县	Panxian	32.84	4	2.0	327	69	44819	13	13.1
红花岗区	Honghuagang	9.07	59	1.1	448	15	23986	38	11.8
汇川区	Huicuan	8.44	67	5.0	430	22	20559	45	11.3
遵义县	Zunyi	60.97	1	8.0	556	5	118429	1	22.5
桐梓县	Tongzi	29.17	8	1.1	481	8	46145	11	12.5
绥阳县	Suiyang	27.23	11	7.1	574	4	45573	12	12.2
正安县	Zhengan	25.76	13	-12.6	466	11	53801	5	19.4
※道真县	Daozhen	13.37	37	-11.0	437	21	32420	27	10.3
※务川县	Wuchuan	17.04	29	-8.9	426	24	25656	33	9.0
凤冈县	Fenggang	17.22	28	-2.2	439	18	35745	22	-2.8
湄潭县	Meitan	25.06	16	2.2	586	3	32887	26	4.8
余庆县	Yuqing	19.09	22	2.7	706	1	37412	19	10.5
习水县	Xishui	28.61	9	2.7	464	12	49461	10	14.2
赤水市	Chishui	14.99	33	3.5	672	2	29422	31	13.6
仁怀市	Renhuai	25.62	14	-4.0	469	10	52600	7	13.0
西秀区	Xixiu	20.86	20	0.9	351	57	35665	23	12.5
平坝县	Pingba	10.77	49	4.7	385	31	15300	60	18.2

23-38续表1(continued)

县(市、区)名 称	County (City,Section)	粮食产量（万吨）Output of Grain (10000 tons)	位次 Order	2005年比2004年增长（%）Increase Rate in 2005 over 2004(%)	人均粮食产 量（公斤）Per Capita Output of Grain (kg)	位次 Order	肉类产量（吨）Output Meat (ton)	位次 Order	2005年比2004年增长（%）Increase Rate in 2005 over 2004(%)
普定县	Puding	11.79	42	3.2	306	79	15934	55	16.1
※镇宁县	Zhenning	10.96	48	1.9	339	64	12177	71	15.3
※关岭县	Guanling	11.13	47	2.4	355	54	15000	62	20.5
※紫云县	Ziyun	11.59	44	-0.2	348	59	19927	49	21.6
铜仁市	Tongren	12.22	40	-8.1	514	7	22104	43	16.2
江口县	Jiangkou	9.01	60	0.9	444	16	18276	51	19.6
※玉屏县	Yuping	4.32	82	1.2	368	41	11831	72	9.7
石阡县	Shiqian	17.29	27	-1.6	471	9	33866	25	8.3
思南县	Sinan	22.40	19	-7.6	383	33	52034	8	33.1
※印江县	Yinjiang	13.74	35	-10.5	352	55	37260	21	12.2
德江县	Dejiang	16.02	30	-7.8	389	30	30504	29	14.0
※沿河县	Yanhe	15.83	31	-12.7	291	84	37277	20	17.2
※松桃县	Songtao	23.06	18	-9.6	370	40	38378	18	13.5
万山特区	Wanshan	1.77	85	-0.6	374	38	3661	85	11.6
兴义市	Xingyi	25.21	15	-1.2	406	28	68101	2	7.6
兴仁县	Xingren	17.50	26	3.9	413	26	31264	28	4.3
普安县	Puan	8.72	62	3.6	319	74	10437	76	16.8
晴隆县	Qinglong	8.88	61	1.8	337	67	12296	70	3.9
贞丰县	Zhenfeng	11.52	45	1.5	343	61	17100	53	8.7
望谟县	Wangmo	8.55	66	5.3	310	76	14833	63	30.2
册亨县	Ceheng	6.42	75	1.6	305	81	15431	59	5.4
安龙县	Anlong	17.52	25	3.1	438	19	25120	35	2.6
毕节市	Bijie	40.94	2	2.5	398	29	63296	3	6.3
大方县	Dafang	31.82	6	3.6	352	55	35546	24	10.0
黔西县	Qianxi	31.11	7	5.2	416	25	38890	16	7.5
金沙县	Jinsha	26.49	12	3.8	538	6	44048	14	5.3
织金县	Zhijin	32.77	5	5.0	375	37	49487	9	13.1
纳雍县	Nayong	28.11	10	3.0	383	33	39788	15	10.1
※威宁县	Weining	35.47	3	3.9	343	61	55428	4	9.8

23-38续表2(continued)

县(市、区)名称	County (City,Section)	粮食产量（万吨）Output of Grain (10000 tons)	位次 Order	2005年比2004年增长（%）Increase Rate in 2005 over 2004(%)	人均粮食产量（公斤）Per Capita Output of Grain (kg)	位次 Order	肉类产量（吨）Output Meat (ton)	位次 Order	2005年比2004年增长（%）Increase Rate in 2005 over 2004(%)
赫章县	Hezhang	20.50	21	3.3	327	69	24332	36	7.4
凯里市	Kaili	9.73	57	-7.0	339	64	22241	42	13.5
黄平县	Huangping	10.43	51	-7.7	321	72	13342	65	8.4
施秉县	Shibing	6.13	76	0.2	438	19	7668	82	6.5
三穗县	Sansui	5.83	77	1.0	308	78	12739	68	8.3
镇远县	Zhenyuan	8.69	63	-2.2	410	27	15974	54	9.4
岑巩县	Cengong	7.12	71	2.7	356	53	11572	73	11.2
天柱县	Tianzhu	13.50	36	3.7	372	39	20072	48	12.9
锦屏县	Jinping	6.69	73	1.1	338	66	12787	66	11.6
剑河县	Jianhe	6.79	72	-7.1	306	79	14672	64	11.1
台江县	Taijiang	4.61	81	2.7	357	52	7016	84	15.2
黎平县	Liping	15.68	32	2.1	334	68	22357	41	4.2
榕江县	Rongjiang	9.77	55	0.9	321	72	12771	67	11.4
从江县	Congjiang	11.81	41	5.0	385	31	18197	52	7.7
雷山县	Leishan	5.07	80	2.0	364	45	7165	83	11.7
麻江县	Majiang	7.17	70	-2.7	361	48	8638	79	12.4
丹寨县	Danzhai	5.33	79	1.9	368	41	8046	81	11.6
都匀市	Duyun	9.89	54	3.5	324	71	22618	39	12.9
福泉市	Fuquan	11.71	43	1.6	456	13	15530	58	9.9
荔波县	Libo	5.58	78	3.7	362	47	9548	77	26.2
贵定县	Guiding	8.66	64	1.8	360	49	11014	75	4.8
瓮安县	Wengan	18.30	24	0.1	452	14	38585	17	35.4
独山县	Dushan	11.18	46	1.4	366	43	20217	47	6.9
平塘县	Pingtang	10.20	52	5.5	345	60	15632	56	17.9
罗甸县	Luodian	10.62	50	5.0	358	50	24035	37	5.2
长顺县	Changshun	9.91	53	5.8	427	23	12552	69	11.9
龙里县	Longli	8.18	68	3.7	443	17	9445	78	16.8
惠水县	Huishui	14.97	34	4.0	383	33	21900	44	17.6
※三都县	Sandu	9.40	58	4.1	304	82	15580	57	16.5

23-39 各县(市、区)油菜籽、烤烟产量及位次(2005)

Output of Rapeseed and Flue-cured Tobacco and Its Order by County(City,Section)(2005)

县(市、区)名 称	County (City,Section)	油菜籽产量(吨) Output of Rapeseed (ton)	位次 Order	2005年比2004年增长(%) Increase Rate in 2005 over 2004(%)	烤烟产量(吨) Output of Fluecured Tobacco (ton)	位次 Order	2005年比2004年增长(%) Increase Rate in 2005 over 2004(%)
南明区	Nanming						
云岩区	Yunyan						
花溪区	Huaxi	2406	66	-4.2	117	63	515.8
乌当区	Wudang	4889	51	6.7			
白云区	Baiyun	1137	74	3.2			
小河区	Xiaohe	16	85				
开阳县	Kaiyang	23267	7	1.2	11911	7	2.4
息烽县	Xifeng	10236	22	13.2	2000	44	56.5
修文县	Xiuwen	8855	29	9.4	2329	41	17.8
清镇市	Qingzhen	10368	21	-1.6	4275	34	27.6
钟山区	Zhongshan						
六枝特区	Liuzhi	5658	44	4.8			
水城县	Shuicheng	85	84	46.6	4521	32	22.5
盘 县	Panxian	598	77	37.8	5107	30	14.7
红花岗区	Honghuagang	8239	32	10.6	35	65	持平
汇川区	Huicuan	9694	23	3.9	2157	42	55.9
遵义县	Zunyi	69132	1	7.2	12598	6	10.8
桐梓县	Tongzi	16243	12	-1.3	7595	16	4.5
绥阳县	Suiyang	33970	3	6.9	7853	15	21.8
正安县	Zhengan	22676	8	-2.0	9000	12	5.1
※道真县	Daozhen	7487	35	-22.2	8884	13	-8.6
※务川县	Wuchuan	10561	19	-5.0	13025	5	4.0
凤冈县	Fenggang	19857	10	-7.2	7485	17	20.1
湄潭县	Meitan	28610	5	-0.1	8100	14	6.4
余庆县	Yuqing	20246	9	1.7	9623	9	6.2
习水县	Xishui	5125	50	0.1	162	60	500.0
赤水市	Chishui	532	79	-31.2			
仁怀市	Renhuai	12316	15	4.2	3337	36	-5.8
西秀区	Xixiu	29096	4	-3.5	7229	20	24.9
平坝县	Pingba	10837	18	0.7	1064	55	72.4

23-39续表1(continued)

县(市、区)名　称	County (City,Section)	油菜籽产量(吨) Output of Rapeseed (ton)	位次 Order	2005年比2004年增长（%）Increase Rate in 2005 over 2004(%)	烤烟产量(吨) Output of Fluecured Tobacco(ton)	位次 Order	2005年比2004年增长（%）Increase Rate in 2005 over 2004(%)
普定县	Puding	11631	17	3.3	147	61	-9.3
※镇宁县	Zhenning	9361	27	1.5	144	62	800.0
※关岭县	Guanling	4472	54	4.4			
※紫云县	Ziyun	5392	47	-3.0	2066	43	53.9
铜仁市	Tongren	6960	36	7.1	341	57	409.0
江口县	Jiangkou	4425	56	28.1	1893	45	14.0
※玉屏县	Yuping	4408	57	16.5			
石阡县	Shiqian	11843	16	6.1	5469	29	11.0
思南县	Sinan	16966	11	10.8	7201	21	2.2
※印江县	Yinjiang	10535	20	5.8	6040	25	6.1
德江县	Dejiang	9624	24	2.8	7250	19	1.2
※沿河县	Yanhe	6831	39	7.2	6044	24	29.0
※松桃县	Songtao	14054	14	6.3	2835	38	360.2
万山特区	Wanshan	817	75	7.4			
兴义市	Xingyi	8310	31	-6.7	10501	8	14.8
兴仁县	Xingren	4208	61	0.5	6250	23	30.7
普安县	Puan	750	76	3.2	5616	27	46.4
晴隆县	Qinglong	581	78	-2.2	1262	54	-1.0
贞丰县	Zhenfeng	3766	63	-4.5	2547	39	8.6
望谟县	Wangmo	1915	72	-8.5			
册亨县	Ceheng	2062	71	38.5			
安龙县	Anlong	4548	53	34.3	1843	46	35.0
毕节市	Bijie	4297	59	5.4	17831	2	30.6
大方县	Dafang	7932	33	8.0	24092	1	16.4
黔西县	Qianxi	51952	2	1.1	16182	3	21.0
金沙县	Jinsha	27571	6	2.4	9141	11	0.2
织金县	Zhijin	9549	25	7.0	5927	26	87.0
纳雍县	Nayong	106	82	持平	5609	28	-15.6
※威宁县	Weining	119	81	-20.1	16148	4	1.0

23-39续表2(continued)

县(市、区)名 称	County (City,Section)	油菜籽产量(吨) Output of Rapeseed (ton)	位次 Order	2005年比2004年增长(%) Increase Rate in 2005 over 2004(%)	烤烟产量(吨) Output of Fluecured Tobacco(ton)	位次 Order	2005年比2004年增长(%) Increase Rate in 2005 over 2004(%)
赫章县	Hezhang	99	83	30.3	9381	10	36.3
凯里市	Kaili	2787	65	15.0	1473	53	24.7
黄平县	Huangping	5860	42	7.7	1538	50	48.3
施秉县	Shibing	4006	62	5.0	4480	33	-3.2
三穗县	Sansui	2214	68	6.0	29	66	-66.7
镇远县	Zhenyuan	6931	37	6.7	3003	37	2.5
岑巩县	Cengong	4333	58	6.6	599	56	45.4
天柱县	Tianzhu	4840	52	33.7	199	58	7.6
锦屏县	Jinping	4426	55	7.5			
剑河县	Jianhe	2087	70	-3.5	25	67	-19.4
台江县	Taijiang	2141	69	6.6			
黎平县	Liping	8419	30	5.9			
榕江县	Rongjiang	5616	45	2.0			
从江县	Congjiang	5158	49	17.0			
雷山县	Leishan	404	80	15.4			
麻江县	Majiang	3624	64	2.2	1750	48	24.3
丹寨县	Danzhai	1293	73	4.6	178	59	-14.0
都匀市	Duyun	6851	38	28.3	1504	52	48.6
福泉市	Fuquan	9172	28	0.2	4966	31	37.2
荔波县	Libo	5433	46	4.1	72	64	-27.3
贵定县	Guiding	5917	41	12.4	1594	49	20.5
瓮安县	Wengan	15058	13	-5.5	7285	18	18.9
独山县	Dushan	7774	34	23.9	2393	40	25.7
平塘县	Pingtang	9388	26	-2.0	3533	35	13.9
罗甸县	Luodian	2297	67	14.4			
长顺县	Changshun	6538	40	5.8	6357	22	15.9
龙里县	Longli	5299	48	8.3	1839	47	42.0
惠水县	Huishui	4209	60	13.2	1524	51	5.6
※三都县	Sandu	5830	43	9.5			

23-40 各县(市、区)乡镇企业主要指标(2005)

Major Indicators of Township and Village Enterprises by County(2005)

县(市、区)名称	County (City,Section)	企业单位数(个) Number of Enterprises (unit)	年末职工人数(人) Staff and Workers (year-end) (person)	营业收入(万元) Operating Revenue (10000 yuan)	实交国家税金(万元) Taxes Paid (10000 yuan)	利润总额(万元) Total Profits (10000 yuan)
南明区	Nanming	3236	27000	993080	18486	25214
云岩区	Yunyan	2163	30767	801442	21366	27035
花溪区	Huaxi	1344	26575	336641	6755	15706
乌当区	Wudang	5236	31949	596040	4510	48270
白云区	Baiyun	1962	28863	737824	9141	43333
小河区	Xiaohe	165	21804	361457	6011	10854
开阳县	Kaiyang	9370	36224	602123	11159	48757
息烽县	Xifeng	314	16324	336708	3852	20435
修文县	Xiuwen	5854	22320	267541	5882	23207
清镇市	Qingzhen	9422	40489	457835	5022	28767
钟山区	Zhongshan	22210	65256	537468	18709	62456
六枝特区	Liuzhi	16763	77756	397025	6958	27945
水城县	Shuicheng	4582	38410	331983	27216	14364
盘 县	Panxian	20406	114275	840209	43507	83129
红花岗区	Honghuagang	7828	35225	676932	12709	35389
汇川区	Huichuan	3471	29014	282740	11880	48333
遵义县	Zunyi	18255	79649	947844	17980	80121
桐梓县	Tongzi	10190	53581	378430	5876	22951
绥阳县	Suiyang	5672	20844	160712	2086	18577
正安县	Zhengan	5293	32070	160039	2143	7387
※道真县	※Daozhen	6823	26857	97343	2008	8557
※务川县	※Wuchuan	9651	25074	90173	883	9108
凤冈县	Fenggang	8185	26862	117449	1805	6353
湄潭县	Meitan	9611	34511	371335	3944	33623
余庆县	Yuqing	6619	21542	157455	2022	12612
习水县	Xishui	5206	23132	132900	3257	12095
赤水市	Chishui	8598	47194	368966	4734	11770
仁怀市	Renhuai	9322	57357	581202	9678	54339
西秀区	Xixiu	8891	39429	355185	4482	18980
平坝县	Pingba	4830	35257	240020	7122	13597

23-40续表1(continued)

县(市、区)名 称	County (City,Section)	企业单位数（个）Number of Enterprises (unit)	年末职工人数（人）Staff and Workers (year-end) (person)	营业收入（万元）Operating Revenue (10000 yuan)	实交国家税金（万元）Taxes Paid (10000 yuan)	利润总额（万元）Total Profits (10000 yuan)
普定县	Puding	6250	27378	265455	4935	39118
※镇宁县	Zhenning	2365	13981	87775	6529	11492
※关岭县	Guanling	3723	24503	92987	2799	4305
※紫云县	Ziyun	3497	15205	43808	1319	4161
铜仁市	Tongren	8928	23201	230080	2749	12984
江口县	Jiangkou	51	1874	6247	460	469
※玉屏县	Yuping	118	9337	67760	3393	4696
石阡县	Shiqian	374	7198	29650	797	1712
思南县	Sinan	6013	22829	93262	1460	6865
※印江县	Yinjiang	892	6569	21500	572	1846
德江县	Dejiang	6325	20493	51415	1140	2433
※沿河县	Yanhe	5830	21149	58947	832	5996
※松桃县	Songtao	1937	22642	60153	2138	3672
万山特区	Wanshan	305	2562	61174	2642	1662
兴义市	Xingyi	11590	88745	471246	11732	43919
兴仁县	Xingren	1935	23611	105280	8958	10485
普安县	Puan	1959	21723	63894	7273	10797
晴隆县	Qinglong	3953	23200	41100	1620	3007
贞丰县	Zhenfeng	1617	18071	55925	3156	5604
望谟县	Wangmo	4333	13522	26328	1159	1967
册亨县	Ceheng	5527	14311	19026	551	585
安龙县	Anlong	4104	23295	80109	5571	7072
毕节市	Bijie	15380	51877	412457	3880	35589
大方县	Dafang	9006	39876	155485	4403	18229
黔西县	Qianxi	8366	36281	164759	3362	15174
金沙县	Jinsha	7321	36011	496480	9128	60362
织金县	Zhijin	4003	35288	179455	4243	28607
纳雍县	Nayong	6715	53601	259085	6878	33788
※威宁县	※Weining	7994	34402	232045	18959	8885

23-40续表2(continued)

县(市、区)名 称	County (City,Section)	企业单位数(个) Number of Enterprises (unit)	年末职工人数(人) Staff and Workers (year-end) (person)	营业收入(万元) Operating Revenue (10000 yuan)	实交国家税 金(万元) Taxes Paid (10000 yuan)	利润总额(万元) Total Profits (10000 yuan)
赫章县	Hezhang	9108	39237	255617	7520	19803
凯里市	Kaili	5471	34061	204896	5770	5316
黄平县	Huangping	2406	8814	28644	526	2948
施秉县	Shibing	2774	10377	53661	2623	4157
三穗县	Sansui	2055	10516	30183	757	1448
镇远县	Zhenyuan	2894	82523	70107	2290	1780
岑巩县	Cengong	1866	4498	24153	1072	1046
天柱县	Tianzhu	3790	11711	41469	822	1592
锦屏县	Jinping	2906	12279	33895	652	2776
剑河县	Jianhe	1191	8461	49437	785	2188
台江县	Taijiang	14	1643	13066	469	741
黎平县	Liping	5391	16695	66068	1226	2335
榕江县	Rongjiang	1717	5229	56276	314	877
从江县	Congjiang	2529	6440	38176	509	2222
雷山县	Leishan	57	5282	22515	886	2313
麻江县	Majiang	2282	12759	73368	2821	2013
丹寨县	Danzhai	1838	4881	39845	898	3308
都匀市	Duyun	4551	29829	285845	3262	6927
福泉市	Fuquan	6992	27326	255926	5546	23975
荔波县	Libo	2393	8896	91197	4186	6301
贵定县	Guiding	3175	13901	70093	1833	6274
瓮安县	Wengan	3643	14676	186989	4472	15806
独山县	Dushan	6998	18860	177614	3940	13108
平塘县	Pingtang	288	4331	19378	672	213
罗甸县	Luodian	2683	15043	89654	3396	6086
长顺县	Changshun	2491	13138	58580	2100	4834
龙里县	Longli	2799	14774	233398	9372	10616
惠水县	Huishui	2992	20715	89147	2129	4611
※三都县	※Sandu	1628	14335	38331	885	1904

注：本表资料由省乡镇企业局提供的快报数（未包含各地、州、市开发区的数据）。

Note:Data in this table are obtained from Township and Village Enterprise Burea.

23-41 各县(市、区)规模以上工业总产值及位次(2005)

Total Gross Industrial Output Value and Its Order above Designated Size by County(City,Section)(2005)

单位:万元 (10000 yuan)

县(市、区)名称	County (City,Section)	工业总产值 Total Gross Industrial Output Value	位次 Order	轻工业产值 Output Value of Light Industry	重工业产值 Output Value of Heavy Industry
南明区	Nanming	712667	4	206580	506087
云岩区	Yunyan	1545879	1	961454	584425
花溪区	Huaxi	244836	15	53209	191627
乌当区	Wudang	609460	6	203844	405616
白云区	Baiyun	882806	3	69276	813530
小河区	Xiaohe	423228	11	128795	294433
开阳县	Kaiyang	321740	13	5584	316156
息烽县	Xifeng	419686	12	37976	381710
修文县	Xiuwen	148053	20	87488	60565
清镇市	Qingzhen	489751	9	45735	444016
钟山区	Zhongshan	1035472	2	13316	1022157
六枝特区	Liuzhi	110336	21	2711	107625
水城县	Shuicheng	222592	16	696	221896
盘 县	Panxian	566235	7	2137	564098
红花岗区	Honghuagang	682582	5	84485	598097
汇川区	Huicuan	160146	19	84266	75880
遵义县	Zunyi	423855	10	66384	357471
桐梓县	Tongzi	77627	23	5907	71720
绥阳县	Suiyang	30660	24	21107	9553
正安县	Zhengan	19402	26	11781	7621
※道真县	Daozhen	13184	29	5011	8173
※务川县	Wuchuan	7525	30	299	7226
凤冈县	Fenggang	15992	27	11286	4706
湄潭县	Meitan	15992	27	11286	4706
余庆县	Yuqing	20865	25	2156	18709
习水县	Xishui	190367	17	25157	165210
赤水市	Chishui	172106	18	15606	156500
仁怀市	Renhuai	500496	8	487776	12720
西秀区	Xixiu	264023	14	70379	193644
平坝县	Pingba	80998	22	13520	67478

23-41续表1(continued)

单位:万元(10000 yuan)

县(市、区)名 称	County (City,Section)	工业总产值 Total Gross Industrial Output Value	位次 Order	轻工业产值 Output Value of Light Industry	重工业产值 Output Value of Heavy Industry
普定县	Puding	174850	4	1230	173620
※镇宁县	Zhenning	56275	12	8044	48231
※关岭县	Guanling	35278	17	69	35209
※紫云县	Ziyun	19313	21	137	19176
铜仁市	Tongren	147438	5	15736	131702
江口县	Jiangkou	11137	26	218	10919
※玉屏县	Yuping	133239	6	4003	129236
石阡县	Shiqian	9125	27	5147	3978
思南县	Sinan	14908	23	3215	11693
※印江县	Yinjiang	14511	24	4439	10072
德江县	Dejiang	18592	22	5168	13424
※沿河县	Yanhe	12288	25	4934	7354
※松桃县	Songtao	120118	8	177	119941
万山特区	Wanshan	44148	16	107	44041
兴义市	Xingyi	522054	1	67491	454563
兴仁县	Xingren	50126	14	431	49695
普安县	Puan	45441	15	269	45172
晴隆县	Qinglong	19368	20	186	19182
贞丰县	Zhenfeng	53558	13	3071	50487
望谟县	Wangmo	5267	29	1068	4199
册亨县	Ceheng	6900	28	131	6769
安龙县	Anlong	57177	11	1105	56072
毕节市	Bijie	120234	7	14593	105640
大方县	Dafang	24919	19	205	24714
黔西县	Qianxi	65858	10	750	65108
金沙县	Jinsha	339541	2	19401	320140
织金县	Zhijin	26463	18	739	25724
纳雍县	Nayong	254830	3	244	254586
※威宁县	Weining	117108	9	2046	115062

23-41续表2(continued)

单位:万元(10000 yuan)

县(市、区)名 称	County (City,Section)	工业总产值 Total Gross Industrial Output Value	位次 Order	轻工业产值 Output Value of Light Industry	重工业产值 Output Value of Heavy Industry
赫章县	Hezhang	57857	10	140	57718
凯里市	Kaili	348401	2	21880	326521
黄平县	Huangping	6769	28	2030	4739
施秉县	Shibing	66738	9	102	66636
三穗县	Sansui	15723	23	5987	9736
镇远县	Zhenyuan	85453	6	4591	80862
岑巩县	Cengong	44203	13	712	43491
天柱县	Tianzhu	21410	18	245	21165
锦屏县	Jinping	10332	27	3119	7213
剑河县	Jianhe	2709	29	114	2595
台江县	Taijiang	18012	19	84	17928
黎平县	Liping	33348	16	897	32451
榕江县	Rongjiang	14114	24	2026	12088
从江县	Congjiang	13300	25	300	13000
雷山县	Leishan	17501	20	341	17160
麻江县	Majiang	49667	12	111	49556
丹寨县	Danzhai	17214	21	1554	15660
都匀市	Duyun	190266	3	45342	144923
福泉市	Fuquan	440579	1	2048	438530
荔波县	Libo	26597	17	410	26187
贵定县	Guiding	38570	15	10742	27828
瓮安县	Wengan	74155	7	4459	69696
独山县	Dushan	67136	8	3732	63405
平塘县	Pingtang	17105	22	1553	15552
罗甸县	Luodian	50149	11	28437	21712
长顺县	Changshun	41149	14	197	40952
龙里县	Longli	176857	4	86323	90534
惠水县	Huishui	96771	5	12713	84058
※三都县	Sandu	13120	26	714	12406

23-42 各县(市、区)社会消费品零售总额(2005)

Total Retail Sales of Consumer Goods by County (City, Section)(2005)

单位:万元(10000 yuan)

县(市、区)名称	County (City,Section)	社会消费品零售总额 Total Retail Sales of Consumer Goods	市、县 City and County	县以下 Below County Level	位次 Order
南明区	Nanming	645324	645324		2
云岩区	Yunyan	829947	829947		1
花溪区	Huaxi	72011	72011		14
乌当区	Wudang	42379	42379		19
白云区	Baiyun	69053	69053		16
小河区	Xiaohe	148087	148087		8
开阳县	Kaiyang	71752	41956	29796	15
息烽县	Xifeng	39235	28054	11181	21
修文县	Xiuwen	41617	17589	24028	20
清镇市	Qingzhen	73101	52144	20957	13
钟山区	Zhongshan	309875	309875		4
六枝特区	Liuzhi	74072	64665	9407	12
水城县	Shuicheng	37366	6440	30926	25
盘 县	Panxian	159313	83990	75323	6
红花岗区	Honghuagang	402002	402002		3
汇川区	Huicuan	159332	159332		5
遵义县	Zunyi	144963	48673	96290	9
桐梓县	Tongzi	48661	19464	29197	17
绥阳县	Suiyang	38070	22795	15275	23
正安县	Zhengan	30324	13949	16375	28
※道真县	Daozhen	18518	8250	10268	30
※务川县	Wuchuan	28154	12951	15203	29
凤冈县	Fenggang	32155	17242	14913	26
湄潭县	Meitan	37627	22576	15051	24
余庆县	Yuqing	48491	33881	14610	18
习水县	Xishui	78034	51350	26684	11
赤水市	Chishui	38756	29727	9029	22
仁怀市	Renhuai	117316	53016	64300	10
西秀区	Xixiu	149624	96874	52750	7
平坝县	Pingba	31946	12894	19052	27

23-42续表1(continued)　　单位:万元(10000 yuan)

县(市、区)名 称	County (City,Section)	社会消费品零售总额 Total Retail Sales of Consumer Goods	市、县 City and County	县以下 Below County Level	位次 Order
普定县	Puding	21817	11280	10537	20
※镇宁县	Zhenning	26434	13770	12664	16
※关岭县	Guanling	26740	11403	15337	15
※紫云县	Ziyun	23649	11287	12362	18
铜仁市	Tongren	89961	67858	22103	2
江口县	Jiangkou	18027	11304	6723	24
※玉屏县	Yuping	18883	10786	8097	23
石阡县	Shiqian	20906	8676	12230	21
思南县	Sinan	44260	20359	23901	8
※印江县	Yinjiang	22322	14274	8048	19
德江县	Dejiang	28322	17382	10940	14
※沿河县	Yanhe	30551	16004	14547	13
※松桃县	Songtao	37897	21143	16754	11
万山特区	Wanshan	5900	3606	2294	29
兴义市	Xingyi	237653	163981	73672	1
兴仁县	Xingren	39895	23138	16757	10
普安县	Puan	14157	7401	6756	26
晴隆县	Qinglong	14685	10260	4425	25
贞丰县	Zhenfeng	19292	13270	6022	22
望谟县	Wangmo	10091	4541	5550	27
册亨县	Ceheng	7509	4976	2533	28
安龙县	Anlong	24513	13306	11207	17
毕节市	Bijie	78164	59317	18847	3
大方县	Dafang	57162	24054	33108	4
黔西县	Qianxi	43877	24132	19745	9
金沙县	Jinsha	47251	25187	22064	6
织金县	Zhijin	49902	19335	30567	5
纳雍县	Nayong	37881	17472	20409	12
※威宁县	Weining	44558	19500	25058	7

23-42续表2(continued)

单位:万元(10000 yuan)

县(市、区)名 称	County (City,Section)	社会消费品零售总额 Total Retail Sales of Consumer Goods	市、县 City and County	县以下 Below County Level	位次 Order
赫章县	Hezhang	30550	13202	17348	6
凯里市	Kaili	165465	129951	35514	1
黄平县	Huangping	19724	10262	9462	18
施秉县	Shibing	15462	10154	5308	24
三穗县	Sansui	25518	15857	9661	11
镇远县	Zhenyuan	25758	13665	12093	10
岑巩县	Cengong	20776	12681	8095	17
天柱县	Tianzhu	35947	18084	17863	5
锦屏县	Jinping	24697	15053	9644	12
剑河县	Jianhe	17282	10683	6599	23
台江县	Taijiang	11001	6763	4238	28
黎平县	Liping	39561	20196	19365	4
榕江县	Rongjiang	23197	14124	9073	14
从江县	Congjiang	21188	11067	10121	16
雷山县	Leishan	10982	6437	4545	29
麻江县	Majiang	14693	7033	7660	25
丹寨县	Danzhai	11232	8265	2967	27
都匀市	Duyun	117058	104270	12788	2
福泉市	Fuquan	44839	19895	24944	3
荔波县	Libo	19113	12124	6989	20
贵定县	Guiding	24181	14579	9602	13
瓮安县	Wengan	29825	19431	10394	8
独山县	Dushan	29880	14558	15322	7
平塘县	Pingtang	14504	9074	5430	26
罗甸县	Luodian	19440	10765	8675	19
长顺县	Changshun	18947	10638	8309	22
龙里县	Longli	19021	11412	7609	21
惠水县	Huishui	26496	17275	9221	9
※三都县	Sandu	22775	9791	12984	15

23-43 各县(市、区)财政一般预算收入及位次（2005）

Revenne of Local Government and Its Order by County(City, Section)(2005)

县(市、区)名　称	County (City,Section)	财政一般预算收入(万元) Revenue of Local Governments (10000 yuan)	位次 Order	2005年比2004年增长(%) Increase Rate in 2005 over 2004(%)	人均财政一般预算收入(元) Per Capita Revenue of Local Governments(yuan)	位次 Order
南明区	Nanming	52542	2	24.6	1034.87	4
云岩区	Yunyan	53471	1	19.3	965.84	5
花溪区	Huaxi	18548	19	20.8	571.59	6
乌当区	Wudang	32280	5	31.7	1046.30	3
白云区	Baiyun	30887	7	20.0	1766.70	2
小河区	Xiaohe	22193	15	16.4	1853.18	1
开阳县	Kaiyang	18933	16	16.4	430.80	13
息烽县	Xifeng	11909	29	36.7	456.01	12
修文县	Xiuwen	10491	32	17.8	339.89	25
清镇市	Qingzhen	22317	14	26.9	427.94	14
钟山区	Zhongshan	23591	13	102.2	544.07	9
六枝特区	Liuzhi	12123	28	2.7	188.33	42
水城县	Shuicheng	16505	21	44.4	216.88	36
盘　县	Panxian	45004	3	45.3	381.73	20
红花岗区	Honghuagang	30115	9	20.3	559.39	7
汇川区	Huicuan	16081	22	27.5	475.28	11
遵义县	Zunyi	26601	10	23.7	229.47	33
桐梓县	Tongzi	9500	34	37.9	142.51	56
绥阳县	Suiyang	6501	49	3.2	126.27	65
正安县	Zhengan	5109	61	1.7	83.71	85
※道真县	Daozhen	4150	69	2.5	121.42	67
※务川县	Wuchuan	4558	66	2.4	106.90	74
凤冈县	Fenggang	4241	68	1.5	101.51	77
湄潭县	Meitan	7009	46	16.7	145.95	53
余庆县	Yuqing	7813	42	13.5	263.80	30
习水县	Xishui	9043	37	20.0	129.17	63
赤水市	Chishui	9450	35	13.3	300.10	28
仁怀市	Renhuai	33875	4	26.2	555.58	8
西秀区	Xixiu	31289	6	29.5	375.15	21
平坝县	Pingba	8544	38	25.2	240.72	32

23-43续表1(continued)

县(市、区)名 称	County (City,Section)	财政一般预算收入(万元) Revenue of Local Governments (10000 yuan)	位次 Order	2005年比2004年增长(%) Increase Rate in 2005 over 2004(%)	人均财政一般预算收入(元) Per Capita Revenue of Local Governments(yuan)	位次 Order
普定县	Puding	9097	36	12.0	218.50	35
※镇宁县	Zhenning	5660	56	9.7	160.73	48
※关岭县	Guanling	4966	62	32.8	150.52	51
※紫云县	Ziyun	2955	77	10.7	85.34	84
铜仁市	Tongren	13322	27	15.6	386.14	18
江口县	Jiangkou	3002	75	13.1	131.83	60
※玉屏县	Yuping	7242	44	2.4	506.11	10
石阡县	Shiqian	5380	59	11.3	138.16	57
思南县	Sinan	8005	41	22.3	124.18	66
※印江县	Yinjiang	4870	64	9.6	115.83	72
德江县	Dejiang	5952	52	10.0	130.04	62
※沿河县	Yanhe	5866	54	15.8	103.08	76
※松桃县	Songtao	6179	50	20.9	94.99	83
万山特区	Wanshan	1518	88	33.7	226.82	34
兴义市	Xingyi	30598	8	22.5	407.89	16
兴仁县	Xingren	11907	30	40.8	254.17	31
普安县	Puan	10209	33	22.8	349.86	24
晴隆县	Qinglong	5119	60	25.3	175.41	46
贞丰县	Zhenfeng	7005	47	21.7	199.01	39
望谟县	Wangmo	2782	79	16.7	96.79	80
册亨县	Ceheng	2161	85	18.6	95.98	81
安龙县	Anlong	8297	40	14.0	189.90	41
毕节市	Bijie	24419	12	13.9	187.25	43
大方县	Dafang	15409	23	29.1	155.95	50
黔西县	Qianxi	14434	26	22.4	171.78	47
金沙县	Jinsha	24759	11	30.5	415.80	15
织金县	Zhijin	18865	18	34.7	199.43	38
纳雍县	Nayong	15037	24	20.3	193.38	40
※威宁县	Weining	14648	25	16.8	131.66	61

23-43续表2(continued)

县(市、区)名 称	County (City,Section)	财政一般预算收入(万元) Revenue of Local Governments (10000 yuan)	位次 Order	2005年比2004年增长(%) Increase Rate in 2005 over 2004(%)	人均财政一般预算收入(元) Per Capita Revenue of Local Governments(yuan)	位次 Order
赫章县	Hezhang	7189	45	61.7	109.65	73
凯里市	Kaili	18086	20	15.1	393.26	17
黄平县	Huangping	3436	72	10.7	96.93	79
施秉县	Shibing	5688	55	40.5	361.62	23
三穗县	Sansui	2669	80	14.6	127.09	64
镇远县	Zhenyuan	7250	43	17.7	278.42	29
岑巩县	Cengong	2603	82	23.5	116.20	71
天柱县	Tianzhu	4931	63	9.3	119.23	69
锦屏县	Jinping	3283	73	6.6	145.27	54
剑河县	Jianhe	2520	83	17.6	103.28	75
台江县	Taijiang	2172	84	9.5	148.11	52
黎平县	Liping	3462	71	5.8	67.98	88
榕江县	Rongjiang	2783	78	12.4	83.54	86
从江县	Congjiang	3087	74	10.4	95.57	82
雷山县	Leishan	1782	86	25.1	117.79	70
麻江县	Majiang	3002	75	9.6	134.83	59
丹寨县	Danzhai	1625	87	12.7	98.22	78
都匀市	Duyun	18902	17	20.5	384.42	19
福泉市	Fuquan	11630	31	20.1	372.28	22
荔波县	Libo	5556	57	12.9	326.26	27
贵定县	Guiding	5901	53	-11.3	202.24	37
瓮安县	Wengan	8470	39	16.6	182.05	44
独山县	Dushan	5515	58	16.6	156.27	49
平塘县	Pingtang	3709	70	21.9	120.66	68
罗甸县	Luodian	4762	65	9.2	143.14	55
长顺县	Changshun	4491	67	9.0	179.87	45
龙里县	Longli	6882	48	20.0	331.26	26
惠水县	Huishui	5970	51	15.6	136.59	58
※三都县	Sandu	2639	81	14.3	79.80	87

23-44 各县(市、区)财政一般预算支出及位次（2005）

Expenditures of Local Government and Its Order by County(City, Section)(2005)

县(市、区)名　称	County (City,Section)	财政支出(万元) Expenditures of Governments (10000 yuan)	位次 Order	2005年比2004年增长(%) Increase Rate in 2005 over 2004(%)	人均财政支出(元) Per Capita Expenditures of Govern ments (yuan)	位次 Order
南明区	Nanming	57725	5	22.4	1136.95	4
云岩区	Yunyan	58629	4	9.6	1059.01	6
花溪区	Huaxi	31068	36	20.4	957.41	7
乌当区	Wudang	52931	11	28.0	1715.67	3
白云区	Baiyun	32884	32	20.3	1880.93	2
小河区	Xiaohe	24086	64	21.5	2011.25	1
开阳县	Kaiyang	39053	23	29.4	888.60	10
息烽县	Xifeng	27760	47	31.0	1062.96	5
修文县	Xiuwen	28287	45	21.6	916.45	9
清镇市	Qingzhen	40023	22	29.8	767.46	17
钟山区	Zhongshan	35714	28	74.4	823.66	13
六枝特区	Liuzhi	44385	16	27.2	689.52	19
水城县	Shuicheng	46968	15	33.6	617.16	25
盘 县	Panxian	80759	1	25.8	685.00	21
红花岗区	Honghuagang	47525	14	11.0	882.79	11
汇川区	Huicuan	26291	53	30.9	777.04	15
遵义县	Zunyi	74429	2	37.9	642.04	24
桐梓县	Tongzi	36394	27	33.3	545.95	29
绥阳县	Suiyang	31519	34	17.8	612.19	27
正安县	Zhengan	32320	33	20.2	529.55	30
※道真县	Daozhen	24735	61	29.8	723.70	18
※务川县	Wuchuan	28526	44	28.5	669.02	22
凤冈县	Fenggang	25767	55	29.4	616.76	26
湄潭县	Meitan	33070	30	35.9	688.60	20
余庆县	Yuqing	24106	63	30.5	813.93	14
习水县	Xishui	41808	20	24.4	597.20	28
赤水市	Chishui	27744	48	25.0	881.06	12
仁怀市	Renhuai	56735	6	31.0	930.51	8
西秀区	Xixiu	55699	7	32.8	667.81	23
平坝县	Pingba	27573	49	36.7	776.83	16

23-44续表1(continued)

县(市、区)名 称	County (City,Section)	财政支出(万元) Expenditures of Governments (10000 yuan)	位次 Order	2005年比2004年增长(%) Increase Rate in 2005 over 2004(%)	人均财政支出(元) Per Capita Expenditures of Govern ments (yuan)	位次 Order
普定县	Puding	25257	58	22.5	606.64	21
※镇宁县	Zhenning	24649	62	21.3	699.99	13
※关岭县	Guanling	23858	66	17.2	723.13	11
※紫云县	Ziyun	22952	70	45.4	662.84	17
铜仁市	Tongren	29376	38	33.7	851.48	4
江口县	Jiangkou	18528	80	26.1	813.65	6
※玉屏县	Yuping	17157	84	7.9	1199.02	2
石阡县	Shiqian	28831	42	33.9	740.41	9
思南县	Sinan	40186	21	30.9	623.39	20
※印江县	Yinjiang	28043	46	28.6	666.96	15
德江县	Dejiang	29152	40	24.6	636.91	19
※沿河县	Yanhe	36543	26	37.9	642.16	18
※松桃县	Songtao	38776	24	41.3	596.13	23
万山特区	Wanshan	11030	88	46.4	1648.09	1
兴义市	Xingyi	53662	9	20.7	715.35	12
兴仁县	Xingren	31497	35	29.5	672.35	14
普安县	Puan	23382	68	25.9	801.28	7
晴隆县	Qinglong	21187	75	16.0	726.01	10
贞丰县	Zhenfeng	23451	67	29.6	666.25	16
望谟县	Wangmo	22047	73	26.8	767.01	8
册亨县	Ceheng	19215	77	31.2	853.46	3
安龙县	Anlong	26370	52	33.9	603.54	22
毕节市	Bijie	60779	3	23.6	466.06	29
大方县	Dafang	49743	12	44.4	503.42	26
黔西县	Qianxi	41822	19	36.5	497.71	27
金沙县	Jinsha	49234	13	26.0	826.83	5
织金县	Zhijin	54709	8	34.6	578.34	24
纳雍县	Nayong	41855	18	10.0	538.25	25
※威宁县	Weining	53513	10	32.9	480.98	28

23-44续表2(continued)

县(市、区)名 称	County (City,Section)	财政支出(万元) Expenditures of Governments (10000 yuan)	位次 Order	2005年比2004年增长(%) Increase Rate in 2005 over 2004(%)	人均财政支出(元) Per Capita Expenditures of Govern ments (yuan)	位次 Order
赫章县	Hezhang	38388	25	48.6	585.49	29
凯里市	Kaili	35137	29	23.9	764.01	22
黄平县	Huangping	22889	71	28.8	645.73	27
施秉县	Shibing	17532	83	35.2	1114.62	1
三穗县	Sansui	18462	81	39.6	879.14	10
镇远县	Zhenyuan	21306	74	32.2	818.20	17
岑巩县	Cengong	18889	78	33.8	843.25	11
天柱县	Tianzhu	28765	43	38.3	695.52	24
锦屏县	Jinping	23130	69	27.8	1023.50	7
剑河县	Jianhe	26568	50	51.4	1088.85	4
台江县	Taijiang	15399	87	17.9	1050.05	6
黎平县	Liping	32888	31	23.1	645.81	26
榕江县	Rongjiang	26105	54	34.8	783.64	20
从江县	Congjiang	26558	51	37.5	822.17	14
雷山县	Leishan	16056	86	28.4	1061.33	5
麻江县	Majiang	18246	82	39.8	819.50	16
丹寨县	Danzhai	16094	85	34.5	972.75	8
都匀市	Duyun	44243	17	34.8	899.80	9
福泉市	Fuquan	25606	56	36.2	819.65	15
荔波县	Libo	18595	79	27.8	1091.93	3
贵定县	Guiding	23996	65	32.9	822.38	13
瓮安县	Wengan	29873	37	32.8	642.09	28
独山县	Dushan	29201	39	31.5	827.44	12
平塘县	Pingtang	24936	60	31.6	811.23	18
罗甸县	Luodian	25444	57	21.6	764.84	21
长顺县	Changshun	20228	76	33.4	810.13	19
龙里县	Longli	22731	72	37.6	1094.13	2
惠水县	Huishui	28968	41	28.0	662.76	25
※三都县	Sandu	25136	59	31.8	760.05	23

23-45 各县(市、区)城乡居民储蓄存款余额及位次(2005)

Jrban and Rural Resident Savings Deposit Balance and Its Order by Cou nty(City, Section)(2005)

县(市、区)名 称	County (City,Section)	城乡居民储蓄存款(万元) Urban and Rural Resident Savings Deposit(10000 yuan)	位次 Order	人均储蓄(元) Per Capita Savings Deposit(yuan)	位次 Order
南明区	Nanming				
云岩区	Yunyan				
花溪区	Huaxi	209637	8	6460	5
乌当区	Wudang	169854	9	5506	6
白云区	Baiyun				
小河区	Xiaohe	295065	5	24639	1
开阳县	Kaiyang	102999	18	2344	15
息烽县	Xifeng	69134	23	2647	12
修文县	Xiuwen	67686	24	2193	18
清镇市	Qingzhen	163622	10	3138	10
钟山区	Zhongshan	530317	2	12231	3
六枝特区	Liuzhi	128292	14	1993	21
水城县	Shuicheng	13371	27	176	27
盘 县	Panxian	284384	6	2412	14
红花岗区	Honghuagang	979875	1	18201	2
汇川区	Huicuan	326622	4	9653	4
遵义县	Zunyi	269454	7	2324	16
桐梓县	Tongzi	134411	13	2016	19
绥阳县	Suiyang	101212	19	1966	22
正安县	Zhengan	90144	20	1477	24
※道真县	Daozhen	75673	22	2214	17
※务川县	Wuchuan	54058	26	1268	26
凤冈县	Fenggang	56663	25	1356	25
湄潭县	Meitan	118777	16	2473	13
余庆县	Yuqing	83016	21	2803	11
习水县	Xishui	115652	17	1652	23
赤水市	Chishui	148060	12	4702	8
仁怀市	Renhuai	121683	15	1996	20
西秀区	Xixiu	443921	3	5322	7
平坝县	Pingba	161420	11	4548	9

23-45续表1(continued)

县(市、区)名 称	County (City,Section)	城乡居民储蓄存款(万元) Urban and Rural Resident Savings Deposit(10000 yuan)	位次 Order	人均储蓄（元） Per Capita Savings Deposit(yuan)	位次 Order
普定县	Puding	41561	24	998	22
※镇宁县	Zhenning	47929	20	1361	14
※关岭县	Guanling	51134	17	1550	10
※紫云县	Ziyun	27391	26	791	27
铜仁市	Tongren	196812	3	5705	1
江口县	Jiangkou	46197	22	2029	5
※玉屏县	Yuping	47486	21	3319	3
石阡县	Shiqian	48145	18	1236	18
思南县	Sinan	89368	8	1386	13
※印江县	Yinjiang	75981	11	1807	7
德江县	Dejiang	51201	16	1119	20
※沿河县	Yanhe	73950	12	1300	15
※松桃县	Songtao	83459	10	1283	17
万山特区	Wanshan				
兴义市	Xingyi	352704	1	4702	2
兴仁县	Xingren	66370	15	1417	12
普安县	Puan	47961	19	1644	8
晴隆县	Qinglong	42259	23	1448	11
贞丰县	Zhenfeng	34466	25	979	23
望谟县	Wangmo	22857	28	795	26
册亨县	Ceheng	24699	27	1097	21
安龙县	Anlong	70053	14	1603	9
毕节市	Bijie	293935	2	2254	4
大方县	Dafang	117209	5	1186	19
黔西县	Qianxi	108312	6	1289	16
金沙县	Jinsha	119232	4	2002	6
织金县	Zhijin	92487	7	978	24
纳雍县	Nayong	73115	13	940	25
※威宁县	Weining	87373	9	785	28

23-45续表2(continued)

县(市、区)名　称	County (City,Section)	城乡居民储蓄存款(万元) Urban and Rural Resident Savings Deposit(10000 yuan)	位次 Order	人均储蓄（元）Per Capita Savings Deposit(yuan)	位次 Order
赫章县	Hezhang	80850	7	1233	24
凯里市	Kaili	347421	2	7554	1
黄平县	Huangping	66159	10	1866	16
施秉县	Shibing	30863	25	1962	15
三穗县	Sansui	47601	16	2267	11
镇远县	Zhenyuan	53810	13	2066	13
岑巩县	Cengong	35433	21	1582	18
天柱县	Tianzhu	93188	5	2253	12
锦屏县	Jinping	60864	11	2693	4
剑河县	Jianhe	57981	12	2376	9
台江县	Taijiang	34345	22	2342	10
黎平县	Liping	75927	8	1491	20
榕江县	Rongjiang	47918	15	1438	22
从江县	Congjiang	28230	26	874	29
雷山县	Leishan	25403	28	1679	17
麻江县	Majiang	32627	24	1465	21
丹寨县	Danzhai	26043	27	1574	19
都匀市	Duyun	351480	1	7148	2
福泉市	Fuquan	107372	4	3437	3
荔波县	Libo	45393	17	2666	5
贵定县	Guiding	71514	9	2451	6
瓮安县	Wengan	112249	3	2413	8
独山县	Dushan	85530	6	2424	7
平塘县	Pingtang	39949	19	1300	23
罗甸县	Luodian	33972	23	1021	27
长顺县	Changshun	24863	29	996	28
龙里县	Longli	41246	18	1985	14
惠水县	Huishui	50806	14	1162	26
※三都县	Sandu	39424	20	1192	25

23-46 各县(市、区)教育事业基本情况(2005)

Basic Conditions of Education by County(City,Section)(2005)

县(市、区)名 称	County (City,Section)	普通中学 Regular Secondary Schools			小学 Primary Schools		
		学校数(所) Number of Schools (unit)	在校生数(人) Students Enrollment (person)	专任教师数(人) Full-time Teachers (person)	学校数(所) Number of Schools (unit)	在校生数(人) Students Enrollm ent (person)	专任教师数(人) Full-time Teachers (person)
南明区	Nanming	53	31265	2165	87	61921	2605
云岩区	Yunyan	39	19229	2518	80	47302	2272
花溪区	Huaxi	39	20115	1221	121	33450	1739
乌当区	Wudang	33	15036	1079	112	32070	1700
白云区	Baiyun	16	14670	926	58	21823	1128
小河区	Xiaohe	10	8697	569	36	15870	688
开阳县	Kaiyang	24	28259	1409	154	47897	2084
息烽县	Xifeng	19	14763	742	104	25099	1322
修文县	Xiuwen	26	18723	944	71	26696	1552
清镇市	Qingzhen	38	29759	1435	183	58863	2336
钟山区	Zhongshan	53	40524	1913	109	64959	2492
六枝特区	Liuzhi	50	36790	1791	200	80560	3087
水城县	Shuicheng	56	40516	1801	348	107369	3505
盘 县	Panxian	79	92245	4054	428	161163	5091
红花岗区	Honghuagang	45	39018	2012	92	54853	2094
汇川区	Huicuan	39	25993	1447	76	34548	1476
遵义县	Zunyi	95	84860	4313	395	132010	5421
桐梓县	Tongzi	55	46993	1957	217	77776	2489
绥阳县	Suiyang	37	30369	1726	212	58284	2289
正安县	Zhengan	43	35083	1620	185	66154	2165
※道真县	Daozhen	25	20020	1085	142	28769	1541
※务川县	Wuchuan	28	27372	1249	222	57924	2258
凤冈县	Fenggang	29	30389	1289	124	52601	1824
湄潭县	Meitan	27	29407	1513	130	52967	2096
余庆县	Yuqing	18	18620	889	113	27472	1051
习水县	Xishui	51	53482	2619	245	75095	2847
赤水市	Chishui	19	12977	850	88	23638	1415
仁怀市	Renhuai	37	43498	2013	211	86502	3302
西秀区	Xixiu	57	58073	2672	268	98925	3733
平坝县	Pingba	24	22607	1138	150	37938	1778

23-46续表1(continued)

县(市、区)名 称	County (City,Section)	普通中学 Regular Secondary Schools			小学 Primary Schools		
		学校数(所) Number of Schools (unit)	在校生数(人) Students Enrollment (person)	专任教师数(人) Full-time Teachers (person)	学校数(所) Number of Schools (unit)	在校生数(人) Students Enrollm ent (person)	专任教师数(人) Full-time Teachers (person)
普定县	Puding	15	24373	1201	192	56254	2206
※镇宁县	Zhenning	19	20589	937	137	45647	1742
※关岭县	Guanling	18	22195	851	154	44964	1679
※紫云县	Ziyun	20	18079	731	143	55762	1881
铜仁市	Tongren	26	31221	1378	135	38901	1943
江口县	Jiangkou	16	16402	792	124	23731	1043
※玉屏县	Yuping	10	9037	532	71	12082	554
石阡县	Shiqian	25	27288	1376	111	44147	1986
思南县	Sinan	40	43568	1890	278	83359	2745
※印江县	Yinjiang	22	27041	1438	133	45298	2219
德江县	Dejiang	30	31219	1541	211	62291	2189
※沿河县	Yanhe	27	35770	1683	213	84167	3006
※松桃县	Songtao	37	42220	2158	314	89394	3449
万山特区	Wanshan	6	3613	229	36	5010	355
兴义市	Xingyi	53	57261	2817	222	86205	3722
兴仁县	Xingren	31	30752	1525	183	61834	2065
普安县	Puan	22	22430	961	109	40926	1543
晴隆县	Qinglong	19	19239	727	102	36322	1451
贞丰县	Zhenfeng	18	22396	1041	147	47073	1729
望谟县	Wangmo	19	14437	588	123	43896	1532
册亨县	Ceheng	21	13525	670	70	29916	1074
安龙县	Anlong	34	32742	1547	180	53525	2404
毕节市	Bijie	94	87829	3793	429	171242	5395
大方县	Dafang	57	69776	2787	371	128865	3834
黔西县	Qianxi	45	50413	2379	319	96933	3561
金沙县	Jinsha	35	34460	1903	248	58391	3246
织金县	Zhijin	51	59328	2639	321	124620	4441
纳雍县	Nayong	40	49387	1926	220	107185	3696
※威宁县	Weining	51	57984	2061	346	172168	3785

23-46续表2(continued)

县(市、区)名 称	County (City,Section)	普通中学 Regular Secondary Schools 学校数(所) Number of Schools (unit)	在校生数(人) Students Enrollment (person)	专任教师数(人) Full-time Teachers (person)	小学 Primary Schools 学校数(所) Number of Schools (unit)	在校生数(人) Students Enrollm ent (person)	专任教师数(人) Full-time Teachers (person)
赫章县	Hezhang	49	35732	1567	267	128076	3091
凯里市	Kaili	41	35122	1953	154	48012	2400
黄平县	Huangping	13	21203	851	130	35873	1489
施秉县	Shibing	11	9869	476	75	17285	823
三穗县	Sansui	13	12424	686	69	18606	977
镇远县	Zhenyuan	18	16296	881	83	21730	1067
岑巩县	Cengong	15	15467	725	112	24804	1025
天柱县	Tianzhu	33	29098	1478	150	38704	1748
锦屏县	Jinping	18	15780	828	162	22936	1112
剑河县	Jianhe	13	13510	703	177	25926	1158
台江县	Taijiang	11	7272	429	68	16605	847
黎平县	Liping	29	35106	1467	254	59148	2395
榕江县	Rongjiang	18	20469	1055	170	42903	1788
从江县	Congjiang	21	18940	965	111	41738	1614
雷山县	Leishan	9	8632	446	72	15369	845
麻江县	Majiang	11	14293	748	86	21092	1021
丹寨县	Danzhai	11	10339	589	40	14810	855
都匀市	Duyun	38	31246	1638	149	42706	2114
福泉市	Fuquan	20	21623	1067	125	33642	1635
荔波县	Libo	12	12253	657	96	18044	1148
贵定县	Guiding	15	15409	771	102	35058	1534
瓮安县	Wengan	28	31388	1269	152	46985	2062
独山县	Dushan	25	25798	1223	165	40146	1643
平塘县	Pingtang	18	18309	839	138	36059	1471
罗甸县	Luodian	24	19063	1006	119	36434	1716
长顺县	Changshun	18	14993	693	102	30289	1422
龙里县	Longli	15	12059	647	100	23644	1213
惠水县	Huishui	28	25515	1152	154	55450	2031
※三都县	Sandu	19	20035	818	140	40628	1604

24

全国各省资料

National Main Statistic Informations Grouped by Provinces

Twenty-Four

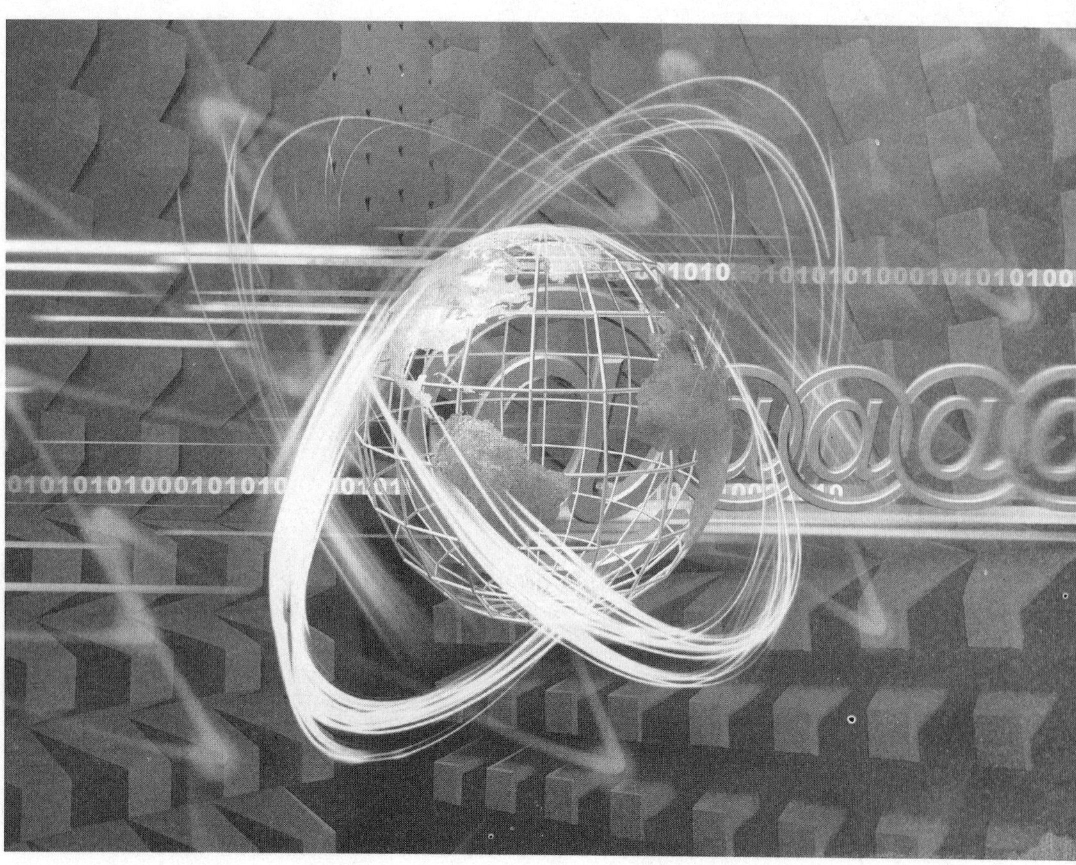

24-1 全国各省(市、区）主要经济指标排序（一）(2005)

The Orders of Major Economic Indicators by Province (City,Region)in China(1)(2005)

单位：‰

地 区	Region	总人口(万人) Total Population (10000 persons)	位次 Order	出生率 Birth Rate	位次 Order	死亡率 Death Rate	位次 Order	自然增长率 Natural Growth Rate	位次 Order
全 国	**National Total**	**130756**		**12.40**		**6.51**		**5.89**	
北 京	Beijing	1538	26	6.29	31	5.20	27	1.09	29
天 津	Tianjin	1043	27	7.44	28	6.01	18	1.43	28
河 北	Hebei	6851	6	12.84	10	6.75	5	6.09	12
山 西	Shanxi	3355	19	12.02	14	6.00	20	6.02	13
内蒙古	Inner Mongolia	2386	23	10.08	20	5.46	25	4.62	20
辽 宁	Liaoning	4221	14	7.01	30	6.04	17	0.97	30
吉 林	Jilin	2716	21	7.89	26	5.32	26	2.57	26
黑龙江	Heilongjiang	3820	16	7.87	27	5.20	27	2.67	25
上 海	Shanghai	1778	25	7.04	29	6.08	15	0.96	31
江 苏	Jiangsu	7475	5	9.24	24	7.03	3	2.21	27
浙 江	Zhejiang	4898	10	11.10	19	6.08	15	5.02	19
安 徽	Anhui	6120	8	12.43	12	6.23	12	6.20	11
福 建	Fujian	3535	18	11.60	17	5.62	24	5.98	15
江 西	Jiangxi	4311	13	13.79	9	5.96	21	7.83	8
山 东	Shandong	9248	2	12.14	13	6.31	10	5.83	16
河 南	Henan	9380	1	11.55	18	6.30	11	5.25	17
湖 北	Hubei	5710	9	8.74	25	5.69	23	3.05	22
湖 南	Hunan	6326	7	11.90	15	6.75	5	5.15	18
广 东	Guangdong	9194	3	11.70	16	4.68	31	7.02	10
广 西	Guangxi	4660	11	14.26	8	6.09	14	8.16	6
海 南	Hainan	828	28	14.65	6	5.72	22	8.93	5
重 庆	Chongqing	2798	20	9.40	23	6.40	9	3.00	23
四 川	Sichuan	8212	4	9.70	22	6.80	4	2.90	24
贵 州	**Guizhou**	**3931**	**15**	**14.59**	**7**	**7.21**	**1**	**7.38**	**9**
云 南	Yunnan	4450	12	14.72	5	6.75	5	7.97	7
西 藏	Tibet	277	31	17.94	1	7.15	2	10.79	3
陕 西	Shanxi	3720	17	10.02	21	6.01	18	4.01	21
甘 肃	Gansu	2594	22	12.59	11	6.57	8	6.02	13
青 海	Qinghai	543	30	15.70	4	6.21	13	9.49	4
宁 夏	Ningxia	596	29	15.93	3	4.95	30	10.98	2
新 疆	Xinjiang	2010	24	16.42	2	5.04	29	11.38	1

24-2 全国各省(市、区)

The Orders of Major Economic Indicators

地 区	Region	地区生产总值 Gross Domestic Product	位次 Order	第一产业 Primary Industry	位次 Order	第二产业 Secondary Industry
全 国	**National Total**	**182320.60**		**22718.40**		**86207.60**
北 京	Beijing	6814.5	10	95.7	27	2100.5
天 津	Tianjin	3663.9	21	109.4	26	2050.3
河 北	Hebei	10116.6	6	1453.9	4	5324.2
山 西	Shanxi	4121.2	16	257.9	25	2307.9
内蒙古	Inner Mongolia	3822.8	19	600.1	18	1685.1
辽 宁	Liaoning	8005.0	8	853.6	12	3906.8
吉 林	Jilin	3614.9	22	607.0	17	1605.1
黑龙江	Heilongjiang	5510.0	14	672.5	15	2970.8
上 海	Shanghai	9144.0	7	79.7	28	4475.9
江 苏	Jiangsu	18272.1	3	1388.6	5	10342.7
浙 江	Zhejiang	13365.0	4	872.6	11	7147.3
安 徽	Anhui	5375.8	15	940.7	9	2234.2
福 建	Fujian	6560.1	11	828.8	13	3224.9
江 西	Jiangxi	4056.2	18	770.0	14	1914.9
山 东	Shandong	18468.3	2	1927.6	1	10620.3
河 南	Henan	10535.2	5	1843.0	2	5539.3
湖 北	Hubei	6484.5	12	1069.8	8	2774.4
湖 南	Hunan	6473.6	13	1255.0	7	2604.6
广 东	Guangdong	21701.3	1	1374.6	6	10747.2
广 西	Guangxi	4063.3	17	902.6	10	1505.0
海 南	Hainan	893.1	28	301.1	23	218.5
重 庆	Chongqing	3069.1	24	463.4	20	1258.3
四 川	Sichuan	7385.1	9	1495.7	3	3052.7
贵 州	**Guizhou**	**1979.1**	**26**	**362.5**	**22**	**826.6**
云 南	Yunnan	3472.3	23	656.2	16	1449.7
西 藏	Tibet	250.6	31	47.9	31	59.5
陕 西	Shanxi	3674.8	20	418.6	21	1849.0
甘 肃	Gansu	1928.1	27	300.0	24	836.6
青 海	Qinghai	543.2	30	62.8	30	264.6
宁 夏	Ningxia	599.4	29	69.8	29	277.8
新 疆	Xinjiang	2639.6	25	506.2	19	1225.5

主要经济指标排序(二)(2005)

by Province(City,Region)in China(2)(2005)

单位：亿元 (100 million yuan)

位次 Order	第三产业 Tertiary Industry	位次 Order	地区生产总值比上年增长(%) Increase Rate of GDP in 2005 over 2004(%)	位次 Order	人均生产总值(元/人) Per Capita GDP (yuan/person)	位次 Order
	73394.60		**9.9**		**13985**	
16	4618.4	5	11.1	26	44441	2
17	1504.1	19	14.5	3	35234	3
6	3338.5	7	13.4	6	14811	11
14	1555.4	17	12.5	12	12321	15
20	1537.6	18	21.6	1	16067	10
8	3244.6	8	12.3	14	19022	8
21	1402.8	21	12.0	17	13350	13
11	1866.7	15	11.6	20	14467	12
7	4588.4	6	11.1	27	51583	1
3	6540.9	2	14.5	4	24518	5
4	5345.2	4	12.4	13	27369	4
15	2201.0	14	11.8	18	8810	27
9	2506.4	13	11.3	25	18613	9
18	1371.3	22	12.8	7	9437	24
2	5920.4	3	15.2	2	20030	7
5	3152.8	9	14.1	5	11265	17
12	2640.3	11	11.4	24	11390	16
13	2614.1	12	11.6	22	10264	20
1	9579.4	1	12.5	11	23674	6
22	1655.7	16	12.7	8	8746	28
30	373.6	28	10.1	30	10819	19
24	1347.4	24	11.5	23	11002	18
10	2836.7	10	12.6	9	9020	26
27	**790.0**	**27**	**11.6**	**21**	**5052**	**31**
23	1366.5	23	9.0	31	7826	29
31	143.3	31	12.2	15	9074	25
19	1407.2	20	12.6	10	9908	23
26	791.6	26	11.7	19	7455	30
29	215.8	30	12.2	16	10030	22
28	251.8	29	10.3	28	10087	21
25	908.0	25	10.2	29	13184	14

24-3 全国各省(市、区)主要经济指标排序(三)(2005)

The Orders of Major Economic Indicators by Province (City,Region)in China(3)(2005)

单位：亿元 (100 million yuan)

地 区	Region	地方财政收入 Local Financial Revenue	位次 Order	地方财政收入比上年增长(%) Increase Rate of Local Financial Revenue in 2005 over 2004(%)	位次 Order	#增值税 Value-added Tax	位次 Order
全国总计	**National Total**	**15092.00**		**19.8**		**10793.90**	
北 京	Beijing	919.2	6	23.5	19	97.60	9
天 津	Tianjin	331.9	16	34.8	4	64.24	15
河 北	Hebei	515.7	9	26.5	14	121.03	6
山 西	Shanxi	368.3	14	43.7	1	102.70	8
内蒙古	Inner Mongolia	277.5	20	41.0	2	48.45	20
辽 宁	Liaoning	675.3	7	27.5	11	113.06	7
吉 林	Jilin	207.2	24	24.6	17	39.53	22
黑龙江	Heilongjiang	318.2	17	9.9	31	85.02	11
上 海	Shanghai	1417.4	2	28.1	8	226.12	3
江 苏	Jiangsu	1322.7	3	34.9	3	265.57	2
浙 江	Zhejiang	1066.6	5	32.3	5	204.23	4
安 徽	Anhui	334.0	15	21.6	23	57.72	17
福 建	Fujian	432.6	11	29.7	6	73.13	12
江 西	Jiangxi	252.9	23	22.9	21	33.87	24
山 东	Shandong	1073.1	4	29.6	7	193.00	5
河 南	Henan	537.7	8	25.4	15	87.97	10
湖 北	Hubei	375.5	13	21.0	24	65.91	14
湖 南	Hunan	395.3	12	23.3	20	58.93	16
广 东	Guangdong	1807.2	1	27.4	12	323.59	1
广 西	Guangxi	283.0	19	19.0	27	39.33	23
海 南	Hainan	68.7	28	20.4	25	9.74	28
重 庆	Chongqing	256.8	22	28.0	10	33.65	25
四 川	Sichuan	479.7	10	24.3	18	71.07	13
贵 州	**Guizhou**	**182.5**	**25**	**22.2**	**22**	**31.37**	**26**
云 南	Yunnan	312.6	18	18.7	28	56.02	18
西 藏	Tibet	12.0	31	20.1	26	1.18	31
陕 西	Shanxi	275.3	21	28.1	8	55.34	19
甘 肃	Gansu	123.5	27	18.6	29	25.33	27
青 海	Qinghai	33.8	30	25.3	16	7.84	30
宁 夏	Ningxia	47.7	29	27.4	12	8.73	29
新 疆	Xinjiang	180.3	26	15.8	30	42.94	21

24–4 全国各省(市、区)主要经济指标排序(四) (2005)

The Orders of Major Economic Indicators by Province (City,Region)in China(4)(2005)

单位：亿元 (100 million yuan)

地 区	Region	#营业税 Operation Tax	位次 Order	财政支出 Financial Expenditure	位次 Order	财政支出比上年增长(%) Increase Rate of Financial Expenditure in 2005 over 2004(%)	位次 Order
全国总计	**National Total**	**4232.60**		**24932.40**		**18.3**	
北 京	Beijing	383.76	3	1058.31	9	17.8	28
天 津	Tianjin	96.45	12	442.12	26	17.9	27
河 北	Hebei	105.28	11	979.16	10	24.6	7
山 西	Shanxi	60.70	22	668.75	17	28.8	4
内蒙古	Inner Mongolia	78.27	15	681.88	16	20.9	18
辽 宁	Liaoning	164.68	7	1204.36	6	29.3	3
吉 林	Jilin	47.59	25	631.12	19	24.3	9
黑龙江	Heilongjiang	59.56	23	787.79	12	12.9	31
上 海	Shanghai	512.93	2	1646.26	3	19.1	23
江 苏	Jiangsu	342.82	4	1673.40	2	27.5	5
浙 江	Zhejiang	324.33	5	1265.53	5	19.1	23
安 徽	Anhui	78.10	16	713.06	15	18.5	26
福 建	Fujian	124.61	9	593.42	21	14.9	30
江 西	Jiangxi	62.84	21	563.95	22	24.2	10
山 东	Shandong	217.79	6	1466.23	4	23.3	14
河 南	Henan	111.60	10	1116.04	7	26.8	6
湖 北	Hubei	91.33	14	778.72	13	20.5	20
湖 南	Hunan	94.25	13	873.42	11	21.4	17
广 东	Guangdong	555.77	1	2289.07	1	23.5	13
广 西	Guangxi	68.38	19	611.48	20	20.5	20
海 南	Hainan	23.68	28	151.24	31	18.9	25
重 庆	Chongqing	70.20	17	487.35	25	23.2	16
四 川	Sichuan	134.76	8	1082.18	8	20.9	18
贵 州	**Guizhou**	**46.31**	**26**	**520.73**	**23**	**24.5**	**8**
云 南	Yunnan	67.64	20	766.31	14	15.5	29
西 藏	Tibet	4.87	31	185.45	28	38.6	1
陕 西	Shanxi	69.27	18	638.96	18	23.8	11
甘 肃	Gansu	31.59	27	429.35	27	20.3	22
青 海	Qinghai	10.02	30	169.75	29	23.6	12
宁 夏	Ningxia	15.76	29	160.25	30	30.3	2
新 疆	Xinjiang	47.67	24	519.02	24	23.3	14

24-5 全国各省(市、区)主要经济指标排序(五)(2005)

The Orders of Major Economic Indicators by Province (City,Region)in China(5)(2005)

单位：亿元 (100 million yuan)

地区	Region	#挖潜改造支出 Innovation Funds	位次 Order	#科技三项费用 Science and Technology Promotion Funds	位次 Order	#农业支出 Expenditure for Agriculture	位次 Order
全国总计	**National Total**					**1776.3**	
北京	Beijing	44.33	5	9.61	7	27.64	14
天津	Tianjin	29.12	10	10.86	6	8.75	27
河北	Hebei	21.13	16	7.40	13	32.27	10
山西	Shanxi	1.66	28	4.36	19	22.84	20
内蒙古	Inner Mongolia	29.13	9	4.35	20	24.21	18
辽宁	Liaoning	37.75	6	23.37	4	43.48	5
吉林	Jilin	21.73	15	4.57	17	21.40	22
黑龙江	Heilongjiang	32.23	7	8.34	9	29.55	12
上海	Shanghai	237.00	1	2.91	25	24.61	16
江苏	Jiangsu	63.33	2	27.13	3	66.22	1
浙江	Zhejiang	57.29	4	34.08	2	57.90	3
安徽	Anhui	23.30	13	3.77	21	28.93	13
福建	Fujian	22.04	14	8.23	10	20.33	23
江西	Jiangxi	16.24	18	2.51	26	26.83	15
山东	Shandong	57.30	3	19.42	5	64.18	2
河南	Henan	29.39	8	9.23	8	35.38	8
湖北	Hubei	12.45	21	7.93	12	32.23	11
湖南	Hunan	16.89	17	8.16	11	40.28	7
广东	Guangdong	26.60	11	52.69	1	45.14	4
广西	Guangxi	14.38	19	3.64	22	23.15	19
海南	Hainan	0.50	30	0.75	30	5.80	31
重庆	Chongqing	9.79	22	4.90	16	13.03	26
四川	Sichuan	24.09	12	7.18	14	41.62	6
贵州	**Guizhou**	**5.02**	**24**	**3.36**	**24**	**24.59**	**17**
云南	Yunnan	14.10	20	5.75	15	33.64	9
西藏	Tibet	0.33	31	0.44	31	5.99	30
陕西	Shanxi	9.62	23	4.38	18	21.75	21
甘肃	Gansu	4.53	25	2.31	27	13.66	25
青海	Qinghai	1.37	29	0.82	29	6.27	29
宁夏	Ningxia	3.34	27	1.27	28	6.59	28
新疆	Xinjiang	3.67	26	3.57	23	19.05	24

24-6 全国各省(市、区）主要经济指标排序（六）(2005)

The Orders of Major Economic Indicators by Province(City,Region)in China(6)(2005)

单位：万平方米 (10000 sq.m)

地区	Region	建筑业总产值（亿元）Gross Output Value of Construction (100 million yuan)	位次 Order	施工面积 Floor Space under Construction	位次 Order	竣工面积 Floor Space Completed	位次 Order
全国总计	**National Total**	**34745.8**		**348969.1**		**150166.5**	
北京	Beijing	1894.3	5	15452.7	6	4906.5	8
天津	Tianjin	725.3	17	3770.3	22	1318.0	25
河北	Hebei	1268.4	9	12622.1	10	4814.7	11
山西	Shanxi	792.3	15	3802.0	21	1342.1	24
内蒙古	Inner Mongolia	366.4	24	2796.8	26	1388.9	23
辽宁	Liaoning	1472.0	8	9914.1	14	4338.7	13
吉林	Jilin	485.2	22	2829.4	25	1601.1	20
黑龙江	Heilongjiang	572.3	19	4465.4	20	2249.8	18
上海	Shanghai	1893.0	6	13587.0	8	4761.2	12
江苏	Jiangsu	4365.1	2	50721.7	2	26132.6	1
浙江	Zhejiang	4620.3	1	59168.5	1	23072.0	2
安徽	Anhui	961.6	13	9609.9	15	4815.3	10
福建	Fujian	804.0	14	10296.8	13	3413.1	16
江西	Jiangxi	543.4	20	6592.4	16	3604.4	15
山东	Shandong	2490.8	3	25122.4	4	12481.9	3
河南	Henan	1055.9	12	10322.3	12	4297.3	14
湖北	Hubei	1247.8	10	13890.4	7	6415.3	6
湖南	Hunan	1177.2	11	13507.7	9	5929.8	7
广东	Guangdong	2067.4	4	26244.3	3	8569.3	5
广西	Guangxi	410.1	23	5309.5	17	2126.4	19
海南	Hainan	59.5	30	666.7	29	242.0	29
重庆	Chongqing	784.6	16	10775.7	11	4816.8	9
四川	Sichuan	1478.4	7	17710.7	5	9070.3	4
贵州	**Guizhou**	**271.2**	**27**	**3152.8**	**23**	**1149.5**	**27**
云南	Yunnan	502.1	21	4466.1	19	2325.5	17
西藏	Tibet	35.5	31	138.0	31	55.1	31
陕西	Shanxi	594.1	18	4936.7	18	1584.1	21
甘肃	Gansu	276.3	26	2892.7	24	1439.5	22
青海	Qinghai	87.9	29	400.0	30	190.1	30
宁夏	Ningxia	111.1	28	1079.2	28	551.7	28
新疆	Xinjiang	343.3	25	2773.1	27	1273.3	26

24-7 全国各省(市、区)

The Orders of Major Economic Indicators

地 区	Region	城镇固定资产投资额(亿元) Investment in Fixed Assets(100 million yuan)	位次 Order	房地产投资(亿元) Real Eatate Development (100 million yuan)	位次 Order
全国总计	**National Total**	**75096.5**		**15759.3**	
北 京	Beijing	2595.4	10	1525.0	2
天 津	Tianjin	1367.5	24	327.5	16
河 北	Hebei	3361.7	7	390.5	14
山 西	Shanxi	1671.9	19	174.6	23
内蒙古	Inner Mongolia	2563.5	11	162.1	24
辽 宁	Liaoning	3669.7	5	873.5	7
吉 林	Jilin	1595.9	21	195.7	22
黑龙江	Heilongjiang	1638.2	20	267.6	20
上 海	Shanghai	3198.6	8	1246.9	5
江 苏	Jiangsu	6211.9	2	1526.9	1
浙 江	Zhejiang	4757.0	4	1454.5	4
安 徽	Anhui	2140.0	14	459.4	11
福 建	Fujian	1970.1	15	540.4	9
江 西	Jiangxi	1933.9	16	300.7	17
山 东	Shandong	7274.8	1	974.3	6
河 南	Henan	3528.3	6	388.5	15
湖 北	Hubei	2433.2	12	448.0	12
湖 南	Hunan	2174.9	13	447.5	13
广 东	Guangdong	5760.7	3	1498.3	3
广 西	Guangxi	1554.3	22	287.0	19
海 南	Hainan	351.5	29	70.8	29
重 庆	Chongqing	1786.4	17	517.7	10
四 川	Sichuan	2989.6	9	699.3	8
贵 州	**Guizhou**	**916.1**	**26**	**154.1**	**25**
云 南	Yunnan	1550.2	23	233.8	21
西 藏	Tibet	187.2	31	6.0	31
陕 西	Shanxi	1761.2	18	297.9	18
甘 肃	Gansu	790.2	27	85.8	27
青 海	Qinghai	312.6	30	29.1	30
宁 夏	Ningxia	382.7	28	74.7	28
新 疆	Xinjiang	1210.1	25	101.7	26

主要经济指标排序(七)(2005)

by Province(City,Region)in China(7)(2005)

房屋施工面积(万平方米) Floor Space under Construction(10000 aq.m)	位次 Order	房屋竣工面积(万平方米) Floor Space Completed (10000 aq.m)	位次 Order	商品房销售面积(万平方米) Floor Space of Commercial Houses(10000 aq.m)	位次 Order
164445.0		**48792.5**		**55769.1**	
10748.5	4	3770.9	3	3123.4	7
3470.6	18	1479.2	14	1402.3	17
3710.8	17	899.2	19	1292.2	19
2160.0	23	480.3	26	667.0	25
2119.0	24	853.6	20	1081.7	21
7042.8	9	2365.1	8	2518.3	8
1890.7	25	479.3	27	667.9	24
2631.1	22	1305.7	17	1244.9	20
10462.4	5	3095.7	6	3158.9	5
15182.7	2	4671.2	1	4740.2	2
15596.7	1	3780.3	2	5299.6	1
5306.9	11	1816.9	10	1907.2	10
6231.6	10	1713.1	11	1894.9	11
4239.8	15	1356.0	16	1527.3	16
10359.5	6	3162.1	5	3608.4	4
4903.8	13	1371.5	15	1724.8	13
4804.4	14	1627.0	12	1708.0	14
4952.0	12	1520.9	13	1815.8	12
15010.8	3	3421.7	4	4686.7	3
4056.0	16	1298.8	18	1556.8	15
911.9	29	165.5	29	257.9	29
7485.2	8	2208.1	9	2015.4	9
8261.3	7	2378.8	7	3148.9	6
2698.6	**21**	**615.0**	**23**	**872.7**	**23**
2717.9	20	630.4	22	1348.9	18
32.7	31	16.3	31	4.4	31
3181.2	19	753.5	21	891.6	22
1449.7	26	338.9	28	473.4	27
418.4	30	102.2	30	116.8	30
1049.5	28	567.5	24	378.0	28
1358.4	27	547.9	25	634.9	26

24-8 全国各省(市、区）主要经济指标排序（八）(2005)

The Orders of Major Economic Indicators by Province (City,Region)in China(8)(2005)

地 区	Region	农林牧渔业总产值（亿元）Gross Output Value of Farming, Forestry, Animal Husbandry and Fishery (100 million yuan)	位次 Order	农林牧渔业总产值比上年增长(%) Increase Rate of Gross Agriculture Output Value in 2005 over 2004(%)	位次 Order	粮食产量(万吨) Output of Grain (10000 tons)	位次 Order
全国总计	**National Total**	**39450.9**		**5.7**		**48402.2**	
北 京	Beijing	268.8	26	0.3	29	94.9	29
天 津	Tianjin	258.4	27	4.5	22	137.5	27
河 北	Hebei	2600.8	3	6.5	13	2598.6	8
山 西	Shanxi	483.8	24	-2.8	30	978.0	20
内蒙古	Inner Mongolia	980.2	18	11.2	2	1662.2	13
辽 宁	Liaoning	1671.6	9	7.5	6	1745.8	12
吉 林	Jilin	1050.5	17	11.7	1	2581.2	9
黑龙江	Heilongjiang	1294.4	14	10.2	3	3092.0	4
上 海	Shanghai	233.4	28	-10.5	31	105.4	28
江 苏	Jiangsu	2577.0	4	3.7	24	2834.6	5
浙 江	Zhejiang	1428.3	12	2.4	25	814.7	23
安 徽	Anhui	1666.2	10	1.4	28	2605.3	7
福 建	Fujian	1396.1	13	2.2	26	715.2	24
江 西	Jiangxi	1143.0	15	6.8	10	1757.0	11
山 东	Shandong	3741.8	1	5.2	19	3917.4	2
河 南	Henan	3309.7	2	7.5	5	4582.0	1
湖 北	Hubei	1775.6	8	4.2	23	2177.4	10
湖 南	Hunan	2056.2	7	5.8	17	2678.6	6
广 东	Guangdong	2447.6	6	4.8	21	1395.0	16
广 西	Guangxi	1448.4	11	7.4	7	1487.3	15
海 南	Hainan	475.9	25	6.7	11	153.0	26
重 庆	Chongqing	662.2	21	5.2	20	1168.2	17
四 川	Sichuan	2457.5	5	6.5	14	3211.1	3
贵 州	**Guizhou**	**571.8**	**22**	**5.9**	**16**	**1152.1**	**18**
云 南	Yunnan	1068.6	16	6.9	9	1514.9	14
西 藏	Tibet	67.7	31	1.9	27	93.4	30
陕 西	Shanxi	730.7	20	8.1	4	1043.0	19
甘 肃	Gansu	521.5	23	6.6	12	836.9	22
青 海	Qinghai	94.0	30	5.3	18	93.3	31
宁 夏	Ningxia	138.0	29	6.2	15	299.8	25
新 疆	Xinjiang	831.1	19	7.4	8	876.6	21

24-9 全国各省(市、区）主要经济指标排序（九）(2005)

The Orders of Major Economic Indicators by Province (City,Region)in China(9)(2005)

单位：万吨 (10000 tons)

地区	Region	油料产量 Oil-bearing Crops	位次 Order	肉类产量 Output of Pork, Beef and Mutton	位次 Order	水产品产量 Aquatic Products	位次 Order
全国总计	**National Total**	**3077.1**		**7743.1**		**5106.1**	
北京	Beijing	2.5	30	66.7	25	6.4	26
天津	Tianjin	1.3	31	57.8	27	33.8	18
河北	Hebei	152.7	7	571.9	4	98.9	13
山西	Shanxi	21.3	25	68.2	24	3.8	28
内蒙古	Inner Mongolia	122.2	9	229.5	15	8.3	23
辽宁	Liaoning	36.8	21	347.9	8	425.3	5
吉林	Jilin	54.4	15	260.2	12	11.9	21
黑龙江	Heilongjiang	60.6	14	173.5	18	43.0	16
上海	Shanghai	6.9	28	31.3	28	35.4	17
江苏	Jiangsu	216.0	6	352.3	7	388.7	6
浙江	Zhejiang	50.1	17	165.3	20	483.8	4
安徽	Anhui	270.7	4	340.1	9	177.6	10
福建	Fujian	27.4	24	165.9	19	602.2	3
江西	Jiangxi	76.1	12	237.1	14	168.7	11
山东	Shandong	363.9	2	753.9	1	736.1	1
河南	Henan	449.6	1	685.9	2	51.7	15
湖北	Hubei	293.9	3	327.3	10	318.2	7
湖南	Hunan	141.0	8	523.5	5	179.2	9
广东	Guangdong	77.0	11	384.3	6	695.2	2
广西	Guangxi	63.2	13	242.9	13	284.2	8
海南	Hainan	8.5	27	58.2	26	150.0	12
重庆	Chongqing	42.7	19	178.0	17	25.1	19
四川	Sichuan	232.3	5	653.6	3	98.2	14
贵州	**Guizhou**	**84.9**	**10**	**187.0**	**16**	**9.5**	**22**
云南	Yunnan	36.2	22	298.6	11	23.8	20
西藏	Tibet	6.1	29	21.5	31		
陕西	Shanxi	45.4	18	102.8	22	7.4	25
甘肃	Gansu	50.3	16	82.1	23	1.6	29
青海	Qinghai	31.9	23	25.8	30	0.1	30
宁夏	Ningxia	12.2	26	26.2	29	5.8	27
新疆	Xinjiang	38.9	20	143.3	21	7.9	24

24-10 全国各省(市、区)主要经济指标排序(十)(2005)

The Orders of Major Economic Indicators by Province (City,Region)in China(10)(2005)

地区	Region	规模以上工业增加值(亿元) Gross Industrial Added Value (100 million yuan)	位次 Order	工业增加值比上年增长(%) Increase Rate of Gross Industrial Added Value in 2005 over 2004 (%)	位次 Order	发电量(亿千瓦时) Electricity (100 million kwh)	位次 Order
全国总计	**National Total**	**66425.2**		**16.4**		**24747.0**	
北京	Beijing	1705.4	15	13.1	28	209.0	29
天津	Tianjin	1783.0	13	20.4	12	365.7	23
河北	Hebei	3219.0	7	22.9	6	1324.1	6
山西	Shanxi	1712.0	14	19.3	14	1272.7	7
内蒙古	Inner Mongolia	1135.5	20	30.9	1	1069.3	9
辽宁	Liaoning	3007.4	8	20.1	13	904.0	11
吉林	Jilin	1200.8	19	11.0	30	412.1	22
黑龙江	Heilongjiang	2166.3	10	15.3	26	596.0	17
上海	Shanghai	3994.7	5	12.5	29	728.7	14
江苏	Jiangsu	8054.0	3	22.5	10	1789.5	3
浙江	Zhejiang	4904.7	4	18.1	20	1353.0	5
安徽	Anhui	1373.9	17	22.7	8	645.7	15
福建	Fujian	2235.2	9	17.4	22	778.3	13
江西	Jiangxi	828.5	24	23.6	3	349.3	24
山东	Shandong	8411.9	1	28.4	2	2001.6	2
河南	Henan	3228.0	6	23.3	4	1419.9	4
湖北	Hubei	1847.9	12	19.3	14	1257.2	8
湖南	Hunan	1535.9	16	20.6	11	630.3	16
广东	Guangdong	8290.0	2	17.0	24	2163.4	1
广西	Guangxi	833.1	23	22.8	7	417.2	21
海南	Hainan	138.0	30	18.6	17	81.6	30
重庆	Chongqing	716.4	25	17.1	23	234.0	27
四川	Sichuan	2034.4	11	23.0	5	958.0	10
贵州	**Guizhou**	**585.9**	**27**	**17.0**	**24**	**786.8**	**12**
云南	Yunnan	1018.1	21	8.4	31	578.5	18
西藏	Tibet	17.4	31	14.9	27	13.3	31
陕西	Shanxi	1267.2	18	18.7	16	504.9	19
甘肃	Gansu	601.8	26	18.6	17	485.1	20
青海	Qinghai	179.5	29	22.7	8	213.2	28
宁夏	Ningxia	202.3	28	18.5	19	312.9	25
新疆	Xinjiang	933.3	22	17.8	21	290.5	26

24-11 全国各省(市、区）主要经济指标排序（十一）(2005)

The Orders of Major Economic Indicators by Province (City,Region)in China(11)(2005)

单位：万吨 (10000 tons)

地 区	Region	成品钢材 Products Steel	位次 Order	原煤 Coal	位次 Order	水泥 Cement	位次 Order
全国总计	**National Total**	**39691.5**		**219000**		**106400.0**	
北 京	Beijing	966.2	14	810.7	22	1160.9	24
天 津	Tianjin	1661.1	6			519.2	28
河 北	Hebei	6464.4	1	7956.4	8	8850.0	3
山 西	Shanxi	1341.2	9	43963.0	1	1920.8	18
内蒙古	Inner Mongolia	747.8	16	22064.5	2	1519.1	21
辽 宁	Liaoning	3206.1	3	6152.8	10	2614.6	15
吉 林	Jilin	478.6	21	2487.2	16	1598.5	19
黑龙江	Heilongjiang	232.3	26	7253.4	9	1113.3	25
上 海	Shanghai	1964.2	5			720.0	26
江 苏	Jiangsu	4328.3	2	2817.6	14	9579.2	2
浙 江	Zhejiang	717.0	18	41.3	27	8829.4	4
安 徽	Anhui	1141.6	12	8434.5	7	3217.8	11
福 建	Fujian	729.7	17	1331.7	21	2713.6	13
江 西	Jiangxi	1017.8	13	1620.8	20	3477.0	10
山 东	Shandong	3008.5	4	14029.8	4	13986.8	1
河 南	Henan	1337.4	10	18761.4	3	6210.7	6
湖 北	Hubei	1585.9	7	478.1	25	4512.5	7
湖 南	Hunan	961.3	15	3646.5	12	3571.1	9
广 东	Guangdong	1365.8	8	234.8	26	8031.7	5
广 西	Guangxi	515.5	19	637.4	23	3177.5	12
海 南	Hainan	14.9	29			442.6	29
重 庆	Chongqing	294.7	25	1957.8	19	2100.7	16
四 川	Sichuan	1172.7	11	5219.1	11	4194.7	8
贵 州	Guizhou	214.9	27	10615.2	6	1558.0	20
云 南	Yunnan	480.1	20	2190.2	18	2644.4	14
西 藏	Tibet			3.4	28	128.2	31
陕 西	Shanxi	337.1	23	10810.7	5	1972.1	17
甘 肃	Gansu	452.3	22	3326.8	13	1326.0	22
青 海	Qinghai	48.5	28	554.9	24	370.6	30
宁 夏	Ningxia	9.2	30	2589.8	15	567.6	27
新 疆	Xinjiang	322.3	24	2435.1	17	1201.6	23

24-12 全国各省(市、区)主要经济指标排序(十二)(2005)

The Orders of Major Economic Indicators by Province (City,Region)in China(12)(2005)

地 区	Region	农用化肥(万吨) Chemical Fertilizers (10000 tons)	位次 Order	移动电话机(万部) Mibile Telephone (10000 units)	位次 Order	程控交换机(万线) Program-controlled Exchange (10000 lines)	位次 Order
全国总计	**National Total**	**5219.7**		**30354.2**		**7720.9**	
北 京	Beijing	5.9	29	8948.4	1	3652.2	1
天 津	Tianjin	16.9	28	6310.1	2	4.0	11
河 北	Hebei	208.9	10			3.0	13
山 西	Shanxi	283.5	6	0.2	14		
内蒙古	Inner Mongolia	64.6	20	98.9	11		
辽 宁	Liaoning	87.7	16	102.0	10	15.4	9
吉 林	Jilin	17.1	27				
黑龙江	Heilongjiang	39.7	25			0.1	16
上 海	Shanghai	3.1	30	1939.5	6	796.6	3
江 苏	Jiangsu	284.6	5	2846.0	4	95.9	6
浙 江	Zhejiang	59.5	23	2791.3	5	156.8	5
安 徽	Anhui	204.1	11				
福 建	Fujian	60.3	22	1166.0	8	0.4	15
江 西	Jiangxi	47.6	24			3.6	12
山 东	Shandong	665.1	1	1232.0	7	224.1	4
河 南	Henan	396.6	3				
湖 北	Hubei	375.5	4	586.9	9	0.1	16
湖 南	Hunan	257.6	9			14.8	10
广 东	Guangdong	36.5	26	4183.9	3	2646.2	2
广 西	Guangxi	81.4	19	94.4	12		
海 南	Hainan	62.7	21				
重 庆	Chongqing	118.0	14				
四 川	Sichuan	428.8	2			19.30	8
贵 州	**Guizhou**	**268.3**	**7**	**54.9**	**13**	**0.0**	**18**
云 南	Yunnan	263.1	8			0.5	14
西 藏	Tibet						
陕 西	Shanxi	122.9	13			87.9	7
甘 肃	Gansu	85.4	17				
青 海	Qinghai	158.9	12				
宁 夏	Ningxia	83.9	18				
新 疆	Xinjiang	99.8	15				

24-13 全国各省(市、区)主要经济指标排序(十三)(2005)

The Orders of Major Economic Indicators by Province (City,Region)in China(13)(2005)

单位：亿元 (100 million yuan)

地区	Region	工业企业产品销售收入 Sales Revenue of Industrial Enterprises	位次 Order	工业企业利润总额 Total Profits of Industrial Enterprises	位次 Order	工业企业亏损企业亏损额 Loss of Loss-making Enterprises	位次 Order
全国总计	**National Total**	**244593.4**		**14362.0**		**1923.0**	
北京	Beijing	7151.7	10	391.1	10	94.0	6
天津	Tianjin	6865.2	11	520.2	9	70.0	8
河北	Hebei	10707.0	6	692.1	7	77.5	7
山西	Shanxi	4626.1	15	264.9	17	42.0	18
内蒙古	Inner Mongolia	2973.8	20	225.9	18	16.8	27
辽宁	Liaoning	10570.6	7	349.2	14	213.6	2
吉林	Jilin	3576.6	18	138.3	22	63.1	10
黑龙江	Heilongjiang	4649.4	14	1065.1	5	60.5	11
上海	Shanghai	16346.1	5	939.6	6	179.2	3
江苏	Jiangsu	32129.5	2	1386.5	3	153.8	4
浙江	Zhejiang	21702.5	4	1072.8	4	98.4	5
安徽	Anhui	4599.5	16	203.0	20	32.3	21
福建	Fujian	7676.9	9	377.0	13	50.2	15
江西	Jiangxi	2883.1	21	115.5	24	20.3	24
山东	Shandong	29910.8	3	2138.2	1	69.5	9
河南	Henan	10049.4	8	668.0	8	49.0	17
湖北	Hubei	5977.9	12	335.8	15	53.6	14
湖南	Hunan	4496.6	17	188.2	21	23.6	23
广东	Guangdong	34033.3	1	1457.6	2	238.7	1
广西	Guangxi	2448.7	24	132.7	23	19.5	25
海南	Hainan	426.4	30	37.5	29	6.1	30
重庆	Chongqing	2516.4	23	112.1	25	18.3	26
四川	Sichuan	5928.1	13	321.9	16	35.4	19
贵州	**Guizhou**	**1577.2**	**27**	**70.8**	**26**	**33.2**	**20**
云南	Yunnan	2532.6	22	223.2	19	27.6	22
西藏	Tibet	22.1	31	3.7	31	0.2	31
陕西	Shanxi	3175.6	19	385.9	12	58.5	12
甘肃	Gansu	1924.3	26	63.0	28	53.7	13
青海	Qinghai	450.0	29	69.3	27	8.1	29
宁夏	Ningxia	639.2	28	20.1	30	13.4	28
新疆	Xinjiang	2102.9	25	388.6	11	49.7	16

24-14 全国各省(市、区)主要经济指标排序(十四)(2005)

The Orders of Major Economic Indicators by Province(City,Region)in China(14)(2005)

地区	Region	工业企业税金总额(亿元) Total Taxes of Industrial Enterprises (100 million yuan)	位次 Order	总资产贡献率(%) Ratio of Total Assets to Industrial Output Value(%)	位次 Order	社会消费品零售总额(亿元) Total Retail Sales of Consumer Goods (100 million yuan)	位次 Order
全国总计	**National Total**	**10967.5**		**12.7**		**67176.6**	
北京	Beijing	257.6	17	7.1	31	2902.8	11
天津	Tianjin	240.6	18	14.3	8	1190.1	23
河北	Hebei	476.3	7	14.5	7	2952.9	10
山西	Shanxi	363.3	12	11.5	17	1401.2	17
内蒙古	Inner Mongolia	192.1	21	12.7	10	1344.1	19
辽宁	Liaoning	441.2	8	8.1	29	2999.0	6
吉林	Jilin	203.0	20	9.1	26	1460.8	16
黑龙江	Heilongjiang	402.0	10	30.9	1	1760.1	15
上海	Shanghai	605.6	5	11.2	19	2973.0	8
江苏	Jiangsu	1001.3	2	11.3	18	5699.9	3
浙江	Zhejiang	805.4	4	12.5	11	4631.7	4
安徽	Anhui	265.4	16	10.8	21	1765.0	14
福建	Fujian	273.1	15	11.7	14	2345.8	13
江西	Jiangxi	160.2	23	11.6	16	1236.2	21
山东	Shandong	1258.1	1	18.5	4	6126.4	2
河南	Henan	534.4	6	16.0	5	3358.4	5
湖北	Hubei	369.2	11	9.9	25	2964.6	9
湖南	Hunan	357.4	13	14.1	9	2459.1	12
广东	Guangdong	940.8	3	10.7	22	7882.6	1
广西	Guangxi	156.7	24	11.7	15	1397.0	18
海南	Hainan	32.1	30	12.2	12	268.6	28
重庆	Chongqing	141.0	25	10.0	24	1215.8	22
四川	Sichuan	326.4	14	10.1	23	2981.4	7
贵州	**Guizhou**	**89.3**	**27**	**10.9**	**20**	**606.9**	**27**
云南	Yunnan	415.4	9	18.9	3	1034.4	24
西藏	Tibet	2.4	31	8.3	28	73.1	31
陕西	Shanxi	236.4	19	14.5	6	1322.4	20
甘肃	Gansu	120.3	26	8.4	27	632.8	26
青海	Qinghai	36.5	28	12.1	13	160.5	30
宁夏	Ningxia	33.4	29	7.4	30	174.3	29
新疆	Xinjiang	165.3	22	22.3	2	637.8	25

24–15 全国各省(市、区）主要经济指标排序（十五）(2005)

The Orders of Major Economic Indicators by Province (City,Region)in China(15)(2005)

单位：亿美元 (USD 100 million)

地 区	Region	海关进出口额 Total Exports and Imports	位次 Order	#出口额 Exports	位次 Order	#进口额 Imports	位次 Order
全国总计	**National Total**	**14219.0**		**7619.5**		**6599.5**	
北 京	Beijing	1255.1	4	308.7	7	946.4	4
天 津	Tianjin	532.8	8	273.8	8	259.0	7
河 北	Hebei	160.7	10	109.2	10	51.5	10
山 西	Shanxi	55.5	19	35.3	18	20.2	22
内蒙古	Inner Mongolia	48.8	21	17.7	25	31.0	16
辽 宁	Liaoning	410.1	9	234.4	9	175.7	9
吉 林	Jilin	65.3	17	24.7	23	40.6	12
黑龙江	Heilongjiang	95.7	11	60.7	11	35.0	14
上 海	Shanghai	1863.4	3	907.2	3	956.2	3
江 苏	Jiangsu	2279.2	2	1229.7	2	1049.6	2
浙 江	Zhejiang	1073.9	5	768.0	4	305.9	6
安 徽	Anhui	91.2	12	51.9	12	39.3	13
福 建	Fujian	544.1	7	348.4	6	195.7	8
江 西	Jiangxi	40.6	25	24.4	24	16.3	24
山 东	Shandong	767.4	6	461.2	5	306.1	5
河 南	Henan	77.2	16	50.9	13	26.4	18
湖 北	Hubei	90.5	13	44.3	16	46.3	11
湖 南	Hunan	60.0	18	37.5	17	22.5	20
广 东	Guangdong	4279.6	1	2381.6	1	1898.1	1
广 西	Guangxi	51.8	20	28.8	20	23.0	19
海 南	Hainan	25.4	27	10.2	27	15.2	26
重 庆	Chongqing	42.9	24	25.2	22	17.7	23
四 川	Sichuan	79.0	15	47.0	15	32.0	15
贵 州	**Guizhou**	**14.0**	**28**	**8.6**	**28**	**5.4**	**28**
云 南	Yunnan	47.4	22	26.4	21	21.0	21
西 藏	Tibet	2.1	31	1.7	31	0.4	31
陕 西	Shanxi	45.8	23	30.8	19	15.0	27
甘 肃	Gansu	26.3	26	10.9	26	15.4	25
青 海	Qinghai	4.1	30	3.2	30	0.9	30
宁 夏	Ningxia	9.7	29	6.9	29	2.8	29
新 疆	Xinjiang	79.4	14	50.4	14	29.0	17

24-16 全国各省(市、区）主要经济指标排序（十六）(2005)

The Orders of Major Economic Indicators by Province (City,Region)in China(16)(2005)

地 区	Region	国际旅游外汇收入(亿美元) Foreign Exchange Earnings (USD 10000)	位次 Order	国际旅游接待人数（万人次）Number of International Tourists Received (10000 person-times)	位次 Order	#外国人 Foreigners	位次 Order
全国总计	**National Total**	**292.96**		**12029.20**		**2025.50**	
北 京	Beijing	36.19	2	362.9	4	311.6	3
天 津	Tianjin	5.09	10	74.0	16	67.5	15
河 北	Hebei	2.09	20	62.7	19	57.4	18
山 西	Shanxi	1.16	24	42.2	23	25.4	25
内蒙古	Inner Mongolia	3.52	14	100.2	12	99.6	9
辽 宁	Liaoning	7.38	8	130.2	10	111.1	7
吉 林	Jilin	1.20	23	37.3	24	30.7	22
黑龙江	Heilongjiang	3.40	15	82.2	15	76.4	11
上 海	Shanghai	35.56	3	444.5	2	379.9	2
江 苏	Jiangsu	22.60	4	378.3	3	262.2	4
浙 江	Zhejiang	17.16	5	348.1	5	232.9	5
安 徽	Anhui	1.86	21	63.3	18	41.1	20
福 建	Fujian	13.05	6	197.4	6	72.4	13
江 西	Jiangxi	1.04	25	37.3	25	13.6	27
山 东	Shandong	7.80	7	155.1	7	124.8	6
河 南	Henan	2.16	19	60.1	20	34.7	21
湖 北	Hubei	2.76	17	82.6	14	62.7	16
湖 南	Hunan	3.90	12	72.0	17	60.9	17
广 东	Guangdong	64.57	1	1897.0	1	476.5	1
广 西	Guangxi	3.59	13	147.7	9	88.7	10
海 南	Hainan	1.28	22	43.2	22	26.9	24
重 庆	Chongqing	2.64	18	52.4	21	41.8	19
四 川	Sichuan	3.16	16	106.3	11	68.3	14
贵 州	**Guizhou**	**1.01**	**26**	**27.6**	**28**	**9.3**	**29**
云 南	Yunnan	5.28	9	150.3	8	99.7	8
西 藏	Tibet	0.44	29	12.1	29	11.1	28
陕 西	Shanxi	4.46	11	92.8	13	74.6	12
甘 肃	Gansu	0.59	28	28.9	27	17.2	26
青 海	Qinghai	0.11	30	3.5	30	1.5	30
宁 夏	Ningxia	0.02	31	0.8	31	0.7	31
新 疆	Xinjiang	1.00	27	33.1	26	29.0	23

24-17 全国各省(市、区)主要经济指标排序(十七)(2005)

The Orders of Major Economic Indicators by Province (City,Region)in China(17)(2005)

单位：元 (yuan)

地区	Region	职工平均工资 Average Wage of Staff and Workers	位次 Order	城镇居民人均可支配收入 Per Capita Annual Disposable Income of Urban Households	位次 Order	农民人均纯收入 Per Capita Annual Net Income of Rural Residents	位次 Order
全国	**National Total**	**18405**		**10493.0**		**3254.9**	
北京	Beijing	34191	1	17653.0	2	7346.3	2
天津	Tianjin	25271	5	12638.6	5	5579.9	4
河北	Hebei	14707	24	9107.1	16	3481.6	10
山西	Shanxi	15645	18	8913.9	17	2890.7	18
内蒙古	Inner Mongolia	15985	15	9136.8	14	2988.9	17
辽宁	Liaoning	17331	9	9107.6	15	3690.2	9
吉林	Jilin	14409	28	8690.6	19	3264.0	11
黑龙江	Heilongjiang	14458	25	8272.5	24	3221.3	12
上海	Shanghai	31940	2	18645.0	1	8247.8	1
江苏	Jiangsu	20957	7	12318.6	7	5276.3	5
浙江	Zhejiang	25896	4	16293.8	3	6660.0	3
安徽	Anhui	15334	21	8470.7	22	2641.0	22
福建	Fujian	17146	11	12321.3	6	4450.4	7
江西	Jiangxi	13688	31	8619.7	21	3128.9	13
山东	Shandong	16614	13	10744.8	8	3930.5	8
河南	Henan	14282	30	8668.0	20	2870.6	19
湖北	Hubei	14419	26	8785.9	18	3099.2	15
湖南	Hunan	15659	17	9524.0	10	3117.7	14
广东	Guangdong	23959	6	14770.0	4	4690.5	6
广西	Guangxi	15461	20	9286.7	12	2494.7	24
海南	Hainan	14417	27	8123.9	27	3004.0	16
重庆	Chongqing	16630	12	10243.5	9	2809.3	20
四川	Sichuan	15826	16	8386.0	23	2802.8	21
贵州	**Guizhou**	**14344**	**29**	**8147.1**	**26**	**1877.0**	**31**
云南	Yunnan	16140	14	9265.9	13	2041.8	29
西藏	Tibet	28950	3	9431.2	11	2077.9	27
陕西	Shanxi	14796	23	8272.0	25	2052.6	28
甘肃	Gansu	14939	22	8086.8	29	1979.9	30
青海	Qinghai	19084	8	8057.9	30	2151.5	26
宁夏	Ningxia	17211	10	8093.6	28	2508.9	23
新疆	Xinjiang	15558	19	7990.2	31	2482.2	25

贵州风采 GUIZHOU ELEGANT APPEARANCE

2006

贵州省民族事务委员会

Guizhou Province Ethnic Affairs Commission

2005年，在省委、省政府的领导下，省民委（省宗教局）坚持以邓小平理论、“三个代表”重要思想和科学发展观为指导，以学习贯彻胡锦涛总书记视察贵州时的重要讲话和中央民族工作会议精神为主线，着力推动民族工作再上新台阶；以贯彻实施《宗教事务条例》为重点，切实加强抵御境外利用宗教进行渗透的工作，努力推动重点、难点问题的解决，各项工作取得了新的进展，为努力开创“十一五”时期民族、宗教工作新局面打下了扎实基础。

一、抢抓机遇，推动中央民族工作会议精神的贯彻落实

全力推进中央民族工作会议精神和国务院《若干规定》的贯彻落实工作。认真学习领会中央民族工作会议精神实质，增强贯彻落实的自觉性。开展广泛深入的调查研究，为省委、省政府提供决策依据。与省委统战部共同牵头，从省直有关部门抽调力量组成调研组，分别由厅级领导干部带队，对各地2000年以来的民族工作情况进行了深入调研。及时筹备召开全省民族工作会议。加强协调工作和督促检查，推动全省民族工作会议精神和黔党发〔2005〕16号文件的贯彻落实。

二、围绕民族工作主题，促进少数民族和民族地区经济社会全面发展

努力推动少数民族和民族地区“三个基本”问题的解决。会同省发展改革委起草的《贵州省“十一五”扶持人口较少民族（毛南族）发展专项建设规划》已经省长办公会议讨论并原则通过。大力加强民族文化、教育工作。成功举办了全省第三届少数民族文艺会演。建成贵州民族文化宫被省委、省政府确定为2006年10件实事之一。启动实施“百优助学工程”。举办了全省民族教育管理干部培训班。积极推动民族法制建设，促进社会和谐稳定。进一步加大少数民族干部培训力度。

三、以贯彻实施《宗教事务条例》为重点，切实加强抵御境外渗透工作

贵州省民族事务委员会党组书记、主任
贵州省宗教事务局局长　郝桂华
The secretary and director of Guizhou Province Ethnic Affairs Commission Party group, the director of Guizhou Province Religious Affairs Bureau Haoguihua

广泛开展《宗教事务条例》培训，积极争取省人民政府举办的全省学习贯彻《条例》培训班。全省共培训党政干部、宗教工作干部、宗教界人士和信教群众1.77万人次。编印《条例》、《宗教活动场所设立审批和登记办法》及有关宣传资料3.8万份，在《贵州民族报》开辟了专栏。宗教事务行政执法主体建设取得初步成效。贵阳、遵义、六盘水、安顺、黔西南、毕节、铜仁等7个市（州、地）编委行文明确同级民族宗教工作机构为“民族事务局”，加挂“宗教事务局”牌子。切实做好抵御境外渗透工作，会同有关部门对境外基督教在我省的渗透情况进行了全面调查，对基督教私设聚会点情况开展了专题调研。加强宗教事务的依法管理，维护宗教领域稳定，依照《条例》规定，规范了宗教活动场所设立审批程序。积极推进爱国宗教团体建设。

全省民族工作会议
The provincial national work conference

贵州民族文化宫新貌
New look of Guizhou Cultural Palace of Nationalities

贵州省宗教事务局

Guizhou Province Religious Affairs Bureau

In 2005, under the leadership of provincial committee and government, the provincial Ethnic Affairs Commission (provincial Bureau of Religious Affairs) insisted on taking Deng Xiaoping Theory and the important thought of "three representatives" and scientific development concept as guides, took the study and implementation important speech of general secretary Hu Jintao inspection Guizhou and the central national work conference spirit as the main line, promoted national work to a new level; Took the implementation of the "religious affairs regulations" as the focus, and strengthened the work of resistance outside use religion making the infiltration, and strove to promote the solution of major and difficult issues, and achieved new progress in all fields, laid a solid foundation for striving to create ethnic, religious work new phase in the period of "Eleventh Five".

First, to seize the opportunity, and promote the implementation of the central national work conference spirit

To spare no effort to promote the spirit of Central Nationalities Work Conference and implementation works of the State Council's "certain provisions". Conscientiously studied and grasped the spirit essence of the central national work conference to enhance implementation consciousness. Opened extensive in-depth investigation and study, provided the decision-making basis for provincial Party committee and government. Jointly took the lead with provincial Party committee United Front Department, composed the investigation team transferred power from provincial related organs, the departmental cadres respectively led to carry out in-depth studies to the nation work situation in various parts since 2000. To prepare holding provincial national work conference in time. Enhanced coordination and supervision and inspection, upgraded provincial national work conference spirit and implemented Qian Party Sending [2005] No.1 6 document.

Second, around the theme of the national work, promoted national and regional economic and social development in a comprehensive way

The minorities and ethnic areas "three basics" problems were advanced settlement in great efforts. Within the Provincial Development and Reform Committee drafting the "Guizhou Province 'Eleventh Five' Support Less National Population (Maonan Autonomous) Development Special Construction Planning", has been discussed and approved in the governor official meeting. Vigorously strengthened national culture, education works. The Third Provincial Minority Theatrical Festival was successfully held. Guizhou Cultural Palace of Nationalities which was determined the one of 10 things in 2006 by provincial Party committee and provincial government was built. The "100 superior assistance study projects" was started implementation. The provincial national education management cadre training class was held. Actively advanced the national legal system construction, and promoted social harmony and stability. The training capability of minority cadres was further enhanced.

Third, to take the implementation of the "religious affairs regulations" as the focus, and strengthen the work of resistance foreign infiltration

Extensively opened the training of the "religious affairs regulations", actively sought provincial government to hold the provincial study and implementing the "Regulations" classes. Party cadres, religious cadres and religious people and religious masses were totally trained 17.7 thousand person-time. Produced the "Regulations", "The establishment and registration procedures of religious activity place" and related publicity materials 38,000 copies, has opened special column in the "Guizhou National Paper". Religious affairs administrative law enforcement main building achieved initial successes. The boards of Guiyang, Zunyi, Liupanshui, Anshun, Qianxinan, Bijie, Tongren seven cities (states, prefectures) cleared the same-level ethnic and religious work organ to set up "Ethnic Affairs Bureau" and increase "Religious Affairs" brand. Conscientiously did well work of resistance outside infiltration, and with the departments concerned, conducted a comprehensive survey on foreign Christianity infiltration in our province, set up a special research to the Christian privately gather point situation. To strengthen the management of religious affairs according to law, safeguard the stability of the area of religions, and standardize the establishment procedure for religious activity place in accordance with the "Regulations" provision. The patriotic religious group building was actively promoted.

省民委郝桂华主任（左二）在贵州民族学院进行调研
The director of Province Ethnic Affairs Commission Haoguihua (the second from left) surveyed in Guizhou National Academy

在第三届全省少数民族文艺会演上省民委主任郝桂华（第二排左三）与演职人员合影
The director of Province Ethnic Affairs Commission Haoguihua (the third from left of the second row) had a group photo taken with performance staff in the third provincial minority nationality theatrical festival

回眸“十五”贵州交通　有力地推动

Looking Back "tenth five" Guizhou traffic　promoting economy and

清镇至黄果树高速公路红枫湖特大桥　邓望庐摄
Qingzhen to Huangguoshu Highway, Hongfenghu Great Bridge
Photographer　Deng Wanglu

清镇至黄果树高速公路　邓望庐 摄
Qingzhen to Huangguoshu Highway
Photographer　Deng Wanglu

农村公路加快发展促进新农村建设　田刚 摄
The development of rural road accelerating for the new rural construction
Photographer　Tian Gang

实施“安保工程”后的国道210线娄山关段　李黔刚 摄
The implementation of the "security project" after Loushanguan s
the State Road 210 Line
Photographer　Li Qiangang

全省经济社会的快速协调健康发展

society to rapid coordinated and healthy development effectively

凯里至麻江高速公路　　李黔刚 摄
Kaili to majiang Highway
Photographer　Li Qiangang

崇溪河至遵义高速公路　　邓望庐 摄
Chongxihe to Zunyi Highway
Photographer　Deng Wanglu

路运输业加快发展方便了老百姓出行　　李黔刚 摄
he accelerated development of road transport facilitating ordinary
eople getting around
hotographer Li Qianggang

整治后的赤水河航道呈现繁忙景象　　李黔刚 摄
A busy scene after the rectification of Chishui River Channel
Photographer Li Qianggang

落实科学发展观 努力实现

Implementation the scientific developing concept Efforts

红枫湖大桥
Hongfenghu Bridge

贵毕西溪
GuiBi Xixi

贵州高速公路开发总公司是专门从事高速公路和高等级公路建设管理的国有独资大型企业，公司的主要职责是按照国家的规划从事高速公路、高等级公路及其它交通基础设施项目的融资、建设和经营管理。公司采取"国家投资、地方筹资、社会融资、银行贷款、引进外资"等方式，多渠道筹措高速公路建设资金。

为规范公路建设市场和加强项目管理，贵州高速公路开发总公司逐步建立和完善现代企业管理制度，在所有在建项目上严格执行项目法人制、招投标制、工程监理制和合同管理制，初步建立起了"统一、开放、竞争、有序"的高速公路建设市场。公司制定了"质量、进度、成本、安全、廉政、环保"的十二字工作方针和"更新更快更好"的管理理念。广大职工解放思想、锐意进取，公司诚实守信，不断做强做大。省内高速公路和高等级公路的快速发展，初步改变了贵州公路交通的落后面貌，有力促进了贵州经济和社会的发展。

"十五"是新世纪的第一个五年期，总公司在省委、省政府的领导下，在省国资委、省交通厅的大力支持下，认真贯彻落实党中央、国务院一系列重大战略部署，牢牢抓住中央实施西部大开发的历史机遇，落实科学发展观，求真务实，圆满地完成了各项工作任务。

"十五"期间共完成高等级公路建设投资304亿元，年均增长9.7%；建成高等级公路八条，共计1022公里，比"九五"建成的301公里增长239.5%。"十五"期间建成了我省标准最高的清镇至黄果树高速公路，享有"贵州第一路"的盛名，建成了"具有世界级难度"的崇溪河至遵义高速公路，实现了西南出海通道的全线贯通。截止2005年底，我省高速公路通车里程达576公里，在建里程504公里，"一横一纵四联线"骨架正在加快形成。

（文字提供：车世武）

（图片提供：钟蔚 邓望庐）

崇遵红花岗遂道
ChongZun Honghuagang Tunnel

Guizhou Expressway Development Corporation is belonged to the state-owned large enterprise which is devoted to the construction management of express highway and high-

高速公路建设历史性跨越

to achieve the historic leap in highway construction

关兴公路北盘江大桥
Beipanjiang Bridge in GuanXing Road

grade highway. The primary responsibility of the corporation is engaged in finance, construction and management for express highway and the high-grade highway and other transportation infrastructure projects in accordance with the planning of State. The corporation raises multi-channel funds for highway construction taking ways of "national investment, local finance, community support, bank loans, introduction of foreign investment".

For standard highway construction market and enhancement project management, Guizhou Expressway Development Corporation gradually established and improved the modern enterprise management system, strictly built the executive project legal system, bidding system, engineering supervision system and contract management system in all projects, initially established a "united, open, competitive and order" express highway construction market. The corporation developed the policy "quality, progress, cost, security, honest and clean, environmental protection" and the management idea "updated, faster and better". Workers emancipated the mind and forged ahead, the corporation was honest and trustworthy, continually grew in size and strength. The rapid development of provincial express highway and high-grade highway, which initially changed the backward image of Guizhou road traffic, has promoted Guizhou economic and social development.

"Tenth Five" is the first period of five-year in the new century, under the leadership of provincial committee and government, and the strong support of the Provincial Stated-owned Assets Supervision and Administration Commission and the Provincial Communication Department, the corporation conscientiously implemented a series of major strategic plans of the Party Central Committee and the State Council, firmly grasped the historic opportunity of the West Development, implemented the scientific development concept, sough truth and dealt with concrete matters, successfully fulfilled all tasks.

During the period of "Tenth Five", the corporation totally completed the high-grade highway construction investment of 30.4 billion yuan, an annual average growth of 9.7%; Eight high-grade highways have been completed with a total of 1,022 kilometres, up 239.5% than 301 km completed in "Ninth Five". During the "Tenth Five", the corporation built the highest standard Qingzhen-Huangguoshu Express Highway of the province, that enjoyed the fame "the first way in Guizhou", and constructed the "having world-class difficulty" Chongxihe-Zunyi Express Highway. The southwest access to the sea has been opened to traffic. By the end of 2005, the province's highway traffic mileage reached 576 km, 504 km in building, the structure "one vertical, one horizontal, and four united lines" was taking shape at an accelerating pace.

(Writing: Che Shiwu)

(Photo: Zhong Wei Deng Wanglu)

贵新公路
GuiXin Highway

水黄路
ShuiHuang Road

贵州省工商

Administration for Industry and

2005年，贵州省工商行政管理局全面落实科学发展观，深入开展保持共产党员先进性教育活动，正确处理监管执法和优质服务的关系，深入整顿和规范市场经济秩序，继续推进监管制度改革创新，充分发挥工商行政管理在促进经济社会协调发展中的职能作用，努力提高执法能力和执法水平，各项工作取得了新的成绩。

一是保持共产党员先进性教育活动成效明显

省工商局机关10个党支部167名共产党员参加了先进性教育活动，党员参与率达到100%，群众满意度达100%，针对查找出的问题和群众建议，认真制定了整改措施并逐步落实整改；组织开展了一系列有益于提高党员素质、加强基层组织、服务人民群众的活动；“七一”期间，对省局机关2003年至2005年度的优秀共产党员、党务工作者及先进党支部和在此次先进性教育活动中的先进单位进行了表彰；召开了全系统保持共产党员先进性长效机制研讨会，制定了《省工商系统保持共产党员先进性长效机制的意见》；在省委先教活动领导小组召开的座谈会上，被指定作了经验交流发言，并两次被推荐为中央督导组调研单位之一，得到中央督导组的充分肯定。

二是为促进经济社会发展作出了新的贡献

积极引导支持各类市场主体健康发展。扶持非公有制经济加快发展。鼓励和支持个体私营企业参与国有企业改制、参与农业开发，认真落实各项优惠政策；围绕建立以明晰产权为目标的现代企业制度，大力支持国有企业改革，积极做好引进外资工作；积极为企业做好服务工作，主动培训企业经营管理人员；积极推进“诚信贵州”建设，完成了企业信用体系建设任务并创建了贵州省合同信用促进会；继续为服务“三农”扎实工作，认真贯彻落实中央和省委的1号文件，围绕农业增效、农民增收开展服务“三农”工作。全年共查处农资案件1211件，总案值942.89万元，为农民挽回经济损失387.78万元；积极支持电煤安全生产。

三是整顿和规范市场经济秩序取得了新的成效

全省各级工商行政管理机关认真履行市场监管和行政执法的职能，不断加大案件查处力度，依法严厉查处各类违法违章行为，努力维护正常的市场经济秩序。共查处各种案件25504件，案值122839.84万元。继续深入开展食品安全专项整治。建立了食品安全预警防范和快速反应机制，确保各类食品市场安全有序。全年共检查食品经营户29万余户，查处假冒伪劣食品案件4780件；深入开展了保护商标专用权行动。大力加强商标注册保护，支持引导企业实施商标战略，充分发挥商标在促进经济发展中的重要作用。全年共查处商标侵权案件276件；扎实做好猪链球菌病和“禽流感”防控工作。全省各级工商机关制订并启动了市场监管应急预案，加强了市场监管，受到了省政府的肯定；加大了打击商业欺诈行为的力度。围绕“打虚假树诚信”主题，开展打击虚假违法广告专项整治行动；严厉打击传销和变相传销违法行为；深入开展对不正当竞争行为和垄断性行业限制竞争行为的专项执法行动。切实维护经营者、消费者的合法权益和公平竞争的市场秩序；认真受理消费者申诉，维护了消费者的合法权益。

四是坚持加强党的建设、队伍建设和党风廉政建设相结合，努力提高依法行政、执法为民的能力

认真做好班子届中考察和管理工作；狠抓了干部选拔任用、调配录用和管理、教育培训工作，全系统干部队伍素质进一步提高；狠抓了基层执法干部队伍建设和基层工商所的党组织建设，基层建设的整体水平有新的提高；扎实推进党风廉政建设和反腐败斗争；切实加强财务管理工作，严格执行“收支两条线”制度；加强法制建设，促进依法行政。

4月19日至20日，肖永安副省长在省工商局局长杨正国陪同下，对黔东南州基层工商系统“保持共产党员先进性”教育活动及工作开展情况进行了专题调研

19 to 20 April, accompanied by the secretary of Provincial Commerce and Industry Administration Yang Zhengguo, the provincial deputy governor Xiao Yongan, carried out specific topics studies to the Qiandongnan state grassroots level industrial and commercial system "maintain the advanced nature of Party members" educational activities and works

省工商局党组书记、局长杨正国同志率局领导成员到黔南州龙里县摆省乡访贫问苦

The provincial Party secretary of the Commerce and Industry Administration, the Dirctor comrade Yang Zhengguo led the other leader members to Baisheng township Longli county Qiannan state visiting the poor and the suffering

贵阳市消费者协会在贵阳市百货大楼广场举行“3.15”健康维权大型宣传活动

Guiyang City Consumer Association held "3.15" healthy safeguard-right major publicity campaign in the department store plaza of Guiyang city

行政管理局
Commerce of Guizhou Province

In 2005, the Administration for Industry and Commerce of Guizhou Province fully implemented the scientific development concept, to conduct maintaining advanced education activities of Party members in-depth and correctly handle the relationship between regulation and law enforcement and quality service, in rectifying and regulating market economic order, and continued to promote regulatory reform and innovation, gave full play the functions of industrial and commercial administration in promoting coordinated economic and social development, and made efforts to enhance capabilities and the level of law enforcement, and made new achievements on all kinds of works.

Firstly, to make marked success on maintaining advanced education activities of Party members.

167 Party members of 10 Party branch of Provincial Administration of Industry and Commerce organ attended the Party advanced educational activities, the participation rate of 100% of Party members, satisfied rate of 100% of the masses, seriously formulated rectification measures and gradually implemented rectification in accordance with the problems and suggestions of the masses; Organized a series of beneficial activities to improve the quality of Party members, strengthening grass-roots organizations, service of the masses; "71" period, the provincial administration organ in 2003 to 2005 annual outstanding Party members and Party workers and advanced Party branches and the advanced units on advanced educational activities were conducted; Held a system-wide mechanism for long seminar on maintaining the advanced nature of Party members, formulated the "the views of long-standing mechanism on maintaining the advanced nature of Party members of provincial industrial and commercial system"; On the forum of holding by Provincial committee advanced educational activities leader group, has been designated to address by the exchange of experience, and two were recommended to the one of the investigation units of the Central Supervision Group, has been fully affirmed by the Central Supervision Group.

Secondly, to make new contribution for promoting economic and social development.

To guide support the healthy development of the main parts in the market actively. To support acceleration development of non-public ownership economy. To encourage and support individual and private enterprises to participate reform in state-owned enterprises, participate in agricultural development, and seriously implement the preferential policies; Focusing on establishing the modern enterprise system taking a clear property right as the goal, to support the reform of state-owned enterprises strongly, and actively carry out the introduction of foreign capital; To carry out services for enterprises actively, and train business management members initiatively; To promote "good faith Guizhou" construction actively, complete enterprise credit system construction tasks and establish Contract Credit Promoting Union of Guizhou Province; To continue service for "three agriculture" works. To implement the No.1 document of the Party Central and Provincial Committee seriously, carry out service "three agriculture" works on surrounding agriculture increased efficiency and peasants increased incomes. And investigated agricultural resources of the year, a total of 1,211 cases, with a total value of 9.4289 million yuan, retrieving economic losses for farmers 3.8778 million yuan; To support electricity coal safety production actively.

Thirdly, to achieve new results on rectifying and regulating market economic order.

The provincial industrial and commercial administrative organs fulfilled conscientiously market regulation and administrative law enforcement functions, increasing the enhancement of the cases investigated, and severely punished all kinds of activities that violate the law, hardly kept the normal order of the market economy. To investigate 25,504 various cases, the value of 1228.3984 million yuan. To continuously carry out food safety special renovation. And established the food security early warning and rapid reaction mechanism to ensure that all food market safety and order. The annual food business operators were inspected 290 thousand households, and 4,780 pieces of counterfeit and shoddy food cases; To carry out protection activities of exclusive rights of trademarks in-depth. Vigorously strengthening the protection of trade marks registration, supporting to guide enterprises implementation trademarks strategic, and gave full play an important role of trade marks in promoting economic development. Annual a total of 276 trademark infringement cases were investigated; To control the pig streptococcus disease and the "avian flu" precautions. The provincial industrial and commercial organs developed and activated the market contingency plans and strengthened the market supervision confirmed by the provincial government; To intensify efforts to combat commercial fraud. Focusing on the theme of "fight falseness & set faith", to fight against false advertising special-operations; To crack down illegal pyramid schemes and disguised pyramid schemes; To carry out special enforcement actions of the acts of unfair competition and monopoly industries restrictions competitive conduct. To safeguard the legitimate rights and interests of operators and consumers, and fair competition in the market order; To handle consumer complaints and safeguard the legitimate rights and interests of consumers conscientiously.

Fourthly, to strengthen party building, team building and build a clean and honest government to enhance the capacity of administration according to law and law enforcement for the people.

To do a job of team-term investigation and management conscientiously; To grasp selection and appointment of cadres and the works of management, education and train to further improve the quality of the whole system cadres; To seize the teem construction of primary level law enforcement cadres and the Party organizations construction of the grass-roots level industrial and commercial stations, and the overall construction of grass-roots having a new improvement; To improve Party conduct and the anti-corruption struggle solidly. To strengthen financial management and strictly implement the system of "two lines of revenue and expenditure", and strengthening the legal system constructions, to promote administration according to law.

烧毁假冒伪劣商品
The fake and shoddy goods are burning

辉煌"十五"

Drawing the national taxation

团结奋进的领导班子
The united and advanced leadership group

精神文明建设卓有成效，国税社会形象与地位显著提升
The building of spiritual civilization has fruitful efforts, the image and status of the national taxation increased significantly

贵州省国家税务局系统组建于国家实施分税制财政体制改革的1994年，主要负责征收管理增值税、消费税、外商投资和外国企业所得税、中央企业和新办企业所得税、车辆购置税、个人储蓄存款利息所得税等。现辖9个市（州、地）局、95个县（市、区、特区）局、214个基层分局（所）。现有在职人员8514人，平均年龄39.22岁，大专以上学历的占87.58%。截止2005年底，全省国税系统管理的纳税人共249801户，其中企业47261户，占18.9%，个体工商户202540户，占81.1%。

"十五"时期，全省国税系统紧紧抓住国家实施"西部大开发"战略的历史机遇，围绕"聚财为国、执法为民"的税务工作宗旨和"强基固本抓关键，创新务实促发展"的工作基调，大力推进依法治税、深化税收改革、强化科学管理、加强队伍建设，实现了全省国税税收收入的协调高速增长："十五"期间，全省国税收入在"九五"期末只有82.27亿元的基础上，先后跃上了100亿元和200亿元台阶，2005年达到了206.47亿元，比2000年翻了近一番半，税收占GDP的比重也由8.39%提高到了10.6%；五年累计组织税收收入703亿元，是"九五"期间税收总量的2.03倍，年均增长达到19.9%，比"九五"时期提高9.7个百分点。同时，全省国税工作得到各级党委政府及社会各界的高度评价，省局机关等6个单位被评为"全国精神文明建设工作先进单位"，1个基层单位被评为"全国文明单位"，全系统被命名为全省文明行业，8个市州地局成为当地的文明行业，省局在省委省政府的目标管理考核中连续5年获得一等奖，且名列中央在黔单位榜首，全系统先后有96个单位、20名个人获得省部级的荣誉称号。

现代科学技术是国税事业腾飞的翅膀
The modern science and technology is the wings of rapid development of national taxation cause

全社会依法诚信纳税意识日益提高
The tax payment consciousness of the whole society according to law are getting higher day by day

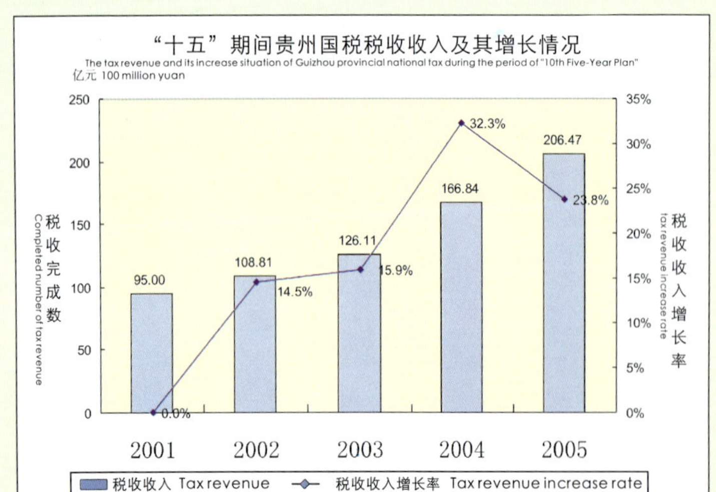

绘就国税新篇章

new chapter in the glorious "Tenth Five"

The system of Guizhou Provincial National Taxation Administration, was founded in 1994, that the state implemented the reform of tax fiscal system, is mainly responsible for the collection and management of value-added tax, consumption tax and foreign investment and foreign enterprise income tax, central enterprise and new-build enterprise income tax, vehicle purchase tax, interest income tax on personal savings deposit. It currently has jurisdiction over 9 cities (prefectures and states) branches, 95 counties (cities, districts, special zones) branches, 214 primary level branches (offices), and has 8,514 serving officers, and their average age was 39.22 years old, college education or higher accounting for 87.58%. By the end of 2005, the taxpayers in the provincial national taxation system management totaled 249,801 households, of which 47,261 enterprises, accounting for 18.9%, and 202,540 individual industrial and commercial households, accounting for 81.1%.

During "10th Five-Year Plan" period, the system of provincial national taxation firmly seized the historic opportunity of the State implementation the "western development" strategy, focused on the taxation work purpose of "the accumulation of wealth for country, law enforcement for people" and the work keynote of "strengthening the foundation to grasp the key, innovating and dealing with concrete matters to promote the development", vigorously promoted regulation tax according to law, deepened reforms, strengthened scientific management, and strengthened team construction, achieved the coordinate, rapid growth on the tax revenue of provincial national tax: "10th Five-Year Plan" period, on the basis of only 8.227 billion yuan of the end of "Ninth Five-year Plan" period, the tax revenue of provincial national tax has leaped 10 billion yuan and 20 billion yuan successively, reached 20.647 billion yuan in 2005, nearly increased double half than that of 2000, the proportion of tax revenue accounting for the GDP increased from 8.39% to 10.6%; Totaled 70.3 billion yuan tax revenue in five years, 2.03 times than the total tax revenue of "Ninth Five-Year Plan" period, with average annual growth 19.9%, more 9.7 percentage points than "Ninth Five-Year" period. Meanwhile, the work of provincial national taxation was got the high evaluation by Party committees and governments at all levels and social all circles, the provincial administration organ and other six units were rated the

优化纳税服务，构建和谐征纳关系
Better service for taxpayers and building a harmonious relationship of imposing and payment

实施科学化精细化管理成为新时期国税工作的主题
Implementation scientific careful management has become the theme of national tax work in the new period

落实税收优惠政策，促进经济社会健康发展
Implemented the tax preferential policy to promote economic and social healthy development

超常规培训工程使国税干部综合素质明显提高
Unconventional training project markedly improved the comprehensive quality of the national taxation cadres

"National Spiritual Civilization Construction Work Advanced Unit", one grassroots unit was rated the "National Civilization Unit", the whole system has been named the province's cultural industry, 8 cities, prefectures, states branches became the local cultural industry, the provincial administration won the first prize in the goal management assessment of provincial Party committee and government for consecutively five years and ranked the top among the Central units in Guizhou, 96 units and 20 individuals of whole system successively awarded the honor title of provincial-level and ministerial-level.

贵州省中小企业局（省非公有制经济办公室）

Guizhou Province Medium-sized and Small Enterprises Bureau (Provincial Non-public Economy Office)

为确保先进性教育活动取得实效，贵州省中小企业局（贵州省非公有制办公室）龙超亚局长（主任）率全局党员和干部职工赴非公有制企业——贵州西洋肥业调研，听取企业对省中小企业局（省非公办）履行工作职责的意见和建议

For ensuring that advanced educational activities making good results, the chief (director) of Guizhou Province Medium-sized and Small Enterprises Bureau (Guizhou Province Non-public Economy Office) Long Chaoya led the party members and cadres and workers of the bureau went to non-public-owned enterprise -- Guizhou Xiyang Fertilizer Industry to research, listen to the suggestions and opinions of enterprise to Province Medium-sized and Small Enterprises Bureau (Guizhou Province Non-public Economy Office) performed job duties

2005年中小企业、非公有制经济发展情况

——新办企业增加。2005年，全省工商企业注册总数为9.49万户，比上年增长19.19%，私营企业达到4.15万户，比上年增长22.38%，占全部企业数的43.72%，个体工商户超过43万户。全省规模以上私营企业数达到805户，比上年增加161户，占全省规模以上工业企业增加数的86.1%。

——经济总量扩大。个体和私营等非公有制经济增长率高于全省GDP的平均增长率，全省经济第一次经济普查的数据表明，非公有制经济在全省经济总量中的比例已达27.8%。中小企业资产规模比上年增加18.7%。

——企业自主创新能力增强。全省中小企业和非公有制经济在自主创新和新产品开发方面能力不断增强。1985年至2005年，我省非公有制企业申请职务发明占全省的43.02%，授权职务发明占全省的40%。

——创造就业岗位能力提高。全省非公有制经济去年新增就业岗位15.49万个，占全省新增就业岗位的80%，比上年提高6.51%。中小企业和非公有制经济已成为吸纳劳动力的主渠道。

——对外贸易扩大。贵州省一批有实力的中小企业和非公有制企业已走出国门，成为实施“走出去”战略的新生力量。

——经济效益提高。全省中小企业实现总产值1067.48亿元，同比增长22.4%，实现利润21.07亿元，同比增长8.38%。

贵州省中小企业局召开全省中小企业、非公有制经济工作会议

Guizhou province Medium-sized and Small Enterprises Bureau held the provincial medium-sized and Small enterprises and non-public-owned enterprises economic work forum

贵州省中小企业局召开全省非公有制企业座谈会

Guizhou province Medium-sized and Small Enterprises Bureau held the provincial non-public-owned enterprises forum

贵州省中小企业局召开省中小企业发展专项资金2005年度项目申报工作会

Guizhou Province Medium-sized and Small Enterprises Bureau convened provincial medium-sized and small enterprises development special funds 2005 annual project report work meeting

广东省委副书记、省长黄华华在第二届中博会贵州省组委会领导的陪同下，亲临中博会贵州展区参观，并与贵州的参展代表进行亲切交谈
The deputy secretary of the Guangdong Provincial Party Committee and the governor Huang Huahua accompanied by the leader of the Second Chinese Fair Guizhou Organization Committee, visited Guizhou show area, and the talked with Guizhou exhibition enterprises delegates

省中小企业局龙超亚局长在“中小企业市场化发展”专题报告会上致辞
The director of Provincial Medium-sized and Small Enterprises Bureau Long Chaoya addressed in "medium-sized and small enterprises market development" symposium

The development situation of medium-sized and small enterprises, non-public economy in the year of 2005

--New business increased. 2005, the total number of businesses registered 94.9 thousand, 19.19% higher than the previous year, private enterprises reached 41.5 thousand, 22.38% higher than the previous year, accounting for 43.72% of the total number of enterprises, individuals households over 430 thousand. The private enterprises above designated size of the province reached 805 households, 161 households increase over the previous year, accounting for 86.1% of added number in industrial enterprises above designated size.

--Economic output expanded. The growth rate of individual and private and other non-public economy were higher than the average growth rate of the provincial GDP, the data of the first economic census in the province showed that the proportion of the non-public ownership economy in total economy reached 27.8%. The asset size of medium-sized and small enterprises increased 18.7% than the previous year.

--Ability to innovate their business increased. The capacity of medium-sized and small enterprises and the non-public ownership economy in independent innovation and new product development has strengthened. 1985-2005, the province's non-public-owned enterprises applied their invention accounting for 43.02% in the province, 40% of the authorized invention in the province.

--Capacity to create jobs improved. The non-public economy increased 154,900 jobs last year, accounting for 80% of the new jobs, more 6.51% than last year. The medium-sized and small enterprises and the non-public economy have became the main channel to absorb the labor force.

--External trade expanded. A number of strong medium-sized and small enterprises and the non-public enterprises of Guizhou province had gone out into the world and became the newly emerging force of implementation the strategy of "going out".

--Economic efficiency increased. The medium-sized and small enterprises achieved output value of 106.748 billion yuan, up 22.4% than the same time of last year, 2.107 billion yuan in profits, an increase of 8.38%.

贵州省中小企业局局长下基层到企业进行调研
The director of Guizhou Province Medium-sized and Small Enterprises Bureau studied to enterprises at the grassroots level

贵州省中小企业局干部职工赴息烽集中营开展保持党员先进性教育活动，接受革命传统教育
All cadres and workers of Guizhou Province Medium-sized and Small Enterprises Bureau went to Xifeng camps to carry out maintaining Party member advanced education activity, and the acceptance revolutionary traditional education

林树森代省长到公安厅视察工作

The Acting Governor Lin Shusen Went to the Public Security Department to Inspect Work

林省长亲切会见省公安厅领导及有关处室负责人
The governor Lin kindly met with the leaders and the persons in charge of offices concerned of the Provincial Public Security Department

省委常委、省公安厅厅长刘光磊向林省长汇报公安工作
The member of the Standing Committee of the Provincial Party Committee and the director of the Provincial Public Security Department Liu Guanglei reported to the governor Lin on the public security work

8月2日下午，贵州省代省长林树森同志在有关领导的陪同下，到我厅视察工作并作重要讲话。代省长林树森充分肯定我省各级公安机关为维护我省社会稳定，打击犯罪、促进经济发展所做出的贡献，同时他强调：一、我省各级公安机关作为社会稳定的主力军，要坚决维护社会的稳定。二、加强公安队伍建设，不断提高民警的综合素质，适应形势发展的需要。三、不断加大对公安机关的投入，使从优待警落实到实处。

In the afternoon of August 2, the acting governor of Guizhou province comrade Lin Shusen accompanied by the leaders concerned, went to our department to inspect the work and gave an important speech. The acting governor Lin Shusen fully affirmed our provincial public security organs at all levels made contribution for safeguard social stability, cracking down on crime, promoting economic development. Meanwhile, he also stressed: First, as the main force in the social stability, our provincial public security organs at all levels will resolutely safeguard social stability. Second, ought to strengthen the public security team construction and constantly improve the overall quality of people's police to meet the needs of the situation developing. Third, ought to constantly enlarge the input to the public security organs and give favored treatment to people's police.

省委常委、省公安厅厅长刘光磊向林省长汇报公安工作
The member of the Standing Committee of the Provincial Party Committee and the director of the Provincial Public Security Department Liu Guanglei reported to the governor Lin on the public security work

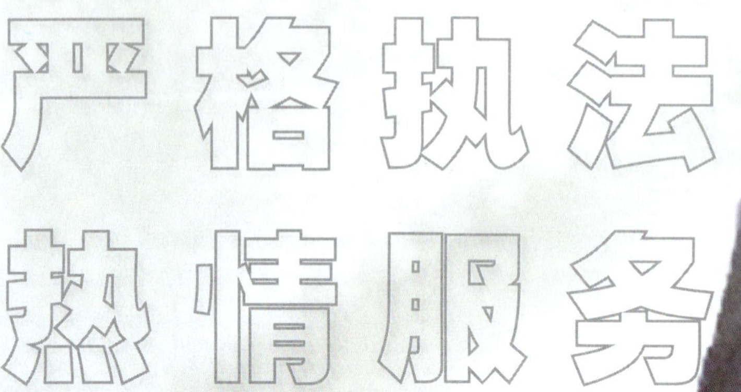

贵州省公安交通警察总队

Guizhou Province Public Security Traffic Police General Team

2005年，贵州交警部门在各级党委、政府和公安机关的领导下，坚持以邓小平理论和“三个代表”重要思想为指导，深入贯彻党的十六届四、五中全会、省委九届五、六次全会和全省公安局长会议精神，树立和落实科学发展观，努力提高预防交通事故能力、维护公路治安能力、服务经济社会发展能力和为民执法能力，不断促进公安交警队伍的规范化建设。紧紧围绕“降事故、保安全、保畅通”的工作目标，结合《中华人民共和国道路交通安全法》的全面实施，深化“五整顿”、“三加强”各项工作措施的落实，大力加强交通安全源头管理，全面整顿路面行车秩序，广泛开展交通安全宣传“五进”活动，深入排查治理道路安全隐患，不断构建和完善责任制体系，形成了“政府领导，公安部门主抓，各相关部门负责，全社会共同参与”的预防道路交通事故工作长效机制，最大限度的预防和减少道路交通死亡事故及重、特大交通事故，在机动车和驾驶员快速增长，道路通车里程不断延伸，客、货运输总量急剧增加的严峻形势下，取得了近10年来道路交通事故全面下降的优良成绩，为实现贵州经济社会协调快速可持续发展做出新的贡献。

In 2005, under the leadership of all levels Party committees, governments and public security organs, Guizhou traffic police departments insisted on taking Deng Xiaoping Theory and the important thought of "three representatives" as the guide, thoroughly implemented the spirit of Party's 16th Conference 4th, 5th Plenary Session, the ninth provincial Party committee 5th, 6th Plenary Session, and the province's public security director meeting, established and implemented the scientific development concept, strove to enhance the capacity to prevent traffic accidents and the capacity of maintenance road public order, the capacities of service economic and social development and law enforcement for people, continuously promoted the standardization construction of the public security police team. Closely focus on the work objective "reducing accidents, ensuring safety, ensuring unblocked", combining the full implementation "PRC road traffic safety law," Guizhou traffic police departments deepened the implementation of "five rectifications", "three enhancements" various working measures, strengthened traffic safety initial management, rectified the driving order, extensively opened traffic safety propagate "five advancements" activities, deep investigated governance road safety dangers, and constantly built and improved responsibility system, and formed the prevention road traffic accident work long-effect mechanism of "government leading, public security departments grasping, relevant departments in charge, society common participation", prevented and reduced road traffic fatalities and heavy and serious traffic accidents in full play, in critical situation of motor vehicles and drivers rapid growth, roads traffic mileage continue expansion, passenger cars and goods wagons transport volume sharp increase, achieved excellent performance of road traffic accidents overall decline in past 10 years, and made new contributions for achieving Guizhou economy and society rapid coordinated sustainable development.

贵州省委常委、省公安厅厅长刘光磊（中）查看交警电子测速系统

The standing member of Guizhou provincial Party committee and the director of the Provincial Public Security Department Liu Guanglei (middle) was checking traffic test speed electronic system

贵州省副省长刘鸿庥（左二）在省公安厅、省交警总队领导的陪同下检查交通秩序整治活动

Liu Hongxiu, vice governor of Guizhou province (the second from left) accompanied by the leadership of the provincial Public Security Department, the Provincial Traffic Police General Team, was inspecting traffic order rectification activity

贵州省公安厅副厅长王泽洪（右三）指导高速公路交通事故预防工作

The deputy director of Guizhou Province Public Security Department Wang Zehong (the third from right) was guiding highway traffic accidents prevention work

贵州省公安厅交警总队总队长施长征为长途车乘客发放宣传资料

The head of Guizhou Province Public Security Department Traffic Police General Team Shi Changzheng was issuing publicity materials for long-distance vehicle passenger

贵州省公安消防总队

Public Security Fire Fighting General Team of Guizhou Province

省委常委、常务副省长王正福在张高潮总队长的陪同下，深入商场市场检查消防安全工作
The member of the standing committee of provincial Party committee and executive vice governor Wang Zhengfu, accompanied by the captain of general team Zhang Gaozhao in-depth inspection fire fighting safety work in the market

2005年，贵州省公安消防部队在公安部消防局和贵州各级党委、政府、公安机关的领导下，深入贯彻落实胡锦涛总书记视察贵州消防部队时的重要讲话精神，按照总队党委"一二三四五"的工作思路和构建"八大工作体系"的目标，全面推进"161"工程，进一步加强和改进消防工作，认真开展保持共产党员先进性教育活动，大力加强部队基层正规化建设，着力夯实基础工作，积极扑救各类火灾，参与灾害事故处置和抢险救援，保持了火灾的相对稳定和部队稳定，为贵州全面建设小康社会、构建和谐社会创造了良好的消防安全环境。

2005年，全省共发生火灾2299起，死97人，伤62人，直接财产损失17085040元，未发生群死群伤等社会影响较大的火灾。全省消防部队共接警出动4794次，出动车辆7291辆次，出动官兵41452人次，抢救遇险群众354人，安全疏散群众15700余人，挽回经济损失9486万余元，出色完成了各类火灾扑救和急、难、险、重抢险救援任务，涌现出了以"全国优秀人民警察"、"全省十大杰出青年"张学富为代表的先进个人和公安部"2004年度人民满意公安基层单位"贵阳市公安消防支队特勤大队为代表的先进集体，总队连续六年荣获贵州省公安机关目标管理工作一等奖，荣获"全国精神文明建设工作先进单位"荣誉称号，被省公安厅评为保持共产党员先进性教育先进集体。

消防特勤装备 鏖战化工火灾
The equipment of fire fighting special service To engage in fierce battle of chemical fire

2005, under the leadership of Fire Fighting Bureau for Ministry of Public Security and Guizhou Party committees and governments, public security organs at all levels, in-depth implementation the spirit of the important speech of the General Secretary Hu Jintao visited Guizhou fire forces, according to the work thought "12345" of general team Party committee, and construction the objective "systems of eight work", Guizhou province public security fire forces comprehensively promoted the project "161" and further strengthened and improved fire fighting work, seriously carried out maintaining the Party members advanced nature educational activities, strengthened the grass-roots forces regularization, solidly tamped the basic work, and actively fought the fire, partook rescue in disaster and relief, maintained relatively stable fire and teems stability, created a good fire fighting safety environment for Guizhou comprehensive building a comfortable and harmonious society.

In the year of 2005, a total of 2299 fires in the province, 97 people died and 62 injured, and direct property losses of 17085040 yuan, without affecting society such as the larger fires. The fire fighting team of the province totally received warning and dispatched 4,794 times, dispatched vehicles 7,291 times a year, dispatched troops 41452 person times, rescued distress masses 354 persons, safely evacuated over 15,700 people, and more than 94.86 million yuan of economic losses were recovered and splendidly fulfilled various fire fighting and urgent, difficult, dangerous and heavy rescue mission, emerged in advanced individual taking Zhang Xuefu, the "National Outstanding People's Police" and "Provincial Ten Outstanding Young Persons" as representative and advanced collective team taking the Ministry of Public Security "people satisfaction with the public security grass-roots unit in 2004 annual" Guiyang City Public Security Fire Fighting Team Special Service Detachment as representative. The general Team consecutively won six the first prizes of Guizhou Province Public Security Organs Target Management Work, awarded the title of "National spiritual Civilization Construction Work Advanced Unit", and awarded the title of Advanced Collective in Maintaining the Party Members Advanced Nature Education by Provincial Public Security Department.

省委常委、公安厅厅长刘光磊在"贵州省119青年志愿者在行动启动仪式"上为志愿者授旗
The member of the standing committee of provincial Party committee and director of the Public Security Department Liu Guanglei was presenting flags for volunteers in "start ceremony of Guizhou Province 119 youth volunteers in action"

贵州省科学技术厅

Guizhou Province Science and Technology Department

常委、省委秘书长、原副省长张
会见德国能源咨询公司客人
anding member of Provincial
Committee, secretary-general
vincial Party Committee, former
ty governor Zhang Qunshan was
ng the guests of Germany Energy
e Consulting Company

省科技厅厅长于杰陪同科技部党组成员、纪律检组长吴忠泽视察汇通华城楼宇科技有限公司
The director of the Provincial Department of Science and Technology, Yu Jie accompanied the Parly group member of the Ministry of Science and Technology, the headman of Commission for Discipline Inspection Wu Zhongze inspecting Huitong Huacherng Building Science and Technology Ltd, Co.

贵州省科学技术厅是主管全省科技工作的省人民政府组成部门。“十五”期间，全省科技发展环境进一步改善、科技创新能力有所增强、科技集成攻关和产业化成效明显，科技综合实力在得到明显提高的同时，对经济社会发展推动作用日渐显现。主要表现在：

科技发展环境进一步改善

科技政策法规体系逐步完善，促进科技发展导向进一步树立；科技投入进一步加大，为科技工作发展提供了较有力的保障；科普和科技宣传深入开展，对提高全民科技意识发挥了积极作用。

科技创新基础进一步增强

科技体制改革有效推进，为科技创新打下了良好的体制基础；科技研发平台建设得到加强，为科技创新提供了条件支持；科技合作深入开展，为科技创新提供了交流平台；科技人才队伍建设进一步加强，为科技创新奠定了人才基础；科技服务体系逐渐完善，为科技创新和成果转化提供了服务保障。

科技创新能力增强，产出水平提高

科技成果数量、质量和专利创造明显上升；高新技术创新能力不断增强，提高了产业发展水平；农业科技攻关推动了优良品种选育和种植技术水平的提高；医药卫生领域取得一批成果，为人口健康水平的提高提供了支撑。

高新技术园区和产业化基地的辐射、带动作用明显

高新技术产业园区发展步伐加快，辐射和带动了全省高新技术产业和农业发展；科技产业化基地建设取得阶段性成果，加快了优势产业和农业的可持续发展。

科技创新和成果转化推动了经济社会的发展

高新技术及产业发展加快，具有比较优势的高新技术及产业初步形成；企业技术创新力度加大，成为高新技术产业发展的重要力量；优良品种推广成效明显，为粮食产量的提高和农业产业结构调整提供了保障；高新技术在农业生产中的应用成效初显，推动了农业经济增长方式的转变；农业科技成果推广成效显著，有力促进了农村经济的发展；喀斯特石漠化综合治理成效明显，为喀斯特脆弱生态区可持续发展奠定了技术基础；科技扶贫工作力度进一步加大，推动了贫困地区的发展。

Guizhou Province Science and Technology Department which is the component of the provincial government is responsible for the scientific and technological. During the period of "Tenth Five", the development environment of science and technology in the province further improved, the capability of technological innovation has enhanced, the results of integrated brainstorm project and industrialization of science and technology were evident, the comprehensive strength of science and technology has been markedly improved, while the increasingly obvious role in promoting economic and social development. Expression mainly in:

Further improved the development environment of science and technology

Gradually improved the legal system for science and technology policy, promoting scientific and technological development guidance further establishment; Further enhanced scientific and technological input to provide stronger protection for the development of scientific and technological work; Carrying out in-depth scientific and technological information propaganda, has played a positive role to enhance the popular scientific and technological consciousness.

Further enhanced scientific and technological innovation foundation

The system reform of science and technology effectively promoted to lay a good system foundation for scientific and technological innovation; Research platform construction has been strengthened, provided the conditions support for scientific and technological innovation; Carried out in-depth scientific and technical cooperation to provide a platform of exchange for scientific and technological innovation; Further strengthened the building of scientific and technological talent to lay the foundation of talent for science and technology innovation; Technological service system gradually improved to provide service guarantee for scientific and technological innovation and results transferring.

Scientific and Technological innovation capacity and output level increased

Scientific and technological achievements quantity, quality and patent creation markedly increased; Increasing high-tech innovation capability, enhanced the level of industrial development; Agricultural scientific and technologic brainstorm project promoted the improved variety breeding and the raising of cultivation technology level; The field of medical and health achieved a batch of results to provide support for the improvement of people health level.

High-tech Park and industrialization bases had visible role in radiation and lead aspect

The development pace of high-tech industrial park accelerated, radiation and lead the province's high-tech industrial and agricultural development; Science and technology industrialization bases building achieved stage results, and accelerated the sustainable development of superiority industrial and agriculture.

Scientific and technological innovation and results transferring promoted the economic and social development

The high-tech industrial was accelerated development, the comparative advantage and high-tech industrial have begun to take shape; The innovation capability of enterprise technology would be increased and became an important force in the development of high-tech industrial; Fine varieties promotion was effective, provided protection for increase grain yield and agricultural restructuring; The application of high-tech in agricultural production, promoted the change in the pattern of agricultural economic growth; Performance achievements in agricultural science and technology were effective and powerful, promoted the development of rural economy; Karst stone-desert comprehensive management was successful, laid the technical foundation for sustainable development of karst fragile ecological zones; Technological work for aid the poor further improved to promote the development of poor areas.

以民为本 为民解困 Taking service people as the foundation Settlement difficulty for people

——2005年贵州民政工作简介

The Brief Introduction of the Work of Guizhou Civil Affairs of 2005

省慰问团慰问省军区机关
Provincial consolation group conveyed the provincial military command organs

副省长肖永安检查特困群众生活情况
Deputy governor Xiao Yongan was inspecting living conditions of the poor masses

郭厅长慰问抗战老战士
Director Guo was extending his regards to veterans of War of Resistance Against Japan

为确保农村特困群众及时得到特困救助款，全省在有条件的地方推开了社会化发放
For ensuring the particularly rural poor masses giving timely salvation charges, the province dealt out socialized relief in the conditional places

民政部门是政府主管社会行政事务的职能部门，主要工作包括社会救助、社会福利、慈善、老龄、拥退伍军优抚安置、村民自治和城市社区建设、行政区划地名边界管理、民间组织管理、殡葬管理、婚姻和收养登记等。2005年，贵州民政各项工作取得良好成效。

(1) 社会救助体系建设取得较大突破。农村特困群众救助制度全面建立实施，全省94.5万因病因残疾丧失劳动能力的农村特困群众纳入了定期救助范围。城市低保对象扩大到49.2万人，基本做到动态管理下的应保尽保和分类施保。救灾工作机制进一步健全，累计救助灾民531.5万人次。五保供养10.94万人。实施城乡医疗救助近17万人。救助城市生活无着流浪乞讨人员1.7万人次。

(2) 双拥优抚安置工作取得多项突破。普遍建立优抚对象抚恤补助标准自然增长机制。城镇退役士兵自谋职业安置改革试点县稳步扩大到50个，自谋职业率提高到43.2%。

(3) 社会福利和慈善事业发展步伐加快。全年累计接收慈善捐款1212万元，实施助医、助学、济困项目受益2.5万人。实施孤残儿童手术康复明天计划，完成手术319例。发行社会福利彩票3.96亿元。老龄工作进一步加强，出台《贵州省优待老年人暂行办法》。

(4) 城乡基层民主建设稳步深入。全省第六届村居委会换届选举顺利完成，村务公开民主管理制度进一步健全，村民自治示范创建取得新成绩，城市社区建设继续深入，社区服务设施4704个，服务网点12004个。

(5) 社会行政事务管理不断加强。殡葬改革深入推进，火化率提高到14.24%。社会团体和民办非企业单位发展到4547个。启动地名公共服务工程，完成省内市州地接边县107条边界联检。办理婚姻登记20余万对。

2005年，全省民政事业费预算160824.3万元，达历史最高，比上年增加41.3%。

The civil affairs department is the function department of government in charge social administrative affairs, major works including social salvation, social welfare, charity, elderly welfare, giving special care and settlement to demobilized solders, and village self-administration and urban community building, administrative division geographic name border management, folk organizations management, funeral management, marriage and adoption registration. In 2005, the Guizhou civil affairs has made good results at various works.

(1) The social assistance system has achieved greater breakthroughs. The salvation system of rural poor masses was comprehensively implemented, 945,000 rural poor people of disability because of illness and deformity of province were brought into a regular salvation range. The number of persons receiving the lowest cost-of-living in urban area expanded to 492,000, which has accomplished dynamic management in the main. The rescue mechanism was further improved and total salvation victims of 5.315 million person-time supported five-guarantees of 109,400 people, implemented urban and rural medical assistance nearly 170 thousand people, rescued wanderer in urban of 17thousasnd person-time.

(2) The work of double-support and giving special care settlement made a number of breakthroughs. The universal mechanism of compensation allowance standard natural growth for giving special care to persons was established. The number of reform pilot counties of urban servicemen for self-employment steadily expanded to 50, self-employment rate increased to 43.2%.

(3) The social welfare and charity cause accelerated pace of development. Annual charitable donations were received 12.12 million yuan to implement medical help, assistance in schooling, and relief project with benefiting 25,000 people. The plan of Recovery Tomorrow for orphan was implemented, and completed 319 surgical operations. Social welfare lottery ticket was issued 396 million yuan. The work of old age was further strengthened, and promulgated the "Interim Procedure for Giving Favored Treatment to Old People of Guizhou Province."

(4) The urban and rural grass-roots democracy-building steadily improved. The sixth village and neighborhood committees election successfully completed, the democratic management system further improved, and the establishment of villagers self-government model has made new achievements, the building of urban communities continued to deepen, community service facilities of 4,704 and service points of 12,004.

(5) The management of social administrative affairs has been continuously strengthened. The reform of the funeral was improved, cremation rate increased to 14.24%. The number of Community groups and civilian-run non-enterprise units developed to 4,547. The project of geographical name public service was started, completed joint inspection of 107 boundaries within the city to the state of province. The number of marriage registration was 200,000 pairs.

In 2005, the budget of provincial civil affairs expenditure reached 1608.243 million yuan, up to the highest level in history, an increase of 41.3% over the previous year.

贵州省人事厅

Personnel Department of Guizhou Province

2005年11月5日国家人事部副部长侯建良，贵州省省委常委、省委组织部部长张少农，副省长蒙启良，省委组织部副部长、省人事厅厅长李先忧视察省人才市场

November 5, 2005, the deputy minister of the State Ministry of Personnel Hou Jianliang, the member of the standing committee of Guizhou Provincial Committee and the director of Provincial Organization Department Zhang Shaonong, the deputy governor Meng Qiliang, the deputy director of the Provincial Organization Department and the director of the Provincial Personnel Department Li Xianyou inspected provincial personnel market

2005年人事人才工作总的要求是：以邓小平理论和“三个代表”重要思想为指导，深入贯彻党的十六大和十六届三、四中全会精神，全面贯彻落实全国全省人才工作会议和全国人事厅局长会议精神，大力实施人才强省战略，以能力建设为核心，加强公务员和专业技术队伍建设，以公务员法出台为契机，健全完善公务员制度；以转换用人机制为重点，积极稳妥地推进事业单位人事制度改革；以规范收入分配秩序为突破口，深化工资分配制度改革；以健全法制为保障，加快人才市场建设步伐；以建立长效机制为目标，切实做好军队转业干部安置和部分企业军转干部解困维稳工作。

保持共产党员先进性教育活动期间，贵州省人事厅全体党员参观息烽集中营，缅怀革命先烈，接受革命传统教育，举行新党员宣誓，老党员重温入党誓诗的活动

During the period of maintaining Party members advanced educational activities, all Party members of Guizhou Province Personnel Department visited Xifeng concentration camp, recalled revolutionary martyrs, accepted revolutionary education, held the activities of new Party members oath and old Party members backing into vow poetry

In 2005, the personnel work in general requirements were : taking Deng Xiaoping Theory and the "three representatives" as the guide, thoroughly implemented the spirit of the Party's 16th National Congress and the Party's 16th National Congress of 3th,4th Plenary Session, and fully implemented the spirit of national provincial talent work conference and the National Personnel Department director conference, vigorously implemented talent strong province strategy, took capacity-building as the core, enhanced the construction of public servant and professional technical teem, taking the public servant law promulgation as an opportunity to improve and perfect the system of service; took change employment mechanism as focus, actively and steadily pushed forward the reform of the personnel system of public institutions; took standard income distribution order as a breakthrough to deepen improvement the wage distribution system reform; took the perfect legal system as protection to accelerate the pace of the construction of talent market; Took establishing a lasting mechanism as the objective to earnestly do a good job on settlement demobilized military cadres and some enterprises demobilized military cadres overcoming the difficulty and guard stabilization .

由国家人事部与贵州省政府共同组建的综合性国家级人才市场——中国贵州人才市场于2005年11月5日在贵阳正式揭牌

A comprehensive national talent market jointly established by the State Ministry of Personnel and the Guizhou Provincial Government —— China's Guizhou Talent Market was formally inaugurated in Guiyang on November 5, 2005

贵州省文化厅

Guizhou Province Cultural Department

[基本情况] 截止2005年底，全省文化部门共有机构1670个，从业人员8297人。2005年全省文化事业财政拨款为18730.9万元，比上年增加2922.5万元，增长18.5%。2005年度，全省文化（文物）事业单位基本建设投资新建及在建项目71个，累计完成投资9047.2万元，新增固定资产2500.3万元。本年全部建成交付使用的项目21个。

[开展保持共产党员先进性教育活动] 在保持共产党员先进性教育活动中，各地结合文化工作开展了丰富多彩的主题实践活动。

[大型民族歌舞《多彩贵州风》]《多彩贵州风》按照文化与旅游结合的方式，以音乐和舞蹈为主线，表现了积淀已久的优秀的民族民间文化，已演出70余场，观众6万余人次，收入250余万元。

[文物保护单位修缮工作]完成了全国重点文物保护单位地坪风雨桥修复设计方案，并获国家文物局批准；完成全国重点文物保护单位安顺文庙石质文物保护工程设计方案；完成镇远青龙洞、黄平飞云崖大佛殿抢险、兴义何应钦故居等一批重要文物保护单位的修缮工程。

[基本建设的文物考古调查与抢救性发掘]完成习水、兴义、大方等25个基本建设项目的文物考古调查任务，调查面积100余平方公里，发现文物点143处。弥补了贵州考古的区域空白，为贵州史前文化、夜郎文化，以及贵州早期对外交往等方面的研究提供了重要材料。

[博物馆事业]新建和改扩建一批博物馆。它们是：独山深河桥抗战纪念园、荔波邓恩铭陈列馆、安龙县博物馆和贵阳市投资2200余万元，完成息烽集中营旧址革命历史纪念馆二期改扩建工程和陈列改造。

[文化产业]进一步落实文化产业贷款贴息项目资金，共安排了7个文化产业贷款贴息项目，贴息114万元。

[对外及对港澳台文化交流] 2005年，我省对外及对港澳台文化交流项目共22起，248人次。涉及新加坡、法国、意大利、澳大利亚、新西兰、文莱、美国、加拿大等国家和香港、澳门、台湾地区。

多彩的贵州民族民间文化
The rich and colorful Guizhou national folk culture

《多彩贵州风》剧照
The photo of "Colorful Guizhou Wind"

《多彩贵州风》剧照
The photo of "Colorful Guizhou Wind"

[Basic situation]By the end of 2005, the total cultural departments have 1,670 institutions, employing 8,297 people. In 2005 financial allocation for cultural undertaking in the province was 187.309 million yuan, increased 29.225 million yuan than the previous year, an increase of 18.5%. The year of 2005, the provincial cultural (relics) undertaking units in the public construction investment new-build and building of 71 projects, accumulated investment 90.472 million yuan, new-added fixed assets of 25.003 million yuan. 21 projects have been completed and made available to the users of this year.

[Open maintaining the Communist Party member advanced educational activity] In the maintaining the Communist Party member advanced educational activity, all the places integrated cultural work to carry out the rich theme practice activities.

[Large national dance "Colorful Guizhou Wind"] "Colorful Guizhou Wind", according to a combination of culture and tourism, taking music and dance as the main line, showed long outstanding the national folk culture, has performed more than 70 times, the audience more than 60,000 people, 2.5 million yuan of income.

[Cultural relics protection unit repair work] To complete national focus cultural relics protection unit Fengyu Bridge of Diping rehabilitation design programme which was approved by the National Heritage Board; to complete national key cultural relics protection unit Wen Temple of Anshun stone cultural relics protection engineering design programme; to complete Qinglong Hole of Zhenyuan, rescue of Feiyunya Large Buddhist Temple of Huangping, He Yingqin former residence of Xingyi, and a number of important cultural relics protection units repair engineering.

[Cultural relics archeological investigation and rescue exploration of infrastructure] Completed Xishui, Xingyi, Dafang, 25 infrastructure projects cultural relics archeological survey mission to investigate the area more than 100 square kilometres and find 143 cultural relics points. Filled the gaps in Guizhou archaeological regions, provided important materials for research Guizhou prehistoric culture, Yelang culture, and Guizhou in the early exchanges with the outside world.

[Museum cause] New-built and expanded a number of museums. They were: Shenheqiao War of Resistance against Japan Memorial Garden of Dushan, Deng Enming Exhibition Hall of Libo, Anlong county Museum, and completed Xifeng Concentration Camp Site Revolutionary History Memorial Hall phase II expansion project and display transformation which was invested more than 22 million by Guiyang city.

[Cultural Industry] Further implemented the cultural industry loan subsidiary interest project funds, a total of seven cultural industrial loans subsidiary interest projects with 1.14 million yuan.

[External and the Hong Kong, Macao Taiwan cultural exchanges] In 2005, the province's external and the Hong Kong, Macao and Taiwan cultural exchanges totaled 22 times, 248 person times, involving countries as Singapore, France, Italy, Australia, New Zealand, Brunei, the United States, Canada and Hong Kong, Macao, Taiwan regions.

贵州省乡镇企业局

Rural Enterprise Administration of Guizhou Province

天方药业
Tianfang Pharmaceutical Company

2005年，全省乡镇企业继续保持持续、健康发展的良好势头。据统计，到2005年底止，全省完成乡镇企业增加值418.5亿元，同比增长12.3%；完成乡镇工业增加值216.4亿元，同比增长12.8%；实现利润143.6亿元，同比增长11.9%；上交税金49.2亿元，同比增长18.6%；完成建设项目投资129.1亿元，同比增长22%，其中引进资金62亿元，占建设项目投资总额的48%；从业人员累计达到234.9万人，同比增长5.5%；累计支付劳动者报酬142.2亿元，农民人均从乡镇企业获得的工资性收入达到490.5元，同比增长9.9%。经过多年的积累和发展，乡镇企业固定资产总值增加到633亿元，同比增长19.2%，“十五”期间年均增长15.4%。

一、二、三次产业增加值结构调整为1.7：61.2：37.1。一年来，有16家企业的产品获得绿色食品证书、10个产品被评为省级名牌产品、13个产品（项目）被评为省级优秀新产品暨优秀技术创新项目。经过我局的引导，有11家企业通过了ISO9000质量管理体系认证、13家企业建立了HACCP食品安全管理体系，22家企业的农产品基地通过无公害产地认定。

全省各类乡镇企业培训机构共对3.8万（人次）乡镇企业从业人员进行了培训，乡镇企业职工中大专及以上文化程度人数达到9.7万人。目前，全省生产总值的22%，工业增加值的30%，财政总收入的13%来自于乡镇企业。

乡镇企业已经成为促进我省农民就业增收和全面建设小康社会的重要力量，成为推进农村工业化、城镇化和财政增收的重要载体，成为促进全省国民经济持续健康发展的重要组成部分。

安泰药业
Antai Pharmaceutical Company

The year of 2005, the township and village enterprises have continued to maintain a sustained and healthy development momentum. According to statistics, by the end of 2005, the added value of township and village enterprises of the province completed 41.85 billion yuan , 12.3% more than last year; Added value of industry of township and village finished 21.64 billion yuan, grew 12.8%; profit of 14.36 billion yuan, 11.9% more than last year, paid taxes of 4.92 billion yuan, increase of 18.6%; The investment of construction projects completed 12.91 billion yuan, up 22%, including the introduction funds of 6.2 billion yuan, accounting for 48% of total investment of construction projects; Staff and workers reached 2.349 million people, 5.5% more than last year; The payment of workers compensation totaled 14.22 billion yuan, per capita wage of farmers receiving from the town and township enterprises reached 490.5 yuan , grew 9.9%. After years of accumulation and development, the total value of township and village enterprises in fixed asset increased to 63.3 billion yuan, up 19.2%, average annual growth rate of 15.4% during the period of "Tenth Five".

The structure of the primary, secondary and tertiary industry added value have been adjusted 1.7:61.2:37.1. Over the past year, products of 16 enterprises have been gained green food certificate, 10 products have been awarded the provincial brand name, 13 products (projects) were awarded provincial outstanding new products cum outstanding technological innovation projects. After guidance of rural enterprise administration, 11 enterprises passed the ISO9000 quality management system certification, 13 enterprises established HACCP food safety management system, the agricultural base of 22 enterprises passed non-public nuisance origin identification.

The training institutions of township and village enterprises in the province trained practitioners total of 38,000 (person times), the number of post-secondary and higher education of township and village enterprises reached to 97,000 people. Currently, 22% of the province's GDP, 30% of industrial added value, 13% of the total fiscal revenue were from township and village enterprises.

Township and village enterprises have became the major force for improvement province's farmers employment & increase-income and comprehensive building a well-to-do society, became an important carrier of promoting rural industrialization, urbanization and finance increase income, and became the important components of promoting sustained and healthy development of national economy in the province.

绿太阳药业
Green Sun Pharmaceutical Company

“十五”税收铸辉煌和谐发展谱新章

Tax of "Tenth Five" Creating Brilliant And Writing the New chapter in Harmonious Development

“十五”期间，全省地税机关组织的税收收入实现了跨越式发展，地方税收事业取得了辉煌成就。

“十五”税收收入实现新突破

全省地税机关共组织税收收入377.22亿元，年均增长19.43%，2005年达到107.69亿元。为促进全省经济的快速发展、全面建设小康社会、构建社会主义和谐社会提供了强大的财力保障。

“十五”税收收入亮点纷呈

各税种、各地区收入规模进一步扩大。“十五”期末，全省有营业税、企业所得税、个人所得税、城市维护建设税4个税种收入超过10亿元，其中，企业所得税、个人所得税收入接近20亿元。

主体税种增长强劲，税收收入以营业税、所得税为主的格局更加稳固。营业税，内资企业企业所得税、个人所得税收入年均递增分别为17.9%、24.74%和32.47%，营业税对税收收入贡献率达到43%，成为地税机关征管的第一大税种，个人所得税、企业所得税以17.93%和17.78%贡献率成为地税机关征管的第二、三大税种。以上三税合计占全省税收收入的比重高达78.71%，与“九五”期末相比提高了近8个百分点，三税在税收收入中的主体地位更加稳固。

产业税收与经济协调增长，重点行业对税收增长的拉动作用明显。各重点行业中，建筑业税收总量和增量继续保持首位，实现税收收入58.34亿元，年均增长21.19%，占全省税收收入的比重为15.47%。从增幅上看，房地产业、采矿业和电力、燃气及水的生产和供应业位居各行业前列，分别增长35.14%、31.86%、23.84%。上述重点行业对全省税收收入增长的贡献超过70%，对税收增长的拉动作用明显。

内资企业股份公司、私营企业强劲增长，带动了税收收入增长提速。“十五”期间内资企业股份公司、国有企业、个体经营占税收收入比重由“十五”初年的31.81:31.19:21.21变化为“十五”末年的38.34:25.69:17.91。

认真签订目标管理责任书
Seriously signed target management responsibility book

积极表彰先进典型
Positively commended advanced model

国家税务总局党组书记、局长谢旭人同志（右二）到贵州看望慰问税务干部

The secretary of Party group of the State Administration of Taxation and the director of the Administration comrade Xie Xuren (the second from right) went to Guizhou comforting the tax cadres

"Tenth Five" period, the tax revenue of provincial local tax organs achieved leapfrog development, and local taxes cause made glorious achievements.

"Tenth Five" achieved a new breakthrough in tax revenue

The provincial local tax organs organized 37.722 billion yuan tax revenue, an average annual increase of 19.43%, in 2005, reaching 10.769 billion yuan, providing the strong financial support for promoting the rapid development of provincial economy and overall building the prosperous society, and construction a harmonious socialist society.

Tax revenue in "Tenth Five" was intricate

All taxes and regions further expanded the scale of income. The end of "Tenth Five", the tax revenue of the business tax, enterprise income tax and personal income tax, urban safeguarding construction tax four taxes exceeded one billion yuan in the province, of which, tax revenue of enterprise tax and personal income tax revenue nearly to 2 billion yuan.

The main tax grew strongly, and the structure of tax revenue taking business tax, income tax as main was more stable. Business tax, domestic-funded enterprise income tax and personal income tax revenue respectively increased at an average rate of 17.9%, 24.74% and 32.47%, the business tax contribution rate to all tax revenues reaching to 43%, becoming the first major tax in local organs, the contribution rate of personal income tax and enterprise income tax respectively took 17.93% and 17.78% to become the second, third major taxes. Above total of three taxes accounted for 78.71% of the provincial tax revenue, and nearly increased eight percentage points than the end of "Ninth Five", the main status of three taxes in the tax revenue was more stable.

Industrial tax revenue and economy was coordinate growth, the leading role of revenue growth in key industrials was obvious. In the key industrials, the total and incremental revenue in the building industry maintained the first, achieved tax revenue 5.834 billion yuan, with an average annual increase of 21.19%, accounting for 15.47% of the tax revenue in the province. From the perspective in increase, the real estate industry, mining industry, production and supply industry of electricity, gas and water occupied the front row among various industrials, respectively growth of 35.14%, 31.86% and 23.84%. The contribution rate of above-mentioned key industries to the growth of provincial tax revenue exceeded 70%, having an obvious role to growth of the tax revenue.

Domestic-funded enterprise stock company, private enterprise had strong growth to accelerate growth in tax revenue. "Tenth Five" period, the proportion of domestic-funded enterprise stock company, the state-owned enterprise, self-employed accounting for tax revenue changed from 31.81:31.19:21.21 at the first year of "Tenth Five" to 38.34:25.69:17.91 at the last year of "Tenth Five".

贵州旅游产业稳步发展

Guizhou Tourism Industry in Steady Developing

丹寨苗族服饰
Miao minority nationality costume of Dan stockade village

音寨
Yin stockade village

近年来，贵州省旅游局取得了可喜的成绩。

一、以交通和配套服务为主的基础设施明显改善

全省以交通为重点的旅游基础设施和配套服务设施建设取得了突破性进展。据统计，2005年全省共接待入境旅游者27.62万人次，同比增长19.55%，收入外汇10141.31万美元，同比增长26.45%；接待国内旅游者3099.46万人次，同比增长24.96%，国内旅游收入242.83亿元，同比增长51.54%；实现旅游总收入251.14亿元，同比增长49.85%。

二、以构建和谐社会为宗旨，大力发展乡村旅游

十多年来，贵州省旅游局始终坚持从实际出发，把旅游产业发展与促进贫困地区农民脱贫致富和产业结构调整紧密结合起来。贵州省委、省政府和黔西南州委、州政府、贵州省旅游局先后于2004年10月15日-17日、2005年10月3日-5日在贵阳和兴义举办了“中国·贵州乡村旅游国际论坛”；编制了《贵州省乡村旅游发展规划》并已通过中期评估；出版了首届《中国·贵州乡村旅游国际论坛论文集》；实施了“巴拉河乡村旅游国际示范项目”。

三、充分利用红色旅游资源优势，大打红色旅游牌

贵州红色旅游资源十分丰富，具有中国革命转折意义的遵义会议、出奇制胜的“四渡赤水”等重大历史事件也都发生在这里。中央红军长征历时一年零九天，在贵州转战的时间就达五个月零八天，留下了大量的革命文物和遗址、遗迹，以及一些极富传奇色彩的动人故事，构成了贵州不可多得的红军长征文化旅游资源，为贵州进一步开发红色旅游资源、开展红色旅游提供了有利条件。因此，从2003年开始，贵州省旅游局就利用两位英国青年重走长征路这一举动组织媒体大力宣传并率先在遵义会议会址内举行了“贵州红色之旅启动仪式”。今年以来，贵州红色旅游屡宣热潮，成为贵州新的旅游亮点，仅春节、五一、十一三个黄金周的统计，全省几个主要红色旅游景区（点）就接待旅游者60多万人次，旅游收入也有较大幅度增长。

In recent years, Guizhou Provincial Tourism Administration achieved gratifying results.

First, The infrastructure mainly on transport and support service has markedly improved

The construction of tourism infrastructure taking the traffic as the focus and support service facility has made breakthrough progress in the province. According to statistics, in 2005 the province received 276,200 person-time of entry tourists, grew 19.55% than the same period of last year, and foreign exchange income of 101.4131 million USD, an increase 26.45%; received 30.9946 million person-time of domestic tourists, grew 24.96%, domestic tourism income of 24.283 billion yuan, up 51.54%; achieved total tourism revenue 25.114 billion yuan, up 49.85%.

Second, taking to create a harmonious society as the purpose, vigorously developed rural tourism

In 10 years, Guizhou Provincial Tourism Administration has always insisted on proceeding from reality, closely integrated the tourism industry development with promotion shaking off poverty and becoming prosperous in poor areas and industrial structure adjustment. Guizhou provincial Party committee and government and Qianxina state Party committee and government, Guizhou Provincial Tourism Administration respectively held "China · Guizhou Rural Tourism International Forum" in Guiyang on October 15-17,2004 and in Xingyi on October 3-5,2005; worked out the "Guizhou province rural tourism development planning" which has been adopted the medium-term assessment; published the first session "China · Guizhou Rural Tourism International Forum Colloquia"; implemented the "Balahe Rural Tourism International Demonstration Project".

Third, to take full advantage of the Red tourism resources, fighting red tourism card

Guizhou has rich red tourist resources. Zunyi Conference, having China revolution turning significance, "Crossing Chishui River Four Times", winning by surprise, and other major historical events have taken place here. Central Red Army's Long March lasted one year and nine days, fought the time of five months and eight days in Guizhou, that leaving a large number of cultural relics and revolutionary sites, monuments, as well as some highly legendary touching story, formed a rare Red Army's Long March Guizhou cultural tourism resources, provided favorable conditions for the further development Guizhou red tourism resources and promotion red tourism. Thus, from the beginning of 2003, making use of two British youths going to Long March Road again, Guizhou Province Tourism Administration organized media to vigorously publicize and took the lead in holding "Start Ceremony of Guizhou Red Tourism" in the site of Zunyi Conference. Since the beginning of this year, Guizhou repeatedly unfolded a great upsurge in red tourism, which became new tourism spot in Guizhou. Only statistics of the Spring Festival, 1st May, and 1st Oct. three Golden Week, the number of major red tourism scenic spots (points) received more than 600 thousand person-time tourists and tourism income grew sharply.

黎平肇兴田园风光
Rural scenery in Zhaoxing Liping

贵州省畜牧局

Guizhou Province Animal Husbandry Bureau

六盘水兴隆养殖基地养鸡场
Xinglong breeding base chicken farm of Liu Panshui

2005年，全省肉类总产量187.01万吨、禽蛋产量11.11万吨、奶类产量3.75万吨；畜牧业产值达194.2亿元，占农业总产值的比重提高到34%，比上年提高1.83个百分点，畜牧业增加值占农业增加值的比重提高到33.13%。畜牧业规模化程度提高，规模养殖场达5390个，建成10户以上连片畜禽养殖小区1268个，已投资建设90个优质畜产品基地。畜牧业结构逐步优化，优良品种和牛羊肉比重上升，牛奶产量持续增长。畜牧业生产方式进一步转变，产业化经营带动作用增强，畜牧业发展投入增加，动物防疫基础设施建设得到完善，重大动物疫病防控工作取得明显成效，兽医管理体制改革稳步推进，饲草饲料生产迅速发展，人员培训和科技推广应用力度加大。实施生态畜牧业统计监测结果显示：我省畜牧业继续保持全面增长，为新农村建设奠定了良好的基础。

山羊
The goats

In 2005, the province produced 1.8701 million tons of meat, eggs yield of 111,100 tons, 37,500 tons of milk production; Animal husbandry output value reached 19.42 billion yuan, the proportion of accounting for agricultural output value increased to 34%, up 1.83 percentage points over the previous year, the proportion of animal husbandry added value accounting for the agricultural added value increased to 33.13%. Further to expand livestock scale, the scale livestock farms amounted to 5,390, and built 1,268 animal breeding areas consisted of more than 10 families, 90 high-quality animal products bases have been invested to build. Livestock structure gradually optimized, improved the high quality varieties and increased the proportion of beef and mutton, milk production continued growth. Further to change in way of livestock production, industrialization leading role enhanced, and livestock development increased investment, animal epidemic prevention infrastructure was improved, the control work of major animal disease achieved a remarkable success, veterinarian management system reformed steadily, and the rapid development of forage production, personnel training and the use of promoting science and technology increased. Implementation ecological livestock statistical monitoring results showed: animal husbandry of the province continued to maintain the overall growth, laid a good foundation for the new rural building.

种公牛
The breeding bulls

威宁草地畜牧业 Grassland animal husbandry of Weining

奶牛
The cows

贵州省通信管理局
Guizhou Province Communication Administration

贵州省通信管理局是由信息产业部派出的对贵州省电信业实施行业管理的政府部门，负责对省内电信、移动、联通、网通、铁通、卫通等基础电信运营企业和增值电信业务经营者进行监管。主要管理职能：电信市场准入、电信设备进网、电信服务资费与服务质量、通信与信息安全、党政专用通信、战备应急通信、行业统计及行业信息发布等。下设贵州省通信工程质量监督站和通信行业职业技能鉴定中心，分别负责全省的通信工程质量监督与管理核发通信行业职业资格证书。

“十五”末，经过全行业的共同努力，全面完成“十五”计划目标，全省通信业实现跨越式发展。全省电话用户数达到975.9万户、完成电信业务收入74.07亿元、电话普及率达到25部/百人、互联网用户数约109万户。特别在发展农村通信方面，为全省17240个行政村开通电话，电话村通比例达到85%，基本实现全省乡乡通宽带，为农村信息化建设做出了突出的贡献。

Guizhou Province Communication Administration which sent by the Ministry of Information Industry is the government department of implementation trade management to Guizhou province telecommunication industry, is responsible for controlling telecommunication, Mobile, Unicom, Netcom, Tietong, Satcom basic telecommunication operation enterprises and value-added telecom operators in the province. Major management functions: telecommunication market access, telecommunication equipment into the network, telecommunication service fee and the quality of service, communication and information security, the Party special communication, war preparedness emergency communication, industry statistics and trade information dissemination. Subordinated Guizhou Province Communication Engineering Quality Supervisor Station and communication industry Vocational Skill Certification Center, which are respectively responsible for the provincial supervision of communication engineering quality and management issuing communication industry vocational qualification certificate.

At the end of "Tenth Five", through hard working, the whole trade fully completed the "Tenth Five" plan objective, the communication industry achieved a leap development in the province. The telephone number of users reached 9.759 million, the completion of the telecommunication operating income 7.407 billion yuan, the telephone universal rate reached 25 telephones / 100 people, about 1.09 million Internet users in the province. Particularly in the development of rural communication, opened the telephone for 17,240 administrative villages to reach 85% in the proportion of opened phone village, basically achieved all the townships to open broadband in the province, made outstanding contributions for rural informatization building.

2005年11月25日，贵州省委常委、省委秘书长，原副省长张群山（左一）在“村村通电话”工程新闻发布会现场拨测村通电话
November 25, 2005, the standing member of Provincial Party Com-mittee, secretary-general of Provincial Party Committee, former deputy governor Zhang Qunshan (the first from left) was dialing the test telephone in the press conference scene of "opened phone in villages" project

贵州省通信管理局领导班子：中，局党组书记、局长李德明；右，局党组成员、副局长江兰；左，局党组成员、省专用通信局局长郭智翰
Leadership of Guizhou Province Communication Administration: middle, the secretary and director of the Administration Li Deming; Right, the board member and deputy director of the Administration Jiang Lan; Left, the board member of the Administration and the director of the Provincial Special Communication Bureau Guo Zhihan

贵州省通信管理局行政审批“一个窗口”
"A window" administrative examination and approval of Guizhou Province Communication Administration

贵州省通信管理局办公大楼
Office building of Guizhou Province Communication Administration

2005年贵州烟草商业发展情况

The Situation of Guizhou Tobacco Commercial Development of 2005

2004年8月，国家烟草专卖局局长姜成康（左二）在贵州省副省长禄智明（右二）、贵州省烟草专卖局局长张建华（中）陪同下检查烤烟生产情况

In August 2004, the director of the State Tobacco Monopoly Administration Jiang Chengkang (the second from left), accompanied by the vice governor of Guizhou Province Government Lu Zhiming (the second from right), the director of Guizhou Province Tobacco Monopoly Administration Zhang Jianhua(middle), to inspect the situation of flue-cured tobacco production.

2005年，全省烟草商业坚持以科学发展观统领发展全局，以在加快发展之中夯实基础、在夯实基础之上加快发展、提高发展质量为基本方针，突出抓好三个重点，切实做好七项工作，各项工作取得明显成效。

经济效益创历史新高。实现税利31.78亿元，同比增长26.87%。烟草出口创汇4350万美元。

专卖管理力度进一步加大。查处案件1.09万起，查没卷烟3010.69件，烟叶、烟丝1021.17吨。

烤烟保持平稳发展。收购烟叶671.1万担，同比增加103.5万担。销售烟叶661.34万担，同比增加141万担。烟农收入32.1亿元（含煤炭补贴），同比增加7.1亿元。

卷烟销售稳步提升。全省基本实现了访送分离和城乡一体的运行模式，电话订货率达93.01%，电子结算率达43%。全省销售卷烟95.97万箱，同比增加2.26万箱。完成销售收入73.52亿元，同比增加11.98亿元。

企业组织结构调整加快。省局（公司）机关完成了新一轮机构改革，在机关和全省选拔了7名副处级干部，对一般干部职工实行双向选择。各分公司整合了内部机构，优化了人力资源配置。

科技兴烟取得新成效。省局（公司）年度科技项目经费突破1000万元。省烟草科研实验大楼及金阳试验基地建设正式启动。烟草航天育种在第一年区域试验中，表现优良。“部分替代进口烟叶生产示范”和“以成熟度为中心配套生产技术试验示范与推广”取得较好效果。完成了全省通信平台、分公司与县局局域网、“1号工程”和烟叶收购信息系统的建设。

两个文明建设取得新成绩。认真组织开展了保持共产党员先进性教育活动。省局（公司）机关和9个市、州、地局（分公司）共捐资200多万元，修建10所金叶希望学校。开展了烟农、零售户、烟叶客户满意度和基层对省公司机关满意度的调查。

In 2005, provincial tobacco business insisted on taking the scientific development concept to guide the development overall situation, implemented foundation in the acceleration development, accelerated development in the implementation foundation, improved the quality of development as the basic policy, grasped three focus, did seven practical works, and the work achieved remarkable results.

Economic benefits created a record high. The profit and tax achieved 3.178 billion yuan, up 26.87% than last year. Tobacco export gained foreign exchange 43.5 million U.S. Dollars.

Monopoly management further increased.10,900 cases were investigated and treated, and 3010.69 pieces cigarettes, and tobacco leaf, pipe tobacco of 1021.17 tons were investigated and confiscated.

Flue-cured tobacco was stable development. 6.711 million dans tobacco leaf were purchased, more 1.035 million dans than last year. Sales of tobacco leaf were 6.6134 million dans, more 1.41 million dans than the same period of last year. The income of tobacco peasants was 3.21 billion yuan (including coal subsidy), an increase of over 710 million yuan than last year.

Cigarette sales have steadily improved. The province achieved the operational model of the separation of call on and delivery and the integration of urban and rural, rate of telephone orders was up to 93.01%, electronic clearing rate of 43%. The province sold 959,700 cases of cigarettes, an increase of 22,600 cases than the same period. The sales income completed 7.352 billion yuan, an increase of 1.198 billion yuan over the same period.

Organizational restructuring of enterprises accelerated. Organs of provincial administration (company) completed a new round of institutional reform and selected 7 deputy department level cadres in organs and the province, carried out two-way choice to general cadres and workers. Each branch reorganized the internal institution, and optimized the allocation of human resources.

Science and technology thriving cigarettes made new achievements. Provincial administration (company) annual broke through 10 million yuan of technology project funds. Provincial tobacco research laboratory building and Jinyang testing base construction officially started. The performance of space breeding tobacco was fine in the first year regional test. "Some substitute import tobacco leaf production model" and "support production technical test demonstration and promotion taking maturity as center" achieved the better results. The building of communications platform, branches and counties administrations LAN, "No.1 Project" and tobacco purchase information system were completed.

Two civilizations constructions have made new achievements. Carefully organized and maintained the Party member advanced educational activities. The organs of provincial administration (company) and nine cities, states, and boards (branches) contributed a total of more than 2 million yuan to build 10 Jinye Hope Schools. The satisfaction survey to the provincial company organs were launched in tobacco peasant, retail customer, tobacco leaf customer and grassroots.

贵州烟草商业科技创新大会

Guizhou tobacco commercial science and technology innovation conference

2004年6月，贵州省烟草专卖局职工捐建的威宁哈喇河乡金叶希望小学落成典礼

In June 2004, the inauguration of Jinye Hope Primary School of Halahe township of Weining contributed by the workers of Guizhou Province Tobacco Monopoly Administration

图片摄影：赵智阳 Photo: Zhao Zhiyang

人民银行贵阳中心支行概述

The Summary of People's Bank of China Guiyang Branch

2005年下半年，中国人民银行在贵州省进行农民工银行卡特色服务试点：贵州外出农民工在异地用工行\农行(限省内发行的卡)的银行卡存款后，回家后在当地农信社即可就近取款，今年中国人民银行已确定在全国12个省市推广。图为2005年12月29日，中国人民银行和贵州省政府等领导出席开通仪式，人民银行贵阳中支王平行长讲话

The second half of 2005, the People's Bank of China engaged in farmer workers bank card characteristic service pilot in Guizhou province: farmers worker who went out Guizhou deposited using bank cards of Industrial and Commercial Bank\Agricultural Bank (allowing the cards issued by the province) in other places, can draw money in the nearby local rural credit cooperatives after going home, this year, the People's Bank of China has decided to promote in the 12 provinces and cities. Photograph shows on December 29 of 2005, the leaders of People's Bank of China and the Guizhou provincial government attended the opening ceremony, the president of the People's Bank of China Guiyang Branch Wang Ping gave a speech

2005年，中国人民银行贵阳中心支行按照总行、分行的总体要求和部署，积极探索人民银行工作的规律和特点，结合贵州省实际，狠抓措施落实。特别是下半年，在总行督导组指导下，大力开展先进性教育活动，上下统一思想认识，跟上形势发展需要，调整工作布局，做到两不误、两促进，各项工作都取得了新的成绩。

2005年，全省金融运行平稳，货币信贷保持合理稳定增长，国家宏观调控政策措施进一步到位，信贷结构有所改善。全省本外币存款余额2777.3亿元，比年初增加418.9亿元，增长17.8%；本外币各项贷款余额2303.9亿元，比年初增加334.6亿元，增长17%。信贷总量的合理增长，促进了我省国民经济的较快发展。以改革为契机大力推进农村信用社改革试点，全省农村信用社各项存款余额360.1亿元，不良贷款比率11.3%，比改革前下降16.78个百分点，全省农村信用社实现利润1.97亿元，比改革前增加2.14亿元。积极推动社会各方共同参与地方金融生态环境建设。金融稳定、征信管理和反洗钱工作稳步发展。外汇管理的改进和加强适应了新形势发展的需要。金融服务水平进一步提高，按照上级行要求，金融服务必须贴近现代金融服务的需求，着重在提高水平和确保安全、高效运行上下功夫。

In 2005, according to the requirements and plans of the head office and branch, People's Bank of China Guiyang Branch actively explored work characteristics and laws of the People's Bank, combined Guizhou provincial actuality, vigorously implemented the measures. Especially in the second half of the year, under the guidance of the head office steering group, vigorously promoted advanced educational activity, unified ideological understanding, kept up with the needs of the situation development, adjusted the layout of work, did two no-neglect and two promoting, made new achievements in all fields of works.

In 2005, the provincial financial operation was stable, monetary credit maintained a reasonable steady growth, the state macro-control policies and measures made further to be in place, the credit structure has improved. The deposits balance of provincial currency and foreign currency was 277.73 billion yuan, more 41.89 billion yuan than the beginning of the year, an increase of 17.8%; the loans balance of currency and foreign currency was 230.39 billion yuan, more 33.46 billion yuan than the beginning of the year, an increase of 17%. The credit total reasonably increased to promote our provincial national economic rapid development. Took reform as the opportunity to vigorously promote rural credit cooperatives reform pilot, the deposits balance of the provincial rural credit cooperatives totaled 36.01 billion yuan, the ratio of non-performing loans was 11.3%, decrease 16.78% than before the reform. The profit of provincial rural credit cooperatives realized 197 million yuan, increase 214 million yuan than before the reform. Actively promoted society of all circles jointly participating in local financial ecological environment building. The works of financial stability, credit management and anti-wash money were steady development. The reform and improvement of foreign exchange management fit in with the needs of the new situation development. Further raised the level of financial services, according to aims of higher level, financial services must be close to the needs of modern financial services, focusing on raising standards and to ensure the safety and efficient operation.

今年全省已清理核查基本存款帐户72857户，销户3094户

This year the province had cleared and verified basic deposit 72,857 accounts, canceled 3,094 accounts

国家开发银行贵州省分行

The situation of the National Development Bank Guizhou

国家开发银行行长陈元与省长石秀诗会谈
The chief of the National Development Bank Chen Yuan talked with the governor of Guizhou Province Shi Xiushi

国家开发银行行长陈元赴遵义调研，参观遵义会议会址并提词
The chief of the National Development Bank Chen Yuan went to Zunyi to research, and visit the Zunyi Conference and draw the words

2005年是“十五”计划最后一年，回顾过去五年，国家开发银行贵州省分行紧紧围绕贵州省“十五”发展规划，积极应对体制缺损和发展瓶颈，扎实推进西部大开发战略的贯彻落实，鼎力支持贵州省经济社会发展，取得了良好的经济效益和社会效益。

自2002年成立以来，贵州分行累计承诺和发放各类贷款已分别达到535.08亿元和274.1亿元，有力支持了贵州交通基础设施、“西电东送”、城市规划建设、生态环境治理、特色产业等经济社会发展的瓶颈领域，为“富民兴黔”事业增添了强劲动力。

“十五”期间，分行对“西电东送”项目累计发放贷款130.25亿元，占贷款发放总额的47.52%，项目用款需求满足率达到100%；对公路行业累计发放贷款36.2亿元，占发放总额的13.21%；对城市基础设施建设项目累计发放贷款80.79亿元，占发放总额的29.48%；对新农村建设、中小企业、红色旅游和县域经济等累计发放贷款26.9亿元，占发放总额的9.80%。分行贷款余额已达267亿元，是成立之初近3倍，年均增长近40%，累计本息回收率99.75%，不良贷款率0.11%。

目前，开发银行贷款支持的一批项目已经竣工投产。据统计，目前已有539.4万千瓦装机建成发电，约占目前贵州建成装机总量的50.7%；公路项目已建成通车527公里；煤炭项目新增原煤生产能力585万吨；“三农”和中小企业项目，提供就业岗位1050个，带动2万农户5万农民增收。

贵州省人民政府和国家开发银行开发性金融合作座谈会
The opening financial cooperation forum of Guizhou province government and the National Development Bank

支持的“西电东送”重点项目洪家渡水电站
The major project "electricity transfer from the west to the east" Hongjiadu Hydropower Station by support

“十五”期间支持贵州建设情况

Branch support Guizhou construction during the period of "Tenth Five"

城市河道建设——“南明河三年变清”工程
Urban river construction - project "Nanming River change-clean by three years"

贵阳市中心环线——大营坡立交桥
The center link line of Guiyang city -- Dayingpo Overpass

The year of 2005 was the last year of "Tenth Five" Plan, recalling the past five years, the National Development Bank Guizhou Branch closely surrounding Guizhou province "Tenth Five" development planning, actively dealt with the system defect and development bottleneck, solidly improved the western development strategy implementation, supported Guizhou province in economic and social development, and made good economic and social benefits.

Since its foundation in 2002, the commitment and payment loans of Guizhou Branch have respectively reached 53.508 billion yuan and 27.41 billion yuan, to strongly support Guizhou transport infrastructure, "electricity transfer from the west to the east", urban planning and construction, ecological environment governing, special industries and other economic and social development bottleneck fields, added a strong impetus for the cause of "enriching people and thriving Guizhou"

During the period of "Tenth Five", the Branch accumulated payment loan of 13.025 billion yuan to the project "electricity transfer from the west to the east", accounting for 47.52% of total loans, the needs met rate for the project using loan reached 100%; cumulatively paid loans of 3.62 billion yuan to highway industry, accounting for 13.21% of total payment; cumulatively paid loans 8.079 billion yuan to urban infrastructure construction project, accounting for 29.48% of total payment; accumulated payment loans 2.69 billion yuan to the new rural development, middle and small enterprises, red tourism and county economy, accounting for 9.80% of total payment. The loans balance of the Branch has reached 26.7 billion yuan, was nearly three times of the foundation, the average annual growth of nearly 40%, the recycled rate of cumulative capital and interest was 99.75%, the rate of bad loans was 0.11%.

Currently, a number of projects that were supported by the loans of Development Bank have been completed and produced. According to statistics, there were 5.394 million kilowatts installed and electrified, about accounting for 50.7% of the current installed amount in Guizhou; highway projects have been built with 527 km; coal projects added raw coal production capacity 5.85 million tons; projects of "three agricultures" and middle and small enterprises, provided 1,050 posts, to lead 20,000 farmer households with 50,000 peasants increase incomes.

“黔电送粤”主要通道（图为贵州500千伏变电站）
"Guizhou electricity transfer to Guangdong" major corridor (Photograph shows Guizhou 500 kV transformer substation)

中国农业发展银行

农发行行长李光
The president of the China Agricultural Development Bank Guizhou Branch Li Guang

2005年，中国农业发展银行贵州省分行紧密结合贵州实际，加大信贷支农力度，年底各项贷款净增加10.6亿元，增幅达21.4%，增长比例居全国农发行系统第6名。其中，发放各级储备贷款11.8亿元，支持以西部地区最大的粮食储备库中央储备粮贵阳直属库等为主体的各级粮油储备体系建设，保证了国家宏观调控目标的实现和粮食安全；发放化肥储备贷款1.2亿元，支持建立化肥储备11万吨，增强了各地政府对农资市场的宏观调控能力；针对贵州粮食资源相对短缺的实际，发放预购订金和收购贷款1.5亿元，重点在仁怀、惠水等优质稻米和有特殊用途粮食品种的主产县倡导推广订单农业，得到了省委、省政府的充分肯定；审批发放贷款1.7亿元，支持17个农业产业化龙头企业、加工企业发展，有力地推动了当地农村经济的发展，带动了当地及周边地区农民大幅增收；相继与黔西南州、遵义市签订了政府信用合作协议，支持两个地区新农村建设，首批信用合作协议贷款项目已经启动。

2005年，农发行贵州省分行按照农发行总行打造现代农业政策性银行的要求，强化风险管理，信贷资产质量大幅提高，不良贷款绝对额和占比持续实现“双降”；加大经营绩效考核力度，强化经营核算，全行经营效益大幅提高；进一步加强内部管理，顺利完成全省系统三级行的调整改革工作。同时，积极响应省委、省政府加强扶贫工作的号召，确立了以救助贫困失学儿童为主要内容的智力扶贫工作思路，广泛动员全省系统力量，共筹集资金50多万元，援建了将军山农发行希望小学，得到了萧克将军、各级政府和社会各界的大力支持和高度评价。

2006年，中国农业发展银行贵州省分行将立足支持贵州社会主义新农村建设，紧紧围绕粮食生产、收购、加工、销售、转化五个环节，大力支持粮食产业链和粮油产业化发展，巩固传统粮油信贷业务；结合贵州实际，把酒、烟、药、种养业等全省重点支柱产业和粮油基地建设作为重点，加大信贷投入力度。同时，进一步深化内部综合改革，狠抓精细化管理的落实，增强执行国家宏观调控政策、产业政策和区域发展政策能力，使农发行成为市场经济条件下引导全省农业和农村资源配置的重要平台，充分发挥在推进新农村建设中的职能作用；大力培育“至诚服务、有效发展、以人为本、构建和谐”的企业文化核心理念，把农发行办成“建设新农村的银行”，为贵州省建设社会主义新农村作出新的更大贡献。

中国农业发展银行贵州省分行领导班子：

党委书记、行长：李光

党委副书记、副行长：樊荣

党委委员、副行长：刘定华

党委委员、副行长：胡世财

党委委员、副行长：胡天禄

In 2005, China Agricultural Development Bank Guizhou Branch in close connection with the Guizhou province practice, increased the intensity of agro-credit, net increase of the loans of 1.06 billion yuan at the end of the year, an increase of 21.4%, the proportion of increase ranking the No.6 in national agricultural development banking system. Among them, granted 1.18 billion yuan at all levels reserve loan to support grain reserve system construction at all levels taking the greatest food reserve the central reserve grain Guiyang granary in the western region as the main, ensured that the realization of national macro-control objectives and food security; Granted fertilizer reserve loans 120 million yuan, to support the establishment of reserves 110,000 tons of fertilizer to enhance the macro-control ability of governments at all levels to agricultural materials market. To the reality of Guizhou food resources relative shortfall, granted advance payment for future purchases and purchasing loans 150 million yuan, advocated and improved orders farming in Renhuai, Huishui and other counties which mainly produced quality rice and special-uses grain varieties, that gained the fully confirmation of the provincial Party committee and government; And examined and approved the issuance of 170 million yuan of loans to support the development of 17 farming industrial leading enterprises and processing enterprises, and have effectively promoted the local rural economic development, leading substantial increase income of local and surrounding areas farmers; Successively with Qianxina state, Zunyi city signed the credit agreement to support two regional new rural building, and the first credit cooperation agreement loan project has been activated.

建设新农村的银行

In 2005, according to the claim of building modern agricultural policy bank by the General Bank, Guizhou Branch strengthened risk management, substantially increased credit assets quality, and bad loans absolute value and accounting for the proportion achieved sustained "double down"; Increased business performance appraisal, strengthened business accounting, the business benefits of the bank significantly improved; further strengthened their internal management and the successfully completed the adjustment and reform work of the provincial system three-level bank. At the same time, positively responded to the call of provincial Party committee and the provincial government to strengthen help-the-poor work, established the work thought of intellectual helping the poor taking relief the poor out-of-school children as the main, mobilized the forces of the system to raise funds over 500 thousand yuan building the General Hill Agricultural Development Bank Hope Primary School, gained the support and highly appraise of general Xiao Ke, all levels of government and social all circles.

In 2006, China Agricultural Development Bank Guizhou Branch will be based to support building Guizhpu socialist new rural areas, centering on five links of food production, purchase, processing, marketing, and transformation, support food industries chain and grain industrial development, consolidate the traditional grain credit operation; Integrated Guizhou reality, take provincial key pillar industries such as wine, tobacco and medicine, cultivation and breeding industry and grain bases building as the key to enlarge credit input. At the same time, further deepening the internal reform, grasp the implementation of meticulous management, and strengthen the implementation capacity of national macro-control policy, industrial policy and regional development policy, become an important platform to guide the resources allocation in provincial agriculture and rural under the market economy condition, and give full play the functions in promoting new rural building; Vigorously cultivate the enterprise culture core concept of "good service, effective development, and people first, building harmony", make the Branch to become "the bank of building new rural", and make new and greater contributions for Guizhou province building socialist new rural areas.

The leadership group of China Agricultural Development Bank Guizhou Branch:

The secretary of the Party committee and the president of the bank: Li Guang

The deputy secretary of the Party committee and the vice president of the bank: Fan Rong

The member of the Party committee and the vice president of the bank: Liu Dinghua

The member of the Party committee and the vice president of the bank: Hu Shicai

The member of the Party committee and the vice president of the bank: Hu Tianlu

贵州省副省长吴嘉甫（纪念碑左执线者）、萧星华将军（纪念碑右执线者）为将军山农发行希望小学纪念碑揭幕。李光行长（右五）、樊荣副行长（左一）、胡世财副行长（左二）出席

The vice governor of Guizhou province government Wu Jiafu (the left holding line from monument), and general Xiao Xinghua(the right holding line from monument) unveiled for General Hill Agricultural Development Bank Hope Primary School. The president Li Guang (the fifth from right), the vice president Fan Rong, (the first from left), and the vice president Hu Shicai (the second from left) attended.

李光行长（左二）、胡世财副行长（右一）在丹寨县就养殖业发展信贷支持和开展农业政策性保险等进行调研

The president Li Guang (the second from left), and the vice president Hu Shicai (the first from right) investigated on development credit support and carrying out agricultural policy insurance for breeding industry in Danzhai county.

地址：贵阳市神奇路32号

Address: No.32 Shenqi road Guiyang city

联系电话(Contact telphone)： (0851) 5874965

邮政编码(Post Code)：550002

中国工商银行贵州省分行

INDUSTRIAL AND COMMERCIAL BANK OF CHINA GUIZHOU BRANCH

包克辛副省长（中）及贵州银监局局长邓瑞林（右一）到工行省分行基层网点视察工作（左一为省分行行长黄再红）
The deputy governor Bao Kexin (center) and the director of Guizhou Banking Supervision Bureau Deng Ruilin (the first from right) went to the GuiZhou Branch grassroot spot to inspect work (the first from left, the president of Guizhou Branch Huang Zaihong)

工行省分行行长黄再红（左三）视察工行贷款支持的清黄公路项目建设现场
The president of Guizhou Branch Huang Zaihong (the third from left) was visiting the construction site of Qing Huang road project, supported by loan of industrial and commercial bank

2005年，工行贵州省分行认真落实工总行各项工作部署，以建设现代化商业银行、社会主义和谐银行和西部精品银行为目标，紧密结合贵州经济发展实际，努力推动各项业务全面协调发展，圆满完成了“十五”发展目标，迈出了实现“再造贵州分行”宏伟目标的坚实一步。

全行经营效益持续提升，实现经营利润12.62亿元，同比增加3.3亿元，增幅达35.41%，资产利润率、人均利润、成本收入比等主要财务指标全面优化。资产质量大幅改善，年末不良贷款余额为6.2亿元，比年初下降49.36亿元；不良贷款占比为1.18%，比年初下降9.54个百分点；不良贷款余额和不良贷款率在总行排名中处于较好位置；不良贷款拨备覆盖率和信贷资产应计拨备覆盖率均达到100%。有效规模稳步扩大，人民币各项存款余额647.6亿元，比年初增加68.59亿元，增幅13.44%，人民币各项贷款余额为521.58亿元，还原剥离因素实际比年初增加54.8亿元，增长10.67%，全行经营规模和人均有效规模进一步扩大。中间业务、新业务发展态势良好，全年实现中间业务收入15989万元，同比增加3325万元，增幅达26.25%；中间业务收入占比进一步提升。电子银行交易额达到2495亿元，电子银行业务量在总业务量中的占比达到24%。信用卡新增有效卡109886张，信用卡发卡量增幅、信用卡存款增量、透支余额增量、风险控制率、各项收入计划完成率等5项指标进入全国工行前10名。在全国工行系统省级分行行长经营绩效考评中，工行贵州省分行经营级次为B，排名第5位，继续保持了在工行系统内靠前的排名。

工行贵州省分行与中国华融资产管理公司贵阳办事处签订不良资产转让协议
Guizhou Branch and China Huarong Asset Management Corporation Guiyang Office signed the transfer agreement of bad assets

In 2005, ICBC Guizhou Branch seriously implemented the work plan of ICBC, took building the modern commercial bank, socialist harmonious bank and the West excellent bank as target, closely connected with the Guizhou economic development reality, made great efforts to promote all businesses comprehensive coordinated development, successfully completed the development goal "Tenth Five", toke a solid step forward realization grand objective "Construction Guizhou Branch Again".

The Branch operation efficiency continued improvement to achieve operation profit of 1.262 billion yuan, 330 million yuan more than the same period of last year, an increase of 35.41%, the major financial indicators such as the rate of asset profit, per capita profit, cost and revenue ratio were overall optimized. Assets quality improved substantially, the saving bad loans of 620 million yuan of the end of the year, fall 4.936 billion yuan than the beginning of the year; the ratio of bad loans of 1.18%, down 9.54 percentage points than the beginning of the year; The saving bad loans and the rate of bad loans were in a better position in the ranking of the ICBC; The assigning covering rate of bad loans and the calculated assigning covering rate of credit assets all reached 100% . Effective size of the steady expansion, the saving deposits of all kinds totaled RMB 64.76 billion yuan, more 6.859 billion yuan than the beginning of the year, an increase of 13.44%, the saving loans of RMB 52.158 billion yuan, the actual increased 5.48 billion yuan than the beginning of the year, growth 10.67%, the scale of business and per capital effective scale of the Branch further expanded. The trend of intermediate business and new business development was well, the revenue of intermediate business annual achieved 159.89 million yuan, 33.25 million yuan more than the same period of last year, an increase of 26.25%; the ratio of intermediate business further enhanced. The transactions amount of electronic bank reached 249.5 billion yuan, the ratio of the electronic bank business amount in total business amount reached 24%. New increased 109886 effectively credit cards, five indicators of the credit card issuing quantity increase, the credit card deposits increment, overdraft balance increment, risk control rate, the completed rate of revenue plan entered the first ten places in ICBC. In the operation performance examination of the president of the provincial branch of ICBC, the Guizhou Branch operation-class was the B-class, ranked the fifth, and continued to maintain in the front place in ICBC.

中国农业银行贵州省分行
Agricultural Bank of China Guizhou Branch

农行贵州省分行致力为广大客户提供灵活多样的电子金融业务，开办自助银行、完善网上银行、建立客户服务中心，使客户享受全方位、全时段的现代商业银行服务。图为该行的"95599"服务热线中心。

Guizhou Branch devoted to provide flexible and variety electronic financial businesses to customers, offering self-service bank, perfecting Internet bank, building customer service center, making customers to enjoy the modern commercial bank service on enjoy side and time interval. The picture shows the "95599" service hotline center.

2005年，农行贵州省分行牢固树立科学发展观，深化改革，强化管理，抢抓机遇，加快发展，各项工作取得了显著成效。在全国农行系统综合绩效考评中跃居B类行第一名。

截止到2005年末，全行本外币各项存款余额达到531.31亿元，比年初增加69.88亿元，其中储蓄存款余额达248.01亿元，比年初增加38.07亿元。本外币各项贷款余额达535.42亿元，较年初增加47.95亿元，其中优良客户贷款较年初上升8.91个百分点。全行本外币业务实现经营利润8.65亿元，同比增盈3.1亿元，位列全国农行十大账面盈利行之一，人均创利10.19万元，超过全国农行平均水平。

在加快有效发展的过程中，农行贵州省分行进一步完善市场营销机制，调整优化信贷结构，重点支持电力、煤炭、交通等优势行业和项目。加大对地方经济的支持力度，与毕节行署及17个县市签订银政合作协议，意向性支持信用280亿元。加大对教育事业的支持力度，建立了从小学到大学"一条龙"的金融服务体系。加快个人业务的发展，建立个人理财中心，在各二级分行所在地成立个贷审查中心，实行集约化经营，强化风险控制，提高个人业务发展质量。同时加快柜台传统结算业务向网上银行、电话银行、ATM、自助银行等新型业务的迁移推广。开通了B2C电子商务业务，创建了集网上银行、电话银行、客户服务于一体的"95599在线银行"，实现了24小时不间断服务，综合服务水平跃上一个新的平台。

农行贵州省分行注重加强企业文化建设，丰富员工的业余文化生活。图为该行举行的"农行颂"文艺晚会。

Guizhou Branch strengthened the enterprise culture construction, enriching spare-time cutural life of employees. The picture shows the Branch holding "the Ode of Agricultural Bank" cultural evening party.

农行贵州省分行积极探索新型政银合作关系，在助推地方经济增长的同时中加快自身有效发展步伐。2005年，农行贵州省分行先后与毕节地区行署及六枝特区、盘县、正安、道真、镇远等县级政府签订了政银合作协议。图为与毕节地区行署签署"政银全面合作"暨"十一五"100亿元项目贷款框架协议。

Agricultural bank of China Guizhou branch explores new governance partnership in boosting local economie growth and accelerating its own effective development. In 2005, the bank signed cooperation agreement between governments and banks with Bijie prefecture and Liuzhi special zone , Panxian, Zhengan, Daozhen, Zhengyuan and other county governments.The picture shows signing ceremony of "government and bank comprehensive cooperation" and "Eleventh Five" RMB 10 billion yuan of loan framework between the bank and Bijie prefecture.

In 2005, Agricultural bank of China Guizhou branch achieved remarkable success by fastening a view of scientific development, deepening reform, strengthening management, seizing opportunity, accelerating development. Ultimately got the first pride in category B in the integrated performance appraise for the whole branches.

By the end of 2005, the balance of the bank's total deposits reached RMB 53.131 billion yuan, an increase of RMB 6.988 billion yuan over the prior year, the balance of Renminbi savings deposits reached RMB 24.801 billion yuan an increase of 3.807 billion yuan over the prior year. The balance of the bank's total loans reached RMB 53.542 billion yuan, an increase of 4.795 billion yuan, excellent customer loans reflected an increase of 8.91 percentage points over the prior year. The profit of the bank's business reached 865 million yuan, 310 million yuan more than last year. The bank ranked the one of the 10 paper profits in all branches, per profit amounted to RMB 101.9 thousand yuan, over the average level.

The bank redoubled their efforts related to product innovation marketing activities and loan structure in their corporate banking business. Provided strong financial support to electricity, coal, transportation and other advantage projects. The bank signed government and bank cooperation with Bijie prefecture and other 17 county governments indicative supported RMB 28 billion credit. Also, from primary school to university level, the bank conducted a coordinated financial service for education. In personal banking business, the bank set up a personal financial management center and personal credit review center in prefectural level branches, conducted intensive operation, strengthened risk management, ultimately accelerate the personal business. At the same time, the bank changed some traditional counter business to new types, such as online banking, telephone banking, self-service banking, ATM and other types. The bank also opened B2C e-commerce operation and "95599 Online Bank" which integrated a system included network bank, telephone bank and clients service, achieved 24-hour uninterrupted service, which presented a kind of new type.

人保财险贵州省分公司保费收入突破10亿元

The Premium of PICC Property and Casualty Company Limited Guizhou Branch exceeded 1 billion yuan

人保财险总公司刘政焕副总裁与贵州省分公司领导班子合影（左起：汪旗副总经理、刘强副总经理、刘政焕副总裁、吕如庆总经理、孙广建副总经理）

PICC Property and Casualty Company Limited Liu Zhenghuan, deputy CEO and Guizhou Branch leadership group had a group photo taken (from the left: Wang Qi vice-general manager, Liu Qiang vice-general manager, Liu Zhenghuan deputy CEO and Lu Ruqing general manager, Sun Guanjian vice-general manager)

人保财险贵州省分公司吕如庆总经理

PICC Property and Casualty Company Limited Guizhou Branch Lu Ruqing general manager

中国人保财险贵州省分公司保险机构和代理网点遍及全省各县（市），是目前贵州省境内最大的国有控股商业性财产保险公司。该公司始终坚持以市场为导向，以客户为中心，求真务实，锐意改革，不断推出创新服务举措，取得了较好经营业绩。2005年，该公司保费收入103,356万元，承担保险责任总额2100多亿元，保费收入突破10亿元。“十五”期间，累计支付各类保险赔款22.4亿元，上交国家税收2.6亿元，为稳定企业经营，安定人民生活发挥了重要作用。

“铸金牌服务，为梦想护航”，2005年中国人保财险成为北京2008年奥运会唯一保险合作伙伴。我们将继续秉承“求实、诚信、拼搏、创新”的企业精神，以新思想、新举措、新作风、新方式适应公众公司的新规则、新要求，不断提升公司价值，提高盈利水平，努力建设成为国内领先、国际一流的知识型、现代化非寿险公众公司，为发展壮大贵州保险业，振兴贵州经济建设做出新贡献。

2005年11月15日，毕节威宁发生死17人重伤3人特大交通事故，人保财险公司及时兑现保险赔款38万元。

November 15, 2005, Weining Bijie happened especially big traffic accident, 17 people died and 3 people serious injury, the company timely paid 380,000 yuan insurance compensation.

PICC Property and Casualty Company Limited Guizhou Branch extends agencies and agent points all over the counties (cities) in the province, is the largest state-controlled commercial property insurance company within the boundaries of Guizhou province. The company always taking market as guide and taking customer as center, sought truth and dealt with concrete matters, and reformed with keen determination, constantly improved the innovation service action, achieved the better business performance. In 2005, the premium of the company was 1033.56 million yuan, assumed over 210 billion yuan total liability insurance, the premium exceeded 1 billion yuan. The period of "Tenth Five", the cumulative payment of insurance compensation reached 2.24 billion yuan, turned over taxes to the state of 260 million yuan, and played an important role for stabilizing the business and settling people's lives.

"Casting Gold Service, Escorting For Dream", in 2005, PICC Property and Casualty Company Limited became the only insurance partner in Beijing Olympic Games of 2008. We would continue to take the enterprise spirit "truth-seeking, honesty, hard work, innovation", take the new idea, new action, new style, new way to fit the new rule, new requirement of public company, and continually improve the value of the company, raise profit level, and strive to build a domestic leading and international first-class knowledge-type, modernized non-life insurance public company, make new contributions to grow Guizhou insurance industry and vitalize Guizhou economic construction.

铸金牌服务　为梦想护航

Casting Gold Service　Escorting For Dream

地址：贵州省贵阳市遵义路30号
Address of the company: No.30 Zunyi road Guiyang city Guizhou province
邮编(Post Code)：550002
电话(Tel)：0851-5570272　传真(Fax)：0851-5577364
服务专线(Service hotline)：95518

在改革中腾飞的中国人寿贵州省分公司
Rising China Life Insurance Company Guizhou Branch

中国人寿贵州省分公司班子“全家福”
右二：省分公司主持工作的副总经理柳福青；左二：省分公司纪委书记李方玲；右一：省分公司总稽核曾渊德；左一：省分公司副总经理金香国
The photograph of China Life Insurance Guizhou Branch leader group
The second from right: the vice general manager who takes charge of works of the provincial branch company, Liu Fuqing The second from left: the secretary of discipline committee of provincial branch company, Li Fangling The first from right: general auditor of provincial branch company, Zeng Yuande The first from left: the vice general manager of the provincial branch company, Jin Xiangguo

2005年，中国人寿贵州省分公司新班子立足系统实情，着力加快发展，提出了“一年初见成效、两年基本变样、三年改变面貌”的三年发展规划和“举旗帜、抓班子、带队伍、上管理、促发展”的五项工作措施，以“跳出贵州看贵州”的视角重新定位自身的发展，为贵州国寿制定了全面发展的蓝图，将远景和阶段性目标有机结合在一起，开拓创新，求真务实开创了贵州国寿新的业务发展期。

2005年，通过思想解放大讨论，员工观念得到空前转变、核心战斗力明显增强；通过卓有成效的人力资源制度改革以及薪酬体制改革，经营管理水平显著提高、业务支撑有效改善、市场竞争力不断提升。

2005年，贵州国寿实现保费收入138,474万元，同比增长50.75%，市场份额提高了6.6个百分点。全面超额完成了总公司下达的各项经营绩效考核指标，在全国系统六项发展指标排名中，贵州省分公司拿到了总保费收入、风险型保费、投资性保费、长险首年保费、意外险首年保费增幅五项第一名，首年期交保费第四名，已从二类B级公司跨入了一类AAA级公司。

作为一家服务于社会经济，诚信为本、稳健经营的民族寿险企业，中国人寿贵州省分公司秉承“成己为人、成人达己”的企业文化理念，在市场竞争中不断调整发展的节奏和步伐，以改革促发展、以管理出效益、以服务博信任，为地方经济的发展作出自己应有的贡献。

The year of 2005, based the truth situation of system , new leader group of China Life Insurance Company Guizhou Branch took great pains to accelerate development, proposed three-year development plan "initial success of one-year, fundamental change of two-year, turning outlook of three-year" and five measures "holing the flag, grasping the leader group, leading the team, running management, and promoting the development", took view of "jump Guizhou see Guizhou" as repositioned its own development, established the overall development blueprint for Guizhou China Life, combined long-range planning with phase goals, explored and created, sought the truth and dealt with concrete matters to open new business development period for Guizhou China Life.

2005, through the discussion of liberation thought, the sense of staff got unprecedented change, core strength has increased markedly; Through effective reform of human resource system and pay system, the management level has markedly improved, and effectively perfected operational support, market competitiveness has advanced.

2005, the Guizhou China Life achieved premium income of 1384.74 million yuan, 50.75% more than last year, increased 6.6 percentage points in market share. Fully overfulfilled operating performance targets assigned by the general corporation, in the ranking of national system six development indexes, Guizhou Branch got 5 the first in total premium income, risk insurance premium, investment insurance premium, long-term insurance first year premium, accident insurance first year premium increase, and the fourth in first year payment premium, has entered the class I AAA company from the class B-class company.

As a service for the social economy, integrity-based, stable national life insurance enterprise, China Life Guizhou Branch commanded the enterprise culture concept "help personal for other people, help other people for personal", constantly adjusted their development pace and rhythm in market competition, taking reform to promote development, taking management to realize efficiency, taking service to win trust, and made contributions for local economic development.

公司地址：贵州省贵阳市遵义路30号
Company address: No.30 Zunyi road, Guiyang city Guizhou province
邮编(Post code)：550002
全国统一服务电话(National unified service Tel)：95519
传真(Fax)：0851-5572110

贵州省分公司柳总与贵阳分公司总经理王永健签定2006年工作目标责任状
The general manager Liu of Guizhou Branch and the general manager Wang Yongjian of Guiyang Branch signed objective warrant of 2006

中国人寿贵州省分公司召开2006年工作会议（会场）
China Life Guizhou Branch held the work meeting of 2006 (the site of meeting)

天安保险股份有限公司
TIANAN INSURANCE COMPANY LIMITED OF CHINA

诚信服务月宣传活动
The propaganda activities of faith service month

天安保险股份有限公司是全国首家由企业出资组建的股份制商业保险公司，成立于1994年10月，总部设在上海浦东，现注册资本金5.015亿元。公司主要经营中国保险监督管理委员会核准的人民币、外币各种财产保险、责任保险、信用保险、水险、人身意外保险、健康保险、金融服务保险、再保险、法定保险和资金运用保险等业务。

公司成立十年来，已从一个区域性中小保险公司迅速成长为全国性的大型现代保险公司，实现了产、寿险兼营，奠定了集团化经营的基础。2005年实现保费收入65.3亿元，成为中国企业500强。公司现拥有700余家营业网点，机构遍布全国各地。

公司始终把“建设中国保险第一品牌”作为战略目标，不但热衷于为客户提供专业化的风险咨询评估，还悉心向客户提供科学的“程式化”的风险管理跟踪服务。

公司在国内率先建立了与国际接轨的“承保人制度”，实现了全系统核心业务的电子化管理和以预警为核心的实时内控系统，并顺利通过了ISO9002、ISO9001：2000国际质量管理体系和ISO14001国际环境管理体系标准的认证。在产品创新上，国内首创了医疗责任、建设工程监理责任、律师责任（乙种）、幸福家庭财产综合保险、幸福女性保险计划等新险种。公司承保了一大批在国内外颇具影响力的重大项目，如上海黄浦江上的4座著名大桥、上海地铁、渝湛高速公路等一大批重大项目，参与共保了亚太卫星、中卫1号、鑫诺中星8号、铱星等14次航天保险。

2003年10月，贵州省分公司正式成立。为天安客户提供专业化的全程服务和周全完善的风险保障，这是天安保险贵州省分公司向社会和所有的客户作出的承诺。

依法合规经营专题讲座
The symposium for business according to law

天安保险保障每一天
Tianan Insurance insures every day

Tianan insurance company limited of China, is the first national stock commercial insurance company which is invested by enterprises, was established in October 1994, with headquarters in Shanghai Pudong, now registered capital of 501.5 million yuan. The company operated the main businesses of Renminbi and foreign currencies property insurance, liability insurance, credit insurance, marine insurance, personal accident insurance, health insurance, financial services insurance, reinsurance, statutory insurance and funds operations insurance, approved by the China Insurance Supervision Management Commission.

During decades foundation, the company rapidly grew up the national large-scale modern insurance company from a regional middle-small insurance company, achieved property insurance and life insurance operations, and laid the foundation for the Group operations. The year of 2005, the company realized 6.53 billion yuan of premium income and became China's top 500 enterprises. The company owned 700 more business networks and institutions throughout the country.

The company always put "building the first brand of China Insurance" as a strategic objective, not only keen to support professional risk advice and estimation, and also to provide good services of scientific "procedures" risk management following for clients.

The company took the lead in establishing the "insurer system" getting along with internation in the country and achieved electronic management of a system-wide core business and real-time control system taking early warning as the core. The company successfully passed the ISO9002, ISO9001:2000 international quality management system and ISO14001 international environmental management system standard certification. In product innovation, the company pioneered some new insurances in domestic market, such as medical responsibility insurance, construction supervision responsibility insurance, the responsibility of lawyers (B types) insurance, happy family property comprehensive insurance, and insurance plans of female happiness. The company underwrote a large number of influential major projects at home and abroad, such as 4 famous bridges in Shanghai Huangpu River, Shanghai subway, Yu Zhan highway, and jointly insured 14 space insurances, such as satellite in the Asia-Pacific, the No.1 Chinese satellite, the No.8 Xinruozhong satellite and Iridium satellite.

October 2003, Guizhou Branch was formally established. Providing comprehensive professional service and perfect risk protection, that is the promise of Tianan Insurce Guizhou Branch to social and all customers.

转型中的

The transition of

作为贵州省主要通信运营企业，贵州电信始终坚持立足于贵州，服务于贵州，服从于贵州社会经济发展的大局，不断加快发展。2005年，全省电信用户突破400万，在西部地区率先实现“宽带到乡镇”，整体通信能力和服务水平迈上了一个新台阶。在百年的发展道路上，贵州电信不畏艰难，励精图治，勇于创新，走出了一条具有自我特色的发展之路，为贵州的地方经济、科学信息发展做出了不可磨灭的贡献。

同时，企业转型业务正在快速拓展。2005年，在中国电信集团大力支持下，全国首创与业界知名软件开发商、系统集成商、设备制造商共同组建艾玛特信息超市项目开发有限公司，开始研发和建设跨PSTN网、PHS网和IP互联网的综合信息处理平台，探索灵活、快速响应市场的事业部经营模式。贵州电信以综合信息服务统领各项业务发展，提高业务自主创新、持续创新能力，着力通过技术、业务和网络的有机融合，不断创造有独特优势的业务。在激烈的市场竞争中，贵州电信树立“稳健经营，持续提升企业价值”和“回报社会，做有责任心的企业公民”的理念，以满足客户需求为中心，建立和完善了大客户、社区经理、农村统包及10000号四个营销服务渠道，开创了电话、互联网、上门、自助、流动等多元化的服务方式，使用户足不出户即可享受电信全方位的服务。

与此同时，贵州电信以企业管理和机制创新为突破口，全面推进企业内部改革。公司以上市为契机，由传统的基础网络运营商向现代综合信息服务提供商转型，转变增长方式和发展模式，由原来的计划、技术和规模导向转变为市场、客户和效益导向，企业管理从粗放向精确转变，不断创新薪酬激励、绩效考核、职业发展、竞争上岗和教育培训机制。

服务是企业永恒的主题。贵州电信建立了服务质量事故领导责任追究制度，对各分公司进行服务质量分等级评定，服务问题实行内部报纸、网站的曝光制度。在集团公司组织的与当地其他运营商服务热线第三方同城拨测评比中，电信10000号从2005年年初的第三名提升到连续三个月排名第一，全年综合评定第一。

近年来，贵州省电信公司先后荣获中华全国总工会授予的2004年度全国“五一劳动奖状”，全国先进劳动争议调解组织，2004年度“贵州省十佳服务单位”、“贵州省最具影响力企业”称号，中国消费者协会2005年度全国“诚信维权”单位等多种荣誉。

电信办公大楼
Telecommunications office building

网管大楼机房
Machine room in network-management building

10000号
No.10000

贵州电信

Guizhou Telecomm

As a major communications business enterprise in Guizhou province, Guizhou Telecom always based on Guizhou, serviced in Guizhou, subordinated to the overall situation of Guizhou economic and social development, continuously accelerates development. In 2005, the telecommunications users exceeded 4 million in the province, took the lead in achieving the "broadband to the township" in the western region, the overall communication capabilities and services have climbed to a new level. In a hundred years development path, Guizhou Telecom defied difficulties, made great efforts, braved in innovation, went a way of self-feature development, made an indelible contribution for the local economy, the development of scientific information of Guizhou.

At the same time, the business of the company rapidly expanded. In 2005, under the support of the China Telecom Group, the company initiated Airmart Information Supermarket Project Development Ltd. jointly organized with renowned software developers, system integration contractors, equipment manufacturers, began developing and building cross-PSTN networks, PHS networks and IP networks integrated information processing platform, and explored business style with flexible, rapid response to the market. Guizhou Telecom took integrated information services to guide all the businesses development, enhanced independent innovation, continuous innovation ability of the business, adopted organic integration of technology, business and network to constantly create business with unique advantage. In the fierce market competition, Guizhou Telecom established a "moderate business, continue improvement the value of enterprise" and "social returns, do responsible corporate citizenship" concept, took satisfied customer needs as the center, established and perfected four market service channels as the big client, community manager, rural and No.10,000, opened the multivariate services such as telephone, Internet, home, self-help, mobile, so that users can enjoy telecommunication services on every side even staying indoors.

In the meantime, Guizhou Telecom took the enterprise management and mechanism innovation as breakthrough point to comprehensively promote the enterprise internal reform. The company took listed as an opportunity to make the traditional basic network operator to transfer a modern integrated information service provider, changed the increase style and development model from the original plans, technology and scale to market, customer and efficiency, the enterprise management was changed from the extensiveness to the preciseness, continuously innovated incentive pay, performance appraisal, career development, competition and the education and training system.

Service is an eternal theme of enterprise. Guizhou Telecom established the service quality accident leadership responsibility system, made the grade evaluation of service quality to all branches, carried out the exposure system of inside newspaper, website in service problem. In the service hotline third-party evaluation organized by China Telecom Corporation with other local operator, telecommunications No.10,000 upgraded the first consecutive three months from the third in the beginning of 2005 , the first in the comprehensive assessment of the whole year.

In recent years, Guizhou Telecom has successively won the prize of the 2004 annual national "1st May labor citation" awarded by All-China Federation of Trade Unions, National Advanced Labor Dispute Mediation Organization, 2004 annual "Ten Best Service Unit of Guizhou Province", title "Guizhou Province Most Influential Enterprise", Chinese Consumer Association 2005 annual national "Integrity Faith Defended Right" unit, and many other honors.

贵州信息港
Guizhou Information Port

耐心为客户服务
Patience for customer service

贵州联通人坚持的服务理念 The insistent concept of service by the people of Guizhou Unicom
——“联通你我，真诚服务”
- - "connecting you and me, with sincere service"

都匀剑江中路大十字营业厅2005年3月被授予全国用户满意电信服务明星班组；2005年5月获全国青年文明号
The Grand Cross Business Hall of Jianjiangzhong road of Duyun was awarded the National User Satisfaction Communication Service Star Group in March of 2005, and theNational Youth Civilization Name in May of 2005

服务是通信企业生存和发展的根本所在。十五期间，随着企业的不断壮大，用户规模的不断增长，贵州联通也在不断创新服务工作，努力提升服务水平，以差异化的服务优势和诚信服务的理念，打造企业新的服务品牌，获得了广大用户的积极认可。

贵州联通一直以来都将服务工作作为企业发展的首要工作，从联通公司成立之初首创“低柜台”和“即买即通”等多种概念新颖、体现亲情的人性化服务开始，公司不断引入新的服务理念，创新服务措施，服务质量有了大幅度的上升。共有20多人次获得省部级劳动模范、先进工作者、全国用户满意服务明星、科技进步奖、优秀质量QC小组、知识型员工等荣誉。

通过一系列改善服务的措施，服务质量得到明显改进，公司在2004年的民主评议行风活动中被评为优秀，2005年“3.15”期间，公司被贵州省消费者协会授予“诚信单位”荣誉称号。

The service is essential for the survival and development of communication enterprise. During the period of Tenth Five, with the growing enterprise, the growing size of the user, Guizhou Unicom also continued to innovate the service work, and strived to improve the level of service, took the different service advantages and the concept of honest and credit service, built the new service brand of the enterprise, so gave the active approval of majority users.

Guizhou Unicom has been taking service work as the priority work for enterprise development, pioneering the "low counter" and "instantly buy instantly open", and many other innovative concepts, embodiment affection humanity service from the beginning of the foundation of the company, the company continued to introduce new service ideas, innovated service measures, so quality of service has significantly increased. A total of more than 20 person times awarded the honors of the provincial and ministry labor model and the advanced worker, the national client satisfaction service star, the progress prize of science and technology, the outstanding quality QC group, and the knowledge worker.

Through a series of measures to improve service, the quality of service has markedly improved, the company was assessed outstanding in 2004 democratic assessment activity, in the period of "3.15" of 2005, the company was awarded honor title of "honest and credit unit" by Guizhou Province Consumer Association.

联通一家亲——毕节联通帮扶层台镇青春村小学场景
The close family of the Unicom -- the scene of Bijie Unicom helping Qingchun village primary school of Cengtai town

优质的服务赢来了顾客的高满意度
High-quality service to win high satisfaction for customer

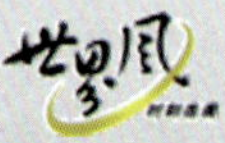

让一切自由连通

中国铁通集团有限公司
China Tietong Corporation Guizhou Branch

中国铁通集团有限公司的前身是铁道部通信信息有限责任公司，成立于2000年12月26日，是中国六家大型基础电信运营商之一，铁通贵州分公司（以下简称“贵州铁通”）是中国铁通集团有限公司的下属省级机构，成立于2001年3月20日，负责贵州省境内的公众电信业务和铁路专网通信服务，在授权范围内自主经营、独立发展，同时接受贵州省电信行业主管部门的行业管理。

贵州铁通在贵州境内下设9个地、州（市）分公司和1个为铁路运输通信服务的铁道通信中心，共有1300余名员工。

贵州铁通目前已经形成覆盖全省9个地州的长途通信网、本地交换网、数据网、寻呼网等，在网络的完整性、覆盖面，技术装备水平等方面具有较强的竞争优势。贵州铁通享有贵州省境内铁路通信网的统一管理与指挥权，承担全省范围内基础电信运营商的责任与义务。

贵州铁通成立5年来，大力开拓公众电信市场，取得了较好的经济效益和社会效益。贵州铁通开通了“10050”统一客服平台，建立了计费中心和全国客户服务体系，是贵州第一家可向用户提供市话详单的电信运营企业，并于2005年顺利通过ISO9001:2000质量管理体系认证。

中国铁通贵州分公司解兵总经理
The general manager of China TieTong Corporation Guizhou Branch Xie Bing

面向未来，贵州铁通为建设效益、合力、和谐铁通和贵州经济腾飞作出贡献。

国资委邵宁副主任给外部董事颁发聘书
The deputy director of China-MOR Shao Ning was issuing the letter of appointment to outside director

庆祝三十六届世界电信日暨三周年巡回演出
Making a performance for celebration the 36th World Tele communications Day cum the Third Anniversary

China TieTong Corporation Guizhou Branch, the predecessor is China-MOR Communication Information Limited Liability Company, was established on December 26 of 2000, and was the one of China's six major foundation telecommunications operators. TieTong Guizhou Branch (hereinafter referred to "Guizhou TieTong") is the subordinate provincial agency of China TieTong Holdings Limited Corporation, was established on March 20 of 2001. Guizhou TieTong is in charge of public telecommunication service and rail special-net communication service in the province, makes its own managerial decision and independently develops in the scope of authority, meanwhile, receives the trade management of telecommunications industry competent department of Guizhou province.

Guizhou TieTong administrated nine areas, prefectures (cities) and one railway communication center serviced for rail transportation communicationin Guizhou boundary, having a total of 1,300 staff.

Guizhou TieTong has now established the long-distance communication network, local exchange network, data network, and paging network, that covering with nine areas, prefectures (cities) in the province, and has a strong competitive superiority in the integrity of the network, coverage and the level of technical equipment. Guizhou TieTong enjoys unified management and command right of railway communication network in Guizhou boundary, and assumes the responsibility and obligation of basis telecommunications operators in the province.

Since foundation five years, Guizhou TieTong devoted major efforts to open up public telecommunications market, and achieved the good economic efficiency and social benefits. Guizhou TieTong launched "10050" unified customer-service platform, established the cost center and the national customer service system. Guizhou TieTong was the first telecommunication operation enterprise provided city-telephone detailed list to users in Guizhou, and successfully passed ISO9001:2000 quality management system certification in 2005.

Face to the future, Guizhou TieTong will contribute to build efficiency, united, harmony TieTong and Guizhou economy rising.

贵州省交通规划勘察设计研究院
GUIZHOU COMMUNICATION DESIGN INSITUTE

老猫冲隧道
Laomaochong tunnel

抚溪江桁式组合拱桥
Purlin-type combined arched bridge of Fuxi river

贵新公路大良田立交桥
Daliangtian overpass of Guixin road

贵州省交通规划勘察设计研究院始建于1958年，隶属贵州省交通厅，是国家甲级工程项目建设总承包单位，持国家工程勘察综合类甲级、公路全行业甲级（公路、特大隧道、特大桥梁、交通工程）、市政公用行业（桥隧）甲级、地质灾害危险性评估、地质灾害防治工程勘查、设计、施工、监理甲级、工程咨询甲级、交通基本建设工程监理甲级、水运行业（航道、港口）、市政公用行业（道路）乙级等资格证书，获ISO9001：2000版质量体系认证。承担高速公路、等级公路、桥梁、隧道、岩土工程、交通工程、港口、航道、地质灾害治理等工程项目的规划、可行性研究、勘察设计、施工监理、技术咨询业务。

我院立足贵州、面向全国、走向世界。曾在援老挝、布隆迪、西藏及支闽、支滇、支前（线）的公路勘察设计中，分别获得交通部、外经部、总参谋部嘉奖。八十年代以来，完成贵阳至黄果树、贵阳至遵义、贵阳至新寨、崇溪河至遵义、凯里至麻江、玉屏至铜仁、玉屏至三穗、三穗至凯里、镇宁至水城、镇宁至胜境关等十余条（段）高等级公路勘察设计，获交通部、省政府表彰。四十多年来，共完成国内外各等级公路勘察设计40000余公里以及赤水河、乌江、南北盘江、红水河等河流整治的勘察设计。先后获国家、部、省级优秀勘察设计和科技进步奖共60余项。

我院经过四十多年的发展建设，现拥有四个公司、三个研究所、四个公路测设处、一个航道测设处、一个地质勘察设计处、一个规划经济室、一个试验检测中心。现有职工371人，各类专业技术人员256人，是一支专业设置齐全、技术力量雄厚、业务水平精良、测设手段先进、思想作风过硬的多功能规划勘察设计科研队伍。

我院于1999年被国家科委列为“全国CAD示范企业”；2000年被交通部授予“全国交通系统档案工作先进集体”；2001年被交通部授予“全国交通系统先进集体”；2002年被贵州省人民政府授予“省级文明单位”等荣誉称号。

边坡加固新材料的研制与开发
Research and development of border slope reinforced new materials

Guizhou Communication Design Institute was established in 1958, is under the jurisdiction of Guizhou Province Communication Department, is the state class A engineering project construction total contract unit, held the certificates of the state engineering survey comprehensive project class A, road industry-wide class A (roads, extraordinary tunnel, extraordinary bridges, traffic engineering), municipal public utility industries (bridge and tunnel) class A, geological disaster risk assessment, geological disaster prevention engineering in survey, design, construction, and supervision class A, engineering consulting class A and transport infrastructure engineering supervision class A, and water transport industry (channel, port), the municipal public industry (road) class B, awarded ISO9001:2000 version quality system certification. The institute bears the businesses of engineering projects planning, feasibility study, survey design, construction supervision, technical advisory in highway, grading road, bridge, tunnel, geotechnical engineering, traffic engineering, port, channel, geological disaster administration.

The institute based on Guizhou, faced to the country and went to the world. In the roads survey designs in aiding to Laos, Burundi, and Tibet and support Fujian, Yunnan and the frontline, the institute respectively has awarded the prizes of the Ministry of Communication, the Ministry of International Business and Economic and the Headquarters of the General Staff. Since 1980s, the institute has completed over 10 high-grade highway survey designs such as Guiyang to Huangguoshu, Guiyang to Zunyi, Guiyang to Xinzai, Chongxihe to Zunyi, Kaili to Majing, Yuping to Tongren, Yuping to Sansui, Sansui to Kaili, Zhengning to Shuicheng, Zhengning to Shengjinguan, and awarded the honor of the Ministry of Communication and the provincial government. For 40 years, the institute has completed all the grade road survey designs of over 40,000 kilometres at home and abroad and realignment river works survey designs such as Chishui River, Wu River, Nanbeipan River, Hongshui River, and successively awarded over 60 items outstanding survey design and scientific and technological progress prizes of the State, ministry, and province.

After 40 years development, the institute now has four companies, three research institutes, four road test departments, a tunnel test department, a geological survey design department, a planned economy office, a pilot-testing center, 371 existing workers, professional and technical staff of 256 people, is a multifunctional planning survey design research team with professional installation complete, strong technical force, good business level, advanced test level, and hard ideological style.

The institute was placed the "National CAD Model Enterprise" by the State Science and Technology Commission in 1999; was awarded the honor of "National Transport System Files Work Advanced Collective" by the Ministry of Communication in 2000; was awarded the honor of "National Transport System Advanced Collective" by the Ministry of Communication in 2001; was given the honor of "Provincial Civilized Unit" by Guizhou Provincial People's Government in 2002.

底图为六广河特大桥
Photograph shows the Liuguanghe extraordinary bridge

贵州赤天化集团公司 Guizhou Chi Tianhua Corporation Group
贵州赤天化股份公司 Guizhou Chi Tianhua Stock Corporation

贵州赤天化集团有限责任公司是贵州省最大氮肥生产企业，其主体生产装置是我国七十年代初从国外引进的十三套大型化肥装置之一。1974年10月破土动工，1978年10月建成投产。公司拥有从美国、荷兰引进的全套大型化肥生产装置和相应的技术力量。现装置年生产能力36.6万吨合成氨，64万吨尿素，为国有大（一类）型企业。

“十五”期间，公司累计生产合成氨181.67万吨、尿素311.67万吨，实现销售收入53.74亿元，实现利税8.77亿元，人均GDP 4.64万元，人均劳动生产率8.29万元，为支援农业生产，发展贵州经济做出了积极的贡献。

2005年公司生产合成氨36.67万吨。尿素63.04万吨，销售收入13.5亿元，实现利税2.82亿元，再创赤天化历史最好水平。其中股份公司实现净利润1.75亿元。公司再获全国用户满意企业殊荣，“赤”牌尿素两次荣获国家免检产品称号，企业创造了连续24年无死亡事故，连续21年无各类重大事故，千人负伤率为零的好成绩。

公司与贵州宏福总公司携手合作，共同出资组建的贵州天福化工有限责任公司于2005年12月28日举行了奠基暨挂牌仪式，标志着企业发展迈出新的重大步伐。

现场生产装置（局部）
The site of production device (part)

产品质量免检证书

CERTIFICATE FOR PRODUCT EXEMPTION FROM QUALITY SURVEILLANCE INSPECTION

经审查

贵州赤天化集团有限责任公司

赤牌农业用尿素符合《产品免于质量监督检查管理办法》规定，批准免检，特此证明。

中华人民共和国国家质量监督检验检疫总局

“赤”牌尿素产品质量免检证书
The urea product quality free-inspection certificate of "Chi" brand

年产30万吨合成氨，15万吨二甲醚装置奠基场面
The scene of devices laying a foundation of annual producing 300,000 tons of synthetic ammonia and 150,000 tons of dimethyl ether

公司董事长、党委书记郑才友
The chairman of corporation, secretary of the Party committee Zheng Caiyou

Guizhou Chi Tianhua Corporation Group Ltd., Co. is the largest nitrogenous fertilizer production enterprises in Guizhou province, its main production devices is one of the 13 sets of large-size fertilizer installation from abroad at the early in 1970s. The corporation was started in October 1974, completed and went into production in October 1978. The corporation owns full set of large-size fertilizer production devices from the United States and the Netherlands and the corresponding technical strength introduced. Annual production capacity of now devices is 366,000 tons of synthetic ammonia and 640,000 tons of urea. The corporation has become a state-owned large-size (class 1) enterprise.

During the period of "10th Five-Year Plan", the corporation accumulatively produced 1.8167 million tons of synthetic ammonia, urea of 3.1167 million tons, and realized 5.374 billion yuan of sales income, profit and tax of 877 million yuan, 46,400 yuan of per capita GDP, per capita labor productivity of 82.9 thousand yuan. The corporation has made positive contributions to support agricultural production and economic development of Guizhou.

In 2005, the corporation produced 366,700 tons of synthetic ammonia, 630,400 tons of urea, and finished 1.35 billion yuan of sales income, realized 282 million yuan in profit and tax, set the best level of Chi Tianhua on record again, among which, the stock company achieved net profit 175 million yuan. The corporation won the honor of National User Satisfaction Enterprise again. The urea of "Chi" brand twice awarded the title of National Free-examination Product. The corporation created a good result of continuous 24 years without fatality, consecutive 21years of no major accidents, rate of being wounded per 1,000 persons of the zero.

The Corporation co-operated with Guizhou Hong Fu Controlling Company to jointly invest building Guizhou Tianfu Chemical Industry Limited Liability Company, which held the ceremony of laying a foundation cum listing the plate on December 28, 2005, that marked enterprise development striding a new major step.

公司总部地址：贵阳市环城北路157号
Address of Headquarters: No.157 Huangcheng north road Guiyang city 邮编(Post Code)：550001
电话(Tel)：(0851) 6822187 传真(Fax)：(0851) 6822387
销售公司电话(Tel of Sales)：(0851)6822156
传真(Fax of Sales)：(0851) 6822130
公司基地地址：贵州省赤水市化工路
Address of Corporation Base: Huagong road Chishui city Guizhou province 邮编(Post Code)：564707
电话(Tel)：(0852) 2878001 传真(Fax)：(0852) 2878333

贵州天福化工有限责任公司

Guizhou Tianfu Chemical Industry Limited Liability Company

贵州省委常委、省总工会主席、贵州大学党委书记龙超云
The standing member of Guizhou provincial Party committee, the presiden of Provincial Federation of Trade Unions, the secretary of Guizhou University Party committee Long Chaoyun

贵州赤天化集团公司党委书记、董事长郑才友
The secretary of Guizhou Chitianhua Group Company Party committee, chairman Zheng Caiyou

贵州宏福总公司党委书记、董事长何浩明
The secretary of Guizhou Hongfu Controlling Company Party committee, chairman He Haoming

贵州天福化工有限责任公司是按照《公司法》和现代企业与项目法人治理结构的要求设立的大型煤炭---能源---化工---一体化的现代企业。它是由我省最大的两家化工企业——贵州赤天化股份有限公司和贵州宏福实业开发有限总公司联合出资组建的，是我省建设的第一个充分发挥贵州丰富的煤、磷、水等资源的综合优势，加快贵州煤、磷化工产业的发展，将贵州的资源优势转化为产业优势和经济优势的大型现代煤化工项目。也是我省第一个规划建设的采用当今世界上最先进的洁净煤气化技术、煤化工工艺技术和装备、环境友好的循环经济型磷煤化工生态工业试点项目。

雄关漫道真如铁、而今迈步从头越。放眼明天，贵州天福化工有限责任公司将为繁荣西部地区经济和发展贵州省煤化工产业做出越来越大的贡献。

Guizhou Tianfu Chemical Industry Limited Liability Company is the large-scale coal--energy--chemical industry--integration modern enterprise, is established in according with the aim of "Law of Company" and the administration structure of moden enterprise and project legal person. It is jointly invested building by Guizhou Chitianhua Stock Ltd, Co. and Guizhou Hongfu Industry Controlling Company, and they are the two largest chemical industry companies in Guizhou province. And it is the first large-scale modern coal chemical industry project our province constructed which sufficient exerted Guizhou's comprehensive resources advantage including rich coal, phosphorus, water power and so on, speeded up the development of Guizhou's coal, the phosphorus chemical industry and transformed resources advantage into industrial predominance and economic predominance. It also is the first environment friendly circulation economical phosphorus coal chemical ecology industry experimental project of Guizhou which is to adopt most advanced pure gasification technology, the coal chemical craft technology and the equipment.

Great pass and long road likes iron is hard, but we will start our work at the present day. Looking ahead, the Guizhou Tianfu Chemical Industry Limited Liability Company will make the more and more contribution for flourishing the western area economy and developing the Guizhou province coal chemical industry.

省、州、市领导参加开工典礼
The leaders of the province, state, and city participated the beginning ceremony

贵州天福化工有限责任公司董事长李文贵(左)与总经理何秦(右)一起揭牌
Guizhou Tianfu Chemical Limited Liability Company chairman Li Wengui (left) and the general manager HeQin (right) were uncovering the plate together.

年产30万吨合成氨、15万吨二甲醚项目

开工典礼

董事长：李文贵
The chairman of company: Li Wengui
总经理：何秦
The general manager: He qin
地址：贵州省福泉市马场坪 邮编(Post code)：550501
Address: Machangping, Fuquan City, Guizhou Province
电话(Tel)：0851-2188606
传真(Fax)：0854-2188804

绿色家园　避暑胜地

The Green Homeland, the Queen of Summer Resorts

人民广场
The Peoples Square

贵阳市因位于贵山之南而得名，地处中国西南云贵高原东部，是贵州省的政治、经济、文化、旅游中心，全市辖10个区县市，总面积8034平方公里，市中心平均海拔1000米，总人口340万。

贵阳是国内首个国家森林城市，全市森林覆盖率达35%，有“森林之城”的美誉。贵阳在2006年中国避暑旅游城市排行榜评选中，入选中国十佳避暑旅游城市，并名列第一，荣获“中国避暑之都”特别称誉。

——森林之城贵阳

——The City of Forest Guiyang

南明河一景
A view of Nanming River

Guiyang was named based on its location to the south of Gui Mountain. Guiyang lies in the eastern Yunnan-Guizhou Plateau in Southwest China. Guiyang is the center of polity, economy, culture and tourist of Guizhou province. It governs 10 districts, counties and cities, with a total area of 8,043 square kilometres, the city center is 1000 metres above sea level. The population of Guiyang is 3,400,000.

Guiyang is the first national forest city in nation, the forest covering rate of the city is up to 35%, it enjoys a reputation of "the City of Forest". In the appraisement and election of 2006 China Summer Resorts Tourist Cities, Guiyang was selected the Ten Best Summer Resorts Tourist Cities in China, and ranked No. 1, won the special praise of "the City of Summer Resorts in China".

绿色家园　避暑胜地

The Green Homeland, the Queen of Summer Resorts

六广河峡谷金银瀑布
Jinyin waterfalls of Liuguang River Gorge

百花湖
Baihua Lake

花溪公园
Huaxi Park

开阳南江峡谷
Nan River Grand Canyon of Kaiyang

红枫湖
Hongfeng Lake

——森林之城贵阳

—— The City of Forest Guiyang

黔灵公园
Qianling Park

天河潭
Tianhe Pool

花溪河风光
A scence of Huaxi River

绿色家园　避暑胜地

The Green Homeland, the Queen of Summer Resorts

青岩古镇
The ancient town of Qingyan

翠微阁
Cuiwei Tower

文昌阁
Wenchang Tower

弘福寺
Hongfu Temple

石头寨
The stone Village

——森林之城贵阳

—— The City of Forest Guiyang

息烽集中营旧址纪念碑
atues in memory of Xifeng Concentration Camp

玄天洞
Xuantian Cave

布依人家
The Buyi house

布依村民在簸箕上作画
The Buyi farmer draw picture on the dustpans

香纸沟古法造纸作坊
The ancient art of paper making mill in Xiangzhi Gully, the farmers make paper which is used for worshipping ceremonies

绿色家园　避暑胜地

The Green Homeland, the Queen of Summer Resorts

大南门广场
Dananmen Square

雪涯桥
Xueya Bridge

贵州饭店
Guizhou Hotel

神奇金筑大酒店
Guiyang Plaza Hotel

——森林之城贵阳

—— The City of Forest Guiyang

小车河秋色
Xiaoche River in autumn

香火岩瀑布
Xianghuo Rock Waterfall

金阳新区行政中心
The municipal administrative center of Jinyang New District

绿色家园　避暑胜地

The Green Homeland, the Queen of Summer Resorts

中国振华集团科技股份有限公司二三极管生产线
The semiconductor production line of China Zhenhua Group Science and Technology Stock Co., Ltd.

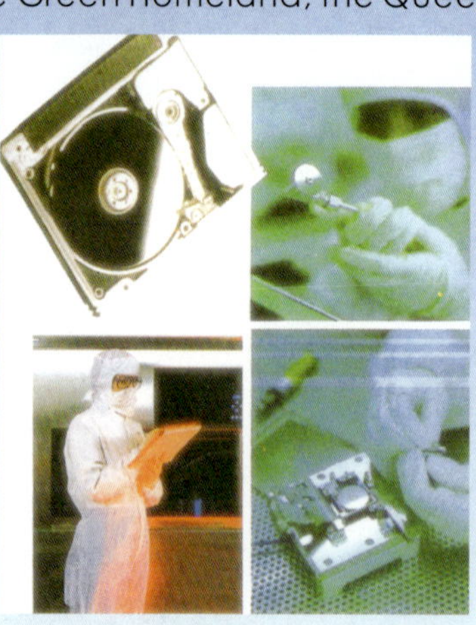

世华数码生产的微硬盘产品
The micro hard disk products produced in Shihua Digit

京瓷振华通信设备有限公司生产的CDMA手机
CDMA Mobil phones produced in Jingci Zhenhua Communications Equipment Co., Ltd.

开阳磷化工（国家）生态工业示范基地规划论证会
The planning argumentation meeting of Kaiyang phosphorus chemical industry (national) eco-industrial demo base

生态村
Ecological village

生态科技农业园区一瞥
A glimpse of Ecological science and technology agricultural park

金阳新区会展中心
The Exhibition Center of Jinyang New District

——森林之城贵阳

—— The City of Forest Guiyang

金阳新区贵阳行政中心
Guiyang Administrative Center of Jinyang New District

金阳南湖别墅
The Nanhu Villa of Jinyang New District

中国凉都
China Cool City

白鹤高架桥
Baihe viaduct

六盘水市明湖高架桥
Minghu viaduct of Liu Panshui city

凉都·六盘水位于贵州西部，地处长江上游水系和珠江上游水系的分水岭地带，位于川、黔、滇、桂结合部，乌蒙山脉南端。是六十年代中期国家“三线建设”开发的，以煤炭、冶金、电力、建材为主要经济支柱的一座重要新兴能源和原材料工业城市，享有“江南煤都”和“中国凉都”之美誉，是“南（宁）贵（阳）昆（明）经济区”的重要组成部分，是贵州省发展区域经济的重点城市之一，发展潜力巨大。

全市幅员面积9914平方公里，境内居住着汉、苗、彝等37个民族，2005年年末总人口302.7万人，全市属低纬高海拔地区，最高海拔2900.3米，最低海拔580米，年平均气温13—14℃，冬无严寒，夏无酷暑，雨热同季。六盘水市辖钟山区、六枝特区、盘县、水城县四个区、特区、县。

“十五”计划实施的五年，是六盘水市解放思想、抢抓机遇、团结拼搏的五年，是实现改革新突破、经济新发展、社会新进步的五年。五年来，六盘水市抢抓西部大开发机遇，有针对性地采取一系列政策措施，坚持发展是硬道理的理念，国民经济和社会发展取得巨大成就。

经济实力明显增强，产业结构逐步优化。五年来，我市国民经济保持持续、快速、健康的发展态势，地区生产总值从“九五”期末的87.61亿元，增至2005年的207.93亿元，年均增长14.2%，比“九五”期间平均每年9.5%的增速高4.7个百分点。人均GDP达到6892元，于2004年提前一年完成人均GDP 4206元的目标。经济增长连续四年保持两位数增长的好成绩，增幅分别高于全国、全省平均水平。经济总量连上台阶，经济实力明显增强。经济总量由2000年的81.5亿元连续跨上100亿元和200亿元台阶。经济结构进一步改善，三次产业协调发展，一、二、三产业占地区生产总值的比重由“九五”期末的15.15：49.3：35.55转变为2005年的9：56.3：34.7，三次产业得到全面协调发展，“二三一”格局继续得到巩固，第二产业的龙头支柱地位日益显现。在经济发展的同时，财政收入也实现大幅度的增长，2005年全市财政总收入达到27.39亿元，比2004年增长42.7%，年均增长27.6%，地方财政收入达到13.23亿元，比2004年增长36.4%，年均增长24.9%，人均地方财政收入达到439元。

农业经济结构得到初步调整，粮食产量创历史最好水平。积极推进农业产业结构调整，加大科技扶持力度，农业经济步入稳定发展之路。粮食产量在2000年迈上70万吨大关后，2005年粮食产量达77.86万吨，比2004年增长2.7%，比2000年增加7.23万吨，年均增长2%；优化种植业结构，扩大经济作物种植比例，经济作物播种面积占总播种面积的比重由2000年的7.87%提高到21.72%，提高13.85个百分点。突出发展畜牧业，努力提高畜牧业在农业中的比重。2005年肉类总

六盘水市南编组站
South yard station of Liu Panshui city

——六盘水
—— Liu Panshui

北盘江大桥，长468.2米，主跨236米，高280米
Beipanjiang Bridge, 468.2 meters of length, the main span of 236 meters, 280 meters of height

险峻的盘山公路
Dangerous road winding around the mountain

产量达到10.24万吨，比2004年增长13.81%，年均增长12.8%，畜牧养殖业在农业总产值中的比重由2000年的27.19%提高到2005年的36.13%。林业生产进一步发展。近年来，加大了植树造林和天然林保护工作，全市森林覆盖率达到27%。

工业经济快速发展，工业结构优化升级。2005年全部工业增加值实现104.15亿元，比2004年增长16.2%，年均增长14.1%，成为推动经济快速增长和产业结构调整的主要因素。“十五”期间，国有企业改革不断深化，坚持改革、改组、改造和加强管理，国有大中型企业重新焕发生机和活力，一些不适应市场变化、污染严重的企业被关停并转。立足资源优势，以煤炭、冶金、电力、建材为主的四大支柱产业在经济发展中的支撑作用越来越显著。2005年四大支柱产业对规模工业的贡献率达到84.5%。产品产量大幅度增长。与2000年相比，发电量增加57.31亿千瓦，增长128.5%，原煤增加2339.97万吨，增长1.6倍，钢材增加49.54万吨，增长37%。

固定资产投资高速增长，基础设施建设取得明显成效。“十五”期间我市固定资产投资力度加大，固定资产投资分别迈上50亿元和100亿元台阶，2005年全社会固定资产投资完成121.4亿元（不含跨地区工程），比2004年增长41.3%，五年固定资产投资总额累计完成326.37亿元，比“九五”增加209.01亿元，年均增长29.3%。

以交通为重点的基础设施建设明显加快，水黄高等级公路建成通车，镇胜高速公路及一批高等级公路相继开工建设，基本实现乡乡通公路、通电、通电话。加快西部大开发步伐，大力发展电力工业，努力把我市建设成为贵州“西电东送”重要的基地之一，盘南电厂、野马寨电厂（三台机组已发电）、发耳电厂等一批重点电力工程正在建设中，建成后我市将新增电力装机容量420万千瓦，为西部大开发奠定了一个良好的基础。

六盘水市市委、市政府着力打造“中国凉都”城市品牌。在2005年第二届“凉都·六盘水消夏文化节”期间，成功举办了玉舍国家森林公园之旅、奇石盆景展、全国汽车拉力赛、黔菜美食文化节、全国青少年自行车锦标赛、移动杯篮球赛、煤雕艺术作品展、彝族民间火把节、甲A篮球邀请赛等项目。通过消夏文化节的举办，提高了六盘水市的城市品味和知名度，搭建了经济、文化交流与合作的平台。

“十一五”期间，中央、省的关心、支持下，在海内外各界的支持、帮助下，通过全市人民的共同努力，凉都·六盘水的明天会更美好。

盘县电厂
Pan County Plant

发耳电厂（效果图）
Faer Power Plant (result figure)

中国凉都

China Cool City

Cool City · Liu Panshui is located in the west of Guizhou, in the watershed area of upper reaches of Yangtze River and Pearl River, in the joint of Sichuan, Guizhou, Yunnan and Guangxi, in the south of Wumeng Mountain. The city was developed in the mid of 1960s the state "three-line construction", is a major emerging energy and raw material industry city taking the coal, metallurgical, electrical, building materials as the main economic pillars, enjoying the reputation of "Coal City in the south of Yangtze River" and "China Cool City", is an important component of "Nan (ning) Gui (yang) Kun (ming) economic zone", is one of the major cities to develop regional economy of Guizhou province, has great development potentials.

The area of the city is 9914 square kilometers. There lives 37 nationalities as the Han, Miao, Yi in the territory, at the end of 2005 the total population of 3.027 million people. The city belongs to the low altitude and high elevation area, the highest elevation of 2900.3 metres, the lowest elevation of 580 metres, and the average temperature of 13 --14 degrees. There is no bitter cold in winter and no intense heat in summer, and summer is rainy season. Liu Panshui city governs four districts, special district and counties as Zhongshan district, Liuzhi special district, Pan county, Shuicheng county.

The five years of implementation "Tenth Five" plan, that Liu Panshui city liberated the thought, seized the opportunity, united and struggled, to achieve a new breakthrough in the reform, new economic development, social new progress. Over the past five years, Liu Panshui city seized opportunity from the West Developing, took a series of targeted policy measures and adhered to the idea that development was the hard reason, and made the great achievements in economic and social development.

Economic strength has markedly increased, and the industrial structure has gradually optimized. Over the past five years, our city national economy has maintained sustained, rapid and healthy development momentum, and the local GDP increased to 20.793 billion yuan of 2005 from the end of "Ninth Five-year Plan" period of 8.761 billion yuan, an average annual increase of 14.2%, more 4.7 percentage points than the average annual growth rate of 9.5% of the "Ninth Five-Year Plan" period. Per capita GDP reached 6,892 yuan, advanced one year to complete the goal of per capita GDP of 4,206 yuan in 2004. The economic growth maintained good results with double-digit growth for four consecutive years, and the range of growth was respectively higher than the national and the provincial average level. The amount of economy continued increase, and the economic strength has increased markedly. The amount of economy continued to step the 10 billion yuan and 20 billion yuan level from 8.15 billion yuan of 2000. Further improvement the economic structure, the three industries coordinated development, the proporation of the first, second, third industries accounting for local GDP changed from 15.15:49.3:35.55 of the end of "Ninth Five" to 9:56.3:34.7 of 2005, the three industries were fully coordinated development, "231" pattern continued to be consolidated, the second industry leading pillar position increasingly appeared. At the same time, financial revenue also achieved substantial growth, in 2005, the city's financial revenue reached 2.739 billion yuan, growth of 42.7% than in 2004, an average annual increase of 27.6%, the local revenue reached 1.323 billion yuan, growth of 36.4% than in 2004, an

市林业局茶叶基地
The tea base of Forestry Bureau of Liu Panshui City

六枝特区梭嘎厂苗族跳花节
Miao nationality Jumping Flower Festival of Suogachang of Liuzhi special district

六盘水市火车站广场
The station square of Liu Panshui city

六盘水市世纪广场
The century plaza of Liu Panshui city

——六盘水
—— Liu Panshui

average annual increase of 24.9%. Per capita financial revenue reached 439 yuan.

Agricultural economic structure has gained the preliminary adjustment, and grain yield reached a record level. The readjustment of the structure of agriculture was actively promoted, increasing technology support, following a stable agricultural economic development path. After the grain production of 700,000 tons in 2000, the grain yield in 2005 amounted to 778,600 tons, growth of 2.7% than in 2004, an increase of 72,300 tons than in 2000, the average annual growth 2%; optimized the cultivation structure, and expanded economic crops cultivation proportion, the proportion of economic crops sown area accounting for the total sown area increased from 7.87% of 2000 to 21.72%, up 13.85 percentage points. Prominence development livestock industry, strived to improve the proportion of animal husbandry in agriculture. In 2005 meat yield reached 102,400 tons, 13.81% growth than 2004, an average annual increase of 12.8%, the proportion of livestock breeding industry accounting for agricultural output increased from 27.19% of 2000 to 36.13% of 2005. Forestry production further developed. In recent years, the work of afforestation and natural forest protection was increased, and the rate of forest covering was up to 27%.

Industrial economy developed rapidly, optimization and upgrading in industrial structure. In 2005 total industrial added value realized 10.415 billion yuan, growth 16.2% than in 2004, an average annual increase of 14.1%, becoming the main factor to promote rapid economic growth and industrial restructuring. "Tenth Five" period, deepening the reform of state-owned enterprises, insisted on the reform, reorganization, transformation, and strengthening management, the large medium-sized state-owned enterprises renewed vigor and vitality, and some enterprises that didn't fit market changes and had serious pollution were closed down. Based resources superiority, the support role in economic development of four pillar industries main as coal, metallurgical, electrical, building materials was increasingly significant. In 2005 the contribution rate of four pillar industries for industry above designated size was up to 84.5%. The output of product grew by a big margin. Compared with 2000, generating capacity increased 5.731 billion kilowatts, growth 128.5%, an increase of 23.3997 million tons of raw coal, up 1.6 times, increase 495,400 tons of steel, an increase of 37%.

Rapid growth in fixed asset investment, infrastructure building achieved a remarkable success. During the period of "Tenth Five" investment in fixed assets of the city increased, respectively

果树基地
The base of fruit tree

盘县柏果林
Boguo forest of Pan county

reached to a new level of 5 billion yuan and 10 billion yuan, fixed assets investment in 2005 completed 12.14 billion yuan (not excluding trans-regional projects), 41.3% growth than in 2004, the cumulative total of five years of fixed asset investment completed 32.637 billion yuan, increase 20.901 billion yuan than "Ninth Five", an average annual increase of 29.3%.

The infrastructure construction taking communications as focus has accelerated markedly, Shuihuang high-grade road was opened to traffic, Zhensheng highway and a number of high-grade road construction have started, basically realized opening rural township-roads, electricity, telephone. Speeded up the pace of West Developing and vigorously developed the power industry, and strived to build the city becoming the one of the important base of "transfer electricity from the west to the east" in Guizhou, a number of key power projects as Pannan Power Plant, Yemazai Power Plant (three units have generated electricity), Faer Power Plant were constructing, the city would new-increase electricity generating capacity 4.2 million kilowatts after completion, lay a good foundation for the development of the western region.

Liu Panshui city Party committee and government vigorously created the city brand of "China Cool City". In the period of the second "Cool City · Liu Panshui Summer Cultural Festival" of 2005, successfully held the projects as the trip of Yushe national forest park, Exotic Stone Potted Landscape Show, the National Automobile Rally, Guizhou Food Festival, the National Youth Cycling Championship, Mobile-cup Basketball Game, Coal Carving Art Exhibition, the Yi Nationality Folk Torch Festival, the first A basketball invitational tournament. Through the activities in Summer Cultural Festival, Liu Panshui city raised its taste and visibility, built economic and cultural exchanges and cooperation platform.

"Eleventh Five" period, under the concern and support of the central, province, under the support and help of all circles at home and abroad, by the joint efforts of the people, the tomorrow of Cool City · Liupanshui will become more beautiful.

黔中崛起——安顺市

Rising in the Middle of Guizhou -- "Tenth

城区中心景区
The scenery in city center

虹山湖景
The scenery of Hongshan Lake

凯旋水会
Triumphal water Party

开发区广场
Plaza of development zone

全国甲级旅游开放城市——安顺市位于贵州省中西部，地处长江水系乌江流域和珠江水系北盘江流域的分水岭地带，是世界上典型的喀斯特地貌集中地区。全市国土面积9264平方公里，2005年末总人口264.25万人，有苗、布依、回、仡佬等39个少数民族，少数民族人口占总人口的38.4%，是一个多民族聚居的地区。

撤地设市以来的五年，是我市全面实施“十五”计划的五年，全市各族人民在市委、市政府的领导下，坚持以邓小平理论和“三个代表”重要思想为指导，全面贯彻落实科学发展观和构建社会主义和谐社

"十五" 建设成果

Five" Building Results of Anshun City

黄果树宾馆
Huangguoshu Hotel

关兴公路北盘江大桥
Beipan river Bridge of Guangxing Road

黄果树机场
Huangguoshu Airport

贵黄公路
Guihuang Highway

黔中崛起——安顺市

Rising in the Middle of Guizhou -- "Tenth

"西电东送"重要通道——安顺变电站
An "electricity transfer from west to east" important channel -- Anshun Transformer Station

我国首批"西电东送"水电建设项目之一引子渡电站（3×12万千瓦）
The one of the first "electricity transfer from west to east" hydroelectri construction projects Yinzidu Power Station(360 thousand kilowatts)

贵州省民族制药企业三强之一，贵州百灵制药集团
The one of three strong national pharmaceutical enterprises of Guizhou province, Guizhou Bailing Pharmaceutical Group

兴伟国际家具城旅游商品市场
Xingwei International Furniture City Tourism Commodity Market

会的重大战略思想，牢牢把握抢抓机遇、加快发展这个富民兴安的第一要务，聚精会神搞建设，一心一意谋发展，经济持续发展，经济实力明显增强，社会各项事业全面进步，人民生活水平不断得到改善和提高。"十五"期间，我市抢抓实施西部大开发和新阶段扶贫开发战略的机遇，认真落实中央宏观控制的各项政策措施，大力实施"农业稳市、旅游兴市、环境立市、工业强市"战略，经济保持持续较快增长的良好态势，GDP总量跃上100亿元的历史新台阶，经济结构趋向合理。2005年GDP达到106.03亿元，比2000年的60.50亿元增加45.53亿元，"十五"期间年均增长10.98%。其中，第一产业增加值

"十五"建设成果

Five" Building Results of Anshun City

湘大骆驼饲料有限公司
Xiangda Camel Fodder Co., Ltd.

华泰食品有限公司
Huatai Food Co., Ltd.

年均增长4.92%；第二产业增加值年均增长12.87%；第三产业增加值年均增长12.44%。三次产业结构比2000年的31.96:34.17:33.87调整为2005年的22.64:38.57:38.79，产业排序由"二、三、一"改变为"三、二、一"。

在未来的"十一五"期间，安顺人民信心百倍，将把安顺建设成为环境舒适、人与自然相互协调、经济社会高质量发展的全国旅游开放城市，成为贵州省实施西部大开发战略重点建设的能源基地和新兴工业城市。随着安顺经济技术开发区和黎阳高新技术工业园区的建设发展，安顺将成为大开发进程中接纳经济发达地区产业和资本转移的热点区域。

双阳飞机制造厂：中国生产歼击机的主机厂之一
Shuangyang Aircraft Manufacture Factory: the one of main machine factories production fighter plane of China

黔中崛起——安顺市

Rising in the Middle of Guizhou -- "Tenth

无公害优质大米生产基地
No-environmental pollution quality rice production base

赛牛会
Cattle race match

油菜大坝
Cole dam

The national Class A tourism open city -- Anshun city is located in the central and west of Guizhou province, in the watershed region of Yangtze River system Wu River basin and Pearl River system Beipan River basin, is a typical Karst geography concentrated area in the world. The land area of the city is 9264 square kilometres, at the end of 2005 the total population was 2.6425 million people, has 39 minorities as Miao, Buyi, Hui, Gelao,etc, minority populations accounted for 38.4% of the total population, is a multi-nationality region.

The five years of dismissal prefecture and foundation city, that our city comprehensively implemented the "10th Five-Year Plan", under the city Party committee and government leadership, the people of all nationalities insisted on taking Deng Xiaoping Theory and the "three representatives" as the guide, comprehensively implemented the concept of scientific development and built the major strategic thought of harmonious socialist society, firmly grasped to seize the opportunity, to accelerate development the primary task of rich people and thriving Anshui, preoccupied construction, wholeheartedly developed and sustained economic development, the economic strength has increased markedly, social progress and people's living standards have been improved and enhanced. "Tenth Five-year Plan" period, the city seized the

养鸡场
Chicken farm

"十五"建设成果

Five" Building Results of Anshun City

云山屯一角
A corner of Yunshantun

opportunities of implementation the West Developing and the support poverty development strategy in new stage, seriously implemented all the policies and measures macro-controlled by the central, vigorously implemented the strategy of "agriculture steady city, tourism thriving city, environmental establishment city, industry strong city", sustained rapid economic growth in a good trend, the total GDP has entered 10 billion yuan with a new stage of history, the economic structure was reasonable. In 2005 GDP reached 10.603 billion yuan, increase 4.553 billion yuan than 6.05 billion yuan of 2000, during the period of "Tenth Five", average annual growth rate was 10.98%. Of which, the first industrial added value annual average increased 4.92%; the second industrial added value average annual increased 12.87%; the third industrial added value annual average increased 12.44%. The proporation of three industrial structures adjusted from 31.96:34.17:33.87 of 2000 to 22.64:38.57:38.79 of 2005, industrial classification changed from "231" to "321".

In the future "Eleventh Five" period, Anshun people are full of confidence, will make Anshun building into a national tourism open city with comfortable environment, human and natural coordination, economic and social high

号营山庄一景
A corner of Haoying Mountain Villa

种猪繁育场
Breeding pig reproduction farm

黔中崛起——安顺市

Rising in the Middle of Guizhou -- "Tenth

黄果树大瀑布
Huangguoshu Great Waterfall

链坠潭瀑布
Yinlianzhuitan Waterfall

漩塘景区
Xuantang Pond beauty spot

“十五”建设成果

Five" Building Results of Anshun City

地球裂缝花江大峡谷
The earth crack Huajiang Grand Gorge

千古之谜红崖天书
An Ancient Mysterious Red-Crag-Carving

面积的海百合化石屏风
lily fossil screen with the largest area in
d

quality development, become an energy base and emerging industrial city of important building in Guizhou province implementation the Western Development strategy. With building and development of Anshun economic and technological development zone and Liyang high-tech industrial park, Anshun will become a hot region admitting economy developed areas industrial and capital transfer in the Developing.

龙宫中心景区
The center of Dragon Palace beauty spot

格凸河
Getu River

锦绣黔南五十载

The glorious Qianann in the 50th anniversary

2006年8月8日，是黔南布依族苗族自治州建州50周年之日，一个充满蓬勃生机和无限活力的绿色黔南正展现在人们面前。

2005年，全州生产总值达到168.27亿元，是1956年的27.39倍。人均GDP 4260元，是1956年的11.71倍。财政总收入22.23亿元，是1956年2555万元的86.99倍，年均增长9.54%。“十五”期间，财政亿元县(市)从3个增加到8个。城镇居民人均可支配收入7393元，比1956年增加7300元，年均增长9.34%。农民人均纯收入达到1846元，是1956年63元的29.21倍，年均增长7.13%。金融机构存款余额167.22亿元，是1956年1404万元的1191倍。三次产业结构逐步趋于合理，2005年三次产业结构为28.5：37.1：34.4。

——农村经济稳步发展。2005年，全州农业产值达到79.48亿元，是1956年的6.22倍。粮食总产量达128.6万吨，比1956年增长2.22倍。畜牧业发展迅速，2005年，总产值达到31.16亿元，是1956年的19.25倍，占农业总产值的39.2%，成为农民增收的大头。农民人均纯收入由1956年的63元增加到2005年的1846元。

——工业经济快速发展。初步形成了冶金、化工、电力、煤炭、建材、酿酒等支柱产业。2005年全州规模以上工业有306个，工业总产值达到123.25亿元，工业增加值达到50.26亿元，占地区总产值的29.9%。出现了宏福、天福、川恒、苎麻、棉麻、建材、农用车等知名企业和农产品、药业加工群。

——非公经济迅速发展。2005年，全州有私营企业1892户，注册资金25.33亿元，有个体工商户4.4万户，注册资金5.36亿元。

——商品购销两旺，城乡市场活跃。2005年全州社会消费品零售总额达到38.61亿元，是1956年的61.46倍。

——基础设施明显改善。2005年，全州社会固定资产投资52.21亿元，是1956年的1249.31倍。50年全州固定资产投资累计369.48亿元，年均增长15.66%，其中，基本建设投资累计达到162.13亿元，占总投资的43.88%，主要用于交通、水利、能源、通讯等基础设施建设。

August 8 of 2006, is the date of the 50th anniversary that Qiannan Buyi Minority Miao Minority Autonomous Prefecture was established. A boundless vitality and full of vigor of the green Qiannan is now spreading out before people.

In 2005, prefectural GDP reached 16.827 billion yuan, increase 27.39 times than in 1956. Per capita GDP was 4,260 yuan, growth 11.71 times than the year of 1956. Financial revenue was 2.223 billion yuan, growth 86.99 times than 25.55 million yuan of 1956, the average annual growth 9.54%. "10th Five-Year Plan" period, the financial 100 million counties (cities) increased from 3 to 8. Per capita disposable income of urban residents was 7,393 yuan, 7,300 yuan more than in 1956, an average annual increase of 9.34%. Per capita net income of farmers reached 1,846 yuan, increase 29.21 times than 63 yuan of 1956, an average annual increase of 7.13%. Financial institutions deposit balance was 16.722 billion yuan, growth 1191 times than 14.04 million yuan of 1956. Three industrial structure has also gradually become rational, the proportion of three industrial structure of 2005 was 28.5:37.1:34.4.

--Rural economy developed steadily. In 2005, the gross output value of prefecture's agriculture reached 7.948 billion yuan, increase 6.22 times than that of 1956. The yield of grain was 1.286 million tons, growth 2.22 times than in 1956. The animal husbandry industry rapidly developed, in 2005, the output value reached 3.116 billion yuan, 19.25 times more than that in 1956, accounting for 39.2% of agricultural gross output value, becoming the major part of peasant increase incomes. Per capita net income of peasants increased from 63 yuan of 1956 to 1,846 yuan of 2005.

--Industrial economy rapidly developed. Initially formed metallurgical, chemical industry, electricity, coal, building materials, wine-making and other pillar industries. In 2005 the prefecture had 306 industries above designated size, the gross output value of industry reached 12.325 billion yuan, the added value of industry reached 5.026 billion yuan, accounting for 29.9% of regional GDP. There has grown Hongfu, Tianfu, Chuanheng, ramie, cotton-linen, building materials, agricultural vehicles, and other famous enterprises and agricultural products, pharmaceutical processing groups.

--Non-public economy has developed rapidly. In 2005, the prefecture had 1892 private enterprises with registered capital of 2.533 billion yuan, and 44000 individual industrial and commercial households with registered capital of 536 million yuan.

--Commodity market of purchase and sale was flourishing, the market of urban and rural was active. In 2005 the prefecture's total retail sales of consumer goods reached 3.861 billion yuan, growth 61.46 times than in 1956.

--Infrastructure has markedly improved. In 2005, the social fixed assets investment of the prefecture was 5.221 billion yuan, growth 1249.31times than in 1956. 50-year fixed asset investment of the prefecture totaled 36.948 billion yuan, the average annual growth of 15.66%, of which investment in capital construction has reached 16.213 billion yuan, accounting for 43.88% of total investment, mainly used for transportation, water conservancy, energy, communications and other infrastructure construction.

黔南首府都匀
Duyun of Qiannan capital

工业经济发展日新月异

The industrial economic development changed for the better day by day

工业经济发展初具规模。工业企业由过去不足百家，增长到“十五”末期的279家，全部工业总产值增长到139.4亿元，50年翻了近8番，固定资产规模达150亿元，实现利税9.82亿元。初步形成以磷化工、冶金、医药、烟草、能源、建材、特色食品为支柱的多元化产业结构；企业规模得到发展壮大，形成了宏福、神奇、龙腾、永红等龙头企业。

工业更新改造投资力度加大，50年投资近100亿元。1976年全州工业更新改造投资仅581万元，“十五”期间，共投入46.7亿元，相当于过去45年的总和。2005年，全州工业固定资产投资25亿元，同比增长46%；全社会更新改造投资20.2亿元，同比增长80%。

工业经济效益水平不断提高。1978年全州工业企业利润总额仅为2148万元，2005年达3.5亿元。

产业结构调整步伐加快，工业园区规模不断壮大。“十五”期间组建的龙里谷脚工业园区、独山麻尾工业园区、惠水长田工业园区已初具规模，2005年工业产值分别达16.3亿元，工业固定资产4.2亿元。

非公有制经济取得积极进展。截止2005年，全州非公经济工业企业从业人数为99036人，规模以上非公有制工业户数达173户，2005年完成工业产值64.4亿元，占全州规模工业总产值的52.3%。固定资产投资19亿元，占全州固定资产投资总数的74.6%。

Industrial economic development was taking shape. Industrial enterprises increased from inadequate 100 to 279 of the end of "Tenth Five", all industrial output value increased to 13.94 billion yuan, nearly 8 times for 50 years, the scale of fixed assets amounted to 15 billion yuan, realized 982 million yuan in profits and taxes. Initially formed diversified industrial structure taking phosphorus chemical industry, metallurgical, pharmaceutical, tobacco, energy, building materials, specialty food as the main pillar; the scale of enterprises has grown and formed Hungfu, Shenqi, Longteng, Yonghong, and other leading enterprises.

Upgrading industrial investment increased, invested nearly 10 billion yuan for 50 years. In 1976 prefecture's industrial investment for renovation and transformation was only 5.81 million yuan, the period of "Tenth Five", totaled investment of 4.67 billion yuan, equivalent to the sum of the past 45 years. In 2005, the industrial fixed assets investment of the prefecture was 2.5 billion yuan, up 46% than pervious time; the society investment for renovation and transformation was 2.02 billion yuan, up 80%.

Industry has constantly increased economy benefit level. In 1978 prefecture's total profits of industrial enterprises were 21.48 million yuan, reaching to 350 million yuan in 2005.

The industrial restructuring speeded step, the scale of industrial park size has grown. Gujiao Industrial Park of Longli, Mawei Industrial Park of Dushan, Changtian Industrial Park of Huishui which were founded during the period of "Tenth Five" have begun to take shape, in 2005, the industrial output value respectively amounted to 1.63 billion yuan and the industrial fixed assets was 420 million yuan.

Non-public ownership economy has made positive progress. Closing 2005-year, the employee number of prefecture's non-public economic industry enterprises was 99,036 people, the number of non-public industry above designated size reached to 173 enterprises, in 2005 industrial output value completed 6.44 billion yuan, accounting for 52.3% of total industrial output value above designated size of the prefecture. The investment in fixed assets was 1.9 billion yuan, accounting for 74.6% of the prefecture's total investment in fixed assets.

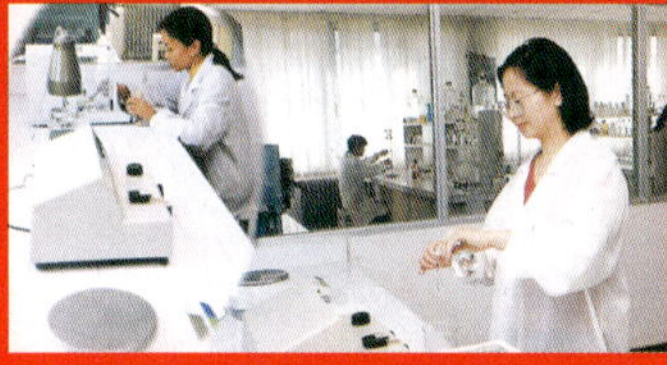

欣欣向荣的贵州龙里正大集团公司
The thriving Guizhou Longli Zhengda Group Corporation

天麻胶囊的生产车间
The production workshop of Rhizoma Gastrodiae capsule

气势宏大的黔南钙肥厂——威顿公司
The momentum Qiannan calcium fertilizer plant --Weidun Company

亚洲最大的磷化工基地——宏福
The largest phosphorus chemical industry base in Asia— Hongfu

发展中的黔南农业

Qiannan agriculture in developing

建州50年来，黔南农业发生了巨大变化，与建州时的1956年相比，2005年全州粮食总产量达128.6万吨、增长了2.22倍；油菜籽总产量8.38万吨，增长了16.4倍。农业科技不断进步，促进了黔南农业的发展。

农村沼气池建设成效显著，取得了显著的生态、经济和社会效益，为“绿色黔南”建设做出了积极贡献。

初步建成粮、油、菜、果、茶、药、烟规模生产基地300万亩。发展种植业龙头企业140个、农业合作经济组织245个，初步形成了经销商、企业、农民协会有组织、有批量、成规模、多渠道、多形式的农产品购销网络。

Since foundation prefecture 50 years, agriculture has taken place tremendous changes, compared with the foundation of 1956, total yield of prefecture's grain of 2005 reached 1.286 million tons, an increase of 2.22 times; Rapeseed yield totaled 83,800 tons, an increase of 16.4 times. Agricultural science and technology has constantly progress to promote Qiannan agricultural development.

Rural methane pit building made effectiveness, and achieved significant ecological, economic and social benefits to make a positive contribution for "green Qiannan" building.

Initially built 3 million mu grain, oil, vegetables, fruits, tea, medicine, tobacco scale production bases. Developed 140 plantation industry leading enterprises, 245 agricultural cooperative economic organizations, initially formed the organization, lot size, and a large scale, multi-channel, and multi-form agricultural marketing network in distributor, enterprises, farmer associations.

销往欧盟市场的法国细刀豆正在装罐
French small sword beans which are sold to the EU market are packing into tinning

2005年杂交玉米推广达到113万亩
In 2005 hybrid maize promoting reached to 1.13 million mu

2005年示范种植超级稻2200亩获得成功，最高亩产达931.8公斤，平均亩产677.6 公斤。图为副州长吴军参加超级稻产量现场验收
In 2005, 2,200 mu model super rice cultivation awarded success, the maximum yield amounted to 931.8 kg/mu, an average of 677.6 kg/mu. Photograph shows the vice-governor Wu Jun took part in super rice production site acceptance

图为即将竣工的沼气池
Photograph shows the methane pit is about to complete

交通建设突飞猛进

Transportation construction making a spurt of progress

建州五十年来，黔南交通建设事业取得了令人瞩目的成就。到2005年底，全州公路通车里程约为1.5万公里，为建州前的21.6倍。全面完成了以“二纵一横四联线”为重点的全州公路骨架网络。实现了州府都匀到各县（市）行车时间最长不超过4小时的目标。全州57.9%的乡镇通油路或水泥路，93%的行政村通公路。

Since foundation prefecture 50 years, the traffic construction of Qiannan has made remarkable achievements. By the end of 2005, the prefecture's highway mileage was about 15,000 km, increase 21.6 times than before prefecture foundation. Fully completed a highway skeleton network taking "two vertical and one horizontal four-line" as the focus in the prefecture. Realized target that maximum travel time of capital Duyun to each county (city) didn't exceed four hours. 57.9% of the prefecture's townships opened pitch or cement roads, 93% of the administrative villages opened roads.

贵新公路贵定段
Guiding section of Guixin Road

通村公路苗二河至米寅通车
The opening village road Miaoerhe to Miyin

贵新路都匀北匝道口
Duyun north ring road junction of Guixin Road

江界河大桥
Jiangjie River Bridge

省道S101线罗甸七道拐段
Qidaogual section of Luodian of provincial road S101 line

文化事业成就斐然

Cultural undertakings attainableness achievements

建州五十年来，我州文艺精品层出不穷，其中获国家级各类奖项68个。我州文化基础设施建设取得一定的成效。基本达到县县有图书馆和文化馆。目前，我州国家级非物质文化遗产代表作名录4个；省级非物质文化遗产代表作名录14个。全州共有255个文物保护单位，其中，国保2处，省保30处，县（市）223处。截止到2005年底，全州有各类文化产业经营单位、经营户1634户，从事各项文化产业人员3529人，各类文化产业经营项目固定资产已达1.1亿元。

Since foundation prefecture 50 years, our prefecture's literature and art fine works were emerging one after another, of which 68 works were awarded national prizes.

黔南民族师范学院
Qiannan National Teachers College

黔南州新落成的体育馆
New stadium of Qiannan

Our prefecture's cultural infrastructure construction has made success. Basically achieved that each county has library and cultural center. Currently, Our prefecture has 4 national and 14 provincial non-material cultural heritage representative work directories. The prefecture has a total of 255 heritage preservation units, of which the state level of 2, the provincial level of 30 and the county (city) level of 223. By the end of 2005, the prefecture has 1,634 various cultural industry business units, operating households with employment of 3,529 persons, the fixed assets in various cultural industries has reached 110 million yuan.

蓬勃发展的旅游业

Thriving tourism

州领导考察水族民族文化
The leader of the prefecture investigated the national culture of Shui Minority

椰木水寨
Langmushui Village

石板街布依婚礼
Buyi wedding of Slabstone Street

黔南山川秀丽，景色迷人，是世界中亚热带喀斯特地貌上原生性森林植被保存较完好的地方。50年来，黔南旅游业逐步发展成为黔南经济的支柱产业。

州内拥有国家级风景名胜区两个。分别是荔波樟江风景名胜区和斗篷山和都匀剑江风景名胜区。其中荔波茂兰国家级自然保护区，享有“地球上喀斯特地区独一无二的绿色宝库”的盛誉，被列为“世界自然”遗产。

2005年，全年旅游接待总人数达到291.07万人，同比增长了31.6%，实现旅游总收入18.7亿元，同比增长了28.2%。

Qiannan has beautiful mountains and rivers, and charming scenery, is the intact place that pro-tophyte forest vegetation of subtropical karst topography of the world are conserved. Over the past 50 years, Qian-nan's tourism gradually deve-loped becoming the pillar industry of Qiannan economy.

The prefecture has two national scenic areas. Respectively are Libo Zhangjiang scenic area and Doupeng Hill and Duyun Jianjiang scenic area. Of which Libo Maolan state-level nature reserve area, enjoying "the unique green treasure house of karst areas of the earth" reputation, is classified "the world nature" heritage.

In 2005, the total number of tourist reception reached 2.9107 million person times, an increase of 31.6%, achieved total tourism revenue of 1.87 billion yuan, an increase of 28.2%.

甲茶瀑布（作者：杨邦贤）
Jiacha Fall (author : Yang bangxian)

拉雅瀑布
Laya Fall

深河桥抗日纪念馆
The memorial hall of Anti-Japanese War of Shen River Bridge

瑶族铜鼓
The bronze drum of Yao Minority

铜仁地区“十·五”建设成就图片展示

The pictures show of "Tenth Five" construction achievements of Tongren Area

渝怀铁路过境铜仁
Yuhuai railway passing through Tongren

贵州红星发展大龙锰业有限责任公司
Dalong Manganese Industry Liability Co., Ltd. of Guizhou Hongxing Development

“十·五”时期，铜仁地区各族人民高举邓小平理论和“三个代表”重要思想伟大旗帜，全面贯彻落实科学发展观，深入实施“三个重点、三个带动”发展战略，抢抓机遇，深化改革，求真务实，开拓创新，保持了全区经济社会的快速发展，在迈向全面建设小康社会的征程上实现了新的飞跃。现将全区“十·五”期间完成或开工建设的一些重大项目进行集中展示。

我们深信：进入“十一·五”，站在一个新的历史起点上，回顾“十·五”辉煌成就，展望“十一·五”美好前景，将更加激发全区人民发展铜仁的热情，坚定全区人民建设开放铜仁、创新铜仁、和谐铜仁的信心和决心。在地委、行署的坚强领导下，全区各族人民将更加振奋精神，团结拼搏，开拓创新，用智慧和勤劳谱写铜仁经济社会发展历史性跨越的崭新诗篇。

During the period of "Tenth Five", the peoples of Tongren area held high the great banner of Deng Xiaoping Theory and "three representatives" important thinking, comprehensively carried out the scientific development concept, and in-depth implemented the development strategy of "three key points, three leads", seized the opportunity, deepened reform, sought the truth and dealt with concrete matters, developed and innovated, maintained the area's rapid economic and social development, achieved a new leap in the journey towards full of building a moderately prosperous society. The area's some major items which have been completed or were building during the period of "Tenth Five" now are centralizing show.

We are convinced: entering the "Eleventh Five", standing on a new historical starting point, recalling "Tenth Five" brilliant achievements, and looking forward to "Eleventh Five" magnificent prospects, will arouse all people's fervor of development Tongren, firm all the people's confidence and determination on building an open, innovation and harmonious Tongren. Under the strong leadership of prefectural Party committee, administrative office, the people of all nationalities will further inspire spirit, make concerted efforts, develop and innovate, and use the wisdom and industriousness to write a new poetry of the historic leape of Tongren conomic and social development.

铜仁机场
Tongren Airport

铜仁至大龙高等级公路
Tongren to Dalong high-grade road

通往铜仁机场的二级公路
The second level road leading to Tongren Airport

松桃道塘水库
Daotang Reservoir of Songtao

大龙火电厂
Dalong Fire Power Plant

正在施工中的思林电站
Silin Power Station in constructing

江口梵净山公路
Fanjing Mountain road of Jiangkou

强本 创新 领先
Strengthening Innovation Leading

都匀供电局
Duyun Power Supply Bureau

都匀供电局领导班子（左起）副局长许良柱、副局长刘培德、党委书记张帆、局长肖永、副局长程庆、纪委书记、工会主席潘健
The leader group of Duyun Power Supply Bureau (from left) the vice-director Xu Liangzhu, the vice-director Liu Peide, the secretary of the Party Committee Zhang Fan, the director Xiao Yong, the vice-director Cheng Qing, the secretary of the Commission for Discipline Inspection and the president of Labour Union Pan Jian

都匀供电局成立于1972年，现隶属于中国南方电网有限责任公司贵州电网公司，现有职工767人。全局肩负着向黔南和黔东南两个少数民族自治州的八县两市的供电重任。

都匀供电局以南方电网公司大政方针统揽全局，按照“完善、规范、巩固、提高”的总体要求和“强本、创新、领先”的工作思路，加快都匀电网发展，确保黔南州、黔东南州八县两市经济社会发展用电需求，为西电东送和构建“责任南网”、“和谐南网”主动承担更多的社会责任。

截至2005年底，都匀电网已形成了以500千伏福泉变为中心，220千伏输电线路为主网架，110千伏电网辐射各县市的供电格局，城市配电系统供电可靠率99.87%，安全生产保持稳定局面。

都匀供电局坚持“两手抓，两手都要硬”的方针，在抓物质文明建设的同时，注重精神文明的建设。供电服务由规范服务向品牌服务提升，电网建设得到进一步加强，满足了负荷发展和市场的需要，为地方社会经济发展提供了有力的先行保障。

都匀供电局以“优质、方便、规范、快捷”的供电服务方针服务人民
Duyun Power Supply Bureau takes power supply services policy of "high-quality, convenient, standardized and efficient" to service people

Duyun Power Supply Bureau, was founded in 1972, is under the jurisdiction of China Southern Power Network Limited liability Company Guizhou Power Network Company, having 767 workers. The bureau undertakes the power supply mission to eight counties and two cities of Qiannan and Qiandongnan ethnic minority autonomous prefectures.

Duyun Power Supply Bureau took Southern Power Network Company general policies as controlling the overall situation, according to the general requirements of "perfect, standardization, consolidation, improvement" and the work thought of "strengthening, innovative, leading", accelerated the development of Duyun power grid, ensured eight counties and two cities of Qiannan prefecture and Qiandongnan prefecture in economic and social development electricity needs, initiatively undertook more social responsibility for transmitting electricity from west to east and building the "Responsibility South Network", "Harmony Southern Network".

By the end of 2005, Duyun electricity network has formed the pattern of power supply taking 500-kilovolt Fuquan transformer as the center, 220-kilovolt transmission line as the main grid, 110-kilovolt power grid radiation cities and counties, the rate of cities reliable electricity distribution system was 99.87%, safe production remained stability.

Duyun Power Supply Bureau adhered to the principle of "grasping in two respects, two respects all insistence", at the same time on grasping the building of material civilization, paid attention to spiritual civilization construction. Power supply services upgraded from standardizing services to brand services, power grid construction has been further strengthened to meet the load development and the needs of the market, to provide the first effective protection for local socio-economic development.

坚强、健康的都匀电网
The strong, healthy Duyun Network

都匀电网调度管理中心
The Electricity Network Dispatch Management Center of Duyun

五年拼搏明珠添彩，

Five years hard work as pearl adding luster,

——思南县“十五”建设

The building results of "Tenth Five" and the develop

“十五”期间，全县人民在县委、县人民政府的正确领导下，以建设乌江中下游电力能源中心、水陆交通枢纽、文化教育中心和生态畜牧业大县为目标，奋力拼搏，经济建设和社会发展取得了突破性的成就。

经济总量迅速增加，产业结构调整取得实效。2005年实现生产总值17.1亿元，比上年增长15.6%，十五期间年均增长9.3%，一、二、三产业的结构从“九五”期末的70.5:15.9:13.6调整为55.6:25.7:18.7。财政总收入突破亿元大关，地方财政收入突破8000万元，分别比“九五”期末增长64.7%、69.8%，年均分别增长10.5%、11.6%。

固定资产投资力度加大，基础设施明显改善，县域经济发展后劲增强。“十五”期间累计完成固定资产投资22.66亿元，年均增长47.5%。总投资78亿元的思林电站顺利实现围堰截流，县域小水电开发全面启动，建成投产后全县境内装机将达到105万千瓦以上。提级改造干线公路243公里，修造通村公路446公里，目前县内通车里程达到3000余公里，70%的村和30%的村民组通了公路。县城总体规划已修编完成，白鹭洲宾馆、青少年活动中心等一批旅游服务设施和娱乐场所相继建成，县城主要街道全面得以改造，河西旧城改造全面启动，城南、城北扩容正在加紧实施。

科技兴农战略着力调整农业结构，农业基础设施地位进一步夯实。“十五”期间全县以实施优质高产示范工程和“食品无公害行动计划”，加大农产品种植的科技含量，大力培育和发展农业产业支柱。年粮食生产规模已达到26万吨，油菜籽生产规模已达到1.8万吨；肉猪出栏规模已达到50万头，肉类总产量5.5万吨。畜牧业已成为全县农村经济发展和农民增收的重要支柱产业，2005年畜牧业总产值已达到53559万元，占农林牧渔业总产值的38.6%。中药材和苦丁茶生产是全县农村经济发展的后续特色产业，目前已初具规模。农业生产条件进一步改善，生态环境逐步好转。“十五”期间，全县新增和改善灌溉面积3.1万亩，恢复灌溉面积1.16万亩，森林覆盖率达到32.68%，对20个乡镇中居住生存环境恶劣的农户实施了易地扶贫搬迁安置。农民人均纯收入已达到1506元。

经济体制改革不断深化，对外开放水平提高。全县共引进项目59个，引资4亿元，非公有制经济发展加快，全县有个体工商户7900户，私营企业98家。

“十一五”期间，全县经济社会发展的总体目标是：保持经济持续快速健康发展，综合实力明显增强，农业产业化建设、扶贫开发，基础设施建设、生态环境建设、文化教育事业取得新突破，电力工业成为重要支柱产业，生态畜牧业、农产品加工业、建筑建材业、城镇经济、劳务经济快速发展，旅游产业、文化产业初步形成。思南成为乌江中下游水陆交通枢纽、电力能源中心、文化教育中心和生产畜牧大县的格局基本形成。

预期目标是：生产总值年均增长15%，一、二、三产业结构调整为43:37:20；财政总收入达到2亿元，全社会固定资产投资年均增长25%以上，城镇居民人均可支配收入达到7000元以上，农民人均纯收入2000元以上。

县委书记　晏世忠
The secretary of the county Yan Shizhong

During the period of "Tenth Five", under the correct leadership of the county Party committee and county government, the people in the county took building Wu River middle-downstream electric energy centre, land and water transport hub, cultural educational center and ecological animal husbandry major county as goals, worked hard and made breakthrough achievements in economic and social development.

Rapid increase in the economy total, the adjustment of the industrial structure achieved good results. In 2005, the GDP realized 1.71 billion yuan, 15.6% higher than the previous year, the average annual growth of 9.3% during the Tenth Five, the structure of the first, second and third industry adjusted from 70.5:15.9:13.6 of the end of "Ninth Five"to 55.6:25.7:18.7. Financial revenue broke through 100

思南县全景
Full view of Sina county

振奋精神再绘蓝图

Bracing up spirit to drawn blueprint again

成果和“十一五”发展规划

ment planning of "Eleventh Five" of Sinan County

县长 戴亮

The governor of the county Dai Liang

million yuan in total, the local revenue exceeded 80 million yuan, respectively growth 64.7%, 69.8% than the end of "Ninth Five", respectively an average annual growth of 10.5%, 11.6%.

Fixed assets investment increased, the infrastructure has markedly improved, strengthened county economic development. Period of "Tenth Five" completed fixed assets investment of 2.266 billion yuan, with an average annual increase of 47.5%. Silin Power Station with a total investment of 7.8 billion yuan has been smoothly dammed river, small hydropower development was in fully opened up, after it completion, the county will reach installed capacity1.05 million kilowatts above. Upgraded 243 km of trunk roads, constructed 446 km of roads through the village, traffic mileage of the current county reached 3,000-plus kilometers, 70% of the villages and 30% of the villager groups linked road. The overall plan of the county has been completed. Bailuzhou Hotel, Youth Activity Center, and a number of tourism service and entertainment facilities have been completed. Main streets of the county were comprehensively transformed, the transformation of the Hexi old city was in fully started, the expansion of the south and north of the city were stepping up implementation .

思南县土家族花灯

Tujia minority lantern of Sina county

The strategy of science and technology thriving agriculture stressed to adjust the agricultural structure, to further consolidate the status of the agricultural infrastructure. "Tenth Five" period, the county implemented the good quality, high-yield demonstration projects and "food non-pollution action plan", and increased agricultural products cultivation of scientific and technological content, and enlarged to cultivate and develop agricultural industrial pillar. Annual grain production scale has reached 260,000 tons, rapeseed production scale has reached 18,000 tons; slaughtered scale has reached nearly 500,000 heads, meat output of 55,000 tons. The animal husbandry has became an important pillar industry in rural economic development and the increase income of peasants in the county, in 2005 output value of livestock product has reached 535.59 million yuan, accounting for 38.6% of the amount of farming, forestry, animal husbandry, fishery industry. Chinese herbal medicine and Kuding tea production were the follow-up special industries for rural economic development in the county, which has begun to take shape. Further improved agricultural production conditions, ecological environment gradually improved. During the period of "Tenth Five", new increase and improvement irrigation areas of the county were 31 thousand mu, renewed irrigation area of 11.6 thousand mu, the coverage rate of forest reached 32.68%, farmers living difficult environment were implemented relocation help poverty settlement in 20 villages. Per capita net income of farmers reached 1,506 yuan.

The reform of economic system constantly deepened to improve the level of opening up. A total of 59 projects in the county were attracted with 400 million yuan, non-public ownership economy accelerated to development, the county has 7,900 individual industrial and commercial households, 98 private enterprises.

"Eleventh Five" period, the overall objectives of the county's economic and social development are : to maintain sustained, rapid and healthy economic development, markedly increase overall strength, make new breakthroughs in agricultural industrialization building, help poverty development, infrastructure construction, ecological environment construction, and cultural educational undertakings, power industry becomes an important pillar industry, the ecological animal husbandry, agricultural product processing industry, building materials industry, town economy, labour service economy rapidly develop, the tourism industry and cultural industry begin to take shape. The structure that Sina will become the Wu River downstream land and water transport hub, electric energy center, cultural and education center and production animal husbandry major county basically forms.

Targets are: the average annual growth of GDP of 15%, the first, second and third industrial restructuring to 43:37:20; financial revenue reaching 200 million yuan, the average annual growth of 25% above in total fixed asset investment, average disposable income of urban residents reaching 7,000 yuan more, the per capita net income of peasants 2,000 yuan or more.

贵定县
Guiding County

《欢腾的音寨》（三等奖） 刘磊摄
"Rejoicing Yin Village" (the third prize) Photographer Liu Lei

（一）区域概况

贵定县行政区域面积1631平方公里，耕地总面积11928公顷，辖8镇12乡，95个行政村，15个社区居委会，年末常住总人口29.3万人，少数民族人口占总人口比重52.35%（公安人口）。人口出生率14.74‰，自然增长率8.068‰，计划生育率95.47%，城镇化率达31.02%。主要矿藏有电石石灰石矿、煤矿、铁矿、粉石英矿、铅锌矿、高岭土和重晶石等。全年植树造林1900公顷，森林覆盖率达48%。

（二）经济概况

1、国民经济持续健康运行。2005年，贵定生产总值171132.57万元，增长13.03%。其中第一产业增加值30730万元，所占比重17.96%，第二产业增加值90172.53万元，所占比重是52.69%，第三产业增加值50230.04万元，所占比重29.35%。工农业总产值231702万元，其中：工业总产值181226万元，增长13.19%。农林牧渔业总产值完成50476万元，增长5%。乡镇企业产值74586万元，增长17.95%。全社会消费品零售总额21825万元，增长10.8%。完成财政收入17680万元，增长10.8%。完成固定资产投资36507万元，增长30.32%。农民人均纯收入1872元，增长8.9%。

2、旅游收益稳步上升。全年接待游客近70万人次，比去年增加50万人次，旅游收入2100万元，比去年增加1520万元。特别是由于"金海雪山"旅游文化节和"金海雪山"盘江冰脆酥李节的成功举办，盘江音寨景区接待游客近50多万人（次），签约20多个项目，签约资金突破5个亿，有效拉动了第三产业的发展。目前音寨已被列为"全国农业旅游观光示范点"和省旅游局重点打造的乡村旅游"示范村寨（群）"。

3、招商引资取得较好成绩。2005年，引进实际到位资金22004万元，增长21.97%。新建、续建项目52个。

4、城镇基础设施建设稳步推进。加大县城基础设施建设，城市服务功能进一步加强，城市面貌正向净化、亮化、绿化方面发展。加快沿山商贸新区和环镇道路建设，有效带动了小城镇建设的发展。

5、金融、保险业保持较好发展态势。全年各项存款余额创历史新高，达105413万元，增长18.23%，各项贷款余额37654万元，其中支农贷款达13187万元，有力支持了农村经济发展。保险业务稳步发展，完成保费收入2163.7万元。

6、交通运输业和通讯业稳步发展。全年新改建公路125.4公里，其中油路25.4公里。公路通车里程972公里。邮政业务收入382.4万元，电信业务收入3833.6万元，本地电话用户53757户，国际互联网用户1953户,移动电话用户33250户。

7、教育、文化、卫生、环保等社会事业进一步发展。教育事业稳步发展，全县现有各类学校151所，在校生59215人，毕业生15930人，招生人数17481人，教职工数2945人，专任教师2583人，学龄儿童入学率99.80%。文化事业稳步发展。广播人口覆盖率93%，电视人口覆盖率81%。全县20个乡镇，98个行政村均实现了乡乡通电视、村村通广播。卫生事业平稳发展。公共环境得到改善，城市建成区面积5.4平方公里，绿化覆盖率18.3%。工业废气、废水、废渣处理率不断改善，年内分别达到75.78%、91.36%、55.41%，为全县人民提供了良好的人居环境。

《游春》 孙跃摄
"Spring Tour" Photographer Sun Yue

《金海雪山》——贵定音寨春色
"Gold Sea and Snow Mountain"-the spring scenery of Yin village of Guiding

(First) Regional overview

The administrative region area of Guiding county is 1631 square kilometres, the total area of 11,928 hectares of arable land, the county governs 8 towns 12 townships and 95 administrative villages, 15 community neighborhood committees, end of the year of the total population of 293,000 people, minority populations accounted for 52.35% of the total population (resident population). The birth rate is 14.74‰, and the natural growth rate is 8.068‰, 95.47% rate of family planning, the rate of urbanization is up to 31.02%. There are major mineral resources as acetylene limestone mine, coal, iron ore, quartz powder mine, lead zinc ore, kaolin and barite. The area of annual afforestation is 1900 hectares, with the rate of the forest coverage reaching 48%.

(Second) Economic background

Firstly, the national economy sustained healthy operation. In 2005, the GDP of Guiding county was 1711.3257 million yuan, an increase of 13.03%. among which, the first industrial added value was 307.3 million yuan with the proportion of 17.96%, the second industrial added value was 901.7253 million yuan with the proportion of 52.69%, the third industrial added value was 502.3004 million yuan with the proportion of 29.35%. Industrial and agricultural total output value was 2.31702 billion yuan, of which: 1.81226 billion yuan of industrial output value, 13.19% growth. The total ouput value of farming, forestry, animal husbandry and fishery completed 504.76 million yuan, an increase of 5%. Township enterprises output value was 745.86 million yuan, an increase of 17.95%. All retail sales of consumer goods amounted 218.25 million yuan, an increase of 10.8%. The financial revenue completed 176.8 million yuan, an increase of 10.8%. The investment in fixed assets completed 365.07 million yuan, an increase of 30.32%. Per capita net income of peasants was 1,872 yuan, an increase of 8.9%.

Secondly, a steady rise in tourism income. Annual received tourists nearly 700 thousand person times, increase 500 thousand person times than last year, tourism revenue was 21 million yuan, increase 15.2 million yuan than last year. Especially by successfully held "Gold Sea and Snow Mountain" Tourism Cultural Festival and the "Gold Sea and Snow Mountain" Panjiang Ice Crisp Plum Festival, Panjiang Yin village scenic zone received nearly 500 thousand person (times), signed more than 20 projects with contracted funds of over 500 million yuan, effectively drew the development of the tertiary industry. Yin village currently has been classified as "National Agricultural Tourism Model Point" and rural tourism "Model Village (group)" building by Provincial Tourism Bureau.

Thirdly, the introduced business and attracted investment made better results. In 2005, the actual available fund was 220.04 million yuan, an increase of 21.97%. 52 projects were new-built and reconstructed.

Fourthly, the urban infrastructure construction advanced steadily. Increased county infrastructure building, urban service function further strengthen, the urban landscape developed towards to purification, brightness and green. The construction of Yanshan trade new district and Huanzhen road was accelerated, to effectively lead the development of small town building.

Fifthly, finance, and insurance remained better development trend. Annual deposits balance created a record, amounting to 1.05413 billion yuan, an increase of 18.23%, and the loan balance was 376.54 million yuan, of which agro-loans amounted to 131.87 million yuan, strong support the development of the rural economy. The business of insurance steadily developed, completed premium income of 21.637 million yuan.

Sixthly, the transport and communications industry steadily developed. Annual 125.4 kilometres roads were new built, of which pitch roads of 25.4 km. 972 km roads were opened to traffic. Post operation income was 3.824 million yuan, and operation income of telecommunications was 38.336 million yuan, with local phone users of 53757 households, 1,953 households of Internet users, mobile telephone users of 33250 households.

Seventhly, education, culture, health, environmental protection and other social undertakings further developed. Education cause steadily developed, the county now had 151 schools with 59,215 school students, graduates 15,930 persons, 17,481 enrolment persons, teaching and administrative staff of 2945 workers, 2583 full-time teachers. The rate of school-age children enrolment was up to 99.80%. Cultural undertakings have been developing steadily. The coverage rate of broadcasting population was 93%, coverage rate of 81% of television population. 20 townships, 98 administrative villages of the county have achieved opening the television in all towns and opening the broadcasting in all villages. The public health undertaking was stable development. Public environment was improved, with urban built area of 5.4 square kilometres, green covering rate of 18.3%. The disposing rate of industrial emissions, waste water, waste residue continued to improve, respectively reached 75.78%, 91.36%, 55.41% within the year, provided a good living environment for the people of the county.

《孤独牧人》 郭登鸣 摄
"Lonely Shepherd" Photographer Guo Dengming

《鲵群》 金连儒 摄
"Salamander Group" Photographer Jin Lianru

修文县

Xiuwen County

旅游文化多姿多彩
The colorful and varied tourist cultural

修文县地处黔中腹部，属贵阳市管辖，总面积1071平方公里。辖4镇6乡，有217个村民委员会、12个居民委员会。2005年末全县总人口309600人，出生率为8.99‰，计生率94.3%。

2005年，全面完成“十五”计划各项目标任务。全年完成地方生产总值200071万元，同比增长22.8%，三次产业结构由2000年的“一、三、二”转变为2005年的“二、三、一”，比重由38：25：37变为26：40：34。完成固定资产投资17亿元，同比增长38.7%，“十五”期间年均增长40.09%。财政总收入达20977万元，同比增长24.2%，其中：地方财政收入完成12828万元，同比增长23.36%。引进投资项目31个，到位资金36520万元，同比增长35%。城镇居民人均可支配收入达8053元，同比增长14.99%；农民人均纯收入2702元，同比增长13.05%。

“三农”工作取得新成绩。以农民增收为核心，突出发展特色农业和生态农业，重投入夯基础，重扶持促带动，积极推进产业化经营，“菜、畜、果、药”四大特色产业不断发展壮大，农业综合生产能力不断提高，农村经济社会保持良好的发展势头。2005年，完成农业总产值76264万元，同比增长11.12%。

工业经济的主导地位已经形成。扎佐医药工业园13家药业全部通过GMP改造，全年实现医药产值85230万元，占规模以上工业产值的57.57%。成功打造“十里工业走廊”，搭建新的工业经济发展平台。技改力度加大，传统产业优势不断提升。全年完成规模以上工业总产值148053万元，占工业总产值的50%以上，二产在三次产业结构中的比重达53.33%。

第三产业迅猛发展。加大开发力度，配套完善景区景点设施，积极打造精品旅游线，全省唯一的森林野生动物园落户扎佐建设，黔中旅游休闲胜地的雏形已初步形成；作为辐射黔北、黔西北和承接南贵昆的物流中枢扎佐物流园区规划建设已纳入省、市“十一五”规划；交通、电信、餐饮、房地产等产业逐步发展壮大。成功举办了第三届国际阳明文化节，充分展示“王学圣地、世外桃源”的旅游形象。全年累计接待游客近20万人次，实现旅游收入2890万元；完成全社会消费品零售总额41617万元，“十五”期间年均增长14.87%。

社会各项事业全面进步。在全省首家组建了修文（畜牧）“三农”专家服务中心；新型合作医疗制度改革试点全面完成；文明县创建工作顺利推进，城市品位和管理水平不断提升；广播电视人口覆盖率达95%以上；实现村村通移动电话；“平安修文”创建成效明显，实现“一降一升”目标；信访案件同比下降21.1%。其他各项社会事业持续快速健康发展。

中国·贵阳(修文)第三届国际阳明文化节开幕盛典
China · Guiyang (Xiuwen) the opening inaugural ceremony of the Third International Yangming Cultural Festival

城市建设日新月异
The urban construction change rapidly

医药产业蓬勃发展
The flourishing pharmaceutical industry

Xiuwen county is located in the abdomen of the middle of Guizhou, is the jurisdiction of Guiyang city, with a total area of 1,071 square kilometers. The county governs 4 towns, 6 townships, 217 villagers committees, 12 residents committees. The total population of the county was 309,600 people at the end of 2005, the birth rate is 8.99‰, family planning rate is 94.3%.

In 2005, the county completed the objectives and tasks of "10th Five-Year" plan. Annual completed local GDP of 2.00071 billion yuan, growth 22.8% than last year, three industrial structure changed from "one, three, two" of 2000 to "two, three, one" of 2005, the proportion changed from 38:25:37 to 26:40:34. The fixed assets investment completed 1.7 billion yuan, increase of 38.7%, average annual growth 40.09% during the period of "10th Five-Year Plan". Total financial revenue reached to 209.77 million yuan, increase of 24.2%, of which: local financial revenue finished 128.28 million yuan, increase of 23.36%. The county introduced 31 investment projects, available funds of 365.2 million yuan, increase of 35%. The per capita disposable income of urban residents reached 8,053 yuan, an increase of 14.99%; the per capita net income of farmers was 2,702 yuan, an increase of 13.05%.

"Three agricultures" works made new achievements. Took increase incomes for farmers as the core to stress development characteristics agriculture and ecological agriculture, attached importance to investment and laid foundation, attached importance to support and promoted lead, actively promoted industrial operations, "vegetables, livestock, fruits, medicines" the four major characteristic industries continuously grew and developed, the comprehensive agricultural production capacity continued to improve, the rural economy society maintained a good momentum of development. In 2005, the total output value of agriculture completed 762.64 million yuan, increase of 11.12%.

Industrial economy has become the dominant position. 13 pharmaceutical companies of Zazo medicine industrial park have all passed GMP reform, annual medicine output value realized 852.3 million yuan, accounting for 57.57% of industrial output value above designated size. The county successfully built "ten li industrial corridor" to erecting a new platform for the development of industrial economy, technological transformation were intensified, the advantage of traditional industries was constantly upgraded. The total industrial output value above designated size finished 1.48053 billion yuan, accounting for more than 50% of industrial total output value, the proportion of the secondary industrial in three industrial structure reached to 53.33%.

The tertiary industry rapidly developed. Enlarged development capability, to form a complete set of perfect scenic facility and to positively create fine tourist routes, the province's only forest wild animal park is located in Zazo, tourist resort of the middle of Guizhou has been initially formed. The planning and construction of Zazo Logistics Park which is took for the logistics hub of radiation Qianbei, Qianxibei and continue Nanning - Guiyang - Kunming has been brought into provincial, city "11th Five-Year" plan; Transportation, telecommunication, catering, real estate and other industrials gradually grew and developed. Successfully held the Third International Yangming Cultural Festival, fully showed its tourist image as "the Holy Land of Wang Learning, A heaven of peace and happiness". Annual total received tourists of nearly 200 thousand person times and achieved tourism revenue 28.9 million yuan; retail sales of social consumer goods total completed 416.17 million yuan, average annual growth 14.87% during the period of "10th Five-Year Plan".

The social various undertakings made overall progresses. The provincial first Xiuwen (livestock) "three agricultures" expert service center was established; The pilot of new cooperative medical system reform was fully completed; The building work of civilization county was smoothly improved and continuously upgraded urban grade and the level of management; Radio and television covering rate reached to 95% above; Every village realized the opening of mobile phone; "Peace Xiuwen" creation made remarkable results to achieve aim of "one drop one raise"; Petition cases decreased 21.1% than last year. And all other social undertakings maintained sustained, rapid and healthy development.

乳业产业初具规模
The dairy industry is beginning to take shape

万亩梨园硕果累累
10 thousand mu pear garden of countless rich fruits

贵阳市小河区

Xiaohe Districtof Guiyang City

贵阳市小河区全面完成了“十五”计划的各项目标任务。

经济发展持续加快，综合实力明显增强。“十五”期间，地区生产总值年均增长17.5%，实现地区生产总值24.1亿元。“十五”期末，实现财政总收入5.38亿元，年均增长29.51%。招商引资实际到位资金达22.7亿元，年均增长45.4%。

经济结构明显优化，质量和效益显著提高。“十五”时期，小河区采取积极措施，推进了经济结构的优化升级。2005年，工业增加值完成11.63亿元，占地区生产总值的48.3%，非公有制经济的比重由26%上升到40%。

切实加强“三农”工作，农村经济全面发展。呈现出农业增效、农民增收和农村稳定的可喜局面。2005年农民人均纯收入达到4079元，是2000年的1.56倍。

固定资产投资增长强劲，城市面貌明显变化。“十五”时期全社会固定资产投资年均增长48.6%，累计完成80亿元。以交通为重点的基础设施建设取得突破性进展。

各项改革稳步推进，对外开放成效显著。五年来累计引进项目700余个，合同资金210亿元，实际到位资金71亿元，实际利用外资3232万美元；与40余个国家和地区发展了贸易和技术合作关系，贸易总额年均增长25%，2005年达7079万美元。出口创汇年均增长38.6%，2005年达5468万美元。

社会各项事业全面进步，和谐社会建设开创新局面。“十五”时期，城镇居民人均可支配收入年均增长11.7%，2005年达到9925元，,农民人均纯收入年均增长9.2%，2005年达到4079元。社会消费品零售总额年均增长15%，2005年达到14.63亿元。城镇登记失业率均控制在4%以内，五年累计统筹城乡就业17395人。建立健全了突发性公共事件预防机制。科技工作扎实推进。教育事业蓬勃发展。计划生育率保持在98%以上。积极推进医疗卫生体制改革。大力推进精神文明建设。行政许可法深入实施。

2006年是实施“十一五”规划的第一年，主要预期目标是：地区生产总值增长17%以上；全社会固定资产投资增长20%；财政总收入和地方财政收入增长15%；招商引资实际到位资金增长20%，实际利用外资增长15%；城市居民人均可支配收入增长10%，农民人均纯收入增长10%；城镇登记失业率控制在4%以内，人口自然增长率控制在8‰以内，万元生产总值能耗下降5%左右；区委、区政府拟为民办好八件实事。

Xiaohe district of Guiyang city has fully completed all the objectives of "Tenth Five" plan.

Continuing to accelerate economic development, comprehensive strength has increased markedly. "Tenth Five" period, the average annual growth of 17.5% in GDP, realized regional GDP of 2.41 billion yuan. The end of "Tenth Five" period, achieved financial revenue of 538 million yuan, an average annual increase of 29.51%. Actual capital attracted investment amounted to 2.27 billion yuan, an average annual increase of 45.4%.

The economic structure was optimized, and significantly improved the quality and efficiency. "Tenth Five" period, Xiaohe district took positive measures to promote the optimization and upgrading of the economic structure. In 2005, 1.163 billion yuan in industrial output added value was completed, accounted for 48.3% of GDP in region, the proportion of non-public ownership economy rose to 40% from 26%.

Strengthened the works of "three agricultures", the rural economy comprehensively developed. The district showed the gratifying situations on agricultural efficiency, peasants increase incomes and rural stability. In 2005, per capita income of farmers reached 4,079 yuan, 1.56 times of the year of 2000.

Fixed asset investment has greatly grown, the city has changed significantly. "Tenth Five" period, all social investment in fixed assets grew 48.6% in average annual, accumulated 8 billion yuan. The infrastructure taking communications as the focus has made a breakthrough development.

Various reforms steadily improved to make notable results in opening up. Since five years, totally introduced 700 items with the contract funds 21 billion yuan, 7.1 billion yuan of funds actually in place, the actual utilization of foreign capital 32.32 million USD; With more than 40 countries and territories developed trade and technological cooperation, trade volume amounted to 70.79 million USD in 2005, an average annual growth 25%. Export foreign exchange amounted to 54.68 million USD in 2005, an average annual growth 38.6%.

All the social undertakings have made comprehensive progresses and created a new situation in the construction of harmony social. "Tenth Five" period, average annual growth 11.7% of disposable income of urban residents, reached 9,925 yuan in 2005, average annual growth 9.2% of per capita net income of farmers, reached 4,079 yuan in 2005. Total retail sales of consumer goods of average annual growth 15%, reached 1.463 billion yuan in 2005. And the registered unemployment rate in urban areas was controlled within 4%, accumulated making overall planning by settlement urban and rural employment of 17395 persons in five years. The mechanism to prevent the sudden public events was established. Science and technology work solidly improved. Education courses were flouring. The rate of Family Planning maintained 98% above. The health system reform was actively promoted. The construction of spiritual civilization was vigorously promoted. The Administrative Permission Law was in-depth implemented.

The year of 2006 is the first year to implement "Eleventh Five" plan, the main targets are : more than 17% growth in GDP; total fixed asset investment growth 20%; government revenue and local revenue growth 15%; investment actual capital growth 20%, actual utilization of foreign investment growth 15%; 10% growth in per capita disposable income of urban residents, and per capita net income of peasants growth 10%; controlling the registered unemployment rate in cities and towns within 4%, the rate of natural population growth controlling within 8‰, the consumption of per 10 thousand yuan GDP decline about 5%; the district Party committee and government to be run eight things for people.

西部开发工业园区
The west development industrial park

开发大厦
Development building

外资企业先进生产设备
Advanced production equipment of foreign capital enterprise

黎平县
Liping County

省长石秀诗（右二）在州、县领导的陪同下视察黎平会议会址
The governor Shi Xiushi (the second from right) accompanied by the leaders of the prefecture and the county to inspect the site of Liping Conference

黎平县位于贵州省东南边缘，地处黔、湘、桂三省（区）交界处。全县辖25个乡镇403个村，总面积4441平方公里，总人口51.7万，其中侗族人口36.01万，占全县总人口的71%，是全国侗族人口聚居最多的县。

全县经济社会各项事业继续保持快速健康发展。2005年，全县国民生产总值实现113179万元，其中，第一产业完成47902万元，同比增长6.40%；第二产业完成21925万元，同比增长17.30%；第三产业完成28950万元，同比增长13.70%。2005年工业总产值完成43698万元，同比增长18.94%。农业总产值完成9.4亿元，同比增长7.0%。财政总收入实现历史新高，2005年达到5738万元，财政支出完成32888万元。农民人均纯收入1702元，同比增长5%。全县社会固定资产投资完成50349万元。社会消费品零售总额完成37850万元，同比增长16.22%。

各项社会事业取得新的成就。以交通为重点的基础设施建设取得历史性突破，黎平机场建成并顺利通航；黎平是革命老区、国家级风景名胜区、国家级森林公园、中国首批民族民间文化保护试点单位和贵州省优先发展重点旅游区，2005年实现旅游收入7438万元；招商引资共引进项目19个，到位资金1.1亿元；教育、科技、文化、卫生等社会事业全面进步，精神文明和民主法制建设不断加强，社会保持稳定。

随着黎平机场建成通航和交通、城镇等基础设施的不断完善，黎平作为贵州东线的民族文化与生态旅游大县，正以崭新的姿态迅速崛起。

Liping county is located in the edge of southeast of Guizhou province, in the junction of Guizhou, Hunan and Guangxi three provinces (autonomous regions). The county governs 25 townships, 403 villages, with a total area of 4,441 square kilometres and a total population of 517,000 people, of which population of 360,100 people of Dong nationality, accounted for 71% of the county's total population, which is the county with the most population of Dong nationality of the nation.

The economic and social undertakings of the county continued to maintain rapid and healthy development. In 2005, the GDP of the county realized 1.13179 billion yuan, of which the completion of the primary industry of 479.02 million yuan, growth 6.40% than last year; the completion of the secondary industry of 219.25 million yuan, an increase of 17.30%; the completion of the tertiary industry of 289.5 million yuan, growth 13.70%. In 2005, total output value of industry completed 436.98 million yuan, increase 18.94% than last year. Agricultural output value completed 940 million yuan, up 7.0% than last year. Financial revenue in 2005 realized the highest record of 57.38 million yuan, expenditure completed 328.88 million yuan. Per capita net income of peasants was 1,702 yuan, an increase of 5%. The county's fixed assets investment completed 503.49 million yuan. Retail sales in social goods completed 378.5 million yuan, an increase of 16.22%.

All social undertakings made new achievements. The infrastructure construction taking communications as the focus made historic breakthrough, Li Ping airport was built and smoothly opened to air traffic; Liping is an old revolutionary area, national scenic area, national level forest park, the first batch of Chinese folk culture protection pilot unit and Guizhou province priority development key tourist area, tourism revenue in 2005 realized 74.38 million yuan; A total of 19 projects were introduced, actually placed funds were 110 million yuan; Education, science and technology, culture, health, and other social undertakings made overall progresses, the construction in spiritual civilization, democracy legal system have been continuously strengthened, and maintained the society stability.

With Liping airport navigation and the improved transport, urban infrastructure, Li Ping, as a Guizhou eastern nationality cultural and eco-tourism large county, is rapidly rising with new posture.

黎平机场于2005年11月6日建成通航，首航飞机飞抵黎平
Liping Airport was built and opened to air traffic on November 6 of 2005, the first aircraft arrived in Liping.

县城新区夜景一角
A corner of night scene of new district in the county

玉屏侗族自治县国民经济和社会发展状况

The National Economic and Social Development Situation of Yuping Dong Nationality Autonomous County

中国华电集团大龙发电公司一景
A view of China Huadian Group Da Long Power Company

上海至瑞丽高速公路玉屏段
Yuping section in Shanghai to Ruili Highway

"十五"时期，玉屏侗族自治县保持了经济持续快速健康协调发展和社会的稳定。

一、"十五"时期经济和社会发展情况

2005年实现生产总值12.0519亿元，是"九五"期末的3.86倍。经济结构调整取得重要进展，"九五"期末一、二、三产业排序为42.76：28.05：29.19，2005年已调整为19.7：48.69：31.61。全社会固定资产投资总额2005年达到13.968亿元，是"九五"期末的4.4倍。地方财政收入2005年实现7242万元，是"九五"期末的2.64倍。工农业总产值2005年实现17.2亿元，是"九五"期末的5.17倍。在规模以上工业企业中，非公经济占经济总量的60%以上，比"九五"期末提高30个百分点，非公企业数占全县企业总数的80%。招商引资取得阶段性成果。2005年城镇居民人均可支配收入8000元左右，年均增长9%。农民人均纯收入2005年达到2300元，年均增长6.8%。人民生活得到不断改善。城镇化进程加快。城镇登记失业率控制在4%以内。医疗卫生事业发展迅速。人口自然增长率控制在8‰以内。卫生文明县城、社会主义精神文明和民主法制建设不断加强。2005年森林覆盖率达到39.8%，比2000年提高5个百分点。治理水土流失面积达到58平方公里。环保治理投入达到6000多万元。

二、"十五"经济和社会发展取得的成就

实现了由温饱社会向总体小康社会跨越。2005年实现人均GDP8800元，在全省88个县（市、区）中名列前茅。实现了产业结构由以农业为主导向以工业为主导跨越。2005年工业在经济结构中的比例已由"九五"期末的28.05%上升到48.69%，农业由42.76%下降到19.7%。经济和社会发展实现了四个转变。传统农业向效益型农业转变。2005年实现农林牧渔总产值3.9亿元。实现农民收入由单一依靠种植业向主要依靠副业、林果业和畜牧养殖业的历史性转变。城镇建设由低层次向大框架、高品位转变。到"十五"期末，城镇建成区已达到10.4平方公里。交通由低等级向高等级渐次发展。玉铜高等级公路竣工通行，实现了铜仁地区高速公路"零"的突破，基本实现村村通公路。第三产业由缓慢发展向实现新的崛起转变。2005年三产实现增加值3.8亿元，为2000年的3.56倍。基本形成了特色农产品、畜禽产品、果品菜蔬和日用百货四大市场体系。旅游业发展起步较快。

三、"十一五"时期总体发展思路和发展目标

未来五年，玉屏自治县面临着如何采取超常规措施，转变经济增长方式，优化产业结构，增强自主创新能力和核心竞争力，实现经济社会快速发展的重大考验。未来五年，更是加快工业化、城镇化和经济发展转型的重要战略机遇期，也是由总体小康向全面小康迈进的重要阶段，有着前所未有的机遇和良好的发展条件。

玉屏国际箫笛文化艺术节上一名萧笛爱好者正在吹奏萧笛
A bamboo flute fan was playing the bamboo flute in Yuping International Bamboo Flute Cultural Festival

现代化综合农业开发
Modern comprehensive agricultural development

"Tenth Five-Year Plan" period, Yuping Dong nationality autonomous county maintained economic sustained, rapid, healthy coordination development and social stability.

First, the economic and social development situation in "Tenth Five-Year Plan" period

The GDP of 2005 realized 1.20519 billion yuan, 3.86 times of the end of "Ninth Five". Has made important progress in economic restructuring, the arrangement in primary, secondary, and tertiary industries have been adjusted from 42.76:28.05:29.19 of the end of "Ninth Five" to 19.7:48.69:31.61 of the year of 2005. Total fixed asset investment of 2005 reached 1.3968 billion yuan, 4.4 times of the end of "Ninth Five". Local financial revenue of 2005 realized 72.42 million yuan, 2.64 times of the end of "Ninth Five". The output value of industry and agriculture of 2005 realized 1.72 billion yuan, 5.17 times of the end of "Ninth Five". In industrial enterprises above designated size, non-public economy, which accounted for more than 60% of the total economy, up 30% than the end of "Ninth Five", the number of non-public enterprises accounting for 80% of total number of enterprises of the county. Introduced business and attracting investment achieved substantive results. In 2005 per capita disposable income of urban residents was about 8,000 yuan, an average annual increase of 9%. Per capita net income of farmers reached 2,300 yuan in 2005, an average annual increase of 6.8%. People's lives were constantly improving. The process of urbanization was accelerated. Urban registered unemployment rate was controlled within 4%. Medical and health undertakings have developed rapidly. Natural population growth rate was controlled the within 8‰. The constructions of health civilization county, the socialist spiritual civilization, democracy and legal system have been continuously strengthened. The rate of forest coverage was up to 39.8% in 2005, increased 5% than 2000. Management soil erosion area reached 58 square kilometres. Environmental management input to more than 60 million yuan.

Second, the achievements in economic and social development of "Tenth Five" period

The step from the community of food and clothing to the overall well-off society was achieved. Per capita GDP of 2005 achieved 8800 yuan, came out in front in the 88 counties (cities and districts). The industrial structure achieved the step from taking agriculture as lead to taking industry as lead. In 2005, the proportion of industry in the economic structure increased from the end of "Ninth Five" of 28.05% to 48.69%, declined from 42.76% to 19.7% of agriculture. Economic and social development achieved four changes. Traditional agriculture changed to benefit agriculture. The output value of agriculture, forestry, animal husbandry, fishery of 2005 realized 390 million yuan. Achieved historic change in farmer incomes from relying on a single farming industry to rely mainly on the sideline, forestry and fruit industries and livestock. Urban construction changed from low level to the big framework, high grade. By the end of "Tenth Five-Year Plan" period, urban areas have reached 10.4 square kilometres. Traffic developed from low level to high grade. Yutong high-grade road completed, which realized the "zero" breakthrough in Tongren region highway, realizing all villages having access road. The tertiary industry changed from slow development to achievement new rising. The added value of the tertiary industry realized 380 million yuan of 2005, 3.56 times of 2000. The four market systems as feature agricultural products, animal products, fruits and vegetables and articles of daily use were basic formed. Tourism industry development started fast.

Third, the overall development thought and development goals of "Eleventh Five" period

In the next five years, Yuping autonomous county faces the major tests how to make unconventional measures to change the mode of economic growth, and optimize the industrial structure and enhance self-innovation and core competitiveness, and achieve rapid economic and social development. In the next five years, is not only an important strategic opportunity period to accelerating industrialization, urbanization and change economic development, but also the important stage stepping from the main well-off to overall well-off, with unprecedented opportunities and good development conditions.

小桥元洞母子峰
Mother and Son Mountain of Xiaoqiaoyuan Hole

习水县
Xishui County

习水地处黔北、渝西、川南交汇地带，全县总面积3127平方公里，总人口68万人，辖24个乡镇（区）。习水紧靠遵义、贵阳，面向成都、重庆，是黔北文化和巴蜀文化的汇集地，黔北国酒文化、生态旅游和红色旅游的链接点及黔北通江达海的前沿窗口。

资源富集的宝地。地下矿藏已探明的有铜、镁、重晶石、石英砂等26种，其中煤炭总储量47.8亿吨，享有“黔北煤海”的盛誉。境内赤水河、习水河、桐梓河等河流蕴藏着丰富的水能资源，开发潜力巨大。

避暑休闲的佳境。习水属中亚热带季风气候区，年降水量1010mm，年均气温为13.8℃，森林覆盖率35.2%，万物滋生，拥有1800多类物种。境内丹霞地貌罕见独特，有世界上最大的桫椤群落，是国家级常绿阔叶林保护区，国家级森林公园和省级风景名胜区。

寻幽访古的去处。习水古称习部，已有两千多年人类生息的历史，繁衍着汉、苗、彝等14个民族，积淀了厚重的民俗、民间文化，密布着珍奇的历史文物古迹。境内有蜀汉章武三年摩崖石刻望仙台，有清代实业家袁锦道创办的48家工厂遗址，是贵州早期工业文明的发祥地。

红色革命的沃土。1935年中央红军在习水转战两个多月，足迹遍及全县，数十处革命遗迹熠熠生辉，其间发生了著名的红军四渡赤水战役，一、二、四渡就在习水。土城青杠坡战役因新中国的两代领导核心、一任开国总理、三任国防部长、七大元帅、上百位将军共同在此浴血奋战，并由此拉开四渡赤水的序幕而成为古今中外的战争奇观。

习水是一片充满机遇的土地。县委、政府以优惠的政策和良好的投资环境，欢迎有识之士前来发展。

Xishui county, is located in the convergence zone of the north of Guizhou, the west of Chongqing, the south of Sichuan, the total area of 3,127 square kilometres, the total population of 680 thousand, governs 24 towns (districts). Xishui county closely adjoins Zunyi, Guiyang, faces to Chengdu, Chongqing, is the collected place of Qianbei culture and Bashu culture, the link of Qianbei nation wine culture, eco-tourism and red tourism and the forward window of going to river and sea of Qianbei.

Xishui is the treasure-place of concentration resources. Underground deposits have proven 26 kinds such as copper, magnesium, barite, quartz sand, of which coal reserves total 4.78 billion tons, enjoying reputation "sea of coal of Qianbei". The county has rich resources in hydropower development potential in Chishui River, Xishi River, Tongzi River and other rivers.

The county is the most enjoyable summer resort. Xishui belongs subtropical monsoon climate zone, and annual precipitation of 1010 mm, the annual average temperature of 13.8 degrees, 35.2% of forest cover rate, having more than 1,800 species. The county has rare and unique Danxia landscape, having largest spinulose trees in the world, is national level evergreen broad-leaf forest protected area, national level forest park and provincial level scenic area.

The county is a nice place to search serene and visit historic site. Xishui, named Xi Bu in ancient times, has over 2,000 years of human history to live and work, lives and multiplies 14 nationalities Han, Miao, Yi, etc, leaves a thick, and heavy folk, folk culture, covers rare historical monuments. There has Maya Stone Wangxian Tower of three years in the kingdom of ShuHan Zhangwu, and 48 factories sites founded by industrialist Yuan Jindao of Qing Dynasty, is the birthplace of Guizhou early industrial civilization.

The county is the red revolution fertile soil. The year of 1935, Central Red Army were in Xishui foght in two months, footsteps across the county, stayed a lot of bright revolutionary relics, during which occurred the famous Red Army Crossing Four Times Chishui Campaign, the first, second, forth were in Xishui. Tucheng Qinggangpo Campaign, the new China's two generations leadership core, one founding prime minister, three ministers of Defence, 7 generalissimos, and more than 100 generals fought in this battle together, and thus began the prelude of Crossing Four Times Chishui to become classical and modern marvellous battle.

XiShui is full of opportunity of land. The county committee and government take preferential policies and good investment environment to welcome people with breadth of vision to development.

习水县高坪村实现耕作田园化
Gaoping village of Xishui county achieved farming field and gardens style

习水县大力发展生态鸡
Xishui county vigorously developed ecological chicken

国家级自然保护区、国家级森林公园——三岔河风景区“水漫丹霞”景观
The state-level nature protection zone, national level forest park -- "water came up Danxia" landscape of Sanchahe scenic area

德江县情简介

The Summary of Dejiang County Situation

德江商业步行街夜景
Commercial pedestrian street night scene of Dejiang

德江县位于黔东北铜仁地区西部，乌江水流从南至北纵贯其境。总面积2071.9平方公里，辖5个镇15个乡355个村3个社区8个居委会2918个村民组，2005年末总人口467958人。

“十五”期间，全县各项工作取得了长足发展，呈现出蓬勃向上的良好势头。

一、全县经济整体推进，综合实力明显增强。“十五”期末全县地方生产总值为142041万元,比“九五”期末（下同）增长54.96%。全县三次产业结构比从“九五”期末的76.1:9.2:14.7调整为55.3:14:30.7。

二、农业结构调整力度加大。全县农、林、牧、渔业增加值比例为65.4:4.8:28.8:1.1。森林覆盖率33.6%，比“九五”期末提高8.6个百分点。畜牧业增加值占农业增加值比重由“九五”期末的24.1%上升到“十五”期末的34.8%。

三、工业生产快速增长。建材、能源、农产品加工三大行业协调发展，工业企业保持良好发展势头。“十五”期末全县全部工业增加值12076万元，比“九五”期末增长113.56%。

四、固定资产投资平稳较快增长。“十五”期末全县固定资产投资完成55584万元，比“九五”期末增长407.06%。累计完成投资29608万元，增长323.82%。

五、交通运输邮电通讯业蓬勃发展。“十五”期末，交通运输仓储电信业实现增加值6030万元，比“九五”期末增长104.9%。全县通车里程1852.14公里，比“九五”期末增加752.14公里。全年邮政业务总量257万元，增长131.11%；电信业务总量1125万元，增长111.86%；移动业务总量1801万元，增长8.09倍。

六、消费品市场稳中有旺。全县实现社会消费品零售总额28146万元,比“九五”期末增长101.3%。

七、财政收入稳定增长，金融事业发展较快。全年财政总收入7427.2万元，地方财政预算内收入5951.7万元，比“九五”期末增长60.13%。全县金融机构年末各项存款余额62750万元，比“九五”期末增长210.63%。各项贷款余额46030万元，增长94.44%。全年保费收入1711万元，比“九五”期末增长171.16%。

八、城乡居民收入稳定增长，社会福利事业不断改善。2005年农民人均纯收入1538元，比“九五”期末增长27.95%。单位从业人员劳动报酬16097.6万元，增长100.44%。全县有敬老院13所，城镇低保人数3419户8005人，共发放低保金733.8万元。农村特困群众定期救助8010户21685人。

复兴黄牛
Yellow ox of Fuxing

Dejiang county is located in the weste of Tongren district of northeast of Guizhou, Wu River running through its territory from south to north. Total area is 2071.9 square kilometres, governs 5 towns 15 Townships 355 villages 3 communities 8 neighborhood committees 2,918 villagers groups, the total population of 467958 people in the end of 2005.

During the period of "Tenth Five", the county has made significant progress and has shown a vigorous good momentum.

First, the county economy improved as a whole, comprehensive strength has increased markedly. The end of "Tenth Five", the GDP of the county was 1420.41 million yuan, more 54.96% than the end of "Ninth Five" (the same below). The structure proporation of three industries in the county adjusted from 76.1:9.2:14.7 of the end of "Ninth Five" to 55.3:14:30.7.

Second, the adjustment of the agricultural structure has been increased. The ratio of the added value of agriculture, forestry, animal husbandry, fishery in the county was 65.4:4.8:28.8:1.1. Forests cover rate of 33.6%, grew 8.6 percentage than the end of "Ninth Five". Added value of animal husbandry accounting for the added value of agriculture from 24.1% of the end of "Ninth Five" rose to 34.8% of the end of "Tenth Five".

Third, industrial production has rapidly grown. Three major industries as building materials, energy resources and farm produce processing coordinated the development, industrial enterprises have maintained a good momentum of growth. Added value of all the industries of the county was 120.76 million yuan at the end of "Tenth Five", growth 113.56% than the end of "Ninth Five".

Fourth, investment in fixed assets grew steadily and rapidly. The county completed 555.84 million yuan of investment in fixed assets at the end of "Tenth Five", growth 407.06% than the end of "Ninth Five". Accumulated investment was 296.08 million yuan, increasing 323.82%.

Fifth, the development of transport telecommunications industry was flourishing. The end of "Tenth Five", transport storage telecommunications industry achieved added value of 60.3 million yuan, growth 104.9% than the end of "Ninth Five". Traffic mileage of 1852.14 km in the county increased 752.14 km than the end of "Ninth Five". Annual postal business totaled 2.57 million yuan, growth 131.11%; telecommunication business totaled 11.25 million yuan, growth 111.86%; 18.01 million yuan of total mobile operations, growth 8.09 times.

Sixth, the consumer market was stable and prosperous. Total retail sales of consumer goods in the county achieved 281.46 million yuan, growth 101.3% than the end of "Ninth Five".

Seventh, government revenue grew steadily, the financial undertakings developed fast. The annual government financial revenue was 74.272 million yuan, local budgets revenue of 59.517 million yuan, growth 60.13% than the end of "Ninth Five". Financial institutions deposit balance in the county was 627.5 million yuan, more 210.63% than the end of "Ninth Five". The loans balance was 460.3 million yuan, growth 94.44%. The annual premium income of 17.11 million yuan, grew 171.16% than the end of "Ninth Five".

Eighth, the steady growth of the income of urban and rural residents, constantly improved social welfare. In 2005 the per capita net income of peasants was 1,538 yuan, growth 27.95% than the end of "Ninth Five". The remunerations of employee were 160.976 million yuan, an increase of 100.44%. There were 13 old people homes throughout the county, the numbers of towns minimal assurance were 3419 households with 8005 persons, totaled funds of 7.338 million yuan minimal assurance. The special poor masses rescue of regularly in rural were 8010 households with 21685 persons.

波尔山羊
Boer goat

平坝县
Pingba County

平坝位于贵州省中部，全县行政区域总面积998.9平方公里，耕地面积1.75万公顷。辖6镇4乡（其中2个民族乡）、193个村民委员会、5个居民委员会、1个社区，有汉、苗、回、布依、仡佬等26个民族。县境内主要河流7条，流域面积755平方公里，径流总量50.34亿立方米，年平均气温14.7℃，降雨量1298mm，无霜期273天，地貌形态为溶蚀作用为主的喀斯特地貌。2005年，全县总人口35.62万人，其中非农业人口7.6万人，少数民族9.7万人。人口出生率14.2‰，自然增长率7.5‰，计划生育率87.41%。主要矿藏有煤、铁、铜、铝土等。森林覆盖率34%。

2005年，初步测算：全县生产总值（GDP）完成197653万元，比上年增长11.9%；农林牧渔业总产值完成50708万元，比上年增长10.55%；工业总产值完成40314万元，比上年增长21.74%。财政总收入17288万元，比上年增长43.9%；其中地方财政收入8617万元，比上年增长25%。县属全社会固定资产投资完成26659万元，比上年增长58.2%。社会消费品零售总额完成46298万元，比上年增长19.2%。农民人均纯收入为1976元，比上年增长5.5%。

Pingba county is located in the middle of Guizhou province, a total area of county administrative region is 998.9 square kilometres, 17,500 hectares of arable land. The county governs 6 towns, 4 townships (including 2 national townships), 193 villager committees, 5 resident committees, 1 community, and has 26 nationalities as the Han, Miao, Hui, Buyi and Gelao. The county has 7 major rivers, covers 755 square kilometres, the total runoff 5.034 billion cubic meters. The average temperature of the county is 14.7 degrees, and rainfall of 1298mm, frost-free period of 273 days. The landscape pattern is karst topography in main. In 2005, the total population of the county was 356,200 persons, including non-agricultural population of 76,000 persons, minorities of 97,000 persons. The population birth rate was 14.2‰, the rate of natural growth was 7.5‰, the rate of family planning was 87.41%. There are major deposits such as coal, iron, copper, bauxite and others. The rate of forest covering is 34%.

In 2005, preliminary estimates : the GDP of the county completed 1976.53 million yuan, increased 11.9% than last year; the total output value of farming, forestry, animal husbandry, fishery industry completed 507.08 million yuan, increased 10.55% than last year; total industrial output value completed 403.14 million yuan, 21.74% higher than the previous year. Financial revenue reached 172.88 million yuan, increased 43.9% than last year; among which local revenue was 86.17 million yuan, increased 25%. The fixed-assets investment of the county completed 266.59 million yuan, 58.2% higher than the previous year. The total retail sales of consumer goods completed 462.98 million yuan, 19.2% higher than the previous year. Per capita net income of peasants was up to 1,976 yuan, 5.5% higher than the previous year.

2005年，平坝县招商引资工作迈出了新步伐。2005年共引进贵州家喻集团平坝生产基地、贵州平坝浩森生物工程有限公司、中外合资“佳力美”公司等13个项目，协议引资39765万元。

In 2005, the work of introduced business and attracted investment in Pingba county has made new step. A total of 13 projects such as Guizhou Jiayu Group Pingba Production Base, Guizhou Pingba Haosen Biological Engineering Limited, Sino-foreign "Jialimei" Company were introduced with agreement attracting 397.65 million yuan in 2005.

为宣传屯堡文化，2005年8月26日，平坝县积极筹办了屯堡文化实景组诗《大地诗章》系列活动，实景组诗《大地诗章》应用现代诗歌语言与交响式的音乐和原生态的村民表演，参加演出的村民演员有220余人。

For promoting Tunbao culture, on August 26, 2005, Pingba county actively organized series of activities of Tunbao cultural views poems "earth poetry chapter", which applied the modern poetry language and symphonic music and the original ecological villagers performance, and villagers actors in participate performance of over 220 persons.

中共平坝县委书记　余显强
The secretary of the CPC Pingba County Party Committee Yu Xianqiang
中共平坝县纪委书记　杨文惠（女，布依族）
The secretary of the CPC Pingba County Discipline Committee Yang Wenhui (female, Buyi minority)
平坝县人大常委会主任　徐静波
The director of the Standing Committee of the NPC of Pingba County Xu Jingbo
平坝县人民政府县长　王 跃
The governor of Pingba County Government Wang Yue
政协平坝县委员会主席　谢发忠（白族）
The Chairman of the CPPCC of Pingba County Xie Fazhong (Bai minority)

最具有开发潜力的“金三角”——织金欢迎您

"Golden Triangle" of having the most development potentiality -- Zhijin welcomes you

县人民政府副县长张智了解经济普查工作进展情况
The deputy governor of the county government Zhaog Zhi inquired about the situation of economic census work

县经济普查办工作人员在聚精会神工作
The staffs of economic census office in the county were working with great attention

天峰（织金洞出口）
Tian mountain (export of Zhijin Hole)

织金县“十一五”工业发展建设规划项目表 Item table of Zhijin County "Tenth Five" industry development construction plan

单位:亿元 (Unit: 100 million yuan)

项目名称 Name of item	建设规模及内容 Scale and content of construction	"估算 Estimate 总投资 total investment"
（一）煤炭开采 Coal mining		
1、戴家田矿井 Daijiatian Mine	180万(ten thousand)t/a	4.3227
2、三甲矿井 Sanjia Mine	90万(ten thousands)t/a	1.7689
3、文家坝一矿 No.1 mine of Wenjiaba	240万(ten thousand)t/a	6.3734
4、文家坝二矿 No.2 mine of Wenjiaba	240万(ten thousand)t/a	6.305
5、肥田矿井 Feitian Mine	300万(ten thousand)t/a	8.6691
6、官寨矿井 Guanzhai Mine	90万(ten thousand)t/a	1.7129
7、中寨矿井 Zhongzhai Mine	240万(ten thousand)t/a	6.4111
8、碾子边矿井 Nianzibian Mine	240万(ten thousand)t/a	6.2561
9、阿弓矿井 Agong Mine	300万(ten thousand)t/a	8.6788
10、红梅矿井 Hongmei Mine	90万(ten thousand)t/a	1.794
11、三坝矿井 Sanba Mine	300万(ten thousand)t/a	8.7369
12、开田冲矿井 Kaitianchong Mine	180万(ten thousand)t/a	4.3078
（二）煤电联营 Joint operation coal electricity		
1、国电织金火电厂 Zhijin Heat -engine Plant of China Guodian Corporation	4×600MW	106.00
（三）煤化工 Coal chemical industry		
1、甲醇、二甲醚生产线 Production line of carbinol, dimethyl ether	合成氨、甲醇、二甲醚、醋酸等化工产品100-200万t/a Synthetic, carbinol, dimethyl ether, acetic acid and other chemical industry products 1-2 million t/a	100-200
2、煤（液化）制油 Coal(liquefaction)petroleum	100-300万(ten thousand)t/a	100-300
（四）磷化工及稀土开发 Phosphorus chemical industry and rare-earth development"	矿石采选 250万t/a，磷精矿153万t/a，稀土精矿1660t/a，磷铵80万t/a（其中DAP60万t/a，MAP20万t/a，磷酸10万t/a，磷酸一、二、三钠等相关产品各2万t/a。 Ore select 2.5 million t/a, phosphorus fine ore 1.53 million t/a, rare -earth fine ore 1660t/a, phosphorus ammonium 800 thousands t/a (including DAP 600 thousand t/a, MAP200 thousandt/a), phosphoric acid 100 thousand t/a,sodium dihydrogen phosphate,sodium hydrogen phosphate dodecahydrate, sodium phosphate and relevant products respective 20 thousand t/a.	80
（五）新建织金水泥厂 New-building Zhijin Cement Plant	30万(ten thousand)t/a	0.8000
1、电解铝厂 Electrolysis aluminium manufacturer	30万(ten thousand)t/a	30.00
2、炼铁厂 Iron mill	10万(ten thousand)t/a	0.6000
3、电石厂 Acetylene plant	1万(ten thousand)t/a	0.2000
4、硅铁厂 Silicoferrite mill	1万(ten thousand)t/a	0.2000
5、水泥厂 Cement plant	30万(ten thousand)t/a	0.8000
6、石墨电级糊厂 Graphite electrode plant	1万(ten thousand)t/a	0.3800
三、农副产品加工 Processed farm and sideline products		
1、绿肥蛋白饲料加工 Green manure egg white feed processing	30万(ten thousand)t/a	0.1850
2、竹荪多糖蛋白口服液 Zhusun polysaccharide egg white oral liquid	100万（瓶）盒(ten thousand bottles boxes)/a	0.1500
3、矿泉水加工厂 Mineral water processing plant	50万桶(ten thousand barrels)/a	0.5000
4、肉联厂 Meat joint operation factory	1000t/a	0.1200

织金关
Zhijin Pass

册亨县
Ceheng County

省委书记在州县主要领导的陪同下检查指导册亨县的社会主义新农村建设
The secretary of the provincial Party committee, accompanied by the principal leaders of the prefecture and the county to inspect and guide the socialist new rural building of Ceheng county

册亨县位于贵州的南部。总面积2598平方公里。辖9镇5乡，10个居委会，185个村委会，994个村民组。居住着布依、汉、苗、壮、满等10多个民族，全县总人口21.8万人，少数民族占全县总人口的80%，其中布依族占74.6%，是一个以布依族为主体民族的边远山区县。

在县委、县政府的领导下，全县经济和社会事业迅猛发展。2005年国内生产总值完成50265万元，比上年增长10.32%，财政收入完成3108万元，比上年增长24.92%，农民人均纯收入提高到1453元，比上年增长8.63%，金融机构各项存款余额52861万元，增长34.82%，全社会固定资产投资15215万元，同比增长9.26%。全县工业总产值达17658万元，比上年增长15.32%，工业化水平进一步提高。基础设施建设成效显著，程控电话、移动电话快速发展，通讯条件显著改善。县城旧城改造全面结束，新区建设速度加快，城市面貌焕然一新，小城镇建设初见成效。县乡公路等级进一步提高，全县通车里程达到1201.06公里，县、乡、村公路网络基本形成。农村基础设施建设力度加大，基本实现通水、通电、通电视，农田水利建设全面铺开，农村生产生活条件得到改善，发展后劲增强。

册亨县的矿产生物资源丰富，发展潜力巨大。目前已初步探明黄金储量23吨，锑储量57万吨，镁储量163万吨，汞、砷、褐铁矿、冰洲石、水晶石、大理石、石灰石等均有分布。全县水资源总量为13.67亿立方米，水能蕴藏量93901千瓦，总开发量18957千瓦。全县旅游资源有：古罗马王国遗址、古土司府遗址等。

册亨县的特色产业初步形成，产业结构不断优化。早熟蔬菜业，时令水果业，畜牧业，有色金属深加工业，建材加工业等特色产业已初具规模。

Ceheng county is located in the south of Guizhou. Total area is 2,598 square kilometres. The county governs 9 towns 5 townships and 10 neighborhood committees and 185 village committees, 994 villager groups. The county lives Buyi, Han, Miao, Zhuang, Man and more than 10 nationalities, the total population of 218,000 people in the county, minorities accounted for 80% of the county's total population, of which Buyi minority accounted for 74.6%, is a remote hill county as main nationality of Buyi minority.

Under the leadership of county Party committee and government, the economy and social cause of the county achieved the rapid development. In 2005, the GDP completed 502.65 million yuan, 10.32% higher than the previous year, the completion of 31.08 million yuan financial revenue, increased 24.92% than last year, the per capita net income of farmers increased to 1,453 yuan, 8.63% higher than the previous year, the deposits balance in financial institutions of 528.61 million yuan, an increase of 34.82%, 152.15 million yuan in total fixed asset investment, grew 9.26%. The industrial output value of the county amounted to 176.58 million yuan, 15.32% higher than the previous year, and the level of industrialization has been further enhanced. Infrastructure construction achieved achievements, program--controlled telephone, mobile phone of rapid development, significant improvements in terms of communication. The old city of the county finished comprehensive transformation, to speed up the new district building, urban landscape took an entirely new look, the building of small towns has achieved the initial results. The road grade of the county was further enhanced, traffic mileage was up to 1201.06 km, the road network of county, township and village has been basically formed. Rural infrastructure building has been intensified to basically realize the opening of water, electricity, communication and television, agricultural water conservancy construction carried out in an all-round way, and improved rural production and living conditions, enhanced development momentum.

Ceheng county has rich mineral biological resources with huge development potential. Now has preliminary proven gold reserves of 23 tons, antimony reserves of 570,000 tons, 1.63 million tons of magnesium reserves, mercury, arsenic, brown iron ore, Iceland spar, crystal stone, marble, limestone, etc. are all distributed. The total water resources of the county are 1.367 billion cubic metres, hydropower potential of 93,901 kW, with a total development volume of 18,957 kW. The tourist resources of the county have: relics of ancient Rome Kingdom, ancient Tusi Home.

The special industries of Ceheng county have begun to take shape, constantly optimized the industrial structure. Maturing vegetable industry, fruit industry, animal husbandry industry, nonferrous metal deep processing industry, building materials processing industry, and other special industries have begun to take shape scale.

县委孟祥熙书记在县委常委县水利局局长王永忠，冗渡镇党委书记张显文的陪同下检查油菜育苗移栽
The secretary of the county Party committee Meng Xiangxi accompanied by the Standing member of county Party Committee and the director of Water Conservancy Bureau of County Wang Yongzhong, the secretary of Rongdu town Party committee Zhang Xianwen to inspect young cole breeding and transplant seedlings

旅游胜地——江口

The Tourist famous scenic spot -- Jiangkou

省级风景名胜区——太平河上风雨桥
The provincial scenic area — Fengyu Bridge on the Taiping River

江口县地处贵州省铜仁地区东部，国土总面积1869平方公里，下辖9个乡镇71个行政村，总人口23万，其中土家、苗、侗、羌等少数民族占总人口的52%。

江口县具有得天独厚的旅游资源优势。中国五大佛教名山之一、省级风景名胜区、国家级自然保护区、联合国“人与生物圈”保护网成员、地球同纬度地区唯一的“绿洲”——梵净山座落在县境西北，它集奇、峻、秀于一体，古朴而有灵气，被誉为“黔山第一”、“镇黔之宝”，有“名岳之尊、武陵之源”的美称。此外，境内还有太平河风景名胜区、神龙洞、凯里沟大峡谷、黄鹄山、百水洞等。是集佛教文化、生态文化、民族民俗文化于一体的难得的旅游胜地。

近年来，江口县依托梵净名山优势，积极实施强农稳县、旅游强县、兴工富县“三个重点”和招商引资带动、旅游牵动、项目和投资拉动“三动”战略，有力地促进了地方经济社会发展。2005年全县生产总值完成69152万元，比上年增长11.7%，其中第一产业增长7.8%，第二产业增长17.4%，第三产业增长14.7%，粮食总产量达9.01万吨，增长0.9%；财政总收入完成3873万元，增长15%，其中地方财政收入完成3002万元，增长13.1%；农民人均纯收入1670元，实际增长7.8%。

Jiangkou county is located in the east of Tongren region of Guizhou province, covers 1,869 square kilometers, governs 9 towns and 71 administrative villages with a total population of 230,000, of which TuJia, Miao, Dong, Qiang nationalities and other minorities accounted for 52% of the total population.

Jiangkou county enjoys exceptional advantages in tourist resources. Fanjin Mountain, the one of China's five major Buddhist famous mountains, the provincial scenic area, national nature conservation area, the member of the United Nations "MAB" Protection Network, the only "oasis" in the same latitude on the earth, is located in the northwest of the county, with the integration of strange, steep and pretty, simplicity and polish, is famed as "the first of the mountains of Guizhou", "precious of Guizhou", having the reputation of "the respect of Five Mountains, the source of Wuling". In addition, there are Taiping River scenic area, Shenlong Hole, Kaili Gap Grand Canyon, Huanghu Hill, Baishui Hole and other sceneries. It is the rare tourist destination with the integration of Buddhist culture, ecological culture and national folk culture.

In recent years, Jiangkou county relied on the advantages of famous Fanjin Mountain, and actively implemented strong agriculture steady county, tourism strong county, thriving industry and rich county "three keys" and introduced business and attracted investment leading, tourism affecting, projects and investment drawing "three leadings" strategy, effectively promoted local economic social development. In 2005 the GDP of the county completed 691.52 million yuan, 11.7% higher than the previous year, of which the primary industry grew 7.8%, the secondary industry grew 17.4%, 14.7% growth in the tertiary industry, the grain output reached 90,100 tons, an increase of 0.9%; the financial revenue completed 38.73 million yuan, growth 15%, of which local revenue completed 30.02 million yuan, an increase of 13.1%; per capita net income of farmers was 1,670 yuan, actual growth of 7.8%.

亚洲第一洞内石瀑——神龙洞
The first stone waterfall in the hole of Asia -- Shenlong Hole

昆明卷烟厂江口县烟叶生产基地
Jiangkou county tobacco leaf production base of Kunming Cigarette Plant

建设中的桃映小城镇 Taoying small town in building

正安概况

The Brief Introduction of Zhengan

县委书记韦圣福
The secretary of the county Wei Shengfu

县长宋霖
The governor of the county Song Lin

正安县幅员2595平方公里，辖19个乡镇，人口59.4万。地处黔北大娄山脉东麓，是贵州襟联重庆的前沿。素有“中国野木瓜之乡”、“小说之乡”、“群众文化之乡”、“油桐之乡”称誉。正安气候温和，风物长宜，属中亚热带湿润季风气候，冬无严寒，夏无酷暑，雨热同季。

正安，山川秀丽，资源丰富。有九道水省级森林公园，尹珍墓、务本堂等景点；有耕地116万亩，林地138万亩，森林覆盖率达36%，草地70万亩，河网密度0.68千米/平方公里，立体农业气候明显。现有植物资源2500余种，有野木瓜、茶叶、方竹笋、橙子、蜜李等农特产品，其中：中药材品种就有1500多种。野生动物70余种，以苏门羚、穿山甲、大鲵(娃娃鱼)最为著名。矿产资源有铁、铝土、含钾页岩、萤石、重晶石、煤等矿藏16种。

正安，历史源远，文化深厚。这里是贵州文化鼻祖尹珍先生故居，曾为古黔北经济文化的中心，具有深厚的文化底蕴，民间文艺纷纭繁荣。

“十五”期末，地区生产总值完成17.56亿元，年均增长10.9%。人民生活水平进一步提高，经济社会不断发展，城乡面貌日新月异，基础设施建设突飞猛进，县域经济实现新发展。展望“十一五”，全县各族人民将在县委、县政府的正确领导下，为建设富裕、和谐、文明、开放的新正安而努力奋斗。

The area of Zhengan county is 2,595 square kilometers. The county governs 19 towns and total population of 594,000. It is located in the east of Dalou Mountain of Qianbei, is the forefront of Guizhou overlapping Chongqing. The county is known as reputation of "the hometown of China wild papaya", "the hometown of novels", "the hometown of mass culture", "the hometown of oil tung tree". The climate of Zhengan is mild, and it belongs to middle subtropical humid monsoon climate. There's no bitter cold in winter or intense hot in summer, the rainy season is in summer.

Zhengan has beautiful mountains and rivers and rich resources. There are Jiudaoshui provincial level Forest Park, Yinzhen Tomb, Wuben Hall and other scenery spots; There are 1.16 million mu of farmland and 1.38 million mu of forest land, the rate of forest covering of 36% and 700 thousand mu grassland, the density of network of waterways of 0.68 km/km^2, with obvious stereo agro-climatic. There are now more than 2,500 plant resources, such us wild papaya, tea, square bamboo shoots, oranges, honey plum, and other agricultural special products, including over 1500 sorts of Chinese medicinal materials. There are over 70 species wild animals, among which, Sumen antelope, pangolin, and giant salamander are the most famous. There are mineral resources such as iron, bauxite, potassium shale, fluorite, barite, coal and other 16 kinds of minerals.

Zhengan has a long history and the deep culture. Here was the former residence of Mr. Yinzhen who was the cultural originator of Guizhou, was the economic and cultural center of ancient Qianbei, with deep cultural foundation and prosperous folk art and literature.

By the end of "Tenth Five", the GDP of Zhengan completed 1.756 billion yuan, an average annual increase of 10.9%. Further improved the people's living standards, economic and social developed constantly, urban and rural landscape changed with each passing day, infrastructure construction developed quickly, and the economy of the county achieved new development. Prospects for "Eleventh Five", under the correct leadership of county Party committee and government, the people of various nationalities of the county are working hard for building new Zhengan of prosperity, harmony, civilization, and open.

九道水森林公园
Jiudaoshui Forest Park

城市新貌
The new outlook of the city

安龙县概况

The Survey of Anlong County

安龙县地处贵州西南部，隶属黔西南布依族苗族自治州。全县国土总面积2237平方公里，辖11镇5乡，289个村民委员会，9个居委会，2005年末总人口43.18万人，其中少数民族人口20.44万人，非农业人口3.4人，人口较多的少数民族有布依族、苗族。已探明的矿产主要有煤、黄金、硫铁矿、水晶、石英砂、石灰石等20多种矿藏，其中煤炭储量12.28亿吨，黄金储量22.4吨；硫铁矿储量900万吨；石灰石10000万吨以上。森林覆盖率为40%。

2005年，全县生产总值完成14.91亿元，比上年增长(下同)14.69％；财政总收入1802万元，增长12.48%，固定资产投资完成9.6亿元，增长128.57%；社会消费品零售总额3.43亿元，增长11.90%；农民人均纯收入1852元，增加126元；城镇居民人均可支配收入5500元，增加500元；金融机构存贷款余额分别为116922万元和70053万元。全年实施基本建设项目75个，总投资126670万元。县通车里程达1900公里。通信覆盖率85%以上。全年接待游客13.3万人次。

2005年，安龙县工业在国民经济中的比重迅速增加，其主导作用进一步凸现，国民经济三次产业结构比为32∶39∶29，全县经济社会实现持续快速协调发展。

建设中的重化工基地一期工程
Phase I engineering of heavy chemical industry base in building

Anlong county is located in the southwest of Guizhou, is subordinate to Qianxinan Buyi & Miao MinorityAutonomous State. The county cover 2,237 square kilometers, governs 11 towns 5 townships, 289 villag committees, 9 neighborhood committees. The total population of the en of 2005 is 431,800, including 204,400 ethnic minority population, the non agricultural population of 34000 people, Minorities nationalities with large population are Buyi and Miao minority. Proven minerals mainly are coal gold, pyrite, crystal, quartz sand, limestone and other more than 20 kinds including coal reserves of 1.228 billion tons, 22.4 tons of gold reserves; pyrite reserves of 9 million tons; limestone reserves of over 100 million tons. The rate of forest covering is up to 40%.

In 2005, the county completed GDP of 1.491 billion yuan, more 14.69% than the previous year (the same below);the financial revenue was 18.02 million yuan, an increase of 12.48%, the investment in fixed asset completed 960 million yuan, growth 128.57%; Total retail sales of consume goods were 343 million yuan, an increase of 11.90%; per capita net income of farmers was 1,852 yuan, increased 126 yuan; per capita disposable income of urban residents was 5,500 yuan, an increase of 500 yuan; balance of deposits and loans of financial institutions were 1.16922 billion yuan and 700.53 million yuan respectively. Annual 75 infrastructure projects were implemented with a total investment of 1.2667 billion yuan. Traffic mileage in the county was up to 1,900 kilometers. The rate of communication covering was over 85%. The county annually received visitors of 133000 person times.

In 2005, the proportion of industry in the national economy increased rapidly, and its leading role in the further advancement, three industrie structure proportion of the national economy was 32:39:29, the economi society in the county achieved sustained, rapid and coordinated development.

招堤十里荷花一角 A corner of 10 li lotus in Zhaod

罗甸县概况

The Profile of Luodian County

全县总面积3013万平方米，耕地面积1.68万公顷，年末总人口31.97万人，其中少数民族21.79万人，人口较多的少数民族是布依族和苗族。主要矿藏有硅石、铁矿、辉绿岩、米黄色大理石等20余种，森林覆盖率34.6%。2005年，实现国内生产总值110893万元，比上年增长11%；农林牧渔业总产值72106万元，比上年增长4.58%；工业总产值65000万元，比上年增长3%；财政总收入8686万元，比上年增长14.05%，其中地方财政收入4762万元，比上年增长9.17%，财政总支出25444万元，比上年增长21.63%；社会消费品零售总额19440万元；农民人均纯收入1648元；固定资产投资50000万元，同比增长15.92%。

The total area of the county is 30.13 million square meters, 16,800 hectares of arable land, a total of population at the end of the year is 319,700, of whom minority population of 217,900, the more minority population are Buyi and Miao minorities. The main mineral resources are silica, iron ore, diabase, buff marble and other more than 20 kinds, the forest coverage rate is 34.6%. In 2005, the GDP realized 1.10893 billion yuan, an increase of 11%;the output value of agriculture, forestry, animal husbandry, and fishery was 721.06 million yuan, growth 4.58% over last year; the output value of industry was 650 million yuan, an increase of 3%; the financial revenue totaled 86.86 million yuan, an increase of 14.05%, of which the local revenue was 47.62 million yuan, an increase of 9.17%, the financial expenditure was 254.44 million yuan, an increase of 21.63%; the total retail sales of consumer goods were 194.4 million yuan; the per capita net income of peasants was 1,648 yuan; the investment in fixed assets was 500 million yuan, an increase of 15.92%.

罗甸县大小井一角
A corner of the big and small Wells of Luodian county

在建的银河电站
Yinhe Power Station in constructing

投产发电的雷公滩电站
Leigongtan Power Station was going into operation and generating power

装机容量达12万千瓦的蒙河流域双河口电站
Shuanghekou Power Station in Meng River basin with generation capacity of 120 thousand kilowatts

中国银行业监督管理委员会贵州监管局

China Banking Regulatory Commission Guizhou Regulatory Bureau

贵州银监局党委书记、局长邓瑞林
The secretary of Party committee of the Guizhou Banking Regulatory Bureau and the director of the Bureau, Deng Ruilin

经中国银行业监督管理委员会批准，中国银行业监督管理委员会贵州监管局自2003年10月16日起正式履行职责。贵州银监局下设办公室、政策法规处（研究室）、银行监管一处、银行监管二处、银行监管三处、股份制银行监管处、非银行金融机构监管处、合作金融机构监管处、统计处、财务会计处、监察室、人事处、机关党委等13个部门。

贵州银监局主要职责：

制定监管法规、制度方面的实施细则和规定，负责对辖内银行业金融机构业务的监督管理；审查和批准辖内银行业金融机构及其分支机构的设立、变更、终止及业务范围；负责组织实施对辖内银行业金融机构的现场和非现场监管，依法对金融违法、违规行为进行查处；审查和批准辖内银行业金融机构及其分支机构高级管理人员任职资格；负责统计、分析、上报辖内银行业金融机构的有关数据、信息，并依据银监会授权进行信息披露；负责对辖内的金融风险进行分析、研究，并会同有关部门及时提出辖内存款类金融机构紧急风险处置意见和建议，以及承办银监会交办的其他事项。

Upon approval of the China Banking Regulatory Commission, China Banking Regulatory Commission Guizhou Regulatory Bureau performed its duty since October 16, 2003. Guizhou Banking Regulatory Bureau consists of office, policy and regulation department (research center), the first department of banking supervision, the second department of banking supervision, the third department of banking supervision, joint-stock banking supervision department, non-bank financial institution supervision department, cooperative financial institution supervision department, the statistical office, financial accounting office, monitoring room, personnel department, Party committee 13 departments.

Guizhou Banking Regulatory Bureau main duties:

Carry out implementation rules and regulations in aspects of regulatory law and system, responsible for banking financial institutions supervision management in Guizhou; Review and approval establishment change, termination and business scope of banking financial institutions and their branches in Guizhou; responsible for organizing implementation on scene or not on scene of banking financial institutions regulatory, investigate and punish violations financial crimes according to law; review and approval of senior managers qualification of the banking financial institutions and their branches in Guizhou; Responsible for statistics, analysis, report relevant data, information of banking financial institutions in Guizhou, and disclosure information authorized by CBRC; responsible for the financial risk analysis study, research, and cooperate with the relevant departments timely submission the emergency risk disposal observation and recommendation of deposit financial institutions in Guizhou, as well as undertake other matters handle by CBRC.

联系地址 Contact address：贵阳市中华南路203号海天商厦 Haitian commercial building No.203 Zhonghua south road Guiyang city
邮政编码 Post code：550002 联系电话 Contact Tel：0851-5811528 传真 Fax：0851-5861569

贵州宏福实业开发有限总公司

Guizhou Hongfu Industry Development Controlling Corporation Limited

贵州宏福实业开发有限总公司于1994年6月成立，由总投资58.5亿元的矿肥结合项目——贵州瓮福矿肥基地改制组建，是中国目前最大的磷矿肥企业，占地面积8平方公里，在岗员工2591人，具有专业技术职称的1435人，固定资产64亿元。生产能力：磷矿石400万吨/年，磷精矿210万吨/年，磷酸80万吨/年，硫酸200万吨/年，磷酸二铵120万吨/年，磷酸一铵48万吨/年；拥有3万千瓦/年热电厂和年吞吐能力为345万吨的铁路专用线。

主要产品：磷酸二铵、磷酸一铵、三聚磷酸钠、工业级磷酸一铵、食品级磷酸、黄磷、磷石膏水泥调凝剂、磷石膏砌块。其中磷酸二铵、磷酸一铵，分别于2003年和2005年获“中国名牌产品”称号；2004年双双列为“质量免检产品”。

公司引进世界先进的采矿、制酸制肥工艺技术和设备，采用先进DCS和PLC控制系统，建有国家级技术开发中心和我国磷化工企业首家博士后科研工作站，自主研发的湿法磷酸净化等核心技术已通过国家鉴定。

公司发展目标：从2005年起，力争在10年内建设成为销售收入100亿元、利税10亿元的企业集团。

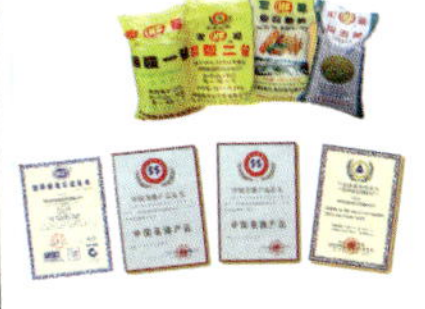

瓮福磷肥厂夜景 Night scene in Wengfu Phosphate Fertilizer Plant

Guizhou Hongfu Industry Development Controlling Corporation Limited was established in June 1994, reconstructed by a total investment of 5.85 billion yuan of the mine fertilizer project -- Guizhou Wengfu Mine Fertilizer Base, is the currently the largest phosphate fertilizer enterprise in China, covering eight square kilometers, post staff 2591 people, with professional and technical titles 1435 people, fixed assets of 6.4 billion yuan. Capacity of production: phosphate ore 4 million tons/year, phosphorus purified ore 2.1 million tons/year, phosphoric acid 800,000 tons/year, sulphuric acid 2 million tons/year, Di-ammonium Phosphate 1.2 million tons/year, Powder Mono-Ammonium Phosphate 480,000 tons/year; having thermal power plant with 30 thousand kilowatts/year and the railway special line with annual handling capacity of 3.45 million tons.

Main products: Di-ammonium Phosphate, Powder Mono-Ammonium Phosphate, poly-phosphate sodium, industrial-grade Powder Mono-Ammonium Phosphate, food-grade phosphoric acid, yellow phosphorus, phosphorus gypsum cement-embodied agents, phosphorus gypsum small pieces. Of which Di-ammonium Phosphate, Powder Mono-Ammonium Phosphate, respectively awarded the title "China Brand-name" in 2003 and 2005; both were placed the "free-check product" in 2004.

The corporation introduced the world's advanced technology and equipment of mining, making acid and making fertilizer, used advanced DCS and PLC control system, built national technology development center and our country phosphate chemical enterprise first postdoctoral research station, the independent research and development of core technologies such as wet phosphoric acid purification passed national identification.

Development goals of the corporation: from 2005, will strive to become an enterprise group with 10 billion yuan of sales income and 1 billion yuan of profits and taxes for 10 years.

地址 Address：贵州省福泉市马场坪镇 Machangping town Fuquan city Guizhou province 邮编 Post Code：550501 联系电话 Contact Tel：0854-2187329
网址 Http：www.wengfu.com E-mail:wf_office@wengfu.com 网络实名：宏福 瓮福 磷铵 Network name: Hongfu Wengfu Linan

贵州商业高等专科学校

Guizhou Commercial Higher Junior College

国家教育部部长周济部长(左一)视察我校酒店管理专业实训室
The minister of the Ministy of Education Zhou Ji(the first from left) visited our college hotel management professional train room

领导班子
Leader group

贵州商业高等专科学校位于贵阳市市区，前身系1947年创建的“贵阳市尚信高级会计职业学校”。学校现有教职工505人，其中专任教师380人，副教授以上职称人员90人，各类在校生1万余人。建校50年多来，学校已为国家和地方经济发展培养和输送了经济、管理类专门人才4万多名，毕业生就业率一直居全省高校前列。

学校先后受到中共中央组织部、中共中央宣传部、教育部、解放军总政治部、国家武警部队政治部、国内贸易部的表彰；1999年被中央精神文明建设指导委员会授予“全国精神文明建设工作先进单位”称号。学校党委和学校连续四届荣获省委、省人民政府授予的“全省先进基层党组织”和“省级文明单位”称号；是全国首批国家级高职高专示范实训基地建设单位（12家）之一（贵州省唯一一家）。

学校现有贸易经济系等11个教学系部，市场营销、酒店管理等26个专业，其中国家级高职高专精品专业（建设项目）1个，教育部教学改革示范专业2个，贵州省教学改革示范专业3个；学校图书馆共有各类图书文献60多万册；各类教学实验设备总值3200万元，固定资产原值总额2.5亿元。办有面向全国公开发行的《贵州商专学报》。

学校已形成高专、高职、成人教育及联办本科教育、研究生课程教育的多层次办学格局。为了培养出更多的高级技术应用性专门人才，和贵州经济社会及中国商贸业的发展作出贡献。

Guizhou Commercial Higher Junior College is located in the urban area of Guiyang city, the predecessor is "Guiyang City Shangxin High Accounting Vocational School" which was founded in 1947. The college now has 505 teachers and administrative staffs, of whom 380 of full-time teachers and above vice professor title of 90 staffs, more than 10,000 students in all types. Since foundation 50 years, the college has educated and delivered more than 40,000 economy and management professionals for national and local economic development, and the employment rate of graduates ranked the front in provincial colleges and universities.

The college was successively awarded the praises of the CPC Central Committee Organization Department, the Central Propaganda Department, the Ministry of Education, the PLA General Political Department, the State Armed Police Department, the Ministry of Domestic Trade; and awarded the title of "national spiritual civilization construction work advanced unit" by the Central Spiritual Civilization Construction Steering Committee in 1999. The college and its Party committee four consecutively won the title of "provincial grass-roots advanced Party organization" and "provincial civilized units" by provincial Party committee and provincial government, was the one of (the only one in Guizhou province)first state-level high vocation & high college model train base construction unit (12 units).

The college now has 11 teaching departments such as department of trade and economy, 26 professionals as the marketing, hotel management, etc, including 1 national high college professional (construction project), 2 teaching reform model professionals of the Ministry of Education, 3 Guizhou province educational reform model professionals; The library of the college has more than 600 thousand copies of books literature; various teaching laboratory equipment worth 32 million yuan, having an original total 250 million yuan of fixed assets. The college manages the "Guizhou Commercial Higher College Journal" that is faced to the nation public issue.

The college has formed multilevel school pattern with high school, vocational school, adult education and joint conduct undergraduate education, postgraduate education. The college devotes its contribution to cultivate more high technology application expertise talents, and the development of Guizhou economy and society and Chinese commercial and trade industry.

学术报告
The academic report

强化学生英语训练
Strengthen students to train English

贵州灵达房地产开发股份有限公司
Guizhou Lingda Real Estate Development Stock Co., Ltd.

贵政大厦 Guizheng Building

新华苑 Xinhua Gaden

贵州灵达房地产开发股份有限公司始建于一九九三年六月，主营房地产开发。十多年来，先后开发建设了“灵达新苑”建筑群体，建筑面积50200平方米；“电台街住宅小区”10000余平方米；“华宫新苑”建筑面积8000余平方米等，已全部交付使用。修建了可容纳200余人的集餐饮、娱乐、会议、休闲为一体的“百花湖灵达度假中心”。

近年来，公司在原开发项目的基础上，继续开发建设了“贵政大厦”（8000余平方米）；“新华苑”建筑群体（10000余平方米）以及“智亿大厦”（40000余平方米）等项目。

Guizhou Lingda Real Estate Development Stock Co., Ltd., was founded in June 1993, operates the real estate development in the main. Since 10 years, the company has developed the "Lingda New Garden" building group with building area of 50,200 square meters; the "Diantai Street residential district" with building area of more than 10,000 square meters; the "Huagong New Garden" with building area of more than 8,000 square meters, which all have already been made available for use. The company constructed the "Lingda Holiday Center of Baihua Lake" which can accommodate more than 200 people integration restaurant, entertainment, convention and leisure.

In recent years, on the basis of the original development project, the company continued to develop the "Guizheng Building" (over 8,000 square meters); the "Xinhua Gaden" building group (over 10,000 square meters), and the "Zhiyi Building" (more than 40,000 square meters) and other projects.

智亿大厦 Zhiyi Building

水城钢铁（集团）有限责任公司
Shui Cheng Iron and Steel (Group) Co., Ltd.

水钢党委书记：赵松桓
The secretary of the Party committee: Zhao Songhuan

水钢总经理：张槐祥
The general manager: Zhang Huaixiang

水钢始建于1966年，现有在岗职工2.3万人，资产总额85亿元。主要产品有普线、高线、螺纹钢，具备年产280万吨铁、300万吨钢、180万吨钢材的综合生产能力。按照水钢调整产品结构，发展循环经济《规划》，将于2007年实现销售收入100亿元；"十二五"期间达到年销售收入200亿元。

Shui Cheng Iron and Steel (Group) Co., Ltd. was built in 1966, 23 thousand workers in existing and assets total 8.5 billion yuan. It had annual production capacity of 2.8 million tons of iron, 3 million tons steel, 1.8 million tons of steel products with main products of common and high-speed linear, screw-steel. According adjustment product structure and development cycle economy "planning" of Shui Steel, it will realize sales income of 10 billion yuan in 2007, and reach sales income of 20 billion yuan in the period of "Twelfth Five".

水钢主要产品之一——螺纹钢
The one of main products of Shui Steel--screw-steel

水钢文化艺术节
Shui Steel cultural festival

水钢煤焦化分公司生产现场一隅
A corner of production site in Coal Coking Branch Company of Shui Steel

水钢三号高炉雄姿
The majestic appearance of No.3furnace of Shui Steel

中国航空工业标准件制造有限责任公司
China Aviation Industry Standard Parts Manufacturing Co., Ltd

表面处理生产线
Surface treatment production line

车铣加工中心
Mill processing center

冷镦成型机
Cold upset shaped machine

五轴联动加工中心
Five shafts gearing processing center

中国航空工业标准件制造有限责任公司是我国航空工业唯一的整机、全系列标准件、高强度紧固件及小零件的专业化科研生产基地。公司组建于1993年12月，由始建于二十世纪六十年代中期的原安湖机械厂和庆文机械厂合并异地搬迁而成。在贵州省贵阳市白云区白云经济技术开发区内拥有14万平方米的生产经营场地，在职职工1400余人，其中科研、管理人员289人（其中：中高级职称187人），现拥有固定资产21200万元，资产总值36600万元，拥有各类主要生产检测设备800余台（套），其中从美、德、法、日、瑞典、瑞士等国家引进的先进设备占固定资产总值的60%以上。

公司相继通过ISO9000-2000版和QS9000/VDA6.1质量体系认证，并通过了德国大众、上海大众、一汽大众、五羊本田、上汽通用五菱等汽车、摩托车行业的质量检查与评审。在全系列、大批量生产经营航空、航天标准件的同时，亦大量生产汽车、摩托车、工程机械高强度紧固件、齿轮齿条式汽车转向器，集科研、生产、检测为一体。多年来，为飞机、航空发动机、火箭、民用航空及汽车、摩托车、工程机械、纺织机械、化工、制冷压缩机与各类柴、汽油发动机等行业（专业）的发展做出了卓越的贡献。公司航空标准件的制造技术、加工设备居国内领先地位，特别是关键技术、关键检测手段、关键加工设备已经接近或达到了国际同行业的先进水平。

公司全体员工奉行“航空报国追求第一”的理念，发扬“团结敬业拼搏进取”的精神，始终坚持“市场至上、以质取胜、管理创优、科技领先、持续改进”的质量方针，依托强大的技术力量和一流的员工队伍，衷心为新老客户提供一流的产品与服务。

The China Aviation Industry Standard Parts Manufacturing Co., Ltd which lies in Baiyun economic and technical development area of Guiyang Guizhou province is the only professional manufacturer for the standard parts, high-strength fasteners and small spare parts of aerospace industry in China. We have gone into business for 37 years. The capital belongs to state-owned assets. The occupation of plant area is 140000 sqs. There are over 1400 employees, including 289 management persons (187 of them are holding medium/senior professional titles) now. The company owns the fixed assets of RMB 212 million (about USD 26 million), and the total assets of RMB 366 million (about USD 45 million). It is provided with more than 800 pieces /sets of various kinds of equipment for testing and manufacturing, which the imported ones (from USA, Germany, Japan, France, Sweden and Switzerland) account for 60% (in terms of the fixed assets).

It has passed the quality system certification of ISO9000 (version 2000), QS9000/VDA6.1, and the quality examination of many automotive manufacturers, such as Volkswagen (Germany), Shanghai Volkswagen, FAW-Volkswagen, WUYANG-HONDA, and GE-WULING, etc. Its large-scale production and business are now covering the product ranges of the standard parts for aerospace industry, and the high strength fasteners and pinion-and-track steering units for automobile, motorcycle and engineering machinery, textile machinery, petrochemical machinery, refrigeration compressor, and diesel engine, etc. Technology and equipments which manufactured standard parts lie leading status in civil. The special technology, special inspecting methods and special equipments have had access to or achieved the advanced level of the international same trade.

We pursue the ideality and faith of Dedicate Ourselves to the Aviation of Our Motherland, Purse No.1. We develop the spirit of Solidarity, Work hard, Struggle, Enterprise. We insist on the quality policy of Market is foremost, Get victory with quality, Management create benefit, Science and technology set the pace, Keep on improving. We are ready for supply first grade products and service to both old and new customers.

地址：中国贵州贵阳市白云区　　邮编（Post Code）：550014
Add: Baiyun district Guiyang city Guizhou province China
信箱：中国贵州省贵阳市白云区220号信箱
Mailbox: No.220 mailbox Baiyun district Guiyang city Guizhou province China
电话（Tel）：0851-4894088
传真（Fax）：0851-4485721
网址：Http://www.zhb3117.com
电子信箱(Email): zhb3117sckf@sinavip.sina.com

“金三角下的一颗明珠”——盘江煤电(集团)有限公司

"A pearl of Golden Triangle"——PanJiang Coal Electricity (Group) Co., Ltd.

公司技术中心 Technology center of the company

盘江煤电(集团)有限公司是大一型国有省属煤炭工业企业，在2005年全国100强煤炭工业企业中排名第44位。公司位于六盘水市盘县境内，由于地处中国“攀西——六盘水”这个资源富集的“金三角”的最南端，又以丰富的煤炭资源称冠江南，被誉为“金三角下的一颗明珠”。盘江矿区资源丰富，交通便利，现已发展成为北通巴渝，南接八桂的西南和西部大开发中的一个交通及能源输出重镇。

盘江煤电(集团)有限公司前身为盘江矿务局，始建于1966年。经过近40年的开发建设，现已发展成为以煤炭生产、洗选加工为主导，融建井施工、土建安装、地质勘测、机械制修、设备租赁、建材、发电、养殖、种植、商饮服务为一体的大型煤炭工业企业集团。公司原煤生产能力和洗选加工能力均已超过1000万吨，发电装机容量为7.5万KW，现有在册职工2.8万人。

盘江矿区面积706平方公里，地质储量94.8亿吨，远景储量383亿吨，炼焦煤储量占贵州省炼焦煤总储量的47.9%。盘江煤质量好，品种齐全，低灰、低硫、微磷、发热量高，是理想的冶金、化工和动力用煤。

盘江矿区原煤生产现已全部实现机械化，生产原煤全部入选洗加工，产品主要销往国内9个省、市、区，还出口日本等地。2005年盘江煤电(集团)公司共生产原煤865万吨，商品煤576万吨，实现销售收入26.6亿元，创利7275万元，主要生产经营指标均创历史最好水平。

公司现有六对生产矿井，两对控股矿井，即：一期设计能力400万吨、与盘南电厂配套的响水煤矿和设计能力240万吨的松河煤矿)；有四座大型洗煤厂，一个上市公司(盘江精煤股份公司)。根据规划，盘江矿区原煤生产2006年将达到1000万吨水平，2010年左右，将形成1500~2000万吨的生产规模，2015年原煤产量将突破3000万吨，精煤产量达到1250万吨，非煤产业形成一定规模，盘江煤电(集团)公司将发展成为西部地区高产高效、煤与非煤产业协调发展的跨行业、跨地区的特大型企业集团。

企业地址：贵州省六盘水市盘县红果经济开发区干沟桥 邮 编(Post Code)：553536

Address of enterprises: Gangou bridge Hongguo economic development zone Pan county Liupanshui city Guizhou province

法人代表：张世新 Legal representative: Zhang Shixin

联系电话(Contact Tel)：(0858)3700035 传 真(Fax)：(0858)3700800

联系人：王永强 Contact person : Wang Yongqiang

火铺矸石发电厂
Fire gangue power plant

井下综采工作面
Comprehensive collected work flat under the mine well

Panjiang Coal Electricity (Group) Co., Ltd. the large class 1 state-owned coal indust enterprise in the province, ranked 44 in the year 2005 National 100 strong coal industry enterprise The company is located in the place of Pan coun of Liupanshui city, because in the most south China "Panxi--Liupanshui" which is the abunda resources "Golden Triangle", also rich in co resources championed Jiangnan, is famed the " pearl of Golden Triangle." Panjiang mine district rich in resources and convenient in transport, hc been developed into a major transportation an energy export town of the West Developmen connected Sichuan and Chongqing to north an the southwest of Bagui to south.

Panjiang Coal Electricity (Group) Co., Ltc formerly was Panjiang Mine Bureau, was built in 196 After nearly 40 years of development an construction, has now developed into a large coc industry group main in coal production and washing selected processing, and integration whole c sinking construction, installation of LBAC, geologic surveying, mechanical repair, equipment leasing building materials, electric power generation breeding, cultivation and commercial and caterin services. The capacity of raw coal production an washing-selected processing of the company have both over 10 million tons. The installed capacity o generating power is 75,000 KW. The company ha existing employees 28,000 people in the book.

The area of Panjiang mine district is 706 square kilometres, the geological reserve of 9.48 billior tons, vision reserve of 38.3 billion tons, coking coa reserve accounting for Guizhou province coking coal total reserve of 47.9%. The coal of Panjiang i of good quality, satisfactory variety, low ash, low sulphur, little phosphorus, high heating value, which is the ideal coal for making metallurgy chemical industry and power.

The raw coal production of Panjiang mine district has fully achieved mechanize, raw coal production all selected washing processing, and products are mainly sold in domestic nine provinces, cities, districts, also export to Japan and other areas. In 2005 Panjiang Coal Electricity (Group) Co., Ltd. produced a total of 8.65 million tons of raw coal, 5.76 million tons of commercial coal, and its sales revenue of 2.66 billion yuan, the profit of 72.75 million yuan, mainly production targets were the highest in history.

The company now has six pairs of production mine wells, two pairs of holding mine wells, namely: Phase I design capacity 4 million tons of Xiangshui Coalmine, assembled with the Pannan Plant, and design capacity of 2.4 million tons of Songhe Coalmine); There are four major washing coal plants, one listed company (Panjiang Purified Coal Stock Company). According to the plan, raw coal production of Panjiang mine district in 2006 will reach 10 million tons, about in 2010, will form the production scale of 15~20 million tons, output of raw coal in 2015 will exceed 30 million tons, output of purified coal will reach 12.5 million tons, non-coal industries form a certain scale, Panjiang Coal Electricity (Group) Co., Ltd. will be developed into a cross-trades and trans-regional super-large enterprise group with high-yield and high-efficiency of the western region, coal and non-coal industries in the coordination development.